Warman's

FIFTEENTH ANTIQUES AND THEIR PRICES

Edited by P.S. Warman

An authoritative guide to comparative prices for collectors and dealers

Published by
E. G. WARMAN PUBLISHING, INC.
Uniontown, Pennsylvania

First Printing
—1980—

Additional copies of this book may be obtained directly from the publisher . . . E.G. Warman Publishing, Inc.
540 Morgantown Road, Uniontown, Pa. 15401

Printed in the United States of America
by the Kingsport Press Inc., Kingsport, Tennessee

Library of Congress Catalog Card Number 79-56808
ISBN 0-911594-01-9

INTRODUCTION

Whether you are a collector or a dealer. . .beginner or experienced. . .this book will be most helpful to you. Price data was personally compiled with an experienced staff. Information was gathered from every available source nationwide. . .including major shows, sales, auctions and trade publications. Additional research ranged from visits in private shops to conversations with individual collectors. Prices depend on area, availability, demand and condition. We attempted to arrive at average retail prices with all due respect and consideration. . .to bring you more realistic figures. Our goal, and the goal of this book, is to serve as a GUIDE to prices, not as a final authority. The final authority is YOU.

There are two primary reasons for continuing growth of interest in art and antiques. . .aesthetic and monetary. At this point in time, investment in the arts (including antiques) is sound; but is the monetary priority beginning to overshadow pure aesthetic values and historical significance? A recent industry report indicates a 25% annual gain over the previous year. Chinese ceramics alone have appreciated at a compound rate of 19.1% . . .outperforming other investments such as stocks and bonds; and keeping well ahead of double digit inflation. Understanding how these rates and figures are compiled is important. Many speculators inflate prices for their own gain and seldom show appreciation or affection for their acquisitions. This self-serving attitude will eventually destroy the market for all who wish to live with antiques for a combination of aesthetic reasons. . .beauty, heritage, nostalgia or pride of ownership.

Yes, antiques are a good investment; but let us not lose sight of the human and historical values of antiques and collectibles. In the "throw-away society" of the 1980's, it will be more important than ever to cherish and protect antiques for future generations; so that they will have an opportunity to examine and experience our heritage, values and dignity of life.

No matter what or why you collect (for financial growth, lasting beauty or combination of the two), the universal advice to all is the same. . .QUALITY! Do not buy or collect simply because an item is old, a bargain or part of a trend. Antiquity alone does not hold merit. . .a bargain price is soon forgotten and trends fade. Beauty is virtuous. . .the best will always hold its own. Addendums to this basic advice should be. . .RESPECT contemporary artifacts of beauty and seek REPUTABLE dealers.

With the growth of interest in collecting, new trends continue to develop. Today, small scale furniture and miniatures are in demand due to 'limited' living space. Contrarily, massive American and English Empire furniture is gaining strength in the market, now that earlier period furniture is priced beyond the average buyer's means. Nineteenth and twentieth century porcelain plus art pottery (regardless of origin) have taken command. Persian and Chinese rugs (pre-1940) are appreciated and appreciating in value. American prints (19th and 20th century) are favored. Pressed pattern glass wares are experiencing a revival and Art Nouveau and Art Deco art glass is holding well due to international favor. Additional trends include Victorian silverplate, stoneware, contemporary paperweights, English furniture, Victorian jewelry, hand-wrought metal items and hand-crafted textiles. There are a number of nostalgia categories that cannot be classified as 'true' antiques; but are collectible for personal reasons. . .beer cans, Norman Rockwell items and comic books are good examples. Limited editions such as plates and figurines should be approached with caution. . .if bought with monetary intent only. They will increase in value; but should be considered long-term investments.

Experienced collectors do not need to be reminded to continue learning; however for beginners, our recommendation is: "Learn everything possible in your chosen subject or categories, attend shows and sales, direct questions to collectors and dealers, enroll in educational programs and seminars and read. . .valid references, plus Price Guides!"

It is virtually impossible and impractical to list all the various categories deemed important in today's diversified market. We have focused on representative listings of the most desirable and sought-after antiques and collectibles.

Every effort has been made to record accurate information. In the event of clerical, typographical or any other error, we decline all responsibility. Regretfully, we are unable to reply to the many requests for information we receive from individuals. We sincerely welcome and appreciate constructive criticism of this book from all who share our goal of better informing others of the value, merit and joy of collecting . . .

ACKNOWLEDGMENTS

Adirondack Memories, Glen Falls, NY
Gloria J. Albrecht, Cincinnati, OH
Andrews Antiques, Pittsburgh, PA
Antiques & Collectables, Sharon, PA
The Antique Lady, Allison Park, PA
Bette M. Apt Antiques, Pittsburgh, PA
Mr. & Mrs. David Arman, Danville, VA
Elizabeth Austin, Charleston, SC
Tom Bastian, Denbo, PA
Bill Baxter, Batesville, IN
Mayme Black, Uniontown, PA
Elsie Blair, Hopwood, PA
Mrs. R.E. Bloch, Brookline, MA
Brass Lantern Antiques, Wiley Ford, WV
Briar Hill Manor Antiques, Kittanning, PA
Martha Brown, Pittsburgh, PA
Thomas Brown, McMurray, PA
Buckles & Jugs Antique Shop, Hopwood, PA
The Butterbaugh's, Harrison City, PA
Candlewood Antiques, Monroeville, PA
Carney's Fine Antiques, Clarksburg, WV
Carney Station Antiques, Latrobe, PA
Century House Antiques, Findlay, OH
Peter Chillingworth, Scenery Hill, PA
D.S. Clarke, Ft. Lauderdale, FL
Mr. & Mrs. Thomas Clawson, Buckhannon, WV
Collectors II, Loveland, OH
Connoisseur Art Glass, Hermitage, PA
Dave Cooper, Bentleyville, PA
Country Antiques, Keedysville, MD
Country Shop Antiques, McClellandtown, PA
The Country Squires, Sewickley, PA
Crandall's Antiques, Rocky River, OH
Crazy Horse Antiques, Lenox, MA
Richard J. D'Aiuto, Mentor, OH
Hal Day, Clearwater, FL
Sally Ann Decker, Morgantown, WV
Dr. Denes de Torek, Bridgeville, PA
Frank Dey, Los Angeles, CA
The Double "O" Antiques, Washington, PA
Leon Dryfoos, Erie, PA
Thos. Gillingham Antiques, Belle Vernon, PA
East End Galleries, Pittsburgh, PA
Emmeraude Antiques, Birmingham, MI
Paul Engelke, Miami Shores, FL
Fischer and Strassler, Pittsburgh, PA
Rufus Foshee, Camden, ME
Faye C. Free, New Stanton, PA
Jean and Jack Frost, Columbus, OH
Mr. & Mrs. Robert Fulton, Uniontown, PA
Betty Gaines Antiques, Alexandria, VA
Gallery of Yesterday, Belle Vernon, PA
James Gebhardt, Sycamore, OH
Gem Antiques, New York, NY
Goebel's Antiques, St. Albans, WV
Barbara Gould, New Kensington, PA
Gray's Antiques, Bridgeville, PA
Green Acres Antiques, Williamsville, NY
Grover Antiques, Naples, FL
Handlebar Antiques, Los Angeles, CA
Michael & Linda Hall, Maidsville, WV
John S. Heller, Newcomerstown, OH
Donald K. Helmick, San Diego, CA
Hillsway House, Charleston, WV
Gladyse H. Hilsdorf, Fayetteville, NY
Hi-Wheel Antiques, Cumberland, MD
Betty Hleba, Munhall, PA
Holly Hill Antiques, Reading, PA
Billie Hoskins Antiques, Wheeling, WV
Imperial Antiques, Shadyside, OH
Kay's Antiques, New Stanton, PA
Olin M. King, Cleveland Hts., OH
Kinzle Galleries, Duncansville, PA
Kocevar's Antiques, Manheim, PA
Kopps Antiques, York, New Salem, PA
Jorge Kripinsky, Richeyville, PA
Ruth Van Kuren, Clarence Center, NY
Edward Kveder, Fredericktown, PA
Laura's Antiques & Curios, Coraopolis, PA
Robert D. Leath, Troy, OH
Mac's Antiques, Terra Alta, WV
Kenneth & Ida Manko, Donora, PA
Manor House Antiques, Mt. Pleasant, PA
Helen Matzie, N. Huntingdon, PA
Marge McMillan, Pittsburgh, PA
Melick's Antiques, Worthington, OH
H. L. Melick, Centerburg, OH
Merry Street Antiques, Milan, OH
Charles & Grete Miller, Canonsburg, PA
Paul B. Miller, Akron, OH
Minor-Roberts Antiques, Bethesda, MD
Charles Momchilov, Jr., Jeromesville, OH
Thomas Moore Antiques, Canal Winchester, OH
Mountain Laurel Antiques, Johnstown, PA
Margaret Mutschler, Leetsdale, PA
Mrs. John C. Nader, Greenwich, CT
D.B. Neal-Sergio Rivera, Philadelphia, PA
E. Thomas Neville Antiques, Quincy, IL
Noll & McGee, Harlansburg, PA
Nonessentials, Bloomfield Hills, MI
North Branch Antique Country Store, Milan, PA
Olde Attic Antiques, Zelienople, PA
Old Line State Antiques, Deer Park, MD
Old Pike Antiques, Addison, PA
H. Meredith Palmer, Uniontown, PA
Past-Times Antique Shoppe, Spring Church, PA
Nancy Peeples Antiques, Westlake, OH
Pilgrim's Pride, Batesville, IN
Piper's Antiques, Jefferson, OH
Plain & Fancy, Columbus, OH
Pot Luck, Rockdale, MD
Robert Blake Powell, Hurst, TX
Shirley Powell, Lum, MI
Primarily Primitives, Western Springs, IL
Patricia Anne Reed, Newcastle, ME
Nancy M. Regner, Chatham, NJ
Resh's Antiques, Lancaster, PA
Pick Richardson "Ann" Company, Reynoldsburg, OH

ACKNOWLEDGMENTS

Steve & George Romanoff, Washington, PA
Rush House Antiques, Farmington, PA
Opal Sallee, Kokomo, IN
M & L Saul, Washington, PA
The Schaefers Antiques, Smoketown, PA
Joan H. Schmunk, Farmington, PA
Florence Schwartz, Pittsburgh, PA
L.H. Selman, Ltd., Santa Cruz, CA
Robert E. Shobe Antiques, Funkstown, MD
Mrs. Robert Sickles, Uniontown, PA
Ken Sinko, Denbo, PA
Bob Smith, Ft. Lauderdale, FL
Ernie Smith, Jr., Grindstone, PA
Snuggery Farms Antiques, Sewickley, PA
William S. Snyder, Orange, CA
M.B. Squires Co., Pittsburgh, PA
Standing Stone Antiques, Huntingdon, PA
Stephen A. Steckbeck, Ft. Wayne, IN
Stewart Interiors, Verona, PA
Lillian C. Stigliano, Sharon, PA
Jayne Stoll, Gibsonia, PA
June Stout, Prosperity, PA
Stratford Manor Antiques Shows, Northfield, IL
Frank Swala, Morgantown, WV
Sy's Antiques, Youngstown, OH
Jabe Tarter, Akron, OH
Sally Thomas, Brighton, MI
Gerald W. Thompson, Shepherdstown, WV
Tom's Gun Shop, Eighty-Four, PA
John Toohill, Monroeville, PA
Treasures & Trash, Connellsville, PA
Jim & Lorraine Tucker, Pittsburgh, PA
Ethel Vallos, Youngstown, OH
H. Alan Wainwright, Medina, OH
Walker Valley Antiques, Walker Valley, NY
Ward's Antiques, Fairmont, WV
Jim Welch, Canton, OH
John West, Halltown, MO
Westchester Enterprises, Rye, NY
Western Reserve Antiques, Chagrin Falls, OH
The Whartons Antiques, Wheeling, WV
White Dolphin Antiques, Ft. Lauderdale, FL
Sue & Jim Widder, Cincinnati, OH
Virginia Williams, Cincinnati, OH
Oscar Wilkins Antiques, Mt. Pleasant, PA
Edward G. Wilson, Inc., Philadelphia, PA
Wilson's Antiques, Hickory, PA
Thelma Wolk Antiques, Pittsburgh, PA
Mrs. John Wood, III, Uniontown, PA
The Wooden Bridge Antiques, Flourtown, PA
Jane & Bill Woodring, Westfield, OH
Doris Woodward, Imlay City, MI
Betty Wyatt, Bridgeport, WV

COVER & ILLUSTRATIONS: Charles S. Kovach, Uniontown, Pa.
PHOTOGRAPHS: John K. Gates, Uniontown, Pa.

A 'special' thanks to our dedicated staff. . .the dynamic force that combined experience, energy and enthusiasm to make this book possible. If we neglected acknowledging the effort of anyone who contributed; it was not intentional. . .our sincerest apologies and grateful thanks.

AMERICAN PATTERN GLASS

The method for producing pressed mold glass objects was first patented in the United States in 1829. In the mid 1800's, pressed pattern glass production began to flourish. Early American Pattern Glass (E.A.P.G.) was made of flint glass. The glass formula contained lead that gave the final product its characteristic bell-tone ring or 'ping' when tapped. The higher the content of lead; the more brilliant the glass and clearer the ring. Most E.A.P.G. was produced in limited table settings . . .goblets, wines and the four piece set (butter, creamer, sugar and spooner.)

When the Civil War erupted in 1861, lead was needed for ammunition. Soda lime replaced the lead in glass making. This glass is known as non-flint. Numerous non-flint patterns were made from thereon until the early 1900's. Although some connoisseurs of early American glass will only collect flint glass patterns . . .design should be taken into consideration. "American Coin," one of the most valuable, is a non-flint glass pattern.

The information given on dates, provenances and reproductions are from investigative sources. Reported reproductions are noted. More probably exist or are in the making. It is virtually impossible to keep current. But when is a reproduction not a reproduction? Many times a collector will say, "It must be a reproduction! It's too heavy, the color is not right, the size is wrong, etc." One must be aware that molds became worn or sold to other manufactuerers. The maker may have varied the glass formula or the pattern slightly. These are not reproductions; but reissues.

SECTION ONE — "Clear Glass Patterns" contain listings of patterns that were primarily made in clear only. A few patterns such as "Herringbone" were also made in one other color. These patterns are listed herein and noted as to the color and its related price.

SECTION TWO — "Colored Glass Patterns" list patterns made originally in clear and colors.

All quotations are retail prices for items in mint condition. Prices on items marked (*) 'reproduced' are for the old and not the reproduction.

SECTION ONE

CLEAR GLASS PATTERNS

ACORN VARIANTS
(Acorn, Acorn Band, Acorn Band with Loops, Panelled Acorn Band)
Non-flint. C. 1870's.

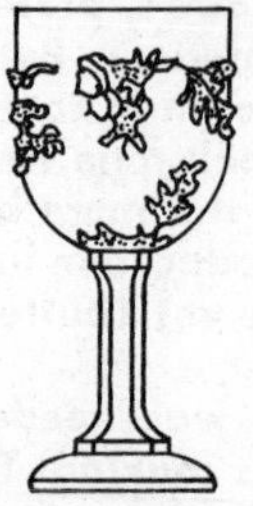

Butter, Covered .... $	27.50
Celery	22.50
Creamer	25.00
Compotes	
Covered	50.00
Open	25.00
Egg Cup	17.50
Goblet	25.00
Pitcher, Water	50.00
Sauces	
Flat	6.00
Footed	12.00
Spooner	18.50
Sugars	
Covered	35.00
Open	25.00

ACTRESS
(Theatrical)
Made by Labelle Glass Co., Bridgeport, Ohio. C. 1870's. Prices listed are for clear and frosted. SEE NOTE:

Bowl. 6", Footed .... $	45.00
Butter, Covered	80.00
Cake Stand. 10"	125.00
Celery. Pinafore	145.00
Cheese, Covered	175.00
Compotes	
Covered. 7". High standard	50.00
Open. 7". Low standard	35.00
Open. 12". High standard	100.00
Creamer	60.00
*Goblet	75.00
Marmalade Jar	100.00
Mug. Pinafore	32.50
*Pickle. "Love's Request is Pickles"	35.00
Pitchers	
Milk	80.00
Water	165.00
Sauces	
Flat	15.00
Footed	20.00
Spooner	55.00
Sugar, Covered	75.00
Tray, Bread. Pinafore	60.00

NOTE: All clear 25% less.
***Reproduced Item**

ALABAMA
(Beaded Bull's Eye and Drape)
Non-flint made by U.S. Glass Co., C. 1898

Butter .... $	30.00
Celery	20.00
Compote, Open. 5"	25.00
Creamer	28.50
Cruet. Stoppered	37.50
Nappy	12.50
Pitcher, Water	45.00
Relish	18.00
Sauce, Flat. 5"	15.00
Spooner	15.00
Sugar, Covered	28.50
Syrup	35.00
Toothpick	20.00

ALASKA
(See Colored Glass Section)

ALMOND THUMBPRINT
(Pointed Thumbprint, Finger Point)

An early flint glass pattern with variants in flint and non-flint. The prices are for flint. Non-flint items are approximately 50% less.

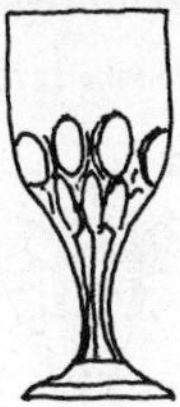

Butter, Covered	$ 85.00
Celery Vase	65.00
Champagne	65.00
Compotes, Covered	
High standard, 7″	55.00
High standard, 10″	85.00
Low standard, 4¾″	40.00
Creamer	65.00
Cruet, Footed	65.00
Egg Cup	32.00
Goblet. All types	50.00
Salts	
Individual	12.00
Large, Flat	20.00
Footed, Covered	40.00
Sugar, Covered	65.00
Sweetmeat jar. 6″. Covered	95.00
Tumbler	40.00
Wine	30.00

AMAZON
(Sawtooth Band)

Non-flint made by Bryce Bros., Pittsburgh, Pa., late 1870's-1880.

Banana Stand	$ 55.00
Bowl. 8″	27.50
Butter, Covered	40.00
Cake Stand. 9¼″	40.00
Celery	25.00
Champagne	30.00
Compotes	
Jelly, 5½″	30.00
Open, 9½″. High standard	45.00
Creamer. Regular	35.00
Goblet	22.50
Nappy, Lion handle	20.00
Pitchers	
Syrup	40.00
Water	50.00
Salts	
Individual	6.00
Master	20.00
Sauces	
Flat	6.50
Footed	10.00
Shakers, Pair	27.50
Spooner. Regular	22.00
Sugar, Covered	35.00
Toothpick	22.50
Tumbler	15.00
Wine	25.00

AMBERETTE
(See KLONDIKE Colored Glass Section)

ANTHEMION

Non-flint made by Model Flint Glass Co., Findlay, Ohio, C. 1890-1900.

Bowl. 8″	$ 25.00
Butter, Covered	42.50
Cake Plate, 9¼″	35.00
Celery	18.50
Creamer	22.50
Marmalade Jar	17.50
Pitcher, Water	50.00
Plates	
10″	15.00
10″. Curled rim	20.00
Sauce. Square	10.00
Spooner	25.00
Sugar, Covered	35.00
Tumbler	25.00

APOLLO

Non-flint first made by Adams & Co., Pittsburgh, Pa., C. Late 1870's. Later by McKee Bros., Pittsburgh, Pa., about 1895.

Bowls	
8″	$ 15.00
9½″	17.50

Butter, Covered	45.00
Cake Stand	35.00
Celery Vase. Etched	30.00
Compote. Open. 7". Low standard	25.00
Creamer	30.00
Goblet	22.50
Lamp. 10" high	40.00
Pitcher, Water	40.00
Sauces	
Flat	8.50
Footed	12.00
Spooner	22.50
Sugar, Covered	35.00
Sugar Shaker. Original top	30.00
Tray, Water	37.50
Tumbler	22.50
Wine	20.00

ARABESQUE

Non-flint produced by Bakewell, Pears & Co., Pittsburgh, Pa. C. 1870's.

Butter, Covered $	50.00
Celery	35.00
Compotes, Covered	
6". High standard	47.50
8". High standard	55.00
8". Low standard	50.00
Creamer, Applied handle	42.50
Goblet	25.00
Pitcher, Water. Applied handle	50.00
Sauce, Flat	8.50
Spooner	25.00

Sugars	
Covered	47.50
Open	27.50

ARCHED GRAPE

Flint and non-flint of the 1870's-late 80's. Prices listed for flint.

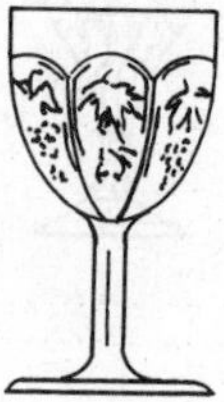

Butter, Covered $	65.00
Celery	50.00
Compotes, Covered	
High standard	75.00
Low standard	60.00
Cordial	25.00
Creamer	55.00
Goblet	35.00
Pitcher, Water	75.00
Sauce	15.00
Spooner	40.00
Sugar, Covered	60.00
Wine	35.00

ARGUS

Bakewell, Pears & Co. made this thumbprint-type pattern in flint glass at Pittsburgh, Pa., in the early 1870's.

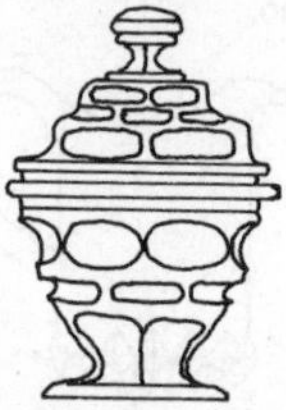

Bitters Bottle $	60.00
Bowl, 5½"	50.00
Butter, Covered	85.00
Celery. Cut	60.00
Champagne	65.00
Cordial	30.00
Creamer	60.00
Decanters	
Pint	75.00
Quart	90.00

Egg Cup	29.50
Goblet	38.50
Lamp, Footed	75.00
Pitcher, Water. Applied handle	185.00
Salt, Open	25.00
Sauce	25.00
Spooner	50.00
Sugar, Covered	75.00
Tumblers	
Footed	45.00
Whiskey, Handled	35.00
Wine	35.00

ART

(Teardrop, Diamond Block, Job's Tears)

Non-flint produced by Adams & Co., Pittsburgh, Pa., in the 1870's. Reissued by U.S. Glass Co. in the early 1890's.

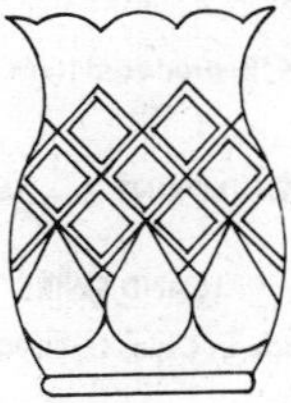

Banana Stand. (scarce)	$ 125.00
Basket, Fruit	75.00
Bowl, Berry, 8"	35.00
Butter, Covered	50.00
Cake Stand, 10"	55.00
Celery	35.00
Compotes	
Covered, Footed. 7"	65.00
Open, Footed. 7½"	45.00
Open, 10"	58.00
Cracker Jar	38.50
Creamer	35.00
Cruet	30.00
Goblet	38.00
Mug	25.00
Pitcher, Water	60.00
Plate, 10"	50.00
Relish	18.00
Sauce, Footed	12.00
Spooner	22.50
Sugar, Covered	40.00
Tumbler	18.50
Wine	20.00

ASHBURTON

A popular pattern produced by several factories from the 1840's to the late 1870's with many variations. Originally made in flint by Bakewell, Pears, New England Glass Co., and others. Later produced in non-flint. Prices listed are for flint.

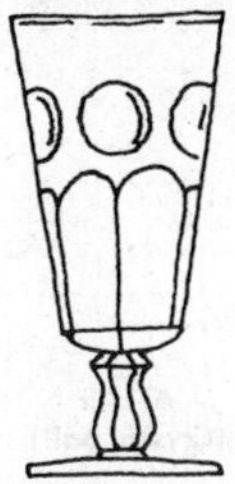

Ale Glass, 5"	$ 75.00
Celerys	
Plain top	75.00
Scalloped top	100.00
Champagne. Cut	85.00
Claret. 5¼"	55.00
Creamer. Applied handle. (scarce)	175.00
Decanters	
Pint. Stoppered	125.00
Quart. Bar lip	85.00
Egg Cup	30.00
Egg Cup, Double	75.00
Goblet, Barrel	40.00
Sauce, Flat	12.00
*Sugar, Covered	110.00
Tumblers	
Flat	65.00
Footed	55.00
Whiskey. Applied handle	80.00
*Wine	50.00

*Reproduced Item

ATLANTA

(Clear Lion Head, Square Lion Head)

Produced by Fostoria Glass Co., Moundsville, W. Va., C. 1890's.

Bowl, Berry. 8½"	$ 22.50
Butter, Covered	48.50
Cake Stand. Large	60.00
Celery	32.50
Compotes	
Covered. 7"	47.50
Open. 7"	37.50

Creamer	40.00
Goblet	38.50
Marmalade Jar	30.00
Relish	16.00
Salt	12.50
Sauce	12.00
Spooner	26.50
Sugars	
Covered	50.00
Open	27.50
Tumbler	35.00

ATLAS
(Crystal Ball)

Non-flint clear glass pattern and occasionally ruby stained made by Bryce Brothers, Mt. Pleasant, Pa. in 1889.

SEE NOTE:

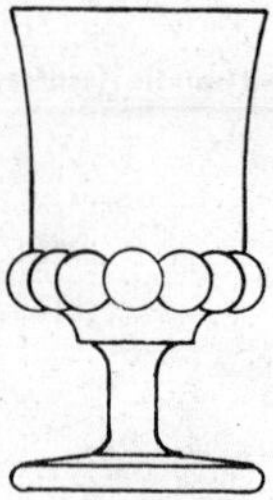

Bowl. 7"	$ 15.00
Butter, Covered	35.00
Cake Stand. 10"	25.00
Celery	12.00
Compotes	
Covered. 8". High standard	85.00
Open. 7". Low standard	30.00
Cordial	20.00
Creamer	25.00
Goblet	20.00
Marmalade Jar, Covered	50.00
Pitchers, Water. Both types	35.00
Salt, Master	20.00
Sauce, Footed	10.00
Spooner	25.00
Tumbler	20.00
Wine	25.00

NOTE: Ruby stained add 100% to price of clear.

BABY FACE
Non-flint. C. 1870

Butter, Covered	$ 165.00
Cake Stand	125.00
Celery Vase	75.00
Compotes	
Covered. 5¼". High standard	125.00
Open. 8". High standard	95.00

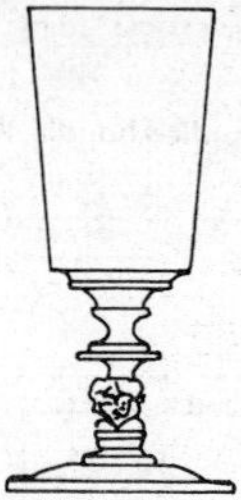

Creamer	125.00
*Goblet	95.00
Pitcher, Water	225.00
Salt	35.00
Sauce, Footed	35.00
Spooner	72.50
*Sugar, Covered	150.00
*Wine	60.00

*Reproduced Item

BABY THUMPRINT, See DAKOTA

BALL AND SWIRL

Made in Ohio. C. 1890's.

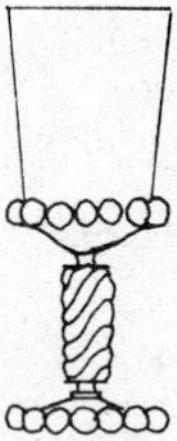

Butter, Covered	$ 25.00
Cake Stand	30.00
Celery	20.00
Compote. Open, High standard	30.00
Cordial	25.00
Creamer	29.50
Decanter. Quart	30.00
Goblet	22.50
Mugs	
Large	15.00
Small	12.50
Pitchers	
Syrup	40.00
Water. Tankard	55.00
Sauce, Footed	10.00
Spooner	20.00
Sugar. Open	22.50
Tumbler	13.50
Wine	17.50

BALTIMORE PEAR

(Twin Pear, Double Pear, Maryland Pear, Fig, Gipsy)

Non-flint originally made by Adams & Co., Pittsburgh, Pa. in the 1880's. Also made by the U.S. Glass Co., in the 1890's. Heavily reproduced.

Bowl, Berry, 9"	$ 28.50
Butter, Covered	50.00
Cake Stand. 9"	45.00
Celery	32.50
Compotes	
Covered. 7". High standard	80.00
Covered. 8¼". Low standard	75.00
Open, Large	50.00
Creamer	45.00
Goblet	35.00
Pickle	20.00
Pitchers	
Milk	50.00
Water	75.00
Plates	
8½"	35.00
10"	50.00
Sauces	
Flat	10.00
Footed	13.50
Spooner	22.50
Sugars	
Covered	50.00
Open	25.00
Tray. 10½"	50.00

BAMBOO

Made in the late 1800's by Pioneer Glass Co., Pittsburgh, Pa. SEE NOTE:

Butter, Covered	$ 35.00
Celery	17.50
Compotes, Covered	
7"	35.00
8"	40.00
9"	45.00
Creamer	25.00
Pitcher, Water	35.00
Relish, 8"	12.50
Sauce, 4"	8.50
Shakers, Pair	27.50
Spooner	15.00
Sugars	
Covered	30.00
Open	15.00
Tumbler	20.00

NOTE: Ruby stained indentations add 100%.

BARBERRY

(Pepper Berry)

Non-flint made in Ohio in the early 1880's.

Butter, Covered. 8" diam	$ 55.00
Butter Pat	6.00
Cake Stand	35.00
Celery	35.00
Compotes	
Covered. 8". Low standard	42.50
Open. 8¼". High standard	30.00
Creamer	45.00
Cup Plate	17.50
Egg Cup	27.50
Goblet	26.50
Pitchers	
Syrup, Pewter top	65.00
Water. Applied handle	75.00
Plate. 6"	26.50
Relish	20.00
Salt, Footed	20.00
Sauces	
Flat	10.00
Footed	13.50
Spooner	22.50
Sugar, Covered	55.00
Wine	20.00

BARLEY

Non-flint originally made by Campbell, Jones and Co. C. 1882 in clear and colored. Possibly by others in varied quality. SEE NOTE:

Butter, Covered	$ 30.00
Cake Stand, 9"	29.50
Celery	20.00
Compotes	
Covered, 8½"	47.50
Open, 6"	20.00
Creamers	
Covered	28.00
Open	15.00
Goblet	22.50
Honey	7.50
Marmalade Jar. (scarce)	50.00
Pitcher, Water	35.00
Plate, 6". (scarce)	50.00
Salt, Master. Wheelbarrow	50.00
Sauces	
Footed, 4"	8.50
Footed, 5"	13.50
Spooner	18.50
Sugars	
Covered	32.00
Open	15.00
Wine	20.00

NOTE: Add 100% for color.

BARRED FORGET-ME-NOT

(See Colored Glass Section)

BASKETWEAVE

(See Colored Glass Section)

BEADED ACORN MEDALLION

Non-flint. C. 1860's-1870's.

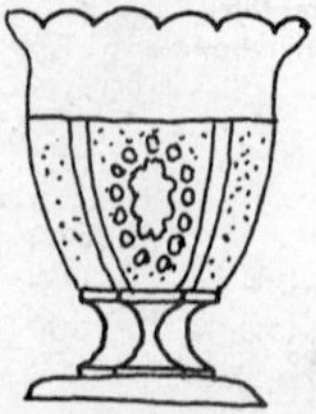

Butter, Covered	$ 50.00
Champagne	35.00
Compotes, Covered	
High standard	55.00
Low standard	45.00
Creamer	50.00
Egg Cup	27.50
Goblet	30.00
Pitcher, Water	55.00
Plate, 6"	25.00
Relish	18.00
Salt, Footed	17.50
Sauce, Flat	10.00
Spooner	20.00
Sugar, Covered	50.00
Wine	20.00

BEADED BAND

C. 1884

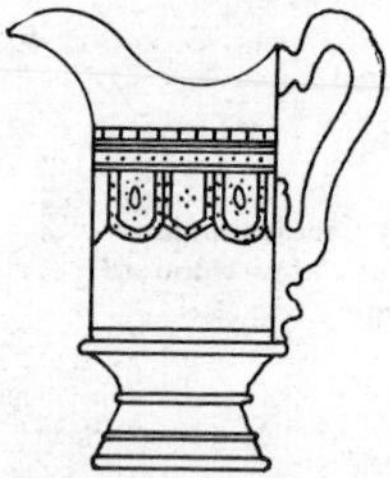

Butter, Covered	$ 35.00
Cake Stand	30.00
Compote, Covered	55.00
Creamer	25.00
Goblet	25.00
Pickle, Covered	45.00
Pitchers	
Syrup	40.00
Water	50.00
Relish. Double	18.00
Sauces	
Flat	7.00
Footed	12.00
Spooner	25.00
Sugars	
Covered	35.00
Open	20.00
Wine	20.00

BEADED DEWDROP

(Wisconsin)

Non-flint made in Pittsburgh, Pa. in the 1880's, Later made by U.S. Glass Co., Indiana in 1898-99.

Bowls	
7½". Panelled	$ 20.00

Oblong, covered	35.00
Butter, Covered	55.00
Cake Stand. 10"	50.00
Celery Tray	17.50
Celery Vase	25.00
Condiment Set, 4-piece in holder	85.00
Creamers	
Large	37.50
Small	25.00
Cruet	25.00
Cup and Saucer	35.00
Goblet	45.00
Mug. Large	27.50
Pitchers	
Syrup	47.50
Water	65.00
Plate. 7", Square	25.00
Salt, Master	25.00
Sauce, Flat. 4"	10.00
Shakers	
Salt and Pepper. Pair	40.00
Sugar	45.00
Spooner	25.00
Sugars	
Large, Covered	55.00
Small	25.00
Toothpick Holder	25.00
Tumbler	35.00
Wine	37.50

BEADED GRAPE
(California)

Non-flint made by U.S. Glass Co., Pittsburgh, Pa. C. Late 1880's. SEE NOTE:

Bowls	
4x7¼" $	12.50
5½"	20.00
6x8½"	22.50
8"	22.50
Butter, Covered	50.00
Cake Stand. 9"	55.00
Celerys	
Tray	27.50
Vase	37.50
Compotes, Covered.	
6½". High standard	55.00
8½". High standard	65.00
Compotes, Open	
4¾". Low standard	45.00
7". High standard	35.00
Creamer	50.00
Cruet, Stoppered	40.00
Egg Cup	18.50
*Goblet	40.00
Pickle	15.00
Pitchers	
Round	55.00
Square	50.00
*Plate. 8½"	22.50
Platter. 7x10"	30.00
*Sauces	
4"	10.00
4½", Handled	15.00
Shakers, Pair	36.50
Spooner	30.00
Sugar, Covered. Flat base	45.00
Toothpick	25.00
*Tumbler	32.50
*Wine	26.50

NOTE: Emerald Green, add 60% to price of clear.

*Reproduced Item

BEADED GRAPE MEDALLION-BANDED

Non-flint made by Boston Silver Glass Co., Cambridge, Mass., C. 1869.

Bowl. 7" $	35.00
Butter	50.00
Celery	35.00
Compotes, Covered	
7¼", 8¼" High standard.	75.00
Low standard	60.00
Creamer	45.00
Egg Cup	29.50

Goblets	
Lady's	25.00
Regular	30.00
Pitcher, Water	90.00
Plate, 6"	22.50
Relish. Dated	25.00
Salts	
Footed, Master	20.00
Oval, Flat	13.50
Round, Flat	12.50
Sauce, Flat	10.00
Spooner	30.00
Sugars	
Covered	65.00
Open	35.00

BEADED LOOP
(Oregon)

Non-flint first made in the 1880's. Re-issued in 1907 as one of the state series.

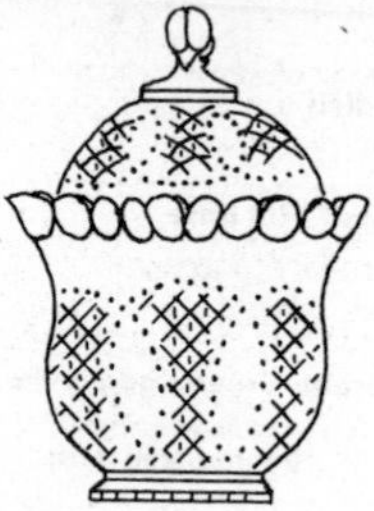

Bowl. 8"	$ 18.50
Butter, Covered	40.00
Cake Stand	37.50
Celery	22.50
Compote, Open. 9"	25.00
Cordial	15.00
Creamer	22.50
Goblet	30.00
Mug	25.00
Pitchers	
Milk	30.00
Syrup	35.00
Water	45.00
Relish	12.50
Sauce, Flat	6.00
Shakers. Salt and Pepper, Pair	35.00
Spooner, Footed	20.00
Sugars	
Covered, Flat	22.50
Covered, Footed	28.50
Open, Footed	15.00
Toothpick Holder	15.00
Tumbler	24.50
Wine	25.00

BEADED TULIP
(Andes)

Non-flint made by McKee Bros., Pittsburgh, Pa. C. 1894

Bowl. Oval	$ 20.00
Butter, Covered	40.00
Compote. Covered, High standard	45.00
Cake Stand	55.00
Creamer	25.00
Goblet	35.00
Marmalade Jar	25.00
Pickle. Oval	20.00
Pitchers	
Milk	45.00
Water	55.00
Plate, 6"	25.00
Sauces	
Flat	10.00
Footed	12.50
Spooner	19.50
Sugar, Covered	40.00
Tray, Water	40.00
Wine	35.00

BEARDED MAN
(Old Man of the Woods, Neptune, Santa Claus, Old Man, Queen Anne)

Non-flint made by LaBelle Glass Co., Bridgeport, Ohio. C. 1879

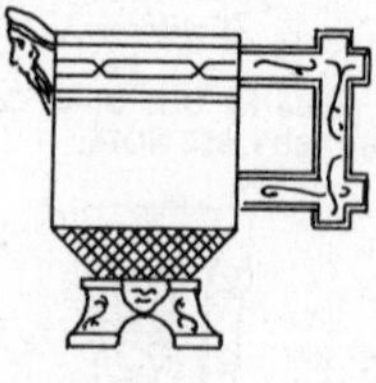

Butter, Covered	$ 50.00
Celery	25.00
Compotes	
Covered	50.00
Open	25.00
Creamer	30.00

Pitcher, Water 65.00
Sauce, Footed, 4½" 20.00
Spooner 19.50
Sugars
  Covered 40.00
  Open 20.00

BELLFLOWER

A fine flint glass pattern first made in the 1830's and attributed to Boston and Sandwich. Later, produced by other firms for many years. There are many variations of this pattern . . .single vine, double vine, fine and coarse rib, knob and plain stems, rayed and plain bases. Type and quality must be considered when evaluating.

Butter, Covered. SV-FR ....$ 100.00
Castor Set. 5-bottle. SV. Pewter stand 250.00
Celery. SV-FR 145.00
Champagnes
  DV-FR. With cut bellflowers 250.00
  SV-FR. Knob stem. Rayed base. Barrel-shaped 120.00
Compotes, Open
  6½" diam. SV-FR 75.00
  7" diam. SV-FR. Scalloped top, Low standard 85.00
  8" diam. SV-CR. High standard .. 60.00
Cordial. SV-FR. Knob stem. Rayed base. Barrel-shaped 75.00
Creamer. SV-FR 150.00
Egg Cups
  DV. With cut bellflowers 225.00
  SV-CR 22.00
  SV-FR 30.00
Decanter. Pint. SV-FR. Bar lip 125.00
Goblets
  DV-FR. With cut bellflowers 250.00
  SV-CR. Barrel-shaped 32.00
  SV-CR. Straight sides 32.00
  SV-FR. Knob stem, Barrel-shaped 50.00
  *SV-FR. Plain stem. Rayed base. Barrel-shaped 30.00
Hat. SV-FR 350.00
Honey. SV-FR 10.00
Lamp, Whale Oil. SV-FR. Brass stem, Marble base 125.00
Mug. SV-FR 225.00
Pitchers
  Milk. DV-FR .... 400.00+
  *Milk. Quart. SV-CR 175.00
  Syrup with lid. SV-FR. Applied handle 225.00
  *Water. SV-FR 250.00
Plate. 6". SV-FR 75.00
Salt, Master. SV-FR. Footed 25.00
*Sauce. Flat. SV-FR 10.00
Spooner. SV-FR 35.00

Sugars
  Covered. SV-CR 60.00
  Open. DV-CR 45.00
  Open. SV-FR 32.00
Tumblers
  DV-CR 65.00
  SV-FR. Footed 150.00
  SV-FR. With cut bellflowers 250.00
Whiskey. 3½". SV-FR 95.00
Wines
  DV-FR. With cut bellflowers. Barrel-shaped 250.00
  SV-FR. Knob stem. Rayed base. Barrel-shaped 85.00
  SV-FR. Straight sides. Plain stem. Rayed base 65.00

*Reproduced Items

BIGLER

Flint. C. 1850's

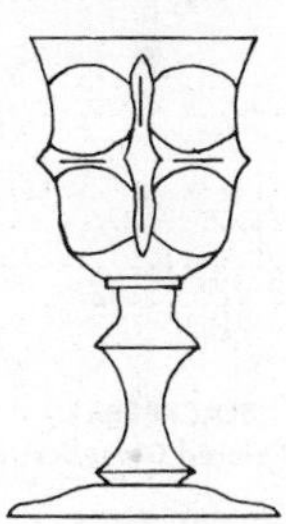

Celery ....$ 75.00
Champagne 85.00
Cordial 85.00
Creamer 75.00
Decanter. Quart 60.00
Egg Cup. Double 45.00
Goblet 40.00
Mug. Applied handle 65.00
Plate, Toddy 50.00

Sauce	12.00
Tumblers	
Water	50.00
Whiskey	55.00
Wine	50.00

BIRD AND STRAWBERRY
(Bluebird)

Non-flint. C. 1890's.

Bowls	
5"	$ 22.50
7½". Footed	45.00
9½". Footed, Oval	50.00
10½". Footed	50.00
Butter, Covered	75.00
Candy. Heart-shaped	50.00
Cake Stand 10"	60.00
Celery Vase	35.00
Compotes, Covered	
High standard, 6½"	85.00
Low standard, 6"	70.00
Creamer	45.00
Goblet	50.00
Pitcher, Water	150.00
Plate. 12"	125.00
Punch Cup	20.00
Sauces	
Flat	15.00
Footed	20.00
Sugars	
Covered	65.00
Open	35.00
Tumbler	28.50
Wine	32.00

BLACKBERRY
(See Colored Glass Section)

BLAZE

Flint made by New England Glass Co., C. 1860.

Bowl. 8"	$ 35.00
Butter, Covered	65.00
Celery	65.00
Champagne	55.00
Cheese, Covered	60.00

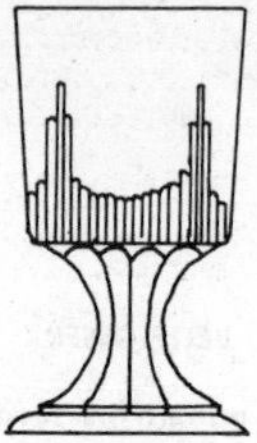

Compotes	
Covered. Low standard, 6"	65.00
Open. High standard, 8"	65.00
Open. Low standard, 8", 9"	50.00
Cordial	55.00
Creamer	75.00
Egg Cup	35.00
Egg Cup. Handled	45.00
Goblet	50.00
Plates, 6", 7"	30.00
Salt. Rectangular	30.00
Sauces, 4", 5"	12.50
Spooner	39.50
Sugar, Covered	85.00
Tumblers	
Footed	45.00
Lemonade	40.00
Wine	55.00

BLEEDING HEART

Non-flint. C. 1870-80's.

Bowl. Waste	$ 30.00
Butter, Covered	55.00
Cake Stand. 10"	65.00
Compotes	
Covered. High standard. 8½"	65.00
Covered. Low standard. Oval	50.00
Open. Low standard. 8½"	25.00
Creamer. Applied handle	50.00
Egg Cup	35.00
Goblets	
Knob stem	35.00
Plain stem	30.00
Mug. 3¼"	28.50

Pitcher, Water. Applied handle	125.00
Platter. Oval	65.00
Relish. 4-sections	65.00
Sauces	
Flat	8.50
Flat, oval	25.00
Spooner	25.00
Sugar, Covered	65.00
Tumbler, Footed	32.50
Wine	75.00

BLOCK AND FAN
(Romeo)

Non-flint made by Richards & Hartley Glass Co., Tarentum, Pa., late 1880's. SEE NOTE:

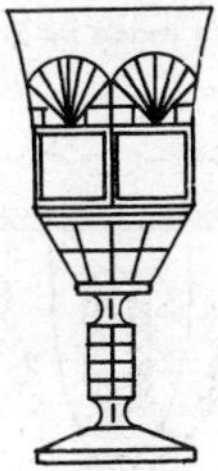

Bowls	
7½" ... $	17.50
10"	20.00
Butter, Covered	37.50
Cake Stand, 10"	32.50
Celery Tray	15.00
Celery Vase	17.50
Compote, Open. 8". High standard	30.00
Cracker Jar	40.00
Creamer	22.00
Cruets, Stoppered	
Large	35.00
Small	20.00
Goblet	45.00
Pitchers	
Milk	25.00
Water	35.00
Plate, 10"	22.50
Relish, Oblong	15.00
Sauces	
Flat, 3¾"	5.00
Footed	9.00
Square	6.00
Shakers	
Salt and Pepper, Pair	50.00
Sugar	35.00
Spooner	22.50
Sugar, Covered	35.00
Tumbler	25.00
Wine	35.00

NOTE: Ruby stained add 100%.

BOW-TIE

Non-flint made by Thompson Glass Co., Uniontown, Pa., C. 1888-1890.

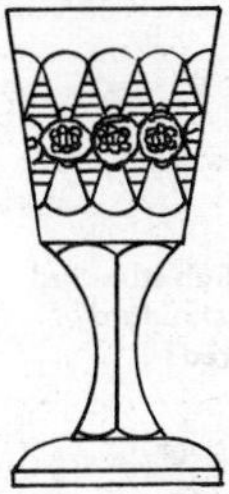

Bowls	
4" ... $	25.00
8"	35.00
10" deep	65.00
Butter, Covered	65.00
Cake Stand. Large, 9" diam	50.00
Compotes, Open	
High standard, 10"	85.00
Low standard, 6½"	45.00
Creamer	45.00
Goblet	45.00
Honey, Covered	55.00
Marmalade Jar	45.00
Pitchers	
Milk	40.00
Water	65.00
Relish, Rectangular	25.00
Salt, Individual	12.00
Sauce, Flat	15.00
Spooner	30.00
Sugars	
Covered	65.00
Open	40.00

BROKEN COLUMN
(Irish Column, Rattan and Notched Rib)

Made in Findlay, Ohio about 1891-92 by Columbia Glass Co. Later made by U.S. Glass Co. SEE NOTE:

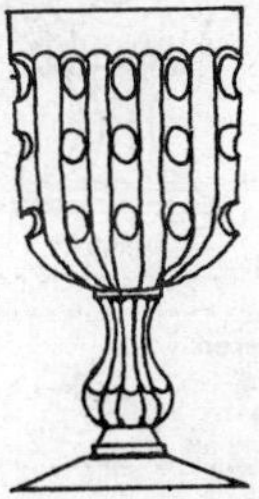

Banana Stand ... $	75.00

Basket. Applied handle, 12x 15"	85.00
Bowls	
6" Covered	35.00
7½"	35.00
Butter, Covered	45.00
Cake Stand, 9"	55.00
Carafe, Water	50.00
Celery, Oval	15.00
Celery Vase	35.00
Champagne	55.00
Compotes	
Covered. 10", High standard	50.00
Open. 7", High standard	30.00
Cracker Jar, Covered	75.00
Creamer	30.00
Cruet	35.00
*Goblet	35.00
Marmalade Jar, Covered	55.00
Mug	40.00
Pickle Castor-Tongs	75.00
Pitchers	
Syrup	50.00
Water	55.00
Punch Cup	20.00
Relish. 5x8"	18.50
Salt, Footed	5.00
Shakers, Pair	35.00
Sugar, Covered	45.00
Tumbler	30.00
Wine	45.00

NOTE: Red notches add 100%.

*Reproduced Item

BUCKLE

A flint and non-flint made by Gillinder & Sons in Philadelphia, Pa., in the 1870's. Possibly made earlier by Sandwich Glass Co., in Massachusetts. SEE NOTE:

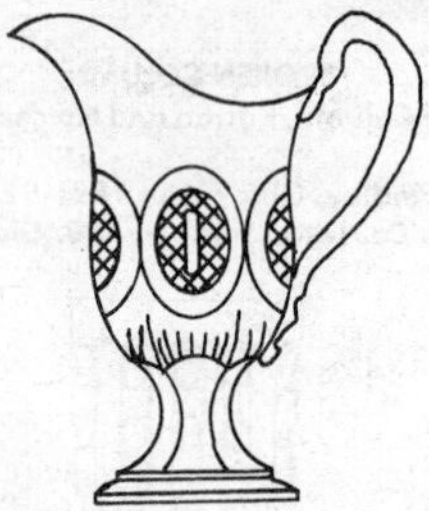

Butter, Covered $	55.00
Champagne	75.00
Compotes, Covered	
High standard	75.00
Low standard	65.00
Creamer	25.00
Egg Cup	18.00
Goblet	25.00
Pickle	20.00
Pitcher, Water	500.00
Salts	
Individual	12.50
Master, Footed	25.00
Sauce	7.50
Spooner	17.50
Sugars	
Covered	30.00
Open	22.50
Tumbler	37.50
Wine	50.00

NOTE: Add 50% for flint.

BUCKLE, BANDED
(Union)

Flint and non-flint made by King, Son & Co. C. 1875. SEE NOTE:

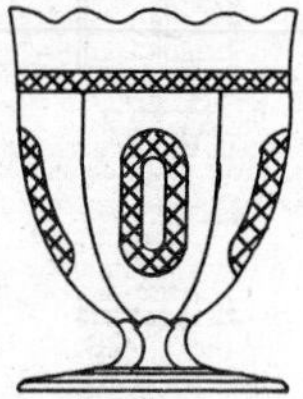

Butter, Covered $	50.00
Compote, Covered	60.00
Cordial	22.50
Creamer	22.50
Egg Cup	22.00
Goblet	28.50
Pickle, Oval	15.00
Pitchers	
Syrup	35.00
Water	165.00
Salt, Master. Footed	18.50
Sauce	10.00
Spooner	18.50
Sugar. Open	20.00
Tumbler, Bar	32.50
Wine	25.00

NOTE: Add 50% for flint.

BUCKLE, LATE
(Belt Buckle, Jasper)
Non-flint. C. 1880's.

BUCKLE WITH STAR
Non-flint. C. 1880's. SEE NOTE:

Bowls	
6". Covered $	20.00
8". Oval	15.00

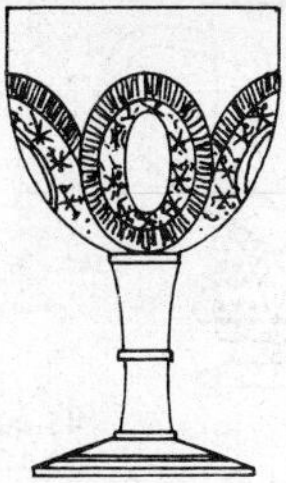

BUCKLE, LATE **BUCKLE WITH STAR**

10". Oval	25.00
Butter, Covered	32.50
Cake Stand	30.00
Celery	25.00
Compotes	
Covered. 7". High standard	50.00
Open. 9½". High standard	30.00
Open. 9". Low standard	20.00
Creamer	35.00
Goblet	25.00
Pitchers	
Syrup	40.00
Water	45.00
Relish	10.00
Salt, Footed	15.00
Sauces	
Flat, 4"	8.50
Footed	12.00
Spooner	20.00
Sugar. Open	15.00
Tumbler	20.00
Wine	17.50

NOTE: Prices for both patterns . . .same value.

BUDDED IVY

Non-flint. C. 1870 SEE NOTE:

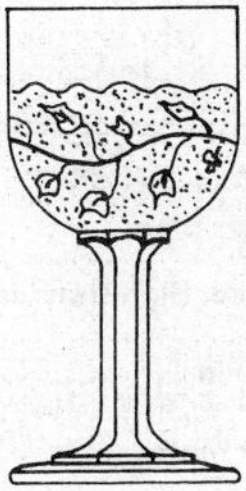

Butter, Covered	$ 42.50
Compotes	
Covered. High standard	45.00
Open. High standard	25.00
Creamer	40.00
Egg Cup	20.00
Goblet	30.00
Pitchers	
Syrup	30.00
Water. Applied handle	50.00
Relish	17.50
Salt, Footed	17.50
Sauce, Flat	7.50
Spooner	25.00
Sugar, Covered	45.00

NOTE: Stippled Ivy is a contemporary of Budded Ivy . . .prices comparable.

BULL'S EYE
(Lawrence)

Flint made by New England Glass Co. in the 1850's.

Butter, Covered	$ 150.00
Carafe. Quart	65.00
Celery	65.00
Champagne	85.00
Cologne Bottle	85.00
Creamer	125.00
Decanter. Quart. Bar lip	125.00
Egg Cup	50.00
Egg Cup, Covered	165.00
Goblet	65.00
Pitcher, Water	85.00
Relish. Oval	45.00
Salt Dip	35.00
Salt, Master. Footed	50.00
Spooner	45.00
Sugar, Covered	110.00
Tumbler, Flat	85.00
Whiskey	87.50
Wine	45.00

BULL'S EYE WITH DIAMOND POINT
(Owl)
Flint. C. 1850's.

Butter, Covered	$ 200.00
Celery	100.00
Champagne	125.00
Cologne Bottle	125.00
Cordial	100.00

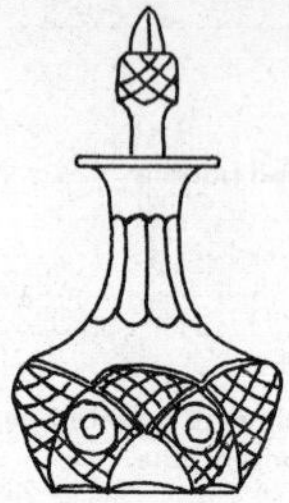

Creamer	175.00
Decanters	
Bar lip, Quart	175.00
With stopper, Quart	225.00
Egg Cup	85.00
Goblet	95.00
Honey	35.00
Pitcher, 10¼". Tankard	225.00
Spooner	70.00
Sugar, Covered	150.00
Tumbler	100.00
Tumble-up	225.00
Wine	65.00

BULL'S EYE WITH FLEUR-DE-LIS

Flint. C. 1850

Butter, Covered	$ 175.00
Celery	87.50
Cordial	75.00
Creamer (scarce)	250.00
Decanter. Quart. Bar lip	150.00
Goblet	75.00
Mug, Handled	150.00
Pitcher, Water. (scarce)	275.00
Salt, Master. Footed	60.00
Sugar, Covered	135.00
Wine	55.00

BUTTON ARCHES

Clear and clear with ruby stained tops, non-flint, C. 1890's. Prices listed are for clear only. SEE NOTE:

Bowl. 8"	$ 20.00

Butter, Covered	45.00
Cake Stand, 9"	32.50
Compote, Jelly	17.50
Creamer	15.00
Custard Cup	6.50
Goblet	25.00
Mug, Small	10.00
Pitchers	
Milk	30.00
Water, Tankard	55.00
Shakers. Original tops. Pair	20.00
Sauce	5.00
Sugar, Covered	35.00
Toothpick	12.50
Tumbler	20.00
Wine	15.00

NOTE: Ruby stained items demand approximately 25% more than clear. Exception: Souvenir-types less 25%.

CABBAGE LEAF (CLEAR)

Non-flint. C. 1880's. SEE NOTE:

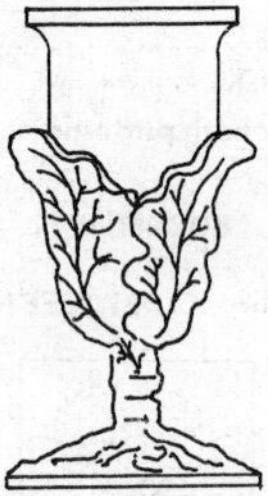

Butter, Covered	$ 85.00
Celery	55.00
Cheese, Covered	75.00
Compote, Covered. High standard	100.00
Creamer	45.00
Pickle. Leaf-shaped	30.00
Pitcher, Water	75.00
Plate. 8". Rabbit center	45.00
Sauce. 3½"	15.00
Spooner	30.00
Sugar, Covered	75.00

NOTE: Add approximately 20% for frosted. Heavily reproduced in both forms and also in color.

CABBAGE ROSE

Non-flint made in Wheeling, W. Va. C. 1870-1881.

Basket, Handled. 12x14" ....$	75.00
Bowl, Berry. 8½". Oval	27.50
Butter, Covered	65.00
Cake Stands	
9"	40.00
11"	62.50
Celery Vase	47.50
Champagne	27.50
Compotes	
Covered. High standard. 6", 7" ..	55.00
Covered. High standard. 8", 9" ..	65.00
Open. High standard. 7½"	35.00
Creamer. Applied handle	57.50
Egg Cup	35.00
*Goblet	42.50
Pitcher, Water	100.00
Relish. 5x8½"	20.00
Salt, Master. Footed	22.00
Sauces, Flat	
4"	7.50
7"	12.50
Spooner	35.00
Sugars	
Covered	57.50
Open	25.00
Tumbler	40.00
Wine	40.00

*Reproduced Item

CABLE

Flint. C. 1850's. SEE NOTE:

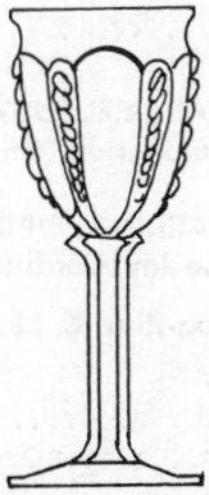

Butter, Covered ....$	85.00
Celery	75.00
Champagne	125.00
Compote, Open	40.00
Creamer. (rare)	350.00+
Decanters	
Pint	100.00
Quart. Ground stopper	175.00
Egg Cups	
Covered	225.00
Open	45.00
Goblet	60.00
Lamps	
All glass	125.00
Hand lamp	100.00
Marble base	85.00
Pitchers	
Syrup	125.00
Water (rare)	300.00+
Plate. 6"	75.00
Salts	
Flat	15.00
Footed	45.00
Sauce, Flat	10.00
Spooner	50.00
Sugar, Covered	85.00
Tumbler, footed. (rare)	150.00+
Wine	125.00

NOTE: Rare as in opaques.

CANADIAN

Non-flint. C. 1870's.

Butter, Covered ....$	50.00
Celery	37.50
Compotes	
Covered. 7". High standard	50.00
Open. 7". High standard	30.00
Creamer	40.00
Goblet	40.00
Marmalade Jar	35.00
Pitcher, Water	65.00
Plates	
6"	25.00
10". Handled	32.50
Sauce, Flat	10.00
Spooner	32.50

Sugars	
Covered	50.00
Open	22.50
Wine	35.00

CANDLEWICK
(Barred Raindrops, Banded Raindrops, Cole)

Non-flint. C. 1880's. SEE NOTE:

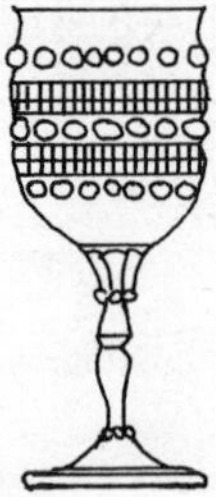

Butter, Covered $	35.00
Celery	20.00
Compote. Covered. 7". High std.	45.00
Creamer	22.50
Cup and Saucer	25.00
Goblet	20.00
Pitcher, Water	40.00
Plate. 5x9"	25.00
Relish, Square	20.00
Sauce, Flat	6.50
Shakers, Pair	28.50
Spooner	18.50
Sugar, Covered	35.00

NOTE: Rare in color.

CANE
(See Colored Glass Section)

CANE AND ROSETTE
(Flower Panelled Cane)

Non-flint. C. Mid-1880's.

Bowl, Covered. Octagonal $	25.00
Butters	
Covered, Footed	30.00
Flat	20.00
Cake Stand. Large	25.00
Compote, Covered. 8". High std.	40.00
Creamer	25.00
Egg Cup	17.50
Goblet	14.00
Pitcher, Water	30.00
Sauce, Footed	7.50
Sugar, Covered	30.00
Wine	15.00

CAPE COD

Non-flint. C. 1870's.

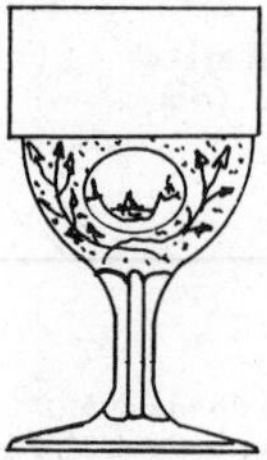

Bowl. Small. 6", Handled $	20.00
Butter, Covered	50.00
Celery	30.00
Compotes, Covered	
7". High standard	50.00
12". High standard	75.00
Compote, Open. 7". High standard	25.00
Creamer	27.50
Cup and Saucer	27.50
Goblet	35.00
Marmalade Jar	40.00
Pitchers	
Milk	35.00
Water	50.00
Plates	
8". Open handles	25.00
10". Handled	35.00
Sauces	
Flat, 4"	10.00
Footed, 4"	12.00
Spooner	27.50
Sugar, Covered	50.00
Wine	30.00

CARAMEL SLAG
(See General Section "Greentown")

CARDINAL BIRD
(Blue Jay, Cardinal)

Non-flint. C. 1870

Butters	
Covered $	55.00
3-Birds	65.00

Cake Stand	45.00
Creamer	37.50
Goblet	40.00
Pitcher, Water	100.00
Sauces	
Flat, 4″	15.00
Footed, 4½″	17.50
Footed, 5½″	20.00
Spooner	27.50
Sugars	
Covered	55.00
Open	22.50

CATHEDRAL
(See Colored Glass Section)

CHAIN

Non-flint made by R.B. Curling and Sons, Fort Pitt Glass Works, Pittsburgh, Pa. in the 1880's.

Butter, Covered $	42.00
Cake Stand. 9″	28.50
Compote, Covered	35.00
Cordial	25.00
Creamer	17.50
Goblet	20.00
Pitcher, Water	35.00
Plate. 7″	15.00
Relish, Oval	15.00
Sauces	
Flat	10.00
Footed	14.00
Spooner	18.50
Sugar, Covered	40.00
Wine	25.00

CHAIN WITH STAR

Non-flint. C. 1880's.

Butter, Covered $	35.00
Cake Stand. 10½″	30.00
Compotes	
Covered. High standard	45.00
Open. Low standard	27.50
Creamer	35.00
Goblet	18.50
Pickle, Oval	15.00
Pitcher, Water	40.00
Plates	
7″	22.50
13½″, Handled	35.00
Sauces	
Flat	8.50
Footed	12.50
Spooner	22.50
Sugars	
Covered	35.00
Open	18.00
Wine	22.50

CHANDELIER
(Crown Jewels)

Non-flint by O'Hara Glass Co., Pittsburgh, Pa. C. 1880's.

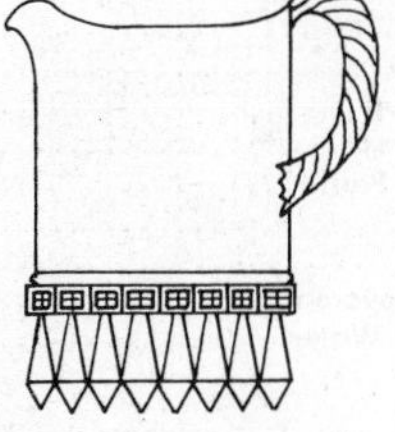

Butter, Covered $	60.00
Cake Stand. 10″	75.00
Celery	35.00
Compotes	
Covered. High standard	75.00
Open. High standard	40.00

Creamer	40.00
Goblet	65.00
Pitcher, Water	75.00
Salt	12.00
Sauces	
Flat	12.50
Footed	18.50
Shakers. Pair	45.00
Spooner	30.00
Sugars	
Covered	50.00
Open	28.50
Tray, Water	55.00
Tumbler	25.00
Wine	30.00

CHECKERBOARD

Non-flint made by Westmoreland Glass Co. and Specialty Co., Pa., in the 1900's. Heavily reproduced in clear and colors.

Butter, Covered	$ 25.00
Celery Tray	12.50
Celery Vase	20.00
Cheese, Covered	22.50
Creamer	20.00
Goblet	15.00
Honey, Square, Footed, Covered	25.00
Pitchers	
Milk	25.00
Water	35.00
Plate, 10"	17.50
Punch Cup	7.50
Sauce, Flat	6.00
Shakers, Pair	20.00
Sherbet	10.00
Spooner	16.50
Sugar, Covered	25.00
Tumbler, Water	12.00
Wine	12.50

CHERRY

Clear and milk glass pattern made by Bakewell, Pears & Co., Pittsburgh, Pa. in the 1870's. SEE NOTE:

*Butter, Covered	$ 55.00
Compotes	
Covered. High standard	55.00
Open. High standard	40.00
*Creamer	40.00
*Goblet	28.50
Sauce, Flat	12.00
Spooner	25.00
*Sugars	
Covered	55.00
Open	32.50

NOTE: Milk glass extremely rare . . .add 100% plus.

*Reproduced Item

CLASSIC

Clear and frosted non-flint produced by Gillinder & Sons, Philadelphia, Pa., in the late 1870's-80's.

Butter, Covered	$ 175.00
Celery	125.00
Compotes	
Covered	150.00
Open	100.00
Creamer	100.00
Goblet	175.00
Pitcher, Water	250.00
Plates	
Portrait	195.00
Warrior	150.00
Sauce	25.00
Sauce, Log feet	32.50
Spooner	85.00

Spooner. Log feet	100.00
Sugars	
Covered	150.00
Open	95.00
Sweetmeat	85.00

CLEAR DIAGONAL BAND

Non-flint. C. 1880's

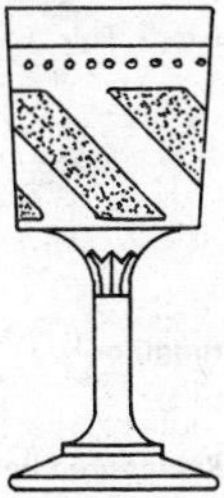

Butter, Covered $	37.50
Celery	22.00
Compotes	
Covered. High standard	38.50
Covered. Low standard	30.00
Creamer	25.00
Goblet	22.50
Marmalade Jar	25.00
Pitcher, Water	27.50
Plate. 7"	16.50
Platter. "Excelsior"	40.00
Sauces	
Flat	5.00
Footed	10.00
Spooner	18.50
Sugar, Covered	37.50
Wine	15.00

CLEAR RIBBON

Non-flint. C. 1880's.

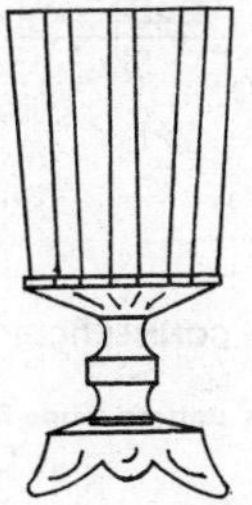

Butter, Covered $	27.50
Celery	17.50
Compote, Covered. Large	35.00
Creamer	27.50
Goblet	17.50
Pitcher, Water	32.50
Relish	10.00
Sauce, Footed	10.00
Spooner	15.00
Sugar, Covered	30.00
Tray, Bread, "Give Us. . ."	25.00

CLEMATIS

Non-flint. C. 1876.

Butter, Covered $	35.00
Creamer	35.00
Goblet	27.50
Lamp, 12". Iron base	35.00
Pitcher. Applied handle	42.00
Relish	12.00
Sauce, Flat	10.00
Spooner	25.00
Sugars	
Covered	40.00
Open	25.00

COIN-COLUMBIAN
(Spanish Coin)

Non-flint. C. 1890's. Prices listed for clear. SEE NOTE:

Butter, Covered $	125.00
Cake Stand	40.00
Celery	75.00

Compotes	
Covered. 8″	75.00
Open. 7″	55.00
Creamer	65.00
Cruet	100.00
*Goblet	55.00
Pitchers	
Syrup	65.00
Water	65.00
Sauce	12.00
Shakers, Pair	50.00
Spooner	45.00
Sugars	
Covered	60.00
Open	35.00
*Toothpick	25.00
Tray, Water	40.00
*Tumbler	25.00

NOTE: Frosted demands approximately 3 times price of clear.

*Reproduced Item

COIN-U.S.

Non-flint frosted and clear pattern made in Wheeling W. Va. in 1892 for three or four months. Production was stopped by U.S. Treasury because real coins were used in the molds.

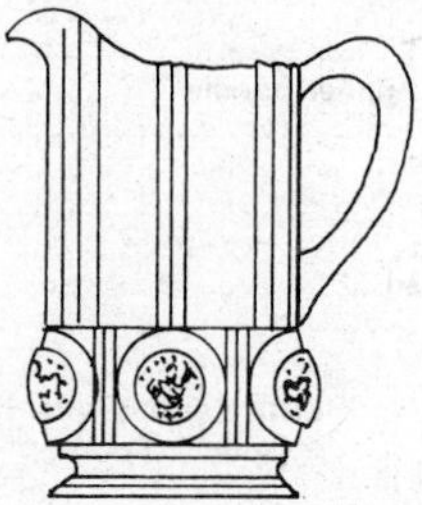

Bowls	
6″	$ 300.00
9″	500.00
Waste	250.00
Cake Stand. 10″	375.00
Celery Tray	200.00
Celery Vase	325.00
Champagne	300.00
Claret	300.00
Compote, Covered. 7″. High std.	400.00
Compotes, Open.	
7″. High standard	225.00
8″. High standard	325.00
Creamer	375.00
Cruet. Stoppered	500.00
Epergne	500.00
Goblets	
Flair top	325.00
Regular	275.00
Lamps	
Round font	300.00
Square font	350.00
Mug, Handled	350.00
Pickle	175.00
Pitchers	
Syrup	500.00
Water	500.00
Sauces	
Flat	110.00
Footed	150.00
Shakers. Original tops. Pair	325.00
Spooner	225.00
Sugars	
Covered	300.00
Open	125.00
*Toothpick	125.00
Trays	
Bread. 7x 10″	350.00
Water. 8″. Rectangular	300.00
Tumbler	225.00
Wine	250.00

*Reproduced Item

COLORADO

(See Colored Glass Section)

COMET

Flint made by Boston and Sandwich Glass Co. in the late 1840's, early 1850's. Horn of Plenty is sometimes referred to by the same name, but is not related in design.

Goblet	$ 75.00
Pitcher, Water	375.00
Tumblers	
Water	125.00
Whiskey	125.00

CONNECTICUT

Non-flint States' pattern made by U.S. Glass Co. C. 1895.

Bowls	
4″	$ 10.00

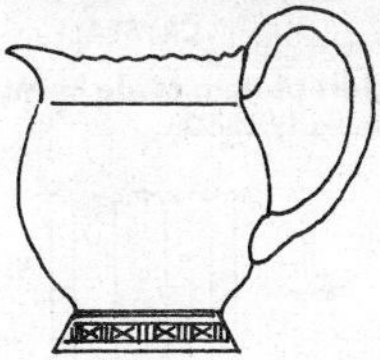

8″	15.00
Butter, Covered	22.50
Cake Stand. 10″	22.50
Celery Tray	12.00
Celery Vase	15.00
Creamer	16.50
Pitchers	
½ Gallon	30.00
Milk	22.50
Relish	10.00
Shakers, Pair	15.00
Tumblers	
Lemonade	10.00
Water	8.50

CORD AND TASSEL

Non-flint of the early 1870's, made by various companies.

Butter, Covered $	45.00
Cake Stand. 9½″	37.50
Celery	32.50
Compotes	
Covered. 10″. High standard	75.00
Open. Low standard	35.00
Creamer	40.00
Egg Cup	25.00
Goblet	30.00
Lamp. Handled	60.00
Pitchers	
Syrup	60.00
Water. Applied handle	55.00
Sauce, Flat	8.00
Spooner	27.50
Sugar, Covered	42.00
Tumbler, Water	25.00
Wine	25.00

CORDOVA

Non-flint made by O'Hara Glass Co., Pittsburgh, Pa. in the early 1890's.

Butter, Covered $	25.00
Cake Stand. 9″	27.50
Celery	20.00
Compotes	
Covered. High standard	30.00
Open. High standard	25.00
Creamer	22.50
Cruet	18.50
Pitchers	
Milk	28.00
Syrup	25.00
Water	35.00
Sauce, Flat	7.50
Spooner	15.00
Sugar, Covered	25.00
Toothpick	12.50
Tumbler	15.00

COSMOS

(See General Section)

COTTAGE

(Dinner Bell, Fine Cut Band)

Non-flint made by Adams & Co., Pittsburgh, Pa. in the late 1870's. SEE NOTE:

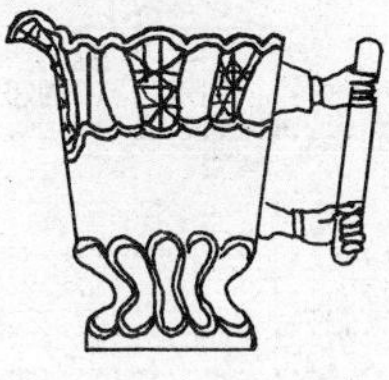

Banana Stand $	25.00
Bowls	
7″	20.00
9½″, Oval	22.50
Butter, Covered	28.50
Cake Stand. 9″	30.00
Celery Vase	20.00
Compotes	
Jelly	17.50

Open, 7". Low standard	25.00
Creamer	18.50
Cruet	25.00
Cup and Saucer	22.50
Goblet	18.50
Pitchers	
Milk	27.50
Water	35.00
Plates	
6", 7"	15.00
8", 9"	20.00
Relish	10.00
Sauces	
Flat	6.50
Footed	10.00
Shakers, Pair	20.00
Spooner	18.00
Sugar, Covered	27.50
Tray, Water	22.50
Tumbler	18.00
Wine	16.50

NOTE: Scarce in dark green

CROESUS
(See Colored Glass Section)

CROW FOOT
(Turkey Track, Yale)

Non-flint made by McKee Glass Co. C. Late 1880's-90's.

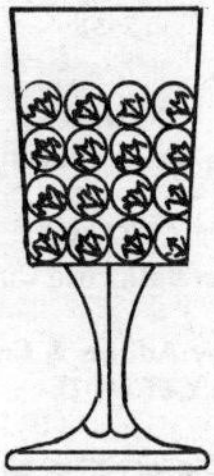

Butter, Covered $	30.00
Cake Stand	30.00
Celery	20.00
Compotes	
Covered	35.00
Open	20.00
Cordial	15.00
Creamer	22.50
Goblet	25.00
Pitchers	
Syrup	22.50
Water	35.00
Sauce, 5½"	9.50
Shakers, Pair	25.00
Spooner	18.50
Sugar, Covered	30.00
Tumbler	15.00

CRYSTAL

A flint glass pattern made by McKee Bros., Pgh., Pa. in the early 1860's.

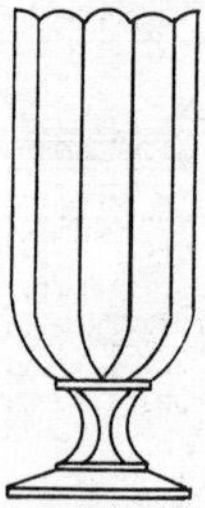

Ale Glass $	35.00
Bowls	
8"	50.00
10"	65.00
Butter, Covered	65.00
Celery	50.00
Champagne	35.00
Compotes	
6", Covered. High standard	50.00
8", Covered. High standard	65.00
10", Open. High standard	60.00
Cordial	32.50
Creamer	65.00
Decanter. Quart	60.00
Egg Cup	30.00
Goblet	35.00
Pitcher, Water	85.00
Sauce	15.00
Spooner	35.00
Sugar, Covered	75.00
Tumblers	
Bar	28.50
Footed	50.00
Wine	40.00

CRYSTAL QUEEN

Non-flint made by Northwood Co., Indiana, Pa., later by Cambridge Glass Co. C. Late 1890's-1900.

Bowl. 8" $	18.50
Butter, Covered	38.50
Celery Tray	18.50

Celery Vase	22.50
Compote, Covered. 9". High std.	45.00
Creamer	20.00
Cruet, Stoppered	22.50
Pitchers	
Syrup	20.00
Water	30.00
Spooner	16.50
Sugar, Open	22.00
Tumbler	10.00

CRYSTAL WEDDING
(Crystal Anniversary, Collins)

Non-flint made by Adams Glass Co., Pittsburgh, Pa. in the late 1880's. SEE NOTE:

Banana Bowl	$ 55.00
Bowl. 8"	25.00
Butter, Covered	39.50
Cake Stand. 10"	65.00
Celery Vase	28.50
Compotes	
Covered. High standard	75.00
Covered. Low standard	55.00
Open. Low standard	35.00
Creamer	32.50
Goblet	27.50
Pitcher, Water	50.00
Sauces	
Flat	7.50
Footed	10.00
Shakers, Pair	30.00
Spooner	25.00
Sugar, Covered	45.00

NOTE: Also found in frosted and ruby stained . . .add 100%. Heavily reproduced in clear, milk glass and enamel trim.

CUPID AND VENUS
(Guardian Angel, Minerva)

Non-flint made by Hartley Glass Co., Tarentum, Pa. in the late 1870's.

Bowls	
7½". Footed	$ 30.00
8". Covered, Footed	55.00
9". Oval	27.50
10". Footed, Scalloped rim	45.00
Butter, Covered	60.00
Celery Vase	42.50
Champagne	55.00
Compotes	
Covered. 8". High standard	57.50
Covered. 9½". Low standard	50.00
Open. 7½". Low standard	35.00
Open. 9½". High standard	50.00
Cordial	50.00
Creamer	40.00
Cruet, Stoppered	37.50
Goblet	55.00
Marmalade Jar	50.00
Mugs	
2½"	27.50
3½"	30.00
Pitchers	
Milk	50.00
Water	65.00
Plate. 10"	29.50
Relish	18.00
Sauces	
Flat	8.50
Footed, 3½"	7.50
Footed, 4"	8.50
Footed, 4½"	10.00
Spooner	30.00
Sugar, Covered	55.00
Tray, Bread	35.00
Wine. (scarce)	72.50

CURRANT

Non-flint. C. 1870's.

Butter, Covered	$ 55.00
Cake Stand. 9½"	60.00
Celery Vase	42.50

Compotes, Covered	
8". High standard	55.00
8". Low standard	50.00
Cordial	32.50
Creamer. Applied handle	50.00
Goblet	28.50
Pitcher, Water	60.00
Plates, Oval	
5x7"	25.00
6x9"	30.00
Relish	12.50
Salt. Footed	20.00
Sauces	
Flat	8.50
Footed	12.50
Spooner	27.50
Sugar, Covered	50.00
Tumbler. Footed	28.50
Wine	32.50

CURRIER AND IVES

Non-flint made by Bellaire Glass Co. at Findlay, Ohio in the late 1880's. Although named after the famous printmaker of its era, there was no connection between the companies. SEE NOTE:

Bowl, Oval. 10" $	30.00
Butter, Covered	50.00
Compotes	
Covered	50.00
Open	40.00
Cordial	22.50
Creamer	25.00
Cup and Saucer	30.00
Egg Cup	18.50
Goblets	
Knob stem	22.50
Plain stem	18.50
Lamp. 9½" high	65.00
Pitchers	
Milk	30.00
Water	37.50
Plates	
8"	20.00
10"	30.00
Relish	12.00
Sauces	
Flat	8.50
Oval	15.00
Shakers, Pair	40.00
Spooner	20.00
Sugar, Covered	45.00
Tray, Water. "Bulky Mule"	50.00
Wine	17.50

NOTE: Rare in color.

CURTAIN
(Sultan)

Non-flint produced by Bryce Bros., Pittsburgh, Pa., in the 1870's through early 1880's.

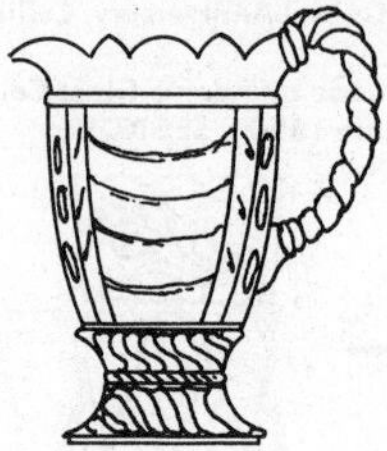

Bowls	
8" $	15.00
Waste	16.50
Butter, Covered	45.00
Cake Stand. 9½"	30.00
Celery Vase	27.50
Compotes	
Covered. High standard	40.00
Open. High standard	25.00
Creamer	35.00
Goblet	26.00
Mug, Large	17.50
Pitchers	
Milk	25.00
Water	50.00
Plate, 7". Square	19.50
Sauce, Footed. Collared	12.50
Shakers, Pair	25.00
Spooner	27.50
Sugars	
Covered	38.50
Open	17.50
Tumbler	23.50

CUT LOG
(Cat's Eye and Block, Ethol)

Non-flint. C. 1880's.

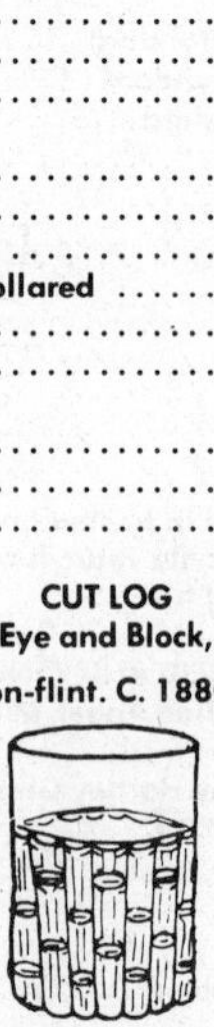

Bowls	
7"	15.00

10". Deep, Footed, Scalloped	50.00
Butter, Covered	40.00
Cake Stands	
Large	60.00
Small	28.50
Celery Vase	28.00
Compotes	
Covered. 5½". High standard	40.00
Covered. 7½". High standard	55.00
Open. 7". Low standard	20.00
Open. 8". High standard	35.00
Open. 10". High standard	47.50
Cracker Jar	30.00
Creamers	
3"	12.50
5"	30.00
Cruet. Original patterned stopper	40.00
Goblet	35.00
Honey. Square	30.00
Mug	17.50
Mustard Jar, Covered	22.50
Nappy. 5". Handled	16.50
Pitcher, Water. Applied handle	50.00
Relish	20.00
Sauces	
Flat	7.50
Footed	12.00
Shakers, Pair	50.00
Spooner	25.00
Sugar, Covered	45.00
Tumbler	25.00
Vase. 16½"	25.00
Wine	22.00

DAHLIA
(See Colored Glass Section)

DAISY AND BUTTON
(See Colored Glass Section)

DAISY AND BUTTON WITH CROSS BARS
(See Colored Glass Section)

DAISY AND BUTTON WITH NARCISSUS
(Daisy and Button with Clear Lily)
(Often found with original flashing)

Non-flint. Late 1890's.

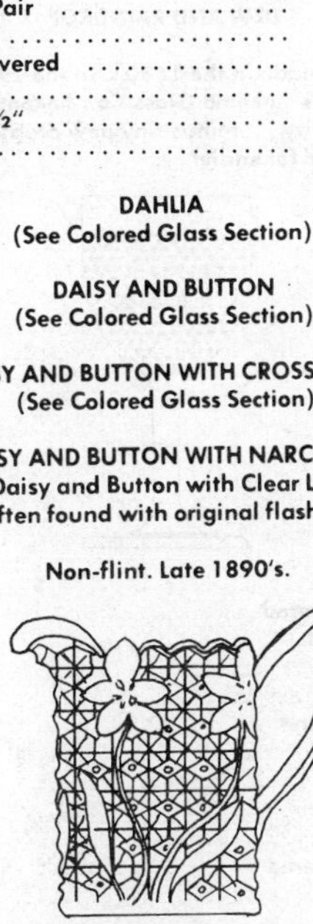

Bowl. 6x9½" oval. Footed	$ 40.00
Butter, Covered	35.00
Celery	22.50
Compote, Open	27.00
Creamer	18.00
Decanter, Stoppered	32.00
Goblet	20.00
Pitcher, Water	40.00
Punch Cup	8.00
Sauces	
Flat	6.00
Footed, 4"	8.00
Shakers, Pair	25.00
Spooner	20.00
Sugar, Covered	28.50
Tray. 10"	25.00
Tumbler	15.00
*Wine	13.50

*Reproduced Item

DAISY AND BUTTON WITH "V" ORNAMENT
(See Colored Glass Section)

DAKOTA
(Baby Thumbprint, Thumbprint Band)

Non-flint made by Doyle & Co., Pittsburgh, Pa. in the late 1880's and early 1890's. Later, reissued by U.S. Glass Co. The prices listed are for etched "Fern and Berry." Plain items command 50% less.

Bowl. 8"	$ 25.00
Butter, Covered	60.00
Cake Stand. 10½"	60.00
Celery	35.00
Compotes	
Covered, 12"	85.00
Open, 6". High standard	35.00
Creamer. Applied handle	60.00
Cruet	45.00
Egg Cup	22.00
Mug	30.00
Pitcher, Water	72.50
Sauces	
Flat	10.00
Footed	17.50
Shakers, Pair	65.00
Spooner	32.50
Sugars	
Covered	65.00

Open	25.00
Tumbler	30.00
Wine	30.00

DEER AND DOG
(Frosted dog finial and etched)
Non-flint. C. 1870's.

Butter, Covered	$ 125.00
Celery Vase	75.00
Compotes	
Covered. 13". High standard	125.00
Open. 7½". High standard	65.00
Creamer	65.00
Goblets	
Straight sides	50.00
U-Shaped	75.00
Marmalade Jar, Covered	100.00
Pitcher, Water. Applied handle	135.00
Sauce, Footed	20.00
Spooner	55.00
Sugar, Covered	125.00
Wine	40.00

DEER AND PINE TREE
(Deer and Doe)

Non-flint pattern originally attributed to Boston & Sandwich Glass Co. Later made in the Pittsburgh area in the 1880's. Although this pattern is reported to have been made also in colors, it is seldom encountered except the platters. SEE NOTE:

Butter, Covered	$ 65.00
Cake Stand	70.00
Celery Vase	50.00
Compotes, Open	
7x 9". High standard	55.00
8", Square. High standard	45.00
Creamer	50.00
*Goblet	40.00
Marmalade Jar, Covered	45.00
Mugs	
Large	35.00
Small	25.00
Pickle	22.50
Pitcher, Water	75.00
Platter. 8x13"	50.00
Sauces	
Flat	12.50
Footed	20.00
Spooner	40.00
Sugar, Covered	50.00
Tray, Water. 9x 15"	75.00
Waste Bowl	30.00

NOTE: Add approximately 50% more for colors.
*Reproduced Item

DELAWARE
(See Colored Glass Section)

DEW AND RAINDROP

Non-flint made in the 1880's. In the 1900's reissued by the Kokomo Glass Co., Kokomo, Ind. of lesser quality . . .minus tiny dew drops on stem. Prices listed for earlier.

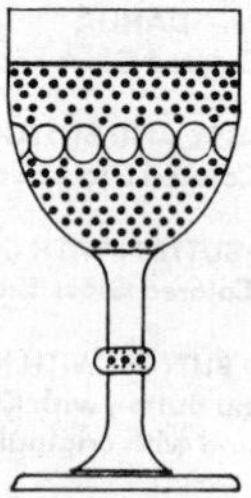

Bowl. 8"	$ 39.50
Butter, Covered	52.50
Cake Stand. 9"	40.00
Creamer	35.00
*Goblet	35.00
Pitcher, Water	60.00
Punch Cup	10.00
Sauce, Flat	10.00
Shakers, Pair	40.00
Spooner	25.00
Sugar, Covered	45.00
Tumbler	22.50
Wine	25.00

*Reproduced Item

DEWDROP
(See Colored Glass Section)

DEWDROP IN POINTS

Non-flint made by Brilliant Glass Works, Brilliant, Ohio in the 1870's, and Greensburg Glass, Greensburg, Pa. after 1889.

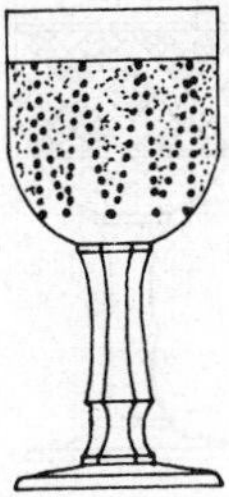

Cake Stand. Rimless .... $	35.00
Compotes	
Covered	35.00
Open	22.50
Creamer	20.00
Goblet	25.00
Pickle	15.00
Pitcher, Water	35.00
Platter, Handled. 9x11¾"	28.50
Sauces	
Flat	7.50
Footed	10.00
Spooner	17.50
Sugars	
Covered	32.50
Open	18.00
Wine	17.50

DEWDROP WITH STAR

Non-flint made by Campbell, Jones & Co., Pittsburgh, Pa. in the late 1870's.

Bowl. 7" .... $	18.50
Butter, Covered	55.00
Cake Stand. 9"	55.00
Celery	45.00
Compotes	
Covered. High standard	75.00
Covered. Low standard	65.00
Open. High standard	50.00
Creamer	38.00
Honey, Covered	85.00
Lamp. Patent mark 1876	100.00
Pitcher, Water	75.00
Plates	
4½"	16.50
*7"	20.00
9"	25.00
Relish. 8"	12.50
*Salt, Footed	20.00
Sauces	
Flat	10.00
*Footed	12.50
Spooner	25.00
Sugar, Covered	42.50
*Tray, Bread. 11". Sheaf of Wheat .	30.00

*Reproduced Item

DEWEY
(See Colored Glass Section)

DIAGONAL BAND AND FAN

Non-flint. C. 1880's.

Butter, Covered .... $	35.00
Celery	20.00
Champagne	18.00
Compotes	
Covered. High standard	35.00
Open. Low standard	25.00
Creamer	25.00
Goblet	22.50
Marmalade Jar	20.00
Pickle	15.00
Pitchers	
Milk	25.00
Water	35.00
Plates	
6"	10.00
7"	15.00
8"	18.00
Sauce, Footed	9.50

Shakers, Pair	25.00
Spooner	20.00
Sugar, Covered	32.00
Wine	15.00

DIAMOND AND SUNBURST

Non-flint. C. 1860's.

Butter, Covered $	35.00
Butter Pat	8.00
Cake Stand	30.00
Celery	20.00
Compote, Covered. High standard	40.00
Creamer. Applied handle	30.00
Egg Cup	15.00
Goblet	20.00
Pitcher, Water. Applied handle	50.00
Relish	12.00
Salt. Footed	12.00
Sauce, Flat	7.50
Spooner	16.00
Sugar, Covered	30.00
Tumbler	15.00
Wine	15.00

DIAMOND CUT WITH LEAF

Non-flint. C. 1880's . SEE NOTE:

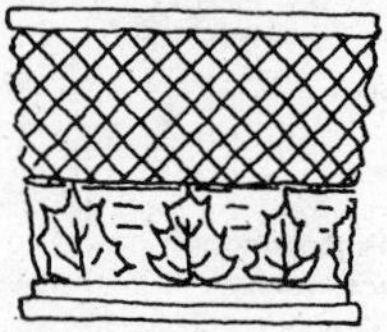

Butter, Covered $	35.00
Cordial	22.00
Creamer	20.00
Goblet	25.00
Mug, Small	15.00
Plates	
7″	15.00
9½″	20.00
Sugars	
Covered	30.00
Open	17.50
Spooner	15.00

NOTE: Scarce in color. Add 100% to clear.

DIAMOND MEDALLION

(Grand, Fine Cut and Diamond)

Non-flint. C. 1880's.

Butter, Covered. Flat $	25.00
Butter, Covered. Footed	35.00
Cake Stands	
8″	17.50
10″	30.00
Celery Vase	18.50
Compotes	
Covered. 7″. High standard	35.00
Open. 9″. High standard	25.00
Creamer	15.00
Goblet	20.00
Pitchers	
Syrup	50.00
Water	35.00
Plate. 10″	18.50
Relish. 7½″, Oval	10.00
Sauces	
Flat	7.50
Footed	10.00
Spooner	17.50
Sugar, Covered	20.00
Wine	20.00

DIAMOND POINT

Flint originally made by Boston and Sandwich Glass Co. in the 1830-40 period. Rare in color - add 400%. Milk white-add 200%.

Bowls	
Covered, 7″, 8″ $	60.00
Open, 7″, 8″	40.00
Butter, Covered	80.00
Cake Stand. 14″	185.00
Celery. K-S	65.00
Champagne	75.00
Claret. K-S	60.00
Compotes	
Covered. 6″. High standard	85.00

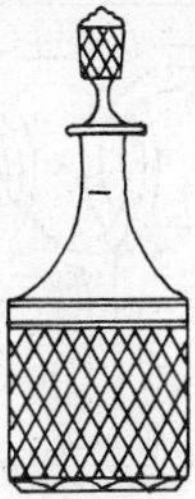

Covered. 8". High standard	100.00
Open. 7½". Low standard	48.00
Creamer	125.00
Decanters	
Bar lip, Pint	55.00
Bar lip, Quart	75.00
Stoppered, Pint	75.00
Stoppered, Quart	100.00
Egg Cup	40.00
Goblet	50.00
Honey	20.00
Pitchers	
½ Pint	55.00
Pint	75.00
Quart	125.00
3 Pints	100.00
Syrup	75.00
Plates	
6"	30.00
8"	50.00
Salt, Master	50.00
Sauces. 5¼"	15.00
Spooner	55.00
Sugar, Covered	100.00
Tumblers	
Bar	60.00
Jelly	35.00
Whiskey, Handled	80.00
Wine	50.00

DIAMOND QUILTED
(See Colored Glass Section)

DIAMOND THUMBPRINT
(Diamond Concave)

Flint attributed to Boston and Sandwich Glass Co. and other factories from 1840 to the 1850's.

Bowl, Waste $	85.00
Butter, Covered	145.00
Celery	175.00
Champagne (scarce)	225.00
Compote Open. 8". Low std. Scalloped	65.00
Cordial	175.00
Creamer	150.00

Decanters	
Pint. No stopper	75.00
Quart. Original stopper	150.00
Goblet (rare)	350.00+
Honey	15.00
Pitcher, Water. (scarce)	300.00+
Sauce	15.00
Spooner	75.00
Sugar, Covered	160.00
Tumblers	
Water	100.00
Whiskey. 3"	125.00
Whiskey, Handled	300.00
Wine (scarce)	225.00

DOLPHIN
(Codfish, Frog, Turtle)

Non-flint. C. 1880's.

Bowl. 8" $	100.00
Butter, Covered	150.00
Compote, Open. High standard	85.00
Creamer	100.00
Goblet	95.00
Pitcher, Water	150.00
Spooner	75.00
Sugar, Covered	100.00
Toothpick	35.00

DOUBLE RIBBON
Non-flint C. 1870's.

Butter, Covered $	40.00
Celery	27.50
Compotes	
Covered. High standard	45.00

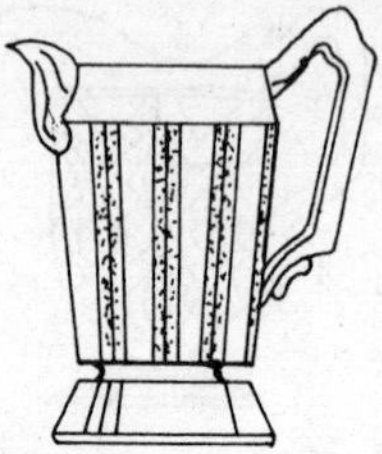

Open. High standard	25.00
Creamer	27.50
Egg Cup	22.50
Goblet	32.50
Pitcher, Water	45.00
Relish	15.00
Sauce, Footed	10.00
Spooner	27.50
Sugar, Covered	28.50
Tray, Bread	35.00

DOUBLE SPEAR

Non-flint. C. 1880's.

Butter, Covered. Flat	$ 27.50
Celery	20.00
Compote, Covered. High standard	40.00
Creamer	25.00
Egg Cup	16.50
Goblet	18.50
Pickle	12.50
Pitcher, Water	40.00
Sauce, Footed	12.50
Spooner	17.50
Sugar, Covered	25.00

DOUBLE WEDDING RING

Flint. C. 1860's.

Champagne	$ 75.00
Creamer	65.00
Decanter	125.00
Goblet	55.00
Syrup, Original top	75.00

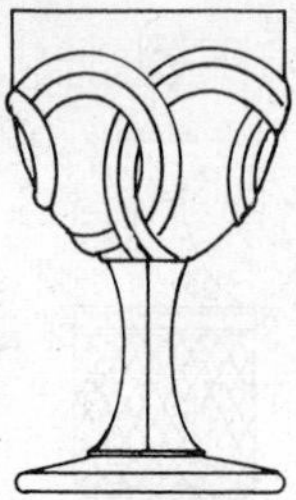

Tumbler, Bar	67.50
Wine	40.00

DRAPERY
(Lace)

Non-flint made by Doyle & Co., Pittsburgh, Pa. in the 1870's. Reportedly made by Sandwich Glass Co. at an earlier period.

Butter, Covered	$ 45.00
Creamers	
Applied handle	35.00
Molded handle	18.50
Egg Cup	18.50
Goblet	26.50
Pitcher, Water	45.00
Plate. 6"	20.00
Sauce, Flat	8.50
Spooner	28.50
Sugar, Covered	37.00

EGG IN SAND
(Bean)

Non-flint. C. 1880's.

Butter, Covered	$ 40.00
Cake Stand	40.00
Compote, Covered	45.00
Creamer	22.50
Goblet	30.00
Pitchers	
Milk	30.00
Water	42.50
Relish	17.50
Sauce, Flat	7.50

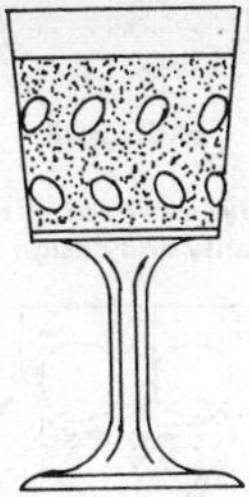

Shakers, Pair	35.00
Spooner	25.00
Sugar, Covered	35.00
Trays	
Bread	30.00
Water	37.50
Tumbler	17.50
Wine	20.00

EGYPTIAN
(Parthenon)

Non-flint. C. 1870's.

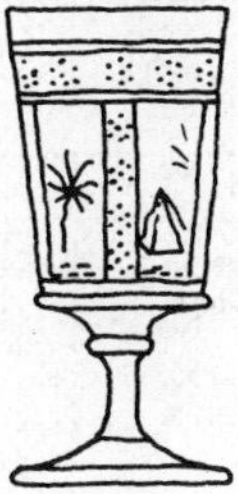

Butter, Covered	$ 55.00
Celery Vase	40.00
Compotes	
Covered, 7". High standard	75.00
Open, 6". Low standard	50.00
Creamer	40.00
Goblet	40.00
Honey	14.50
Pickle, Oval	27.50
Pitcher, Water	100.00
Plate. 12". Handled	40.00
Sauce, Footed, 4½"	17.50
Spooner	35.00
Sugar, Covered	45.00
Trays, Bread	
9x12". "Cleopatra"	50.00
"Salt Lake Temple"	250.00+

EIGHTEEN-NINETY

Made by Beaver Falls Glass Co., Beaver Falls, Pa., in the 1890's.

Bowl. 8", Deep	$ 15.00
Butter, Covered	25.00
Celery	15.00
Creamer	17.50
Pitcher, Water	25.00
Shakers	
Salt and Pepper. Pair	20.00
Sugar	18.50
Spooner	13.50
Sugar, Open	12.50

EMERALD GREEN HERRINGBONE
See PANELLED HERRINGBONE

ESTHER-TWO

Non-flint made by Riverside Glass Works of Wellsburgh, W. Va. C. 1896. SEE NOTE:

Bowl. 8"	$ 25.00
Butter, Covered	65.00
Cake Stand. 10½"	45.00
Celery Vase	35.00
Compotes	
Covered. 5". Low standard	40.00
Open. 6". High standard	30.00
Creamer	85.00
Cruet, Stoppered	50.00
Goblet	35.00
Pitcher, Water	100.00
Sauce, Footed	15.00
Spooner	30.00
Sugar, Covered	45.00
Toothpick	30.00
Tumbler	20.00
Wine	25.00

NOTE: Add 100% for Emerald Green.

EUGENIE

Flint made by McKee Glass Co., Pittsburgh, Pa. C. 1850's.

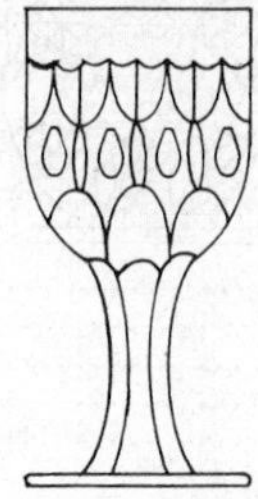

Butter, Covered ....$	75.00
Castor Bottle	25.00
Celery	75.00
Champagne	55.00
Compote, Covered. High standard	100.00
Cordial	45.00
Egg Cup	45.00
Goblet	50.00
Sauce, Flat	18.50
Sugar, Covered. Dolphin finial	150.00+
Tumbler	40.00
Wine	45.00

EUREKA

Made in Pittsburgh, Pa. in the late 1860's.

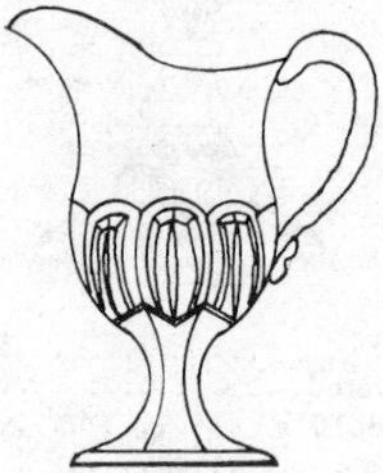

Bowl. 8" ....$	30.00
Butter, Covered	65.00
Compotes	
Covered. 7", 8". High standard	85.00
Open. 7", 8". Low standard	45.00
Cordial	35.00
Creamer	65.00
Egg Cup	32.50
Goblet	30.00
Plate, Bread	40.00
Salt, Footed	20.00
Sauce	12.50
Spooner	30.00
Sugar, Covered	55.00
Tumbler, Footed	25.00
Wine	35.00

EXCELSIOR

Flint made by several firms from the 1850's-60's. Quality and design vary.

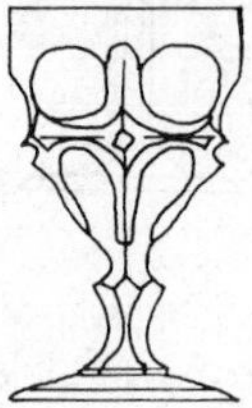

Bowl. 10" Open ....$	125.00
Butter, Covered	100.00
Candlestick	125.00
Celery Vase	95.00
Claret	45.00
Compotes	
Covered, Low standard	125.00
Open, High standard	85.00
Cordial	40.00
Creamer	100.00
Egg Cups	
Double	50.00
Single	35.00
Goblets	
Plain. Either size	40.00
With Maltese Cross	50.00
Pitchers	
Milk (scarce)	200.00+
Syrup	125.00
Water (scarce)	300.00+
Salt, Footed	35.00
Spooner	75.00
Sugar, Covered	85.00
Tumblers	
Bar	35.00
Footed	55.00
Jelly	35.00
Whiskey, with Maltese Cross	65.00
Wine	40.00

EYEWINKER
(Crystal Ball, The Winking Eye, Cannon Ball)

Non-flint made in Findlay, Ohio. C. 1890's. SEE NOTE:

*Banana Dish ....$	65.00
Bowl. 9"	35.00
*Butter, Covered	50.00
Cake Stand	62.50
Celery	45.00

*Compotes	
Covered. 6"	28.50
Jelly	20.00
*Creamer	30.00
Cruet	30.00
*Lamp	50.00
*Pitchers	
Milk	35.00
Syrup. Original lid	75.00
Water	50.00
Plate. 7½"	25.00
*Sauce, Flat	8.50
*Shakers, Pair	45.00
*Spooner	19.50
Sugars	
Covered	50.00
Open	22.50
*Toothpick	15.00
*Tumbler	17.50

NOTE: Other items reproduced also in clear and colors.

*Reproduced Item

FANS WITH DIAMOND

Non-flint. C. 1870's.

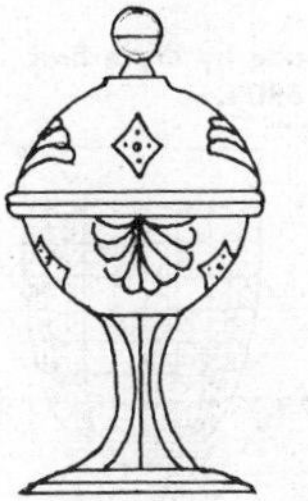

Butter, Covered	$ 35.00
Compotes	
Covered. High standard	45.00
Covered. Low standard	35.00
Cordial	17.50
Creamer	28.50
Egg Cup	17.50
Goblet	22.00
Pitcher, Water	35.00
Relish	15.00
Sauce, Flat. 4"	10.00
Spooner	22.50
Sugars	
Covered	28.50
Open	17.50
Wine	20.00

FEATHER

(Finecut and Feather, Indiana Swirl)

Non-flint made in Indiana in 1896. Later, the pattern was reissued with variations and quality. Also made in green. Prices listed are for quality clear. SEE NOTE:

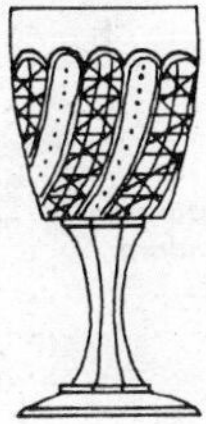

Banana Dish	$ 55.00
Bowl. 8". Square	25.00
Butter, Covered	55.00
Cake Stands	
8"	30.00
9½"	45.00
Celery Vase	35.00
Compotes	
Covered. 8¼". Low standard	50.00
Open. High standard	35.00
Jelly. 4½"	20.00
Cordial	65.00
Creamer	22.50
Cruet. Stoppered	38.50
Goblet	65.00
Marmalade Jar	100.00
Pitchers	
Milk	45.00
Water	55.00
Plate. 10"	35.00
Relish	15.00
Sauces	
Flat. 4"	10.00
Footed. 5½"	17.50
Spooner	17.50
Sugar, Covered	30.00
Toothpick	35.00
Tumbler	35.00
Wine	30.00
Wine. Scalloped	40.00

NOTE: Green approximately 3 times price of clear.

FESTOON

Non-flint. C. Late 1880's.

Bowls	
4½"	$ 10.00
7"	16.50
9". Rectangular	20.00
Butter, Covered	40.00
Cake Stand. 10"	35.00
Celery	22.00
Compotes	
Covered. High standard	50.00
Open. High standard	28.50
Creamer	27.50
Goblet	27.50
Pickle Jar	40.00
Pitcher, Water	50.00
Plates. 7¼", 8½". (scarce)	35.00
Sauce, Flat. 4½"	8.50
Spooner	20.00
Sugars	
Covered	50.00
Open	30.00
Tray, Water. 10"	35.00
Tumbler	25.00
Wine	17.50

FINE CUT

(See Colored Glass Section)

FINE CUT AND PANEL

(See Colored Glass Section)

FINE RIB

Flint made by New England Glass Co. in the 1860's. Later made in non-flint. Prices listed are for flint.

Bitters Bottle	$ 65.00
Bowl. 7". Covered	85.00
Butter, Covered	100.00
Castor Bottle	25.00
Celery	65.00
Champagne	50.00
Compotes.	
Covered. 7", 8". High standard	125.00
Covered. 7", 8". Low standard	100.00
Open. 7", 8". Low standard	65.00
Open. 9", 10". Low standard	75.00

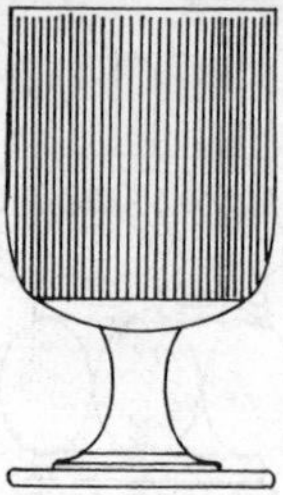

Cordial	60.00
Creamer. Applied handle	125.00
Decanters	
Bar lip. Pint	55.00
Bar lip. Quart	65.00
With stopper. Pint	100.00
With stopper. Quart	135.00
Egg Cup	45.00
Goblet	50.00
Lamp	150.00
Mug	55.00
Pitcher, Water	175.00
Plates. 6", 7"	50.00
Salts	
Covered. Footed	85.00
Individual	20.00
Sauce	16.50
Spooner	60.00
Sugar, Covered	85.00
Tumbler, Bar	40.00
Tumble-up	125.00
Whiskey. Handled	85.00
Wine	45.00

FISHSCALE
(Coral)

Non-flint made by Bryce Bros., Pittsburgh, Pa., in the mid 1880's.

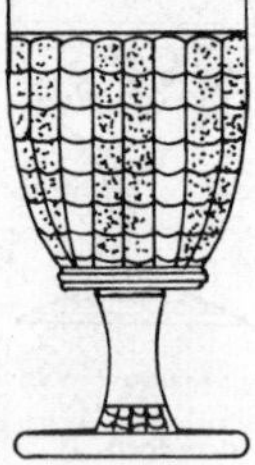

Bowls	
7¾". Covered	$ 37.50
8". Open	20.00
Butter, Covered	45.00
Cake Stands. 9", 10½"	35.00

Celery	25.00
Compote, Jelly	22.50
Creamer	30.00
Goblet	29.50
Lamp, Finger	75.00
Mug, Large	35.00
Pitchers	
Milk	30.00
Water	40.00
Plates	
7", Round	25.00
8", Square	30.00
Sauces	
Flat, Round	6.50
Flat, Square	10.00
Footed	15.00
Shakers, Pair	50.00
Spooner	20.00
Sugar, Covered	40.00
Tumbler	22.50

FLAT DIAMOND
(Lippman)

Non-flint. C. 1870's.

Butter, Covered	$ 47.50
Celery	35.00
Creamer	36.50
Goblet	27.50
Pitcher, Water	45.00
Sauces	
Flat	8.50
Footed	12.50
Spooner	26.50
Sugars	
Covered	35.00
Open	25.00
Wine	20.00

FLOWER POT
(Flower Plant, Potted Plant)

Non-flint. C. 1880's.

Butter, Covered	$ 50.00
Cake Stand. 10½"	50.00
Compote. 7". Covered	45.00
Creamer	35.00
Pitchers	
Milk	35.00

Water	50.00
Sauces	
Footed	10.00
Square	10.00
Spooner	27.50
Sugars	
Covered	45.00
Open	25.00
Tray, Bread	40.00

FLUTE

Research has proven there were more than 15 Flute variants produced in flint and non-flint glass, from the 1850's through the 1880's. Some of the flint variants are Banded Flute, Bessimer Flute, New England Flute, etc . . .all with comparable prices. Prices listed are for flint examples.

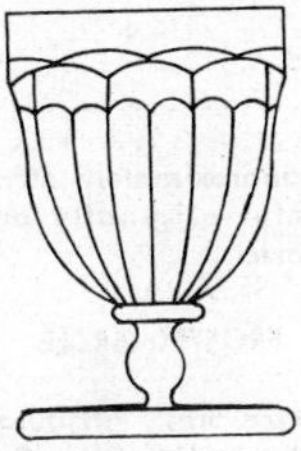

Ale Glass	$ 22.50
Candlesticks. 4". Pair	35.00
Champagne	26.50
Compote. Open. 8¼". Low standard	30.00
Creamer	35.00
Decanter. Bar lip. Quart	45.00
Egg Cups	
Double	25.00
Single	17.50
Goblet	25.00
Lamp. Whale Oil	65.00
Mug	40.00
Pitchers	
Milk	30.00
Water	50.00
Sauce, Flat	8.50
Sugar, Open	25.00
Tumbler	20.00
Whiskey, Handled	20.00
Wine	20.00

FROSTED ARTICHOKE

Non-flint. C. 1890's. SEE NOTE:

Bowl. 8"	$ 45.00
Bowl, Finger. With underplate	30.00
Butter, Covered	75.00
Cake Stand	55.00
Celery	38.50
Compotes	
Covered	85.00
Open. Scalloped edge	50.00
Creamer	50.00
Lamp. Large	100.00
Pitcher, Water. Tankard	75.00
Sauces	
Flat	8.50
Footed	12.00
Spooner	26.50
Sugar, Covered	75.00
Tray, Water	50.00
Tumbler	25.00

NOTE: Clear approximately 50% less. Reportedly no goblet originally produced, but reproductions exist.

FROSTED CIRCLE

Produced by Bryce Bros., Pittsburgh, Pa. in the late 1870's. Later by U.S. Glass Co. in the early 1890's.

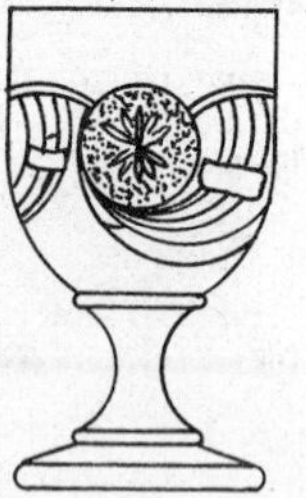

Bowls	
Covered. 7", 8"	$ 30.00
Open. 8", 9"	20.00
Butter, Covered	45.00
Cake Stand. 10"	50.00
Compotes	
Covered. 7", 8". High standard	65.00
Open. 10". High standard	45.00
Creamer	42.50
Cruet. Stoppered	55.00
*Goblet	35.00
Pitchers	
Syrup	55.00
Water	65.00
Plates	
4"	16.50
7"	25.00
9"	28.50
Relish, Oval	20.00
Sauces	
Flat	10.00
Footed	12.50
Shakers, Pair	50.00
Spooner	27.50
Sugar, Covered	45.00
Tumbler	20.00
Wine	35.00

*Reproduced Item

FROSTED LEAF

Flint. C. 1850's

Butter, Covered	$ 150.00
Celery Vase	125.00
Champagne	175.00
Compote, Covered	250.00
Creamer	125.00
Decanter. Stoppered. Quart	250.00
Egg Cup	95.00
*Goblet	85.00
Pitcher, Water. (very scarce)	350.00+
Salt	50.00
Sauce	25.00
Spooner	75.00
Sugars	
Covered	125.00
Open	65.00
Tumbler	150.00
Wine	135.00

*Reproduced Item

FROSTED RIBBON

Non-flint made by Bakewell, Pears & Co., Pittsburgh, Pa. in the 1870's. Later made by Geo. Duncan & Sons, Pittsburgh, Pa.

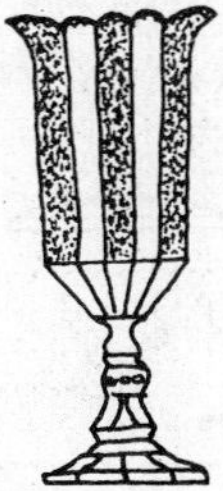

Butter, Covered	$ 30.00
Celery	27.50
Champagne	22.50
Compotes	
Covered. High standard	35.00
Open. Low standard	17.50
Creamer	32.50
Egg Cup	22.50
*Goblet	25.00
Pitcher, Water*	27.50
Salt, Footed	15.00
Sauce, Footed	8.50
Spooner	22.50
Sugar, Covered	35.00
Tumbler	22.50
Wine	20.00

*Reproduced Item

FROSTED STORK

Non-flint made by Crystal Glass Co., Bridgeport, Ohio, C. 1880. Now reproduced.

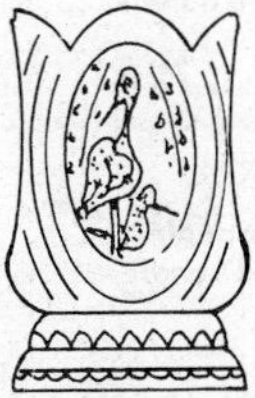

Butter, Covered	$ 65.00
Creamer	75.00
Goblet	55.00
Marmalade Jar	55.00
Pitcher, Water	125.00
Platter. 9"	55.00
Sauce, Flat	15.50
Spooner	55.00
Sugar, Covered	85.00
Trays	
Bread. 9"	45.00
Water	75.00
Waste Bowl	42.00

GARFIELD DRAPE

Non-flint pattern issued in 1881 by Adams & Co., Pittsburgh, Pa., after the assassination of President Garfield.

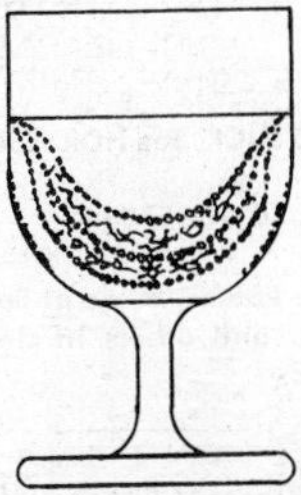

Bowl. 6"	$ 25.00
Butter, Covered	65.00
Cake Stand. 9½"	55.00
Celery	40.00
Compotes	
Covered. 8". High standard	65.00
Open. 8½". Low standard	32.50
Creamer	50.00
Goblet	32.50
Pitchers	
Milk	50.00
Water	65.00
Plates	
11". Memorial	50.00
11". Star center	40.00
Relish, Oval	18.00
Sauces	
Flat	9.50
Footed	12.00
Spooner	25.00
Sugars	
Covered	50.00
Open	20.00
Tumbler	22.50

GIBSON GIRL
(Goddess of Liberty)

Non-flint. C. Early 1900's.

Butter, Covered	$ 65.00
Creamer	50.00
Pitcher, Water	85.00
Plate. 10"	80.00
Spooner	50.00

Sugar, Covered	55.00
Tumbler	40.00

GOOD LUCK, See HORSESHOE

GOOSEBERRY

Non-flint of the 1880's. Made at Boston & Sandwich Glass Co. and others in clear and milk glass. SEE NOTE:

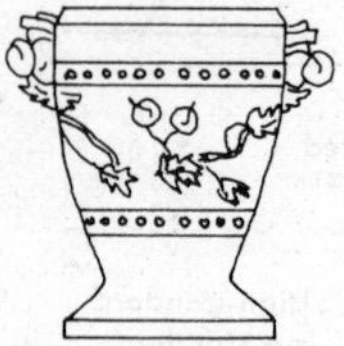

Butter, Covered	$ 42.50
Compote, Covered. 6". High std.	50.00
Creamer	35.00
Goblet	26.50
Mug	20.00
Pickle	15.00
Pitchers	
Syrup. Applied handle	65.00
Water	55.00
Sauce, Flat	8.00
Spooner	22.50
Sugars	
Covered	35.00
Open	20.00
Tumbler	25.00

NOTE: Reproduced in Milk Glass.

GOTHIC

Flint made by McKee & Bros., in the 1860's; possibly reissued in the 1870's.

Bowl. 8"	$ 50.00
Butter, Covered	75.00
Castor Bottle	20.00
Celery Vase	80.00
Champagne	75.00
Compotes	
Covered. 8"	150.00
Open. 7"	85.00
Cordial	55.00
Creamer	85.00
Egg Cup	32.00
Goblet. Either type	60.00
Sauce, Flat	15.00
Spooner	50.00
Sugar, Covered	75.00
Tumbler	45.00
Wine	85.00

GRAPE AND FESTOON-STIPPLED LEAF

Non-flint made by Doyle & Co., Pittsburgh, Pa. in the early 1870's.

Butter, Covered	$ 40.00
Celery Vase	27.50
Creamer. Applied handle	35.00
Egg Cup	18.50
Goblet	20.00
Lamp, Oil. 7½"	50.00
Mug	18.00
Pitchers	
Milk. Applied handle	50.00
Water. Applied handle	65.00
Plate. 6"	20.00
Relish	12.50
Salt, Footed	17.50
Sauce, Flat. 4"	7.50
Spooner	22.50
Sugar, Covered	35.00
Wine	20.00

GRAPE BAND

Issued in flint glass in the late 1850's; non-flint

in the late 1860's. Prices listed herein are for non-flint glass; flint glass prices are approximately 100% more.

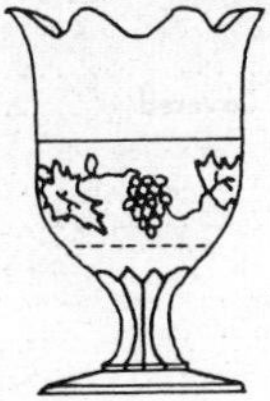

Butter, Covered $	35.00
Compotes, Covered	
High standard	40.00
Low standard	28.00
Creamer	25.00
Egg Cup	15.00
Goblet	18.50
Pickle	12.50
Pitcher, Water	50.00
Salt, Footed	12.50
Sauce, Flat	7.50
Spooner	20.00
Sugars	
Covered	35.00
Open	17.50
Wine	17.50

GRAPE WITH THUMBPRINT BAND

Non-flint. C. 1890's.

Butter, Covered $	30.00
Celery	22.50
Creamer	25.00
Goblet	18.50
Pitchers	
Syrup	27.50
Water	37.50
Sauce, Flat	7.50
Spooner	15.00
Sugar, Covered	30.00

GRASSHOPPER
(Locust, Long Spear)

Butter, Covered $	50.00

Celery	27.50
Compote, Covered. 8½". High std.	55.00
Creamer	27.50
Pickle	16.00
Pitcher, Water	55.00
Sauce, Footed	12.00
Spooner	22.50
Sugars	
Covered	40.00
Open	20.00

HAIRPIN

Flint made by Boston & Sandwich Glass Co. in the 1850's. SEE NOTE:

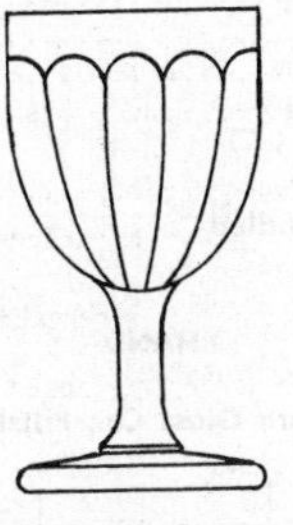

Butter, Covered $	75.00
Celery	60.00
Champagne	50.00
Compote, Covered	85.00
Creamer	72.50
Egg Cup	28.50
Goblet	35.00
Pitcher, Water	125.00
Salt, Footed	18.50
Sauce, Flat	12.50
Spooner	35.00
Sugars	
Covered	60.00
Open	35.00
Wine	40.00

NOTE: Add 100% for Milk Glass

HAMILTON

Flint. C. 1860's

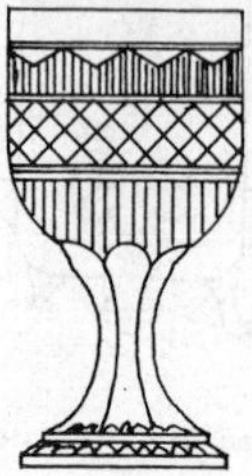

Butter, Covered	$ 75.00
Celery	65.00
Compotes	
Covered. High standard	115.00
Open. Low standard	55.00
Cordial	50.00
Creamers	
Applied handle	75.00
Molded handle	50.00
Egg Cup	32.00
Goblet	40.00
Honey	15.00
Pitcher, Water	150.00
Plate. 6"	45.00
Salt, Footed	30.00
Sauce, Flat	15.00
Spooner	35.00
Sugar, Covered	65.00
Tumblers	
Water	55.00
Whiskey. Handled	85.00
Wine	55.00

HAND

Made by O'Hara Glass Co., Pittsburgh, Pa., C. 1880's.

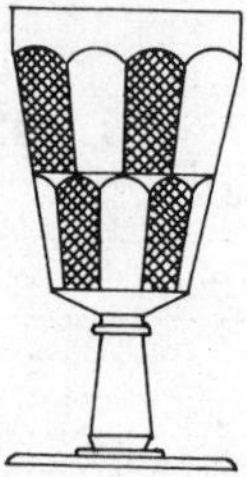

Bowls	
8"	$ 22.50
10"	27.50
Butter, Covered	50.00
Cake Stand	38.00
Celery	32.50
Compotes	
Covered. High standard	50.00
Open. High standard	30.00
Creamer	40.00
Goblet	30.00
Marmalade Jar, Covered	38.50
Pickle	17.50
Pitcher, Water	57.00
Platter. 8x10½"	29.50
Sauces	
Flat	10.00
Footed	12.50
Spooner	25.00
Sugar, Covered	45.00
Wine	50.00

HARP

Flint made by Bryce Bros., Pittsburgh, Pa. in the late 1840's, early 1850's.

Butter, Covered	$ 175.00
Compote, Covered. 6". Low std.	175.00
Goblet. Either type (rare)	350.00+
Honey	20.00
Lamp, Hand	75.00
Salt, Footed	38.50
Spillholder	60.00

HEART WITH THUMBPRINT
(Bull's Eye in Heart)

Non-flint. C. 1899. SEE NOTE:

Banana Boat	$ 37.50
Bowls	
7". Flared	25.00

9". Berry	35.00
Butter, Covered	40.00
Carafe, Water	48.50
Car Tray	17.50
Celery	28.50
Compote. 8½". High standard	48.00
Creamers	
Individual	18.00
Regular	35.00
Goblet	32.00
Hair Receiver, Metal lid	28.50
Ice Bucket	65.00
Nappy	15.00
Pitchers	
Syrup	32.50
Water	45.00
Plates	
6"	22.00
10"	32.00
12"	37.50
Punch Cup	15.00
Rose Bowl	25.00
Sauce, Flat	8.50
Sugars	
Individual. Open	18.00
Regular. Covered	50.00
Toothpick	20.00
Tumbler	25.00
Vases	
6"	17.50
10"	22.50
Wine	35.00

NOTE: Rare in emerald green and cobalt blue. Add 100%. Occasionally found stained. Add 200%.

HEAVY PANELLED FINE CUT
(Panelled Diamond Cross, Fine Cut Four Panel)

Made by Geo. Duncan & Sons, Pittsburgh, Pa., C. 1880's.

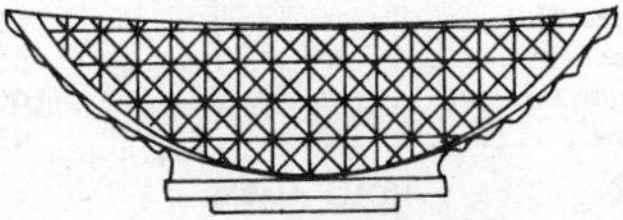

Bowls, Berry	
8" $	17.50
10"	22.00
Butter, Covered	22.50
Castor Set. 5-Bottle	100.00
Compote, Covered. 8". High std.	35.00
Creamer	12.00
Goblet	14.50
Pitcher, Water	60.00
Spooner	18.00
Sugar, Covered	22.50
Tumbler	15.00

HERRINGBONE
(See Panelled Herringbone)

HIDALGO
(Frosted Waffle)

Non-flint made by Adams & Co., Pittsburgh, Pa. in the early 1880's.

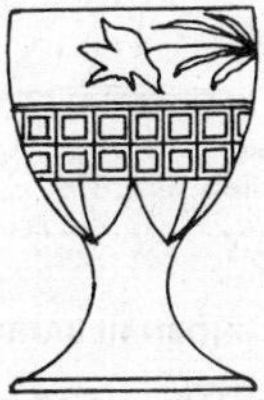

Bowls	
7½", Square $	15.00
10", Square	17.50
Butter, Covered	35.00
Celery Vase	18.50
Compotes	
Covered. High standard	35.00
Open. Low standard	20.00
Goblet	16.50
Pitchers	
Milk	30.00
Syrup	25.00
Water	40.00
Plate. 10"	22.50
Sauces	
Flat	5.00
Footed	10.00
Handled	10.00
Shakers	
Salt and Pepper, Pair	17.50
Sugar	15.00
Spooner	16.50
Sugar, Covered	32.50
Tray, Water	25.00
Tumbler	15.00

HINOTO
(Diamond Point with Panels)

Flint made by Boston & Sandwich Glass Co., in the 1850's.

Butter, Covered $	75.00
Celery	65.00
Champagne	40.00
Creamer	70.00
Egg Cup	37.50
Goblet	45.00
Spooner	30.00
Sugar, Covered	65.00

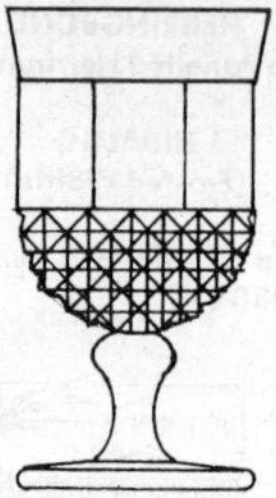

Tumbler, Footed	30.00
Whiskey, Handled	50.00
Wine	40.00

HOBNAIL BAND

Non-flint. C. 1900's.

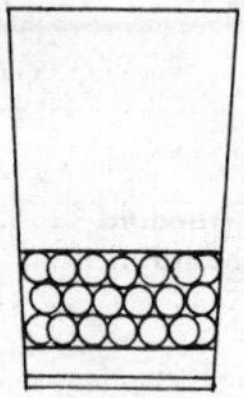

Bowls	
8½"	$ 16.00
9½"	18.50
Butter, Covered	30.00
Candlesticks. Ball top. Pair	35.00
Celery Tray	22.50
Champagne	17.50
Coaster	7.50
Creamer	22.00
Cup and Saucer	18.00
Custard Cup	10.00
Goblet	16.00
Pitcher, Water	32.00
Plates	
7⅜"	12.00
8", Handled	15.00
11"	20.00
Relish, Divided	12.50
Sauce, Flat	6.50
Shakers, In matching holder. Set	20.00
Spooner	16.50
Sugar, Covered	25.00
Tumblers	
Juice	8.50
Water	10.00

HOBNAIL, FAN TOP

(See Colored Glass Section)

HOBNAIL, OPALESCENT

(See General Section "OPALESCENT GLASS")

HOBNAIL, PANELLED

(See Colored Glass Section)

HOBNAIL, POINTED

(See Colored Glass Section)

HOBNAIL, PRINTED

(See Colored Glass Section)

HOBNAIL, THUMBPRINT BASE

(See Colored Glass Section)

HOLLY

Non-flint made by Boston & Sandwich Glass Co., late 1860's, early 1870's.

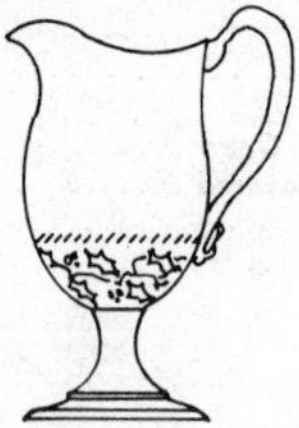

Butter, Covered	$ 125.00
Cake Stand. 11"	85.00
Celery Vase	75.00
Compotes	
Covered. High standard	125.00
Open. Low standard	50.00
Creamer. Applied handle	85.00
Egg Cup	55.00
Goblet	65.00
Pitcher, Water	100.00
Salt, Footed	25.00
Sauce, Flat	15.00
Spooner	55.00
Sugar, Covered	100.00
Wine	45.00

HOLLY AMBER

(See Colored Glass Section)

HONEYCOMB

A popular pattern made in flint and non-flint glass by numerous firms, C. 1860-1900. The prices recorded below are for non-flint glass. Prices on flint glass items would be considerably higher.

Ale Glass	$ 15.00
Bottles	
Barber	22.50

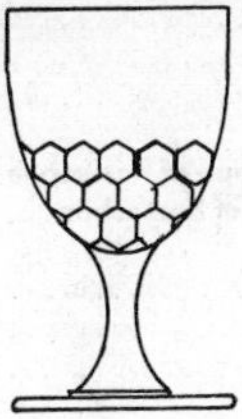

Castor	10.00
Bowls	
6". Covered	18.50
8"	15.00
10"	22.50
Butter, Covered	35.00
Celery Vase	27.50
Champagne	25.00
Compotes	
Covered. High standard	45.00
Covered. Low standard	40.00
Open. Low standard	25.00
Creamer. Applied handle	25.00
Decanters	
Pint	18.50
Quart. Stoppered	29.50
Egg Cup	16.50
Goblet	17.50
Honey, Covered	25.00
Lamps	
All glass	45.00
Marble base	30.00
Mug. ½ Pint	15.00
Pitcher, Water	40.00
Plate. 6"	12.50
Pomade Jar	15.00
Salts	
Covered, Footed	20.00
Open, Footed	13.50
Sauce	7.50
Shakers, Pair	22.50
Spooner	15.00
Sugar, Covered	28.50
Tumblers	
Flat	12.50
Footed	15.00
Lemonade	16.50
Wine	12.50

HONEYCOMB AND STAR
(Starred Honeycomb)

Non-flint made by Fostoria Glass Co., C. 1905.

Butter, Covered	$ 30.00
Cake Stand	30.00
Celery	20.00
Compote, Covered. High standard	37.50
Creamer	22.00
Cruet	16.50
Sauce, Flat	6.00

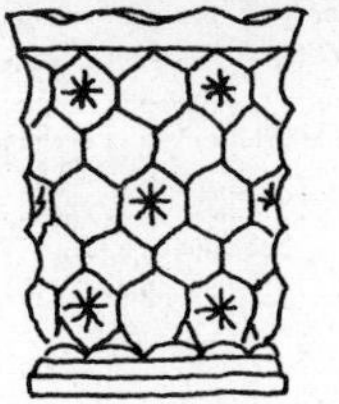

Spooner	18.50
Sugars	
Covered	20.00
Open	15.00
Tumbler	12.00

HORN OF PLENTY

A fine flint glass pattern reputed to have been first made by Boston and Sandwich in the 50's. Later made in flint and non-flint by other firms. Prices listed are for flint.

Bowl. 8½". Flat	$ 100.00
Butters, Covered	
Conventional knob	125.00
Washington's head	500.00
Celery	100.00
Champagne	125.00
Compotes, Open	
7". Low standard	65.00
7". Scalloped rim	125.00
8". High standard	100.00
10½". High standard	135.00
Cordial	95.00
Creamers	
Large	150.00
Regular	250.00
Decanters	
Pint	125.00
Quart. Stoppered	150.00
Egg Cup	50.00
*Goblet	75.00
Honey, Covered. Rectangular	500.00+
Lamps	
*All glass	165.00
Marble base	100.00
Mug	150.00

Pitcher, Water	300.00
Plate. 6"	85.00
Relish. 5x7"	30.00
Salt, Master. Oval	75.00
Sauces	
3½"	10.00
4½"	15.00
5"	27.50
Spillholder	50.00
Spooner	50.00
Sugar, Covered	115.00
Tumblers	
*Water	80.00
Whiskey, 3"	85.00
Wine	125.00

*Reproduced Item

HORSESHOE
(Good Luck, Prayer Rug)

Non-flint made by Adams & Co., and others in the 1880's.

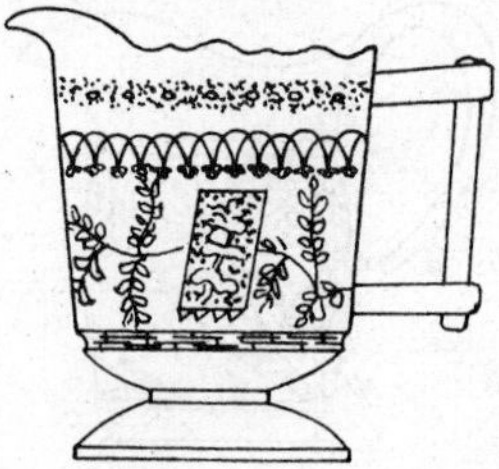

Bowls	
7". Covered	$ 35.00
7". Open	20.00
8x5", Oval. Covered	125.00
9x6", Oval. Open	30.00
Finger	20.00
Waste	40.00
Butter, Covered	65.00
Cake Stands	
8"	30.00
9"	40.00
10"	55.00
Celery. Plain stem	35.00
Cheese, Covered. Scenic base	175.00
Compotes	
Covered. 7". High standard	65.00
Open. 8". High standard	35.00
Creamer	32.50
Goblet	
Knob stem	35.00
Plain round stem	30.00
Marmalade Jar, Covered	50.00
Pitcher, Water	60.00
Plates	
7"	35.00
9"	45.00
10"	50.00
Relish. 5x7"	15.00
Salts	
Individual, Shape of horseshoe	17.50
Master, Shape of horseshoe	55.00
Sauces	
Flat. 4½"	9.00
Footed. 5"	11.50
Spooner	25.00
Sugars	
Covered	48.50
Open	20.00
Trays, Bread	
Double. 10x14". Horseshoe hdls	55.00
Single. Horseshoe handles	40.00
Wine. (rare)	150.00

HUBER
(Straight Huber)

Flint made by Boston and Sandwich Glass Co. and Bakewell, Pears and Co., Pgh., Pa. C. 1860's. SEE NOTE:

Bitters Bottle	$ 25.00
Bowls	
6"	20.00
7". Covered	35.00
Butter, Covered	50.00
Celery	28.50
Compotes, Covered	
High standard, 8"	65.00
Low standard, 8"	50.00
High standard, 10"	75.00
Compotes, Open	
High standard, 8½"	45.00
High standard, 11"	55.00
Cordial	25.00
Creamer	45.00
Decanter	
Bar lip. Pint	35.00
Bar lip. Quart	50.00
Stoppered. Pint	50.00
Stoppered. Quart	65.00
Egg Cups	
Handled	35.00
Regular	20.00
Goblet	25.00
Mug	20.00

Pitcher, Water 50.00
Plate. 7½" 22.50
Salts
  Footed 20.00
  Individual 7.50
Sauce, Flat 10.00
Spooner 20.00
Sugars
  Covered 40.00
  Open 18.50
Tumblers
  Jelly 15.00
  Lemonade 17.50
  Water 15.00
  Whiskey, Handled 25.00
Wine 15.00
NOTE: Barrel Huber. Same values

HUMMING BIRD
(See Colored Glass Section)

ICICLE

Non-flint. C. 1870's. SEE NOTE:

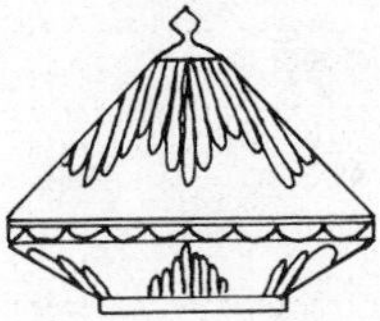

Butters
  Covered, Flat $ 45.00
  Covered, Footed 55.00
Compotes
  Covered. 6". High standard 50.00
  Covered. 8". High standard 60.00
  Open, 8". Low standard 35.00
Creamer 35.00
Goblet 35.00
Lamp, Hand. 5". Complete 50.00
Pickle 20.00
Pitcher, Water 50.00
Salt, Master 20.00
Sauce, Flat 12.50
Spooner 30.00
Sugar, Covered 45.00
NOTE: Milk Glass add 100% more.

ILLINOIS

Non-flint . One of the States' patterns made by U.S. Glass Co., in 1907.

Bowls
  6" $ 18.50
  8" 15.00

Butter, Covered 30.00
Candlestick 15.00
Celerys
  Tray, 11" 17.50
  Vase 25.00
Cheese, Covered 35.00
Creamers
  Large 20.00
  Small 15.00
Cruet 15.00
Olive 10.00
Pitchers
  Milk 32.00
  Water, Square 75.00
  Water, Tankard 35.00
Plates
  7", Round 15.00
  7", Square 17.50
Relish 10.00
Shakers
  Salt and Pepper, Pair 22.50
  Sugar 16.50
Spooner 15.00
Sugar, Open 15.00
Toothpick 17.50
Tray, Ice Cream 18.50
Tumbler 8.50

INVERTED FERN
Flint. C. 1860's.

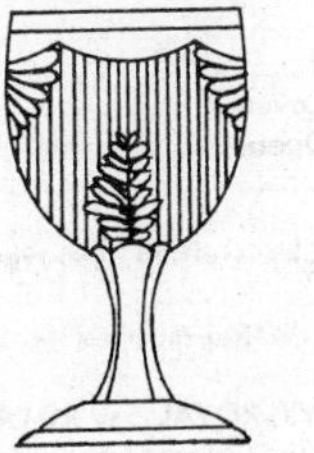

Butter, Covered $ 75.00
Compote, Open. 8" 55.00
Creamer. Applied handle 85.00
Egg Cup 30.00
Goblets
  Plain base 28.50
  Rayed base 37.50

Honey	12.50
Pitcher, Water	250.00
Salt, Footed	25.00
Sauce, Flat	12.00
Spooner	37.50
Sugars	
Covered	65.00
Open	25.00
Tumbler, Water	60.00
Wine	65.00

INVERTED STRAWBERRY

Non-flint. C. 1890's.

Bowl. 9" $	35.00
Celery Tray, Handled	35.00
Compote, Open. 5". High standard	38.00
Cup, Punch	15.00
Goblet	40.00
Mug	18.50
Nappy	27.50
Pitchers	
Milk	55.00
*Water	75.00
Plates	
9½". Rolled rim	30.00
10"	35.00
Relish. 4½x7"	17.50
Rose Bowl	40.00
Sauce, Flat. 4"	8.50
Sugars	
Individual	35.00
Regular, Covered	35.00
Regular, Open	35.00
Toothpick	6.50
*Tumbler	30.00
Tumbler, Ruby stained. (Souvenir-type)	25.00

*Reproduced Item

IVY, ROYAL, See ROYAL IVY
(See Colored Glass Section)

IVY IN SNOW
(Forest Ware)

Non-flint made by Cooperative Flint Glass Co., Beaver Falls, Pa., in the late 1880 period and continued by other firms. SEE NOTE:

Bowl. 8" $	26.50
Butter, Covered	50.00
Cake Stand, Large	50.00
Celery	30.00
Compotes, Covered. High standard	
Small	32.50
Medium	55.00
Large	75.00
Creamer	22.00
Goblet	20.00
Marmalade Jar	32.50
Pitcher, Water	45.00
Plates	
6"	20.00
8"	25.00
10"	30.00
Relish	15.00
Sauce, Flat. 4"	10.00
Spooner	27.50
Sugars	
Covered	45.00
Open	25.00
Tumbler	20.00
Wine	24.00

NOTE: Reproduced in clear and milk white.

JACOB'S COAT

Non-flint. C. 1880's. SEE NOTE:

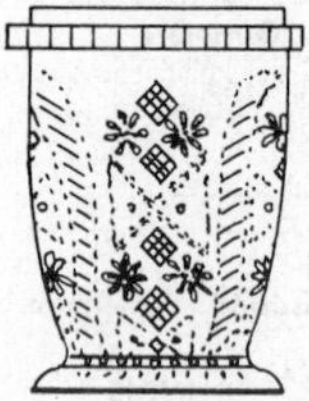

Bowl. 8" $	25.00
Butter, Covered	35.00
Celery	25.00
Creamer	25.00
Goblet	28.50
Pitcher	45.00
Relish	15.00

Sauce, Flat	6.50
Spooner	18.50
Sugar, Covered	25.00

NOTE: Amber add 50% to clear.

JACOB'S LADDER
(Maltese)

Non-flint made by Byrce Bros., Pittsburgh, Pa. in the 1870's. Reissued in 1890's; but of inferior quality.

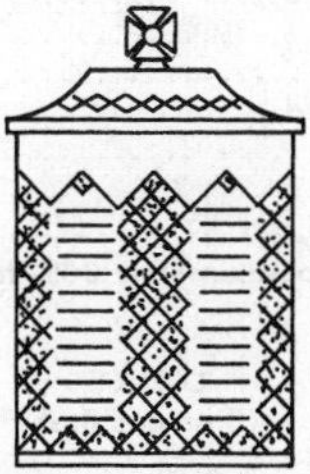

Bowls	
7¼", Footed	$ 20.00
10"	30.00
Butter, Covered	50.00
Cake Stand. 9½"	35.00
Castor Bottle	12.50
Celery	30.00
Compotes, Open	
7". Low standard	25.00
9". High standard	35.00
12". Low standard	75.00
Dolphin standard. (scarce)	250.00
Creamer	40.00
Goblet	55.00
Honey	12.50
Honey, Covered	65.00
Marmalade Jar	50.00
Pitchers	
Syrup, Knight's head knob	85.00
Syrup, Plain top	40.00
Water	125.00
Plate. 6½"	25.00
Platters	
8"	18.50
9¾"	25.00
Relish. Maltese Cross handles	18.00
Sauces	
Flat, 3½", 4"	10.00
Footed, 4½"	12.50
Spooner	27.50
Sugars	
Covered	55.00
Open	25.00
Tumbler, Bar	55.00
Wine	35.00

JEWEL AND DEWDROP
(Kansas)

Non-flint originally produced by Cooperative Flint Glass Co., Beaver Falls, Pa. Later produced by U.S. Glass Co. under the name of "Kansas" in 1907.

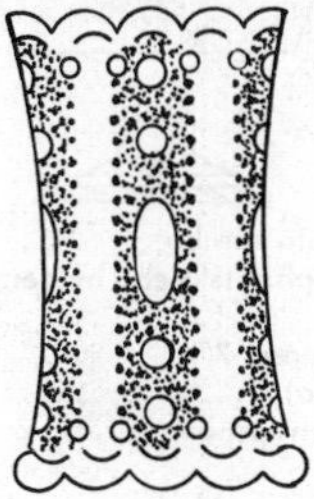

Banana Stand	$ 45.00
Bowls	
6½"	20.00
7½"	22.50
Butter, Covered	55.00
Cake Stands	
8"	35.00
10"	45.00
Celery	35.00
Compotes, Open	
6½". Low standard	20.00
9½". High standard	40.00
Cordial	28.50
Creamer	25.00
*Goblet	30.00
*Mug	20.00
Pitchers	
Milk	40.00
Syrup	65.00
Water	35.00
Relish	20.00
Sauce, Flat	10.00
Shakers, Pair	60.00
Spooner. (scarce)	35.00
Sugar, Covered	40.00
Toothpick	35.00
Tray, Bread	35.00
Tumbler, Water	26.50
Wine	30.00

*Reproduced Item

JUMBO AND BARNUM

A non-flint novelty pattern made by Canton Glass Co., Canton, Ohio in 1870's. The unique motif was used to commemorate P.T. Barnum's famous "Jumbo". Later, numerous unrelated patterns with the elephant motif were made . ."Plain Jumbo" and "Elephant."

Butters	
Covered. Barnum's Head	$ 300.00

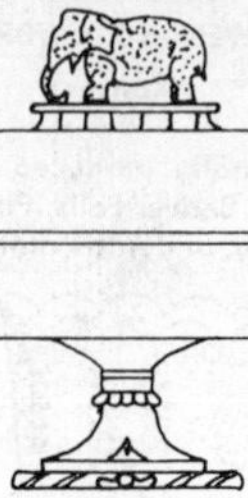

Oblong. (Plain Jumbo)	225.00
Castor Set. Elephants' Head holder.	
With bottles	350.00
Compote, Covered. 7".	
(Plain Jumbo)	200.00
Creamer. (Plain Jumbo)	85.00
Goblet. (Rare)	350.00+
Spooner. Barnum's Head	100.00
Spoon Rack. Barnum's Head	125.00
Sugars	
Covered. Barnum's Head	250.00+
Open. (Plain Jumbo)	65.00
Toothpick. (With box on back)	55.00

KING'S CROWN
(Ruby Thumbprint when stained with red)

A non-flint pattern made by Adams & Co. and others from the 1890's. Made in clear, clear with gilt, ruby-stained, and rare in green and blue. Clear and ruby stained are the most prevalent. Practically every piece has been reproduced. SEE NOTE:

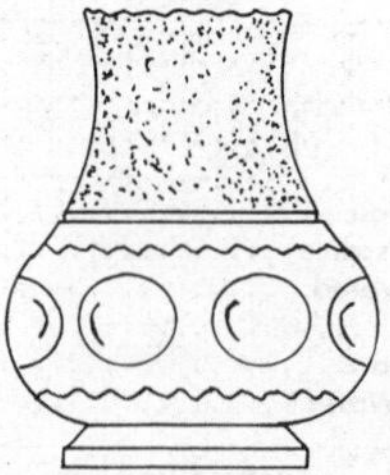

Banana Stand ....$	225.00
Bowls	
7½", Berry	42.50
10", Oval, Scalloped	65.00
Butter, Covered	60.00
Cake Stand. 9"	55.00
Castor Set. All Glass, 4-bottles,	
complete	150.00
Celery Vase	55.00
Champagne	35.00
Cheese, Covered	195.00
Compote, Open. 7". High standard	45.00
Creamer, Regular	400.00
Creamer and Sugar, Individual	55.00
Cup and Saucer	50.00
Goblet	30.00
Olive Dish. Round, Handled	25.00
Pitchers, Water	
Bulbous	125.00
Tankard	100.00
Plate. 8", Square	35.00
Sauces	
Boat-shaped	17.50
Scalloped top	15.00
Shakers, Pair	50.00
Spooner	35.00
Sugar, Covered	65.00
Toothpick	18.50
Tumbler	20.00
Wine	25.00

NOTE: Add approximately 30% for gilt or ruby stained.

LATTICE
(Diamond Bar)

Non-flint made by King, Son & Co., Pittsburgh, Pa., C. 1880.

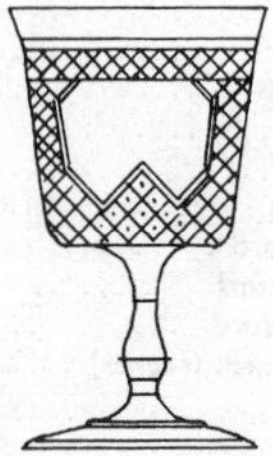

Bowl. 9½", Deep ....$	20.00
Butter, Covered	45.00
Cake Stand. 12½"	50.00
Celery	27.50
Compote, Covered. 7½" High std. . .	40.00
Creamer	30.00
Egg Cup	18.50
Goblet	25.00
Pitchers	
Milk	30.00
Syrup	40.00
Water	45.00
Plates	
6"	10.00
7"	15.00
10", Bread	32.50
Relish	15.00
Sauces	
Flat	8.50
Footed	15.00

Spooner	22.50
Sugar, Covered	35.00
Wine	18.50

LIBERTY BELL
(Centennial)

Made by Gillinder & Co., Philadelphia, Pa. for the Philadelphia Centennial, Exposition, 1876.

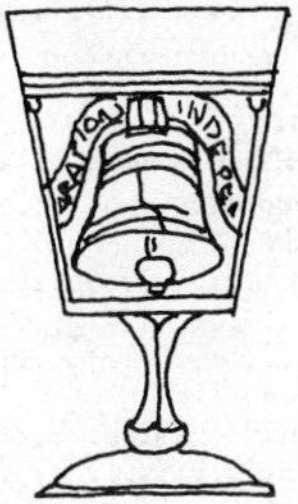

Bowls, Footed	
6″	$ 100.00
8″	135.00
Butter, Covered	150.00
Compote, Open. 8″	110.00
Creamer, Applied handle	150.00
Goblet	65.00
Mug. Snake handle, (rare)	275.00+
Pickle, 5½ x 9½″. With 13 colonies	65.00
Pitcher, Water. Applied handle	500.00+
Plate	
6″. With 13 colonies	75.00
8″. With 13 colonies	95.00
10″. With 13 colonies	125.00
Platters, Bread	
Clear. 9½x13⅜″. No signatures	125.00
Milk White. 7x11½″.	
John Hancock	250.00+
Milk White. 9½x13½″	300.00+
Salt, Individual	35.00
Sauces	
Flat	30.00
Footed	40.00
Shakers, Pair	250.00
Spooner	100.00
Sugars	
Covered	135.00
Open	75.00

LILY OF THE VALLEY

Non-flint pattern made in the 1870's in two forms. . .plain stem and three-legged. Attributed to Boston and Sandwich Glass Co.

Butter. Either type	$ 55.00
Cake Stand	65.00
Celery	42.50
Compote, Covered. 8″. High std.	85.00

Creamer. Either type	47.50
Cruet. Stoppered	50.00
Egg Cup	39.50
Goblet	37.50
Pitchers	
Milk. Plain-type	75.00
Water. Plain-type	85.00
Relish. 5x8″	16.50
Salt, Covered. Legged	45.00
Spooner	26.50
Sugar, Covered. Legged	60.00
Wine. (scarce)	50.00

LINCOLN DRAPE

Flint. C. 1860's.

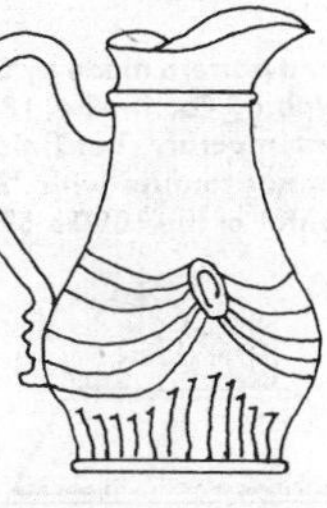

Butter, Covered	$ 100.00
Celery	85.00
Compotes	
Covered. 8½″. High standard	150.00
Open. 6″. Low standard	65.00
Open. 8″. High standard	85.00
Creamer	125.00
Egg Cup	50.00
Goblet	75.00
Honey	20.00
Lamp. Marble base	125.00
Pitchers	
Syrup	100.00
Water	350.00
Salt, Footed	40.00
Sauce, Flat. 4½″	20.00
Spillholder	50.00
Spooner	60.00
Sugar	
Covered	125.00

Open	50.00
Wine	50.00

LINCOLN DRAPE WITH TASSEL

Flint. C. 1860's. Contemporary of Lincoln Drape.

Butter, Covered $	135.00
Compote, Open. 6". Low standard	100.00
Egg Cup	65.00
Goblet	100.00
Spooner	80.00
Sugar, Covered	165.00

LION

Clear and frosted pattern made by Gillinder and Sons, Philadelphia, Pa. in the 1870's. "Lion's Head" is a contemporary; but finials are lion's heads only. Do not confuse with "Square Lion's Head" or "Atlanta" of the 1890's. SEE NOTE:

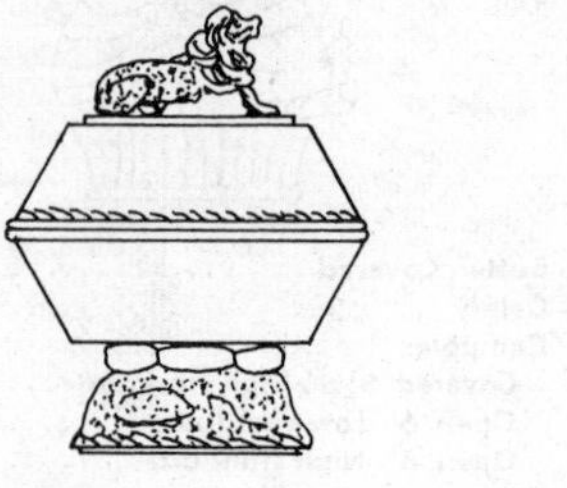

Butters, Covered	
Lion head finial $	85.00
Rampant finial	100.00
Celerys	
Etched	100.00
Plain	60.00
Champagne, Frosted	200.00
Cheese, Covered. Rampant finial	350.00+
Compotes, Covered	
6". Low standard. Rampant finial	85.00
7". High standard. Rampant finial	125.00
9". Oval. Collared base. Rampant finial	100.00
10". Low standard. Rampant finial	100.00
Compote, Open. 8". Low standard	65.00
Creamer	65.00
Egg Cup, Frosted	80.00
Goblet, Frosted	60.00
Marmalade Jar. Rampant finial	85.00
Paperweight	150.00
Pitchers	
Milk	350.00+
Syrup	250.00
Water	225.00
Plate, Bread. 10"	75.00
Relish, Frosted. Lion handles	45.00
Salt, Master. Footed	150.00
Sauces, Footed	
4"	15.00
5"	20.00
Spooner	50.00
Sugars, Covered	
Lion head finial	65.00
Rampant finial	85.00
Sugar, Open	38.50
Wine, Frosted	150.00

NOTE: Reproductions abound.

LOG CABIN

Non-flint made by Central Glass Co., Wheeling, W. Va., C. 1875.

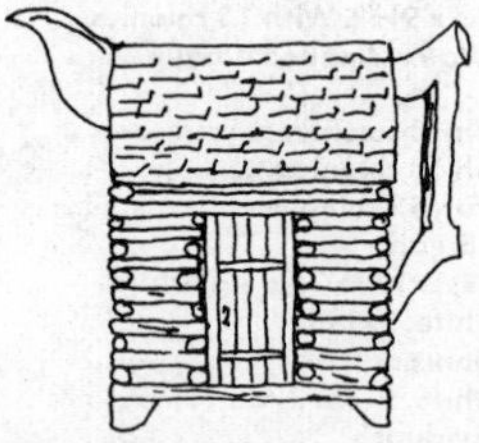

Butter, Covered $	200.00
Compote, Covered. 4x6". High std.	225.00
Creamer	125.00
Pitcher, Water	225.00
Sauce, Flat.	35.00
Spooner	100.00
Sugar, Covered	150.00

LOOP
(Seneca Loop)

Flint of the 1850-60's. Made by several firms Later produced in non-flint. Yuma Loop is a contemporary with comparable values. Prices listed are for flint.

Bowl. 9" $	50.00
Butter, Covered	65.00

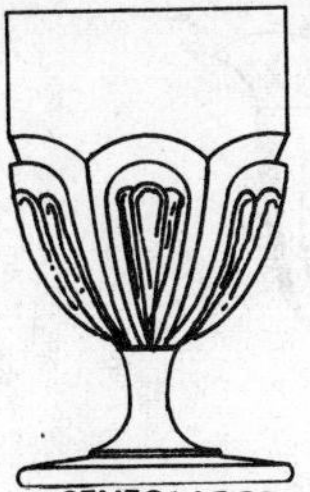

SENECA LOOP

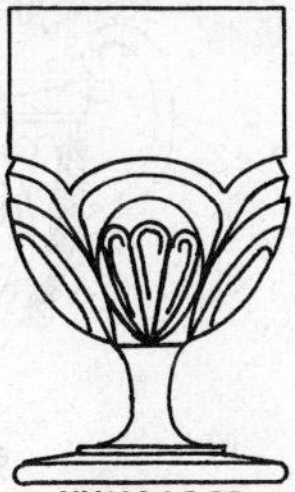

YUMA LOOP

Cake Stand	75.00
Celery	50.00
Champagne	27.50
Compotes	
Covered. 8". High standard	60.00
Open. 8". Low standard	35.00
Creamer	60.00
Egg Cup	27.50
Flip	40.00
Goblet	25.00
Pitcher, Water	75.00
Salt, Master	20.00
Spooner	30.00
Sugars	
Covered	60.00
Open	35.00
Wine	30.00

LOOP AND DART

Non-flint clear and stippled pattern of the 1860's with many variants. . .Loop and Dart with Diamond Ornaments, Loop and Dart with Round Ornaments, Double Loop and Dart, Leaf and Dart and others. Prices for all are comparable.

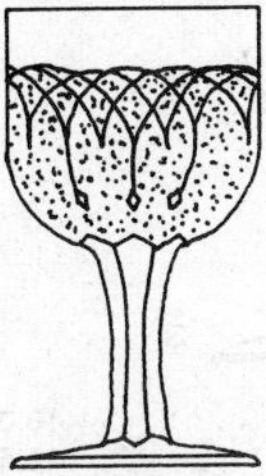

LOOP AND DART

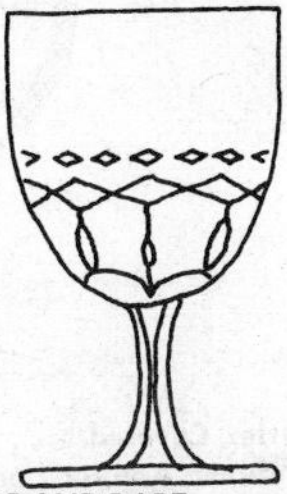

LOOP AND DART WITH DIAMOND ORNAMENTS

Bowl. 6x9", Oval	$ 20.00
Butter, Covered	45.00
Cake Stand. 10"	35.00
Celery	45.00
Compotes	
Covered. 8". High standard	60.00
Open. 8". Low standard	30.00
Creamer, Applied handle	45.00

DOUBLE LOOP AND DART

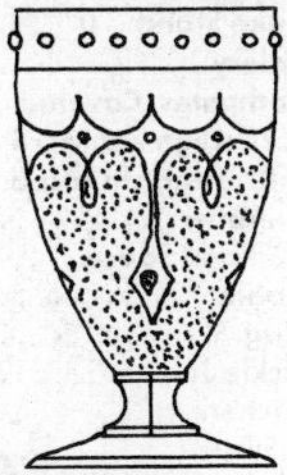

LOOP AND DART WITH ROUND ORNAMENTS

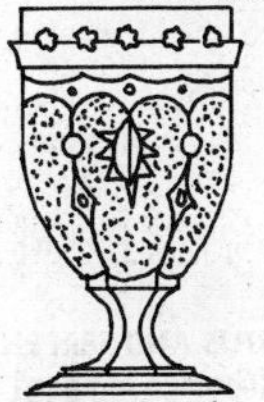

LEAF AND DART

Egg Cup	20.00
Goblet	30.00
Pitcher, Water	65.00
Plate. 6"	25.00
Relish	15.00
Salt, Master	30.00
Sauces	
Flat	7.50
Footed	10.00
Spooner	25.00
Sugars	
Covered	45.00
Open	22.50
Tumbler, Footed	25.00
Wine	20.00

LOOP WITH DEWDROPS

Early maker unknown. Reissued by U.S. Glass Co. in 1892 and later in 1898.

Bowl. 8"	$ 18.50
Butter, Covered	35.00

Cake Stand. 10"	42.00
Celery	25.00
Compotes, Covered	
7". High standard	35.00
8". High standard	45.00
Creamer	30.00
Cup and Saucer	25.00
Goblet	22.50
Mug	12.50
Pickle Jar	20.00
Pitchers	
Syrup	35.00
Water	32.50
Sauces	
Flat, 4"	7.50
Footed, 4"	12.00
Shakers, Pair	25.00
Spooner	20.00
Sugar, Covered	32.00
Tumbler	17.50
Wine	25.00

LOTUS AND SERPENT
(Garden of Eden)

Non-flint. C. 1870's.

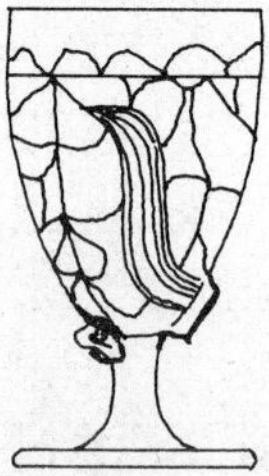

Bowl. 4½x7", Oval $	17.50
Butter, Covered	60.00
Cake Stand. 11½"	50.00
Compote, Covered. 10" High std.	75.00
Creamer	50.00
Goblet	60.00
Mug	38.50
Pickle, Oval	20.00
Plate. 6½", Handled	20.00
Salt, Master	30.00
Sauce, Flat	12.00
Spooner	25.00
Sugars	
Covered	50.00
Open	27.50
Tray, Bread	40.00

MAGNET AND GRAPE-FROSTED LEAF

Flint. C. 1860's. SEE NOTE:

Butter, Covered $	135.00
Celery Vase	195.00
Champagne	115.00
Compote. Open. 7". High standard	125.00
Cordial	150.00
Creamer	115.00
Decanter, Quart. Original stopper	250.00
Egg Cup	75.00
Goblets	
American Shield. (rare)	150.00+
Knob stem	65.00
Low stem	85.00
Salt, Footed	45.00
Sauce, Flat	15.00
Sugar, Covered	125.00
Tumblers	
Water	100.00
Whiskey	125.00

NOTE: Reproductions reported.

MAGNET AND GRAPE-STIPPLED LEAF

Non-flint. C. 1870's.

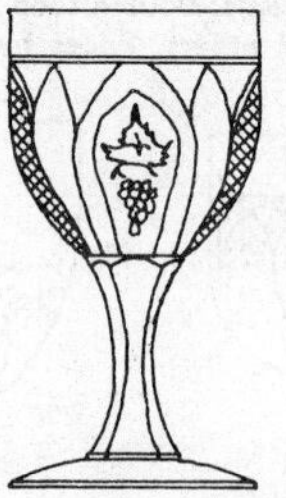

Butter, Covered $	40.00
Creamer, Applied handle	42.50
Egg Cup	22.50
Goblet	25.00
Mug	22.50
Pitchers	
Syrup, Spring lid	50.00
Water, Applied handle	75.00
Relish, Oval	15.00
Salt, Footed	15.00
Sauce, Flat. 4"	7.50
Spooner	25.00

Sugar, Open	22.50
Tumbler	20.00
Wine	25.00

MAINE
(Stippled Panelled Flower)

Non-flint made by U.S. Glass Co., Pittsburgh, Pa., C. 1890's.
SEE NOTE:

Bowls	
6x8"	$ 22.50
8"	27.50
Cake Stand	60.00
Celery	28.50
Creamer	22.50
Mug	20.00
Sauce, Flat	10.00
Sugars	
Covered	28.50
Open	18.00
Toothpick	18.50

NOTE: Goblets were not made. Items are sometimes found with enamel trim, and in emerald green. Green-add 100%.

MAIZE
(See Colored Glass Section)

MANHATTAN
Non-flint made by U.S. Glass Co., C. 1902. SEE NOTE:

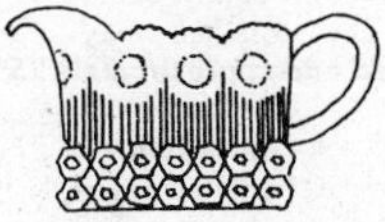

Bowls	
7"	$ 12.50
8½"	15.00
10"	20.00
12½"	25.00
Cake Stand. 10"	35.00
Celery	12.50
Compote, Covered. 9½". High std.	35.00
Creamers	
Individual	10.00
Regular	16.50
Goblet	12.50
Pitcher, Water. Tankard	45.00
Plates	
6"	12.00
10½"	17.50
Punch Cup	5.50
Punch Set. 14 pieces	150.00
Sauce Flat. 4½"	6.00
Sugars	
Covered	27.50
Open, Individual	12.50
Tumbler	12.00
Wine	12.00

NOTE: Reproduced in clear and color.

MAPLE LEAF
(See Colored Glass Section)

MARQUISETTE
Non-flint made by Cooperative Flint Glass Co., Beaver Falls, Pa., C. 1880.

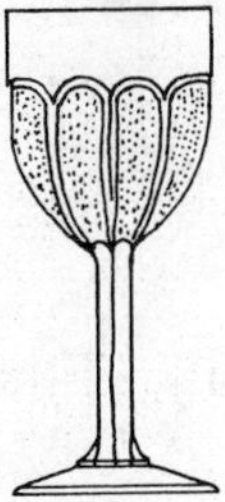

Butter, Covered	$ 60.00
Celery	32.50
Champagne	30.00
Compotes	
Covered. High standard	65.00
Open. Low standard	35.00
Creamer, Applied handle	55.00
Goblet	25.00
Pitcher, Water. Applied handle	65.00
Sauce, Flat. 4"	12.00
Spooner	25.00
Sugar, Covered	55.00
Wine	25.00

MASCOTTE
Non-flint made by Ripley & Co., Pittsburgh, Pa., in the 1870's. Reissued by U.S. Glass Co. in 1898.

Bowl. 8"	$ 17.50
Butter, Covered	45.00
Cake Basket with handle	85.00
Cake Stand. 10½"	35.00

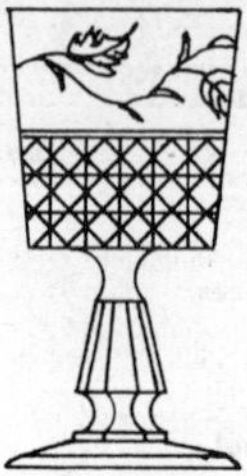

Celery Vases

Etched	35.00
Plain	25.00
Cheese, Covered	55.00
Compotes	
Covered. 8″. High standard	75.00
Open. 8″. Low standard	40.00
Creamer, Etched	35.00
Goblet, Etched	30.00
Marmalade Jar, Covered. Pat'd. May 20, 1873.	55.00
Pitchers	
Milk	17.50
Water	37.50
Sauces	
Flat	7.50
Footed	15.00
Shakers, Pair	30.00
Spooner, Etched	25.00
Sugar, Covered	35.00
Tray, Water. Etched	45.00
Tumbler	17.50
Wine	22.50

MASONIC

Non-flint made by McKee Glass Co., Jeannette, Pa., C. 1894.

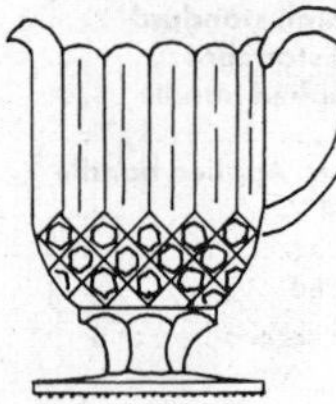

Bowl. 8″ $	25.00
Butter, Covered	40.00
Cake Stand	38.50
Celery	17.50
Creamer	32.50
Pitcher, Water	55.00
Sauce, Flat	8.00
Spooner	15.00
Sugar, Covered	37.50
Tumbler	18.50

MEDALLION

(See Colored Glass Section)

MELROSE

Non-flint made by Brilliant Glass Works, Brilliant, Ohio. C. 1887. SEE NOTE:

Banana Stand $	30.00
Bowl. 8″	20.00
Butter, Covered	32.50
Cake Stand. 10″	35.00
Celery	20.00
Compotes	
Covered. 6″. High standard	37.50
Covered. 8″. High standard	45.00
Open. 7″. Low standard	25.00
Creamer	18.00
Goblet	18.00
Mug	12.50
Pickle	12.50
Pitchers	
Milk	30.00
Water	40.00
Plates	
8″	10.00
9″	12.00
10″	13.50
Sauce, Footed	7.50
Spooner	15.00
Sugars	
Covered	25.00
Open	15.00
Tray, Water	35.00
Wine	15.00

NOTE: Etched add approximately 25%

MICHIGAN

(Panelled Jewel)

Non-flint made by U.S. Glass Co., C. 1893.

Bowls	
8½″ $	18.50
10″	25.00
Butter, Covered	35.00
Champagne	27.50
Creamers	
Individual	20.00
Regular	28.50

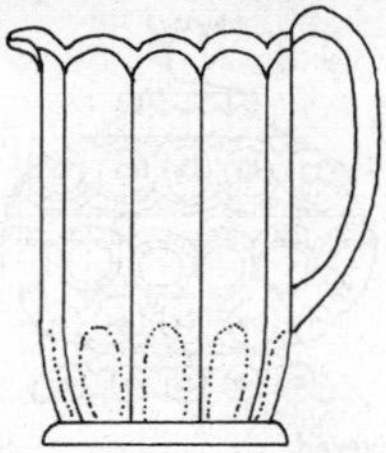

Cruet, Stoppered	25.00
Goblet	25.00
Pitchers	
Milk	35.00
Water	55.00
Sauce	8.00
Shakers, Pair	30.00
Spooner	20.00
Sugar, Covered	30.00
Water Bottle	28.50
Wine	25.00

MIKADO
(Late Butterfly)

Non-flint made by Indiana Glass Co., Dunkirk, Indiana in the early 1900's.

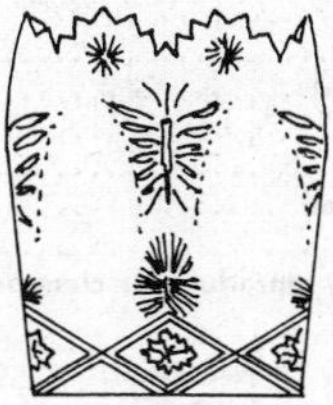

Bowls. Various sizes	$15.00-20.00
Butter, Covered	25.00
Celery	15.00
Compotes. Various sizes	20.00- 35.00
Creamer	17.50
Goblet	15.00
Pitchers	
Milk	20.00
Water	25.00
Punch Cup	7.50
Sauce	5.00
Spooner	13.50
Sugars	
Covered	17.50
Open	12.50
Tumbler	10.00
Wine	12.00

MINERVA
(Guardian Angel)

Non-flint made by Boston and Sandwich Glass. Co.

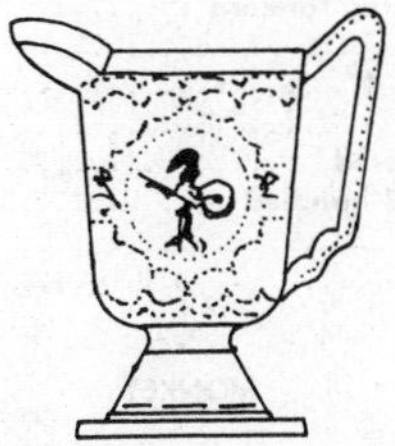

Butter, Covered	$ 80.00
Cake Stands	
9″	68.50
13″	100.00
Compote, Covered. 7″. High std.	85.00
Creamer	45.00
Goblet. (rare)	85.00
Marmalade Jar, Covered	75.00
Pickle, Inscribed	40.00
Pitcher, Water	100.00
Plates	
9″, Closed handles	55.00
11″	65.00
Platter. 9x13″	60.00
Relish. 5x8″	25.00
Sauces	
Flat	15.00
Footed	20.00
Spooner	30.00
Sugar, Covered	65.00

MINNESOTA

Non-flint made by U.S. Glass Co. in the late 1890's.

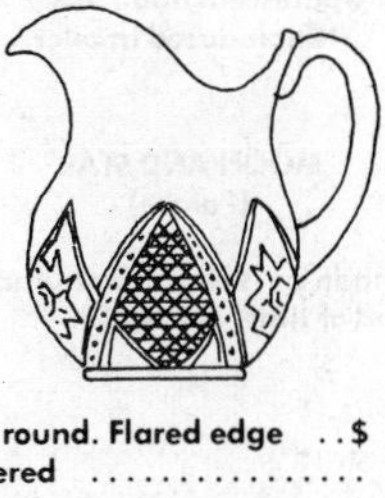

Bowl. 8½″, round. Flared edge	$ 30.00
Butter, Covered	45.00
Celery Trays	
10″	25.00
13″	30.00
Compotes, Open	
9″, Square. Low standard	28.50

10", Flared edge. High standard	65.00
Creamer	30.00
Goblet	20.00
Mug	12.50
Nappy	10.00
Pitcher, Water. Tankard	45.00
Relish	15.00
Sauce, Flat. 4"	8.50
Spooner	18.00
Sugar, Covered	37.50
Toothpick, 3-handled	30.00
Tumbler	15.00
Wine	18.50

MONKEY

Non-flint pattern made by George A. Duncan & Sons, Washington, Pa., C. 1880's. SEE NOTE:

Bowl. 8½"	$ 100.00
Butter, Covered	150.00
Creamer	100.00
Mug	65.00
Pitcher, Water	175.00
*Spooner	95.00
Sugars	
Covered	150.00
Open	75.00
*Toothpick	65.00
Tumbler	75.00
Waste Bowl	85.00

NOTE: Fiery Opalescent add 75%.
*Reproduced in color

MOON AND STAR
(Palace)

Non-flint made by several manufacturers: over a long period of time. SEE NOTE:

Bowls	
6"	$ 17.50
8"	25.00
12½"	35.00
Butter, Covered	55.00
Cake Stand. 9"	55.00
Celery	35.00
Champagne	50.00

Cheese, Covered	65.00
Compotes	
Covered. 7". Low standard	40.00
Covered. 8". High standard	55.00
Covered. 10". High standard	75.00
Open. 9". High standard	37.50
Creamer	50.00
Cruet	65.00
Egg Cup	35.00
Goblets	
Clear	35.00
Frosted	42.50
Lamp, Tall	65.00
Pickle, Oval	20.00
Pitchers	
Syrup	65.00
Water	100.00
Salt Dip	7.50
Sauces	
Flat	8.50
Footed	15.00
Shakers, Pair	45.00
Spooner	25.00
Sugar, Covered	50.00
Toothpick	17.50
Tray, Water	45.00
Tumbler, Footed	45.00
Wine	32.50

NOTE: Heavily reproduced in clear and color.

NAILHEAD
(Gem)
Non-flint. C. 1880's.

Butter, Covered	$ 40.00
Cake Stands	
9"	30.00
12"	45.00
Celery	27.50

Compotes
  Covered. 8". High standard 50.00
  Open. 9½". High standard 35.00
Cordial 25.00
Creamer 25.00
Goblet 22.50
Pitcher, Water 50.00
Plates
  Round, 9" 17.50
  Square, 7" 22.50
Sauce, Flat 8.00
Spooner 22.50
Sugar, Covered 30.00
Tumbler 18.00
Wine 16.50

NEVADA

Non-flint made by U.S. Glass Co.

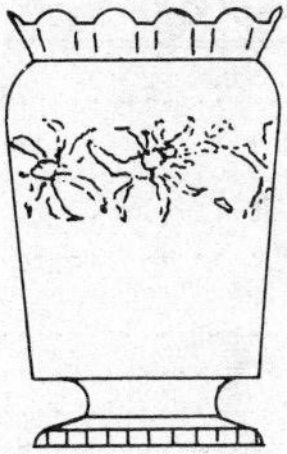

Bowl. 8" ....$	15.00
Butter, Covered	28.50
Cake Stand. 10"	25.00
Celery	17.50
Compotes	
Covered. 8". High standard	35.00
Open. 6". Low standard	25.00
Creamer	17.50
Cruet	15.00
Pickle, Oval	10.00
Pitchers	
Syrup	18.50
Water, Tankard	30.00
Salts	
Individual	5.00
Master	8.50
Sauce	6.50
Shakers, Pair	20.00
Sugar, Covered	22.50
Toothpick	10.00
Tumbler	10.00

NEW ENGLAND PINEAPPLE

(Pineapple, Loop and Jewel)

Flint made by Boston and Sandwich Glass Co. in the early 1860's.

Castor Bottle ....$	28.50

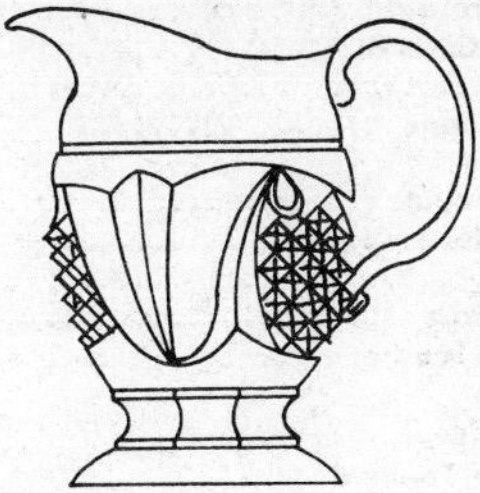

Castor Set. 4-Bottle, complete	350.00
Champagne	100.00
Compotes, Open	
7". High standard	65.00
8½". High standard	80.00
Cordial	75.00
Creamer	175.00
Decanters	
Pint. No stopper	75.00
Quart. Stoppered	125.00
Egg Cup	37.50
Goblet. Either size	39.50
Mug	175.00
Pitcher, Water	300.00
Plate. 6"	85.00
Salt, Master	40.00
Sauce, Flat	15.00
Spooner	40.00
Sugars	
Covered	85.00
Open	35.00
Tumblers	
Bar	85.00
Water	75.00
Whiskey, Handled	125.00
*Wine	75.00

*Reproduced Item

NEW HAMPSHIRE

(Bent Buckle)

Non-flint made by U.S. Glass Co.

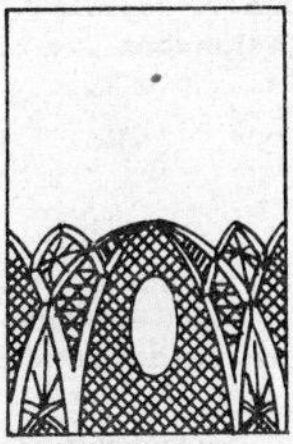

Bowls	
Flared. 6½", 7½", 8½" ....$	15.00
Round. 6½", 7½", 8½"	17.50

Square. 6½", 7½", 8½"	20.00
Butter, Covered	30.00
Celery	22.50
Champagne	17.50
Creamers	
Individual	15.00
Regular	22.50
Goblet	18.50
Mug, Large	15.00
Nappy, Square	8.50
Pitchers	
Syrup	35.00
Water, Tankard	30.00
Punch Cup	10.00
Sugars	
Covered	27.50
Individual	20.00
Toothpick	15.00
Tumbler	12.50
Wine	15.00

NEW JERSEY
(Loops and Drops)
Non-flint made by U.S. Glass Co.

Bowls	
8", Flared $	18.50
10", Oval	25.00
Butter, Covered	35.00
Cake Stand. 8"	30.00
Celery Tray	15.00
Celery Vase	25.00
Compotes	
Jelly. Covered, 5"	28.50
Open. 8". High standard	35.00
Creamer	18.50
Cruet	20.00
Goblet	28.50
Pickle	12.00
Pitchers	
Syrup	25.00
Water, 1 Gallon. Applied handle	65.00
Water, ½ Gallon. Molded handle	35.00
Plates	
8"	18.50
10½"	25.00
12"	28.50
Sauce, 4"	7.50
Shakers, Pair	35.00
Spooner	20.00
Sugar, Covered	30.00
Toothpick	10.00
Tumbler	18.50
Wine	20.00

NIAGARA

Non-flint made by Fostoria Glass Co. in the 1900's.

Bowl. 8" $	15.00
Butter, Covered	25.00
Celery Vase	18.50
Creamer	16.50
Cruet, Stoppered	18.50
Pitchers	
Syrup	20.00
Water, Tankard	32.50
Sauce, 4"	7.50
Shakers, Pair	25.00
Spooner	12.50
Sugar, Covered	22.50
Tumbler	10.00

OAK, ROYAL
(See Royal Oak in the Colored Glass Section)

ONE HUNDRED ONE

Non-flint made by Bellaire Goblet Co., Findlay, Ohio in the late 1870's.

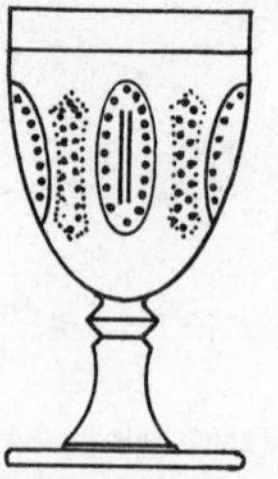

Butter, Covered $	60.00
Cake Stand. 9"	50.00
Celery	50.00

Compote, Covered. Low standard	60.00
Creamer	36.50
Goblet	35.00
Lamp, Hand	85.00
Pitcher, Water	100.00
Plates	
7″	18.50
9″	22.50
11″	40.00
Relish	15.00
Sauces	
Flat	10.00
Footed	13.50
Spooner	40.00
Sugars	
Covered	45.00
Open	25.00

OPALESCENT HOBNAIL

(See General Section "Opalescent Glass")

OPEN ROSE

C. 1870's

Bowls	
Berry, Handled. Scalloped	$ 30.00
Oval, 6x9″	22.50
Butter, Covered	55.00
Celery	35.00
Compotes	
Covered. 9″. High standard	65.00
Open. 7½″. Low standard	30.00
Creamer	40.00
Egg Cup	25.00
Goblet	25.00
Pitcher, Water. Applied handle	175.00
Relish	15.00
Salt, Master	17.50
Sauce, Flat. 4″	7.50
Spooner	25.00
Sugar, Covered	55.00
Tumbler	35.00

OVAL MITRE

Flint. C. Late 1850's

Butter, Covered	$ 75.00

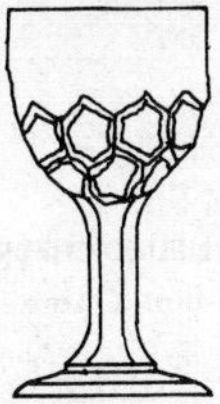

Creamer, Applied handle	60.00
Compotes	
Covered. 6″. High standard	55.00
Open. 7″. High standard	45.00
Open. 10″. High standard	65.00
Goblet	40.00
Sauce, 4″	10.00
Spooner	35.00
Sugar, Covered	65.00

PALMETTE

(Spades, Hearts and Spades)

Non-flint. C. Late 1870's

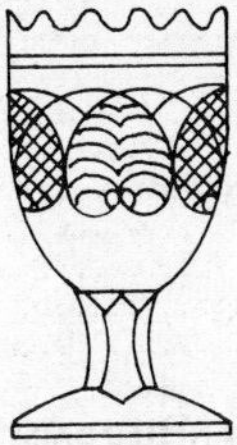

Bowl. 8″	$ 12.50
Butter Chip. 2″	7.50
Butter, Covered	50.00
Cake Stand	38.50
Castor Bottle	15.00
Celery Vase	30.00
Compotes	
Covered. 8½″. High standard	55.00
Open. 7″. Low Standard	25.00
Cordial	25.00
Creamer, Applied handle	50.00
Egg Cup	27.50
Goblet	26.50
Lamp, Oil	60.00
Pitchers	
Syrup, Applied handle	50.00
Water, Applied handle	75.00
Relish Scoop	17.50
Salt, Master. Footed	18.50
Sauces	
4″	7.50
6″	15.00
Spooner	25.00
Sugar, Covered	35.00

Tumblers	
Bar	45.00
Footed	30.00
Wine	22.50

PANELLED CHERRY

Non-flint. C. Late 1880's

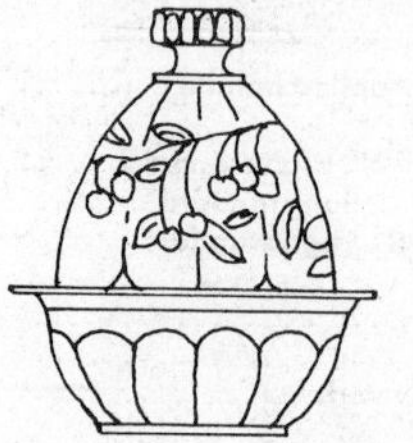

Bowl. 8" $	25.00
Butter, Covered	45.00
Creamer	32.50
Goblet	30.00
Pitchers	
Syrup	28.50
Water	45.00
Sauces	
Flat	6.50
Footed. Ruby stained	15.00
Spooner	22.50
Sugar, Covered	32.50
Toothpick	10.00
Tumbler	18.00

PANELLED DAISY

(Brazil, Oval Medallion)

Non-flint made by Bryce Bros., Pittsburgh, Pa., in the late 1870's.

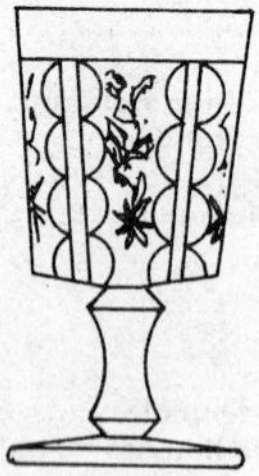

Bowls	
5x7", Oval $	16.50
9", Square	22.50
10½", Open	27.50
Waste	20.00
Butter, Covered	45.00
Cake Stands	
8", 9"	40.00
10", 11"	50.00
Celery Vase	35.00
Compotes	
Covered 5", 6", High standard	37.50
Covered. 7", 8". High standard	45.00
Covered. 10", 11". High standard	65.00
Open. 11". High standard	50.00
Creamer	40.00
*Goblet	30.00
Mug	25.00
Pickle, Handled	17.50
Pitchers	
Syrup	50.00
Water	60.00
Plates	
Round, 7"	22.50
Square, 9"	27.50
Relish. 5x7"	15.00
Sauces	
Flat	10.00
Footed	15.00
Shakers	
Salt and Pepper, Pair	38.50
Sugar	32.50
Spooner	25.00
Sugar, Covered	45.00
Tray, Water	42.50
*Tumbler	26.00

*Reproduced Item

PANELLED DEWDROP

(Stippled Dewdrop)

Non-flint. C. Late 1870's

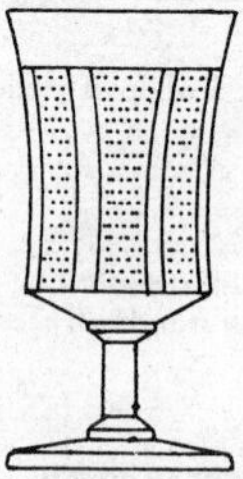

Bowls	
6½" $	15.00
8½", Oval	17.50
11", Oval, Footed	22.00
Butter, Covered	57.50
Celery Vase	32.50
Cheese, Covered	67.50
Compote, Covered. 8". High std.	55.00
Creamer, Applied handle	42.00
Goblets	
Dewdrops on base	36.00
Plain base	32.00

Lemonade Glass, Applied handle	40.00
Marmalade Jar, Covered	35.00
Mug, Applied handle	35.00
Pitcher, Water	50.00
Plates	
6"	18.00
10"	25.00
Platter, Bread. "Give Us..."	55.00
Relish. 5x7"	12.50
Sauces	
Flat	6.00
Footed	10.00
Spooner	35.00
Sugar, Covered	45.00
Wine	22.50

PANELLED DIAMOND POINT

Flint. C. 1860's

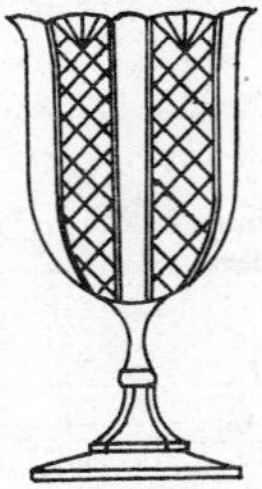

Butter, Covered	$ 80.00
Celery Vase	55.00
Creamer	50.00
Goblet	45.00
Pitcher, Water	85.00
Sauce	15.00
Spillholder	35.00
Spooner	35.00
Sugar, Covered	65.00

PANELLED FORGET-ME-NOT

(See Colored Glass Section)

PANELLED GRAPE

(Heavy Panelled Grape)

Non-flint made in Indiana, Pa., C. 1880-1900. This pattern has been heavily reproduced.

Ale Glass	$ 20.00
Bowl. 12", Crimped	30.00
Butter, Covered	45.00
Celery	25.00
Compotes	
Covered. 5"	35.00
Open. 6½". Low standard	26.50
Creamer. Vine handle	50.00
Goblet	35.00
Mug	18.50

Pitchers	
Syrup	55.00
Water	62.00
Plate. 10"	25.00
Salt	15.00
Sauces	
Oval	15.00
Round, 4¼"	13.50
Sherbet	18.50
Spooner	17.50
Sugar, Covered	50.00
Toothpick	20.00
Tumblers	
Jelly	27.50
Lemonade	25.00
Water	30.00

PANELLED GRAPE, LATE

Non-flint. C. 1890's.

Bowl. 12"	$ 29.50
Butter, Covered	47.50
Creamer	25.00
Goblet	25.00
Pitchers	
Milk	45.00
Syrup	38.50
Water	50.00
Sauce	12.50
Spooner	22.50
Sugar, Covered	35.00
Tumbler	15.00
Wine	18.50

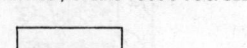

PANELLED HERRINGBONE
(Florida, Emerald Green Herringbone)

Made by U.S. Glass Co., C. Late 1800's-90's. SEE NOTE:

Bowls	
6"	$ 22.50
9"	30.00
Butter, Covered	35.00
Cake Stand	30.00
Celery	15.00
Compotes, Open	
5½"	22.50
6½". High standard. Square	35.00
Cordial	22.00
Creamer	17.50
Cruet	30.00
Goblets	
Buttermilk	20.00
Regular	15.00
Pitchers	
Milk	18.50
Syrup	25.00
Water	40.00
Plates	
7½", Square	10.00
9¼"	20.00
Relishes	
6", Square	12.00
8½", Square	15.00
Shakers, Pair	25.00
Sauce	10.00
Spillholder	22.50
Spooner	22.50
Sugars	
Covered	27.50
Open	20.00
Tumbler	17.50
Wine	12.50

NOTE: Green is approximately two times price of clear. Reproduced.
Also made in Milk Glass. Add 150% to price of clear.

PANELLED THISTLE

Non-flint made by J.P. Higbee Glass Co., Bridgeville, Pa., in the early 1900's. This pattern has been heavily reproduced.

Banana Stand	$ 55.00
Basket	35.00
Bowls	
7¼"	25.00
8" with bee	30.00
Butter, Covered	40.00
Cake Stand. 9"	25.00
Celerys	
Tray	18.50
Vase	25.00
Compotes, Open	
5". Low standard	18.50
8". High standard	25.00
Cordial	25.00
Creamer with bee	30.00
Cruet, stoppered	35.00
Egg Cup	22.50
Goblet	35.00
Honey, Covered. Square with bee	50.00
Pitchers	
Milk	40.00
Water	50.00
Plates	
7", Square	25.00
9"	20.00
10" with bee	32.00
Punch Cup with bee	32.00
Relish, 8" with bee	22.50
Rose Bowl. Large	50.00
Salts	
Dip	10.00
Master with bee	20.00
Sauces	
Flared with bee	15.00
Flat	10.00
Footed	12.00
Shakers, Pair	50.00
Spooner	20.00
Sugars	
Covered	38.50
Open	18.50
Toothpick with bee	30.00
Tumbler, Water	25.00
Vases	
5"	20.00
9". Trumpet-shaped	30.00
Wine	25.00
Wine with bee	30.00

PAVONIA
(With Pineapple Stem)

Non-flint made in Pittsburgh, Pa., C. 1880's

Bowls	
9", Plain	$ 28.50
Waste, Etched	32.00
Butter, Covered. Etched	50.00
Cake Stands	
Large, Etched	50.00
Small, Plain	30.00
Celery Vases	
Etched	28.00
Plain	20.00
Compotes	
Covered. 6". High std., etched	45.00
Open. 8". High standard, plain	32.00
Creamers	
Etched	32.50
Plain	18.50
Goblets	
Etched	35.00
Plain	22.50
Pitchers	
Etched	50.00
Plain	35.00
Salt, Individual	7.50
Sauces	
Flat	8.50
Footed	12.00
Spooner, Plain	20.00
Sugar, Covered. Etched	47.50
Tumblers	
Etched	18.50
Plain	12.00
Wines	
Etched	32.00
Plain	18.50

PEACOCK FEATHER
(Georgia, Peacock Eye)

Originally a Sandwich pattern, but reissued by several glass factories, including U.S. Glass Co. in 1907 as part of their States' series.

Bowl. 8"	$ 27.50
Butter, Covered	40.00
Cake Stand. 11"	40.00
Celery Tray	25.00
Compotes	
Jelly	25.00
Open, 8". High standard	30.00
Creamer	30.00
Cruet, Stoppered	30.00
Lamps	
7", Hand	40.00
9"	60.00
Pitchers	
Syrup	45.00
Water	60.00
Plate. 5¼"	25.00
Relish. 8", Oval	15.00
Sauces	
4½"	8.50
6½", Flared	22.50
Shakers, Pair	40.00
Spooner	22.50
Sugar, Covered	38.50
Tumbler	25.00

PENNSYLVANIA
(Balder)

Non-flint made by U.S. Glass Co., C. 1898

Bowls	
Berry. 8"	$ 20.00
Punch. 12"	65.00
Square. 8"	22.50
Butter, Covered	35.00
Carafe	25.00
Celery Tray	15.00
Champagne	17.50
Cheese, Covered	35.00
Creamer	22.50

Cruet, Stoppered	15.00
Goblet	20.00
Pitchers	
Syrup	22.50
Water, Tankard	40.00
Punch Cup	12.00
Sauces	
Round	7.50
Square	9.50
Shakers, Large. Pair	40.00
Spooner	25.00
Sugar, Covered	25.00
Tumblers	
Juice	9.50
Water	10.00
Wine	15.00

PICKET
(London)

Non-flint made by the King Glass Co., Pgh., Pa., in the late 1800's.

Butter, Covered	$ 55.00
Celery	30.00
Compote	
Covered. 6". High standard	45.00
Covered. 8". High standard	55 00
Open. 8". High standard	35.00
Creamer	32.50
Goblet	35.00
Marmalade Jar, Covered	30.00
Pitcher, Water	50.00
Salts	
Individual	10.00
Master	18.50
Sauces	
Flat	8.50
Footed	12.00
Sugar, Covered	38.50
Toothpick	25.00
Tray, Water	45.00
Waste Bowl	20.00

PINEAPPLE AND FAN
(Cube With Fan, Holbrook)

Non-flint made by Adams & Co., Pittsburgh, Pa., later by U.S. Glass Co., in 1891.

Bowls	
8"	$ 22.50
12", Punch	60.00
Waste	10.00
Bucket, Ice	35.00
Butter, Covered	35.00
Cake Stand. 9"	25.00
Celery Vase	30.00
Creamers	
Individual	18.50
Regular	28.50
Cruet, Stoppered	25.00
Cups	
Custard	15.00
Punch	10.00
Decanter, Stoppered	35.00
Goblet	18.50
Pitchers	
Milk	27.50
Water, Tankard	40.00
Plate. 6½"	15.00
Sauce, Flat. 4"	7.50
Spooner	20.00
Sugars	
Individual	20.00
Regular, Covered	30.00
Tumblers	
Water	12.50
Whiskey	15.00
Wine	20.00

PLEAT AND PANEL
(Derby)

Non-flint made by Bryce Bros., Pittsburgh, Pa., C. 1870-1880.

Bowls	
5x8", Covered	$ 45.00
Waste	37.50
Butter, Covered	50.00
Cake Stands	
9"	40.00
10"	55.00
Celery Vase	40.00
Compotes	
Covered. 6". High standard	40.00

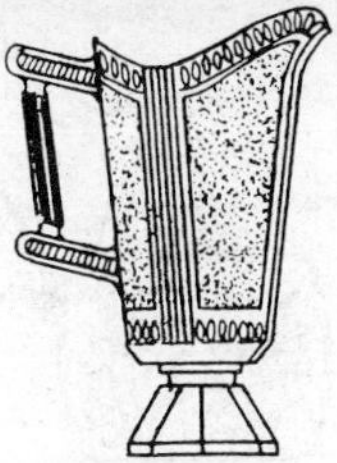

Covered. 8″. High standard	50.00
Open. 8″. High standard	25.00
Creamer	35.00
*Goblet	22.50
Marmalade Jar, Covered	40.00
Pitchers	
Milk	35.00
Water	50.00
Plates	
6″	17.50
*7″	15.00
8″	25.00
Relish. 5x8½″	15.00
Salt, Master	20.00
Sauces	
Flat	8.00
Handled	12.50
Shakers, Pair	40.00
Spooner	22.50
Sugar, Covered	42.00
Trays	
Bread, Closed handles	30.00
Bread, Open handles	35.00
Water (scarce)	65.00
Wine (scarce)	40.00

*Reproduced Item

PLUME

Non-flint made by Adams Glass Co., Pittsburgh, Pa., C. 1874.

Bowls	
6″	$ 25.00
8″, Shallow	17.50
Butter, Covered	42.00
Cake Stand. 10″	36.50
Celery	27.50
Compotes, Open	
6″. Low standard	25.00
7″. High standard, Flared	30.00
9″. High standard	35.00
Creamer	22.50
*Goblet	35.00
Lamp, Hand	60.00
Pickle	15.00
Pitcher, Water	45.00
Sauces	
Flat	10.00
Footed	15.00
Spooner	20.00
Sugar, Covered	40.00
Tumbler	17.50

*Reproduced Item

POLAR BEAR
(Iceberg, Artic, North Pole)

Non-flint made by Crystal Glass Co., Bridgeport, Ohio, C. 1880.

Bowls	
Ice, Clear	$ 85.00
Waste, Frosted	75.00
Goblets	
Clear	90.00
Frosted	100.00
Pitchers, Water	
Clear	150.00
Frosted	185.00
Trays	
Bread, Frosted	100.00
Water, Frosted. Oval	150.00

POPCORN

Non-flint. C. 1870's.

Butter, Covered	$ 65.00
Cordial	50.00
Creamer	50.00
Goblets	
With ear	55.00
Without ear	42.50
Pitcher, Water	75.00

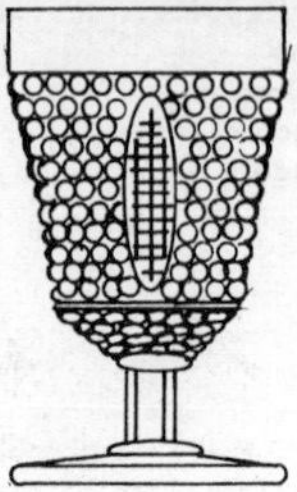

Sauce	17.50
Spooner	30.00
Sugar, Covered	60.00
Wine	30.00

POWDER AND SHOT
(Powderhorn and Shot)

Non-flint made by Boston and Sandwich Glass Co. C. 1870's

Bowl. 5", Footed and Handled ... $	45.00
Butter, Covered	85.00
Castor Bottle	35.00
Celery	55.00
Compotes	
Covered. High standard	85.00
Open. Low standard	50.00
Creamer. Applied handle	72.50
Egg Cup, Flint	55.00
Goblet	45.00
Goblet, Flint	55.00
Salt, Footed	27.50
Sauce	17.50
Spooner	40.00
Sugars	
Covered	75.00
Open	35.00

PRESSED LEAF

Non-flint first made by Sandwich Glass Co.; McKees Bros. in 1868, Central Glass Co., Wheeling, W. Va. in 1881.

Butter, Covered ... $	40.00

Champagne	42.00
Compotes, Covered	
6". High standard	50.00
7", 8". High standard	60.00
7", 8". Low standard	55.00
Cordial	20.00
Creamer, Applied handle	45.00
Egg Cup	19.50
Goblet	24.00
Lamp, Hand	50.00
Pitcher, Water. Applied handle	75.00
Salt, Master	22.50
Sauce, Flat	10.00
Spooner	25.00
Sugar, Covered	50.00
Wine	35.00

PRIMROSE
(See Colored Glass Section)

PRINCESS FEATHER
(Rochelle, Lacy Medallion)

Non-flint made by Bakewell, Pears & Co., in the late 70's, later by U.S. Glass Co., in 1880. SEE NOTE:

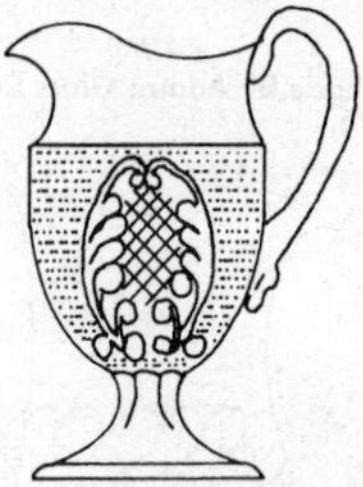

Bowl, Covered. 7½" ... $	35.00
Butter, Covered	65.00
Cake Stand. 8"	27.50
Celery Vase	37.50
Compotes	
Covered. 6". High standard	50.00
Covered. 8". High standard	60.00
Open. 8". Low standard	25.00

Creamer, Applied handle	50.00
Egg Cup	28.50
Goblet	30.00
Honey	12.00
Lamp, Kerosene	75.00
Pitcher, Water. Applied handle	65.00
Plates	
6"	25.00
7"	27.50
9"	35.00
Relish. 5x7"	20.00
Salt, Master	22.50
Sauce, Flat	8.50
Spooner	25.00
Sugars	
Covered	55.00
Open	25.00

NOTE: Add 100% for Milk Glass

PRINTED HOBNAIL
(See Colored Glass Section)
HOBNAIL, PRINTED

PRISCILLA
(Alexis, Sun and Star, Steele)

Non-flint made by Dalzell, Gillmore & Leighton Co., Findlay Ohio in the late 1890's. SEE NOTE:

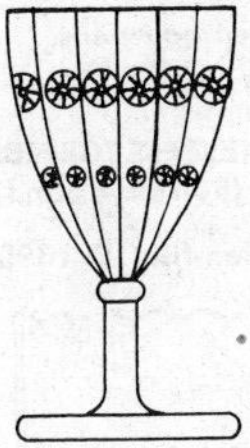

Biscuit Jar, Covered	$ 45.00
Bowl. 10¾"	25.00
Butter, Covered	45.00
Celery	25.00
Compotes	
Jelly, Covered	35.00
Open. 9". High standard	45.00
Creamer	28.50
Cruet, Stoppered	35.00
Cup and Saucer	35.00
Goblet	25.00
Mug	15.00
Plate. 10½", Turned-Up edge	35.00
Relish	15.00
Rose Bowl	25.00
Sauce, 4½"	7.00
Spooner	20.00
Sugar, Open	20.00
Syrup	50.00
Toothpick	25.00
Tumbler	15.00
Wine	25.00

NOTE: Reproduced in clear, color and opalescent.

PRISM AND FLUTE

Non-flint made by Bakewell, Pears, Pittsburgh, Pa., in the late 1870's.

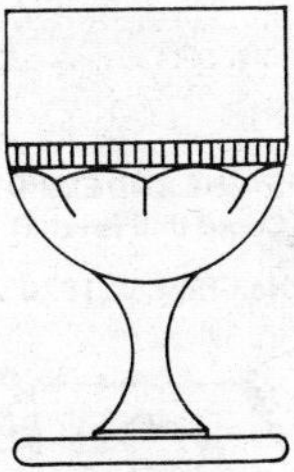

Butter, Covered	$ 50.00
Cake Stands	
9"	35.00
10½"	45.00
12½"	65.00
Celery Vase	30.00
Compotes	
Covered. 8". High standard	55.00
Open. 8". Low standard	35.00
Cordial	30.00
Creamer	37.50
Egg Cup	25.00
Goblet	25.00
Pitcher, Water	75.00
Salt, Master	17.50
Sauce, Flat	7.50
Tumbler, Footed	25.00
Wine	28.50

PRISM WITH DIAMOND POINTS

Flint made by Boston and Sandwich Glass Co.

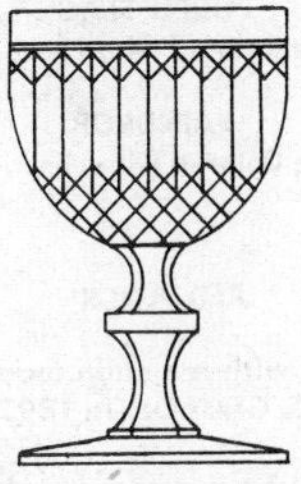

Butter, Covered	$ 75.00
Compote, Covered. 6". High std.	95.00

Creamer	65.00
Egg Cups	
Double	45.00
Single	35.00
Goblet	50.00
Pitcher, Water	100.00
Salt, Master	30.00
Sauce	15.00
Spooner	35.00
Sugar, Covered	55.00
Tumbler	40.00
Wine	50.00

PSYCHE AND CUPID
(Cupid and Psyche)

Non-flint. C. 1870's

Butter, Covered	$ 65.00
Celery	40.00
Creamer	30.00
Goblet	35.00
Pitcher, Water	60.00
Sauces, Footed	
3¾"	10.00
4½"	12.50
Spooner	30.00
Sugars	
Covered	42.50
Open	22.50
Wine	25.00

PURPLE SLAG
(See Colored Glass Section)

RAINDROP
(See Colored Glass Section)

RED BLOCK

Clear non-flint with red stain made by Doyle & Co.; later by U.S. Glass Co., in 1892.

Bowl. 8"	$ 65.00
Butter, Covered	75.00
Celery	45.00

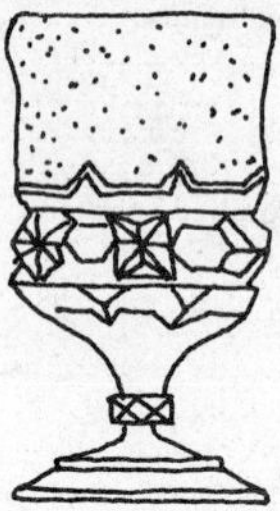

Creamers	
Individual	45.00
Regular	60.00
Decanter. 12", Stoppered	85.00
Goblet	45 00
Mug	35.00
Pitcher, Water	95.00
Rose Bowl	55.00
Sauce, Flat. 4½"	25.00
Shakers, Pair	85.00
Spooner	35.00
Sugars	
Covered	60.00
Open	35.00
Tumbler	30.00
Wine	40.00

NOTE: Many reproductions.

REVERSE TORPEDO
(Bull's Eye Band)

Non-flint. C. 1890's

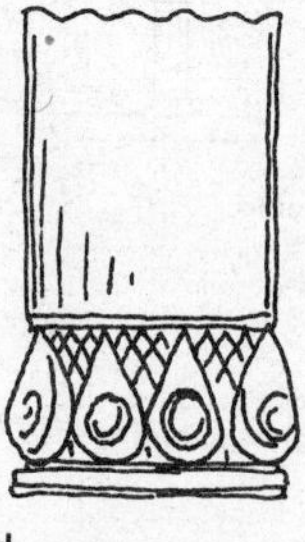

Banana Stand	$ 100.00
Bowls	
6"	30.00
7½", Crimped	55.00
Butter, Covered	72.50
Cake Stand. 9½"	75.00
Compotes	
Jelly, Covered	75.00
Open, 6". High standard	50.00
Goblet (rare)	75.00
Pitcher, Water. Tankard	95.00

Sauce	12.50
Sugar, Covered	55.00
Tumbler	25.00

RIBBED GRAPE

Flint. C. early 1860's. SEE NOTE:

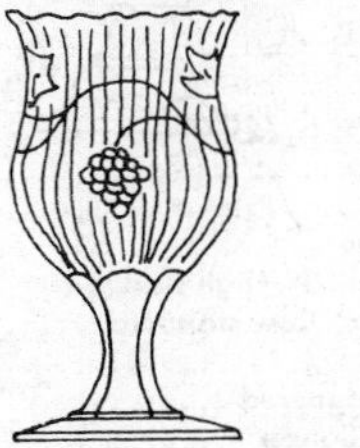

Butter, Covered	$ 85.00
Celery	50.00
Compotes	
Covered. 6"	150.00
Open. 8". Low standard	65.00
Creamer, Applied handle	125.00
Goblet	50.00
Pitcher, Water	175.00
Plate. 6"	50.00
Sauce	22.50
Spooner	35.00
Sugar, Covered	85.00

NOTE: Rare in cobalt blue, green and milk white.

RIBBED IVY

Flint. C. Late 1850's

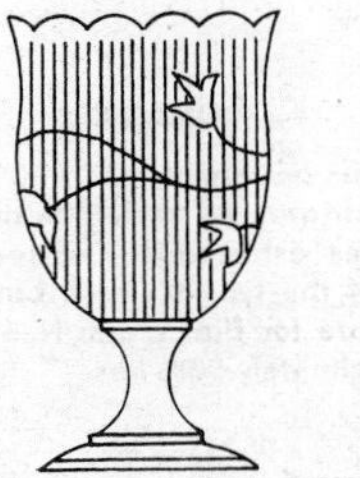

Butter, Covered	$ 95.00
Castor Bottle	35.00
Celery (rare)	300.00+
Champagne	100.00
Compotes	
6". Jelly. Covered	130.00
8". Open. Low standard, Scalloped edge.	65.00
9". Open. High standard, Scalloped edge	175.00
Creamer	125.00
Decanters	
½ Pint, Without Stopper	75.00
Quart, Stoppered	125.00
Egg Cup	35.00
Goblet	50.00
Hat	350.00+
Honey	15.00
Salts	
Master, Covered	135.00
Master, Open. Beaded rim	55.00
Open, Scalloped rim	40.00
Sauce	12.50
Spooner	35.00
Sugar, Covered	85.00
Sweetmeat, Covered. On standard	125.00
Tumblers	
Water	75.00
Whiskey, Handled	75.00
Wine	95.00

RIBBED PALM

(Acanthus, Sprig, Oak Leaf, Royal)

Flint made by McKee & Bros., Pgh., Pa. C. 1868 .

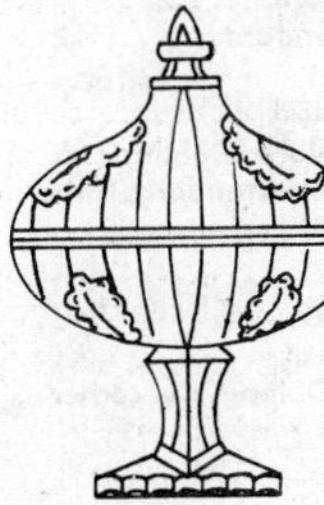

Bowl. 8"	$ 40.00
Butter, Covered	85.00
Castor Set. Pewter base	150.00
Celery Vase	75.00
Champagne	75.00
Compotes	
Covered. 6"	125.00
Open. 8". High standard	65.00
Open. 10". High standard	85.00
Open. 7". Low standard	50.00
Creamer, Applied handle	100.00
Egg Cup	38.50
Goblet	37.50
Lamp. All glass	85.00
Pitcher, Water (scarce)	175.00
Plate. 6"	50.00
Salt, Footed	30.00
Sauce, Flat	16.00
Spillholder	40.00
Spooner	35.00
Sugar, Covered	65.00

Tumbler	75.00
Wine	55.00

RIBBON

Non-flint clear and frosted pattern made by Bakewell, Pears, Pittsburgh, Pa., in the late 1860's.

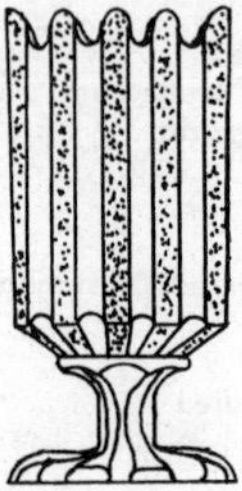

Butter, Covered $	65.00
Cake Stand. 8½"	30.00
Celery	42.00
Cheese, Covered	85.00
Compotes, Covered	
6", Low standard	30.00
7½", High standard	50.00
Compotes, Open	
7", Low standard	40.00
10½". Silverplated Dolphin std.	100.00
Oblong, Dolphin standard, Large	300.00
Oblong, Dolphin standard, Small	175.00
Creamer	45.00
*Goblet	30.00
Pitcher, Water	65.00
Platter. 9x13". Oblong, Cut corner	62.50
Sauces	
Flat	10.00
Footed	18.50
Handled	20.00
Spooner	30.00
Sugar, Covered	65.00
Tray, Water. 15x16¼"	100.00
Waste Bowl	30.00
Wine. (scarce)	85.00

*Reproduced Item

RIBBON CANDY
(Double Loop, Figure Eight, Bryce)

Non-flint made by Bryce Bros. Pittsburgh, Pa., in the 1880's. Reissued by U.S. Glass Co. in 1890's.

Bowls	
5", Covered $	22.50
7", Covered	30.00
8", Open	20.00
Butter, Covered	35.00
Cake Stands	
8"	25.00

10½"	45.00
Celery	22.50
Compotes	
Covered. 5". High standard	32.50
Open. 6". Low standard	20.00
Creamer	20.00
Cruet, Stoppered	35.00
Cup and Saucer	20.00
Goblet	22.50
Honey, Covered	30.00
Lamp, Oil	75.00
Pitchers	
Milk	35.00
Syrup	47.50
Water	55.00
Plates	
8½"	17.50
10½"	30.00
Relish	12.00
Sauce, Flat	6.50
Shakers, Pair	50.00
Spillholder	22.50
Spooner	17.50
Sugars	
Covered	30.00
Open	18.50
Tumbler	20.00
Wine	17.50

ROMAN KEY

A flint glass pattern of the 1860's but made in several variants by different glass factories. Sometimes erroneously called Greek Key because of the typical Greek band. The prices recorded are for flint glass. Non-flint variants are approximately 50% less.

Bowl 8" $	35.00
Butter, Covered	75.00
Cake Stand. 12"	95.00
Celery Vase	65.00
Champagne	50.00
Compote, Open. 7". Low standard	45.00
Creamer, Applied handle	75.00
Decanter, Stoppered	150.00
Egg Cup	35.00
Goblet	45.00
Pitcher, Water	225.00
Salt, Footed	40.00

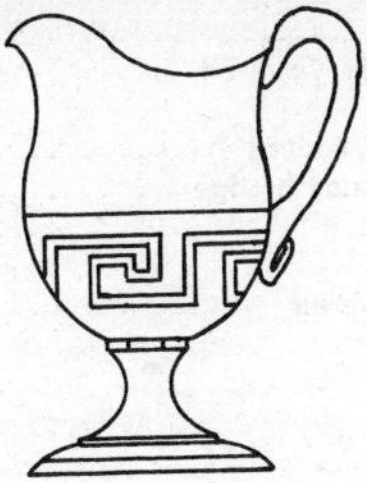

Sauce	15.00
Spooner	45.00
Sugar, Covered	65.00
Tumbler	50.00
Wine	45.00

ROMAN ROSETTE

Non-flint made by Bryce, Walker & Co. between 1875-1885. Reissued by U.S. Glass Co. in 1892 and 1898.

Bowls	
6"	$ 20.00
8½"	25.00
Butter, Covered	45.00
Cake Stand. 9"	55.00
Castor Set, Glass	75.00
Celery	32.50
Compotes	
Covered. 6". High standard	65.00
Open. 7½". High standard	35.00
Cordial	45.00
Creamer	32.50
*Goblet	28.50
Mug. 3"	17.50
Pickle	20.00
Pitchers	
Milk	40.00
Syrup	45.00
Water	65.00
Plate. 7¼"	40.00
Sauces	
Flat	10.00
Footed	15.00
Shakers, Pair	35.00
Spooner	25.00
Sugar, Covered	40.00
Tray, Bread	35.00
Wine	35.00

*Reproduced Item

ROSE-IN-SNOW

(See Colored Glass Section)

ROSE SPRIG

(See Colored Glass Section)

ROSETTE

Non-flint originally made by Bryce Bros., Pgh., Pa. in the late 1870's. Continued by U.S. Glass Co. Later made in Ohio 1898.

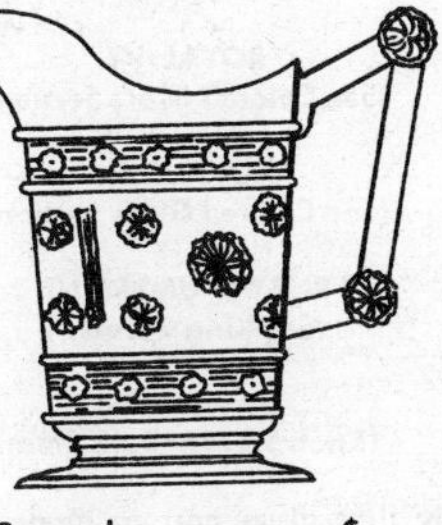

Bowl. 7¼", Covered	$ 35.00
Butter, Covered	32.50
Cake Stand. 11"	30.00
Celery	25.00
Compotes	
Covered. 6". High standard	48.50
Open. 7". High standard	40.00
Creamer	22.50
Goblet	26.50
Pitchers	
Milk	25.00
Water	45.00
Plates	
7"	25.00
9", Handled	35.00
Relish	15.00
Sauce, Flat	8.00
Shakers, Pair	35.00
Spooner	20.00
Sugar, Covered	25.00
Wine	20.00

ROSETTE AND PALM

Non-flint. C. late 1880's

Banana Stand	$ 35.00
Butter, Covered	28.50
Cake Stand. 9½"	22.50
Celery	20.00
Goblet	20.00
Relish	17.50
Sauce	6.50

Spooner	15.00
Sugar, Covered	22.50
Wine	18.00

ROYAL IVY
(See Colored Glass Section)

ROYAL OAK
(See Colored Glass Section)

RUBY THUMBPRINT
(See King's Crown)

SAWTOOTH
(Knob Stem or Bulb Stem)

An early flint glass pattern made in the late 1850's by the New England Glass Co. Later made in non-flint. Prices given are for flint.

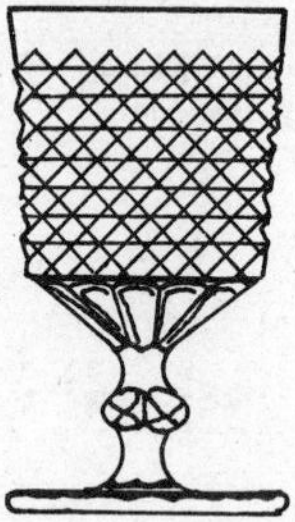

Butter, Covered ....$	85.00
Cake Stand. 10"	85.00
Celery Vase. 10"	65.00
Champagne	65.00
Compotes	
Covered. 8". Low standard	75.00
Covered. 9½". High standard	125.00
Open. 8". Low standard	50.00
Creamer	85.00
Cruet. Acorn finial	100.00
Decanter, Quart. Stoppered	125.00
Egg Cup	45.00
Goblet	45.00
Pitchers	
Milk	65.00
Water	95.00
Pomade Jar, Covered	50.00
Salts	
Covered, Footed	55.00
Open, Smooth edge	25.00
Sauce, Flat. 4"	15.00
Spooner	35.00
Sugar, Covered	80.00
Tumblers	
Flat	35.00
Footed	45.00
Wine	55.00

SAWTOOTH AND STAR
(Ruby Star)

Non-flint. C. 1890's. SEE NOTE:

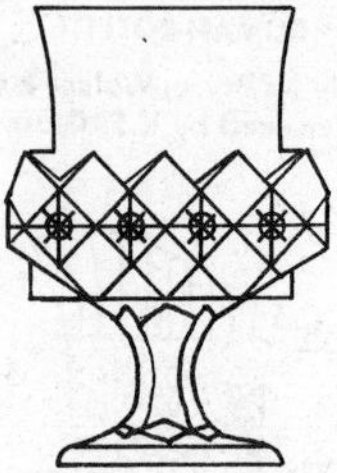

Butter, Covered ....$	30.00
Creamer	22.50
Cruet	20.00
Cup and Saucer	20.00
Goblet	22.50
Pickle	17.50
Pitcher, Syrup	25.00
Plate. 10"	17.50
Sauce, Flat	7.50
Shakers	
Salt and Pepper, Pair	25.00
Sugar	20.00
Spooner	20.00
Sugar, Covered	25.00

NOTE: Ruby stained add 100%.

SAWTOOTHED HONEYCOMB
(Diamond, Serrated Block and Loop)

Non-flint pattern made by Steimer Glass Co., Buckhannon, W. Va. C. 1904-1908. Molds sold to Morgantown Glass Co. about 1921.

Bowls, Berry	
8" ....$	30.00
9"	35.00
Butter, Covered	55.00
Compote. 9½". High standard	40.00
Creamer	20.00

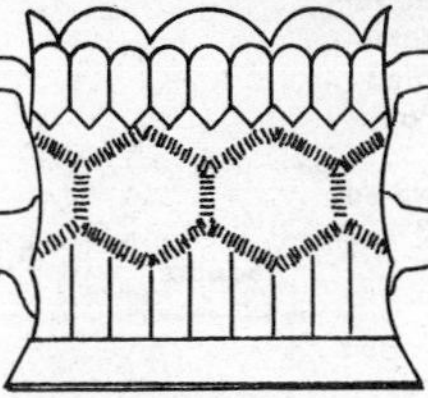

Cruet	45.00
Goblet	15.00
Nappy	30.00
Pitchers	
Milk. 7″. Bulbous, Applied handle	40.00
Milk. 8″. Tankard	45.00
Water. 10″. Bulbous, Applied hdl.	50.00
Sugar, Covered	30.00
Toothpick	15.00

SAXON

Non-flint. C. 1870's.

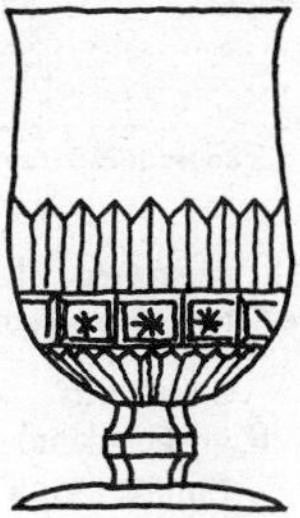

Bowl. 8″	$ 25.00
Butter, Covered	47.50
Celery	32.00
Creamer	30.00
Egg Cup	25.00
Goblet	22.50
Pitcher, Water	45.00
Plate. 6″	25.00
Relish	15.00
Salt	10.00
Sauce, Flat	7.50
Spooner	20.00
Sugar, Covered	35.00
Sweetmeat Jar, Covered	40.00
Tumbler	18.50

SCROLL

(Taunton, Stippled Scroll)

Non-flint. C. 1870's.

Butter, Covered	$ 35.00
Celery	27.50

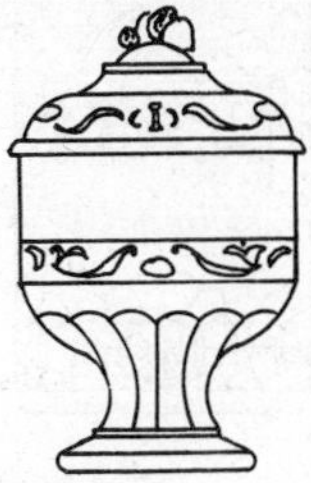

Compotes	
Covered. High standard	38.50
Open. High standard	25.00
Creamer	20.00
Egg Cup	18.50
Goblet	20.00
Pitcher, Water	45.00
Salt, Footed	15.00
Sauce, Flat	7.50
Spooner	18.50
Sugar, Covered	35.00
Tumbler, Footed	15.00
Wine	15.00

SCROLL WITH FLOWERS

Non-flint made by Central Glass Co. in the 1870's; then later by Northwood. SEE NOTE:

Butter, Covered	$ 35.00
Cake Plate, Handled	35.00
Celery	30.00
Cordial	30.00
Creamer	35.00
Egg Cup, Double	25.00
Goblet	25.00
Mustard Jar, Covered	35.00
Pickle, Handled	18.00
Pitcher, Water	45.00
Salt, Footed	15.00
Sauce	10.00
Spooner	20.00
Sugar, Covered	35.00
Wine	25.00

NOTE: Occasionally found in color.

SHELL AND JEWEL

(Victor)

Non-flint made by Westmoreland Glass Co., C. 1893. SEE NOTE:

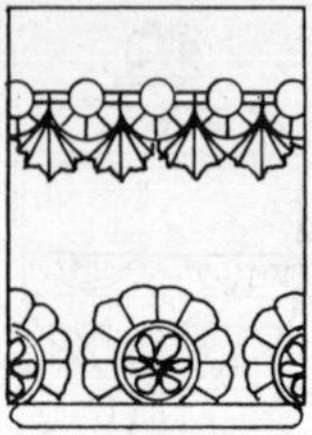

Banana Stand	$ 36.50
Bowl. 8"	25.00
Butter, Covered	38.50
Cake Stand. 10"	35.00
Compote. Open. 7". High standard	35.00
Creamer	25.00
Pitcher, Water	35.00
Relish	20.00
Sauce	10.00
Spooner	20.00
Sugar, Covered	28.50
Tray, Water	28.50
Tumbler	15.00

NOTE: Also made in blue and green but seldom seen. Add 100%.

SHELL AND TASSEL
(Shell and Spike)

Non-flint glass made by George A. Duncan & Sons, Pittsburgh, Pa. in the 1880's. Two forms were issued. . .square with shell-shaped finials and later, round with dog finials. Also made in azure blue, amber and canary; but extremely rare.

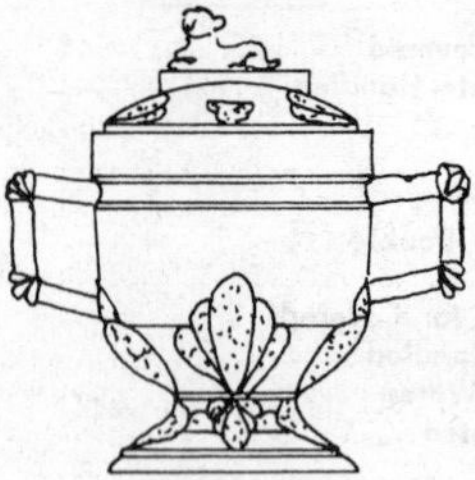

Round

Bowls	
10", Oval	$ 45.00
12", Oval. Deep	60.00
Butter, Covered	45.00
Celery Vase	45.00
Creamer	32.50
*Goblet	35.00
Marmalade Jar	50.00
Pitcher, Water	40.00
Sauce, Footed	12.50
Shakers, Pair	100.00
Spooner	25.00
Sugar, Covered	75.00
Tray. 9x13"	45.00

Square

Bowl. 5x8"	20.00
Butter, Covered	75.00
Cake Stands	
8"	45.00
12"	65.00
Celery Vase	35.00
Compotes	
4½", Jelly	45.00
8". Open	40.00
10". Open	50.00
Creamer	45.00
*Goblet	35.00
Pitcher, Water	55.00
Platter. 9x13"	40.00
Salt, Shell-shaped	15.00
Sauces	
Flat. Shell-shaped	10.00
Footed	12.50
Spooner	35.00
Sugar, Covered	85.00

*Reproduced Item

SHERATON
(See Colored Glass Section)

SMOCKING
(Plain Smocking)

Flint. C. 1850's

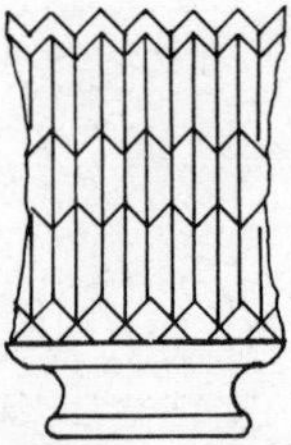

Bottle, Bar. Blob top	$ 100.00
Bowl, Berry. 9"	75.00
Butter, Covered	75.00
Compote. Covered. 7". Low std.	60.00
Creamer, Applied handle	87.50
Egg Cup	50.00
Goblet	60.00
Lamp. 9"	125.00
Spillholder	45.00
Spooner	40.00

Sugars	
Covered	75.00
Open	50.00
Tumblers	
Water	50.00
Whiskey	75.00
Vase. 10"	75.00
Wine	35.00

SNAIL
(Compact, Idaho)

Made by George Duncan & Sons, Pittsburgh, Pa., C. 1880.

Banana Stand $	100.00
Bowls	
Berry. 8"	35.00
Open. 6x9"	28.00
Butter, Covered	65.00
Cake Stand. 10"	75.00
Celery Vase	65.00
Cheese, Covered	65.00
Compotes. High standard	
Covered. 10"	75.00
Open. 8"	60.00
Creamers	
Individual	25.00
Regular	35.00
Cruet, Stoppered	40.00
Finger Bowl	25.00
Goblet	40.00
Pitchers	
Syrup	45.00
Water, Tankard	85.00
Plate. 7"	40.00
Punch Cup	20.00
Relish. 7", Oval	22.50
Rose Bowl	48.50
Salt	12.00
Sauce, 4"	15.00
Shakers	
Salt and Pepper, Pair	40.00
Sugar	35.00
Spooner	28.50
Sugars	
Individual, Covered	20.00
Regular, Covered	45.00
Open	30.00

Tumbler	35.00
Wine	30.00

SOUTHERN IVY
Non-flint. C. 1880's

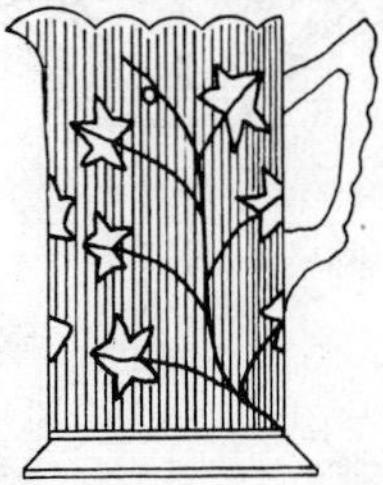

Bowl. 8" $	18.50
Butter, Covered	25.00
Creamer	25.00
Cruet, Stoppered	25.00
Pitcher, Water	30.00
Sauce, Flat	5.00
Spooner	17.00
Sugars	
Covered	25.00
Open	15.00

SPIRALLED IVY
Non-flint. C. 1880's

Butter, Covered $	39.50
Creamer	30.00
Pitchers	
Milk	35.00
Water	45.00
Sauce, Flat	7.50
Spooner	20.00
Sugars	
Covered	30.00
Open	18.50
Tumbler	18.00

SPIREA BAND
(See Colored Glass Section)

SPRIG
(Indian Tree, Panelled Sprig)

Non-flint made by Bryce, Higbee & Co., Pittsburgh, Pa., C. mid 1880's.

Bowls	
5x7" $	20.00
10", Footed, Scalloped	35.00
Butter, Covered	40.00
Cake Stand. 8"	40.00
Celery	32.00
Compotes	
Covered. High standard	45.00
Open. High standard	32.50
Open. Low standard	28.50
Creamer	35.00
Goblet	30.00
Pickle	15.00
Pitcher, Water	45.00
Platter	35.00
Sauces	
Flat	10.00
Footed	12.00
Spooner	25.00
Sugar, Covered	35.00
Tumbler	20.00
Wine	25.00

STAR ROSETTED

Non-flint made by McKee & Bros., Pittsburgh, Pa., C. 1875.

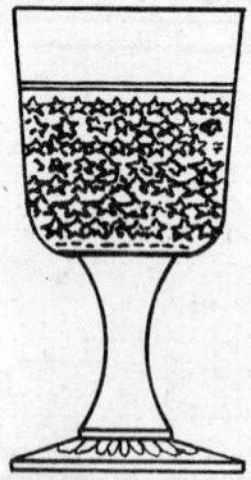

Butter, Covered $	35.00
Compotes	
Covered	55.00
Open	30.00
Creamer	28.50
Goblet	22.50
Pickle	10.00
Pitcher, Water	40.00
Plates	
7"	15.00
10". "A Good Mother. . ."	40.00
Relish. 9"	15.00
Sauces	
Flat	6.50
Footed	10.00
Spooner	18.50
Sugars	
Covered	35.00
Open	25.00

STATES, THE

Non-flint made by U.S. Glass Co. in 1905.

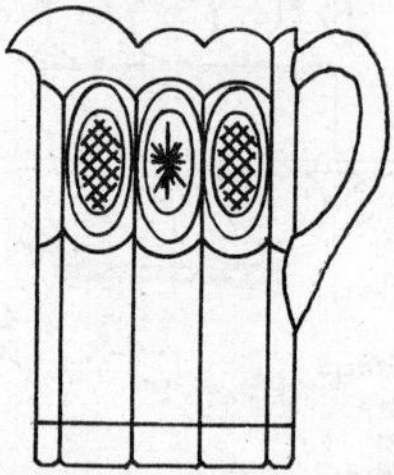

Bowl. 9" $	32.50
Butter, Covered	35.00
Celery Vase	17.50
Compote, Open. 7". High standard	25.00
Creamer	18.50
Goblet	22.00
Pitcher, Water	40.00
Punch Cup	10.00
Relish. 6½", 3-handled	25.00
Sugar, Covered	25.00
Toothpick, Earred	35.00
Tumbler	15.00
Wine	18.50

STEDMAN

Flint glass. C. 1860's

Celery $	60.00
Champagne	55.00
Cheese, Covered	60.00
Compotes	
Covered. 7", 8". High standard	75.00
Open. 8". Low standard	50.00
Creamer	75.00
Egg Cup	35.00
Goblet	50.00
Plate. 6"	30.00
Salt, Master	30.00
Sauce	12.50
Spooner	39.50

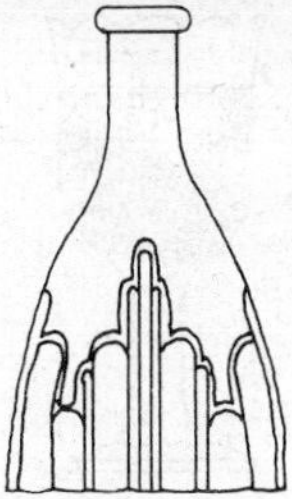

Sugar, Covered	85.00
Tumbler	35.00
Wine	50.00

STIPPLED BAND
(Panelled Stippled Bowl)

Non-flint. C. 1870's.

Butter, Covered $	40.00
Celery	25.00
Compotes, High standard	
Covered. 9″	45.00
Open. 8″	30.00
Creamer, Applied handle	30.00
Goblet	18.50
Pitcher, Water. Applied handle	40.00
Salt, Footed	15.00
Sauce, Flat	6.50
Spooner	18.50
Sugars	
Covered	30.00
Open	18.00
Tumbler, Footed	20.00

STIPPLED CHAIN

Non-flint made by Gillinder & Sons, C. 1870's

Biscuit Jar $	75.00
Butter, Covered	45.00
Creamer, Applied handle	28.50
Egg Cup	18.50
Goblet	20.00
Pickle	15.00
Pitcher, Water. Applied handle	42.50
Salt, Footed	15.00
Sauce	8.00

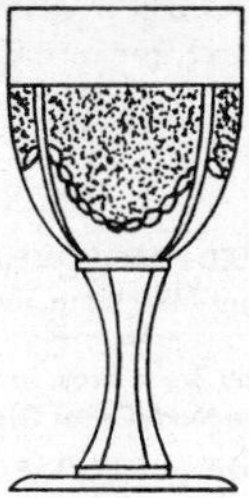

Spooner	20.00
Sugar, Covered	35.00

STIPPLED CHERRY

Non-flint reportedly made by Lancaster Glass Co. in the 1880's.

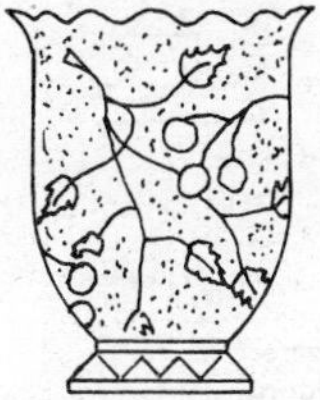

Bowl. 8″ $	25.00
Butter, Covered	40.00
Celery	25.00
Creamer	25.00
Pitcher, Water	35.00
Plates	
6″	18.50
9¼″, Bread	30.00
Sauce, 4″	10.00
Spooner	15.00
Sugar, Covered	28.50
Tumbler	18.50

STIPPLED DAISY

Non-flint. C. 1890's

Compote, Open. 8¼″. High std. $	35.00
Creamer	25.00

Pickle	15.00
Pitcher, Water	40.00
Sauce, Flat. 4¼"	8.50
Spooner	18.50
Sugar, Covered	30.00

STIPPLED FORGET-ME-NOT
(Forget-Me-Not in Snow)

Non-flint made by Bryce Bros. in the 1880's and after 1891 by the Model Flint Glass Co.

Butter, Covered ......$	50.00
Cake Stands	
9"	35.00
12"	50.00
Celery	45.00
Compotes, Covered	
6". Low standard	45.00
8". High standard	60.00
Creamer	35.00
Cup and Saucer	30.00
Goblet	35.00
Mug	20.00
Pitchers	
Milk	42.50
Syrup	40.00
Water	50.00
Plates	
7". Star center	30.00
9". Kitten center	40.00
Relish, Oval	18.50
Salt, Master	25.00
Sauces	
Flat	10.00
Footed	15.00
Spooner	25.00
Sugar, Covered	35.00
Toothpick, Hat-shaped	75.00
Trays	
Bread	35.00
Water, Aquatic center	45.00
Tumbler	30.00
Wine	35.00

STIPPLED GRAPE AND FESTOON

Non-flint made by Doyle & Co., Pittsburgh, Pa., C. 1870.

Butter, Covered ......$	72.50
Celery	40.00
Compote, Covered. 9". Low std.	60.00
Creamer, Applied handles	45.00
Egg Cup	22.50
Goblet	30.00
Pickle	15.00
Pitchers, Applied handles	
Milk	60.00
Water	85.00
Sauce, Flat	12.00
Spooner	30.00
Sugar, Covered	45.00
Wine	25.00

STIPPLED PEPPERS

Non-flint made by Boston and Sandwich Glass Co. in the 1870's.

Creamer, Applied handle ......$	32.50
Egg Cup	20.00
Goblet	27.50
Pitcher, Water. Applied handle	45.00
Salt, Footed	15.00
Sauce	8.50
Spooner	25.00
Sugar, Covered	35.00
Tumbler, footed	18.50

STIPPLED STAR

Non-flint made by Gillinder & Sons, in the 1870's.

Butter, Covered ......$	55.00

Celery	45.00
Compotes, High standard	
Covered. 12″	65.00
Open. 8″	45.00
*Creamer	45.00
Egg Cup	25.00
*Goblet	30.00
Pickle	15.00
Pitcher, Water	75.00
Sauces	
Flat	10.00
Footed	15.00
Spooner	35.00
*Sugar, Covered	45.00
Tumbler	20.00
*Wine	25.00

*Reproduced Item

STRAWBERRY
(Fairfax)

Non-flint pattern first made in the late 1860's and attributed to Boston & Sandwich Glass Co. SEE NOTE:

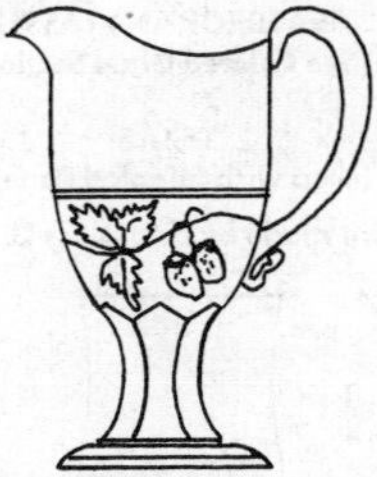

Butter, Covered $	55.00
Compotes, Covered	
8″. High standard	75.00
8″. Low standard	65.00
Creamer, Applied handle	40.00
*Egg Cup	25.00
*Goblet	25.00
Pitchers, Applied handles	
Syrup	40.00
Water	65.00
Relish, Oval	20.00
Salt, Footed	25.00
Sauce, Flat	15.00
Spooner	25.00
Sugar, Covered	40.00

NOTE. Milk Glass add approximately 100%.

*Reproduced Item

STRAWBERRY AND CURRANT
(Currants and leaves on reverse)

Non-flint. C. 1880's. SEE NOTE:

Butter, Covered $	50.00
Celery	40.00
Cheese, Covered	50.00
Creamer	40.00
*Goblet	30.00
Pitchers	
Milk	45.00
Water	55.00
Sauce, Footed	12.00
Spooner	30.00
Sugars	
Covered	45.00
Open	30.00
Tumblers	30.00

NOTE: Goblet has been reproduced in clear, amber, blue, green and opalescent.

SUMMIT

Produced by Thompson Glass Co., Uniontown, Pa., in the early 1890's.

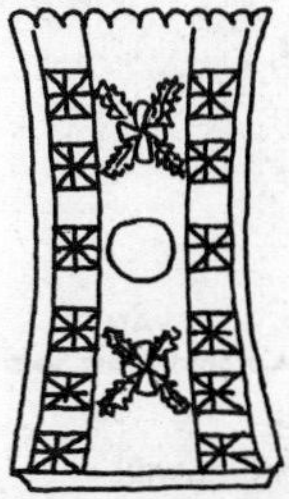

Bowl. 7¼″, Pie crust edge $	28.50

Butter, Covered	65.00
Celery	35.00
Compote. Open. 8", High standard.	
Pie crust edge	55.00
Creamers	
Individual	25.00
Regular	40.00
Pitcher, Water. Tankard	75.00
Relish, Handled	25.00
Spooner	28.50
Sugar, Open	40.00
Tumbler	26.50

SUNBURST

Non-flint. C. 1880's

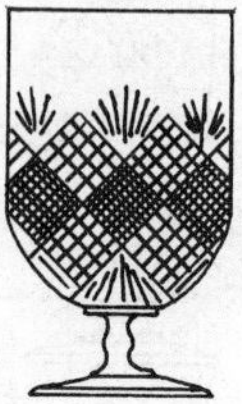

Bowl. 5"	$ 15.00
Butter, Covered	40.00
Cake Stand. 9"	30.00
Celery	30.00
Cordial	18.50
Creamer	25.00
Cruet, Stoppered	25.00
Egg Cup	15.00
Goblet	20.00
Marmalade Jar, Covered	28.50
Pitchers	
Milk	35.00
Water	45.00
Plates	
6"	13.50
11"	20.00
11". Bread, with motto	30.00
Relish, Double	20.00
Salts	
Individual	6.50
Master	20.00
Sauce, Handled	10.00
Spooner	20.00
Sugar, Covered	30.00
Tumbler	12.00
Wine	15.00

SWAN

(See Colored Glass Section)

SWIRL

(See Colored Glass Section)

SWIRL AND STAR

(Spiral, Texas Star, St. Louis Star, Frosted Star)

Non-flint pattern made by Steimer Glass Co., Buckhannon, W. Va. C. 1903-1908.

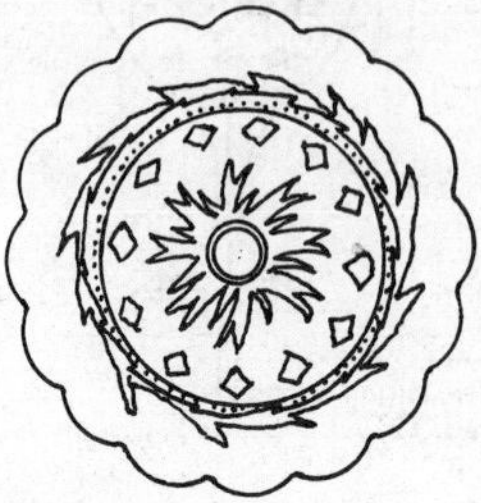

Bowls	
6"	$ 30.00
9½"	45.00
Creamer and Sugar, Open. Bulbous	45.00
Cup, Punch	12.00
Nappy. 5"	35.00
Pitchers	
Milk, Bulbous. Applied handle	50.00
Syrup	50.00
Water, Tankard. Applied handle	60.00
Plates	
8"	30.00
11". Cake	40.00
Shakers	
Salt and Pepper, Pair	25.00
Sugar	40.00
Toothpick	15.00
Tumbler	12.50

TEARDROP AND TASSEL

(See Colored Glass Section)

TEXAS

(Loop with Stippled Panels)

Non-flint made by U.S. Glass Co. C. 1900.

Bowls	
Flat. 7½", 8½", 9½"	$ 20.00
Footed. 7½", 8½", 9½"	25.00

Scalloped. 6", 7", 8"	20.00
Butter, Covered	40.00
Cake Stand. 10"	50.00
Celerys	
Tray	15.00
Vase	25.00
Compotes	
4". Open. Low standard	22.50
5". Open. High standard	30.00
8". Covered. High standard	50.00
*Creamers	
Individual	20.00
Regular	22.50
Cruet, Stoppered	25.00
Goblet	25.00
Pitcher, Water	40.00
Plate. 9"	20.00
Relish	15.00
Salt, Master	22.50
Sauce. 4"	10.00
Spooner	20.00
*Sugars	
Individual	20.00
Regular, Covered	35.00
Regular, Open	20.00
Toothpick	15.00
Tumbler	25.00
Wine	20.00

*Reproduced Item

THE STATES, SEE STATES, THE

THISTLE

Non-flint. C. 1870's.

Bowl, 8"	$ 30.00
Butter, Covered	60.00
Cake Stand	55.00
Compotes, Covered	
High standard	55.00
Low standard	45.00
Cordial	45.00
Creamer, Applied handle	55.00
Egg Cup	30.00
Goblet	35.00
Pitcher, Water	55.00
Relish	20.00
Salt, Footed	18.50
Sauce, Flat	15.00
Spooner	25.00
Sugar, Covered	50.00
Tumbler	35.00
Wine	37.50

THOMPSON NO. 77

Made by the Thompson Glass Co., Uniontown, Pa. in 1892. Some items were ruby stained and-or etched.

Butter, Covered	$ 55.00
Cordial	25.00
Creamers	
Individual	22.50
Regular	35.00
Spooner	25.00
Sugars	
Individual	22.50
Regular, Open	27.50
Syrup	40.00
Toothpick	18.50
Tumbler	28.50
Waste Bowl	30.00

THOUSAND EYE

(See Colored Glass Section)

THREE FACES

(Three Sisters)

Non-flint made by Duncan & Miller Glass Co., Pittsburgh, Pa. in 1878. SEE NOTE:

Butter, Covered	$ 150.00
Cake Stands	
8", 9"	100.00
10", 11"	150.00
Celery	100.00

Champagnes	
Hollow stem	250.00+
Saucer-type	150.00
Claret	150.00
Compotes	
Covered. 4"	125.00
Covered. 6½"	150.00
Open. 8"	100.00
Cracker Jar (rare)	500.00+
Creamer (with face)	100.00
Goblet	80.00
Lamp, Oil	150.00
Marmalade Jar	100.00
Pitchers	
Milk	300.00
Water	250.00
Salt Dip	35.00
Sauce, Footed	30.00
Shakers, Pair	75.00
Spooner	75.00
Sugar, Covered	125.00
Tumbler	55.00
Wine	100.00

NOTE: Heavily reproduced.

THREE-IN-ONE
(Cut Diamond, Diamond Band, Fancy Diamonds)

Non-flint. C. Early 1900's

Bowl. 8", Fluted	$ 22.50
Butter, Covered	38.50
Cake Stand. 9"	28.50
Celery	26.50
Compotes	
Covered. 6". High standard	25.00
Open. 10", Fluted. High standard	40.00
*Cracker Jar	50.00
Creamers	
Individual	18.50
Regular	25.00
Goblet	20.00
Pickle	17.50
Pitcher, Water	30.00
Shakers, Pair	25.00
Spooner	20.00
Sugars	
Individual	18.50
Regular, Open	25.00
Toothpick	15.00
Wine	15.00

*Reproduced Item

THREE-PANEL
(See Colored Glass Section)

THUMBPRINT, EARLY
(Giant Baby Thumbprint)

Flint made by several factories in various forms. C. 1850-1860.

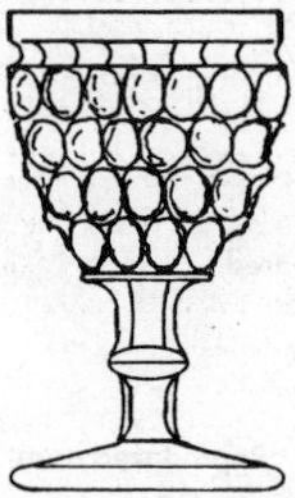

Castor Bottle	$ 30.00
Celery Vases	
Pattern base	125.00
Plain base	100.00
Compotes	
4". Covered	75.00
8". Open. Flared and scalloped top, Pattern base	95.00
8½". Open. Pattern base	175.00
Creamer	65.00
Egg Cup	40.00
Goblet. Barrel-shape, Baluster stem	75.00
Honey	20.00
Plate. 8"	65.00
Salt, Master. Footed	35.00
Sugars	
Covered	95.00
Open	45.00
Tumbler	55.00
Tumble-Up	400.00
Wine. Barrel-shape. Baluster stem	65.00

TORPEDO
(Pygmy, Fisheye)

Non-flint made by Thompson Glass Co., Uniontown, Pa., in 1889.

Banana Stand	$ 75.00
Bowls	
7" Open, Flared rim	30.00

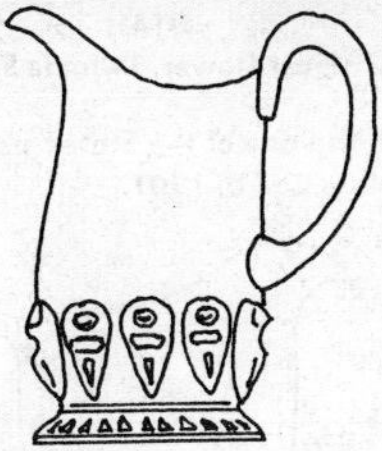

8". Covered	38.50
9½". Flared rim. Open.	35.00
Butter, Covered	75.00
Cake Stand. 10"	65.00
Celery. Scalloped top	40.00
Compotes	
4". Covered, Jelly	55.00
5". Open, Flared rim	35.00
6". Covered, High standard	65.00
8". Covered, High standard	85.00
9". Open, Flared rim, High std.	55.00
Creamer	40.00
Cruet, Stoppered	45.00
Cup and Saucer	40.00
Decanter, Stoppered	65.00
Goblet	50.00
Honey. 6", Covered	50.00
Lamps	
3⅜", Handled	45.00
8", Plain base, Pattern on bowl	65.00
Marmalade Jar, Covered	55.00
Pitchers	
Milk. 8¾"	60.00
Syrup	55.00
Water. 10½"	95.00
Rose Bowl	60.00
Salts	
Individual	10.00
Master	25.00
Sauces	
3½", Flat	12.50
3½", Collared base	16.50
4¼", Collared base	20.00
Shakers, Pair	50.00
Spooner, Scalloped top	30.00
Sugar, Open	50.00
Trays, Water	
10", Round	95.00
11¾", Clover-shaped	75.00
Tumbler	40.00
Waste Bowl	35.00
Wine	28.50

TREE OF LIFE

(Pittsburgh Tree of Life, Tree of Life With Hand) Non-flint made by Duncan and Sons, Pittsburgh, Pa., in 1884.

Bowls	
8", Oval	$ 25.00

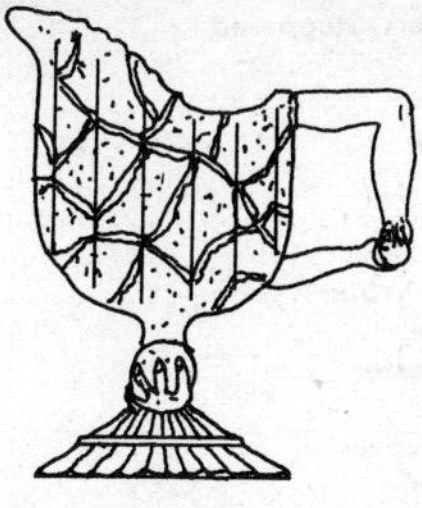

10"	35.00
Butter, Covered	75.00
Cake Stands	
8¾"	60.00
10"	100.00
Celery	40.00
Compote, Covered. 6". High std.	85.00
Compotes, Open	
5". Low standard	50.00
9". High standard	65.00
10½". High standard	95.00
Creamer	50.00
Finger Bowl	16.50
Goblet	40.00
Mug	30.00
Pitcher, Water	75.00
Plate. 7"	20.00
Punch Cup	17.50
Sauce, Footed	15.00
Spooner	35.00
Sugar, Covered	65.00
Tray, Ice Cream	40.00
Tumbler	27.50
Wine	30.00

TULIP

Flint. C. late 1850's

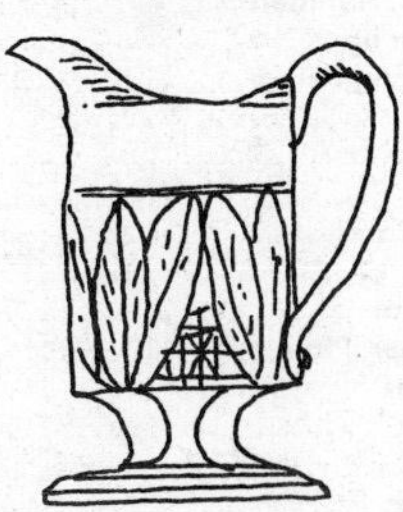

Butter, Covered	$ 125.00
Celery Vase	75.00
Compotes	
Covered. 7". High standard	135.00
Open. 7". High standard	100.00
Creamer	85.00
Cruet, Stoppered	85.00

Decanters, Stoppered

Pint	85.00
Quart	150.00
Egg Cup	35.00
Goblet	50.00
Honey	20.00
Mug	65.00
Pitcher, Water	250.00
Plate. 6″	65.00
Salt, Master	30.00
Spooner	50.00
Sugar, Covered	100.00
Tumbler	38.00

TULIP WITH SAWTOOTH

Originally made in flint glass by Bryce Bros., Pittsburgh, Pa. in the 1860's; later made in non-flint. Prices listed represent flint.

Butter, Covered	$ 125.00
Celery	60.00
Champagne	75.00
Covered. 6″. High standard	85.00
Open. 9″. High standard	100.00
Creamer	100.00
Cruet	60.00
Decanters, Handled	
Pint, Bar lip	55.00
Quart, Stoppered	150.00
Egg Cup	50.00
Goblet	45.00
Mug	85.00
Pitcher, Water	175.00
Plate, 6″	50.00
Pomade Jar	45.00
Salt, Master. Plain edge	25.00
Sauce, Flat	15.00
Spooner	35.00
Sugars	
Covered	95.00
Open	45.00
Tumbler, Footed	50.00
*Wine	42.50

*Reproduced Item

TWO PANEL

(See Colored Glass Section)

UTAH

(Frost Flower, Twinkle Star)

Non-flint and one of the States' patterns made by U.S. Glass Co., in 1901.

Bowls	
Covered. 6″, 7″, 8″	$ 20.00
Open. 6″, 7″, 8″	15.00
Butter, Covered	35.00
Cake Plates	
9″	20.00
11″	25.00
Cake Stands	
8″	20.00
10″	28.50
Celery	17.50
Compote. Covered. 6″. Jelly	25.00
Goblet	15.00
Pickle	12.00
Pitcher, Water	30.00
Sauce, 4″	7.50
Shakers	
Salt and Pepper, Pair	25.00
Salt and Pepper, In holder, Pair	30.00
Spooner	13.50
Sugar, Covered	25.00
Tumbler	15.00

VICTORIA

Flint made by Bakewell, Pears & Co., in the early 1860's.

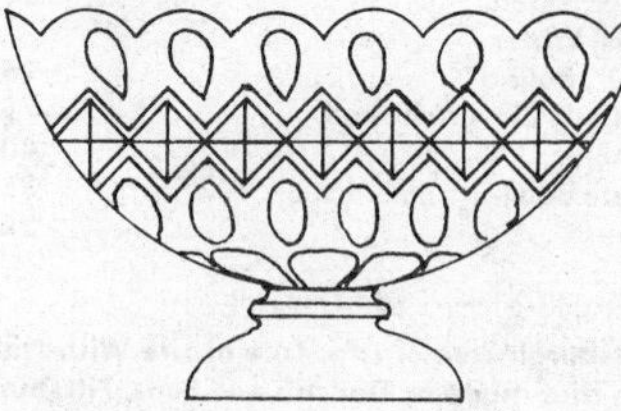

Butter, Covered. Footed	$ 100.00
Cake Stands	
9″	75.00

15"	135.00
Compotes	
Covered. 6". High standard	55.00
Covered. 8". High standard	65.00
Covered. 8". Low standard	55.00
Open. 10". High standard	65.00
Open. 10". Low standard	60.00
Creamer	85.00
Spooner	50.00
Sugar, Covered	135.00

VIKING

(Old Man of the Mountains, Bearded Head, Prophet)

Non-flint. C. 1880's

Bowls	
7"	$ 25.00
9"	35.00
Butter, Covered	60.00
Cake Plate. 10", Footed	47.50
Celery Vase	42.50
Compotes, Covered	
8". Low standard	65.00
8". Oval. Low standard	55.00
Creamer	38.50
Egg Cup	35.00
Mug	45.00
Pickle	25.00
Pitcher, Water	75.00
Salt, Master	25.00
Sauce, Footed	15.00
Spooner	30.00
Sugars	
Covered	45.00
Open	27.50
Tray, Bread. "Cupid Hunt"	50.00

VIRGINIA

(Galloway, Late Block, Foster, Mirror)

Non-flint made by the U.S. Glass Co., C. 1901.

Bowls	
Flared, 7½", 8½", 9½"	$ 22.50
Straight, 6", 7", 8"	20.00
Butter, Covered	38.50

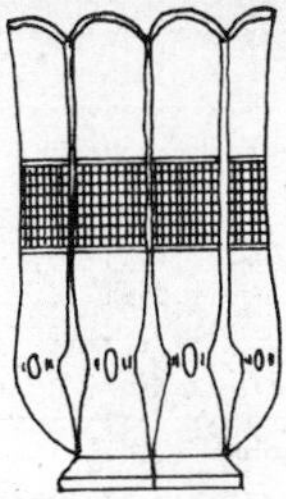

Carafe	25.00
Celery Vase	25.00
Creamers	
Individual	20.00
Regular	25.00
Cruet, Stoppered	22.50
Goblet	25.00
Pitcher, Water. Tankard	40.00
Relish	15.00
Sardine	20.00
Sauces	
Flared, 4"	15.00
Straight, 4", 4½"	10.00
Spooner	25.00
Sugars	
Covered	35.00
Covered, Individual	20.00
Toothpick	15.00
Tumbler	25.00
Wine	28.50

WAFFLE

Flint made by Boston and Sandwich Glass Co. in the mid 1800's. Later by Bryce, Walker & Co., Pittsburgh, Pa.

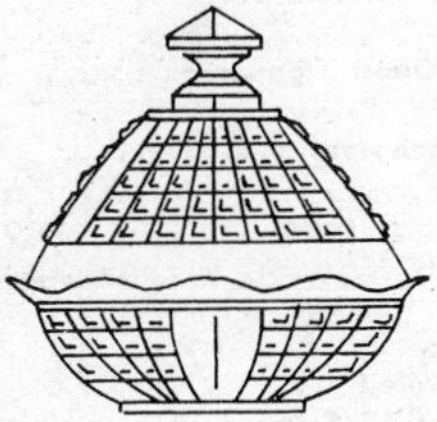

Butter, Covered	$ 125.00
Celery. 9½", Footed	75.00
Champagne	100.00
Compotes	
Covered. High standard	125.00
Open. High standard	65.00
Cordial	75.00
Creamer	110.00
Decanter, Stoppered	100.00
Egg Cup	40.00

Goblet	55.00
Lamps	
All glass	175.00
Marble base	125.00
Plate. 6"	45.00
Salt, Master	30.00
Sauce, Flat	15.00
Spooner	50.00
Sugar, Covered	95.00
Tumblers	
Water	60.00
Whiskey, Handled	85.00
Wine	65.00

WAFFLE AND THUMBPRINT

Flint made by New England Glass Co. and Boston and Sandwich Glass Co. C. 1850-60's. Later by Bryce, Walker & Co., Pittsburgh, Pa.

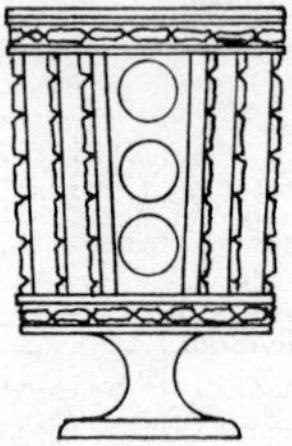

Butter, Covered $	150.00
Celery. Knob stem	82.50
Champagne	75.00
Claret	85.00
Compotes	
Covered, High standard	165.00
Open, High standard	125.00
Open, Low standard	85.00
Creamer	125.00
Decanter, Quart, Stoppered	125.00
Egg Cup	45.00
Goblet. Knob stem	60.00
Lamp. 9½"	100.00
Pitcher, Water. (rare)	250.00+
Salt, Master	40.00
Spillholder	55.00
Spooner	65.00
Sugar, Covered	125.00
Sweetmeat, 6", Covered, High standard. (rare)	150.00
Tumblers	
Water, Footed	75.00
Whiskey	65.00
Wine	65.00

WASHINGTON (EARLY)

Flint made by New England Glass Co. C. 1860's.

Bowl. 6¼x9¼", Oval $	75.00
Bottle, Bitters	75.00
Butter, Covered	175.00
Celery	95.00
Champagne	100.00
Compotes, Covered	
6". High standard	95.00
10". High standard	175.00
Cordial	150.00
Creamer	200.00
Decanter, stoppered	150.00
Egg Cup	75.00
Goblet	75.00
Pitcher, Water	250.00+
Salt, Master	55.00
Sauce. 4½"	25.00
Spooner	65.00
Sugar, Covered	125.00
Tumbler	85.00
Wine	100.00

WASHINGTON (LATE)

Non-flint made by U.S. Glass Co., Pgh., Pa.

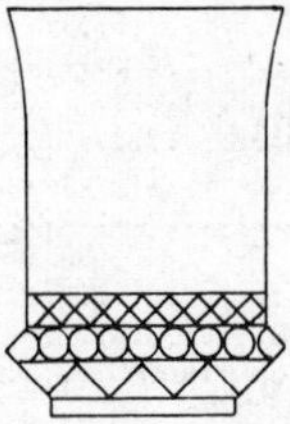

Bowls	
5", 6". Covered $	13.50
7", 8". Covered	15.00
8". Open	13.50
Butter, Covered	22.50
Cake Stands	
8"	22.50
11"	27.50
Celery Tray	16.00
Champagne	13.50
Claret	13.50

Compotes	
Covered. 6"	20.00
Open. 8"	25.00
Cordial	13.50
Creamer	18.50
Cruet, Stoppered	15.00
Goblet	15.00
Pickle	8.50
Pitchers	
Milk	20.00
Water	27.50
Water, ½ Gallon	35.00
Plates	
6"	10.00
8"	12.50
10"	15.00
Sauces	
3"	7.50
4"	8.50
Spooner	13.50
Sugar, Open	18.50
Toothpick	8.50
Tumbler	10.00
Wine	13.50

WASHINGTON CENTENNIAL
(Chain with Diamonds)

Made by Gillinder & Co., Philadelphia, Pa.

Butter, Covered	$ 100.00
Cake Stands	
8½"	60.00
10"	85.00
Celery Vase	60.00
Champagne	65.00
Compotes	
Covered, 9"	75.00
Open, 8"	50.00
Creamer	75.00
Egg Cup	50.00
Goblet	45.00
Pitcher, Water	100.00
Platters	
"Carpenter's Hall"	125.00
"George Washington"	150.00
"Independence Hall"	125.00
Relish. "Bear Paws" handles. Dated	50.00
Salt, Master	45.00
Sauce. 4"	15.00
Spooner	55.00
Sugars	
Covered	75.00
Open	40.00
Wine	55.00

WESTWARD-HO
(Pioneer, Tippecanoe)

Non-flint made by Gillinder & Sons, Philadelphia, Pa. in the late 1870's. This popular pattern has been reproduced in clear and colors.

Butter, Covered	$ 165.00
Celery Vase	125.00
Compotes, Covered	
4". Low standard	125.00
5". High standard	250.00
5". Low standard	175.00
6". Low standard	150.00
8". High standard	225.00
Cordial	150.00
Creamer	100.00
Goblet	85.00
Marmalade Jar, Covered	175.00
Pitcher, Water	200.00
Platter, Bread. Oval	100.00
Sauces, Footed	
3½"	25.00
4½"	30.00
Spooner	85.00
Sugar, Covered	145.00
Wine	135.00

WHEAT AND BARLEY
(See Colored Glass Section)

WILDFLOWER
(See Colored Glass Section)

WILLOW OAK
(See Colored Glass Section)

WINDFLOWER

Non-flint. C. late 1870's.

Butter, Covered .... $	50.00
Celery	32.50
Compotes	
Covered, High standard	65.00
Open, Low standard	35.00
Cordial	38.00
Creamer	35.00
Egg Cup	22.50
Goblet	30.00
Pickle	20.00
Pitcher, Water	45.00
Salt, Master	25.00
Sauce, Flat	8.50
Spooner	22.50
Sugar, Open	25.00
Tumbler	27.50
Wine	30.00

WISCONSIN, See BEADED DEWDROP

ZIPPER
(Cobb, Late Sawtooth)

Non-flint made by Richards & Hartley, Tarentum, Pa., C. 1880's.

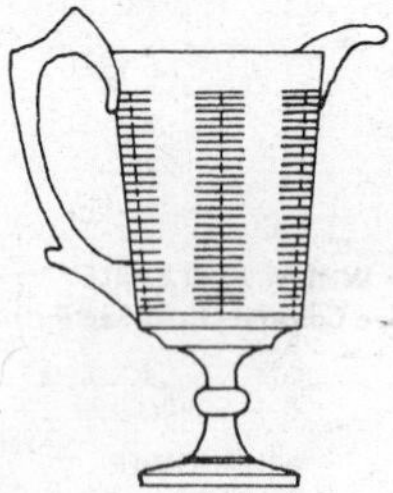

Banana Stand .... $	55.00
Bowl. 7"	15.00
Butter, Covered	30.00
Celery	18.50
Compote, Covered. 8". Low std.	35.00
Creamer	20.00
Cruet, Stoppered	25.00
Egg Cup	18.50
Goblet	18.50
Lamp, Oil	40.00
Marmalade Jar, Covered	28.50
Pitchers	
Milk	25.00
Syrup	20.00
Water	35.00
Relish	12.50
Salt Dip	10.00
Sauces	
Flat	6.00
Footed	7.00
Spooner	16.50
Sugars	
Covered	25.00
Open	15.00
Sugar Shaker	26.00
Toothpick	15.00
Wine	18.50

COLORED GLASS PATTERNS

ALASKA
(Lion's Leg)

One of three patterns named for Alaska. Made by Northwood Glass Co., from 1897 to 1910.

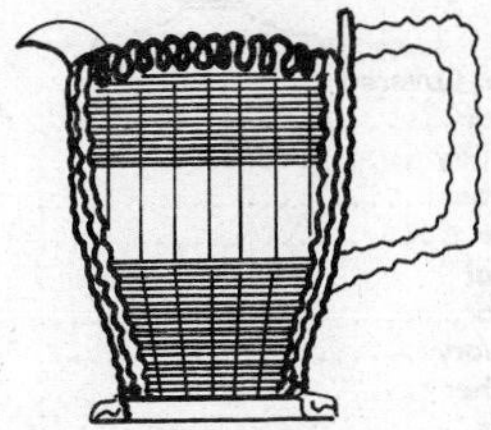

Bowl. 9"	
Emerald Green	$ 35.00
Pearl Clear	50.00
Pearl Yellow	60.00
Pearl Blue	75.00
Butter, Covered	
Emerald Green	150.00
Pearl Clear	200.00
Pearl Yellow	250.00
Pearl Blue	300.00
Creamer	
Emerald Green	55.00
Pearl Clear	80.00
Pearl Yellow	95.00
Pearl Blue	115.00
Pitcher, Water	
Emerald Green	150.00
Pearl Clear	225.00
Pearl Yellow	250.00
Pearl Blue	300.00
Rose Bowl	
Emerald Green	45.00
Pearl Clear	68.00
Pearl Yellow	80.00
Pearl Blue	95.00
Sauce	
Emerald Green	22.50
Pearl Clear	35.00
Pearl Yellow	42.00
Pearl Blue	55.00
Shakers. Pair	
Emerald Green	40.00
Pearl Clear	55.00
Pearl Yellow	72.00
Pearl Blue	85.00
Spooner	
Emerald Green	50.00
Pearl Clear	75.00
Pearl Yellow	90.00
Pearl Blue	110.00
Sugar, Covered	
Emerald Green	65.00
Pearl Clear	100.00
Pearl Yellow	125.00
Pearl Blue	150.00
Tray, 4½x9"	
Emerald Green	55.00
Pearl Clear	80.00
Pearl Yellow	98.00
Pearl Blue	120.00

AMBERETTE, See KLONDIKE

BARRED FORGET-ME-NOT

Made by Canton Glass Co., Canton, Ohio. C. 1883.

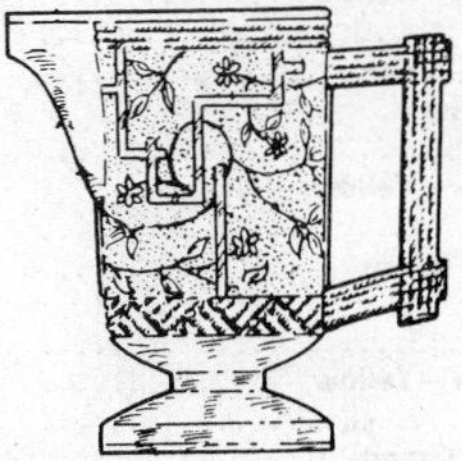

Butter, Covered	
Clear	$ 35.00
Amber—Yellow	50.00
Blue	52.50
Apple Green	60.00
Cake Stand, Large	
Clear	30.00
Amber—Yellow	42.00
Blue	46.50
Apple Green	55.00
Celery	
Clear	30.00
Amber—Yellow	42.50
Blue	45.00
Apple Green	50.00
Compote, Covered. High standard	
Clear	40.00
Amber—Yellow	56.00
Blue	65.00
Apple Green	75.00
Compote, Open. Low standard	
Clear	25.00
Amber—Yellow	37.50
Blue	42.50
Apple Green	48.00

Creamer	
Clear	25.00
Amber—Yellow	35.00
Blue	38.50
Apple Green	46.00
Goblet	
Clear	22.50
Amber—Yellow	32.00
Blue	35.00
Apple Green	40.00
Pitcher, Water	
Clear	35.00
Amber—Yellow	50.00
Blue	55.00
Apple Green	65.00
Plate, Handled. 9"	
Clear	25.00
Amber—Yellow	35.00
Blue	40.00
Apple Green	48.00
Relish, Handled	
Clear	15.00
Amber—Yellow	22.50
Blue	25.00
Apple Green	27.50
Sauce, Flat	
Clear	7.50
Amber—Yellow	10.50
Blue	12.50
Apple Green	15.00
Spooner	
Clear	20.00
Amber—Yellow	29.00
Blue	30.00
Apple Green	37.50
Sugar, Covered	
Clear	25.00
Amber—Yellow	35.00
Blue	42.00
Apple Green	50.00
Wine	
Clear	20.00
Amber—Yellow	28.00
Blue	30.00
Apple Green	36.50

BASKETWEAVE

Non-flint. C. 1880's

Bowl. 9"	
Clear	$ 28.50
Canary	40.00
Amber	52.00
Blue	58.00
Bowl, Covered. 8"	
Clear	35.00
Canary	50.00
Amber	60.00
Blue	70.00

Butter, Covered	
Clear	35.00
Canary	50.00
Amber	62.00
Blue	75.00
Cordial	
Clear	25.00
Canary	37.50
Amber	45.00
Blue	52.00
Creamer	
Clear	28.50
Canary	40.00
Amber	52.00
Blue	60.00
Cup and Saucer	
Clear	25.00
Canary	35.00
Amber	47.50
Blue	55.00
Egg Cup, Single	
Clear	16.00
Canary	22.50
Amber	30.00
Blue	32.50
***Goblet**	
Clear	20.00
Canary	28.50
Amber	36.00
Blue	40.00
Mug	
Clear	18.50
Canary	26.00
Amber	35.00
Blue	40.00
Pickle	
Clear	15.00
Canary	22.00
Amber	27.00
Blue	30.00
Pitcher, Milk	
Clear	45.00
Canary	62.50
Amber	75.00
Blue	85.00
Pitcher, Syrup	
Clear	45.00
Canary	65.00
Amber	80.00
Blue	90.00

*Pitcher, Water	
Clear	50.00
Canary	75.00
Amber	92.00
Blue	125.00
Plate. 9"	
Clear	22.50
Canary	32.00
Amber	45.00
Blue	47.50
Salt Dip	
Clear	7.50
Canary	10.50
Amber	14.00
Blue	16.50
Sauce, Flat	
Clear	8.50
Canary	12.00
Amber	16.00
Blue	18.50
Shakers, Pair	
Clear	30.00
Canary	42.00
Amber	55.00
Blue	60.00
Spooner	
Clear	18.50
Canary	26.00
Amber	37.50
Blue	40.00
Sugar, Covered	
Clear	32.50
Canary	50.00
Amber	58.50
Blue	65.00
*Tray, Water. 12"	
Clear	30.00
Canary	42.00
Amber	57.50
Blue	65.00
Tumbler	
Clear	18.00
Canary	26.00
Amber	32.50
Blue	38.00
Wine	
Clear	20.00
Canary	28.00
Amber	36.00
Blue	45.00

*Reproduced Item

BLACKBERRY

Non-flint pattern made by Hobbs, Brockunier & Co. in the late 1870's. Later reissued by Phoenix Glass Co.

Bowl, Covered. 7½"	
Clear	$ 45.00
Milk Glass	85.00

Butter, Covered	
Clear	65.00
*Milk Glass	125.00
Celery Vase	
Clear	75.00
*Milk Glass	200.00
Compote, Covered. 8". High standard	
Clear	85.00
Milk Glass	175.00
Creamer	
Clear	55.00
*Milk Glass	100.00
Egg Cup, Double	
Clear	40.00
Milk Glass	100.00
Goblet	
Clear	40.00
*Milk Glass	75.00
Honey	
Clear	16.50
Milk Glass	45.00
Pitcher, Water (scarce)	
Clear	150.00
*Milk Glass	500.00+
Relish	
Clear	25.00
Milk Glass	55.00
Salt, Master	
Clear	28.50
Milk Glass	65.00
Sauce	
Clear	15.00
Milk Glass	30.00
Spooner	
Clear	50.00
Milk Glass	85.00
Sugar, Covered	
Clear	60.00
*Milk Glass	110.00
Tumbler	
Clear	25.00
Milk Glass	45.00

*Reproduced Item

CANE

Non-flint pattern made by Gillinder Glass Co. and McKee Glass Co., C. 1875-85. SEE NOTE:

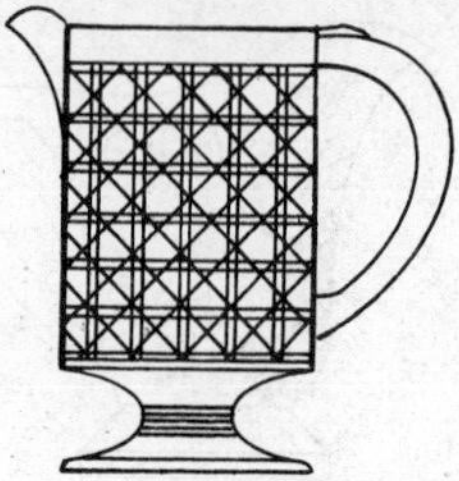

Bowl. 7½"	
Clear	$ 22.50
Apple Green	36.00
Amber	42.00
Blue	45.00
Butter, Covered	
Clear	40.00
Apple Green	65.00
Amber	72.00
Blue	80.00
Creamer	
Clear	25.00
Apple Green	40.00
Amber	45.00
Blue	55.00
Finger Bowl	
Clear	15.00
Apple Green	25.00
Amber	27.00
Blue	30.00
Goblet	
Clear	22.50
Apple Green	38.00
Amber	45.00
Blue	47.50
Pickle	
Clear	15.00
Apple Green	25.00
Amber	28.00
Blue	30.00
Pitcher, Water	
Clear	30.00
Apple Green	48.50
Amber	55.00
Blue	65.00
Plate, Toddy. 4½".	
Clear	10.00
Apple Green	16.00
Amber	20.00
Blue	22.00
Salt Dip	
Clear	10.00
Apple Green	17.50
Amber	18.00
Blue	21.50
Sauce, Flat	
Clear	7.50
Apple Green	12.00
Amber	14.00
Blue	15.00
Sauce, Footed	
Clear	10.00
Apple Green	16.50
Amber	18.00
Blue	20.00
Shakers, Pair	
Clear	30.00
Apple Green	48.50
Amber	55.00
Blue	62.50
Spooner	
Clear	20.00
Apple Green	32.50
Amber	36.00
Blue	40.00
Sugar, Covered	
Clear	35.00
Apple Green	55.00
Amber	65.00
Blue	75.00
Toothpicks	
Clear	20.00
Apple Green	32.50
Amber	35.00
Blue	40.00
Tray, Water	
Clear	35.00
Apple Green	55.00
Amber	62.50
Blue	72.00
Tumbler	
Clear	18.50
Apple Green	30.00
Amber	34.00
Blue	38.50
Wine	
Clear	25.00
Apple Green	42.50
Amber	46.00
Blue	50.00

NOTE: Apple Green is the most common color in this pattern.

CARAMEL SLAG

(See General Section "Greentown")

CATHEDRAL
(Orion)

Non-flint pattern made by Byrce Bros., Pgh., Pa., C. 1880's.

Bowl, Berry. 7", 8"	
Clear	$ 25.00
Amber—Canary	35.00
Blue	48.00
Amethyst	65.00
Butter, Covered	
Clear	55.00
Amber—Canary	75.00

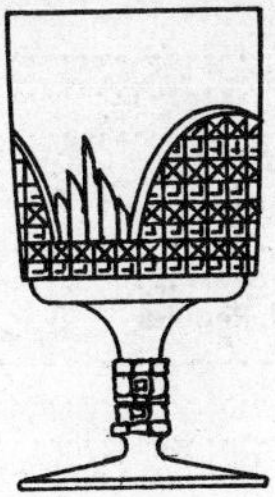

Blue 100.00
Amethyst 135.00

Cake Stand
- Clear 38.50
- Amber—Canary 55.00
- Blue 70.00
- Amethyst 100.00

Celery
- Clear 30.00
- Amber—Canary 42.00
- Blue 55.00
- Amethyst 75.00

Compote, Covered. 8". High standard
- Clear 50.00
- Amber—Canary 75.00
- Blue 95.00
- Amethyst 125.00

Compote, Open. 7". Low standard
- Clear 25.00
- Amber—Canary 35.00
- Blue 46.50
- Amethyst 65.00

Creamer
- Clear 40.00
- Amber — Canary 55.00
- Blue 75.00
- Amethyst 98.00

Egg Cup
- Clear 25.00
- Amber—Canary 34.50
- Blue 45.00
- Amethyst 65.00

Goblet
- Clear 35.00
- Amber—Canary 50.00
- Blue 62.50
- Amethyst 90.00

Pitcher, Water
- Clear 55.00
- Amber—Canary 75.00
- Blue 100.00
- Amethyst 140.00

Sauce, Flat. 4"
- Clear 10.00
- Amber — Canary 15.00
- Blue 18.00
- Amethyst 25.00

Sauce, Footed. 4"
- Clear 15.00
- Amber—Canary 21.50
- Blue 28.00
- Amethyst 40.00

Spooner
- Clear 25.00
- Amber—Canary 36.50
- Blue 46.00
- Amethyst 65.00

Sugar, Covered
- Clear 45.00
- Amber—Canary 65.00
- Blue 85.00
- Amethyst 115.00

Tumbler
- Clear 25.00
- Amber—Canary 36.50
- Blue 45.00
- Amethyst 65.00

Wine
- Clear 30.00
- Amber—Canary 42.50
- Blue 55.00
- Amethyst 75.00

COLORADO
(Lacy Medallion)

Non-flint pattern made by U.S. Glass Co., C. 1897. SEE NOTE:

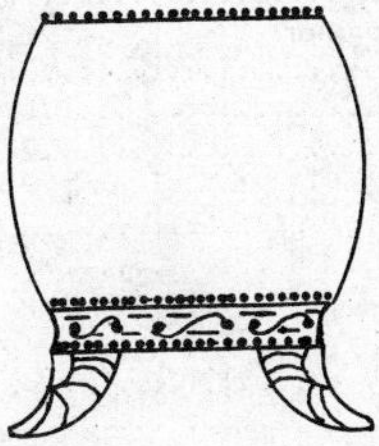

Banana Stand
- Clear ....$ 25.00
- Green 37.50
- Blue 50.00

Bowl. 6"
- Clear 12.50
- Green 20.00
- Blue 26.00

Bowl. 7½", Footed
- Clear 20.00
- Green 32.50
- Blue 44.00

Bowl. 8½", Footed
- Clear 45.00
- Green 70.00
- Blue 95.00

Bowl. 10", Footed, Flared
- Clear 55.00
- Green 82.50
- Blue 112.00

Butter, Covered
- Clear 50.00
- Green 76.00
- Blue 105.00

Cake Stand
- Clear 55.00
- Green 85.00
- Blue 115.00

Candy. 6"
- Clear 15.00
- Green 22.50
- Blue 35.00

Celery
- Clear 32.50
- Green 48.00
- Blue 65.00

Compote, Open. 6". Low standard
- Clear 27.50
- Green 42.00
- Blue 60.00

Compote, Open. 9½". Low standard
- Clear 35.00
- Green 55.00
- Blue 80.00

Creamer, Individual
- Clear 20.00
- Green 35.00
- Blue 42.00

Creamer, Regular
- Clear 32.50
- Green 50.00
- Blue 75.00

Mug
- Clear 18.50
- Green 28.50
- Blue 42.00

Nappy
- Clear 20.00
- Green 36.00
- Blue 41.50

Plate. 6", Square
- Clear 22.50
- Green 35.00
- Blue 45.00

Punch Cup
- Clear 12.00
- Green 18.50
- Blue 25.00

Salt
- Clear 10.00
- Green 16.50
- Blue 22.00

Sauce, Footed
- Clear 15.00
- Green 20.00
- Blue 32.50

Spooner
- Clear 22.00
- Green 32.50
- Blue 46.00

Sugar, Individual
- Clear 22.50
- Green 35.00
- Blue 45.00

Sugar, Covered, Regular
- Clear 45.00
- Green 68.00
- Blue 95.00

Toothpick
- Clear 20.00
- Green 32.00
- Blue 45.00

Tray, Card
- Clear 16.00
- Green 25.00
- Blue 35.00

Tumbler
- Clear 18.00
- Green 30.00
- Blue 37.50

Vase. 12"
- Clear 35.00
- Green 55.00
- Blue 75.00

Vase. 14"
- Clear 40.00
- Green 62.50
- Blue 85.00

NOTE: Reportedly made in Ruby—Clear and Amethyst, but seldom encountered.

CROESUS

Made by Riverside Glass Works, Wheeling W. Va., C. 1897.

Bowl. 6¾", Footed
- Clear .... $ 75.00
- Emerald Green 152.50
- Amethyst 225.00

Butter, Covered
- Clear 100.00
- *Emerald Green 215.00
- *Amethyst 300.00

Celery Vase
- Clear 65.00
- Emerald Green 135.00
- Amethyst 195.00

Compote, Jelly
- Clear 85.00
- Emerald Green 165.00
- Amethyst 250.00

Creamer, Individual
- Clear 35.00
- Emerald Green 72.00
- Amethyst 105.00

Creamer, Regular
- Clear 65.00
- Emerald Green 140.00
- Amethyst 200.00

Cruet, Stoppered
- Clear 75.00
- Emerald Green 155.00
- Amethyst 230.00

Pitcher, Water
- Clear 90.00
- Emerald Green 185.00
- Amethyst 265.00

Relish
- Clear 35.00
- Emerald Green 72.00
- Amethyst 100.00

Sauce
- Clear 20.00
- Emerald Green 39.50
- Amethyst 60.00

Shakers, Pair
- Clear 45.00
- Emerald Green 95.00
- Amethyst 150.00

Spooner
- Clear 40.00
- Emerald Green 85.00
- Amethyst 120.00

Sugar, Covered
- Clear 85.00
- Emerald Green 175.00
- Amethyst 250.00

Toothpick
- Clear 40.00
- *Emerald Green 82.50
- *Amethyst 125.00

Tumbler
- Clear 30.00
- *Emerald Green 65.00
- *Amethyst 95.00

*Reproduced Item

DAHLIA
(Stippled Dahlia)

Non-flint. C. 1880's.

Bowl. 5x7"
- Clear .... $ 15.00
- Blue — Green 22.50

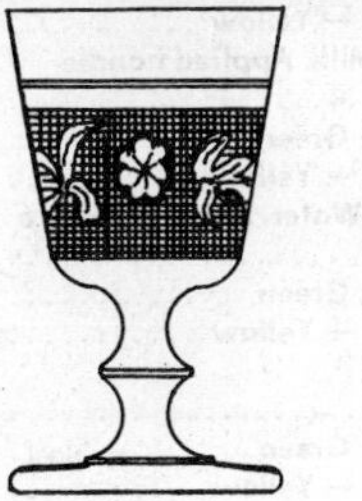

- Amber — Yellow 28.50

Butter, Covered
- Clear 45.00
- Blue — Green 68.00
- Amber — Yellow 80.00

Cake Stand. 10"
- Clear 30.00
- Blue — Green 46.50
- Amber — Yellow 55.00

Champagne
- Clear 45.00
- Blue — Green 65.00
- Amber — Yellow 80.00

Compote, Covered. 7". High standard
- Clear 55.00
- Blue — Green 85.00
- Amber — Yellow 100.00

Compote, Open. 8". High standard
- Clear 30.00
- Blue — Green 45.00
- Amber — Yellow 57.00

Cordial
- Clear 30.00
- Blue — Green 46.50
- Amber — Yellow 55.00

Creamer
- Clear 22.50
- Blue — Green 32.50
- Amber — Yellow 40.00

Egg Cup, Double
- Clear 45.00
- Blue—Green 65.00
- Amber — Yellow 80.00

Goblet
- Clear 35.00
- Blue — Green 55.00
- Amber — Yellow 65.00

Mug, Large
- Clear 37.50
- Blue — Green 55.00
- Amber — Yellow 65.00

Mug, Small
- Clear 30.00
- Blue — Green 42.50
- Amber — Yellow 55.00

Pickle
- Clear 18.00
- Blue—Green 27.50

Amber — Yellow 32.50
Pitcher, Milk. Applied handle
Clear 35.00
Blue — Green 55.00
Amber — Yellow 66.00
*Pitcher, Water. Applied handle
Clear 60.00
Blue — Green 95.00
Amber — Yellow 110.00
Plate. 7"
Clear 25.00
Blue — Green 37.50
Amber — Yellow 45.00
Plate, Cake. 9", Closed Handles
Clear 30.00
Blue — Green 45.00
Amber — Yellow 60.00
Platter. 8x12"
Clear 28.00
Blue — Green 42.00
Amber — Yellow 50.00
Salt, Footed
Clear 20.00
Blue — Green 30.00
Amber — Yellow 35.00
Sauce, Flat
Clear 5.00
Blue — Green 8.50
Amber — Yellow 10.00
Sauce, Footed
Clear 10.00
Blue — Green 15.00
Amber — Yellow 18.50
Spooner
Clear 25.00
Blue — Green 40.00
Amber — Yellow 50.00
Sugar, Covered
Clear 40.00
Blue — Green 58.00
Amber — Yellow 72.00
Wine
Clear 35.00
Blue — Green 52.00
Amber — Yellow 62.50

*Reproduced in color

DAISY AND BUTTON

Non-flint pattern made from the 1870's by several companies in many different forms. Practically every item in this pattern has been reproduced in a variety of colors.

Bowl. 9", Octagonal
Clear .... $ 22.50
Amber — Yellow 32.50
Blue 40.00
Bowl. 11", Scalloped
Clear 60.00

Amber — Yellow 85.00
Blue 98.00
Butter Chip
Clear 5.50
Amber — Yellow 8.00
Blue 10.00
Butter, Covered. Round
Clear 65.00
Amber — Yellow 90.00
Blue 105.00
Butter, Covered. Square
Clear 100.00
Amber — Yellow 145.00
Blue 175.00
Canoe. 4"
Clear 8.00
Amber — Yellow 12.50
Blue 14.00
Canoe. 8½"
Clear 15.00
Amber — Yellow 21.50
Blue 26.00
Canoe. 12"
Clear 20.00
Amber — Yellow 28.50
Blue 34.00
Canoe. 14"
Clear 25.00
Amber — Yellow 35.00
Blue 39.50
Castor Set. Glass holder, 3-Bottle.
Clear 50.00
Amber — Yellow 75.00
Blue 90.00
Castor Set. Metal holder, 5-Bottle
Clear 100.00
Amber — Yellow 145.00
Blue 175.00
Celery, Square
Clear 25.00
Amber — Yellow 35.00
Blue 42.50
Compote, Covered. 6". High standard
Clear 20.00
Amber — Yellow 28.00
Blue 35.00
Compote, Open. 8". High standard
Clear 40.00
Amber — Yellow 58.00

Blue 65.00

Creamer

Clear 20.00
Amber — Yellow 28.50
Blue 35.00

Cruet, Stoppered

Clear 25.00
Amber — Yellow 35.00
Blue 42.50

Egg Cup

Clear 15.00
Amber — Yellow 22.50
Blue 25.00

Goblet

Clear 20.00
Amber — Yellow 28.00
Blue 35.00

Hat, Various sizes

Clear ....10.00— 30.00
Amber — Yellow ....15.00— 45.00
Blue ....20.00— 60.00

Inkwell

Clear 30.00
Amber — Yellow 42.50
Blue 48.00

Parfait

Clear 20.00
Amber — Yellow 27.50
Blue 35.00

Pickle Castor. Complete

Clear 75.00
Amber — Yellow 110.00
Blue 135.00

Pitcher, Syrup

Clear 30.00
Amber — Yellow 45.00
Blue 52.50

Pitcher, Water. Bulbous

Clear 95.00
Amber — Yellow 135.00
Blue 155.00

Pitcher, Water. Tankard

Clear 50.00
Amber — Yellow 65.00
Blue 95.00

Plate. 5", Leaf-shaped

Clear 8.00
Amber — Yellow 12.00
Blue 15.00

Plate. 6", Round

Clear 6.50
Amber — Yellow 10.00
Blue 12.50

Plate. 7", Square

Clear 10.00
Amber — Yellow 15.00
Blue 18.50

Platter, Handled. 9x13", Oval

Clear 22.00
Amber — Yellow 32.50
Blue 37.50

Punch Bowl. 10", With stand

Clear 85.00
Amber — Yellow 125.00
Blue 150.00

Salt, Master

Clear 10.00
Amber — Yellow 15.00
Blue 18.50

Sauce, Various sizes and shapes

Clear ....7.50— 15.00
Amber — Yellow ......10.00— 20.00
Blue ....15.00— 30.00

Shakers, Pair

Clear 20.00
Amber — Yellow 28.00
Blue 35.00

Slipper. 5"

Clear 18.50
Amber — Yellow 26.00
Blue 30.00

Slipper, Scuff-type. 11½"

Clear 100.00
Amber — Yellow 145.00
Blue 170.00

Spooner

Clear 15.00
Amber — Yellow 22.00
Blue 25.00

Sugar, Covered

Clear 35.00
Amber — Yellow 50.00
Blue 60.00

Sugar, Open

Clear 25.00
Amber — Yellow 37.50
Blue 45.00

Toothpick. Urn-shaped

Clear 10.00
Amber — Yellow 15.00
Blue 17.00

Tray, Various shapes and sizes

Clear ....20.00— 35.00
Amber — Yellow ......30.00— 50.00
Blue ....35.00— 60.00

Tumbler

Clear 12.00
Amber — Yellow 18.00
Blue 22.50

Wine

Clear 10.00
Amber — Yellow 15.00
Blue 17.50

DAISY AND BUTTON WITH CROSS BARS

Non-flint pattern made by Richards & Hartley, Tarentum, Pa. C. 1888.

Bowl. 6", Open

Clear ....$ 18.50

Amber — Yellow	26.00
Blue	30.00
Bowl. 9", Open	
Clear	22.50
Amber — Yellow	32.50
Blue	38.50
Butter, Covered. Flat	
Clear	75.00
Amber — Yellow	100.00
Blue	125.00
Butter, Covered. Footed	
Clear	85.00
Amber — Yellow	120.00
Blue	138.50
Celery	
Clear	30.00
Amber — Yellow	42.00
Blue	50.00
Compote, Covered. 8". High standard	
Clear	45.00
Amber — Yellow	65.00
Blue	78.50
Compote, Open. 8". High standard	
Clear	30.00
Amber — Yellow	45.00
Blue	50.00
Creamer, Individual	
Clear	20.00
Amber — Yellow	28.00
Blue	35.00
Creamer, Regular	
Clear	28.50
Amber — Yellow	40.00
Blue	48.00
Cruet, Stoppered	
Clear	32.50
Amber — Yellow	45.00
Blue	55.00
Goblet	
Clear	25.00
Amber — Yellow	36.50
Blue	45.00
Pitcher, Milk	
Clear	35.00
Amber-Yellow	52.00
Blue	60.00
Pitcher, Syrup	
Clear	35.00
Amber — Yellow	50.00
Blue	58.00
Pitcher, Water	
Clear	55.00
Amber — Yellow	80.00
Blue	90.00
Sauce, Flat	
Clear	10.00
Amber — Yellow	15.00
Blue	20.00
Sauce, Footed	
Clear	15.00
Amber — Yellow	22.50
Blue	25.00
Shakers, Pair	
Clear	25.00
Amber—Yellow	38.50
Blue	42.50
Spooner	
Clear	22.50
Amber — Yellow	32.50
Blue	45.00
Sugar, Covered	
Clear	40.00
Amber — Yellow	55.00
Blue	65.00
Toothpick	
Clear	15.00
Amber — Yellow	22.50
Blue	27.50
Tray, Water	
Clear	35.00
Amber — Yellow	50.00
Blue	58.00
Tumbler	
Clear	15.00
Amber — Yellow	22.50
Blue	28.50
Wine	
Clear	20.00
Amber — Yellow	28.50
Blue	35.00

DAISY AND BUTTON WITH "V" ORNAMENT

Made by A. J. Beatty & Co., C. 1886-1887.

Bowl. 9"	
Clear	$ 22.50

Amber — Yellow 35.00
Blue 42.50

Bowl. 10½"
Clear 25.00
Amber — Yellow 38.50
Blue 45.00

Butter, Covered
Clear 75.00
Amber — Yellow 110.00
Blue 125.00

Celery
Clear 30.00
Amber — Yellow 42.00
Blue 50.00

Creamer
Clear 28.50
Amber — Yellow 40.00
Blue 48.00

Goblet
Clear 25.00
Amber — Yellow 36.50
Blue 45.00

Mug
Clear 15.00
Amber — Yellow 22.50
Blue 27.50

Pickle Castor, Complete
Clear 85.00
Amber — Yellow 122.50
Blue 135.00

Pitcher, Water
Clear 40.00
Amber — Yellow 55.00
Blue 68.50

Punch Cup
Clear 7.50
Amber — Yellow 12.50
Blue 18.00

Sauce. 5"
Clear 10.00
Amber — Yellow 15.00
Blue 18.50

Spooner
Clear 22.50
Amber — Yellow 32.50
Blue 40.00

Sugar, Covered
Clear 40.00
Amber — Yellow 60.00
Blue 75.00

Toothpick
Clear 12.50
Amber — Yellow 18.50
Blue 25.00

Tray, Water
Clear 35.00
Amber — Yellow 50.00
Blue 65.00

Tumbler
Clear 15.00
Amber — Yellow 24.50
Blue 28.00

DELAWARE
(Four-Petal Flower)

Non-flint pattern made by U.S. Glass Co. C. 1899. SEE NOTE:

Bowl. 9"
Clear ....$ 25.00
Green, Gilted 45.00
Rose, Gilted 55.00

Bowl, Banana
Clear 40.00
Green, Gilted 48.50
Rose, Gilted 55.00

Butter, Covered
Clear 75.00
Green, Gilted 100.00
Rose, Gilted 125.00

Creamer
Clear 35.00
Green, Gilted 40.00
Rose, Gilted 50.00

Cruet, Stoppered
Clear 42.50
Green, Gilted 50.00
Rose, Gilted 60.00

Cup and Saucer
Clear 35.00
Green, Gilted 45.00
Rose, Gilted 50.00

Pitcher, Water
Clear 60.00
Green, Gilted 75.00
Rose, Gilted 100.00

Sauce
Clear 20.00
Green, Gilted 25.00
Rose, Gilted 30.00

Spooner
Clear 50.00
Green, Gilted 65.00
Rose, Gilted 75.00

Sugar, Covered
Clear 65.00
Green, Gilted 85.00
Rose, Gilted 100.00

Toothpick
Clear 20.00
Green, Gilted 30.00
Rose, Gilted 40.00

Tumbler

Clear	30.00
Green, Gilted	35.00
Rose, Gilted	45.00

NOTE: Amethyst scarce.

DEWDROP

Non-flint. C. 1870's.

Butter, Covered

Clear	$ 50.00
Canary	67.00
Amber	75.00
Blue	87.50

Cake Stand. 9½"

Clear	30.00
Canary	42.50
Amber	45.00
Blue	57.50

Compote, Covered. 9¼". High std.

Clear	50.00
Canary	65.00
Amber	72.50
Blue	85.00

Creamer

Clear	30.00
Canary	40.00
Amber	46.50
Blue	55.00

Goblet. Plain base

Clear	20.00
Canary	26.50
Amber	30.00
Blue	38.00

Goblet. Dewdrop base

Clear	35.00
Canary	45.00
Amber	55.00
Blue	62.50

Mug, Applied handle

Clear	25.00
Canary	32.50
Amber	39.50
Blue	45.00

Pitcher, Water

Clear	50.00
Canary	68.50
Amber	75.00
Blue	90.00

Relish, Double

Clear	25.00
Canary	32.50
Amber	38.50
Blue	45.00

Sauce, Flat

Clear	10.00
Canary	12.50
Amber	16.50
Blue	21.50

Sugar, Covered

Clear	40.00
Canary	55.00
Amber	62.50
Blue	67.50

DEWEY
(Flower Flange)

Made by Indiana Tumbler & Goblet Co., Greentown, Indiana, 1894. Later by U.S. Glass Co. until 1904.

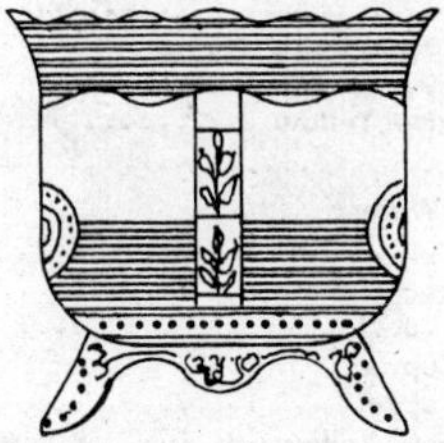

Butter, Covered

Clear	$ 37.50
Green—Yellow	75.00
*Caramel	125.00

Creamer

Clear	26.50
Green — Yellow	50.00
*Caramel	78.00

Cruet, Stoppered

Clear	40.00
Green — Yellow	75.00
Caramel	115.00

Mug

Clear	35.00
Green — Yellow	65.00
Caramel	98.00

Pitcher, Water

Clear	45.00
Green — Yellow	85.00
Caramel	135.00

Plate. 7½", Footed

Clear	25.00
Green — Yellow	50.00

Caramel	80.00
Sauce	
Clear	12.00
Green — Yellow	20.00
Caramel	30.00
Shakers, Pair	
Clear	32.00
Green — Yellow	60.00
Caramel	92.50
Spooner	
Clear	20.00
Green — Yellow	35.00
*Caramel	55.00
Sugar, Covered	
Clear	35.00
Green — Yellow	60.00
*Caramel	95.00
Tumbler	
Clear	22.50
Green — Yellow	40.00
*Caramel	65.00

*Reproduced Item

DIAMOND QUILTED

Non-flint. C. 1880's.

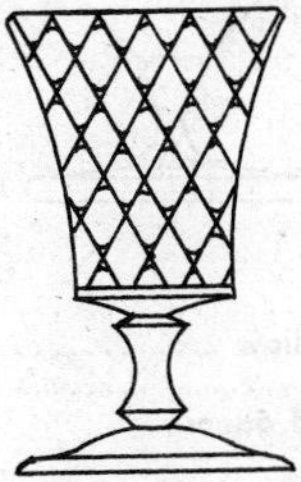

Butter, Covered	
Clear	$ 40.00
Yellow	85.00
Ambers, Blues, Amethyst	125.00
Amethyst, Dark	165.00
Celery	
Clear	27.50
Yellow	60.00
Ambers, Blues, Amethyst	75.00
Amethyst, Dark	110.00
Champagne	
Clear	25.00
Yellow	65.00
Ambers, Blues, Amethyst	78.00
Amethyst, Dark	110.00
Compote, Covered. High standard	
Clear	45.00
Yellow	87.50
Ambers, Blues, Amethyst	120.00
Amethyst, Dark	175.00
Compote, Open. High standard	
Clear	30.00
Yellow	65.00
Ambers, Blues, Amethyst	78.00
Amethyst, Dark	125.00
Creamer	
Clear	25.00
Yellow	55.00
Ambers, Blues, Amethyst	75.00
Amethyst, Dark	100.00
***Goblet**	
Clear	25.00
Yellow	52.50
Ambers, Blues, Amethyst	65.00
Amethyst, Dark	110.00
Pitcher, Water	
Clear	35.00
Yellow	72.50
Ambers, Blues, Amethyst	85.00
Amethyst, Dark	140.00
Sauce, Flat	
Clear	10.00
Yellow	25.00
Ambers, Blues, Amethyst	30.00
Amethyst, Dark	42.50
Sauce, Footed	
Clear	18.00
Yellow	37.50
Ambers, Blues, Amethyst	48.50
Amethyst, Dark	72.00
Spooner	
Clear	25.00
Yellow	55.00
Ambers, Blues, Amethyst	65.00
Amethyst, Dark	98.00
Sugar, Covered	
Clear	30.00
Yellow	62.50
Ambers, Blues, Amethyst	75.00
Amethyst, Dark	125.00
Tray	
Clear	30.00
Yellow	65.00
Ambers, Blues, Amethyst	80.00
Amethyst, Dark	125.00
***Tumbler, Water**	
Clear	15.00
Yellow	32.50
Ambers, Blues, Amethyst	40.00
Amethyst, Dark	62.50
Wine	
Clear	15.00
Yellow	35.00
Ambers, Blues, Amethyst	42.50
Amethyst, Dark	65.00

*Reproduced Item

FINE CUT

Made by Bryce Bros., Pittsburgh, Pa., C. 1870's.

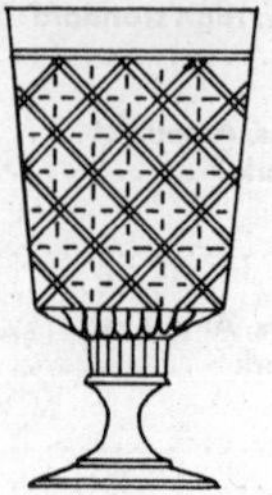

Butter, Covered	
Clear	$ 40.00
Amber — Yellow	55.00
Blue	68.50
Creamer	
Clear	26.50
Amber — Yellow	37.50
Blue	45.00
Finger Bowl. Footed	
Clear	16.50
Amber — Yellow	25.00
Blue	28.50
Goblet	
Clear	25.00
Amber — Yellow	34.00
Blue	42.50
Pickle	
Clear	15.00
Amber — Yellow	20.00
Blue	25.00
Pitcher, Water	
Clear	40.00
Amber — Yellow	52.00
Blue	65.00
Plate. 6"	
Clear	20.00
Amber — Yellow	28.50
Blue	35.00
Plate. 7"	
Clear	22.50
Amber — Yellow	30.00
Blue	38.00
Plate. 10"	
Clear	30.00
Amber — Yellow	42.00
Blue	50.00
Sauce	
Clear	8.50
Amber — Yellow	12.50
Blue	14.50
Spooner	
Clear	30.00
Amber — Yellow	39.50
Blue	48.00
Sugar, Covered	
Clear	32.50
Amber — Yellow	45.00
Blue	55.00
Sugar, Open	
Clear	25.00
Amber — Yellow	38.00
Blue	45.00
Tray, Bread	
Clear	25.00
Amber — Yellow	35.00
Blue	42.00
Tray, Water	
Clear	35.00
Amber — Yellow	48.00
Blue	55.00

FINECUT AND PANEL
(Nailhead and Panel)

Non-flint pattern made by many Pittsburgh factories in the 1880's. Reissued in the early 1890's by U.S. Glass Co.

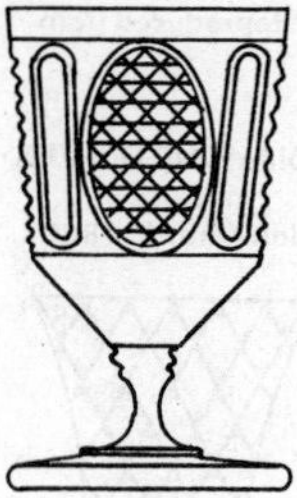

Bowl. 7"	
Clear	$ 17.50
Amber — Yellow	26.50
Blue	35.00
Butter, Covered. Square	
Clear	40.00
Amber — Yellow	60.00
Blue	82.50
Cake Stand. 10"	
Clear	30.00
Amber — Yellow	48.00
Blue	65.00
Compote, Open. High standard	
Clear	35.00
Amber — Yellow	55.00
Blue	72.50
Cordial	
Clear	20.00
Amber — Yellow	32.50
Blue	45.00
Creamer	
Clear	25.00
Amber — Yellow	37.50
Blue	50.00
Goblet	
Clear	25.00
Amber — Yellow	40.00

- Blue. (scarce) 100.00

Pitcher, Water
- Clear 35.00
- Amber — Yellow 45.00
- Blue 75.00

Plate. 6¼″
- Clear 15.00
- Amber — Yellow 22.50
- Blue 32.50

Plate. 7¼″
- Clear 17.50
- Amber — Yellow 25.00
- Blue 35.00

Platter
- Clear 45.00
- Amber — Yellow 67.50
- Blue 95.00

Relish
- Clear 17.50
- Amber — Yellow 25.00
- Blue 36.50

Sauce, Footed, Square
- Clear 10.00
- Amber — Yellow 15.00
- Blue 22.50

Spooner
- Clear 25.00
- Amber — Yellow 40.00
- Blue 55.00

Sugar, Open
- Clear 22.50
- Amber — Yellow 35.00
- Blue 47.50

Tray, Water. 12″
- Clear 45.00
- Amber — Yellow 68.50
- Blue 95.00

Tumbler
- Clear 16.00
- Amber — Yellow 25.00
- Blue 35.00

Wine
- Clear 20.00
- Amber — Yellow 30.00
- Blue. (scarce) 85.00

FRANCESWARE

Made by Hobbs, Brockunier and Co., Wheeling, W. Va. in the 1880's. A clear, frosted hobnail or swirl pattern glass with amber stained top rims. It may be pressed or mold blown.

Bowl, Hobnail. 4″
- Clear .... $ 42.50
- Frosted 65.00

Bowl, Hobnail. 7½″
- Clear 60.00
- Frosted 89.50

Box, Hobnail, 5½″, Round, Covered
- Clear 50.00
- Frosted 75.00

Butter, Covered Hobnail
- Clear 85.00
- Frosted 135.00

Creamer, Hobnail
- Clear 50.00
- Frosted 72.50

Pitcher, Hobnail. 8½″
- Clear 125.00
- Frosted 180.00

Pitcher, Hobnail. 11″
- Clear 200.00
- Frosted 295.00

Pitcher, Syrup. Swirl
- Clear 65.00
- Frosted 95.00

Sauce, Hobnail. 4″, Square
- Clear 25.00
- Frosted 38.00

Shaker, Sugar. Swirl
- Clear 85.00
- Frosted 125.00

Shakers, Pair. Hobnail
- Clear 55.00
- Frosted 82.50

Shakers, Pair. Swirl
- Clear 65.00
- Frosted 95.00

Spooner, Hobnail
- Clear 45.00
- Frosted 65.00

Sugar, Covered. Hobnail
- Clear 65.00
- Frosted 98.00

Sugar, Open. Hobnail
- Clear 40.00
- Frosted 65.00

Toothpick, Hobnail
- Clear 35.00
- Frosted 52.50

Tray, Leaf-shaped. 12″
- Clear 85.00
- Frosted 125.00

Tumbler, Hobnail
- Clear 35.00
- Frosted 55.00

GREEN HERRINGBONE
(See Clear Glass Section
Panelled Herringbone)

HOBNAIL, FAN TOP

Non-flint. C. 1880's.

Bowl, Berry	
Clear	$ 30.00
Amber	48.00
Blue	55.00
Butter, Covered	
Clear	45.00
Amber	68.50
Blue	80.00
Celery	
Clear	27.50
Amber	42.00
Blue	55.00
Creamer	
Clear	30.00
Amber	45.00
Blue	55.00
Goblet	
Clear	25.00
Amber	40.00
Blue	48.50
Salt, Individual	
Clear	8.50
Amber	14.50
Blue	17.50
***Sauce**	
Clear	12.00
Amber	20.00
Blue	25.00
Sugar, Covered	
Clear	35.00
Amber	58.50
Blue	25.00
Sugar, Covered	
Clear	35.00
Amber	58.50
Blue	67.50
Tray. 8x 12"	
Clear	22.50
Amber	35.00
Blue	45.00

*Reproduced Item

HOBNAIL, OPALESCENT
(See General Section
"Opalescent Glass")

HOBNAIL, PANELLED

Non-flint pattern made by Bryce Bros., Pgh. Pa., C. 1875-1885.

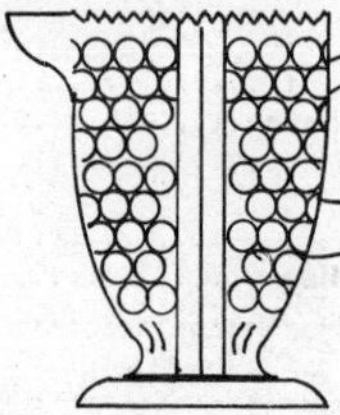

Bowl. 8"	
Clear	$ 25.00
Amber — Yellow	38.50
Blue	45.00
Butter, Covered	
Clear	40.00
Amber — Yellow	65.00
Blue	75.00
Celery Vase	
Clear	30.00
Amber — Yellow	46.50
Blue	55.00
Compote, Open. High standard	
Clear	35.00
Amber — Yellow	55.00
Blue	68.50
Creamer	
Clear	25.00
Amber — Yellow	40.00
Blue	46.50
Goblet	
Clear	22.50
Amber — Yellow	38.50
Blue	42.00
Plate. 4½"	
Clear	15.00
Amber — Yellow	25.00
Blue	30.00
Plate. 7"	
Clear	20.00
Amber — Yellow	32.00
Blue	38.50
Sauce, Flat	
Clear	8.50
Amber — Yellow	15.00
Blue	20.00
Spooner	
Clear	20.00
Amber — Yellow	30.00
Blue	35.00
Sugar, Covered	
Clear	35.00

Amber — Yellow 57.50
Blue 65.00

Wine
Clear 15.00
Amber — Yellow 25.00
Blue 29.50

HOBNAIL, POINTED

Non-flint. C. 1880's. SEE NOTE:

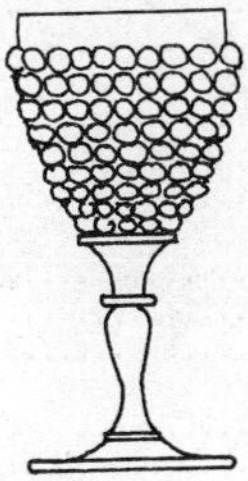

Bone Dish
Clear ....$ 20.00
Amber 25.00
Blue 30.00

*Bowl. 8"
Clear 25.00
Amber 32.50
Blue 50.00

Butter, Covered
Clear 35.00
Amber 60.00
Blue 75.00

Cake Stand. 10"
Clear 40.00
Amber 50.00
Blue 65.00

Celery Vase
Clear 30.00
Amber 37.50
Blue 50.00

Compote, Open. 8". High standard
Clear 40.00
Amber 55.00
Blue 65.00

Cordial
Clear 25.00
Amber 35.00
Blue 40.00

Creamer
Clear 30.00
Amber 40.00
Blue 45.00

Goblet
Clear 28.50
Amber 37.50
Blue 45.00

Inkwell
Clear 25.00
Amber 45.00
Blue 55.00

Pickle
Clear 15.00
Amber 22.50
Blue 28.50

*Pitcher, Water
Clear 40.00
Amber 55.00
Blue 75.00

Plate. 7"
Clear 20.00
Amber 28.50
Blue 35.00

Salt, Individual
Clear 5.00
Amber 10.00
Blue 12.50

*Sauce, Flat
Clear 10.00
Amber 12.50
Blue 15.00

*Shakers, Pair
Clear 25.00
Amber 35.00
Blue 40.00

Spooner
Clear 25.00
Amber 35.00
Blue 48.50

*Sugar, Open
Clear 25.00
Amber 35.00
Blue 42.50

Tray, Pen
Clear 15.00
Amber 25.00
Blue 28.50

Tray, Water. 11½"
Clear 30.00
Amber 50.00
Blue 65.00

*Wine
Clear 15.00
Amber 22.00
Blue 30.00

NOTE: Rare in Apple Green, Dark Green and Yellow.

*Reproduced Item

HOBNAIL, PRINTED

Non-flint. C. 1880's-1890's.

Butter, Covered
Clear ....$ 35.00
Amber — Yellow 58.00
Blue 65.00

Celery Vase
Clear 28.50
Amber — Yellow 45.00

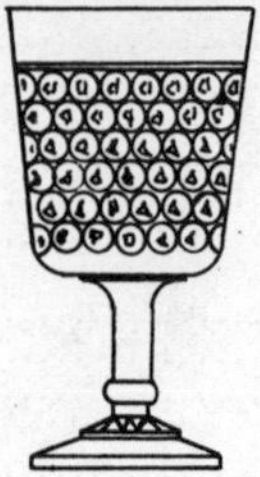

Blue	55.00
Creamer	
Clear	22.50
Amber — Yellow	35.00
Blue	45.00
Goblet	
Clear	20.00
Amber — Yellow	32.50
Blue	40.00
Mug	
Clear	17.50
Amber — Yellow	28.50
Blue	35.00
Pitcher, Water	
Clear	35.00
Amber — Yellow	60.00
Blue	75.00
Sauce	
Clear	8.50
Amber — Yellow	15.00
Blue	18.00
Spooner	
Clear	20.00
Amber — Yellow	35.00
Blue	42.50
Sugar, Covered	
Clear	30.00
Amber — Yellow	50.00
Blue	55.00
Tumbler	
Clear	15.00
Amber — Yellow	24.00
Blue	28.50
Wine	
Clear	16.50
Amber — Yellow	28.00
Blue	32.50

HOBNAIL, THUMBPRINT BASE

Non-flint pattern originally made by Doyle & Co., Pittsburgh, Pa. in the 1880's. Later by several other companies between 1893-1898.

Bowl, Berry. 9", 10"	
Clear	$ 35.00
Amber	55.00
Blue	75.00

Butter, Covered	
Clear	40.00
Amber	62.50
Blue	85.00
Celery	
Clear	35.00
Amber	55.00
Blue	75.00
Creamer	
Clear	32.50
Amber	50.00
Blue	68.00
Mustard Jar	
Clear	18.50
Amber	30.00
Blue	38.50
Pitcher, Water	
Clear	50.00
Amber	78.00
Blue	110.00
Salt, Individual	
Clear	12.00
Amber	18.50
Blue	25.00
Spooner	
Clear	32.50
Amber	50.00
Blue	65.00
Sugar, Covered	
Clear	35.00
Amber	55.00
Blue	75.00
Tray, Water	
Clear	30.00
Amber	47.50
Blue	62.50

HOLLY AMBER
(Golden Agate)

Made by Indiana Tumbler & Goblet Co., Greentown, Indiana from January 1 to June 13, 1903.

Bowls	
7½"	$ 650.00
8½"	750.00
*Butter, Covered	1250.00
Cake Stand	1750.00
*Compote, Jelly. 4¼", Covered	750.00
*Creamer	600.00
*Cruet, Stoppered	1250.00
*Mug, 4", Handled	500.00

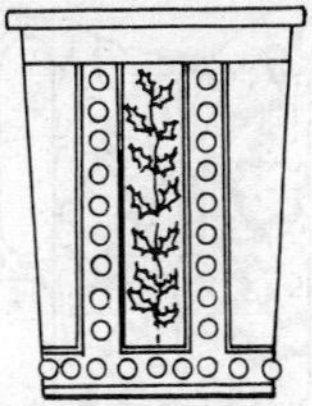

*Nappy	550.00
Parfait. 6″	550.00
Pitchers	
Syrup	750.00
Water. 10″	2250.00
Plate. 7½″, Round	500.00
Relish	500.00
Sauce, 4″	225.00
Spooner	500.00
Sugars	
*Covered. 4¼″	500.00
Open. 3¾″	400.00
Toothpicks	
*Flat	250.00
Footed. (rare)	750.00
Tray, Water. 9¼″	1000.00

*Reproduced Item

HUMMING BIRD

(Flying Robin, Bird and Fern, Thunder Bird)

Non-flint. C. 1880's.

Bowl, Finger	
Clear	$ 20.00
Canary	28.00
Amber — Blue	35.00
Butter, Covered	
Clear	50.00
Canary	72.00
Amber — Blue	86.50
Celery	
Clear	35.00
Canary	48.50
Amber—Blue	62.50
Creamer	
Clear	35.00
Canary	50.00
Amber — Blue	65.00
Goblet	
Clear	30.00
Canary	42.50
Amber — Blue	55.00
Pitcher, Water	
Clear	50.00
Canary	75.00
Amber — Blue	90.00
Sauce, Flat	
Clear	10.00
Canary	15.00
Amber — Blue	18.50
Sauce, Footed	
Clear	15.00
Canary	22.50
Amber — Blue	26.50
Spooner	
Clear	25.00
Canary	36.50
Amber — Blue	42.50
Sugar, Covered	
Clear	45.00
Canary	65.00
Amber — Blue	78.50
Tray, Water	
Clear	50.00
Canary	72.50
Amber — Blue	85.00
Wine	
Clear	32.50
Canary	45.00
Amber — Blue	55.00

KLONDIKE

(Amberette, English Hobnail Cross)

A non-flint pattern issued in the 1880's to commemorate the Alaskan Gold Rush. The frosted panels depict snow; the amber bands, gold. It can be found clear, frosted, with or without scrolls depending on the maker. SEE NOTE:

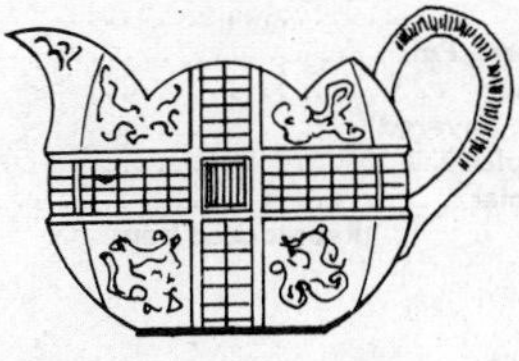

Bowl, Berry.8″	$ 250.00
Butter, Covered	350.00
Cake Stand. 8″, Square	500.00
Celery	200.00
Champagne	400.00
Cruet, Stoppered	550.00
Goblet	250.00
Pitchers	
Syrup	350.00
Water	600.00

Punch Cup	125.00
Sauce, Flat	85.00
Shakers, Pair. Original tops	250.00
Spooner	175.00
Sugars	
Covered	300.00
Open	225.00
Toothpick	225.00
Tray, 5½", Square	150.00
Tumbler	175.00
Vase. 8"	350.00

NOTE: Prices listed are for frosted. Clear panels, approximately 30% less.

MAIZE

A milk-white novelty glass designed by Joseph Locke and made by Libbey & Son, Toledo, Ohio, C. 1889.

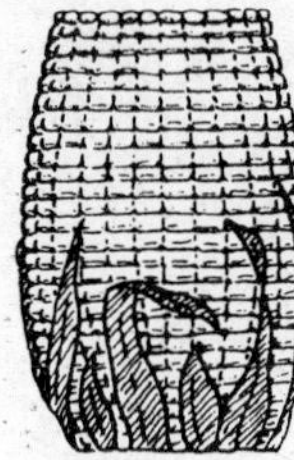

Bowls	
5"	$ 125.00
9"	175.00
Butter, Covered	395.00
Celery Vase	135.00
Creamer	165.00
Cruet, Stoppered	175.00
Mustard, Covered	95.00
*Pitcher, Water	275.00
Sauce	45.00
*Shakers, Pair	165.00
Spooner	100.00
Sugar, Covered	295.00
Toothpick	160.00
*Tumbler	100.00

*Reproduced Item

MAPLE LEAF

Non-flint pattern made by Gillinder & Sons, C. 1880's. SEE NOTE:

Bowl. 6x 9"	
Clear	$ 25.00
Frosted	30.00
Amber — Yellow	35.00
Blue	38.50
Green	45.00
Bowl. 6x10", Footed.	
Clear	28.50
Frosted	35.00
Amber — Yellow	42.50
Blue	48.50
Green	55.00
Butter, Covered	
Clear	45.00
Frosted	55.00
Amber — Yellow	65.00
Blue	75.00
Green	85.00
Cake Stand. 11"	
Clear	40.00
Frosted	50.00
Amber — Yellow	62.50
Blue	75.00
Green	85.00
Celery	
Clear	30.00
Frosted	37.50
Amber — Yellow	45.00
Blue	55.00
Green	65.00
Compote, Covered. 9". High standard	
Clear	75.00
Frosted	95.00
Amber — Yellow	125.00
Blue	140.00
Green	150.00
Compote, Jelly	
Clear	30.00
Frosted	37.50
Amber — Yellow	45.00
Blue	50.00
Green	57.50
Creamer	
Clear	32.50
Frosted	40.00
Amber — Yellow	48.00
Blue	60.00
Green	65.00
Goblet.	
Clear	35.00
Frosted	50.00
Amber — Yellow	65.00
Blue	75.00
Green	85.00

Pitcher, Milk
Clear 40.00
Frosted 50.00
Amber — Yellow 62.50
Blue 75.00
Green 85.00

Pitcher, Water
Clear 55.00
Frosted 65.00
Amber — Yellow 80.00
Blue 90.00
Green 100.00

Plate, "Grant Peace." 10"
Clear 35.00
Frosted 45.00
Amber — Yellow 55.00
Blue 60.00
Green 75.00

Platter. 10½"
Clear 30.00
Frosted 37.50
Amber — Yellow 45.00
Blue 55.00
Green 65.00

Relish
Clear 12.00
Frosted 15.00
Amber — Yellow 18.50
Blue 22.50
Green 25.00

Sauce. 5", 6", Footed
Clear 10.00
Frosted 13.50
Amber — Yellow 16.50
Blue 22.50
Green 25.00

Spooner
Clear 20.00
Frosted 25.00
Amber — Yellow 30.00
Blue 35.00
Green 40.00

Sugar, Covered
Clear 35.00
Frosted 45.00
Amber — Yellow 50.00
Blue 60.00
Green 65.00

Tumbler
Clear 20.00
Frosted 25.00
Amber — Yellow 30.00
Blue 32.50
Green 35.00

NOTE: Heavily reproduced in clear and colors.

MEDALLION
(Spades, Hearts and Spades)

Non-flint. C. 1880's.

Butter, Covered
Clear .... $ 35.00
Amber — Canary 45.00
Blue — Green 60.00

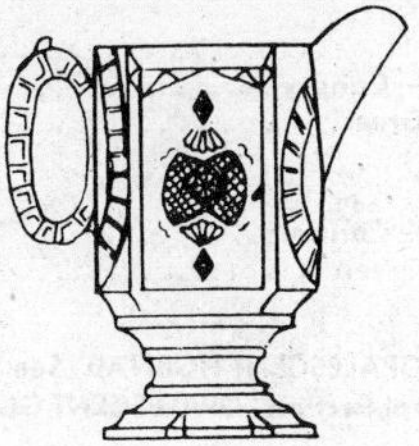

Castor Bottle
Clear 10.00
Amber — Canary 12.50
Blue — Green 15.00

Celery
Clear 25.00
Amber —Canary 35.00
Blue — Green 45.00

Compote, Covered. High standard
Clear 40.00
Amber — Canary 57.50
Blue — Green 75.00

Creamer
Clear 25.00
Amber — Canary 36.00
Blue — Green 45.00

Egg Cup
Clear 18.00
Amber — Canary 22.50
Blue — Green 31.50

Goblet
Clear 25.00
Amber — Canary 32.50
Blue — Green 40.00

Pickle
Clear 15.00
Amber — Canary 20.00
Blue — Green 28.00

Pitcher, Water
Clear 50.00
Amber — Canary 65.00
Blue — Green 85.00

Sauce, Flat
Clear 7.50
Amber — Canary 10.00
Blue — Green 13.50

Sauce, Footed
Clear 10.00
Amber — Canary 15.00
Blue — Green 18.00

Spooner
Clear 20.00
Amber — Canary 26.00
Blue — Green 35.00

Sugar, Covered
Clear 30.00
Amber — Canary 38.50
Blue — Green 5.00

Tumbler

Clear	18.50
Amber — Canary	25.00
Blue — Green	28.50

Wine

Clear	20.00
Amber — Canary	27.50
Blue — Green	35.00

OPALESCENT HOBNAIL, See General Section "OPALESCENT GLASS"

PANELLED FORGET-ME-NOT

Non-flint pattern made by Bryce Bros., Pgh., Pa., C. 1870's. SEE NOTE:

Butter, Covered

Clear	$ 40.00
Amber	55.00
Blue — Green	75.00

Cake Stand. 9½"

Clear	35.00
Amber	55.00
Blue — Green	65.00

Celery

Clear	30.00
Amber	47.50
Blue — Green	55.00

Compote, Covered. 8". High standard.

Clear	55.00
Amber	85.00
Blue — Green	100.00

Creamer

Clear	25.00
Amber	37.50
Blue — Green	42.50

Goblet

Clear	30.00
Amber	42.50
Blue — Green	50.00

Marmalade Jar, Covered

Clear	35.00
Amber	50.00
Blue — green	65.00

Pickle

Clear	15.00
Amber	22.50
Blue — Green	27.50

Pitcher, Water

Clear	35.00
Amber	50.00
Blue — Green	68.50

Sauce, Flat

Clear	10.00
Amber	14.50
Blue — Green	17.50

Sauce, Footed

Clear	15.00
Amber	22.50
Blue — Green	26.50

Spooner

Clear	25.00
Amber	37.50
Blue — Green	50.00

Sugar, Covered

Clear	35.00
Amber	50.00
Blue — Green	62.50

Wine

Clear	35.00
Amber	55.00
Blue — Green	65.00

NOTE: Amethyst. Add 200% to clear.

PRIMROSE

Non-flint pattern made by Canton Glass Co., Canton, Ohio, C. 1880's. SEE NOTE:

Bowl, 8"

Clear	$ 20.00
Amber — Yellow	26.50
Blue	32.50

Butter, Covered

Clear	40.00
Amber — Yellow	55.00
Blue	68.50

Cake Stand. 10"

Clear	35.00
Amber — Yellow	48.50
Blue	55.00

Celery

Clear	25.00
Amber — Yellow	32.50
Blue	40.00

Compote, Covered. 6". Low standard

Clear	28.00
Amber — Yellow	37.50
Blue	45.00

Creamer
- Clear 30.00
- Amber — Yellow 37.50
- Blue 47.50

Egg Cup
- Clear 20.00
- Amber — Yellow 25.00
- Blue 32.50

Goblet. Knob stem
- Clear 26.50
- Amber — Yellow 35.00
- Blue 45.00

Goblet. Plain stem
- Clear 19.50
- Amber — Yellow 25.00
- Blue 32.50

Pickle
- Clear 12.50
- Amber — Yellow 16.50
- Blue 20.00

Pitcher, Milk
- Clear 35.00
- Amber — Yellow 45.00
- Blue 55.00

Pitcher, Water
- Clear 32.00
- Amber — Yellow 42.50
- Blue 50.00

Plate. 4½"
- Clear 10.00
- Amber — Yellow 12.50
- Blue 14.50

Plate. 6"
- Clear 15.00
- Amber — Yellow 20.00
- Blue 25.00

Sauce, Footed
- Clear 12.00
- Amber — Yellow 15.00
- Blue 18.50

Spooner
- Clear 18.00
- Amber — Yellow 25.00
- Blue 30.00

Sugar, Covered
- Clear 30.00
- Amber — Yellow 42.50
- Blue 55.00

Toothpick
- Clear 17.50
- Amber — Yellow 22.50
- Blue 28.50

Tray, Water
- Clear 30.00
- Amber — Yellow 42.50
- Blue 50.00

Waste Bowl
- Clear 20.00
- Amber — Yellow 25.00
- Blue 32.50

Wine
- Clear 20.00
- Amber — Yellow 26.50
- Blue 32.50

NOTE: Scarce in Apple Green. Add 100% to clear.

PRINTED HOBNAIL See HOBNAIL, PRINTED

PURPLE SLAG

Challinor, Taylor and Company, Tarentum, Pa. was probably the largest producer of this glass. Also made by other factories in America and England in the 1880's. Being reproduced but obvious to the knowledgeable.

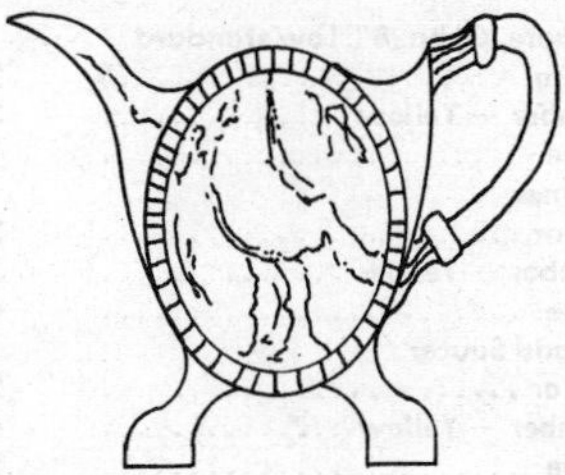

Bowls
- Acanthus. 9½". Atterbury .... $ 125.00
- Basketweave. 5½ x 8" 125.00
- Raindrop. 5" 50.00

Butter, Covered 225.00

Cake Stand. 9". Ring 150.00

Celery Vases
- Fluted, 8¼" 110.00
- Jewel, 8½" 125.00

Compotes
- 7". Open, High std. Basketweave 150.00
- 8". Covered, High std. Fluted 225.00

Creamers
- Acanthus 125.00
- Flower Panel 125.00
- Sunflower 150.00

Match Holder. Ring 75.00

Pitcher, Water. Raindrop 225.00

Plates
- Basketweave. 8½" 85.00
- Lattice Edge. 10" 125.00

Salt. Kettle-shaped 65.00

Sauce, Flat 50.00

Spooners
- Acanthus 85.00
- Flower Panel 100.00
- Flute 85.00

Sugar, Open. Acanthus 100.00

Toothpicks
- Acanthus 85.00
- Boot 65.00
- Picket 60.00

RAINDROP

Non-flint. C. 1880's. SEE NOTE:

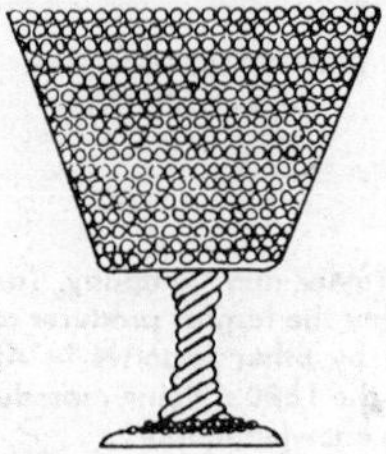

Compote, Open. 8". Low standard	
Clear $	22.00
Amber — Yellow	37.50
Blue	45.00
Creamer	
Clear	22.50
Amber — Yellow	38.50
Blue	45.00
Cup and Saucer	
Clear	25.00
Amber — Yellow	40.00
Blue	50.00
Egg Cup, Double	
Clear	25.00
Amber — Yellow	39.50
Blue	48.50
Finger Bowl	
Clear	15.00
Amber — Yellow	25.00
Blue	32.00
Pickle	
Clear	18.00
Amber — Yellow	28.50
Blue	35.00
Pitcher, Syrup	
Clear	35.00
Amber — Yellow	50.00
Blue	65.00
Pitcher, Water	
Clear	35.00
Amber — Yellow	55.00
Blue	75.00
Plate, Cake	
Clear	28.50
Amber — Yellow	45.00
Blue	55.00
Sauce, Flat	
Clear	8.00
Amber — Yellow	13.50
Blue	15.00
Sauce, Footed	
Clear	12.00
Amber — Yellow	20.00
Blue	25.00
Tray, Water	
Clear	35.00
Amber — Yellow	55.00
Blue	75.00

NOTE: Scarce in Apple Green

ROSE-IN-SNOW

Non-flint pattern made by Bryce Bros., Pgh. Pa. in the square form, C. 1880's. Also made in the round form by the Ohio Flint Glass Co.

Bowl. 4"	
Clear $	12.50
Amber — Canary	15.00
Blue	20.00
Butter, Covered. Round.	
Clear	40.00
Amber — Canary	50.00
Blue	65.00
Butter, Covered. Square	
Clear	50.00
Amber — Canary	65.00
Blue	75.00
Cake Stand. 9"	
Clear	75.00
Amber — Canary	100.00
Blue	125.00
Compote, Covered. 8". High std.	
Clear	65.00
Amber — Canary	80.00
Blue	100.00
Compote, Covered. 7". Low standard	
Clear	50.00
Amber — Canary	65.00
Blue	75.00
Compote, Open. 6". Low standard	
Clear	25.00
Amber — Canary	32.50
Blue	52.00
Creamer, Round	
Clear	35.00
Amber — Canary	45.00
Blue	55.00
Creamer, Square	
Clear	40.00
Amber — Canary	48.50

Blue 60.00
*Goblet
Clear 32.50
Amber-Canary 40.00
Blue 50.00
Marmalade Jar, Covered
Clear 50.00
Amber — Canary 60.00
Blue 75.00
*Mug. "In Fond Remembrance"
Clear 35.00
Amber — Canary 45.00
Blue 55.00
Pickle. 8¼x7", Double (scarce)
Clear 85.00
Amber — Canary 100.00
Blue 125.00
Pickle. Oval, Handles at ends
Clear 21.50
Amber — Canary 27.50
Blue 32.50
Pitcher, Water. Applied handle
Clear 100.00
Amber — Canary 125.00
Blue 150.00
Plate. 6½"
Clear 25.00
Amber — Canary 32.50
Blue 38.50
*Plate, 10", Handled
Clear 35.00
Amber — Canary 47.50
Blue 55.00
Sauce, Flat
Clear 9.00
Amber — Canary 12.50
Blue 16.00
Sauce, Footed
Clear 15.00
Amber — Canary 18.00
Blue 22.50
Spooner, Round
Clear 25.00
Amber — Canary 32.50
Blue 40.00
Spooner, Square
Clear 32.50
Amber — Canary 40.00
Blue 48.00
Sugar, Covered. Round
Clear 38.50
Amber — Canary 48.50
Blue 60.00
Sugar, Covered. Square
Clear 45.00
Amber — Canary 55.00
Blue 70.00
Tumbler, Applied handle
Clear 35.00
Amber — Canary 42.50
Blue 50.00
Vegetable, 7x10"
Clear 65.00
Amber — Canary 80.00
Blue 105.00

*Reproduced Item

ROSE SPRIG

Non-flint pattern made by Campbell, Jones & Co., Pittsburgh, Pa. C. 1886.

Cake Stand. 9", Square
Clear ....$ 37.50
Amber — Yellow 47.50
Blue 55.00
Celery
Clear 30.00
Amber — Yellow 38.50
Blue 47.50
Creamer
Clear 32.50
Amber — Yellow 40.00
Blue 50.00
Goblet
Clear 30.00
Amber — Yellow 37.50
Blue 45.00
Lemonade Glass
Clear 35.00
Amber — Yellow 42.50
Blue 50.00
Nappy. 6", Square
Clear 15.00
Amber — Yellow 18.50
Blue 22.50
Pitcher, Water
Clear 45.00
Amber — Yellow 55.00
Blue 65.00
Plate. 8"
Clear 25.00
Amber — Yellow 30.00
Blue 37.50
Plate. 10"
Clear 30.00
Amber — Yellow 37.50
Blue 45.00
Relish. Boat-shaped
Clear 25.00

Amber — Yellow	32.50
Blue	38.00
Salt, Sleigh	
Clear	22.50
Amber — Yellow	30.00
Blue	40.00
Sauce, Footed	
Clear	10.00
Amber — Yellow	15.00
Blue	20.00
Spooner	
Clear	22.50
Amber — Yellow	27.50
Blue	32.50
Sugar, Covered	
Clear	42.50
Amber — Yellow	50.00
Blue	60.00
Tray, Water	
Clear	45.00
Amber — Yellow	55.00
Blue	68.50
Tumbler	
Clear	25.00
Amber — Yellow	30.00
Blue	37.50
Wine	
Clear	30.00
Amber — Yellow	37.50
Blue	45.00

ROYAL IVY OR ROYAL OAK

Contemporary non-flint patterns made by Northwood Glass Co., Martins Ferry, Ohio, C. 1889-1890. The upper portion is tinged with a light cranberry stain that fades into the lower half of the clear body. Prices are comparable for both patterns.

Bowl. 7½"	$ 135.00
Butter, Covered	200.00
Creamer	120.00
Cruet	200.00
Dresser Jar. 5½" high	75.00
Finger Bowl	65.00
Pitcher, Water	200.00
Sauce	35.00
Shakers	
Salt and Pepper, Pair	125.00
Sugar	125.00
Spooner	100.00
Sugar, Covered	150.00
Toothpick	65.00
Tumbler	75.00

RUBY THUMBPRINT

(See King's Crown in Clear Glass Section)

SHERATON (Ida)

Non-flint pattern made by Bryce, Higbee & Co., Pittsburgh, Pa. C. 1880's.

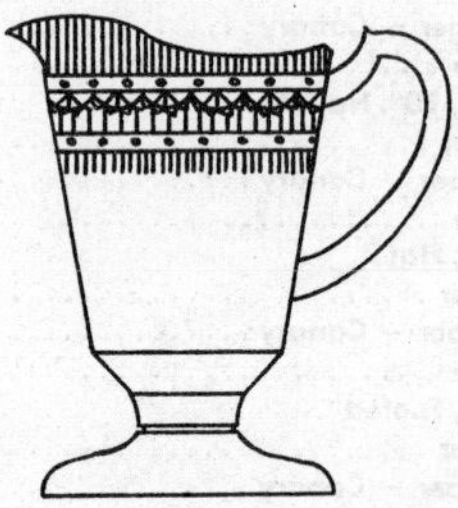

Bowl. 8x10"	
Clear	$ 20.00
Amber	35.00
Blue	40.00
Butter, Covered	
Clear	30.00
Amber	50.00
Blue	60.00
Celery Vase	
Clear	20.00
Amber	32.50
Blue	38.50
Compote, Open. 7". Low standard	
Clear	25.00
Amber	42.50
Blue	50.00
Creamer	
Clear	20.00
Amber	32.50
Blue	40.00

Goblet
Clear 20.00
Amber 35.00
Blue 42.00

Pitcher, Milk
Clear 20.00
Amber 32.50
Blue 40.00

Pitcher, Water
Clear 29.50
Amber 50.00
Blue 65.00

Sauce, Flat
Clear 10.00
Amber 18.00
Blue 22.00

Spooner
Clear 16.00
Amber 28.50
Blue 32.50

Sugar, Covered
Clear 27.50
Amber 42.00
Blue 55.00

Tray, Bread
Clear 20.00
Amber 36.50
Blue 42.00

Wine
Clear 15.00
Amber 25.00
Blue 30.00

SPIREA BAND
(Square and Dot, Earl)

Non-flint pattern made by Bryce, Higbee & Co., Pgh., Pa. C. 1885

Bowl. 8"
Clear .... $ 20.00
Green — Yellow 32.50
Amber — Blue 40.00

Butter, Covered
Clear 34.00
Green — Yellow 50.00
Amber — Blue 65.00

Cake Stand. 11"
Clear 30.00
Green — Yellow 45.00
Amber — Blue 65.00

Celery
Clear 25.00
Green — Yellow 37.50
Amber — Blue 48.50

Compote, Covered. 7". High std.
Clear 40.00
Green — Yellow 60.00
Amber — Blue 85.00

Cordial
Clear 25.00
Green — Yellow 35.00
Amber — Blue 48.50

Creamer
Clear 22.50
Green — Yellow 32.50
Amber — Blue 45.00

Goblet
Clear 17.50
Green — Yellow 25.00
Amber — Blue 35.00

Pitcher, Water
Clear 28.50
Green — Yellow 40.00
Amber — Blue 55.00

Platter. 10½"
Clear 20.00
Green — Yellow 30.00
Amber — Blue 42.00

Relish
Clear 18.50
Green — Yellow 27.50
Amber — Blue 35.00

Sauce, Flat
Clear 8.50
Green — Yellow 13.50
Amber — Blue 16.50

Sauce, Footed
Clear 12.50
Green — Yellow 18.50
Amber — Blue 25.00

Spooner
Clear 20.00
Green — Yellow 28.50
Amber — Blue 38.50

Sugar, Open
Clear 20.00
Green — Yellow 20.00
Amber — Blue 42.50

Wine
Clear 17.50
Green — Yellow 25.00
Amber — Blue 32.50

SWAN
Non-flint. C. 1880's.

Bowl, Covered. 7½x10", Oval
Clear .... $ 50.00
Amber — Canary 72.50
Blue 85.00

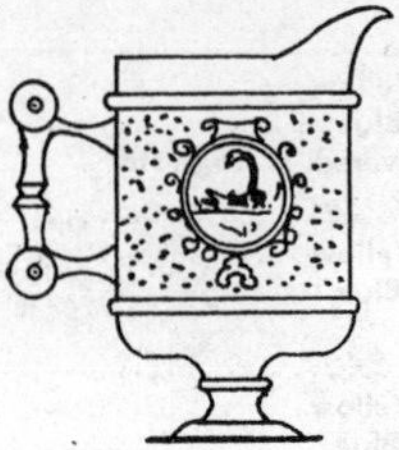

Butter, Covered
- Clear 85.00
- Amber — Canary 125.00
- Blue 150.00

Celery
- Clear 40.00
- Amber — Canary 55.00
- Blue 68.50

Creamer
- Clear 45.00
- Amber — Canary 65.00
- Blue 78.50

Goblet
- Clear 55.00
- Amber — Canary 75.00
- Blue 95.00

Pitcher, Water
- Clear 100.00
- Amber — Canary 150.00
- Blue 175.00

Sauce, Flat
- Clear 12.00
- Amber —Canary 17.50
- Blue 22.00

Sauce, Footed
- Clear 15.00
- Amber — Canary 22.50
- Blue 27.50

Spooner
- Clear 32.50
- Amber — Canary 48.50
- Blue 55.00

Sugar, Covered
- Clear 65.00
- Amber — Canary 85.00
- Blue 100.00

Sugar, Open
- Clear 45.00
- Amber — Canary 65.00
- Blue 78.50

SWIRL
(Jersey Swirl)

Non-flint pattern made by Windsor Glass Company, Pittsburgh, Pa. C. 1887. SEE NOTE:

Butter, Covered
- Clear .... $ 40.00
- Canary 55.00
- Amber — Blue 65.00

Cake Stand. 9"
- Clear 35.00
- Canary 50.00
- Amber — Blue 58.50

Celery
- Clear 26.50
- Canary 35.00
- Amber — Blue 48.50

Creamer
- Clear 30.00
- Canary 40.00
- Amber — Blue 47.50

Goblet
- *Clear 28.50
- Canary 37.50
- Amber — Blue 42.50

Pitcher, Water
- Clear 35.00
- Canary 50.00
- Amber — Blue 60.00

Plate. 6"
- Clear 18.50
- Canary 22.50
- Amber — Blue 30.00

Plate. 8"
- Clear 25.00
- Canary 32.50
- Amber — Blue 40.00

Plate. 10"
- Clear 30.00
- Canary 40.00
- Amber — Blue 50.00

Salt, Individual
- Clear 8.50
- Canary 12.50
- Amber — Blue 15.00

Salt, Master
- Clear 18.50
- Canary 22.00
- Amber — Blue 27.50

Sauce
- Clear 10.00
- Canary 12.50
- Amber — Blue 16.50

Spooner
- Clear 20.00
- Canary 35.00
- Amber — Blue 38.50

Sugar, Covered

Clear	35.00
Canary	45.00
Amber — Blue	55.00

Tumbler

Clear	16.50
Canary	20.00
Amber — Blue	25.00

Wine

Clear	20.00
Canary	35.00
Amber — Blue	40.00

NOTE: Heavily reproduced in color.

*Reproduced Item

TEARDROP AND TASSEL
(Sampson)

Non-flint pattern made by the Indiana Tumbler & Goblet Co. C. 1890's.

Bowl. 7½"

Clear	$ 40.00
Green Tint	48.50
Green — Blue	55.00
Green Milk Glass	75.00

Butter, Covered

Clear	55.00
Green Tint	65.00
Green — Blue	80.00
Green Milk Glass	100.00

Compote, Covered. 7". High std.

Clear	75.00
Green Tint	95.00
Green — Blue	110.00
Green Milk Glass	145.00

Compote, Open. 8". Low standard

Clear	45.00
Green Tint	55.00
Green — Blue	65.00
Green Milk Glass	85.00

Creamer

Clear	35.00
Green Tint	45.00
Green — Blue	55.00
Green Milk Glass	70.00

Goblet (scarce)

Clear	60.00
Green Tint	75.00
Green — Blue	85.00
Green Milk Glass	125.00

Pickle

Clear	17.50
Green Tint	22.50
Green — Blue	27.50
Green Milk Glass	35.00

Pitcher, Water

Clear	65.00
Green Tint	80.00
Green — Blue	95.00
Green Milk Glass	125.00

Sauce, Flat

Clear	12.50
Green Tint	15.00
Green — Blue	18.50
Green Milk Glass	22.50

Shakers, Pair

Clear	100.00
Green Tint	125.00
Green — Blue	145.00
Green Milk Glass	195.00

Spooner

Clear	30.00
Green Tint	36.50
Green — Blue	45.00
Green Milk Glass	55.00

Sugar, Covered

Clear	50.00
Green Tint	65.00
Green — Blue	75.00
Green Milk Glass	95.00

Tumbler

Clear	30.00
Green Tint	38.00
Green — Blue	45.00
Green Milk Glass	55.00

Wine (scarce)

Clear	65.00
Green Tint	80.00
Green — Blue	95.00
Green Milk Glass	125.00

THOUSAND EYE
(Plain standard)

Non-flint pattern made by Adams C. 1875 and by Richards & Hartley, C. 1888, and New Brighton Glass Co., New Brighton, Pa. in the late 1880's. SEE NOTE:

Butter, Covered. Footed

Clear	$ 50.00
Amber — Yellow	65.00
Blue — Dark Amber	80.00
Apple Green	100.00

Celery. Hat-shaped

Clear	40.00
Amber — Yellow	48.50
Blue — Dark Amber	60.00
Apple Green	75.00

Cologne Bottle

Clear	25.00
Amber — Yellow	32.50
Blue — Dark Amber	40.00

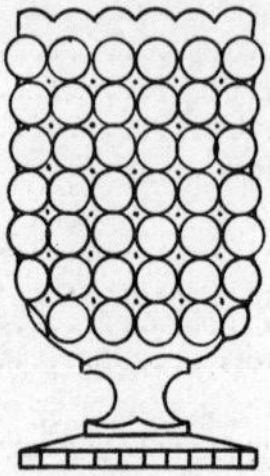

Apple Green	50.00
Compote, Covered. 6″. High std.	
Clear	65.00
Amber — Yellow	80.00
Blue — Dark Amber	100.00
Apple Green	125.00
Cordial	
Clear	25.00
Amber — Yellow	32.50
Blue — Dark Amber	40.00
Apple Green	48.50
Creamer	
Clear	40.00
Amber — Yellow	50.00
Blue — Dark Amber	60.00
Apple Green	75.00
***Cruet**	
Clear	30.00
Amber — Yellow	37.50
Blue — Dark Amber	46.50
Apple Green	58.50
Egg Cup (rare)	
Clear	50.00
Amber — Yellow	65.00
Blue — Dark Amber	80.00
Apple Green	115.00
***Goblet**	
Clear	30.00
Amber — Yellow	37.50
Blue — Dark Amber	45.00
Apple Green	55.00
***Hat**	
Clear	15.00
Amber — Yellow	20.00
Blue — Dark Amber	24.00
Apple Green	29.50
Lamp, Handled	
Clear	55.00
Amber — Yellow	75.00
Blue — Dark Amber	85.00
Apple Green	100.00
Lamp, High standard	
Clear	85.00
Amber — Yellow	100.00
Blue — Dark Amber	125.00
Apple Green	160.00
***Mug**	
Clear	15.00
Amber — Yellow	20.00
Blue — Dark Amber	25.00
Apple Green	30.00
Pickle. 9¼″	
Clear	25.00
Amber — Yellow	30.00
Blue — Dark Amber	38.50
Apple Green	48.50
Pitcher, Syrup, Pewter top	
Clear	55.00
Amber — Yellow	65.00
Blue — Dark Amber	80.00
Apple Green	100.00
Pitcher, Water	
Clear	65.00
Amber — Yellow	80.00
Blue — Dark Amber	100.00
Apple Green	125.00
***Plate. 6″**	
Clear	20.00
Amber — Yellow	25.00
Blue — Dark Amber	28.50
Apple Green	38.50
***Plate. 8″**	
Clear	25.00
Amber — Yellow	30.00
Blue — Dark Amber	37.50
Apple Green	48.50
***Plate. 10″**	
Clear	30.00
Amber — Yellow	36.50
Blue — Dark Amber	45.00
Apple Green	55.00
Platter. 8x11′, Oblong	
Clear	35.00
Amber — Yellow	47.50
Blue — Dark Amber	55.00
Apple Green	75.00
Sauce, Flat	
Clear	10.00
Amber — Yellow	12.50
Blue — Dark Amber	16.50
Apple Green	20.00
Sauce, Footed	
Clear	12.00
Amber — Yellow	15.00
Blue — Dark Amber	19.50
Apple Green	22.50
Shakers, Pair	
Clear	35.00
Amber — Yellow	45.00
Blue — Dark Amber	50.00
Apple Green	65.00
Spooner	
Clear	20.00
Amber — Yellow	25.00
Blue —Dark Amber	28.50
Apple Green	42.50
Sugar, Covered	
Clear	42.00
Amber — Yellow	50.00
Blue — Dark Amber	62.50
Apple Green	85.00

Tray, Water. 14", Oval
Clear 55.00
Amber — Yellow 65.00
Blue — Dark Amber 82.50
Apple Green 110.00
Tray, Water. 12½" diam.
Clear 50.00
Amber — Yellow 60.00
Blue — Dark Amber 75.00
Apple Green 95.00
*Tumbler, Water
Clear 22.00
Amber — Yellow 27.50
Blue — Dark Amber 32.50
Apple Green 40.00
*Twine Holder
Clear 25.00
Amber — Yellow 32.50
Blue — Dark Amber 40.00
Apple Green 50.00
*Wine
Clear 20.00
Amber — Yellow 26.50
Blue — Dark Amber 32.50
Apple Green 40.00

NOTE: Knob standard add 25% to price of plain. Scarce in Opalescent; rare in Opaque Blue.

*Reproduced Item

THREE PANEL

Non-flint pattern made by Richards & Hartley Co., Tarentum, Pa. C. 1888.

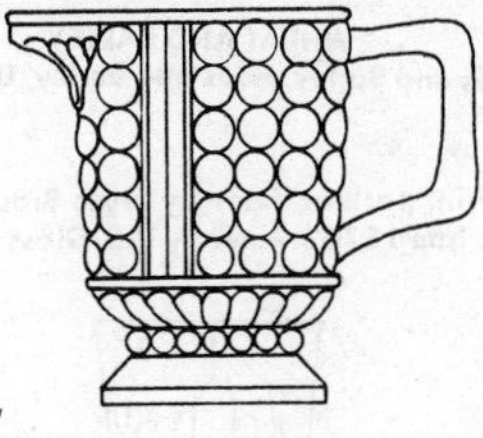

Bowl. 8½"
Clear .... $ 17.50
Amber — Yellow 25.00
Blue 30.00
Bowl. 10"
Clear 25.00
Amber — Yellow 35.00
Blue 42.50
Butter, Covered. Plain
Clear 37.50
Amber — Yellow 50.00
Blue 60.00
Compote, Open. 7". Low standard
Clear 25.00
Amber — Yellow 35.00
Blue 42.50
Compote, Open. 10". Low standard
Clear 40.00
Amber — Yellow 55.00
Blue 65.00
Creamer
Clear 25.00
Amber — Yellow 35.00
Blue 42.50
Goblet
Clear 25.00
Amber — Yellow 35.00
Blue 42.50
Mug
Clear 17.50
Amber — Yellow 25.00
Blue 30.00
Pitcher, Water. ½ Gal.
Clear 45.00
Amber — Yellow 65.00
Blue 75.00
Sauce, Footed
Clear 12.00
Amber — Yellow 16.50
Blue 20.00
Spooner
Clear 20.00
Amber — Yellow 28.50
Blue 32.50
Sugar, Covered
Clear 35.00
Amber — Yellow 48.50
Blue 55.00
Tumbler
Clear 18.00
Amber — Yellow 25.00
Blue 30.00

TWO PANEL

Non-flint pattern made by Richards & Hartley Glass Co., Tarentum, Pa. in the early 1880's.

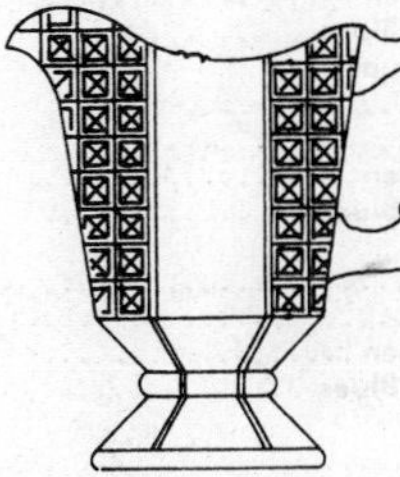

Bowl. 5½x7"
Clear .... $ 20.00
Canary 28.50
Apple Green 35.00
Amber — Blues 40.00
Bowl. 8x 10"
Clear 30.00
Canary 42.50
Apple Green 50.00
Amber — Blues 58.50

Butter, Covered
- Clear 38.50
- Canary 55.00
- Apple Green 65.00
- Amber — Blues 75.00

Celery
- Clear 25.00
- Canary 37.50
- Apple Green 42.50
- Amber — Blues 55.00

Creamer
- Clear 25.00
- Canary 35.00
- Apple Green 40.00
- Amber — Blues 50.00

*Goblet
- Clear 22.50
- Canary 32.50
- Apple Green 39.50
- Amber — Blues 45.00

Lamp
- Clear 50.00
- Canary 75.00
- Apple Green 90.00
- Amber — Blues 110.00

Mug, Large
- Clear 20.00
- Canary 29.50
- Apple Green 35.00
- Amber — Blues 40.00

Pitcher, Water
- Clear 45.00
- Canary 65.00
- Apple Green 80.00
- Amber — Blues 100.00

Relish. 4½x7"
- Clear 10.00
- Canary 16.50
- Apple Green 18.50
- Amber — Blues 20.00

Salt, Individual
- Clear 5.50
- Canary 8.50
- Apple Green 10.00
- Amber — Blues 12.00

Salt, Master
- Clear 18.50
- Canary 25.00
- Apple Green 32.50
- Amber — Blues 38.50

Sauce, Flat
- Clear 10.00
- Canary 15.00
- Apple Green 17.50
- Amber — Blues 20.00

Sauce, Footed
- Clear 12.50
- Canary 18.50
- Apple Green 22.50
- Amber — Blues 25.00

Shakers, Pair
- Clear 35.00
- Canary 50.00
- Apple Green 60.00
- Amber — Blues 75.00

Spooner
- Clear 25.00
- Canary 35.00
- Apple Green 40.00
- Amber — Blues 50.00

Sugar, Covered
- Clear 30.00
- Canary 45.00
- Apple Green 55.00
- Amber — Blues 65.00

Tray, Water
- Clear 35.00
- Canary 45.00
- Apple Green 60.00
- Amber — Blues 70.00

Tumbler
- Clear 15.00
- Canary 22.50
- Apple Green 27.50
- Amber — Blues 30.00

Waste Bowl
- Clear 22.50
- Canary 32.50
- Apple Green 40.00
- Amber — Blues 47.50

*Wine
- Clear 20.00
- Canary 28.50
- Apple Green 35.00
- Amber — Blues 40.00

*Reproduced Item

WHEAT AND BARLEY
(Oats and Barley, Hops and Barley, Duquesne)

Non-flint pattern made by Bryce Bros., Pgh., Pa. in the late 1870's. Later by U.S. Glass Co.

Bowl. 8", Covered
- Clear .... $ 30.00
- Amber — Yellow 42.50
- Blue 55.00

Butter, Covered
- Clear 40.00
- Amber — Yellow 60.00
- Blue 75.00

Cake Stand. 8"
Clear 18.50
Amber — Yellow 28.50
Blue 35.00
Cake Stand. 10"
Clear 35.00
Amber — Yellow 50.00
Blue 65.00
Compote, Covered. 7", 8". High std.
Clear 36.50
Amber — Yellow 55.00
Blue 62.50
Compote, Jelly. Open, High std.
Clear 17.50
Amber — Yellow 27.50
Blue 35.00
Creamer
Clear 22.50
Amber — Yellow 32.50
Blue 40.00
Goblet
Clear 25.00
Amber — Yellow 37.50
Blue 42.50
Mug
Clear 20.00
Amber — Yellow 28.50
Blue 35.00
Pitcher, Milk
Clear 35.00
Amber — Yellow 50.00
Blue 58.00
Pitcher, Water
Clear 30.00
Amber — Yellow 48.50
Blue 55.00
Plate. 7"
Clear 22.50
Amber — Yellow 30.00
Blue 35.00
Plate. 9", Closed handles
Clear 25.00
Amber — Yellow 35.00
Blue 42.50
Sauce, Flat
Clear 9.00
Amber — Yellow 13.50
Blue 15.00
Sauce, Footed. 4"
Clear 12.00
Amber — Yellow 17.50
Blue 20.00
Shakers, Pair
Clear 30.00
Amber — Yellow 45.00
Blue 48.50
Spooner
Clear 20.00
Amber — Yellow 30.00
Blue 35.00
Sugar, Covered
Clear 30.00
Amber — Yellow 45.00
Blue 55.00
Toothpick
Clear 12.00
Amber — Yellow 17.50
Blue 20.00
Tumbler
Clear 20.00
Amber — Yellow 28.50
Blue 35.00

WILDFLOWER

Non-flint pattern made by Adams & Co., Pittsburgh, Pa. C. 1874; also by U.S. Glass Co. C. 1898. This popular pattern has been heavily reproduced.

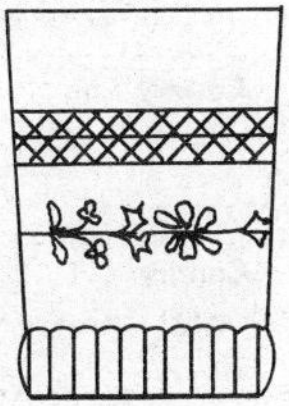

Bowl. 6", Round
Clear .... $ 15.00
Amber, Light 18.50
Amber, Dark — Canary 25.00
Blue — Green 28.50
Bowl. 8", Square
Clear 22.00
Amber, Light 27.50
Amber, Dark — Canary 35.00
Blue — Green 40.00
Butter, Covered. Collared base
Clear 37.50
Amber, Light 45.00
Amber, Dark — Canary 60.00
Blue — Green 68.50
Butter, Covered. Flat
Clear 30.00
Amber, Light 37.50
Amber, Dark — Canary 48.50
Blue — Green 55.00
Cake Stand. 9½"
Clear 40.00
Amber, Light 50.00
Amber, Dark — Canary 65.00
Blue — Green 72.50
Celery Vase
Clear 28.50
Amber, Light 35.00
Amber, Dark — Canary 45.00
Blue — Green 52.00
Champagne
Clear 35.00
Amber, Light 45.00

Amber, Dark — Canary	55.00
Blue — Green	62.50
Compote, Covered. 8" High std.	
Clear	45.00
Amber, Light	58.00
Amber, Dark — Canary	72.50
Blue — Green	80.00
Compote, Covered. 8". Low standard	
Clear	37.00
Amber, Light	55.00
Amber, Dark — Canary	60.00
Blue — Green	65.00
Compote, Open. 8". Low standard	
Clear	28.50
Amber, Light	35.00
Amber, Dark — Canary	45.00
Blue — Green	52.50
Cordial	
Clear	28.00
Amber, Light	35.00
Amber, Dark — Canary	45.00
Blue — Green	50.00
Creamer	
Clear	25.00
Amber, Light	32.50
Amber, Dark — Canary	40.00
Blue — Green	50.00
Goblet	
Clear	25.00
Amber, Light	34.50
Amber, Dark — Canary	40.00
Blue — Green	45.00
Pitcher, Syrup	
Clear	50.00
Amber, Light	65.00
Amber, Dark — Canary	80.00
Blue — Green	90.00
Pitcher, Water	
Clear	40.00
Amber, Light	50.00
Amber, Dark — Canary	65.00
Blue — Green	75.00
Plate. 8"	
Clear	18.50
Amber, Light	22.50
Amber, Dark — Canary	28.50
Blue — Green	32.50
Plate. 10", Square	
Clear	30.00
Amber, Light	37.50
Amber, Dark — Canary	45.00
Blue — Green	52.50
Platter. 10", Oblong	
Clear	30.00
Amber, Light	38.50
Amber, Dark — Canary	47.50
Blue — Green	55.00
Relish. 8"	
Clear	20.00
Amber, Light	24.50
Amber, Dark — Canary	30.00
Blue — Green	35.00
Salt, Turtle	
Clear	45.00
Amber, Light	55.00
Amber, Dark — Canary	70.00
Blue — Green	80.00
Sauce, Flat. Round or square	
Clear	8.50
Amber, Light	10.00
Amber, Dark — Canary	13.50
Blue — Green	15.00
Sauce, Footed. 4", Round	
Clear	12.00
Amber, Light	15.00
Amber, Dark — Canary	18.50
Blue — Green	22.50
Shakers, Pair	
Clear	40.00
Amber, Light	48.50
Amber, Dark — Canary	65.00
Blue — Green	75.00
Spooner	
Clear	25.00
Amber, Light	32.50
Amber, Dark — Canary	40.00
Blue — Green	45.00
Sugar, Covered	
Clear	35.00
Amber, Light	45.00
Amber, Dark — Canary	55.00
Blue — Green	62.50
Tray, Water	
Clear	40.00
Amber, Light	50.00
Amber, Dark — Canary	65.00
Blue — Green	75.00
Tumbler	
Clear	20.00
Amber, Light	26.50
Amber, Dark — Canary	32.00
Blue — Green	35.00
Wine	
Clear	35.00
Amber, Light	45.00
Amber, Dark — Canary	55.00
Blue — Green	65.00

WILLOW OAK

(Oak Leaf, Acorn, Thistle, Wreath, Stippled Daisy, Sunflower)

Non-flint pattern made by Bryce Bros., Pgh., Pa. C. 1880's.

Bowl. 7", Covered	
Clear	$ 30.00
Amber	42.50
Blue	55.00
Bowl. 8"	
Clear	25.00
Amber	37.50
Blue	50.00

Butter, Covered
- Clear 50.00
- Amber 72.50
- Blue 95.00

Cake Stand 8½"
- Clear 28.50
- Amber 42.50
- Blue 55.00

Celery Vase
- Clear 30.00
- Amber 42.50
- Blue 55.00

Compote, Covered. 7½". High std.
- Clear 45.00
- Amber 65.00
- Blue 85.00

Creamer
- Clear 25.00
- Amber 38.50
- Blue 47.50

Goblet
- Clear 28.50
- Amber 40.00
- Blue 50.00

Mug
- Clear 25.00
- Amber 38.00
- Blue 48.50

Pitchers, Milk or Water
- Clear 40.00
- Amber 65.00
- Blue 85.00

Plate. 7". (rare)
- Clear 30.00
- Amber 42.50
- Blue 55.00

Plate. 9", Closed handles
- Clear 25.00
- Amber 40.00
- Blue 50.00

Sauce, Flat. Handled
- Clear 10.00
- Amber 15.00
- Blue 18.50

Sauce, Footed. 4"
- Clear 20.00
- Amber 28.50
- Blue 38.50

Shakers, Pair
- Clear 40.00
- Amber 55.00
- Blue 75.00

Spooner
- Clear 25.00
- Amber 37.50
- Blue 48.50

Sugar, Covered
- Clear 40.00
- Amber 55.00
- Blue 75.00

Tray, Water. 10½", Round
- Clear 40.00
- Amber 58.00
- Blue 78.50

Tumbler
- Clear 20.00
- Amber 28.50
- Blue 38.50

Waste Bowl
- Clear 20.00
- Amber 28.50
- Blue 39.50

ABC PLATES

These plates were made especially for children with the alphabet around the outer rim. Center decorations often consisted of animals, great men, maxims and nursery rhymes. They were made of various materials; including glass, pewter, porcelain, pottery and tin.

Pottery. 7¼". Brown transfer on white ground. "Nations of the World." Tunstall, England $35.00

GLASS

Child's Head. Amber. 6" .... $	35.00
Child's Head. Frosted. 8"	45.00
Clock. Amber. 7"	35.00
Clock. Amethyst. 7"	55.00
Daisy. Clear. 6"	32.50
Deer. Frosted. 6"	60.00
Dog's Head. Blue. 6"	35.00
Dog's Head. Clear. 6"	28.50
Ducks, Two. Amber. 6"	35.00
Elephant. Clear. 6"	25.00
Hen and Chicks. Clear. 6"	25.00
Heron Palm trees. Clear and frosted. 6"	30.00
Little Bo-Peep with numerals. Clear. 7½"	45.00
Mary Had a Little Lamb. Clear. Deep. 6"	40.00
Numbers 1 thru 10. Clear. 6"	25.00
Rabbit. Clear. 6"	25.00
Sancho Panza and Dabble. Clear and frosted. 6"	40.00
Star. Clear. 6"	28.00

PORCELAIN or POTTERY

Artist at Easel. H-P. 8" .... $	50.00
B is for Billy. 7"	32.50
Bathing Scene at Beach. 6½"	60.00
Birds, Three. 6"	35.00
Boatman. 7". England	30.00
Capitol at Washington. 7¾"	35.00
Cat and Four Kittens. 7¼"	35.00
Children, Four. Transfer. 6¾". Germany	55.00
Clock, Months, etc. Allerton. 8"	55.00
Cow. 7"	32.50
Dancing Master, The. 7¼"	28.50
David and Goliath. 5"	30.00
December. Old man, holly, etc. Green. 7"	35.00
Dog pulling children in cart. 6¾". Early Staffordshire	45.00
Elephant. Fishing. 8". Staffordshire-type	35.00
Elves. 8". Marked 3-Crown. Germany	40.00
Emma. 6¼"	25.00
Eye of God. Harps. Cherubs. 4-line verse. Ironstone. 7"	45.00
First Nibble, The. 8"	30.00
Football scene. Meakin. 7¼"	40.00
Franklin. Maxim. 5½"	38.50
Gleaners, The. 6"	50.00
Graces, The. Mulberry. 6"	50.00
Guardian, The .7". Staffordshire ..	50.00
Horse racing. 7"	30.00
Hunters and dogs. 7¼"	35.00
Kittens, Three. 7"	35.00
Little Bear, The. 7¼"	45.00
Little Bo-Peep. 8"	45.00
Little boys playing marbles. 6"	28.50
Little Jack Horner. 7¼"	40.00
Little Jockey. 7"	35.00
Lord's Prayer, The. Transfer. 6½" ..	45.00
Miss Muffet. 6¼"	35.00
Mother and Daughter. Dear to Each. Transfer. 8". Early Staffordshire ..	65.00
New Pony. Transfer. 7¼". Staffordshire	35.00
Our Donkey and Foal. 6"	30.00
Owl. Sign language around border. 6¼"	45.00
Playing Lovers. 7¾"	35.00
Potter's Art, The. 7"	35.00
Punctuality. 8"	30.00
Puss-in-Boots. 7"	35.00
Rabbit. Sign language around border. 8"	50.00
Red Riding Hood. Late Delft. 8½" ..	30.00
Red Riding Hood Meets the Wolf. 7¼"	35.00

Reuben interceding with brethren for life of Joseph. 6" 32.50
Robinson Crusoe. 8". England 40.00
Rooster, 3 chickens. Color transfer. 6¼". Germany 45.00
See Saw, Margy Daw. Blue transfer. 7½" 40.00
Swing Swong. White and blue transfer. 7½" 47.50
Those Children, etc. 6" 30.00
Tired of Play. 7" 32.50
Whittington and His Cat. 8" 35.00
Youth, Woman, Child and Fowl. Black transfer. 8" 40.00

TIN

Birds. Animals. 8" ....$ 25.00
Cock Robin. 7" 35.00
Girl on Swing. 6¼" 25.00
Hey Diddle Diddle. 9" 35.00
Jumbo. 6¼" 27.50
Liberty. 5½" 50.00
Numerals. 6¼" 30.00
Victoria-Albert. 5½" 30.00
Washington. 5½" 60.00

ADAMS

ADAMS

(See "Flow Blue," "Jasperware," "Staffordshire.")

ADAMS ROSE

This early ware is decorated with brilliant red roses and green leaves on a white ground. It was made by William Adams in the early 1800's in the Staffordshire district of England. A variant of the pattern was made later by G. Jones and Sons, also in England, until 1908. This type is referred to as Late Adams Rose.

Bowls
6". Early ....$ 135.00
6". Late 40.00
Creamers
Early 150.00
Late 75.00
Cups and Saucers
Early Scalloped edge 165.00
Late. Plain edge 30.00
Pitcher. 7" high. Late 85.00
Plates
7½". Early 65.00
7½". Late 25.00
8½". Early 75.00
8½". Late 30.00
9½". Early 175.00
9½". Late 85.00

Plate. 7½". Late $25.00

10". Soup. Early 175.00
10½". Early 185.00
Sugar, Covered.
Early 400.00
Late 125.00
Teapots
Early 500.00
Late 125.00
Wash Set. Bowl. 10½" diam. Early 850.00

ADVERTISING SIGNS

Letters. Pine. Approximate 8" high. Each $8.50

"Baxter's Drum 5c Cigar." 10x14". Tin. Red, white and blue. C. 1910 ....$ 25.00
"Big 6 Gin." 13x16". Wooden. Barroom scene in color. C. 1910 .... 300.00
"Bull Durham." 14x22". Cardboard 35.00
"Buster Brown Bread." 22x30". Tin. Embossed frame. C. 1920 ...... 200.00
"Campbell's Soup." 16x24". Porcelain 150.00
"Coke."-SEE "Coca Cola Items"

"Columbian Beer." 12x16." Tin. Columbia on label. C. 1915 .... 30.00

"Cooks Beer." 12 x 21". Tin. Cop. Horseless carriage 75.00

"Diamond Wedding Whiskey." 12".Tin. Self-framed. Lady in red. C 1905 .... 150.00

"DuBois Budweiser." 13x21". Tin. C. 1920 .... 15.00

"Enjoy Bacardi Rum & Coca-Cola." 72" long. Cardboard. Blonde in swimming pool 60.00

"Fill-Em Fast Gasoline." 9x16". Porcelain. Bright orange and yellow. 20.00

"Gayoso Gin." 15x15". Tin. C. 1900. Mint 95.00

"Hires Root Beer." 12x28". Paper. Framed. C. 1926 .... 40.00

"Hudepol Beer." 8x12". Tin. Bottle of beer. C. 1930 .... 45.00

"Ice Card." 9". Cardboard 3.00

"Kellogg's Corn Flakes." 13 x 19" Tin. Baby in wicker basket. C. 1910. Worn 75.00

"Kool's." 4x12". Tin. C. 1930 ...... 10.00

"Korbel Sec." 13x19". Tin. Girl holding grapes. C. 1910 .... 135.00

"Lipton's Tea." 9x19". Tin. Two sided. C. 1915 .... 30.00

"Mail Pouch Tobacco." 2¾x12". Porcelain 35.00

"Mail Pouch Tobacco." 11x36". 'Treat Yourself to the Best." Porcelain 75.00

"Moxie." 23" square. Cardboard. Soda fountain table top 50.00

"Nehi Soda Pop." 4x18". Tin. Vivid colors. C. 1920's 10.00

"Nehi." 14x20". Cardboard. Ladies. C. 1930 .... 15.00

"Old Dutch Cleanser." 3x5". Cardboard, 2-sided ceiling fan. Yellow, blue and red. C. 1930 .... 5.00

"Old Dutch Cleanser." 9x13". Cardboard. Yellow, red and blue. C. 1930 .... 15.00

"Popsicle." 12x28". Tin. Embossed. C. 1930 .... 30.00

"Prudential Insurance Co. of America." 12x15". Brass 75.00

"Quaker Oats." 30x60". Tin. Framed. C. 1910 .... 250.00

"Sky Chief". 12x18". Porcelain 15.00

"E. R. Weethee, Bootmaker." 32". Wooden. Original red paint 150.00

"Welch." 13x19". Tin. C. 1931 .... 30.00

"Whitman's Chocolates." 13x18". Velvet. C. 1920 .... 50.00

ADVERTISING TRADE CARDS

These cards are a small thin cardboard printed with a name of a product extolling its merit and bearing the name and address of a merchant. With the invention of lithography, colorful trade cards became a popular advertising media of the late 19th and early 20th century.
Most advertising trade cards are relatively inexpensive ranging in price from $1.00 to $5.00. A few command higher prices because of subject matter, artist or scarcity. Some were made in sets and present a challenge to collectors.

Clothing

C. E. Longley Co. Conn. 5" round cards. Comics of owls, cat, monkey, etc ....$ 2.50

Soller's & Co. Cat and kitten dressed like women 1.50

Max Stadler & Co. NJ. Comic of father and twins 1.50

Food Products

Bovine Beef Extract. Lithophane. Mint 10.00

Campbell's Soup 25.00

Cocoa. Runkel Bros., NY. Three little girls 1.25

Coffee

Arbuckle Bros., Co. Patagonia. People. Animals 3.00

McLaughlin & Co. Little girl with cats and parrot 5.00

William A. Scull Co., NJ. "Champion Coffee". Set of 4 old fashioned dressed children. Attributed to Kate Greenaway. C. 1800's. Set 20.00

Woolson Spice Co. Easter with 3 girls and lamb. C. 1891 .... 6.00

Condensed milk. A&P Tea Co., Ohio. Cow and calf. C. 1890 .... 1.50

Extracts. Chas. S. Yale Bros. Lovely lady at well. C. 1889 .... 1.50

Flour. Washburn-Crosby Mills. Cathedral, boats. Silver gilt .... 2.50.

Lard. N.K. Fairbank & Co. Comic of 2 pigs 2.50

Tea. Union Pacific Tea Co., Children with egg cart 1.50

Yeast

E.W. Gillett Mfg. Co. Cupids riding fish. C. 1893 .... 1.50

Northwestern Yeast Co. Battleship, "Texas" 3.00

Royal Yeast Co, Bord. Rose. Kids skating 2.00

Medicine

Burdocks Blood Bitters. Girl with ostrich plume hat 3.00

Curtis Davis & Co. "Welcome Soap" $1.00

Dr. Jaynes Medicine. Granny and children. Vermifuge 2.50
H.T.L. Hoods Pill. Children scene. Copyright 1888 .... 5.00
Lutted Cough Drops. Old fashioned little girl 1.75
Lydia E. Pinkham Co. Vegetable Compound. Scenic. Snow scene .. 2.00
Standard Family Medicine. "Take Quaker Bitters." Victorian tot in a wooden barrel. Sepia. 3.50
Rumford Chemicals. Acid Phosphate. Fat little baby 4.00
Warner's Safe Cure. Autumn leaves 2.00

Musical
Emerson Piano Co. NYC. Hunter. Hounds. Cottage 1.50
Newby-Evans Co. Boy and girl skipping daisy rope 1.50
J. C. Woods Co. Little Lord Fauntelroy with banjo 2.50

Sewing Machines
Household Sewing Machine Co. Boy and girl with fishnet, with sailing ship in background. C. 1895 .... 2.50
Royal St. John Co. Miss. River 2.50
Singer Sewing Machine Co. Algerian man. C. 1892 .... 3.00

Soap
Curtis Davis & Co. "Welcome Soap." Nurse. Infant. Father 1.00
Fairbanks's Soap Co. Comic of man with soap in his eyes 2.00
Ivorine Soap-Cleaner. Three children. Music 1.50
Kendall Mfg. Co. RI. Cat, dressed in lace ribbons 2.00

Stoves
Raymond Mfg. Co., PA. Boy blue with horn 3.50
W. C. Wilson, MO. Comic of farmer with hoe 1.50
Webster Stove Co., VT. Girl. Roses. Lacy border 3.50

Thread
Beldings Silk Co. Bird eggs 1.00
Clark Thread Co. Baby. Bonnet. Rattle.................... 2.00
Clark Thread Co. King Humbert-Italy. Castle 2.50
J&P Coats Co. Girls. Robins and snow subject 2.00
Merrick Thread Co. Cherub riding spool drawn by butterflies 3.00

Tobacco
C.A. Jackson Co., VA. Crescent Chewing Tobacco. Set of 6 comic cards of black man and mule. Set 30.00
Lucky Strike Tobacco Co. Cut Plug. Actress Constance Gilchrist 2.50
Old Judge Cigarettes. Metamorphis. "An interesting interview." Dated 1888 .... 7.50

Shirrell's Kulliyun. "Washing Crystal" $1.50

Miscellaneous
Bon Ami Co., NYC. Girls. Boys. Mice 1.50
Alexander Dining Saloon. Fish on platter 1.00
Deering Harvester. Litho of boy being spanked. Reverse full picture of Deering All-Steel Harvester 5.00
Ivans & Bros., Phila. Ladies shoe with flowers 2.00
Metropolitan Life Ins. Grecian type boy and girl 2.00
John Wanamaker, Phila. Girl in stylish coat, button shoes, muff, hat with feather of 1800's 7.50

Waterbury Watch Co. Three oriental girls 3.50

ADVERTISING TRAYS

Tip. "Resinol Soap and Ointment" $45.00

"Camel Cigarettes." Tip ....$ $7.50
"Coke"-SEE "Coca Cola Items"
"Coors"-SEE "Coors"
"Cortex Cigars." Tip. No litho mark. 1905-1915 .... 30.00
"Climax." (stoves, furnaces) Roman soldier holding torch. 1910 ...... 75.00
"Dick's Beer." Tip 65.00
"Enterprise Brewery." No litho mark. 1900-1910 .... 25.00
"Franklin Life Insurance." Tip. Ben Franklin. No litho mark. 1915.... 25.00
"Genesee." "Ask For Jenny" Girls head 7.50
"Gloria Ice Cream." Rectangular. (Palmer Cox Brownies) Mfg. by H.D. Beach. 1905-1915 .... 35.00
"Hires Root Beer." Brunette. 1910 .. 85.00
"Liberty Ice Cream." Round. (Sacramento) Mfg. by American Art Works. 1900-1910 .... 25.00
"Miller's." Girl on Moon 15.00
"Moxie." Tip. Mfg. by Beach. 1900-1910 .... 25.00
"Muriel Cigar." Tip. Gypsy girl. 1910 .... 35.00
"Old Reliable Coffee." Tip. Mfg. by American Art Works. 1907 ...... 20.00
"Orange Julep." Rectangular. No litho mark. 1920 .... 30.00
"Piels." 1961 .... 7.50
"Quandt." Rectangular. 1937 .... 45.00
"Quandt." Tip 20.00
"Ranier Brewer." Mfg. by Bachrach. 1903 .... 45.00
"Red Raven Splits." Victorian lady hugging red raven. 1910 ...... 65.00
"Resinol Soap." Tip. Center has picture of girl with pink roses 45.00
"Ruhstaller's Lager." Tip. Barmaid with steins 50.00
"Ryans Beer." Tip. Brunette 45.00
"Schlitz." 1955.................. 7.50
"Stanton." 1941 .... 15.00
"Stemaier Brewing Co." Tip. Hand with 4 bottles 25.00
"Strohs Bohemian Beer." Square. Mfg.by Beek. 1901-1909........ 45.00
"Sweetwater Ice Cream." Lady eating ice cream. 1921 .... 110.00
"Tom Moore Cigars." Tip 28.00
"Universal Stoves." Tip. Mfg. by Shonk. 1910-1920 .... 15.00
"White Rock." Tip. Mfg. by Shonk. 1905-1915 .... 30.00
"Wrigleys Gum." Glass change tray in shape of arrow 20.00

ADVERTISING ITEMS, MISCELLANEOUS

Ashtray. "Security National Bank, Trenton, NJ. 1927." High brown glaze. New Jersey Porcelain Co., Inc. ....$ 15.00
Calendar. "Alka Seltzer." 10x13". 1942. Original envelope 3.50
Calendar. "Blatz Beer." Victorian girl in pink dress. 1904 .... 150.00
Calendar. "Jacob Ruppert Beer." 10x15". Elves and beer cans. 1937 .... 10.00
Corkscrew. "Anheuser Busch." 3". Ad on brass plate. 1900 .... 20.00
Doll. "Kellogg's, Daddy Bear." 12" high. Stuffed. 1920's 35.00
Match Books. Advertising candy, soda, beer, food, etc. 1930's. Each 1.00
Fan. "Moxie." 6x7". 2-sided. Dated 1922 .... 20.00
Mug. "Anheuser Busch." 6" high. Emblem monogrammed. 1930-1940 .... 15.00
Opener. "Duquesne Beer." 4" high. Litho. Tin. Bottle shaped. 1940's .. 3.00
Pin. "Heinz Pickle." Green 3.00

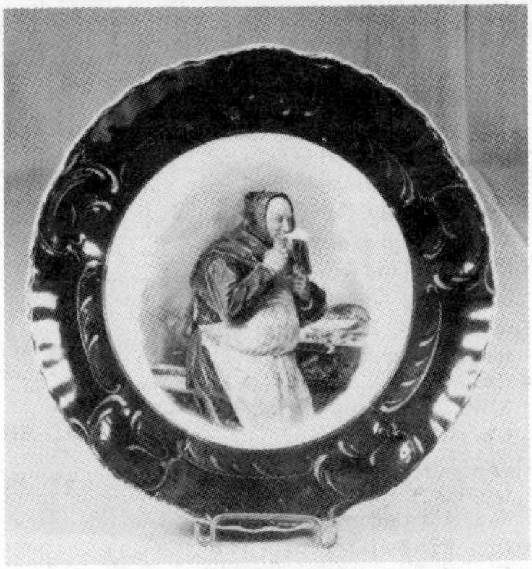

Plate. 9¼". "Roberts The Home Furnishers. Market and Locust St., Johnstown, Pa." Monk center. Dark green rim. Gold trim. Dresden China in wreath $27.50

Salt and Pepper Shakers. "Schlitz Beer." Miniature bottles. Mkd. Muth Pat. Pend. Buffalo. Set 25.00
Statue. "Miller's Beer." 6½" high. Girl. 1930's 28.00
Thermometer. "Landis Leaf Tobacco Co." 5½x24". Wood. Shape and color of leaf 135.00
Thermometer. "Mail Pouch Tobacco." 8x39". Porcelain 50.00
Thermometer. "Old Dutch Root Beer." 7x26". Two Wind Mills 25.00
Thermometer. "Dr. Pepper." 17".... 25.00

AGATA GLASS

Joseph Locke of the New England Glass Company, Cambridge, Mass. is credited with producing this art glass in the 1880's. The characteristic mottling of Agata glass was obtained by spraying alcohol on the colored glass before it was tempered.

Bowls
- 3" diam. .... $ 1500.00
- 4½" diam. Handled 1800.00
- 5" diam. Tricorn top 1250.00
- 5½" diam. Crimped top 1350.00

Celery 1650.00
Cruet 1500.00
Pitcher. 6¾" high. Square mouth .. 3500.00
Toothpick Holders
- Crimped top 750.00
- Square top 500.00
- Trefoil top 600.00

Bowl. 5". Tricorn top $1250.00

Tumbler 800.00
Vases
- 4½" high, 3½" diam. Pinched sides. Crimped top 1000.00
- 4½". Two handles. Square top .. 1800.00
- 7¾". Lily-shaped 1650.00

AKRO AGATE GLASS

The Akro Agate Company was established in Akron, Ohio in 1911, relocating in Clarksburg, West Virginia in 1914 for economic reasons. They were the largest marble producing company in America, supplying over three-fourths of the market.

In the early 1930's, when competition came from another marble producer "Master Marbles", Akro Agate began to diversify. Ashtrays, advertising items and children's play dishes were introduced. The unfortunate burning of The Brilliant Glass Products of Ohio in 1936, became Akro Agate's fortune. They acquired all their "Westite" molds, material and John Henderson, the plant's general manager. It was then, their garden line was added.

During World War II, due to lack of Japanese imports and the scarcity of metal, Akro Agate literally controlled the children's doll dish market. Sets were produced in every conceivable color spectrum; opaque, marbleized and clear in a variety of shapes and sizes.

Occasionally, Akro Agate contracted work from specific firms for advertising purposes or containers for their products; namely cosmetics.

The company prospered until 1948. Due to financial difficulties the firm was dissolved and in 1951 the factory was sold to Clarksburg Glass Company.

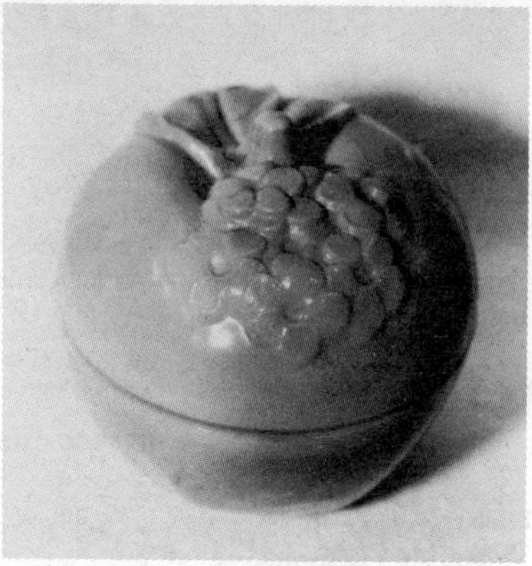

Powder Jar. "Apple." Pumpkin coloring $150.00

Ashtrays
  3x4". Leaf-shaped. Blue marbleized .... $ 6.00
  4". Rectangular. Orange marbleized 12.50
*Basket. Two handles. Opaque white 22.50
*Bell. 5½". Opaque white 35.00
Bowls
  5". Opaque white 10.00
  9" o.d. Tab handles. Orange marbleized 25.00
Children's Dishes
  7 pieces. Lemonade Set. Opaque green pitcher. Opaque white tumblers. "Stacked Disc." Set 40.00
  17 pieces. "The Little American Tea Set." Opaque three colors. Original box. Octagonal. Set 75.00
  28 pieces. Opaque mixed colors. Large size. Octagonal. Set 200.00
Cup and Saucer, Demi. Green marbleized 15.00
Flower Pots
  3½". "Ribbed Tops." Green marbleized 12.00
  5½". "Ribs and Flutes." Smooth top. Opaque green 15.00
  5½". "Stacked Disc." Orange marbleized 18.50
Lamp. 14" high. No shade. Brown marbleized 75.00
Marbles.
  Set of 10. Original cardboard box 7.50
  Set of 50. Original cardboard box 30.00
Planters
  3x6". Oval. Flowers in relief. Metal frame with bail handle. Opaque white 30.00
  6". Rectangular. Blue marbleized 10.00
  8". Rectangular. Scalloped top. Opaque yellow 15.00
Powder Jars
  Apple. Pumpkin coloring 150.00
  Colonial Lady. Opaque blue 50.00
  Mexicali. Opaque green 40.00
  Ivy. Green marbleized 35.00
  Scotty Dog. Opaque pink 50.00
Smokers Set. Holder and two ashtrays. Opaque cobalt. Set 25.00
Vases
  3¼". Cornucopia. Green marbleized 15.00
  3¼". Urn-shape. Square base. Orange marbleized 15.00
  4½". Lily decor. Opaque green 22.50
  6". Ribbed. Scalloped top. Opaque green 30.00
  8". Ribbed and fluted. Green marbleized 35.00

*Reproduced Item

ALMANACS

An almanac (almanack) is a small booklet containing calculated and pertinent facts regarding astronomical data, weather forecasts and other useful and sometimes entertaining information. In the late 18th and during the 19th century, the yearly almanac was religiously consulted by people as a guide to planting their fields, arranging family outings and other daily activities. . .yesteryears horoscope!?! Almanacs published after 1900 were plentiful and sold in the $3.00 to $5.00 range.

1776-North American Almanac, Samuel Sterns .... $ 40.00
1783-Bickerstaff's New England Almanac, Norwich 35.00
1791-N. Strong, Almanac, Hartford 30.00
1794-The New England Almanack, Nathan Daboll, New London 35.00
1796-Nehemiah Strong's Almanac, Hartford 25.00
1797-Hagerstown Town & Country Almanack, First Edition 100.00
1799-Farmer's Leap Year Issue. In Old Kyng's English 30.00
1805-New England Almanac, Nathan Daboll, New London 30.00
1808-New England Almanac, Nathan Daboll, New London 30.00
1808-The Virginia Farmer's Almanac, Benjamin Bates, Richmond 27.50
1810-New England Almanac, Nathan Daboll 30.00

1916. "Poor Richards Almanac." Wilmer Atkinson Co., Philadelphia $5.00

1812-Low's Boston	15.00
1813-New England Almanac, Nathan Daboll	25.00
1820-New England Almanac, Nathan Daboll	25.00
1828-The Farmer's Dairy, Ontario Almanac, Oliver Loud, Canandaigua	20.00
1829-Western Almanac, Oliver Loud, Rochester, NY	17.50
1834-Poor Richard's Almanac, Tobias Ostrander, Rochester	20.00
1837-American Anti-Slavery Almanac, Boston	35.00
1843-Presbyterian Almanac, Pgh ..	10.00
1848-Farmer's Almanac, Boston	10.00
1850-Hagerstown Town and Country Almanac	15.00
1853-Ayers American Almanac	10.00
1867-Pinney's Calendar or Western Almanac, Geo. R. Perkins	15.00
1869-Hagerstown Town & Country Almanac	10.00
1871-Miner's Almanac, Pittsburgh	7.50
1872-Tarrytown Argus Almanac, Tarrytown, NY	7.50
1874-Hostetter's United States Almanac, Pgh. Pa..	7.50
1880-Hagerstown Town & Country Almanac, J. Gruber, Hagerstown	10.00
1882-Brown's Iron Bitters. Lithographed cover	15.00
1886-Mandrake Bitters	7.50
1887-Kendall. Doctor at Home. Humans and Horses	10.00
1888-Williams & Clark Fertilizers. Colored litho cover	15.00
1888-Wright's Pictorial Family Almanac	7.50
1889-Burdock Blood Bitters and Key to Health	10.00
1895-Ayer's American Almanac ..	6.50
1897-Home Almanac	6.50
1902-The Ladies' Birthday Almanac	10.00
1902-Swamp Root	5.00
1906-Ayer's American	3.00
1908-Diamond Dye No. 6	10.00
1911-Dr. Ayer's. German	5.00
1912-Ranson's	5.00
1912-Royster's	3.50
1917-Ayer's American	3.00
1917-The Ladies Birthday Almanac	5.00
1918-Herrick's	3.50
1919-International Harvester	3.50
1919-Poor Richard's	5.00
1923-Hood Farm	3.50
1931-Dr. Miles	3.00
1934-Foleys	3.00

ALUMINUM, HAND WROUGHT

Aluminum is a light weight, malleable silvery metal that resists corrosion.

In the mid 20th century, hand wrought aluminum tablewares were made by several manufacturers in various patterns. These accessories became acceptable to the modest, modern homemaker and were popular gifts.

Due to the lack of present day production, hand wrought aluminum wares are becoming collectible. . .and are still relatively inexpensive to obtain.

Tray. 9½x16½" long including handles. Flying geese decor. Unmarked . . $15.00

Ashtray. 7". "Chrysanthemum." Continental ....$ 3.00

Baskets
- 9½". Buenulum 3.50
- 13". "Raspberry." Farberware.... 5.00

Bowls
- 11". "Dogwood." Everlast 4.00
- 14". "Leaf Scroll." Admiration.... 6.00

Candy Dish. 7" diam. Covered, with glass insert. 10" underplate. Bail handle. "Fruit and Flowers." Hand-Finished 6.50

Casserole Holder and Lid. 9½". Buenulum 4.00

Coasters. (6) In holder. "Tulip." Hodney Kent. Set 5.00

Cocktail Shaker. "Chrysanthemum." Continental 15.00

Cream and Sugar, Covered. "Chrysanthemum." Continental Set 10.00

Ice Buckets
- Open. 5". Bail handle. Unmarked 3.50
- With lid. "Chrysanthemum." Continental 10.00

Lazy Susan. 14½". "Fruits and Flowers." Cromwell 7.50

Percolator. Lucite handles. Original cord. "Chrysanthemum." Continental 30.00

Pitcher. Quart size. Loop handle. Plain. Buenulum 6.50

Plate. 8". Plain. Hodney Kent 2.50

Server. Two-tiered. 17½" diam. "Acorn." Continental 10.00

Silent Butler. "Fruits and Flowers." Cromwell 3.50

Tray, Bread. 7½x13". Bail handle. "Chrysanthemum." Continental .. 8.50

Trays
- 9x11". "Pines and Mountains." Cylinder handles. Arthur Armour 10.00
- 11½x16½". Two handles. "Bird." Lehman 5.00
- 12" diam. Center dip dish and cover. "Tulip". Hodney Kent 7.50
- 14½" diam. Two handles. "Fruit Tree." Unmarked 6.00
- 15" diam. Two handled. "Acorns." Continental 7.50
- 20" diam. "Daffodils." Unmarked 10.00

AMBERINA GLASS

Amberina or "Rose Amber" glass was first made by the New England Glass Company, Cambridge, Mass., in 1883. The trade name "Amberina" was devised by Edward J. Libbey, head official of the company. The characteristic shading of the glass from ruby to amber occurred in its making. Gold was added to the glass batch in the pot. The glass was then amber colored when blown or molded. The ruby color developed when the item was reheated to the correct temperature. The practice was to reheat one end of the product and then the other. Eventually the idea was conceived to reheat only one end of the items to produce a two-colored glass.

Mug. 2½" high. Baby Thumbprint. Clear applied ribbed handle........$165.00

Bottle, Water. 8" high. ITP. Applied clear rigaree on neck ....$ 225.00

Bowls
- 3¾" diam. DQ. With underplate 150.00
- 4½" diam. Diamond Optic 125.00
- 5" Square 60.00
- 7" diam. Ruffled. Signed "Libbey" 350.00
- 7" diam., 3" high. Swirled. Ribbed body. Applied gold 350.00
- 8" diam. DQ 250.00
- 9" Square, 2¾" deep. Daisy and Button 300.00
- 11¼" diam. Punch 750.00
- 13" high. Covered. Ovid. ITP 1000.00

Butter. Covered 350.00

Butter Pat. Daisy and Button 75.00

Candlesticks. 10" high. Pair 250.00

Canoe. 14" long. Daisy and Button 350.00

Carafe. 6" high. Trefoil top. Bulbous body, 4 dimples. Applied amber rigaree at shoulder 500.00

Celery Vases
- 4½" high. DQ. Scalloped. Square top 275.00
- 6½" high. DQ. Ribbed 295.00
- 6½" high. Three amber leaf feet. Bulbous base. Crimped top with rigaree 350.00
- 6½" high. Venetian Diamond .. 175.00

Cologne. 8" high. Stoppered. Pedestal base. Signed Libbey 500.00

Creamers
- 2¼" high. Ribbed body. Trefoil top, Amber reeded handle 150.00
- 3⅛" high. ITP. Applied reeded handle ....

Creamers and Sugars
- Amber handles, Square tops. Set
- Melon ribbed. Clear handles 350.00

Cruets
- 4" high. Applied clear glass handle. Amber stopper 295.00
- 7" high. Applied amber handle. Ground stopper 350.00

Cups
- Punch. DQ. Applied reeded amber handle 135.00
- Punch. ITP. Clear applied handle 100.00

Epergne. One lily. 7½" diam. Bowl, 8½" high. Signed "Libbey" 1250.00

Ice Bucket. 6½" diam., 3½" high .. 375.00

Mustard Pot. Pewter top 150.00

Pitchers
- 5¾". Hobnail. Square top 625.00
- 7". ITP. Applied handle. Bulbous body 275.00
- 7½". DQ. Applied reeded handle 275.00
- 8½". Tankard-shape. DQ 450.00
- 10". Bulbous. Square top. Enameled floral decor 300.00
- 11". Enameled 325.00

Plates
- 7" 100.00
- 7". Expanded Diamond 150.00
- 9½". Floral decor 175.00

Rose Bowl. 4½" high. Egg-shaped. Ribbed. Three green applied feet 275.00

Salt, Master. 1¼" high, 3½" diam. On pedestal. Ruffled edge 100.00

Sauces
- 4". DQ 65.00
- 5". Square. Daisy and Button 100.00

Shakers
- Salt. Enameled decor 75.00
- Salt. ITP 65.00
- Sugar. ITP Pewter top 200.00

Sherbet 100.00

Spoonholder. 6" high. Swirled 125.00

Syrup. Silverplated collar. Handle .. 300.00

Toothpick Holders
- Daisy and Button 200.00
- DQ 150.00
- ITP 225.00
- Square top 150.00
- Trefoil top 195.00

Tumblers
- Juice. ITP 100.00
- Lemonade. Handled 100.00

Water
- DQ. Ground pontil 100.00
- Enameled floral decor 85.00
- Expanded Diamond 100.00
- ITP 85.00
- Swirl 125.00

Whiskey. DQ 100.00

Tray. 1¼x8½x13½". Daisy and Button 500.00

Vases
- 4½". Signed "Libbey" 325.00
- 5¼". DQ. Applied rigaree on neck 200.00
- 6". Hobnail 250.00
- 6½". DQ. Bulbous 175.00
- 6½" high, 3¾" diam. ITP 225.00
- 7". Jack-in-the-Pulpit 195.00
- 7½". Lily in plated holder. Swirl. Tufts, Boston 250.00
- 9". Ribbed. Trefoil top 250.00
- 10¼". Jack-in-the-Pulpit. Swirl .. 300.00
- 14" high, 8½" diam. Crimped top 275.00
- 16". Jack-in-the-Pulpit. Signed "Libbey" 500.00

AMBERINA GLASS-PLATED

Plated Amberina glass was a product of the New England Glass Company, Cambridge, Mass. Its characteristic coloring of deep amber shading to deep cranberry is enhanced by vertical ribbing and a fiery opalescent white lining. A cased Wheeling glass of similar appearance has an opaque white lining, but is not opalescent and the body is not ribbed.

Cruet. 6¾" high $3800.00

Bowl. 8" diam., 3½" high ...... $ 6000.00
Cup, Punch 2000.00
Pitchers
3¾". Trefoil top 3500.00
4½". Syrup. Embossed silver band. Handle 4000.00
6" 5000.00
9" 7500.00
Shaker, Salt 500.00
Tumbler 2500.00

AMPHORA

AMPHORA AUSTRIA

"Made in Czecho-Slovakia" AMPHORA

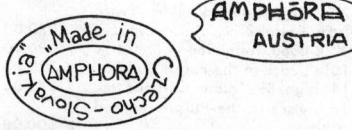

The dictionary defines amphora as a two-handled vessel with a narrow neck used by the ancient Greeks to hold wine, water or oil.
The Amphora wares found on today's market were made in Austria in the late 1800's. They are usually marked Amphora with a crown. Occasionally a piece is cross-indexed with Tillowitz and signed twice.

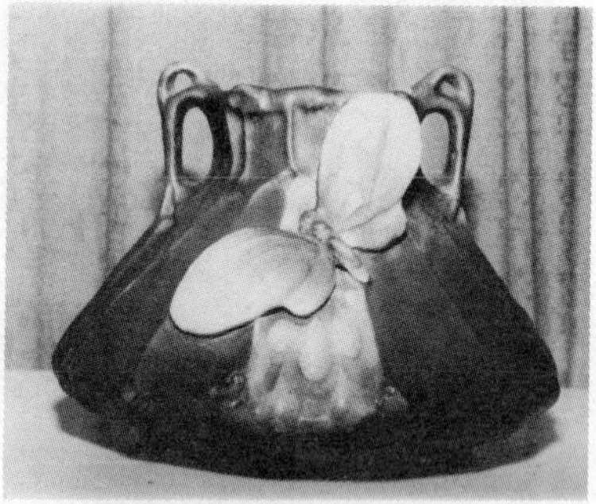

Vase. 6". Dragonfly decor. Signed $75.00

Baskets
6x7". Incised with flowers in relief. Predominately blue .... $ 65.00
7x11". Floral and cupid decor. Signed "Amphora" with crown .. 195.00
Bowls
5" diam., 5" high. Owl decor in relief. Blue. Signed 75.00
10" diam. Represents bird's nest with pheasant. All over embossing in earth tones. Signed 375.00
Urns
9x9½". Figure of boy with cauldron decor 150.00
12x14". Green glaze. Purple highlights. High relief gold flowers. Signed "Amphora" with crown.......................... 275.00
Vases
7½". Checkered shield decor. Matte green with mottled green ground. Silvered black lustre. Signed 100.00
8". Gold, green with pink leaves, gold pine cones. Signed 125.00
8". Man and lion decor. Blue, yellow and ivory. Signed "Amphora" with crown 175.00
9". Beige, green gold, basketweave with flowers in relief 125.00
9½". Gold ground, yellow and green flowers. Artist signed and marked "Amphora" with crown .. 195.00
10½". Tannish-green with lavender and purple seawood decor. 4-handled. Gold trim 225.00
11". Maroon, white, green, blue floral decor. Signed 225.00
13½". Gold on bronze. Signed "Amphora" with crown 250.00

ANIMAL DISHES, COVERED

Covered animal dishes were a popular product of glass manufacturers in the late 1800's. Although hens were the most plentiful, (they were distributed as premiums) the subjects were as varied as the type of glass used and the combinations of colors. The majority of these novelties were made in America, but several types were produced in foreign countries.
McKee of Pittsburgh, Pa. probably produced some of the finest examples. The famous and well known Atterbury ducks were a patented (March 15, 1887) product of the Atterbury Company, also of Pittsburgh, Pa.
Also see "Milk Glass" and "Vallerystahl" for additional listings.

Caution! Reproductions abound.

Camel. White milk glass .... $ 85.00
Cats
Cobalt Carnival. 8". Limited edition 40.00
White milk glass. Atterbury 150.00
White milk glass. Blue ribbed base. 5½" long................ 85.00
Chicken on sleigh. White milk glass. 4" long 50.00
Chicken and eggs on nest. White milk glass. Atterbury 150.00
Chicks with chicken. Round. Basket base. Frosted................. 100.00

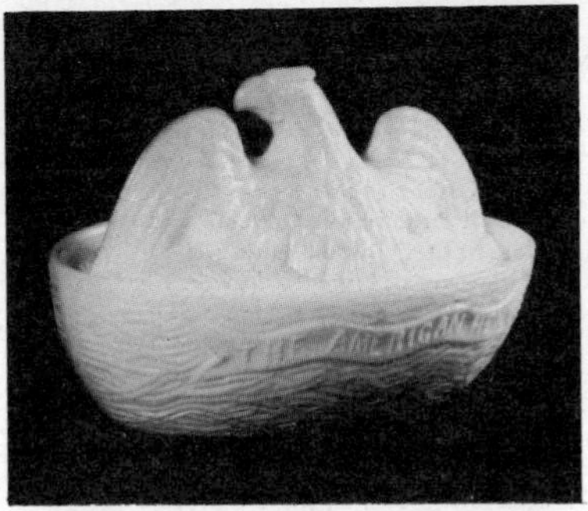

Eagle. 6⅛" ovoid. White milk glass. "The American Hen, Puerto Rico, Cuba, Phillipines." $125.00

Cockatoo. Painted. Staffordshire. 3½" 85.00
Cows
Amber Glass. Ribbed base. 6". 40.00
Frosted. 6" 95.00
Dogs
Blue milk glass. White head. 5½" 125.00
Green milk glass. Fringed mat. Embossed flowers. 5" 85.00
White milk glass. 5" 100.00
Doves
Amber. Ribbed base. 6" 35.00
White milk glass. Basketweave base. McKee. 4x4¼" 250.00
Ducks
Aqua. Clear. 5" 75.00
Blue milk glass with white head 22.50
Blue milk glass without eyes. Atterbury. Rare 500.00
Clear glass. 6½" 50.00
Cobalt Carnival. 8". Limited edition 40.00
Frosted. 6½" 60.00
Frosted. 7½" 65.00
*White milk glass. Amethyst head. Atterbury 225.00
*White milk glass. Atterbury 150.00
Eagle. White milk glass 125.00
Fish. White milk glass. Atterbury 175.00
Fox. Ribbed 100.00
Hens
Parian. 7" 175.00
White milk glass. 6½" 125.00
Hens, Colored glass
*Amber. Dark 50.00
Amber. Light. 6½" 75.00
Cobalt Carnival. Limited edition 20.00
Purple Carnival. Limited edition 25.00
Hens, Staffordshire
2½". Painted 50.00
3½". Painted 75.00
6½". Painted 125.00
8". White. Brown basket base 150.00
Lamb. White milk glass. McKee 175.00
Lions
Blue milk glass with white head on blue ribbed base 100.00
White milk glass. Lacy base. Atterbury 165.00
Owl. White milk glass. Red eyes. Atterbury 150.00
Quail. White milk glass. 5" 75.00
Rabbits
*White milk glass 75.00
White milk glass. Atterbury 175.00
White milk glass. Blue ribbed base 175.00
White milk glass. Greentown 225.00
Robins
*Milk glass. Indiana Goblet and Tumbler Co. 125.00
*Pink glass. 6" 25.00
*Vaseline glass. 6" 25.00
Roosters
White milk glass. Blue head 75.00
*White milk glass. Ribbed base 75.00
Squirrel. White milk glass. Ribbed base. McKee 150.00
Swans
*Blue milk glass. 5" 125.00
Clear glass. Frosted head and neck. Sandwich 6½" 150.00
Staffordshire. 6" 225.00
White milk glass. Closed neck. 5" 85.00
White milk glass. Open neck. Atterbury. 7" 125.00
White milk glass. Spread wings. 5½" 150.00
Turkeys
Leeds. 9" 275.00
White milk glass. McKee. 5" 175.00
White with brown nest. Staffordshire. 8" 200.00
Turtle. Clear glass. 6" 25.00

***Reproduced Item**

APOTHECARY ITEMS

Yesteryear's apothecary shop was quite removed from today's version of the modern drugstore which sells everything from gift items to prescriptions from corporate manufacturers. The early pharmacist concocted the doctor's shotgun prescriptions in a mortar and pestle, rolled the pills by hand, percolated the cough syrup, sold over-the-counter remedies and in the time of need, acted as the country doctor, neighborhood psychiatrist, and checker partner.
Therefore, these fixtures of a bygone era are being collected for nostalgia. . .especially by those involved in the medical field.

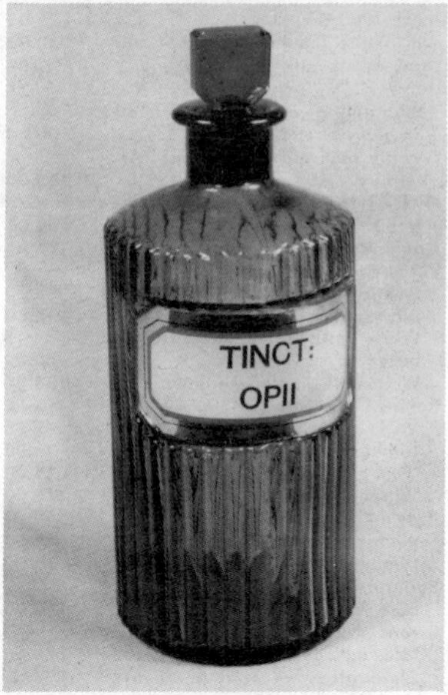

Bottle. "Tinct OPII", 8" high. Recessed label. Ribbed emerald green. Ground stopper $30.00

Bottles

6" high. Clear. With stopper . . . . $	12.50
6½" high. Emerald. Ribbed. Recessed panel for label. Glass stopper	35.00
6½" high. Embossed "Fayette Drug Co., Uniontown, Pa."	7.50
7½" high. Round. Ground glass finger pull stopper. Label in recessed panel with gold border	25.00
7½" high, 5½" diam. Free blown. Clear	30.00
8½" high. Square. Clear. Ground stopper. "Tr. Opii Camph."	30.00
8½" high. White porcelain. Floral decor. "Azahar."	30.00
8½" high. 3¼" diam., 1¼" stopper	25.00
9½" high. Clear. Round. Ground stopper. Label has wide red border	32.50
11" high. 4½" diam., 2¼" stopper. Wide mouth	40.00
12" high. Ground stopper	50.00
14" high. Bulbous. Fancy ITP pedestal and base	65.00
15" high. Round. Slender. Thumbprint base and cover	75.00

Container. Ice cream topping. 7" diam. White ceramic with nickel-plated hinged top	25.00
Cork Press. 8¼" long. Lever-type. Black cast iron, 4 different size corks	50.00
Display Cases	
"B-D Thermometers." Wood and glass front. Original lining	30.00
"Parke Davis." Tin. Two drawers . .	75.00
Funnels. 24½" o.h., 6½" top diam. Clear glass mounted on 9" square wooden base. Pair	100.00
Globes	
Hanging. 22" high. Clear glass. 3 chains. C. 1891	195.00
Standing. 13" high. 3" diam. base. 3-tier, top section green glass. Bottom clear	50.00
Graduate. 5" diam. base. 24" high. Cylindrical, 2000cc size. Pre-1940	50.00
Labels. Blank. Early 1900's. Set of 12	1.00
Label Dispensers	
Cabinet. 7x8x24". Oak. 4 drawers. 12 brass label dispensers per drawer	150.00
McCourt Label Cabinet Company. Oak and brass. Holds 48 labels . .	75.00
McCourt Label Cabinet Co., Bradford, Pa. Pat. June 11, 1912. 3x6x6". Brass. Top hinges open, dispenses roll of 2½" width labels. Embossed sides	50.00
Literature	
"American Druggists Journals" 1932-1937. Ads and illustrations. Each	1.50
"Druggist" catalog. 1911	2.50
"Handbook of Pharmacy & Therapeutics". Eli Lilly. Hardback, 336pp. C. 1897	20.00
"The Pharmaceutical Era". Complete list of drugs and preps. From the 1905 U.S.P. First edition, 85 pp. Pocketsize	12.50
"The Pharmacopeia of the U.S." and "National Formulary with Comments." 250pp. Soft leather covers. C. 1916. Set	25.00
Mortars and Pestles	
Brass. 4"	60.00
Brass. 5"	75.00
Lignum Vitae. 7"	75.00
Maple. 6". Hand turned	65.00
Pine. 5". Hand turned	35.00
Porcelain. 5"	35.00
Percolator. 7½" diam., 15" high. Pre-1900	60.00
Pill Roller. 7x14". 2-pc. Walnut and brass. Makes 24 pills	75.00

Scales. Counter top-type. Cast iron with porcelain pans. American $65.00

Scale. Counter-top. Wood base. Marble top. Two large brass pans, full set of brass wgts 125.00

Suppository Mold. 1x1¼x1¼". Brass. 12 suppository size, 30 grain. "S. Maw & Son & Thompson, London." 65.00

Tumbler. 4". White porcelain. Top has clock face. "Ace Tumbler Cover & Dose Indicator." Sharon Mfg. Co., Phila., Pa. Patd. Nov. 17, 1896 .... 15.00

ART DECO

The Art Deco period was named for an exhibition held in Paris in 1927, "L'Exposition Internationale des Arts Decoratifs." It is a later period than Art Nouveau but sometimes crosses since they are relatively close in time and are often confused with the flowing and sensuous female forms of the earlier era. The designs of Art Deco are angular and of simple lines. This was the period of skyscrapers, movie idols and the cubist work of Picasso and Legras. It was used for every conceivable object being produced in the 1920's-1930's, including ceramics, furniture, glass and metals, not only in Europe but in America as well.

This is a special market for the "new" collector and the best of this style is now commanding prices comparable to earlier periods.

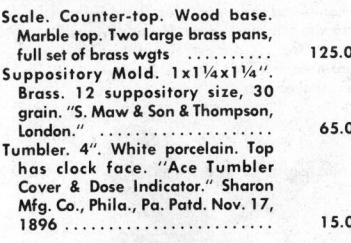

Andirons. Brass. Square column tapering to step tops. Pair ......$ 250.00

Ashtray. 5¼" square. Bronze. Footed base, kneeling Egyptian woman 125.00

Biscuit Jar. 6" high. "Valamour." Off white 35.00

Inkwell. 7" diam. Double. Glass inserts. Tin with bright blue painted top $25.00

Bookends. 6x8." Bronzed metal. Nude girl sitting on open book. Signed K&Co. Pair 75.00

Bottles, Perfume

- 5" high. Emerald green. Stylized cut. Stoppered 25.00
- 6" high. Crystal 25.00
- 6½" high. Cobalt. Geometric cutting 40.00
- 10" high. Crystal. Cone-shaped with 7" long twisted and pointed stopper 85.00

Bowl. 8" square. Black enamel, H-P red flowers with gold edging 100.00

Box, Powder. 6" diam., 3" high. Frosted pale green glass. Molded cubic designs 25.00

Bust. 7". Mouth is cigarette lighter. Signed Arturo Levi 85.00

Candelabra. 15" high. Bronze. Three-lite, straight line. Signed E. Hurley 500.00

Cigarette Case. Chrome trim on simulated tortoise shell 10.00

Cigarette Case with attached lighter. "Ronson." Simulated tortoise. Chrome trim. Original flannel bag 20.00

Compacts

- 3". Sterling and 14K gold. Hangs from 6" chain 75.00
- 3½". Enameled. Turquoise and lime green. Simulated diamond in center. Fitted interior 20.00
- 4". Enameled. Black with bust of woman on cover in relief. Chain handle 35.00
- 4". Sterling. All over engraving .. 50.00

Demitasse Set. 4 cups and saucers. Creamer and sugar. Geometric pattern of leaves in green, black, platinum on white ground. Marked Empire Ivory Ware. "Grosvenor." Set 100.00

Desk Calendar. 4" high, 6⅜x6⅝" base. Bronze finish. Ornate initial in circle. C. 1930 .... 50.00

Desk Set. Inkwell, paper clip, rocking blotter, triple stamp box. "Bradley Hubbard." Set 250.00

Figurines

11¼" high. Nude. Carved French ivory. (Chryselephantine Sculpture.) 650.00

12¾" high. Woman. Porcelain. Yellow, blue, brown. Austria 200.00

Flower Frogs

6½". Seated nude. Light blue glass 35.00

8". Woman in long dress, trailing flowers, 2-piece. White porcelain 50.00

Furniture-See "Furniture"

Lamps

8¾" high. Gilted metal nude, afghan hound. Hobnail glass shade 100.00

9" high. Gilt bronze oriental dancer base, holds Millefiore globe. (Chryselephantine Sculpture).... 1500.00

10½" high. Bronze. Mushroom-shaped with silver decor. "Henitz" 300.00

11" high. Bronze. Dancing girl on marble plinth. Brass shade, crystal prisms. Signed Braved Austria 650.00

13" high. Bronzed metal with 3 standing nudes. Arms raised, holding globe-shaped marigold shade with geometric sculptured design 175.00

13½" high. Galleon silvered metal base. Shade of multicolored glass fruit 175.00

15½" high. Desk-type. Adjustable. Brass 195.00

Porringer. 5¼" diam. Sterling. Handle set with Carnelian stone. "Greif." 175.00

Screen, Radiator. 27" high, 52" long. Three panelled pierced brass. Wood frame 500.00

Shoe Buckles. 1½" steel backs and clips. Late 1930's. Assorted styles. Pair 10.00

Smoking Set. One side holds cigarettes; other, 3 ashtrays, match box. Sterling trim on bronze 95.00

Tazza. 4½x6". Sterling. Pierced border. Set with 3 cabochon jade stones. "Grief" 300.00

Vases

6". Pear-shaped. Flared rim. Enamel blue and yellow stylized pussy willows on clear ground. Signed Goupy 250.00

8½". Flying geese. Blue, green, yellow. Signed Boch 175.00

12". Parrot. Allover enamel. Marked "Keramis." "Made in Belgium." 150.00

ART NOUVEAU

The French term for the new art, "Art Nouveau," had its beginning in the 1890's and swept the continent and America for almost 40 years. Some of its more recognized artists were Galle', Lalique and Tiffany. But there were other artists of the period, not as proficient or promoted, and knowledgeable collectors are now searching out their works. Art Nouveau can be identified by its flowing and sensuous lines, floral forms, insects, and the feminine form. These designs were incorporated on almost everything produced at that time; from art glass to furniture, to silver, to personal objects.

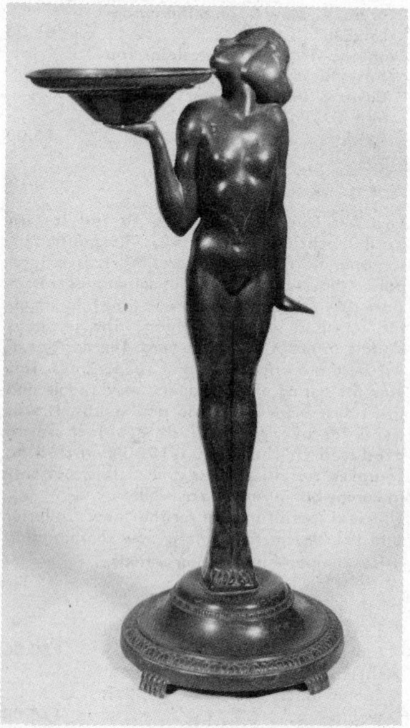

Ash Tray. Figural floor-type. 26½" high. Bronzed pot metal $95.00

Bookends

Brass. Reclining nudes with arched backs and flowing hair. Pair ... $ 100.00

Brass. Frog in tailcoat, carrying top hat. Pair ... 75.00

Bronze. 6¼" high. Nude. Pair ... 100.00

Boxes

3x5". Pewter design on top. Red acid finish. Signed. M. Hess ... 100.00

Ring. Goldplated. Lined ... 20.00

Button Hook. 6½" long. Sterling .. 30.00

Candlesticks

10" high. Flowers with intertwined stems. Silverplated ... 40.00

15" high. Man, woman, butterflies. Silverplated. Pair ... 175.00

Chamberstick. 6" high. Battery operated. Bronze finish. "Candle" Pat. 1915 ... 35.00

Dresser Set. Two brushes, comb mirror. Sterling. Unger Bros. Set ... 250.00

Figurine. Girl, Dancing. 9" high. Bronze. Ivory face and hands ... 300.00

Hand Mirror. Sterling. Sculptured woman's head with flowing tresses; irises, swans and rising sun. Unger Bros ... 125.00

Hair Brush. 9½". Sterling. Handle in form of woman, roses and cupid at top ... 125.00

Lamps

11" high. Gilded nymph supporting pedestal with ball shade of cased spatter glass in red, yellow and white ... 150.00

15" high. Cobra-shaped base. Jeweled shade. Gilted metal ... 300.00

16" high. Red lustre glass in bronze holder shape of flowers, leaves and vines ... 300.00

18" high. Bronzed base with 3" medallion of woman's head. 10" diam. art glass shade. Amber mottling on yellow ground ... 375.00

Letter Holder. 4½x5½". Two sections, 4 ladies, side profiles with long flowing hair. Long stemmed, floral decor. Bronzed ... 60.00

Pitcher. 12" high. Pewter. Handle in form of female figure. Bearded man decor. Signed ... 300.00

Stamp Case. Sterling ... 20.00

Tea Strainer. Pierced corner. Fits over cup. 7" long. Sterling ... 35.00

Trays

3x5". Flowing-haired woman. Flowers in relief. Sterling ... 35.00

4x8". Girl watching sunrise. Bronze. "Maxim." ... 175.00

6x7". Oval. Sterling ... 50.00

Crumber. Brass. Embossed gargoyle, horn of plenty, sheaf of wheat ... 50.00

Vases

8". Floral motif. Pewter. Kayserzinn ... 150.00

9". Vividly colored stylized floral decor. Signed Corona-Holland .. 250.00

9½". Girl with flowing hair. Flowers. Handled. Metal ... 75.00

10½". Panelled. Blue opalescent to emerald green. Heavy enameled poppies ... 125.00

10½". Lady with flowing hair. **Signed Asch. Royal Bonn ... 250.00**

17½". Angels. Green and maroon leaves. Dore' female figures. Bronze. Signed ... 500.00

Wax Letter Seal. Sterling ... 35.00

AURENE GLASS

This type of art glass was invented by Frederick Carder, an Englishman. The name "Aurene" was bestowed upon the glass by the originator from the Latin "Aureus"—a Roman gold coin. Aurene glass has a smooth, uniform, iridescent, goldlike surface, although some is either silvery or dark blue. It was manufactured by the Steuben Glass Works from about 1904 to 1930. Most items were permanently marked in ink under glaze with the word "Aurene", others bore only a paper label.

Basket. 8x8". Flared top. Iridescent gold and blue. Applied handle .. $ 450.00

Biscuit Jar. Straight sides. Gold. Signed ... 500.00

Bottles, Cologne

4½" high. Gold. Signed ... 350.00

6½" high. Blue blossom stopper .. 400.00

6½" high. Melon ribbed body. 3 shell feet. Blue. Signed and no'd. 750.00

6½" high, 2½" diam. Pedestal base. Iridescent blue. Original stopper ... 600.00

Bowls

7" diam., 2" high. Blue. Footed. Folded-in rim. Signed and no'd .. 300.00

9½" diam., 4" high. Peacock blue. Flared. Collar base. Steuben ... 650.00

10" diam., 5" high. 5" base. Blue swirl. Signed and no'd ... 395.00

12½" diam., 2" high. Gold. Rollover rim ... 500.00

13" diam., 3" high. Blue roll-over rim ... 550.00

Box. 4". Gold. Copper wheel

Vase. 4½". Gold. Ruffled top. Signed and numbered, 121. .... $350.00

engraving. Yellow enamel decor on cover 250.00

Candlesticks

7" high. Gold. Signed Steuben .. 300.00

8" high. Gold. Double twist stem. Signed and no'd. Pair 600.00

10" high. Gold. Signed 450.00

Compotes

7". Blue. Twisted standard. Steuben 400.00

7". Gold. Steuben. Signed and no'd 600.00

8½" high, 6" diam. Blue. Unsigned 395.00

Cordial. 5". Gold 150.00

Cordial Set. 10¼" decanter with six 2¼" cordials. Swirl pattern. Gold. Set 1500.00

Cup with underplate. Signed 200.00

Cuspidor, Ladies'. Gold. Signed 350.00

Goblet. Blue. Twisted stem. Signed 250.00

Lamp Shades-SEE-"Lamp Shades"

Parfait. 4½" high. Signed "F. Carder" 350.00

Plate. 5½" diam. Gold 165.00

Rose Bowl. 4" diam. Blue. Steuben 400.00

Salt. 1½" high. Gold. Signed 150.00

Vases

3¾". Gold. Dimpled base. Signed Steuben 195.00

4". Gold with green leaves, white florals. Signed Steuben 1450.00

5½". Blue. Optic rib. Signed 300.00

6¼". Blue tree trunk or bark style. Signed and no'd 675.00

6¼". Gold. Wafer base. Flared. Ruffled rim. Unsigned 250.00

8". Blue. Stick-type bud vase. Signed and no'd.................. 300.00

8". Gold. Balustered-shape. Applied green rigaree. Signed Steuben...................... 450.00

10½". Green drape pattern. Floral form on platinum iridescence 1200.00

12". Bud. Gold. Wafer based. Flared top. Signed and no'd 750.00

13". Blue iridescent. Steuben 1500.00

Wine. 4½" high. Gold. Twisted stem. Signed.................. 175.00

AUSTRIAN WARE

During the late 19th and early 20th centuries, much fine porcelain and pottery were produced in Austria. Although Carlsbad (known as Karlsbad after World War I when Austria became a part of Czechoslovakia) was the center of the industry, other factories existed. These factories were either held or supported by American monies; thus, their wares were produced mainly for export to the United States. The U.S. firm of Lazarus and Rosenfeldt imported large amounts of porcelain from Czechoslovakia after World War I, marked "Victoria." For additional listings, see specific manufacturers listed alphabetically in this book.

Plate. 6". White ground with blue and green floral decor. Gold rim. Marked Imperial Crown China. $18.50

Bowl. 5¾" diam. H-P border of yellow roses. Artist signed ....$ 25.00
Cache Pot. 6½" diam., 3¼" high. Handled. Fluted. Small sprays in pink. Lustre touches 35.00
Cake Set. 9¾" serving plate. Six-6¾" plates. H-P vintage decor. Gold trim. Pierced rims. Artist signed. Set 165.00
Cream and Sugar, Covered. Eggshell porcelain with pale blue and shaded red fruit decor gold trim. Set 40.00
Cups and Saucers
Hexagonal-shaped bases. White with pink roses, eagle. Gold band. "MZ. Austria." Set of six 75.00
White with pink roses. Green leaf trim. Imperial 12.50
Dresser Set. 4 pieces. Bluebird under glaze. Victoria 60.00
Hair Receivers
Gold scroll edging. Tiny rose decor. Victoria 18.50
Rust to yellow with roses. Victoria 18.50
Pitcher, Syrup. 5½" high. Rose decor. Underplate. Victoria 40.00
Plates
8¾". Geese flying against white moon. Pale blue ground. Dark blue rim. "MZ. Austria." 20.00
9½". H-P pink, yellow roses. Tinted background. Victoria 25.00
Sardine. Pink floral. Sardine handles. Victoria 25.00
Ramekins with underplates. White porcelain. Gold trim. Victoria. Set of 6 .... 75.00
Salt and Pepper Shakers. H-P florals. Pair 20.00
Salt Dips. H-P with pink roses. Gold feet and trim. Set of 6 .... 35.00
Vases
8¼". Floral decor on medallion. Green and white. Pair 75.00
12". Pink and yellow floral decor on ivory ground. Gold trim. Footed and handled. Bisque finish 75.00

AUTOGRAPHS

An autograph is a person's own signature. This is one field of collecting that the law of supply and demand does not seem to apply. The abundance of a particular person's signature doesn't seem to affect the value if universal interest exists.

The novice autograph collector should seek the counsel of knowledgeable and reputable dealers. . .forgeries abound in the market.

The following abbreviations denote type of autographed material:

ADS. . .Autograph Document Signed
ALS. . .Autograph Letter Signed
AMsS. . .Autograph Manuscript Signed
ANS. . .Autograph Note Signed
AQS. . .Autograph Quotation Signed
CS. . .Card Signed
DS. . .Document Signed
FDC. . .First Day Cover
LS. . .Letter Signed
MCS. . .Magazine Cover Signed
PS. . .Photograph Signed
S. . .Signed
SO. . .Signature Only
TLS. . .Typed Letter Signed
TMsS. . .Typed Manuscript Signed

Baseball. Pittsburgh Pirates. C. 1960's $75.00

Agnew, Spiro. MCS ....$ 20.00
Alexandra. SO. Queen Consort of Edward VII. Closing lines of ALS .. 20.00
Barnard, Dr. Christian. MCS 5.00
Barnum, Phineas T. ALS. To a collector 25.00
Barrymore, Lionel. 8x10". PS. Dated '35 .... 25.00
Bates, Edward. Attorney General under Lincoln. Printed Report. 20th Congress 1828. 35pp 50.00
Best, Charles H. SO. Canadian Physiologist. Co-discoverer of insulin 10.00
Burns, George. 8x10". PS 10.00
Busoni, Ferruccio. SO. Italian Composer 20.00
Carnegie, Andrew. ALS 100.00

REVERSE OF BASEBALL

Chian Kai-shek. SO. Chinese General and Statesman. In Chinese 20.00
Cisco Kid. (Duncan Renaldo) 8x10". PS 15.00
Cooper, Peter. SO, American Philanthropist. Founded Cooper Union, Member of American Hall of Fame 15.00
Coward, Sir Noel. 4⅛x5¼". PS 20.00
Crosby, Bing. CS 10.00
Dempsey, Jack. 8x10". PS 15.00
Doyle, Sir A. Conan. SO. Creator of Sherlock Holmes. From ALS 45.00
Eisenhower, Dwight D. LS. Supreme Headquarters Allied Expeditionary Force, 1944 .... 75.00
Eden, Anthony. SO 10.00
Emmich, Otto Von. German Gen. WWI. Post Card picture in uniform. Pencil autograph note .. 25.00
Ford, Gerald R. SO 35.00
Frantz, Robert. SO. German Composer 10.00
George III. SO. King of Great Britain. "Our Last King" 35.00
Grey, Zane. Bank check filled in and signed. 1936 .... 25.00
Groener, Wilhelm. SO. German General WWI 10.00
Hamilton, Alexander. SO. 1757-1804. Am. Statesman. First Secretary of Treasury. Killed by Burr in duel 150.00
Hammerstein, Oscar. ALS. Director of Manhattan Opera House 25.00
Harding, Warren G. President. DS. Twice as W.G. Harding, 1 full page, proof of legal publication, May 7, 1892 .... 65.00
Hemingway, Ernest. Unsigned Autograph Note, 3 lines. Original envelope addressed by Hemingway, his signature "E. Hemingway" and return address. Included is a LS by Mrs. Ernest Hemingway (Mary Hemingway) explaining the note. New York 1976. Three items 160.00
Hilton, Conrad, MCS 5.00
Holmes, Oliver Wendell. ALS to a collector 15.00
Hoover, J. Edgar. SO 20.00
Hubbard, Elbert G. Bank check filled in and signed. June 22, 1904 .... 15.00
Humphrey, Hubert. MCS 20.00
Hussein, King. MCS 15.00
Johnson, Lady Bird. CS 5.00
Johnson, Lyndon. PS 50.00
Karloff, Boris. SO 50.00
Kennedy, Robert. MCS 50.00
Kissinger, Henry. MCS 15.00
Laurier, Sir Wilfrid. LS. Canadian Prime Minister. Ottawa. 1901 .. 17.50
Lee, Gypsy Rose. LS 20.00
Livermore, Mary A. SO. American Suffragette and Reformer 10.00
Longfellow, Henry Wadsworth. CS .. 25.00
Loren, Sophia. 3x5". PS 10.00
Marshall, George C. LS. Washington, 1953 .... 20.00
Marx, Groucho. LS. Expressing his feeling regarding his son's ambition to become the fourth "Marx" 20.00
Meir, Golda. MCS 35.00
Merrill, Robert. 8x10". PS 5.00
Michener, James A. SO 10.00
Monroe, James. S. Land Grant 1822 with seal intact 125.00
Monroe, Marilyn. 8x10". PS 150.00
Namath, Joe. 8x10". PS. Quarterback for University of Alabama .. 20.00
Nicklaus, Jack. MCS 5.00
Peary, Robert E. LS. American Arctic Explorer, discovered North Pole. Washington, 1912 .... 35.00
Pons, Lily. SO 10.00
Presley, Elvis. SO. 45 RPM cover of his, "Rags to Riches" 150.00
Roebuck, Alvan C. SO. Co-founder of Sears, Roebuck Co. 25.00
Roosevelt, Elliott. ANS. 1934 ...... 5.00
Roosevelt, F.D. TLS. With envelope. Written from Warm Springs, GA. Re: his victory as Gov. of New York, 1928 .... 50.00
Salinger, Pierre. SO 15.00
Shaw, George Bernard. ANS. "GBS". Post card addressed by Shaw, containing a printed request to strike

his name from lists of available speakers. "When the Rotary movement..." 50.00
Stevenson, Adlai E. 8x10". PS 17.50
Strauss, Richard. SO. In pencil 40.00
Tennyson, Lord Alfred. ALS 50.00
Truman, Harry. PS 40.00
Vanderbilt, Cornelius, Jr. SO. Dated, 1934 .... 5.00
William II. SO. Emperor of Germany. The Kaiser 50.00
Wilson, Harold. 4¾x6¾". PS. With Mrs. Wilson 15.00

AUTOMOBILE ITEMS

Carbide Tank. For running board. Brass plated ....$ 150.00
Clock, Dash. Stevens Duryea. Brass. Bevelled case. 8-day. Key wind. Hoffecker Co., Boston. Running .. 75.00
Emblems. Each .... 15.00 to 30.00
Gear Shift Knobs
- Orange and white marbleized .. 18.50
- Red and white agate 50.00

Hood Ornaments
- Buick. Blue glass 50.00
- Mack Truck. Bulldog 20.00
- Nude. Chrome 50.00
- Pontiac. Chief 25.00

Horns
- Brass. English. "King of the Road." No. 34 .... 150.00
- Bulb-type. Brass. Early.......... 125.00
- Plunger-type. Early 65.00

Head light, "Presto" 7¼x9¾" diam. Brass. C. Early 1900's..........$75.00

Hubcaps. Each .... 10.00 to 20.00
Jack. Ford, Model "T" 50.00
Lamps
- "Adlake Balanced Draft." 8½" high. Original brackets. Hubmobile 75.00
- "Dietz Eureda." 7½" high. Clear lens in front. Red glass in rear. Brass 125.00
- "E. & J. Model 12". Two side lamps. One rear lamp. Brass with beveled glass. Refinished. C. 1910-12. Set of 3 .... 300.00
- "Everready Mazada." Original bulbs. C. 1910 .... 25.00
- Interior. Electric car.Brass. Bevelled glass panels, 2¾x5". Pair 150.00

License Plates
- California World's Fair 1939. Pair 35.00
- Enameled.Early. Each .... 10.00 to 20.00
- N.Y. World's Fair 1939. Pair 35.00
- Porcelain. Early 1900's. Each.................. 25.00 to 50.00

Lights
- Cadillac, 1913. Headlights. Pair.. 200.00
- Dodge, 1928. Tail light 25.00
- Ford, Model T, 1915. Tail light. Brass. Pair 50.00
- Lucas, King of the Road. Two side lights. One tail light. Brass with original glass. Signed. Set 150.00

Literature
- "American Motorist." Jan. 1930 .. 10.00
- "Audel's Automobile Guide." 1915 .... 50.00
- "Auto Accessories." Willis, Co., N.Y. 1912 .... 20.00
- "Auto Blue or Green Books." Early 1900's .... 10.00 to 20.00
- "Automobile Engineering." 5 volumes. 1920 .... 75.00
- "Automobile Oddities." 40 pages. 1932 .... 25.00
- "Auto Parts." 1931 Calendar. 16x40". Picture of Pirate girl 25.00
- "Buick." 1954. Shop manual 20.00
- "Fix Your Ford." 1964. Talboldt, Goodheart. 288 pages.......... 5.00
- "Franklin." 1918. Sales catalog. Hard cover. 77 pages 75.00
- "Official Handbook." 1929. 6x9" prints of most vehicles. Hard cover, 189 pages 75.00
- "Packard." 1953. Shop manual .. 25.00
- "Reo." 1912. Shop manual 25.00
- "Rolls and Bentley." 1931. Brochure, 2 pages. Specs and photographs of models 15.00
- "Studebaker, Big 6 and Special 6." 1923. Owners manual 25.00

Magneto. Ford Model "N", for 4-

cylinder engine	100.00
Motor Meters	
1916 Boyce	50.00
1916 Dodge	50.00
Parasol. Touring car accessory. Silk, yellow with green trim	35.00
Pump, Tire. "Ford". New base	25.00
Seats, Leather. 1922. Packard Coupe. Set of two	200.00
Spark Coil. For early car	50.00
Spark Plugs. 1906 Model T. Mounted on wood block. Set of four	25.00
Steering Wheel. 1925 Durant	85.00
Tools. "Ford." Set of 12	35.00
Vases. (Used to hold flowers in electric cars)	
Black Satin Glass. Tiffin. Pair	75.00
Green. 7½". Pressed glass with bracket	25.00
Pink glass. No bracket	20.00
Pink glass. 8". "Woodpeckers." Pair	35.00

AUTOMOBILES

In 1947 the Antique Automobile Club of America (AACA) devised a system or car classification to assist in the preservation and restoration of old cars. They classify any land motor vehicle made prior to 1930 (including buses, motorcycles, fire trucks, etc.) as an authentic antique vehicle.

The Classic Car Club of America (CCCA) recognizes some luxury models from 1925 through 1948 as authentic classics. Some vehicles manufactured from 1948 to 1964 are classified by the Mile Stone Club (MSC) as Milestone cars.

Prices are for unrestored, good unrestored and restored. An unrestored vehicle is one that requires considerable rebuilding, but is not a basket case. A good, unrestored is a complete, drivable car, but is in need of cosmetic repairs (paint, upholstery, chrome, etc.) to bring it up to show quality. A point system is used in classifying restored cars for varying degrees of restoration.

The prices listed herein are for vehicles in good, unrestored condition unless otherwise noted.

AMX. 1968. Sports. Hard Top $	1850.00
Auburn. 1931. 4-Door Sedan	7500.00
Bricklin. 1974. Sports Hard Top	7000.00
Buick. 1928. Club Sedan	3000.00
Buick. 1942. Formal Sedan	4800.00
Buick. 1948. Roadmaster. Sedan	1300.00
Cadillac. 1919. Touring	10000.00
Cadillac. 1930. V-16. Limousine	25000.00
Cadillac. 1939. Convertible Sedan. V-16	15000.00
Cadillac. 1939. 4-Door Sedan	6500.00

AMX. 1968. Sports. Hard Top $1850.00

Cadillac. 1946. Model 62 Club Coupe	1800.00
Cadillac. 1948. Fleetwood Limousine	2500.00
Cadillac. 1961. Coupe DeVille	450.00
Cadillac. 1963. Convertible	1100.00
Chevrolet. 1913. Touring Car	4500.00
Chevrolet. 1936. Master	2500.00
Chevrolet. 1947. Convertible	3500.00
Chevrolet. 1951. Convertible	1800.00
Chevrolet. 1955. Bel-Air, V-8 Hard Top, 2-Door	1500.00
Chevrolet. 1955. Bel-Air. 4-Door	1200.00
Chevrolet. 1957. Corvette. Restored	8500.00
Chevrolet. 1961. Impala, 4-Door Hard Top	500.00
Chevrolet. 1963. Corvette. Roadster with extras. Restored	8000.00
Chevrolet. 1963. Corvette. Roadster with extras; plus fuel injection, KO wheels, factory air	11000.00
Chrysler. 1928. 2-Door Sedan	3000.00
Chrysler. 1932. Imperial. 8-Cylinder. 7-Passenger Sedan	9500.00
Chrysler. 1958. New Yorker. 4-Door Hard Top	500.00
Cord. 1936. Phaeton	19000.00
Dodge. 1938. 4-Door Sedan	1000.00
Dodge. 1962. 8-80, 4-Door Sedan	450.00
Duesenberg, J. 1934. Convertible Sedan	150,000.00
Edsel. 1958. Citation. Convertible	2200.00
Edsel. 1960. 2-Door, Hard Top	850.00
Ferrari. 1964. 330-GTC V-12	10000.00
Ford. 1914. Model T. Dixie Suspension	5500.00
Ford. 1919. Model T. Coupe	2800.00
Ford. 1920. Touring Car	3000.00
Ford. 1925. Roadster	3500.00
Ford. 1926. 4-Door Sedan	3000.00
Ford. 1929. Model A. Sports Coupe. Rumble seat	2800.00
Ford. 1930. Model A. 2Door Sedan	2500.00
Ford. 1931. Model A. 4-Door Sedan	3000.00
Ford. 1936. Convertible Sedan	7500.00
Ford. 1942. Station Wagon. V-8	3800.00
Ford. 1947. Deluxe Coupe	1500.00
Ford. 1949. Coupe	2000.00

Duesenberg. 1932. Murphey Convertible Coupe. Restored . . $175000.00+

Ford. 1957. Thunderbird. Convertible	6000.00
Ford. 1959. Convertible Sunliner	2000.00
Ford. 1962. Galaxie 500. 2-Door Hard Top	400.00
Ford. 1963. Thunderbird. Restored	6000.00
Ford. 1965. Mustang. Convertible	1500.00
Franklin. 1932. 4-Door Sedan	3750.00
Hudson. 1946. Super 6 Brougham	1500.00
Hudson. 1950. Pace Maker Coupe	750.00
Hudson. 1955. Custom Hornet Sedan	1200.00
Jaguar. 1948. Mark IV Saloon	4500.00
Jaguar. 1953. XK 120 Coupe	3800.00
Jaguar. 1961. Mark IX. 4-Door Sedan	3000.00
Kaiser-Darrin. 1954. Sports Roadster	10500.00
Kaiser-Manhattan. 1951. Sedan	1200.00
Lincoln. 1928. 7-Passenger Touring	25000.00
Lincoln. 1933. V-12 Club Sedan KA	7000.00
Lincoln. 1941. Coupe Continental	6000.00
Lincoln. 1956. Continental Mark II	5500.00
Lincoln. 1959. Mark IV. Convertible	2000.00
Lincoln. 1963. Convertible Sedan	3000.00
Lincoln. 1963. 4-Door Sedan	750.00
Mercedes-Benz. 1952. 300 Coupe	7500.00
Mercedes-Benz. 1956. 300 Convertible Sedan	10000.00
Mercedes-Benz. 1961. 190 SL Roadster	3100.00
Nash. 1928. Deluxe Sedan	2500.00
Nash. 1940. Lafayette Sedan	1800.00
Oldsmobile. 1956. 88. 2-Door Hard Top	700.00
Oldsmobile. 1960. 98 Convertible	1500.00
Oldsmobile. 1962. Starfire Coupe	600.00
Packard. 1933. V-12 CLB Sedan	20000.00
Packard. 1940. Custom Super 8 Limousine	9500.00
Packard. 1950. Super 8. 2-Door	4400.00
Packard. 1955. Clipper. 4-Door	1800.00
Packard. 1958. 4-Door Sedan	850.00
Plymouth. 1937. 4-Door Sedan. Restored	3500.00
Plymouth. 1947. Special Deluxe. 4-Door Sedan	1250.00
Plymouth. 1948. Station Wagon	3500.00
Plymouth. 1950. Convertible Coupe	2000.00
Plymouth. 1960. Fury, 2-Door Hard Top	400.00
Plymouth. 1963. Belvedere. 2-Door Hard Top	400.00
Pontiac. 1939. Coupe. 2-Door	2000.00
Rolls Royce. 1932. Brewster Limousine	18000.00
Rolls Royce. 1940. Wraith. 5-Passenger	8000.00
Rolls Royce. 1947. Silver Wraith Deville	11000.00
Rolls Royce. 1955. Silver Cloud I, 4-Door	10000.00
Rolls Royce. 1960. Silver Cloud II, Sedan	12000.00
Studebaker. 1942. Coupe	1800.00
Studebaker.. 1947. Starlight Com. Coupe	1000.00
Studebaker. 1948. 4-Door	800.00
Studebaker. 1953. Champion Regal Coupe	1200.00
Studebaker. 1963. Avanti	4800.00

MISCELLANEOUS

Fire Engines	
1928. Chevrolet	$ 1500.00+
1931. Diamond T Pumper	2000.00+
1935. Ford Hook and Ladder. Complete	2500.00+
1944. Mack	1250.00+
Trucks	
1931. Ford. ½-Ton Pick-up	2800.00
1932. Chevrolet. ½-Ton Pick-Up	850.00
1934. Ford. V-8 Pick-up	3000.00
1939. Diamond T. ¾-Ton Pick-Up	1000.00
1940. International. 1½-Ton Stake	850.00
1949. Dodge. ½-Ton Pick-up	750.00
Willys.	
1949. Jeepster	1500.00
1955. Jeep Ambulance. ¼-Ton. Military Wheels	1500.00

AUTUMN LEAF PATTERN

The only exclusive premium line pattern produced by Hall China, East Liverpool, Ohio. The "Autumn Leaf" pattern was designed for the Jewel Tea Company in 1933 by Arden Richards. At first, this Hall-Jewel design had no name and in the early years was called "Hall-Jewel or Autumnal". Then in April 1942 it was designated "Autumn". Finally, in 1960, it was called "Autumn Leaf".

It remains Jewel property to this day. Although the Jewel catalog has not listed any "Autumn Leaf" since 1977, the pattern has not been officially discontinued. There is some doubt as to whether it will be re-introduced in the future.

Tid-bit Tray. 3-graduated tiers, 6¼" diam., 7¼" diam., 10" diam. Metal center post $22.50

Bean Pot. Two handled	$ 45.00
Bowls	
6½"	8.00
8½"	10.00
10½". Divided	15.00
Butters, Covered	
¼ pound	25.00
1 pound	65.00
Cake Plate. Footed. Metal base	10.00
Cake Server. Metal	30.00
Canisters	
Round. Plastic cover	7.50
Square. Metal. Set of 4	50.00
Casserole, Covered. Tab handles	12.50
Coffee Server. 8"	28.50
Cookie Jar, Covered. Tab handles	35.00
Creamers and Sugars	
1934	30.00
1940	15.00
Cup and Saucer	6.50
Custard Cup	4.00
Flour Sifter, Metal	20.00
Gravy Boat	12.00
Marmalade Jar, Covered	20.00
Pie Plate. 9½"	6.50
Pitcher, With ice lip	17.50
Place Mats	15.00
Plates	
7¼"	5.00
10"	8.00
Platter. 13"	12.00
Salt and Pepper Shakers, Pair	12.00
Table Cloth. 56x81"	50.00
Tea Pot. Aladdin, With insert	25.00
Tea Towels. 16¼x33¼"	12.00
Toaster Cover, Plastic	10.00
Tumbler. 14 oz. Frosted	12.50

BACCARAT GLASS

Baccarat glass was established by royal decree from Louis XV in 1764. The factory was located in Alsace-Lorraine, France. Since its very beginning up to the present, Baccarat glass has always been of the finest quality and highly regarded by all connoisseurs of crystal.

During the Classic Era of Paperweights (1845-1860), Baccarat was one of the major producers of exquisite weights. In 1953 Baccarat again re-entered the paper-weight market with an assortment of limited editions. Also see "Paperweights."

Vase. 6⅛". Cobalt with white lace decor $250.00

Bobeches. Signed. Pair	$ 50.00
Bottles, Perfume	
3½" high. Pyramid. Sphinx stopper.	

Signed	65.00
4½" high. "Guerlain." Signed	25.00
6" high. Gold stripes. Gold star on cut stopper. Signed	75.00
8" high. "Houbigant.' Gold stopper. Signed	85.00
Bowls	
5½". Scalloped edge. Footed. Swirl. Signed	75.00
7½x19". Centerpiece. Amberina Swirl. Ornate gold color holder. Signed	450.00
10". Cut from ruby to pale rose	375.00
Box. 1¾x2⅛x3⅝". Covered. Rose Tiente. Signed	65.00
Candelabra. 10". 3-arm. With prisms. Pair	250.00
Candlesticks. 8¾" high. Cobalt. Gothic design with gold decor. Hexagonal sockets and bases. Pair	350.00
Champagne. 7" high. Engraved	35.00
Compotes	
Open. 2x3¼" diam. Crystal. Swirl. Signed. Late	25.00
Open. 8" diam. Amber Block. 1890. Signed	175.00
Cordial	25.00
Creamer and Sugar. 3x3" with 5x9" handled tray. Crystal. Set	85.00
Cruet. Amberina Swirl	125.00
Cup and Saucer	75.00
Decanters	
8½" high. Original stopper	85.00
10½" high. Applied fleur-de-lis and scroll work. Stoppered	150.00
Epergne. 13" high. Single lily	225.00
Figurine. Turtle. 1½x2½x4". Crystal	50.00
Inkwells	
Crystal bowl with 4 green leaves. Brass top	150.00
Crystal. Swirl. Sterling top	150.00
Jars	
Biscuit. Brass cover and bail. Cranberry on frosted. Signed	200.00
Jam, Covered. Amberina Swirl. Signed	75.00
Knife Rest. 4" long. Crystal with frosted "Baby Heads." Signed	65.00
Letter Opener. 9" long. Signed	45.00
Pitchers	
8¼". Diamond Quilted. Crystal. Applied handle	150.00
10¼". Taupe and white mottling	175.00
Relish. 3½x9½". Rose Teinte	85.00
Rose Bowl. 3½". Cut crystal with gold, blue, white forget-me-nots	150.00
Shade, Lamp. 5" high. 6" top opening. Vaseline. Diamond Point. Signed Baccarat Depose	100.00
Sugar, Open. Daisy and Leaf. Crystal	65.00
Toothpick Holder. Crystal	35.00
Tumbler, Water. Swirl	25.00
Tumble-Up with plate. Set	175.00
Vases	
5". Lacy. C. 1870	200.00
10". Cameo cut. Chartreuse yellow to frosted. Bronze bases. Paper label. Pair	750.00
11½". Cameo cut. Cranberry flowers and leaves. Gold trim. Pair	750.00
Whiskey. Cut crystal	15.00

BANKS-GLASS

Lincoln Bottle. Tin top $15.00

Barrel. Embossed staves. Bands	$ 7.50
Baseball. Mobil giveaway	5.00
Bear. 8"	7.50
Beehive Coke Oven. Green. Commemorative	15.00
Brick. "Pittsburgh Paints."	10.00
Charlie Chaplain. 3¾"	50.00

House. "Save with Pittsburgh Paints." 3"	20.00
Independence Hall. 7½"	85.00
Kewpie	65.00
Liberty Bell. Carnival glass. Marigold	22.50
Liberty Bell. 5". Tin screw base marked "Robinson & Loeble, Phila., Pa." Amber and milk glass	35.00
Lincoln. "Pure Fruit Flavored Orange Syrup." Tin top	15.00
Log Cabin Syrup	15.00
Lucky Joe. Painted	25.00
Radio	15.00

BANKS, MECHANICAL

Banks which display some type of action when a coin is inserted are known as mechanical banks. The majority of the approximately 325 different known banks were manufactured between 1850 and 1935. The prices listed herein are for unrepaired banks in good condition and will vary upwards or downwards, depending upon the individual condition of the bank. Free reader's service on pricing and selling old mechanical banks is available from Stephen A. Steckbeck, Collector, 200 W. Superior St., Ft. Wayne, Indiana 46802.

*Acrobat	$ 950.00
Afghanistan	830.00
African Native	1500.00
*Always Did 'Spise' a Mule. Darky sitting on bench in front	300.00
*Always Did 'Spise' a Mule. Darky riding mule	300.00
*Artillery. 4-sided block house	240.00
Artillery. 8-sided block house	1000.00
Atlas	900.00
Automatic Savings Bank	900.00
*Bad Accident	500.00
Bamboula Bank	350.00
Bank of Education & Economy	600.00
Bank Teller	6000.00
*Bear. Slot in chest. No lettering	450.00
Bear. Tin	1800.00
*Bear with paws around tree	390.00
*Bill E. Grin. Bust	400.00
*Bird on Roof of Church	800.00
Bonzo. Tin	1000.00
Bowery	7500.00
Bowing Man in Cupola	2500.00
Bowling Alley	10000.00
*Boy on Trapeze	500.00
*Boy robbing bird's nest	750.00
*Boy Scout Camp	900.00
Boy Scout with tray. Tin	750.00
*Boy Stealing Watermelons	600.00
Breadwinner	3000.00
British Lion. Tin	1500.00

Calumet Bank. Tin $125.00

*Buffalo butting	1200.00
*Bull and Bear	3000.00
Bureau. Wood	400.00
Bureau. Wood. Serrill	800.00
Burnett Postman. Tin	600.00
Butting Ram	1600.00
*Cabin	180.00
*Calamity or Football	2500.00
Called Out	5000.00
Calumet Bank. Tin	125.00
*Camera or Kodak	1500.00
*Cannon, U.S. & Spain	900.00
*Cat and Mouse	525.00
Cat jumps for mouse. Springing Cat. Lead	4300.00
Chandlers Bank	350.00
Chandlers Bank. Clock	750.00
*Chief Big Moon	500.00
"Child's Bank." Wood	300.00
*Chimpanzee	950.00
Chinaman in Boat. Lead	6000.00
Chinaman reclining on log. Reclining Chinaman	1200.00
Chinaman with Cue. Tin	1200.00

Goat, Butting $425.00

Clown Bust. English	3000.00
Chocolat Menier. Tin	240.00
Circus	3300.00
*Circus Ticket Collector w-Barrel	900.00
Clever Dick. Tin	1200.00
Clock Registering. Dime	300.00
Clown & Dog. Tin	1800.00
Clown Bank. Tin	200.00
Clown on Bar. Iron and tin	5000.00
*Clown on Globe	600.00
Coin Registering Bank	500.00
Columbian Savings Bank	120.00
*Columbus World's Fair Bank	450.00
Confectionery Store	2400.00
*Cow. Milking or Kicking	1400.00
*Creedmore	200.00
Crescent Cash Register	500.00
Crowing Rooster. Tin	600.00
Cupola Bank	1000.00
Dapper Dan	330.00
*Darktown Battery	500.00
Darky Bust. Tin	300.00
Darky Fisherman. Lead	8000.00
*Dentist	1450.00
Dinah with sleeve	140.00
Dinah with no sleeve. Aluminum	100.00
Ding Dong Bell. Tin	5000.00
Dog Barking. Safe	440.00
Dog Jumping. Wood and tin	3000.00
*Dog, Bull. Standing	300.00
Dog, Bull. Savings Bank	1000.00
*Dog Charges Boy	400.00
*Dog on Oblong Base	330.00
Dog on Turntable	190.00
Dog trees cat	12500.00
*Dog, Trick	290.00
*Dog, Trick. Modern w-solid base	180.00
*Dog with tray	1500.00
Doghouse. Watch Dog Savings. Wood	800.00
Droste's Spaar. *Automaat	400.00
*Eagles and Eaglets	290.00
Electric Safe	400.00
Elephant, Baby. Open at X o'clock. Lead	4500.00
*Elephant. Jumbo on wheels. Small	750.00
*Elephant. Light of Asia	1200.00
*Elephant. Modern	100.00
*Elephant. Man in Howdah	200.00
Elephant and three clowns	475.00
*Elephant with locked howdah	900.00
*Elephant. 3 stars	280.00
*Elephant. Small. On small wheels with tusks	1200.00
Elephant. Made in Canada	800.00
*Elephant. Wiggles	60.00.
English Bulldog. Tin	1500.00
Five-Cent Adding Bank	650.00
Football Bank	1200.00
Football. 1 black player with watermelon.	10000.00
Fortune Horse Race. Tin	2500.00
*Fortune Teller. Building. Automatic Coin Savings Bank	500.00
Fortune Teller. "Drop a coin and I will tell your fortune."	1200.00
Fortune Teller. Safe	440.00
Fowler. Hunter shoots bird	2200.00
Freedman's Bank. Desk	15000.00
"Freedman's Bureau," chest	1500.00
*Frogs. Two	400.00
Frog on Arched Track. Tin	6500.00
Frog on Rock	200.00
Frog on round lattice base	140.00
Frog, or Toad. On stump	240.00
Frog and Serpent. Tin	6000.00
Fun Producing Savings Bank	750.00
*Gem	240.00
Germania Exchange	4300.00
Giant	4800.00
Giant in Tower. English	3000.00
*Girl in Victorian Chair with dog on lap	1950.00
*Girl Skipping Rope	3900.00
"Give Me A Penny."	1200.00
*Goat, Butting	425.00
*Goat, Frog and Old Man	1200.00
Goat, Little Billy	1500.00
Golden Gate Key. Aluminum	200.00
Guessing Bank	1750.00
Guessing Bank. Woman's figure. Pot metal	5250.00
Hall's Excelsior	95.00
Hall's Lilliput	180.00
*Harlequin, Clown & Columbine	10000.00
Harold Lloyd. Tin	1250.00
Hen. Setting	675.00
Hillmann Coin Target Bank	1500.00
*Hindu with Turban	500.00
*Hold the Fort	1000.00
Home Bank	350.00
Home Bank. Lithographed tin. Ejects receipt	160.00
Hoop-La	350.00
*Horse Race. Race Course	1200.00
*Humpty Dumpty	275.00
Ideal Bureau. Tin	500.00
Indian Chief. Aluminum	4000.00

*Indian Shooting Bear	500.00
Initating Bank. First Degree	2200.00
Jack Horner (Weedens.) Tin	5000.00
Japanese Ball Tosser. Tin	5000.00
Jocko, Musical. Tin	1800.00
Joe Socko Novelty	300.00
John Bull's Money Box	3600.00
Jolly Joe Clown Bank. Tin	950.00
*Jolly N	100.00
*Jolly N. Aluminum, English Bust	100.00
*Jolly N. Bust. Fixed eyes	100.00
*Jolly N. Butterfly Tie	100.00
*Jolly N. Moves ears. High hat. Aluminum	175.00
*Jolly N., Shepherd	100.00
*Jolly N., Stevens	100.00
*Jolly N., with Fez. Aluminum	300.00
*Jolly N., with High Hat. Iron	125.00
*Jonah and the Whale	600.00

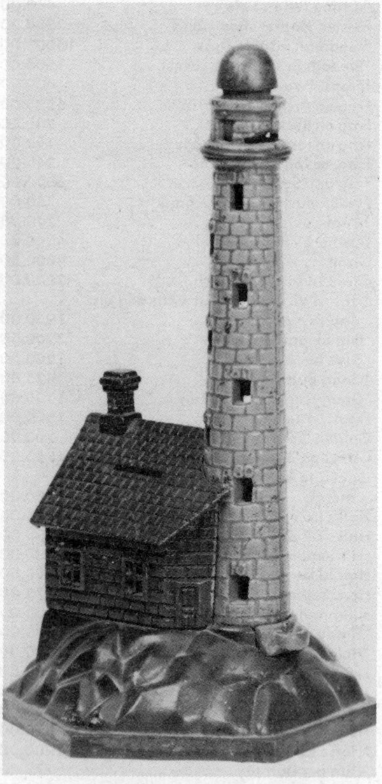

Lighthouse $490.00

Jonah and the Whale. Jonah emerges from mouth	12500.00
*Katzenjammer Kids	2000.00
Kick Inn	440.00
Kiltie Bank	750.00
*Leap Frog	650.00
Liberty Bell	550.00
Lighthouse	490.00
*Lions & Monkeys	300.00
Lion Hunter	1200.00
Little Hi Hat	650.00
*Little Joe	100.00
*Little Mo	700.00
Locomotive Savings Bank	500.00
Lucky Wheel Money Box. Tin	550.00
*Magic	350.00
Magic. Tin	750.00
Magic Safe. Tin	600.00
*Magician	750.00
Mammy and Child	625.00
*Mason and Hod Carrier	690.00
Merry-Go-Round	6000.00
Mickey Mouse. Tin	1800.00
Mikado	6500.00
Minstrel. Tin	200.00
Minstrel. Cross-legged. Tin	480.00
Model Savings Bank.Tin	3500.00
*Monkey and Coconut	600.00
*Monkey and Organ Grinder	200.00
Monkey and Parrot. Tin	200.00
Monkey with Tray. Tin	320.00
Monkey and Tray, Coin in stomach	1300.00
Mosque	330.00
Motor Bank, Trolley	5000.00
*Mule Entering Barn	325.00
Mule Bucking	600.00
*Mule Bucking. Miniature	375.00
Music Bank. Tin	900.00
Musical Savings Bank	1200.00
Musical Savings Bank. Wood House	1200.00
National Bank	700.00
New Bank	340.00
New Bank. Lever in front center	440.00
*North Pole. Flag pops up	4800.00
*Novelty	190.00
Old Woman That Lived in a Shoe	12500.00
*Organ Bank, Cat and Dog	260.00
*Organ Bank, Monkey, Boy & Girl	350.00
Organ Bank with monkey only	275.00
Organ Bank, Tiny. With monkey on top	450.00
*Organ Grinder & Dancing Bear	1200.00
*Owl. Head turns	160.00
Owl with Book. Slot in book	195.00
Owl with Book. Slot in head	300.00
*Paddy and His Pig	450.00
Panorama Bank	1450.00
Pascall Savings Bank. Tin	330.00
Patronize the Blind	1600.00
*Pegleg Beggar	850.00
Pelican. Arab	500.00

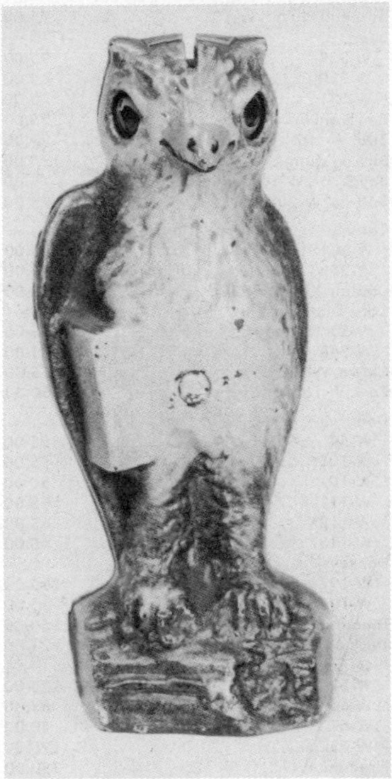

Owl with book. Slot in head . . $300.00

Pelican. Feed the Goose	300.00
Pelican. Mammy	400.00
Pelican. Man Thumbs Nose	350.00
Pelican. Rabbit in Mouth	550.00
*Perfection Registering	2200.00
*Piano. Plays music	1850.00
Picture Gallery	1600.00
*Pig. Bismark	1000.00
Pig in High Chair	300.00
Pistol. Cast Iron	650.00
Pistol. Stamping	300.00
*Pony, Trick	350.00
Popeye Knockout Bank	300.00
Preacher in Pulpit	10000.00
*Presto. Mouse on Roof	4800.00
*Presto. Small building	160.00
Presto. Penny changes to quarter	4500.00
*Professor Pugfrog	1650.00
Pump and Bucket	790.00
Punch and Judy. Iron and tin	1200.00
Punch and Judy. Tin	500.00
*Punch and Judy. Small letters	350.00
*Punch and Judy. Large letters	350.00
Queen Victoria. Bust	4800.00
Rabbit. Standing. Round base	290.00
*Rabbit. Standing. Rectangular base	390.00
Rabbit in Cabbage	250.00
Railroad Ticket Vendor	600.00
Red Riding Hood	7500.00
Regina Musical Bank	1200.00
Rival	6000.00
Robot. Aluminum	1500.00
Roller Skating Rink	4500.00
Rooster	180.00
Royal Trick Elephant Bank. Tin	1500.00
Safe Deposit Bank. Tin elephant	2600.00
Safe. Top springs open. U.S. Bank	850.00
Sailor Face. Tin	600.00
Saluting Sailor. Tin	750.00
Sam Segal's Aim to Save	1800.00
Sambo	560.00
*Santa Claus at Chimney	400.00
Savo Bank. Tin	125.00
Schley. "Admiral Schley Bottling Up Cevera."	3800.00
Schoolmaster (Weedens.) Tin	5000.00
Scotchman. Tin	300.00
Seek Him Frisk	12500.00
Sentry Bank. Tin	690.00
Sentry Bugler. Tin	500.00
*Sewing Machine. American	2000.00
*Shoot the Chute	5000.00
Shoot That Hat Bank	3500.00
Signal Cabin. Tin	375.00
Snap-It	190.00
Speaking Dog	300.00
Squirrel and Tree Stump	800.00
"Stollwerck Bros." Vending. Tin	150.00
"Stollwerck's Victoria Savings." Tin	225.00
*Stump Speaker	490.00
Sweet Thrift Bank. Tin	200.00
*Tabby Bank	390.00
*Tammany	150.00
Tank & Cannon	400.00
Target. Fort and Cannon	4300.00
*Teddy and the Bear	400.00
10-Cent Adding Bank	900.00
Thrifty Animal Bank. Tin	400.00
Thrifty Tom. Tin Jigger Bank	350.00
Tiger. Tin	1200.00
Time is Money	1800.00
Time Lock Savings Bank	1500.00
"Time" Registering. Mechanical Clock	350.00
Tommy	1500.00
Tower Bank. Lehmann. Tin	2500.00
Treasure Chest Music Bank. Pot metal	1200.00
Trick Savings Bank. Wood	160.00
Try Your Weight Scale Bank	1200.00
Turtle	4800.00
20th Century Savings Bank	800.00

Two Ducks in a Pond. Pot metal	600.00
*Uncle Remus	1295.00
U.S. Bank	995.00
*Uncle Sam	495.00
*Uncle Sam. Bust	550.00
*Uncle Tom	100.00
Viennese Soldier	3500.00
Volunteer Bank	220.00
Watch Bank	500.00
Watch Bank. Dime disappears	700.00
Weedens Plantation. Tin	450.00
*William Tell	300.00
William Tell. Cross bow	900.00
Wimbledon	2300.00
Winner Savings Bank. Tin	5500.00
Wireless. Tin	195.00
Woodpecker	1800.00
*World's Fair Bank	450.00
World's Banker. Tin	990.00
*X-Ray Bank. Smyth	800.00
*Zoo	600.00

*Reproduced Item

BANKS-STILL METAL

Banks with no mechanical action are known as Still Banks. They were usually cast of metal in the shapes and forms of animals, buildings, figures, etc. Numbers refer to "Whiting."

Horse Shoe. W-83 ....$125.00

Auto. W-157	$ 375.00
Banks, Buildings	
W-111	55.00
W-307	45.00
W-411	55.00
W-412	35.00
W-442	95.00
Baseball Player. W-10	95.00
Bears	
W-329	95.00
W-330	60.00
W-331	75.00
Ben Franklin. W-313	25.00
Bird. W-107	30.00
Bird on stump. W-209	175.00
Boy Scout. W-14	75.00
Buffalo. W-208*	75.00
Camels	
W-201	125.00
W-202	75.00
Captain Kidd, W-38	325.00
Cats, Seated	
W-53	65.00
W-248*	100.00
Clown. W-29*	75.00
Cow. W-188	150.00
Dogs	
W-54	85.00
W-105*	55.00
W-107	50.00
W-111	95.00
W-112*	65.00
W-113	40.00
Donkeys	
W-197	115.00
W-198	85.00
Dreadnaught. (Battleship) W-363	550.00
Duck. W-323	75.00
Elephants	
W-59	125.00
W-60*	65.00
W-67	40.00
W-75	125.00
Fireman. W-9	250.00
Geese	
W-211	75.00
W-213	300.00
W-214	125.00
Hat, W.W.I. W-167	125.00
Horse, Prancing. W-77	40.00
Horseshoe Good Luck. W-83	125.00
House. W-355	45.00
Lambs	
W-191	450.00
W-192	85.00
Lions	
W-57	65.00
W-89	75.00
W-91	35.00
W-92	45.00
Mail Boxes*	
W-121	35.00
W-123	50.00
W-126	30.00
Mammy. W-17	65.00
Mutt & Jeff. W-13	100.00
Owl. W-204	250.00
Pershing, General. W-312	100.00

Pigs	
W-176*	125.00
W-182	75.00
W-184*	75.00
Rabbits	
W-96*	125.00
W-99	95.00
Radios	
W-137	50.00
W-140	55.00
Rhino. W-252	275.00
Rooster. W-187	85.00
Safe. W-374	50.00
Sailor. W-16	125.00
Seal. W-199	225.00
Sharecropper. W-18	75.00
Sheep. W-191*	65.00
Statue of Liberty. W-269	75.00
Turkey. W-193	65.00
Woman, Two faced. W-44	75.00

*Reproduced Item

BANKS, STILL POTTERY

Die. 2¾" square. Ochre coloring	$32.50

Acorn. "Acorn Stoves." 3". Light brown glaze	$ 32.50
Apple. Red. 3½	27.50
Barrel. Gilt hoops. 4"	25.00
Bear, Sitting. 6"	35.00
Beehive. 4½". Brown mottled slipware	35.00
Bell. 5½". Heavy unglazed red ware	30.00
Black face. With turban. 4½"	60.00
Boy's head. With cap. Painted	27.50
Cash Register. White-yellow glaze	40.00
Cask. "Kentucky Wild Cat-I'm Thirsty." 3¼"	35.00
Cat. White, yellow, on green and white cushion	55.00
Corn. 6"	60.00
Dwarf Head. Brown high glaze	50.00
Elephant, Seated. 3" Slipware	40.00
Frog. 4"	25.00
Globe. 5".Chicago World's Fair	25.00
Gourd. 4"	50.00
Jug. 4". Brown glaze	25.00
Lion, Standing. 6"	30.00
Lion's Head	35.00
Monkey. Mottled yellow, brown	35.00
Pig. Rockingham-type glaze	50.00
Pig in green pocketbook	60.00
Pig. Mottled slipware	50.00
Pig. 5". Gray	30.00
Pig. 10". Pennsylvania red slipware. Early	200.00
Poodle Head. 3¾ x 4½". Staffordshire-type. Black collar-ears. Gold lock	60.00
Ram. Rockingham-type glaze	50.00
Rooster, Standing. 4½"	35.00
Scarecrow. Rockingham-type glaze	75.00
Shoe. High button. 5". Tan glaze	85.00
Tree Stump. 3½x4½"	25.00
Turnip. Marked "Charity."	40.00
Walrus. Rockingham-type glaze	75.00
Watermelon Slice. 4x9½". Hanging-type	60.00

BAROMETERS

A barometer is an instrument for measuring atmospheric pressure which, in turn, aids in the forecasting of weather. For example, low pressure indicates the coming of rain, snow or a storm, while high pressure indicates fair weather. They were popular home accessories in Victorian England and later in America.

Banjo-type	
"John Berringer". Mahogany	$ 350.00
English. Rosewood	300.00
Desk-type. English. 4" diam. Dial. Brass	65.00
Stick-type	
"D. E. Lent, Rochester, N.Y." American	225.00
"Widdenfield & Co., Boston." American	250.00
Wheel-type	
"Air Guide." 18". Walnut. Brass dial. Vertical thermometer	175.00
"Anaroid." 27". Oak. With thermometer	165.00
"F. Aprile, New Market Warranted." 39". Mahogany. Swan neck crest. Hydrometer dial. Fahrenheit thermometer. Silvered dial. C. 1860	350.00

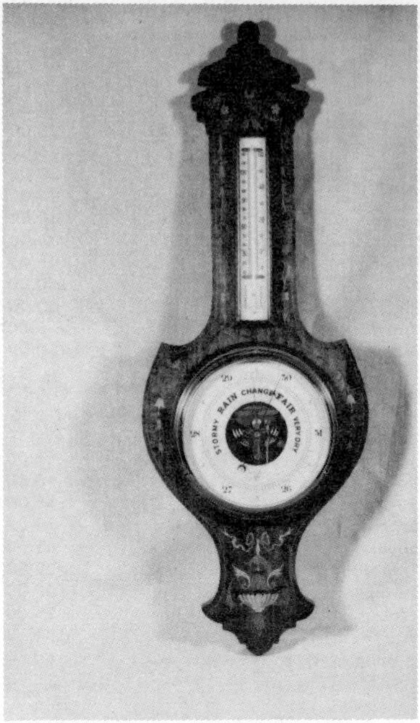

"Short & Mason. London TYCOS #2468." Inlaid mahogany. Fahrenheit and centigrade. 12½x33½" long $1250.00

"G. Bianchi, Salisbury Warranted." 22". Inlaid mahogany. Swan neck crest. Hydrometer, Thermometer and barometer dials. C. 1860 .. 350.00

"Georgian-style". 36". Mahogany. Broken arch crest. Silvered dial. Thermometer. English 650.00

"C. Maspela, Manchester." 47". Inlaid MOP mahogany. Hydrometer dial. Rectangular thermometer. Engraved barometer dial. Spirit level. C. 1850 .... 500.00

BASALT

This type of black vitreous pottery was originally made in ancient times and re-discovered in the latter part of the 18th century by Josiah Wedgwood. It was later produced by other English potters.

Atomizer. 4" high, Including sterling top. Classical decor in white. Wedgwood, England .... $ 125.00

Cup and Saucer. Classical decor in relief. Signed Wedgwood only $195.00

Bowls
- 8x 3½" deep. EPNS rim. Wedgwood, England 125.00
- 8". Figures in relief. Wedgwood .. 395.00
- 9½". Acorn border 225.00

Busts
- Myron. 13" high. Wedgwood. C. 1860 .... 1000.00
- Mercury. 18" high. Wedgwood .. 1000.00
- Paris. 18" high. C. 1800's 1200.00
- Washington. 9" high 195.00

Candlesticks. 12". Pair 250.00

Chalice. 3" deep, beaded pedestal base. Wedgwood 275.00

Coffee Pot. 8½". Engine turned 195.00

Creamers
- 2¼". Glazed interior, molded handle. Wedgwood, England .. 25.00
- 3¾". Drape decor. C. 1800-1820 95.00
- 4½". Classical decor. Wedgwood 150.00

Cups and Saucers
- Classical decor. Wedgwood, England 65.00
- Plain. Wedgwood 175.00

Foo Dog. 3" high. On base 50.00

Inkwell. Wedgwood 175.00

Medallion. 2¼ x 2¾". Wedgwood and Bentley. 750.00

Pitchers

5¼". Helmet-shape. C. 1800	150.00
6½". Relief of Flaxman figures around base with border of leaves and bunches of grapes at top. Wedgwood	195.00
8". Ribbed top, scrolled bulbous center	175.00
Teapot. 4¾x 7½" long. "Widow" finial. Wedgwood	225.00
Inkwell. Wedgwood	85.00
Medallion. 2¼x2¾". Wedgwood and Bentley	500.00

BASKETS

Basketry is a form of textile art in that it is woven. Baskets are often classified as hard textiles.

Baskets were invented when man first required containers to gather, store and transport goods. Thusly, basketry is probably one of the earliest indigenous crafts of all cultures. There are egg baskets, cheese baskets, market baskets and even bed baskets for infants. Baskets were made in a variety of shapes and sizes all to fulfill a specific need. Methods and techniques used in construction. . .coiling, plaiting, wicker-type, rib cage, etc. . .mainly depended on the raw materials available or intended usage.

Enthusiastic collectors of baskets prefer to view basketry more than a craft but as an art form; which it rightfully deserves.

Split hickory. 9x21" diam. Open handles $65.00

Baby cradle with hood. 36" long. Splint ....$	175.00
Cheese. 25" diam., 9" deep	225.00
Clothes basket. 21" diam. Two handles	75.00

Willow. Darning basket. 12" diam $30.00

Egg. 10x13". 12" high including handle. Central Pennsylvania ..	65.00
Fruit. Oval, ½ bushel	35.00
Indian	
Apache. 8x9½"	165.00
California. 3½x7"	35.00
Hupa. 4½x7"	150.00
Maine	
7x11½x16". Splint. Red painted flowers	100.00
11x13x22". Covered. Splint. Painted with stencils of red and yellow circles	150.00
Papago	
10" diam. top. 8" high. Pot-shaped	195.00
12" diam. Drying-type. Two handles	45.00
36" diam. Shallow dish-type. Coiled construction	100.00
Japanese. 7½" diam. Brown and tan finely woven reeds	75.00
Lunch. 5x8". Double handles	35.00
Nantucket	
7" diam. Brass ears	300.00
14" diam. Handled	150.00
Wall-type. 10x29". 3-compartments. Early	250.00

BATTERSEA ENAMELS

Battersea enamel is a generic name for painted enamels on metal.

Stephen T. Janssen first explained this method of transferring prints from engraved copper plates onto enamelled surfaces in the early

1750's at the York House in Battersea, London. In 1756, financial difficulties forced the enterprise to be discontinued. All materials, including the copper plates were sold and subsequently used by other firms. . .mainly in the Staffordshire district.

Small 'gift boxes' of Battersea-type enamels are currently being produced in France and available in fine retail outlets at a fraction of the cost of the earlier examples.

Heart-shaped box. "And tighter the knot, the farther apart." Yellow base $ 500.00

Boxes	
"And tighter the knot, the farther apart." Heart-shaped. Yellow base ....$	500.00
"Angel." 1¾x3"	400.00
"Coaching." Shield-shape. Pink base	500.00
"Esteem the Giver." Yellow with rust colored bird on nest	500.00
"Fishing Scene."	450.00
"Floral". 4" square. Blue and yellow...........................	350.00
"Fox Hunt." 2x4"	500.00
"Garden Scene". 1½x2"	395.00
"Lay Hold on Time While in Your Prime." 1x2", round. Blue base ..	500.00
"Love is Eternal." Blue base......	600.00
"Mother."	400.00
"Pixies." 2x3"	600.00
"Racing and You See the Race." 1½x2½". Robin-egg blue base ..	500.00
"Success to the Fleet." Blue base. Heart-shaped	500.00

BAVARIAN CHINA

Bavaria was an important porcelain production center in Germany, similar to the Staffordshire districts in England. However, very little of the production from this area was imported into the United States before 1870. The term covers the products of several companies operating there.

Fruit plate. 7½". Gold rose decor on black ground. Gold trim. Made in Germany $10.00

Atomizer. 3". Garden scene ......$	32.50
Bowls	
7". White with gold trim. Reticulated sides	35.00
10". Rose decor on white	50.00
Cake Set. Plate 11" diam. Six serving plates. 7½" diam. Fruit decor center. Pierced edges. Gold trim. Set	100.00
Celery. 5" wide, 12" long. Lavender blossoms on white ground. Lustre edge	25.00
Cream and Sugar, Covered. H-P iris decor. Heavy gold trim. Set	50.00
Cup and Saucer. Cream with maroon. Baker's Chocolate. Portrait decor	25.00
Dinner Set. Service for 8, plus 5 serving pieces. Gray leaves on pale gray ground, gold edge. Schwarzenback, Winterling. 45 pieces ..	350.00
Dresser Set. Box. 2 perfume bottles	50.00
Hat Pin Holder	22.50
Marmalade Set. Bowl with underplate and saucer. H-P fruit decor. Artist signed	20.00
Plates	
7½". Portrait of seated maiden,	

cupid and arrows. Rose sprays and gold embossed areas 20.00

8¼". Fruit and flowers in multicolors cover most of the surface 50.00

8½". Portraits. George and Martha Washington. J&C. Louise Bavaria. Pair................. 60.00

9½". Scalloped. Pierced border. Multicolored floral design. Gold trim. Schumann, Arzberg 75.00

13". Dark green shading to white ground, pink, yellow, white mums, gold trim. Crown mark Bavarian 95.00

Shakers

Salt and Pepper. 3" high. White "Swirl" with gold trim. Pair...... 25.00

Sugar. 4½" high. H-P pink and blue florals 25.00

Sugar. 4" high. White ground with pink roses. Gold trim 18.50

Syrup with Underplate. Covered. Pastel. Gold trim. Set 35.00

Tea Set. Teapot, sugar and creamer. Panels divided by narrow black vertical panels. Pink roses in panels. Set 85.00

Tray, Pin. Blue forget-me-nots in center and on sides. Much gold. Pierced border. Schumann 12.50

Vase. 6½". Floral decor. Gold trim.. 25.00

BEER CANS (AMERICAN)

Beer cans are one of the newest collectibles. and one of the fastest growing hobbies. After a little over ten years of interest, it is reported that there are over a half million collectors in the United States alone. How or why this 'fad' began will remain as much a mystery as the reason for any collection.

Beer in cans is a relatively new phenomenon. Before prohibition, beer was stored and shipped in kegs and dispensed in returnable bottles. When the Prohibition Act was repealed in 1933, only 700 of the 1700 breweries resumed operation. The law of 'supply and demand' created the need for an inexpensive container that would permit beer to be stored longer and shipped safely. Cans were the answer.

The first patent for a suitable lined can was issued to the American Can Company on September 25, 1934 for their "Keglined" process. Gottried Kruger Brewing Co., Newark, New Jersey was the first brewery to use the can. Pabst was the first major company to join the canned beer movement.

In 1935 Continental Can Co. introduced the cone-top beer can. Schlitz was the first brewery to use this type of can. The next major change in beer can design was the aluminum pop-top in 1962.

Beer can collectors not only seek the early examples for historical reasons; but also cans made after 1962 for their unique names, far away countries or limited availability.

The following abbreviations have been used to conserve space: CT-cone type, FT-flat top, PT-pull top, ML-malt liquor.

"Olde Frothingslosh." 12 oz. Pittsburgh Brewing Co., Pittsburgh, Pa. Yellow. PT $3.00

7 oz.

Coors. Gold Band. Golden, CO. (FT) ....$ 2.00

National Bohemian. Baltimore, MD. (FT)........................ 12.00

Rolling Rock, Spring label. Latrobe, PA. (PT) 2.00

8 oz.

Colt 45 M.L. National, 4 cities. (PT) 1.00

Miller. 3 cities. (PT) 2.00

Schlitz M.L. (1963) Paper label. Milwaukee, WI (FT) 5.00

10 oz.

Budweiser. Anheuser-Busch. 4 cities. (PT) 4.00

Colt 45 M.L. National. 4 cities. (PT) 2.00

Tuborg. Carling. Baltimore, MD. (PT) 8.00

12 oz.

ABC. Los Angeles, CA. (FT) 25.00

American. Baltimore, MD. (CT) .. 50.00

Ballantine Ale. (1935) Newark, NJ. (FT) 15.00

"Schell's." 12 oz. August Schell Brewing Co., New Ulm, Mn. Black. PT $3.00

Bavarian's Select. Associated. 3 cities. (PT) 6.00
Black Label. Carling. Cleveland, OH. (PT) 2.00
Blatz Pilsener. (1945) Milwaukee, WI. (FT) 7.00
Blatz Select Lager. Milwaukee, WI. (CT) 18.00
Busch Bavarian. Anheuser-Busch. 4 cities. (FT) 4.00
Carling's Red Cap Ale. B.C. of America. Cleveland, OH. (CT) .. 50.00
Cook's. Associated. 3 cities. (PT) .. 3.00
Dixie. New Orleans, LA. (PT) .... .50
Duke. Duquesne. Pittsburgh, PA. (PT) 3.00
Encore. (1970) Schlitz. 8 cities. (PT) 4.00
Falstaff. 8 cities. (PT) 1.00
Fort Pitt. Smithton, PA. (PT) 8.00
Genesee. Rochester, NY. (FT) 5.00
Iron City, 1973 Steelers, Offensive. Pittsburgh. Pittsburgh, PA. (PT) 5.00
Iron City 1974. Barnegat Light House, New Jersey Series. Pittsburgh. Pittsburgh, PA. (PT). Each 2.00
Iron City. 1974 Sport Series. Pittsburgh. Pittsburgh, PA. (PT) Each 3.00
Lucky Lager. Falstaff. 6 cities. (PT) . 1.00
Metz, Red label. Omaha, NB. (FT) 12.00
National Bohemian Bock. 4 cities. (PT) 10.00
Old Export. Cumberland, Cumberland, MD. (FT) 5.00
Old Frothingslosh. Pittsburgh. Pittsburgh, PA. (PT)
- Blue 8.00
- Brown, Yellow 3.00
- Orange 10.00
- Purple, white, silver 2.00

Old German Style. Renner. Youngstown, OH. (CT) 50.00
Old Milwaukee. (1962) Schlitz. Milwaukee, WI. (PT) 4.00
Ortlieb's. 1976 Bicentennial Series. Philadelphia, PA. (PT) Each 5.00
Pearl. 1975 Texas Football Series. (PT) Each 5.00
Pfeiffer. 1960. Outdoor Series. Detroit, MI. (FT) Each 30.00
Rhinelander Export. Rhinelander, WI. (CT) 18.00
Rolling Rock. Latrobe, PA (PT) 2.00
Schaefer. New York, NY. (FT) 15.00
Schmidt Draft-Wildlife Series. Associated. St. Paul, MN. (PT) Each 10.00
Schmidt's Drafting-Bicentennial Series. 2 cities. (PT) Each 2.00
Sterling. Gold. Evansville, IN. (FT) 12.00
Sunshine Premium. Reading, PA. (CT) 40.00
Valley Forge. Norristown, PA. (FT) 15.00
Wiedemann. Slogan Series. Newport, KY. (FT) Each 6.00
Ye Tavern. Lafayette. Lafayette, IN. (CT) 60.00

16 oz.

Ballantine Ale. Newark, NJ (PT) 6.00
Champagne Velvet. Associated. 3 cities. (PT) 5.00
Heidelberg. Carling. Tacoma, WA. (PT) 8.00
Krueger. New York, NY. (CT) 125.00
Narragansett. 1966. Cranston, RI. (PT) 7.00
Ortlieb's. 1976 Bicentennial. Philadelphia, PA. (PT) Each...... 2.00
Rheingold. 2 cities. (PT) 1.50
Skol. Atlas. Chicago, IL. (FT) 30.00

32 oz.

Ballentine's Ale. Newark, NJ. (CT) 60.00
English Lad Ale. Prima. Chicago, IL (CT) 75.00
Pabst Blue Ribbon. Milwaukee, WI. (CT) 12.00
Schmidt's Light. Philadelphia, PA. (CT) 50.00

Gallons

Ballantine Draught Beer. Newark, NJ 30.00

Koch's Draft. Dunkirk, NY 15.00
National Draft. Baltimore, MD .. 60.00
102 Draught. Maier. Los Angeles, CA 100.00
Sterling Draught Ale. Associated. Evansville, IN. 80.00

BELLEEK

Belleek is a thin, ivory colored, almost iridescent-type porcelain made in County Fermanagh, Ireland from 1857. The company continued production until World War I. . .discontinued operation for a period of time. . .resumed operation. . .continuing today. The Shamrock pattern may be the most familiar, but other patterns were made.
Several different identifying marks were used including the Harp and Hound (1865-1880) and Harp, Hound and Castle (1863-1891). Some items are marked Belleek Co., Fermanagh. After 1891 the word Ireland or Eire was added. Serious collectors can identify the circas by these marks.
A Belleek-type porcelain was made in America by several firms. The first was Ott and Brewer Co., Trenton, New Jersey in 1884. They were succeeded by Cook Pottery Co. in 1894. Another early manufacturer was Willets. Other American firms and their years of establishment were The Ceramic Art Co. (1889), American Art China Works (1892), Columbian Art Co. (1893) and Lenox, Inc. (1904). See "Lenox."
There is an Irish saying. . .if a newly married couple receive a gift of Belleek, their marriage will be blessed with lasting happiness.

Baskets
- 6½". Fermanagh ....$ 150.00
- 10½". Fermanagh 275.00

Bowls
- 3½". Coral. 2nd BM 195.00
- 4½". Shamrock. 2nd BM 65.00
- 5½". Shell. 1st BM 125.00

Coffee Pot. Limpet. 3rd BM 250.00

Creamers
- Lotus. 3rd BM 37.50
- Rathmore. 1st BM 75.00
- Shamrock. 2nd BM 50.00
- Shell. 2nd BM 75.00

Creamers and Sugars
- Limpet. 3" high. 3rd BM 100.00
- Neptune. 2nd BM 150.00
- Shamrock. 2nd BM 100.00
- Shell. 3rd BM 125.00
- Souvenir of "Cork International Expo 1903." 2nd BM 125.00

Honey Pot. 4¾x5x6¼" to top of finial. "Shamrock." 2 BM $265.00

Cups and Saucers
- Artichoke. Farmer's. 1st BM 125.00
- Erne. 2nd BM 75.00
- Handpainted. Floral decor. Willets 75.00
- Limpet. Demi. 3rd BM 50.00
- Neptune. 2nd BM 75.00
- Shamrock. 2nd BM 45.00
- Shell. 2nd BM 85.00
- Waffle. Ott and Brewer 65.00

Hat Pin Holder. 5". Swirled flowers, silver overlay. Willets 100.00
Jug. 9½". Aberdeen. 2nd BM 650.00
Juice Set. Pitcher. Four matching tumblers. Raised enameled fruit, flowers. Willets 350.00

Mugs
- 5" high. Landscape scene. Three handles. C.A.C. 200.00
- 5½" high. Portrait of cavalier. Artist signed. Willets 150.00
- 5½" high. Vintage decor. Gold trim. Willets 100.00
- 7½" high. Berries and branches. Black and gold trim 125.00

Mush Set. Bowl and creamer. 1st BM 150.00
Mustard, Covered. Shamrock. 2nd BM 60.00

Pitchers
- 5" high. Ivy. Handled. 1st BM 125.00
- 6". H-P berries, flowers, and leaves. C.A.C. 135.00
- 6" high. Neptune. 3rd BM 150.00
- 14½" high. Tankard. H-P vintage motif. Willets 450.00

Plates
6". Grasses. 1st BM 50.00
6¼". Shamrock border. 2nd BM . . 55.00
7½". Wild flowers with gold trim. Willets 75.00
10½". Cake. Shamrock. 2nd BM. . 125.00
Platters
9". Shamrock. 2nd BM 95.00
12". All white. 1st BM 150.00
Salts, Individual
Coral. 2nd BM 45.00
Shamrock. 2nd BM 25.00
Sugar
Neptune. 2nd BM 85.00
Shamrock. Covered. 2nd BM 75.00
Shamrock. Open. 2nd BM 50.00
Teapots
Basketweave. Shamrock. 3rd BM 150.00
Cone. 2nd BM 195.00
Echinus. 2nd BM 325.00
Grasses. 1st BM 325.00
Hexagon. 2nd BM. 175.00
Neptune. 2nd BM 250.00
Tridacna. 2nd BM 225.00
Tea Sets
Coral. Teapot, covered sugar, creamer. 4 each. Cups, saucers, and plates, 2nd BM. 16 pcs 650.00
Neptune. Teapot, creamer, sugar, 2 cups and saucers. 2nd BM. 8 pcs. 350.00
Shamrock. 7 pieces. 2nd BM 300.00
Tridacna. 7 pieces. 2nd BM 325.00
Tray. 12½x15½". Echinus. 1st BM. . 275.00
Trays, Bread
Limpet. 3rd BM 75.00
Neptune. 3rd BM 85.00
Tridacna. 1st BM 65.00
Tub. 4½" high. Shamrock. 3rd BM . . 75.00
Vases
3". Open water lily. Willets 100.00
4¾". Flying fish. 1st BM 300.00
6". Aberdeen. 3rd BM 125.00
6¾". Lily Spill. 2nd BM 250.00
7". Dolphin. 2nd BM. 475.00
7". Shamrock. 3rd BM 100.00
8". Owls. 3rd BM 150.00
10½". H-P. Portraits of Arabian equestrians. Artist signed. Willets. 395.00
13". Hollyhocks on pale green to lavender background. Willets 225.00
15". Decorated with two parrots. Willets 250.00
16". Mermaid holding child. Willets 400.00

BELLS

Bells have played an important part in the life of man since ancient times. He has had many uses for them. . .they have called him to worship, tolled at his death, struck the time, summoned him to school, warned; him of the approach of enemies, invited him to dinner, bade him to assemble. . .and the lowly alarm clock has urged him to arise and be about his daily work.

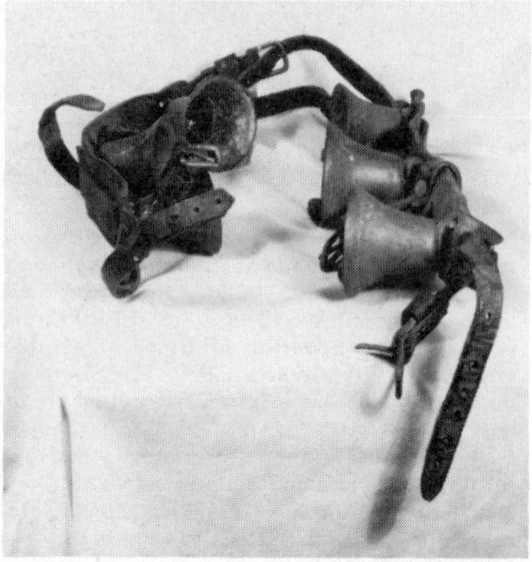

Horse Bells. 6-3" long brass bells on leather strap. All original $125.00

Church
22" high. Bronze. "Troy N.Y. 1871." Complete . . . . $ 1500.00
22" high. Iron. "American Bell Foundry, Northville, Michigan, U.S.A." 500.00
Conestoga Wagon. 5 brass half bells on arched frame. C. 1850-1865 . . 150.00
Cow
Brass 40.00
*Iron 25.00
"Cutter." Nickel, with iron strap. Set of three 85.00
Desk. 3½" high. Brass 12.50
Desk-type. Hotel. Nickelplated. Marble base 30.00
Donkey
Brass. 10 bells on leather strap . . 165.00
Brass. 22 bells on leather strap. Refinished 250.00
Elephant. Brass 50.00
Farm
Iron. 14" across bottom. #2 size. Hanger. All original 200.00
20" with yoke and bracket. C. B. Bell Co., Hillboro, Ohio. Dated 1866 . . . . 275.00
Figurals
Dutch Girl. 3½" high. Brass. Knitting sock. Embossed design 35.00
Soldier, Roman. 3½" high. Brass 35.00

Sleigh Bells. 30-1" diam. brass bells on leather strap $275.00

Turtle. Tortoise top. Iron legs and head. Wind-up type, bell rings when head or tail is pressed. Germany	75.00
Woman, Standing. 3½" high. Balloon skirt. Embossed decor. Sterling. Vermeil work	150.00
Goose. Double clapper. Original strap	30.00
Hame. Swedish. Set of 5	125.00
Liberty. Bronze. 4½" high, marked "Colonial 1832-1925"	75.00
Locomotive	
12". Activated by air. Complete . .	395.00
17". Brass. "Great Northern." Complete	650.00
17". "Union Pacific." Vertical mounting from front. Complete . .	750.00
School	
Brass. 6" high	35.00
Brass. 8" high. Turned handle	45.00
Brass. 11½" high	75.00
Ship, U.S.N. Brass with side mount. Dated 1898. Eagle finial. Brunswick, Ga.	250.00
Sleigh	
16 bells. Brass. 1⅛" diam. Brass lug in back to fit "S" lock hook. Unstrung	100.00
17 bells. Burnished brass. Restrung on old strap	175.00
25 bells. Graduated sizes. Brass cleaned. Good leather strap	250.00
27 bells. Brass, on strap. Small . .	175.00
30 bells. Iron. 1¼" diam.	125.00
32 bells. Nickel plated brass. Graduated	175.00
Tea. 4½" high. Sterling 950	35.00
Temple, Japanese. Lizard handles. Engraved with dragons and flowers. 5¼" high	75.00
Trolley Car. Iron. 6" diam. Complete	150.00

*Reproduced Item

BELLS, GLASS

Although bells made of metal are more practical, glass bells were produced in England and in the United States in the early 1800's. They can be found in clear or colored glass, large or small. Some were made for use on the tea tray or dining table, while others were purely decorative, an example of the glass blower's talent and the glass manufacturer's product.

Glass bells are still being manufactured. Be careful of the reproductions which are coming in from Europe.

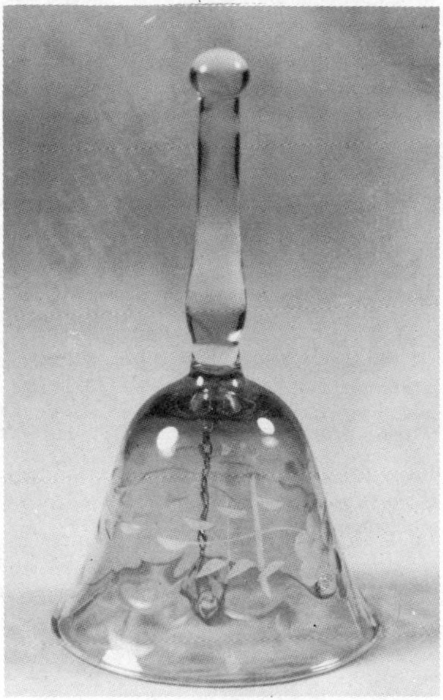

Amber. 5". Clear handle. Etched floral decor $22.50

Bristol. 11½" high . . . .$	100.00
Bristol. Wedding bell. 13¼". Red barrel in swirl pattern. Clear swirl handle. 4-ball finial. With clapper.	125.00
Columbian Exposition 1893. Swirled handle. Metal clapper . .	75.00

Cranberry. 11" high. Clear applied handle. English 175.00
Custard. Souvenir "Seaside Pavillion Corpus Christi." 35.00
Milk Glass. 5½" high. Chain links form handle. Metal clapper...... 65.00
Ruby. 12" high. Clear handle...... 50.00
Venetian. 4¼" high. Latticinio 150.00

BENNINGTON POTTERY

J. NORTON
BENNINGTON
VT.

The two potteries located in Bennington, Vermont were Norton Pottery and Fenton Pottery; owned and operated independently.
When Captain John Norton began making pottery in 1793, he offered only crocks and jugs. As the firm progressed; parian, stoneware, colored porcelains and much more were produced. They were marked with several different names; J.&E. Norton, E. & L.P. Norton, L. Norton Co. and others. The pottery existed as a family business until 1894.
In 1845 Christopher Fenton entered the business. Being enterprising, he increased production and introduced additional lines including the Rockingham glaze. (It is incorrect to associate this mottled dark brown glaze only with Bennington. Rockingham. . .named from a similar type produced in England was only a limited line of Fenton's products. Its popularity demanded other large potteries in the United States to duplicate the effect.) By 1847, Fenton was on his own. Assisted by associates he produced a wide array of English imitated ceramics including the animal forms, until 1858. Fenton also used several different marks, Fenton's Works, United States Pottery Co., U.S.P. and others.
NOTE: "Rebecca At The Well" teapot, first made by Samuel Alcott & Co. of England and then by E. & W. Bennet of Baltimore was not made at Bennington.

NORTON

Beer Bottle. 8" high. Joe Norton ..$ 35.00
Chamber Pot. Grey stoneware. Julius Norton 100.00
Cream Pot. Covered. 1 qt. Blue cobalt floral. J&E. Norton 125.00
Crocks
- 4-gal. Yellow-brown with "4" impressed with cobalt blue. L. Norton & Co.................... 280.00
- 5-gal. Blue cobalt on incised flower. J. Norton 150.00

Inkstand. 6". J. Norton & Co. 160.00
Jar. Covered. 1-gal. Preserve-type. Blue cobalt 200.00
Jugs
- 2-gal. Blue cobalt maple leaf impressed. J. & E. Norton 150.00
- 2-gal. Two handled.Blue cobalt rabbit. J. Norton & Co........... 650.00
- 4-gal. Blue cobalt floral decor. E. Norton & Co.................. 100.00

Pitcher. 11". Hexagonal. Brown. Birds and flowers. Norton & Fenton 250.00

Bennington-type Cuspidor. 3¾x7¼" diam. $75.00

FENTON

Bottle. Cologne. 8". Parian. Grape and Leaf ....$ 95.00
Bowls
- 8½". Tulip.................... 75.00
- 10½". Mixing. Flint enamel 95.00

Box, Jewelry. 5½". Parian 50.00
*Creamer, Cow. 4". Open. Upright stand. Flint enamel 185.00
Cuspidors
- 6". Lady's. Flint enamel. Mottled brown. Tan glaze. C. 1849 ...... 150.00
- 9½" base, 7½" top, 4½" diam. .. 195.00

Door Knobs
- Single. Rockingham glaze 20.00
- Double. Complete. Flint enamel .. 125.00

Drawer Pulls. Rockingham glaze. Each 10.00
Ewers
- 6". Parian. Blue and white 110.00
- 10½". Parian. Grape and Leaf .. 150.00
- 11". Parian. Twisted handle. Grape and Leaf............... 180.00

Figurines
- Autumn. 10". Standing woman with grapes. Parian 400.00

Eagle. 4½". Parian 150.00
Greyhound. Lying. 2" long. Black graniteware 130.00
Little Red Riding Hood. Parian. C. 1854............ 350.00
Poodle ;Holding Basket. 8". Rockingham glaze 300.00
Praying Girl. 5¼". Parian 280.00
Spaniel, Lying. 3" long. White graniteware 125.00
Flask, Pocket. Pint. Rockingham glaze 75.00
Flower Pot. 8¼". Solid brown slip .. 65.00
Frames
5½" square. Flint enamel 55.00
8¼" oval. Rockingham glaze 75.00
18" square. Rockingham glaze .. 180.00
Inkwell. Greyhound, Lying. 3½" long. Gold graniteware 150.00
Lamp Base. 13" high. Pedestal-type. Yellow ware 525.00
Pitchers
10". Tulip and Sunflower. Blue and white porcelain 300.00
*10½". Dead Game. Hound handle. Rockingham glaze 350.00
14". Virginia & Paul. Blue and white porcelain 435.00
19". Pond Lily. Blue and white porcelain 400.00
*Plate. 8¼".Rockingham glaze 75.00
Syrup Jug. U.S.P. 395.00
Tobacco Jar. 10". Covered. Marked 129B Bennington 350.00
Tobys
Bank. 5¼". Yellow ware. Glazed. Flat bottom 575.00
Bottle. 12". Coachman 125.00
Jug. Duke of Wellington. C. 1850 395.00
Pitcher. 5¾". Boot handle. Flat bottom. Rockingham glaze 350.00
Snuff Jar. 3⅞". Flint enamel. Flat bottom 680.00

BENNINGTON-TYPE

Bed Pan .... $ 125.00
Bowls
7½" 65.00
10"............ 85.00
Churn, Butter 250.00
*Creamer. Cow. Covered.......... 150.00
Cup, Custard 25.00
Flasks
Book. "Departed Spirits" 195.00
Tavern Scene............ 150.00
Foot Warmer 135.00
Mugs
Frog in bottom 150.00
Parrots in relief 75.00
Pitchers
10". Castle scene 250.00
11". Frog in bottom 250.00
Plate. 9". Pie............ 65.00
Pudding Mold 65.00
Vase. 7". Pond Lily 150.00
Wash Board 250.00

*Reproduced Item

BISQUE

Bisque or biscuit china is the name applied to wares that have been fired once and are not glazed. Some were decorated with colors. The body is soft and porous. (Hint: To clean bisque, do not submerge in water. Use a sponge or cotton balls that has been dampened with an ammonia based detergent solution.)
Bisque figurines and busts were popular during the Victorian era. They were made by numerous potteries in the United States and abroad. Bisque wares are being produced today in Japan.

Figurine. "Two Tots Sharing a Pot." 4" high. Hamk............$35.00

Box. Egg-shaped. Footed. Windmill scene in relief ....$ 45.00
Bust. 5½" high. Girl with blonde hair, blue hat and blouse, gold trim 75.00
Figurines
Boy. 6¼" high. Dressed in nightgown, holding doll. "Germany." 50.00
Boy. 9¾" high. Cream trousers, jacket and hat. Leaning against tree. "Heubach." 100.00

Cherub on Sleigh. Appr. 8½" long. Pink, white. Gold trim 65.00
Farmer. 12¾" high. With scythe. "Heubach." 165.00
Hunter. 8" high. With gun and dog 65.00
Madonna. 9" high. Undecorated .. 45.00
Tennis Players. 15" high. Decorated. Pair 150.00
Match Holders
  Dutch girl holding pitcher. 3½" .. 35.00
  Girl holding doll. 5½" 45.00
  "Happy Hooligan." 8" 55.00
*Piano Babies. Also see "Dolls"
  5½" long. Boy reclining 125.00
  6" long. Girl lying on stomach. Germany 150.00
  8" long. Holding toy doll. Decorated 125.00
  13" high. Girl sitting 275.00
Shoes
  4½" long. Blue flower with yellow center. Lavender frill 50.00
  6¼" long. Two white love birds at top. Three blue birds on side 65.00
Toby, Hanging. 3x3" 40.00
Vase. 5". Blossoms and leaves 40.00

*Reproduced Item

BLOWN THREE MOLD GLASS

Although the method of producing blown mold glass objects was known to the Ancients, it was not practiced in America until the early 1800's. The glass maker placed a quantity of molten glass on the tip of a hollow rod or tube and literally blew air into it to form the article. Free blown glass did not use a mold. Blown molded glass used a pre-designed mold that usually consisted of two, three or more hinged parts. The term Blown Three Mold (BTM) indicates a three part mold; but the key word to all blown glass is 'blown' and not 'three'. The impressed decorations on blown mold glass are usually reversed, i.e. what is raised or convexed on the outside will be concave on the inside. This is one of its identifying factors. New methods for producing glass items continued to be developed. By 1850 American made glasswares were in relatively common usage which necessitated greater production by mechanical means. Small glass producers either abandoned the trade or became large industrial factories. Two important firms were Boston and Sandwich and the New England Glass Co.
The numbers used refer to "American Glass" by George L. and Helen McKearin.

Bird Drinking Font. 7" high. Clear. Fitted with amethyst blown glass ball top. Free Blown ....$ 250.00

GIII-21. Bowl, 1⅞" deepx5" diam. Clear rayed base $225.00

GII-16. Decanter. 7⅜" high. Golden amber. Pint. $550.00

Bottles
  Blacking
    227-7. Deep olive-amber. 4½". Without label 35.00
    228-13. Brilliant olive-amber. 4⅛" Eight panels 55.00
  Castor. 6¼". Clear. Conical-shape. Matching stopper. Teardrop-shaped air trap 50.00

Gemel. 10⅛". Clear with applied threading 150.00
Toilet Water
GI-7. Purple blue 250.00
GI-7, type 5. Amethyst. 6⅝". With original stopper. Ribbed .. 250.00
GI-7, type 5. Medium blue. 6". Twelve panel. B & S Co. 175.00
GI-7, type 5. Sapphire blue. 5½". Ribbed 225.00
Vinegar
GI-3, type 1. Deep cobalt blue. Original stopper 250.00
Clear. Twelve sided design with ring around neck. Minus stopper. B & S Co. 175.00

Bowls
GII-21. Clear. 5" 125.00
GII-21. Clear. 5¾" 125.00
GII-21. Clear. 7" 150.00
GIII-21. Clear. 5" diam., 1⅞" deep. Rayed base 225.00
GIII-24. Clear. 6" 100.00

Castor Sets
GI-13. Clear. 5-bottle. Israel Trask pewter holder 250.00
"Diamond Sunburst." 4-bottle. Red painted metal stand 325.00

Celery Vase. 10½". Eight rib pillar molded. "Riverboat." 100.00

Compote. 7x8¾" diam. Opaque white. Blue scalloped rims and knob ring. Attributed to Pgh. Glass Co. 750.00

Cruet, Stoppered. 6¼". Cobalt blue. Hollow blown applied handle. Free Blown and pattern molded .. 225.00

Decanters
G-29. Quart. Original stopper .. 175.00
GII-16. Pint. Golden amber 550.00
GII-18. Pint. Clear. Original stopper 275.00
GII-18. Quart. Clear. Polished flange 175.00
GIII-6. ½ pint. Clear. Stoppered .. 150.00
GIII-15. Quart. Clear. Three
GIII-15. Quart. Clear. Three rigaree rings 275.00
GIII-20. Pint. Clear. Original hollow stopper 150.00
GIII-24. Quart. Clear 250.00
GIV-6. Quart. Clear 175.00
GV-9. Quart. Clear. Applied lip .. 175.00
Miniature. Clear. No stopper 365.00
Miniature. Clear. With penny stopper. Free blown 75.00
Quart. Clear. "Drapery." With stopper 175.00
Quart. Clear. Nailsea-type. Applied lip. Pittsburgh 600.00

Decanter Set. (4) with stoppers. Brandy, Wine, Gin, Rum. Set 1500.00

GI-7, Type 5. Toilet Water Bottle. 6⅝" high. Amethyst. Original stopper. Ribbed $250.00

Flips
GII-18. 4¾" 180.00
GII-18. 5¾" 150.00

Hats
GIII-4. Clear 150.00
GIII-7. Clear 150.00
GIII-23. Clear. Rayed base 225.00
GIII-24. Cobalt blue 350.00
GIII-25. Clear. Concentric base .. 225.00

Inkwells
GII-18. Olive-amber 160.00
GII-29. Olive-green 150.00

Pitchers
Miniature. GIII-12. Clear 250.00
1¾". Light green. Applied handle. New York State. C. 1830. Free Blown 225.00
3⅝". Brilliant cobalt blue. Eighteen vertical ribs. Applied handle. Free Blown and pattern molded 250.00
4⅝". GI-29. Violet cobalt. Applied handle 275.00
8". Clear. Graceful form with

wide lip. Applied handle. Quadruple crimp at bottom. Free Blown 125.00

Salt Cellars

GII-21. Cobalt blue 450.00

GIII-3. Clear 135.00

GIII-20. Clear 135.00

GIII-26. Brilliant cobalt blue 325.00

String Holder. 4¼ x 4⅜" diam. Clear with applied cobalt blue rim and ornament at top. Attributed to B & S Co. 225.00

Whiskey Tasters

8-panel. 3½". Aqua green. Rough pontil 50.00

8-panel. 3½". Sapphire blue. Rough pontil 50.00

12-rib. Medium blue. Vertical ribbing, swirled to top. Slightly flared rim 50.00

"Sunburst." Clear 275.00

Vase. 10". Light green with opaque white loopings. South Jersey. Free Blown 250.00

BOHEMIAN GLASS

The once independent country of Bohemia, now a part of Czechoslovakia, produced a variety of fine glassware. . .etched, cut overlay and colored. Their glasswares were first imported into America in the early 1820's and continue today. Perhaps Bohemia is best known for their 'flashed' glass that was not only produced in the familiar ruby color, but also in amber, green, blue and black. Common patterns include "Deer and Pine Tree", "Deer and Castle" and "Vintage." Most of the Bohemian glass encountered in today's market is of the 1875-1900 period.

A Bohemian-type glass was also made in England, Switzerland and Germany.

*Bell. 4½" high. "Deer and Castle." Ruby. Clear glass handle. Clear clapper on chain..............$ 85.00

Bottles

5". Perfume. "Vintage." Ruby. Original stopper 50.00

6¼". Cologne. "Deer and Castle." Green. Original stopper 85.00

8". Cologne. Panels of forget-me-nots and other etched flowers. Amber 100.00

Bowls

Finger. "Vintage." Ruby 50.00

3½x9" diam. "Deer and Pine Tree." Amber. Three legged........ 75.00

Butter, Covered. "Deer and Castle." Ruby 150.00

Castor Set. 14½" high. Ruby and clear frosted. Three bottles. Stoppered. Sheffield-type holder 175.00

Celery. "Deer and Castle." Ruby. C. 1875 .... 75.00

Chalice. 10" high. Enameled overlay. Amber................ 150.00

Compotes

7" high. Open. "Deer and Castle." Ruby 75.00

9" high. Covered. "Vintage." Ruby 35.00

10" high. Covered. "Deer and Pine Tree." Ruby 150.00

15" high. Covered. "Deer and Pine Tree." Ruby 175.00

Cordial. "Vintage." Ruby 20.00

Cordial Sets

Decanter and 4 cordials. "Deer and Castle." Ruby 200.00

Decanter, Tray, 4 cordials. "Lily of the Valley." Amber 300.00

Decanters. 11¼" high. "Deer and Castle." Ruby with clear stoppers. Pair $135.00

Cruet. 6" high. "Deer and Pine Tree." Ruby. Clear handle 85.00

Cuspidor, Ladies'. "Deer and Castle." Ruby 75.00

Decanters

10" high. "Vintage." Ruby 50.00

12½" high. "Vintage." Ruby 75.00

15" high. "Deer and Castle." Ruby. Stoppered. C. 1850 ...... 150.00

Door Knobs. Ruby. Set 75.00

Goblet. "Vintage." Ruby. Knob stem 75.00

Lamp. 12" high. Cobalt overlay 175.00

Pitcher, Water. "Vintage." Ruby.... 150.00

Plate. 8¾". "Deer and Castle." Ruby 60.00

Salt. "Vintage." Ruby. Three ribbed. Scroll feet. Gold trim 20.00

Salt and Pepper Shakers. "Deer and

Castle." Ruby Ornate silverplated frame. Set ... 100.00
Sugar, Covered. Etched hunting scene. Amber ... 150.00
Tumble-Up. "Vintage." Ruby ... 95.00
Tumblers
  Juice. "Bird and Castle." Ruby ... 30.00
  Water
  "Deer and Pine Tree." Green ... 40.00
  "Flowers and Birds." Amber ... 45.00
  "Vintage." Ruby ... 35.00
  "Vintage." Ruby. Footed ... 50.00
Urn. Covered. 14" high. "Deer and Pine Tree." Ruby ... 150.00
Vases
  5". "Castle and Deer." Ruby ... 75.00
  5¼". "Wildlife." Ruby ... 100.00
  9½". "Deer and Castle." Ruby. Tapered. Gourd-shaped ... 125.00
  10¼". "Castle and Bird." Ruby. Cone-shaped ... 125.00
  12¼". "Flowers and Birds." Ruby ... 120.00
  12½". "Castle and Deer." Ruby ... 150.00
  13". Amethyst to clear with heavy gold overlay ... 250.00
  13½". Green, enameled grapes, gold leaves. Fluted top. Pedestal base ... 125.00
  19½". "Deer and Castle." Ruby ... 175.00
Wine. "Vintage." Ruby ... 30.00
Wine Set. "Deer and Castle." Ruby. Decanter and six glasses ... 300.00

*Reproduced Item

BONE

Items carved from dried animal bones are desirable collector's items. Caution: Some bone items are being misrepresented as ivory on today's market.

Snuff box. 2¼" diam. Convex glass top. Brass bezel ... $25.00

Apple Corer. 4". Early ... $ 25.00
Back Scratcher. Chinese. Late ... 25.00
Clothes Pin. Early ... 15.00
Knives and Forks. 6 each. In lined wooden case. Set ... 150.00
Letter Opener. Carved figure at top. ... 25.00
Napkin Rings
  Ornate ... 15.00
  Plain ... 10.00
Posey Holder. Hand carved. Oriental. Late 18th century ... 100.00
Scoop. Flour. Early ... 30.00
Sled. 6" long. Leather lacing ... 30.00
Spoons
  5¼" long ... 15.00
  8" long ... 20.00

BOOKENDS

Bookends are props placed at the end of a row of books to keep them upright. They have and are made of every conceivable shape, size, form and material imaginable. Very popular in the early 1900's; those of Art Nouveau and Art Deco designs are highly collectible and command high prices.

Mahogany with brass bases. Carved jade inserts. 6" high. Pair ... $150.00

Brass
  Art Nouveau decor. 27". Expansion-type ... $ 75.00
  Dog. Marble base. Pair ... 100.00
  Owl. Expandable. Pair ... 75.00
Bronze
  Buffalo. 5x5". Pair ... 195.00
  Geisha Girl. 4½". Pair ... 150.00
  Lily Pad with Frogs. Pair ... 150.00
  Napoleon Bust. Armour. Artist signed ... 75.00
  Oriental figurine. On green marble base. Pair ... 185.00
  Scottie Dog. Signed Edith Parsons. Pair ... 225.00
  Shepherd. German. 5" high. C. 1900-1920. Pair ... 50.00
Cast Iron
  Elephant. Pair ... 50.00
  Lincoln Cabin. 4". Pair ... 100.00

Pirate. 7" high. Painted light green. Pair 50.00
Ship, Pirate. Painted. Pair 50.00
Jade. Foo Dog. 3x5". Ebony bases. Pair 850.00
Plaster of Paris, Bronzed. Female. Art Nouveau. Pair 100.00
Porcelain. Male and female figures. 5½"high. Japan. C. 1930. Pair .. 40.00
Pottery. Lion. 5x7x10". Ohio Pottery. Late 19th century. Pair........ 250.00
Rose Quartz. Birds on stepped brass bases. Hand-carved. Pair........ 200.00
Soapstone. Urn and flowers. Pair .. 65.00
Teakwood. Elephant head, 10" high. Ivory trim. Pair 100.00
Wood, Petrified. 5½x8". Cut and polished bases. Twelve pounds. Pair 75.00

BOOKS, FIRST EDITIONS

Jermey Collier said, ". . .books are a guide in youth and an entertainment for age." Collecting books can be a very satisfying experience. Some collectors limit their collections to first editions. A first edition of any book can be readily identified by a small mark on the lower right corner of the back cover. Early books were marked with a black circle. In recent years a small depression or blind stamp is used.

In pricing used books, the 'condition' is of utmost importance. Dust jackets are a valuable part, rebound copies bring less than original bindings, autographed copies command two to four times the average price.

The following list of first editions is limited and of more recent publications. For a more complete guide to buying and selling books, consult "3rd Value Guide to Old Books." This book lists alphabetically over 6,000 books by author with a concise description. Available from: E. G. Warman Publishing, Inc., 540 Morgantown Road, Uniontown, PA 15401.

Auchincloss, Louis. "The Winthrop Covenant." Boston, 1976. First trade edition. Damaged jacket. Mint........$ 7.50
Baldwin, Faith. "Take What You Want." New York. 1970. Slightly chipped jacket. Very fine........ 10.00
Baldwin, James & Margaret Mead. "A Rap On Race." Philadelphia, 1971. Dust jacket. Fine 10.00
Barta, Alvin. "Timetable of Civilizations." New York, 1958. Very fine 10.00
Burroughs, Edgar Rice. "Tarzan and the Foreign Legion." Tarzana, 1947. Chipped jacket. Fine 25.00
Capote, Truman. "In Cold Blood." New York, 1965. Dust jacket. Mint 35.00
Carroll, Lewis. "Feeding The Mind." London, 1907. Gray flexible boards and cloth. Mint........ 50.00
Cheever, John. "The Brigadier and the Golf Widow." New York, 1964. Soiled jacket. Fine 10.00
Cheever, John. "The Housebreaker of Shady Hill and Other Stories. New York, 1958. Near fine jacket. Fine 35.00
Cheever, John. "The World of Apples." New York, 1973. Dust jacket. Fine 15.00
Costain, Thomas B. "The Moneyman." Garden City, 1947. Cloth. Near fine 15.00
Ferber, Edna. "Giant." Garden City, 1952. Scuffed 10.00
Gardner, John W. "No Easy Victories." New York, 1968. Damaged jacket 5.00
Gardner, Leonard. "Fat City." New York, 1969. Dust jacket. Very fine 20.00
Harrington, Alan. "The Immortalist." New York, 1969. Dust jacket. Very fine 15.00
Harte, Bret. "Poems." Boston, 1871. Green cloth. Very good 35.00
Hersey, John. "The Marmot Drive." New York, 1953. Dust jacket. Very fine 20.00
Higgins, Jack. "The Last Place God Made." New York, 1971. Dust jacket. Very fine 10.00
Huxley, Aldous. "Brave New World Revisited." New York, 1958. Slightly worn. Chipped jacket. Very fine 10.00
Kimbrough, Emily. "Water, Water, Everywhere." Drawings by Vasiliu. New York, 1956. Very fine 20.00
Longfellow, Henry Wadsworth. "The Divine Tragedy." Boston, 1871. Original cloth. Small type edition, with Bayard Christy bookplate. Near fine 25.00
Mailer, Norman. "Of A Fire On The Moon." Boston, 1970. Dust jacket. Mint 15.00
Markey, Gene. "Literary Lights, A Book of Caricatures." New York, 1923. Damaged jacket. Near fine 35.00
Marks, Peter. "Collector's Choice." New York, 1972. Dust jacket. Fine 10.00
Michener, James A. "The Drifters." New York, 1971. Dust jacket. Mint 15.00
Miller, Arthur. "After The Fall." New York, 1964. First trade edition. Very fine 15.00

Mitford, Jessica. "The Trial of Dr. Spock." New York, 1969. Dust jacket. Very fine 5.00
Morely, Christopher. "The Powder of Sympathy." Garden City, 1923. Cloth-backed boards. Bookplates. Very good 15.00
Nash, Ogden. "The Private Dining Room." Boston, 1953. Worn jacket. Very fine 20.00
Nathan, Robert. "But Gently Day." New York, 1943. Green cloth. Very fine 15.00
Nin, Anais. "A Spy In The House Of Love." New York, 1954. First American edition. Dust jacket. Near fine 10.00
O'Hara, John. "The Ewings." New York, 1973. Dust jacket. Mint 10.00
Ruark, Robert. "Something Of Value." Garden City, 1955. Very good 5.00
Sandburg, Carl. "Home Front Memo." New York, 1943. Fine .. 10.00
Saroyan, William. "My Name Is Aram." New York, 1940. Chipped jacket. Fine 25.00
Saroyan, William. "Not Dying." New York, 1963. Dust jacket. Very fine 25.00
Slaughter, Frank G. "The Stubborn Heart." Garden City, 1950. Very fine 15.00
Stone, Irving. "Love Is Eternal." Garden City, 1954. Fine........... 15.00
Tarkington, Booth. "Mary's Neck." Garden City, 1932. Fine 12.00
Tully, Jim. "Biddy Brogan's Boy." New York. 1942. With Cecil B. DeMille's bookplate. Very fine .. 20.00
Updike, John. "A Month of Sundays." New York, 1975. Dust jacket. Mint 12.00
Updike, John. "On The Farm." New York, 1965. Dust jacket. Very fine 35.00
Uris, Leon. "Exodus." Garden City, 1958. Very good 12.50
Vidal, Gore. "Myron." New York, 1974. Dust jacket. Near mint 12.50
Watson, John B. "The Ways of Behaviorism." New York, 1928. Very good 25.00
Wells, H.G. "The War of the Worlds." New York, 1898. First American edition. Cloth slightly faded. Fine 100.00
Whittier, John Greenleaf. "The Vision of Echard and Other Poems." Boston, 1878. Original cloth. Gilt top. Very good........ 25.00
Wilner, Herberf. "Dovisch In The Wilderness and Other Stories." Indianapolis, 1968. Dust jacket. Mint 15.00
Wouk, Herman. "Marjorie Morningstar." Garden City, 1955. Near fine 15.00
Wouk, Herman. "Youngblood Hawke." Garden City, 1962. Worn jacket. Fine 10.00

BOOT JACKS

Various types of boot jacks were made to facilitate the removal of boots, the useful footwear of the past and fashionable today. Some were constructed of wood while others were made of metals such as brass or iron. Two of the popular designs were "Beetle" and "Naughty Nellie."

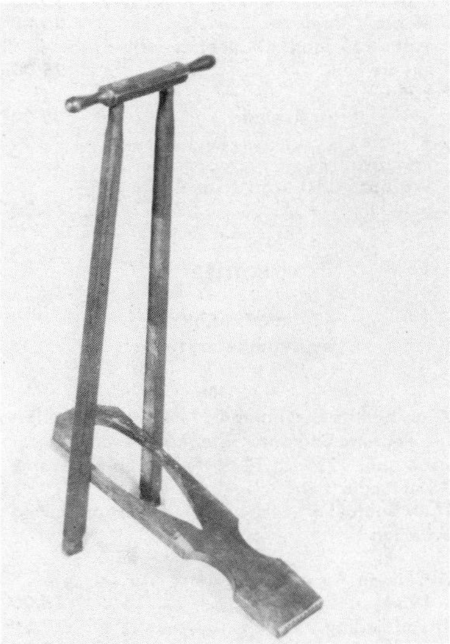

Wooden. Stand up-type. 19½" long, 28½" high. Portable $50.00

Brass
- Beetle. 10" ....$ 85.00
- Naughty Nellie............... 85.00

Cast Iron
- Advertising
  - Downs & Co. 13". Center design 30.00
  - "Try It." 25.00
  - "Use Musselman's Boot Jack Plug." 35.00
- *Beetle. 11½" 50.00
- Bowed-type. 7". "C. Hull, Bir-

mingham" on back, and "Regd. Boot Jack." 25.00
Buggy Wrench. Pittsburgh Novelty Works 50.00
Cap Pistol. 8½" double barrel. Legend. "American Bull Dog Boot Jack" 65.00
Double. Ornate. Pat. 1869 ...... 50.00
Horseshoe 25.00
Mechanical. Carpet covered. Movable jaws to grip boot. Pat. 1850 .... 50.00
*Naughty Nellie 50.00
Shoe sole. 15". With maple wood. Pat. 1859 .... 35.00

Wooden
Advertising-type. 13" long. "Fye & Co., The popular shoe for Men, Zanesville, Ohio." 25.00
Cow Horns.................. 40.00
Maple. 7" long 25.00
Pine. 25" long. Oval ends with square nails 25.00

Portable
2½x5". Brass riveted 35.00
8". Pine 40.00
Primitive. 16" 25.00
Walnut. Cast iron frame. Carpeted top 45.00

*Reproduced Item

BOTTLES

APOTHECARY

(See "Apothecary Items")

AVON

Avon had its beginning in 1886 as the California Perfume Company. The name Avon was not used until 1929. In 1939 the company became Avon Products, Inc.
Their figural bottles are of interest to specialized collectors.

American Beauty Fragrance Jar, 1934 ....$ 35.00
*Avon Calling, 1969 .... 12.50
Avon Classic, 1969 .... 7.50
Bath Urn. Milk glass, 1973 .... 5.00
*Bay Rum Jug, 1962 .... 12.50
Boots
Gold top, 1966 .... 3.50
Silver top, 1965 .... 7.50
Bud Vase, 1965 .... 7.50
*Bud Vase, 1968 .... 8.00
Bullet, 1965 .... 10.00
Cable Car, 1974 .... 7.50
Candlestick, Silver, 1966 .... 12.00
*Captain's Choice, 1964 .... 10.00
*Casey's Lantern, Amber or red, 1966 .... 15.00
Christmas Ornaments

Golf Car. Green $25.00

*Balls, Red or silver, 1967 ...... 6.00
Bell, 1968 .... 3.50
*Sparkler, 1968 .... 12.50
*Tree, Red, green or silver, 1968 .. 5.00
Crystal Glory, 1962 .... 12.50
Demi Cup, Gold top, 1968 .... 12.50
*Dolphin, 1968 .... 7.50
*Dutch Girl, 1973.............. 4.50
*Eiffel Tower, 1970 .... 5.00
Eight Ball, 1973 .... 2.00
Fan Rocker, 1962 .... 5.00
First Edition, 1967 .... 7.50
Freddy the Frog, 1969 .... 4.00
*Futura, 1969 .... 15.00
*Gavel, 1967 .... 15.00
Gold Cadillac, 1969 .... 7.50
Indian Head Penny, 1972 .... 3.50
King Pin, 1969 .... 2.50
*Mallard, 1967 .... 10.00
*Ming Cat, 1971 .... 6.50
*Opening Play, 1968 .... 15.00
Orchard Blossom, 1941 .... 60.00
Peanuts Mug, 1969 .... 6.50
*Pipe Dream, 1967 .... 17.50
Precious Owl, 1972 .... 5.00
Quaintance, Boxed, 1948 .... 50.00
Snoopy and Dog House, 1969...... 4.50
Splash Down, 1970 .... 3.50
Stein, Silver, 1965 .... 10.00
*Sterling Six Car, 1968 .... 6.50
*Straight Eight Car, 1969 .... 5.00
Strawberries and Cream, 1970 .... 10.00
Swinger Golf Bag, 1969 .... 5.00
To A Wild Rose, 1950 .... 12.50
Town Pump, 1960 .... 7.50
*Twenty Paces, Blue box. Pair, 1967 100.00
Volkswagon, Black, 1970 .... 7.50
*Weather Vane, 1969 .... 6.00
Miscellaneous:
Books
1967. Avon Beauty Book 3.00
1967. Cosmetics by Avon 3.50
1971. Color Perfect 1.00

*Discontinued Item

BARBER

These bottles were used to hold and dispense men's toilet preparations; such as hair tonics and shaving lotions. The town barber bought his supplies in bulk and would refill the shelf bottles as necessary for convenience. He knew what each unlabeled bottle contained by its color. Therefore, most barber bottles came in sets of two or three.

Barber bottles were made in almost every conceivable style-of-the-day glass . . .spatter, opalescent, crystal, milk glass, etc. Corklined pewter tops or "squirts" were furnished with the bottles. Porcelain bottles usually had matching "squirts."

Before World War I, most of these bottles were imported from European glass makers. The majority of the American bottles were made in Glassboro, New Jersey.

There are reproductions; primarily in the Swirl pattern, Thumbprint, Hobnail, Opalescent-type and others.

"Hobnail" Opalescent. 8¼" high. Cranberry. Silvered cork stopper $135.00

Bohemian. 8½". Ruby. Enamel floral decor . . . . $ 65.00

Blown
- Amber. DQ 75.00
- Amethyst. Enamel decor 100.00
- Blue. Sapphire. Thumbprint 100.00
- Blue. Cobalt. Enamel decor 125.00
- Clear. Paneled 50.00
- Green. Emerald. DQ 75.00
- Green. Olive. Enamel decor 65.00

Bristol. 9½". Black enamel decor . . 45.00
Camphor. "Witch Hazel" 75.00
Carnival. Marigold 75.00
Clambroth. 7". "Witch Hazel" 50.00
Cranberry. ITP. Pair 175.00
Crystal. Sterling-topped cork with pull ring 45.00

Cut Glass
- Pewter top. 5" 35.00
- Sterling top 75.00

End-of-Day Glass. Amber-white . . 65.00
Frosted glass. Pottery dispensers. "Water" & "Witch Hazel." Pair . . 65.00

*Hobnail
- Amber 85.00
- Cobalt 100.00
- Cranberry 75.00
- Vaseline 85.00

Mary Gregory
- Amethyst. Girl 185.00
- Cobalt. Boy playing tennis 185.00

*Milk Glass
- Blue. 10". Enameled decor. Late . . 35.00
- Green. 11". Handpainted 85.00
- White. Handpainted 75.00

*Opalescent
- Stripes 85.00
- Swirl 85.00

Porcelain. Handpainted blue birds. Square base 55.00

Satin Glass
- 10¼". Cranberry with white looping. Pewter stopper 225.00
- 10½". DQ, MOP. One pink. Other pale blue. Original pewter stoppers. Pair 800.00

Spanish Lace. 8½". Cranberry 85.00
Sterling. Cone-shaped, 10". 2" base 150.00
Wedgwood. Tri-color. Four cameos of classical scenes 750.00

*Reproduced Item

BEER

Beer was bottled in the United States as early as 1860. Perhaps the earliest beer containers were hand thrown pottery, later blown glass and eventually mass produced machine made.

Bock. Quart. Stoneware . . . .$ 65.00
Carnival-type. 16 oz. 20.00
Coors. Miniature 7.50
Ginger Beer. Stoneware. C. 1915 . . 20.00
Home Brew. Pint. Amber 2.50

Embossed "Blatz Milwaukee", 12 oz. Clear $7.50

Home Brew. Quart. Light green	10.00
Milk Glass. 16 oz.	15.00
Miller's High Life. 12 oz. C. 1935	7.50
Schlitz. 7 oz. Ruby red	15.00
Tennessee Brewing Co. 12 oz. Paper label	7.50

BITTERS

The bottles originally contained various concoctions of herbs which were mixed with alcohol and sold as tonics from about 1860 to 1900. "Old timers" have stated that many ardent W.C.T.U. members, in the early days of the Prohibition Movement, returned home exhausted after fighting "demon rum" at the local meeting house. They regained their strength and stability by taking a liberal dose of a favorite bitters tonic which, unknown to them, had an alcohol content of 75% to 80%.

African Stomach Bitters. Amber. Cylindrical, ¾-quart . . . . $	30.00
Allen's, William. Congress Bitters. Green. Watson's 4	295.00

Pottery. "Mein flussiges Kapital" (My liquid Capital) Germany. C. 1920's $30.00

Angelica Bitter Tonic. Jos. Triner, Chicago. Amber	50.00
Angostora Bark. Amber. ½ pint	50.00
Atwood's Jaundice Bitters. Aqua. 12-sided. 3½"	15.00
Atwood's Jaundice Bitters. Aqua. 6"	5.00
Augauer Bitters. Light green. Original label. 8"	75.00
Baker's Orange Grove Bitters. Amber. Square. Rope corners. ¾-quart	125.00
Barry's Tricopherous. O.P.	40.00
Bell's Cocktail Bitters. Amber. Lady's legs. Pint	250.00
Big Bill Best. Amber. ¾-quart	85.00
Bismarck. Bitters, W.H. Miller, N.Y., U.S.A. ½ pint	50.00
Black Bear	125.00
Brown's Castilia Bitters. Amber. 10"	75.00
Brown's Celebrated Indian Herb Bitters. Amber. Watson's 57. Figural Indian Queen	375.00
Burdock's Blood Bitters. Clear. 8½"	25.00
Burdock's Blood Bitters. Aqua. 8½"	40.00
Caldwell's Herb Bitters. Amber. Triangular	175.00
Clarke's Vegetable Sherry Wine Bitters. Aqua. Pontil, 8"	75.00

Claw Bitters. Amber. 4¾″	35.00
Climax Bitters. Amber. 9½″	75.00
DeWitt's Stomach Bitters. Amber	40.00
Dr. Flint's Quaker Bitters, Providence, R.I. Aqua. 9½″	50.00
Dr. Harter's Wild Cherry Bitters. Amber. Filled	35.00
Dr. Henley's Wild Grape Root Bitters. Cylindrical. Aqua, "IXL" in oval. 12″	60.00
*Dr. J. Hostetter's Stomach Bitters. Square. Amber, 9″	15.00
Dr. Langley's Root & Herb Bitters. Aqua	45.00
Dr. Loew's Celebrated Stomach Bitters. Green. 9½″	175.00
Dr. Petzold's. Light amber. 6¾″	95.00
Dr. C. W. Roback's Stomach Bitters. Dark brown	100.00
Dr. Vonhoph's Curaco Bitters. Dark reddish amber	75.00
Doyle's Hops Bitters. Cabin-shape 1872 on roof. Amber. 9¼″	35.00
Drake's Plantation. Cabin-shape. 5-logs. Light amber. ¾-quart	175.00
Drake's Plantation. Cabin-shape. 6-logs. Amber	60.00
Drake's Plantation. Cabin-shape. 6-logs. Olive green	100.00
Electric Bitters. Square with depressed panels. H.E. Bucklew & Co., Chicago, Ill. Amber	50.00
English Female Bitters. Clear. 8½″	60.00
Fish Bitters, The. Amber. ¾-quart. Watson's 125	150.00
Greeley's Bourbon Bitters. Amber. 9½″	150.00
Hart's Star Bitters. Aqua. 9¼″	85.00
H.P. Herb Wild Cherry Bitters. Log cabin-shape. Rope corners. Amber. ¾-quart. Watson's 148	125.00
Higby, J.T. Tonic Bitters. Golden amber	35.00
Holtzermann's Stomach Bitters. Amber. Watson's 172	195.00
Kelly's Old Cabin Bitters. Amber. Watson's 199	350.00
Lash's Kidney & Liver Bitters. Amber. 9½″	25.00
Leak Kidney & Liver Bitters. Amber.	65.00
Malt Bitters Co., Boston, Mass	25.00
Mills Bitters. Lady's leg. Amber	65.00
National Bitters. Figural ear of corn. Amber. Watson's 236	295.00
Old Homestead Cabin Bitters. Amber, 9½″	150.00
Old Sachem, Barrel. Amber. Watson's 244	200.00
*Perrine's Apple Ginger Bitters. Log cabin-shape. Rope corners. Amber. ¾-quart	75.00
Peruvian Bitters. Amber	60.00
Petzold's Genuine German Bitters. Amber. Watson's 256	125.00
Prickley Ash Bitters. Square. Beveled corners. ¾-quart	60.00
Professor Geo. J. Byrne, New York. Lady's leg neck. 12″	55.00
Ramsey's Trinidad Bitters. Dark olive. 8¼″	75.00
Rex Bitters Co., Chicago. Clear. 10¼″	35.00
Richardson's. S.O. Bitters. Aqua	50.00
Romaine's Crimean Bitters. Amber. Watson's 282	195.00
Sarsparilla & Tomato Bitters. F.F. Brown, Boston. Aqua. Pint	60.00
*Suffolk Bitters. Yellow pig. Watson's 332. Scarce	750.00
Tippecanoe Bitters. Amber	85.00
Travellers Bitters. Amber	65.00
Ulmar Mt. Ash Bitters. Aqua. 7″	100.00
*Warner's Safe Kidney & Liver Cure. Picture of safe on front. "Rochester, N.Y." below. Dark amber. 9½″	75.00
Wheeler's Tonic Sherry Wine Bitters, with label. Aqua. Watson's 518	350.00
White's Stomach Bitters	50.00
Whitewell's Temperance Bitters. Aqua. 7″	85.00
Yerba Buena Bitters. Coffin-shaped. Amber	85.00

*Reproduced Item

COLOGNE

The cologne bottles listed are mainly early American pressed glass (unless noted) made prior to 1850 at the Boston and Sandwich Glass Co. and in the Pittsburgh, Pa. area.

Amethyst	
4¾″. Twelve-panel. McKearin 243-4	$ 175.00
6⅞″. Bulbous. Twelve panel	275.00
11″. Twelve panel	250.00
Amethyst, Bright. 5″. Applied salamander and white enamel and gold leaf decor. French	175.00
Amethyst, Light. 5″. Twelve panel	90.00
Aqua. 10½″. Hexagonal with "Gothic Arch."	110.00
Clear. 5⅛″. Hexagonal. "Loop" with gold presentation decoration. C. 1840-50	150.00
Cobalt Blue	
"Violin"	225.00
4¼″. Bulbous. Ten panel	175.00
7⅜″. Bulbous. Twelve panel	175.00
7½″. Twelve panel	245.00
Cobalt Blue, Brilliant. 5⅞″. Hexagonal-shape. Fine gold decoration. French	150.00

Cobalt blue. "Violin" $225.00

Cobalt Blue, Deep
- 4¼". Replaced clear stopper 75.00
- 5¾" Eighteen panels. Replaced stopper. BTM 150.00

Emerald Green
- "Violin" 275.00
- 4¼". Waisted. B & S 275.00
- 4¾". Twelve panel. McKearin 243-4 .... 165.00
- 4⅞". Twelve panel. B & S 185.00
- 5". Bulbous. Twelve panel 245.00
- 5⅝". Twelve panel 185.00

Fiery Opalescent. 5½". Decor of large rose and other flowers. Original stopper 100.00

FIGURALS

Bottles which are shaped in any recognizable form; such as animals, objects, people, etc., are known as figural bottles.

Antelope. Horn-shaped, 15". Twisted ....$ 35.00
Baby, Crying. Bust. French 35.00
Bear, Black. 11". Kummel-type 50.00
Belt and Mail, Gloved hand. 8½", 3" diam. at base. Clear. Patd. 1877. E.R. Durkee & Co., N.Y. 20.00

Knockwurst. 6½" long. Pottery. Natural coloring $25.00

Cat. Porcelain. Painted 20.00
Clowns
- 3". Porcelain, Decorated. "Perfume." 17.50
- 8½". Bisque. German 35.00

Crane. 14½". Clear glass 25.00
Cucumber. 6". Pottery. Green and tan glaze 30.00
Dog, Standing on hind legs. 13". Clear glass 20.00
Guitar. 16". Amber, with cork 20.00
Hand with revolver. Depose's. French 65.00
Hands. French 65.00
Hessian Soldier. 7¼". Clear glass . 40.00
Japanese Gods, Seven. Painted 25.00
Leprechaun 15.00
Madonna. 12". Aqua 20.00
Mail Box, U.S. Clear glass 110.00
Man, Black. 11½". Dressed in high hat and tails, playing banjo. Ceramic 65.00
Man, German. 7½". Impressed Star and Crown 50.00
Monkey. Wrapped around green bottle 15.00
Moses, Poland. Water. Quart. Green 30.00
Mr. Pickwick. 9". Clear 10.00
Nude. Plump, draped. 13". Partially frosted 50.00
Pig. 4". "Something in a Hog and He Won't Squeal." 50.00
Potato. 5" long. Screw top. Embossed "World's Fair 1893." 35.00
Pretzel. 6". Ceramic. Natural coloring 35.00

Queen Elizabeth. Bust 30.00
Saddle. 9". Amber. Applied ring. Open pontil 125.00
Sailor Boy. 13". Clear 15.00
Santa Claus. Red Satin Glass. 1973 100.00
Scotsman. 17" 40.00
Shoe. 5" long. "Perfume." Crystal .. 40.00
Skeleton in Shroud with 5 skull cups. "Poison." Mdk. Shofu 50.00
Taylor's Castle 12.50
Totem Pole. Porcelain. German 45.00
Victorian Lady. Milk glass. 11" 25.00
*Violin. 9". Blue 45.00
Washington, Bust of Jacquin. Cobalt. Miniature 20.00
*Washington, George. 9½". Clear glass 10.00

*Reproduced Item

FOOD

Milk bottles, ½ pint. Garner Dairy Co. $1.00

Heinz Ketchup. 7". Urn-shaped. Blob top ....$ 10.00
Jumbos
- Bank-type. Figural. Castle Products, Newark 15.00
- Peanut Butter. 1 lb. Embossed elephant 10.00

Lee and Perrins. 11½". Glass stopper 7.50
Milk
- Baby Face. Embossed. Quart 7.50
- Baby Face. Painted. Quart 5.00
- Cream-top. Embossed. Quart 4.00
- Embossed. Pint. Quart. Each 1.00
- Tin closure. Pint. Quart. Each 6.50

Pepper sauce.
- 7½". Cathedral Arches. Aqua .. 35.00
- 8". E.R.D. & Co. Patent Feb. '77. Green 25.00

Pickles.
- 7½". Cathedral Arches. Square. Aqua 65.00
- 10½". Goofus. Embossed floral. Ground mouth 20.00
- 11". Cathedral Arches. Square. Rolled lip. Aqua 125.00

FRUIT JARS

Fruit jars or canning jars made of glass for preserving foods, had their beginning in France. In 1829, Thomas W. Dyott was promoting his glass jars in Philadelphia. It was his advertising that brought about the name "fruit jars."

John Landis Mason was responsible for the screw-type glass jar which was patented on November 30, 1958. This date on a jar does not indicate its age, but refers to the patent date. Thousands of fruit jars have been manufactured with various closures, colors and embossings.

Acme. ½ gallon. Shield with stars, stripes. Clear ....$ 12.00
Anchor Hocking Mason. Various sizes 2.00- 5.00
Atlas E-Z Seal. Quart. Amber 25.00
Atlas Good Luck. Embossed clover front. gallon, ½ gallon, quart and pint. Amber. Each 10.00-15.00
Atlas Mason Patent. Nov. 30th, 1858. ½ gallon. Zinc lid. Green .. 10.00
Atlas Mason Patent. Pint. Aqua 3.00
Automatic Sealer, 1895. Quart. Aqua. Glass lid with bail 20.00
Ball Ideal. ½ pint. Clear 10.00
Ball Ideal. Quart. Clear 1.00
Ball Improved. Quart. Aqua 6.50
Ball Perfect Mason. ½ gallon. Amber 30.00
Ball Sure Seal. Quart. Blue 1.00
Banner. Pat'd. February 9, 1864. Aqua 35.00
Beaver. Quart. Glass lid. Zinc ring. Made in Canada 35.00
Best. Quart. Clear 25.00
Best Wide Mouth. Quart. Clear. Glass insert 5.00
Bold. Quart. Aqua 15.00
Boyd Perfect Mason. Pint. Green .. 5.00
Brown, Geo. D. Pint. Clear 60.00
Canton Domestic. Quart. Clear 50.00
Clarke Fruit Jar Co. 1886. Quart. Aqua. Glass lid with bail 50.00

Drey Square Mason. Embossed. Zinc lid. ½ pint $2.00

Cohansey Glass Mfg. Co. Pint, Aqua. Pat'd. Feb. 12, 1868	40.00
Crystal. Quart. Clear	25.00
Double Safety. Quart. Clear	1.00
Easy Co. Pint. Clear	15.00
Economy. Quart. Amethyst	10.00
Electric. World in center. Quart. Glass lid. Wire clamp	75.00
Electroglass Mason. Quart. Amber	7.50
Empire. Stippled Cross. Quart	10.00
Eureka. Quart. Aqua. Pat. Dec. 27, 1864	65.00
Family. Quart. Clear	15.00
Genuine Mason. In flag. Pint. Aqua	8.00
Glenshaw Mason. Screw band. Gallon. Quart or pint. Each	7.50-10.00
Globe. Quart. Amber	50.00
Hazel. Quart. Aqua	20.00
Improved Crown. Pint. Aqua	7.50
Keystone. In circle. Mason. Quart. Aqua	10.00
Kline. Quart. Aqua	20.00
Kline. Oct. 27, 1863. ½ gallon. Stoppered	100.00
Lamb Mason. Quart. Amber	10.00
Lightning	
Amber. ½ gallon. Quart	35.00
Aqua. Quart	10.00
Mason. Patd. Nov. 30, 1858. Quart. Aqua	5.00
Masons Cross. Pat. Nov. 30, 1858. Quart. Light green	15.00
Masons Improved. ½ gallon. Aqua	3.00
Masons Star. Quart. Pint. Clear	1.00
Millville. Atmospheric. Quart. Aqua. Glass lid. Metal clamp. Patd. June 18, 1861	45.00
Millville Improved. Quart. Aqua	25.00
New Gem. Quart. Clear	8.00
Presto. ½ pint. Clear	6.00
Quick Seal. Dated. Quart. Clear	5.00
Royal. Quart. Clear	7.50
Standard Mason. In flag. Quart. Aqua	5.00
Sun. Pint. Aqua	40.00
The Hero. Quart. Aqua	15.00
The Ideal. Quart. Aqua	25.00
Victory. On milk glass lid. Quart. Clear	7.00
Whitall-Tatum. Pint. O.P.	30.00

INK

Early ink bottles were made of ceramics and glass, designed to be 'tip proof.' Most were imported. They were first used in America in the early 1800's.

3" high. Aqua. Round. Applied lip and collar. C. 1880 ....$8.50

Billing & Co. 2". Aqua. Embossed "B" ....$	15.00

Carter's.
- 2¼". Label. Aqua 5.00
- 3⅝". "Ma and Pa.". Pair 75.00
- Pint. Cathedral. Embossed. Cobalt 45.00
- 32 oz. Machine made. Label. Cobalt 15.00

Farley's. 2x2". Deep olive green. Open pontil. C. 1850 200.00

Hover, Philadelphia. 2⅛x2¼". Umbrella-shape. 8 panels. Aqua 200.00

Improved Process Blue Co.
- 2½". Cone. Aqua 6.50
- 2½". Label. Clear 3.00
- 2½". Round. Cobalt 5.00
- 2½". Square. Cobalt 5.00

Sanfords. 1¾x2¼". #6. Clear 3.00

Stanford. 2x2". Machine made 7.50

Travel. Turtle. 2x4". Aqua 75.00

Travel. Umbrella. No pontil. Blue 25.00

Underwood's. 9¾". Pinch spout. Cobalt 40.00

MEDICINES

Home remedies were first made in England in the early 1700's. In America not all medicines were patented. The first patent was issued in 1796.

The popular "medicine man" of the 1880's was a traveling showman. He traveled from town to town in a horse-drawn wagon, shouting the virtues of his tonics, which the patient soon learned were mostly alcoholic. With the passing of the Food and Drug Act in 1907, another era faded.

Astol Hair Coloring Restorer. 5½". Cobalt $ 45.00

Ayer's Cherry Pectoral. 7¼". Aqua 20.00

Ayer's Pills. 2½". Square. Clear 2.50

Bayer Aspirin. 2½". Clear. Machine made 2.50

Berry Bros., N.Y. 11¼". Aqua 5.00

Castor Oil, Pure. 5¼". Machine made 2.50

Castoria. 5½" 5.00

Cod Liver Oil. 9". With fish. Amber 7.50

Dr. A. Boschee's German Syrup. 6¾". Aqua 5.00

Dr. Cumming's Vegetine. 9¾". Aqua 6.00

Dr. Harter's Iron Tonic. 9". Amber 17.50

Dr. Jayne's Arabian Balsam. 4¼". Aqua 5.00

Dr. Jayne's Expectorant. 5½". Aqua 5.00

Dr. B. J. Kendall's Quick Relief. 5". Aqua 7.50

Dr. Kilmer's Swamp Root 12.50

Dr. R. V. Pierce, Extract of Smart-Weed. 7". Light olive green 20.00

Dr. Sanford's Liver Invigorator. 7½". Aqua 7.50

Dr. Wistar's Balsam of Wild Cherry 25.00

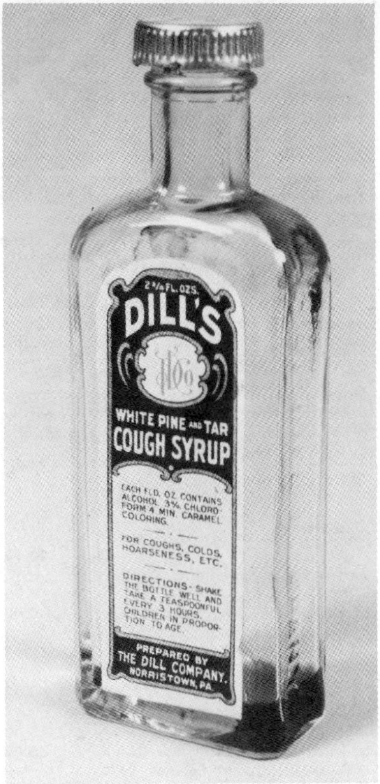

Dills Cough Syrup. Paper labeled front. Embossed side and back. Clear $8.50

Foley's Honey & Tar. 5¼". Aqua 8.00

Hall's Balsam for the Lungs. 7¼". Aqua 7.50

Johnson & Johnson Oil. 5". Aqua 3.50

Larkin Co. 4¼". Clear 3.50

Lediard's Morning Call. Qt. Olive green 95.00

Life Plant. Quart. Original contents 25.00

Paine's Celery Compound. 10". Aqua 25.00

Physician's Traveling Bottle. 2½". Clear blown glass 5.00

Phillips Milk of Magnesia. 7". Light blue 5.00

Smelling Salts. 2½". Cobalt. Early 40.00

Taylor's Cherokee Remedy 8.50

Tobias' Venetian Liniment. Aqua 20.00

Vapo-Cresolene. 4". Aqua 7.50

Vaseline. 3". Amber 3.50

Warner's Safe Cure

Amber, ½ Pint	85.00
Amber, Pint	65.00
Green, ½ Pint	125.00
Green, Pint	75.00
Red. Melbourne, ½ Pint	100.00
Red. Rochester, ½ Pint	25.00
Wine of Life. C.W. Beggs, Sons & Co. Original contents, sealed	25.00
John Wyeth & Bro. 6½". Cobalt	15.00

MINERAL WATER

Mineral water is the natural spring water found beneath the earth's surface. In the 1850 to 1900's, health conscious people favored this water for drinking.

Many resorts were built around a natural spring. Several establishments had special bottles produced to ship and store their mineral water.

Today, "Perrier," a naturally carbonated water of France, is a fashionable drink.

Buffalo Lithia. Embossed. Aqua. ½ gal. $	20.00
Buffalo Lithia. Paper label. Aqua. ½ gal.	10.00
Clark & White. Olive green. Pint	30.00
Congress & Empire Spring Co. Olive green. Quart	30.00
Empire Spring Co. E. Saratoga, N.Y. Dark green. Quart	30.00
Hathorn Spring. Saratoga, N.Y. Blue green. Pint	28.50
Middletown Springs. Amber. Quart	35.00
Oak Orchard Acid Springs. H.W. Bostwick. Teal green. Quart	45.00
Saratoga Red Spring. Dark green. Quart	40.00
Veronica. California. Amber. Quart	10.00
Watchung Spring, N.Y. Green. Quart	20.00

NURSING

Early nursing bottles were of the blown-type. First used in the mid 19th century; increased popularity and demand necessitated improved design and production . . .machine made, embossed, graduated . . .disposable!

Blown. 8¾". Ovid tooled mouth. Pontil $	225.00
Embossed. 7". Bear	7.50
Embossed. 7". Happy Baby	10.00
Hygienic Feeder. 8 oz. Semi-turtle	25.00

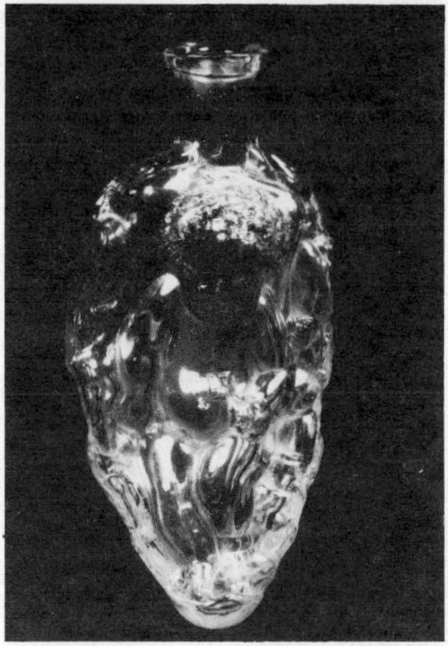

Figural-type. 4½" long. Baby in center. Clear $50.00

POISON

Poison bottles were designed to warn and prevent accidental intake or misuse of their poisonous substances, especially in the dark of the night.

Poison bottles were generally made of colored glass, embossed with the word "POISON", a skull and crossbones, ribbed, ghastly shaped . anything to call attention to their deadly contents.

Coffin-shaped. 5". Amber $	95.00
"Not to be Taken." Embossed, 7¾". Cobalt	40.00
Poison, Embossed	
Diamond-shaped. 3⅝". Amber	10.00
Lattice. 11½" high. Green	50.00
Ribbed. Cobalt	50.00
Skull and Crossbones. 8". Clear. Germany	20.00
Skull and Crossbones. 3¼". Light amber. "Tincture of Iodine."	10.00

SARSAPARILLA AND SODA

Sarsaparilla was a soft, sweet drink made from natural roots of plants for flavoring. It was the forerunner of the currently popular soda or 'pop' drink . . .Pepsi, Coca Cola, etc. Early bottles for carbonated drinks had their own characteristics. With today's 'pop-top' cans, these bottles are now considered collectible.. Commemorative bottles are now being made for various events.

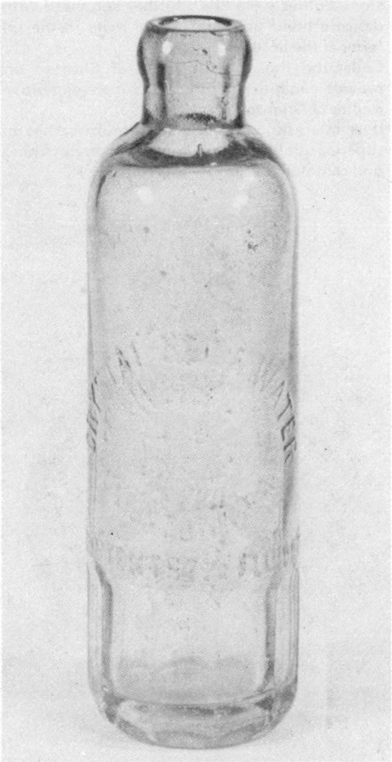

Crystal Soda Water Works. Embossed. 7½ oz. $7.50

Ayer's Compound Extract. Pint . . . . $ 7.50
Babcock's 50.00
Beard, Luke. Boston. Green. Pontil . . 50.00
Bristol's. Quart. Aqua 25.00
Brown, H.L. & J.W. Connecticut. Blob top. Dark green 75.00
Brown's Jamaica Ginger. 9". Aqua 12.50
Canada Dry Ginger Ale. Carnival glass 10.00
Coca Cola - SEE - "Coca Cola Items"
Dr. Green's. Pint. Aqua 18.50
Dr. Larohah's 15.00
Dr. Pepper
- Baylor Bears 8.50
- Embossed 3.50
- Fat Stack Show 7.50
- Miami Dolphins 15.00
- Texas vs Oklahoma 7.50

Dr. Townsend's. Quart. Green 125.00
Gay-ola-Cola 7.50
Grapette. Painted 3.00
Hood's 5.00
Joy's 25.00
Kuck, Henry. Green. C. 1878 ...... 25.00
Moxie
- Embossed. Pat'd. Stopper 20.00
- Labeled 15.00

Nehi Lemon 2.50
Nu-Grape 2.50
Orange Crush. Embossed 7.50
Pepsi Cola
- Amber, 16 oz. Embossed 6.50
- Cincinnati Reds World Champs . . 7.50
- Dallas Cowboys 8.50
- #1Mountain State, W. Va. 7.50
- States, Bicentennial. Each 7.50

Ranier Soda & Bottling Works. Seattle. Stoppered 22.50
Royal Crown
- 12 oz. 3.50
- Governor Cup #1 and #2. Each . . 5.00
- Kentucky Derby 10.00
- Pittsburgh World Champs
  - Empty 7.50
  - Full 10.00

Raft Race, Michigan 3.50
Schlieper, C.W. St. Louis, Mo. Pontil 20.00
Seven-Up
- Cincinnati Bengals 5.00
- Cleveland Browns 5.00
- Farm Fest, Minnesota 5.00
- Indiana University, 1976 ...... 5.00
- Ohio State Buckeyes 5.00
- Oklahoma Sooners, 1976 ...... 5.00
- U.C.L.A. 5.00

Soda & Mineral Co., Warren, Pa 15.00
William & Severance. Squat. Cobalt. Pontil 65.00
Witmer & Helt. Squat. Lykens, Pa. Teal Blue 35.00

SCENT

The scent bottles listed are early American pressed glass made prior to 1850, mainly of the New England provenance.

Amber. "Violin." Pewter top ...... $ 125.00
Amethyst. 2½". Rosetted molding. Embossed eagle on top. Original pewter screw top. B &S 150.00
Amethyst, Black. With pewter rose top 110.00
Amethyst, Deep. 2½". Pewter screw top. Chamfered corners 95.00
Blue cut to clear. 3". Double cut overlay. Gourd-shaped 125.00

Black Amethyst with pewter rose top $110.00

Blue, Powder. "Violin", Pewter top . .	175.00
Clear with white stripes. Seahorse-form	95.00
Cobalt Blue, Deep. 2⅜". Unusual form, minus pewter top. Attributed to B&S	125.00
Cobalt Blue. Ribbed. Stiegel-type. C. 1765	225.00
Fiery Opalescent with brown slag. Tin top	110.00
Fiery Opalescent. Gothic-shaped and panelled	75.00
Opaque Opalescent, Blue. 2½". Without pewter top. B &S	70.00
Opaque Opalescent, Blue. 2⅝". Original pewter screw top. Rosetted molding around lower edge. Embossed eagle on top. B&S	150.00
Slag. Dark blue. Eagle top	110.00
White. Corkscrew-shape. Ribbed. Broken pontil. Cork top	95.00

SNUFF

Although tobacco is indigenous to America, the Europeans were soon introduced to its use and eventually in the late 16th century; the Chinese. For some reason, they preferred to grind the dried leaves into a powder and to 'sniff' it into their nostrils. The elegant Europeans carried their 'snuff' in boxes and took a pinch with their finger tips. The Chinese upperclass, because of their lengthy fingernails, found this inconvenient and devised a bottle with a fitted stopper and attached spoon more suitable.

In the Chinese manner, these utilitarian objects soon became objects d' art. Beautiful snuff bottles were fashioned from precious and semi-precious stones, glass, porcelain and pottery, wood, ivory and metals. Glass and transparent stone bottles were often further enhanced with delicate hand paintings, some done in the interior of the bottle.

Collecting these small works of Chinese art provide examples of larger and more expensive realms of Oriental art.

It is interesting to note; that snuff bottles of superior quality are being made today in China and command relatively high prices.

Cinnabar red, 3½" high. Persimmon decor on front and back. Late 19th century $85.00

Agate. Polished exterior . . . .$	250.00
Amber	
Carved	85.00
Smooth finish. Early 19th century	400.00
Amethyst. 2". Carved	300.00
Argonaut. Carved	150.00
Beetlenut. Carved. Bird and flower motif	125.00
Chalcidony. Carved. Tapered	450.00
Cinnabar. Red with white jade top	250.00
Cloisonne	
Autumn foliage on blue ground. Cloisonne stopper.	275.00
Dragons. 2½"	300.00

Mongolian. 2¾". "China"	175.00
Crystal, Rock. Carved monkey. Tiger eye stopper	225.00
Famille Rose. 19th century	350.00
Hornbill. 2½". Carved. 19th century	700.00
Ivory	
Figures and flowers. 2½". Rings on each side	85.00
Shape of man's head. 2½"	150.00
Jade	
2". On teakwood stand. White	350.00
2½". Mottled brown. Carved landscape. Seal bottom. 19th century	500.00
3". Carved. Urn-shaped with lion finial	350.00
3". Pebble-shaped. Coral stopper. Wooden spoon	300.00
Lapis Lazuli	
Carved	175.00
Oval. Flattened	100.00
Malachite	
2¼". Carved Bonsai tree	175.00
2½". Carved bird	200.00
Mother of Pearl	
Carved	100.00
Ovate. Scenic	75.00
Opal. Carved	395.00
Painted Interiors	
3¾". Birds, flowers, etc. Unsigned. 19th century	500.00
3¾". Landscape. Artist signed. C. 1895	750.00
Peking	
2½". Birds and flowers. Red on white	400.00
3". Black, white to deep red. Carved with flora, fauna. 19th century	750.00
Porcelain	
3½". White ground with green and orange decor	250.00
Blue, gray and red underglaze. Two poems	500.00
Blue and white. Vase-shaped on teakwood stand. Stopper and spoon	350.00
Dragons on yellow. C. 1850	350.00
Rose Quartz. 3½". Carved mother and child	1000.00
Turquoise. 2½". Carved Chinese decor	350.00
Wood. Black lacquered, MOP inlay	50.00

WHISKEY, EARLY

Some of the earliest whiskey bottles made in America were blown by pioneer glass makers in the 18th century. The first bottles designed specifically for whiskey are the Bininger's (1820-1880's.). The cylinderical 'fifth' was used by many distillers from the 1860's on. The first embossed brand name bottle was the amber E.G. Booz Old Cabin Whiskey bottle which was issued in 1860. Many stories have been told about this classic bottle and unfortunately most are untrue. The only substantiated research proves that the term 'booze' was a corruption of the words 'bouse' and 'boozy' from the 16th and 17th centuries. It was only a coincident that the Philadelphia distributor was also named Booz. Over the years, this bottle has been reproduced repeatedly.

With the onset of Prohibition (1920-1933) the whiskey industry came to a stand still. Whiskey was marketed for 'medicinal purposes only' and distributed by 'private' distillers in unmarked or paper labeled bottles.

Sizes and shapes of whiskey bottles are fairly standard. Colors are limited to amber, clear, green and rare Cobalt blue. Corks were the common closures, although inside screw types were used in the 1890-1910 period.

Bottles made prior to 1880 are rare and command high prices. Bottles from 1880 to 1920 and from the Prohibition era are also collectible to bottle specialists.

Middletown Golden Rye. Clear. Stoppered $35.00

Bininger's. 19 Broad St. New York. 9½". Amber ....$	350.00
Bininger's Traveler. ½ pint. Flask-shape. Amber	200.00
Casper's. 10½". Cobalt blue	350.00
Cheatham & Kinney. Chestnut. Amber. 4" squat. Machine made	20.00
Crown. 8½". Amber. Machine made. Pinch-type	15.00
Fitzgerald, John F. Quart. Clear	15.00
Fleming's. Quart. Clear. "Bottled Expressively for Family & Medicinal Purposes."	50.00
Golden Wedding. Fifth. Carnival glass with label	20.00
Mount Vernon Pure Rye Whiskey. 4½". Patented March 25, 1890. Amber	35.00
Old Bridgeport Pure Rye Whiskey, Brownsville, Pa. Clear. Original contents. Prohibition-type	50.00
Old Velvet. Prescription. Clear. 17 years old	175.00
Vinol. Violin-form. Plain without label	45.00
Wharton's. Pint. Union oval. Plain Strap handle. Clear	25.00

WHISKEY

BEAM, JIM

The Beam Distillery was established in Kentucky by Jacob Beam in 1788. About 1880, Colonel James Beam (Jim Beam) began working at the family distillery making bourbon, which later was to bear his name.

The company began the novelty bottle business in 1953 when a cocktail shaker decanter was designed for the Christmas trade. It was an immediate success. In 1955, the 160th anniversary of the concern, the first bottle of the present executive series, in the shape of a decanter, was issued.

Centennial Series. First issue, 1960

1960-Santa Fe ....$	250.00
1960-Civil War. North	35.00
1960-Civil War. South	65.00
1964-St. Louis Arch	25.00
1966-Alaska Purchase	12.50
1967-Antioch	10.00
1967-Cheyenne	8.00
1967-St. Louis Arch	18.00
1968-Laramie	8.50
1968-Reno	8.50
1968-San Diego	7.50
1969-Baseball	10.00
1969-Lombard Lilac	6.50
1969-Portola Trek	6.50

JIM BEAM. Portrait. Composer Series. Chopin $7.50

1969-Powell Expedition	8.50
1970-Preakness	6.50
1970-Riverside	12.50
1971-Chicago Fire	17.50
1971-Indianapolis Sesquicentennial	6.50
1972-Colorado Springs	8.50
1972-Dodge City. Boothill	7.50
1973-Reidsville	10.00
1975-Preakness	10.00
1976-Washington Bicentennial	18.50
Club Specialties	
Akron Club	30.00
Amvets	7.50
Bartenders Guild	7.50
Bowling Proprietors	8.50
BPO Does	6.50
Conventions	
1st-Denver	17.50
2nd-Anaheim	45.00
3rd-Detroit	27.50
4th-Lancaster	40.00
5th-Sacramento	20.00
6th-Hartford	20.00
7th-Louisville	20.00
8th-Chicago	25.00

Ducks Unlimited. #1, 2, 3, 4. Each	15.00
Elks. 1978	20.00
101st. Airborne	15.00
PGA	7.50
Shriners	
El Kahir Temple	18.50
Indiana	6.50
Moila with Camel	17.50
Moila with Sword	28.50
Rajah Temple	25.00
Sports Car Club	15.00
Trout Unlimited	20.00
VFW	20.00

Customer Specialties. First issue, 1956

1956-Foremost. Black and Gold	200.00
1956-Foremost. Grey and Gold	225.00
1956-Speckled Beauty	650.00
1957-Harold's Club. Man in barrel. #1	475.00
1958-Harold's Club. Man in barrel. #2	275.00
1963-Harold's Club Nevada Silver	175.00
1963-Harrah's Club Grey	750.00
1963-Harrah's Club Silver	1000.00
1964-First Nat'l. Bank Chicago	3000.00
1965-Harold's Club Pinwheel	75.00
1967-Harold's Club VIP Exec	55.00
1968-Harold's Club VIP	55.00
1969-Harold's Club VIP	185.00
1970-Harold's Club VIP	65.00
1971-Harold's Club VIP	75.00
1972-Harold's Club VIP	42.50
1973-Harold's Club VIP	35.00
1975-Harold's Club VIP	30.00
1976-Harold's Club VIP	35.00
1977-Harold's Club VIP	42.50
1978-Harold's Club VIP	40.00

Executive Series. First issue, 1955

1955-Black Porcelain	450.00
1956-Royal Gold	140.00
1957-Royal DiMonte	87.50
1958-Cherub, Gray	400.00
1959-Tavern Scene	80.00
1960-Cherub, Blue	150.00
1961-Chalice, Gold	75.00
1962-Flower Basket	55.00
1963-Royal Rose	50.00
1964-Gold Diamond	55.00
1965-Marbled Fantasy	75.00
1966-Majestic	42.50
1967-Prestige	20.00
1968-Presidential	10.00
1969-Sovereign	10.00
1970-Charisma	15.00
1971-Fantasia	15.00
1972-Regency	15.00
1973-Phoenician	12.50
1974-Twin Cherubs	15.00
1975-Reflections	18.50
1976-Floro de Oro	25.00
1977-Golden Jubilee	20.00
1978-Yellow Rose	25.00

Glass Specialities. First issue, 1953

1953-Cocktail Shaker	7.50
1954-Pyrex Coffee Warmer	12.00
1955-Ducks & Geese	8.00
1956-Pyrex Coffee Warmer	5.00
1957-Royal Opal	8.50
1958-Royal Emperor	7.50
1959-Pinch	100.00
1960-Olympian	5.00
1962-Cleopatra. Yellow	15.00
1963-Delft Blue	6.50
1963-Delft Rose	7.50
1963-Dancing Scot. Short	87.50
1963-Dancing Scot. Tall	12.50
1964-Smoked Crystal "Geni"	10.00
1965-Cameo Blue	6.50
1966-Pressed Crystal Scotch	12.00
1967-Pressed Crystal Ruby	15.00
1968-Pressed Crystal Emerald	6.50
1969-Pressed Crystal Opaline	7.50
1971-Pressed Crystal Blue	6.50
1972-Crystal Marbleized	5.00
1972-Mark Anthony	20.00
1973-Sapphire	7.50
1974-Sunburst(s) Each	6.00
1975-Sunburst. Glo (s) Each	5.00
1976-Sunburst (s) Each	5.00

Regal China Series. First issue, 1955

1955-Ivory Ashtray	25.00
1956-Black Canasta	15.00
1962-Seattle World's Fair	25.00
1964-N.Y. World's Fair	25.00
1966-Turquoise Jug	7.50
1967-Redwood	10.00
1968-Antique Trader	8.50
1968-Cable Car	8.50
1970-Bell Ringer, Plaid #1	10.00
1970-German Series. Each	8.50
1970-London Bridge	7.50
1970-Submarine. Redfin	6.50
1971-New Hampshire Eagle	45.00
1972-Oldsmobile	75.00
1974-Hawaii Aloha	8.50
1974-Expo	12.50
1975-Bonded-Silver	6.50
1977-Gold Loving Cup	37.50

State Series. First issue, 1958

1958-Alaska	85.00
1959-Hawaii	65.00
1959-Colorado	50.00
1959-Oregon	50.00
1960-Kansas	70.00
1963-Idaho	75.00
1963-Montana	90.00
1963-Nevada	65.00
1963-New Jersey. Yellow	60.00
1963-West Virginia	225.00
1964-North Dakota	100.00
1965-Wyoming	75.00

1966-Ohio	15.00
1967-Hawaii. Reissue	55.00
1967-Kentucky. White	25.00
1967-Nebraska	12.00
1968-Arizona	7.50
1968-Florida. Shells	5.00
1968-Illinois	10.00
1970-Maine	7.50
1970-South Carolina	7.50
1972-Michigan	7.50
1972-New Mexico	17.50
1977-Washington. Apple	15.00
Trophy Series. First issue, 1957	
1957-Duck	35.00
1958-Ram	175.00
1959-Dog	75.00
1960-thru 1968. Pheasants. Each	25.00
1961-thru 1968. Horses. Each	25.00
1963-thru 1967. Does. Each	35.00
1965-Fox	45.00
1966-Eagle	16.50
1967-Cat(s) Each	12.50
1967-Fox	35.00
1968-Cardinal. Male	50.00
1969-Bird (s). Each	10.00
1970-Poodle. Grey	10.00
1971-Wisconsin Muskie	20.00
1974-Blue Gill	12.00
1976-Great Dane	10.00
1976-Rabbit. Gold	35.00

BISCHOFF

BISCHOFF-Canteen, fruit $17.50

Amber Flower	$ 30.00
Amphora (s). Each	25.00
Bell House	40.00
Canteen, Fruit	17.50
Cat, Black	15.00
Chinese Man — Woman. Each	40.00
Chariot. Urn	25.00
Christmas Tree	60.00
Clown. Low — Tall. Each	40.00
Emerald Rose	50.00
Fish. Ashtray	20.00
Fruit Bowl	28.50
Geese	30.00
Mask (s). Each	20.00
Pirate	20.00
Rose, Red	50.00
Silver (s). Each	35.00
Vase, Yellow	25.00
Venetian (s). Each	30.00
Wild Geese. Ruby — Topaz. Each	32.00

BOLS

BOLS-Teapot . Delft #68076 ....$12.00

Animals. Miniatures. Each	$ 10.00
Ballerina	15.00
Crock (s). Each	12.50
Dutch Boy — Girl. Each	20.00
Dutch Lady. Miniature	150.00
Gendarme	75.00
Lobster Claw. Miniature	15.00
Radio	85.00
Tea Pot. Delft	12.00

BROOKS, EZRA

American Legion. Hawaii — Miami Beach. Each	$ 10.00

BROOKS, EZRA. Jester. Original box $8.00

American Legion. Texas	55.00
Arizona	7.50
Basketball Player	7.50
Beaver	8.50
Big Bertha. Elephant	7.50
Big Red-Football #1	27.50
Big Red-Football #2	16.50
Big Red-Football #3	16.50
Birthday Cake. 100th Award	15.00
Brahma Bull	15.00
Bucket of Blood	7.50
Cable Car. Set of 3	15.00
CB Convoy	10.00
Cheyenne	7.50
Chicago Fire	25.00
Churchill	10.00
Clowns. Accordion—Balloons Each	12.50
Decanters. 64—65. Each	15.00
Decanters. 66—67—68. Each	7.50
Dice	7.50
Eagle, Gold	12.50
Elk	25.00
Fire Engine	12.50
Ford Thunderbird	25.00
Fresno Grape. No gold	60.00
Gators. #1,2, 3. Each	17.50
Gold Panner	10.00
Hereford	12.50
Historical Flasks. Set of 4	16.00
Idaho Skier	12.50
Indian, Ceremonial	18.00
Indianapolis 500 Race Car "21"	20.00
Iowa Farmer	75.00
Japanese Pistol, Dueling	30.00
Jayhawk	6.50
Kachina Doll #1, 1971	150.00
Kachina #2, 1973	50.00
Kachina, #3, 4,5, 6. Each	25.00
King	8.50
Laurel—Hardy. Each	15.00
Lighthouse	16.50
Lobster	20.00
Longhorn Steer	16.50
Mule, Gold	28.50
Oil Gusher	12.00
Ontario Racer#10	15.00
Panda	12.50
Phonograph	15.00
Queen	7.50
Ram	22.50
Saddle, Silver	25.00
Salmon	20.00
Senator, Gold	25.00
Ski Boot	12.50
Slot Machine	20.00
Snowmobile	12.00
Sprint Racer #21	18.50
Telephone	12.00
Tennis Player	10.00
Ticker Tape	10.00
Tonopah	15.00
Turkey, Gold	45.00
Turkey, White	18.00
W. Va. Mountain Man	85.00
W. Va. Mountain Lady	20.00

DANT, J.W.

DANT, J. W. Washington at Delaware $7.50

Alamo	$ 7.50
Atlantic City	6.50
Boeing 747	15.00
Boston Tea Party, Eagle	12.50
Constitution	7.50
Field Birds. Each	10.00
Ft. Sill	12.00
Indianapolis 500	6.50
Paul Bunyan	8.00
Pot Belly Stove	8.00
San Diego	5.00
Washington at Delaware	7.50

DICKEL, GEO.

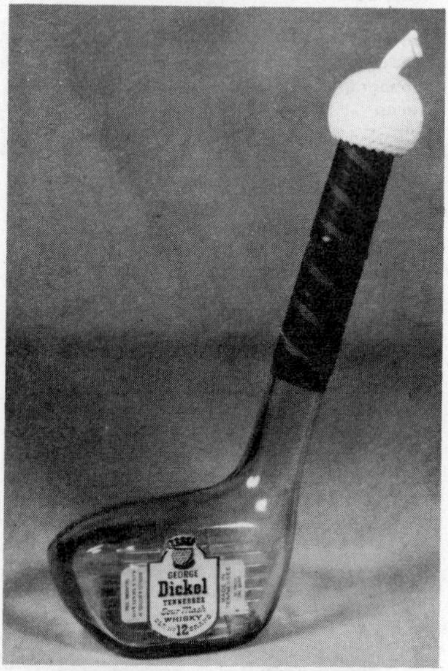

DICKEL, GEO. Golf Club $10.00

Golf Club	$ 10.00
Golf Club. Miniature	5.00
Jug. White. Reissued	10.00
Powder Horn	10.00
Powder Horn. Miniature	5.00

DOUBLE SPRINGS

Bentley	$ 28.50
Bicentennial	12.50
Buick	50.00
Bull, Red	18.50
Cadillac, Gold	55.00
Chicago Water Tower	18.50

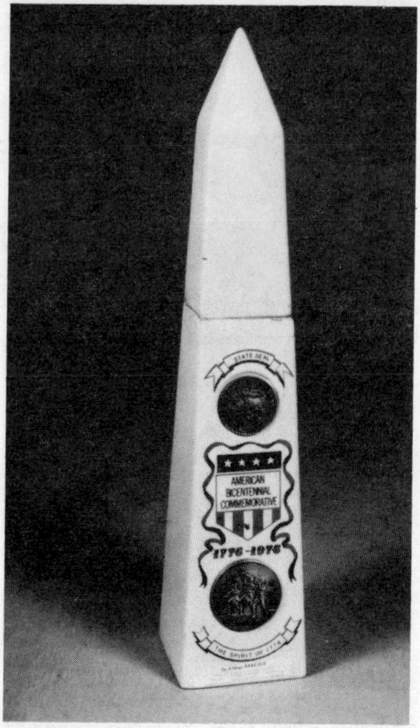

DOUBLE SPRINGS. Bicentennial. Iowa Seal $12.50

Duffers. Each	10.00
Ford. 1910	25.00
Georgia Bulldog	12.50
Golden Coyote	12.50
Kentucky Derby. With glass	10.00
Matador	16.50
Mercedes Benz	30.00
Mercer	27.50
Owls. Brown — Red. Each	20.00
Peasant. Boy — Girl. Each	10.00
Pierce Arrow	35.00
Rolls Royce	35.00
Stanley Steamer. 1911. 1971 issue	35.00
Stutz Bearcat	30.00
Tiger. On football	12.50
Wild Catter	7.50

GARNIER (FRANCE)

Acorn	$ 35.00
Alladins Lamp	47.50
Baby Foot	12.50
Bacchus	12.50
Baseball Player	20.00

Indian $15.00

Birds. Miniature. Each	6.00
Candlestick #134	40.00
Cars. Each	17.50
Cat. #52	75.00
Clown's Head	75.00
Coffee Pot	35.00
Dogs. Each	15.00
Greyhound	75.00
Drunkard "Milard"	18.50
Duckling	40.00
Eiffel Tower	22.50
Elephant #183	25.00
Flower Bouquet	17.50
Giraffe	18.50
Indian Princess	12.50
Jockey	22.50
Locomotive	15.00
Maharajah	75.00
Painting	25.00
Parrot	25.00
Partridge #177	35.00
Pheasant	28.50
Policemen. Each	15.00
Poodle. Black — White. Each	13.50
Sheriff "Cowboy"	15.00
SS France	125.00
Taxi, Paris	30.00
Violin	20.00
Watch. Blue — Tan. Each	25.00
Watering Can	16.50

GIN

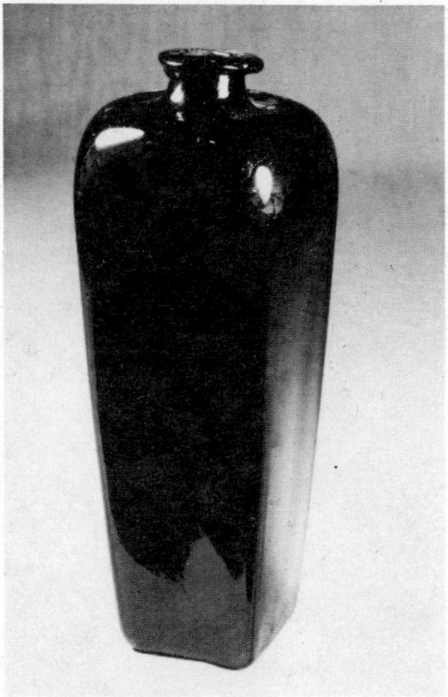

Case. 9½". Amber. Broken pontil $95.00

Bininger Dewitt. ¾-quart. Tapered square. Olive green ....$	850.00
Bininger. Old London Dock. No. 17 Broad St. ¾-quart. Light olive	75.00
Bininger. Old London Dock. No. 19 Broad St. ¾-quart. Yellow amber	50.00
Bininger. Old London Dock. No. 338 Broad St. ¾-quart. Olive green	40.00
Brown. 9". Olive amber. Flared mouth	25.00
Blown. 19". Square. Rolled mouth. Olive amber	550.00
Burnett, Sir Robert. Miniature. Aqua	7.50
Case. 10". Applied seal. Embossed. Olive	55.00
Case. 10". No label. Deep olive	15.00
Case. 10". Paper label. Olive	25.00
Gordon & Co's. Dry Gin. Bear's head	15.00
London Jockey, Clubhouse. ¾-quart. Collared mouth. Emerald green	250.00
Morley's Buchlin. 12" square	20.00

Park & Tillford. Quart. Embossed.	
Aqua. Glass stopper	10.00
Tipstaff, Stephen. 9". Stoneware	150.00

GRENADIER

Pancho Villa,
General $25.00

Arabian Horse	$ 35.00
Bicentennial Series. Set of 12	275.00
Custer, General	25.00
Firechief	35.00
Grenadier, Corporal	22.50
Joan Of Arc, Club	85.00
Lafayette	35.00
MacArthur, General	30.00
Maryland-2nd. (1777)	55.00
Miniatures. Each	17.50
Napoleon	75.00
Pancho Villa. Bookends. Set of 6	175.00
Pennsylvania-1st	50.00
Santa Claus. Green Sack	40.00
Texas Ranger	30.00
Thoroughbred	35.00
Washington on Horse	28.50

HARPER, I.W.

Barrel	$ 15.00
Croquet Player	20.00
Flags of Nations	10.00
Grand Prize	10.00
Man. Blue — Gray. Each	25.00
Man. White	5.00
Roman Coins	8.00
Tip Bottle	15.00

HOFFMAN

Women's Lib. Pair ..$20.00

Aesops Fables. Each	$ 35.00
Doggie Series. Miniatures. Musical. Set of 6	100.00
Ducks. Miniature. Each	20.00
Eagle and Fox. Musical	55.00
Generation Gap. Miniature. Each	20.00
Guns. Miniature. Each	20.00
Leprechaun Series. Each	35.00
Mr. Mini Set. #1, 2, 3. Each Set	75.00
Race Car Series. Each	35.00
Rodeo Series. Each	47.50
Russel Series. Each	35.00
Wildlife Series. Musical. Each	55.00
Exceptions:	
1976-Eagle	75.00
1977-Eagle	65.00
Women's Lib. Miniature. Pair	20.00

HOUSE OF KOSHU

Angel with Book. 7 oz	$ 7.50
Blossom Woman. Miniature	6.00
Boy, Naughty	30.00
Crown	20.00

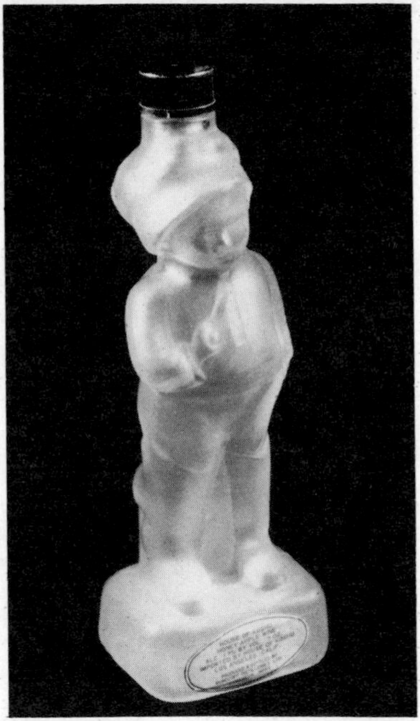

Sailor $7.50

Annie Oakley $35.00

Geisha Series. (Floral). Each	22.00
Kokeshi Doll. 12¾"	15.00
Lantern, Stone	50.00
Lionman. Red	25.00
Mask, Noh: Okame	35.00
Pagoda. Green — White. Each	12.50
Playboy	15.00
Two Lovers	30.00

LIONSTONE

Annie Oakley ....$	35.00
Bar Scene. #1, 2,3,4. Each	125.00
Bar Scene. #2. Nude and framed	350.00
Bartender. Miniature	11.00
Baseball Player	35.00
Bath	40.00
Betsy Ross	45.00
Bluebird. Eastern — Western. Each	27.50
Boxers	35.00
Buccaneer	45.00
Call House Madam	60.00
Camp Cook	32.00
Cardinal	37.50
Cowboy	17.50
Dance Hall Girl	75.00
Doctor	20.00
Dogs. Miniature	
#1	85.00
#2	80.00
#3	65.00
Fireman. #1. Yellow hat	65.00
Football Players	35.00
Frontiersman	25.00
Gambler. Miniature	12.00
Golfer	30.00
Hockey Players	30.00
Indian, Casual	15.00
Jesse James	22.50
Judge, Circuit	20.00
Mailman	32.50
Meadowlark	25.00
Photographer	45.00
Rainmaker	40.00
Riverboat Captain	22.50
Secretariat	50.00
Sheepherder	100.00
Telegrapher	25.00
Tinker	35.00
Tropical Birds. Miniatures. Each	25.00
Turbo Car. STP	
Gold	55.00

Red	20.00
Silver	55.00
Washington	38.50
Woodpecker	45.00

LUXARDO (ITALY)

Apothecary Jar $15.00

African Head	$ 18.00
Amphora. Miniature	20.00
Apple. Miniature	28.00
Bacchus	17.50
Candlestick. Alabaster	27.50
Cannon. Brass wheels	25.00
Cellini. 1952	40.00
Chess Horse. Quartz	40.00
Coffee Pot	15.00
Dinosaur	15.00
Duck. Green	37.50
Eagle. Onyx	57.50
Fish. Quartz	38.50
Fish. Gold — green. Each	35.00
Gondola. Miniature	5.00
Mayan. 1960	20.00
Owl. Onyx	45.00
Penguin	35.00
Pheasant. Black	175.00
Pheasant. Quartz	42.50
Puppy on base	32.50
Sphinx	15.00
Squirrel	37.50
Tamburello	30.00
Venus	17.50
Wobble Bottle	15.00
Zodiac	27.50

McCORMICK

Train. Wood tender $35.00

Air Race. Propeller	$ 17.50
Austin, Stephen F	35.00
Barrel with stand	12.50
Bell, Alexander G	35.00
Bicentennial Series. Each	30.00
Confederate Series. Each	30.00
Confederate Series. Miniatures. Each	15.00
Football Mascot Series. Each	15.00
Frontiersman Series. Each	25.00
Gunfighter Series. Each	25.00
Rogers, Will	35.00
Shriner. "The Noble"	27.50
Train Series. Each	35.00

O.B.R.

Fields, W. C. Top Hat	$ 15.00
Football. NFL	17.50
Hockey Series. Each	10.00
Transportation Series	
Ballon	12.00
Caboose	15.00
Fifth Avenue Bus	17.50
Pierce Arrow	20.00
River Queen. Gold	25.00
Santa Maria	20.00
Train	20.00

Big Red Football Player . . $12.00

Trolley Car	35.00
Wagon, Covered	15.00

OLD FITZGERALD

America's Cup	$ 22.50
Blarney Stone	16.50
Candlelite. 1955	18.00
Classic	7.50
Diamond. 1959	10.00
Executive	8.50
Fleur-de-Lis	15.00
Gold Web	17.50
Irish Luck	17.50
Leprechaun	22.50
Man of War	8.50
Memphis Sesquicentennial. 1819-1969	15.00
Pilgrim Landing	15.00
Rip Van Winkle	45.00
Rip Van Winkle. Green Suit	25.00
Son of Erin	15.00

Decanter. Thomas Jeffersons Monticello. $8.50

Tree of Life	6.50
Vermont	17.50
West Virginia. Forest Festival	20.00

SKI COUNTRY

Barnum, P.T.	$ 30.00
Basset	40.00
Blue Jay	45.00
Bonnie — Clyde. Each	32.50
Burro	45.00
Canadian Goose	45.00
Cave Man	27.50
Dove	45.00
Ducks	
Bluetail	40.00
Mallard	55.00
Redheaded	45.00
Unlimited	55.00
Wood	85.00
Eagles	
Majestic	165.00
Gallon	600.00
Miniature	60.00
Mountain	60.00
Miniature	65.00
On Drum	75.00
Horse. Palomino	40.00

Lady. Blue $25.00

Indian. Cigar Store	25.00
Indian on Horse. #1,2. Each	50.00
Lind, Jenny. Yellow	50.00
Peacock	45.00
Ringmaster	30.00
Skiers	
Blue	30.00
Gold	115.00
Red	20.00
Skiers. Miniature. Each	18.00
Swan. Black	35.00
Tom Thumb	27.50
Woodpecker. Gila	70.00
Woodpecker. Ivory bill	42.50

WHEATON-NULINE

The original glass firm of Wheaton was established in 1888. At that time, they produced hand blown and pressed glass wares. As automation of the industry took hold, they added a line of molded containers for pharmaceutical and food suppliers as well as "antique" bottles for gift shops.

Since 1975 Wheaton-Nuline commorative bottles of limited editions have been made by the Wheaton Craft Guild: Holly City Bottle, Millville, New Jersey. In 1979, the firm became known as Millville Art Glass.

Charles A. Lindbergh $7.50

Apollo 11	$ 20.00
Apollo 12	45.00
Apollo 12. Flint	300.00
Apollo 13. Flint	350.00
Apollo 13 thru 16. Each	8.50
Apollo 17	15.00
Christmas. 1971	12.50
Christmas. 1972	50.00
Christmas. Flint. 1973	500.00
Christmas. 1973 thru 1977. Each	10.00
Edison, Thomas A	7.50
Eisenhower, General	7.50
Ford, Gerald	7.50
Kennedy, John	35.00
Kennedy, John. 15 Year Memorial. Light green. First run	125.00
King, Martin L	7.50
Lincoln, Abraham	10.00
Nixon, Richard	10.00
Nixon-Agnew '68	12.00
Presidents. Miniature. Set #1, 2,3. Per set	12.00

Queen Elizabeth. Silver Jubilee. Amethyst. First run	150.00
Ross, Betsy	9.50
Ross, Betsy. Flint	450.00
Saint Series. Each	15.00
Sky Lab Series. #1, 2, 3. Each	7.50
Washington	30.00
Washington, George	7.50
Watergate. Amethyst. First run	200.00

WILD TURKEY

Wild Turkey with Poult $100.00

Number 1. Male. 1971	$ 300.00
Number 2. Female	200.00
Number 3. On wing	100.00
Number 4. With poult	100.00
Number 5. With flags	45.00
Number 6. Striding	35.00
Number 7	35.00
Number 8	45.00

PITCHERS

Small water pitchers bearing the product's name were given as premiums to tavern keepers by whiskey salesmen. These were placed on the bar for the convenience of the patron and also as an advertising media.

Black Velvet $15.00

Ballentine	$ 15.00
Beefeater	15.00
Bischoff	12.50
Bischoff. Alpine	20.00
Black Velvet	15.00
Bols	15.00
Boodle Gin	25.00
Cutty Sark	12.50
Four Roses	10.00
Garnier	17.50
Hennessey	12.50
House of Koshu. 7 oz. Clear	7.50
Imperial	15.00
Johnnie Walker	10.00
Kentucky Tavern	10.00
Luxardo. Burma	15.00
Old Grandad	15.00
Seagrams VO	7.50
Teachers	12.00
Vat 69. White	7.50
W.C. Fields	22.50
White Satin Gin	15.00
Wild Turkey	30.00

WINES (ITALIAN)

Angel. ½-gallon ....$	10.00
Arche of Triumphe	12.00
Baby Bottle. Miniature	6.50
Bacchus........................	15.00
Bagpiper	8.00
Barrel with barrel straps	7.50
Bird, Red	10.00
Canary	7.50
Cannon, Florentine	15.00
Car Series. Miniatures. Each	10.00
Cat, Black	10.00
Dice, Lucky. Pair	10.00
Dog, Poodle. Leather Covered......	25.00
Donkey, Leather	17.50
Eiffel Tower	14.00
Elk-BPOE-1869-1969	25.00
Harlequin	10.00
Horse..........................	25.00
Lamp. Hurricane. Round	7.00
Lamp. Hurricane. 6 sided	15.00
Leaning Tower	10.00
Lion	20.00
Manger Scene	30.00
Peacock........................	10.00
Penguin with hat	8.50
Political Series. Each	8.00
Rooster. White — Red Specks	15.00
Santa Claus	18.50
Santa Maria Ship	10.00
Snow White & 7 Dwarfs. Miniature. Set	450.00
Turkey, Ceramic	15.00
Turkey, Leather	30.00
Vase, Artisca Series. Each	16.00

BRANDING IRONS

A branding iron is an iron shaft used to brand or mark animals for identification purposes. They were first used by early ranchers in the western part of the United States. Branding livestock is still being practiced today. The early hand forged irons are collectible as "Primitives" or "Americana."

Initials. Wood handle $25.00

Average Price

Wrought Iron. "Initials." .. $25.00 to $35.00

BRASS

Brass is a durable, malleable and ductile metal alloy consisting mainly of copper and zinc. It was and continues to be used by many cultures to make a variety of utilitarian and decorative objects.

Also see specific categories: i.e. Bells, Candlesticks, Fireplace Equipment, etc.

Bed Warmer. 46" long. Pine handle $175.00

Anvil. 5" long. 2¼" high ....$	25.00
Ashtray. 5". Ball feet. Foliage decor. "India."	5.00
Bed Warmers	
*46" Long. Pine handle	175.00
9½", including handle	75.00
Bird Cage. 15" high..............	65.00
Bowls	
7¾", 2¾" deep. Dragon decor. Impressed seal signature. "Made in China."	50.00
12" diam. Etched dragon design. Teakwood base stand	85.00

Candlesticks. 9". "Beehive." Push-ups. Pair. $150.00

14" diam. Hand hammered. Early ... 150.00
Box. 2½ x7x7" 35.00
Buckets
11" diam. Iron bail. Polished 65.00
13½" diam 9¾" deep. Iron bail. "E. Miller and Co." Meriden, Conn ... 85.00
18½" diam. 12" deep. Iron bail .. 125.00
Bullet Mold. Hinged ... 65.00
Candelabras
11". 3-branch ... 125.00
18". 7-branch. Arms turn separately ... 200.00
20". 7-branch. Adjustable ... 250.00
*Candleholder. Chamber-type 4½" diam. saucer ... 50.00
*Candle Snuffer. With scissors. Tray 50.00
*Candlesticks
7¾". Heavy. "India." Pair ... 20.00
9". Beehive. Push-ups. Burnished. Pair ... 150.00
10". Faceted. Push-ups. English. Pair ... 75.00
11½". Push-ups. "The 1901." Pair 200.00
11½". Queen of Diamonds. Pair .. 225.00
Chafing Dish and Tray. Two quart. Late ... 125.00
*Chestnut Roaster. 18" Long. Brass handles ... 85.00
Coffee Pot. 7¼". high. Tankard-shape ... 65.00
Cuspidors
8½". Granite liner ... 55.00
12" ... 75.00
Turtle-shaped ... 100.00
*Dipper. 6" diam. Early ... 50.00

Door Latches
Chippendale-style. Scrolled 45.00
Wallace Nutting ... 85.00
Easel, Floor. 62" high. Triangular-shape. Acorn finials. C. 1880 .... 150.00
Ferner. On 3 ball feet ... 65.00
Fireplace Items. SEE "Fireplace Equipment."
Foot Warmer. Oval-shaped ... 65.00
Forks
18". Shakespeare on handle. English ... 45.00
20". Owl decor ... 40.00
Hand Warmer. 5x7". Wood handle. French ... 50.00
Heel Plates. Pennsylvania Dutch. Heart cutouts. Pair ... 50.00
Horn, Canal. 24". Polished and lacquered. Horse Bit ... 15.00
*Horse Brasses
American. Symbols ... 15.00
English
Diamond Jubilee ... 30.00
Edward VIII ... 30.00
George V ... 35.00
Golden Jubilee ... 35.00
Ice Tongs ... 30.00
Jardinieres
5x5". Hand hammered ... 50.00
8" high. 10" diam. 3 ball feet. Polished ... 75.00
10". Stag head handle ... 150.00
*Key. Large ... 7.50
*Ladles
3½" bowl. 15" handle ... 35.00
5½" bowl. 14" iron handle. Marked "F.B. Co., Canton, Ohio. Patd. Jan. 20, '88" ... 50.00
Mustache Curling Iron. With alcohol burner. Repousse' decor on handle and stand ... 50.00
Oil Can. 11" spout ... 35.00
Pancake Turner. Long. Iron handle .. 25.00
*Pans
9" diam. Two open handles 65.00
18" diam. 7" deep. Two handles ... 85.00
Paper Clips
Bird. "China." ... 20.00
Hand-shaped ... 35.00
Plaques
22x24". William Shakespeare bust in high relief. Inlaid ornamented ebony frame ... 100.00
24" diam. Tavern scene in center. Ornate border ... 125.00
Powder Horns. SEE "Powder Flasks and Horns"
Roasting Jack. Iron wheel. Hooks. English ... 125.00
Scoops
3x5½". With 3" handle ... 30.00
5¼" x 8¾". With 3¾" handle .. 35.00

7x11". With 4½" handle	50.00
Skimmer. 7¾" diam.	65.00
Slide Bolt. Embossed decor	25.00
Stove, Hand. Warming. Portable. Charcoal burning	100.00
*Teakettles	
Acorns and raised leaves decor. Stand and burner	125.00
Dovetailed. Early American	250.00
Gooseneck. Button feet. Wooden handle	75.00
Tie Backs	
Arm-type. Victorian. Pair	75.00
3⅝" diam. "Rosette." Pair	35.00
Trays	
7½x11½". Scalloped rim. Marked "China."	25.00
8½" diam. Late	25.00
11½" diam. Etched decor of figures, foliage, etc. "India."	25.00
14x21". Open handles	65.00
15" diam. Late	50.00
*Umbrella Stand. Lion ring handles	75.00
Urns. 16" high. Ornate. Pair	200.00
Watch Holder. Centered on embossed round tray	75.00
Whistle, Steamboat. 10½" high	150.00

*Reproduced Item

BREAD PLATES

"Our Father who art in Heaven, give us this day our daily bread . . " Bread is known the world over as the staff of life. From the mid 1800's, special serving plates were made in a variety of materials. The majority were of pressed glass, others of porcelain, pottery, metal and wood. Many were made honoring heroes, celebrations, famous places and some were inscribed with words of "Thanks."

Also see Pattern Glass Sections I and II for specific patterns.

Declaration of Independence. 1776-1876 ....$85.00

American Eagle. 8½"	$ 25.00
Banner. Amethyst	150.00
Banner. Clear	85.00
Bible	50.00
Bread is the Staff of Life	40.00
Bunker Hill Monument	60.00
Cleveland	165.00
Columbus Pilot. Wheel border	60.00
Constitution	80.00
Crying Baby	65.00
Dancing Bears. Teddy Roosevelt	125.00
Dog Cart	50.00
Elaine	65.00
Faith, Hope and Charity	65.00
First in War. Washington	125.00
Fitz Hugh Lee. 5½"	25.00
Garden of Eden	35.00
Garfield. Star border	50.00
Garfield Memorial. 11"	65.00
"Give Us This Day, Etc." Wheat center	45.00
Gladstone	30.00
G.O.P. Commemorative	100.00
Grant, General. Patriot & Soldier	55.00
Harrison, Morton	175.00
Hendricks	175.00
Independence Hall	85.00
In Remembrance	55.00
Iowa City. Frosted	55.00
"It Is Pleasant to Labor for Those We Love." 12½"	50.00
Kittens	55.00
Knights of Labor. Amber	200.00
*Last Supper	25.00
*Little Miss Muffet	45.00
Little Red Riding Hood	50.00
McCormick Reaper	75.00
McKinley. "It Is God's Way. His Will Be Done."	50.00
Mitchell, John	150.00
Nellie Bly	175.00
Niagara Falls. 11½x16". Frosted and clear	125.00
Old Statehouse. Phila	75.00
Pacific Fleet	350.00
Pioneer Flour. Minneapolis	65.00
Pittsburgh Commandery. 8½". "The Milkmaid"	75.00
Pope Leo XIII	25.00
Prescott, Stark, Warren, Putnam, 1776-1876	50.00
Queen Victoria	45.00
Railroad. Transcontinental	85.00
Rock of Ages. Milk glass center	125.00
Sailing Ship. Rising sun	45.00
Salt Glaze. 13" diam	100.00
Three Graces	65.00
Three Presidents	65.00
Virginia Dare	65.00
Warrior. Frosted	100.00
Waste Not, Want Not	45.00

Wheat 45.00

*Reproduced Item

BRIDE'S BASKETS

The bride's basket derived its name in that it was a popular wedding gift of the 1880-1910 era. The glass bowls, usually with a ruffled edge, were made by many American and European glass makers . . .from the finest art glass to the style of the day glass. The metal holders, most often silverplated, were fitted with a bail handle; thus resembling a basket. Reproductions exist; especially the glass bowls.

Prices listed include accompanying silver plated holder unless otherwise stated.

Pink cased with clear ruffled edge. 11" diam. bowl. Silverplated frame $150.00

Amethyst ....$ 175.00
Cased
- Amberina 275.00
- Apricot. 9¼" diam. 200.00
- Green. 6x8". Oblong 175.00
- Pink 150.00
- Rose. Applied clear rigaree 165.00
- Spatterware. 11½" diam. 185.00

Cranberry
- Hobnail 225.00
- Inverted Thumbprint. 7" diam. .. 150.00
- Overlay. Enameled decor 180.00
- Undecorated 125.00

Mt. Washington. 16" diam. Melon ribbed bowl in shades of pink, hobnails and enameled floral decor. Ornate silverplated frame with cherubs 1250.00

Peachblow. New Martinsville 85.00
Pigeon Blood. 9¼" diam. Resilvered frame 275.00
Satin Glass. 7" diam. Blue. Enameled decor. 175.00
Threaded. Pink threads on ruby, vaseline colored rigaree 150.00
Vasa Murrhina. Oval. Beige 200.00

BRISTOL GLASS

Bristol glass is the generic name applied to a variety of semi-opaque glasswares made in America and Europe during the 19th and 20th centuries.

Bristol glass was originally the product of several glass houses in Bristol, England in the 18th century. Bristol was once the glass center of England.

Vase. 12¼". Cream ground with bird and water decor in green, yellow and blue $95.00

Bottles, Dresser
- 4⅛" high. Blue with matching stopper. Gold floral decor. Gold trim ....$ 100.00
- 8½" high. Original stopper. Pink with gold, rose, black enamel trim 40.00
- 9" high. Tan with multicolor

enamel decor. Gold trim 55.00
Bowl, Punch. Covered. Enameled floral and gold decor 175.00
Boxes
3½". Dark blue glass. Lid decorated with children 75.00
5½". Rectangular. Blue. Brass chamfered corners. Early 19th C... 300.00
Candlesticks. 10". Green. Shape of ducks. Pair 125.00
Cracker Jar. 5¼x7¼" high. Enameled flowers. Silverplated top. Rim and bail 135.00
Decanters
7¾" high. Bird decoration in gold on blue. Gold tops. Pair 125.00
9" high. Enameled flowers on white. Pair 85.00
Dresser Set. Pair of 10" bottles and covered powder jar. White with gold trim. Set 150.00
Ewer. 8½" high. Green, floral and butterfly decor. Ruffled top. C. 1845 .... 75.00
Mugs
3¼". Floral decor. Applied handle. "Remember Me." 50.00
4". Blue. "Think of Me." 45.00
Pitchers
4" high. Blue, white enamel decor. Applied handle. "Remember Me" in gold 55.00
5½" high. Gray with blue handle and gold decoration 75.00
Plate. 12" diam. Handpainted decor 65.00
Ring Tree. 3" high. Blue with gold trim 40.00
Shades. 14" diam. For hanging lamp:
Red rose decor on white 100.00
Spray of purple morning glories on white 100.00
Smoke Bell. 7" high. Applied ruby self-ring at top. Original brass chain 30.00
Tumbler. White with black transfer. Peasant scene 20.00
Urn. 19" high. Covered. Decorated in heavy enamel with cupids and lady. Cream ground 195.00
Vases
5". Ruffled overlay pink edge. Handpainted bird on branch 40.00
6". Caramel. Enameled decor 30.00
6½". Frosted custard with flying ducks. Pair 85.00
7¼". Beige with enameled daisies. Ruffled top 40.00
8". Stick-type. Handpainted flowers, leaves and stems 50.00
9". Enameled scenic medallion on white 45.00
10½". "The Gleaners." 85.00
10¾". Cylinder-type. White with painted brown hen and rooster .. 40.00
11". Gold and copper lustre on chartreuse. Pair 85.00
11¾". Urn-shaped. Multicolored flowers, branches on white 65.00
13". Pink with red, white and green strawberries and flowers in enamel. Pair 150.00
15". White, handpainted orange and blue floral decor. Ruffled top 85.00
24". Blue with white casing. Multicolored flowers and gold leaf decor 150.00

BRONZE

Bronze is any of the various alloys of copper and -or tin sometimes with traces of other metals. Bronze has been used since Biblical times for utilitarian and decorative purposes. A period of human culture between the Stone Age and Iron Age is known as the Bronze Age, characterized by the use of bronze for weapons and implements. After a decline in the Middle Ages, bronze was revived in the 17th century and continues today.
Bronze animals, figurines, busts and other objects d'art of the 19th and 20th centuries are considered as a highly sophisticated form of art. Prices of works of recognized artists have reached new highs.
Do not confuse a bronzed object that is either made of a white metal base or weighted Plaster of Paris finished to resemble bronze with a true casted bronze. Some desirable works are being restruck by contemporary foundries.
There are also 'signed' reproductions. Know your bronzes or know your dealer!

ANIMALS

Alligator. 7½". Barye ....$ 650.00
Bear. 6¾". Marble ball and base .. 350.00
Bird. 5x7". Pautrot 600.00
Birds, Battling. 9½x12". DeLabrierre 1000.00
Bird. Fish in mouth. 5x6½". DeLabrierre 500.00
Bird. Partridge. 6½x7". Moigniez .. 475.00
Bisons, Battling. 25" long. Tiffland 1250.00
Bull. 3½x5½." Perrin 450.00
Bull. 5½x7½". Barye 950.00
Bull. 13". Rosa Bonheur 150.00
Bull Fighting Dog. 4½x7½". DeLabrierre 550.00
Calf. 6x9". Walking over fallen tree log. I. Bonheur 1000.00
Camel. 9x10". Unsigned 325.00
Chickens, Seven. 6½x10". Basket. Cain 600.00

Beethoven at Piano. Black wooden base. 9¼" high. Kauba. #4156 ..... $850.00

Boy with ram. 4" high. Barye $750.00

Cow. 3½x5½". I. Bonheur 550.00
Cow nursing calf. 9¼x13". P.J. Mene 1500.00
Dog. 1½x3½". Tail in mouth. Savage, Gorham Co 375.00
Dog. Hound. 12¼". I. Bonheur 950.00
Dog. Retriever. 6½" long. Barye .. 650.00
Dog. Retriever. 6½ x 12". Mene 850.00
Dog. Retriever. 8 x 12½". Moigniez 900.00
Dog. Scottie. 5x7". E.B. Parsons 600.00
Dog. Setter. 6¼". Fremiet 300.00
Dog. Spaniel. 3½x5½". Mene 500.00
Dog. Terrier. 4x8". Three rats and bucket. A. Leonard 450.00
Dogs. German Police. (2) 11x15". Green marble base. A. Varnier .. 1650.00
Dogs. Two. "At the Sound of the Gun." Lemaitre 3500.00
Elephant. 5x7". Fratin 550.00
Elephant. 6½x8". Valton 750.00
Ewe. Reclining. 8½". Rosa Bonheur 900.00
Fox. 4¼x5". Peeking over rock at rabbit. Masson 650.00

Gazelles. 8x13x15". Moigniez 1650.00
Goat. 6x10". Mene 750.00
Horse. Rearing. 13x15½". Costou .. 500.00
Jaguar. 7½x9½". Barye 850.00
Lion. 12x22". Holding rabbit in jaws. DeLabrierre 1850.00
Lion. Female. Stalking. 8x16". Barye 750.00
Lion. With captured gazelle. 4x9½". "Barye-7" 750.00
Lion and Serpent. 6x8½". Barye 875.00
Panther of Tunis. 4½ x 7¾". Barye 550.00
Pheasant. 5½x9". Pautrot 650.00
Pheasant. 7" long. Mene 650.00
Ram. 8x10". Lanceray 1750.00
Seal on Rocks. 5" high. E. Angela, Gorham & Co 500.00
Stag. Attacked by three hounds. 12x17". P.J. Mene 1750.00

Busts

Indian Head. 4x4¼". Headdress. Mouth open. Renevez 850.00
Joan of Arc. 18" high. Chapu. 1500.00
Lincoln. 7" high. G.O. Bissell 500.00
Lincoln. 11" high. L. Volk, Gorham .. 750.00
Man. 10" high. Marble column. Unsigned 350.00
Napoleon. Larger than life size 1000.00
Queen Victoria. 9½" high. Joseph Boehm 400.00
Woman. 4" high. Russian. T. Teneszezok 950.00
Woman. 6¼" high. Victorian. Barthoz 350.00

Figurines

Arab. 2" high. Riding camel with woman hostage, etc. 19th C	2500.00
Athlete. 15" high. Nude in balancing position. Hammerman......	1500.00
Basketball Player. 13½" high. About to throw ball. Gornik	500.00
Boy. 10½" high. Drinking from goblet. Kovalzenski	650.00
Camel with Master. 12½x13". Oasis scene. Greb.............	1750.00
Cavalier. Standing. 6½" high. Guillot	325.00
Cossack on Horse. 5x9x9". Lanceray	2500.00
Dancer, Flamenco. 16½" high. H. Gaudet. C. 1900	1250.00
Dancer, Okina. 12" high. Japanese	275.00
Farmer. 16½" high. Charles Levy ..	1750.00
Gibson Girl. 9x12½". Sitting on bench. Der-Stretton	750.00
Harlequin. 35" high. DuBois	1500.00
Huntsman, Persian. 17x22". With lions, gazelles. Dubucand	2500.00
Huntsman, Scottish. 20" high. Mene	200.00
Indian. 4½" long. Kneeling with bow and arrow. Marble base. C. Kauba	850.00
Indian Chief. 6½" high. "Swift Dog." Marble base. Kauba	1000.00
Jockey. 13¼" high. "Derby Winner." Mene	1650.00
Maidens. Farm. Two 33" high. Moreau	2500.00
Mephistopheles. 11½" high. Troubadour playing musical instrument. DeWever	1500.00
Michelangelo. 4x11½". Savage....	600.00
Mozart. 13" high. "Don Juan" score. Pilet	550.00
Race, The. 7x8". Boyer............	3000.00
Raphael. 13¼" high. Duchoieselle	750.00
*Sergeant. 11" high. Restrike. 138—2000. Remington	1500.00
Slave Girl. Nude. 16" high. Bouraine	900.00
Slaves. Semi-nude. 11½x14½". Carrying sedan carriage with lady. Enamel work. Originally lamp base. Nam Greb	2500.00
Soldiers. Group with rabbit. 6½x7". Barye.........................	750.00
St. Michael Slaying the Dragon. 11½" high. E. Fremiet	950.00
Venus de Milo. 17½" high. French. C. 1880	600.00
Woman. 10½" high. Nude, running. Marble base. German. C. 1880	500.00
Woman. 21½" high. Art Deco design. Garnier	2000.00
Woman. 22" high. "Triumph of Labor." Marble base. Lugerth	2250.00

*Reproduced Item

Miniatures

Antelope. 1¼x2". On base. Tiffany Studios	100.00
Bull. 2½x4¼". Vienna	150.00
Camel. 2½x3½". On oval base. Tiffany Studios	125.00
Cat. 3". Arched back. Vienna	100.00
Dogs	
Bloodhound. 2½x5". Vienna	150.00
Bull. 1¼x3". Upper half shown inside lady's glove. Vienna........	125.00
Dachshunds. 1x1⅛". Two puppies peeking out of knapsack. Vienna	125.00
Scottie. 1x1½". Vienna	50.00
Hippopotomus. 1¼x2½". On base. Tiffany Studios	100.00
Kitten. With boot. 2½ x 3½"	125.00
Lion. Standing over wounded lioness. 3x4¾". Polychrome decor. Vienna	175.00
Magpie. 1½". Vienna	50.00
Monkey. 4¼" high. Holding large half walnut shell in paws. Vienna	250.00
Rabbits. Two. 1" high, sitting in 2-handled woven basket, 1¼x2½". Vienna	150.00
Rooster and three Hens. 1½" rooster. Vienna. Set	150.00
Seal. 3¼" high. Simulated tree trunk, mouse crawling up with bird sitting on top of trunk. Unsigned	50.00
Turtle. 1¾x3½". Unsigned........	65.00
Young Black Boy. Lying prone and looking at kettle hanging from tripod. Vienna	200.00

Miscellaneous

Ashtray. 4". Art Nouveau decor ..	75.00
Bowl. 11¼" diam. Aqua marbled. Grape handles. Sorenson	75.00
Candleholders. 12½" high. Lady holding socket. Pair	150.00
Paper Clip. Eagle's head. Glass eyes	50.00
Planter. 6¼" diam. W. Henning ..	125.00
Plaques	
Garfield, President. 12x18". Robertson	750.00
Lincoln, Abraham. 6½" diam. Oak frame. Nock 1914	300.00
Woman and Child. 10¼". German	150.00
Salver. 5x13". Footed. "John the Baptist." C. 1880. Emile Picault ..	1000.00
Urns. 17" Cherubs. Unsigned. 19th C. Pair	1000.00

Vases

5¼″. Cherubs, butterflies, dragonfly 150.00

10½″. Applied dancing couple. Garland with crossed swords. Ruff Bessereich. 19th C 450.00

11½″. Foliage decor 250.00

15″. Leaves form fountain, grotesque head pours water. Les Curieuses, Geschutz 950.00

BUFFALO POTTERY

Information regarding the beginning of Buffalo Pottery, Buffalo, N.Y. is sketchy. It is believed that the establishment commenced business about 1903. The company made a series of quart jugs in a variety of shapes. The decorations were underglaze in hand-tinted colors. The subjects were from history and literature and included John Paul Jones and Robin Hood. In 1908 the company introduced Deldare ware. It has a rich olive-green body. The underglaze decorations were "The Fallowfield Hunt" and "Ye Olden Times." In 1911 Emerald Deldare was introduced. It had varied center scenes banded with stylized designs, the most popular pattern being "The Tours of Dr. Syntax." The firm also issued a series of commemorative plates depicting various scenes of historic interest. In 1940, the company reorganized to make hotel china.

Bowls

5½″ diam. Floral center banded $ 25.00

6″ diam. Roosevelt Bears 125.00

Butter Pat. Willow 5.00

Butter Tub. Tab handles. Fern Rose pattern 45.00

Cream and Sugar. Wedding Band .. 25.00

Cup, Farmer's. "Take Ye a Cuppe O' Kindness For Auld Lang Syne" .. 50.00

Cups and Saucers

Demitasse. Gold banded on white with handled metal holder. C. 1923 .... 25.00

Willow 17.50

Game Set. 15″ platter. Four 9″ plates. Deer scenes. Artist signed, Beck. 5 pcs 275.00

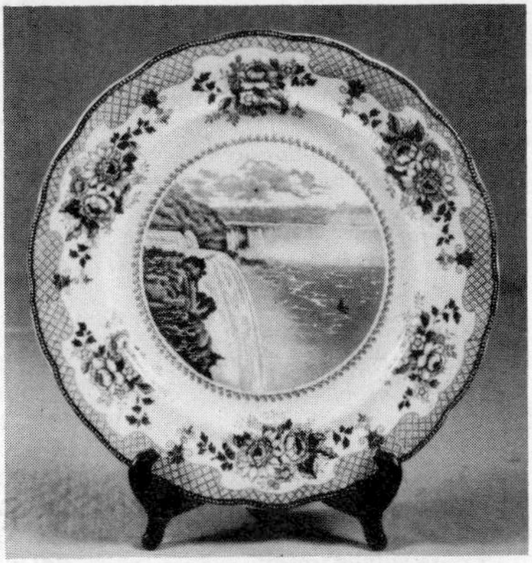

Plate. 10″. "Niagara Falls." Blue transfer on white $40.00

Gravy Boats

LaFrancerosa 27.50

Willow 15.00

Jugs

George Washington 350.00

New Bedford 250.00

Triumph 175.00

Wild Duck 175.00

Luncheon Set. Service for 6. Bluebird. Dated 1919. Set 225.00

Mug. Shaving. Wildroot 75.00

Pitchers

4″ high. Roosevelt Bears. 1907 .. 125.00

4½″. high Bluebirds 40.00

6½″ high. Bulbous. Blue Geranium. 1905 .... 85.00

7″ high. Pink mums on white 50.00

9¼″ high. Blue Gloriana.1907-1909 .... 250.00

Buffalo Hunting Scene. Green and white. Undated 250.00

George Washington one side, Mt. Vernon other side. Blue and white. 1907 .... 225.00

Sailor's & Lighthouse. 1906 ...... 300.00

Plates

Child's. Boy bringing candy to girl who has fallen 30.00

7½″. Grant's Tomb 40.00

7½″. Niagara Falls 25.00

9″. Pike. Gold border 45.00

9″. The Gunner 60.00

9″. Wild Ducks. Turquoise ground 75.00

10″. Faneuill Hall 40.00

10″. Independence Hall 40.00

10″. Mount Vernon 40.00

10″. Niagara Falls 40.00

10″. U.S. Capitol 40.00

10". White House 40.00
11". George Washington. C. & O. Railroad 225.00

Teapot. Blue and white argyle. 1914 .... 65.00

Vase. 10½". Two-handled. Scalloped top. Bulbous. Handpainted 100.00

Vegetables, Covered
- Wedding Band 40.00
- Willow 50.00

Deldare Ware

Bowls
- 6½". "Ye Olden Days" 100.00
- 8". "The Death" 295.00
- 8". "Dr. Syntax-His Tour" 300.00
- 8". "Ye Lion Inn" 225.00
- 9". Breaking Cover." 400.00
- 9". "Fallowfield Hunt." 325.00
- 9". "Village Scene." 300.00
- 9". "Ye Village Tavern" 300.00
- 12". "Breakfast at the Three Pigeons." 400.00

Candlestick. 9½". "Village Scenes." 225.00

Creamers
- "Dr. Syntax Dairymaid" 300.00
- "Village Scenes" 150.00

Cream and Sugar. Covered. "Breaking Cover." 425.00

Cups and Saucers
- "Fallowfield Hunt" 225.00
- "Ye Olden Days" 200.00

Humidor, Tobacco. "At Ye Lion Inn" 350.00

Mugs
- "Breakfast at the Three Pigeons" 200.00
- "The Death" 250.00
- "Dr. Syntax Made Free of the Cellar" 250.00
- "Fallowfield Hunt" 200.00
- "Ye Lion Inn" 200.00

Creamer. "Village Life in Ye Olden Days." C. 1909. ....$150.00

Pitchers
- 5¾". "Which He Returned with a Courtsey.". 225.00
- 6". "His Manner of Telling Stories." 250.00
- 6¼". "To Demand My Annual Rent." 295.00
- 6½". "Ye Olden Days" 265.00
- 6½". "Fallowfield Hunt." 325.00
- 7". "Breaking Cover." 375.00
- 8". "Demand Annual Rent" 375.00
- 9". Tankard. "Village Scenes." .. 375.00
- 12½". Tankard. "Hunt Supper." Signed 500.00

Plates
- 6¼". "At Ye Lion Inn." 135.00
- 6½". "Fallowfield Hunt." 100.00
- 6½". Advertisement. "Hand Painted Deldare Ware Underglaze." Marked and dated 1908 on base 300.00
- 6½". "Dr. Syntax Presenting a Floral Offering." 225.00
- 6½". "Fallowfield Hunt" 145.00
- 7½". Fallowfield Hunt." 195.00
- 8½". "The Death." 200.00
- 8½". "The Town Crier." 165.00
- 9½". "Dr. Syntax Loses His Wig." 275.00
- 9½". "Ye Olden Times." 175.00
- 9½". "The Start." 225.00
- 10". "Breaking Cover." 250.00
- 10". "Ye Village Gossips" 300.00
- 12" "Breakfast at the Three Pigeons." Hanging-type 400.00
- 14". "Fallowfield Hunt" 400.00
- 14". "The Start." 475.00
- 14". "Ye Olde Lion Inn." Sgnd. .. 425.00

Sauce. 6". "The Fallowfield Hunt." Sgnd 125.00

Sugar, Covered. "Scenes of the Village Life." 250.00

Teapot. "Village Life in Ye Olden Days" 375.00

Tiles
- "The Death" 250.00
- "Traveling in Ye Olde Days." 250.00

Trays
- 7¾". "Fallowfield Hunt." 225.00
- 9x12". "Ye Olde Lion Inn." 425.00
- 9¼x12½". "Dancing Ye Minuet." 400.00
- 10¼" x 12½". "Heirlooms" 425.00

BURMESE GLASS

Burmese glass, first named 'Bermise', is an art glass originated and manufactured by the Mt. Washington Glass Co., New Bedford, Mass., from 1885 to approximately 1891. It was discovered accidentally when Fred Shirley, the new manager of the plant, was making a small pot of ruby glass. He added gold but the metal sank quickly to the bottom without mixing with the glass. He then added a quantity of Uranium

Oxide which was used in making canary yellow glass. The reaction, when the item was reheated, produced a soft yellow shading to flesh pink. The blending of the colors was so gradual that it was difficult to determine where one color ended and the other began.

Although some of the glass has a surface that is glossy, most of it is acid finished. The majority of items have no pattern, but some have a ribbed, hobnail or diamond-quilted design. The pontil mark was often hidden by a "berry-shaped" piece of glass which is an added means of identification.

The only other factory licensed to make it was Thos. Webb & Sons in England. Out of deference to Queen Victoria, they named their wares "Queen's Burmese."

Plate. 6". Glossy finish. Unmarked $325.00

Basket. 8¼" high. Footed. Applied reeded handle. Acid finish. Mt. Washington ....$ 1000.00

Bell. 6" high. Pale amber reeded loop handle. Crimped edge. Glossy finish. Unmarked 450.00

Bobeches

2½" diam. Acid finish. Pair....... 250.00

3¼" diam. Glossy finish. Pair 275.00

Bottle, Perfume. 4¾". Irish spray decor. Silver top with hallmarks. Webb.......................... 500.00

*Bowls

4½" diam. Scalloped edge. Webb 500.00

5x2½". Ruffled edge. Sgnd. "Queens". Thomas Webb 625.00

6x3". Ruffled top. Unmarked 325.00

10" diam. Reeded feet. Berry pontil. Mt. Washington 850.00

Condiment Set. 3 pieces. Salt, pepper and mustard. Acid finish. Silvered holder. Unmarked. Webb 750.00

*Creamers

2½" high. Applied handle. Acid finish. Unmarked. Webb 300.00

3½" high. Enameled daisy decor. Gold trim. Acid finish. Mt. Washington 400.00

*Cruet. Acid finish. Mt. Washington 750.00

Cups

Custard. Acid finish. Unmarked .. 250.00

Punch. Acid finish. Mt. Washington 350.00

*Cups and Saucers.

Demitasse. Acid finish. Unmarked 450.00

Regular. Acid finish. Unmarked .. 600.00

*Epergne. 26" high. Large ruffled bottom bowl, 15" diam., 10" diam. center bowl and 7" diam. third bowl. Acid finish. Unmarked 2500.00

*Lamps, Fairy

3¾" high. Clear Clarke base. Webb.......................... 400.00

5" high. Clarke base. Webb 550.00

Lemonade Set. 9" Tankard. Six tumblers Glossy finish. Unmarked .. 2000.00

Mustard Pot. 3½" high. Ribbed. Acid finish.................... 350.00

Nappie. 5" diam. Acid finish. Mt. Washington 350.00

*Pitchers

6¾" high. Bulbous. Acid finish. Mt. Washington 1000.00

9" high. Tankard-shape. Acid finish. Mt. Washington 1250.00

Plates

5". Acid finish. Unmarked 300.00

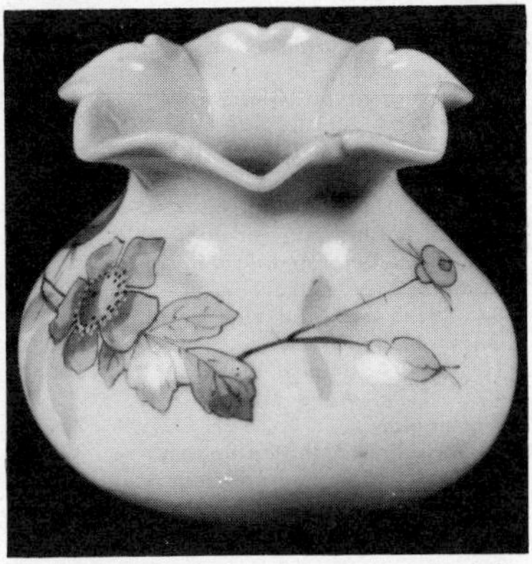

Vase. 2½". Petal top. Blossom decor. Glossy finish. Webb..........$750.00

6". Glossy finish. Unmarked 325.00

Rose Bowls

2¼" high. Decorated with polychrome acorns and leaves. Acid finish. Unmarked 325.00

3¾" high. Applied rigaree. Acid finish. Mt. Washington 500.00

4" high. Egg-shaped. Applied ruffle foot. Acid finish. Mt. Washington 500.00

6" high, 5" diam. Acid finish. Footed. Berry pontil. Mt. Washington 750.00

*Salt and Pepper Shakers. Ribbed. Acid finish. Unmarked. Pair 450.00

Sauce. 4½". Crimped top. Unmarked 225.00

Shade, Lamp. 16" diam. Approx. 5" deep. Three ormolu rosettes. Finial. Acid finish 3000.00

Sherbet. Footed. Acid finish. Mt. Washington 375.00

*Toothpick Holders

Diamond. Acid finish. Mt. Washington 325.00

Hexagonal top. Glossy finish. Mt. Washington 225.00

Square top. Enameled decor. Acid finish. Mt. Washington 250.00

*Tumblers

Juice. Ivy decorated. Acid finish. Webb 250.00

Lemonade. DQ. Handled. Glossy finish. Mt. Washington 350.00

Water. Acid finish. Mt. Washington 450.00

*Vases

3½". Corset-shape with 5-point rolled star top. Thomas Webb & Co., "Queen's Burmese" incised on bottom 500.00

4". Nosegay-type. Glossy finish. Unmarked 250.00

7". Lily-shaped. Glossy finish. Unmarked 300.00

7½". Jack-in-the-Pulpit. Crimped edge. Acid finish. Unmarked 400.00

7½". Stick. Decorated. Acid finish. Unmarked 400.00

8". Stick. Leaf and vine decor. Original label. Webb 1000.00

10". Stick. Acid finish. Webb 500.00

17". Lily. Acid finish. Mt. Washington 750.00

Wine. Acid finish. Mt. Washington 375.00

*Reproduced Item

BUSTS

The portrait bust originated from pagan and Christian traditions. The first were mainly of Roman heroes. Later, images of Christian saints were made for reliquaries. It was not until the Renaissance that it was deemed proper that 'ordinary' man should be represented. Busts of notable persons were popular adornments in the 18th and 19th-century home libraries. Considering the number of library pieces produced, a collector can still find excellent examples at reasonable prices based on artist, subject and material.

By the very nature of their simplicity, busts can add a very spectacular image to the most modern setting. Also see "Bronzes" and "Parian."

"William Penn". 8½" high. Bronze. Signed Greil $275.00

Burns, Robert. 13". Parian ......$ 195.00

Clytie. 12". Parian 125.00

Duke of Wellington. 6". Wax. Framed. Green velvet background 95.00

Edward VII and Alexandra. 6½". Parian on marble base. Impressed "Prince and Princess of Wales." Pair 250.00

Franklin, Ben. 9½". Parian 185.00

Gladstone. 25½". Terra Cotta 150.00

Goethe. Philosopher. 22½". Parian 275.00

Judith. 7". Bronze. Art Nouveau .. 125.00

King George V. 7½". Clay by L. Harradine. Doulton-Lambeth 150.00

Lady. 20½". Mitchell." C. 1856 .... 300.00
Mozart. 6". Square pedestal. Parian. Herco 35.00
Onenone. 11½". Crystal Palace Art Union. "Copeland" 495.00
Penn, William. 8". Parian 75.00
Queen Alexandra. 10½". 1884-Crystal Palace Art Union. Terra Cotta. "Copeland" 550.00
Queen Victoria. 23". "Copeland" .. 550.00
Rebecca at the Well. 16½". Bronze. "Villanis" French 650.00
Scott, Sir Walter. 6". Parian. Germany 35.00
Sumner, Charles. 12¼". Polychrome. Emblem of Boston Sculpture Co 85.00
Washington, George. 7". Parian .. 35.00
Washington, George. 8". Modeled by Enoch Wood. Impressed Washington on base. C. 1800-10 350.00

BUTTER MOLDS

(See "Food Molds")

BUTTER STAMPS

Butter stamps or prints differ from butter molds in that they are of one-piece construction. They were used to decorate the top of the butter after t was molded. The earlier ones were handcraf-ed, including the print design. Later ones were factory made with the print design forced into the wood by a metal die. Once again butter stamps have gained favor in the kitchen for decorating butter, cookies, cheese, etc. Needless to say, watch for reproductions!

Leaf. 3½" diam $30.00

Bird. 4¼" diam. Hand carved ....$ 225.00
Eagle. 4¼" diam 325.00
Floral. 3½" diam 30.00
Flora. 4" diam. Hand carved 150.00
Leaf. 3½" diam 30.00
Sheaf of Wheat. 3¾" diam........ 25.00
Swan. 3½" diam. Hand carved 100.00
Teazel. 4¾" diam. Hand carved .. 150.00
Tulip with stars. 4¾" diam. Hand carved. Handle missing 125.00

CALENDAR PLATES

Calendar plates were first made in England in the late 1800's. They became popular in the United States after 1900. The majority were of the advertising-type and made of porcelain or pottery. Occasionally some were made of glass or tin.

1909.-9½". Advertising-type. Portrait center $35.00

1907-9¼". Santa & Holly ....$ 50.00
1907-Tin. Advertising-type 45.00
1909-8". Red roses in center 25.00
1909-9¼". Full figure of girl in sailor dress. Fruit and flower border 30.00
1909-9¼". Santa on sleigh. Whip in hand. Four reindeer 45.00
1910-7½". Holly with gold trim .. 30.00
1910-8". Dog with calendar 25.00
1910-8½". Betsy Ross center 40.00
1910-8½". Old man with scythe. Oyster shells, holly leaves and berries. 28.00
1911-"Should Auld Acquaintances" 35.00
1912-8". Airplane in center 32.50
1912-8¾". "Kitty Hawke." Advertising-type 30.00

1912-9½". Presidents Lincoln, Garfield and McKinley 50.00
1913-7½". Girl on rock 25.00
1913-9¼". Aircraft over coastal town 27.50
1914-7½". Scene of horse woman. Advertising-type 25.00
1914-8". Betsy Ross center 35.00
1914-9¾". Washington Tomb 50.00
1915-7¾". Map of Panama Canal crossed with flags 35.00
1916-Indian in canoe 45.00
1918-9". Birds in border, 2 deer, trees and stream in center 28.50
1920-7¼". War and Peace. Flags .. 35.00
1921-8½". Calendar with bluebirds and pink flowers in border. U.S. flag in center 28.50
1923-8½". Calendar with blue, yellow and red flowers at top. Trees and stream in center 30.00
1928-Red, pink, yellow roses. Mkd. "Harker." 35.00
1929-9". Boy with dog center...... 30.00

CALLING CARD CASES

During the Victorian era, the habit of leaving a personal calling card was a social custom. The engraved cards were carried in a proper case. Card cases were made of various materials . . . silver, gold, ivory, mother of pearl, etc; many were handsomely monogrammed. This gracious custom passed into oblivion after World War I.

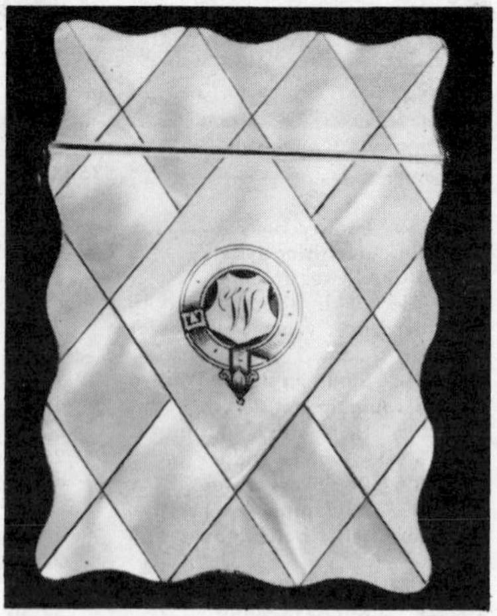

Mother of Pearl and Tortoise. 3x4". Monogrammed $50.00

Ivory. 2½x4½". Carved flowers and vines ....$ 75.00
Lacquer. Black 25.00
Mother of Pearl................. 50.00
Silver
- Chinese. Applied dragon. Signed 100.00
- Coin 50.00
- English. 2¾x4". Embossed scroll work 145.00
- Plated. 2½x4½" 35.00
- Sterling. Embossed 65.00
- Sterling. Embossed. Chain handle 75.00
- Sterling. Enameled 85.00

Tortoise Shell
- Monogrammed................ 65.00
- With ivory separator. C. 1900.... 50.00

CAMBRIDGE GLASS

Cambridge Glass Company, Cambridge, Ohio was incorporated in 1901. In the beginning their main line was clear tableware. Later, they expanded into colored, etched and engraved glass. Over 40 different hues were produced in their fine blown and pressed glass. Five different marks were employed during the production years, but not every piece was signed.
In 1954, the plant closed its doors. The molds were later sold to the Imperial Glass Company, Bellaire, Ohio.

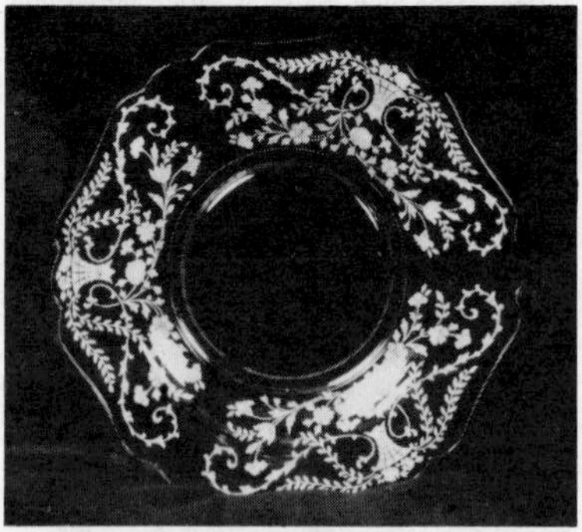

Plate. 8½". "Portia." Crystal $10.00

Ashtrays
- 3". Seashell. Amber ....$ 6.00
- 4". Seashell. Crystal. 3 feet 6.00
- 7". Crown Tuscan 30.00

Baskets
- 5½" high. Ritz blue with Farber chrome holder. Handled 37.50
- 11" high. Tomato. Satin finish .. 125.00

Bon Bons
5½". Decagon. Ebony 15.00
7". Gadron. Crystal. Silver deposit 20.00
Bookends
Eagle. Crystal. Pair 150.00
Scottie. Crystal. Satin finish. Pair 125.00
Bowls
5". Jenny Lind. Amber 35.00
6½". Thistle. Nearcut 18.00
7". Everglade. Crystal 15.00
10". Caprice. Pink. 4 feet 22.50
10". Ram's head. Helio 225.00
10". Seashell. 3 feet. Crown Tuscan 100.00
12". Gold Wheat. Azurite 125.00
12". Portia. Crystal. Crimped edge. 4 feet 25.00
12". Rosepoint. Crystal 40.00
16". Everglades. Indian and Buffalo. Moonlight blue. Satin finish 150.00
Candelabras
Elaine. Crystal. Pair 35.00
Rosepoint. Pair 45.00
Candlesticks
2½". Caprice. Blue. Pair 35.00
8¾". Nude. Crown Tuscan. Pair 200.00
9½". Dolphin. Amber. Pair 200.00
Rams Head. Dark green. Pair 75.00
Champagne. Nude. Crystal stem. Amethyst bowl 48.00
Cigarette Boxes
Crown Tuscan. H-P roses 30.00
Ebony with silver deposit 80.00
Seashell. Dolphin feet. Crown Tuscan 55.00
Cocktail. Rosepoint. Crystal 22.50
Cocktail Set. Farberware. 12½" shaker. 6 glasses (Mixed hues) Tray, 12x18½" 150.00
Compotes
5½". Nude stem. Flat shell, Crown Tuscan 95.00
6". Seashell. Crown Tuscan 50.00
7". Caprice. Crystal with silver deposit 20.00
8¼". Carmen top. Clear nude stem and base 75.00
Cordials
Farber holder. Amethyst 12.00
Rosepoint. Crystal 35.00
Wildflower. Crystal 22.50
Cracker Jar. Feather. Near cut 100.00
Creamers and Sugars
Chantilly. Crystal 22.50
Rosepoint. Crystal 35.00
Wedding Ring. Crystal 20.00
Cruet. Buzz Saw. Crystal 25.00
Cup and Saucer. Decagon. Pink 7.50
Cups
Custard. Feather. Crystal 10.00
Punch. Daisy. Crystal 12.50
Decanter. 8". Farberware. Amber 30.00

Epergne. Crystal. Two 3-branch candelabra with prisms. Two 8" vases, one bird figural 150.00
Flower Blocks
6". Bashful Charlotte. Apple green 65.00
8". Draped Lady. Crystal 40.00
8½". Draped Lady. Mandarin gold 135.00
8¾". Herron. Crystal 65.00
9". Bashful Charlotte. Amber 70.00
9½". Seagull. Crystal 40.00
Goblets
Aurora. Amethyst with crystal 10.00
Diane. Crystal 12.00
Rock Crystal. Lynbrook. Crystal 7.50
Rosepoint. Crystal. Orig. label 25.00
Roxanne. Crystal 18.00
Ice Bucket. Cleo. Ebony. Farber ware 35.00
Ice Tea Set. No. 3400. 80 oz. ball jug. Six 12 oz. tumblers 500.00
Ivy Balls
8½" high. Ribbed Optic. Green. Footed 45.00
9½" high. Nude. Crystal 75.00
Lamp Bases
5" globe vase. Apple Blossom. Amber. Mounted in brass base and brass socket fittings. Original cord and bulb 100.00
11½". Flashed green on ivory. Ebony base. C. 1920-25 .... 600.00
Nappy. Farberware. Light green 12.50
Nut Dish. 3". Mandarin Gold 12.00
Pitchers
32 oz. Caprice. Moonlight blue 50.00
62 oz. Honeycomb. Covered. Rubina 595.00
62 oz. Nautilus. Cobalt. Clear handle 65.00
80 oz. Rosepoint. Crystal 100.00
80 oz. Silver Deposit. No. 3400. Cobalt 275.00
Plates
6". Ebony 6.50
8". Rosepoint. Crystal 25.00
8½". Portia. Crystal 10.00
Punch Set. Tally Ho. Crystal with Carmen. 13" bowl, 17½" tray, 8-cups. 10 pieces. Set 450.00
Relishes
5½". Rosepoint. Gold 35.00
9". Portia. Three part. 4 feet 35.00
Salt and Pepper Shakers. 3¼". Empress. Crystal. Pair 20.00
Shell Dish. 7¼". H-P flowers. Crown Tuscan 65.00
Sherbets
Decagon. Crystal 6.00
Rosepoint 20.00
Wedding Ring. Crystal 8.00

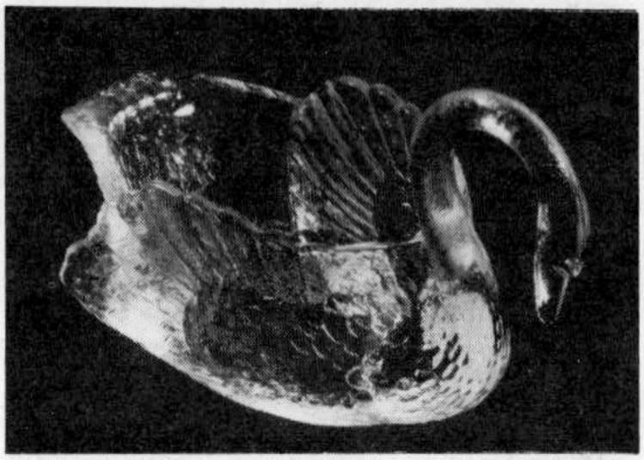

Swan. 3½". Crystal. Signed $25.00

Sugar, Creamer and Tray. Caprice. Moonlight. Set 40.00

Swans, Signed
- 2½". Crown Tuscan 32.50
- 3". Heatherbloom 75.00
- 3". Light pink 35.00
- 3½". Apple Green 35.00
- 3½". Crystal 25.00
- 3½". Dianthus 35.00
- 3½". Mandarin Gold 40.00
- 5". Crystal 60.00
- 6½". Ebony 100.00
- 7". Dianthus 65.00
- 8½". Charleton. Orig. label 275.00
- 8½". Mandarin Gold 100.00
- 11¾". Ebony 200.00

Swans, Unsigned
- 3½". Crystal 18.00
- 3½". Dianthus 25.00
- 3½". Emerald 50.00
- 3½". Mandarin Gold 30.00
- 8½". Crystal 40.00
- 10". Crystal 65.00

Trays
- 11". Apple Blossom. Mandarin Gold 30.00
- 13". Ebony with silver. Two-handled 75.00
- 16". Everglades 45.00

Tumblers
- Caprice. Blue 22.50
- Nearcut 15.00
- Rosepoint 18.50

Vases
- 3½". Cornucopia. Four shell pebble base. Crown Tuscan 55.00
- 5". Bulbous. Apple Blossom. Mandarin Gold 27.50
- 8". Ebony with silver 85.00
- 8". Martha Washington. Crystal ... 12.50
- 9½". Cornucopia. Crystal 15.00
- 10". Cornucopia. Shell foot. Crown Tuscan 150.00
- 10". Rosepoint. Trefoil 55.00
- 10½". Bud. Crystal. Nude stem .. 65.00
- 12". Japonica. Carmen 1250.00
- 12". Portia. Etched in gold. Ring stem. Crown Tuscan 225.00
- 12" high, 4¼" diam. Rosepoint. Keyhole-type 35.00

Water Set. 80 oz. ball jug, 6—12 oz. tumblers. Amethyst and clear. 7 pieces. Set 75.00

Wines
- Diane. Crystal 12.50
- Gloria. Crystal 10.00
- Nude. Ebony 65.00

CAMBRIDGE POTTERY

CAMBRIDGE

The Cambridge Art Pottery was incorporated in Ohio in 1900. Between1901 and 1909, the firm produced the usual line of jardinieres, tankards and vases with underglazed slip decorations and glazes similar to other Ohio potteries. Their line names included "Terrhea," "Oakwood," "Otoe" and others. In 1904, the company introduced Guernsey kitchenwares. It was so well received that it became the plant's primary product and in 1909 the name was changed to Guernsey Earthenware Company. All wares were marked.

Bowls
- 8". Berry motif. Glossy brown glaze .... $ 65.00
- 8". Terrhea. Standard glaze 55.00
- 9½". Floral slip decor. Glossy brown glaze 75.00

Candlesticks. 4". Terrhea. Standard glaze. Pair 30.00

Cookie Jar. 14" high. Brown glaze 60.00

Tankard. 12". Oakwood 125.00

Vases
- 3½". Bulbous. Floral decor. Standard glaze 65.00
- 8". Berry motif. 2-handled. Artist signed 175.00
- 8". Otoe 75.00
- 8". Terrhea 100.00
- 10". Acorn 85.00
- 10¾". Cherry spray. High brown glaze 125.00
- 11". Floral slip decor. Standard glaze 95.00
- 11". Oakwood 100.00
- 13". Bulbous base, slender neck. Artist signed. 250.00

CAMEO GLASS

Cameo glass is a form of cased glass. A shell of glass was prepared; then another layer of glass of a different color was faced to the first. A design was then cut through the outer layer leaving the inner layer exposed.

This type of art glass originated in Alexandria, Egypt, C. 100-200 A.D. The oldest and most famous example of Cameo glass is the Barberini or Portland vase which was found near Rome in 1582. It contained the ashes of Emperor Alexander Serverus who was assassinated by his own soldiers in 235 A.D.

Emile Galle', son of a French glassmaker, is probably one of the best known artists of Cameo glass. He established his factory at Nancy, France in 1884. Although much of the glass bears his signature, some he only designed while his many assistants did the actual work . . .even to signing his name. Glass made after his death in 1904 has a star before the name Galle'. Other makers of Cameo glass located in France included D'Argental, Daum (Bros.) Nancy, LeGras, DeLatte (1920's), etc. The majority of Cameo glass found on the market today was made in the 1884-1900 period. It is being reproduced in limited quantities in France; but being very inferior, it will not confuse a knowledgeable collector.

Atomizers

5¾". Sable colored on honey ground. Galle' .... $ 300.00

7½". Scenic. G. Ray Miller 350.00

Bottle. Perfume. 4". Lavender to pink. Daum Nancy 275.00

Bowls

4". Gold foil spatterings between layers of orange colored glass. Daum Nancy 250.00

4¾". Gray body. Purple overlay cut with blossoms and foliage. Galle' with star.................. 325.00

4¾". Trefoil. Yellow. Gray overlaid with orange, brown cut anemone blossoms. Galle' 650.00

5½". Scenic, ducks and oriental style medallions. Martin Luneville 450.00

7½ x 11" long. Purple and green on camphor ground. Daum Nancy 750.00

Box. 2¾x5". Scenic. Carved and enameled band on lid. LeGras .. 350.00

Ewer. 10½". Yellow overlaid with white, cut foliage, butterflies. Silver mounts. Unsigned Webb .. 1250.00

Inkwells

2¼x2¾". Blue. Green frosted ground, lavender flowers, green leaves. Floral trimmed decor on lid. Daum Nancy 325.00

Atomizer. 9". Cobalt floral decor. Signed Muller Fres Luneville $475.00

2¾" high. Gray ground with floral and French mottos. Four openings for pens. Faience 350.00

Jars

Cracker. Camphor colored glass with burgundy ivy. Brass rim, lid and bail. LeGras 500.00

Dresser. 4x5½". Complete with top cover in cameo. Deep rose color ground with leaves. Vines in maroon. D'Argental 450.00

Lamp Bases

9". Baluster-shape. Leaves and blossoms in two shades of burgundy on off-white ground. Round base. Galle' 300.00

9½". Rose ground with green shadings, blue and green butterflies, also enameled. LeGrass 500.00

13". Sailboat and trees on lake scene in colors of dark brown on pale amber. Muller Fres Luneville 500.00

13¼". Lake with orange skyline. LeGras 350.00

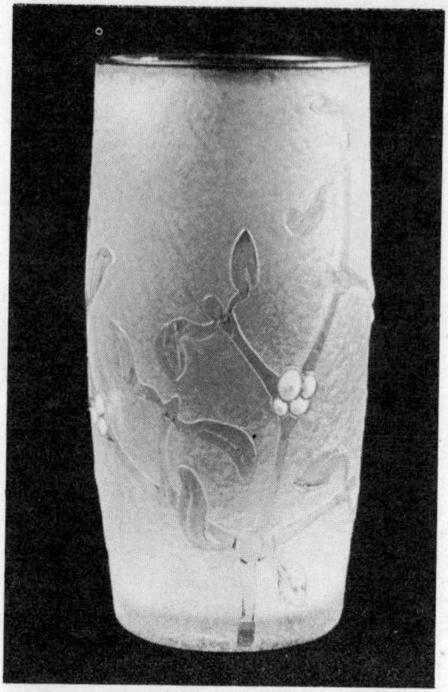

Vase. 4¾". White. Frosted ground. Floral decor. Gold trim. Daum Nancy $500.00

16". Baluster-shape. Light green. Cut with water lily and foliage. Metal mounts. Daum Nancy ... 500.00
16". Burgundy grapes against mottled yellow ground. LeVerre Francais. Charder 650.00
17¾". Forest scene in dark blue. Muller Fres Luneville 750.00

Pitchers
8" high. Yellow with grapes and leaves in tan and red. Galle' 400.00
11" high. Blue, green, reds. LeVerre Francias 500.00

Plaque. 5½x9". Woodland valley scene. Jacques Gruber 350.00

Rose Bowls
4¾x5". Green ground. Flowers and leaves with gold trim. LeGras 450.00
6x6". Yellow iridescent ground. Pink flowers. Window technique. Galle'.......................... 850.00

Salts
1¼x2". Summer scene. Daum Nancy 175.00
1¾x2¼". Hallmarked silver mount. Five petaled pink flowers, leaves and stems with gold enameled silver spoon 2" long. Webb 250.00

Toothpick Holder. 2¼x2½". Dark flowers on satin light green ground. St. Louis Nancy 225.00

Tumblers
4¼" high. Dutch girl dancing. Crystal and enamel. Galle' 250.00
5" high. Cut gold leaves and white berries on cranberry acid cut frosted ground. Daum Nancy 275.00

Vases
3¼". Clair de Lune ground. Goose girl, four geese. Enameled. Daum Nancy 500.00
3½". Baluster-shape. White satin ground with cobalt flowers, foliage. Richard 375.00
4". Blue ground with pink sunset, river and green hanging leaves with cypress trees. DeVez 400.00
4". Pillow-shape. Winter scene. Daum Nancy 500.00
4½". Carved flowers. Yellow ground. Allover decor. Webb 795.00
5½". Orange ground. Pine boughs in two shades of brown. E. Rigor 350.00
5½". Bulbous. Frosted amber ground. Wine cut rose. Scalloped top. Degue' 400.00
5⅝" high x 5" wide. Scenic. Beige ground. Pink clouds in sky. Purple, navy. Three acid cuts. Muller Fres Luneville 650.00
6". Baluster-shape. Olive green and orange leaf cuttings on frosted amber. D'Argental 650.00
6". Three cuttings in rich autumn colors of gold, orange, brown. Acid wheel carved. Galle' 850.00
6". White on cranberry. Butterfly on back. English 1950.00
6¼". Top flares to 8¼", 4¾" base. Cobalt cut to clear. Webb 650.00
6¾". Stick. Maroon berries, leaves on frosted ground. Traces of light green on bottom. Galle' 550.00
7¼" high x 7" diam. Three cuts. Flowers, foliage in blue on lighter blue frosted ground. Muller Fres Luneville 1200.00
7¼". Three cuts. Mountains, water, island, buildings, tree with defined robin. DeVez 750.00
7½". Flared, peach ground. Allover cutting. Enameled. Harbour scene. LeGras 595.00
8". Kelly green. Deeply acid cut in silver, gold. Monte Joye 350.00
9½". White on citron. Underside dated. English 2000.00

10". Ovoid-shape. Berries and leaves of magenta on frosted amber ground. D'Argental 850.00
10". Fruit, leaves, flowers in shades of pink, red. Gold ground. Galle' 1250.00
11½". Rampant lion on front in gold. Green ground. Daum Nancy 500.00
13¾". Peach to beige. H-P enameled decor in cranberry, green leaves. LeGras 725.00
14". Gold cameo cut border at top. Enameled pink, white flowers, purple centers. Frosted ground. Gold leaves, stems. Monte Joye .. 500.00
17". Three acid cuts. Frosted gold ground, flowers in pink, rose, deep burgundy. Galle' 2500.00
18". Burnt Amber. Trees on scenic ground. D'Argental 1250.00

CAMERAS

Photographica. . .the collecting of cameras and related items is still in its infancy. With the acceptance of photography as a recognized art form, interest in old cameras is increasing.
In the early 1900's, there were over 40 firms manufacturing cameras in the United States alone. Some of the pioneer makers; i.e. Graflex, Graphic, Leica, Zeiss, etc. because of the many models issued, have become special categories in themselves. Cameras, like automobiles, are now classified by collectors as antique, classic and collectible.

Kodak, Eastman. Brownie. #2A $25.00

Adlake Plate. C. 1903 ....$ 85.00
Agfa
Memo. f3.5-50mm 80.00
Plenax 25.00
Ansco
No. 3A Folding Buster Brown 27.50
Novelette. 4x5". 3 speed. Mahogany case. C. 1887-1898 .. 175.00
Argus
A2; Ilex f4.5-50mm 25.00
K; Ilex f4.5-50mm 135.00
Bolsey. Model C; Wollensak f3.2-44mm 45.00
Century View. With tripod 125.00
Ciroflex; Wollensak. f3.5-83mm .. 135.00
Contax I; with Tessar f2.8-5mm 250.00
Compass; Kern. f3.5-35mm 875.00
Cycle Poco. C. 1896 .... 50.00
Daguerreotype. Full plate. C. 1840 3500.00
Exakta A; Biotar f2.0-80mm 175.00
Graflex
National, Series II Tessar f3.5-75mm 175.00
No. O Graphic; 127 roll film 175.00
Graphic 35; Graflar f3.5-50mm.... 45.00
Kodaks
Bantam f4.5 Flash 35.00
Box. Various types .... 5.00++
Daylight. Model "B". C. 1892 .... 400.00
Folding Pocket (first model) C. 1898 .... 150.00
Folding. Various types .... 7.50++
Original. C. 1888 .... 2200.00
Recomar 33 .... 60.00
Retina f3.5-50mm 60.00
Stereo Brownie No. 2. C. 1905 .. 200.00
Super 620 (first automatic exposure) C. 1938 .... 1000.00
Mercury I; Tricor f3.5-35mm 40.00
Minolta 35 Model II; Tokkor f2.8-45mm 100.00
New Model View (Rochester Optical Co.) C. 1870's 100.00
Premo (Rochester Optical Co.) 3¼x4¼". C. 1895. .... 45.00
Robot. Luftwaffe; Tele-Xenar f3.5-75mm 300.00
Seneca Improved. Brass barrel lens 5x7" 75.00
Tourist Hawk-Eye (Blair) C. 1898 .. 175.00
Voigtlander Bessa II; Heliar f3.5-105mm 225.00
Miscellaneous
Safe Light. Kerosene 20.00
Tweety Bird. C. 1890 .... 50.00

CAMPAIGN ITEMS

Since the time of the campaign of William Henry Harrison for President of the United States in 1840, souvenirs have been distributed during the campaigns to advertise or win favor for the various candidates.

Badges
Bryan. Gilded white metal ....$ 40.00

Democratic National Convention, 1976. U.S. Representative 10.00
Progressive. National Convention, 1916. Messenger 30.00
Progressive National Convention, 1916. Press 40.00
Uncle Joe Cannon, 1908. Speaker of the House 25.00
Wilson. New York State Tammany Democratic Convention, Syracuse 1912 30.00

Bandanas
Harrison, B. 19x20". Silk 75.00
Roosevelt, T. Red. Portrait and slogan 40.00
Wilson, W 15.00

Books, Song
Garfield campaign. C. 1880 25.00
Lincoln campaign. C. 1860 50.00

Bowtie. Kennedy 12.50
Brooch. Official White House (given to guests). Enameled metal 25.00
Buckle, Belt. LBJ 5.00

Bumper Stickers
J.F. Kennedy 5.00
Wilkie-Wilson 8.50

Pin. Hoover. Red, white, blue ..$20.00

Buttons
Bryan-Kern 35.00
Bryan-Sewall 25.00
Bryan-Stevenson 40.00
Carter. "The Grin Will Win" 2.00
Carter-Mondale. "Goober Peas" 5.00
Dewey-Warren 7.50
Eisenhower-Nixon. 'They're for You" 20.00
Ford. "Happy Days Are Here Again-Fordzie" 2.00
Garfield, Arthur 15.00
Harding 10.00
Johnson-Kennedy, R 5.00
Landon 12.00
Landon-Knox 28.50
McGovern-Shriver. "Give Peace A Chance." 35.00
McKinley-Hobart 15.00
Nelson-Thomas 15.00
Nixon-Agnew. Inauguration 7.50
Parker-Davis 40.00
Rockefeller For President 10.00
Roosevelt, F.-Wallace 15.00
Roosevelt, T.-Fairbanks 22.50
Stevenson-Sparkman. "Go Forward..." 15.00
Taft 15.00
Taft-Sherman 30.00
Willkie-McNary 4.00
Wilson. "United Behind the President" 10.00
Wooley, J. C. Prohibition Party 50.00

Cane. McKinley 85.00
Catalogue. Roosevelt, T. Campaign Supplies, 1904 125.00
Cigar. Nixon, 10" 12.00
Cigarettes. McGovern 12.50
Clicker. Nixon 8.50

Flashers
Eisenhower. "I Like Ike". 2½" 5.00
GOP National Convention, 1964. "I Was There" 5.00
Johnson 5.00
Nixon. "I'm For Nixon" 10.00
Stevenson. "All the Way With Adlai" 1.50

Fobs
Republican National Convention, Phila., Pa. June 19, 1900 25.00
Republican National Convention, San Francisco, 1964 10.00
Roosevelt, T. GOP elephant, "Protection, Prosperity..." 50.00

Hat. Wallace. Straw, red-white-blue band 15.00
Invitation, Inaugural. Nixon, 1969 7.50

Lanterns
4"h. Brass. Bulbous with jet bulleyes. C. Early 1900's 65.00
Paper. Garfield, Arthur 65.00

License Plate Attachment. Willkie. "Hope of Our Country" 15.00
Matchbook. Nixon. "Now" 1.00
Medal. McKinley. Inauguration. Red-white-blue ribbon 35.00

Mugs
Delany, R.E. National Convention, Atlantic City, 1911 35.00
Hoover. 5½x7'' toby-type. Ceramic 95.00

Pencil. Al Smith for President, 1928. Figural head 22.00

Pins
Cox. Pewter 12.00
Eisenhower. "Ike with 5 Stars." 15.00
Kennedy, J.F. PT boat. Brass 15.00
McClellan. Bronze 28.00
National Alliance 7.50
Roosevelt, T. ⅞" 10.00
Smith. Red-white-blue enamel 5.00
Wilkie. Elephant head. Brass 18.50

Plate. 6¼" oval. "A Good Deal for a Tasty Meal". C. 1932 10.00
Program. Johnson-Humphrey. Inaugural Ceremonies 10.00

Ribbon. Cleveland-Hendricks, 1884.
  Silk floral, 6" 28.00
Sewing Kit. Hoover-Curtis, VP. Cardboard 10.00
Stickpins
  Cleveland. Rooster 10.00
  Roosevelt, T. White metal 15.00
Studs
  Cox. "I Will Crow in November." Raised letters 20.00
  Harrison, B. Celluloid with metal frame 20.00
  McKinley-Roosevelt, T. 22.50
Tabs
  Donkey 2.00
  Humphrey 1.50
  Johnson. Yellow-black 1.50
  Kennedy 4.00
  McGovern 1.00
Ticket. Democratic National Convention, 1920 .... 5.00
Tie Tac. Eisenhower 3.00
Tokens
  Garfield. Gilt metal, 25mm 15.00
  Grant. Brass. 26mm. C. 1880 .... 15.00
  Grant. Bronze. 60mm. C. 1868 .... 45.00
  Harrison. Brass. 28mm. C. 1840 .... 13.50
  Jackson, A. Brass. 25mm. "Hero of New Orleans". C. 1824 .... 40.00
  McClellan. Gilt metal. 25mm. "Union Must and Shall be Preserved." 15.00
  Parker-Davis. Gilt metal. 32mm 30.00
  Roosevelt-Fairbanks. Bronze, 30mm 30.00
T-Shirt. Carter. "Peanut Power" 5.00
Umbrella. McKinley-Hobart 200.00

CAMPHOR GLASS

Camphor glass derives its name from the color. It has a cloudy white appearance, similar to gum camphor. This was accomplished by treating the glass with hydrofluoric acid vapors.

Basket. 4" o.h. ....$ 15.00
Bookends. 7" long. Horse heads. Pair 85.00
Bottles
  4" high. Stoppered 14.50
  6½" high. Stoppered 25.00
Boxes
  3x5¼x5¾". Scroll design 30.00
  4". Powder. Hinged cover 30.00
  4½". Shallow. Enameled floral decor 25.00
  5". Hinged. Enamel holly spray 75.00
Candlesticks. 7" high. Centennial Expo, Phila. 1876. Pair 150.00
Compotes
  7" diam. Embossed running horses 50.00

Vase. 8". Fan-shaped. Frosted with clear leaf design and rim $75.00

  11¾" diam. Enameled pink and yellow leaves 65.00
Console Set. Compote 8½" high, 8½" diam. at top. 7¼" high candlesticks. Stems are seated cherubs. Set 100.00
Creamer. Individual. Wild rose and bowknot decor 15.00
Cruet. Enamel decor 30.00
Hands. Grapes and leaves at wrists 35.00
Owl. Standing. 3½". Green glass eyes 25.00
Pitchers. Water. Hobnail. Applied handle. Ground pontil 125.00
Plates
  6½". Easter greetings 18.50
  7¼". Fleur-de-lis decor 20.00
  7¼". Owl 20.00
Playing Card Holder. 3¾". Four feet 15.00
Rose Bowl. 4". Handpainted blue forget-me-nots. Gold trim 35.00
Shoes
  Boot. 2½" high 18.50
  Lady's. 5" long. "Made by Libbey Glass Co., Toledo, Ohio for 1893 World's Fair." 30.00
Toothpick Holders
  Plain 12.00
  Swirled. Ruffled top 27.50
Trays
  8x10½". Wild rose. Bowknot decor 18.50
  Pin. Blue and silver trim 10.00
Vases
  5". Handpainted red tulips, daisies 28.50

8½". Bulbous. Floral motif. 3 feet ... 35.00

10" high. 4½" diam., at ruffled turned-down top. H-P decor of pink and blue flowers, gold leaves and butterfly. Pedestal base 60.00

CANARY LUSTRE

(See, "English Yellow-Glazed Earthenware")

CANDLE MOLDS

Candles were a necessity of life in the past and candle making a major household chore.

First, a supply of animal fat had to be collected. The fat was then purified by boiling with water. The resulting tallow rose to the top and was skimmed off.

There were two methods used to make the final product. . .dipping and molding. Dipped candles were made by repeatedly dipping the wick in and out of the tallow until the desired size was formed. Molded candles were made in a tubular mold. The wick was threaded through the center of the tube and securely fastened. Then, the tallow was poured into the mold and allowed to harden. Candle molds were usually made of tin in various sizes. . .from a single candle mold to a grouping that made dozens of candles at a single time.

16-candle. Unusual circular grouping. Early tole $350.00

1-candle. 9¾" ....$	30.00
1-candle. 15"	75.00
4-candle	35.00
6-candle	50.00
8-candle	65.00
12-candle	85.00
16-candle. Pewter with wood frame	600.00
18-candle	125.00
18-candle. Pewter with wood frame	850.00
24-candle	125.00
24-candle. Pewter. Signed Webb ..	1250.00
48-candle	250.00
50-candle	300.00

CANDLESTICKS

A candlestick or candleholder is a portable holder with a hollow cup or spike to support a single candle.

Although candlelight has always played an important role in civilization. . .basic lighting, religious ceremonies, gracious hospitality; the wax tapers as we know them today were not developed until the 11th century and the candlestick has existed since. Man's imagination and creativity has improvised the once simple utilitarian form into a myriad of shapes, sizes and materials.

Also see "Sandwich Glass" and other specific categories.

Glass. 8½". Medium blue. Acid finish. Corinthian stem. Clambroth petal top. (Lee 186-3) $275.00

Brass

5". Marble bases. Pair ....$ 40.00
6". Square bases, shafts. Late Georgian. Pair 150.00
11½". "Queen of Diamonds." Pair 225.00
12". Stepped square base. English. Late 18th century 150.00
12½". "King of Diamonds." Pair .. 265.00
19". Hexagonal bases. Twisted shafts. Pair 275.00

Glass

6¾". Clear pressed square base. Double knob. Free blown socket .. 200.00
7¼". Cranberry shades with ornate silverplated holders. Victorian. Pair 250.00
7¼". Dolphin on scalloped base. Hexagonal top. Translucent blue. (McKearn 196) 375.00
7½". Medium blue. Attributed to NEG Co. (McKearn 200-29) 395.00
8½". Deep emerald green. Hexagonal base and top. NEG Co. (un-recorded) 700.00
8½". Medium blue. Acid finish. Corinthian stem. Clambroth petal top. (Lee 186-3) 275.00
10½". Dolphin. Clambroth base. Jade green petal top. Acid finish 1500.00
11½". Crucifix. Pale smoky lavender 500.00

Iron

5". Hogscraper. Pat'd 1853 ...... 65.00
6½". Hogscraper. Hanging-type 85.00
9". Hogscraper. Signed Shaw 135.00

Wood

8". Turned oak. Pair 50.00
8¾". Sheraton-style. Square base. Sharp turned shaft 50.00
11½". Turned mahogany. Pair .. 50.00

CANDY CONTAINERS

At the turn of the 20th century, candy makers used glass containers shaped like automobiles, boats, etc. for packaging small candies. These were popular 'what did you bring me' children's gifts. After the candy was eaten, the child still had a toy remaining.
Highly collectible. . .therefore, reproductions!

Airplane. "Spirit of Good Will." ..$ 45.00

Autos

Limousine 55.00
Pierce Arrow 40.00
Stream Line 35.00
Volkswagon 18.50
Zeppelin-type. Repainted tin bottom and wheels 35.00

Ball Player 35.00
Beau Brummel 45.00

Rooster. 8" high. Clear $45.00

Betty Boop 25.00
Boat, Speed 25.00
Building. "1914" 25.00
Bull Dog 25.00
Bus, Greyhound 35.00
Buster Brown with Tige 50.00
Carpet Sweeper 30.00
Charlie Chaplin, by barrel 65.00
Chick, Baby. Standing 35.00
Chicken on basket 45.00
Cigar. 5½" long 37.50
Clock, Alarm 45.00
Clock, Mantle 45.00
Clown on horse 65.00
Dirigible. "Los Angeles" 55.00
Dog, Sitting. 3" high 18.50
Donkey pulling cart 37.50
Duck on basket 50.00
Elephant, GOP 85.00
Fire Engine. Metal wheels 50.00
House 25.00
Kewpie, standing next to barrel ... 85.00
Lantern, R.R. 25.00
Liberty Bell 50.00
Locomotive #1026 .... 30.00
Moon Mullins, Plastic hat 25.00
Motorcycle 35.00
Nursing Bottle 8.00
Opera Glasses 40.00
Pistol. Amber 45.00
Rabbit. 5½" high 35.00
Rabbit with Eggshell 45.00
Radio. "Tune-In" 65.00
Revolver. 8" 25.00
Rolling Pin 30.00

Santa Claus. Climbing down chimney. Tin closure 60.00
Satchel with handle 25.00
Scotty Dog 25.00
Spark Plug 85.00
Submarine 40.00
Tank 25.00
Telephone. Candlestick with pewter top and wooden receiver 55.00
Telephone. Dial-type. Victory Glass Co. 20.00
Top, Spinning 30.00
Trolley, Toonerville 75.00
Trumpet. Milk glass 40.00
Trunk. Milk glass 75.00
Turkey 35.00
Wheelbarrow 40.00
Windmill 35.00

CANES

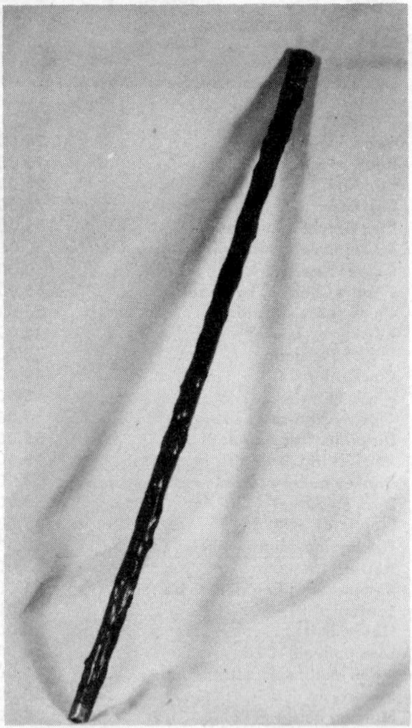

Walking Stick. Briar. 33¼". Silvered top and tip. $30.00

Bottle Cane. Glass inside liner for holding liquor. Removable head exposes cork. 36" long .... $ 150.00

Glass
- 35" long. Clear glass with blue-red swirl ribbon inside 165.00
- 48" long. Green 65.00
- 60" long. Green 85.00

Horn handle. Personalized 75.00
Horseman's Special. English 85.00
Parade. Political-type. Elephant head 50.00

Sword Canes
- 35" long. Horn handle in shape of dog's head 150.00
- 38" long. Bone and wooden handle 75.00

Umbrella Cane. 34" long. Black umbrella. Wood case 85.00

Walking Sticks
- Gold Head. 14K. Scrolled and monogrammed 100.00
- Hickory. Carved dog's head 135.00
- Sterling Silver Head. Monogrammed 75.00

Handles Only

Amethyst. 12½". Cut glass with tortoise shell 195.00
Gold. 14K. Plain 75.00
MOP and Gold 60.00
Sterling. Walking stick top 30.00

CANTON CHINA

Canton is a type of oriental porcelain made in Canton, China for export to America from the 1820's to the present. These wares were hand-decorated in light to dark blues underglaze on white, with simple scenes of houses, mountains and a bridge in the center panel. Borders on earlier Canton feature a rain-and-cloud motif; while later pieces usually have the straight-line border. The Canton pattern has the second greatest variety of forms found in Chinese export porcelain. The markings "Made in China" and "China" indicate wares made after 1891.

Bottles, Water
- 8½" .... $ 325.00
- 10" 375.00

Bowls
- 4½". Waste 75.00
- 6" 95.00
- 9¼". Fruit with underplate, reticulated. 750.00

Butter Dish. 3 pieces 750.00
Cache Pot. 5x8" 750.00

Chargers
- 16" 450.00
- 18" 500.00
- 20" 700.00

Coffee Pots
- 9". Dome lid 750.00

Bottle, Water. 10″ $375.00

Cup and Saucer. Loop handle .. $50.00

Cups and Saucers	
Cross handle	75.00
Loop handle	50.00
Fish-shaped dish. 6″ long. Late	75.00
Garden Seat. 19″ high. Octagonal-shaped	1250.00
Ginger Jars, Covered	
3″	75.00
6″	175.00
9″	350.00
Hot Water Dish. 9″ octagonal	275.00
Lamp. 6½″. Ginger jar base. Brass fittings	350.00
Leaf-shaped dish. 5½x7″	150.00
Mug	225.00
Pitchers	
4″	150.00
8″	275.00
10″	450.00
Plates	
7″	60.00
8½″	70.00
8½″. Soup	65.00
9½″	100.00
10¼″. Square	250.00
Platters	
7x10″	150.00
8x10½″	175.00
14½x17½″	275.00
16½x20½″	350.00
Posset Cup. 3″. Polychromed	150.00
Sugar, Covered. Loop handles	195.00
Tea Caddy. Hexagonal	750.00
Teapots	
4″, 4″ square base	550.00
6¼″	600.00
Tile. 6″ square	225.00
Vegetable Dishes, Covered	
8″ oval. Late	100.00
11½″ oval. Strawberry finial. Scalloped rims	475.00
12″ oval. Boar Head handles. C. 1810	850.00

CAPO-DI-MONTE CHINA

Capo-di-Monte porcelain was originally made in Italy from 1743 to 1760 in a soft paste and again from 1770 to 1834 in a hard paste. Since then other factories in France, Germany, Hungary and Italy have produced Capo-di-Monte-style porcelain including the famous "Crown" with "N" mark.

It is estimated that more than 90% of the wares encountered on the market today are of this later period and should be designated as "Capo-di-Monte-Type."

*Bell. 4½″ .... $	35.00
Boxes	
2x3x4″. Heart-shaped. Cupid with garland of flowers	150.00
3¼x4½x11″. Early	450.00
3½″. diam. King Neptune, two horses, flowers on side	125.00
4¼x6″. Children in relief	125.00

Plaque. Neptunes Maidens. 11x16¾" including frame. 18th century. $275.00

Creamer. 3½". Bacchus 135.00
Cups and Saucers
Chocolate. Portrait 100.00
Tea. Cherubs with flower garlands, maidens 75.00
Ewer. 11" high. Allover decor of cherubs, people, animals 350.00
*Fairy Lamp 50.00
Figurines
6x7". Three dogs and bull under tree 500.00
7". Flower girl and boy. Pair 350.00
8". Lady and Gentleman 95.00
15". Madonna and Child 150.00
Pitchers. 7". Masked faces in relief. Female form handle 300.00
Plaques
3x4¼". Five children playing in flower garden. Brass frame 125.00
5½x7¼". Lady in shell boat drawn by dolphins, surrounded by cherubs 250.00
11x15". Group of satyrs with Bacchus on mule. Early 800.00
Plate. 10½". Cupid border. Floral center on cobalt ground. Fatto A. Anno. 1818 .... 150.00
Teapot. Figures of lady with mirror and her maiden in relief. Serpent spout 195.00
Urns
7". Typical colors. Early 250.00
10". Covered. Late. Pair 150.00
11½". Covered. Cupids, men, women, etc. Early 19th century. Pair 500.00
14". Karamos. Late 195.00

*Reproduced Item

CARLSBAD CHINA

This porcelain was made at Carlsbad, Austria, by a number of factories. Most of the items found in shops and collections today were made after 1891.

Plate. 8½". Portrait center. Green border. Gold trim $45.00

Bowls
3¼". Cream ground with flowers in red, green and gold .... $ 30.00
6". Classic figures decor 40.00
Chocolate Pot. 9". Blue bachelor's buttons on violet ground. Gold trim 100.00
Cups and Saucers
Demitasse. Lady and gentleman decor 40.00
Demitasse. Portrait. "Meditation." Heavy gold trim 100.00
Tea. Pink and yellow roses on white ground. 1" gold scroll with blue top border 35.00
Ewer. 11" high. Picnic scene. Tan ground 50.00
Mayonnaise Set. Portrait. Green with gold 50.00
Pitchers
5½" high. Helmet-shaped. Leaf decor with bird 45.00
10½" high. Helmet-type. Cream ground, white lilies. Gold handle and trim 75.00
11½" high. Pink ground with cobalt blue band at top and bottom. Gold floral decor. Gold handle 85.00
Plates
8½". Oyster. Scalloped gold rim. Violet decor 37.50
8½". Portrait center. Green border with gold trim 45.00
11½". Hanging-type. Dark green

border with gold gilt. Center scene of two ladies at tea, gentleman visitor 75.00
Platter. 15¼" long. Blue floral decor. Gold trim 75.00
Tea Caddies
Pink to white background. Woman with cupid decor........ 75.00
Portrait of lady on side.......... 85.00
Tray. 6½x9½". Pin compartments. Crimped border with sepia, green florals on white. Gold trim 28.50
Tureen. Covered. 7½x12". Violets, daisies and leaves. Gold trim 50.00
Vase. 7". Cupids. Gold trim 65.00

CARNIVAL GLASS-AMERICAN

Carnival glass, sometimes referred to as "Taffeta Glass" or "Poor Man's Tiffany," was made during the 1900-1925's. The majority was manufactured near Wheeling, W. Va. Carnival glass has been reproduced profusely in various patterns and colors. Imperial Glass Co. of Ohio, one of the largest producers of 'new' Carnival glass, was purchased by the Lenox China Co. Lenox intends to discontinue some of Imperial's line and re-introduce others. These discontinued patterns are now collectible.

ACORN BURRS

Berry Set. 7 pieces. Marigold ....$ 175.00
Butter, Covered. Green 200.00
Punch Bowls with bases
Marigold 300.00
Purple 475.00
Table Set. 4 pieces. Green 500.00

APPLE TREE

Water Sets. 7 pieces
Blue ....$ 425.00
Marigold 250.00

BIRDS AND CHERRIES

BonBon. Marigold ....$ 37.50
Bowl. 9". Green 195.00
Compotes
Marigold 35.00
Purple 65.00

BLACKBERRY SPRAY

Bowls
6½." Slag red ....$ 200.00
9". Green 65.00
10". Marigold 25.00
Compote. Small. Pastel 60.00

Tumbler. "Grape" (Northwood). White $125.00

Hats
Marigold 22.50
Pastel........ 100.00
Purple 30.00
Slag red........ 125.00

CHERRY (NORTHWOOD)

Bowls
7½". Flat. Marigold ....$ 28.50
10". Footed. Marigold 57.50
Butter, Covered. Purple 275.00
Compote. Purple 75.00
Table Set. 4 pieces. Marigold 400.00

CIRCLED SCROLL

Berry Set. 5 pieces ....$ 75.00
Butter. Marigold 100.00
Creamer. Purple 75.00
Hat. Marigold 45.00
Spooner. Marigold 50.00
Sugar. Marigold 45.00

COIN DOT

Bowls
7½". Marigold ....$ 16.50
8½". Aqua. Opalescent 85.00
8½". Purple 30.00
Pitcher, Water. Marigold 100.00
Water Set. 7 pieces. Marigold...... 275.00

CORN

Vases
- Blue $ 225.00
- Marigold 275.00
- Pastel Green 185.00
- Purple 225.00

CRAB CLAW (IMPERIAL)

Bowl. 9". Marigold $ 25.00
Pitcher, Water. Marigold 275.00
Sauce. Marigold 13.50
Tumbler. Marigold 35.00

DAHLIA

Bowl. 9". Marigold $ 45.00
Butter, Covered. Marigold 175.00
Cream and Sugar, Covered. Purple 165.00
Sauce. Pastel 35.00
Water Sets. 7 pieces
- Marigold 850.00
- Purple 1000.00

DANDELION

Mugs
- Aqua $ 300.00
- Blue 175.00
- Marigold 135.00
- Marigold. "Knights Templar" 250.00

Water Sets. 7 pieces
- Green 650.00
- Ice Blue 1650.00
- Marigold 450.00
- Purple 800.00

FASHION

Bowls
- Punch. 2 pieces. Marigold $ 100.00
- Rose. Marigold 50.00

Cream and Sugar. Individual size.
- Marigold. Set 60.00

Pitcher, Water. Purple 285.00
Punch Set. 8 pieces. Marigold 225.00
Tumbler. Marigold 37.50
Water Set. 7 pieces. Marigold 295.00

FLUTE

Bowl. 9". Purple $ 65.00
Butter, Covered. Marigold 95.00
Creamers and Sugars
- Green 65.00
- Purple 100.00

Goblet. Marigold 15.00
Punch Set. 8 pieces. Marigold 250.00
Salt, Footed. Marigold 35.00
Toothpicks
- Green 55.00
- Marigold 40.00
- Purple 75.00

Water Set. 7 pieces. Marigold 250.00

GRAPE (IMPERIAL)

Berry Set. 7 pieces. Purple $ 150.00
Bowls
- 7½". Marigold 18.50
- 9". Marigold 25.00
- 9". Purple 40.00

Cups and Saucers
- Green 85.00
- Marigold 55.00

Plates
- 6". Marigold 28.50
- 8½". Ruffled. Purple 55.00

Punch Sets
- 8 pieces. Marigold 175.00
- 8 pieces. Purple 325.00

Wine. Marigold 20.00

GRAPE (NORTHWOOD)

Berry Set. With Thumbprint. 7 pieces. Purple $ 250.00
Bowls
- 7". Pastel 95.00
- 11". Marigold 100.00

Butters, Covered
- Marigold 195.00
- Pastel 525.00
- Purple 250.00

Candlestick. Purple 195.00
Cologne. Stoppered. Pastel 450.00
Cracker Jar. Purple 375.00
Creamer. Purple 150.00
Dresser Trays
- Blue 225.00
- Green 225.00
- Marigold 175.00

Hat Pin Holders
- Green 150.00
- Marigold 125.00

Pitchers, Tankard
- Green 450.00
- Marigold 300.00

Powder Jar. Green 85.00
Punch Cup. Pastel 50.00
Spooner. Purple 175.00
Tumbler. With Thumbprint. Purple 35.00
Water Sets
- Marigold. 7 pieces 325.00
- Purple. 7 pieces 400.00

Whimsey. Purple 200.00

GRAPE AND LATTICE (FENTON)

Pitcher, Water. Purple $ 300.00
Plates
- 7". Marigold 25.00

7". White	40.00
Tumbler. Marigold	22.50
Water Sets	
5 pieces. White	600.00
7 pieces. Marigold	225.00

HEART AND VINE (FENTON)

Bowls	
7". Purple. Candy ribbon rim $	50.00
8½". Blue. Candy ribbon rim	40.00
8½". Green	40.00
8½". Marigold	25.00
Plates	
9". Blue	115.00
9". Purple	135.00
Vase. 7½". Green	45.00

INVERTED STRAWBERRY

Berry Set. 7 pieces. Green $	275.00
Bowls	
8½". Purple	95.00
9". Marigold	60.00
Creamer. Marigold	65.00
Pitcher. Marigold	350.00
Powder Jar. Marigold	65.00
Tumbler. Marigold	40.00

KITTEN

Banana Dish. Marigold $	75.00
Bowls	
4½". Marigold	55.00
5". Pinched. Purple	80.00
Cup and Saucer. Marigold	125.00
Spooner. Marigold	75.00

LION (FENTON)

Bowls	
7". Blue $	125.00
7". Marigold	75.00
Plate. 6". Marigold	195.00

LUSTRE ROSE (IMPERIAL)

Bowls	
8". Footed. Marigold $	20.00
9". Marigold	17.50
Butter, Covered. Marigold	45.00
Cream and Sugar. Marigold	60.00
Creamer. Purple	75.00
Pitchers	
Milk. Marigold	20.00
Water. Green	150.00
Plate. 9". Amber	50.00
Rose Bowl. Marigold	28.50
Table Sets. 4 pieces	
Marigold	150.00
Purple	400.00

Tumblers	
Clambroth	30.00
Green	27.50
Marigold	15.00
Purple	35.00

ORANGE TREE (FENTON)

Bowls	
7". Pastel $	60.00
9". Blue	40.00
9". Green	50.00
9". Red Slag	275.00
10". Footed. Marigold	65.00
11". Footed. Purple	85.00
Butter, Covered. Blue	165.00
Creamers and Sugars, Individual Size	
Blue	75.00
Marigold	50.00
Pastel	100.00
Hat Pin Holder. Marigold	75.00
Mugs	
Blue	47.50
Marigold	25.00
Red Slag	150.00
Plates. 9"	
Blue	65.00
Marigold	45.00
Pastel	100.00
Purple	75.00
Punch Sets. 8 pieces	
Blue	350.00
Marigold	250.00
Pastel	450.00
Rose Bowl. Marigold	27.50
Sherbet. Marigold	20.00
Water Sets. 7 pieces	
Blue	475.00
Marigold	375.00
Pastel	750.00
Wines	
Blue	40.00
Marigold	25.00

ORIENTAL POPPY

Plate. 9". Pastel $	250.00
Water Sets. 7 pieces	
Green	800.00
Marigold	450.00
Pastel	1250.00

PEACOCK AT FOUNTAIN (NORTHWOOD)

Berry Sets. 7 pieces	
Blue $	275.00
Marigold	175.00
Purple	250.00
Bowl. 10". Footed. Marigold	125.00
Butters, Covered	
Green	265.00
Marigold	110.00

Creamers and Sugars, Covered

Blue	195.00
Marigold	125.00
Purple	175.00
Punch Sets. 8 pieces	
Marigold	350.00
Purple	475.00
Spooner. Purple	80.00
Sugar, Covered. Pastel blue	200.00
Water Sets. 7 pieces	
Blue	475.00
Marigold	325.00
Pastel	850.00
Purple	450.00

SINGING BIRD (NORTHWOOD)

Berry Set. 7 pieces. Purple	$ 275.00
Butter, Covered. Marigold	125.00
Creamer. Purple	70.00
Mugs	
Blue	65.00
Green	65.00
Marigold	40.00
Purple	65.00
Pitcher, Water. Marigold	195.00
Sauce. Marigold	18.00
Sugar, Covered. Marigold	60.00
Tumblers	
Green	35.00
Marigold	27.50
Purple	37.50

SPRINGTIME (NORTHWOOD)

Butters, Covered	
Marigold	$ 135.00
Purple	195.00
Cream and Sugar. Green	125.00
Sauce. Purple	30.00
Spooner. Marigold	55.00
Water Set. 7 pieces. Marigold	375.00

VINTAGE

Berry Set. 7 pieces. Marigold	$ 75.00
Bowls	
7½". Marigold	15.00
9". Purple	27.50
10". Footed. Marigold	65.00
Compote. Green	45.00
Nut Dish. 6". Marigold	30.00
Plate. 7". Blue	42.50
Powder Box. Covered. Marigold	50.00
Punch Cup. Marigold	12.00
Rose Bowl. Pastel	100.00
Wines	
Marigold	17.50
Purple	27.50

WINDFLOWER

Bowls 8½"	
Amber	$ 100.00
Blue	45.00
Marigold	20.00
Purple	40.00
Plate. 9". Marigold	45.00
Sauce Boat. Marigold	30.00

CAROUSEL FIGURES

When, where or how the carousel originated is truly unimportant when compared to the excitement and joy of riding the Merry-Go-Round. Prancing steeds, snarling tigers and graceful swans set to calliope music and scintillating lights can transfer all. . .young and old into the Magic Kingdom.

Early figures were usually hand crafted by superior craftsmen and artists. The prices listed can serve only as a guide as condition is extremely important.

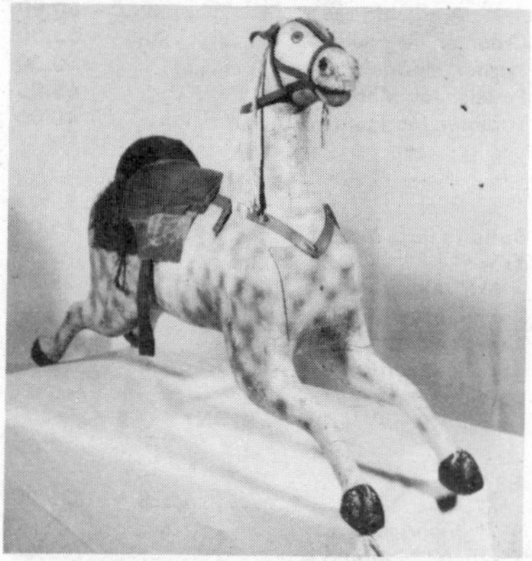

Horse. 46" long. All original including leather saddle and halter. Unknown maker. C. 1850. ....$850.00

Camel. French	$ 3000.00
Cat. French	3500.00
Deer. Muller	4000.00
Dog. Spillman	2000.00
Goat. Spillman	3000.00
Horses	
Dentzel	1000.00
Loott. Jeweled	3000.00
Muller	3000.00
Parker	1000.00
Parker. Jeweled	1500.00
Spooner	2000.00

Spillman. Jumper. Jeweled	1350.00
Spillman. Standing	1750.00
Stein and Goldstein	3500.00
Tiger. Heyn	5000.00

CASTLEFORD

Castleford is a soft paste porcelain made in Yorkshire, England in the early 1800's for the American trade. The ware has a warm white ground, scalloped rims (resembling castle tops) and trimmed with deep blue. Occasionally, pieces were further decorated with a coat-of-arms, eagles or "Liberty". Few pieces, if any, are marked.

Sugar, Covered..............$225.00

Bowl. 5" diam ....$	175.00
Creamer	275.00
Spill Holder	150.00
Sugar, Covered	225.00
Teapot	275.00

CASTOR SETS

A castor set is a set of matched condiment bottles held within a frame or holder. Most castor sets consisted of three to five pressed glass bottles in a silverplated frame. Some consisted of cut glass bottles and a sterling silver holder. Occasionally, an all-glass set is encountered. Although castor sets were known as early as the 1700's, most found today are from the Victorian period when they were quite popular.

6-bottle. Silverplated holder ..$175.00

3-Bottle. Square cut glass bottles in silverplated Sheffield holder ..$	125.00
3-Bottle. Ribbed. Silverplated holder. English	50.00
3-Bottle. Ribbed Palm. Pewter tops, frame.......................	100.00
4-Bottle. Cut glass. Silverplated round holder	75.00
4-Bottle. Pressed glass bottles in glass holder. Metal ring post	65.00
4-Bottle. Rubina cut glass bottles. Footed square silverplated holder with center post	195.00
4-Bottle. Square silverplated holder. English	150.00
5-Bottle. Button Band. Silverplated holder	150.00
5-Bottle. Clear glass bottles. Blue glass holder with center post	175.00
5-Bottle. Cut and etched bottles in silverplated holder	145.00
5-Bottle. Flint glass bottles with pewter holder	200.00
5-Bottle. Gothic. Pewter holder. "Israel Trask."	175.00
5-Bottle. Honeycomb. Resilvered holder. Meriden #39	175.00

5-Bottle. Matching bottles. Replated tops and holder 125.00
6-Bottle. Cut Diamond. Oval silver-plated holder 175.00
6-Bottle. Grey cut bottles. Silver-plated revolving holder 150.00
8-Bottle. Cut glass. Sterling tops and holder. Ground stoppers. Hallmarked and documented. C. 1733 .... 3500.00
8-Bottle. Pressed glass bottles. Silverplated tops and holder. Simpson H. Miller Co 225.00

CATALOGUES AND MAGAZINES

Catalogues and magazines of yesteryears are of interest today for various reasons. They are not only entertaining; but are an invaluable source of information in many fields. . .antiques, architecture, fashion and the performing arts. There is another important reason: the covers themselves are highly collectible for their art-work. Many of these covers were executed by talented and now recognized artists. True, the covers may be lithographs, but nonetheless . . . limited editions.
Condition of the covers and text is IMPORTANT. The listed prices should be consulted as a guide.

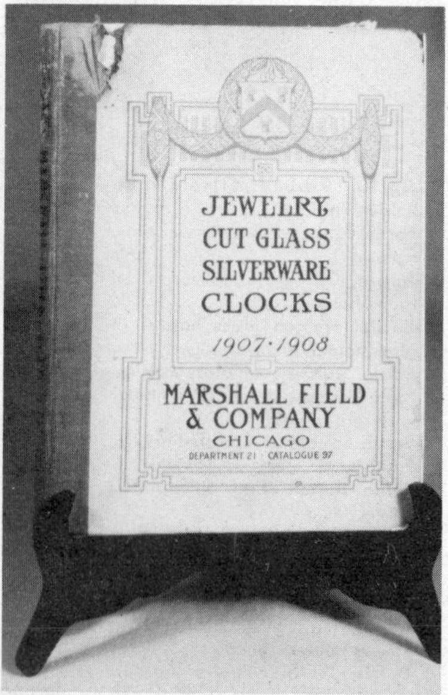

Catalogue. "Marshall Field & Co., Chicago." 1907-1908 ....$50.00

Magazine. "Woman's Home Companion." July 1939. ....$5.00

American Flyer Manufacturing Co. 8pp. 1920's ....$ 25.00
Antiques
1922-1927. Each 15.00
1928-1940. Each 5.00
1941-1958. Each 3.50
Atwater Kent Radio. 30pp. 1927 .. 15.00
Baseball Digest. 1947-1964. Each .. 2.50
Bennet Bros. Blue Book. 616pp. 1952 .... 15.00
Better Homes & Gardens
1946-1956. Each 4.00
1957-1968. Each 2.50
Boy Scouts of America
Equipment. 34pp. 1932 .... 10.00
Manual. 1930 .... 5.00
Burgess Seed and Nursery. 48pp. 1922 .... 5.00
Butterick Fashions. 20pp. 1907 .... 7.50
Cutprice Pharmacy. 1898 .... 25.00
Etude Music. 1905-1945. Each 2.00
Fisher Carriage Co. 33pp. 1903 .... 25.00
Fortune
1930-Vol. 1#1 .... 50.00
1930-1936. Each 15.00
1937-1956. Each 7.50
1957-1964. Each 5.00
Fostoria Glass Co. 96pp. 1965 .... 100.00
Good Housekeeping
1903-1932. Each 15.00
1933-1944. Each 5.00
1945-1956. Each 3.00

Gourmet
1945-1956. Each 5.00
1957-1968. Each 2.50
Higginbotham-Bailey Co. Christmas, 84pp. 1967 .... 15.00
International Harvester Co. Almanac and Encyclopedia. 96pp. 1911 .... 10.00
Jack 'n Jill. 52pp. 1945. Each 5.00
Kenner Products Co. 64pp. 1967 .. 6.00
Larkin Co.
1930. Fall-Winter. 220pp 35.00
1937. Spring-Summer. 176pp. .. 20.00
Life
1936-Vol. 1, No. 1 .... 75.00
1936-Vol. 1, No. 2, 3. Each 25.00
1936-1946. Each 5.00
1947-1966. Each 3.50
Look. 1941-1951. Each 8.50
McCalls
1913-1919. Each 15.00
1920-1939. Each 7.50
1940-1964. Each 3.50
Model Engineer and Light Machinery Review, The. 1920's. Each 4.00
Montgomery Ward. Fall-Winter. 1024pp. 1954-55 .... 20.00
Movie Theater
1920-1930. Each 20.00
1930-1950. Each 7.50
National Bellas Hess (fashions). 60pp 1934 .... 5.00
National Geographics
1899-1900. Each 40.00
1900-1910. Each 20.00
1911-1920. Each 10.00
1921-1950. Each 5.00
Ostermoor & Co., N.Y. (beds, cribs, etc.) 60pp. 1903 .... 35.00
Popular Mechanics, Popular Science
1914-1920. Each 10.00
1921-1924. Each 7.50
1925-1940. (Popular Science) Each 5.00
1941-1968. Each 3.00
Popular Photography, Modern Photography
1937-Vol. 1, #1,2. Each 10.00
1938-1949. Each 5.00
1950-1969. Each 2.50
Punch. 1887-1895. Each 5.00
Saturday Evening Post
1888 .... 20.00
1900-1930. Each 12.50
1931-1950. Each 6.00
Saturday Evening Post (Leyendecker or Rockwell covers)
1900-1945. Each 35.00
1946-1969. Each 15.00
Sears Roebuck
1928-1929. Fall-Winter. 1104pp 30.00
1958. Spring-Summer. 1426pp .. 15.00
Siegel Cooper Co. (music boxes, instruments, etc.) 264pp. 1905 .... 50.00
Singer Mfg. Co., The. 1930 .... 12.00
Spiegels. Spring-Summer. May Stern Co. 272pp. 1935 .... 15.00
Sport. 1947-1960. Each 4.00
Sports Illustrated. 1955-1973. Each 4.00
Taiyo Trading Co. (Oriental merchandise) 64pp. C. 1930's 60.00
Tell City Furniture Co. 1934 ...... 20.00
Thayer & Chandler (artists' china and supplies) 36pp. 1918 ...... 15.00
Time
1923-1925. Each 15.00
1926-1940. Each 7.50
1941-1956. Each 3.50
Winchester World's Standard Guns & Ammunition. 88pp. 1925 .... 50.00
Worcester Royal Porcelain Co. Ltd., The. 32pp. 1955 .... 20.00

CELADON

Celadon is an Oriental porcelain with a characteristic of pale grey-green glaze. The name was taken from the character Celadon in D'Urfe's "L'Astree" of the 17th century. The ware has been made for centuries in China, Japan and Korea.

Bowl. 7''. Shallow and footed. Polychromed decoration. C. 1810 ....$250.00

Bowls
10¼'', 2½'' high. 19th century ....$ 650.00
15¾'', 5'' high. Turned-up rim .. 1200.00

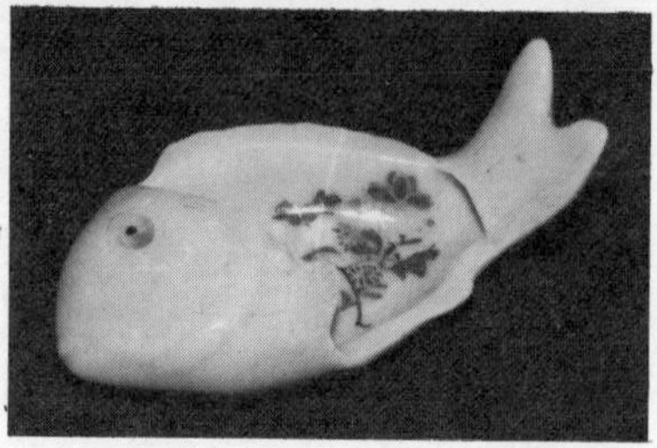

Condiment. 5½" long. Fish-shaped $55.00

Charger. 14½". Birds, insects, mums, etc 375.00
Condiment. 5½" long. Fish-shaped 55.00
Creamer. Foliage design with gold 175.00
Cup and Saucer, Demitasse. Typical decor 45.00
Inkwell. 2x3½x3¾". Openwork sides. Simulated bamboo cross pieces 75.00
Jar. Covered. 7" high. Floral decor .. 75.00
Plates
7". Collar base. Scalloped rim. 19th century 150.00
7¼". Birds, butterflies and florals 65.00
9". Square. Typical decor. 19th C. 150.00
10". Flowers, butterflies, etc. 19th century 225.00
Platters
6½x8". Floral decor with birds, butterflies. 19th century 250.00
8x11". Leaf-shaped. Insects and florals 275.00
Soap Dish. 3½x4x5". Hanging-type 75.00
Sugar. 5". Loop handles 125.00
Teapot. 5" high. Bulbous. Covered. Raised pastel floral decor 225.00
Umbrella Holder. 8½x24½". Typical decor of flowering tree, etc. 750.00
Vases
7¾". Underglaze decor panels. Ears. Late 150.00
9". Applied Foo Dog and small animal near top. Early 600.00
9¼". Floral decor with bird on front. Squirrel handles with gold 300.00
9½". Hexagonal shape. Bird and floral decor. Late 150.00
11". Hexagonal. Pink and white flowers. 19th century 375.00
12¾". Bulbous, Dragon draped part way around center 500.00

CELLULOID ITEMS

Celluloid is the trade name for a material made of nitrocellulose and camphor invented just before 1870. It was used mainly in making toilet articles; but also as an inexpensive material for figurines, jewelry, vases, etc. to simulate the more expensive amber, bone, ivory or tortoise shell.

Jewelry Box. 2¼x3¾x6". Hinged lid $12.50

Album, Photo. Approximately 8½x 12" ....$ 25.00
Baby Rattle. 2½" diam 6.50
Bank. "My Own Bank." Clock-shaped 15.00
Boxes
Collar. Lined 20.00
Glove. 3x4x12". Mottled green with decor of flowers. Lid has center panel showing two children with lamb. Original lining 40.00
Jewelry. 7½x12x14½". Interior lined with red velvet. Mirrored lid. Slant front 50.00
Powder. 2x4" 6.50
Trinket. Covered. 2½" diam. Transfer on lid and front. Man and woman 12.00
Bracelet. Bangle-type 7.50
Comb. 8⅝" 5.00
Dresser Sets
5 pieces. Tray, mirror, hair receiver, comb and brush 35.00
8 pieces. Long box, round box with glass insert, nail buffer, nail file, button hook, scissors, shoe horn and mirror 50.00
Elephant. 6" long. Nodding. Natural color with beige blanket on back 18.50
Hair Brush 3.50
Hair Receiver. 3 pieces 6.50
Hand Mirror. 4" diam. Ring handle 8.00
Manicure Set. 14 pieces. Leather roll case 32.50

Manicure Tools. Various implements. Each 2.00
Napkin Rings
Figural 7.50
Plain 5.00
Ram. 3½x4½" 7.50
Shoe Horn 3.50
Tray, Dresser. 7½x11¼" 7.50
Vase. 6½" 10.00

CHALKWARE

Chalkware figurines are made of Plaster-of-Paris and decorated with water base paints. The animal forms are imitations of the Staffordshire and other Europen models.
There exists a discrepancy among collectors and dealers concerning the origin of chalkware. Some say that it was developed from the folk art of the Pennsylvania Dutch or Germans. Others insist that the figurines were made and sold in America by Italian immigrants during the mid-nineteenth century.

Ewe and Lamb. 7" $300.00

Cat. 4½" .... $ 150.00
Dogs
3" base. White. Black trim. Red dots 125.00
4". Reclining. Original black and brown paint. Early. Pair 450.00
12" high. Staffordshire-type. White with black markings 300.00
Dove. 6" high 125.00
Eagle, Spread. 9½" high, 12½" wide. Late 200.00
Ewe and Lamb. 7" 300.00
Hen. 6½" high 225.00
Lamb. 8½". Grey body, tail and ears. Red inside ears 300.00
Rabbit, Sitting. 8½" high 175.00
Roosters
6½" high. Multicolored gold trim. Late 50.00
11" high. Painted. Late 225.00
Squirrel. 9" high 225.00
Stag. 15" high, 17" long 450.00

CHARACTER AND PERSONALITY ITEMS

Nostalgia. . .a longing for the past. . .is the fastest growing area in the collecting field. It has resulted in a new market for items which were offered by candy, cereal and other companies as premiums to children. Most of them have been issued within the last thirty years. Many of the articles are presently selling for one hundred to one thousand times their original value.

Mug. 3". Orphan Annie. (Beetle Ware) $20.00

Train. Tin. Wind-up. Walt Disney Characters $20.00

Andy Gump. Mirror and brush .... $ 15.00
Batman. Glass milk mug 6.50
Beatles. Lunch box. Tin 25.00
Betty Boop. Tambourine. 6". Tin.... 35.00
Billiken. Salt Shaker. Glass. Pewter top 25.00

Brownies

- Book. "The Brownies in the Philippines." 144 pp 30.00
- Box. Pin. Figural 20.00
- Cup. Child's. Silverplated Brownie figures 50.00
- Cup and Saucer. Porcelain 35.00
- Dolls, Paper. Set of 12 ..... 35.00
- Spoon, Demitasse. Sterling with gold-washed bowl. Enameled Brownie 28.50
- Tile. 6" square. Dated 1895. A. E. Tiling Co. 50.00

Buffalo Bill. Trade card. 1910 ..... 5.00

Buster Brown

- Cards, Playing. Complete deck 27.50
- Clicker 5.00
- Dictionary. 1927 ..... 45.00
- Figurine. Cast iron. Original paint 17.50
- Hand Mirror 15.00
- Knife, Fork and Spoon. Silverplated 40.00
- Waffle-maker. Cast iron, dated 1906 ..... 50.00

Campbell Kids. Spoon. Silverplated 7.50

Captain Midnight

- Decoder. 1949 ..... 20.00
- Glass. Ovaltine 17.50

Captain Video

- Ray gun, space map 17.50
- Space Helmet. Original box. 1950 ..... 18.00

Charlie McCarthy

- Doll. 16". Plaster of Paris. Painted 30.00
- Spoon. Silverplated 12.50

Davy Crockett and Indian. Plate 7.50

Donald Duck

- Book. Big Little Book 35.00
- Cookie Jar 30.00
- Figurines
  - 3". Bisque 25.00
  - 5½". Seiberling Hard Rubber 65.00
- Toothbrush Holder. Early 50.00

Dopey. Figural. 5½". Marked Walt Disney, Seiberling Latex, Made in U.S.A. #13 ..... 55.00

Flash Gordon

- Compass, Wrist. C. 1940's 15.00
- Kite. Packaged 12.50
- Puzzle. Copyright 1951, K.F.S. 10.00

Flintstones. Lunch box. C. 1950's 6.00

Gene Autry. Lunch box. Tin. Litho 15.00

Hopalong Cassidy

- Lunch Box with Thermos 12.50
- Picture Gun and Theater. 7 films. Original box 40.00
- Wall Lamp. Gun in holster form. Marked Aladdin 50.00

Howdy Doody

- Beanie Kit. Leather 10.00
- Doll. 4" high. Plastic 7.50

Jiggs. Wooden. Moveable arms and legs. Marked "Jiggs". Copyright K.F.S. 25.00

Lone Ranger Pistol. 10½" long. Tin, cork 15.00

Mickey Mouse

- Bells. For Christmas lights. Walt Disney. Original box. Set of 8 ..... 50.00
- Book. The Big Little Book. Walt Disney 35.00
- Cookie Cutter. 4". Aluminum 10.00
- Figurines
  - 3". Seiberling Hard Rubber 50.00
  - 6". Seiberling Hard Rubber Black 125.00
- Fork and Spoon. Silverplated. Set 20.00
- Lunch Box. Tin. Thermos included 20.00
- Popcorn Popper 75.00
- Radio. Emerson 450.00
- Sharpener, Pencil 5.00
- Telephone 100.00

Orphan Annie

- Decoder Badge 25.00
- Dress Up Kit. 8x12". Dated 1968 ..... 25.00

Planters Peanut

- Ashtray. 50-Year Anniversary 15.00
- Car. 5" long. Small peanut-shaped with Mr. Peanut driver. Red, hard plastic. C. 1940's 25.00
- Clock, Alarm. 1960's special offer. Boxed 25.00
- Cookie Cutters. Plastic, 2 different shapes, blue 7.50
- Jacket, Official. Worn by workers. Embroidered 35.00
- Jar. 15". Four peanuts in relief. Peanut finial. Embossed 95.00
- Marbles. C. 1955. Set of 10 ..... 5.00
- Matches, Book 15.00
- Mug, Baby. Silverplated 50.00
- Nightlight. 9" high. Electric. Plastic 35.00
- Nut Dishes. One large, 4 small. Tin. Original mailing box. Set 12.50
- Pencil, Mechanical. Figure at end is floating in oil 12.50

Popeye. Figural. 2½". Metal. Made in U.S.A. Copyright 1929 E.F.S. 20.00

Roy Rogers

- Cap Pistol 10.00
- Deputy badge. Tin. C. 1950's 4.00
- Membership card. Fan Club. C. 1940 ..... 3.00

Shirley Temple

- Books
  - Captain January and Little Colonel. H-B 15.00
  - Heidi. H-B 15.00
  - Poor Little Rich Girl 25.00
  - Shirley at Play. 1935 ..... 15.00
- Bowl 20.00
- Creamer 20.00
- Pocket Mirror 5.00

Records. 78RPM in album. All the songs she sang in movies. Story and pictures of Shirley inside 50.00
Snoopy. Lunch box. C. 1959 ...... 12.50
Superman. 1965 Movie Viewer. Two films 12.00
Yellow Kid. Button. Pinback. C. 1890 .... 10.00

CHELSEA

Chelsea is a fine English porcelain which was made to compete with Dresden. The factory began operating in the Chelsea area of London, England in the 1740's. The products can be divided into four periods: (1) Early period, 1740's, with incised triangle and raised anchor mark. (2) The 1750's, with red raised anchor mark. (3) The 1760's, the gold anchor period. (4) The Derby period from 1770-1783. In 1924, a large number of the molds and models of figurines were found at the Spode-Copeland Works and many items were brought back into circulation.

Letter Holder. 4" high. Fan top. Pale blue floral decor on white ground $225.00

Bowl. 6½". Molded leaves on exterior. Floral spray in center. Red anchor ....$ 1000.00
Candlesticks. 10¾" high. Birds. Gold anchor. Pair 2000.00
Cup and Saucer. "Ladies". Late 17.50
Figurines
- 4⅜" high. Pantaloon. Italian comedy. Red anchor 1500.00
- 7" high. Tyrolean Dancers. Red anchor 2500.00
- 8½" high. Woman with tray. White ground with rust, red and blue decor. Late 250.00
- 9" high. Woodsman and Milkmaid. Late. Pair 500.00

Jardiniere. 11" high. Covered. Hexagonal-shape. Red anchor .. 1275.00
Plates
- 7½". Floral decor. Late 40.00
- 8½". Fruit decor. Late 75.00
- 9⅜". Floral decor. Red anchor 875.00

Tureens, Covered
- 5¼". Molded as cauliflower with natural coloring. Red anchor 1000.00
- 15". Blue. Gold anchor 1800.00

"CHELSEA" GRANDMOTHER'S WARE

Wares decorated with the familiar grape, sprig or thistle pattern in relief and lustred are erroneously called Chelsea. These wares were not made in Chelsea, but in the Staffordshire district of England in the early 1880's. There is a movement to rename this decorated porcelain "Grandmother's Ware."

Pitcher. 6¾". "Scrolls & Medallions" $55.00

Bowl. 10". Grape ....$ 50.00
Butter Pat. Grape 7.50
Creamers
- Grape 25.00
- Thistle 45.00

Cups and Saucers
- Grape. Bouillon 20.00
- Grape. Handled 20.00
- Grape. Handleless 50.00
- Thistle. Handled 27.50

Egg Cup 16.50
Plates
- 4". Grape 9.50
- 7". Grape 15.00
- 9". Grape 25.00

Sauce Boat. Grape 25.00
Sugars, Covered
- Grape 75.00
- Sprig 135.00

Teapots, 9"

Grape	125.00
Thistle	150.00

CHILDREN'S DISHES

During the late 19th and 20th centuries, tablewares designed especially for children's personal use and playtime were very much in vogue. Even major pottery and glass firms catered to the demand. Today these children's items are very collectible and sometimes command higher prices than their adult counterparts. Also see "Children's Glass Dishes."

Feeding dish. 6¾". "Beach Baby". P.K. Unity Germany $35.00

Tea Set, 14 pieces. "Azalea." Noritake $175.00

Baking Set. Tin. 9 pieces ....$ 18.50

Bowls. 7½". Children at play. Limoges. Set of six 85.00

Canister Set. 2¾x2¾x4½". Dutch children and floral decor. 4 pieces 35.00

Coffee Pot with underplate. Tin. "Little Bo Peep" 15.00

Cookware. Aluminum. C. 1930. 12 pieces 20.00

Cream and Sugar. "Ribbed." Silver Lustred 50.00

Creamers
- "Bunnykins." 4". Royal Doulton .. 27.50
- Clown with rabbit. 2½". Germany 16.50
- "Cow Jumping over the Moon." 2". U.S. 10.00

Cups and Saucers
- "Brownies". Germany 15.00
- "Jack and Jill." Tin. Germany 15.00

Feeding Dishes
- 7". Boy, toy animals, etc. center. ABC and numeral border. Germany 28.50
- 7¼". Woman holding child. Pink lustre. C. 1840 .... 35.00
- 7½". "Campbell Kids." Buffalo Pottery 50.00
- 7½". Dutch woman with two children. Edwin M. Knowles 15.00
- 7½". Warming-type. Child in snowsuit. Nickel plated. G.W. Co. 17.50
- 9". Warming-type. "Sing a Song of Sixpence." 35.00

Feeding Sets
- 2 pieces. 6½" bowl. 6½" plate. Frolicking animals. James Kent Ltd. 30.00
- 3 pieces. 6⅝" bowl, 7¾" plate, 2½" mug. Children's scenes. "Arabia". Made in Finland 20.00
- 3 pieces. "Simple Simon". Warwick 40.00
- 3 pieces. "This is The Cow, etc." Edward Knowles Co. 40.00

Molds, Food. Tin. 5 pieces 15.00

Mugs
- Bunnykins. 3½". Royal Doulton .. 15.00
- Sterling Silver. 2½". Monogrammed and dated. Poole Silver Co. . . 30.00
- Sterling Silver. 2½". "Rose" Steiff 40.00

Plates
- 4⅛". "Mother Goose" center. U.S. 8.50
- 4½". "Miss Muffet." Reticulated border 15.00
- 6". "Faint Heart Never Won Fair Lady." Austria 17.50
- 6½". Monkey with high hat carrying candy cane and ice cream cone. Edward Knowles Co. 17.50
- 7". Child with rabbit. Czeckoslovakia.................. 32.50

7½". Two Sunbonnet babies playing with lamb. Imperial China 20.00
8½". Children's scenes. Maroon and floral border. French. Set of six 100.00
10½". Children (2) standing in rural road. Handled. Limoges 40.00

Platters
"Blue Onion." 2½x3". Open handles. Unmarked 20.00
"Blue Willow." 3¾x4x6¼". Japan 12.50

Tea Sets
9 pieces. Cats and dogs. Red and blue. Tin. Germany 50.00
10 pieces. "Cinderella." Tin...... 20.00
11 pieces. Aluminum 35.00
12 pieces. White porcelain. Unmarked 85.00
13 pieces. Scenic decor. Orange lustre. Japanese 35.00
13 pieces. Red, white, blue linear decor. Unmarked 65.00
15 pieces. "Little Bo Peep." Tin .. 40.00
16 pieces. Each plate with different blue transfers of boy, animals, and titles. Staffordshire. C. 1860 .... 250.00
21 pieces. Pink roses on white porcelain. Germany 150.00
21 pieces. Violet decor on white porcelain. Japanese 50.00
21 pieces. Multicolored flowers, green band on white porcelain. Noritake 200.00
23 pieces. "Ring Around the Rosy". Austrian........ 100.00
23 pieces. Birds, branches. Blue on white. Japanese 65.00

Tureen, Covered. 2½x5¼". "Blue Willow." Japanese. C. 1920 .... 25.00

CHILDREN'S GLASS DISHES

Children's glass dishes evolved in the 1900's by a recycling process. Glass manufacturers had a surplus problem stemming from producing only two new patterns a year. To remedy the waste, the manufacturers began to produce dishes for children. The dishes were used as premiums with grocery items and were also sold to the Sears Roebuck and Montgomery Ward catalog houses.

Berry Sets
Flute. 6 pcs........ $ 55.00
Lacy Daisy. 7 pcs 75.00
Whirligig. 6 pcs. 95.00

Bowls
Diamond Fine Cut 20.00

Butter, Covered. "Tappan" $38.00

Inverted Strawberry, Large 35.00
Lacy Daisy. Large 15.00
Nursery Rhymes. Small 27.50

Butters
Diamond Flute 30.00
Drum 85.00
Flattened Diamond & Sunburst .. 25.00
Lamb 100.00
Lion 100.00
Nursery Rhymes 85.00
Oval Star 30.00

Cake Stands
Baby Thumbprint. Large 45.00
Hawaiian 32.50
Rexford 30.00
Ribbon Candy 37.50

Candlesticks. Pairs
Colonial........ 25.00
Flute 15.00
Swirl 15.00

Castor Sets
American Shield 95.00
Drape........ 85.00
English Hobnail 50.00
Square Block 85.00

Creamers and Sugars
Colonial. Heisey 75.00
Oval Star 45.00
Puritan 60.00

Creamers
Daisy and Button 12.00
Drum 65.00
Grapevine with Ovals. Blue 45.00
Hobnail 22.50
Hook 37.50
Inverted Strawberry 50.00
Owl 60.00
Sawtooth 40.00
Vines and Beads 35.00
Whirling Star 25.00

Cup and Saucer. Lion 100.00

Dinner Set. 14 pcs. Cherry Blossom. Pink 175.00

- Mugs
  - Grape Leaf and Fruit 35.00
  - Ribbed Cherry 35.00
  - Three Birds 40.00
- Punch Sets. 7 pieces
  - Flattened Diamond & Sunburst .. 65.00
  - Inverted Strawberry. Cambridge 150.00
  - Tulip and Honeycomb 80.00
  - Wheat Sheaf 85.00
  - Whirligig 75.00
- Spooners
  - Fish. Blue 65.00
  - Kittens 85.00
  - Lion 85.00
- Sugars, Covered
  - Lion 100.00
  - Sawtooth 45.00
  - Tappan 25.00
  - Tulip and Honeycomb 25.00
- Table Sets. 4 pieces
  - Arrowhead-in-Ovals 85.00
  - Clear & Diamonds Panels 150.00
  - Colonial
    - Cambridge 125.00
    - Heisey 150.00
  - Lion. Frosted 350.00
  - Nursery Rhymes 300.00
  - Oval Star 75.00
  - Pennsylvania 125.00
  - Sawtooth 125.00
  - Sweetheart 125.00
  - Tappan 75.00
  - Tulip and Honeycomb 85.00
  - Whirligig 75.00
- Water Sets. 7 pieces
  - Colonial. Cambridge 65.00
  - Oval Star 85.00
  - Pattee Cross 95.00
  - Virginia 100.00

CHILDREN'S ITEMS

This list consists of miscellaneous items related to children. Also see individual categories, i.e. "Children's Dishes," "Doll Furniture," "Games," etc.

- Blocks
  - 4". Telescoping. Lithographed. Nine pieces ....$ 25.00
  - 7". Telescoping. Lithographed. Nine pieces 45.00
- Books
  - ABC. Linen. 12pp 10.00
  - Book About Animals. 2½x3¼". Ten woodblock prints. Rufus Merril 12.50
  - Child's Book of Songs, The. 4x6". Seven woodblock prints. Meriam and Merril. 12.50
  - Father Tuck's Wide Awake Series. Raphael Tuck & Sons. C. 1890. Each 15.00
  - Greedy Ben. 3½x4½". "One Cent Book." McLaughlin Bros. C. 1870 15.00
  - Hymns For Children in Prose. 1¾x2¾". Woodblock prints. S. Babock 18.00

Book. "Three Little Pigs." Charles E. Graham & Co.................$10.00

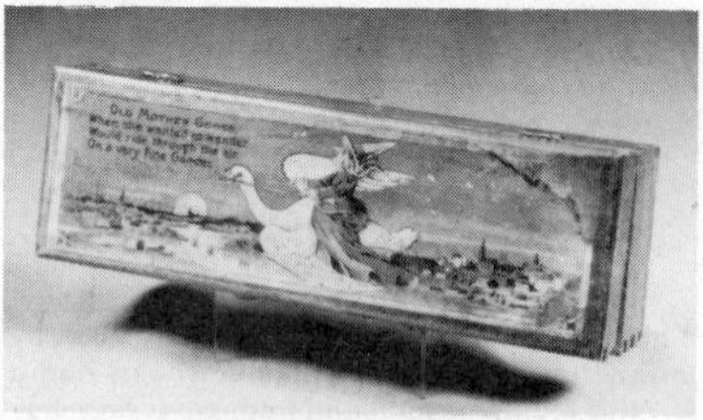

Pencil Box. 2½x7¾". Wood. Interior divided. Lithographed lid $12.50

  - Mother Goose Nursery Rhymes. 5x9". Illustrated by G.M. Burdt Violet Moore. Higgins 10.00
  - Nursery Rhymes. Prudential Insurance Co. C. 1908 .... 7.50
  - Peter Rabbit. 5¼x9¼". Color plates. Chas. E. Graham 10.00
  - Punch and Judy Series. Color covers, B-W illustrations. McLaughlin Bros. C. 1903. Each .. 15.00

Raggedy Ann Series. Hardcovers. Color plates. C. 1916. Each 18.50
School Books. C. 1860-70's. Each 3.00
Sleepy Time Stories. 17 plates. Autographed, "Maud Humphrey." C. 1911 .... 55.00
Tale of O.N.T., A. Grandmother's story. Booklet issued by Clark 6.50
Tale of Peter Rabbit, The. 5¼x6½". Linen, 24pp. Color cover. 12 color plates. Saalfield. C. 1910 .... 25.00
Teddy Bears, The. Hard cover. Saalfield. C. 1907 .... 17.50
Uncle Wiggly Apple Roast. Illustrated by Lang Campbell. C. 1927 .... 8.50

Bubble Pipe. Tin. C. 1880 .... 12.00
Cookie Roller. 11". Maple 18.50
Dog. 9". Glass eyes. "Steiff." 32.50
Doll Dishes
6 pieces. Serving. Blue and white floral borders. Country scene center 85.00
21 pieces. Pink floral on white. Gold trim. C. 1880 .... 65.00
Flatware. 13 pieces. Tin, original box........................ 15.00
Ice Cream Freezer. 5x7". Wooden barrel. Iron handle 35.00
Paper Toy. 6¼x9". Lithographic sheet, uncut. Approximately 30 items. C. 1865 .... 25.00
Pencil Boxes
6". Hinged. Burnt and colored .. 15.00
8½". Paper decorated 10.00
Rattles, Baby
6". Drum rattle. Porcelain whistle. C. 1860 .... 65.00
8". Pewter with wood handle. C. 1840 .... 75.00
Records. Book That Sings. Harper Columbia, Pat'd. 1909.......... 10.00
Rubber Stamps. 1x1½x1¾". Mounted on wooden blocks. C. 1880. Set of 14 .... 20.00
Sewing Machine. C. 1940 .... 12.50
Sleds
36". Log. All wood, including runners 50.00
41". "Steermasters Bob Ski." Oak. Metal rudder. Original label 60.00
Smokey the Bear. 15". Plush, dressed. Voice box. C. 1950-60 ...... 35.00
Teddy Bear. 20". Brown plush body. Glass eyes. Straw filled 75.00
Wagon. 43". "Red Racer." C. 1930 50.00
Wheelbarrow. 8¾x10x29½". All wood, including wheel. Stenciled. 50.00

CHINESE

(See, "Orientalia")

CHRISTMAS ITEMS

There are many reasons why individuals seek Christmas decorations and related items from the past. . .nostalgia, return to the basics, acceptance of traditions. . .or perhaps just insurance that, in this contemporary world, an old-fashioned Christmas will always be in vogue.

Tree Stand. Cast iron. 5¾x9½" square. Cut out bells and scroll work $50.00

Books
"Miracle of Christmas." Hallmark, 1968 ....$ 6.00
"The Life and Adventures of Santa Claus." Julie Lane. Santa Claus Pub. Co., 1932 .... 25.00
Pop-Up. Santa Claus. 1949 ...... 8.00
Santa Claus. 47" high. Wooden. Handpainted 150.00
Stocking. 31" long. Printed cotton. C. 1900 .... 35.00
Tree Lights. Candleholders. 3½"
Amber 10.00
Amethyst 15.00
Cobalt 12.50
Tree Lights. Electric
Ball with holly 4.00
Ball with stars 4.00
Basket of fruit. Milk glass 5.00
Birdcage 5.00
Blue Bird 4.00
Child. Milk glass 6.00
Clown. Milk glass 6.00
Elephant 3.00
Gingerbread Man.............. 8.00
Grapes 3.00
Humpty Dumpty. Milk glass 8.50
Lantern. Occupied Japan........ 3.00
Rose 4.00
Santa Head 8.50
Santa, Standing 15.00
Showman. Milk glass 8.50

Zepplin with flag 10.00

Tree Lights, Sets

Bubble-Lite. Original box 9.50

Lights by Noma. 1936. Original box.......... 12.50

Tree Ornaments

Angel. 4". Wax, brown wig, angel hair wings. Handpainted 50.00

Ball. 5". Amber glass. Original wire 20.00

Bisque. Set of 12 in original box .. 25.00

Canary. Blown glass. Brush tail .. 10.00

Figurals. Occupied Japan. Box of 12 .... 25.00

Figurals. Spun glass. Germany. Box of 12 .... 60.00

Football Player. Celluloid 6.00

Fruit shapes. Blown glass. Each .. 8.00

Icicles. 7¾" long. Glass. Each 1.50

Man-Woman, Dancing. Wooden. Germany. C. 1890 .... 50.00

Peacock. Blown glass. Brushtail .. 15.00

Pinecone. Blown glass. Germany 8.00

Santa. Blown glass 15.00

Tree Stands

Cone-shaped. Tin with decals. Noma 55.00

Musical. Revolving and lighted. "Lador." C. 1935 .... 250.00

CIGAR CUTTERS, POCKET

Pocket-type cigar cutters are not only utilitarian to a smoking man but often a fine piece of jewelry that was attached to his watch chain. With the return of the vested suit and watch chain for the 'well dressed' man, cigar cutters have regained their popularity. They are also currently being made and sold in tobacco shops and jewelry stores.

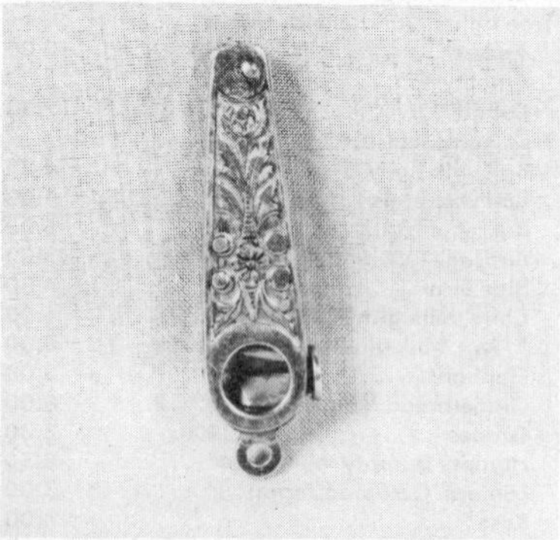

Knife-type. 2" long. Sterling. Embossed $45.00

Bottle-shaped. 2" long. Brass ....$ 15.00

Combination cigar cutter and watch fob. 10K gold 65.00

Horseshoe-shaped. With buckle 35.00

Knife-types

Gold. 10K. Engraved 50.00

Goldplated. Loop 20.00

Silverplated 15.00

Scissors-type

Gold. 10K 55.00

Nickelplated 35.00

Silverplated 35.00

Sterling. Embossed 45.00

CIGAR STORE FIGURES

Cigar store indians, squaws or turks were familiar sights in front of cigar stores and tobacco shops. These figures are now scarce and command a good price when offered for sale. They are being reproduced in various sizes, styles and materials.

Indian. 72" $6500.00

Indian. 24½". Original paint. Bone embellishments. Leather belt. Metal earrings ....$ 2000.00
Indian Brave. 60" 6000.00
Indian Chief. 60" 5000.00
Indian Chief. 84" 7500.00
Indian Maiden. 68". On base. Wheels 6500.00
Indian Princess. 70" 6000.00
Indian Scout. 76". Including base .. 6000.00

CINNABAR

Cinnabar is a ware made of numerous layers of a heavy mercuric sulphide, often referred to as vermillion. It was carved into boxes, buttons, snuff bottles and vases. The best of this ware was made in China.

Box. 2x3¾x5⅝". Floral carvings on red. Black interior $75.00

Boxes
1½x2½x4". Carved bird on lid. Marked "China." ....$ 50.00
1⅝x2⅜". Carved. Marked "China." 32.50
2x4x5". Carved scenic decor. Brass bound edges 75.00
2½x4½". Garden scene 50.00
3½x5½". Chinese figures in garden with flowers and trees 75.00
Figurine. Horses. 10½x13½". Jade with turquoise inlay 2500.00
Plate. 9". Carved scene of people .. 250.00
Snuff Bottle. Red. Carved 125.00
Tray. 8x12". Carved scenic decor .. 200.00
Vases
4". Floral design. Red. Marked "China." 30.00
6½". Carved floral design. Brown 65.00
10½". Dragon design. Early 225.00

CIVIL WAR AND RELATED ITEMS

Civil War items listed here consist mainly of military items issued or used during the war between the states in 1861-1865.

Powder flask. 5" diam. Tin $35.00

Badge, Helmet. Shield and eagle with company number in center $ 35.00
Bags
Carpet. 18x18". Leather handles. Iron lock. Double compartments .. 65.00
Doctor's. 9x11½". Black leather. Two 4x6" flapped pockets on front. Brass mounts. Lock with stars and eagle 250.00
Bayonet and Scabbard. .58 cal 75.00
Bell. 3¾x3¾". For mule team. Brass 45.00
Belt. Leather with brass buckle. Union 75.00
Bill of Rental. Slave. "Jim." 1856 .. 50.00
Bill of Sale. Entire family. Dated 1862 .... 85.00
Boots. Cavalry. Pair 125.00
Canteens
Tin. Drum-shape 100.00
Wood. Cloth covered 65.00
Cartridge Box, Pistol. Brown leather. 36 cal., label "W.C. McClallan & Co.," Springfield, Mass 65.00
Casket Plate. Silver on copper 25.00
Chin strap. Officer's 25.00
Covers
Confederate 25.00
Union 25.00
Discharge Papers. 1st Ohio. Dated 1863 .... 40.00
Drum. 15" high, 17" diam. Eagle design on sides 500.00
Enlistment Papers. Union. Fully signed 35.00
Eye Glasses
Clear. Adjustable frames 25.00
Sun. Sharp shooter's 30.00

Flags
6x9'. United States. 36 stars. 1864-1867 period 500.00
22x28". Swallow Tail. Silk. 2 ties. White with red lettering and a blue 19th Corps insignia. 159th N.Y.S. Volunteer's 750.00

Field Glass. 7½" closed. Brass. Made by Lemaire Fabt., Paris 50.00
Gloves, Officer's. Leather. Pair 75.00
Helmet, Dress. Cavalry. Brass trim with eagle badge. Spike 100.00

Holsters, Pistol
Brown leather with iron flap fastener. Confederate 125.00
Brown leather with push through flap fastener on brown leather belt with roller buckle. Confederate 225.00
Horse Bit 45.00

Images
Confederate. 1-9 plate 65.00
Yankee. 1-6 plate............. 75.00
Yankee. 1-9 plate............. 50.00
Jacket, Shell. Cavalry. Complete with buttons, lining and inspector's marks 350.00
Knife and Spoon. Combination 25.00
Knives, Bowie
Bone handle with scabbard 275.00
Stag handle. Wostenholme address. Etchings of eagles, flags. Leather scabbard. "IXL." 275.00
Wood handle, brass guard. No scabbard 125.00
Leggings. Black leather. Pair 100.00
Letters and Numbers. Brass. Regimental. Each 8.50
Mess Kit. Bone handles. In original case 50.00
Plume, Shako. Cavalry and Artillery. Horse hair 25.00
Ribbon. 1861-1865 blue gray. Lincoln's head surrounded by "With Malice Toward None With Charity for All" 75.00
Saddle. Cavalry. McCullems and Militia types 295.00
Saddle Bags
"Allegheny Arsenal". 1864 ...... 175.00
Virginia. 1st Cavalry 175.00
Shoulder Sling. Brass buckle. Carbine 35.00
Spurs
Brass. Officers. Pair 125.00
Teardrop. 1" rowels with chins. Pair 50.00
Spy Glass. 16". Four sections. Leather-wrapped 65.00
Sword Belt Plate. Union NCO 1861 35.00

Swords
Cavalry. 42" long 150.00
Confederate. 34½" long 225.00
Naval. Cutlass model. Brass grip 150.00
Non-Commissional Officer. Bone grip 175.00
Officer's. Brass trim. Leather scabbard 225.00
Tarpot 125.00

CLAMBROTH GLASS

Clambroth glass derives its name from the color of the glass. The semi-opaque, greyish-white color resembles the broth from clams. This type of glassware was popular in the Victorian period.

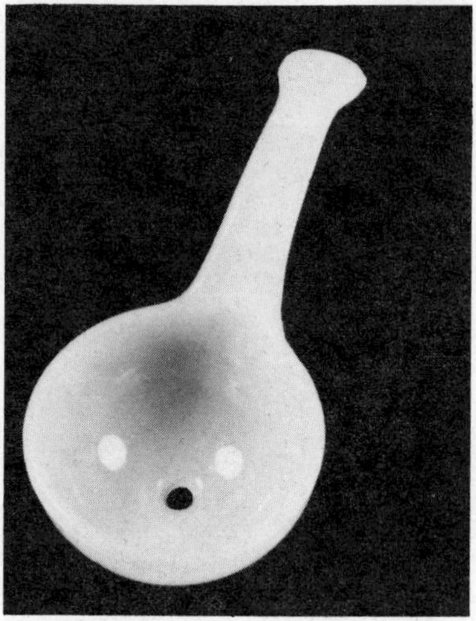

Pickle dipper. 9½" long $22.50

Bottle, Barber. "Bay Rum." Stoppered ....$ 30.00
Goblet. 7" high. Souvenir-type 22.50
Mugs
3½" high. Swans. Ring handle .. 35.00
Birds and wheat. Fence post handle 35.00
Plate. 8½" diam................ 30.00
Toothpick. Souvenir-type 15.00
Tumbler. Souvenir-type 25.00
Vases. 9". Crimped top. Pontil. H-P flowers. Pair 75.00
Whimsey. 2½x2½" high. Green serpent entwining cylinder 45.00

Vases

6". Brass. Made for Weller. C. 1909	225.00
11½". Copper. Green patina. Made for Weller	300.00

CLEWELL POTTERY

Charles Walter Clewell was a metal worker and not a potter. He opened a small shop in Canton, Ohio in the early 1900's to produce metal overlay pottery. Metal on pottery was not a new idea, but Clewell was perhaps the first to completely mask the ceramic body with copper, brass, 'silvered' or 'bronzed' metals.

A limited quantity of his art work exists. . .simply because he operated on a small scale with little outside assistance. He retired at the age of 79 in 1955 and never revealed his technique. Most of his wares are marked. Occasionally, pieces appear with the mark of the pottery blank. . .such as Owens or Weller.

Vase. 11½". Iridescent copper shaded brown. Incised $150.00

Bowl. 6x7". Copper. Ornate floral decor ....$	265.00
Candlesticks. 8". Copper. Pair	100.00
Jardiniere. 9". Copper. Geometric design. C. 1947	285.00
Powder Jar. Copper. Riveted	150.00

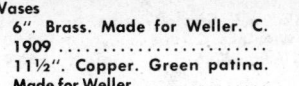

CLIFTON POTTERY

CLIFTON

The Clifton Art Pottery, Newark, New Jersey was established by William A. Long, once associated with Lonhuda Pottery and Fred Tschirner, a chemist.

Production consisted of two major lines. ."Crystal Patina" that resembled 'true porcelain' with a subdued crystal-like glaze and "Indian Ware" or "Western Influence" an adaptation of the American Indians' unglazed and decorated pottery; but with a high glazed black interior. Other lines included "Robin's Egg Blue" and 'Tirrube."

Art pottery production continued until 1911; when porcelain fired, unleaded glazed tiles were introduced. In 1914, success of the tile business necessitated that the firm change its name to Clifton Porcelain Tile Company to reflect their major production.

Marks were incised or impressed. Early pieces may be dated and shape numbers impressed, and Indian wares were further identified by tribes.

Bowl. 3½", 2½" deep. Red clay body with feather design. Glazed black interior. "Indian War." C. 1906. $125.00

Mug. 4". Arkansas Tribal Design. Signed W. A. Long. C. 1905 ....$	85.00
Jar, Covered. 7½". Indian Ware ..	85.00

Teapots

3½ x8¼" o.1. Crystal Patina. Signed W.A. Long. C. 1908	125.00
7½x9". Indian Ware	95.00

Vases

4½". Bulbous. Indian Ware	50.00
5½". Bulbous. Crystal Patina. Green	85.00
6½". Arizona Tribal Design. C. 1906	75.00
9", 5" diam. Tirrube	125.00.
11". Floral overlay. Various shades of green. Signed W. A. Long. C. 1907	250.00
12". Crystal Patina. Yellow green glaze. Silver overlay	600.00

CLOCKS

The sundial was undoubtedly the first man made device for measuring time. Its basic disadvantage is well expressed in the saying: "Do like the sundial, count only the sunny days."

With the need for greater dependability, man developed the water clock, the oil clock and the sand clock respectively. All these clocks worked on the same principle. . .time was measured by the amount of material passing from one container to another. The wheel clock was the next major step toward more accurate time. These clocks can be traced back as far as the 13th century. Many improvements on the basic wheel clock were made and they continued to be the most accurate time piece available until the quartz crystal movement was introduced in 1934.

Recently, an atomic clock that measures time by the frequency of light molecules that only varies one second in a thousand years has been invented.

Has the cycle been completed. . .light source?!?

My sincerest "Thanks" to Mr. Frank Dey, Los Angeles, CA., who so conscientiously assisted in compiling the following lists of clocks, makers and their prices.

ALARM CLOCKS

Big Ben. Nickeled case, 4" black dial and luminous numbers ....$	115.00
German. Ornate oak round case with brass spandrels. Strikes on half hour and hour. 30 hour	135.00
Ingraham. Advertising. "Red Ball."	75.00
Musical. Nickeled case. 4x5x6". Swiss movement. 2-tune	200.00
Thomas, Seth. Cottage. 9" high. Octagonal dial. 30 hour. Patented alarm. T&S	100.00
Thomas, Seth. Oak case. Automatic alarm. 8-day. T&S	135.00

BANJO CLOCKS

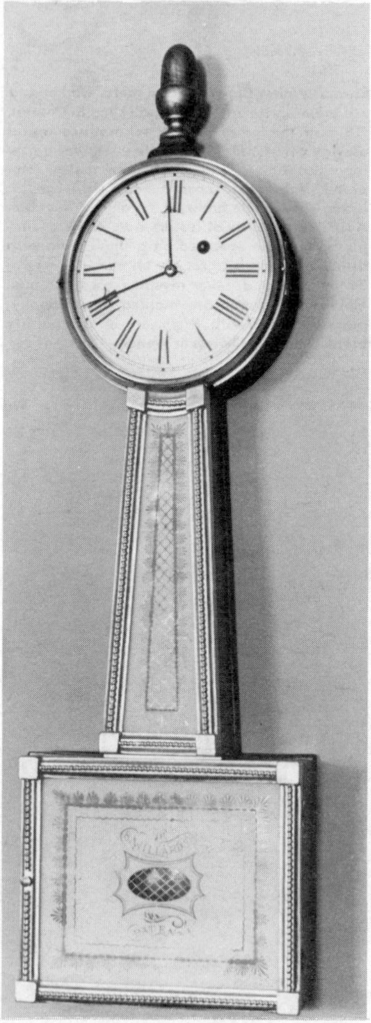

BANJO. Willard,A. "Patent". Mahogany case. Gilt rope molding. 7" dial. Weight driven. Repainted tablets. 8-day, time only $2300.00

Howard. #4. Signed on dial ......$ 2250.00
Howard. #5. Excellent condition .. 1875.00
Howard & Davis. #1. Weight driven. Signed dial. Mint condition 5400.00
Howard-type 850.00
Ingraham. Mahogany case. Original glass. Spring driven 350.00
Ingraham. Ship scene on glass. 8-day spring driven. T&S 250.00
New Haven. Mahogany case. 30" high. Brass eagle and spandrels. 8-day spring movement. T&S.................... 325.00
New Haven. Miniature case. 16" high. 8-day spring movement. T&S.................... 310.00
Noyes, L. Mahogany case. 7" dial. Weight driven. Brass spandrels and eagle. Original glass tablets. Time only 750.00
Sessions. Mahogany case. 9x26". Brass dial. 8-day spring movement. Time only. Restored .. 275.00
Seward, Joshua. Rope front presentation case. Original glasses 2200.00
Stennes. #15. Curtiss-type Girandole. Marriage scene 2750.00
Stotzell, A. & Sons. Mahogany case. 7" dial. Signed. 8-day weight driven. Restored. Charlestown. Mass 950.00
Tifft, H. Weighted. Wooden bezel and wood throat. Early 1575.00
Unsigned. Walnut case. Westminster chime. Original glasses. Brass spandrels and eagle. Good condition.................... 400.00
Unsigned. Weight driven 1050.00
Waltham. Mahogany case. Mt. Vernon glass tablet. Weight driven. All original 1750.00
Waterbury. Mission oak case. Weighted. Heavy porcelain dial. Black, gold glasses 1500.00
Waterbury. Williard-style. Porcelain 'dial. Standard size. 8-day weight movement.............. 1275.00
Williard, A. "Patent". Mahogany case, gilt rope molding. 7" dial. Repainted tablets. 8-day weight driven, time only 2300.00
Williard, A. Jr. Unrestored condition 2750.00
Williard-type. 8-day spring driven. T&S.................... 395.00

BEEHIVE SHELF CLOCKS

Brown, J.C. Walnut case. Ripple front. 8-day, T&S. Original ....$ 975.00
New Haven. Walnut case. Original glass. 8-day, T&S 175.00
Pratt, Daniel. Mahogany case. Frosted tablet, 8-day, T&S 225.00
Terry and Andrews. 8-day, T&S. Restored condition 250.00
Waterbury. Mahogany veneer. Frosted tablet and painted dial. 8-day, T&S.................. 315.00
Waterbury. Walnut case. Frosted glass. 30 hour, T&S 125.00

BRACKET CLOCKS

Boulle. Bronze inlaid tortoise shell case. Silk thread suspension. 40-day ....$ 2750.00
Boulle. Ornate gilt case. 18" high. Porcelain dial. Full strike. Double fuzee. 8-day. Mint condition. C. 1730 .... 4750.00
English. Baroque oak case. 29". Double fuzee. Strikes hours 1575.00
English. Double fuzee. 8-day, T&S .. 850.00
German. Inlaid rosewood case. Full columns. Two train, quarter chime 500.00

CALENDAR SHELF AND WALL CLOCKS

Ansonia. Walnut case. 32". Octagonal. Long drop. 8-day, T&S $ 400.00
Burwell & Carter. Wall, #2. Rosewood case. 31". B. B. Lewis calendar. 8-day weight, time only 950.00
Ingraham. "Gila," shelf. Oak case. Kitchen-type. Barometer and thermometer. 8-day spring movement, T&S. Restored 295.00
Ingraham. "Mosaic," wall. B.B. Lewis calendar, Original dials. 8-day.................... 1000.00
Ithaca. Shelf, #9. Walnut case 22". Cottage-style. Spring movement, T&S..................... 700.00
Ithaca. Shelf, 25½". Library-type. Lever movement. 30-day, time only 900.00
Ithaca. Shelf, #3½. Walnut case with ebony trim. Parlor-type. Black double dials. Crystal pendulum bob 2700.00
Ithaca. "Skeleton." Walnut case with ebony trim. 4½x12x24". Very rare 5500.00
Maranville, Galusha. Wall. Rosewood case. 8-day, T&S 725.00
Prentiss. "Empire." Wall. 38" Heavy movement, 60-day 1500.00
Sessions. "Eclipse." Wall. Oak case. 17x38" Regulator-type. 8-day, time only 375.00
Waterbury. Shelf, #44. Walnut case. 24" high. 8-day, T&S, alarm. Good condition 650.00

CALENDAR SHELF. Ithaca. # 3½, Parlor shelf. Walnut case with ebony trim. 20". Black double dials. Crystal pendulum bob $2700.00

Waterbury. Wall. #33. Oak case. 15x39". 8-day, T&S 1175.00
Welch. Shelf. Rosewood case, 18". 5" day and date dial. B.B. Lewis calendar. Rare 775.00
Welch. E.N.Wall. Rosewood case with gold trim. 24" short drop. Calendar dial. 8-day, T&S 375.00

CARRIAGE CLOCKS

French. Beveled glass case. 5½" high. Porcelain dial. 8-day, T&S $ 600.00
French. Arabic. Repeater. Porcelain dial. T&S 675.00
French. Bronzed case. Porcelain dial. Repeater on the hour. Alarm. T&S 500.00
French. Gold plated and beveled glass case. 5". Porcelain dial. 8-day, Gran Sonnorie Strike. Rare 1800.00
German. Brass with leather case. 3" square 85.00
Musical. "Pepoday." Metal case. 6½". T&S 325.00
Repeater. 5-minute. Rare 1000.00
Waterbury. Miniature brass case. 8-day, time only 165.00

CHINA CASED CLOCKS

Ansonia. Blue, gold and multifloral decor. 8-day, T & S ....$ 275.00
Ansonia. Royal Bonn case. Open escapement. 8-day, T & S 400.00
German Movement. 7¾" high. Delft blue decor on white 200.00
New Haven. Embossed case. Urn-shaped. 8-day, T&S............ 225.00
Waterbury. White china case. 5" porcelain dial. Floral decor. 8-day, T&S........................ 175.00

COTTAGE STYLE CLOCKS

Jerome. Miniature. 9". Painted tablet. 30-hour, T&S ....$ 75.00
Jerome. Walnut case. 12". Label and good tablet. 30-hour 115.00
New Haven. Rosewood case. 8-day 100.00
Thomas, Seth. Rosewood case. 30-hour 100.00
Thomas, Seth. Walnut case. Miniature. Mirror tablet. Seth Thomas hands. 30-hour. 85.00
Waterbury. Rosewood case. 30-hour 85.00
Welch, E.N. Rosewood case. 9" miniature. 30-hour, T&S 110.00

CRYSTAL REGULATOR CLOCKS

Ansonia. Brass, 10½". Open escapement. Beveled glass. Mercury pendulum ....$ 350.00
Ansonia. Green onyx base and top. 11¼". Beveled glass. Open escapement. Mercury pendulum. Brass supports. 8-day, T&S 375.00
Ansonia. Beveled glass and brass case. 6x8x13¾". Four full columns with finials. Open escapement 425.00
Ansonia. Brass, 15½". Open escapement. Beveled glass. Cathedral gong 395.00

French. Alabaster top and base. Enameled columns. Mercury pendulum. Ornate top. Open escapement. Mint condition 1900.00
Thomas, Seth. Plain case. 11". Brass and beveled glass porcelain dial 320.00
Tiffany. Heavily detailed case. Mercury pendulum 475.00
Waterbury. Plain case. 9½" high. Porcelain dial. Beveled glass 250.00

ELECTRIC (BATTERY) DRIVEN CLOCKS

Brille. Wall. Oak case. Master regulator. 14" dial. Sweep seconds. Battery driven. 8-day, time only ....$ 600.00
Bulle'. Shelf. Green marble case. 10". Beveled glass. Battery movement.................... 425.00
Bulle'. Shelf. Glass dome. 11" 265.00
Eureka. Shelf. Wood and glass case. 8" high. Battery movement...... 450.00
Self Winding Clock Co. Wall. Carved mahogany case. 20". Gallery-type. Dry cell battery movement, 8-day, time only 500.00

EMPIRE SHELF CLOCKS

Birge and Peck. Empire case. 3-tier. 32" high. Reverse painted tablets. 8-day weight driven. T&S .....$ 425.00
Goodrich, E.B. Mahogany veneer case. 20" high. 8-day brass movement, T&S 375.00
Hoadley, Silas. 36". Wood movement. Weight driven. 30-hour 500.00
Hoadley, Silas. Upside down. 36". Wood movement. Weight driven. 30-hour, T&A. 600.00
Ives, C.L. 3-tier. Reverse painted tablet. 8-day weight driven, T&S 550.00
Jerome, Chauncey. 2-tier. 18" mini column. Weight driven, 8-day, T&S...................... 350.00
Munger, Asa. "Black Face". Sore finger model. Mirror tablet. 30-hour weight driven. T&S 950.00
Thomas, Seth. Empire case. 8-day weight driven. T&S. Thomaston, Conn 375.00
Thomas, Seth. Walnut case. Painted dial and door glasses. 2-weight. 8-day, T&S. Mint condition. Plymouth Hollow 325.00
Thomas, Seth. Rosewood case. Gilted columns. 8-day weight driven, T&S 450.00
Wadsworth, Dyer. Triple decker. Weight driven. All original. Mint condition 575.00

GALLERY CLOCKS

Ansonia. Oak case. 24". Wood bezel. Seconds bit. 30-day, time only ....$ 475.00
Atkins. Rosewood case. 26". Octagon shape. Ripple front. 2 fuzee. 30-day 1250.00
English. Walnut case, 15". Fuzee movement.................... 315.00
Thomas, Seth. Mahogany case. Square. 11" dial. 8-day, T&S. All original 225.00
Thomas, Seth. Oak case. 18" dial. 30-day. Time only 525.00
Thomas, Seth. Oak case. 19". Original 14" dial. 8-day, T&S 300.00

KITCHEN SHELF CLOCKS

KITCHEN SHELF CLOCK. Ingraham. "Lion". Pressed oak case, 8-day, T&S. All original $300.00

Ansonia. "Army". Oak case. 8-day, T&S. All original ....$ 195.00
Davis, H.J. "Morning Star." Walnut case. 8-day. T&S. Restored 250.00
Ingraham. Oak case. 22". Calendar dial, 8-day, T&S 325.00
Ingraham. "Dewey." Oak case. 8-day, T&S. Restored 350.00
Ingraham. "Lion." Pressed oak case, 8-day, T&S. All original 300.00
Ingraham. "Niagara." 8-day, T&S .. 250.00
New Haven. Oak case. Alarm, 8-day, T&S..................... 175.00
Sessions. "Hiawatha." Oak case. 8-day, T&S..................... 225.00
Thomas, Seth. Plain oak case. 8-day, T&S. 145.00
Waterbury. Oak case. Barometer. Thermometer. 8-day, T&S 200.00
Waterbury. Pressed oak case. 8-day, T&S......................... 165.00
Waterbury. Ornate walnut case. Alarm, 8-day, T&S 225.00
Welch. "Robert E. Lee". Pressed oak case. 8-day, T&S. Original 275.00
Welch. Oak case. Fancy pendulum. Alarm, 8-day, T&S 215.00
Welch. Walnut case. Fancy glass. 8-day, T&S..................... 170.00

MARINE CLOCKS

Chronometer. Ulysee Nardin. Original wooden box ....$ 1150.00

Deck

- Chelsea Mark I. 3-part. Naval Bronze swingout case. 6" black dials. C. 1941 .... 400.00
- Hamilton. Outer protective box .. 325.00
- Longines. Complete 250.00
- Thomas, Seth. Nickled case. 6" silvered dial. Side winder. Lever action 225.00
- Waltham. In gimbaled box 425.00

Ship's Bell

- Chelsea. Heavy brass. 8-day 450.00
- Chelsea. Outside bell. 8-day, T&S 550.00
- Thomas, Seth. Heavy brass case. Outside bell. 8-day, T&S. Early .. 425.00

MIRROR SIDE SHELF CLOCKS

Ansonia. Walnut case. Windsor model. 8-day, T&S. All original ..$ 350.00
Gilbert, Wm. Walnut case. 23". Original cherubs. R&A pendulum. 8-day. Restored 375.00
New Haven. Walnut case. Drawer front. 8-day, T&S. All original 350.00

NEW ENGLAND WALL AND SHELF CLOCKS

Ives, Joseph. Wall. Walnut case. 36". Mirror clock. Conn. Rare ... $ 2700.00
Morill. B. Wall. Wheelbarrow movement. New Hampshire. Mint condition 2200.00
Stennes. Shelf. Mass 1850.00
Tappen. Wall. Mirror clock. 2-weight movement. Time only. New Hampshire. Mint condition 2450.00

O.G. SHELF CLOCKS

Ansonia Brass Co. Rosewood case. Good tablet. 30-hour weight driven, T&S ....$ 150.00
Brown, J.C. Iron dial. 8-day. All original 325.00
Burch, Thomas. 30-day, T & S. Pittsburgh 165.00
Constant & Sperry. Mahogany case. Original glass and dial. 30-hour weight driven 185.00
Davis Clock Co. 30-hour weight driven. All original 175.00
Gilbert, Wm. Miniature, 16". Painted dial and tablet. Spring driven. T&S. Alarm. All original 185.00
Jerome, Chauncey. Labeled. 30-hour, T&S. Bristol, Conn 125.00
Jerome, Chauncey. Original tablet. T&S. Rare weight alarm 275.00
New Haven. 30-hour weight driven. T&S.......................... 125.00
Thomas, Seth. Miniature. 16". Original tablet. 8-day spring driven. T&S. Alarm 225.00
Thomas, Seth. Stylized floral tablet in gold. 30-hour weight driven. Thomaston, Conn 125.00

PILLAR AND SCROLL SHELF CLOCKS

Hopkins and Alfred. Mahogany case. Brass finials. Painted wood dial. 30-hour wood movement. T&S ....$ 950.00
Ives, Chauncey. Cherry case. Wooden finials. Wooden movements. Weight driven. T&S. Labeled. Bristol, Conn 1000.00
Terry, Eli & Sons. Mahogany case. Brass finials and original glass. 2-weights. 30-hour wood movement. T&S 1250.00
Wadsworth, Longsbury and Turner. Walnut case. Standard size. Brass finials and original tablet. 2-weight. Wood movement 875.00

POT METAL AND IRON CASE MANTEL CLOCKS

Ansonia. "Troubadour" Statue clock. 8-day, T&S ....$	385.00
Art Nouveau. 18" high. Statue clock. Marble base. Porcelain dial. Hand painted. 8-day French movement. T&S	650.00
Bradley and Hubbard. "John Bull." Blinking eye. Good paint. 8-day. Time only. Working condition	750.00
Flash Light. "Deposit Box". Pressed steel. Alarm	125.00
Kroeber, F. Iron case. 12" Gothic. MOP inlay. 8-day, T&S	225.00
Kroeber, F. Iron case. Patented 1859. 8-day. T&S	175.00
Mueller. Ornate iron case. 8-day, T&S........................	150.00
Ornate case. 16". Iron front. 30-hour	165.00
River Boat. Pot metal. Side wheeler. No animation	90.00
Rogers, Will. Pot metal. 12". Animated drummers	150.00
Ships Wheel. F.D.R. Pot metal. Animated bartender. C. "Repeal of Prohibition."	125.00
"Steersmen, The." Pot metal. F.D.R., Lincoln, Washington. Animated ..	150.00
Welch, E.N. Iron front case. Labeled. 8-day, T&S....................	200.00

RECTANGULAR SHELF CLOCKS (Early 1900)

Gilbert. "Anniversary." Black marble case. Bell on top. 8-day, T & S.	225.00
Ingraham. Mantle. Black marble case. 8-day, T&S	165.00
Thomas, Seth. Black paint. 8-day, T&S........................	150.00

REGULATOR WALL CLOCKS

Brille. Master Regulator. Sweep second. Battery driven ....$	600.00
English Parliament. Walnut burl case. 11" painted dial. Heavy brass movement. Weight driven, time only	475.00
Gilbert. Oak case. 33" rectangular. 11" dial. Regulator on tablet. T&S. Restored	325.00
Howard, #70. Oak case. Original tablet. 8-day weight driven. Time only. Mint condition	1125.00
Jeweler's Pinwheel. Carved walnut case, 60". Glass door. Porcelain dial. Sweep seconds hand. Lyre pendulum. Weight driven. Time only. Mint condition.	3200.00

REGULATOR WALL CLOCK. Thomas, Seth #2. Walnut case. Original dial. Restored and refinished $750.00

New Haven. Oak case. 15x35". Original face. Brass pendulum. Second bit. Weight driven	695.00
New Haven. Walnut case. 72". Glass door. 14" porcelain dial. Seconds bit. 8-day weight driven. Time only	1500.00
Pinwheel. Porcelain face. Lyre pendulum. Sweep second hand. Weight driven	3200.00

Thomas, Seth, #2. Light oak case. 37". Painted 11" dial, seconds bit. 8-day. Weight driven. Time only. All original 750.00

Thomas, Seth, #20. Oak case. 62". 14" dial. Seconds beat. Graham deadbeat movement. 8-day, time. only 1500.00

Thomas, Seth. "Umbria". 40" high. Original finish. 15-day spring driven, T&S 550.00

Waterbury. Oak case. 30-day spring driven. Time only 350.00

Waterbury. "Pinwheel." Walnut case. 60". Can be mounted on 36" base for floor standing. Porcelain dial. Sweep second hand. Lyre pendulum. Weight driven. Time only 3700.00

SCHOOL HOUSE CLOCKS

American. Cherry case. 22" octagonal. Short drop. 8-day spring movement. T&S. Refinished ....$ 225.00

Ansonia. Small-size. Rosewood case. Calendar dial. 8-day spring movement.................. 425.00

Ansonia. Walnut case. Long drop. Seconds bit. 8-day spring movement. T&S. All original 400.00

Ball. Walnut case. Short drop. Original glass. 11" dial. 8-day. Time only. Regulator-type 325.00

Gilbert. Walnut case. Short drop. Calendar. 8-day spring movement. T&S 425.00

Howard, E., #11. Rosewood case. 31". Keyhole-type. 10" painted dial. Weight driven. Time only. Mint condition 1800.00

Japanese-Korean. Miniature. 8-day spring movement. T&S. All original 175.00

Miniature. Cherry case. Round top. 8-day spring movement. T&S. Mint condition 225.00

New Haven. Octagonal. 12" dial. Short drop. T&S. 250.00

Thomas, Seth. Oak case. Round top with short drop. Time only 250.00

Waterbury. "Bahia". Ionic style mosaic case. 10" dial. Roman numerals. 8-day, T&S. All original 375.00

Waterbury. Oak case. Long drop. 8-day spring movement. Time only. Mint condition 300.00

Waterbury. Oak case. Short drop. Calendar. 8-day spring movement.................. 350.00

Waterbury. Walnut case. Long drop. Wooden bezel. 11" dial. 8-day spring driven, T&S 375.00

Welch. Miniature. Original label. 8-day spring movement, T&S 275.00

Welch. "Verdi". Rosewood case. Painted dial. Strikes gong on hour and bell on ½ hour. Labeled. 8-day spring movement, T&S 475.00

SHELF CLOCKS

Ansonia. "Monarch". Walnut case. Drawer front. Fancy top. Original glass tablet. 8-day spring driven, T&S ....$ 400.00

Brewster and Ingraham. Walnut case. Round gothic onion top with 4 columns and frosted tablet. 8-day, T&S.................. 750.00

Brown, J.C. Ripple front. Round gothic. 4 columns. Painted glass. 8-day, T&S. Mint condition 1500.00

Ingraham. "Grecian." Mahogany case. 8-day, T&S with alarm. Original 325.00

Thomas, Seth. Walnut case and painted dial with Seth Thomas hands. 8-day. T&S with alarm. Original 250.00

Welch, E.N. "Patti". Rosewood case. 6¼x12¼x19" high. 8-day, T&S. All original 950.00

STEEPLE SHELF CLOCKS

Birge and Fuller. Steeple on steeple. Wagon spring movement. 8-day. All original 2500.00

Boardman, C. Walnut case. Painted dial and tablet. 30-hour fuzee movement.................. 425.00

Brewster and Ingraham. Curved gothic steeple. Original brass springs. 8-day, T&S 875.00

Jerome and Co. Mahogany case. Miniature. Painted dial and tablet. 3 o'clock wind. 30-hour, T&S.......................... 165.00

Manrose, Elisha. Steeple on steeple. 23". Double fuzee movement, 8-day 1500.00

Terry and Andrews. Walnut case. Double steeple. Lyre movement. 8-day, T&S.................. 825.00

Welch, E. N. Miniature steeple. Painted dial and tablet. 30-hour. Time and alarm 135.00

SWINGER CLOCKS

Ansonia. "Diana." Small size ....$ 325.00

Ansonia. "Fortuna". Ball movement. 8-day. Time only 2100.00

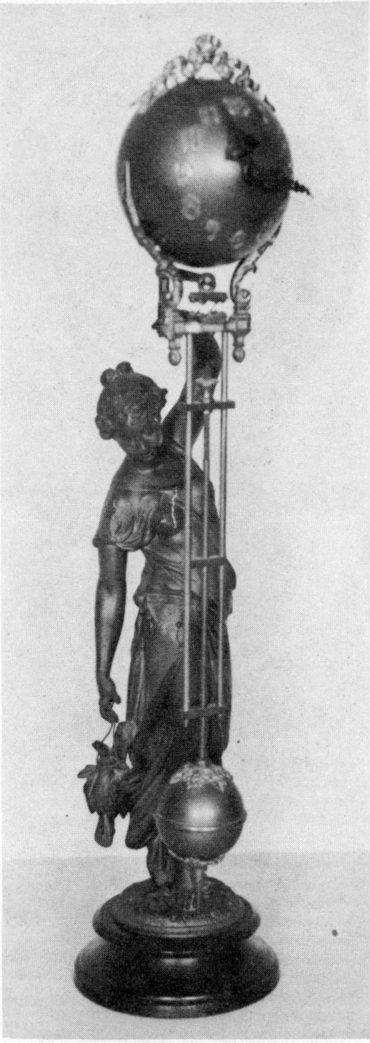

SWINGER CLOCK. Ansonia. "Huntress. "25" high. Ball movement $1100.00

Ansonia. "Gloria." Ball movement. 8-day 1350.00
Ansonia. "Huntress." Ball movement 1100.00
Ansonia. "Juno". Tin can. 8-day movement 1000.00
German. Novelty swinging soldier pendulum. 30-hour. Time only .. 325.00
Jughans. "Elephant." Original 375.00
Kroeber, F. "Swinging Doll". Walnut case. 17". Labeled 525.00

TALL CASE CLOCKS

Aitken. Mahogany case. Painted dial. 8-day. Glasgow, Scotland $ 1650.00
American. Cherry case. Moon dial. Center sweep second hand. Hill, Ohio 5500.00
Benbow. Mahogany case. Moon dial. Three train bells. Northport. American 3750.00
Custer, Jacob D. Cherry case. Broken arch. Moon phase. Painted dial. Signed. 8-day brass movement. T&S. 2-weight. Norristown, Pa. ... 4250.00
Elliot. Mahogany case. Engraved brass dial. Three train bells. London, England 2750.00
English. Mahogany case. Broken arch top. Glass door. Brass moon dial. 8-day weight driven. T&S. 2600.00
English. Oak case. Plain. Painted dial. Wood works. 1-weight. 30-hour, T&S. C. 1780 .... 500.00
Federal-style. Mahogany case. Broken arch. Moon phase. 8-day brass movement. Unsigned. C. 1820 .... 2250.00
Garrett. Cherry case. Rocking-chair. 8-day, T&S (bell). Philadelphia 4250.00
Hoadley, S. Pine grained case. 8-day 2500.00
Hopkins, Asa. Wood works. 30-hour 1800.00
Ithaca. Oak case. Painted white. 8-day spring driven, T&S 1000.00
Morbier. Pegged case. Simple pendulum. 8-day. T&S 1750.00
Pennsylvania. Inlaid cherry case. Hepplewhite-style. Bonnet with broken arch and pediment 4750.00
Pennsylvania. Walnut case with inlay. Moon phase. 8-day, T&S (bell) 4500.00
Scottish. Mahogany veneer and inlay case. Moon dial. Calendar and second hand. Mint dial. C. 1800 .... 2500.00
Scottish. Oak case. Brass dial with spandrels and chapter ring. 8-day, T&S. C. 1785 .... 2200.00
Shriener, Martin. Cherry case. Moon dial. Calendar and sweep second

hand on center arbor. 8-day movement. Very rare. Mint condition. American 6500.00
Speedman. Oak case. Painted dial. 8-day 1750.00
Willard, Simon. Walnut case. Double arch top. Fret work finials. Calendar. Iron dial. Signed. 8-day, T&S 2300.00
Windmills, Joseph. Walnut case. Seconds and calendar. 8-day. C. 1690. London, England 2750.00

TAMBOR SHELF CLOCKS

New Haven. Carved walnut case. Westminster chime. Brass dial. 8-day spring driven ....$ 170.00
Sessions. Westminster chime. 8-day 150.00
Thomas, Seth. Carved mahogany case. Giant. Senora chime. Plays tune on 5 bells 325.00
Thomas, Seth. Oak case. Westminster chime. Silvered dial. 8-day .. 170.00

VIENNA REGULATOR WALL CLOCKS

1-weight. Porcelain dial. 8-day, T&S. Original ....$ 325.00
1-weight. 60 beat. 30-day movement.................. 550.00
1-weight. Black case. 8-day, T&S. Early 300.00
1-weight. Mahogany case. 36". Fancy top. Porcelain dial. Center sweep second hand. 8-day, time only. Rare 700.00
3-weight. Serpentine walnut case. 50" long. Porcelain dial with seconds bit. 8-day, T&S 1450.00
3-weight. Walnut case. 36" long. Brass moon dial. Calendar. Embossed dial. Weights and bob. 8-day, T&S. Mint condition 1600.00
3-weight. Dark mahogany case. 42". Fancy, porcelain dial. Seconds bit. All original......... 2100.00
"R&A". Spring driven. 24" case. Fancy top. 8-day, T&S 275.00
"R&A". Spring driven. Rosewood case. 27". Fancy. Porcelain dial and pendulum bob. 8-day, T&S .. 300.00

MISCELLANEOUS CLOCKS

Advertising

Baird, E. "Guskey's". Ionic-style. All original including dial and paint. 8-day. T&S. ....$ 425.00
"Calumet Baking Powder." Wall. Oak case. 8-day, time only 475.00

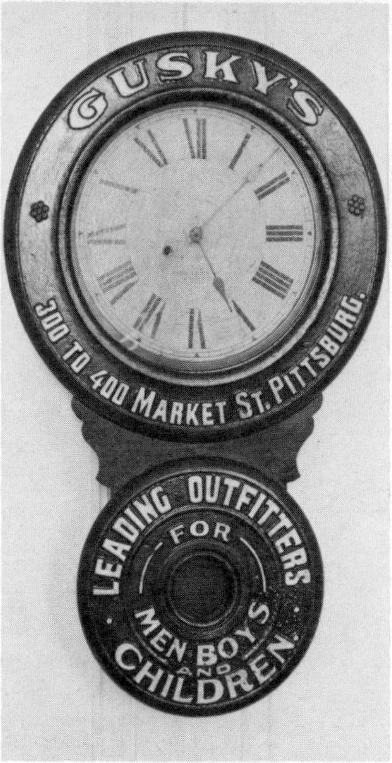

MISCELLANEOUS CLOCKS. Advertising type. Baird, E. "Gusky's." Ionic style. All original including dial and paint. 8-day, T&S $425.00

"Mr.Boston". Wooden case in shape of whiskey flask. Gilbert .. 225.00
"Sauer's Extracts and Flavorings". Regulator. Oak case. 8-day, T&S. All original. New Haven 450.00

Black Forest

Ansonia. "Bobbing Doll." 13" high. Original doll. Time only 600.00
Carved clock peddler. Whistles and head turns 300.00
Wall. 44". Highly carved deer and bird finial. Two weights. C. 1840-1850 .... 2200.00

Gas Light. Waltham 185.00
Gravity. Ansonia. Good condition. All original 225.00
Lantern. Joseph Knibb. London, C. 1650 .... 4250.00

Railroad. Hanging-type. Brass. Faces on opposite sides. French .. 575.00
Rotary. (Briggs)
Early 395.00
Welch, E.N. Glass dome. 30-hour spring driven. Time only. Early .. 395.00
Skeleton
Double fuzee. 11" high. Glass dome. 8-day, T&S, (bell on top), English 850.00
Triple fuzee. Shelf. Glass dome. 8-day. T&S (nest of 8 bells). English. Rare. 8750.00
Tavern. 13". Painted dial. 8-day. Time only. English. C. 1790...... 550.00
Time Recorders
Cincinnati. Oak case. 42". 8-day. Time only..................... 300.00
Dey. Oak case. 20 employees. Records on 7-day drum. Seth Thomas. 8-day movement. Restored 500.00
International. Ornate oak case. All original and working. 8-day. Time only. Restored 575.00
Tower
Morbier. Pinwheel movement only. Short pendulum 1500.00
Thomas, Seth. Movement only. Weights and pendulum not original 1100.00
Wag on Wall. Two weights. Hand-painted face. T & S on the hour. Germany. C. 1825 .... 350.00

CLOISONNE

Cloisonne is a form of enameling on metal. The technique originated in the orient many centuries ago. Fine gold wires were soldered to the surface of the article to build up a wall so that the design could be filled in with smalt. Smalt consists of colored, powdered glass mixed with an adhesive. Although gold wires were originally used, less expensive metals, such as brass were employed later. The cloisonne wares encountered today are most probably from the Victorian era, 1870-1900, and came from China or Japan.

Bowls
2½x4½". Red, yellow flowers over green. Green interior ......$ 65.00
3¼x10". Five claw yellow dragon 500.00
4". Lidded. Black geometric design 85.00
5". Duck-shaped. Cobalt and red. Early 750.00
5½x7". Melon ribbed. Black with medallions, butterfly, mums, etc 375.00

Coaster. 3¾" diam. Oriental decor $35.00

Bird, Wine Vessel. Aqua blue ground with gold, red and yellow decor $700.00

7". Covered. Tan ground. Blues, reds, greens, floral decor. Late .. 175.00
7". Footed. Covered. Black, white, turquoise flowers. Goldstone 275.00
7½". Covered. Floral decor. Foo Dog finial. Late 175.00
12½". Rare colors. Early 750.00
Boxes
2" diam. Jade insert carved into

vase and flower. Pigeon blood with multicolored flowers 300.00
2¾x3¾". "Kyoto Jippo." Multicolored flowers. Symbols with goldstone. Gilt wire scroll pattern on black.................... 500.00
5" diam. Green ground. Multicolored flowers. Marked "China." 75.00

Chargers
12". Turquoise with orange and pink lilies. Butterfly 500.00
12". Scalloped edge. Dragon in center, pearl and floral motif around border. Japanese 500.00
18". Floral and bird decor with goldstone. C. 1870 .... 795.00

Cup and Saucer. Late 75.00
Figurines. Turtles. 3½x6". Light blue with dragons in cobalt. Removable tops. Pair 675.00
Humidor. 8" high. Foo Dog finial. Late 175.00
Incense Burner. 9½" high. Ball-shaped 85.00

Jars, Ginger
3". Floral design with goldstone. Japanese. C. 1880 .... 300.00
9½". Black ground. Multicolored flower motif. Marked "China." .. 175.00
12". Green butterflies, flowers. Marked "China." 225.00

Napkin Ring. 1¼". Floral decor 55.00
Pipe. Opium. 15"................ 250.00
Pitcher. 4". Floral, geometrical pattern. Late 85.00

Plates
6". Floral. Brass base, edging 75.00
7¼". Landscape scene 100.00
11¼". Hanging-type. Flowers and birds on light blue ground 300.00
14". Butterfly, flowers 450.00

Plaque. 7x7½". Framed. Flowers, butterfly. Goldstone............ 225.00
Salt. Typical colors 50.00
Tea Caddy. Late 125.00
Teapot. 5x6". White ground. Floral decor 300.00
Tea Set. Teapot, two gold-lined cups, sugar and creamer. Dragons, black ground. Goldstones 750.00
Toothpick 50.00

Trays
5" square. Yellow ground. Late .. 50.00
7x9". Black ground with flowering plants. 5 butterflies in red, blue, white, green. Chinese. C. 1850 .. 600.00

Vases
3¾". Hexagonal. "Kyoto Jippo." Multicolored flowers. Gilt wire scroll on black 250.00
5½". Dark blue ground. White dragon, decorated in red, green. Late 100.00
6¼". Hexagonal. "Kyoto Jippo." Multicolored flowers. Gilt wire scroll on black. Goldstone. Japanese 375.00
7". Dragon among flames. Goldstone stars. 250.00
7". Turquoise ground. Butterflies, birds, flowers in panels. Late 175.00
8". U.S. and Chinese flags on blue floral background.............. 350.00
8½". Red ground with white wisteria and green leaves. C. 1890 .... 295.00
10½". Yellow dragons on blue. Green leaves and multicolored flowers. Chinese. Pair 400.00
11". Green ground. Decor of flowers, butterflies, birds. C. 1850. Pair 650.00
12". Background in shades of aqua. Flowers, three panels with dragons against black and rust ground. Goldstone 500.00
12". Burgundy ground with turquoise blue, green, red decor. C. 1900 .... 300.00
17". Cobalt ground, pheasants in flower garden. Early. Pair 2250.00

CLOTHING

The ghost of "Fashion Past" usually dwells in attic trunks and thrift shops. **Today this apparition** is casting longer shadows. . .right into chic boutique shops, department stores and designers' drawing boards. Enterprising Salvation **Army and Goodwill outlets have set up special departments called "Annie Hall."**
Retrospective or 'retro' dressing is on the move. Cotton half slips are being worn as skirts, camisoles as suntops, tatted lace collars are stitched to crepe dresses. Even the beaded sweaters, fur stoles and coats of the 1940's and 50's are being recycled. Hang on to that old crepe dress Nanny. . .young Debbie sees it as a fashionable disco outfit!

Apron, Long. White batiste with lace and tucks ....$ 10.00
Boa. 70" long. Yellow marabou 25.00

Bags
Alligator. 8½x12½". Envelope-style. C. 1930's 50.00
Beaded
Blue and black beads. Fringed bottom. Drawstring top 25.00
Carnival beads. Mint condition. C. 1930 .... 45.00

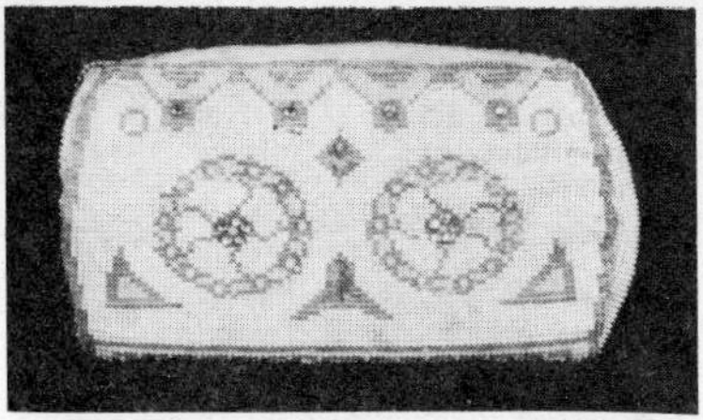

Evening bag. Beaded. Made in Czechoslovakia. C. 1920 ...... $25.00

Petticoat. White batiste. Drawstring top. Scalloped bottom $30.00

Mesh
- Gold colored pouch. Expanding top. C. 1950 .... 35.00
  - Silverplated 35.00
  - Sterling 75.00

Blouse. White batiste. Long sleeves, round neck. Tucks and lace inserts 15.00
Bonnet. Dutch-type. Pleated lace. Ribbon ties 30.00
Camisole. White cotton. Lacy trim .. 10.00

Capes
- Black taffeta. 16". Ruffled collar. C. 1900 .... 15.00
- Seal. Finger tip length 50.00

Coats
- Persian Lamb. ¾ length 100.00
- Persian Paw. ¾ length 75.00
- Raccoon. Man's 850.00
- Sheared Raccoon. Small size 125.00

Collars
- Lace. Ecru 7.50
- Mink. 7" wide 20.00

Dresses
- Batiste. White. High waist. Ankle length. Lace insertions on skirt and puffy sleeves. C. 1912 ...... 50.00
- Beaded. Black on black net. V-neck, sleeveless. Floor length. C. 1925 .... 50.00
- Child's. Size 6. White cotton with lace trim, ribbons. Matching panties 25.00
- Taffeta. Green. Ankle length. Round neck. puffed sleeves, flounced skirt. C. 1925 .... 35.00

Hats
- Flapper. Black felt 3.00
- Opera. Folding-type. Silk. Original box 60.00

Pill Boxes
- Persian Lamb 15.00
- Somali Leopard 25.00

Jackets, Ladies'
- Mink. Matching pill box hat. C. 1950 .... 100.00
- Muskrat 65.00
- Ocelot 85.00
- Sheared Raccoon 75.00

Mantilla. Black lace. Triangular-shape. Scalloped edges. Italian .. 50.00

Neck Pieces
- Fox 25.00
- Mink. 3 skins 30.00

Night Cap. Blue silk. Lace and ribbon trim 15.00
Night Gown, Woman's. White cotton. Lace trim 12.50
Ostrich Plume. 20". Pink 15.00

Parasols
- Linen. White 50.00
- Taffeta. Black-ruffled 35.00

Petticoats
- Long. White cotton, tucks and lace 20.00
- Short. White cotton, flounce bottom 12.50

Shawls
- 44" long. Silk. Melon color. Fringed 85.00
- 48" square. Yellow. Embroidered. 5" fringe 100.00

Shoes
- Child's. Button. Pair 25.00
- Lady's. High. Black leather. Laced. Pair 40.00

Skirt Hoop 20.00
Spats, Motor car. Lady's. Black with black fur trim. Pair 12.50
Stole. Mink. Pastel. Medium size. C. 1950 .... 75.00
"Teddy." One piece suit. White batiste with lace trim 12.50

COALPORT

Coalport porcelain has been made by the Coalport Porcelain Works in England since the late 1700's. It is currently being produced at Stoke-on-Trent. One of their more popular patterns is "Indian Tree."
See "Indian Tree Pattern."

Tureen. 9x10½" o. h. Handled. Imari-type decor. Polychromed finial. C. 1805-1810 ....$850.00

Boxes
  2x1⅛" diam. Fan-shaped. Hinged lid. Floral decor ....$ 65.00
  2¼x4" diam. Pink ground. Jeweled with gold trim 175.00
Chocolate Pot. 6". Tankard-style. Bird and flowers 65.00
Cups and Saucers
  Black, orange floral on white. Gold trim. Late 15.00
  Demitasse. Blue flowers on gold. Gold interior. C. 1891 .... 95.00
  Demitasse. Jeweled 125.00
Mug. 2½". Can-shaped 50.00
Plates
  8½". Green border. Castle scene in center. Gold trim 35.00
  11½". Scalloped edge. Cobalt border. Floral center. Gold trim .. 125.00
Vases
  4". Shell-shaped. Oyster coloring 50.00
  5½". Cobalt with gold trim. Handled. Pair 175.00
  6". Blue. Gold handles. H-P scenic reverse designs on each side. Gold trim. Pair 225.00

COCA COLA ITEMS

The originator of the famed Coca Cola was John Pemberton a pharmacist from Atlanta, Georgia. In 1886, Dr. Pemberton introduced a patent medicine to relieve headaches, stomach disorders and other minor human maladies.
Unfortunately, his failing health and meager finances forced him to sell his interest. In 1888, Asa G. Candler was the sole owner of Coca Cola. Candler improved the formula, increased the advertising budget and widened the distribution. Accidentally, a 'patient' was given a dose of the syrup mixed with carbonated water instead of the usual still water. The result was a tastier, more refreshing drink. Gallon sales went from 9,000 to 1890 to 400,000 in 1900. Candler recognized that the product was more suitable for the soft drink market and began advertising as such. From the beginning, with Dr. Pemberton's appreciation of advertising throughout the growth of Coca Cola, a myriad of advertising items have been issued to invite all to "Drink Coca Cola."
Dates of interest: The first unauthorized Coca Cola tray was issued in 1900. "Coke" was first used in advertising in 1941. The distinctive shaped bottle was registered as a trademark on April 12, 1960.

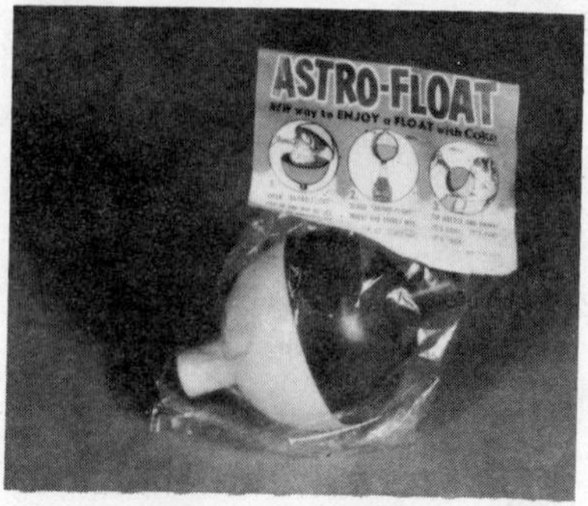

Astro-float. Red and white plastic $6.00

Truck. 12" long. Cast iron. Red . . $75.00

Ashtray. 4½" d. "I Drink Coca Cola." Reg. U.S. Pat. Office. Imprint of Coke Bottle. Tin. Crimped edge, all over ridging . . . . $ 7.50
Blotter. 1940's 5.00
Bottles
  Anniversary, 75th. Various cities. Each 2.50
  Canadian. 6 oz. 3.00
  Cola Clan Convention 15.00
  Dated. 1905 . . . . 10.00
  Dated. WWI, Nov. 16, 1915 . . . . 15.00
  Embossed. Painted label. 6½ oz. C. 1900 . . . . 30.00
  Embossed. 10 oz. Teal green. 1975 . . . . 35.00
  First Throwaway. 9" 6.50
  Israel Exposition. 6½ oz. 1975 . . 7.50
  *Miniature 1.00
  Youngstown, Ohio. Amber 20.00
Cases, Wooden
  6-bottle. 1929 . . . . 25.00
  48-bottle. Lid and latch 150.00
Coaster. 4". Cardboard 1.50
Cigarette Lighter. Bottle-shaped . . 10.00
Door Pull. Bottle-shaped 45.00
Game. "Bingo" 50.00
*Pocket Knife. 2" long 2.00
Route Pads 2.50
Rule. 12". Wooden 7.50
Signs
  "Autumn Leaves." 42" long. Cardboard. 3-sections 65.00
  Bottle-shaped. 10x24". Porcelain 45.00
  "Santa Claus." 19". Cardboard, 1955 . . . . 25.00
Thermometer. 7x16". Tin. Bottle-shaped. 1923 . . . . 55.00
Thimble. C. 1940's 1.50
Trays
  1904. Tip. St. Louis World's Fair . . 135.00
  1904. 13½x16¾". Oval. H.D. Beach 200.00
  1909. Tip 85.00
  1909. American Art Works 100.00
  1914. Oval 145.00
  1914. Rectangular. Passaic Metal Ware 85.00
  1914. Tip. Passaic Metal Ware . . 60.00
  1917. "Elaine." 8½x19". Passaic Metal Ware 85.00
  1917. Tip. Passaic Metal Ware . . 50.00
  1920. Rectangular. No mark 65.00
  1920. Oval 85.00
  *1921. Rectangular. H.D. Beach . . 75.00
  1922 . . . . 125.00
  1923. Rectangular. American Art Works 75.00
  1924. Rectangular. American Art Works 100.00
  1925. Rectangular. American Art Works 60.00
  *1927. Rectangular. Tindeco 45.00
  1932 . . . . 125.00
  1936 . . . . 40.00
  1938. Tip 30.00
  1940 . . . . 40.00
  1943 . . . . 25.00
  1950. Mint 20.00
  1960 . . . . 15.00
  1961. Flower Garden 12.50
Tumbler. 6 oz. Glass 2.00

*Reproduced Item

COFFEE MILLS

Coffee mills or grinders were made in a variety of shapes and sizes. . .from the large cast iron store models to the table top or lap and wall models for the home. The first home-size coffee mill was introduced in the 1890's.

Arcade. Wall-type. Cast iron and glass . . . . $ 45.00
Crystal. Wall-type. Glass container 30.00
Elgin. 27" high. Cast iron. 2-wheels 325.00
Enterprise Mfg. Co. Store-type. 2-wheels 375.00
German. Cast iron. White porcelain jar. Blue Delft-type decor 150.00
Golden Rule Coffee. Wood and metal. Glass insert 75.00
Kenrick. Table-type. Cast iron. One drawer. Porcelain-lined cup 65.00
National Specialty Co., Phila., Pa. Wall-type. Cast iron. Original red scroll with gold decor 75.00
Patent Applied For. Wall-type. Cast iron. Glass jar 35.00
Peugeot, Brevetes, S.G.D.G. 17" high. Cast iron wheel and cup. One drawer. Store-type 200.00
Pride. Wood. One drawer. Iron handle. Lap-type 45.00

Arcade. Table-type. Imperial #1 Mill. Pat. June 5, 1894 ....$55.00

Universal
- Table-type. With clamp 35.00
- Wall-type. Cast iron. Metal container...................... 45.00

Unmarked, Wooden
- 2½x2½x3". Iron cup and crank. One drawer 50.00
- 4½x7x10". Wall-type. Glass dome 40.00
- 5x5½x5⅞". Brass fittings. Refinished 55.00
- 6" square. Dovetailed. Embossed iron top 75.00
- 6" square. Dovetailed. Early pewter cup. Iron crank. One drawer. Refinished 85.00
- 7½x13". Table-type with cast iron. One drawer 75.00

COIN OPERATED ITEMS

A wide variety of coin-operated machines have been made in the past. Games of skill and chance have always held a certain fascination to mankind. Inflation and the decreasing value of the dollar has made the one-cent and nickel-type vending machines obsolete. People are collecting these earlier coin-operated items for nostalgia and entertainment reasons.

GAMES

Advance Electric Shock. C. 1920 ..$ 275.00
Bally Hoo. Pinball. C. 1931 .... 500.00

Game. "Rocket Ship." Pinball. Gottlieb....................$450.00

Booz Barometer. 5-cent 150.00
Buckaroo. Gottlieb. One player pinball. C. 1965 .... 450.00
Charger Target Game. 1-cent...... 200.00
Genco. Hand strength tester 75.00
Grand Tour. Bally pinball. C. 1964 400.00
Hi Score Pool.................... 600.00
Kicker Katcher. 1-cent wood 225.00
Merry-Go-Round. Pinball. Gottlieb. C. 1964 .... 450.00
Smiley. 1-cent counter game 175.00
Steeple Chase. 1-cent counter game 400.00
Turf. Champ. One player pinball. Williams. C. 1958 .... 650.00
Wizard. Mills. Fortune Teller. 1-cent 500.00

VENDING MACHINES

Advance. 1-cent gumball. C. 1912 $ 125.00
Advance. 5-cent nut. C. 1923...... 60.00
Advance. 5-cent package gum. C. 1924 .... 60.00
Belvend. 1-cent candy vendor 50.00
Columbus. 1-cent gumball 85.00
Dixie. 1-cent paper cup dispenser. C. 1913 .... 500.00

Flatbush. 1-cent gumball	125.00
Ford. 1-cent gumball, chrome	50.00
Gas Pump. 1-cent lighter fluid dispenser. Card holder	200.00
Griswold. 1-cent match	175.00
Hawkeye. 1-cent gumball with bell	75.00
Hershey. 1-cent candy	95.00
Imp. 1-cent game with gumball ..	150.00
Masters. 1-cent gumball	75.00
National. 5-cent mint and gum	95.00
Northwestern. 1-cent, 5-cent peanut machine	65.00
Postcard. 25-cents. 3 cards pre-stamped	100.00
Premier. 1-cent card and gum	50.00
Rosebud Ohio match	85.00
Silver Comet. 1-cent cigarette	150.00
Silver King. 5-cent hot nuts	95.00
Spitfire gumball	125.00
Stamp. Vends 1-cent and 3-cent stamps	100.00
Stampmaster. Vends 4-cent stamps	55.00
Star. 1-cent candy	85.00
Victor. 1-cent candy	75.00
Zeno. Gum. Wood case. C. 1908 ..	500.00

MISCELLANEOUS

Astrology by Oak. 25-cent ......$	40.00

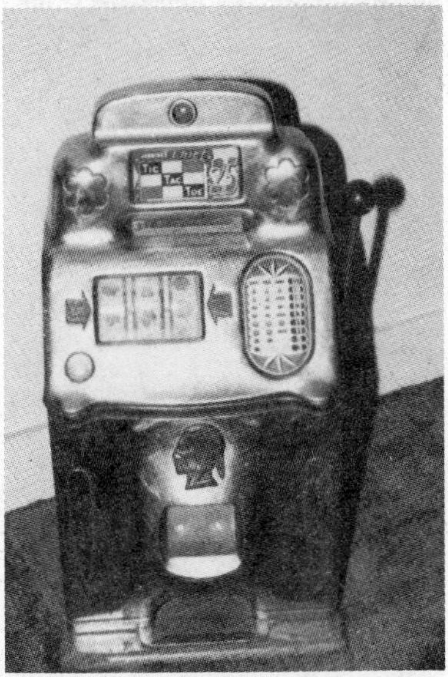

Slot Machine. "Chief". Jennings. 3-reels, 25 cents. $2250.00

Cash Registers	
Michigan. 1-cent to 50-cents	350.00
National. Rings from 1-cent to $3.00. Ornate brass	650.00
Duo-Scope Flip Card. 13x14x19". Spring wound. Electrified	400.00
Juke Boxes	
AMI. Model C. C. 1949	500.00
Seeburg. 100-selections, 45RPM. C. 1958	500.00
Seeburg. 100-selections, 78 RPM. Model M-100-A	600.00
Seeburg. Cylindrical-style. No. 148. C. 1948	550.00
Wurlitzer. 48-selections, 78RPM. Style 1600. Unrestored	550.00
Mutoscopes (Peep Shows)	
64" high. Cast iron stand. C. 1920's	1000.00
76" high. Ornate cast iron stand. "American Mutoscope Reel Co." C. 1905-10	1650.00
Parking Meter. 1-cent with key	50.00
Scale. Vending operator's	65.00
Slot Machines	
Caille. "Doughboy." 5-cent. C. 1930	950.00
English. Vertical wood case. Ornate cast iron trim. 1-cent	350.00
Jennings. "Chief." 3-reels, 10-cents	1750.00
Mills. "Black Knight." 25-cents ..	1000.00
Mills. "Diamond." 50-cents	1000.00
Mills. "Special Award 7-7-7." 1-cent. Restored	1295.00

COIN SPOT GLASS

(See, "Opalescent Glass")

COLLECTORS' PLATES, ETC.

The first collectors' plates were made by Bing and Grondahl in 1895. Royal Copenhagen issued their first Christmas plate in 1908. Since, several potteries, glass factories, mints and artists have been issuing varied items commemorating occasions, events, people, etc. Although once considered a speculative field in the collecting market, with little increase in value, these 'new' collectibles are gaining in popularity and price.

ANRI (ITALY)

Christmas Plates	
1971-FE ....$	78.50
1972	95.00
1973	200.00
1974	75.00
1975	68.50

1968. Bing and Grondahl. Christmas in Church $45.00

1976	135.00
1977	100.00
1978	85.00
Figurines 3″	
Flower Girl	65.00
Free Ride	40.00
Hurdy Gurdy	75.00
Journey	85.00
Spring Arrivals	55.00

BAREUTHER (GERMANY)

1967-Christmas. FE	$ 120.00
1968-Christmas	32.50
1969-Christmas	20.00
1970-Christmas	15.00
1971-Father's Day	22.50
1971-Mother's Day	22.50
1972-Christmas	57.50
1972-Thanksgiving	22.50
1973-Christmas	30.00
1973-Father's Day	30.00
1973-Thanksgiving	25.00
1974-Christmas	25.00
1975-Christmas	27.50
1976-Christmas	27.50
1976-Mother's Day	25.00
1977-Mother's Day	27.50
1978-Christmas	30.00

BERLIN (GERMANY)

1970-Christmas. FE	$ 155.00
1971-Mother's Day. FE	27.50
1972-Bell. FE	22.50
1973-Christmas	42.50
1974-Father's Day	45.00
1975-Christmas	42.50
1976-Christmas	35.00

1975. Hummel, Berta. Christmas Ornament $17.50

1975. Hummel, Goebel. Annual Plate $110.00

1976-Stein. Annual	85.00
1976-Stein. Nautical	175.00
1977-Historical	35.00
1978-Christmas	38.50

BING AND GRONDAHL (DENMARK)

Christmas Plates	
1895-Frozen Window. FE	$ 3250.00

1896-New Moon	2000.00
1897-Sparrows	1250.00
1898-Star and Roses	800.00
1899-Crows	1350.00
1900-Church Bells	800.00
1901-Three Wise Men	425.00
1902-Gothic Church Interior	400.00
1903-Expectant Children	300.00
1904-Frederiksberg Hill	145.00
1905-Christmas Night	175.00
1906-One Horse Sleigh	120.00
1907-Little Match Girl	145.00
1908-St. Petri Church	90.00
1909-Yule Tree	100.00
1910-The Old Organist	100.00
1911-Angels and Shepherds	100.00
1912-Going to Church	95.00
1913-Bringing Home the Tree	100.00
1914-Royal Castle	95.00
1915-Dog Outside Window	135.00
1916-Sparrows at Christmas	85.00
1917-Christmas Boat	85.00
1918-Fishing Boat	95.00
1919-Outside the Window	87.50
1920-Hare in the Snow	85.00
1921-Pigeons	65.00
1922-Star of Bethlehem	75.00
1923-The Ermitage	70.00
1924-Lighthouse	70.00
1925-Child's Christmas	85.00
1926-Churchgoers	70.00
1927-Skating Couple	100.00
1928-Eskimos	75.00
1929-Fox Outside Farm	85.00
1930-Town Hall Square	100.00
1931-Christmas Train	95.00
1932-Lifeboat	87.50
1933-Korsor-Nyborg Ferry	80.00
1934-Church Bell in Tower	68.50
1935-Lillebelt Bridge	78.50
1936-Amalienborg Castle	90.00
1937-Guests Arrival	90.00
1938-Lighting the Candles	125.00
1939-Old Lock-Eye, the Sandman	195.00
1940-Christmas Letters	190.00
1941-Horses	425.00
1942-Danish Farm	185.00
1943-Ribe Cathedral	190.00
1944-Sorgenfri Castle	125.00
1945-The Old Water Mill	145.00
1946-Commemoration Cross	80.00
1947-Dybbol Mill	110.00
1948-Watchman	78.50
1949-Landsoldaten	78.50
1950-Kronborg Castle	170.00
1951-Jens Bang	115.00
1952-Thorvaldsen Museum	85.00
1953-Royal Boat	78.50
1954-Snowman	110.00
1955-Kalundborg Church	115.00
1956-Christmas in Copenhagen	160.00
1957-Christmas Candles	175.00
1958-Santa Claus	110.00
1959-Christmas Eve	155.00
1960-Village Church	235.00
1961-Winter Harmony	125.00
1962-Winter Night	75.00
1963-The Christmas Elf	147.50
1964-The Fir Tree and Hare	55.00
1965-Bringing Home the Tree	65.00
1966-Home for Christmas	47.50
1967-Sharing the Joy	45.00
1968-Christmas in Church	45.00
1969-Arrival of Guests	32.00
1970-Pheasants in Snow	25.00
1971-Christmas at Home	22.50
1972-Christmas in Greenland	22.50
1973-Family Reunion	30.00
1974-Christmas in the Village	22.50
1975-Old Water Mill	30.00
1976-Christmas Welcome	30.00
1977-Copenhagen Xmas	34.00
1978-B&G Xmas Tale	35.00

Mother's Day Plates

1969-Dog. FE	450.00
1970-Bird	40.00
1971-Cat	15.00
1972-Horses	17.50
1973-Duck	18.50
1974-Bear	17.50
1975-Doe	20.00
1976-Swans	20.00
1977-Squirrels	28.50
1978-Heron	25.00

Miscellaneous

1974-Bell, Annual. FE	175.00
1976-Bicentennial U.S.A.	55.00
1978-Thimble. FE	15.00

BOEHM (LENOX)

Annuals

1970	$ 275.00
1978	65.00

Bird Series

1970-Wood Thrush. FE	375.00
1971-Goldfinch	175.00
1972-Mountain Bluebird	100.00
1973-Meadowlark	80.00
1974-Hummingbirds	80.00
1975-Redstart	75.00
1976-Cardinals	70.00
1977-Robins	65.00
1978-Mockingbirds	65.00

Wildlife Series

1973-Raccoons. FE	95.00
1974-Fox	80.00
1975-Rabbits	72.50
1976-Chipmunks	80.00

1977-Beaver	72.50
1978-Whitetail Deer	75.00

DISNEY, WALT (SCHMID)

1973-Christmas. FE $	150.00
1974-Christmas	65.00
1974-Christmas Ornament. FE	10.00
1974-Mother's Day. FE	40.00
1975-Christmas	15.00
1975-Christmas Bell. FE	12.50
1976-Bicentennial	16.50
1977-Mother's Day Bell. FE	10.00
1978-Mickey Mouse. 50th Birthday	30.00

FRANKLIN MINT

Audubon Series (Younger)	
1972 thru 1973. Each $	125.00
Mother's Day (Spencer)	
1972. FE	160.00
1973	135.00
1974	150.00
1975	175.00
1976	180.00
Presidents Series. Each	150.00
Rockwell, See Rockwell, Norman	
Thanksgiving	
1972 thru 1975. Each	150.00
Western America	
1972 thru 1973.	
Gold. Each	2500.00
Silver. Each	200.00
Wyeth, James	
1972	165.00
1973	150.00
1974	165.00
1975	175.00

GORHAM

Christmas Items (other than plates)

Bells	
1976 thru 1978. Each $	15.00
Ornaments	
Angel	25.00
Drummer Boy	25.00
Three Wise Men	28.50
Snowflakes	
1970-Sterling	85.00
1971-Sterling	55.00
1974-Sterling	35.00
1976-Sterling	35.00
1977-Sterling	40.00
1978-Crystal	32.50
Spoons, Sterling	
1972	25.00
1973	25.00
1975	25.00
Santa, demi	25.00

Figurines

Beguiling Buttercup	100.00
Fishing	100.00
Four Seasons. See Rockwell, N.	
Gay Blades	95.00
Grace Before Meals	110.00
Independent	90.00
Missed	125.00
Skating	80.00

Plates

1971-Quiet Waters	25.00
1972-Rembrandt	35.00
1972-1978-Four Seasons. See Rockwell, Norman	
1973-Moppets. Christmas. FE	32.50
1973-Moppets. Mother's Day. FE	25.00
1974-Moppets. Christmas	12.50
1975-Dear Child	150.00
1976-Promises to Keep	75.00
1977-Johnny and Duke	30.00
1977-Patient Ones	45.00

HAVILAND & CO.

1970-Christmas. FE $	275.00
1971-Christmas	42.00
1971-Christmas Ornament. FE	10.00
1972-Gaspee	13.50
1973-Mother's Day, Breakfast. FE	12.50
1975-Christmas	35.00
1975-Mother's Day	32.00
1976-Christmas	38.00
1976-Mother's Day	30.00
1977-Christmas	45.00
1977-Mother's Day	35.00
1978-Christmas	48.00
1978-Mother's Day	40.00

HAVILAND-PARLON (FRANCE)

1971-Unicorn Captivity. FE $	150.00
1972-Madonna. FE	175.00
1973-Madonna	110.00
1974-Madonna	55.00
1976-Mother's Day. Mother and Child. FE	60.00
1977-Lady and Unicorn. FE	65.00
1978-Madonna	55.00

HUMMEL, BERTA (SCHMID)

1971-Christmas. FE $	60.00
1972-Christmas	32.00
1973-Christmas	220.00

1974-Mother's Day	32.50
1975-Christmas	28.50
1975-Mother's Day	30.00
1976-Mother's Day	28.50
1977-Christmas	35.00
1978-Bell. FE	275.00
1978-Christmas Cup	20.00
1978-Paperweight. Crystal. FE	165.00

HUMMEL, GOEBEL (GERMANY)

Annuals	
1971	$ 1100.00
1972	110.00
1973	250.00
1974	145.00
1975	110.00
1976	85.00
1977	195.00
1978	175.00

HUTSCHENREUTHER (GERMANY)

Figurines	
Beagle. 4¼x5½"	$ 58.00
Chihuahua. 4x4"	63.00
Cocker Spaniel. 4¼x5½"	63.00
Colt, lying. 3x5½"	80.00
Donkey, lying. 3¼x4"	55.00
Donkey, standing. 5x6½"	65.00
Fawn, spotted, lying. 4x4¾"	100.00
Fawn, spotted, standing. 5x5½"	138.00
Fawn, standing. Colored foal. 4¾ x 5½"	54.00
Foxes. 7x11"	240.00
Hummingbird, flower. 2¾x4"	75.00
Hummingbird, nest with egg. Matte finish. 2¼ x 3"	85.00
Lizard. 2x3½"	57.00
Stallion. 4x4¼"	45.00
Tammy "Tiger Eye" Cat. 4¼x6¼"	105.00
Miscellaneous	
Birthday	175.00
Christmas Bell. 1978. FE	25.00
Christmas 1978. FE	275.00
Floral Bell. 1978 FE	45.00
Friendship	85.00
Months. Set of 12	800.00
Mother and Child 1978. FE	55.00
"Pansies in a Coffee Tin." Carroll. 1978. FE	75.00
"Princess Snowflake." Valenza. 1978 FE	55.00
Wedding	225.00
"Zinnias in a Sugar Bowl." 1978 FE	68.50
Zodiac. Set of 12	1500.00

NORITAKE (JAPAN)

1971-Easter Egg. FE	$ 90.00
1972-Christmas Bell. FE	17.50
1973-Easter Egg	27.50
1973-Valentine Heart. FE	12.50
1974-Christmas Bell	25.00
1974-Easter Egg	22.50
1974-Valentine Heart	7.50
1975-Christmas Bell	20.00
1976-Easter Egg	17.50
1976-Mother's Day Cup	22.50
1977-Irish Setter	45.00
1978-Easter Egg	25.00
1979-Easter Egg	22.50
1979-Valentine	25.00

PEANUTS-SCHMID

1972-Christmas. FE	$ 65.00
1972-Mother's Day. FE	20.00

1972. Peanuts, Schmid. Mother's Day. FE $20.00

1973-Christmas	80.00
1973-Christmas Bell. FE	25.00
1973-Mother's Day	25.00
1974-Christmas	75.00
1975-Christmas	15.00
1975-Mother's Day	20.00
1976-Bicentennial	15.00
1976-Christmas	18.50
1977-Christmas	20.00
1977-Mother's Day Bell. FE	10.00
1977-Valentine. FE	13.00
1978-Christmas	15.00
1978-Mother's Day	15.00
1979-Valentine	20.00

ROCKWELL

(See, "Rockwell, Norman")

ROYAL COPENHAGEN (DENMARK)

Christmas Plates

1908-Madonna and Child......$	1950.00
1909-Danish Landscape	150.00
1910-The Magi	135.00
1911-Danish Landscape	150.00
1912-Christmas Tree	150.00
1913-Frederik Church Spire	150.00
1914-Holy Spirit Church	145.00
1915-Danish Landscape	115.00
1916-Shepherd at Christmas	90.00
1917-Our Saviour Church	85.00
1918-Sheep and Shepherds	80.00
1919-In the Park	87.50
1920-Mary and Child Jesus	75.00
1921-Aabenraa Marketplace	75.00
1922-Three Singing Angels......	72.50
1923-Danish Landscape	72.50
1924-Sailing Ship	95.00
1925-Christianshavn	82.50
1926-Christianshavn Canal	75.00
1927-Ship's Boy at Tiller	150.00
1928-Vicar Family	80.00
1929-Grundtvig Church	80.00
1930-Fishing Boat	80.00
1931-Mother and Child	85.00
1932-Frederiksberg Gardens	85.00
1933-Great Belt Ferry	105.00
1934-The Hermitage Castle	120.00

1970. Royal Copenhagen. Christmas Rose and Cat. $30.00

1935-Kronborg Castle	140.00
1936-Roskilde Cathedral	140.00
1937-Main Street Copenhagen ..	145.00
1938-Round Church Ostelars	265.00
1939-Greenland Pack Ice	275.00
1940-The Good Shepherd	375.00
1941-Danish Village Church	350.00
1942-Bell Tower	385.00
1943-Flight into Egypt..........	475.00
1944-Danish Winter Scene	160.00
1945-A Peaceful Motif	350.00
1946-Zealand Village Church ..	150.00
1947-The Good Shepherd	250.00
1948-Noddebo Church	165.00
1949-Our Lady's Cathedral	165.00
1950-Boeslunde Church	200.00
1951-Christmas Angel	340.00
1952-Christmas in Forest	130.00
1953-Frederiksborg Castle	115.00
1954-Amalienbord Palace	150.00
1955-Fano Girl	250.00
1956-Rosenborg Castle	200.00
1957-The Good Shepherd	125.00
1958-Sunshine Over Greenland..	130.00
1959-Christmas Night	175.00
1960-The Stag	200.00
1961-Training Ship Danmark	225.00
1962-The Little Mermaid	235.00
1963-Hojsager Mill	100.00
1964-Fetching the Tree	75.00
1965-Little Skaters	75.00
1966-Blackbird	55.00
1967-The Royal Oak	55.00
1968-The Last Umiak	35.00
1969-The Old Farmyard	35.00
1970-Christmas Rose and Cat ..	30.00
1971-Hare in Winter	30.00
1972-In the Desert	27.50
1973-Train Homeward Bound ..	27.50
1974-Winter Twilight	27.50
1975-Queen's Palace	25.00
1976-Waterfall	32.50
1977-Hunter-Hound	25.00
1978-Greenland Scenery	37.50

Mother's Day Plates

1971-American Mother. FE	50.00
1972-Oriental	20.00
1973-Danish..................	17.50
1974-Greenland	20.00
1975-Bird in Nest..............	22.50
1976-Mermaids	22.00
1977-The Twins	25.00
1978-Mother and Child	28.50

VENETO FLAIR (ITALY)

1970-Madonna. Bellini..........$	750.00
1971-Christmas. Three Kings. FE ..	200.00
1972-Mother's Day. Madonna and Child. FE	125.00
1972-Christmas. Shepherds	95.00
1972-1976. Dog Series	
1972-Shepherd	100.00
1973-Poodle	45.00
1974-Doberman	42.50
1975-Collie	45.00

1976-Dachshund	45.00
1972-1976. Last Supper Series. Set of 5	350.00
1973-Easter. Rabbits. FE	110.00
1975-Candleholder. FE	17.50
1975-Christmas Bell. FE	35.00
1975-Diana	85.00
1975-Easter Egg. FE	20.00
1976-Christmas Card. Old North Church	50.00
1976-Mother's Day	60.00
1976-Stein. FE	75.00
1977-Valentine	75.00
1978-Christmas Card. Dutch Christmas	55.00
1978-Easter Egg	18.50
1978-1979. New Years Bell	40.00
1979-Flower Children. FE	65.00
1979-Valentine. FE	60.00

WEDGWOOD (ENGLAND)

1969-Christmas. FE $	285.00
1970-Christmas	25.00
1971-Children's Story. FE	18.50
1972-1976. Bicentennial Series. Set of 6	500.00
1973-Christmas	65.00
1973-Mother's Day	25.00
1974-Christmas	65.00
1974-Mother's Day	32.50
1975-Christmas	50.00
1975-Christmas Mug	45.00
1975-Mother's Day	37.50
1976-Christmas	40.00
1977-Easter Egg. FE	30.00
1977-Innocence. FE	195.00
1977-Mother's Day	45.00

COMIC BOOKS

Through the centuries pictures have been used for visual storytelling. In America, the first comic which became a Sunday feature was published in the New York World in February, 1896. Since that time newspapers have carried comics as a daily and Sunday feature.

In the 1915-30 period, pulp magazines filled the need for adventure reading. However, before World War II, they had reached the saturation point and publishers secured rights and printed many back adventures of comic strip characters, such as Captain Easy, Maggie and Jiggs, Orphan Annie, etc.

The comic book idea caught on and publishers had artists create special adventure plots and situations for such new characters as Air Fighters, Bulletman, Capt. Marvel, Military Comics, Plastic Man, Spy Smasher, Superman, and numerous other titles.

In the 1960's, when interest was shown in collecting comic books, doubters dismissed the happening as a passing fancy. Today, it is a serious hobby or business for several thousand people. Comic books are a part of our history in the arts.

Although the price on average comic books of the 1940-1960 period is approximately a dollar or two, rare and first editions command hundreds of dollars. Condition of the book is one of the main factors in arriving at a price. Remember, children were the main readers and many books are in poor condition. A book in poor condition can affect the price of the same book in mint condition by more than 50%.

The prices listed below are for books in mint condition. The numbers represent issue numbers, i.e., #1 is first edition; #5, fifth issue, #10, tenth issue, etc. Check publishers and numbers. Different publishers published the same title in different years.

Classics Illustrated. "Mutiny on the Bounty," #100. Nordoff & Hall. Gilberton Co. $5.00

Amazing Spider-Man, The. Marvel Comics Group, March, 1963.

Annual #1, 1964 $	15.00
Giant-Size, #1 (7-74)	2.00

America's Biggest Comic Book. Better Publications, 1944. 196 pp. #1. The Grim Reaper, The Silver Knight, Zudo, The Jungle Boy, Commando Cubs, Thunderhoof .. 25.00
Buck Rogers. Golden Key, October, 1964. #1. (10128-410) 3.00
Bugs Bunny, Gold Key. Vacation Funnies, #1. 1951. 112 pp....... 10.00
Classic Comics. Gilberton Publications.
Adventures of Sherlock Holmes .. 75.00
Hunchback of Notre Dame, The .. 25.00
Invisible Man, The 10.00
Oliver Twist 25.00
Ox-Bow Incident, The 5.00
Robinson Crusoe 40.00
Twenty Thousand Leagues Under the Sea 15.00
Donald Duck Beach Party. Dell Publishing Co. 1954. #1 .... 7.50
Frankenstein Comics. 1945. #1. Frankenstein Begins by Dick Briefer 25.00
Journey Into Unknown Worlds. Atlas Comics. #36. Science Fiction 7.50
Jumbo Comics. Fiction House Magazines. 1938. (#1-8 oversized-10½ x 14½"). #6-8. Last black and white issue 100.00
Popeye. Whitman Publishing Co. 1937. All color drawings and text attributed to Segar. Each 50.00
Popular Comics. Dell Publishing Co. Feb., 1936. #50-75. Each 15.00
Santa Claus Funnies. Dell Publishing Co. 4-color, #205-254. Kelly art. Each 25.00
Sparkler Comics. (2nd Series) United Features Syndicate. #28-39. Tarzan covers by Hogarth. Each 25.00
Super Book of Comics. Omar Bread & Pan-Am Motor Oil Co. giveaways. 32pp. #2,5,7,18,21. Each 10.00
Superman. National Periodical Publications. Annual #1 (10-60) 20.00
Uncle Scrooge (Walt Disney) Dell Publishing Co. March, 1952. 4-color #495. (#3) Reprinted in Uncle Scrooge #105 .... 50.00
Wheaties (Premiums, 32 titles) Walt Disney Productions. 1950 & 1951. 32pp. Set A-1 to A-8, 1950. Set .. 50.00

COMMEMORATIVE AND HISTORICAL GLASS

Commemorative and historical items have always been popular in the collectors' field. With the bicentennial celebration of 1976, people are more aware of such items. Some of the old patterns have been reproduced in goblets and bread plates and should be dated 1976.

Also see "Bread Plates," "Campaign Items" and "Commemorative and Souvenir Plates."

Butter Dishes, Covered. "Banner."
Amber ....$ 150.00
Blue 250.00
Clear 85.00
Compote. Jenny Lind. Covered. High standard. Amber 125.00
Cup. Covered. Wm. J. Bryan 55.00
Goblets
Grant-Wilson 225.00
Marguerite. Ale size 75.00
Phila. Centennial 1876 .... 100.00
Shield and Keystone 75.00
Match Holder. "Goddess of Liberty." Wall-type 60.00
Mugs
"E. Pluribus Unum." 13 stars and shield 75.00
"Liberty and the Republic." Amber 85.00
Martyrs. 2½". Clear. Garfield and Lincoln 55.00
Peabody, George. English 50.00
Washington-Lafayette 50.00
Paperweights
Memorial Hall. Gillinder. 1876. Frosted 250.00
Plymouth Rock 40.00
Pickle Dishes
"E. Pluribus Unum." Gillinder & Sons, Philadelphia 85.00
Nellie Bly. 6½x12½" 95.00
Pitcher. Gridley 85.00

Plate. "We Mourn Our Nations Loss" 11½" $65.00

Plates

Automobile Roadster. Lindsey 145	60.00
Cleveland Classic	200.00
Cleveland-Thurman	250.00
50th Anniversary of McKee Glass, Jeannette, Pa. Opalescent blue. 5½"	30.00
Grant Peace Plate. 10½". Green	45.00
Logan Classic	165.00
Peabody, George. 6". Lee-Rose 836	30.00
"Preparedness." Spanish American War	45.00
Prescott-Stark, Warren-Putnam	50.00
Prince and Princess of Wales. 5". Flint	100.00
Santa Maria	50.00
"Simply to Thy Cross I Cling." Milk glass center	65.00
Victoria's Jubilee 1837-1887. 4½". Blue	50.00

Slipper. Gillinder. 1876	45.00

Trays

Constitution. 12½" long	65.00
Niagara Falls. 11x16"	100.00

Tumblers

Bust of Cleveland. Wreath in base	55.00
Louisiana Purchase	20.00
McKinley	35.00
Sampson, Admiral	18.00
Vase. Hand and Torch. Gillinder. 1876	60.00

COMMEMORATIVE AND SOUVENIR PLATES

Plates commemorating special events, places and people and souvenir-types have always ranked high with collectors. During the Philadelphia Centennial in 1876 through the New York's World's Fair in 1939, a series of plates were made by Rowland & Marcellus, Staffordshire, England. These scenic plates should not be identified with the historical Staffordshire made in the early 1800's. Also see "Commemorative and Historical Glass"

Atlantic City. Rowland & Marcellus. Staffordshire, England $	30.00
Capitol at Washington, D.C. R. & M. Co.	45.00
Captayne John Smith, Admiral of New England. R. & M. Co.	35.00
Chicago. 9". Views	35.00
Delaware Water Gap from Winona Cliff. 9½". Staffordshire	40.00
DeSota's Discovery of the Mississippi. 10". R. & M. Co.	40.00
Detroit. R. & M. Co.	25.00
Faneuil Inn. Blue and white. Wedgwood	45.00
Fort Ticonderoga, Lake Champlain. 9¼". Wedgwood	40.00

Plate, deep. 10¼". 'Troy, from Mount Ida, Hudson River." Black transfer **$40.00**

Francis Scott Key. Tin. Shield and flag center. Portrait and 4 stanzas of Star Spangled Banner on border	125.00
Governor Yates House, Schenectady, N.Y. 7½"	35.00
Indian Hunter Menotomy. Blue and white. Wedgwood	45.00
Jefferson, Thomas. B. & M. Co.	45.00
Knights of Columbus. 10" Columbus center. Emblem border. 1905 patent	55.00
Lewis and Clark Centennial. R. & M. Co.	50.00
Longfellow's Home. Portland, Maine. 9". Blue and white. Wedgwood	50.00
McKinley's Home. Blue and white. Wedgwood	40.00
Morse High School. Bath, Maine. Wm. Adams & Co.	30.00
Mt. Vernon. Blue and white. Wedgwood	47.50
New London. R. & M. Co.	30.00
Niagara Falls. 9". Greenish brown. Ridgway	35.00
Old North Church. Wedgwood	40.00
Old South Church, Boston. Reintroduced by Shree, Crump, Low	45.00
Philadelphia City Hall. R. & M. Co.	35.00
Pilgrim Memorial Monument. Blue and white. Wedgwood	40.00
Plymouth, Massachusetts. 10". R. & M. Co.	30.00

Public Library, Boston. Blue and white. Wedgwood 40.00
Waltham Watch Factory, Massachusetts. R. & M. Co 50.00
Witch House. Roger William's House. Blue and white. Wedgwood 45.00

COMMEMORATIVE AND SOUVENIR SPOONS

These spoons were made as mementos of special events, personages or places of interest. Commemorative and souvenir spoons reached their highest peak of popularity in the 1880's-1900's. Many such spoons are currently being made and spoon collecting is regaining favor. The spoons listed are 800-900 silver unless otherwise noted. Abbreviations in regards to size are: D-demitasse, C-citrus, T-teaspoon, X-between a demi and teaspoon or sometimes called a 5 o'clock teaspoon. Reference numbers refer to "American Spoons, Souvenir and Historical" by Rainwater and Felger.

Alaska. (D) Plain bowl. Totem pole and miner on handle ....$ 15.00
Atlantic City. (D) Engraved Lighthouse in bowl. Twisted handle 10.00
Atlantic City. (T) Embossed bowl. Lighthouse on handle 25.00
Benjamin Franklin. (D) Full figure forms half the handle. Hamilton & Diesinger 125.00
Bermuda. (T) Plain bowl. Cut out palm trees on handle 15.00
Boston. (T) Plain bowl. Embossed handle 25.00
Bunker Hill Monument. (D) Plain bowl. Embossed Old South Church and Hub on handle. Stowell & Co. 20.00
Chicago. (D) Embossed view of the Coliseum in bowl. Embossed handle 25.00
Chicago World's Fair. (D) Plain bowl. 1933. Art deco design 20.00
Christmas. (D) Tree engraved in bowl. Embossed holly. Santa Claus handle 50.00
Colorado. (T) Boulder engraved in bowl. Handle spells out Colorado 15.00
Columbian Exposition. (T) R&F 512 25.00
Denver. (D) Form of shovel. 1910 engraved in bowl. Miners pan and head of miner on handle 50.00
Ethan Allen. (T) Plain bowl. R&F 143 35.00
Florida State Seal. (D) Embossed view of the Old City Gate in bowl. Embossed handle. Dec. rev. Alvin 50.00

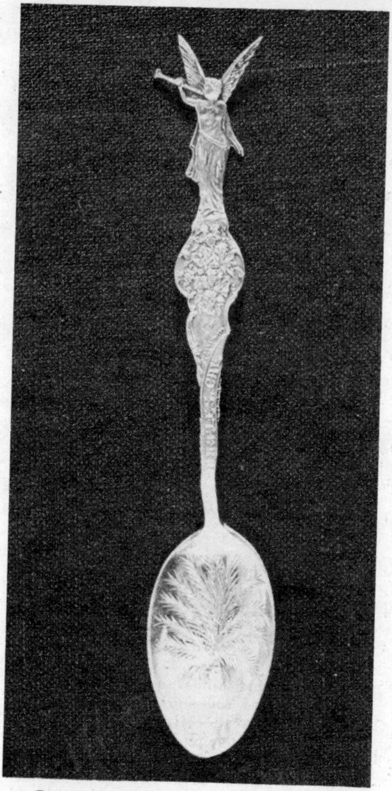

Teaspoon. Los Angeles, Cal. Embossed palm tree in bowl. Sterling $20.00

London. (D) Engraved bowl. Ornate handle with cut out London Crest at the tip 15.00
London (D) Engraved bowl. Twisted handle with cut out of St. Paul's at the tip 25.00
Los Angeles, California. (T) Embossed palm tree in bowl. Handle has roses 20.00
Louisiana Purchase. (D) Embossed view of the Festival Hall & Cascade in bowl. R&F 587 ...... 35.00
Lucerne. (X) Lion embossed in bowl. Handle with enameled crest 45.00
Mexico. (D) Embossed view of National Palace in bowl. Recuerdo de Mexico. Eagle and local views embossed on handle. Dec. rev.... 20.00

Teaspoon. William Penn. "Proclaim Liberty Throughout the Land." Dated 1682 on handle. Sterling $30.00

Michigan. (T) Hastings engraved in bowl. State Seal embossed on handle. Gorham	15.00
Montreal. (D) Gilt embossed bowl of waterfront. Enameled Montreal Crest at the tip of handle	15.00
Napoleon. (X) Engraved view of the Arc de Triomphe in bowl. Ornate handle with full figure. High relief at tip	50.00
New Orleans. (D) Plain bowl. Flower form handle, lettered within a crescent at the tip. Gorham	35.00
Niagara Falls. (T) Bowl of chased and embossed raging water. R&F 673	45.00
Notre Dame. (D) Embossed bowl. Twisted handle with maple leaf. Beaver and Snow Shoe	30.00
Old Faithful. (D) Engraved bowl. Enameled flowers on handle	25.00
Old Man of the Mountains. (T) Plain bowl. R&F 662	35.00
Panama Exposition. (T) Embossed view of Jeweled Tower in bowl. San Francisco 1915	25.00
Paris. (D) Engraved bowl. Handle with bust of Napoleon	30.00
San Francisco. (D) Embossed view of the Golden Gate in bowl. Embossed views on handle including the State Seal	25.00
Saratoga. (T) Plain bowl. R&F 676 ..	45.00
Seattle. (X) Bowl embossed with a panorama of Seattle. Handle form of Alaskan totem pole	45.00
Shakespeare, Wm. (X) Plain bowl. Inscribed handle	20.00
Texas. (T) Capitol Bldg., Austin, Texas. Embossed in bowl. State Seal embossed on handle. Dec. rev	30.00
Tip Top House. (T) Plain bowl. Mt. Washington. R&F 663	30.00
Warwick Castle. (X) Embossed view in bowl. Twisted handle with cut-out standing bear. Warwick Crest	15.00
Washington. (D) Christ Church embossed in bowl. Pedestal handle. Full figure of Washington. R.C. Acton & Son	50.00
Washington, D.C. (T) Embossed view of the Capitol. Profile of Geo. Washington. Dec. rev. Campbell Metcalf Sil. Co.	50.00
Waterloo Monument. (X) Engraved bowl. Ornate handle	15.00

COPELAND

COPELAND & SPODE CHINA

In the third quarter of the 18th century, Josiah Spode founded the Spode Works located in the Staffordshire area of England. In 1843 the firm became Copeland & Garrett and continued under this name until W. T. Copeland & Sons, Ltd. succeeded them in 1847. Production continues today, designated by the mark "Late Spode."

Bowls

3¾". White classical figures in high relief on glossy dark green $	75.00
9". Footed. Scalloped rim. Blue and white. Marked Copeland "Spode's Tower." England	25.00

Tea Set. 3 pieces. Pot 6½" high, creamer 5" long, sugar 6½" long. Brown transfer of farm scene. Impressed Copeland. Set $95.00

11". With underplate. Scalloped rims. Floral decor. Late	50.00
Cake Stand. 3" high, 9½" diam. Blue on white. "Spode's Tower." Late	25.00
Coffee Pot. 9". Cowslip. Late	40.00
Cracker Jar. White classical figures on blue ground	75.00
Creamers	
Floral. Terra cotta and black	75.00
Helmet-shaped. Late	30.00
Wildflower. Late	25.00
Cups and Saucers	
Cabbage Leaf. C. 1829	85.00
Panels of flowers with alternating panels of cobalt. Gold trim. C. 1820	75.00
Figurine. 7". Mistress Campen No. 6. Marked "Chelsea Derby Copeland Spode"	60.00
Jug, Ale. 7½". Vintage decor. Men, verse, "Good Old Ale." Late	95.00
Mug. Washington. Eagles and flags. C. 1876	275.00
Pitchers	
5" high. Imari-type decor. C. 1851-1885	60.00
8". high. Cameo-type. Blue and white	150.00
8¼" high. White with orange peel decor	100.00
10" high. Hunt scene. Bulbous	150.00
Plaque. 10" diam. Underglaze sepia painting. W. Yale. C. 1857	200.00
Plates	
8". Bird center. Black rim with flowers	50.00
8". Octagon-shaped. Floral border and center. White ground. Gold trim. C. 1851-85	50.00
8½". Fighting warriors. Deep orange. Black fluted rim. Late	35.00
10". "British Flowers II". Blue. C. 1850	85.00
10". Peacocks in bold blues, red. Late	35.00
Platters	
10½". Green transfer of parrot, flowers. Enameled	60.00
16½". Blue and white pasture scene. Copeland Spode's "Italian." England	125.00
17½". Imari-type decor. C. 1850	100.00
18". Blue and white transfer	150.00
Sauce Boat. 4x5¾". Cabbage Leaf	125.00
Soup Plate. Brown transfer. Scene in center. Late	25.00
Sugar. Covered. 4½ x 6½". Pineapple-shape. Salt glaze. C. 1847-67	85.00
Teapot. 9½" high. Blue. Gilded handles. Foo Dog finial. Imported from England by Tiffany Co. Late 19th century	250.00
Tea Set. Miniature. Sugar bowl, creamer and teapot. Decor of pink roses and green leaves. Set.	150.00
Tureens. Covered	
Brown transfer. Underplate and ladle	225.00
"Spode's Tower." With underplate	150.00

COPPER

Copper has been an important metal used throughout the centuries. Buckets, pots and pans do not tell the complete story. It was also used for jewelry, plaques, lighting fixtures, weathervanes and decorative items.

*Bed Warmer. 40½" long. Brass lid. Turned wooden handle ....$	150.00
Candle Snuffer. 9¼" long. Scrolled end	15.00
Chafing Dishes	
1-quart. Brass trim. Patented 1902 burner	55.00
2-quart. Copper pan. Brass holder. Wood handle	75.00
2-quart. Ornate handles. Wood grips and knob. Wood handle on burner. 14" tray. Perfection. Manning-Bowman Co. 1901	125.00
Coaching Horn. C. 1845	125.00
*Coal Hod. 10½x10½x18". Iron bail and grip. Handwrought	175.00
Coffee Pot. 10". Burnished and lacquered. Pewter trim.	95.00
Dipper. 9". Wrought iron handle	35.00
Funnel. 10" diam. With brass	30.00

Teakettle, English. Gooseneck. Hollow handle. Gallon size $75.00

Hot Dish. Porcelain liner. 9" 65.00
Hot Water Bottle. 11" oval 60.00
*Kettles
  17" diam. Hand forged handles. Dovetailed. Burnished. C. 1840 .. 300.00
  22" diam., 14" deep 125.00
  23" diam., 18" deep. Hammered bail with heavy mountings 150.00
  25" diam., 16" deep. Wrought iron handle 165.00
Milk Tank. 10-gallon. With spigot .. 125.00
*Pails
  9". Bail handle 55.00
  10½". Bail handle 60.00
  11½".Bailed. Two handles. Two pouring lips 75.00
  15". Covered. Pouring lip 85.00
  24". Bail handle 125.00
*Pans
  5" diam., 3" deep. Dovetailed. Handled 85.00
  7" diam., 5" deep 75.00
  9¼" diam., 5" deep. 12" long handle. Dovetailed 150.00
  10" diam., 5" deep. 11" iron handle. Burnished. Lacquered 100.00
  13" diam., 9" deep 150.00
Pitchers
  1½" high 15.00
  12" high. Hand wrought 65.00
Roaster. 5x10¼x14". Open 75.00
Skimmer. 19" long. Iron handle 60.00
Teakettles
  American. Dovetailed. Fold-down gooseneck spout 275.00
  American. Dovetailed side and bottom. 14" to top of handle 325.00
  Norwegian. Gooseneck spout 100.00
  Swedish. Gooseneck spout 100.00
Thermometer. Candy 30.00
Toast Rack 25.00
Tray. 15x18". Late 50.00
*Umbrella Stand. Brass lion handles 75.00
Wash Boiler. Burnished 75.00
Water Can. 13" high to top of brass handle 65.00
Whiskey Still. 10x21" high. Two handles. Hand wrought 100.00

*Reproduced Item

COPPER LUSTRE

Copper lustred wares were first made in the early 1800's by potters in the Staffordshire district, England. A copper compound added to the glaze resulted in the final metallic-like surface. Quantities were imported into the United States during the 19th century. Reproductions are on the market, especially creamers and the so-called "Polka Jug." The new wares are heavier in appearance and weight when compared to the earlier.

Pitcher. 5½". Blue band with embossed hunting scene decor..........$135.00

Bowls
  4". Blue band with red roses ....$ 55.00
  5". Pedestaled. Blue band 50.00
  5½". Covered. Plain 75.00
  6". Blue band. Leaf decor 65.00
Box. 2¾x3¼x5". Comic black transfer 85.00

Cups and Saucers
- Blue band. C. 1820-40 .... 55.00
- Handpainted design 65.00
- Scalloped rims 60.00

Figurine. Dog. 8" high 85.00

Goblets
- Blue band. Floral decor 65.00
- Blue band. Boy and girl decor 75.00
- Cream band. Green and pink lustre vines 55.00

Mugs
- 3" high. Decorated blue band 55.00
- 3" high. Plain 50.00
- 3¾" high. Orange band. Floral decor 60.00
- 4" high. Pink lustre on rim. Tan band 65.00

Pitchers
- 3". Plain 32.50
- 3½". Blue band with figure of girl and cat 45.00
- 4½". White band. Red scrolls 75.00
- 5". Bulbous. Plain.............. 50.00
- 5½".Sanded band 85.00
- 5½". Stag decor. Dark blue band 135.00
- 6½". Lustre lining. C. 1840...... 125.00
- 6¾". Children dancing on blue band 75.00
- 7". White band. Floral decor 125.00
- 7½". Plain 80.00
- 8". Floral decor. C. 1820-40 .... 175.00

Salts
- Blue band. Pedestaled.......... 32.50
- Plain. Pedestaled 30.00
- Sanded band. Pedestaled 35.00

Sugar Bowl. Open. Raised floral and leaf design on 2" blue band 85.00

Teapots
- 5½" high, 10" long. Plain. C. 1820-40 .... 225.00
- 6" high. Floral and leaf design on 2" blue band, same on lid 175.00

Toby Jug. C. 1820-40 .... 250.00

Toothpick. Sanded band 45.00

Urn. 8½" high. 8" across handles. 3½" green band 175.00

CORALENE

Coralene is an American art glass first made by the New England Glass Company in 1880. Later other firms produced a similar type.
The name Coralene was derived from one of the patterns that resembled natural coral formations. Other recognized patterns are Wheat and Fleur-de-Lis. The designs were formed by applying tiny glass beads to the surface of the object. Most of the base glass was satin finished, but unfrosted glass was also used.
Reproductions are on the market. The beaded decoration on 'new' Coralene is merely glued to the surface, rather than fired on, which is the case with the originals.

Vase. 6½". MOP. Mauve to white with yellow beading $350.00

Bottle, Perfume. 6". Stoppered. Multicolored. "Fleur-de-Lis" on blue glass ....$ 265.00

Rose Bowl. 4". Crystal. "Seaweed" on MOP pink satin glass 250.00

Toothpick. Yellow "Seaweed" on glossy English peachblow 350.00

Tumblers
- 4" high. Blue "Seaweed" on MOP butterscotch satin glass 265.00
- 4" high. Orange "Seaweed" on DQ blue satin glass 225.00

Vases
- 3¼". Crystal "Wheat" on DQ, MOP yellow satin glass 425.00
- 3¾". "Fleur-de-Lis" on yellow MOP satin glass 375.00
- 5⅛". "Star" on DQ, MOP rose satin glass.................. 750.00
- 5½". Yellow "Seaweed" on English peachblow satin finished glass 400.00
- 5¾". Bulbous base. Slender neck. Yellow "Seaweed" on white to yellow satin glass.............. 350.00
- 6". Bluebird and tree coralene on opaline glass. Ruffled blue top 500.00

7½". Gold "Seaweed" on Rainbow satin glass 450.00
8". Multicolored peacock on opalescent crystal. Shell feet. Gold trim 750.00

CORKSCREWS

The corkscrew. . .a utilitarian device used to draw a cork from a bottle was and continues to be made in a variety of shapes, styles and materials.

As early as the 17th century, the figural corkscrew was favored. Mechanical models were popular in the Victorian era. Elaborate examples with handles of Mother-of-Pearl, ivory and sterling proliferated throughout the Art Nouveau period for people with champagne tastes.

Once, collections of corkscrews were found mainly in related establishments. Today, individuals are pursuing this relatively new hobby.

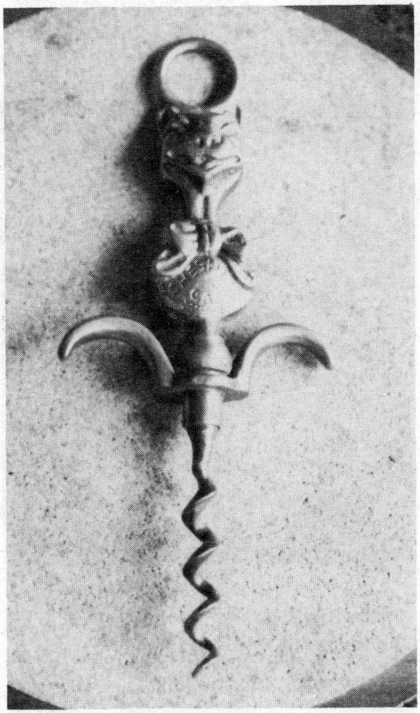

Brass. Cheshire Cat. 6¼" long . . $45.00

Bone. 3¾". Metal capped. English. 45.00

Commemorative. 1893 World's Fair. "Hail Columbia" 10.00
Figural. Scottie. Bronzed metal. German 15.00
Horn. 4¼". Capped with continental silver. English 40.00
Steel
- 2¾". Ring top. American 8.00
- 3". Bar top. American 15.00
- 4½". Flat ring top. American 25.00
- 7". Captain's Key. Germany 35.00

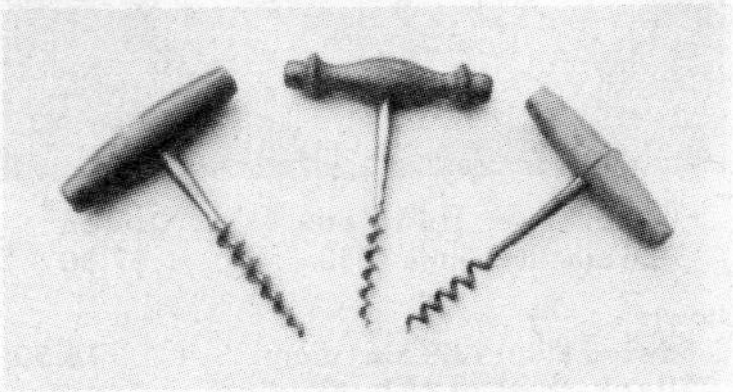

Wood. Turned handles. English. Each $20.00

Wood
- 4". Walnut with ring top. American 20.00
- 4¼". Hand turned walnut handle. English 35.00
- 4½". Hand turned. Black stain. English 30.00
- 5". Hand turned cherry. American 25.00
- 5½". Hand turned walnut with ring top. American 28.50
- 6". Black stained handle. Brass cap. English 35.00
- 6". Black stained handle. Long skirt. Spring plunger. Marked "Hercules." English 55.00
- 6". Burl 25.00

CORONATION ITEMS

From the time of Queen Victoria's coronation to the present ruling monarch of England, souvenir items commemorating the occasions have been made. Although china mugs and plates were the most prevalent; tin boxes, glasswares, silver spoons and a variety of other items were also made and are considered collectible.

Ashtrays. Edward VIII, 1937. Royal Doulton. Set of 4 in holder ...... $ 65.00
Beakers
- Edward VII, 1902. Royal Doulton 35.00
- Edward VIII, 1937 .... 30.00

Bottle, Whiskey. George V and Queen Mary, June 22, 1911. Green and tan. Royal Coat of Arms. Flags 200.00

Ash Tray. Handled. 4½". Queen Elizabeth II, June 1953 .... $7.50

Bowls
- Edward VIII, 1937. 5¼" diam. 18.50
- Elizabeth II, 1953. 7" diam. Meakin 10.00
- Victoria. 1897. Stoneware 50.00

Boxes, Tin
- Elizabeth II, 1953. 3x4" 10.00
- George V, Queen Mary, "Silver Jubilee." 7½x10". Hinged lid 22.50

Cup. George VI and Queen Elizabeth, 1937. Registered and designed by Dame Laura Knight .. 40.00

Cup and Saucer. Victoria and Albert. Purple transfer. Pink lustre trim 75.00

Handkerchief. Elizabeth II, 1953 .. 5.00

Jug. Edward VIII, May 12, 1937. Lion handle, music box in base. ''God Save the King.'' Limited Edition 500.00

Medals
- Edward VIII, May 12, 1937. 2" diam. Bronze. Original case 50.00
- Elizabeth and Philip, 1953. 3¼x4¼". Blue Jasperware. Wedgwood. Framed 250.00

Mugs
- Edward VIII, 1937 .... 35.00
- Elizabeth II, 1953. Staffordshire-type 25.00
- George VI, Queen Elizabeth, 1937 35.00

Pitchers
- Edward VII, 1902. Royal Doulton 150.00
- Elizabeth II, 1953. 5½" high. Worcester 50.00
- Victoria, 1897. 6½" high. Redware. Black glaze 100.00

Plates
- Edward VII, 1902. 8" 25.00
- Edward VIII, 1937. 4x6" 18.50
- Edward VIII. 8½" square 18.50
- Edward VIII, 1937. 10" 20.00
- Elizabeth II, 1953. 4¼" square .. 12.50
- Elizabeth II, 1953. 9" 25.00
- George V, Queen Mary, 1911. 9" 28.00
- George VI, 1937. 10". Glass 22.50
- Victoria, 1897. "Jubilee." 10". Glass 45.00

Spoons
- Elizabeth II, 1953. Demitasse. Silverplated 7.50
- George VI, 1911. Demitasse. Silverplated 12.50
- Victoria. 1837-97. Gold washed bowl. Pierced handle. Sterling .. 30.00

Tea Caddy. George VI, 1937. Rington 35.00

Tray, Pin. Elizabeth II, 1953 ...... 7.50

Tumbler. Edward VII, Alexandra. 1902 .... 28.50

COSMOS GLASS

Cosmos glass is pressed milk glass decorated with the cosmos flower in relief. The flowers were 'stained' or 'flashed' with pale shades of blue, pink and yellow. It is attributed to Dithridge and Son, New Brighton, Pa. C. 1900.

Tumbler $55.00

Butter, Covered. 8" diam., 5¾" high high.........................$ 195.00

Castor Set. Salt, pepper, mustard .. 225.00

Creamer 125.00

Lamp. 8". Base. No shade 125.00

Lemonade Set. Bulbous pitcher with lid. Six mugs with handles 750.00

Pickle Castor. With tongs 250.00

Pitchers
Water. 10" high 250.00
With 6 tumblers. Set 600.00
Shakers, Salt and Pepper. Original tops. Pair 100.00
Spooner 85.00
Sugar, Covered 175.00
Syrup. Original top 150.00
Tumbler 55.00

COWAN POTTERY

Cowan Pottery was founded by R. Guy Cowan, Cleveland, Ohio in 1913. The establishment was in almost continuous operation in the Cleveland area until 1931 when financial difficulties forced closure.

Early production was redware pottery that was later refined to a porcelain-like finish. Special glazes were always emphasized. "Lustreware" and "Crackleware" are two of the most sought. Early marks include an incised "Cowan Pottery" on the redware (1913-1917), impressed "Cowan" and "Lakewood" on others. The imprinted stylized semi-circle with or without the initials R.G. were later.

Commercial type wares marked "Lakeware" were produced from 1927 to 1931.

Ash Tray and match holder combination ....$ 32.00
Bowls
4x8x12". Fruit. Scalloped. Mottled 50.00
9". Footed. Ivory with green interior 15.00
12", 4" deep. Blue iridescent 40.00
Candlesticks
4½". "Seahorse." Blue iridescent. Pair 25.00
7½". Blue iridescent. Pair 35.00
Compote. 3x6". Pink and white. "Seahorse" 30.00
Flower Frog. 8". Nude dancers. Ivory glaze 35.00
Lamp base. 10". 2 handles, band of leaves. Fitted. 110.00
Plate. 7¾". Blue iridescent 15.00
Vases
3½". Larkspur lustre 32.00
6". Iridescent blue 25.00
6". Yellow. "Seahorse" 36.00
8". Bulbous. 4" band of berries. Royal blue 130.00

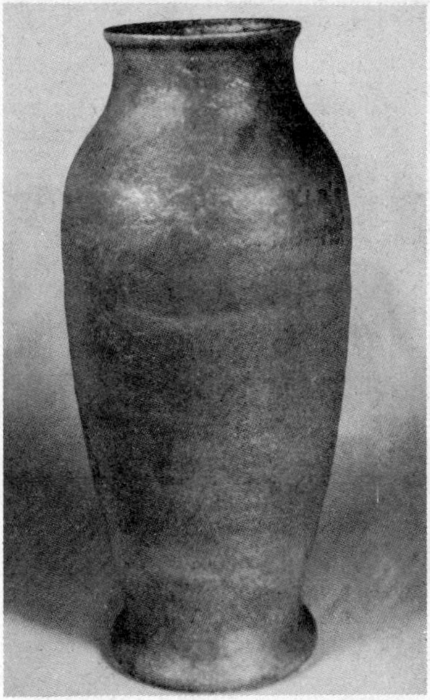

Vase. 12". Redware. Incised Cowan and Cowan's monogram $75.00

12". Art Deco. Nude. Blue lustre 110.00
13". Bulbous. Orange lustre. "Dragonflies" 145.00

CRACKER JARS

The cracker or biscuit jar was the forerunner of the cookie jar. They were made of various materials by many major glass makers and potteries.

Also see individual categories

Amethyst Glass. 6". Silverplated mountings ....$ 95.00
Bella Ware. Yellow and red floral decor. Signed 400.00
Cobalt Glass. Enameled decor. Silverplated mountings 75.00
Crown Milano. 6x7" high. Gold chrysanthemums, pastel flowers, vines on ivory satin glass. Silver rim, bail and melon-ribbed cover. Unsigned 350.00
Meissen-Type. Blue floral decor on white ground. Silverplated lid and bail 150.00

Crown Milano. Bulbous. Multicolored mum decor. Silverplated lid and ornate bail. Signed MW $600.00

Opal Glass. 6½". H-P daisies, violets. Ornate silverplated mountings 150.00

Porcelains

- Floral decor on beige ground. Gold trim. Silverplated lid, bail 125.00
- Floral decor on blue ground with gold trim 75.00
- Floral transfer on white ground .. 75.00
- Golfing scene on shaded green ground 125.00

Satin Glass

- Green shading to white. Pink wild roses decor. Lid and bail resilvered. 175.00
- Pink. Blue and gold decor. Lid and bail resilvered 275.00
- White. Pansies on front and back. A.J. Hall, Meriden, Conn 150.00
- Yellow shading to white. Allover blossom decor. Silverplated lid and bail. Monogrammed........ 150.00
- Staffordshire. Allover poppy decor on white salt glaze. Silverplated lid and bail 195.00

CRANBERRY GLASS

Cranberry is the color of the glass and not the ware. The color was achieved by adding a small amount of gold to a pot of molten glass. The blown or molded objects were first amber in color. When reheated at a low temperature, the cranberry or ruby color developed. Cranberry glass was made by several glass factories in America and Europe. It is currently being produced but the new is not of the same quality as the old.

Pitcher. 8¼". "Ribbed Swirl". Quatrefoil top. Applied clear reeded and lion foot handle $195.00

Bells

- 10¼" high. Clear handle ......$ 95.00
- 12" high. Clear applied handle .. 175.00
- 12" high. Swirl. Opalescent rim. Clear handle................. 295.00
- 20" high, 5½" diam. White handle and clapper 275.00

Bobeches. Ruffled edges. Pair...... 50.00

Bottle, Perfume. 4" high. Crystal ball stopper. Gold enamel flowers and scroll work 85.00

Bowls

- 5½". Fluted rim. Gold threading 50.00
- 5½x6¼". Footed. Applied flowers. Ribbed sides 75.00
- 5½x9½". Milk bowl 165.00

Boxes

- 3" high, 3¼" diam. Florentine cameo portrait of lady on lid. Satin finish 175.00
- 4¾" high, 3" diam. Gold gilted cranberry knob and decor. Scalloped top and base 125.00
- Patch. Gold filigree design 65.00
- Pill. Gold mesh overlay 75.00

Bucket, Ice. 5¼". Enameled lily-of-the-valley decor 125.00

Butter. 6" high to top of crystal ball finial. Underplate 6½" diam. .. 150.00
Celery. 6⅞" high. IVT. Scalloped top. Enamel decor 125.00
Compotes
  5" diam. Clear standard. Blown .. 125.00
  8" diam., 5½" high. Clear standard 150.00
Cordial Set. Tray, decanter, 8 cordials. Undecorated 200.00
Cracker Jar. 6" high, 5" diam. Silverplated lid and bail. Blown .. 175.00
Cream and Sugar. Clear applied handles 150.00
Cruets
  5". Gold and silver enameled decor. Original gold stopper. Applied handle. Blown 175.00
  8½". Original crystal steeple stopper. Applied crystal handle 75.00
Cup and Saucer. 2" high cup, 4¾" diam. saucer. Cut to clear. Gold enameled scrolls 120.00
Cup, Loving. 3½" high. Clear handles. Silver rim 75.00
Decanters
  9". Hobnail 185.00
  9". Paneled. Crystal handle and stopper. Blown 175.00
  11". Clear cut stopper. White lace pattern on upper portion 250.00
Epergnes
  10" high. Single lily. Ruffled top. Satin intaglio flowers, leaves, stems. Set in ornate silver base .. 165.00
  19" high. Single lily. Clear ribbon decor. Opalescent rim 225.00
  21" high. Ruffled base bowl. 10" diam., 2¾" deep. Four lilies with ruffled tops. Crystal petals 350.00
Ewers
  7". Swirl pattern. Ovoid body. Applied crystal handle. Blown 100.00
  8". White threaded neck. Applied crystal handle 125.00
Finger Bowl with underplate 55.00
Gas Shade. 7½" diam. Swirl. Fluted rim 50.00
Goblet, Water. Crystal stem 32.50
Lamps, See "Lamps"
Lustres. 14½" high. Top edged in gold. Enameled gold flowers. 2 rows cut prisms. 7" long. Pair 500.00
Muffineer. 6" high. Silverplated top 55.00
Mustard Jar. Silverplated top and spoon 45.00
Pitchers
  4½". Clear applied handle. Applied clear petal feet 60.00
  4½". Paneled. Bulbous, Clear handle 65.00
  6". Bulbous with swirls. Clear applied handle 85.00
  7½". IVT. Square top. Applied reeded handle. Blown 150.00
  7½". Flared, ribbed top. Clear applied handle. English 100.00
  8½". Bulbous. IVT. Clear applied handle and neck rope 275.00
  8½". Paneled. Clear applied handle 125.00
  10". IVT. Pontil. Clear handle 295.00
Rose Bowl. 5". Undecorated 75.00
Salt and Pepper Shakers. 3½". IVT. Silverplated tops. Pair 75.00
Salt, Master. Sterling holder and spoon 85.00
Sauce Boat. 4½" high. Blown 150.00
Sugar. 9½" o.h. With sterling holder 135.00
Sugar Shakers
  Lattice overlay 75.00
  Paneled 65.00
  Paneled. Enamel decor. Gold top 100.00
Syrup. Silverplated spring lid 75.00
Toothpicks
  Applied ruffled crystal band around middle. Applied feet 75.00
  Gold scrolls 85.00
Tray. 13" long, 2" deep 150.00
Tumblers
  Diamond Quilted 40.00
  Lemonade. Handled 55.00
  Ribbed Swirl 40.00
Tumble-Up. IVT 165.00
Vases
  4". Melon-shaped. Pair 65.00
  6½". Crimped top. Applied white decor. English 95.00
  8¼". Shell pattern. Flared neck .. 135.00
  10½". Applied crystal rigaree .. 95.00
  12". Enameled blue forget-me-nots. Gold trim 150.00
  13¼". Fluted tops. Clear wafer bases. Pair 250.00
Vinaigrette. 2¼". 1" diam. Enamel decor 65.00
Wash Set. Pitcher 7" high. With applied crystal handle. Bowl 7" diam. 1½" deep. Blown, rough pontil. Set 200.00
Water Set. Pitcher 9" with 6 tumblers 450.00
Wines
  Gold decor 32.50
  Plain. Clear foot, stem 28.50
  Swirl. Clear foot, stem 32.50

CROCKS

(See, "Stoneware")

CROWN DERBY,

(See, "Royal Crown Derby")

CROWN MILANO

Crown Milano is an American art glass, with a semi-opaque quality. It is ivory in color, satin finished and delicately embellished with floral sprays, beaded and enriched with gold enamel. The glass was made by the Mt. Washington Glass Company, New Bedford, Mass. from 1886 to 1888. Some of the wares were marked CM on the pontil, others bore a paper label. Biscuit or cracker jars, were usually signed on the underside of the lid with the letters MW.

Vase. 8". Bulbous. Leaf decor in browns and green on ivory ground with gold trim. Unsigned $1200.00

Bowl. 4½". Melon-ribbed. Petal top ....$ 400.00
Bride's Basket. 8" overall height. 6" sq. bowl. Floral pattern. Silverplated holder 1500.00
Biscuit Jars
- Jeweled. Square-shape. Silver lid and bail. Signed MW 600.00
- Pink daisy decor. Square. Silver lid and bail 475.00
- Swirl. Multicolored swirls. Gold lid and bail. Signed MW in lid 650.00
- Waterlilies and Pads. Silver lid and bail. Signed MW in lid. Original paper label 600.00

Creamer. 2¼" high. Floral decor. Applied handle 400.00
Creamer and Sugar. Melon-shaped. Gold mums. Sterling tops 800.00
Cruet. 6⅞" high 750.00
Cup and Saucer. Signed CM 650.00
Ewer. 12¼" high. Dragon decor with phoenix handle 1250.00
Hatpin Holder. 2½x5½". Mushroom-shape. Pink and white chrysanthemums 300.00
Jardiniere. 13x16". Leaf decor in pastels. Signed CM 1500.00
Muffineer. 6" high. Ribbed 350.00
Mustard. Silverplated lid. Signed MW 300.00
Pitcher, Water. Floral decor. Signed CM 1250.00
Rose Bowl. 3½" high. Red holly and beaded decor 450.00
Sweetmeat Jars
- 4¼" high. Swirl. Rose decor. Signed CM on pontil and MW in silverplated cover 750.00
- 4¾" high. Swirl. Pansy decor. Silverplated cover with turtle finial. Signed CM on pontil and MW in lid 875.00

Syrup. Silverplated top 750.00
Toothpick. 2" high. Pansy decor 400.00
Vases
- 6". Blue Forget-me-nots 650.00
- 8½". Oak leaf and acorn decor. Signed 850.00
- 9¾". Floral decor. Signed 1000.00
- 12½", 8¼" diam. base. Stick-type. Gold leaves, flowers, beads. Signed 1250.00

CRUETS

Cruets are small bottles used for storing or serving vinegar and oil. They were introduced to England from Italy in the 17th century. Cruets gained their importance in the American home in the 19th century. Practically every glass manufacturer produced cruets.
Also see specific wares such as Amberina, Cranberry Glass, Cut Glass, Pattern Glass, etc.

Amber
- Applied blue handle and stopper. BTP. Blown ....$ 85.00
- Crackled. Hobbs 150.00
- IVT. Original stopper 75.00

Amethyst. Amber handle and stopper. Melon-shaped 95.00
Blue
- Challinor. #20 .... 75.00
- Cobalt. Clear stopper and handle. 75.00
- Cobalt. Paneled. Amber stopper. Applied amber handle. Blown .. 85.00
- IVT. Clear reeded handle and stopper 75.00
- Milk Glass 55.00

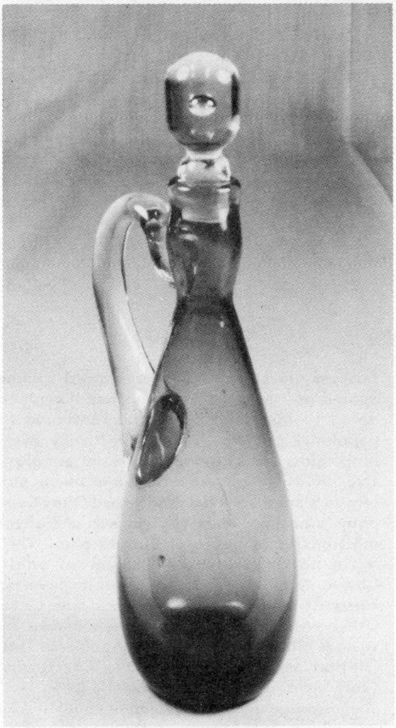

Amethyst. 9½" high. Blown. Clear applied handle. Ground stopper . . $50.00

Clear	
Blue applied handle and ball stopper. Gold trim	85.00
Wild Rose and Bowknot. Frosted . .	85.00
Frosted and Etched. "Vinegar." Sterling stopper. Signed Hawkes	150.00
Green, Emerald. Applied handle. Original stopper. Enameled white daisies	75.00
Pomona-Type. 8". Strawberry decor in color leaves, vines. Gold trim . .	175.00

CUP PLATES

Many early cups and saucers were handleless with deep saucers. The hot liquid was poured into the saucer and sipped from it. This necessitated another plate for the cup. . .the cup plate.

The first cup plates made of pottery were of the Staffordshire variety. In the mid 1830's to 40's, glass cup plates were favored. Boston and Sandwich Glass Co. was one of the main contributors to the lacy glass type.

The numbers listed refer to "American Cup Glass Plates" by Ruth Webb Lee and James H. Rose. Reproductions are on the market.

LR-82. Acorn and Leaves. Silver opaque blue. Fiery opalescent $550.00

Glass

LR-11. Clear. Eastern . . . . $	25.00
LR-46. Black Amber. Unique	1200.00
LR-62. Clear. Eastern	35.00
LR-65. Clear. Eastern	25.00
LR-79. Clear. New England Glass Co.	25.00
LR-82. Acorn and Leaves. Silver opaque blue. Fiery opalescent . .	550.00
LR-147-A. Flower. Bull's Eye border. Clear. Midwestern	30.00
LR-159-A. Clear. Midwestern	45.00
LR-197-B. Lacy. Clear. Midwestern . .	25.00
LR-230-A. Lacy. Clear. Eastern	45.00
LR-262. 12 sides. White fiery opalescent	250.00
LR-343-B. Clear. Eastern	35.00
LR-394. Beehive. Clear	25.00
LR-440-B. Valentine. Cobalt blue . .	300.00
LR-455-B. Heart. Clear	25.00
LR-458-A. Heart. Fiery opalescent . .	95.00
LR-465-J. Heart. Lacy opalescent . .	150.00
LR-467-A. Heart. Canary	500.00
LR-522. Sunburst. Amethyst	150.00
LR-531. Sunburst. Vaseline	150.00
LR-562-A. Henry Clay. Clear	175.00
LR-565-B. Henry Clay. Peacock blue	350.00
LR-568. Harrison. Clear	45.00
LR-576. Victoria. Clear	50.00

LR-592. Log Cabin. Clear	350.00
LR-610-B. Cadmus. Cobalt blue	150.00
LR-610-B. Cadmus. Peacock blue	300.00
LR-612-A. Steamboat. Clear. Midwestern	150.00
LR-628. Livingston. Blue green	500.00
LR-635. Maid of the Mist. Light green. Midwestern	300.00
LR-651-A. Eagle. Fiery opalescent	500.00
LR-654-A. Eagle. Cobalt blue	350.00
LR-670. Eagle. Clear. Midwestern	50.00
LR-679. Eagle. Clear	35.00
LR-692. Lyre. Clear. Midwestern	25.00
LR-699. Hound. Clear	125.00

PORCELAIN OR POTTERY

America Villa. Dark blue	95.00
Battery. Wood	150.00
Cadmus. Wood	165.00
Canova	40.00
Cathedral. Brown	40.00
Franklin Kite	65.00
Kings Rose	95.00
Pink Lustre	30.00
Spatterware. Floral	50.00

CUPS AND SAUCERS

A cup and saucer was a popular gift in the early 20th century. They continue to be a favorite collector or souvenir item today.

Miscellaneous types are listed herein. Please see individual categories for further information.

Farmer's. Floral transfer on white ground.......................$25.00

Farmers

"Cries of London." Adams $	55.00
Ducks. Made in England	40.00
"Take Ye a Cuppa O'Kindness." Staffordshire	55.00

Gift-type

Daddy. Germany	20.00

Hand Painted

Current Sprays	25.00
Figure. Gold trim. French	50.00.
Gold banded and monogrammed	20.00
Holly and berries	30.00
Scenic. Kauffman-type	75.00
Violets	22.50

CUSTARD GLASS

Custard glass is a cream or custard colored opaque pressed or mold-blown glass. It made its debut in the late 1800's and continued its popularity until the 1920's. Practically every major glass factory produced this pattern glass. Over 20 major patterns and some minor patterns are known to exist. Northwood Glass Company, Wheeling, West Virginia was one of the most prolific producers of Custard glass. Their main patterns included Argonaut Shell, Chrysanthemum, Grape and Cable, Inverted Fan and Feather, Louis XV, Sprig and others.

Other well-established companies known for custard glass patterns were Duncan and Sons, "Button and Arches," Fenton's "Cherry and Scale," and Heisey's "Winged Scroll."

Creamer. "Chrysanthemum Sprig" $100.00

Berry Sets

Chrysanthemum Sprig. 7 pieces. $	1300.00

Grape and Gothic Arch. 7 pieces.	500.00
Louis XV. 5 pieces	325.00
Bowls, Berry. Master	
Argonaut Shell	325.00
Beaded Circle	195.00
Chrysanthemum Sprig	195.00
Gem	125.00
Grape and Cable. Northwood	225.00
Intaglio	275.00
Inverted Fan and Feather	225.00
Ivorina	100.00
Jackson	150.00
Butter, Covered	
Argonaut Shell	250.00
Chrysanthemum Sprig	275.00
Geneva	150.00
Georgia Gem	125.00
Intaglio	175.00
Ivorina	165.00
Louis XV	175.00
Maple Leaf. Gold trim	175.00
Paneled Flower	150.00
Ringed Band	175.00
Winged Scroll	275.00
Celerys	
Chrysanthemum Sprig	185.00
Georgia Gem	200.00
Winged Scroll	195.00
Compotes, Jelly	
Argonaut Shell	125.00
Chrysanthemum Sprig	100.00
Strawberry	65.00
Creamers	
Argonaut Shell	110.00
Chrysanthemum Sprig	100.00
Diamond Peg. Souvenir-type	50.00
Georgia Gem	55.00
*Inverted Fan and Feather	175.00
Louis XV	95.00
Maple Leaf	95.00
Nautilus	150.00
Winged Scroll	175.00
Cruets	
Chrysanthemum Sprig	175.00
Intaglio	175.00
Louis XV	175.00
Winged Scroll	225.00
Goblets	
Beaded Swag	65.00
Diamond Peg. Souvenir-type	40.00
Grape and Cable	75.00
Grape and Gothic	65.00
Mugs	
Diamond Peg	50.00
Thistle	65.00
Pitchers, Water	
Argonaut Shell	500.00
Chrysanthemum Sprig	500.00
Grape Arbour	750.00
Plates	
Three Fruits. 7½"	60.00
8". Grape and Cable	75.00
Powder Jars	
Fleur-de-lis. Souvenir-type	65.00
Winged Scroll. Souvenir-type	75.00
Punch Bowl. 14½". Sunburst Cane	500.00
Punch Set. Grape and Cable. 2 piece bowl, six cups	1500.00
Rose Bowl. Persian Medallions	125.00
Salt and Pepper Shakers. Pair	
Argonaut	300.00
Chrysanthemum Sprig. Blue	500.00
Diamond Peg. Souvenir-type	100.00
Iris	500.00
Little Gem	150.00
Louis XV	250.00
Winged Scroll	300.00
Sauce Dishes	
Argonaut Shell	65.00
Beaded Swag	40.00
Chrysanthemum Sprig	75.00
Diamond Peg	35.00
Geneva	55.00
Inverted Fan and Feather	85.00
Louis XV	50.00
Optic	45.00
Wild Bouquet	50.00
Spooners	
Argonaut Shell	150.00
Chrysanthemum Sprig	150.00
Diamond Peg	100.00
Geneva	85.00
Honeycomb	65.00
Louis XV	100.00
Nautilus	85.00
Victoria	75.00
Wild Bouquet	100.00
Winged Scroll	125.00
Sugar, Covered	
Argonaut Shell	225.00
Beaded Circle	150.00
Chrysanthemum Sprig	300.00
Georgia Gem	75.00
Grape and Gothic Arch	150.00
Louis XV	150.00
Paneled Flower	100.00
Syrup Jug. Spider Web	150.00
Toothpicks	
*Chrysanthemum Sprig	165.00
Ring Band	65.00
Vermont	75.00
Tumblers	
Argonaut Shell	125.00
Chrysanthemum Sprig	85.00
Diamond Peg. Souvenir-type	50.00
Geneva	60.00
Intaglio	60.00
*Inverted Fan and Feather	80.00
Louis XV	80.00
Maple Leaf	65.00
Ring Band	65.00
Winged Scroll. Gold	95.00

Water Sets

Chrysanthemum Sprig. Pitcher and 6 tumblers 1000.00
Geneva. Pitcher and 6 tumblers . . 750.00
Intaglio. Pitcher and 6 tumblers . . 750.00
Inverted Fan and Feather. Pitcher and 6 tumblers 1000.00
Louis XV. Pitcher and 6 tumblers 850.00

Wine. Honeycomb 50.00

*Reproduced Item

CUT GLASS

Cut glass is a brilliantly carved and faceted glass with a history dating back to the ancient Romans. The art of ornamenting glass with a hard metal point and a lapidary's wheel was abandoned for several centuries. In the 1600's, the Bohemians revived the art and it quickly spread to other European countries and Great Britain. The popularity of this glass reached its peak in America in the late 1800's to the early 1900's. Most of the fine examples of cut glass encountered in today's antique market are from this era. . .rightfully called "The Brilliant Period."

Cologne Bottle. 4½" high. Sterling. Enameled stopper. French $85.00

Banana Bowls

4x8¼x11½". American Shield. $ 400.00
5x12". Gravic. Signed Hawkes . . 200.00
5x12". Hobstars, Strawberry Diamond, Fan. Signed Maple Leaf. 250.00

Baskets

5x10x15" high to top of double notch cut handle. Flowers, leaves. Harvard border. Sixteen point rayed base 350.00
6½x7½" high. Fan. Buzz and Strawberry Diamond. Notched handle 175.00
8¼x12" high. Brides. Butterflies, flowers and foliage. Ornate silver plated frame. Signed Hawkes . . . 395.00

Bells

4¼". Cornflower and leaves. Unsigned 100.00
6". Strawberry Diamond and Fan. Cut handle 185.00

Bobeches. Unsigned. Pair 65.00

Bowls

8". Crown and Thistle 125.00
8". Harvard 95.00
8". Hobstar. Notched prisms, etc. Signed Libbey. 150.00
8". Maywood 150.00
8". Millicent. Signed Hawkes 175.00
8". Pinwheel 125.00
9". Hobstars. Engraved flowers. Signed Signet 165.00
9". Hobstars. Signed Clarke 225.00
9". Senora. Signed Libbey 175.00
9". Victoria 175.00
10". Hobstars. All over cut. Signed Straus 200.00
11". Hexagonal-shape. All over cut. Signed Hoare. 650.00

Boxes, Glove

Harvard. 4½x8½x11". 500.00
Hobstar, Strawberry Diamond, Fan 125.00

Boxes, Puff

3½". All over cut 150.00
5". Florence 250.00
5". Hobstar. Rayed base. Silver rims 165.00
6½". Gravic. Signed Hawkes 175.00

Butter Dishes, Covered

American Shield 550.00
Harvard. 225.00
Hobstar and Cane 300.00

Butter Pat. Unsigned 25.00

Cake Stand. 12" diam. with gallery. Hobstar and Fan 300.00

Candelabra. 14". 3-branch. Sunburst. Signed P&B 350.00

Candlesticks

Brunswick Variant. 10". Pair 700.00
Gravic. 8½". Unsigned Hawkes. Pair 200.00
Strawberry Diamond, Flute. Notches, rayed bases. 9". Pair 200.00

Carafes

Strawberry Diamond. Signed Maple Leaf 175.00
32 rayed base notched neck. Signed Libbey 165.00

Celerys

Caprice 125.00
Hobstar and Fan. Signed Hawkes 125.00
Joan 125.00
Parisian. Dorflinger 250.00

Champagnes

Cross Cut Diamond, Fan. Notched stem 30.00

Hobstar. Strawberry Diamond, Fan. 24. Rayed base. 35.00
Russian. Teardrop stem. Rayed base 75.00

Cheese and Cracker Dish. 10" underplate, 5" top diam. Cross Cut Diamond 225.00

Clock Case. 5x8x10" long. Signed Fry 350.00

Compotes

4¼" diam., 7½" high. 48-point rayed foot. Hobstar and Cane. St. Louis Diamond cut stem with teardrop 175.00
6" diam., 9½" high. Alladin Star. Pitkin and Brooks. Pair 300.00
6¼" diam., 8½" high. Hobstar, Fan, Crosshatching, etc. Center and stem plain. Rayed base 100.00
8" diam., 5½" high. Kalana Pansy. Hollow stem. Signed Dorflinger 275.00
8" diam., 12" high. Hobstars, Strawberry Diamond, Fan. Notched stem with teardrop 375.00

Cordials

Harvard. Signed Maple City 30.00
Russian 85.00

Creamers and Sugars

Bedford. Bergen. Set 85.00
Geometric. Signed Tuthill. Set .. 350.00
Heart. Oval-shaped. Set 200.00
Hobstar. Hawkes. Set 175.00
Pinwheel. Set 95.00
Renaissance. Set 65.00

Cruets

Allover cut. 24 rayed base. Signed Hawkes 85.00
Middlesex. Dorflinger 75.00
Strawberry Diamond, Hobstars. Rayed base 75.00

Decanters

Pinwheel 175.00
Sussex. Diamond neck. Rayed base 375.00
Thistle. Rayed bottom. Signed Hawkes 250.00

Ferners

Harvard 165.00
Hobstars and Fan 100.00
Pinwheel 75.00

Fingers Bowls

Ellsmere. Signed Libbey 45.00
Lorraine. Signed Dorflinger 30.00
Russian. 48-point rayed base 75.00

Flask, Whiskey. 7¾" high. Silver cap and bottom. Signed Clarke .. 100.00

Goblets

Diamond Cut. Signed Hawkes ... 35.00
Hobstar. Signed Libbey 65.00
Russian 125.00

Strawberry and Fan 65.00
Vintage. Signed Locke 60.00

Humidor. 7" high. Notched prism. Sterling lid. Signed Hawkes 225.00

Ice Buckets

Harvard. 7" diam 350.00
Hobstar Chain, Flashed Fan. 7" diam. Hobstar cluster in Strawberry Diamond. Pointed star in base 275.00

Inkwells

Cane. 4½x4½". 24-point rayed base. 8½" sterling underplate .. 165.00
Harvard. 2½x3½". Millicent variant. Signed Hawkes 150.00

Knife Rests

Hobstars 30.00
Teardrop. Signed Hoare 65.00

Ladles.

Cane, Hobstars, Teardrop. Signed. Pairpoint 350.00
Hobstars, Strawberry Diamond, Fan. Silverplated bowl 150.00

Lamps

12" high, 7" diam. shade. Flowers and leaves, diamond point prisms 500.00
14½" high, 8" diam. shade. 1" band of Cross Cut Diamond, Hobstar top. Variation of Sheriden. Signed Hawkes 850.00
19" high, 11" diam. shade. Hobstar, Fine Diamond, Hobnail, Fan 1250.00
29" high. Harvard and floral with prisms 1500.00

Muffineer. Fine Cut and Panel. Sterling top 100.00

Napkin Ring. Harvard 30.00

Nappies

Hobstar, Crosshatching and Fans. Double Thumbprint handle. Signed Clarke 65.00
Hobstar, Fan, etc. Signed Hawkes 65.00
Pinwheel 50.00
Sultana. Dorflinger 95.00

Perfume Bottle. Lay-down. Cane. Sterling top 85.00

Pitchers

5¼". Strawberry Diamond. Single star base 125.00
8". Harvard. Libbey 200.00
8". Hobnail, Hobstar and Fan. Triple-notched handle 175.00
9½". Cosmos Spray. Signed Fry .. 250.00
10½". Pinwheel, Crosshatching and Fan 125.00

Plates

5¼". Sunburst 60.00
9". Carolyn. Signed Hoare 200.00
10". Brunswick. Signed Hawkes .. 250.00
12". Harvard. Signed Libbey 265.00

Punch Bowls

9" diam. Ribbon and Star. Signed

Tumbler. "Buzz Star and Block Variant" $25.00

Libbey. 2 pieces 850.00
10" diam., 10½" high. Hobstar, Fan, Strawberry Diamond. 2 pieces 500.00
10½" diam., 10½" high. Signed Tuthill. 2 pieces 700.00

Punch Cups
Hobstar, Split Fan, etc 25.00
Imperial. Triple-notched handles. Straus 50.00
Monarch. Signed Hoare 85.00

Relish Dishes
Harvard 100.00
Pinwheel 75.00

Rose Bowl. Harvard. Libbey 325.00

Spooner. 3½" diam., 4½" high. Hobstar, Strawberry Diamond and Fan. 24-point rayed base 125.00

Syrups
Cane. 24-point rayed base. Silverplated mountings............ 175.00
Pineapple, Fan. Silverplated mountings 75.00
Strawberry Diamond, Fan, etc. Silverplated mountings 75.00
Wheeler. Brass mountings 50.00

Toothpicks
Cornflower. Octagonal 50.00
Intaglio cut 35.00
Pinwheel 25.00

Trays
5½x8½". Harvard. Libbey 125.00
7x12". Harvard 175.00
7¼x14". Hobstar, Fan, Crosshatching, etc. Signed Clarke 250.00
9x13". Chain of Hobstar and floral engraving. Signed Hawkes 250.00
10x17". Harvard center. Cornflower ends 250.00

Tumblers
Diamond, Fan. Signed Libbey 37.50
Greek Key Chain. Signed Hawkes 37.50
Harvard 30.00
Hobstar. Signed Hoare 25.00
Middlesex. Signed Hawkes 30.00
Princess. Signed Libbey 35.00
Strawberry Buzz Variant 75.00

Vases
9½" high, 5" top diam. Roses, leaves. Signed Libbey 275.00
10". Brunswick. Signed Hawkes .. 275.00
11½". Trumpet-shape. Cane 200.00
12" high, 5½" diam. Beverly. Meriden 325.00
14". Bullseye and Prism with Hobstar and Diamond. Signed Hawkes 375.00
14". Queens. Signed Hawkes 375.00

Whiskey. Pinwheel 12.50

CUT VELVET

Cut Velvet is a satin-finished art glass made with two layers of glass . . .the outer layer in color with a white liner. The ribbed or diamond-shaped designs were cut in high relief, exposing the white interior. It was a product of several glass manufacturers in the Victorian era, 1870-1900.

Bowl. 5". Deep pink. Crimped, flared top ....$ 225.00

Ewer. 10¼" high. 3-pour top with ruffled rim. Bulbous body. Green with applied white handle 350.00

Pitcher. 5" high. Pink. Applied frosted handle 250.00

Rose Bowl. 4" high. Blue 250.00

Tumbler. Pink 125.00

Vases
6". Blue. Bulbous bottom. Stick-neck 225.00
7½". Apple green 275.00
8". Deep pink 250.00
8½". Stick. Blue 225.00
8½" high, 5" base. Blue. Fluted edge 395.00
10". Lavender 395.00
11¾". Raspberry. Gourd-shaped 350.00
14". Pink shading to red. Ruffled

Vase. 6" Blue. Bulbous bottom. Stick neck $225.00

5" top on 3 rigaree frosted feet. Enamel floral decor	450.00
Water Set. 8" pitcher with 4 tumblers. Butterscotch	1000.00

CZECHOSLOVAKIAN ITEMS

Objects marked "Made in Czechoslovakia" were produced after 1918, when the country claimed its independence from Austria Hungary. The people became more cosmopolitan . . .liberating and expanding their scope of life. They approached the arts on the principle "art for art's sake." Their porcelains, pottery and glasswares reflect many influences. A specific manufacturer's mark may be identified as being much earlier than 1918 but indicates that the factory existed in the Bohemian or the Austrian-Hungarian Empire period.

Ashtrays	
4½" diam. Orange lustre with multicolored Indian-type design. Yellow lustre interior ....$	10.00
2½x3x5". With cigarette box, 1¾x3½x4½". Orange and white lustre. Transfer of cigarettes and matches. Set	15.00
Basket. 4x5". Tan lustre. Black trim	15.00
Coffee Service. Demitasse. 16 pieces. White ground with cobalt and rust Gold-lined cups. Heavy gold trim. Open-handle tray. "Pirkenhammer." Set	175.00

Plate. 8". H-P grape center. Burgandy rim. Gold trim $18.50

Cream and Sugar. Creamer, 4½" high. Sugar, 6½". Peach iridescent, pearlized interior. Black handles, finial. Set	28.50
Cup and Saucer. Demitasse. Multicolored. Set of four	25.00
Invalid Feeder. Aladdin-shape	10.00
Pitcher. 3½". Bulbous. Ribbed. Blue and white lustre	10.00
Plate. 10¾". H–P. "Rembrandt." Heavy gold trim	75.00
Ramekin. Semi-porcelain. Molded fruit design lids	10.00
Vases	
4". Barrel-shaped. Brown lustre exterior with applied flowers, leaves, rings. Buff lustre interior . .	12.50
5¼". Yellow and blue parrot on brown stump. Three openings. Matte finish	15.00
6". Footed, with two handles. Grey, pink and blue lustre. Black trim	12.50
8". Pottery. Frog on tree trunk with bug	25.00
Wall Pocket. Red and blue bird perched on green and brown tree. Matte finish	10.00

DAGUERREOTYPES

Photography evolved slowly . . .daguerreotypes were one of the first methods.

In the 18th century, artists had only the 'camera obscura' to solve their problems of proportion. Experimenting with available light, J.M.

Daguerre and others devised methods to produce lasting printed images. In 1839, Daguerre patented his process in France. His method consisted of covering a copper plate with silver salts, sandwiching the plate between glass for protection and exposing the plate to light and mercury vapors to imprint an image. Rightfully so, this process was called Daguerreotype.

Fox Talbot's method for making paper negatives and prints (calotypes) was patented in Great Britain in 1841. Frederick Scott Archer introduced the wet collodian process in 1851. Dr. Maddox developed dry plates in 1871. When George Eastman introduced the roll film in 1888, the photographic industry emerged. Special cases were made to frame and protect these early prints. Generally classified as daguerreotype cases, they were also used to hold other prints. The majority were made of embossed gutta-percha, padded and lined with fabric and ornamented with metal mounts.

The following sizes represent average plate sizes. Sizes will vary from daguerreotypists and — or origin:

Full plate	6½x8½"
One-half	4¼x6½"
One-fourth	3¼x4¼"
One-sixth	2¾x3¼"
One-eighth	2⅛x3¼"
One-ninth	2x2½"
One-sixteenth	1⅝x2⅛"
CDV	Carte de Viste
TT	Tintypes

¼-Children. Double. Gutta percha case $40.00

Daguerreotypes With Cases

1/6-Child's Portrait. Gutta-Percha case. Bradley, Philadelphia .... $ 65.00

1/6-Couple, Older. Staring intently into camera. Single case. C. 1840-1855 .... 15.00

1/6-Gentleman, Older. Embossed stars on case. C. 1840-1855 .... 25.00

1/6-Lady, Young. Sitting with arm resting on table. MOP case. C.C. Schoonmaker, Troy, N.Y. C. 1840-1855 .... 15.00

1/6-Lady, Young. Wearing cape. Holding child. Case repaired. C. 1840-1855 .... 15.00

1/6-Lady and gentleman. Double. Gutta-percha case. Paper label. Union 40.00

1/4-Lady, Older. Wearing gingham dress. Lace fingerlets. Push button case. C. 1840-1855. 30.00

1/2-Soldier, Confederate. Gutta-percha case with eagle and shields 65.00

1/4-Soldiers, Three Civil War. Single case 50.00

1/2-Lady, Young. Elegantly dressed in sitting pose. Mountain scene for backdrop. MOP case with inlay of flowers, scroll corners. C. 1840-1855 .... 125.00

Daguerreotype Cases Only

Basket of Fruit 15.00

Cherries, Cluster of. Gutta-percha .. 28.50

Children, Three. Playing with toys. Critchlow and Co. 60.00

Cupid and Wounded Stag. Gutta-percha 85.00

Eagle, American 75.00

Faithful Hound. Gutta-percha 75.00

Fireman Saving Child 75.00

Flowers and Scrolls. Holmes, Booth & Hayden 45.00

Fortune Teller 85.00

Geometric. Littlefield & Parsons 30.00

Locomotive 50.00

Scrolled. Gutta-percha. Littlefield & Parsons 40.00

Miscellaneous

Ambrotype

1/6-Angelic young girl sits with hands folded in lap. Delicately tinted cheeks. C. 1856-1900's .. $ 5.00

1/6-Lady and gentleman in sitting pose. C. 1856-1900's 8.00

1/6-Portrait of young gentlemen. Brown case. Scroll design. Littlefield & Parsons 40.00

1/6 —-Three rowdies holding beer bottles. With case. C. 1856-1900's 25.00

1/9 —-Portrait of gentleman. Scroll design. Littlefield & Parsons 28.50

1/9 —-Portrait of gentleman. Papier mache with MOP inlay case 10.00

CDV

2½x4"-British soldier in dress uniform with cross belt. Stamped W. Piper, Camborne. C.1860-1875 .... 7.50

2½x4″-Lady in sitting pose holding photo album. C. 1860-1875 .... 5.00
Tintype. 1/6-Bearded soldier wearing 9 button jacket. ½ pose. Mat with flags, cannons, eagle, etc. Patriotic leather case 25.00

DAVENPORT

DAVENPORT
LONGPORT
STAFFORDSHIRE

DAVENPORT

At first only earthenware was made. 'Flown' blue decorations were used extensively. In the early 19th century, porcelain wares were introduced with cottage-style decorations.

Cup and Saucer. "Clifford" $95.00

Biscuit Jar. 8¾″. Silverplated holder. C. 1870-86............$ 185.00
Bowls
9½″. Stoneware. Floral decor. C. 1850 .... 25.00
13″, 4½″ deep. English scenic view with floral border 150.00
Compote. 5″. Floral decor 85.00
Cup Plates
Sprig 20.00
Teaberry. Pink Lustre 25.00
Cups and Saucers
Cyprus. Mulberry. Handleless 45.00
Imari. Can-shape. C. 1815 ...... 55.00
Pitchers
6¾″. Blue, pink floral decor. C. 1840 .... 85.00
8″. Cathedral. Pink lustre with black transfer 195.00
Plates
7″. Blue Willow. C. 1820 .... 30.00
7″. Embossed daisies on rim. Handpainted scene in center. C. 1825
9″. Handpainted fruit center. Green rim. C. 1885 .... 30.00
10″. Imari. C. 1810 .... 35.00
10½″. Green transfer. C. 1850 .. 40.00
Platters
4x7″. Imari 150.00
9x10¼″. Blue Willow. C. 1810 .. 55.00
9x12¼″. Cyprus. Mulberry 85.00
11x14″. Imari. Anchor mark 100.00
Tea Set. Sprig. 7 pieces 195.00
Tureens
10½″. Cyprus. Mulberry 100.00
12″. Blue Willow 150.00
Vase. 9¾″. Deep blue with gilt trim. Butterfly handles. C. 1870-86 .. 150.00

DECOYS

Decoys are artificial birds or other animals used to lure game into shooting or netting range.

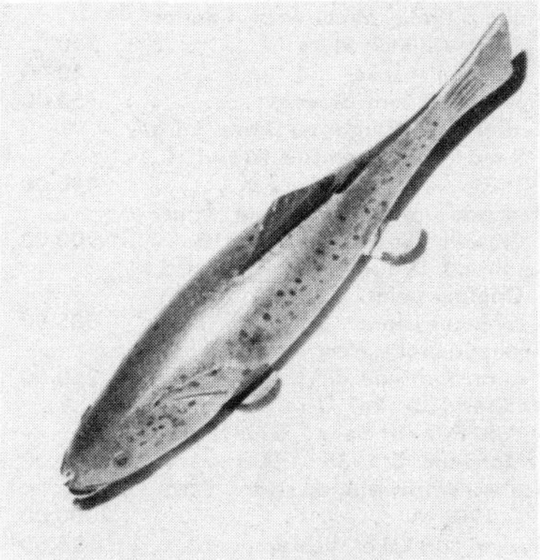

Speckled Trout. 10½″. Attributed to Shalk $150.00

Black Duck. Barnegat Bay. C. 1900. Unsigned ....$ 75.00
Black Duck. Original paint. Minor wear. Canadian Ken Anger, Michigan 425.00
Black Duck. Hollow carved. Original paint. Roswell Bliss, Connecticut 450.00
Black Duck. Paint worn. Minor split. Ira Hudson, Chincofeague, Va .. 185.00
Black Duck. Lloyd Johnson 600.00
Black Duck. Original paint. Joe Lincoln, Illinois River 850.00
Black Duck. Lou Rathmell, Connecticut 1500.00

Black Duck. Doug Jester. Original paint. Dave "Umbrella" Watxon, Delmarva Peninsula	450.00
Bluebill Drake. Ben Holmes, Connecticut. C. 1890	1200.00
Bluebill Duck. Pinched Breast. Ward Brothers. C. 1929	850.00
Bluebill. Scaup. Minor wear. Ben Schmidt, Michigan	165.00
Bufflehead. L. Johnson	600.00
Canadian Goose. L. Parker	250.00
Canvasback Drake. Swan Island Gun Club. Elmer Crowell, Illinois River. C. 1890	1500.00
Canvasback Drake. Original paint. Minor wear. Bert Graves, Illinois River	325.00
Goose. 42" Long. Handcarved and painted	150.00
Goshawk. M. Wavercak	500.00
Mallard Drake. Minor wear. Elmer Crowell, Illinois River. C. 1915-20	1200.00
Mallard Drake. Minor wear. Bert Graves, Illinois River	325.00
Mallard Drake. Minor wear. Charles Perdew, Illinois River	250.00
Perch. Mullet Lake	40.00
Plover Shore Bird. Stevens	150.00
Redbreasted Merganser Drake. Corb Reed, Chincoteague Island. C. 1939	440.00
Redhead Drake. Minor wear. Elmer Crowell, Illinois River. C. 1910	900.00
Redhead Drake. Hollow carved. Original paint. Ira Hudson, Chincoteague Island	385.00
Redhead Drake. Near mint. Ben Schmidt, Michigan	250.00
Redhead Drake. Original paint. Ward Brothers, Crisfield, Maryland. C. 1936	1500.00
Scoter. White-winged. Hans Berry. C. 1900	3000.00
Sucker. Burt Lake, Michigan	125.00
Yellow Legs. Female, 9". Tin. Folding-type. Original paint. New England. Pat. 1874	335.00
Widgeon. Joe Lincoln, Illinois River	1500.00

DEDHAM POTTERY

The Robertson family was actively engaged in pottery making long before Alexander W. Robertson established a pottery in Chelsea, Massachusetts in 1866 known as the Chelsea Keramic Art Works. At first, unglazed red clay flower pots and vases were made. From 1875 to 1889, the firm progressed to more sophisticated lines. In 1891 to 1896 tablewares were introduced. The name was changed to Chelsea Pottery, U.S.A. The pottery was moved to Dedham, Massachusetts in 1895, and again the firm's name was changed to Dedham Pottery Company.

The familiar and famous crackle glaze wares are the best known. It is a high fired, true 'porcelain' with a soft gray glaze with blue inglazed decorations. The mold for the Rabbit plate, which was the first standard design, was first slightly incised for the decorator's ease. Later the molds were made smooth. Over 60 border designs are recorded, but only 13 were considered standard in 1938. The Rabbit pattern is currently being reproduced; but marked accordingly.

The following marks can be used to determine the approximate age of items made by the company; (1) A.W. & H.C. Robertson 1868-1872. (2) Chelsea Keramic Art Works, Name Robertson & Sons, impressed, 1872-1889. (3) CPUS impressed in a cloverleaf, 1891-1895. (4) Foreshortened rabbit, 1895-1932. (5) Conventional rabbit with Dedham Pottery stamped in blue, 1896-1943. (6) Word "Registered" added to rabbit mark, 1929-1943.

Plate. 8½". "Pond Lily" $145.00

Bowls	
Grape. 3x7" diam	$ 195.00
Rabbit. 1½x6" diam	175.00
Rabbit. 1½x10" diam	325.00
Butter. Rabbit	250.00
Candle Snuffer. Butterfly	325.00
Candlesticks	
Azalea. Pair	225.00
Rabbit. Pair	275.00
Celerys	
Elephant	195.00

Rabbit	225.00
Chocolate Pot. Rabbit	295.00
Creamers	
Magnolia. 3"	150.00
Rabbit. 4"	150.00
Cups and Saucers	
Duck	150.00
Elephant	195.00
Polar Bear	175.00
Pond Lily	150.00
Rabbit. Demi-tasse	195.00
Rabbit. Large	135.00
Snowtree	160.00
Egg Cup, Double. Rabbit. 4"	150.00
Mug. Rabbit. 5¼"	195.00
Pitcher. Rabbit. 7"	250.00
Plates	
6". Azalea	75.00
6". Duck	85.00
6". Grape	85.00
6". Magnolia	85.00
6". Mushroom	175.00
6". Polar Bear	250.00
6". Pond Lily	100.00
6". Rabbit	100.00
6". Snowtree	125.00
7½". Azalea	100.00
8½". Butterfly	125.00
8½". Crab	225.00
8½". Duck	125.00
8½". Horse Chestnut. Raised	150.00
8½". Iris	125.00
8½". Magnolia	150.00
8½". Rabbit	100.00
8½". Rabbit. One ear	150.00
8½". Snowtree	150.00
10". Azalea	175.00
10" Duck	225.00
10". Grape	195.00
10". Iris	195.00
10". Lion. Tapestry	500.00
10". Moth	225.00
10". Mushroom	225.00
10". Polar Bear	295.00
10". Pond Lily	175.00
10". Rabbit	145.00
10". Turtle	250.00
12½". Crab	395.00
12½". Rabbit	250.00
Platters	
5x9". Rabbit	195.00
6½x10". Swan	250.00
Shakers, Salt and Pepper. 3½".	
Rabbit. Pair	175.00
Sugar, Covered. Rabbit	175.00
Tiles	
Rabbit	185.00
Swan	225.00

DEGENHART GLASS

John and Elizabeth Degenhart founded Crystal Art Glass in Cambridge, Ohio in 1947. Their privately owned company produced a wide variety of pressed glass objects and John became world famous for his paperweights.

After John's death in 1964 the glass making operation continued under the personal direction of his widow. Elizabeth Degenhart made many innovations; adding new molds and introducing a wide spectrum of colors (many of her own creation.) There are 150 official colors in the Degenhart glass listing; but the actual list of colors is much longer (over 214) because of numerous variations of some colors. Only a few of the available colors could be listed herein.

Elizabeth died in 1978 and the Crystal Art Glass plant closed. The molds were taken by Island Mold Co.; and the familiar trademark of a "D" within a heart was removed. A few molds were left intact and glass will be pressed in these molds specifically to support the pending Degenhart Museum.

NOTE: Special THANKS. . .to Paul B. Miller and Jabe Tarter. . .close friends of Mrs. Degenhart. They have contributed a wealth of information and conscientously assisted in compiling this limited listing of Degenhart glass.

Animal Dishes, Covered	
Hen. 3".	
Basic Colors. Crystal ....$	65.00
Basic Colors. Opaque	125.00
Animal Dishes, Covered	
Hen. Lamb, Robin, Turkey. 5".	
Amberina	350.00
Amethyst	175.00
Chocolate	400.00
Cobalt	125.00
Jabe's Amber	75.00
Peach Blow	100.00
White Milk Glass	60.00
Candleholders. "Wildflower"	
Basic Colors. Crystal	20.00
Ruby	35.00
Compotes, Covered	
"Wildflower." 4" high.	
Basic Colors. Crystal	25.00
Caramel	100.00
Jade	50.00
Rubina	75.00
Creamers and Sugars. Sets	
"Daisy and Button", "Texas"	
Amber	35.00
Amethyst	20.00
Bloody Mary (3 shades)	100.00

Doll. "Priscilla"

Chocolate	135.00
Crystal	10.00
Milk Glass	45.00

Doll, "Priscilla." 7"

Amber	50.00
Boyd Black	75.00
Degenhart Green	100.00
End of Day	125.00
Milk White	60.00
Vaseline	45.00

Drawer Pulls. "Sandwich"

Crystal Clear	35.00
Milk Blue	45.00
Milk White	30.00
Opalescent	65.00

Owls. 3"

Champagne	475.00
Chocolate	225.00
Cobalt	75.00
Crystal Clear	20.00
Crystal Clear, White Carnival Effect	200.00
Frosty Jade	150.00
Lemon Opal	75.00

Owl

Opal	45.00
Smoky	65.00
Violet	60.00
Violet Opaque	165.00

Paperweights

Bubble. Miniature animal or bird inside	225.00
Controlled Cut and Heart. With flowers. All colors	175.00
Controlled Cut and Heart. Without flowers. All colors	135.00
Name	125.00
Novelty	125.00
Overlay. With decorations	750.00
Rose. Footed. All colors	110.00

Pooch Dog. 2½" high.

April Green	30.00
Canary	20.00
Caramel Slag	75.00
Crystal	12.00
Elizabeth Blue	100.00
Ruby	100.00
Snow White	45.00

Portrait Plate. (Elizabeth Degenhart)

Crystal Only

Amberina	75.00
Canary	50.00
Opalescent	85.00
Smoky	100.00

Salt Dips and Salt and Pepper Shakers.

Various Patterns

Amber	10.00
Cobalt	12.00

Crown Tuscan 20.00
Opal 20.00
Peach Blow 45.00

Shoes
Baby Shoe or Tramp Boot All Opaques 55.00
Cat Slipper.
All Crystals 15.00
Colonial Bow Slipper
All Crystals 30.00
Daisy and Button High Shoe and Skate Boot
All Crystals 25.00
All Opaques 45.00
Texas Boot
Crystals and Opaques
Apple Green 12.00
Baby Blue 20.00
Heatherbloom 45.00
Pearl Gray 15.00

Toothpicks
Various Patterns
Crystal 15.00
Custard 45.00
Emerald 20.00
Milk Glass 25.00
White Marble 75.00

Wines, "Buzz Star", "Daisy and Button."
Crystal Clear 12.00
Custard 27.50
Pigeon Blood, Iridescent 150.00
Ruby 50.00
Taffeta 65.00
Vaseline 15.00

Witches Pot. With Lugs.
All Crystals 75.00

Witches Pot. Without Lugs.
All Crystals 25.00
All Mixed Colored Slags 40.00

MISCELLANEOUS

Baby Pottie. All Crystals 10.00
Cup Plates 12.00
Hand 8.00
Heart Jewel Box 20.00
Mug, Child's. Opaque 20.00

DELDARE WARE

(See "Buffalo Pottery")

DELFTWARE

Delftware includes not only the tin glazed pottery produced in Holland in the familiar blue and white "Windmill" scenes for the country market and the finely executed pieces decorated in the Chinese manner; but also other tin glazed pottery produced in England and on the continent. As early as the 16th century the name Delft became synonymous with this particular pottery, when the Dutch designated their city of Delft as a world trade center.

Modern adaptations of Delft blue and white Dutch scenes are common in today's gift market.

Charger. 13½". Stylized basket of flowers in center. Early $275.00

Bowls
8⅞". "Success to Trade." Floral sprays. Blue and white. Liverpool. C. 1750 ....$ 225.00
10¼". "One Bowl More and Then." Blue and white. Lambeth. C. 1760-1780 .... 450.00

Cat, Sitting. 6" Black and white 60.00

Condiment Set. Dutch scene. Blue and white. Hanging salt box, 6 large jars, 6 small covered jars, 2 cruets. 15 pieces 250.00

Creamers
Cow, Reclining. Blue and white .. 65.00
Cow, Standing. Blue and white .. 75.00

Ewer. 6½". Blue and white applied flowers 50.00

Inkwell. 4". Heart-shaped. 3-holder. Blue and white. Late 40.00

Jugs
8". Peacock pattern. Blue and white. Dutch. 18th century 450.00
8¾". "Vinegar." Blue and white. Late 35.00

Plaques
13". Mother and Child. Blue and white. Signed M. Bloomers 250.00
13¼". Scenic. Rim with four panels of flowers. Blue diaper cartouche. Dutch. 18th century 225.00
15". Ship decor with ornate border 125.00
15¾". Mother and Children 295.00

Plates
8". Dutch scene. Blue and white. Late 50.00
9". Floral. Blue and white. Dutch. 18th century 135.00

9". Tulip pattern. Blue and white. Bristol. 18th century 125.00
9¼". Floral. Manganese, within border of pendant festoons. Lambeth. C. 1760-80 .... 150.00
10". Peacock pattern. Polychrome. Dutch. 18th century 195.00
Stein. ½ L. Blue and white. Windmills, sailboats. Inlaid lid, litho bottom. Germany 225.00
Trays
9½x10". Dutch scene. Blue and white. Scalloped edge. Late 65.00
14x18". Dutch scene. Four ball feet. Metal rim 125.00
Urn, Covered. 17". Blue windmill decor on white 165.00
Vases
8½". Dutch scene. Polychromed .. 95.00
11". Windmill scene. Blue and white. Gold trim. Late. Pair 150.00

DEPRESSION GLASS

Depression glass is a general term used to describe the glassware manufactured primarily during the "Depression" years, 1929-1940. It was an inexpensive machine-made glass manufactured by several major glass factories in a wide variety of patterns and colors. More than 100 patterns have been identified and several hundred occasional pieces have been discovered. The glassware was sold in variety stores. Quantities of it were given as prizes at fairs and used as premiums or for sales promotions.

Interest in collecting Depression glass has risen... including the later handmade colored glass of the fifties and sixties. As with most antiques and collectibles, where demand exceeds the supply, reproductions appear on the market. The majority of the reissued patterns are marked accordingly, but there are some deceivers.

ADAM
Jeannette Glass Co. 1932-34

Green
Ashtray. 4¼" ....$ 8.50
Bowls
5¾" 10.00
9". Covered 20.00
10". Oval 12.50
Butter, Covered 200.00
Candlestick. 4" 20.00
Cream and Sugar, Covered 22.50
Cup and Saucer. Square 12.00
Plates
6" 3.00
9". Grill 8.00
Platter. 12" 8.50
Salt and Pepper. Footed. Pair 65.00

"Cherry Blossom." Tumbler. 3¾" high. Footed. AOP. Pink $10.00

"Princess". Water Pitcher. 60 oz. Green $25.00

Tumblers
4½" 8.00
5½". Iced Tea 15.00
Pink
Bowls
5¾" 8.50
10". Oval 11.50
Butter, Covered 50.00

Butter. Sierra 500.00
Candy Jar, Covered. 2½" 25.00
Cream and Sugar, Covered 17.50
Cup and Saucer, Round 35.00
Pitcher. Quart. Round base 17.50
Plates
7¾". Round 22.50
7¾". Square 5.00
9". Grill 6.50
Platter. 12" 8.00
Relish. 8". Divided 5.00
Sherbet. 3" 6.50
Vase. 7½" 38.50

Yellow
Cup and Saucer. Round 200.00
Plate. 7¾". Round 75.00

AMERICAN PIONEER
Liberty Glass Works 1931-34

Crystal
Bowls
5". Handled .... $ 5.00
10¾". Console 17.50
Candlestick. 6½" 12.00
Cream and Sugar. 3½" 12.00
Cup and Saucer 8.50
Goblet.6" 18.50
Ice Bucket. 6" 22.50
Pitcher, Covered. 5" 95.00
Plates
8" 4.50
11½". Handled 5.00
Rose Bowl. 4½". Footed 22.50

Green
Candy, Covered. 1 lb. 75.00
Cream and Sugar. 3½" 15.00
Cup and Saucer 10.00
Dresser Set. 3 pieces 65.00
Lamp. 8½" 55.00
Tumblers
4" 12.00
5" 15.00

Pink
Bowls
8¾". Covered 18.50
9". Handled 6.50
Cheese and Cracker 15.00
Coasters. Set of 4 .... 15.00
Plate. 8" 15.00
Tumblers
4" 10.00
5" 15.00
Vase. 7" 25.00

AMERICAN SWEETHEART
MacBeth-Evans Glass Co. 1930-36

Blue
Cream and Sugar. Open .... $ 165.00
Cup and Saucer 125.00
Plates
8" 85.00
15½". Wedding 300.00
Server. 2-tier. 8", 12" plates 250.00

Cremax
Bowls
6" 10.00
9" 30.00

Monax
Bowls
6" 7.50
9" 22.50
11'. Oval 28.50
Cream and Sugar, Covered 125.00
Cream and Sugar, Open 15.00
Cup and Saucer 10.00
Plates
8" 5.00
12" 12.50
13". Oval 28.50
Salt and Pepper. Footed. Pair 125.00
Server. 3-tier. 8", 12", 15½" plates 75.00

Pink
Bowls
9" 10.00
11". Oval 12.00
Cream and Sugar, Open 10.00
Cup and Saucer 8.50
Plates
6" 3.00
10¼" 9.50
Pitcher. 8" 175.00
Salt and Pepper. Footed. Pair 145.00
Tumbler. 4½" 20.00

Red
Cream and Sugar 175.00
Cup and Saucer 115.00
Plates
8" 75.00
15½. Wedding 250.00
Server. 3-tier. 8", 12", 15½" plates 650.00

BLOCK OPTIC (BLOCK)
Hocking Glass Co. 1929-33

Green—Pink—Yellow
Bowls
5¼" .... $ 5.00
8½" 8.50
Cream and Sugar. All styles 12.00
Cup and Saucer. All styles 6.00
Goblet. 9 oz. Thin 12.50
Ice Bucket 12.50
Pitcher. 8½" 20.00
Plates
6" 2.50
8" 2.50
Sherbet. Low 3.00
Shot Glass 5.00
Tumbler. 9 oz. Flat 6.00

BUBBLE (BULLSEYE, PROVINCIAL)
Hocking Glass Co. 1934-65

Blue	
Bowls	
5¼"	$ 4.00
8¾"	6.50
Cream and Sugar	15.00
Cup and Saucer	4.00
Plates	
6¾"	1.75
9¾". Grill	6.00
12". Oval	6.50
Crystal	
Bowl. 5¼"	1.75
Candlesticks. Pair	12.00
Cup and Saucer	3.50
Pitcher. 64 oz. Ice lip	28.50
Plates	
6¾"	1.50
9½"	3.00
Green, Dark	
Bowl. 8¾"	6.50
Cream and Sugar	9.00
Cup and Saucer	3.75
Plates	
6¾"	1.50
9½"	3.50
Ruby	
*Bowl. 4½"	3.00
Cup and Saucer	5.00
Plate. 9½"	4.00
Server. 2-tier	16.50
Tumblers	
6 oz	5.00
16 oz.	8.50

CAMEO (DANCING GIRL, BALLERINA)
Hocking Glass Co. 1930-34

Crystal	
Bowl. 4¼"	$ 4.50
Cocktail Shaker. Metal lid	75.00
Cup	3.00
Plates	
6"	2.00
8"	4.00
Tumbler. 4"	6.50
Green	
Bottle. "White House Vinegar"	20.00
Candlesticks. 4". Pair	38.50
Cookie Jar, Covered	25.00
Cream and Sugar. 4¼"	16.50
Cup	6.50
Pitcher. 8½"	22.50
Plates	
8"	4.50
8½". Square	15.00
10½". Grill	6.00
Saucer. (Rare)	25.00
Sherbet. 5"	15.00
Tumblers	
4¾". 10 oz. Flat	12.50
5". 11 oz. Flat	15.00
5". 9 oz. Footed	8.50
5¾". 11 oz. Footed	13.50
6½". 15 oz. Footed	75.00
Pink	
Bowl. 11" 3-feet	18.50
Cream and Sugar. 4¼"	100.00
Goblet. 4"	95.00
Ice Bucket	350.00
Plates	
6"	8.50
9½"	15.00
Salt and Pepper. Footed. Pair	300.00
Tumbler. 3¾". 5 oz.	55.00
Yellow	
Bowl. 8¼"	20.00
Butter, Covered	500.00
Cream and Sugar. 3¼"	15.00
Cup and Saucer	7.50
Pitcher. 5¾". 20 oz.	350.00
Plates	
8"	2.75
10½". Grill	4.50
Tumbler. 5". 9 oz. Footed	10.00

CHERRY BLOSSOM
Jeannette Glass Co. 1930-39

Delphite	
Bowls	
4¾"	$ 8.50
9". Handled	12.50
Cream and Sugar, Covered	35.00
Pitcher. 6¾". AOP	100.00
Plate. 6"	10.00
Tumbler. 3¾". Footed. AOP	17.50
Green	
Bowls	
4¾"	7.50
5¾"	15.00
9". Oval	15.00
*Butter, Covered	75.00
Cream and Sugar, Covered	20.00
Cup and Saucer	15.00
Mug. 7 oz.	125.00
Pitcher. 6¾". AOP	32.50
Plates	
6"	4.00
9". Grill	8.50
Platters	
11"	16.50
13". Divided	25.00
*Salt and Pepper. Pair	750.00
Tumbler. 3¾". Footed. AOP	15.00
Pink	
Bowls	
4¾"	6.50
8½"	8.50
9". Handled	7.50
10½". Three-legged	22.50
*Butter, Covered	60.00
Cream and Sugar, Covered	16.00
Cup and Saucer	12.50

Pitcher. 8". 42 oz. PAT	25.00
Plates	
7¾". Soup	22.50
9". Grill	8.50
11". Oval	15.00
Sherbet	7.00
Tumblers	
3¾". Footed. AOP	10.00
4¼". Flat. PAT	6.50

CHERRY BLOSSOM, CHILD'S

Delphite	
Cream and Sugar	45.00
*Cup and Saucer	30.00
Dinner Set. 14 pieces	225.00
Plate. 6"	10.00
Pink	
Cream and Sugar	40.00
*Cup and Saucer	20.00
Plate. 6"	10.00
Set. 14 pieces	175.00

CLOVERLEAF
Hazel Atlas Glass Co. 1930-36

Black	
Ashtrays	
4"	$ 45.00
5¾"	65.00
Cream and Sugar. Footed	17.50
Cup and Saucer	15.00
Salt and Pepper. Pair	65.00
Sherbet. Footed	10.00
Green—Pink	
Bowls	
4"	5.00
8". Deep	20.00
Cream and Sugar. Footed	10.00
Cup and Saucer	6.50
Plate. 8"	3.00
Tumbler. 4". 9 oz.	12.50
Yellow	
Bowl. 5"	10.00
Cream and Sugar. Footed	15.00
Plates	
8"	7.50
10¼". Grill	12.00
Salt and Pepper. Pair	75.00
Sherbet. Footed	6.50
Tumbler. 5¾". 10 oz. Footed	12.50

COLONIAL (KNIFE & FORK)
Hocking Glass Co. 1934-38

Crystal	
Butter, Covered	$ 35.00
Cream and Sugar. Open	15.00
Cup and Saucer	5.00
Green	
Bowls	
4"	5.00
5½"	10.00
9"	12.50
Butter, Covered	40.00
Creamer. 5"	10.00
Plate. 10". Grill	8.50
Sugar, Covered	18.50
Sugar, Open	8.50
Tumbler. 12 oz.	15.00
Pink	
Cup and Saucer	6.50
Pitchers	
7". 54 oz.	30.00
7¾". 68 oz	50.00
Plates	
8½"	3.50
10". Dinner	17.50
10". Grill	5.00
Sherbet	4.00
Tumblers, Footed	
3¼". 3 oz.	6.50
5¼." 10 oz.	8.50
Whiskey. 2½"	6.50

CUBE (CUBIST)
Jeannette Glass Co. 1929-33

Green	
Bowls	
4½". Deep	$ 6.00
6½"	8.00
Candy Jar, Covered. 6½"	20.00
Cream and Sugar. Covered. 3"	15.00
Cup and Saucer	7.50
Plate. 6"	2.50
Sherbet	6.00
Pink	
Coasters. 3¼". Set of 4	10.00
Cream and Sugar. 2"	5.00
Cup and Saucer	5.00
Pitcher. 8¾". 45 oz.	100.00
Powder Box, Covered	12.50
Salt and Pepper. Pair	17.50
Tumbler. 4". 10 oz.	15.00

DAISY (NUMBER 620)
Indiana Glass Co. 1933-40

Amber	
Bowls	
4½"	$ 3.50
7½"	5.00
10". Oval	7.50
Cream and Sugar. Footed	7.50
Cup and Saucer	5.00
Plate. 10½"	3.50
Relish. Divided. 8½"	5.00
Sherbet. Footed	4.00
Tumblers	
9 oz. Footed	6.00
12 oz. Footed	8.50
Crystal	
Bowl. 7½"	3.50
Plates	
6"	1.00
9½"	3.50
11½". Server	5.00

DIAMOND QUILTED (FLAT DIAMOND)
Imperial Glass Co. 1920's-30's

Black—Blue	
Bowls	
5"	$ 4.50
7"	7.50
Candlestick	8.50
Cream and Sugar	17.50
Cup and Saucer	7.50
Plate. 8"	6.50
Server. Center handle	20.00
Sherbet	6.50
Green — Pink	
Bowls	
5"	3.00
7"	4.50
Candlesticks. All styles. Each	7.50
Compote, Covered. 11½"	22.50
Cream and Sugar	7.50
Plates	
7"	1.50
14". Server	6.00
Sherbet	3.00

DOGWOOD (APPLE BLOSSOM, WILD ROSE)
MacBeth-Evans Glass Co. 1929-32

Green	
Bowls	
5½"	$ 12.00
8½"	55.00
10¼"	110.00
Cream and Sugar. 2½". Thin	50.00
Cup and Saucer	12.50
Pitcher. 8". 80 oz. Decorated	500.00
Plates	
8"	3.00
10½". Grill. AOP	10.00
Tumblers	
4". 10 oz. Decorated	25.00
5". 12 oz. Decorated	35.00
Monax—Cremax	
Bowl. 5½"	10.00
Cup and Saucer	35.00
Plates	
6"	20.00
12"	30.00
Pink	
Bowls	
5½"	7.50
8½"	15.00
10¼"	100.00
Cream and Sugar. 3¼". Thick	15.00
Cup and Saucer	7.50
Pitchers	
8". 80 oz. "American Sweetheart"	500.00
8". 80 oz. Decorated	85.00
Plates	
6"	3.00
8"	2.00
9¼"	10.00
10½". Grill. AOP	7.50
12". Oval	135.00
Server. 2-tier. 8", 12" Plates	40.00
Tumblers	
4". 10 oz. Decorated	15.00
5". 12 oz. Decorated	20.00

DORIC
Jeannette Glass Co. 1935-38

Delphite	
Bowls	
4½"	$ 18.50
8¼"	55.00
Pitcher. 6". 36 oz. Flat	115.00
Sherbet	5.00
Green	
Cream and Sugar. Covered	12.50
Cup and Saucer	6.00
Plates	
6"	2.00
9"	6.00
9". Serrated	20.00
Pink	
Bowls	
4½"	3.50
8¼"	8.00
9". Oval	7.50
Butter, Covered	50.00
Candy, Covered. 8"	15.00
Cream and Sugar. Covered	12.50
Cup and Saucer	5.00
Pitchers	
6". 36 oz. Flat	17.50
7½". 48 oz. Footed	350.00
Plates	
7"	5.00
9"	5.00
12". Oval	6.50
Salt and Pepper. Pair	20.00
Trays	
4x4"	3.50
8x8"	5.00
Tumbler. 5". 12 oz	12.00

FLORAGOLD (LOUISA)
Jeannette Glass Co. 1950's

Iridescent	
Bowls	
4½". Square	$ 3.50
5½". Ruffled	3.25
9½". Deep	12.50
12". Ruffled	7.50
Butter. Oblong ¼ #	15.00
Butter. Round	30.00
Cream and Sugar. Covered	10.00
Cup and Saucer	6.50
Pitcher, Water. 64 oz.	20.00
Plates	
8½"	10.00
11¼". Oval	10.00

Tumblers, Footed	
10 oz.	8.00
15 oz.	15.00

FLORAL (POINSETTIA)
Jeannette Glass Co. 1939-40

Delphite	
Bowls	
7½" $	45.00
9". Oval	150.00
Cream and Sugar. Open	50.00
Plate. 9"	45.00
Platter. 10¾"	75.00
Green	
Bowls	
4"	5.50
9". Oval	10.00
Butter, Covered	55.00
Candy Jar. Covered	25.00
Cream and Sugar. Covered	20.00
Cup and Saucer	8.50
Plate. 9". Grill	22.50
Pink	
Bowls	
7½"	6.50
9". Oval	7.50
Butter, Covered	45.00
Candy. Covered	18.50
Cream and Sugar. Covered	15.00
Cup and Saucer	7.00
Pitcher. 8". 32 oz.	15.00
Plates	
8"	4.50
9"	6.00
Salt and Pepper. Pairs	
4". Footed	22.50
6". Flat	25.00
Tray. 6" Square. Closed handles	6.50
Tumblers. Footed	
4"	7.00
5¼"	18.00

FLORENTINE NO. 2 (POPPY NO. 2)
Hazel Atlas Glass Co. 1934-37

Crystal—Green	
Bowls	
4½" $	5.00
8"	10.00
Cream and Sugar. Covered	12.50
Cup and Saucer	6.00
Pitchers	
7½". 28 oz. Footed	15.00
7½". 54 oz.	25.00
8". 76 oz.	85.00
Plates	
8½"	2.50
10". Dinner	4.50
Salt and Pepper. Pair	20.00
Tumbler. 4". 9 oz.	6.50
Pink	
Bowl. 5"	6.50
Plates	
6¼"	6.50
8½"	3.50
10"	6.00
Platter. 11"	7.50
Yellow	
Bowl. 4½"	6.00
Cream and Sugar. Covered	15.00
Cup and Saucer	7.50
Salt and Pepper. Pair	28.50

GEORGIAN (LOVEBIRDS)
Federal Glass Co. 1931-36

Green	
Bowls	
5¾" $	6.50
6½". Deep	22.50
9". Oval	17.50
Butter, Covered	55.00
Cream and Sugar. Open. 4". Footed	15.00
Cup and Saucer	6.50
Plates	
6"	2.25
9¼". Center design	5.00
Platter. 11½". Closed handles	22.50
Sherbet	5.00
Tumblers	
4". 9 oz.	15.00
5¼". 12 oz.	20.00

HOMESPUN (FINE RIB)
Jeannette Glass Co. 1939-40

Pink	
Bowls	
4½". Handled $	5.00
8¼"	8.00
Butter, Covered	35.00
Coaster	3.50
Cream and Sugar, Covered. Footed	7.50
Cup and Saucer	5.50
Plate. 9¼"	6.50
Platter. 13". Handled	7.50
Tumblers	
4". 9 oz.	5.00
5¼". 13 oz.	7.50
6½". 15 oz. Footed	10.00

HOMESPUN, CHILD'S

Crystal	
Dinner Set. 14 pieces $	125.00
Pink	
Cup and Saucer	28.50
Dinner Set. 14 pieces	250.00
Plate	12.50
Teapot, Lidded	75.00

HORSESHOE (NUMBER 612)
Indiana Glass Co. 1930-33

Green—Yellow	
Bowls	
4½"	$ 7.50
7½"	8.50
10½". Oval	15.00
Cream and Sugar, Open	13.50
Cup and Saucer	8.00
Pitcher. 8½". 64 oz.	200.00
Plates	
8½"	5.00
10½"	12.50
10½". Grill	9.00
11¾". Sandwich	7.00
Sherbet	6.50
Tumblers, Footed	
9 oz.	8.50
12 oz.	50.00

IRIS (IRIS AND HERRINGBONE)
Jeannette Glass Co. 1928-32

Crystal	
Bowls	
5"	$ 8.50
8"	17.50
11½". Ruffled	7.50
Butter, Covered	25.00
*Candy, Covered	40.00
Coaster. (Rare)	25.00
Cream and Sugar, Covered	12.00
Cup and Saucer	8.00
Plates	
5½"	2.50
7"	18.50
9"	15.00
11¾". Sandwich	7.00
Tumblers	
4". Flat. PAT	18.50
6". Footed	8.50
7". Footed	10.00
*Vase. 9"	10.00
Iridescent	
Bowls	
4½"	3.75
8"	8.00
Butter, Covered	30.00
Plate. 9"	10.00

LACE EDGE (OPEN EDGE)
Hocking Glass Co. 1935-38

Pink	
Bowls	
6½"	$ 6.50
7¾"	7.50
9½"	7.00
Butter, Covered	30.00
Compote, Covered	18.50
Cream and Sugar	17.50
Cup and Saucer	12.00
Plates	
8¾"	5.50
10½". Grill	6.50
Platter. 13¾". Divided	10.00
Tumbler, Footed. 5". 10 oz.	18.50

MANHATTAN (HORIZONTAL RIBBED)
Anchor Hocking Glass Co. 1939-41

Crystal — Pink	
Ashtray. 4"	$ 5.50
Bowls	
5½". Handled	2.25
7½"	5.00
9"	6.50
Cream and Sugar	7.00
Cup and Saucer	4.00
Compote. 5¾"	3.00
Plates	
6"	2.00
10¼"	5.50
Relish. 14". 5-part	7.50

MISS AMERICA
Hocking Glass Co. 1933-37

Crystal	
Bowls	
6¼"	$ 5.00
10". Oval	7.00
Cream and Sugar	10.00
Cup and Saucer	7.50
Pitcher. 8". 65 oz.	50.00
Plates	
8½"	5.00
10½"	7.00
12". Oval	6.50
*Salt and Pepper. Pair	20.00
Sherbet	6.00
Tumbler. 4½". 10 oz.	10.00
Pink	
Bowls	
8". Curved top	32.50
10". Oval	10.00
*Butter, Covered	350.00
Celery. Flat	7.00
Cream and Sugar	12.50
Goblet. 5½"	25.00
Pitcher. 8". 65 oz.	75.00
Plate. 10½"	12.50
Sherbet	8.00
Tumbler. 4½". 10 oz.	22.50

MODERNTONE (WEDDING BAND)
Hazel Atlas Glass Co. 1934-42

Amethyst—Cobalt	
Bowls	
4¾"	$ 5.50
8¾"	14.50
Cream and Sugar, Open	7.50
Cup and Saucer	6.00
Custard	6.00
Plates	
6¾"	4.50

9″ 6.00
10½″. Server 10.00
Salt and Pepper. Pair 17.50
Sherbet 4.50

Platonite (Fire-on-Colors)
Bowls
4¾″ 3.50
8¾″ 4.50
Cream and Sugar 5.00
Cup and Saucer 3.00
Plates
6¾″ 1.50
9″ 2.25
11″. Oval 4.00
Salt and Pepper. Pair 10.00
Tumblers
5 oz. 2.25
12 oz. 3.50

PATRICIAN (SPOKE)
Federal Glass Co. 1933-37

Amber—Crystal
Bowl. 6″ .... $ 7.50
Butter. Covered 50.00
Cookie Jar. Covered 32.50
Cream and Sugar, Open 8.50
Cup and Saucer 8.50
Pitcher. 8″. 75 oz. 50.00
Plate. 10½″. Grill 5.00
Sherbet 4.00
Tumbler. 4½″. 9 oz. 12.50

Green
Bowl. 6″ 12.50
Cream and Sugar, Open 11.50
Plate. 7¼″ 7.50
Salt and Pepper. Pair 38.50
Sherbet 7.50

Pink
Bowls
8½″ 13.50
12″. Oval 15.00
Butter, Covered 225.00
Cream and Sugar 12.00
Cup and Saucer 9.50
Pitcher. 8″. 75 oz. 95.00
Plates
7¼″ 9.00
10½″ 22.50
Tumblers
4″. 5 oz. 14.00
5¼″. 8 oz. Footed 40.00

PRINCESS
Hocking Glass Co. 1931-35

Amber—Green—Pink—Yellow
Bowls
4½″ .... $ 7.00
9″ 13.50
Cream and Sugar 15.00
Cup and Saucer 5.50
Plates
9½″. Grill 6.50
11½″. Server 6.50
Relish. 7½″. Divided 9.50
Sherbet 7.50
Tumbler. 5¼″. 12 oz. 15.00

RING (BANDED RINGS)
Hocking Glass Co. 1927-32

Crystal
Bowls
5″ .... $ 1.50
8″ 2.75
Cream and Sugar, Open 5.00
Cup and Saucer 2.75
Goblet. 7½″. 9 oz. 6.50
Pitcher. 8″. 60 oz 9.50
Plate. 8″ 1.25
Tumbler. 4¼″. 9 oz. 2.50

Green—Decorated
Bowls
5″ 2.75
8″ 4.00
Cream and Sugar 6.50
Cup and Saucer 5.00
Decanter. Stoppered 18.50
Ice Bucket 10.00
Pitcher. 8½″. 80 oz. 15.00
Plates
6¼″ 1.75
8″ 2.25
Sherbet. 4¾″ 4.50
Tumbler. 4¼″. 9 oz. 3.50

ROYAL LACE
Hazel Atlas Glass Co. 1934-41

Cobalt
Bowl. 10″. 3-footed. Straight edge .... $ 27.50
Cookie Jar, Covered 85.00
Cup and Saucer 18.00
Pitcher. 8½″. 96 oz. 125.00
Plate. 10″ 15.00
Platter. 13″ 27.50
Salt and Pepper. Pair 125.00

Crystal—Pink
Butter, Covered 100.00
Candlesticks. Ruffled. Pair 20.00
Creamer 6.50
Cup and Saucer 7.00
Pitcher. 8″. 68 oz. 30.00
Plate. 10″ 5.50
Soup, Cream. 4¾″ 6.50
Tumbler. 4″. 9 oz. 8.50

Green
Bowl. 10″. 3-footed. Ruffled edge 25.00
Cookie Jar, Covered 32.50
Creamer 8.00
Cup and Saucer 9.50
Nut Dish 50.00

Plate. 8½"	6.50
Sherbet	12.50
Tumbler. 4". 9 oz.	15.00

ROYAL RUBY
Anchor Hocking Glass Co. 1939-60's.
(reissued, 1977)

Green—Red	
Ashtray. 4½". Square	$ 2.75
Bowls	
4¼"	3.50
8½"	10.00
Cream and Sugar. Flat	8.50
Cream and Sugar. Footed	12.50
Cup and Saucer	5.00
Goblet	6.50
Pitcher. 42 oz.	19.50
Plates	
6½"	2.00
9¼"	6.00
Punch Set. 14 pieces	75.00
Rose Bowl. 4"	5.00
Tumblers	
9 oz.	4.50
13 oz.	5.50
Vase. 6½". Bulbous	7.50

SHARON (CABBAGE ROSE)
Federal Glass Co. 1935-39

Amber	
Bowls	
5". Cream soup	$ 10.00
10½"	12.50
Butter, Covered	35.00
Cream and Sugar, Covered	18.50
Cup and Saucer	6.00
Jam 7½"	15.00
Pitcher. 80 oz.	50.00
Plates	
6"	2.25
9½"	4.50
Platter. 12½"	6.50
Salt and Pepper. Pair	25.00
Tumbler, Footed. 6½". 15 oz.	25.00
Green	
Bowl. 9½". Oval	12.00
*Butter, Covered	60.00
Pitcher. 80 oz.	325.00
Plate. 9½"	8.50
Platter. 12½"	10.00
Sherbet	18.00
Tumbler, Footed. 6½". 15 oz.	65.00
Pink	
Bowls	
5"	5.00
8½"	6.00
10½"	13.50
*Butter, Covered	35.00
Cream and Sugar, Covered	22.50
Cup and Saucer	6.00
Plates	
6"	2.50
9½"	7.50
11½". Cake	17.50
Salt and Pepper. Pair	32.50
Sherbet	7.00
Tumblers	
4". 9 oz.	15.00
5¼". 12 oz.	18.50
6½". Footed. 15 oz.	22.50

STRAWBERRY
Jenkins Glass Co. 1929-30

Crystal—Green—Pink	
Bowls	
4"	$ 6.50
7½". Deep	12.50
Butter. Covered	100.00
Cream and Sugar, Covered. Large	30.00
Cream and Sugar, Open. Small	18.50
Pitcher. 8"	95.00
Plate. 7½"	6.50
Sherbet	5.50
Tumbler. 3½". 9 oz.	15.00

TEA ROOM
Indiana Glass Co. 1929-31

Crystal—Pink	
Bowls	
7½"	$ 6.00
8¾". Deep	20.00
9½". Oval	30.00
Candlesticks. Low. Pair	22.50
Cream and Sugar on tray	25.00
Cup and Saucer	16.50
Goblet. 9 oz.	16.50
Ice Bucket	25.00
Parfait	5.00
Plates	
6½"	6.50
8¼"	12.50
10½". Handled	15.00
Relish. Divided	6.50
Vases	
9"	13.50
11". Straight	20.00
Green	
Banana Split	15.00
Bowls	
7½"	8.50
9½". Oval	38.50
Cream and Sugar. Square	17.50
Cup and Saucer	20.00
Goblet. 9 oz.	22.00
Pitcher. 64 oz.	85.00
Plates	
6½"	8.50
8¼"	16.50
Salt and Pepper. Pair	35.00
Tumblers	
6 oz. Footed	15.00
8 oz.	25.00

WINDSOR (WINDSOR DIAMOND)
Jeannette Glass Co. 1936-46

Crystal	
Butter, Covered	$ 22.50
Candlesticks. 3". Pair	12.00
Coasters. 3¼". Set of 4	7.50
Pitchers	
4½". 16 oz.	6.50
6¾". 52 oz.	10.00
Plates	
7"	2.00
9"	3.75
Salt and Pepper. Pair	12.50
Trays	
4". Square	3.50
8x10"	7.50
Tumbler, Footed. 4"	6.50
Green	
Ashtray. 5¾". Round	25.00
Bowls	
5½"	6.00
7x11¾". Oval	20.00
Cream and Sugar. Covered	16.50
Cup	5.00
Plates	
6"	2.50
9"	6.50
13½". Cake	8.50
Pink	
Bowls	
4¾"	3.50
8½"	6.00
12½"	15.00
Butter, Covered	30.00
Cream and Sugar, Covered	12.50
Pitcher. 6¾". 52 oz.	20.00
Plates	
7"	5.50
10¼". Handled	6.50
Platter. 11½"	8.00
Tumbler. 4". 9 oz.	5.50

*Reproduced Item

DESIGN SPATTERWARE

Design Spatterware marks the transition period that bridged Spatterware and Spongeware. Early examples are often confused with Spongeware because they are similar to some degree. The earliest patterns were carefully arranged and generally covered the entire piece. In the next period of this ware, various motifs were created . . .such as a decorated border with a tulip in the center. In the 1850's, Elsmore and Foster in England created the noted Holly Leaf pattern in red and green, and also in purple and green . . .blue bands divide the primary motif arranged in broader bands. Design Spatterware progressed to more definitive designs and finally was limited to only floral . . .much of this type is attributed to Adams. Design Spatterware is primarily in blue. Modes of decoration were applied in several ways, including the so-called 'cut sponge.' Some were hand painted; while other pieces were transferred in an endless variety of colors and designs.

Platter. 16". "Holly Leaf.' Purple and green. Elsmore and Foster. C. 1855 .... $275.00

Bowls	
Earthenware. Heavy. Greens and ochre. Large	$ 245.00
Rainbow. Blue and red. Small	150.00
Serrated Rim. Blue, white, black. 9½". Rare	250.00
Tulip and Pretzels. Small. Damaged	95.00
Butter, Covered. Holly Leaf. Lion finial. Drain	250.00
Charger. 15". Elaboration of Adam's Rose	180.00
Cups and Saucers	
Adam's Rose. Red rosette border	185.00
Blue	185.00
Poppies. Red, blue and green. Mush	145.00
Red	225.00
Jugs	
Diamonds and bands. Blue. Very early form. 5¾"	165.00
Geometric design. Red, green and brown. 4"	65.00
Leaf. Green. Early form. 5½". Damaged	95.00
Rosettes. Blue. Rare barrel-shaped. Fern prongs. 7". Repaired	125.00
Tulip. Blue. 3⅞"	165.00
Mugs	
Blue and Purple. Large	110.00
Holly Leaf. Red and green	65.00
Rosettes. Blue. Green bands	72.00
Tree. Blue	65.00

Plates
- Colombine with Rose Bud and Thistle. 8½". Green. Rosette border 165.00
- Holly Leaf. 8¾". Red and green. Elsmore and Foster 92.00
- Peony. 8¾". Red and green 125.00
- Tree border. 8¾". Red flowers, green leaves 75.00
- Tulip. 8½". Blue 225.00

Plate, Soup. Six tulips in 6 pointed star. Red, blue and purple 155.00

Platters
- Dragoon and Awkward Squads. Red. 14" 185.00
- Holly Leaf. Red and green. Elsmore and Foster. 12" 185.00
- Holly Leaf. Red and green. Elsmore and Foster. 16" 225.00

Sugars
- Large. Red and green 85.00
- Small. Red and green 65.00

Teapot. Blue. Early form. Repaired 265.00

DOLL AND DOLL HOUSE FURNITURE

Although most doll furniture of the past was of primitive construction made by a doting relative; exquisitely detailed furniture was also made. These fine examples are sometimes placed in the category of salesman's samples or miniatures of a cabinetmaker's skill.

Doll houses are primarily enjoyed by children; but it was not unusual for Victorian ladies to exhibit their artistic abilities by furnishing a 'second' home on a small scale.

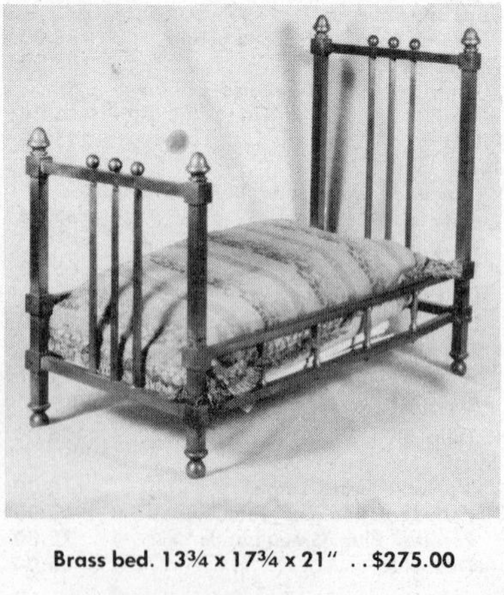

Brass bed. 13¾ x 17¾ x 21" . . $275.00

Beds
- Biedermeier-style. 3¾ x7¼" . . $ 250.00
- Brass. 19 x 29½". Complete with springs, mattress and bolster 275.00
- Cannon Ball. 8" long. Maple. Rope mattress. C. 1890 .... 30.00
- Canopy. 10½ x 15 x 18". Metal .. 40.00
- Empire. 7½ x 8 x 16". Pine. Straw mattress. C. 1870 .... 85.00
- Poster, High. 7½ x 22 x 31". Mahogany 95.00
- Poster, Low. 12½ x 22". Walnut. Scrolled headboard. Blanket roll footboard 75.00
- Victorian. 14½ x 21 x 26". Walnut. Carved flowers 60.00

Bedroom Sets
- 3-pieces. Bed, dresser, rocker. Cast iron. "Arcade." 65.00
- 3-pieces. Bed, dresser, vanity. Painted wood. C. 1920 .... 50.00
- 6-pieces. 1" scale. Two beds, stand with mirror, table, 2 chairs. Metal 125.00

Cabinet, China. 4 x 8 x 11½". Oak. Mirrored back shelves. Glass doors 50.00

Carriages
- Bentwood. 13 x 23 x 26". Stroller-type. Spindled back, arms. Wooden wheels 100.00
- Wicker. Stroller-type. Wooden and wire wheels 125.00
- Wicker. 12 x 21". Wooden wheels 85.00

Chairs
- Arm. 10¼" high. Adirondack fan back. Painted 35.00
- Biedermeier-style. 2 x 4" high .. 50.00
- High Chair. 15" high. Pine. C. 1890 .... 35.00
- Ice Cream Parlor. 5" high. Heart back 15.00
- Rocker. 16" high. Pine. Rush seat 40.00
- Rocker. 17" high. Wicker. Upholstered seat 50.00

Chests
- Curly Maple. 13½ x 15". Two tier top, 3 drawer base. Applied molding. Bracket feet. Pa. C. 1800 375.00
- Oak. 4 x 7 x 9½". Three drawers, wooden pulls 45.00
- Pine. 4 x 5 x 6¾". Three drawers. Carved acorn and leaf pulls. Arched bracket feet 75.00
- Pine. 5 x 7¾ x 8". Three drawers. Bootjack ends. Coped backboard. Chamfered drawers. C. 1870 .... 65.00
- Pine. 13x 20". Hand cut nail construction. New England. C. 1800 150.00
- Walnut. 5½ x 8 x 8¾". Two drawers over 3 long drawers. Oval swivel mirror. Victorian. 75.00

Cradles

Painted. 10 x 11½ x 20". Spindled swinging-type. Original mattress. C. 1880 .... 75.00

Pine. 1 x 3". 3" rockers 10.00

Pine. 9x 18". Dovetailed construction. Natural finish. New England. C. 1880 .... 95.00

Pine. 23½" long. Bonnet-type .. 75.00

Walnut. 10¼ x 25". Slat rails, 4 posters with turned finials. Victorian........................ 75.00

Wicker. 10 x 19". Original mattress, pillow 50.00

Crib. 10 x 16". Wicker 50.00

Cupboard. 15¾ x 28½" high. Painted pine. Step back-type. 2 glazed doors above 2 drawers. Bracket feet. C. 1800................. 250.00

Dining Room Set. 4-pieces. Table 3 x6", chairs 4". Sideboard. Victorian styling. Walnut. Marble tops. Upholstered chairs 150.00

Fireplace. 2¾ x 3 x 5". Pine mantel. Hearth opening 25.00

Ice Cream Parlor Set. 3½" table, 2 heart-shaped chairs with wire mesh seats. C. 1890............ 45.00

Rugs

Braided. 4 x 5" 15.00

Needlepoint. 3½" diam. Scenic .. 20.00

Sled. 3 x 5 x 11" long. Wooden runners. All original. C. 1890 ...... 50.00

Sofa. 3¾ x 7" long. Biedermeier-style 195.00

Spinning Wheel. 4¼" high. Pine. C. 1940 .... 10.00

Stove. 3½ x 4½ x 5½". Cast iron. 3-lids. "Eagle." 75.00

Tables

Cast Iron. 3 x 4". Empire-style.... 35.00

Chestnut. 7½ x 12 x 16½" top. Drop leaf. Swivel top 150.00

Pine. 10 x 15". Turned legs. C. 1880 .... 50.00

Poplar and Maple. 6 x 6 x 10". Drop leaf. Turned legs 65.00

Trunks

5 x 5 x 7". Wooden, dome top. Lithographed paper covering. Tin hinges 28.50

9x 9 x 16". Embossed tin covering over wood. Lift-out tray 45.00

10 x 12 x 21". Wooden. Steamer-type with hangers. C. 1920....... 60.00

DOLLS

Dolls have existed as children's play toys as well as important figurines in the ceremonies of life; in all cultures from pre-historic times. The earliest known examples date to the Babylonians, 3000 B.C.

From the 14th through the 18th century doll making was centered in Europe; namely Germany and France. French dolls were not **primarily play toys; but were elaborately dressed in the latest fashions for milady's approval** of couturiers' designs. All these early dolls had one thing in common . . .they represented adults. It was not until the mid-19th century that the child or baby doll was introduced in England. At this time, the famous Jumeau with swivel head and sawdust-filled kid body had its beginning in France. The Bye-Lo, designed by Grace S. Putnam, was born in the 20th century and was made by firms in Germany and the United States. Doll making in the United States began to flourish in the 1900's with names like Horsman, Effanbee, Alexander, Ideal and others.

Collecting antique dolls is an exciting, educational and rewarding experience . . .a defined artistic category all its own.

Effanbee. Suzanne. 13½" high. Complete with 4 outfits, suit case and bracelet $150.00

A.M.

Boy. 23". Molded hair. Blue sleep eyes. Original dress and bonnet $ 325.00

Character. 18". Sleep eyes, open mouth, wig. Dressed. #985 ...... 450.00

Child. 37". Bisque head. Kid body, ball-jointed, wig. Dressed 950.00

Dream Baby. 12". Blue sleep eyes, closed mouth 300.00

Googly. 9". Toddler, blue glass eyes. #323 .... 650.00
Lady. 12½". Painted bisque head. Composition body. Dressed 500.00
Queen Louise. 27". Blue sleep eyes, human hair wig, jointed body, original lashes. White dress 300.00

ABG
Character. 14". Bisque head, open mouth, sleep eyes. Suitably dressed 195.00
Child. 32". Marked and numbered 450.00
Floradora. 19". Bisque head, ball-jointed body. Blue sleep eyes 195.00

Alexander
Alice in Wonderland. 16". All cloth. C. 1923 .... 375.00
Brenda Starr. All original, boxed. C. 1970 .... 75.00
Butch. 11". Dressed. C. 1940 .... 145.00
Jenny Lind. C. 1969 .... 375.00
Kate Greenaway. 15". C. 1942 .. 200.00
Little Women. 15" 95.00
Madame Pompadour. All original, boxed. C. 1970 .... 375.00
McGuffey, Anna. 15". Mint condition. C. 1936 .... 125.00
Nationality. 8" 30.00
Scarlet O'Hara. 21". Composition jointed body, black wig, green sleep eyes. Dressed in green gown. C. 1937 .... 195.00
Sonja Henie. 14". Human hair wig. Original clothes including shoe skates. C. 1939 .... 175.00
Wendy Ann. 13½". Human hair wig. Dressed including hat 125.00

Belton
12". Brown paperweight eyes. Schmitt-type body 475.00
18". Blue paperweight eyes, closed mouth, pierced ears. Human hair wig. Dressed 750.00

Black
9". Topsy Turvy. All composition, jointed body, three yarn tufts. Unmarked. C. 1940 .... 50.00
15". Campbell Kid. Boy, head and arms composition, molded hair, cloth body. All original clothing. Horsman. C. 1912 .... 95.00
18". Toddler. Composition, jointed body, molded hair, painted eyes. Dressed. Unmarked 60.00
24". Biskoline. Glass sleep eyes, jointed body. Dressed 225.00
Betty Boop. 12". Black dress, wood jointed. Cameo Doll Products Co. C. 1932 .... 275.00

Bru
13". Bisque head, shoulders, limbs, kid body, paperweight eyes, human hair wig. Original clothes plus hat. Marked 2500.00
13". Bisque head, kid body, wood and bisque limbs. All original. Marked .... 3500.00+

Bye-Lo
4". All bisque, painted eyes, pink shoes. Signed 285.00
4½". Bisque, glass sleep eyes, blond wig. Part of paper label on tummy. Dressed in diaper, sacque, bonnet, molded white sox and pink slippers 400.00
10". Bisque head, cloth body, rare brown eyes. Signed 225.00
13". Bisque head, cloth body, blue sleep eyes, original hands. Lace dress. Marked body 300.00

China Heads. Various German makers. C. 19th Century
Bald Head. 14-18". Dressed. Marked with black spot 750.00
Bangs. 16-18". Dressed 175.00
Low Brow. 10-15". Dressed 75.00
Pet Names. 15-20". Dressed 100.00

Effanbee
Historical. 14". "1625." All original, boxed. C. 1940 .... 195.00
Little Lady — Anne Shirley. 18". Original box. C. 1945 .... 150.00
Little Tommy Tucker. 15". Composition head and hands, cloth body. Original clothes. C. 1940 .. 75.00
Patsy Ann. 19". Sleep eyes, molded hair 135.00
Patsyette. 9". All original including bracelet 75.00
Sweetie Pie. 15". Vinyl, all original 25.00

Frozen Charlotte. 13". Blonde 295.00
French Fashion. 18". Bisque head, shoulder, kid body and arms, wired fingers, human hair wig. Dressed. Unmarked 850.00
Fulper. 18". Girl. Toddler, jointed composition body, blue sleep eyes, human hair wig. Marked head 350.00

Heubach
Automaton. 10". Bisque head, painted features, open mouth with 2 molded teeth. Wooden carved body with wooden skis, metal poles. Original clothes 325.00
Character. 10½". Bent-limb body, blue intaglio eyes, molded hair. Dressed in white silk. Marked in square or sunburst. 300.00
Chin Chin. 4". Labeled 150.00
Gypsy. 10". Koppelsdorf 452 .... 300.00

Ideal. Deanna Durbin. 18" $175.00

Piano Baby. Bisque. 11½" high. Signed $425.00

Horsman
- Campbell Kid. 12". Girl. All composition. C. 1948 .... 150.00
- Poor Pitiful Pearl. 17" 35.00

Ideal
- Dianna Durbin. 14". Original sleep eyes and clothes 185.00
- Betsy McCall. 7½". Dark hair with barrettes. Original clothes. Boxed 35.00
- Pinocchio. 8". Composition, fully jointed, molded hat. Marked Ideal for Walt Disney 50.00
- Pinocchio. 12". All wood, jointed 150.00
- Shirley Temple. 13". Composition. All original clothes 175.00+
- Shirley Temple. 19". Vinyl, rooted hair, flirty eyes, jointed body. Original clothes 55.00
- Shirley Temple. 22". Composition. Dressed in all original sailor suit. (Capt. January) 350.00
- Shirley Temple. 27". Composition. All original 400.00

Jumeau
- Bebe. 17". Bisque head, stationary eyes, closed mouth, jointed composition body. Dressed 1800.00
- DEP. 23½". Bisque head, blue sleep eyes, pierced ears, open mouth, brown human hair wig, composition body. Dressed. Marked 750.00
- Fashion. 18". Bisque head and shoulder plate, swivel neck, blue paperweight eyes, original blonde human hair wig and earrings. Gusset jointed kid body. Marked....................... 850.00

Kestner
- 4". Celluloid, blonde hair, jointed, closed mouth, Dressed. Turtle mark 35.00
- 12½". Fully jointed composition body, blue sleep eyes, open mouth, original blonde wig. Dressed in long baby dress, undies, cap. #167 .... 225.00

14". Century baby, laughing face. Head marked. C. 1925 .... 425.00
14". Character baby, gray sleep eyes, molded tongue, light brown human hair wig. #152 .... 295.00
16".Sammy. Original curly wig, brown sleep eyes. #211 .... 350.00
17". Character baby, molded head, open mouth. #151 ...... 375.00
18". Boy, brown sleep eyes, open mouth, human hair wig. All original costume and underwear 275.00
30". Child, jointed composition body, original mohair wig, sleep eyes, open mouth. Old lace dress and undies 450.00

K-R
Baby. 19". Head circum. 14", blue intaglio eyes. Old long dress. #126 .... 500.00
Baby. 25". Blue sleep eyes. Christening gown. #126 .... 550.00
Baby Bumps. 12". Composition. All original. C. 1919-21 .... 100.00
Character. 13". Composition body, original mohair wig. #114 1450.00
Toddler. 22". Brown flirt eyes, ball-jointed BJ body. #126 ...... 500.00

MacArthur, Gen. 18". Composition. Freudnlich Novelty Corp., N.Y. C. 1940 .... 95.00

Paper Dolls, Uncut
Rosemary Clooney. C. 1955 .... 15.00
Dell. With 7 articles of clothing, full color. Feb. 1921 Delineator Magazine 7.50
Forbes Paper Doll. 8''. Lithographed. Boston Sunday Globe. C. 1895 .... 15.00
Betty Grable. C. 1940 .... 25.00
Raphael Tuck. 10", complete with 4 changes. Artist series. C. 1894 .. 95.00

Penny. 10". All wood. Carved head, painted hair, eyes. Jointed body. C. 1910 .... 50.00

Papier Mache. 14". Head. limbs, cloth body, blue paperweight eyes, original blonde wig. Dressed in white gauze chemise and bloomers 195.00

Parian. 24". Blonde molded hair, glass eyes, swivel neck, kid body. Dressed 400.00

Piano Babies. Also see "Bisque"
4" Sitting, White night shirt. Signed Heubach 100.00
7" long. Reclining. Heubach 150.00
10" long. Lying on stomach hugging a pug dog. Bisque. Unmarked 165.00

Simon & Halbig. 29" high. Bisque head, sleep eyes, open mouth, pierced ears. All original except clothing ..$750.00

Pincushion
2½". Blonde hair girl, white bonnet. Holding flowers in hand. Arms away from body. High gloss finish. Germany 95.00
3". Dutch dress. Holding ball of yarn in hand and the rest on arm. Heubach 95.00
4¾". Gray hair. One arm raised. Germany. #5022 .... 30.00
5". Flapper 125.00

Rag
Boy. 13". Printed cloth face. Original blue jumper suit. C. 1890 25.00
Cat. 12". Printed cloth. Dressed like a person. C. 1920 .... 35.00
Mary Had a Little Lamb. 12½". Kelloggs 40.00
Topsy Turvy. 12½". Hand sewn facial features, cotton hair. One doll is blonde, opposite is black .. 37.50
Uncle Wiggley and Nurse Jane. 13". Pair 80.00

SFBJ
Character. 18". Toddler body,

bisque head, composition body, brown eyes. #251 .... 1250.00
Child. 20". Bisque, brown glass sleep eyes, original brown human hair wig, pierced ears, open mouth with teeth. Good composition jointed body, jointed wrists. Dressed. #301 .... 600.00

Schoenhut. See "Schoenhut"

Simon & Halbig
Automaton. Manivelle. 5 figures, two playing stringed instruments, three dancing pirouettes in front. 1500.00
Child. 15". Girl, composition jointed body. #1279 .... 595.00
Lady. 20". Blue sleep eyes, open mouth, pierced ears. Original wig and clothes. #1159. C. 1911 .... 950.00
Little Women-type. 13". #1160 .. 250.00
Oriental. 13¼". Brown eyes, black wig. Costumed. #1329 .... 950.00
Santa. 24". #1249. C. 1900 .... 350.00

Steiner, J.
14". Blue eyes with eyelashes, open mouth, teeth, original blonde mohair wig. All original clothing. Working mama and papa strings. Signed Le Parisien, Paris A78 .... 1850.00
23". Closed mouth, paperweight blue eyes, solid wrists 2500.00
Terri Lee. 16". Hard plastic. Terri Lee Sales Corp. C. 1950-60 ...... 95.00

Three-Face. 12". Bisque head, composition limbs, cloth body. Dressed. Carl Bergner, Germany. Early 20th century 950.00

Vogue
Ginnette, Baby. All original. Complete with bed 35.00
Ginny. 8". All composition, painted eyes, mohair wig, Dressed. Non-walker 50.00
Ginny. 8". Hard plastic, brown hair. Original clothes. Walker 40.00

Wax. 22". Pierotti-type. Cloth body. Suitably dressed. Unmarked. C. 1850 .... 275.00

Wax over composition. 15". Blonde mohair wig, blue sleep eyes. C. 1860 .... 125.00

DOOR KNOCKERS

Before the advent of the mechanical bell, electric buzzer or chimes; a door knocker was considered an essential door ornament to announce the arrival of visitors. Metal was used to cast or forge the various forms.

Brass
Anchor. 4½" long ....$ 30.00
Fox head. 4½ x 7" 50.00

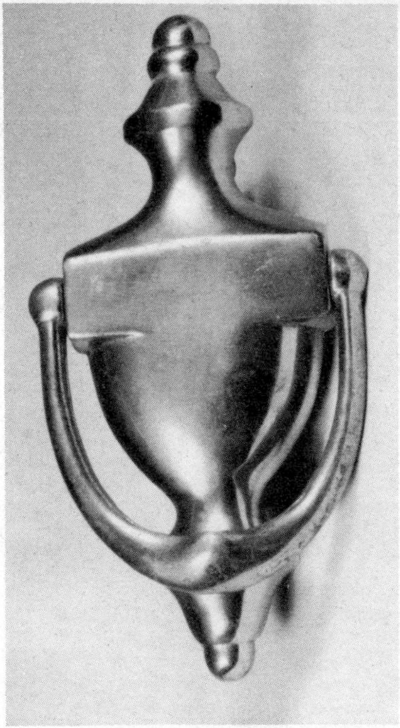

Brass. 7" long. Urn-shaped $25.00

Grapes. 5 x7" 35.00
Hand, holding ball 50.00
Hand with ball and striker 60.00
Lion's head. 4½ x 7" 50.00
William Wordsworth. 2½", with 3" backplate. England 30.00

Bronze
5". Hand with ruffled sleeve 85.00
8". Ship and anchor 100.00

Charles Dickens 85.00
Elephant and Castle 65.00
Grecian Bust 65.00

Iron
Gloved hand 25.00
Hand, holding ball. 2½ x 5½". Original black painted finish. Striker button 35.00
Horseshoe and hammer 28.50
Imp. 1¼ x 3". Bronzed 20.00
Parrot. 2½ x 3¼" 25.00
Spur 30.00
"Trusty Servant." 3¼" 30.00

DOOR STOPS

As the name indicates, door stops were and are used to hold doors in a desired position. They were usually made of cast iron.

Kittens. 7¼" high. Cast iron $35.00

Aunt Jemima. 10" high. Painted . . $	60.00
Cats	
6" high. Painted black	20.00
8½" high. Full figure. Painted black. Green eyes	35.00
9½" high. Tiger, gray	35.00
Child, Female. 6" high	15.00
Cockatoo. 7" high	25.00
Cornucopia. 11" high. With flowers	35.00
Court Jester and Dog. 12" high	45.00
Dogs	
Boxer. 7½". Clipped ears and tail. Brown	35.00
Bulldog. 9x 10½"	40.00
Fox Terrier. 8 x 9½"	28.50
German Shepherd. 13 x 14". Marked Davison Co	45.00
Pointer. 9"	35.00
Scottie. 8"	32.50
Setter. 15" long	45.00
Spaniel. 10½" long	40.00
Eagle. 16" high	50.00
Elephant. 8" long. Painted red	25.00
Flower in Basket. 8" high	28.50
Flowers in Basket. 8". Brass	65.00
Fox, Sleeping. 8" long. Brass	75.00
Frog. 4". Bronze	85.00
Horses	
7¾ x 8½". Black with red saddle	35.00
9 x 10". Saddled with stirrups, head down. Bronzed iron	40.00
Indian with spear on horse. 5½ x 6¼". Four pounds	75.00
Kittens. 7¼" high. Painted yellow with blue ribbons	35.00
Lighthouse. 13". Nine pounds	60.00
Little Red Riding Hood and Wolf. 8" high. Painted	30.00
Parrot. 8¼". Blue, red and yellow . .	30.00
Punch. 12" high	85.00
Rabbit. 10" high	30.00
Snooper. 13½" high	55.00
Squirrel. 6" high	35.00
Sunbonnet Girl. 6" high	35.00
Union Civil War Officer. 7½" high . .	45.00
Wagon, Conestoga. 7" high	40.00
Windmill. 7" high	35.00

DORCHESTER POTTERY

George Henderson founded the Dorchester Pottery Works near Boston, Massachusetts in 1895. At first, bean pots, jugs, jars and industrial containers . . .all of stoneware, were produced. In 1940, a line of decorated pottery in blue and white made from New Jersey clay was introduced. Some of the patterns are: "Blueberry", "Colonial Lace", "Pinecone", "Pussy Willow" and "Scroll".

Since 1940, the potters and decorators sign each piece and the name Dorchester is on each example. This helps dating for collectors . . .as most earlier wares are marked with the name of the company only.

The pottery is still in operation today using the traditional methods of production to maintain the high quality of Dorchester. The stoneware is available only at the pottery . . .it is never shipped or sold in other commercial outlets.

Bowls	
5½x 11 x 13". Shell-shaped. Three scalloped feet . . . .$	175.00
5¾, 2" deep. "Scroll." Artist signed	50.00
Creamers and Sugars	
"Colonial Lace. "Creamer 3" high, sugar 3½" high. Artist signed. Set	95.00
"Scroll. " 3" high with underplates, 4¾" diam. Artist signed. Set	150.00
Crock, Covered. 10" high. Signed Dorchester	65.00
Cups and Saucers, Coffee	
"Grape."	30.00
"Scroll."	50.00
Cups and Saucers, Demi	
"Blueberry."	40.00
"Pussy Willow."	50.00

Foot Warmer. 4 x6 x 10¾". Jug-shaped. Brass screw cap. Impressed Dorchester 125.00

Mugs. 4" high

"Pear." 45.00

"Stripes and Codfish." 50.00

Pitcher. 9". Batter-type. Signed Dorchester 85.00

Plates

"Blueberry." 8" 60.00

"Blueberry." 10" 75.00

"Scroll." 10½". Artist signed 95.00

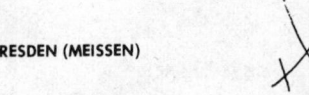

DRESDEN (MEISSEN)

In 1710; Johann Frederick Boettger, an alchemist, accidentally discovered a white clay in the area of Dresden, Germany. When he replaced his red stoneware pots with the white kaolin clay product, he produced the first true porcelain in Europe; and Meissen Porcelain Works had its beginning.

Meissen porcelain is finely molded, decorated with applied floral motifs, enameled and gilted. In the 19th century, the factory reissued versions of their earlier examples. These debased wares are referred to as Dresden to differentiate them from the original Meissen porcelains.

Many marks were used to identify the porcelain. The first was a pseudo-oriental mark in a square. In 1724, the famous crossed swords mark was adopted. The crossed swords mark with a small dot between the hilts was used in the 1763-1774 period. The following years, 1774 to 1814, the dot between the hilts was changed to a star. It has been reported that two new marks are appearing on the modern market ...swords with a hammer and sickle and swords with a crown.

Basket. 1½ x 4". White latticed work. Applied flowers ....$ 65.00

Bowls

6x8". Swan head handles. Garden scene. Pale blue, pink. Gold trim 125.00

9½". White ground. Multicolored floral decor. Gold trim. C. 1860 .. 125.00

12". Shallow. Scenic and floral reserves. Gold trim 175.00

Box. 3½ x 3½ x 5½". Floral decor .. 300.00

Candelabra. 19½" high. 5-lite. Figures of boy and girl. Applied flowers 650.00

Candlesticks. 10". Boy and girl. Applied florals. C. 1900. Pair 450.00

Console Set. Candleabras, 3-lite 10", bowl. 10" diam. Applied florals, cupids. 3-pieces 650.00

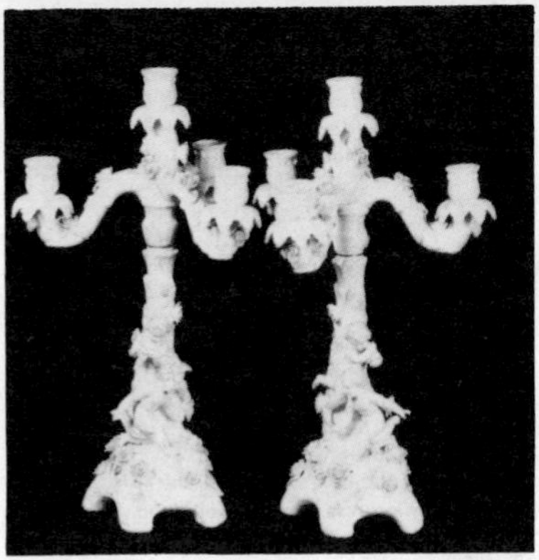

Candelabras. 17" high. 4-lite. Applied pink roses and white cherubs. Crossed swords mark. Pair $750.00

Cups and Saucers

Demitasse. Fluted, multicolored flowers. Gold trim 65.00

Tea. Floral decor on white. Gold trim 75.00

Figurines

Ballerina. 4" 95.00

Ballerina. 7" 175.00

Ballerina. 3 x 8". Volkstedt mark 375.00

Cupid Performing Wedding. 8". #2452. C. 1860 .... 950.00

Drunken Silinus. 8". #2724...... 950.00

Europa and the Bull. 6 x12" 750.00

Gentleman, Colonial. 6½" 400.00

Monika. 5½" 175.00

Monkey Band. 5". Sitzendorf 495.00

Peasant Girl. 5¾" 325.00

Slight on Vanity. 6". C. 1850 .... 600.00

Tea Party. 5 x 7". Volkstedt mark 600.00

Warbler. 7" 135.00

Frames

3½x5". Double portrait frames. Applied flowers. Heavy gold border 150.00

6½ x 9". Scalloped, floral decor on white. Gilt scrolls in relief 195.00

Lamps

5½" high, 5" base diam. Shell-shaped. Applied flowers and cupids 350.00

10" high. Applied cherubs, flowers. Multicolored 650.00

15". Mandarin figure. C. 1860 .. 275.00

Mirrors

Hand. 5½" diam. Scenic. Lavender, white violets. C. 1900 ...... 60.00

Wall. 10 x 12". Oval. Cupids. Applied flowers	375.00
Pen Holder. 2½ x 9" long. Floral decor. Gold trim	65.00
Place Card Holder. 3¾" high. Full figure of girl holding 2-tiered lace skirt	40.00
Plates	
8½". Flower center. Lattice rim	55.00
9". Basketweave rim, 4 floral reserves in shades of blue	85.00
9½". Portrait	125.00
Teapots	
5" high, 8" long. Footed. Floral decor on white. Gilted	150.00
8" high. Cobalt, white with 2 scenic medallions. Rose finial	225.00
17" high. Relief-molded hot water kettle on stand, burner. Gold and white. Late	150.00
Tea Service. Two pots, cream, sugar, 12 cups and saucers. White, cobalt. Gold trim	1250.00
Tea Set. Teapot, sugar and creamer. Floral and gold decor. Swan finial	**375.00**
Toast Rack. White and gold	75.00
Tray. 15". Floral gold decor	225.00
Vases	
5½". Floral decor on white. Scalloped tops, collared bases. Pair	200.00
7½". Turquoise. Jeweled. Portrait signed Richtner "Voluptos."	395.00
9½". Covered. Dragon handles, foo-dog finial. Multicolored birds, flowers	250.00

DUNCAN AND MILLER GLASS

The firm began in Pittsburgh, Pa. in the late 1860's, under the name of George Duncan and Sons. In 1893-94 the glass works moved to Washington, Pa. where they manufactured some of the finest handmade glassware in America for sixty-three years.

It was George Duncan, the founder, who discovered the talents of his designer, John Ernest Miller and recognized him to be the greatest asset to the company. He later became one of the owners, thus the name "Duncan and Miller" glass.

A specialty of the firm was the reproduction of the early American Sandwich Glass; but probably the most famous Miller design was "Three-face" and probably the most beautiful is the Duncan and Miller "Swan."

In 1957 the United States Glass Co. purchased the firm, including its molds, and has continued to produce Duncan-Miller products.

Ashtray. 5½". Patio, Crystal	$ 15.00

Panel. 8x16". Clear and frosted Dogwood blossoms. $20.00

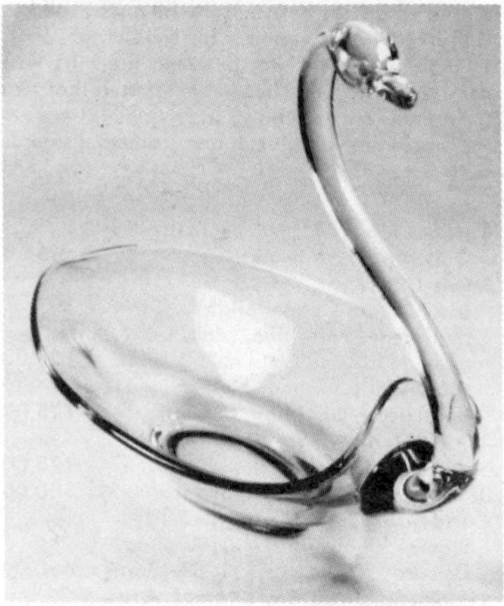

Swan, open back. 11½" long. Blue tint, crystal neck $125.00

Basket. 7¾ x 9¾". Canterbury. Crystal	35.00
Bon-Bon. 4 x7". Caribbean. Blue	42.50
Bowls	
7½" x 5½" high. Hobnail. Pink opalescent	50.00
7½" x 13" high. Wedding. Crystal. Covered	60.00
9". Morano. Chartreuse	40.00
10½" x 3" high. Canterbury. Blue opalescent	45.00
12". Hobnail. Crystal	18.50
12". Sanibel. Pink opalescent	75.00
Box. 3 x 5 x 8". Divided. Crystal with magnolia decor	35.00
Butter, Covered. Beaded Swirl. Green with gold trim	145.00
Candlelabras	
6½" high. 2-lite. Chartruese	25.00
14½" high. 3-lite, prisms. Crystal	125.00
15¼" high. 4-lite with center vase, prisms. Crystal	350.00
Candlesticks	
Hobnail. 4". Crystal	7.50
Teardrop. 5". Crystal	12.50
Champagne. Etched First Love. Crystal	15.00
Compote. 5½ x 7". Etched First Love. Crystal	40.00
Console Set. 12" bowl, pair of 4½" candlesticks. Hobnail. Opalescent pink. Set	100.00
Creamers and Sugars	
Beaded Swirl. Green with gold. Set	100.00
Sandwich. Crystal. Set	15.00
Cruet. 4". Caribbean. Crystal	18.50
Goblets, Water	
Caribbean. Crystal	10.00
First Love. Crystal	15.00
Hat. 4". Hobnail. Blue opalescent	25.00
Ivy Ball. 6" high. Hobnail. Red	45.00
Pitcher, Water. Canterbury. Crystal	25.00
Plates	
7½". Sylvan. Crystal	5.00
8". Sandwich. Crystal	8.50
8½". Sanibel, Cape Cod. Blue opalescent	25.00
13¾". Hobnail, Shell. Pink opalescent	40.00
Punch Cups	
Caribbean. Crystal with blue handle	6.50
Hobnail. Pink opalescent	10.00
Punch Set. Caribbean. Blue. 27 pieces	250.00
Relishes	
Canterbury. Pink opalescent	35.00
Caribbean. 8". Handled. Blue	15.00
First Love. Crystal	20.00
Teardrop, 5-sections	12.50
Rose Bowl. 3½" high. Canterbury. Pink opalescent	35.00
Salt and Pepper Shakers. Teepee. Crystal. Pair	28.50
Souvenir Items	
Creamer. 2⅝". Button Arches. Clambroth	18.00
Goblet. Button Arches. Clambroth	22.50
Tumbler. Button Arches. Gold flashed	25.00
Sugar Castor. 3 x 4". Quartered Block. Crystal	37.50
Swans, Open back	
5". Crystal	20.00
5½". Sylvan. Jasmine yellow opalescent	55.00
7½". Chartreuse	25.00
7½". Crystal	17.50
7½". Crystal with silver overlay	75.00
7½". Sylvan. Pink opalescent	75.00
7½". Ruby bowl	30.00
10½". Green bowl	40.00
10½". Ruby bowl	65.00
12". Ruby bowl	85.00
Swans, Solid back	
3". Crystal	22.50
5". Crystal	25.00
8". Crystal	45.00
Tumblers	
Canterbury. Cape Cod. Blue opalescent	25.00
Mardi Gras	15.00
Sandwich. 9-oz	6.50
Teardrop. 7-oz	4.50
Vases	
3½ x 4" diam. Canterbury, Cape Cod. Blue opalescent	18.50
4". Hobnail. Crystal	10.00
5x7" diam. Canterbury. Blue opalescent	32.00
7". Venetian. Blue. Crimped	25.00
7½ x 4½". diam. Caribbean. Sapphire blue. Pedestaled	22.50
10". First Love. Crystal. Footed	30.00
Whiskey. #42	12.50
Wine. #42	15.00

DURAND

Victor Durand, Sr. reputed to be a descendant of the French family which made Baccarat glass, started a factory in Vineland, New Jersey in the early 1920's.

The art glass resembles Tiffany in some respects, especially the iridescent sheen. The glass was sticker-labeled, "Durand Art Glass." Some items were marked with the letter "V" in the pontil. The factory closed in 1931.

Bowls	
4¾" diam., 2½" high. Flared rim. Gold. Signed $	300.00

Vase. 7½" high. Orange with blue leaves. Unsigned $700.00

7" diam. Shallow, blue. Signed . . 750.00
11" diam. 2" Deep blue. Vaseline colored foot 500.00
Candlesticks
3" high. Amber vase, stem. Green bobeche. "Rose of Brixton" cut into bobeche 150.00
10" high. Blue. Signed 295.00
Compote. 5¾" high. Feather. Baluster stem. Deep red 550.00
Cordial. 4½". Feather. Blue and white. Vaseline stem 250.00
Goblet. Red, gold iridescent loopings 350.00
Plate. 8". Feather 350.00
Rose Bowls
4". King Tut. Green over yellow. Signed "V" 650.00
6". Blue. Threaded 450.00
6". Gold with green leaves. Cream colored lining. Signed "V" and Durand 750.00
Vases
6". King Tut. Gold and green. Inverted rim. Signed "V", Durand and numbered 900.00
7". Pulled Feather. Peach with gold threads. Signed 650.00
7". Vine. White to ecru. Deep orange interior. Cylindrical-shaped 500.00
7¾". Blue with gold threads. Baluster-shaped. Signed "V", Durand and numbered 750.00
8½". Jack-in-the-Pulpit. Gold iridescent 550.00
9". Orange, blue threads 550.00
10". Pulled Feather. Deep red, Ovoid-shaped 600.00
10½". Inlaid silver on deep blue. Signed 1250.00
13". Deep cranberry. White Nailsea-type loopings at base. Signed "V" 1500.00
Wine. 4½". King Tut. Blue. Gold lining 375.00

END-OF-DAY GLASS

End-of-Day glass is a multicolored, mottled glass, sometimes called "spatter glass," made from about 1885 to 1905.
The name "End-of-Day" was derived from the custom of glassblowers using the remains of the day's glass from various pots and blowing or molding objects of their own fancy. Some of the glass was made commercially but was never very popular.

Vase. 8". Bulbous, slim neck. Cased glass. Applied crystal rigaree . . $85.00

Baskets

3½x5". Multicolored with clear thorn handle ....$	95.00
4½ x 6". Blue and yellow. Clear thorn handle	115.00
6½ x 7½". Orange, yellow and pink. Clear thorn handle	125.00
6x 9". Green, white, maroon. Green thorn handle	135.00
Boot. 3⅛ x 5" long. Green and white cased in crystal. Applied crystal rigaree. Opaque white lining	65.00
Bowl. 3 x 7". Multicolored. Black interior. Cased	85.00
Candlestick. 9¼". Multicolored. Cased in clear	75.00
Cracker Jar. 9" high. Cased in white, yellow, red, green. Clear thorn handle	150.00
Cup and Saucer. Demitasse. Red and green. Clear handle	85.00
Marmalade Jar. 7½". Green and blue. White casing. Silverplated frame, lid	85.00
Mug. 4¼" high. Red, yellow, green, blue. Clear glass handle	55.00

Pitchers

5". Tortoise shell coloring. Clear reeded handle	75.00
10". Brown, yellow. Cased in clear. White lining	275.00
Sugar Shaker. Pink and white. Metal top	55.00
Tumbler. Multicolored. Cased in clear	35.00

Vases

4½". Multicolored. Cobalt handles	65.00
6½". Urn-shaped. Cased in clear	75.00
8". Jack-in-the-Pulpit. Crimped ..	65.00
8½". Bulbous, slim neck, fluted top. Pink, white, clear casing	85.00
10". Yellow, pink, orange. Square top, clear glass crimped edge. Cased	95.00
12". Pastel multicolors. White lining	120.00

ENGLISH YELLOW-GLAZED EARTHENWARE

This ware has been called Canary Lustre, but that is a misnomer. Developed mostly at the highest technical moment in English pottery history, English Yellow-Glazed Earthenware embraces the finest quality of Creamware found toward the end of the century of experimentation and into the nineteenth century. Documented pieces date from the 1780's to 1840, including Wedgwood wares as early as 1785.

While many pieces have silver and more rarely copper lustre; some items have none. Examples may be painted in a colorful, free-form manner or transfer decor in black or brick red with or without lustre. Pieces without any decoration are uncommon. The yellow overglaze varies in intensity from canary to a very pale yellow.

Plate. 7". Floral relief border. Rose center $650.00

Basket and Stand, 9". Leeds-type. Open work, painted in red and green ....$	285.00

Bowls

8¼". Paneled border containing floral relief sprays and floral center. Painted in red, green, and brown	750.00
Waste Bowl. Single rose pattern ..	265.00

Jugs

"Faith and Hope." Large	800.00
"Faith and Hope." Small	500.00
"Sir Frances Burnett"	650.00
"Success to the United States." ..	750.00

Mugs

2¼". "A Present for a Good Boy."	275.00
3½". "The Landlord's Caution." ..	400.00
7". Black transfer of babies	600.00
Plate. 7". Floral relief border. Rose center	650.00
Salt. 1¾". No decoration	135.00

EPERGNES

An epergne is an elaborately designed centerpiece for a table; consisting of a number of receptacles for fruits, flowers, candies and or candles.

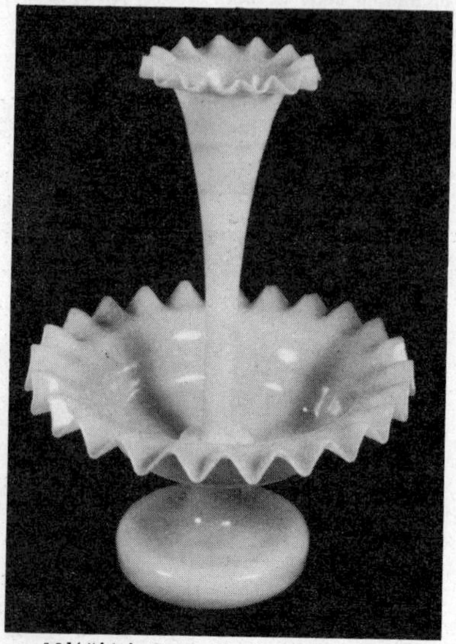

11½" high. Single lily, fluted rims. Pink. Bristol $125.00

9" high, 9" diam. bowl. Single lily. White opaline with cranberry edging. Footed ....$	175.00
11" high, 10¾" ruffled bowl. Single lily. Pink. Silver plated frame	250.00
12½" high. 3-white satin glass bowls with enamel decor. Silver-plated frame..................	450.00
14" high. Single lily. Cranberry	100.00
16" high. Single lily. Cranberry opalescent swirl. Ruffled edge. Crystal rigaree	225.00
16" high, 15" diam., ruffled bowl. Single lily. Cranberry	225.00
17" high, 12" diam. bowl. 4-lilies. Blue opalescent	195.00
19" high. Single lily with two hanging baskets and two stationary baskets. Green to white opalescent..................	295.00
20" high. 3-lilies. Canary and white cased glass	200.00
21" high, 12" diam. bowl. Cranberry with crystal arms, holding two cranberry baskets	325.00
21½" high. Single lily. Ruby glass. English	165.00
22" high, 10" diam. scalloped bowl. Three lilies. Emerald green	300.00
22½" high, 10" diam. bowl. 3-lilies. Cranberry to opalescent to clear with clear rigaree	195.00

FAIRY LAMPS

Fairy Lamps are candle-burning night lights consisting of a clear base and a shaped shade. They were first introduced by the Samuel Clarke Co., England in 1857; but made by many other firms from then on.

A wide array were produced . . .from pressed glass to fine art glass. There are two main classifications. The Fairy Pyramid has a clear glass base and a dome-shaped shade that measure approximately 3½ inches high when assembled. Others are 5 inches or more high and may have in addition to the clear glass candle insert, a saucer that matches the shade.

Floral pyramid. Clear and rose pink petal shade. Cranberry insert. Clear base. Signed Clarke, twice $165.00

Baccarat. 5" high, 6" saucer. Blue Swirl. Clarke insert ....$	295.00
Brass	
4½" high. Jeweled. Ornate filigree shade	150.00
8½" high. Amber and blue glass windows in brass shade	195.00
Bristol. Blue. Enameled floral decor	175.00
Burmese	
Clarke base. Signed Thomas Webb & Sons, Queen's Burmese ..	550.00
5" high. Clarke insert	375.00
Cut Velvet. Rose. Clarke base	250.00

Diamond Point (Pressed)
- Amber. Clarke base 85.00
- Amethyst. 11¼" high. Clear standard. Clarke insert 225.00
- Blue. Clarke base 65.00
- Clear. Clarke base 40.00
- Ruby. Clarke base 50.00

End-of-Day. Rainbow colors. Clarke base 175.00

Lithophane. 7¼" high. Ormolu holder. Blue enamel saucer 350.00

Millefiori. Clarke base 225.00

Satin Glass
- Apricot. Clarke base 250.00
- Butterscotch. Ribbed Swirl Clarkebase 250.00
- Cranberry. 6¾" high. Clear Clarke insert. 395.00
- Pink shading to white. 5" high. Matching crimped deep saucer .. 295.00
- Yellow. Ribbed, Clarke base 250.00

Verre Moire (Nailsea)
- Amber. 5" high. Clarke base 195.00
- Blue. Frosted. Clarke base 400.00
- Chartreuse. Frosted. 12" high, 10" mirrored plateau, with green glass leaves. Frosted standard. Clarke insert 650.00
- Cranberry. Frosted. Clarke base .. 250.00
- Cranberry. Frosted. 5¼" high, 6" saucer. Signed. Clarke clear insert 425.00
- Yellow. Frosted. Clarke base 225.00

FAMILLE ROSE

Famille Rose is a Chinese export porcelain made in the 18th and 19th centuries. The opaque hues of rose, blue and yellow are evident. The decorations are frequently figures, birds and insects in the familiar rose coloring. The porcelain is relatively scarce and therefore commands higher prices than some of the other Chinese export wares of the same era.

Vase. 10½". Figures in reserves. Mandarin. C. 1820 ....$500.00

Bowls
- 5". Three figures. Flowering tree. C. 1880 ....$ 95.00
- 10". Paneled floral bouquets. C. 1780 .... 500.00
- 15". Peacock design. 18th century 2000.00

Chargers
- 13". Octagonal-shaped. C. 1850 350.00
- 15¾". Birds. Floral decor on white. 18th century 500.00

Garden Seat. Mid 19th century 2500.00

Ginger Jar. 9" high. Early 19th century 350.00

Mugs
- 5". Dutchman decor. C. 1780 .... 350.00
- 5½". Floral decor. C. 1800 ...... 300.00

Plaque. 10¾" diam. Bird and floral decor on white. Mid 19th century 500.00

Plates
- 8⅞". Floral decor. C. 1750 ...... 195.00
- 10" Oval. Floral decor. 20th century 85.00

Teapot. 9". Flowers and butterflies. 19th century 350.00

Vases
- 9". Landscape decor. 20th century 75.00
- 11". Floral decor. 20th century .. 65.00
- 12". Figures in reserves. C. 1800 750.00

Wig Stand. 11½" high. 18th century 400.00

FANS

The hand fan was a necessary 'coolant' before the electric fan and central air conditioning. Utilitarian fans made of paper and wood were a popular advertising media distributed to churches, social organizations, meetings, etc. An elaborate fan, fashioned of lace or silk, was an important accessory to milady's costume in the Victorian era.

Celluloid. 7" long. Pierced ......$ 15.00

Feather
- Marabou. 23". Ivory sticks 85.00
- Ostrich. 17x22". Celluloid sticks. 40.00

8". Wood sticks. Red silk $17.50

Ivory. 9". Pierced slats. Handpainted floral design 75.00
Lace. White, pierced ivory sticks. Wedding-type 50.00
Paper
  Advertising-type. Common 6.50
  Centennial. 11". 1876 Philadelphia Horticultural Hall one side, eagle on reverse 100.00
  Chicago Exposition 20.00
  French. Handpainted on heavy paper, 20" opened. Ivory sticks .. 125.00
Silk
  8". Embroidered pastel flowers and birds. Pierced ivory sticks 40.00
  10½". Handpainted pink flowers, forget-me-nots. Carved. Pierced ivory sticks. Wedding-type 85.00
  12¾". Tortoise sticks. Handpainted scenic, sequins. French .. 100.00
  18". Black, carved ebony-type sticks, ribbon trim............ 50.00

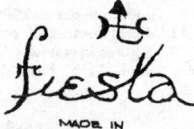

Fiesta
MADE IN USA

FIESTA WARE

Fiesta ware is a pottery dinnerware made by the Homer Laughlin China Co. in 1936, redesigned in 1969 and discontinued in 1973.
It can be distinguished from other brightly colored dinnerware of the same period by its characteristic band of concentric circles beginning at the rim, and the full circle handle on the cups. In 1969, a partial circle handle was used. Most of the wares were incised "Fiesta."

Ashtrays
  Ivory-Yellow .... $ 20.00
  Red 25.00

Cup and Saucer. Red $15.00

Bowls
  4¾". Cobalt-Yellow 6.00
  6". Red 8.50
  7⅝". Yellow-Turquoise 16.50
  8". Flat. Soup. Turquoise 10.00
Candleholders
  Red. Pair 40.00
  Turquoise. Bulbous. Pair 30.00
Carafe. 3 pint. Cobalt 40.00
Coffee Pots
  After dinner. Ivory 75.00
  Regular. Turquoise-Ivory 45.00
Creamer. Ring handle. Ivory 6.50
Cups and Saucers
  Red 15.00
  Yellow 10.00
Egg Cups
  Chartreuse 18.50
  Cobalt 10.00
Marmalade Jar. Metal holder.
  Cobalt 50.00
Mug. Yellow 20.00
Mustards
  Cobalt 65.00
  Ivory 50.00
Nappy. 8½". Green, dark 7.50
Pitchers
  Juice. 30 oz. Yellow 17.50
  Water. Disk. 2 qt. Ivory-Turqoise .. 22.50
Plates
  7¼". Salad. Green-Ivory-Yellow 3.00
  9½". Luncheon. Turqoise-Yellow 3.50
  10". Dinner. Turqoise-Green-Ivory 5.00
  10½". Grill. Regular green 6.50
  15". Chop. Ivory-Yellow 15.00
  15". Chop. Red-Rose 30.00
Relish Tray. 6 pieces. 6 colors 50.00
Salt and Pepper Shakers. Ivory-Turquoise. Pair 10.00
Sauceboat. Cobalt 15.00
Sugar, Covered. Turquoise-Yellow .. 8.50
Teapot. 8 cup. Green, regular...... 30.00

Tray. 5 x 10". Green, regular 10.00
Tumblers
Juice. 5 oz. Ivory 10.00
Water. 10 oz. Ivory 15.00
Vases
8". Yellow-Green 65.00
10". Red 125.00

FIRE EQUIPMENT

In the days before mechanized fire equipment, firefighters utilized man-power for the job of extinguishing fires. Most of the first companies were made up of volunteers. Each member had his own bucket and helmet.
Property owners who carried insurance displayed a firemark made of iron or brass. In the last few years, reproduction firemarks, cast of aluminum have been placed on the market.

Axe. 20". Blade and pick. Painted wood handle ....$ 28.50

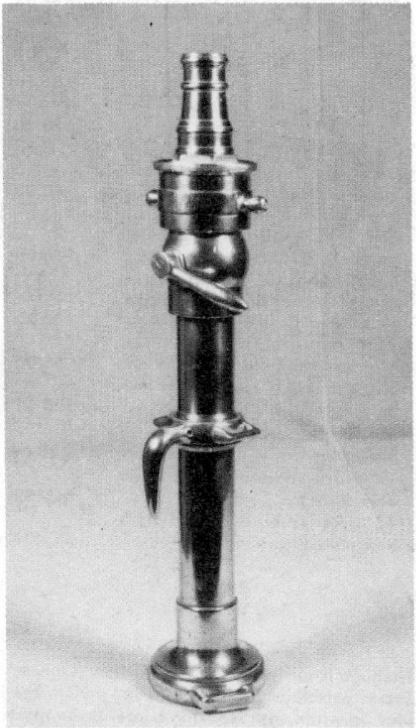

Nozzle. 20". Brass. "The Eastern Coupling Co., Camden, Maine." $125.00

Belt. Red and white. Embossed "Salem"........................ 125.00
Buckets, Leather
English. Replaced handle 150.00
Owner's name. 1807 .... 300.00
Owner's name. Replaced handle. C. 1820 .... 250.00
Pramdee No. 1. New England. 1800 .... 400.00
Extinguishers
14". Brass 20.00
24". Brass 30.00
Fire Horn. Brass 250.00
Fire Marks
Germantown National Fire. 1843 125.00
Hydrant, F.A. 1817 .... 195.00
"Mutual Assurance Co. Phila." Cast iron 125.00
United Fireman's Ins. Co 125.00
Helmets, Brass
American. Eagle finial.......... 250.00
English. C. 1860 .... 175.00
Helmets, Leather
American. Eagle finial. C. 1878 .... 75.00
Trumpet finial 125.00
Nozzles, Hose
5½". Brass. "Elkhart" 25.00
12½". Brass. "Eureka".......... 65.00
25½". Copper with brass fittings, "B.C. Co." 75.00
Pin with ribbon. 1½". Connecticut, 1936 .... 15.00

FIREPLACE EQUIPMENT

Before the advent of central heating, the fireplace was the only source of home heating. The open fire also served for cooking and lighting.

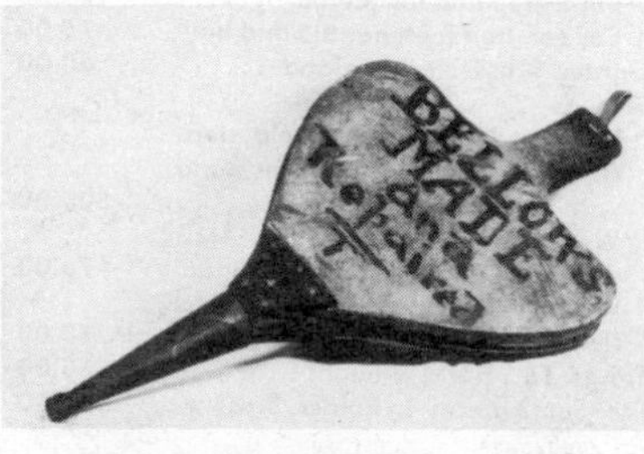

Bellows. Advertising-type. 13¾x24¾". "Bellows Made and Repaired". Wood. Iron nozzle, leather trim $150.00

Andirons (Pairs)
Adams-style. 18". Brass ......$ 100.00

Federal-style. 12". Brass. Lemon tops. Penny feet ... 500.00
Federal-style. 24½". Wrought iron and brass urn finials. Penny feet. C. 1790 ... 750.00
Firedogs. Wrought iron. 19th century ... 200.00
Griggins. 7". Brass ... 125.00
Queen Ann-style. 9½". Brass. 19th century ... 200.00
Queen Anne-style. 17¼". Ball finials. Penny feet. 18th century ... 1500.00

Bellows
Leather. 15". Floral decor ... 65.00
Wood. 18". Ivy leaves in relief. Brass nozzle ... 60.00
Wood. 20". Metal nozzle. Refinished ... 65.00

Boxes, Coal
11½x14x15". Brass plated. Hinged slanted lid, paper picture on front ... 75.00
12x16x17". Brass. Slanted lid. Handled. Ball feet. "Repousse" ... 250.00
12¼ x 18x18". Brass. Ornamental. Lift-off top. Tongs. English ... 225.00
19x20", to top of finial. Cast iron. Green with floral decor. Trimmed in gold. English ... 150.00

Fenders
23". Iron base. Brass rail. C. 1880 ... 200.00
31" long. Iron base. Brass rail ... 250.00
48" long. Brass. Slotted ... 450.00
52½" long. Brass wire work. 3 finials. New York. C. 1810 ... 750.00

Grate. 9x 17½". Cast iron ... 50.00

Hods
Brass. Chinese ... 45.00
*Brass. Delft-type handles ... 100.00
Brass. Helmet-type with scoop. Burnished and lacquered ... 175.00
Copper. Iron feet, handle and bail ... 75.00

Lighter. Brass. New England ... 60.00

Screens
Lacquered. Black with gold stenciling in oriental design. On stand with tripod legs ... 500.00
Wood. Hinged, 3 parts. Arch design on center section. Victorian ... 175.00
Wood. Single panel stenciled floral decor. Late Victorian ... 75.00

Tongs. 15". Hand wrought ... 55.00
Tool Set. 3 pieces, in holder. Brass ... 225.00

Trammels
24". Hand forged iron. Extends to 32" ... 150.00
39". Hand forged. Extends to 60" ... 200.00

Trivet. 12" high. 3 legs. Wood handle. Cast iron ... 125.00

*Reproduced Item

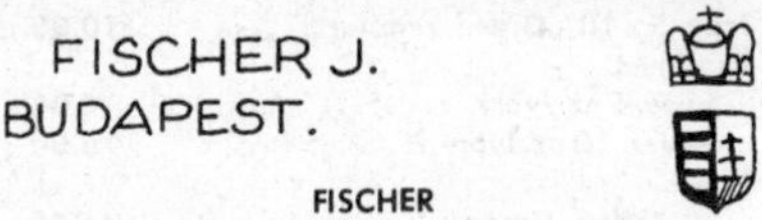

FISCHER

In 1893 Moritz Fischer founded the factory that produced Fischer wares in Herend, Hungary. The porcelain's most outstanding characteristic is its elaborate, allover design in multicolors. The designs and colors are very much like those found in native Hungarian costumes.

Bowl. 6¾". Reticulated edge. Birds, butterflies and floral decor. Late $ ... 45.00

Ewers
15". Brown, green, ivory coloring. Signed and numbered. Late ... 95.00
16". Multicolors ... 225.00
17". Snake handle. Floral decor on collar ... 250.00
20". Reticulated. Pink and green lustred ... 350.00

Figurine. 4". Nude, looking into mirror ... 125.00

Plates
9½". Reticulated and enameled ... 185.00
9½". Handled. Handpainted birds. Late ... 125.00

Vases
3". Gold top, cream bottom. Hand-painted florals. Late ... 40.00
7¾". Reticulated. Decorated with blue florals, green foliage. Gold handles ... 150.00
8¼" high, 3" diam. base. Multicolored enameling, reticulated. Gold trim ... 300.00
9". Triangle top and base. Polychromed. Gold trim. Late ... 65.00
10". Multicolored decor. Reticulated. Gold trim ... 300.00
12". Reticulated. Ornate handles. Multicolored with heavy gold trim ... 325.00
14". Urn-shaped. Reticulated. Blue decor ... 350.00
15". Reds, blues. Gold trim. Reticulated top and bottom ... 395.00

FISH SETS

(See "Game Plates")

FITZHUGH

Fitzhugh is one of the most recognized Chinese Export porcelains of the 1780-1880 period. The blue on white with Nanking border is the most accessible to the collector. The following colors are listed in monetary order . . .orange, green, sepia, mulberry, yellow, black, with gold being the scarcest. Examples with the standard butterfly and honeycomb border are a challenge to the collector. Combinations of colors are rare. Currently, Spode Porcelain Company, England is producing a Fitzhugh pattern in several colors.

Platter. 15¾". Blue $425.00

Bowl. 9½" diam. Quatrefoil rim. Green. C. 1820 ....$	800.00
Brush Box. Blue	575.00
Butter Tub. Covered. Pedestaled. Blue	600.00
Garden Seat. 18½" high. Green. C. 1850	4000.00
Plates. 10".	
Blue	150.00
Green	275.00
Orange	225.00
Sepia	375.00
Yellow	425.00
Platter. 18½" long. Blue	500.00
Vegetable, Covered. 5½ x 8½". Blue	475.00

FLASKS

A flask is a container with a narrow neck, used mainly for liquids. Some whiskey flasks are shaped to fit a pocket. The historical flasks are very desirable collectors' items and therefore demand a good price. SEE NOTE:

Anchor. Quart. Amber ....$	35.00
Chestnut. 5". Amber	100.00
Chestnut. 6". 16 vertical ribs. Aqua	85.00
Chestnut. 6½". 16 swirled ribs. Aqua	75.00
Corn For The World & Baltimore. Quart. Citron	150.00
Cornucopia. ½ pint. Deep olive. (GIII-7)	60.00
Cornucopia & Urn. Pint. Olive (GIII-4)	65.00

Eagle and Cornucopia. ½ pint. Aqua. (GII-18) $350.00

Double Cornucopia. ½ pint. Aqua ..	150.00
Double Eagle. Quart. Aqua. (GII-31)	75.00
Eagle & Cornucopia. ½ pint. Aqua. (GII-18)	350.00
Eagle & For Pike's Peak. Pint. Aqua	75.00
Eagle & Willington Glass Co. Quart. Olive green	125.00
Granite Glass Co. & Stoddard, N.H. Pint. Olive	150.00
Hunter and Dog. Pint. Puce	400.00
Jenny Lind, Glass Works. Quart. Aqua. (GI-103)	100.00
Masonic and Eagle. Pint. Olive amber. (GIV-20)	225.00
Railroad, Eagle. Pint. Amber. (GV-9)	225.00
Ravenna Glass Works. Pint. Aqua. (GII-37)	145.00
Scroll. IP. Quart. Aqua	75.00
Scroll. Two stars. Pint. Amber. (GIX-10)	400.00
Scroll. OP. Pint. Aqua	40.00
Sheaf of Wheat. 'Traveler's Companion." Quart. Amber	100.00
Stoddard & Double Eagle. Pint. Amber	85.00
Success To The Railroad. Pint. Olive. (GV-5)	175.00

Union, Eagle. ½ pint. Aqua 50.00
Washington & Taylor. Quart. Aqua. (GI-51) 75.00
Miscellaneous
Crystal with silverplated base and cap. Monogrammed. Gorham. C. 1950 .... 30.00
Nailsea-type. 6". Red glass with white loopings. South Jersey 295.00
Sterling. Pint. Embossed 85.00
Sterling and leather. Pint 55.00

NOTE: The numbers used refer to "American Glass" by George L. and Helen McKearin.

FLOW BLUE

Flowing, flown, flo or flow blue are all general terms used to describe the type of blue decorations on white earthenwares. The patterns were obviously inspired by Japanese and Chinese designs; but with a compromise between the elegant Oriental to a simple distinct interpretation that was more complimentary to country settings. A popular product of the Staffordshire potteries in the early 19th century, the wares were also produced in Europe and the United States.

Cup and Saucer. "Touraine." Stanley Pottery Co. $42.50

Bowls
Chapoo. 6x 9" oval. J. Wedgwood ....$ 165.00
Delmonte. 9½". Johnson Bros. C. 1900 .... 35.00
Fairy Villas. 8½". Wm. Adams & Co. C. 1891 .... 45.00
Jenny Lind. 8". A. Wilkinson. C. 1895 .... 65.00
Kin Shan. 8½ x 11" oval. E. Challinor. C. 1855. .... 95.00
Non Pareil. 9x 12" oval. Covered. Burgess & Leigh 250.00
Touraine. 7 x 10" oval. Stanley Pottery Co 50.00
Touraine. 10½". Stanley Pottery Co 65.00
Vermont. 12" oval. Burgess & Leigh. C. 1895 .... 75.00
Waverly. 9¼". Grindley. C. 1891 35.00
Butters, Covered
Delmonte. Johnson Bros. C. 1900 65.00
Lancaster. New Wharf Pottery. C. 1891 .... 75.00
Lorne. Grindley 85.00
Touraine. H. Alcock 125.00
Vermont. Burgess & Leigh. C. 1895 .... 75.00
Butter Pats
Argyle. Mayer 15.00
Idris. W. H. Grindley. C. 1910 .... 10.00
Lorraine. Ridgeway. C. 1905 .... 10.00
Non Pareil. Burgess & Leigh. C. 1891 .... 7.50
Olympia. Grindley 12.00
Touraine. H. Alcock 15.00
Virginia. John Maddock & Sons. C. 1891 .... 12.50
Windflower. Burgess & Leigh 12.00
Chamber Pot. Kyber. W. Adams 150.00
Creamers
Corean. P.W. & Co. C. 1850 ...... 65.00
Holland. Alfred Meakin 50.00
LaBelle. Wheeling 65.00
Melbourne. W. H. Grindley. C. 1900 .... 65.00
Simla. Elsmore & Forster. C. 1860 75.00
Touraine. Stanley Pottery Co 75.00
Cups and Saucers
Canton. John Maddock. C. 1850 .. 65.00
Delmonte. Johnson Bros. C. 1900 30.00
Hindustan. J. Maddock. C. 1850 .. 65.00
Jeddo. Wm. Adams & Son. C. 1845 .... 65.00
Manilla . P.W. & Co 65.00
Non Pareil. Burgess & Leigh 40.00
Shanghai. W.H. Grindley. C. 1900 50.00
Touraine. Stanley Pottery Co 42.50
Gravy Boats
Atlanta. W. H. Grindley. . 1900 .. 40.00
Gironde. W. H. Grindley. C. 1900 65.00
Linda. John Maddock & Sons. C. 1896 .... 38.50
Olympia. W. Grindley 55.00
Panama. E. Challinor. C. 1850 .. 55.00
Touraine. H. Alcock 65.00

Plate. "Manilla." 9". P.W. & Co. C. 1845 ....$35.00

Mug. Pekin. 3¼". T. Dimmock. C. 1845 .... 125.00

Pitchers

- **Amoy. 7". Davenport** 200.00
- Corean. 1½-quart. P.W. & Co. C. 1850 .... 85.00
- Fairy Villas. 9½". Adams 125.00
- Indian. 2-quart. F.R. Pratt 275.00
- LaBelle. 2-quart. Wheeling 100.00
- **Melbourne. 1½-quart. W.H. Grindley. C. 1900** 125.00
- Non Pareil. 7" high. Burgess & Leigh 150.00
- Scinde. 2-quart. Alcock 250.00
- Touraine. 8" high 135.00
- Watteau. 2-quart. Doulton 125.00

Plates

- Amoy. 7". Davenport. C. 1845 .. 30.00
- Argyle. 9". Grindley 20.00
- Athens. 10". Meigh 50.00
- Canton. 10½". J. Edwards. C. 1845 .... 70.00
- Coburg. 9". Edwards 45.00
- Chaing. 10" square. J. Gildea. C. 1870 .... 75.00
- Formosa. 10½". Mayer 75.00
- Grace. 6". Grindley 22.50
- Iris. 8". A. Wilkinson. C. 1907 .... 15.00
- Kyber. 10". Adams 45.00
- Lobelia. 9½". Phillips. C. 1845 .. 30.00
- Hong Kong. 10". Meigh 60.00
- Madras. 10". Doulton 35.00
- Manilla. 9". P.W. & Co. C. 1845 .. 35.00
- Non Pareil. 8". Burgess & Leigh. C. 1891 .... 27.50
- Oregon. 9½". T.J. & J. Mayer. C. 1845 .... 50.00
- Poppy. 9". Wedgwood. C. 1908 .. 18.50
- Scinde. 8". J & G. Alcock. C. 1840 40.00
- Temple. 10". P.W & Co 40.00
- Touraine. 6½". Stanley Pottery Co 17.50
- Touraine. 9". Stanley Pottery Co .. 25.00
- Touraine. 9". Alcock 25.00
- Waldorf. 8". New Wharf Pottery. C. 1892 .... 25.00
- Watteau. 9½". Doulton. C. 1900 37.50

Plates, Soup

- Denton. W. Grindley 20.00
- Hyson. J. Clementson. C. 1850 .. 30.00
- Indian Jar. J. & T. Furnival. C. 1843 .... 40.00
- Olympia. W. Grindley 25.00
- Scinde. 10¾". T. Walker. C. 1847 50.00
- Touraine. Stanley Pottery Co 35.00
- Virginia. J. Maddock & Son 25.00

Platters

- Alaska. 9x 12". W. Grindley. C. 1891 .... 35.00
- Amoy. 10x 13½". Davenport 150.00
- Cashmere. 14 x 19". Ridgway and Morley. C. 1840-45 .... 300.00
- **Duchess. 10 x 14¼". W.H. Grindley. C. 1891** 55.00
- Florida. 10x 13½". Grindley. C. 1889 .... 65.00
- LaBelle. 12x 16". Wheeling...... 60.00
- **Le Pavot. 10½ x 14½". W. Grindley** 75.00
- Linda. 12 x 17½". J. Maddock & Sons. C. 1886 .... 75.00
- Madreas. 9x 11". Doulton 65.00
- Manilla. 12 x 16". P.W. & Co. C. 1845 .... 175.00
- Non Pareil. 13x 15½". Burgess & Leigh 100.00
- Pekin. 15x 20". Dimmock. C. 1845 225.00
- Percy. 12 x 16". F. Morley. C. 1850 80.00
- Scinde. 10x 13". Alcock. C. 1840 195.00
- Scinde. 14x 18". Alcock. C. 1840 275.00
- Scinde. 16x 20½". Alcock. C. 1840 .... 325.00
- Shanghai. 10½ x 13½". J.F. & Co. C. 1860 .... 135.00
- Tonquin. 10x 13½." Adams 85.00
- Touraine. 8x 13½". Alcock 50.00
- Touraine. 8½ x 12½". Stanley .. 40.00
- Troy. 14½ x 18". C. Meigh 175.00
- Washington's Vase. 12 x 16". P.W. & Co. C. 1850 .... 100.00
- Watteau. 10x 14½". Doulton 85.00

Sauces

- Argyle. Grindley 16.50
- Fairy Villas. W. Adams 17.50
- Gothic. J. Furnival 22.50
- Non Pareil. Burgess & Leigh...... 17.50
- Oregon. T.J. & J. Mayer. C. 1845.. 18.50
- Touraine. Alcock 16.50
- Touraine. Stanley. C. 1898 ...... 12.50

Sugars, Covered
  Athens. Wm. Adams and Son. C. 1850 .... 125.00
  Floral. W. Ridgway & Co. C. 1850 85.00
  Gladys. New Wharf 60.00
  Lorne. Grindley 85.00
  Manilla. P.W. & Co. C. 1845 .... 150.00
  Non Pareil. Burgess & Leigh. C. 1891 .... 195.00
  Scinde. Alcock 125.00
Syrup. LaBelle. Original lid. Wheeling 85.00
Teapots
  Amoy. Davenport. C. 1844 ...... 225.00
  Argyle. Grindley 195.00
  Iris. Wilkinson 135.00
  Manilla. P.W. & Co. C. 1845 .... 300.00
  Persian. Johnson Bros 150.00
  Shanghai. J.F. & Co. C. 1860 .... 295.00
  Touraine. Alcock 150.00
Tureens, Covered
  Fern. 9½ x 13". W. Adams. C. 1870 .... 95.00
  LaBelle. 7½ x 10½". Wheeling .. 65.00
  Scinde. 10x 13". Alcock. C. 1840 300.00
  Shanghai. 9 x 11½". J.F. & Co. C. 1860 .... 285.00
  Touraine. 9x 12½". Stanley 95.00
  Verona. 9x 12". Wood 150.00

FOOD MOLDS

Molds were made and used for a variety of foods . . .butter, ice cream, custards etc. The main objective was to present the food in an attractive and appealing manner. Early molds were handcrafted. Later, they were machine produced.
Today these molds are being collected, not only for decorative reasons, but also for their original intended usage. Reproductions exist! Also see "Butter Stamps."

BUTTER MOLDS

Acorn. Rectangular. 1# size ......$ 40.00
Acorn, Double. With leaves. 4½" diam 50.00
Cloverleaf. Rectangular. 1# size .. 40.00
Cow. Hand carved 125.00
Dove. Hand carved 75.00
Fern. Rectangular or round. 1# size 45.00
Initialed. Rectangular or round. 1# size 40.00
Maple Leaves, Double. 1# size 75.00
Pineapple. Hand carved 75.00
Plain. 1# size
  Glass. Round 35.00
  Wooden. Rectangular 25.00
Sheaf of Wheat. Rectangular 40.00
Sheaf of Wheat. Round. Hand carved 125.00

Star. ½# size 40.00
Strawberry. 3½" diam. Hand carved 85.00
Swan. 1# size 75.00

CANDY MOLDS
(Tin, Tin and Copper, Etc.)

Candy Mold. Santa Claus. 8". Tin $65.00

Basket. 3½ x 6" ....$ 30.00
Card Suits. 3". Set of four 65.00
Clown. 10". Four pieces 50.00
Eggs, Easter. 5 x7". Three compartments 40.00
Frog. 5" 30.00
Groom. 3½" 20.00
Humpty Dumpty. 5½" 35.00
Lion. 7" 40.00
Rabbits
  6" 30.00
  7½" 35.00
  10" 45.00
Rooster. 5½" 35.00
Rose. 4½" 25.00
Santa Claus. 6¼" 55.00
Snowman. 4" 35.00

Three Wise Men on Horses. Eight pieces	100.00
Witch on Broom. 6″	30.00

ICE CREAM MOLDS
(Pewter)

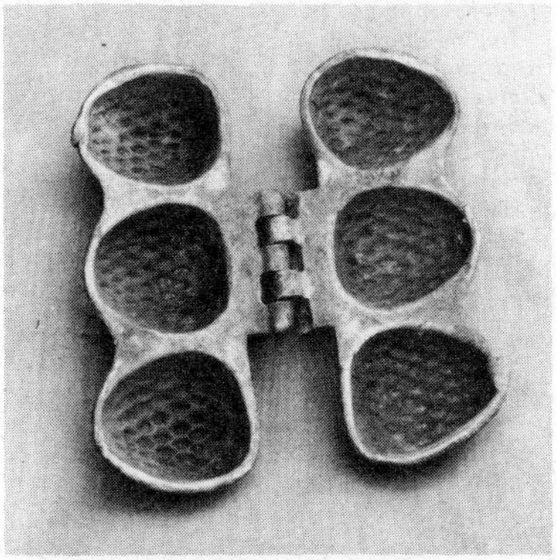

Ice Cream Mold. 3 Strawberries. "M" Pewter. $35.00

Autombile .... $	50.00
Basket, Medallion	35.00
Battleship	45.00
Bear, Teddy	40.00
Beaver	50.00
Bride and Groom	75.00
Cat and Moon	65.00
Chick	22.50
Christmas Tree with Star	55.00
Clover, 4-leaf	32.50
Clown, full figure	60.00
Cupid's face in Rose	35.00
Eagle, American	75.00
Eagle, Medallion	50.00
Elks Head, 3-part	45.00
Engagement Ring	22.50
Fisherman	30.00
Football, 3-part	30.00
Golf Bag, with clubs	60.00
Grapes, Bunch	25.00
Heart and Cupid	35.00
Locomotive	60.00
Melon Slice	15.00
Ocean Liner	35.00
Rabbit, Crouching	30.00
Rose	30.00
Sailboat	55.00
Santa Claus, 1890	50.00
Santa Claus, with pack	65.00
Shriner Emblem	28.50
Star	17.50
Stork	35.00
Swan	40.00
Uncle Sam	65.00
Violin	50.00
Washington, George. Bust	55.00
Wedding Bell with cupid	25.00
Wedding Ring	18.50
Wishbone	20.00
Zeppelin	85.00

POTTERY MOLDS

Asparagus. 3½ x 6 x 8″ .... $	40.00
Ear of Corn. 7″	35.00
Grapes, Cluster. 6½″	35.00
Melon. 5¾ x 7¼″	30.00
Pea Pods. 6½″	35.00
Rabbit. 7½″	50.00

MISCELLANEOUS

Fish. 5 x 11″. Copper .... $	45.00
Grape. 4″. Glass	25.00
Horseshoe. 5½ x 6″. Tole. Early	75.00
Lamb. 12″. Aluminum. C. 1920	20.00
Lamb. 14″. Cast iron	55.00
Marizipan. 3 x 3″. Tin	35.00
Melon. 4 x 5½ x 7″. Tin	10.00
Pear. 2 x 7¾″. Copper	25.00
Pineapple. 4½ x 5 x 7¼″. Copper	60.00
Rabbit. 4½″ Copper	35.00
Santa Claus. 12″. Cast iron	75.00
Sunburst. 2¼ x 8¼″. Copper	25.00

FOSTORIA GLASS

FOSTORIA

Fostoria Glass Company began operations at Fostoria, Ohio in 1887. A few years later they moved to Moundsville, W. Va. where they continue to manufacture quality glassware. Many of their discontinued patterns and items are being collected today.

Bookends, Pairs	
Lyre .... $	45.00
Rearing Horse	50.00
Bowls	
Heirloom. 11″. Green opalescent	22.50
Royal. 10″. Amber. Footed	35.00
Victoria. 8″	20.00
Candlesticks	
Baroque. 2-lite. Pair	30.00
Evangeline. 2-lite. Topaz. Pair	30.00
Rose. 1⅝″. Pair	10.00
Versailles. Topaz. Pair	20.00
Castor Set. 5-bottle. Raleigh	125.00
Champagnes	
Beacon	7.50
Optic	2.50
Rainbow	6.00
Compotes	
Royal. 6″. Green	25.00
Shirley. 5½″	15.00

Console Set. "Heather". Crystal. Bowl, 11½" diam., candlesticks 4⅞" high $65.00

Vase. "Mother of Pearl". 6¾" high. Ruffled and flared top $30.00

Creamers and Sugars
- Buttercup 20.00
- Colony 15.00
- Fairfax. Ruby 35.00
- Wild Rose. Topaz 18.50

Cruet. Cornet etched with Willowmere. Ground stopper 25.00

Cups and Saucers
- Fairfax. Green 10.00
- June. Azure 18.50

Figurines
- Colt. 4" 25.00
- Duck. 4¼". Blue 25.00
- Penguin. 4¼" 40.00
- Seal. 4". Topaz 45.00

Goblets
- June 12.50
- June. Topaz 20.00
- Trojan. Topaz 10.00

Ice Bucket. Versailles. Topaz 30.00

Plates
- Beverly. 8½". Green 4.00
- Fairfax. 9¼". Green 5.00
- Heather. 9½" 18.50
- Holly. 7½" 10.00
- Royal. 9¼". Azure 6.00
- Seville. 8½". Amber 5.00

Sherbet. June 12.00

Tumblers
- American. 4". Footed 4.50
- Priscilla. Green 12.50

Vases
- American. 8" 20.00
- Heirloom. 9". Pink opalescent 25.00
- Rose. 8". Topaz 17.50
- Rose. 13" 22.50

FRAMES

(See "Furniture")

FRANKOMA POTTERY

The original factory was founded in 1936 at Sapulpa, Oklahoma by John N. Frank, an instructor of ceramics at the University of Oklahoma. After a fire in 1938, the factory was re-established in 1943. Although Frankoma pottery is recent, with the increased interest in American art pottery, it is being collected and at reasonable prices.

Bean Pot, Lidded. 6½ x 8½". Green, brown. Block caps .... $ 25.00

Bowl. 12" deep. Mottled brown, yellow 18.50

Clamshell Dish. 7". Footed 7.50

Console Set. Boat-shaped bowl 12" long. Loop-shaped candleholders 5" high. Brown, cream glaze 30.00

Cup and Saucer. Demitasse. Impressed 6.50

Jug. 5½". Green, brown. With cork 20.00

Leaf Dish. 12". Green, brown. Impressed "226" 10.00

Mugs, Political. 1968 to 1977. Each 15.00

Pitchers
- 3⅛". Covered. Mottled blue 6.50
- 8". Green, brown. Ice lip. Impressed "5-D" 18.50

Sugar. "Aztec." One-handle. Block caps 6.50

Jug, Handled. 5½" high. Cork stopper. Green and brown glaze $20.00

Vases
- 4½". Ball-shaped 10.00
- 6". Brown, green. Ram's head handles 12.00
- 7½". Bulbous. Rose. Paper label 12.50
- 10". Cylindrical. Brown. "72" 15.00

Wall Pockets
- Acorn. Tan 7.50
- Girl. Green 8.50
- Indian Brave and Squaw. Pair .. 25.00
- Wagon Wheel. Green 8.50

Water Set. Lidded pitcher, 6 tumblers. Powder blue glaze 50.00

FRUIT CRATE ART

Fruit crate art had its beginning in the 1880's when orange growers in California began using lithographed labels on their wooden crates. Soon other fruit growers followed suit. The earlier labels were romantic and sentimental. Later, the labels became more masculine to appeal to the male wholesale buyer.
Cardboard boxes replaced the wooden crates in the 1940's, thus the end of the colorful labels.
These labels have regained their popularity and are now being framed and displayed in homes and even in museums as a part of the history of American art.

All Year. Lemons. Ventura valley and mountains. Fillmore ...... $ 1.25

Great Northwest Brand. Apples . . $3.50

Annie Laurie. Oranges. Beautiful lady. Strathmore 5.00

Bellboy. Bellboy carrying apples on tray 5.00

Blue Goose. Oranges. Big blue goose. Los Angeles 2.50

Brownies. Lemons. W. & M. Marks, Tulare County, California 5.00

First American. Lemons and oranges. Indian, girl, teepee. Los Angeles. C. 1905 .... 65.00

Foot High. Pin-up against black background with vibrant colors. C. 1940 .... 7.50

Gold Coast. Oranges. Placentia Orchard, California 3.50

Golden Eagle. Oranges. Charles C. Chapman, Fullerton, California .. 3.50

Golden Rod. Oranges. Colorful bunch of golden rod. Rialto Orange Co., California 1.50

Golden Trout. Oranges. Large trout jumping out of water. Orange Cove. C. 1945 .... 12.50

Hesperian. Art Deco image in blue and orange 5.00

Honeymoon. Lemons. Black, orange and white castle in moonlight. Los Angeles 18.50

Indian River Sunshine fruit. Ft. Pierce, Florida 1.50

King Pelican. Pelican, gold outlined on black background. C. 1920's .. 35.00

King Tut. Lemons. Lemonade and fruit cluster. Santa Barbara 10.00

Legal Tender Apples. Design of money. Columbia. C. 1930's 35.00

Marguita. Gavilan Citrus Ass'n., California 6.50

Moon. Oranges. Greenspot Citrus Ass'n., California 5.00

Orbit. Oranges. Exeter Citrus Ass'n, California 3.50

Princess. Grapefruit. Princess in robe. Corona 1.50
Quercus Ranch. Pears. Lake County, California 1.50
Redman Apples. Smiling Indian in war dress 5.00
Rodeo. Cowboys riding in ring 3.50
Sails Apples. Sailing sloop 3.50
Small Black. Grapes. Victor Fruit Growers, California 3.00
Sno Boy Apples. Snowman in top hat 4.00
Stonewall Jackson. Oranges. Full color portrait. Placentia Orchards, California 10.00
Sun. Oranges. Greenspot Citrus Assoc., California 3.00
Sunkist. Grapefruit. Sunkist emblem. Los Angeles 2.00
Sunkist. Oranges. Orange and Sunkist Brand. Los Angeles 1.00
Wolf. Glaring wolf 3.50

Miscellaneous

Kingfish. Asparagus. Fish jumping with mouth open 2.00
King Pelican. Lettuce. F.E. King 1.50
Squaw. Peas. Detailed Indian maidens. C. 1925.............. 3.00

FRY GLASS

The H.C. Fry Glass Company, Rochester, Pa., began operating in 1901 and ceased production in 1933. In the first years, their main products were cut glass items. Later, a fine art glass, "Foval," was introduced and made only for a few months during 1926 and 1927. Fry Foval glass is primarily pearly blue in color and other than a simple Delft blue or Jade green contrasting color trim, the items are no further decorated. Delft blue or Jade green were the only colors commercially produced by Fry. Occasionally, a worker's fancy will be trimmed in pink. Very few examples were ever produced entirely in the blue or green. "Radioware" made in blue or green with festoons is extremely rare. Fry Pearl Art Glass may also display silver or gold deposit designs. These pieces were produced on Fry blanks which were sold to the Rockwell Company and marketed under their name.

Fry's Art Line and Pearl Oven Wares are related in color because of the collodial state of the aluminum oxide present in the formulas, but should not be classified together. The art wares were mold blown and the oven wares pressed. Fry Foval glass was seldom signed . . .perhaps one piece in a thousand.

Also see "Cut Glass."

FOVAL

Bottle, Cologne. 5". Blue stopper . . $ 100.00

Foval. Lemonade Set. Covered pitcher with 6 tumblers. Applied cobalt handles. Set $500.00

Oven Ware. . .Reamer. 7½" diam. $28.50

Bowls
9½" diam., 4½" high. Footed. Blue trim 165.00
10" diam., 3½" high. Footed. Green base, trim. 175.00

Candlesticks
11½". Blue wafers and threading. Pair 295.00
12". Delft blue. Twisted stems. Pair 350.00
12". Looped festoons and wafers. "Radioware." Pair 500.00

Compotes
6x8". Covered. Green finial and stem 185.00

7". Silver overlay. Green stem .. 175.00
9x11½". Blue base ... 225.00
Creamer. 2½". Applied blue handle. Polished pontil ... 75.00
Cup and Saucer. Green handle ... 85.00
Finger Bowl. 4¼", 7" underplate. Blue trim. Set ... 125.00
Lamp. 15" high, 8" diam. shade. Pink loopings. Electrified ... 850.00
Lemonade. Green handle ... 50.00
Pitchers
9½". Jade green trim ... 150.00
11½". Covered. Blue trim ... 250.00
Plate. 9½". Blue trim ... 75.00
Sherbet. Blue stem ... 65.00
Teapot. 6½" high. Green handle, spout and finial ... 225.00
Toothpick Holder. Blue handles ... 65.00
Vases
6". Green wafer ... 100.00
7½". Cobalt handles ... 175.00

OVEN WARES

Bowl. 7½" ... 12.50
Bread Pan ... 16.50
Cake Pan. 9" ... 10.00
Casserole, Covered. 5½ x 7¾". Oval ... 12.50
Custard Cup. 3⅞" ... 5.50
Plates
Grill. 10½". 3-sections ... 35.00
Pie. 10" ... 12.50
Reamer ... 28.50
Teapot on footed hot plate ... 75.00

FULPER POTTERY

The American Pottery Company of Flemington, N.J. made pottery jugs and housewares from the early 1800's. They made Fulper Art Pottery from approximately 1910 to 1930.

Bowls
7½". Yellow to green matte glaze ... $35.00
8". 2¾" deep. Green with blue interior. Stamped ... 28.50
8½". Azure blue crystalline glaze, Leaping fish flower frog ... 80.00
10½". Cobalt blue. Matte glaze. Blue flambe' interior ... 55.00
12" oval. Leopard skin crystalline glaze. Impressed mark ... 95.00
13", 2½" deep. Famille Rose with blues. Crimped edge ... 75.00

Vase, handled. 5". Squat-type. Brown matte glaze ... $35.00

Boxes, Powder
6¼". Lady holding fan. Pink ... 100.00
7½". Spanish lady with shawl, fan ... 85.00
8". Basket-shaped. With floral decor ... 65.00
Candlesticks
4" high x 5" diam. base. Earth colors in crystalline glaze. Side handles. Pair ... 38.50
6¼" high. Figural fish. Black, green crystalline glaze. Anniversary issue. C. 1930. Pair ... 75.00
10½" high. Blue green. Ochre crystalline glaze. Pair ... 95.00
Flower Frog. 7¾" high. Mushroomed-shaped. Famille Rose. Crown inkmark ... 65.00
Lamp Base. 9x 9". Blue with ochre crystalline glaze. Reticulated base and collar. Unsigned ... 100.00
Perfume Lamps
5½" high. Lady, blue ... 150.00
6¼" high. Figure of girl in full skirt. Electrified. Artist signed ... 175.00
Pitcher. 6". Bulbous. Mottled brown flambe' glaze ... 35.00
Vases
3½" high, 2½" diam. Plum drip over cucumber glaze ... 35.00
5". Crystalline green. Snowflakes ... 50.00
6" Ribbed body. 2 handles. Famille rose crystalline glaze ... 35.00
7" Bulbous. Handled. Green crystalline gray green flambe' glaze ... 45.00
8" Cafe au Lait. Snowflakes ... 75.00
10". Blue crystalline glaze over blue wisteria ground ... 100.00
10". Flask-shaped. Green crystalline glaze ... 55.00

FURNITURE

("Please Read")

Prices vary considerably on furniture. The original quality, style, desirability and condition, i.e., original finish, amount of restoration and the quality of the workmanship in the restoration, are all influencing factors in determining prices. An attempt has been made to arrive at an average price on each item listed. This list should only serve as a guide. The above enumerated factors must be taken into consideration in arriving at a final price.

FURNITURE STYLES APPROXIMATE DATES

William and Mary	1688-1710
Queen Anne	1710-1750
Chippendale	1754-1780
Hepplewhite	1786-1800
Sheraton	1790-1810
Empire	1810-1830
Duncan Phyfe	1800-1840
Victorian	
Early	1840-1850
Rococo or Louis XV	1845-1870
Louis XVI	1865-1880
Renaissance	1860-1885
Eastlake	1875-1895

BEDS

Art Deco. Headboard 43¼", Burled demilune contour, stylized mask decor .... $ 350.00

Art Nouveau. Single. Inlaid mahogany, molded cornice, carved supports. Attributed to Louis Marjorelle. C. 1890 .... 2000.00

Brass. Double size.
- Ornate fan-shaped headboard. 62" high. Footboard 42" high. Complete with rails. Polished .. 1500.00
- Standard tubular styling. Burnished 850.00

Brass. Single size. Standard tubular styling 500.00

Brass and Iron. Double size. Ornate headboard and footboard. Complete 500.00

Cannon Ball. Double size. Maple. All original 850.00

Cannon Ball. Single size. Rope-type. Pine. Original red stain 500.00

Day Beds
- American Empire. 22 x 71". Pine. Sleigh front end. Upholstered 150.00
- Queen Anne style. 66½" long. Cherry. Scroll crest, molded slat frame. Cabriole legs, pad feet. Connecticut 4000.00

Eastlake, Victorian. Double size. 7'4" arched headboard. Walnut. Wooden slats. All original $500.00

Eastlake, Victorian. Double size. 7' headboard. Walnut with burled veneer panels. Applied carvings. 500.00

Empire, American. Double size. Turned and block posts, shaped and paneled headboard. Original red paint 650.00

Field
- Double size. Marriage-type. Original painted decor. Attributed to Bavarian origin. C. 1750 ..... 5000.00
- Single size. Maple and pine. OG canopy frame. C. 1810 .... 1500.00
- Tiger maple and poplar. Original finish. Connecticut. 18th century 3500.00

Jenny Lind-style
- Double size. Maple. Original finish 650.00
- Single size. Walnut 300.00
- ¾-size. Walnut 500.00

Oak. Double size. Arched headboard and footboard. Some carving 500.00

Pencil Poster. 79" high. Double size. Cherry. Plain headboard, footboard. Rope-type 3500.00

Renaissance, Victorian
- Double size. Highly carved architectural headboard and footboard. C. 1860 .... 1250.00
- Double size. Walnut. Applied carvings with burled walnut panels. Refinished. C. 1860 .... 150.00

Rococo, Victorian. Double size. Walnut. Finely carved arches, pediments, detailed carvings of people. C. 1840-1850 .... 3000.00
Tester, Flat. ¾-size. Cherry. Turned head, foot posts, arched headboard. New England. C. 1840 .. 1500.00

BENCHES

Saddle Stitchers Bench. 25 x 41" high. Chestnut. $125.00

Carver's. 72" long. Maple ....$ 850.00
Church
 36x48" long. Pine 250.00
 36x60" long. Oak.............. 375.00
Cobbler
 Three drawers. Pine with leather seat. All original 750.00
 12x16½ x19" long. Splayed sides, four drawers. Hand forged strappings. Pine 175.00
 17x44" long. Pine. One piece construction. Refinished 500.00
 20x42" long. Pine. One drawer, leather seat 450.00
Deacon
 90" long. Arrowback. Cherry and poplar. Plain crest rail, turned legs, stretchers................ 1000.00
 Windsor-style. 31 spindles, bamboo turnings, 8 legs. Original finish 3000.00
Fireside. 18x 59" high back. Scalloped top and base. Pine 750.00
Kneeling. 6½ x 48" long. (from church) 75.00
Kneeling. 7½ x8x20" long. Pa 45.00
Mammy
 44". Half spindle back, shaped crest. Repainted and stenciled .. 750.00
 72". 4-chair back. Restenciled with original design. Complete with keeper 1250.00
Park. 54" long. Pine with wrought iron supports. Pa 200.00
River Boat-type. 98" long. Mixed woods, metal arms. Turned spindle back, plain crest 500.00
Tinsmith's. 34x70" long. Oak 500.00
Water
 7½ x 30x32". Pine. two shelves, zinc lined. Old paint 250.00
 18x43x68" high. Cupboard above shelves, shelf and 2 panelled doors below 1500.00
 35x46". Pine. Boot jack ends. Old paint. 175.00

BENTWOOD

In 1856, Michael Thonet of Vienna perfected the process of bending wood using steam. Shortly after, Bentwood furniture became popular. Other manufacturers of Bentwood furniture were Jacob and Joseph Kohn, Philip Strobel and Son, Sheboygan Chair Company and Tidoute Chair Company. Bentwood furniture is still being produced today by the Thonet firm and others.

Chairs
 Arm. Cane seat and high back . . $ 195.00
 Arm. Wooden seat. Signed Thonet 175.00
 High Chair. Child's 150.00
 Rocker, Child's. 22" 75.00
 Rocker, Child's. Signed Thonet .. 250.00
 Rocker, Nursing. Replaced cane seat 195.00
 Rocker. Sleigh. Recaned back and seat 500.00
 *Rocker. Sleigh. Signed Thonet .. 850.00
 *Side. Cane seat 75.00
 *Side. Wood seat 40.00
 Side. Wood seat. Signed Thonet .. 65.00
Cradles
 22" high 275.00
 50" high. On stand with bonnet

top. Swing-type. All original 1500.00
Easel, Artist's 75.00
Hat Racks
9x36½" long. Five swivel pegs. Brass fittings 75.00
28x32" long. Seven pegs. Glove holder 175.00
62" high. Floor model with umbrella holder. Six shaped hangers 300.00
Stool. 26½" high. Cane seat 75.00
*Reproduced Item

BOOK CASES

Oak
17½" square. 42½" high. Five slots, 6 shelves. Revolving-type $ 300.00
29x32x59½" wide. Open. Copper hardware. C. 1910. Signed L. & J. G. Stickley 850.00
46x74" high. With desk. Shaped glass doors. Desk has pigeon holes and drawers. Mirror on side 450.00
Oak, Golden. 48x 58" high. Four shelves, 4 lifting glass doors. C. 1920's 200.00
Walnut
13¼ x 48x74" high. Two drawers below 5 shelves. C. 1870........ 350.00
92" x 102" high. Carved cornice, 4 glazed arched doors above and 4 paneled doors below. Adjustable shelving. Early Victorian 2000.00

BOXES

Ballot
6x8x12½". Maple. Dovetailed. Sliding top ....$ 150.00
6x7x11½". Pine with brass fitting. Pa 65.00
7x7½ x 18¼". Pine. Dovetailed. Carved wooden handles. C. 1850 75.00
8½x11x16". Walnut. Wide dovetailing. Brass hardware 75.00
Band. 12 x 20" high. Oval. Original dark green finish 100.00
Bride's
5½x6x12" long. Dome top, original paper cover. C. 1810 .... 275.00
27" long. Sponge decor. C. 1840 350.00
Candle
4x7x18". Oak. English. C. 1850 .. 125.00
5x5x12". Pine with sliding lid. Dovetailed 80.00
5x7½x15¼". Wall-type. Dovetailed. Original blue paint .. 175.00
8½x14¼x16". Oak. Shaped crest. Hinged lid 100.00
10x13½" long. Walnut. Sliding lid. Refinished 75.00

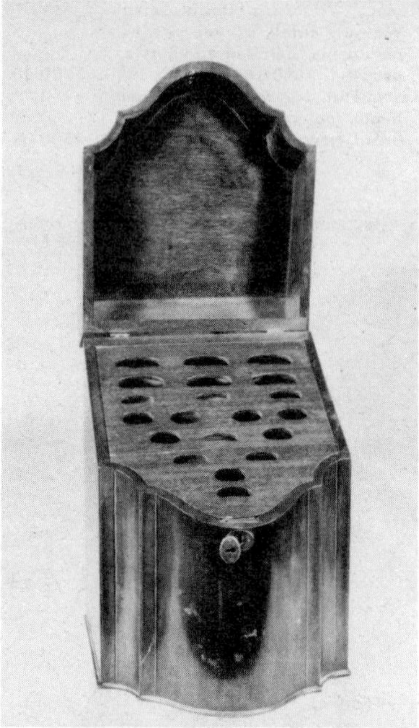

Knife box. Serpentine front. Inlaid mahogany $600.00

Cigar. 4 x 7½ x 12". Mahogany, stripe inlay on lid and base. Zinc lined. Nickelplated hardware .. 75.00
Deed
4½ x 5½x8". Leather cover. Brass studding. Original paper liner. Iron Lock, Key. C. 1850 .... 75.00
6½ x 8½ x 14". Pine covered with black leather, red trim. Brass fittings. C. 1820 .... 150.00
Hat
9½ x 12". Cardboard, covered with floral paper. C. 1880 ...... 35.00
16" square. Pine. Domed top with strap handle 200.00
Knife, Mahogany
Serpentine front. Inlaid. Pair 1200.00
Sheraton. Pair 1500.00
Urn-shaped. Pair 850.00
Pantry
5¾". Hand stitched 40.00
7". Splint wood 35.00
14" oval. Dark wood 75.00
14½", 7" deep. Splint wood, original stain 50.00

25½" oval. Splint wood. Stained 95.00

Spice

Oak

4 drawers. Brass pulls 75.00

8 drawers. Brass pulls 150.00

Pine

4 drawers. Labeled 75.00

4 drawers. Slant lid, all dovetailed. 18th century 300.00

5 drawers. Painted white. Black trim. Porcelain knobs. Labeled. Germany 65.00

8 drawers. Brass pulls. Refinished 100.00

8 drawers. Original green paint 195.00

8 drawers. Porcelain fronts 95.00

9 drawers. Wall-type. Old paint 150.00

Rosewood.

8 drawers. Wood pulls 150.00

Tin

Cylindrical. 6 cans with grater and 2 shakers. All original including stenciling 85.00

Rectangular. Hinged lid. 6 containers. Original paint 65.00

Walnut. 8 drawers. Porcelain labels and pulls 150.00

Trinket

3x4½x6". Pine, carved. One piece construction 95.00

3¼ x 6¾x10". Mahogany. Paper lined. Reverse painting on glass inside lid 75.00

CABINETS

Spool Cabinet. "Brainerd & Armstrongs Spool Silk." Four drawers. Oak $300.00

Curio. 13x 24 x 45" high. Rosewood. Red lacquer, lined with tea paper. Oriental ....$ 1000.00

Dye

Peerless. 10½ x 18½ x 32". Oak, tin front 300.00

Putnam. Slant front, metal and wood. Lithograph of General Putnam 175.00

Hardware Store. 76" high. **80-drawers on 19" base. 12-drawers below. Oak with porcelain pulls** 850.00

Kitchen. Hoosier. Oak with glass doors. Porcelain work surface, flour bin, etc 450.00

Medicine

Pine. 3 shelves. Primitive. Open .. 65.00

5½ x 16x24½". Painted pine. Glazed door, 3 shelves, shaped crest 75.00

Serving

35x 37½" wide. Art Deco. Mirrored glass top. Bronze hardware. One drawer over double cupboard with 3 shelves 750.00

39½ x 48" wide. De Macassar. Maple and ebony. Shaped top, 3 drawers. C. 1930 .... 1000.00

Silver. 18x 28x30". Oriental-style. Black lacquer, MOP Coramandel decor. Fitted interior, lined with felt. Brass fittings, including puzzle locks 1250.00

Spool

Clarks Spool Cotton. 6½ x 15x18". Two drawers. Original porcelain pulls 125.00

Cortecilli. 5 drawers 275.00

Goffs Best Braid. 3 drawers. Original melon-shaped pulls 225.00

Leonard Silk Co. 10 glass front drawers, 2 wooden front doors, beveled mirror sides 500.00

Merrick's. Six Cord. Two large drawers over 2 small drawers. Cherry. Refinished 275.00

Richardson's Spool Silk. 2 drawers 125.00

Star Mercerized. Four glass front doors, logo on sides, gold lettering 100.00

Williamantic. Two drawers. Original pulls 100.00

Watchmaker's. 17x 18¾ x 31" long. Ten drawers complete. Six drawers with 42 scooped out pockets, 4 undivided drawers. Single board construction 350.00

CANDLE SHIELDS

21". Brass with needlepoint and beaded shield. Angel with cherubs decor. French. Pair ....$ 500.00

22". Brass with floral needlepoint shields. Pair 300.00

53". Mahogany. Fabric screen. 18th century 2500.00

CANDLE STANDS

Walnut. 18½ x 18¾x25" high. Zoar. C. 1840. ....$400.00

Ash. 35½" high. Ratchet-type. Adjustable standard, block support. New York. C. 1710 ....$ 1000.00

Cherry
- 15" diam. Ring and vase standard, arched tripod with snake feet 500.00
- 16½" square top, 26½" high. Hepplewhite-style. New York 850.00
- 18" diam. Queen Anne-style. Two board construction top, turned standard, arched tripod, snake feet 750.00

Curly Maple
- 16" diam. Dish top 650.00
- 16" oblong top, one drawer. Vase turned standard, arched tripod base 750.00

Mahogany
- 19½" diam. Tilt top, bird cage support, ring and vase standard, snake feet. Pa. C. 1780 .... 2500.00
- 27" diam. Dish top. Philadelphia. C. 1760 .... 1500.00
- 28" diam. Bird cage. Pa. C. 1770 3500.00

Maple. 26" diam. Tilt top. Mass. C. 1760 .... 1500.00

Pine
- 16½" square. Hepplewhite-style 500.00
- 27" square. Tapered legs 350.00

Walnut
- **Queen Anne-style. Dish top and bird cage support. Pa** 1750.00
- 17" diam. Turned standard, tripod base, serpent feet 350.00

CHAIRS

Child's High Chair. Oak. Pressed back. Painted. $65.00

Arrowbacks
- Full. Plank seat ....$ 225.00
- Half. Plank seat. Original stenciling 200.00
- Half. Rabbit ears. Plank seat 300.00

Art Deco
- Arm. 3" high. Tiger eye maple. Brown leather inserts, red lacquered fretwork 500.00
- **Side. Walnut and black stain.** Shaped back, scrolled side rails, 2 straight legs, 2 cabriole legs, upholsterred seat. Viennese. C. 1930 .... 350.00

Barber Chairs
- Cast iron and oak. Upholstered in velvet. Refinished. C. 1890 ...... 750.00

Renaissance, Victorian. Side chair. Finger molded with nut carved crest. Upholstered $400.00

Cast iron and porcelain. Upholstered. Rough condition	350.00
Belter. Side. Rosewood. Pierced, carved grapes and roses. Upholstered needlepoint seat and back	3500.00
Biedermeier-style. Arm. Fruitwood, lyre splat, shaped seat. C. 1850 ..	225.00
*Captain's. Pine. Roll-back. Refinished	325.00
Children's	
Arm. Ladderback, cane seat	75.00
Arrowback. Plank seat	150.00
Captain's. Plank seat. Hickory. Original finish	175.00
High Chair. Mixed woods. Cane seat, folding-type	150.00
High Chair with stroller. Pine. Spindle back, cane seat. Refinished	225.00
Ladderback. Red paint, rush seat. Oak. Early	225.00
Morris. Oak. Upholstered	95.00
Potty. Pine. Painted and stenciled	65.00
Side. Rush seat, ring turned legs, ball feet. American. C. 1910	125.00
Chippendale-style	
Arm. Dining. Centennial, slip seat	750.00
Corner. Mahogany. Horseshoe rest, turned posts, solid splats, molded seat	750.00
Corner. Mahogany with upholstered slip seat. English	850.00
Country. Slat back, rush seat. 18th century	500.00
Side. Cherry. Centennial, slip seat	500.00
Side. Ribbon back. Upholstered slip seat	750.00
Side. Mahogany. English. C. 1750	750.00
Eastlake, Victorian	
Arm. Walnut. Upholstered back and seat	250.00
Side. Walnut. Small arms, cane seat	150.00
Side. Walnut. Upholstered, tufted back, castors on front legs, small arms	250.00
Empire-style	
Arm. Mahogany. Square back, upholstered seat, brass castors. Eagle terminals on arms. C. 1825	650.00
Side. Walnut. Slip seat	250.00
Folding. Carpet back and seat. Late Victorian	175.00
George II-style. Corner. Mahogany. Slip seat, upholstered with crewel work. C. 1740	1500.00
Gothic-style. Side. Walnut. Upholstered seat	500.00
Hepplewhite-style	
Arm. Mahogany with satin wood inlay. English. C. 1800	1500.00
Side. Upholstered seat. Shield back. New England	1000.00
Side. Mahogany. Rosettes on back of splats.	650.00
Hitchcock. Plank seat. Original paint and stencil. C. 1840	750.00
*Hitchcock-style. Rush seat, original paint and stenciling	250.00
Ladderback	
Cherry. Ruh seat. C. 1880	450.00
Mahogany. Pierced slats. Rush seat	500.00
Maple. Rush seat, ball turned stretcher	375.00
Louis XV-style	
Arm. Walnut. Finger carved, upholstered seat. Victorian	750.00
Side. Walnut. Finger carved frame, scroll and rose carved crest. Upholstered	350.00

Windsor-style. Broad arm. Christmas tree splat. Elm and ash. English $900.00

Morris
Oak. Lion's paw feet and arms. Adjustable back 200.00
Walnut. Ball and claw feet, brass rod. Adjustable back 250.00
Office. (Desk) Arm. Oak, flat spindles, revolving seat. Tilt back. C. 1910 .... 300.00
Oriental
Arm. Heavy carved teak. Japanese 750.00
Side. Heavy carvings, arched top with finials, carved seat. Japanese. C. 1900 .... 500.00
Plank Bottom. 4 half turned spindles, pillow crest, original paint and stenciling 175.00
Pressed Back. Side Oak 50.00
Queen Anne-style
Banister back, split spindle 750.00
Corner. Tiger maple and pine. Pierced slats, scalloped apron 1000.00
Corner. Walnut. Slip seat 1000.00
Country. Bulbous turnings, original ball feet, replaced rope seat 375.00
Side. Walnut. Cabriole legs, pad feet. English 1500.00
Renaissance, Victorian
Arm. Lady's. Walnut. Upholstered. Refinished. C. 1870 .... 500.00
Side. Walnut with maple inlay. Upholstered back and seat. C. 1870 .... 350.00
Rococo, Victorian
Arm. Gentleman's. Finger molded and pierced. Reupholstered. C. 1860 .... 750.00
Arm. Lady's. Refinished and reupholstered 500.00
Side. Cherry. Balloon back, slip seat 250.00
Side. Walnut. Balloon back, upholstered seat 200.00
Sheraton Country. Arm. Cherry. Rush seat 350.00
William and Mary. Banister back. New England. C. 1740 .... 1000.00
Windsor-style
Arm. Bow back, 7 spindles. Bamboo turned. Black with gold trim 1250.00
Arm. Brace back, 9 spindles, bulbous turnings, shaped seat. Original paint 2500.00
Arm. Comb back. Rhode Island. C. 1780 .... 3500.00
Arm. Fan back. Signed Wallace Nutting 1250.00
Side. Bow back. Signed Wallace Nutting 750.00
Side. Brace back, 9 spindles 850.00
Side. Dove cote. 7 spindles. Bamboo turned legs. Original paint .. 500.00
Side. Fan back. 7 spindles. Saddle seat 650.00
Writing Arm. 7 spindles. Conn. C. 1780 .... 3500.00

*Reproduced Item

CHESTS

Blanket Chest. Camphor. 21½x22x42½". Brass hardware. Dovetailed $250.00

Tall Chest. Chippendale-style. 23x37x71½″. Cherry. Pa. C. 1780-1790 .... $4000.00

Blanket
Pine. 20x24x42″ long. Cannonball feet. Refinished ....$ 400.00
Pine. 20x29x45″. Field panels, wrought iron straps, replaced brasses, bracket base. C. 1770 .. 950.00
Poplar. 19x26¾ x 39¼″. Original graining, ball feet. Pa. C. 1840 .. 500.00

Chippendale-style
18x38x45″. Two drawers over four. Tiger stripe maple 2200.00
19x40x56″. Curly maple. Six drawers, original brasses. New England. C. 1800 .... 5000.00
22x29x49″. Blanket. Pine. Strap hinges. Pa. C. 1780 .... 1250.00
22½x40½x66½″. Three drawers over 2 over 5 graduated drawers. Replaced brasses 5500.00
38x60¾″. Mahogany. Molded cornice, three freeze drawers, 5 graduated drawers, bracket feet. Replaced brasses 3000.00
75½″. Highboy. Cherry. Fluted corners, shaped apron, carved ball and claw feet. New York. C. 1770 12500.00
80½″. Highboy. Cherry. Bonnet top. Centennial 200.00

Commode
Mahogany. English Chippendale-style. C. 1820 .... 750.00
Pine. Refinished 300.00
Oak. Machine carvings. One drawer over 2 doors, towel racks 250.00
Walnut. White marble top. Back splash, candle shelves, one drawer over 2 doors. C. 1860 .... 500.00

Dower. 22¼x29x50″. Three drawers. Original finish. Inscribed and dated 1808. Pa 7500.00

Eastlake, Victorian
30″. Oak. Three drawers, machine carvings, white marble top 250.00
32″. Walnut. Three drawers, candle stands, attached mirror, white marble top, machine carved 500.00
48″. Oak. Two drawers over 1 drawer over 2 door cupboard. Back splash, machine carved 500.00

Empire
46″. Cherry with curly maple facade. Four drawers, paneled ends, columns. C. 1835 .... 650.00
47″. Cherry. Four drawers, inlaid. C. 1840 .... 500.00

Hepplewhite
18x30x30″. Mahogany. Bow front, plank ends, brass hardware. Gold tooled leather top. Late 250.00
20¼x36¾x 38¾″. Four drawers. Cherry with pine and chestnut secondary woods. Inlaid, original brasses 3500.00
40″. Mahogany. Band inlaid. Four graduated drawers, fluted columns. Mass. C. 1820 .... 1950.00
46″. Cherry with mahogany strip inlay and shield escutcheons. Five drawers. French feet, original brasses 2500.00

Ice. 36x 50½″. Golden oak. Four paneled doors, original ornate brasses 500.00

Pine
39x48½″. Two drawers over 4. Original brasses. Dovetailed. C. 1810 .... 1850.00
40x42″. Four drawers, plank sides 650.00
42x46½″. Four drawers, plank sides. Maple pulls............. 750.00

Queen Anne-style
Blanket. Cherry and tulip wood. On frame, New England 3000.00
Chest on Chest. 41¼″ wide, 6′ 11″ high. Cherry. Flat top, molded cornice. Three small drawers above 5 graduated drawers. Lower section with 3 small

drawers over 4 graduated drawers. Molded apron, cabriole legs, pad feet. New England. C. 1760-80 .... 8500.00
Highboy. 36½ x 72". Maple. Flat top. Molded cornice over 5 graduated drawers, 3 freize drawers over 3 drawers below. Conn. C. 1750 .... 8500.00
Lowboy. 20x 32x33". Cherry. Original brasses 5000.00

Rococo, Victorian. Walnut. Two small drawers, marble insert over 4 graduated drawers. Attached oval mirror, leaf pulls. C. 1870 ... 650.00
Sea Chest. 12½ x 14½x25½". Strap hinges, handles. Fitted for bottles. Early 19th century 500.00

Sheraton
19x22½x40". Blanket. Curly maple 1250.00
21x40½ x44⅞". Cherry. Two split drawers over 3 graduated drawers. Inlaid escutcheons, replaced brasses. C. 1830 .... 850.00
Silver Chest. 8x 18x 24". Mahogany. Hinged lift top. One drawer below. Silk lined fitted interior. Brass hardware .. 350.00

William and Mary-style. 35½". Walnut and curly maple. Two small drawers, 3 graduated long drawers. Replaced feet. Mass. C. 1740 .... 1850.00

CRADLES

Cherry. 17x40". Shaped ends, hand holds ....$ 225.00
Maple
22x38x40". Windsor-style 350.00
26½x32x51". Folding-type. C. 1880 .... 225.00
Mixed Woods. 38" long. Spindled, arched bentwood top and bottom. Straight spindled sides. Feather mattress 125.00
Pine
13x34". Open sides 175.00
14x37". Hooded. Dovetailed. Refinished 350.00
Walnut
42". Spindle-type. Refinished. C. 1900 .... 350.00
44". Bonnet top 450.00
Walnut and walnut burl veneered. 16x37". On platform. C. 1877 .. 500.00

CUPBOARDS

Corner Cupboard. Walnut. Brass hardware. 18½x52x84". Two 6 glass pane doors over three drawers over two door base $3500.00

Chimney
9¼x38". Hanging-type. Four shelves. Original paint ....$ 1250.00
14x17x74". Two doors. Original paint. Brass hardware 1750.00
Corner
Cherry. 33x83" high. Swan neck, urn-shaped wood finials. Cathedral door with glazed panels, one drawer over single cupboard door. Bracket feet 2500.00
Cherry. 45 x 86" high. Primitive. Two pieces. Pa. C. 1844 .... 4000.00
Cherry. 57½ x 87½" high. Two 8-lite doors above two blind doors below. Two pieces 3500.00
Cherry. 92" high. Cathedral door, blown glass panes, butterfly shelves, Original brass hinges. Two pieces..................... 6500.00

Cherry and Tiger Maple. 96" high. Cathedral door with blown glass panes. Three drawers over 2 doors. Bracket feet 5000.00
Curly Maple. 86" high. Glazed panel door, 16 panes, two drawers over cupboard. C. 1810.. 5000.00
Pine. 35½ x 77½" high. One paneled door over single paneled door. Molded base and cornice .. 1250.00
Pine. 82" high. Two blind doors over 3 drawers over two blind doors. All original 1500.00
Poplar. 40x77" high. Simple cornice. Four panels on single upper door with single paneled door .. 1000.00
Walnut. 78½" high. Art Nouveau. Shaped cornice above shelves. C. 1900 .... 1250.00

Flat Wall
Honduras Mahogany. 5x12x16". Curved glass sides, glass door. C. 1930's 150.00
Oak, Golden. Curved glass sides, glass door, mirrored back, glass shelves 500.00
Oak, Golden. 16½ x37x68". Two glass doors over two drawers, over two blind doors. Machine carved 500.00
Pine. 43½ x 74" high. Molded cornice above two paneled doors. New York. C. 1810 .... 1750.00
Pine. 84" high. Bow front, blind doors, dental molding. "H" hinges. Refinished 2000.00
Walnut. Eastlake. Single panel glazed doors, two drawers over two blind doors. Machine carvings 500.00

Hanging
Cherry. 19¾x25". Two doors with glass panes, brass and porcelain fittings. Orig. condition. C. 1900 125.00
Pine, Painted. 12½ x20¾x33½". Paneled door, three shelves. Original paint. C. 1820 .... 300.00
Poplar. 20x29" high. Painted graining. One shelf, blind door .. 500.00

Jelly
15x33x57½" high. Two doors, four shelves. Gallery top. Original red paint. C. 1850 .... 750.00
27x34x58" high. Single door. Simple molding. Stripped of old paint 300.00

Kas. 53½" high, 54½" wide. Pine. Diamond inlay on doors. Canadian 1500.00

Pie Safe
Pine. Eagle tins 1000.00
Pine. Tulip tins. Original red paint. Country Sheraton 650.00
Poplar. Flower basket tins. Refinished 500.00
Poplar. Pinwheel tins 350.00
Walnut. Pinwheel tins 400.00

DESKS

Chippendale-style
36x43½". Slant front. Curly maple. New England..........$ 4000.00
38x46½". Slant front. Pine. Brass hardware 2500.00
40½x44". Slant front. Ox-bow. Block and Fan interior. Original brasses. Mahogany. C. 1765 .... 8500.00

Davenport
Walnut. Inlaid top, front 500.00
Walnut. Spring operated structure, brass gallery 750.00

Eastlake, Victorian. 35x62". Drop front. Machine carvings, gallery top, fitted interior. Walnut. C. 1890 .... 500.00

Empire, American. Butler's. 44x49". Cherry 650.00

Bookkeepers Desk. 3 pieces. 28x49x90" Pine. Brass hardware. Top with fitted interior, lift top writing surface, over 8 graduated drawers $2850.00

Hepplewhite. Slant front. Mahogany case. Veneered drawer fronts. Original brass bail pulls. Inlaid. C. 1790-1800 .... 3500.00

Lap Desks

8½x11½". Child's. Walnut. Drawing slate, green felt writing surface. Original label. C. 1877 .. 125.00

9x12½". Walnut. Blue velvet lining. Secret compartment. 19th century 125.00

9½x14". Oak 75.00

10x12". Mahogany. Brass fittings and filigree decorations 195.00

Queen Anne-style. 36x42". Slant front. Maple. Fitted interior, one drawer above 3 graduated drawers. Original brasses 6000.00

Renaissance, Victorian. Walnut. Cylinder front, fitted interior, 3 small drawers. C. 1876 .... 2000.00

*Roll Tops

Mahogany. 48". "C" curved 750.00

Oak. 36". "S" curved 600.00

Oak. 50". "S" curved 1500.00

School, Child's. Pine with iron. Folding seat. C. 1930 .... 35.00

Schoolmaster's

Flat top. 26x31x36". Oak. One drawer 150.00

Kneehole-type. 25x59". Mahogany, veneered drawers. Four drawers in each pedestal, fitted interior 650.00

Slant top. 33x37½". Painted pine. Pigeon holes 275.00

Sheraton, Country. 32" wide. Pine. Slant front, one deep drawer, gallery back 1500.00

Store, Country

7½x19x24". Pine. Counter top-type 150.00

72" wide. Pigeon holes. walnut .. 650.00

*Reproduced Item

DOUGH TROUGHS

Cherry. 29x32". Dovetailed, turned legs. Original finish ....$ 750.00

Chestnut. 18x28x28". Pine legs.... 300.00

Maple. 33x38". Set in legs. Sliding top 500.00

Pine

13x24". Table top-type 100.00

28" long. Table top-type. Original graining and dovetailed. C. 1840 185.00

30x32". Splayed legs with stretcher, covered................ 750.00

34x29½". Dovetailed, turned legs 350.00

Walnut. 20x27x39". Dovetailed, splayed legs 350.00

Lancaster, Pa. grain
15x31x33½" $250.00

DRY SINKS

Ash. 17x45½x46". One small drawer over 2 door cupboard. Wooden pulls. Hand decorated. C. 1890 ....$475.00

Butternut. 20x35x42". Two doors, one shelf inside. Original stippling and finish ....$ 350.00

Oak. 19x34x44". Zinc lined. Two doors 450.00

Pine

16½x30x32". One door base 395.00

37x37". One drawer, two doors .. 350.00

44". Original green paint 500.00

42x48". One drawer, two doors below. Copper lined. Redecorated 350.00

66". Painted. All original. Lancaster, Pa 2000.00

Pine and Poplar. 50". Two drawers, two doors below 500.00

Poplar. 36x42". Single drawer, 2 paneled doors. Painted graining 450.00

Walnut. 33x44". One drawer with two doors 375.00

FRAMES

Brass

7x12". Art Nouveau-style. Two oval openings. Easel back ......$ 125.00

8x14". Florentine styling. Easel back 75.00

13x16" oval. C. 1880's 85.00

Brass Plated

2½x3½". Blue enameled decor .. 20.00

7¾x 10¾". Pierced, scrolled, easel back 30.00

Curly Maple. 15x17" 125.00

Gold Gilt

10½ x 12¾". Berries and leaves in relief 75.00

13" oval. Fruit and flowers in relief 75.00

24x28". Shadow box-type. Scrolled. C. 1900 .... 100.00

Leather over wood. 6x6½". Birds, animals, etc. in relief. Folk Art .. 175.00

Mahogany. Gold liner. 35" square .. 100.00

Oak

10½ x 38½" 50.00

20x77". Medallions and bulleyes. 19th century 275.00

Pine. 14x16" 40.00

Porcelain. 10x12". Double openings. Handpainted pansy decor, gold trim. T & V France 75.00

Silver, Sterling

4x6". Easel-type 40.00

5⅝x7". Plain rim 60.00

8x9". Ornate 100.00

Walnut

8¾x 11". Oval 30.00

8x12". Cross bar corners 40.00

11x13½". Oval. Gold liner 50.00

16x19". Oval 75.00

18¼ x 27½". Leaves in relief. Gold liner 100.00

28x32". Shadow box-type. Double liner 125.00

HAT RACKS and HALL TREES

Hall Tree. Walnut. 80" high. Beveled mirror. Brown marble insert. Umbrella holders. Renaissance, Victorian $600.00

Iron, Cast. 10" beveled mirror. 12 hooks, umbrella holders, 4 arched legs. C. 1880 ....$ 225.00

Oak. 60" high. 8 brass hooks. C. 1910 .... 50.00

Oak. Hall Tree. 90" high. Beveled mirror, 4 pegs, hinged seat, umbrella holders at sides 600.00

Pine. Accordion-type. 7 porcelain pegs 40.00

Pine. Accordion-type. 9 turned wooden pegs 50.00

Walnut. Accordion-type. Arched, 14 turned wooden pegs 85.00

Walnut. 27" long mirror with 3 pegs below 50.00

Walnut. Hall Trees. 96½" high. Beveled mirror with wooden pegs, white marble insert, umbrella holders. C. 1870 .... 800.00

ICE CREAM PARLOR FURNITURE

Chairs	
Heart back. Refinished ....$	60.00
Spectacle. Refinished	60.00
Arm. Wood seat	100.00
Stools	
26½" high. Refinished	50.00
30" high, 12" diam. seat. Refinished..................	60.00
Tables	
27" square. Oak top............	175.00
30" diam. Oak top	200.00
Table and 2 chairs. Child's. Table 18" diam., chairs, 9½" diam. seat. Set	195.00
Table and 4 chairs. Table, 30" diam. wood top. Chairs, 14" diam. replaced seats. Refinished. Set ..	450.00

LOVE SEATS

Art Nouveau. 62". Carved mahogany frame. Upholstered $	1000.00
Empire. 48". Mahogany. Re-upholstered	650.00
Hepplewhite. Walnut. Spade feet, bellflower inlay. Refinished and re-upholstered	1250.00
Rennaissance, Victorian. Finger carved, tufted upholstery	500.00
Rococo, Victorian. Walnut frame with rose carving on 3 crests. Refinished and re-upholstered ..	850.00
Sheraton. 52". Refinished. Re-upholstered in velvet, nailhead trim	850.00
Victorian. Early. Walnut. Mirror back	850.00
William and Mary-style. 48". Loose cushion, turned baluster legs, stretcher	750.00

MAGAZINE RACKS

Canterbury	
American. 14½ x 18½x20". Walnut ....$	500.00
American. 17x17½x22½". Acorn finials, one drawer, brass castors	750.00
English. 15½x19½x25". Mahogany	750.00
Eastlake, Victorian	
13½x18". Walnut. Machine carved.......................	50.00
13½x26". Turned posts. Machine carved, pierced sides	85.00
Rococo, Victorian. 13½x23". walnut. Carved leaves, flowers ..	150.00

MANTELS

Marble, Carrara. 70" shelf. Adams-style.........................$	1500.00
Oak. 66x78" high. Carved and scalloped columns	750.00
Pine	
44x47" high	150.00
68". Curved top section. C. 1820	500.00
82". Carved rosettes, round columns. C. 1790	1000.00
82". Chip carved. C. 1800	750.00

MIRRORS

Sheraton. Mahogany frame. Reverse painting on glass tablet. 10x22". C. 1810 ....$300.00

Cheval. 30x57½". Oak, S-supports, paw feet, castors ....$	250.00
Chippendale-style	
13½ x 30¾". Walnut. Original glass	850.00
14x27½". Glass eagle finial. Original glass	1000.00
18x26". Mahogany. English	1250.00
Convex. 27" wide, 34" overall height. Carved, gilted, eagle finial	2000.00

Dining Table. Hepplewhite. Banquet. 10′ long. Mahogany with diamond shaped inlays. Baltimore. C. 1790 .... $4000.00

CLOSE UP VIEW OF INLAY OF ABOVE BANQUET TABLE

Chippendale-style. 43x43″. Maple	1250.00
Duncan Phyfe. 9′4″. Mahogany. D-shaped ends, 3 pedestals with reeded tetrapods, brass paw-castors	3000.00
Georgian-style. 51x98″. Mahogany. C. 1800	8000.00
Hepplewhite. 9′3″. Mahogany. English	5000.00
Queen Anne-style. 36x48″. Elm	1350.00
Queen Anne-style. 51″ oval. Cherry. Gateleg, pad feet	4500.00
Twentieth Century. 45″ diam. Oak. Pedestal base, scrolled feet	600.00
Victorian. 48″ diam. Walnut. Pedestal base, paw feet	750.00
Drop Leaf	
Chippendale-style, Country. 13½x40″, 13½″ leaves. Maple top, birch legs. Painted	450.00

Marble top table. 22½x30x34″. Renaissance, Victorian. Finger carved walnut. White marble $750.00

Chippendale-style. 42″ wide. Mahogany. Ball and claw feet	1750.00
Empire, American. 18x48″, 23″ leaves. Mahogany	350.00
Hepplewhite. 30x60″. Walnut	650.00
Queen Anne-style. 42″. Walnut	3500.00
Sheraton. 18¼x29x46″, 20½″ leaves. Walnut	850.00
Harvest	
5′ long. Pine	650.00
5′5″ long. Pine. Turned legs, spade feet	850.00
6′ long. Walnut	1000.00
Hutch	
40x58″. Pine. Three board top, hinged lid. Painted	400.00
48½″. Pine. Three board top, shoe foot base, trestle feet. Painted	750.00
Library. 23x23x29″. Oak. One shelf	200.00
Marble Top	
14x18″. Walnut. Finger molded, scrolled legs, castors. White marble	395.00
15x20″. Walnut. Machine carvings. Brown marble. Eastlake, C. 1890	300.00
18x22″ oval. Walnut. Finger carved. Center pedestal with 4 supports. White marble	395.00
18½x23″. Walnut. Machine carved. Black marble insert. C. 1890	250.00
24″. Turtle top. Walnut. Molded apron, scrolled balustered supports. White marble	600.00

24x33". Turtle top. Walnut. Carved cabriole legs, stretcher base with urn. White marble 850.00

Papier Mache
- 32" diam. Tilt top. Wood pedestal. Black lacquered floral center. Gold trim. 500.00
- Nest of 3. 15x22" largest. Black lacquer, MOP inlay. C. 1890 .... 450.00

Pembroke
- Chippendale-style. 28x35". English. C. 1770 .... 2500.00
- Hepplewhite. 25x30". Mahogany. Line inlay 650.00
- Sheraton. 18½x30", 11" leaves. Cherry, tiger stripe maple drawer 450.00

Poker. 36" diam. Oak. Swivel iron pedestal base 650.00

Pool. Regulation size, 9' long. Oak. Slate top, webbed leather pockets 1500.00

Tavern
- Maple. 40". Turned spool legs 500.00
- Pine. 48". Country Chippendale-style. Some original red paint 1250.00
- Pine. 48". Cherry turned legs, box stretcher 500.00
- Pine. 60". Maple turned legs, single drawer 600.00
- Walnut. 64". Turned legs, splined top, 2 drawers. C. 1750 .... 3000.00

Tea
- 18¾" diam. Walnut. Dish top. Inlaid with star and circles. Reeded pedestal, serpent feet 750.00
- 26x30" oval. Cherry. Splayed legs, pad feet 1850.00
- 29" diam. Cherry. Tilt top. Birdcage. Pa. C. 1760 .... 1500.00
- 30" diam. Mahogany. Tilt top. Birdcage 1500.00
- 31" diam. Maple. Tilt top. Pie crust top. 750.00
- 36" diam. Mahogany. Tilt top. Tripod base, serpent feet 750.00
- 36" square. Maple. Slipper foot. Pie crust top 1000.00

Work
- Empire. 17½ x 23x30½". Cherry. Two fitted drawers, vase turned pedestal, 3 scrolled legs. New York 500.00
- Hepplewhite. 18½" square. Mahogany. Cherry inlay, 2 drop leaves, splayed legs. C. 1830 .... 300.00
- Hepplewhite, Country. 28½x42". Walnut. Single drawer 200.00
- Oriental. 19x26". Black lacquered, gold stenciling. Ivory fittings 650.00
- Queen-Anne-style, Country. 29x45". Bread board ends, single drawer, turned legs, pad feet. Some original paint 750.00
- Regency. 16x29x32". Mahogany. English 1750.00
- Victorian. 17½" diam. Walnut. Sewing. 1880 .... 300.00

TEA WAGONS

Walnut. D-shaped drop leaves. One drawer, slide out tray. Two large wooden wheels ....$ 295.00

Walnut. D-shaped drop leaves, glass lift off tray top. Two large wooden wheels, castors. Victorian 200.00

WAGON SEATS

Wagon seats cannot be classified with seats from a wagon. Early wagon seats were usually constructed with a double frame and a basketry-type seat. They served a dual purpose .. in the house and in the family wagon for additional seating.

Hickory. Spindle back and arms, leather basketweave seat, 6 legs. 18th century ....$ 750.00

Maple. Slat back, rush seat. Early 19th century 650.00

Pine. Painted. Slat back, rush seat. Connecticut. C. 1830 .... 650.00

Pine. Windsor-type. Spindle back, cut-out heart sides 500.00

WICKER

Rattan, reed and willow are all known as wicker. Wicker items were produced and imported from the Orient as early as the 18th century. It was not until the mid 19th century that wicker furniture was manufactured in the United States. The elaborate, ornate and closely woven designs are from this Victorian era. The plainer and coarser reedings are from the early 1900's.

Bassinet. 18x23" high. Ornate. C. 1890 ....$ 250.00

Chairs
- Arm. Rolled arms, round seat, scrolled curled back 250.00
- Arm. Spring seat, rolled arms. Refinished. C. 1910 .... 150.00
- Rocker, Child's. High fan back, rolled arms. Upholstered slip seat .. 150.00
- Rocker, Child's. Upholstered slip seat. C. 1910 .... 75.00
- Rocker, Lady's. Ornate. Green velvet seat. Refinished. C. 1890 .. 350.00

Foot Stool. 13½x16½" diam. top. Wicker apron $75.00

Rocker. Spring cushion seat. Barrel back	150.00
Side. Ornate. C. 1890	500.00
Carriage. Large wire wheels, rubber tires. Re-upholstered interior, refinished	650.00
Crib. High back. Ornate. Early	500.00
Hall Tree. Floor model. 12 pegs	175.00
Hamper, Corner. 25" high. Hinged lid. C. 1890	55.00
Lamp, Floor. 27" diam. shade, 71" high. Refinished	250.00
Settee. 23x31x50". Tete-tete-type ..	300.00
Sofa. 72" long. Three spring cushions. Closed back	400.00
Tables	
12x22¾". C. 1900	95.00
20x36" oval. Refinished	165.00
Tea Wagon. 31x34". Removable glass serving tray top	250.00
Tray. 8x12" oval. Butterfly and fern under glass	35.00

YARN WINDERS

Double Spool. Rare ....$	275.00
Niddy Noddy. Maple. Hand pegged	45.00
4-spoke. Adjustable. Pine	150.00
6-spoke. Pine. Hand crafted, mortised and pegged	165.00
6-spoke. Pine. Painted and decorated	185.00
6-spoke. Walnut. Complete	175.00

6-spoke. Poplar. All original, complete with counter $185.00

GAME PLATES

A general classification of special plates used to serve game, including fish, is game plates. They were popular in the late 1800's and early 1900's. They were decorated with various species of birds, fish or other game. A set usually consisted of a service platter, individual serving plates and a sauce boat. Many sets have been divided and the individual plates used for wall hangings.

Birds

Plates	
9". Grouse. Heavy gold. Artist signed. Marked Comte' de Artois, Limoges ....$	38.50
9½". Ducks. Limoges	40.00
10⅛". Bird and 2 water spaniels. Crimped gold rim. Signed "R.K. Beck."	65.00

Bird. Platter. 18½" long. Partridge center with dark green border and gold trim. Theodore Haviland, Limoges. Artist signed $250.00

10½". Decal of "Singer of American Wild Game Birds." 27.50
10½". Handpainted game bird. Signed LUS, Limoges 85.00
12½". Handpainted birds, foliage, etc. Artist signed. Limoges 175.00
Platter. 10¾ x 11½". Long-billed duck. Water scene. Scalloped edges with gold trim 150.00
Sets
7 pieces. Game birds. Molded edges with shell decor. Impressed maker's mark. Bonn, Germany .. 250.00
7 pieces. Game birds. Platter, 6-8½" plates. Artist signed. France 295.00
8 pieces. Birds in marsh. Cobalt and gold fluted border. Limoges. H & C Co 425.00

Deer

Sets
5 pieces. Artist signed. "Beck." Buffalo Pottery ....$ 275.00
7 pieces. 18" platter, 6-9¼" plates. Gold trim. Unsigned 175.00

Fish

Plates
8½". Hanging-type. Colorful fish swimming on green shaded ground. Scalloped border, gold trim. Signed "Lancy", "Biarritz, W.S. or S.W. Co., Limoges, France" 30.00
9". Trout. Cobalt border. Signed "Kestler Beehive," (old underglaze mark), M.Z. Austria 45.00
9". Underwater scene of fish, clam, plant life. Embossed and scalloped rim decorated with green and gold seaweed. "T & V Limoges" 35.00
Platters
14". Bass on lure. Signed "R.K. Beck." 85.00
16¼". Bass, waterlilies. Heavily embossed. Signed "MAX", Limoges 125.00
Sets
7 pieces. 16" platter, 6-8¼" plates. Seashells and fish. Limoges 225.00
7 pieces. 15" platter, 6-9" plates. Signed. "R. K. Beck." Buffalo Pottery 325.00
8 pieces. 24" platter. 4 plates. Covered tureen and sauce boat with attached underplate. Rosenthal 350.00
9 pieces. 17" platter, 8-8⅞" plates. Embossed gilted rims. Artist signed, Limoges 375.00
10 pieces. 24" platter, 6-9" plates. Covered casserole. Sauce boat. Handpainted. "Self Bavaria." 375.00
14 pieces. 22" platter, 10-8½" plates. Sauce boat. Covered tureen. Artist signed, Limoges .. 750.00
14 pieces. 23½" platter, 12-8½" scalloped plates. Sauce boat with underliner. Pastel colors. Gold rococo border. T.V. Limoges 400.00
15 pieces. 24" platter. 12-9" plates. Sauce with attached plate, covered tureen. Handpainted. Heavy raised gold design on edges. Gold handles and finial. Artist signed, Limoges 750.00

GAMES

Parlour or home games have regained their importance for home entertainment. Earlier versions of the old 'standbys' are being collected for the quality materials and fine craftsmanship used in their making, such as handcarved wood chess sets and ivory Mah Jong tiles. More recent examples of home games are considered collectible because they are no longer in production, extinction of the manufacturer or for their ingenuity.

Anagrams. Milton Bradley. C. 1940 ....$ 8.00
Authors. Milton Bradley. C. 1908 .. 17.50
Big Apple. Rosebud Art Co. C. 1938 12.50
Blocks, Wood
4" sq. Nine. Colorful animals, numbers, letters, etc. Early 1900's 30.00

"Lotto." McLaughlin Bros. Lithographed box. C. 1880 ....$25.00

7⅛" sq. Nine. Nursery rhymes with scenes 50.00
Bradleys Cavalry. Milton Bradley. Sixty soldiers with stands. C. 1890's 85.00
Chess Set. Carved ivory chess pieces. Leather covered box, brass hardware 450.00
Combination Board. McLaughlin. C. 1905 .... 30.00
Corn and Beans. E.G. Selchow and Righter Co. C. 1875 .... 25.00
Cribbage Board. Carved ivory. Chinese 60.00
Dominoes. Ivory and ebony. Brass pegs. Complete 40.00
Donkey Party. Whitman. C. 1930's 15.00
Five Little Pigs Puzzle, The. 6¾" sq. R. Bliss Mfg. Co. Boxed. C. 1880 .. 17.50
Follow The Leader. 27x 31". Lithographed. C. 1906.......... 50.00
Fortune Teller, The. Milton Bradley. Original box. Copyright 1905 .... 30.00
Funny Face. Ideal Book Builder. C. 1912 .... 35.00
Game of Auction, The. Milton Bradley. C. 1900 .... 15.00
Humpty Dumpty. Parker Bros. C. 1924 .... 35.00
I've Got A Secret. Lowell Toy Mfg. Corp. C. 1956 .... 15.00
Jack Straws. Wood. Milton Bradley Co. C. 1906 .... 15.00
Keno. Milton Bradley. C. 1930's 10.00
Lotto. Wooden box with slide cover. Lithographed cards. C. 1880 .... 25.00
Mah Jong
Bone Tiles. Lacquered box 50.00
Ivory Tiles 300.00
Ivory over wood tiles. C. 1920 .... 75.00
Plastic Tiles. Leatherette box 30.00
Marble Bingo. Wolverine Supply & Mfg. Co. C. 1930's 20.00
Meet The Presidents. Selchow & Righter. C. 1953 .... 20.00
Merry Game of Old Maid, The. McLaughlin Bros. Copyright 1898 35.00
Mother Goose. Milton Bradley. C. 1910 .... 25.00
Nationalities. Fireside Game Co. C. 1897 .... 20.00
New Pretty Village Church Set, The. McLaughlin Bros. C. 1897 ...... 60.00
Parcheesi. Selchow & Righter. C. 1890 .... 15.00
Quiz Kids Radio Question Bee. Whitman. C. 1940 .... 15.00
Ring My Nose. Milton Bradley. Ring toss game. C. 1925 .... 20.00
Tiddly Winks. Lithographed box. 5½" sq. Complete. C. 1890...... 20.00
Tom Hamilton's Football Game, Pigskin. Parker Bros. C. 1946 ...... 30.00
Stamps — A Game for Stamp Collectors. Whitman. C. 1937 ...... 15.00
Toy Money. Milton Bradley. C. 1940's 10.00
Twiggy. Milton Bradley. C. 1967 .. 6.50
Uncle Wiggily. Milton Bradley. C. 1949 .... 8.50
Waterloo. Parker Bros. Pat'd. 1894 35.00
Whist Set. Eight trays in original box. Pat'd. 1900 .... 25.00
Winnie Winkle Glider Race Game. Milton Bradley. C. 1930's 15.00
Wizard, The. Fulton Specialty Co. Boxed. C. 1921 .... 18.00
World Educator, The. W.S. Reed. C. 1919 .... 25.00

GARDEN FURNISHINGS

Garden furniture and accessories, mainly from the Victorian Gingerbread era are being collected for use on patios or for special garden settings. With the current interest in plants, all types of planters and plant stands are being sought by home gardeners and decorators. Many of these items are being reproduced in design.

Benches
34x44" overall length. Cast iron. Ornamental. Painted white ....$ 350.00
40x43" overall length. Wire mesh. Painted white 250.00
Chairs
Arm. 17" diam. Seat, 33" high. Wire mesh. Painted white 150.00
Side. 14" diam. seat, 31" high. Ornate. Cast iron 175.00

Bench. 34" high x 44" long. Cast iron. Ornamental. Painted white . . $350.00

Fence. 39½" high. Cast iron. Ornamental. Painted black. Per lineal foot	25.00
Planters, Urn-shaped	
19x23½" high. Cast iron...........	300.00
21½x42½" high. Cast iron. Ornate handles. Three swan base ..	350.00
28x32" high, on 21½" plinth. Cast iron. Turned-down rim. No handles	350.00
Post Finial. 21" high. Pineapple form. Cast iron	125.00
Stand, Plant. 27x40x44" overall height. Three tiered, wire mesh. 6 legs, porcelain castors	225.00
Sundial. 8½". Brass	150.00

GAUDY DUTCH

Gaudy Dutch is a hand decorated, opaque soft pasteware made in the Staffordshire district of England during the first quarter of the 19th century. It was presumed to have been made as an earthenware imitation of the Imari-type porcelain produced at Derby and Worcester. The glaze is soft with the blue under glaze and the other colors over the glaze. There is no lustre on any of the standard patterns. Most of the wares are unmarked, but occasionally a rare piece may be found impressed Wood or Riley. Reproductions of the patterns have been reported, namely cup plates, but the body of the wares are semi-porcelain and not earthenware; therefore obvious. The known patterns are: Butterfly (two types), Carnation, Dahlia, Double Rose, Dove, Grape, Leaf (scarce), Oyster, Primrose, Single Rose, Strawflower, Sunflower, Urn (two types . . .also known as Vase or Flower Pot), War Bonnet, Zinnia.

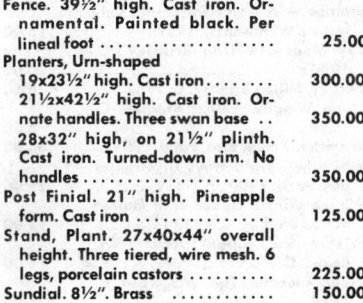

Plate. 9¾". "Butterfly". Wide border band $750.00

Butterfly	
Coffee Pot. 10⅞" ....$	4000.00
Creamer	425.00
Cup and Saucer	650.00
Plate. 8¼"	600.00
Teapot	1750.00
Carnation	
Bowl. 5½"..................	550.00
Cup and Saucer	485.00
Plates	
6½"	295.00
8¼"	450.00
9¾"	650.00
Dahlia	
Creamer	375.00
Cup and Saucer	500.00
Sugar, Covered	500.00
Teapot	1500.00
Double Rose	
Plate. 7½"	450.00
Dove	
Coffee Pot. 11"	3500.00
Cup and Saucer	550.00
Plates	
8¼"	500.00
9¾"	750.00
Grape	
Cup and Saucer	275.00
Sugar, Covered	450.00
Oyster	
Cup and Saucer	450.00
Plate. 8¼"	400.00
Single Rose	
Cup and Saucer	300.00
Plate. 9¾"	650.00

Urn

Cup and Saucer	475.00
Plate. 8¼"	450.00

War Bonnet

Creamer	365.00
Cup and Saucer	550.00
Plate. 9¾"	750.00
Teapot	1500.00

GAUDY IRONSTONE

Ironstone is an opaque, heavy bodied earthenware containing large proportions of flint and slag. Gaudy Ironstone is decorated with some of the patterns bearing resemblance to Gaudy Welsh. The shape, texture and registry marks indicates that the ware was made in England in the 1850's. Most items are impressed "Ironstone."

Plate. 9¾." "Strawberry" $150.00

Coffee Pot. 10" high. Strawberry ..$	500.00
Cracker Jar. Imari-type decor. Silvered lid and bail	95.00
Cups and Saucers	
Blackberry. Demitasse	75.00
Imari-type decor	65.00
Seeing Eye. Niagara-shape	125.00
Strawberry	125.00
Pitcher. 8". Imari-type decor	100.00
Plates	
Grape. 9½"	55.00
Seeing Eye. 9"	95.00
Strawberry. 9"	125.00
Sunflower. 7"	55.00
Urn. 8"	75.00

Platters

Imari-type decor. Leaf-shape. 7¼ x 11"	75.00
Polychrome. 13 x 18"	150.00
Sauce. 6¾". Imari-type decor	35.00
Sugar, Covered. 8½" high. Strawberry	395.00

GAUDY WELSH

Gaudy Welsh is a translucent porcelain that was originally made in the Swansea area of England from about 1830 to 1845. Although the designs resemble Gaudy Dutch, the body texture and weight differ. One of the characteristics is the gold lustre on top of the glaze.

In 1890, Allerton made a similar ware. These items are a heavier, opaque porcelain and usually bear the export mark.

Some of the known patterns are: Daisy and Chain, Flower Basket, Grape, Morning Glory, Oyster, Shanghai, Strawberry, Tulip, Urn and Wagon Wheel.

Creamer. 4" high. "Oyster" $60.00

Daisy and Chain

Creamer ..$	75.00
Sugar, Covered	125.00
Teapot	165.00

Flower Basket (also known as "Urn" or "Vase")

Bowl. 10½"	175.00
Creamer	85.00
Cup and Saucer	75.00
Mug. 4"	65.00
Plates	
7½"	60.00
9"	85.00

Sugar, Covered	95.00
Grape	
Creamer	47.50
Cup and Saucer. Handled	65.00
Cup and Saucer. Handleless	75.00
Morning Glory	
Cup and Saucer	65.00
Pitcher. 6½". Bulbous. Allerton. C. 1890	85.00
Plate. 10"	100.00
Teapot. 5½" to top of finial	150.00
Oyster	
Bowl. 6¼"	40.00
Creamer	60.00
Cup and Saucer	75.00
Mug. 3"	55.00
Plates	
5½"	55.00
7"	65.00
9½"	100.00
Tiles	55.00
Shanghai	
Creamer	95.00
Strawberry	
Creamer	95.00
Plate. 8¼"	85.00
Teapot	175.00
Tulip	
Creamer	75.00
Cup and Saucer	55.00
Pitcher, Milk	150.00
Plate. 6"	40.00
Sugar, Covered	95.00
Teapot	150.00
Wash Set. Miniature. Pitcher, 3¼". Bowl, 4¼".	150.00
Waste Bowl	75.00
Wagon Wheel	
Cup and Saucer	60.00
Mug. 2¾"	55.00
Plates	
5½"	35.00
7"	47.50
8¼"	65.00

GIBSON GIRL PLATES

Charles Dana Gibson, an eminent American artist, produced a series of 24 drawings entitled "The Widow and Her Friends." The Royal Doulton Works at Lambeth, England reproduced the drawings on plates. All the plates are 10½" and have the same blue border. Life Publishing Company copyrighted the plates in 1900 and 1901. Prices for the following range from $65.00 to $75.00 each:

'A Message from the Outside World
A Quiet Dinner with Dr. Bottles
And Here Winning New friends

"She Finds Exercise Does Not Improve Her Spirits."

Failing to Find Rest and Quiet in the Country She Decided to Return Home
Miss Babbles Brings a Copy of Morning Paper
Miss Babbles, The Authoress, Calls and Reads Aloud
Mr. Waddles Arrives Late and Finds Her Card Filled
Mrs. Diggs is Alarmed at Discovering
She Becomes a Trained Nurse
She Contemplates the Cloister
She Decides to Die in Spite of Dr. Bottles
She Finds Exercise Does Not Improve Her Spirits
She Finds Some Consolation in Her Mirror
She Goes into Colors
She Goes into Retreat
She Goes to the Fancy Dress Ball as "Juliet"
She is Disturbed By a Vision
She Looks for Relief Among the Old Ones
Some Think She Has Remained in Retirement
The Day After Arriving at Her Journey's End
They All Go Skating
They Go Fishing
They Take a Morning Run

GIRANDOLES

A girandole is a highly ornamental candlestick. The base is usually of marble and the mountings are cast metal surrounded by cut glass prisms. Girandoles were often made in pairs or a set of three . . . a 3-lite candelabra and two single candlesticks.

Bear and Beehive. 3-lite candelabra, 2 candlesticks. Marble

Basket of Flowers. 3-lite candelabra. Two candlesticks 16¼" high. Brass with marble bases. Set $500.00

bases. Gilted mountings. Prisms suspended from grape cluster bobeches. Set ....$ 500.00

Indians. 3-lite candelabra centerpiece, 18" high. Two candlesticks 16" high. Bronzed with marble bases. Set 650.00

Lady and Gentleman. 14" high. Cast metal. Marble bases. Cut glass prisms. Pair 200.00

Paul and Virginia. 3-lite candelabra. 2 candlesticks. Cast metal. Two step marble bases. Starcut prisms. Original finish. Set. 500.00

People Group. 3-lite candelabra, 20" high. 2 candlesticks. Brass mountings. Marble bases. Starcut prisms. Set 500.00

Warriors. 3-lite candelabra, 16½" high. 2 candlesticks. Gilted metal mountings. Marble bases. Cut glass prisms. Set 750.00

Woman and Child. 20" high. Gilted cast metal. Marble bases. Prisms. Pair 175.00

GONDER POTTERY

Lawton Gonder established the Gonder Ceramic Arts, Inc. Zanesville, Ohio in 1941.

Gonder was experienced in the pottery field having worked at several other factories in the past. He produced good quality pottery of excellent design. New glazes . . .Chinese crackle, gold crackle and a flambe' were introduced. Lamp bases were produced at another factory of Gonder's under the name of Elgee.

The corporation was dissolved in 1957.

Also see "Peters and Reed Pottery," and "Zane Pottery."

Bowls

6½ x 2½" deep. Ribbed. Light blue and pink glossy glaze ....$ 7.50

7¾ x 7" deep. With flower frog. Swirl. Glossy blue and brown glaze 15.00

Cornucopia. 7". Turquoise and brown. Signed E-5 Gonder 10.00

Ewers

6". Mottled blue. Pink interior.... 17.50

12". Swan-shaped 25.00

Vases

5". Dogwood. Signed E-3 Gonder.. 7.50

7½". Flower-shaped. Pink and mottled blue glaze 10.00

8". Swans on base. Lavender and brown glaze. Signed 1-147 USA Gonder 25.00

12". Leaf decor. Glossy yellow with mottled red glaze 30.00

GOOFUS GLASS

Goofus glass, originally called Mexican glass, was first made in the early 1900's. From about 1910 to 1920 it competed with Carnival glass as give-aways or prizes at fairs and carnivals.

Vase. 7½". "Roses." $20.00

The glass is pressed with painted design and lustered. Several factories produced Goofus glass . . .LaBelle Glass Co., Bridgeport, Ohio, Crescent Glass Co., Wellsburg, W. Va., Imperial Glass, Bellaire, Ohio, and Northwood Glass Co., Indiana, Pa.

Bowls
- Carnation. 9" ....$ 17.50
- Grapes. 9¼" 15.00
- Poinsettia. 9¼" 20.00
- Roses. 9" 18.50
- Strawberry. 10½" 22.50
- Water Lily. 10½" 20.00

Bread Tray. "Last Supper." 38.50

Jars, Powder
- Peacocks 20.00
- Roses 18.50

Lamps, Roses
- Miniature 38.50
- Oil. Pedestaled-type 35.00

Plates
- Carnation. 7½" 10.00
- Poppy. 10½" 18.50
- Portrait. 9" 25.00
- Roses. 10" 18.50
- Strawberry. 11" 30.00

Tray. Chrysanthemum. 8x11" 32.50

GOSS CHINA

Goss ceramics were first made by William Henry Goss at Falcon Pottery, Stoke-on-Trent, England in 1858. Cauldon Pottery acquired the factory in 1934 and changed the name to Goss China Company. In 1947, the factory again changed ownership and was resold to Washington Potteries (China Craft) Ltd. in 1951.

The majority of Goss ware is marked . . .impressed W.H. Goss or with the Gosshawk, thus readily identifiable.

Animals
- Cat, Cheshire. Goss, England ..$ 85.00
- Cat, Cheshire. Unglazed. C. 1920 250.00
- Dog, Colored. C. 1920 .... 650.00
- Lion, Standing. C. 1920 .... 500.00
- Rabbit. Small. Goss, England 65.00
- Swan. 2". C. 1920 .... 195.00

Busts
- Burns, Robert. Terra Cotta. C. 1867 .... 400.00
- Scott, Sir Walter. 5½". Parian 195.00
- Shakespeare. 3½". Parian. Colored 125.00
- Shakespeare. 3½". Parian. White 75.00

Mug. 3" high. Shield transfer. Rexet Nostra Jura-Great Yarmouth ..$20.00

Cottages
- Dickens, Charles. Gad's Hill 175.00
- Hathaway, Ann 100.00
- Hathaway, Ann. Night light 225.00
- Shakespeare. Full length 85.00
- Shakespeare. Night light 175.00

Cross. Banbury. White. Goss, England 295.00

Figurines. Goss, England
- Bride 150.00
- Grandmother 200.00
- Lady Rose 225.00
- Mother-in-Law 150.00
- Trusty Servant. Colored 225.00
- Welsh Lady. (Teapot) 125.00

Models
- Bettws-y-coed Kettle. Bath crest .. 25.00
- Canterbury Leather Bottle 20.00
- Chester Roman Vase. Large 25.00
- Dorchester Jug 15.00
- Eddystone Lighthouse. Exeter crest 22.50
- Flemish Milk Pot. Portrush crest .. 30.00
- Irish Wooden Noggin 25.00
- Jersey Fish Basket. Exmouth crest 18.50
- Lanlawren Urn. Small 12.00
- Longships Lighthouse. Lynmouth crest 60.00
- Norwegian Wooden Shoe 40.00
- Swiss Cow Bell. 3". Maldon crest 40.00
- Swiss Milk Bucket. 2¼" 28.50
- Tew Kesbury Urn 15.00
- Welsh Hat 22.50
- Yorick's Skull. Medium. Yellow .. 225.00
- Yorick's Skull. Medium. White 125.00
- Yorick's Skull. Night light. White 250.00

Miscellaneous
- Ash Tray. "Ride a Cock Horse . ."

Goss, England 30.00

Cups

- Egg Cup. Tynemouth crest 35.00
- Tea with saucer 15.00
- Three-handled. Arms of Glastonburg 25.00

Goblet. Libation. Woodbridge crest 17.50

Hat Pin Holder. Bilston crest 30.00

Jug, Cream. 4½". Melon 10.00

Marmalade, Covered. Bag Ware 50.00

Mugs

- 1¼". Windsor Castle 25.00
- 3". Blenheim 30.00

Pitcher. 5¾". Saffron Walden crest 55.00

Teapot. Bag Ware 55.00

Tea Sets. Miniatures

- "Coat of Arms." 10 pieces 250.00
- "Thistle." 8 pieces 300.00

Vase. 1¾". Bag Ware 20.00

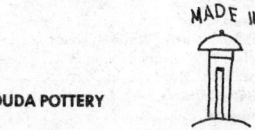

GOUDA POTTERY

Gouda, Holland and the surrounding areas have been known as a pottery center for centuries. The potteries originally produced simple utilitarian Delft-type earthenwares with a tin glaze. But, the story of Gouda pottery began with the making of clay smokers' pipes in the early 1700's. The decline of the pipe making industry in the 1900's led to the introduction of art pottery. Influenced by the Art Nouveau and Art Deco movements, artists expressed themselves with free-form and stylized designs in bold colors to produce the modern or symbolic decor of Gouda pottery. A modern adaptation of Gouda pottery is currently on the market.

Basket. 5¼x8½" high. Turquoise, navy, orange, etc. "Ingeborg." ..$ 125.00

Bowls

- 6". Covered. Stylized leaves. "Schoonhoven." 100.00
- 7½". Multicolors. "Canada." 65.00
- 8½". 2-handles. Multicolored floral decor. "Pelta." 75.00

Box, Covered. 4¼" diam. Black, gold, white. High glaze. "Regina." 150.00

Candlesticks

- 4" high. Floral. Pair 85.00
- 13" high. Blue, gold, black. C. 1910. Pair 165.00

Charger. 12" diam., 2" deep. "Plazuid." Pierced for hanging .. 200.00

Coaster. Grape. C. 1910 .... 35.00

Chamberstick. 3", 6½" diam. Green with yellow, blues and cream decor. Matte finish. Mkd. 0139 DAM III Holland P.C. 1885 ....$95.00

Compotes

- 3" high, 10" wide. 2-handles. Multicolored. "Sluis." 150.00
- 7½" high. Handled. Multicolored floral. C. 1925 .... 95.00

Ewer. 6". Multicolored. Art Deco decor. "Arnhem" 85.00

Inkwell. 3" high. Hexagon-shape. C. 1920 .... 100.00

Jardiniere. 4½". Multicolored florals. C. 1925-35 .... 95.00

Pitcher. 5" high. Lion design. Orange, green. Late 50.00

Plates

- 8". Pastel multicolored. C. 1900 .. 100.00
- 10". Art Deco 125.00

Shoes

- 5". Multicolored. "Lanac." 65.00
- 6". Floral. High glaze 150.00

Tobacco Jars.

- 6½" high. Art Deco decor 150.00
- 11" high. Floral. C. 1910 .... 195.00

Tray. 12½x17". Black ground. High glaze 185.00

Trivet. 4". "Damascus.". C. 1895 .. 200.00

Vases

- 4½". Art Nouveau. Rust, cobalt. C. 1900 .... 65.00
- 6". Floral. Blue, green. C. 1900 .. 95.00
- 7". Stick-type. Multicolored. High glaze. "Arnhem.". C. 1900 ...... 125.00
- 8". Black and white 225.00
- 8½". Tulip. High glaze 145.00
- 10". Art Deco. Multicolored. "Isolde." 175.00
- 12". Art Nouveau design. High glaze. C. 1910 .... 295.00

GRANITEWARE

Graniteware is a type of enameling on metal.

The enamel finish is usually mottled or speckled resembling granite . . .thus the name. The ware, especially in kitchen utensils, was popular after 1900. Green graniteware is earlier than the gray or blue. Graniteware is being reproduced today in all colors.

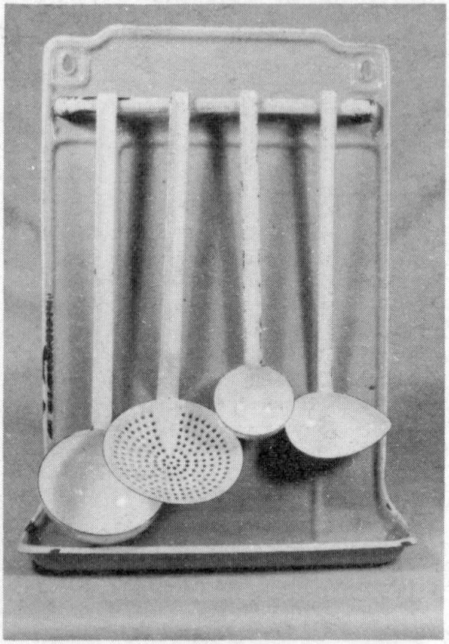

Utensil Rack, hanging-type. Blue rack, white utensils. 13¾" w. x 18" high. Set $50.00

Basin, Wash. 3x12" diam. Gray. Hole for hanging ....$	15.00
Bowls	
Blue. 7" x 6" deep	15.00
Blue. 8½". Shallow	17.50
Gray. 5½"	10.00
Green. 5½"	15.00
Bun Tray. 6½x13". Gray	45.00
Chamberstick. 5" square base. White	20.00
Coffee Pots	
Blue. 11"	25.00
Gray. 10". Tin lid	45.00
Gray. 12". Pewter lid	85.00
Green. 10"	40.00
Colander. 9" diam. Gray	12.50
Cream Cans. Gray	
Half-gallon	50.00
Quart	30.00
Kettles	
Blue. 6½ x 10½"	25.00
Gray. 9x17". Bail handle	35.00
Muffins. Gray	
6-cup	17.50
12-cup	25.00
Mugs	
Blue	10.00
Gray	10.00
Green	15.00
Pan. 3x12" diam. Gray	15.00
Pap Feeder. White with black trim	15.00
Pitchers. Quart	
Blue	25.00
Gray	35.00
Green	45.00
Plates, Dinner	
Blue	10.00
Gray	10.00
Green	15.00
Plates, Pie	
Blue	8.50
Gray	8.50
Green	12.50
Pot, Covered. 6½" diam. x 6½" deep. Gray	18.50
Salt Box. White. Wooden cover	25.00
Skillet. 8½". Gray	20.00
Soap Dish. Blue	8.50
Spoon, Mixing. White with black handle	5.00
Teapots	
Blue	30.00
Brown. Pewter lid	75.00
Gray	30.00
Green	50.00
Utensil Rack. Hanging. Gray. 21" high, 12" wide. Ladle, spoon, strainer, holder. 4 pieces	75.00
Washboard. Blue. Wooden frame	60.00

GREENAWAY, KATE

K.G.

Kate Greenaway was a 19th century English artist. She began her artistic career by illustrating Christmas cards and later, books. Her charming 'children' were adapted as decorations, by several English and German potteries in the 1880-1890 period.

Almanacs	
1884. Routledge and Sons ....$	60.00
1886. Routledge and Sons	60.00
1887. French Edition	50.00
1890	45.00
Books	
A Apple Pie. F. Warner Co	65.00
A Day in a Child's Life. 1881	75.00
Alphabet. C. 1885	65.00
Birthday. F. Warner & Co.	65.00
Language of Flowers. Edmund Evans	85.00

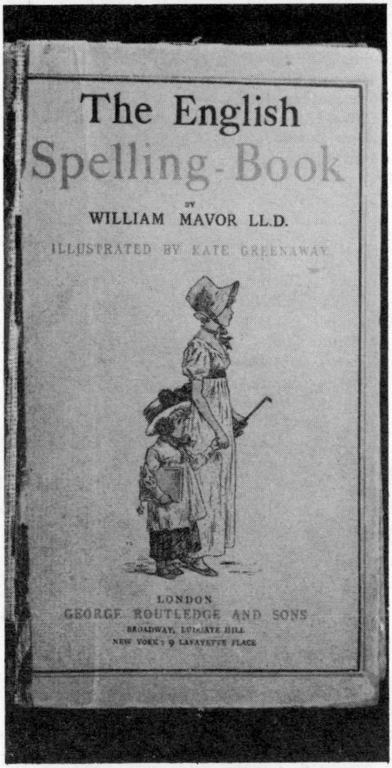

"The English Spelling Book." by William Mavor. Illustrated by Kate Greenaway. 1885 .... $85.00

Little Ann. Edmund Evans. Worn 45.00
Mother Goose. Edmund Evans 75.00
Pied Piper of Hamlin. Edmund Evans. Worn 40.00
Book Plate. 7 x 9½". Lithographed. C. 1881 .... 10.00
Boxes
5". Brass. Embossed figures 85.00
2x 3 x 5" high. Porcelain. Staffordshire 125.00
Bread Plate. "SeaSaw". Glass 75.00
Cake Stand. 9". Doulton 150.00
Calendar of the Seasons. 8 tinted pages. Signed 45.00
Child's Set. Plate, cup, saucer. Germany 125.00
Feeding Dish. 8". Little Jack Horner 55.00
Figurines
5¾". Bisque. Boy and girl in blue and pink outfits. Pair 150.00
6". Boy with top hat, boots, umbrella. White and gold. Staffordshire 85.00
14". Bisque. Boy and girl. Pair 250.00
Inkwell. Bronze. Two figures 225.00
Mug. 2" high. Sterling 65.00
Napkin Rings. See "Napkin Rings"
Plate. 6". Porcelain. Handpainted. Girls under umbrella 45.00
Print. 6 x 8". Outdoor tea party. 15 girls. Signed 100.00
Salt and Pepper Shakers
Girl with muff. Silverplated. Meriden 65.00
3". Boy and girl. Barrel-shaped bodies. Period clothing. Pair 85.00
4½". Boy and girl. Period clothing. Staffordshire. Pair 100.00
Tile. 6". Square. "May" 75.00
Toothpick Holders
Bisque. Boy. Period clothing 50.00
Glass. Blue. Boy and girl 85.00
Silverplated. Boy 150.00
Vases
4½". Porcelain. Green coloring halfway up vase with soft ivorine tones above with 2 little girls at play. Sterling silver rim 125.00
4x 7". Porcelain. Handpainted children. Irises on reverse 125.00
8". Handpainted. Children playing with hoops and dancing 150.00

GREENTOWN

Greentown glass was first made at the Indiana Tumbler and Goblet Company, Greentown, Indiana in 1894. In 1899 the company was reorganized as the National Glass Company, the second largest glass manufacturer in the United States. A factory fire in June, 1903 brought an end to Greentown glass.
The concern produced a variety of pressed glass wares in clear and colored; including the limited "Holly Amber." Their "Cactus" pattern has been heavily reproduced in colors not originally made. Also see PATTERN GLASS SECTIONS for additional patterns.

Animal Dishes, Covered
Cat on Hamper. Chocolate .... $ 200.00
Rabbit on Nest. Amber 100.00
Robin on Nest. Milk white 195.00
Berry Set. Cactus. Chocolate. 7 pieces 225.00
Bowls, Berry
Cactus. Chocolate 125.00
Cord Drapery. Amber 85.00
Geneva. Chocolate 95.00
Butter, Covered. Cactus. Chocolate 225.00

Mug. "Cactus". Chocolate $100.00

Celery. Cactus. Chocolate 125.00
Compote. 5¼". Open. High standard. Cactus. Chocolate 150.00
Cracker Jar. Cactus. Chocolate 195.00
Creamers
  Austrian. Clear 45.00
  Cactus. Chocolate 125.00
  Cord Drapery. Clear 35.00
  Fleur-de-lis. Chocolate 100.00
  Overall Lattice. Clear 40.00
  Shuttle. Chocolate 100.00
Cruets, Stoppered
  Cactus. Chocolate 200.00
  Leaf Bracket. Chocolate 200.00
Mugs
  Cactus. Chocolate 100.00
  Hearts of Loch Lavern. Chocolate 85.00
  Serenade. Milk white 50.00
Nappies
  Austrian. Clear 50.00
  Masonic. Chocolate 150.00
Pitchers, Syrup
  Cactus. Chocolate 135.00
  Cord Drapery. Chocolate 175.00
  Herringbone Buttress. Clear 85.00
Pitchers, Water
  Cactus. Chocolate 250.00
  Cord Drapery. Clear 65.00
  Paneled. Chocolate 200.00
Plates
  Cactus. Chocolate. 7½" 85.00
  Overall Lattice. Chocolate 10" .. 185.00
  Serenade. Milk white. 6" 55.00
Shakers. Cactus. Chocolate. Pair .. 125.00
Spooners
  Austrian. Clear 25.00
  Leaf Bracket. Chocolate 85.00
Stein. Lidded. Elves. Milk white 50.00
Sugars
  Austrian. Clear 25.00
  Cactus. Chocolate. Covered 200.00
  Flower Flange. Chocolate 165.00
  Herringbone Buttress. Clear. Covered 85.00
Toothpicks
  Boot. Chocolate 75.00
  *Cactus. Chocolate 100.00
  Dog's Head. Nile green 140.00
  Wheelbarrow. Nile green 165.00
  Wild Rose. Green 80.00
  Witch's Head. Nile green 125.00
Tumblers
  Austrian. Clear 20.00
  *Cactus. Chocolate 95.00
  Geneva. Chocolate 85.00
  Leaf Bracket. Chocolate 50.00
  Shell. Chocolate 85.00

*Reproduced Item

GRUEBY POTTERY

William Grueby was active in the ceramic industry for several years before he developed his own method of producing matte glazed pottery ...and hence the founding of The Grueby Faience Company, Boston, Massachusetts in 1897.
The art pottery was hand thrown in natural shapes, hand molded and hand tooled. A variety of colored glazes, singly or in combinations, were produced with green being the most prominent. In 1908, the firm was divided into The Grueby Pottery Company and Grueby Faience & Tile Co.; the latter making art pottery until bankruptcy forced closure shortly thereafter.

Bowl. 3". Turned-in rim. Green ..$ 135.00
Candlestick. 5½". Blue 150.00
Scarab. (Paperweight). Blue-green. Molded. 150.00
Tiles
  2x6". Green 30.00
  4½" square. Biblical animal. Multicolored 225.00
Tobacco Jar. 7". Blue. C. 1907 .... 650.00
Vases
  4½". Blue 275.00
  4½". Green. Tooled leaves. Buds in white 395.00

5". Blue. Bulbous 450.00
7". Green. Stick-type 225.00

GUNS

For almost six centuries man has known the value of a gun. He has used it and misused it for pleasure and survival. Guns had their beginning with the discovery of gun powder. Legend says that the first propulsive force of gun powder was developed by a monk in the early 1300's. The invention of the pistol dates back to the 15th century when the matchlock was devised. The pistol was designed for one-hand use. Most authorities agree that the name "pistol" was derived from the town of Pistola, Italy, where many of these first firearms were manufactured. Another explanation of the name is from the word "Pistallo" or "pommell," a weapon used by mounted troops in the 15th century.

Guns have progressed from the early Matchlock to Wheellocks, Flintlocks, Breechloaders, Repeaters and Magazine arms. They continue with more modern manufacturers such as Colt, Remington, Winchester, etc.

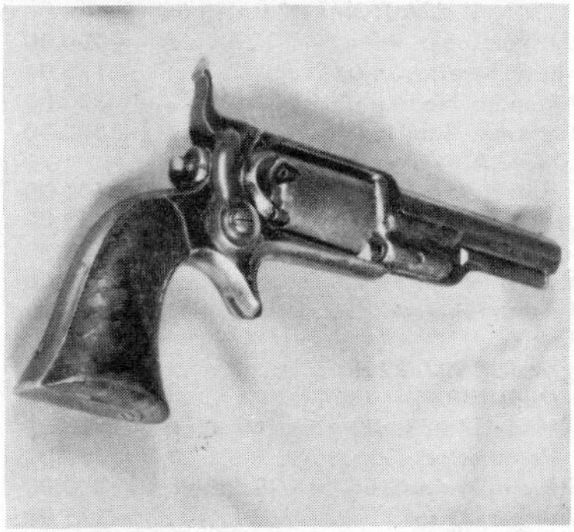

Colt. Gambler's type. 41 cal. Peterson's side lock conversion $550.00

COLT PISTOLS AND REVOLVERS

Army
Model 1860. Converted to 44 cal. Attached shoulder stock. Third type ....$ 1500.00
Model 1860. Converted to 44 cal., 6 shot. c.f. U.S. specimens 800.00
Model 1860. Converted to 44 cal., 6 shot. c.f. (Richards-Mason Conversion) 750.00
Model 1894. 38 cal. c. f 225.00
Model. 1917. 45 cal., 6 shot 150.00

Automatics
Model 1900. 38 cal., 7 shot. Standard model 375.00
Model 1902. 38 cal. Military 325.00
Model 1903. 32 cal., 8 shot. Pocket. Hammerless 200.00
Model 1905. 45 cal., 7 shot. Standard model 300.00
Model 1908. 380 ACP cal., 7 shot. Pocket. Hammerless 185.00
Model 1911-Al. 45 cal. Commercial 275.00

Bisley
Various calibers. c.f. Various barrel lengths. Standard model 400.00
Various calibers, 6 shot. 7½" barrel. Flat top 1750.00

Deringers
First Model. 41 cal., single shot. 2½" barrel. All metal construction 500.00
Second Model. 41 cal., single shot. 2½" barrel. Checkered walnut grips 350.00
Third Model. 41 cal., single shot. 2½" barrel. Standard model 300.00

Dragoon
First Model. 44 cal., 6 shot. Civilian issue 3000.00
First Model. 44 cal., 6 shot. Military issue 3500.00
Second Model. 44 cal., 6 shot. 7½" barrel 2750.00
Third Model. 44 cal., 6 shot. 7½" barrel. Standard model 2000.00
Shoulder stock for Third Model .. 1500.00
Model 1848. Baby. 31 cal., 5 shot. Various barrels 1650.00

Frontier. Model 1878. Various calibers and barrel lengths. D.A. Standard model 325.00

House
41 cal., 4 shot. 3" round barrel. Cloverleaf cylinder 375.00
41 cal., 5 shot. 2⅝" round barrel 275.00

Marine. U.S. Model 1905. 38 cal., 6 shot. 6" barrel. Varnished checkered grips................ 450.00

Navy
Model 1851. 36 cal., 6 shot. 7½" barrel. Fourth model 650.00
Model 1851. Cut for shoulder stock. Second type 2500.00
Model 1851. 36 cal., 6 shot. 7½" barrel. Colt's London 750.00
Model 1861. 36 cal., 6 shot. S.A. 7½" barrel. Standard model 800.00
Model 1889. New Navy. 38 cal. D.A. Swing-out cylinder 275.00

New Line. 38 cal. r.f. 2½" barrel. Rosewood grips 275.00

New Police. "Cop and Thug." 38 cal., 5 shot.................. 600.00

Patterson

Holster Model. 36 cal., 5 shot. Various octagon-shaped barrel lengths. Standard model with attached loading lever 10000.00

Pocket Model. Various calibers, 5 shot. Various barrel lengths 3500.00

Pocket

Model 1848. (Thuer Conversion) 3500.00

Model 1849. 31 cal., 5 shot. Various barrel lengths. Standard model 350.00

Walker. 1847. 44 cal., 6 shot 12500.00

FLINTLOCK PISTOLS

British. Wheellock. 54 cal ....$ 2500.00

Evans, O. & E. 69 cal. 8⅞" barrel. Walnut half stock. Brass mountings. Contract type 4000.00

Harper's Ferry. Model 1806. 54 cal. Converted to percussion 1000.00

Henry, J. 54 cal., 10" barrel. Contract type 2850.00

Kentucky-style. (Pennsylvania) Various calibers, smooth bore. Brass fittings and inlays .... 1500.00+

North, Simeon. Model 1816. 54 cal. Smooth bore 9 1/16" barrel 750.00

Waters and Johnson. Model 1836. 54 cal. Smooth bore 8½" barrel. Iron mountings 650.00

PERCUSSION PISTOLS AND REVOLVERS

Allen & Wheellock. 44 cal., 6 shot. 7½" barrel. Army ....$ 650.00

Alsop. 36 cal., 5 shot. Various barrel lengths. Navy. Standard model .. 550.00

Bacon. 31 cal., 5 shot. 4" barrel. Pocket model 300.00

Butterfield. 41 cal., 5 shot. 7" barrel. Army. Standard model 1200.00

Cooper, J.M. 36 cal., 5 shot. D.A. Various barrel lengths. Navy 400.00

Freeman, Austin T. 44 cal., 7 shot. Army 500.00

Joslyn. 44 cal., 5 shot. 8" barrel. Army. Standard model 500.00

Marston, W.W. 31 cal., 5 shot. Various barrel lengths. Walnut grips. Pocket model 300.00

Massachusetts Arm Co. 28 cal., 6 shot. S.A. Maynard Primed Pocket model 250.00

Metropolitan Arms Co. 36 cal., 6 shot. 7" barrel. Navy 450.00

Pettingill's. 34 cal., 6 shot. Navy. Belt model.................. 650.00

Rogers & Spencer. 44 cal., 6 shot. 7" octagonal barrel. Army 500.00

Savage & North. 36 cal., 6 shot. Figure 8 Model, Third Model 2500.00

Starr Arms Co. 44 cal., 6 shot. D.A. Army 375.00

Starr Arms Co. Model 1858. 44 cal., 6 shot. D.A. Navy 450.00

Walch, John. 31 cal., 10 shot. S.A. 3½" barrel. Pocket model 550.00

Warner, James. 31 cal., 6 shot. S.A. Various barrel lengths. Pocket model 365.00

REMINGTON HAND GUNS

Army. Model 1861. 44 cal., 6 shot. S.A. "Old Model Army."........$ 450.00

Beals Army. 44 cal., 6 shot. 8" octagon barrel. Standard model. C. 1860-1862 .... 1000.00

Beals Navy. 36 cal., 6 shot. S.A. Standard model 500.00

Deringer, Double. Model 95. 41 cal. r.f. short. Type one. C. 1866-1935 450.00

Deringer, Elliot. 41 cal., single shot. r.f 450.00

Pocket. New Model. 31 cal., 5 shot. S.A. Second type 300.00

Police. New Model. 36 cal., 5 shot. Various barrel lengths. Standard model 350.00

Rider. 31 cal., 5 shot. D.A. 225.00

Smoot. New Model. No. 3. 38 cal, 5 shot. r.f. short 275.00

SEMI-AUTOMATIC HAND GUNS

German Luger. 9mm ....$ 400.00

Italian Beretta. 38 cal 175.00

Japanese. Nambu 300.00

Japanese. Baby Nambu 300.00

Luger, Artillery. Adjustable rear sight. 1916-1918 .... 600.00

Luger. 6" barrel. Navy............ 475.00

Luger. 8" barrel 300.00

Mauser. Military 275.00

Russian Tokarev 200.00

Savage

Model 1907. 32 cal 200.00

Model 1907. 45 cal 1500.00

Model 1915. 32 cal., 10 shot. Hammerless 125.00

Stevens. Walnut Hill #417-0. 22 cal 200.00

Walther. 25 cal 175.00

Walther PP. 22 cal 300.00

Walther PP. 32 cal 175.00

Walther PPK. 380 cal 325.00

SHOULDER GUNS

Double Barrel Shotgun. Flintlock. Unmarked ....$ 850.00

Ithaca. 4-E single trap. 12 gauge .. 1500.00

Japanese. 25 cal. Military 225.00

Japanese Take Down Rifle. Rare .. 250.00

Kentucky. Flintlock. C. 1790-1830 .. 1200.00

Kentucky. Percussion. Full stock. Brass patch box. Many inlays 2500.00

Kentucky. Percussion. Full stock. Brass trim. Plain grade 1000.00

Parker. Trojan. 12 gauge. Standard 250.00

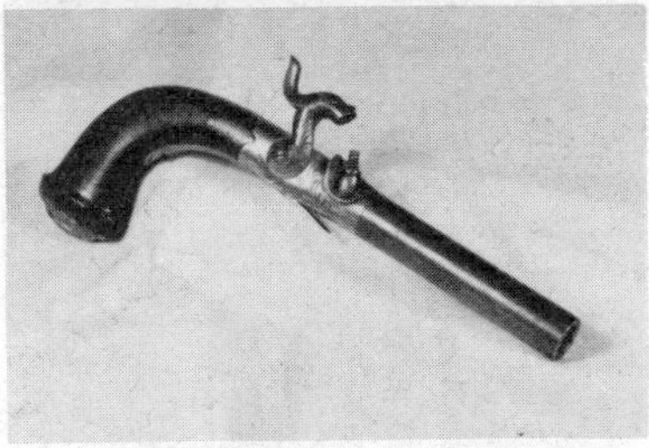

Percussion. Boot pistol. B.B.L. Silver trim. English. C. 1820 ....$225.00

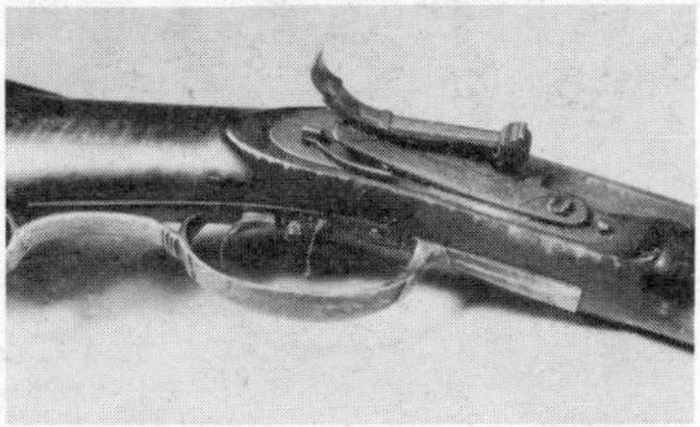

Shoulder Guns. Close-up view of mule ear on muzzle loader ....

Scheutzen. Target. Plain grade 850.00
Sharps. Borchard Model 1878. 45-70 cal. Military. Old Reliable Model 650.00
Springfield
Model 1840. Musket. Flintlock .. 3000.00
Model 1855. 58 cal. Carbine 295.00
Model 1861. Musket 500.00
Model 1863. Percussion 300.00
Model 1863. Rifle. Musket 500.00
Model 1870. 50 cal. Rolling Block 500.00
Model 1873. Carbine 1000.00
Model 1884. Trapdoor Rifle 600.00
Model 1896. Krag.............. 225.00
Model 1903. National Match. First Model 600.00
Model 1922. M-1. 22 cal. 650.00
Model 1922 . M-2. 22 cal 395.00
U.S. Civil War Model. 52 cal. r.f. Spencer 575.00
U.S. Model 1795. Harper's Ferry. Type One 1750.00
U.S. Model 1808. Musket. Contract type 1000.00
U.S. Model 1842. Musket. Percussion. Contract type 650.00
U.S. Model 1855. 52 cal. Percussion. Carbine. Standard model. Sharps 1350.00
U.S. Model 1858. 58 cal. Remington 350.00
U.S. Model 1863. 58 cal. Remington 300.00
U.S. Model 1866. 50 cal. Breechloading 250.00
U.S. Model 1873. Cadet Model. 45-70 cal 600.00
U.S. Model 1917. Remington 225.00
Winchesters
Model 1866. 44 cal. r.f. Fourth model 1250.00
Model 1873. Various calibers 475.00
Model 1873. "One in One Thousand." Rare 12500.00
Model 1876. Plain sporting rifle .. 750.00
Model 1895. Carbine 600.00
Model 1895. Standard Production Model 400.00

SMITH & WESSON HAND GUNS

Hand Ejector, Military & Police First Model. 38 cal., 6 shot. Standard model ....$ 350.00
Ladysmiths First Model. 22 cal., 7 shot 500.00
Ladysmiths Second Model. 22 cal.,7 shot. 3" barrel 400.00
Model No. 1, First issue. 22 cal., r.f. short 2850.00
Model No. 1, Second issue. 22 cal. r.f. short...................... 150.00
Model No. 1½, First issue. 32 cal., r.f.......................... 250.00
Model No. 2. 38 cal. Often called "Baby Russian." 275.00
Model No. 3. "First Model American." 44 cal................ 550.00
Model No. 3. Russian First Model. 44 cal., 6 shot. S.A 500.00
Safety Third Model. 38 cal. D.A..... 200.00

MISCELLANEOUS

Ball and Cap Pistols. 41 cal. 4½" barrels. Deringer. Matched set . . $ 1200.00
Bull Dog Pistol. 44 cal. Connecticut Arms 175.00
Cane Pistol. Various calibers and makers 395.00
Cup Primer. Army Second Model. 42 cal., 6 shot. Brass frame. Plant's Mfg. Co 450.00
Knuckle Duster. "My Friend." 22 cal. James Reid 265.00
Knuckle Duster. 32 cal. Brass frame. James Reid 300.00
Protector Palm Pistol. 32 cal., 7 shot 325.00
Steyr (Kropatschek)
Model 1886. Carbine 85.00
Model 1886. Long Rifle 35.00
Model 1886. Short Rifle 65.00
Model 1894. Straight Pull Rifle. Carbine 50.00

Guns, Miscellaneous Cartridge types

Top . . . "The Defender." English $85.00

Bottom . . . "English Bulldog." . . $85.00

Model 1894. Straight Pull Rifle. Long Rifle 100.00

Model 1912. Automatic Pistol. 9mm. Austrian cartridge. World War I Model 200.00

Model 1912. 08. Automatic Pistol. 9 mm Luger. Nazi proof marked. World War II Model 175.00

GUTTA-PERCHA ITEMS

Gutta-Percha are species of tropical trees that have a milky latex sap. The sap can be used to make a rubbery, leather-like material. Probably the most extensive use of gutta-percha material in the past has been for daguerreotype cases. Also see "Daguerreotypes and Daguerreotype Cases."

Boxes
- 2x3¾ x 13''. Hinged lid. Strawberry decor in relief ......$ 40.00
- 3¼x4¾x4¾". Hinged lid. Ornate scene of deer in woodland 35.00

Brooch. 3¼" key design. Ornate .. 35.00

Buckle. George and Martha Washington decor 75.00

Compote. 7" high. 11½" diam. Turned wooden standard. Inlaid bands of gutta-percha and wooden floral decor and medallion 140.00

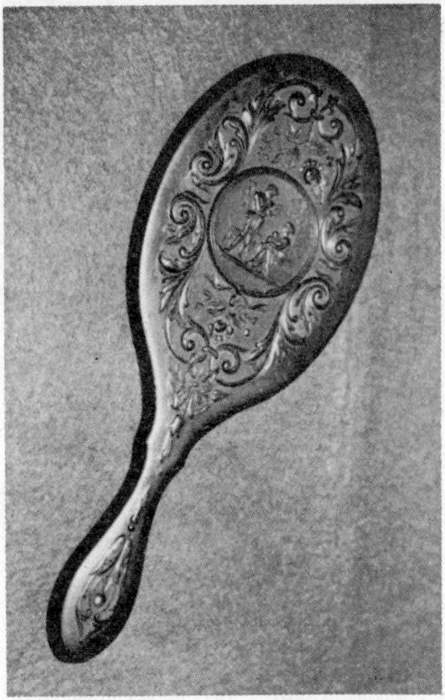

Hand mirror. 9¾" long. Portrait center. Scroll border $30.00

Cross. 3¼" long. Ornate 55.00

Frame. 6x 7¾". Embossed florals. Dated 1868 .... 60.00

Match Safes
- Arm & Hammer 30.00
- Garter crest. Edward VII 75.00

Mirror, Folding. 4¼ x 7". Greek key border. Florals. Portrait center.... 125.00

Mirrors, Hand
- Leaves and berry design. Patd. 1868-78 .... 25.00
- Woodland scene, house. Dated 1872 .... 35.00

HAIR ORNAMENTS

Hair ornaments consist of barrettes, combs and elaborate hair pins to hold or adorn women's hair of all cultures, from the past to the present. They can be had in any material from simple bone or celluloid set with 'brilliants' to precious metals.

Barrette. 4" oval. Bar-type. Tortoise shell-type with rhinestones. C. 1950 ....$ 7.50

Bun Cover. Expandable-type. Metal with attached beads. C. 1940.... 10.00

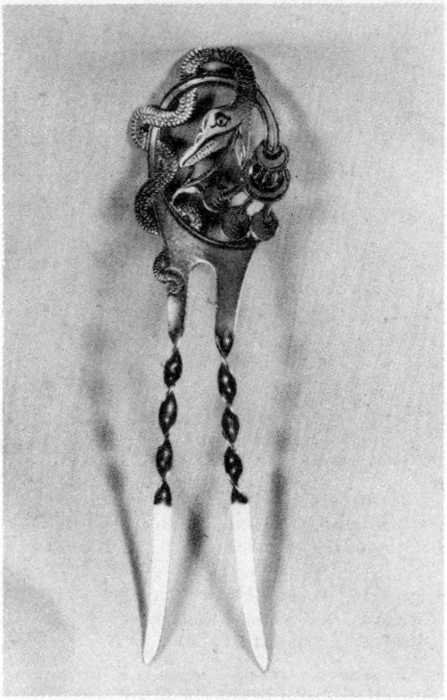

Comb. Sterling silver serpent. 4" long. 2 prong $35.00

Combs	
Gutta-Percha and Cetron Turquoise. 8". Scrolled and pierced floral crest	65.00
Gutta-Percha and Cetron Turquoise. Set with brilliants. "King Tut."	85.00
Silver, Coin. 3½ x 4". Rectangular-shaped. Monogrammed	85.00
Silver, Coin. 3½ x 4½". Wedge-shaped. Chased	65.00
Tortoise Shell. 7". Four-prongs. Set with beads	45.00
Hair Pins	
Tortoise-type. 2" long. 2 prongs. Vine decor	7.50
Tortoise-type. 3" long, 2 curved prongs. Inlaid stones	10.00
Metal, Silvered. 6" long. Attached free swinging bells. Oriental. C. 1960	10.00

HAMPSHIRE POTTERY

James S. Taft founded the Hampshire Pottery Company, Keene, Massachusetts in 1871. In the beginning redwares and stonewares were produced. Majolica wares decorated with colors entered in 1879. A semi-porcelain ware with the Royal Worcester glaze was introduced in 1883. Also in 1883, the recognizable matte glazes were developed.

The factory made an extensive line of utilitarian and art wares including souvenir items until World War I; when the limited demand for such items forced closure. After the war, the firm resumed operation, but only made hotel dinnerware and tiles. The company was dissolved in 1923.

Vase. 3 x 6" wide. Squat. Green matte glaze $65.00

Bowls	
5½", 3½" deep. Scroll work in relief. Green ....$	65.00
6", 2½" deep. Dark blue	55.00
9", 2¼" deep. Florals in relief. Dark blue	85.00
Mug. 4⅛". Landing of the Pilgrims. Tan	75.00
Nappy. 9". Violet on ivory. Artist signed	65.00
Pitchers	
8¼". Ewer-type. Green	65.00
11½". Yankee Doodle. Royal Worcester glaze. C. 1883	350.00
12". Tankard. Browns, greens, cream and pink asters decor	150.00
Planter. 4 x 6½". Cattails in relief. Green	50.00
Vases	
2¼". Pitcher-type. Green	25.00
6½". Pitcher-type. Green	65.00
7". Cylinder. Blue	45.00
7". Molded arches. Mottled blue ..	85.00
7½". Acanthus leaves in relief. Green	85.00
9". Free-form. Mottled blue, brown, green	100.00

HAND PAINTED CHINA

Painting on porcelain or pottery was fashionable in England and the Continent from the middle of the 19th century on; but it did not reach America until after the Civil War. It remained popular until World War I and is currently being revived.

The first American classes in china painting were organized by Edward Lycett in New York City and the most important influence in the spread of this pastime was Benn Pitman's classes at the Cincinnati School of Design in 1875.

During the late 1890's and early 1900's china painting was not limited to gentle women at home; many factories employed artists to hand-paint designs on their own blank porcelain or pottery or blank wares produced by other manufacturers.

A majority of the blanks used by amateurs were imported; but there were also American-made wares. One of the first was A.H. Hews and Co. of Cambridge, Mass. who produced both porcelain and pottery blanks. However, machine-made pottery never gained the popularity of porcelain.

Willets Manufacturing Co., Trenton, New Jersey produced the most varied and extensive supply of white art porcelain blanks for amateur artists. They competed successfully with Dresden, Limoges and Royal Berlin in supplying blanks to painters. China for decorating was also produced by Knowles, Taylor and Knowles in East Liverpool, Ohio.

Prices of hand-painted china vary according to several factors such as origin and type of porcelain blank; and the talent of the artist who used that ware as his canvas. SEE NOTE:

Box, Covered. 7¼" diam. 2-handled. Cherries. Pickard. Artist signed .... $ 45.00
Cream and Sugar. Approx. 2x5". Pink blossoms. Gold handles and trim. Bavarian blanks 40.00
Cup and Saucer. Grapes 18.50
Pitcher. 15". Tankard-shaped. Pink roses on red ground. Gold handle, trim 125.00
Plates
7½". Strawberries. Bavarian 35.00
8½". Grapes. Signed A. Kock 50.00
9¼". Roses. Silesia. Artist signed .. 40.00
9½". Yellow, red roses. Scalloped edge with gold trim 55.00
11½". Strawberries. Reticulated edge with gold trim. Vienna 175.00
Syrup. Floral decor on beige ground. W. & W. Co. English 95.00
Tea Set. Teapot, cream and sugar. Pink roses. Gold trim. Royal Austria. Artist signed 125.00

Powder Jar. 4⅝" diam. "Strawberries." Diamond Quilted iridescent glass. Hinged lid, brass fittings $135.00

Tray. 9x12". Roses. Gold trim 75.00
Vase. 14". Red poppies. Gold trim. Limoges. Artist signed 95.00

NOTE: Also see specific wares, i.e. Bavarian, Limoges, Haviland, Game Plates, etc.

HARDWARE

(See "Ironware")

HAT PINS AND HAT PIN HOLDERS

Hat pins became popular in the closing decades of the 1800's when the vogue developed for oversized hats. Designers used various materials to decorate the pin shaft. . .china, crystal, shells, enamel, gem stones, precious metals and coins. Decorative subjects range from commemorative designs to insects. Occasionally, women used hat pins as a weapon when threatened or as protection against an overzealous suitor. Porcelain containers, designed to hold a collection of these pins, could be found on most dressing tables in the Victorian period. Familiar names such as Wedgwood, Meissen, Limoges and Satsuma are associated with the production of hat pin holders.

HAT PINS

Abalone .... $ 7.50
Brass
Amber set 10.00
Parrot 15.00
Sailors hat with enameled red bow 12.00

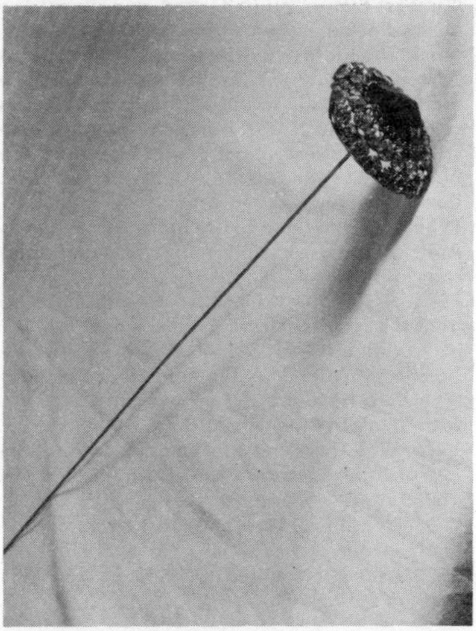

Pin. 12½" long. Amethyst and rhinestones $22.50

Turtle. Enameled green with red eyes	22.50
Carnival Glass. Dragonfly. Blue	17.00
Gold Filled. Moonstone	15.00
Gold, 14K. Embossed designs. 6½"	35.00
Jet Beads. Diamond-cut	14.00
Porcelain	
Portrait. Handpainted	25.00
Roses. Handpainted	18.50
Rhinestone. 1½" diam.	15.00
Scarab. Blue	25.00
Silver, Sterling	
Art Nouveau-style	30.00
Monogrammed	18.00
MOP inset	12.00

HAT PIN HOLDERS

Austrian. Floral decor. Gold trim. Saucer base ....$	25.00
Haviland. White. Undecorated. Petal base	18.50
Limoges. Saucer base. Handpainted rose decor	28.00
Nippon. Handpainted white birds on blue ground	22.50
R. S. Germany. Rose decor	35.00
Silverplated. Combination-type. Hatpin and ring holder, pin cushion base	30.00

Holder. R.S. Germany. 5". Blue floral decor on black ground. Gold trim.$30.00

HAVILAND CHINA

Treasured from generation to generation, Haviland china has never fallen from favor with those who demand the finest in porcelain. The first Haviland was imported in 1842 and production continues to this day. Four generations of the family have maintained a standard of high quality and artistic achievement that is evident in each of many hundreds of patterns and in thousands of variations of those patterns.

The history of Haviland china is complicated and confusing because of the various combinations of partnerships of the Haviland brothers and their sons. David Haviland, a New York china importer, established a china factory at Limoges, France in 1842, under the name of Haviland & Co. Products were sold through the American firm of D.G. & D. Haviland Co., of which David Haviland was a partner.

In 1852, two other brothers were admitted to the firm of D. G. & D. Haviland Co., and the

name Haviland Bros. & Co. was established. The firm was discontinued in 1865.

Chronology of the various Haviland firms and partnerships:

1835-36. Edmund and David Haviland, New York china importers.

1837. David Haviland established his own importing business.

1838. David's brother, Daniel, joined him to establish the American firm of D. G. & D. Haviland.

1842. David Haviland established a factory at Limoges, France under the name of Haviland & Co. His brother Daniel was a silent partner and continued to manage the New York importing firm.

1852. Daniel and David admitted two brothers, Robert and Richard, to the D.G. & D. Haviland firm. The name was then changed to Haviland Bros. & Co.

1858. Chas. Field Haviland, a son of David's brother Robert, married the granddaughter of Francois Alluaud, owner of the Alluaud factory.

1859. Chas. Field Haviland established a decorating shop with blanks furnished by the Alluaud Works.

1863. David withdrew from Haviland Bros. & Co. to devote full time to the Limoges factory.

1865. Haviland Bros. & Co. suspended business as importers and distributors.

1866. Daniel G. Haviland withdrew as a partner from the French Limoges factory.

1870. Chas. Field Haviland & Co. was formed in New York between Chas. Field Haviland and Oliver A. Gager.

1874. David Haviland's sons, Charles Edward Miller and Theodore, entered into partnership with their father as Haviland & Co.

1876. Chas. Field Haviland became manager of Casseau Pottery Works, successor to the Alluaud Pottery. He used the mark "Ch. Field Haviland."

1879. David died and his sons, Charles Edward and Theodore, continued business through 1891.

1881. Chas. Field Haviland retired from manufacturing and sold his interest in Chas. Field Haviland & Co. in New York to Oliver A. Gager who continued in the business until 1889 when he died. Firm name was changed to Haviland & Abbott. Operations ended about the time of World War I.

1892. Brothers, Charles Edward Miller and Theodore, dissolved partnership. Charles continued business under the name of Haviland & Co., while Theodore began operations as LaPorcelaine Theodore Haviland at Limoges, France where he acquired a factory. White ware was marked "Theodore Haviland" in a horseshoe with "France" within, all in green. Decoration marks varied. In 1892 the T. H. monogram with "Limoges France" printed in red, and "Porcelaine Mousseline" above was used. In 1914 the mark was "Theodore Haviland" (in italics) with "Limoges" below and "France" underneath. The mark was usually in red with occasional green coloring. In 1920 the italicizing of the name Theodore was discontinued after his death. The business was then conducted by his son, Wm. David Haviland.

1936. Company decided to make chinaware in America because of tariff regulations and rising costs in France.

1941. Assets of Haviland & Co. were obtained from the French heirs of Charles Edward Miller Haviland by Wm. David Haviland for the Theodore Haviland Co. The mark after 1941 was "Theodore Haviland, New York" in a vignette with "Made in America" below.

1946. Wm. Theodore Haviland modernized factory at Limoges, France with electronically controlled kilns.

1963. New line of Haviland giftware introduced in America.

1970. Issued first edition in a series of Christmas collector's plates.

Gravy Boat with attached underplate.
Conventional Border. No. 278 . . $50.00

Bone Dish. Ranson. #1 . . . . $	12.50
Bowls	
Ranson. #24. Cereal	16.50
Ranson. #24. Soup	18.50
Butter Pats	
Princess	6.50
Ranson. #1	6.50
Chocolate Pot. H-P blue green flowers, leaves. Gold trim	85.00
Cream and Sugar. 3½". H-P florals. Gold trim	65.00
Cups and Saucers	
Drop Rose	75.00
Norma. Coffee	22.50

Princess. Coffee	22.50
Ranson. #1. Coffee	25.00
Ranson. #24. Coffee	35.00
Ranson. #24. Tea	30.00
Decanter. 9". With stopper. H-P floral decor	55.00
Dinner Sets	
Ranson. #24. Service for 12. 120 pieces.	2500.00
Ranson. #1. Service for 12. 100 pieces.	1500.00
Silver Anniversary. Service for 12. 80 pieces	1500.00
Dresser Trays	
7¾x9½". H-P flowers and berries.	45.00
8x9". Leaf-shaped. Baltimore Rose	35.00
Gravy Boats	
Princess	45.00
Ranson. #24	65.00
Silver Anniversary	50.00
Mayonnaise. With underplate. H-P florals	40.00
Pitcher, Water. 7½". H-P yellow roses on white ground. Gold handle, trim	85.00
Plaque. 13½". Indian chief. Full head dress	85.00
Plates	
Dorset. 6⅛"	7.50
Moss Rose. 9½"	18.50
Princess. 9½"	20.00
Ranson. #1. Oyster	37.50
Ranson. #24. 7⅜" (coupe)	18.50
Ranson. #24. 9⅝"	25.00
Silver Anniversary. 9½"	15.00
Platters	
Baltimore Rose. 10½"	45.00
Greek Key. 16"	40.00
Handpainted. 23½". Yellow roses. Satin finish. Artist signed	225.00
Ranson. #1. 16"	28.50
Ranson. #24. 11½"	35.00
Ranson. #24. 18". Two wells	65.00
Ramekin. With underplate. Baltimore Rose	32.50
Relish. Princess	18.50
Sauces	
Baltimore Rose	12.50
Moss Rose	6.50
Ranson. #24	10.00
Silver Anniversary	6.50
Sugars, Covered	
Ranson. #1	25.00
Ranson. #24	35.00
Teapots	
Handpainted. Cupids, florals. Gold trim.	75.00
Moss Rose	50.00
Ranson. #1	65.00
Tea Set. Wedding Ring. 3 pieces	125.00
Tureen. 9½" diam., 10" high. H-P blue flowers	125.00
Vegetables, Covered	
Ranson. #24. Oval	50.00
Silver Anniversary	35.00
Vegetables, Open	
Norma	30.00
Princess	30.00
Ranson. #24	40.00
Waste Bowl. Ranson. #1	25.00

HEISEY GLASS

The A.H. Heisey Glass Company began producing glasswares in April, 1896 in Newark, Ohio. Mr. Heisey was not a newcomer to the field having been associated with the craft since his youth.

Hundreds of crystal patterns for table settings were produced. Heisey also employed colored and opal (custard) glass. Glass figurines were introduced in 1933 and continued until 1957 when the factory ceased production.

Some Heisey molds were sold to Imperial Glass of Bellaire, Ohio and certain items were reissued. These pieces may be mistaken for the original Heisey; but are still acceptable to collectors because of their fine quality.

Not all Heisey glasswares are marked with the familiar "H" within a diamond.

Bowl, shallow. "Orchid." 12½" diam. Etched crystal $95.00

Animals, Crystal	
*Airdale	$ 65.00
Colt. Standing	50.00

*Duck. 4½" high	100.00
Giraffe. Head forward. 11" high.	150.00
Goose. Wings half	125.00
*Goose. Wings up	100.00
*Mallard. Wings up	145.00
*Pheasant	100.00
Pony, Rearing	150.00
Rooster	75.00
*Scotty	85.00
Ashtrays	
Old Sandwich. 2½" square	7.50
Ridgeleigh. 2¾" square	6.50
Basket. Lariat	60.00
Bookends. Horses. Pair	200.00
Bottle, Cologne. Twist. Pink	25.00
Bowls	
Colonial. 9½"	35.00
Crystolite. 13"	25.00
Oceanic. 12". Scalloped. Unsigned	30.00
Orchid. 12"	38.50
Ring Band. Opal. Floral design	125.00
Twist. Flared. Footed. Emerald	40.00
Box, Cigarette. Ridgeleigh	18.50
Butter, Covered	
Colonial	60.00
Plantation. ¼ size	50.00
Ring Band. Opal	295.00
Butter Pat. Colonial	6.00
Candlesticks	
Crystalite. 2". Pair	14.00
Lariat. 2-lite. Pair	37.50
Old Sandwich. 6½". Sahara. Pair	95.00
Orchid. 2-lite. Pair	65.00
Ridgeleigh. 10½". With prisms	85.00
Candy Jar, Covered. Colonial. Gold trim. 3½ x 6⅜" high	30.00
Champagnes	
Minuette. Symphony stem	15.00
Twist	12.00
Cheese. Whirlpool. 8"	15.00
Coasters	
Lariat. 4"	6.50
Ridgeleigh. 3¾"	7.50
Cocktails	
Minuette. Symphony stem	20.00
Orchid	15.00
Compotes	
Colonial. 7½x8½" diam.	40.00
Optic. 4x8" diam. Emerald	55.00
Plantation. 6x12½" diam.	50.00
Cream and Sugars	
Crystolite. Individual. With tray	35.00
Orchid	42.50
Paneled. Marigold	125.00
Ring Band. Opal	275.00
Creamers	
Beaded Swag. Opal. Gold trim	25.00
Waverly	20.00
Cruets	
Colonial. Original stopper	25.00
Greek Key. Original stopper	30.00
Pineapple and Fan. Pineapple-shaped stopper	55.00
Winged Scroll. Opal	450.00
Goblets	
Crystolite	12.50
Ipswich	17.50
Old Sandwich	12.50
Puritan	15.00
Hair Receiver. Near Cut. Silver-plated lid.	32.50
Ice Tubs	
Colonial	32.50
Iris. Silver overlay	55.00
Ladle, Condiment. Pink	8.50
Madonna. 8¾"	125.00
Nut Set. Queen Anne. Sahara master bowl, 6 individual bowls	100.00
Parfait. Minuette, Symphony stem	20.00
Pitchers, Water	
Colonial	45.00
Greek Key	75.00
Plates	
Beehive. 14"	95.00
Crystolite. 8"	12.00
Fancy Loop 8"	25.00
Ipswich. 8" square. Sahara	18.50
Plantation. 8"	18.50
Queen Anne. 8". Alexandrite	75.00
Shaw Dancer. 7¼"	20.00
Platter. 10x13". Colonial	50.00
Punch Cups	
Crystolite	6.50
Ridgeleigh	8.50
Punch Sets	
Colonial. 17 pieces	450.00
Greek Key. 13 pieces	400.00
Lariat. 8 pieces	100.00
Ridgeleigh. 13 pieces	175.00
Relish. Crystolite. 5-sections. 10"	28.50
Salt, Open. Swan-shaped. Paper label	12.50
Sherbets	
Colonial	8.50
Greek Key	7.50
Lariat	8.50
Puritan	7.50
Sugar Castor. Plantation	30.00
Toothpick Holders	
Fancy Loop	55.00
Prince of Wales. Gold trim	75.00
Ring Band. Opal	95.00
Tumblers, Water	
Beaded Swag. Opal	75.00
Fancy Loop	15.00
Ipswich	20.00
Oxford	15.00
Winged Scroll	50.00
Vases	
Colonial. 8". Bulbous	50.00
Ridgeleigh. 4½"	18.50

Warwick. 9". Cornucopia-type ..	30.00
Whirlpool	25.00
Wines	
Colonial	12.00
Minuette. Symphony stem	25.00

*Reproduced Item

HERCULANEUM

Before 1796, known as Worthington, Humble & Holland, this factory was taken over by a more ambitious group in that year; and by modern methods produced a fine cream-colored earthenware.

By 1800, the factory was producing bone china, heavier than most bone china of the period but never the less well potted and with an exceptional glaze. Early examples were rarely marked; but coming later in Liverpool, marked Herculaneum pieces can be found with some frequency. Transfer examples in black and polychrome are appealing and much collected. The factory closed in 1841.

Jug. 6½". Polychrome. C. 1815. $165.00

Jug. 6½". Polychrome ....$	165.00
Plate. 9". Black transfer	185.00
Soup Plate. 9½". Black transfer. Marked	225.00

HITCHING POSTS

(See "Ironware")

HORN

Animal horns have been used to make various utilitarian items such as boxes, spoons and tumblers. Also see "Powder Flasks and Horns."

Tumbler. 2½" $18.50

Fork. Two-tined. Horn handle ....$	5.00
Letter Opener. 7½" long. Figural ..	25.00
Napkin Ring	10.00
Snuff Boxes	
1¼x2½". Hinged lid. Ivory inlay..	50.00
1¾x2¾". Lift top lid. Brass ring ..	35.00
3" oval-shaped. Carved top latch..	50.00
3" long. Hollowed natural horn. Screw top	35.00
Spoon. 9¾" long, bowl 3¼" wide ..	28.50
Tea Caddy Spoon. 5" long	22.50
Texas Longhorn Steer Horn. 40" long. Mounted	1500.00
Tumblers	
2½"	18.50
4"	25.00

HULL POTTERY

In 1905 Addis E. Hull purchased The Acme Pottery Company, Crooksville, Ohio. In 1917 A. E. Hull Pottery Company began making a line of art pottery for florists and gift shops. Also made were novelties, kitchenwares and stoneware. From 1921 to 1929 the firm also imported European pottery to be sold through their outlets. In 1950 the factory was destroyed by fire and re-established in 1952 as Hull Pottery

Company by J. Brandon Hull. The company is currently in operation; but the artline has been discontinued.

The pottery is marked Hull U.S.A., Hull Art U.S., paper labeled and pieces made after 1952 "hull".

Cream and Sugar. 5½" long. "Waterlily" $25.00

Basket. Bow Knot. 10½" ....$	50.00
Bowls, Console	
Butterfly. 11¾" diam. x 4¾" deep	30.00
Ebb Tide. 16" long	20.00
Candlesticks	
Blossomflite. 3". Handled	12.50
Bow Knot	10.00
Cookie Jar. Red Riding Hood	30.00
Cornucopias	
Bow Knot. 7½"	25.00
Magnolia. 8½"	25.00
Waterlily. 9¼"	30.00
Woodland. 11"	30.00
Creamers and Sugars	
Magnolia. Open	22.50
Red Riding Hood	25.00
Rosella	20.00
Demitasse Pot. Pine	32.50
Ewer. Open Rose. 7½"	30.00
Pitchers	
Magnolia. 7"	27.50
Tokay. 8"	25.00
Woodland. 5½"	20.00
Planters	
Duck. 4½x6½"	12.00
Duck, Flying. 8¼x10"	32.50
Lamb. 8"	20.00
Strawberry. 6½". Scalloped top. Pedestaled.	20.00
Swan. 8¾x10¼"	25.00
Salt Box. Ribbed. Wooden cover....	20.00
Shakers, Salt and Pepper. Red Riding Hood. 5". Pair	22.50
Teapots	
Magnolia	32.00
Red Riding Hood	25.00
Tom, The Piper's Son	30.00
Tea Sets	
Bow Knot. 3 pieces	75.00
Woodland. 3 pieces	55.00
Vases	
Bow Knot. 8½"	35.00
Butterfly. 10". Triangular-shaped	32.50
Iris. 4¾". 2 handles	15.00
Magnolia. 8½". 2 handles. Pedestaled	26.50
Rosella. 5"	13.50
Tulip. 6¾"	20.00
Waterlily. 5½"	15.00
Waterlily. 8½"	20.00
Wildflower. 5½"	12.50
Woodland. 7½"	20.00
Wall Pockets	
Duck, Flying	15.00
Whisk Broom. 8" long	13.50

EARLY

1957

1960

© BY W. Goebel W. Germany

1970

HUMMEL ITEMS

Goebel W. Germany CURRENT

Hummel figurines are the original creation of the German artist, Sister Marie Innocentia Hummle (known as Sister Berta), who began drawing rosy-cheeked children as a teenager, before entering a Franciscan convent.

In 1934 W. Goebel Co. of Rodental, Germany began producing 3-dimensional bisque figurines based on Sister Berta's drawings.

During the depression, Schmid Brothers of Randolph, Mass. brought Hummel figurines to America and became Goebel's U.S. distributor.

All authentic Hummels bear both the signature of M. I. Hummel and the Goebel trademark. Various trademarks identify the years a particular item was manufactured. Most desirable marks are the Crown and the Full Bee.

Hummel figurines, even those produced between 1934 and 1945 are not true antiques; but because of their fine workmanship and quality, they are considered to be good collectibles.

In 1967 Goebel began distributing Hummel items in the U.S. and a controversy developed between the two companies. . .also involved are Sister Berta's family and her convent. Prices of Hummel items continue to be affected by this unresolved legal battle.
Recently, certain early Hummel figurines have been "re-instated" by Goebel (from the original molds). No one is quite sure how these items will affect the market in the future. SEE NOTE:

Ashtrays

Boy with Bird. #166 ....$ 65.00
Happy Pastime. #62 .... 55.00
Joyful. #33 .... 30.00
Let's Sing. #144 .... 55.00
Singing Lessons. #34 .... 65.00

Bookends

Apple Tree Boy and Girl. #252-A&B ....$ 125.00
Bookworms. #14-A&B 150.00
Friends, She Loves Me. . .She Loves Me Not. #251-A&B 150.00
Goose Girl and Farm Boy. #60-A&B. 150.00
Little Goat Herder and Feeding Time. #250-A&B 150.00
Playmates and Chick Girl. #61-A&B 150.00

Candleholders

Angel Duet. #193 ....$ 65.00
Angelic Sleep. #25-1 .... 75.00
Angel Trio. 3 Ass't. Sitting with candle. #111-38-0................ 55.00
Christmas Angels. #115-116-117. Set 175.00
Herald Angels. #37 .... 65.00
Lullaby. #24-1 .... 110.00
Silent Night. #54................ 85.00

Candy Boxes

Chick Girl. #111-57 ....$ 75.00
Happy Pastime. #111-69 .... 75.00
Joyful. #111-53 .... 100.00
Let's Sing. #111-110 .... 75.00
Playmates. #111-58 .... 75.00
Singing Lesson. #111-63 .... 75.00

Figurines

Accordion Boy. #185............$ 85.00
Adoration. #23-1 .... 200.00
A Fair Measure. #345 .... 125.00
Angelic Sleep. #25-1 .... 100.00
Angelic Song. #144.............. 80.00
Apple Tree Boy. #142-1 .... 125.00
Apple Tree Boy. #142-V 450.00

Figurine. "Bookworm." #3-1 ..$225.00

Apple Tree Girl. #141-1 .... 125.00
Apple Tree Girl. #141-3-0 .... 65.00
*Auf Wiedersehen. #153-1........ 250.00
Autumn Harvest. #355 .... 95.00
Band Leader. #129 .... 75.00
Barnyard Hero. #195-1 .... 100.00
Barnyard Hero. #195-2-0 .... 75.00
Bashful. #377 .... 65.00
*Birthday Serenade. #218-0 ...... 175.00
Blessed Event. #333 .... 250.00
Bookworm. #3-1 .... 225.00
*Boots. #143-1.................. 175.00
Brother. #95.................... 65.00
Builder. #305 .... 85.00
Busy Student. #307.............. 100.00
*Candlelight. #192 .... 125.00
Chick Girl. #57-0................ 90.00
Chick Girl. #57-1 .... 125.00
Chimney Sweep. #12-1 .... 75.00
Cinderella. #337 .... 110.00
Confidentially. #314 .... 100.00
Congratulations. #17 .... 75.00
Culprits. #56-A 110.00
Doctor. #127 .... 80.00
Doll Mother. #67 .... 110.00
Drummer. #240 .... 65.00

Easter Greetings. #378	100.00
Farewell. #65-1	195.00
Favorite Pet. #61	95.00
Feathered Friends. #344	125.00
For Mother. #257	75.00
Friends. #136-1	85.00
Going to Grandma's. #52-0	125.00
Goose Girl. #47-0	100.00
Goose Girl. #47-11	225.00
Happiness. #56	55.00
Happy Birthday. #176-0	95.00
*Happy Days. #150-1	250.00
Happy Pastime. #69	125.00
Hear Ye! Hear Ye!.#15-0	85.00
Hear Ye! Hear Ye! #15-2	245.00
Heavenly Angel. #21-1	100.00
Heavenly Angel. #21-11	200.00
Heavenly Angel. #21-0-2	85.00
Heavenly Protection. #88-11	300.00
Hello. #124-10	65.00
Homeward Bound. #334	185.00
Joyful. #53	50.00
Joyous News. #27-11	295.00
Kiss Me. #311	135.00
Knitting Lesson. #256	225.00
Let's Sing. #110-0	100.00
Letter To Santa Claus. #340	175.00
Little Cellist. #89-1	80.00
Little Fiddler. #2-0	85.00
Little Goat Herder. #200-1	145.00
Little Helper. #73	75.00
Little Hiker. #16-1	72.50
Little Scholar. #80	85.00
Little Shopper. #96	55.00
*Little Thrifty. #118	95.00
Lullaby. #24-1	195.00
Mail is Here. #226	350.00
Max and Moritz. #123	85.00
Meditation. #13-0	85.00
Meditation. #13-11	300.00
Merry Wanderer. #7-0	125.00
Merry Wanderer. #11-0	75.00
Mischief Maker. #342	125.00
Mother's Helper. #133	85.00
Pharmacist. #323	100.00
Photographer. #178	110.00
Playmates. #58-0	100.00
Playmates. #58-1	125.00
Postman. #119	105.00
Puppy Love. #1	95.00
Retreat to Safety. #201-2-0	85.00
Ride into Christmas. #396	250.00
School Boy. #82-0	85.00
School Boy. #82-2-0	75.00
School Boys. #170-111	1000.00
School Girl. #1-2-0	100.00
School Girls. #177-111	1000.00
Sensitive Hunter. #6-0	85.00
Signs of Spring. #203-2-0	75.00
Singing Lesson. #63	125.00
Sister. #98-2-0	55.00
Skier. #59	100.00
Smart Little Sister. #346	95.00
*Spring Dance. #353-0	450.00
Stitch in Time. #255	95.00
*Telling Her Secret. #196-1	235.00
The Run-a-Way. #327	125.00
*To Market. #49-1	275.00
Trumpet Boy. #97	55.00
Umbrella Boy. #152-A-O	275.00
Umbrella Girl. #152-B-O	275.00
*Village Boy. #51-1	125.00
*Volunteers. #50-0	195.00
Wash Day. #308	100.00
Wayside Devotion. #28	175.00
Wayside Harmony. #111-1	95.00
We Congratulate. #220	85.00
Worship. #84-0	125.00
*Worship. #84-V	1000.00

Fonts

Angel at Prayer. #1-A or -B ......$	55.00
Angel Duet. #146	55.00
Angel with Birds. #22	55.00
Angel with Flowers. #36-0	38.50
Child Jesus. #26	55.00
Devotion. #147	50.00
Good Shepherd. #35-0	38.50
Guardian Angel. #248	55.00
Holy Family. #246	55.00

Lamp Bases (Wired)

Apple Tree Boy. #230 ....$	200.00
Apple Tree Girl. #229	200.00
Culprits. #44-A	250.00
Good Friends. #228	175.00
Just Resting. #225-1	225.00
Out of Danger. #44-B	250.00
She Loves Me, She Loves Me Not. #227	195.00
To Market. #101 (rare)	1250.00
To Market. #223	200.00
Wayside Harmony. #224-1	175.00

Madonnas

Flower Madonna. Color. #10-1 ..$	500.00
Flower Madonna. White. #10-1	225.00
Flower Madonna. Color. #10-111	300.00
Madonna. #214-A-M	55.00
Madonna, Child. 2 pieces. Color. #214-AM&K.	85.00
Madonna Praying. Color. #46-0-6	32.50
Madonna Praying. White. #46-0-W	25.00
Madonna with Halo. White. #45-1-6	50.00

Music Boxes

Little Band. With candle. #388M ..$	175.00
Little Band. Without candle. #392M	150.00

Nativity Components

Angel Serenade. #214-D ....$	25.00
Camel. #HX306-0-6	85.00
Cow. #214-K	25.00
Donkey. #214-J	20.00
Flying Angel. Color. #366	38.50
Flying Angel. White. #366-W	18.00
Infant Jesus. #214-A-K	20.00
King, Kneeling on both knees. #214-N	50.00
King, Kneeling on one knee. #214-M	55.00
King, Standing. #214-L	65.00
Lamb. #214-0	10.00
Little Tooter. #214-H	75.00
Madonna. #214-A-M	55.00
Madonna and Child. 2 pieces. Color. #214-AM & K	85.00
Shepherd Boy. #214-G	40.00
Shepherd with Sheep. 1 piece. #214-F	65.00
Stable. #H-214-S-1	50.00

Nativity Sets

3-pieces. Holy Family. #214......$	135.00
15-pieces. Figures only. #214	850.00
17-pieces. Color. #260	2000.00

Plates (See, "Collectors' Plates, Etc.")

Wall Plaques

Ba Bee Ring. #30-A ....$	90.00
Child in Bed. #137	45.00
Little Fiddler. #93	100.00
Madonna. #48-0	95.00
Merry Wanderer. #92	175.00
Retreat to Safety. #126	125.00
Vacation Time. #125	150.00

*Re-instated Item

NOTE: The slash-mark which appears between numbers on Hummel items was not available from the typesetter; therefore a dash has been substituted. Dash should be read as slash.

IMARI

Japanese porcelain was first produced in the early 17th century near Arita. One of the major types, according to style of decoration, was Imari.

The early Imari was simply decorated and quite unlike the later heavily decorated brocade pattern commonly associated with Imari. Most of the decorative patterns are an underglaze blue and overglaze 'seal wax' red supported by turquoise and yellow. The pattern and colors inspired many English and European potteries, such as Derby, Meissen and others to adapt a similar style of decoration for their wares. Imari-type decorated ceramics are being reproduced.

Vase. 9½". Blue and white . . $125.00

Bowls	
6¾". Blue and white ....$	65.00
7¼". Typical colors. Ribbed. Scalloped rim.	125.00
9", 5½" deep. Octagonal-shaped. Typical colors. Scalloped rim. C. 1830	350.00
12". Typical colors. Collar base. C. 1850	500.00
Box, Covered. 2x3½"	65.00
Chargers	
12". Blue and white	175.00
12". Typical colors. C. 1850	250.00
14½". Typical colors. Four reserves	295.00
18". Typical colors. C. 1850	500.00
22". Typical colors. C. 1830	650.00
Compote. 8x9x12". Oval-shaped ..	250.00
Cups and Saucers	
Handled	55.00
Handleless. C. 1850	65.00
Garden Seats	
Cylindrical. 19" high. Blue and white	1500.00
Octagonal. 20" high. Typical colors	2500.00
Ginger Jars, Covered	
8½". Blue and white	175.00
14". Typical colors	300.00

Plates

- 8¼". Blue and white. Ribbed. Scalloped rim. 45.00
- 8½". Typical colors. C. 1830 .... 75.00
- 9½". Blue and white. Eight reserves. Center medallion 100.00
- 10" square. Blue and white. Chamfered corners. C. 1830 .... 125.00

Platters

- 4½x8¼". Typical colors. C. 1880 135.00
- 11½x14½". Typical colors 275.00

Vases

- 6½". Bottle-shaped. Two medallions. Typical colors 175.00
- 8". Cylindrical. Typical colors. C. 1830 .... 295.00
- 9". Blue and white. C. 1880 .... 125.00
- 10½". Bulbous. Typical colors. C. 1840 .... 400.00

NUCUT

IMPERIAL

NUART

IMPERIAL GLASS

The Imperial Glass Co., organized in 1901 in Bellaire, Ohio, at first produced mainly clear, pressed glass for the "mass market" in abundance. In 1910, they began making the popular, inexpensive lustred ware known as Carnival Glass. Then came NUART, an iridescent ware; followed by pressed glass imitations of hand cut glass under the tradename of NUCUT. In 1916, the company introduced a Lustred Art Glass line. . ."Free-Hand" and "Imperial Jewels," an exquisite iridescent stretch glass that carries the IMPERIAL-cross trademark. Reorganized as Imperial Glass Corporation, in the 1930's this firm continues production to the present. In recent years, Imperial has acquired the molds and equipment of several other glass companies. . .Central, Cambridge and Heisey. Many of the "retired" molds of these companies are once again in use. The resulting reissues are acceptable as such because they are marked accordingly to distinguish them from the originals.

CUT GLASS
(Etched or Engraved)

Bowls

- 5½". Floral spray. Rayed bottom $ 22.50
- 7". Buzz star decor. Rayed bottom 25.00
- 11⅜". Wheat and flower decor. Uranium yellow. "Naome."...... 125.00

Vase. 6". Blue body with white leaf and vine decor. Lustred. "Free Hand" $195.00

Candlesticks. 12". Hand cut. "Naome." Pair. 65.00

Pitchers

- Milk. 6". Butterfly decor 35.00
- Syrup. 12 oz. Rayed. Silverplated lid 25.00
- Water. 9". Daisy decor 45.00

Tumbler. 4". Buzz star decor 12.50

Vases

- 7¼". Wheat and flower 45.00
- 9". Teardrop. Rubigold. "Naome." 85.00
- 13½". Daisy decor. Flared 45.00

JEWELS

Bowls

- 4¼" diam. Turned in top. Pearl Ruby over clear body ....$ 45.00
- 4¾" diam. x 2⅝" high. Pinched flare top. Amethyst with Pearl Ruby lustre 75.00
- 10⅛" diam. x 3" high. Pearl Green over clear body 75.00

Compote. 7⅜" high. Ribbed. Blue with gold 65.00

Plate. 9¼". Amethyst with Pearl Silver lustre 75.00

Vases

- 5½" high x 8" diam. Ruffled top. Pearl Silver over clear 150.00
- 6". Bulb-type. Amethyst with Pearl Ruby lustre 125.00

7". Flared. Ribbed interior. Pearl Green lustre over clear 55.00

LUSTRED
(Free Hand)

Bowl. 11" top diam. x 5½" high. Green loop on clear. Green wafer base ....$ 250.00
Candlestick. 10¾". Orange with blue loop. Blue drip cup and base. 125.00
Rose Bowl. 8". Leaf and vine decor. Dark green 95.00
Vases
6". Green loop over white 95.00
9½". Bulbous bottom. Slender flared top. Gold cased over white. Orange lustre throat 175.00
10". Blue and white marbleized.. 85.00
11½". Transparent green. White threads. Applied base 250.00
14". Crystal. Cut design. Applied cobalt loop handles, rim, base .. 225.00

NUART

Lamp Shades. See "Lamp Shades"
Vases
6½". Apricot lustre over opaque white ....$ 200.00
7". Green crazed iridescent over green transparent 150.00
7½". Green over green transparent 125.00

NUCUT

Bowls
5½"......................$ 12.00
8½" 22.50
12" diam. x 8½" high. Flared scalloped top. Wafer base 45.00
Compotes
4½". Jelly 8.50
9¼". Fruit. High standard 75.00
Cream and Sugar. Open 20.00
Ferner. 7⅜" 40.00
Nappy. 6½". Two handles 15.00
Vases
6" 12.50
10"......................... 25.00

PRESSED PATTERNS

Bowls
Beaded Band and Panel. 9". Reef Aqua ....$ 65.00
Beaded Band and Panel. 5¼". Rosemarie 18.50
Candlewick. 7" 10.00
Cape Code. 6¾" 6.00
Empire. 5" square 5.00
Mt. Vernon. 6" 6.50

Butter, Covered. Mt. Vernon 35.00
Candlesticks
Candlewick. 3½" 7.50
Empire. 2½" 6.50
Celerys
Beaded Band and Panel. 6x12½" long. Rosemarie 25.00
Mt. Vernon. 5½" high 22.50
Mt. Vernon. 10½" long 8.50
Compotes
Beaded Band and Panel. 5" diam. High standard. Rosemarie 20.00
Candlewick. 5½" diam 7.50
Cream and Sugars
Cape Cod. Handled 12.50
Colonial. Individual size 15.00
Mt. Vernon 7.50
Cup, Custard. Colonial. 2¾". Handled 7.50
Cup and Saucer. Candlewick 5.00
Ferner. 7" diam. x 4" deep. 3-feet. Open Rose. Amberina 95.00
Goblets
Cape Cod 6.50
Colonial...................... 12.00
Pitcher. Mt. Vernon. 69 oz 15.00
Plates
Candlewick. 8" 4.00
Candlewick. 12" 10.00
Cape Cod. 8" 5.00
Empire. 7". square 4.00
Empire. 10" round 7.50
Mt. Vernon. 11" 8.50
Ribbed. 7½". Amberina 65.00
Salt, Master. Beaded Band and Panel. Footed and handled 12.50
Shakers, Salt and Pepper. Mt. Vernon. Pair 7.50
Vase. Empire. 10" square 15.00

MISCELLANEOUS

Cigarette or Card Holder. Footed. Decorated ....$ 25.00
Hen on Nest 18.50
Honey Pot. Covered. Shape of beehive 25.00
Swan.......................... 27.50
Tumblers
5 oz. Blown. Decorated 7.50
7 oz. Enameled caricature-type animal decor.................. 6.50
12 oz. Blown. Decorated 12.00

INDIAN ARTIFACTS

Indian artifacts, for the purpose of this listing, are the objects made and-or used by the first inhabitants of America. Also see "Baskets," "Indian Jewelry."

Arrow. Complete. Apache. C. 1890. $ 40.00

Pot. 4½" high. Earth colors. Unglazed. Acoma-type $95.00

Axe. Full grooved. Taos, New Mexico 50.00
Baskets-See "Baskets"
Belts
- 36" long. Beaded. Taos Pueblo. C. 1890 .... 50.00
- 44½" long. Leather. Quill work both sides. Texas. C. 1900 ...... 75.00

Blanket, Saddle. 30x36". Navajo .. 125.00
Bowls, Pottery
- Acoma. 7½ x 8". White, black rust. Signed Sara Garcia 175.00
- Case Grande. 4 x 7". White, black, rust 150.00
- Chaco. 7". Black and white 85.00
- Cochiti. 5". Polychromed. C. 1920 35.00
- Hopi
  - 2½ x 5". Tan with dark brown .. 55.00
  - 3½ x 7½". Tan, black, rust 85.00
- Jemez. 6 x 7". Red, black, white. Signed Mary Tosa 125.00
- Mimbres
  - 8". Black 20.00
  - 9". Banded 50.00
- Santa Clara. 4 x 7". Black. Signed Isabel Pena. C. 1935 .... 185.00
- Zia. 8½ x 9½". White, rust, brown. Signed Sefeina Pina 350.00

Canoe-Model. 20". Birch bark. Great Lakes 40.00
Canteen. Made from gourd. Buckskin sling. Apache 30.00
Dipper. Made from gourd. Taos Pueblo 6.50
Drum. 7 x 9½ x 12" diam. Leather top, handle and laces. Cottonwood. Cochiti 75.00
Fetishes
- Bear, Black. Polished. San Ildefonso. C. 1900 .... 30.00
- Owl. Polychromed pottery. Acoma Pueblo. C. 1920 .... 25.00
- Pack Rat. Polychromed pottery. Cochiti. C. 1900 .... 45.00
- Turtle. Polychromed pottery. Cochiti. C. 1900 .... 25.00
- Water Bird. Black and white pottery. Cochiti 30.00

Gloves. Gauntlet-style. Beaded. Pair 75.00
Headdress. Basket frame. Beaded tradecloth. Turkey feathers. Iroquois Gustoweh 150.00
Knife. 6". White Chert, Illinois 25.00
Knife Case. 7". Full beading. Plaines. C. 1920 .... 50.00
Leggings. Shoshoni. Pair 50.00
Moccasins, Adult
- Apache. Rawhide. Pair 100.00
- Cheyenne. Buckskin with beaded tops. C. 1880. Pair 165.00
- Chippewa. Beaded. Pair 175.00
- Pawnee. Full beaded. C. 1920. Pair 65.00

Moccasins, Child. Beaded. Pair 75.00
Moccasin Tops. Iroquois. C. 1890. Set 30.00
Pipe Bag. 20". Deerskin. Beaded. Fringe bottom. Cheyenne. C. 1880 395.00
Pipes
- Alabama. 4½" 50.00
- Iroquois. 9". Serpent effigy 175.00
- Sioux. 8". Made of catlinite. C. 1930 .... 45.00

Points, Flint
- 2". Birdpoint. California 8.50
- 2¾". Adena. Kentucky 2.50
- 3x5". Notched. No beveling. Ohio 225.00
- 3½". White. Ohio 15.00
- 3½". Speckled. Dovetailed. Kentucky 45.00
- 4¼". Notched. White and brown. Ohio 17.50
- 5". Turkey tail. Indiana 65.00
- 5½". Beaver tail. Allegan County, Michigan. 95.00

Points, Stone. 4½". Dovetailed 125.00
Pots, Pottery
- Huichole. 6x9". Scafito design. Unglazed. Signed R. Mateos 65.00
- Huichole. 9x19". Lidded. Scrafito design. Unglazed. Signed Juan .. 95.00
- Picuris Pueblo. 7x7". One handle. Mica. C. 1870 .... 35.00
- Santa Fe. 10x11" 85.00

Pouches
- Apache. 8½x14". Leather with geometric bead work. Drawstring top. Fringed bottom 195.00

Cheyenne. 3½x3½". Buckskin with multicolored beads. C. 1880. 125.00
Yakina. 6½x8". Floral beading. C. 1920 .... 95.00

Rattle. Made from gourd. Cherokee. C. 1870 .... 65.00

Rugs, Navajo
23x37½". Tans, reds, blue, black and white. C. 1880 .... 350.00
31x41". Yei. Maroon, gray, yellow, red, etc. 500.00
40x60". Black, red and gray 750.00
44x60". Vegetable dyed 2000.00
48½x78". "Eye Dazzler." Red with yellow, brown and greens .. 750.00

Sash. ½" wide, 60" long. Beaded. Plaines. C. 1920 .... 85.00

Tomahawks
Crow Spike iron head. Beaded tradecloth covered handle. Feathers. C. 1870-1890 .... 400.00
Iroquoise stone head. Tuscarora Reserve. C. 1750-1800 .... 175.00
Vest. Moose hide. Geometric beading on front and back. Cree . 125.00

INDIAN JEWELRY

Indian jewelry represents one of the highest standards of native American art.

Several years ago a leading financial reporter predicted that fine turquoise would rival diamonds as an investment medium. . .and today Indian jewelry has fulfilled his promise. 'Old Pawn' or 'Pawn' is the name given to the authentic jewelry made by the Indians for their personal adornment, wealth or collateral. It has come into the market through the peculiar institution of the trading post pawn rooms. The Pawn, along with the contemporary examples of jewelry listed herein, are understood to be made of sterling silver and the stones to be genuine.

Beads, Trade
Earthenware. 28" on straw ....$ 20.00
Heische Shell. 30" on straw...... 30.00

Belt. Concha. 44" long. Six scalloped Conchas. Six butterfly separators and buckle set with coral 1250.00

Bracelets
Contemporary. Large cabochon turquoise stone in center with three coral stones. Signed Tommy Yellowhorse 150.00
Hopi, Pawn
Shadowbox with triangular-shaped turquoise.
Signed Jackson.......... 135.00

Necklace. Squash Blossoms. All silver. Pre-WWII $850.00

Five small oval cabachons of Kingman turquoise.
Signed T. Lee 125.00

Navajo
Cluster of oval cabochons of Royston turquoise. Signed D.W. 400.00
Three bracelets soldered together. Stamped with arc designs. Set with 3 large high cut cabochons of pale green Nevada turquoise. Signed AV .. 175.00
Three cabochons of Persian turquoise. Signed C.M. Yazzie .. 195.00
Ten blossom-shaped mountings set with green turquoise centers. Marked Coin, Handmade Navajo. C. 1927 .... 275.00

Navajo, Pawn
Large turquoise-blue center stone with "Raindrops" bezel. Silver twist and bands 125.00
Cluster of 24 baroque nuggets of Gem Mine turquoise set in the round bezel. Two leaves on each side 375.00
Sand casted with Nevada green cabochon turquoise stone and 2 coral cabochons.......... 75.00

Zuni
Coral inlay cardinal on branch of turquoise and coral inlay. Kingman bands around edges. Signed C. Bowie 200.00

Turquoise chip inlay in channel-style. Signed C. J. 125.00

Zuni, Pawn

Cluster of 77 round and teardrop-shaped turquoise stones .. 325.00

Oval of MOP with inlaid Katchina. High relief leaves. Set with bands of MOP, bone and tortoise shell. Signed Dan Thunderball 71 .... 300.00

Petit pt. 42 blue gem stones .. 850.00

Three rows of turquoise stones with needlepoint work. Signed Begay 275.00

Three oval baroque turquoise with wire twists, bentwork, raindrops and bars. Unsigned .. 150.00

Buckle, Belt. 3¼". Sandcasted. 11 blue Lone Mountain nuggets. Windings between stones. 300.00

Earrings

Heische. 1½" hoop. Birds suspended on turquoise 100.00

Navajo, Pawn. Blossom-shaped mountings set with green turquoise. Unsigned. Pair Zuni. 3¼" long. Total of 26 turquoise stones. Pair 135.00

Necklaces

Contemporary. Five large free form turquoise stones. Silver beads. Signed Tommy Yellowhorse 250.00

Sandcasted. Seven squash blossoms. Sandcasted. Set with turquoise cabochons. Signed D.T.B. 350.00

Heische. 14 green serpentine hand carved birds. 16 pieces of red coral interwoven. 450.00

Navajo. Squash blossom. 10 blossoms. 94 hand engraved beads strung on foxtail. Approximately 500 carats of polished green turquoise. C. 1910 .... 3250.00

Santo Domingo. 21 Kingman turquoise nuggets in graduated size. Strung on Heishi. 33" long .. 500.00

Zuni

Coral, MOP and turquoise inlays. 10" long 550.00

48 handcarved tortoise shell birds. Strung with golden melon Heische 2250.00

35 petit point turquoise. Signed HA C. 1925 .... 375.00

Ring. Navajo. 30 carat. Lone Mountain turquoise. Leaf design 250.00

INDIAN TREE PATTERN

The Indian Tree pattern, derived from the Oriental-type shrub or tree that predominates the design, is a popular pattern for porcelain dinnerware from the last half of the 19th century to the present. The pattern was used by several English potteries including Burgess and Leigh, Coalport, Maddox and others.

Platter. 10½" long. Coalport ..$35.00

Bowl. 7". Coalport ....$ 35.00

Butter, Covered. Coalport 95.00

Chocolate Set. Pot, 6-cups and saucers. 14 pieces.............. 225.00

Cream and Sugar. Open. Coalport.. 50.00

Cups and Saucers

Bouillon. Coalport 25.00

Coffee. Maddox 20.00

Coffee. Minton 25.00

Demitasse. Coalport........... 25.00

Gravy Boat. Underplate. Coalport .. 95.00

Pitchers

5" high. Burgess & Leigh 30.00

6" high. Maddox & Sons 40.00

Plates

6". Coalport 10.00

6". Fluted rim 12.00

7½". Soup. Coalport 12.50

8". Coalport 15.00

9". Fluted 20.00

9½". Maddox & Sons 18.50

10". Johnson Bros. 25.00

10½". Square. Handled 40.00

Platters

10½". Coalport 35.00

13½". Copeland & Spode 40.00

15½". Burgess & Leigh 60.00

19½". Minton 95.00

Sauce. 5". Coalport 7.00

Shakers, Salt and Pepper. Coalport. Pair 50.00

Tea Set. Pot, cream and sugar, 6 cups and saucers. 6-7" plates. Coalport. 23 pieces 295.00

Tureen, Soup. 10". With ladle. Maddox & Sons 125.00
Vegetables, Covered
9". Maddox 40.00
11½". Coalport 20.00
Waste Bowl. Coalport 20.00

INKWELLS

Commercial ink bottles in America date from the early 1800's, inkwells were much earlier. Ever since man began recording his thoughts and experiences with 'pen and ink', a suitable container was needed for the ink. Documented proof exists of an inkwell found in the ruins of the Essences, a group of Holy men believed to have been responsible for some of the writings of the Dead Sea Scrolls; written more than 2000 years ago.
With the advent of the self-contained ink pen, inkwells disappeared from the scene. The majority of the inkwells found in collectors' field today are ornate examples with Victorian or early 20th century styling.
Also see specific categories in regards to material or manufacturer i.e. "Cut Glass," "Limoges," "Tiffany," etc.

Marble. 6¼ x 11½" base. Two wells. Hinged lids $85.00

Basalt. 2" diam., 1⅜" high ......$ 55.00
Brass
Crab. 6½x8" diam. Hinged lid. Glass well. 75.00
Horse. 5½x9½" base. Separates 2 milk glass wells. Pen holder at bottom 100.00
Rococo. 8½". Flowers, butterflies, scrolls. Glass well 125.00
Scrolled. 6¼x6¼". Porcelain well. 75.00
Bronze
Art Deco-style. Pyramid shape. Geometric silver inlay 75.00
Art Nouveau-style. Cloverleaf shape. Woman's head and flowing hair lid 125.00
Bear chained to tree trunk. 3" high. Hinged lid. Glass well 125.00
Bears. Single well. Austrian 175.00
Cat. 6" high. Vienna 125.00
Cloisonne. 6" square. Attached shaped tray 95.00
Delft-type. 2¾" square, 3½" high. Windmill decor. Domed lid. Brass connector 75.00
Faux Malachite. 12" oval. Blown glass well. Brass hinged lid. Ball feet 65.00
Glass
1½" square, 2" high. Hinged glass lid. Brass connector........ 30.00
2½" square, 3½" high. Swirled. Matching lid. Sterling connector .. 65.00
3½" high. Figural. "Scottie Dog." 50.00
Iron
Automobile. 5½x10" long. Two glass wells under hood 150.00
Camel. 6x9" long. Saddle opens to reveal well 145.00
Columbian Expo. Half of globe. Glass well 45.00
Crab. 5". Black enameled 50.00
Mephistopheles. 2½x3". Glass well. Ears as pen holders 75.00
Owl. 4x9½" long. Original paint. Glass well. 85.00
Lacquer, Black. 7½x10" long. Two crystal wells on MOP box. Pen drawer. Chinese 125.00
Milk Glass. Hound dogs. 4" high. Iron base 125.00
Pewter
2½x3¼" diam. 5-quill holes. Hinged top 100.00
5" high. Owl 150.00
Porcelains
2" diam., 2½" high. Melon-shaped. Hand painted floral decor 60.00
4" high. Lady in 18th century dress 45.00
4x6½". Boat-shaped. Hand painted floral decor. Gold trim 150.00
Green leaves. Domed lid. Brass connection 85.00
4½" high. Clown. French. Artist signed 150.00
School Desk-type. Black bakelite top 4.00
Soapstone. 2½x2¾x3". Carved. Pen holder 55.00
Staffordshire
Doves. Cobalt on white. Tulip-shaped pen holder 85.00
Poodles. Polychromed. Tree trunk pen holder 125.00
Wooden
2½x3" diam. Hinged lid. Porcelain well 50.00

7x11" long. Rosewood. Two crystal wells. Center handle and drawer 95.00

INSULATORS

The invention of the telegraph in 1832 and the telephone in 1875 created the need for insulators. The first patent was issued in 1844.

The earlier insulators were threadless. Later threads, drip points and double skirts were introduced as improvements. Because of their single function or purpose. . .to prevent shock or current leakage. . .there is little variation in design of the millions of insulators that have been manufactured.

Dominion. Cobalt $10.00

American Insulator Co. Pat. Sept. 13, 1881. Aqua ....$	15.00
Armstrong. No. 14. Clear	12.00
Bakelite. No name	3.50
Brookfield, W. No. 9. Green	5.00
Cable. No. 2. Green	12.00
Dominion. No. 42. Amber	2.00
Gayner. No. 48-400. Aqua	10.00
Hemingray	
No. 1. High voltage. Pat. May 2, 1893. Aqua	15.00
No. 12. Pat. May 2, 1893. Green	8.50
No. 19. Amber	25.00
No. 21. Aqua	2.00
No. 38. Aqua	7.50
No. 55. Aqua	2.50
Knowles. No. 2 Cable. Aqua	35.00
Locke, F.M. No. 16. Green	12.50
Lynchburg. No. 30. Aqua	10.00
McLaughlin. No. 9. Aqua	5.00
Pottery. Blue. No name	15.00
Pottery. Brown. No name	3.00
Pyrex Corning. No. 661. Marigold. Carnival	35.00
Standard. Amethyst	20.00
Westinghouse. No. 4. Aqua	35.00
Whitall Tatum Co.	
No. 1. Amethyst	10.00
No. 9. Aqua	2.00

IRONS (SMOOTHING, ETC.)

Smoothing irons or hand-pressing irons of the past were probably one of the least popular domestic objects in a woman's life.

The flat iron is sometimes called a 'sad iron.' It derived this name from the obsolete terminology for solid. . .sad. If you have ever lifted one of these heavy irons, you might suspect the housewife would be sad at the end of the ironing day. . .perhaps a better explanation for the name "sad iron!" There were four methods for heating these irons: (1) The slug was heated and attached to the iron. (2) The iron was heated directly on the fire. (3) Hot charcoal was contained within the iron. (4) The self-heating gas iron.

Irons can be found in various shapes and sizes, all of which evolved around the current fashions of the day. . .ruffles, stiff collars, mutton sleeves, etc.

Alcohol Iron. "Laundry Maid" ..$25.00

Box Iron. Cast iron with wood handle. One slug ....$	40.00
Charcoal Irons	
American. 10" long. Wood handle. With trivet	55.00
British. Coat of Arms in brass. One chimney	65.00
Turkish	35.00

Flat Irons
"Dover No. 12.0" Wood handle .. 25.00
"Silvester's No. 5." Hollow iron handle 20.00
Fluting Irons
"American." Dated August, 1879 . 65.00
"Eclipse." Dated 1875 .... 50.00
"Geneva." Dated 1878 .... 45.00
Gas Iron. Coleman. "Good Value Model 4 A" 20.00
Sleeve Iron. "Hub." 17.50
Tailor's Iron 25.00

IRONSTONE

(See "White Patterned Ironstone")

IRONWARE

Iron, a metallic element that occurs abundantly in combined forms, has been known for centuries. Items made from iron range from the utilitarian to the decorative. Early hand-forged ironwares are of considerable interest to collectors of Americana. Also see "Kitchen Collectibles."

Shoe Scraper. "Harp". Cast iron $28.50

Blacksmith tongs. 11". Hand-forged .... $ 100.00
Book Press. 11½x15x17"x9½" diam. Wheel. Weighs 60 lbs. C. 1865 .... 125.00
Boot Scrapers
"Mudder's Little Helper." 13x16" base 35.00
Scroll design. 4" wide x 6¼" high. 25.00
Bunion Stretcher. "Lightning-Fulton." C. 1897 .... 15.00

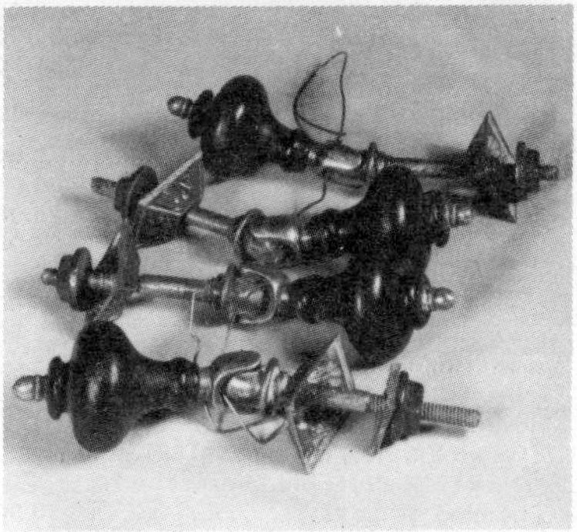

Furniture pulls. "Teardrop." Brass and wood. C. 1850. Set of 4 .... $30.00

Buggy Whip Holder. C. 1868 .... 65.00
Candle Snuffer. Scissors-type 35.00
*Corn Dryer 10.00
Door Knobs. Set 25.00
Door Latches
Butterfly 75.00
Ear-Form. With thumbpiece. Early 19th century 85.00
Heart 50.00
Door Lock. 4x6". Turn handle, complete with key. C. 1840 .... 100.00
Eel Spear. Hand-forged 60.00
Hair Curling Iron 10.00
Hand Cuffs. Chain joint, screw release 45.00
Harpoon. 6'3". Early 150.00
Hay Fork. 34" long 50.00
Hearth Plaque. 15x18½". Weighs 8 lbs. Victorian lady center; cherubs, griffins, etc. Border all in high relief 225.00
Hinges, Strap. Hand wrought
12". Pair 30.00
18". Pair 40.00
36". Pair 85.00
*Hitching Posts
Black Boy. 24". Painted 220.00
Horse's Heads
8" 100.00
36". Mounted on fluted post. 19th century 300.00
Jockey. 38". Painted 350.00
Hooks
Bailing 5.00
Grapple. Hand-forged 10.00
Meat. 18" long 20.00
Shutter. 7". "S" 7.50
Horseshoe 7.50
Ice Skates. Clamp-ons. Racers. Pair . 35.00
Ice Tongs. 12" 12.50

Kettles

5x8" diam.	35.00
5½x9" diam. Three legs, lid	75.00
11x20½". diam. Three legs, bail handle	125.00

Key. 7". Wrought iron	10.00
*Lamp Bracket. Lacy. Complete	60.00
Scissors. 8". Hand-wrought	25.00
Shoelast. Double. "S" shaped	15.00
Shoes. Advertising-type. 10" high. High button-style. Pair	125.00
Snow Bird. 6½"	22.50
Soap Dish. Wall-type. Lacy design	15.00
Spitoon. Tin lid. Cast iron	50.00

Stoves

Crown #8, Troy, N.Y. Pat'd. 1881. 9½x11". Portable. Kerosene burning	50.00
William V. Many, Albany, N.Y. Wood burning	375.00
Radiant Air Blast, German Stove Co., Erie, Pa. 48" high. Parlour-type. Ornate cast iron, nickel plated trim	750.00
Whiteman & Cox, Phila., Pa. 51" high. Dated 1869. Parlour-type	500.00
Sugar Nippers. 9" long. Wrought iron	65.00
Tractor Seat. C. 1910-20	65.00

Traps

Bear	150.00
Beaver. Double spring	85.00
Fox. Hand-forged	125.00
Wolf. Double spring	85.00
Water Pump	100.00

*Reproduced Item

IVORY

True ivory, a yellowish white organic material, comes from the teeth or tusks of animals. Ivory lends itself well to carving because of its basic structure and has been used for centuries, by many cultures, for artistic and utilitarian items. The Endangered Species Act of 1973 that prohibited the importation and sale of antique ivory and tortoise shell was amended in 1978 . . .with limitations. If you deal or collect ivory, familiarize yourself with this law.

Billiard Ball. ½lb	$ 25.00
Boxes	
Jewelry. 2x3¼x6". Heavily carved in lacy decor. Velvet lined. Separate tray	175.00
Opium. 4x4". Carved elephants	295.00
Brush Holder. 3x4½" high. Carved with 5-claw dragons. Pierced	165.00
Button Hook. Ivory handle	20.00

Candlesticks. 9½". Carved. 5 piece construction. Pair $350.00

Card Case. Carving of stag, foliage. Red silk lining	85.00
Chess Set. 4" King. Red and white. C. 1830	400.00
Cigarette Holders, Carved	
3½"	25.00
5"	50.00
7"	75.00
Doctor's Dolls	
8". On base. C. 1925	250.00
15". On base	500.00
Figurines	
Elephant. 1½x2¾" long. Japanese. C. 1890	125.00
Elephant. 2¾x6" long	350.00
Farmer. 9" high. Basket and goose. Signed	500.00
Fisherman. 6½"	295.00
FooDog. 6". Chinese. C. 1890	500.00
Horse. 5" high. Prancing	500.00
Koom Lum. 8½"	250.00
Kwan Yin. 32". With basket of flowers and phoenix bird	2500.00
Lion. 7½" long	400.00
Madonna. 12". Germany	200.00
Mandarin. 4" high. C. 1900	175.00
Warrior on Lion. 2¾x3½". C. 1910	125.00
Knife Rest. 4½" long. Carved heads	45.00

Napkin Rings

Carved	50.00
Plain	25.00
Needle Case. Shape of book	40.00
Scabbard. 16¾" long. Carved oriental warriors	300.00

Shoe Horns

Plain	20.00
6¾" long. Carved birds and serpents	75.00
Spoon. 5" long. Carved handle	45.00
Teething Ring. Plain	25.00

Tusks

Elephant. 17" long. Carved with seven elephants forming bridge	375.00
Elephant. 34½ long. Carved with animals, portrait of Charles I. Coat of Arms. Dated 1641	2500.00
Elephant. 41" long. Carved figures, dragons, etc	3500.00
Wild Boar. 13" long. Carved reptiles. C. 1900	300.00

JACKFIELD POTTERY

Jackfield is a red clay pottery with a high black glaze. It is sometimes decorated with enamels or designs in relief. The ware was first made at the Jackfield Pottery, Stropshire, England in the 18th century. Most Jackfield pottery encountered today is from the 19th century.

Cache Pot. 7½x7½". Enameled classical scenes. Two lion ring handles. Gold trim ....$	175.00
Cat. 12½" high. Glass eyes. Gold neck ribbon	125.00
Coffee Pot. 9½" to top of finial	125.00
Cow. Creamer. 7" long	85.00
Cream and Sugar, Open. 3" high. Plain. Set	75.00
Cup and Saucer. Plain	50.00
Dog. 10" high	75.00
Hen. Covered dish. 8½" long. Some enameling	135.00
Inkwell. 2x3" diam. Three quill holes. Incised and beaded	125.00
Syrup. 7½" high. Pewter lid. Decorated with enameled flowers.	95.00

Teapots

5" high. Squat-type. Basketweave design in relief	85.00
7¼" high. Plain. Pewter lid	95.00
Vase. 4". Beaded band in relief	50.00

JACK-IN-THE-PULPIT VASES

Vases in a form of the "Jack-in-the-Pulpit" flower were in vogue during the late Victorian and early 20th century periods. These vases were made in a wide variety of glass, color and size.

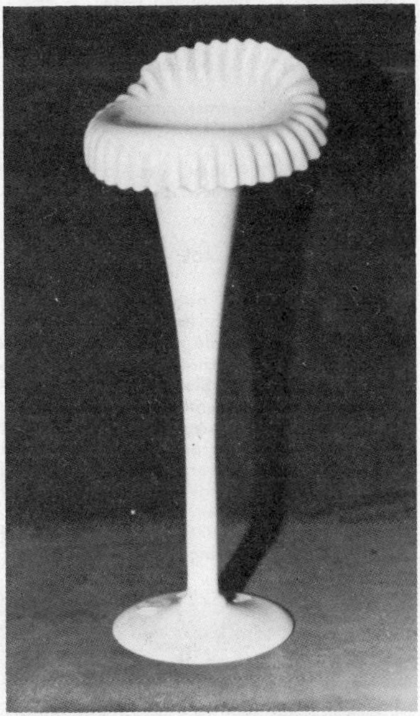

Burmese. New England. Glossy finish. 11" high $950.00

Amberina

8". Plain ....$	150.00
11". Inverted Thumbprint. Amber foot. Gold leaves and enameled florals. Amber ruffled applied edge	275.00

Opalescent

4". Vaseline	65.00
5". White	55.00
7". Vaseline. Hand blown. Applied foot	85.00
11". Vaseline	100.00

Satin

5¼". Yellow to orange. Enameled butterfly and florals	150.00
6". Blue. Cased. 3-camphor feet	175.00
9". Rainbow	195.00
9½". Peach. Cased. 5-camphor feet	250.00
Spatter. 9". Green base with yellow and pink spatters	95.00

Transparent

Amber. 8". Hand blown 55.00

Cranberry. 9". Star-shaped base in crystal. Gold decorated. English. Pair 195.00

Cranberry. 12". Crystal pedestal and wafer foot 125.00

Crystal. 7". Pink enamel spatters 65.00

Green. 6⅞". Opalescent white top. 75.00

Green. 10¾". Ribbed. Swirled pedestal. Gold enameled roses .. 85.00

JADE

Jade is the generic name for two distinct minerals. . .nephrite and jadite.

Nephrite, an amphibole mineral from Central Asia, has a waxy surface and ranges in hues from white to almost a black-green. All jade carvings before the 18th century were of nephrite.

Jadite, a pyroxene mineral found in Burma, has a glassy appearance and comes in various shades of white, green, yellow-brown and violet. Most jade carvings from the 18th century to the present are jadite.

Jade is held in high esteem as a gemstone and lends itself well to carving.

Tree. 10¾" high. Various shades and hues of jadite. Jadite planter .. $350.00

Box. 2¼ diam, 3½" high. Covered. Light green $350.00

Buckle. 4¾". White. Carved dragon 300.00

Dice

English. Pair 50.00

Gold inlaid 'numbers'. Pair 175.00

Figurines

Bird. 4½". Medium green 195.00

Buddha. 6". Light green. C. 1850. 650.00

Carp. 2½". Medium green 175.00

Carp. 3½". Lavender 250.00

Elephant. 4". Medium green 375.00

Foo Dog. 2½". Mutton Fat 275.00

Foo Dog. 3". Green 225.00

Frog. 3". Deep green 295.00

God of Longevity. 6½". Green .. 650.00

Goddess of Mercy. (Kwan Yin) 8". Deep green. 600.00

Griffin. 3½x5½". Medium green 350.00

Horse. 4½". Grey, white 500.00

Lion. 2½x3". Roaring. Green 175.00

Rabbit. 4¾". Medium green 250.00

Rhinoceros. 5". Medium green .. 500.00

Water Buffalo. 3x5½". Rose 500.00

Incense Burner. 6". Carved masks, vines. Mutton Fat 400.00

Letter Opener. 6". Dark green 85.00

Paperweight. 2¾". Pale green 225.00

Pendant. 2½x3¼". Carved florals. Medium green 125.00

Screen. 20x25". Carved birds, lotus flowers, foliage. Green. Mounted on carved teakwood stand 5000.00

Trees

8½" high. Various shades of jadite. C. 1870 .... 275.00

11" high. Various shades and hues of jadite. Cloisonne planter . 650.00

Vase. 7". Carved. Mutton Fat. C. 1810 .... 1250.00

JAPANESE CORALENE
(See, "Moriage")

JAPANESE EXPORT POTTERY

Japanese Export Pottery (J.E.P.), also known as SUMIDA, was first produced in 1890 at kilns along the Sumida River near Tokyo. J.E.P. wares were made throughout the Nippon and 'Made In' eras and continues in production today.

Most of the Japanese Export Pottery, which is hand thrown pottery with molded and applied porcelain characteristics, has a cartouche (seal) or marking indicating the name Ryosai (a family name, likely the original potter).

For some time, SUMIDA pieces such as vases, baskets and teapots have been mistaken for Korean Banko . . .but research reveals little resemblance as the latter is much earlier in

origin and does not bear the 'Ryosai' mark.
There is no reason to believe Japanese Export Pottery prices will decline as a result of new information. . .as collectors continue to find Japanese Export Pottery very appealing and definitely collectible.

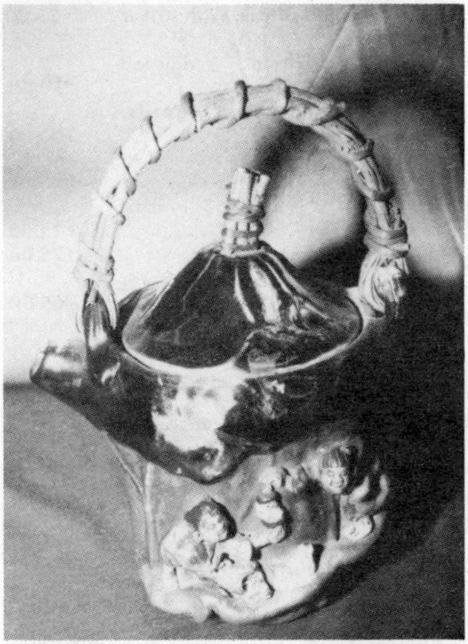

Teapot. 4" high. Two applied figures. Rush handles and finial. Seal signed $325.00

Ashtray. 3¼" diam. Boy climbing into bowl. Impressed signed ....$	55.00
Basket. 10½" high. Seal signed	350.00
Humidor. 7¼". Seal signed	275.00
Lamp Base. 13". Unsigned	150.00
Mug. 5" high. Old man carrying large rock. Seal signed	125.00
Teapot. Two applied figures. Seal signed	325.00
Toothpick. Impressed signed	75.00
Vases	
8". Figure climbing over a bar. Seal signed	175.00
8½". Bottle-shaped. Man with beard in ceremonial robe sitting on throne. Unsigned	100.00
9". Impressed signed	145.00
12". Three figures in high relief. Impressed signed	225.00

JASPERWARE

Josiah Wedgwood described Jasperware as "a fine Terra Cotta of great beauty and delicacy proper for cameos." Jasperware is a hard, unglazed porcelain with a background that varies in colors. . .from the most common blues and greens to lavender, yellow, red or black. The white designs are applied in relief and often reflect classical tradition.
This ware was first produced at Wedgwood Etruria Works in 1775. While Wedgwood was probably the most prolific and recognized maker, other English potteries produced Jasperware. Although Jasperware continues to be made today, most of the ware encountered in todays antique market is from the late 19th century.

Cheese Dish, Covered. Tan. Adams. C. 1820 ....$350.00

Biscuit Jars	
5x 4¼" diam. Blue. Silverplated lid and bail. Adams ....$	100.00
5½ x 4" diam. Blue. Portraits of Franklin, Lafayette and Washington in relief. Silverplated lid and bail. Wedgwood only	450.00
5½ x 4" diam. Lilac. Classical figures. Silverplated lid, bail and ball feet. Wedgwood only	395.00
Bowls	
7". Light green	150.00
9". Dark blue. Silverplated rim. Wedgwood only	250.00
10". Light blue	295.00
11¼". Dark blue. Adams	150.00
Boxes, Covered	
4". Heart-shaped. Light green. Bust of man in relief on cover	100.00
5x 2" deep. Light blue. Wedgwood, England	85.00
Candlesticks	
6½". Dark blue. Dudson Bros. C. 1891. Pair	150.00

Biscuit Jar. 6" high. Tricolor. Classical decor. Silverplated lid and bail $750.00

8". Dark blue. Wedgwood only. Pair 250.00
Cheese Dish, Covered. 9½ x 10¾" high. Dark blue. Wedgwood only 350.00
Chocolate Pot. Light blue 195.00
Cream and Sugar. Dark blue. Adams. Set 100.00
Creamers
2½" high. Bulbous. Dark blue. Wedgwood, England 75.00
4" high. Dark blue. Wedgwood only 95.00
Cup and Saucer. Medium blue. Rope handle. Wedgwood only 95.00
Game Dish, Covered. 10¼" long. Rabbit handles. Animals in relief around body. Wedgwood only .. 295.00
Jam Jars
With matching underplate. Dark blue. Wedgwood only 145.00
4 x 4". Dark blue. Silverplated lid. Adams 65.00
Jardinieres
6¼ x 7¼" diam. Blue. Classic figures, lion heads, garlands in relief. Wedgwood, England 175.00
7½". Light blue. Landing of Columbus. Copeland, England .. 150.00
8". Dark blue. Hunting scene. Adams Brothers 200.00
18". Dark blue. Classical figures. Adams 250.00
Match Holder. 2". Black. With striker 85.00
Medallions
1½ x 2½". Tricolor. Wedgwood only 250.00
2x2⅝". Light blue. Pegasus. Wedgwood only 100.00
Mugs
5½". Green. "Fill This Cup and Drink It Up." Floral garland in relief 125.00
6". Blue. Four seasons 125.00
Mustard Pot. With spoon. Blue. Cupids in relief 65.00
Pitchers
4½". Medium blue. Vintage decor. Samuel Alcock 65.00
5¼". Yellow 250.00
6¾". Light blue. Classical scenes. Rope handle. Wedgwood only .. 75.00
7". Green. Wedgwood only 175.00
8". Dark blue. Tankard 195.00
10". Dark blue. Adams 125.00
Plaques
3x 4½". Green. Applied girl's head 65.00
5¼ x 7¼". Shield-shaped. Green. Vintage border 125.00
18x 48". Green. Classical figures. Gold leafed frame 650.00
Ring Tree. 4¼" diam. x 2¾" high. Green. Wedgwood, England 75.00
Shakers
Salt. Dark blue. Classical figures. Self lid 50.00
Sugar. Dark blue. Classical figures 175.00
Sugars, Covered
Dark blue. Wedgwood only 100.00
Green 125.00
Yellow. Wedgwood only 295.00
Syrup. 5½" high. Blue. Vintage decor. Silverplated lid 150.00
Teapots
Dark blue. Wedgwood, England 95.00
Light blue. Wedgwood only 175.00
Tea Sets
Dark blue. Adams. 3 pieces 175.00
Green. 3 pieces 350.00
Toothpick Holder. Light blue. Angel head medallion 50.00
Tray. 7¾ x 10". Blue. Classic decor. Wedgwood, England 165.00
Vases
5⅛ x 3" diam. Dark blue. Classical decor. Wedgwood only 85.00
6½". Green. Cupid decor 85.00

10½ x 4¼" diam. Black. Classical decor. Wedgwood, England 295.00
12". Black. Classical decor. Wedgwood only 450.00

JEWEL BOXES

The jewel boxes listed herein are mainly from the late Victorian period. The common variety was made of pot metal; cast in an irregular shape with scrolls, flowers, etc. in relief and gilted. The interior was lined with satin or velvet.

Gilted. 5 x 6". Rose decor. Padded and lined in blue silk $40.00

Enamel. 2½x2¾x3¾". Ornate metal feet. Panels decorated with flower sprays. French ....$ 200.00

Gilted
- 2½x3½". Scrolled. Green velvet lining 27.50
- 2½x4". Heart-shaped. Pin cushion top 30.00
- 3x7". Scrolled. Satin lining 37.50

Ormolu with Glass Inserts. 3x6½". Padded bottom. Hinged lid. 19th century 225.00

Silverplated
- 2x5". Lily decor. Pierced sides 35.00
- 2½x7". Engraved. Rogers 65.00
- 3x10". Monogrammed lift-off lid. Velvet lining. Rogers 125.00

JEWELRY

Since ancient times, jewelry has been used as personal adornment or as symbols of wealth and status. Primitive people decorated themselves with bone, seeds or pebbles. Bronze was employed before the discovery of gold. The Greeks and the Romans fashioned elaborate gold pieces and added precious gems to enhance the appearance and value. Beginning in the Victorian period, jewelry became more available to the general populus. Materials, other than costly metals and stones, were adapted. With the advent of modern techniques, artists and craftsmen were able to have their designs duplicated and mass produced. Manufacturers issued illustrated catalogues that brought jewelry to the attention of all, including people residing in rural areas.

Victorian, Art Nouveau and Art Deco jewelry are being reproduced to coordinate with today's fashions.

Beads, Tiger Eye. 24" long. Hand knotted. Goldplated clasp $150.00

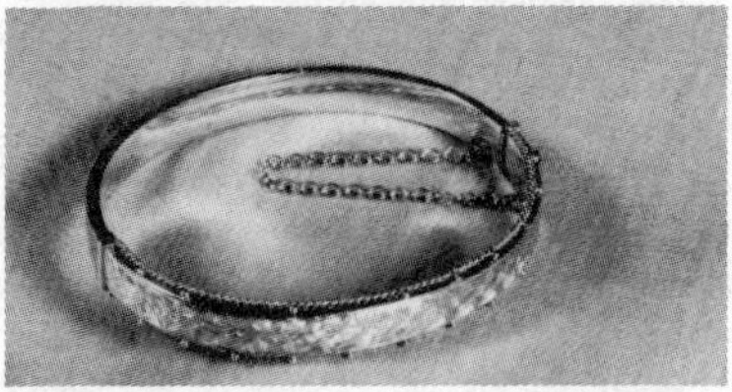

Bracelet, Bangle. 15K gold. Engraved English hallmarked $300.00

Beads
- Agate. 18" long. Mottled orange and white graduated beads ....$ 45.00

Amber. 30" long. 14K gold clasp. Victorian 135.00
Cloisonne. 50 beads, 15mm 225.00
Coral, Angel Skin. 68 graduated beads 200.00
Crystal. 18" long. Faceted. Graduated 50.00
Garnets. Cut. 10" long 35.00
Gold. 14K. 16" long. 72 beads, 10mm 350.00
Jade, Siberia. 16¾" long. 48 graduated beads 300.00
Pearls. Baroque. 16" long, 8½mm 100.00
Pearls, Rice. 16" long 75.00

Bracelets

Bangle. Bamboo design. 14K gold. 18DWT 450.00
Bangle. Engraved. ½" wide. 14K gold 275.00
Charm. Six contemporary charms. 14K gold. 20DWT 500.00
Charm. Thirteen charms. 14K gold. 14DWT 350.00
Cuff. 1¼" wide. Sterling. "Repousse." S. Kirk and Son 65.00
I.D. Link design. 14K gold. 32DWT 800.00

Brooches

Cameo. 1¾" oval. 14K gold mounting 125.00
Diamond. Crest-shaped. Platinum mounting. TW 1.42K 1850.00
Marcasite. 1½x2¼". Diamond-shaped. Initials 20.00
Sterling. 2x3". Flower basket with butterfly 28.50

Buckle, Belt. 2x3". Fishscale cloisonne. Butterfly-shaped 125.00

Chains

Cuban. Link design with religious pendant. 18K gold. 119DWT 3000.00
Flattened curb link. 25" long. 18K gold. 12DWT 275.00
Watch. 23" long. Ladies. Gold filled. Diamond shaped turquoise and pearl slide 55.00

Chatelaines. Sterling

Gorham. Clip with three implements 150.00
Kerr. Clip with two ornate implements. Art Nouveau-style 100.00

Crosses

Amethyst. 2" long, 1¼" wide. Six full cut amethyst. Openwork silver (800) 100.00
Gold. 1" long. 14K gold. Embossed 35.00
Gutta Percha. 3". Anchor overlay. Mourning-type. C. 1850 .... 85.00

Cuff Links. Moonstone insets. 14K gold 45.00

Earrings

Diamonds. 4, TW-.30K; 2 sapphires, TW-.90 K. Old French back. Dangle-type. 14K gold 350.00
Gold. 6mm ornate ball with frame. Pierced. Wires. 14K gold .. 175.00
Pearl. Stud-type. 14K gold 25.00
Sapphire. TW-2.85K. 14K white gold 250.00

Lockets

1" diam. Engraved. 14K gold 50.00
1½" oval. Heavily embossed. 18K gold. 14DWT. C. 1890 .... 350.00
⅝x13-16". Elaborate floral engraving. Pinchbeck gold 30.00
Lorgnette. 27" plus 2" leader. Long and short links. 14K gold .. 150.00

Pendants

Crystal. R. Lalique 350.00
Moonstone teardrop. 1" long, 16" gold chain. 14K gold 195.00

Pin. Lalique. Jet center. Marquisette stones. Sterling mounting ..$300.00

Pins

1". Marcasite. Crown-shape 15.00
1⅛". Bar. Sterling silver with 11 seed pearls 15.00
1½". Bar and circle. Art Deco-style. 9K gold 25.00
1¾". Bar. Leaf and scrolls. 12 seed pearls. 9K gold 27.50
1¾". Oval. Bar. Pressed relief. Diamond chip. 9K gold 50.00

Rings

Diamond

.12K. 10K white gold mounting 175.00
.30K. 18K white gold mounting 350.00
.50K. Mine cut with 4 side diamonds. Platinum mounting 500.00
1.02K. 14K white gold mounting 2500.00

Diamond & Emerald. Dinnertype. 14K white gold. 10 emeralds. TW-.98K; 20 diamonds, TW-.85K 2000.00

Gold

- Mounting-type. Engraved.
  - Georgian 500.00
  - Signet. 18K gold 50.00
  - Wedding. 14K gold. 20DWT .. 425.00
- Hair. ⅛" wide. Mourning-type. Woven band. Channel set. Engraved. Mid 19th century .. 75.00
- Opal. 1.17K with 12 diamonds, TW-.60K. 14K white gold mounting 500.00

*Slides. 14K gold. (approx. ½")

- Amethyst. Oval. 5 chips 40.00
- Diamond chip. Diamond-shaped. 50.00
- Embossed cloverleaf. Oval 20.00
- Pearl, Seed. 3, round 30.00
- Ruby chip. Square 40.00
- Turquoise. Square 25.00

*Stickpins

- Horseshoe-shape. 14K gold...... 20.00
- Lover's Knot. 14K gold 55.00
- Mosaic. ¾" long. Dog with ball design. 14K gold 150.00
- Pearl. 14K gold 25.00
- Sterling. Art Nouveau-style...... 15.00

Watches, See "Watches"

*Reproduced Item

JUGTOWN POTTERY

Pottery making in North Carolina commenced in the mid 18th century and continued through the 19th and 20th centuries. The Jugtown Pottery encountered today began its colorful and somewhat off-beat operation in 1920. Jacques and Juliana Bushbee decided to leave their cosmopolitan world and return to North Carolina to revive the dying craft of pottery making in their native state. They located in Moore County, miles away from any large city and accessible only "if mud permits." They employed a talented young potter, Ben Owen, to turn all the wares. Jacques Bushbee did most of the designing and glazing. Juliana busied herself in promoting.

From 1922 until 1962, with only a few years exception "Jugtown Ware" was made by Ben Owen under the operation of the founders, Jacques and Juliana Bushbee.

Utilitarian and decorative items were produced. Although many colorful glazes were used, orange predominated. A Chinese blue glaze that ranged from light blue to deep turquoise was a prized glaze reserved for the very finest pieces.

Pottery is still being made in North Carolina and marked "Jugtown." At last report, Ben Owen is still turning pottery under his own mark, "Ben Owen, Master Potter."

Bowl. 3 x 4½" diam. Gray. Cobalt trim. Orange peel texture. Impressed signature $32.50

Bowls

- 3". Dark green to blue ....$ 35.00
- 4½". Blue, aqua 40.00
- 5". Handled. Orange 25.00
- 6". Brown 35.00

Chamberstick. 7" diam. saucer.

- Orange glaze 35.00

Cup, Custard. With underplate.

- Orange. "Ben Owen." 25.00

Mug. Orange. "Ben Owen." 20.00

Pitchers

- 5". Green 40.00
- 6½". Covered. Brown 50.00
- 7¾". Covered. Orange 35.00
- 12". Bulbous. Orange 50.00

Planter. 5x5½". Bulbous. Mottled blue, maroon, tan glaze 45.00

Plates

- 5¾". Orange. "Ben Owen." 25.00
- 6". Orange 18.50

Pot. Frog-shaped. Handled 50.00

Sugar, Covered. Orange 25.00

Vases

- 4". Orange 20.00
- 5". Green 32.50
- 6". Brown and orange 30.00
- 7". Rose brown. Speckled white drips 35.00
- 8". Green to tan. 3-handles 50.00
- 8". Rose shading to green. 2-handles 45.00
- 9". Square. Green 50.00
- 9¼". Light green to aqua. Dragon handles 60.00

KPM *K.P.M.*

Meissen originally used this mark, but only for a short time. In 1832 the mark KPM (Koenigliche Porzellan Manufaktur) was used as a trade mark of the Royal Factory in Berlin, Germany. This was the factory that produced the very fine porcelain (Royal Berlin) under the patronage of Frederick the Great from 1763-1786. In the late 19th and early 20th century other factories in Germany also produced this ware.

Bowl. 5¼ x 11¼ x 13¼". Puce on cream ground. Applied flowers. C. 1880 ....$ 350.00
Cache Pot. 7½", 6¼" deep. Pink on white. Handpainted roses. Gold trim 125.00
Cups and Saucers
Chinoiserie decor. Deep saucer. C. 1840 .... 45.00
Molded pattern with handpainted flowers. C. 1870 .... 35.00
Figurines
4". Bear. All white 75.00
4½". Boy with lamb 95.00
6¾". Artist 195.00
8½". Lady in 18th century dress .. 250.00
10¼". Bacchus and Bacchants. C. 1880 .... 300.00
Lithophanes. See "Lithophanes"
Plaques
4¾x6¾". Oval. Portrait of Gypsy girl. Mounted on velvet. Framed .. 1350.00
9x11". Liebesfruhling. (Spring Love) Artist signed 1500.00
11½x13¼". The Sad Magdelaine 3000.00
Plates
10". Cake. Handled. Handpainted floral decor. Gold trim 65.00
12". Service plates. Handpainted decor. Gold trim. Set of 12 ...... 750.00
12½". Floral decor with scrolls. Yellow to orange. C. 1880 ...... 150.00
Teapot. 6½" high. Floral decor. Gold trim 165.00
Tea Set. Blue Morning Glories. Gold trim. 24 pieces 650.00
Tray. 12½". Square. Handpainted flowers, butterflies. Gold rim 225.00
Vases
6¾". Goat head handles. Handpainted scenic decor. Gold trim. Pair 650.00
9½". Pillow-shape. Birds in relief. Satin finish 195.00
10½". Portrait. Gold trim 500.00

Statue. 24" high. Full figure of male and female on round ornate pedestaled base $3500.00

KAUFFMANN, ANGELICA

Marie Angelique Catherine Kauffmann was a Swedish artist (1741-1807). Her paintings were adapted to decorate many porcelains of the 19th century.

Bowl. 9¼". 4 portraits. Cobalt border. Austrian ....$ 65.00

Plate. 8½". Three classical figures in center. Mauve scalloped rim with gold trim. Signed. Beehive mark $50.00

Box. 1¾x2¾". Classical scene 75.00
Candlestick. 5½". Classical scene. Gold trim 65.00
Coffee Set. Coffee pot, creamer, sugar, tray, 4 mugs. Classical decorations. Gold trim. Signed . . 500.00
Cup, Mustache. Lithographed. Signed 75.00
Cup and Saucer. Demitasse. Classical decor. Cobalt border. Gold trim 40.00
Jam Jar, Covered. 5½". Classical decor in green, magenta. Gold trim. Beehive mark. Signed 75.00
Pitcher. 8½". Tankard-shape. Cupid decor. Deep rose ground. Gold trim 85.00
Plates
9½". Classical scene. Austrian . . 55.00
10". Classical center. Gold border 65.00
11". Hanging-type. Multicolored center of two ladies. Green rim. Gold trim. Signed 85.00
11". Portrait center. Green rim . . 75.00
13½". Hanging-type. Garden scene. Irregular-shaped border outlined in gold. Signed 225.00
Tray. 15" long. Classical decor. Pierced gold handles 150.00
Urn. 10½". Classical decor. Dark green ground. Heavy gold trim. Beehive mark. Signed 225.00
Vases
5". Classical decor. Footed and handled 35.00
10". Four classical figures. Green with gold trim. Signed 85.00
11". Portrait. Gold handles. Austrian 100.00

KEW BLAS

Kew-Blas

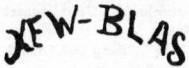

Kew Blas is an art glass made by the Union Glass Company, Somerville, Massachusetts in the late 1890's. The company executed many items for Tiffany and from this we can judge their quality.

Vase. 7". "Pulled Feather." Signed $1500.00

Bowl. 14x5" high. "Pulled Feather" on red. Signed . . . . $ 450.00
Candlestick. 8½". Swirled stem. Iridescent gold 275.00
Compote. 4½" flared top, 3½" high. Gold iridescent. Signed 500.00
Creamer. 2½" high. Bulbous. "Fishnet." 195.00
Goblet. 6". Gold iridescent 250.00
Pitcher. 5". "King Tut." White, green and gold. Blue handle and lining. Signed 1750.00

Plates
- 4". Iridescent gold 165.00
- 6½". Iridescent gold 200.00

Rose Bowl. 4" high. Green and gold "Chain" on gold iridescent 750.00

Tumbler. 5". Gold iridescent 325.00

Vases
- 4½". "King Tut." Gold iridescent. Signed 850.00
- 7". "Pulled Feather." Signed 1500.00
- 7½". Creamy pearl with light green highlights. Gold lining. Scalloped top 850.00
- 8". Gold iridescent. Teardrop-shape 800.00
- 10". Black with gold loopings. Gold lining 2500.00
- 10", 7" diam. Iridescent gold, green and white 1750.00
- 11". Iridescent blue. Gold lining. Signed 1250.00
- 12". Iridescent gold with highlights of rose, blue and green. Signed 1500.00

KING'S ROSE

King's Rose pattern is a hand decorated earthenware made in the Staffordshire district, England in the 1820-1840 period. A large cabbage-type rose is the main decor. The rose may be brick red, pink or pale red. The pink rose is often called "Queen's Rose." Borders are a solid pink band, vined, lined or sectional.

Creamer. Helmet-shaped. Brick red rose $350.00

Coffee Pot. 10½" high. Dome lid. Brick red rose ....$ 1000.00

Creamer. Helmet shaped. Brick red rose 350.00

Cups and Saucers
- Handled. Brick red rose 150.00
- Handleless
  - Brick red rose 225.00
  - Pink rose 200.00
  - Pale red rose 175.00

Plates
- 6½". Brick red rose 225.00
- 8¾". Brick red rose 250.00

Sauceboat. 6" long. Brick red rose .. 225.00

Sugars, Covered
- Scroll work in relief. Brick red rose 400.00
- Pink rose 325.00

Teapot. 5" high. Bulbous. Pink rose . 450.00

KITCHEN COLLECTIBLES

Kitchenwares and allied primitives (of any period. . .18th, 19th and early 20th century) are a vital reminder of family togetherness and the basic creative culinary arts. During the 18th century, cooking was done on the open fire or hearth. Pots were made of iron, copper or brass. Cast iron cooking stoves replaced hearth cooking by the mid-19th century. Iron and copper pots and pans continued to be popular; but in smaller and lighter weight versions. A myriad of kitchen gadgets were invented, patented and made available to help the homemaker. Woodenwares; such as breadboards, cookie rollers, butter stamps and molds; plus pewter and cast iron molds hold nostalgic appeal that few other areas of collecting have. Dealers and collectors note heightening interest and increasing value of these utilitarian and decorative kitchen collectibles.

Also see: "Brass", "Copper", "Graniteware", "Ironwares", "Woodenwares" and other related and specific categories.

*Apple Parers
- 3-gear. Cast iron ....$ 30.00
- 4-gear. Cast iron 40.00
- 16x22". Wooden with wooden gears. Leather belt 125.00

Biscuit Oven. 8x13x14" wide. Tin .. 50.00

Bowls. Also see "Woodenware"
- Curly Maple. 19¼" diam.x6½" deep. Hand turned 275.00
- Maple
  - 11" diam.x4" deep. Lathe turned 40.00
  - 15" diam. Lathe turned. Old worn red paint exterior 95.00
- Pine
  - 10x18". Rectangular. Hand hewn 75.00
  - 17¼x26¼"; 5" deep. Rectangular. Hand hewn. Flange handles. 4 carved feet 125.00

Ice Cream Scoop. Tin $15.00

Bread Board. 9½" diam. Maple. "Bread" carved on border 35.00
Bread Box. 10x11½x14". Tin. Stenciled lettering "Bread." Complete 25.00
Bread Maker. 10½" high. Tin. Complete 25.00
Broiler. 12" diam. Wrought iron. Early 250.00
Butter Churns. Also see "Woodenware."
  Glass. ½ gal. Two geared metal top. 4 wooden paddles. Vented cover 35.00
  Stoneware. 6¼" high. Cream glaze with blue banding 45.00
  Tin. 13" high. Tapering cylinder with side handles. All original and complete. 85.00
  Wooden
    18" high. Cylinder-type with stave construction and brass bandings 100.00
    22½" high. Square. Beveled top edge. Worn red paint 135.00
Butter Crock. Stoneware. "Dragon Fly" decor. Blue and white. Bail handle 65.00
Butter Hands. 8". Hand carved with curling handle 150.00
Butter Paddles
  Burl Walnut. 8". Hand carved with curling handle 150.00
  Curly Maple. 10". Hand carved .. 85.00
  Maple. 8" 12.50
  Pine 7.50
Cake Decorator. 8½" long. Pewter. Turned wooden handle. C. 1840 . 40.00
Carpet Beater. 26" long. Woven wire 25.00
*Cherry Seeder. 13". Clamp-type. Cast iron 32.50
Chimney Cleaner. Wireware 18.50
Cookie Board. 8x15". Walnut. Carved windmill design 125.00
Cookie Cutters
  Advertising-type 5.00
  Animals
    3" 8.50
    4¾". Strap handles. Early 25.00
  Card Suites. 1½". Set of 4 ...... 15.00
  Gingerbread Man. 3x5" 7.50
  Lady. 3½" 10.00
Cookie Roller. 10". Maple 25.00
Cream Beater. 4½x5x10" high. Tin. Complete 75.00
Cutlery Trays
  Pine. 8x12" 35.00
  Pine and maple. 10x13½" 40.00
Dipper. 27". Made from gourd 25.00
Dish Rack. 4x12x16". Wireware. C. 1890 .... 25.00
Dough Scraper. 3¾". Wrought iron 15.00
Egg Beater. Wireware 5.00
Flour Sifter. 2-cup. Tin 7.50
Food Choppers
  Hand wrought iron. 6½" long. C. 1850 .... 25.00
  Steel curved blade. 6" long. C. 1875 .... 10.00
Fork. 11¾". 3-tine. Wrought iron .. 30.00
Graters
  6¾" high. Tin. Hand pierced. Strap handle. Early 45.00
  9¼" high. Tin. Late 6.50
Grinder. Clamp-type. Cast iron 20.00
Ice Card. 8" square. Cardboard. C. 1910-1930 .... 3.50
Ice Cream Freezer. Two quart 50.00
Jar Opener 12.50
Kettles
  8x3" deep. Brass with iron bail handle 45.00
  8x5" deep. Cast iron with bail handle 35.00
  11x6¾" deep. Cast iron with bail handle 65.00

Kraut Cutter. 10" high x 22" long. Oak $55.00

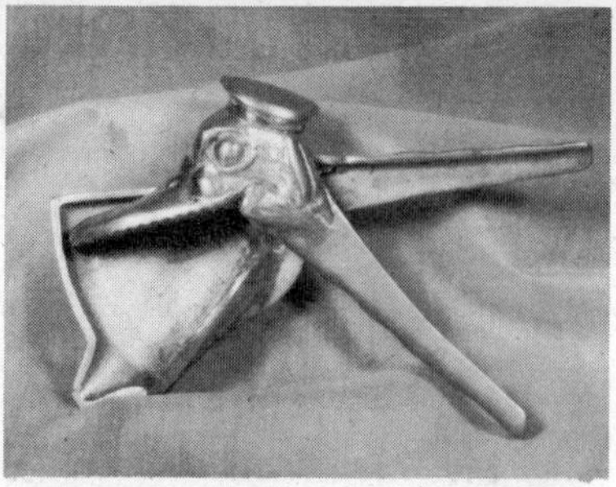

Lemon Squeezer. "Donald Duck". Aluminum. 8" long $10.00

Lunch Bucket. Double. Tin cup top. Bail handle $35.00

14x9" deep. Brass with iron bail handle	75.00
Kraut Cutter. 35". Cherry	95.00
Ladles	
Cast Iron. 15"	10.00
Hand Forged. 22". Pouring lip	125.00
Lemon Squeezer. 11" long. Wood with brass	25.00
Mashers	
Maple. One piece construction	25.00
Maple. Two piece construction	10.00
Pine. One piece construction	10.00
Walnut. One piece construction	25.00
Meat Tenderizers	
Cast Iron	12.50
Wooden	6.50
Milk Strainer. 12" diam. Tin with fine mesh	7.50
Molds. See "Food Molds"	
Noodle Roller. 14". Wooden	50.00
Nutmeg Grater. 4" long. Hand pierced tin	25.00
Oven Peel. 46" long. Wrought iron. Heart and scroll handle	150.00
Pans	
Bread	12.50
Bread. 2-loaf size. Covered	25.00
Bundt. 6½". Copper. Early	75.00
Cake. 8". C. 1920's	3.00
Corn Stick. 7-ear. Cast iron	15.00
Muffin. 6-cup. Tin	5.00
Muffin. 8-cup. Cast iron	25.00
Pastry Boards	
Pine. 14x16". Tongue and groove ends	25.00
Poplar. 18½x20½". Arched top	50.00
Tin. 14x16½". With original rolling pin	125.00
Pastry Cutters	
Brass wheel	25.00
Whale bone wheel	40.00
Pastry Cutters With Crimpers	
Brass and iron. C. 1870	65.00
Wrought iron	30.00
Pea Sheller. Cast iron	25.00
Pie Carrier. 5-pie size. Bentwood	75.00
Pie Lifter. Wireware	18.00
Pineapple Eye Snips. Painted tin	22.50
Pitchers, Stoneware	
"Plain." Tankard. Brown and white	40.00
"Poinsettia." Bulbous. Blue and white	75.00
"Windmill." Tankard. Blue and white	50.00
Raisin Seeder. "Enterprise." Cast iron	35.00
Reamers	
Chrome. Bird-shape. C. 1930's	10.00
Milk Glass. "Sunkist."	10.00
Porcelain. White	12.00
Rolling Pins-Glass	
Amber. Blown	85.00
Clear. Bottle-type. C. 1910	18.50
Milk Glass. 14"	85.00
Nailsea-type. 12"	125.00
Rolling Pin. Ironstone. Turned wooden handles	65.00
Rolling Pin. Stoneware. Blue and white. Wooden handles	125.00
Rolling Pins-Wooden	
Lignum Vitae. 12". No handles	35.00
Pine. 16". Turned handles	12.50
Tiger stripe maple. 19½"	45.00

Salt Boxes

Milk Glass. Wooden lid 40.00

Pine. 5½x7¼". Open. Wall-type. C. 1840 .... 85.00

Stoneware. "Plain." Blue and white. Wooden lid. Stenciled "Salt." 50.00

Sausage Presses

Cast Iron. 8x20½" high. "Enterprise." 45.00

Tin. 20¼". Wooden plunger 30.00

Tin. 30". Two man operation 100.00

Scissors

5½" long. C. 1900's 7.50

8½" long. C. 1880's 12.50

Scoops

Maple. 9½" 22.50

Tin. 10½" 12.50

Skewers. Set of 5 with hanger. Hand forged. 18th century 300.00

Skillets

9½x4¾" deep. 8" handle. 3-legged. Cast iron 75.00

10". Lipped. Cast iron 65.00

12". 14" rat-tailed handle. Wrought iron 85.00

Spatula. 10½". Wrought iron...... 55.00

Spoons

Cherry. 12" 10.00

Maple. 14" 6.50

Wrought Iron. 7½". Taster-type .. 50.00

Strainer. 9" long. Brass bowl. Wrought iron handle. Early 85.00

Strawberry Huller. "Nip-it." Tin 3.50

Tea Ball. Acorn-shaped. Aluminum. 3.00

Tea Kettles-Cast Iron

8" diam. Gooseneck spout. Solid handle 65.00

9x16½" oval; 8" high. Gooseneck spout. Footed. Bail handle 45.00

Tea Kettles-Copper

7½" high. Dovetailed construction. American. Unsigned 275.00

11" high. Brass handle 75.00

Toasters

Hearth. 4x5x13" long. Wrought iron. Two arches. 18th century .. 100.00

Hearth, Rotating. Wrought iron. Four rectangular arches. 18th century 175.00

Utensil Rack. 7½x35". Wall-type. Pine back board with ten iron hooks 85.00

Waffle Irons

Hearth. 4½x6" rectangular plates. 26" long handle. Wrought iron 35.00

Range-type. 8" diam. "American #8." Cast iron 28.50

Range-type. 8" diam. Scroll design. Handled. Cast iron 55.00

Washboard. Galvanized tin. Wooden frame 20.00

*Reproduced Item

KUTANI

Kutani is a Japanese ware first made in the area of Kutani, Japan in the mid 17th century. The early wares (Ko-Kutani) were quite heavy, almost approaching stoneware with simple glazes. The new Kutani (Ao-Kutani) of the 19th century is much lighter, more elaborately designed and glazed with many colors to imitate other Oriental porcelains of the period.

Plate. 8¼". Beige ground with multicolored floral center. Black and red stylized rim with gold. Marked. $75.00

Bowls

2½x8½". Terra Cotta. Ko-Kutani type ....$ 150.00

3½x7". Melon ribbed with scalloped top. Four curved feet. Garden scene with ladies 125.00

3½x8½". Chrysanthemum blossoms and dragon decor. C. 1860 185.00

Box, Covered. 2x2½". Oriental scene 75.00

Chocolate Set. Garden scene. Pot and 4 cups and saucers. Set 150.00

Cup and Saucer. Satsuma-type decor 45.00

Demitasse Set. Bamboo pattern. Green and gold on white. 15 pieces 200.00

Figurines

11" high. Standing man holding scroll and peach 175.00

12" high. Seated man with scroll. 175.00

Incense Burner. 2 x 2½ x3". Diamond-shape. Foo Dog finial. 19th century 65.00

Plates

9½". Bird decor 75.00

12". Floral decor 125.00

Teapots

2¾" high. Classic design. 19th century 75.00

5½" high. Bulbous. Garden scene in panels 110.00

Urns, Covered. 3x3". Decorated with figures. Pair 200.00

Vases

5½". Purple lotus blossoms and green leaves on ochre ground speckled with black. Ko-Kutani .. 325.00

7¼". Birds and flowers in burnt orange, yellows, white and gold. No mark 125.00

8¼". Four rectangular panels with figures and flowers. No mark 125.00

11½". Covered. Garden scene. Foo Dog finial 300.00

12". Floral decor, butterflies. Gold trim 200.00

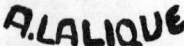

A.LALIQUE

LALIQUE

LALIQUE

Lalique is a quality glass designed in the manner of the Art Nouveau and Art Deco style. It is a combination of blown, molded or pressed and-or engraved glass.

Rene Lalique first produced this glass in France from the 1890's until his death in 1945. Pieces from this era are signed "R. Lalique." Items made after 1945 are marked "Lalique." Script and block letters were used alternately.

Forgeries of the signature on Lalique-type glass are not uncommon. In some instances the "R" has been added to "Lalique" to misrepresent the circa.

Atomizers

5" high. Six nudes in sculptured relief on frosted ground. Gold wash. Silver collar and top. R. Lalique ....$ 475.00

6" high. Cylindrical. Deep emerald green. All original. R. Lalique 275.00

Bookends. 5x7½". Cherubs. Molded in full relief. R. Lalique. Pair 650.00

Bottles, Perfume

3¾". Square. Flat shape. Knotted vine decor. Dome-type stopper .. 85.00

Vase. 10". Bulbous. "Inseparables." Opalescent with satin finish $2100.00

4". Monkey. Blue. R. Lalique 300.00

4". Tulip. Frosted and clear 85.00

4½". "Epines." Thorny branches stained brown. R. Lalique 250.00

5½". Square. Beveled. Woman's profile in center with leaves. Square stopper 125.00

Bowls

4½". Cherries. R. Lalique 65.00

9", 3½" deep. Swirling fish. R. Lalique 650.00

9½". Cherries in relief on underside. R. Lalique 395.00

9½", 3" deep. Opalescent. Starfish. R. Lalique 500.00

10". Flared petal form. Opalescent. R. Lalique 275.00

10". Inverted flowers with purple enamel centers on underside. R. Lalique 400.00

10". Sprays of berries on underside. R. Lalique 250.00

10½". Octagonal. Frosted 1½" border 185.00

Boxes

1¾x3¼x4¼". Blossoms and leaves on lid. Sides in vertical herringbone 125.00

4" diam. "D'Orsay". Brown stain. R. Lalique 175.00

5¼" long. Frosted cupids, flowers. R. Lalique 185.00

Car Mascots

Eagle. 4¼x5½" long. Clear and frosted 575.00

Eagle. 5¾". Clear. R. Lalique 750.00
Rooster. 8" high 350.00
Rooster. 8" high. R. Lalique 500.00
Clock. 4½" square. "Inseparables." Opalescent love birds. Blue stain. R. Lalique 500.00
Compote. 4" high. Cherub standard 165.00
Decanters
10½". Conical form. Geometric stopper. R. Lalique 195.00
14½". Molded nudes at corners. Full female figure stoppers. Pair .. 650.00
Figurines
Bird. 5" 75.00
Dragonfly. 8x8" 250.00
Female. Nude. 9" 250.00
Lion, Reclining. 4". Frosted and clear 175.00
Madonna. 9¾". Heliotrope. Frosted and clear 400.00
Nudes. Embracing. 10½". Frosted. R. Lalique 350.00
Owl. 3" 75.00
Squirrel. 4¾". Opalescent 225.00
Goblet. Clear bowl. Frosted molded stem 35.00
Inkwell. 2¼" high. Triangular-shape. Molded dragonflies. Petal finial 250.00
Knife Rests
Baby-head ends. Clear and frosted 40.00
Clover-leaf ends. Blue 50.00
Lamp Shades. See "Lamp Shades"
Medallions
Flowers head. 1¾" diam. R. Lalique 300.00
Nude. 1⅝" diam. Frosted. Gold fitting for chain. Small diamond at bottom. R. Lalique 450.00
Pin Tray. 2½x5¼". Plain frosted. R. Lalique 50.00
Pitcher. 10". Amber stained band of molded and cut berries, leaves. Applied handle. R. Lalique 275.00
Plates
6½". Leaping fish. Clear with blue stain. R. Lalique 75.00
6¾". Nude center. Garland of flowers. Amber stain. R. Lalique .. 175.00
8½". Grapes. Frosted. R. Lalique 85.00
10¾". Florals, urns, foliage. Frosted. R. Lalique 275.00
12". Fish spiraling. Opalescent. R. Lalique 300.00
15". Engraved with chrysanthemums. Clear 250.00
Tumbler. Frosted band at base 35.00
Vases
5½". "Honfleur." Cylindrical. Molded vine handles with blue stain. R. Lalique 375.00
6¼". Globular. "Lievres". Opalescent. Molded frieze of rabbits. R. Lalique 400.00
7½". Bulbous. Molded fern fronds. Clear. R. Lalique 450.00
7½". Open fan design. Frosted. R. Lalique 250.00
7½". Rose and thorn decor. Brown stain 275.00
8". Clear top. Opalescent cherries in bottom. R. Lalique 375.00
Wine. Figural stem. Molded in shape of rooster 50.00

LAMPS

All oil lamps evolved from the Stone Age lamps which were nothing more than small hollow-out stones in which animal fat was burned.
In 1784 Aime' Argand, a Swiss physicist, patented the first 'modern' oil lamp which bears his name. . .it featured a round, hollow burner with a tubular wick and glass chimney.
After oil was discovered in Titusville, Pa. in 1850, kerosene became the primary lamp fuel. Thomas A. Edison invented the electric light bulb in 1879 and his invention marked the beginning of the end of oil lamps; even though the full impact was not felt for another quarter century. Oil lamps are still used today. However; most lamps from the past are collected because of their artistic qualities and not their usefulness.

Aladdin Lamps
Alacite. Bulbous. Footed pedestal base. Acanthus leaf decor. 21" o.h. ....$ 85.00
Alacite. Electric. Rose decor. Signed. 26" o.h. 50.00
Beehives
Amber, Dark 100.00
Amber, Light 55.00
Clear 30.00
Bennington-type base. Removable font. 14" 65.00
Brass base. Milk glass shade. Electrified 125.00
Model B. "Drape" milk glass shade. Glass font and base. All original 150.00
Angle Lamps
Double. Copper. Embossed. Opalescent shades 450.00
Double. Nickelplated brass. Milk glass chimneys. Frosted glass shades 250.00
Single. Nickelplated brass. Milk glass chimney. Frosted glass shade 135.00
Argand Lamp. Double. Bronzed. Etched shades. Signed 325.00

Gone With The Wind Lamp. 31" high. Handpainted scenic decor. Artist signed. Fostoria burner. All original ..$650.00

Astral Lamp. 34" high. Brass base. Cut and etched shades with prisms. Electrified 850.00
Banner Lamp. 20". Clear glass paneled base. Drum font. #2 chimney 50.00
Banquet Lamps
24½" high. Brass corinthian base. Cranberry font. Cranberry hobnail shade 350.00
25" high. Marble base. Brass stem and font. Frosted geometric design shade with prisms. Electrified 375.00
29" high. Brass. Cherub standing with butterfly in hand. Frosted white shade. Ornate font. Burnished and electrified 350.00
30" high. Silvered base, stem, font. Original shade with berry decor 375.00

Pairpoint Lamp. 12" high. Blue ground with blossom decor base. Matching shade. Signed $750.00

32" high. Wrought iron base. Handpainted ball shade 200.00
37" high. Ornate brass base. Opaque white overlay stem. Brass font with double wick burner. Frosted wheel-cut engraved shade 500.00
Betty Lamps
Iron 125.00
Redware. Sponged 135.00
Tin 85.00
Bicycle Oil Lamp 40.00
Bracket Lamps
Brass. Blown chimney 100.00
Iron. Lacy frame. 9" mercury glass reflector 75.00
*Iron. Frame only 35.00
Lamp only. "Prism" 30.00
Bradley and Hubbard Lamps
Banquet. 20". Brass relief base and font. Missing fringed shade .. 300.00
Banquet. 31½". Onyx and gilted metal base and stem. Complete with shade 650.00
Bracket, Gas. 4" projection. Scrolled brass 100.00
Chandelier. 19x34". Brass. Three gas lights 500.00
Hall. Brass. 7x7". Brass and beveled glass light 200.00

Library. (Center-hanging) 34" long. Embossed brass. 14" dome shade with prisms 750.00
Pendant. 20" closed, 80" extended. Brass. Embosses font. 14" white dome shade 400.00
Piano. Extension-type. 54" to burner. Cast metal. No shade 500.00
Table. 12" to burner. Ornate cast metal. Brass finish. Detachable font 250.00

Carriage Lamp. 20". Painted black metal. Four beveled glass panes. Brass trim 250.00

Chandeliers
Brass. 31" spread, 42" drop. Four glass fonts. Electrified 1500.00
Glass
15" drop. Waterfall-type. All prisms 500.00
36" spread. Frosted and molded panels on gilted metal supports. Molded leaves. Signed Sabino .. 1500.00
36" spread. Glass arms with five lights. Prisms and chains 1000.00

Cruise Lamps
Iron, Wrought. 8½". Double 85.00
Tin, Lapped. 8". Double 175.00

Gone With the Wind Lamps
20½" high. Green ground. Pink and red roses on font and shade. Electrified 350.00
22" high. Puffed with grape decor 450.00
23" high. Lion's head on base and shade. All original 750.00
24" high. Handpainted blossoms. Satin finish 500.00
26" high. Red satin glass. Matching ball shade. Electrified 500.00
28½ high. Red satin glass. Puffed fruits 650.00

Grease Lamps
Iron 100.00
Tin. Handled. Square base tray .. 225.00

Hand Lamps
Glass
Aqua. 3". Free blown. Circular foot. Applied handle. Attributed to South Jersey 350.00
Blue Bristol. Enameled decor. Applied handle. All original .. 100.00
Clambroth. 5". "Waisted Loop." Double burners 295.00
Clear. 4". Blown and cut. Applied handle. Double burner .. 185.00
Cobalt. 3¼". 'Three Printie". Pewter collar. Single drop burner 450.00
Pewter. 3x6". Single brass tube. Early 175.00
Tin. 2x2½". Drum-shaped. Strap handle 65.00

Handel Lamps
7". Boudoir. Scenic shade 650.00
7½". Hanging lantern. Tan slag panels in reticulated metal frame 750.00
8". Tree trunk base. Leaded shade 500.00
15". Domed base. 10" diam. "Chipped Ice" shade with birds .. 1000.00
18". Oriental-style base. Persian border shade.................. 2000.00
18". Tripod base. Art Deco-type shade 1750.00
22". Patina finished base. Leaded floral shade 2000.00
24". Bronze base. Leaded floral shade 2500.00
57". Floor. Patina finished base. "Chipped Ice" shade 2000.00
61". Floor. Double standard base. 20" diam. Leaded shade 3500.00

Hanging Lamps
Central. Brass frame. Cranberry opalescent font and shade 250.00
Central. Brass frame and font. 14" handpainted shade. Prisms. All original 375.00
Country Store. Embossed brass font. 14" diam. tin shade. Complete 250.00
Hall. Brass frame and chains. Cranberry cylindrical shade 175.00
Kitchen. Brass frame. Decorated milk glass shade 275.00
Kitchen. Iron frame. Milk glass shade. Complete. Electrified 175.00
Miniature. 17". Jeweled brass .. 200.00

Jefferson Lamp. Bronzed base. 16" diam. Domed shade with scenic decor. Signed base and shade .. 1000.00

Lacemaker's Lamps
9¾". Clear blown glass. Peg-like font. Hollow stem. Circular foot .. 300.00
16". Cranberry overshot. Brass base 395.00

Pairpoint Lamps
8" high. Apricot floral shade 895.00
8" high. Silvered base. Puffed rose shade 750.00
14½" diam. shade. Silvered base. Reverse painted shade 750.00

Peg Lamps
4" high. Tin asphaltum. Petticoat-type with handle 85.00
5" high. Blown molded globular ribbed panels. Brass fittings 175.00
6½". Clear. "Thumbprint". Brass fittings 75.00
19½" o.h. Shaded pink satin glass. "Beaded Drape." Brass candlestick holder 350.00

Rushlight Holder. 10¼" high. Wrought iron with scrolled balance. Turned wooded base 175.00

Sparking Lamps
Black Amethyst. 4½". Tin burner. Unique 1500.00

Whale Oil Lamp. 8½" high. "Loop." Peacock blue. Square base. Boston & Sandwich $950.00

Blue, Light. Wine glass form. Knob stem. McKearin 189-3 .... 150.00
Clear
2⅛". Free blown. Applied handle. Single drop. Tin burner. McKearin 189-10. .... 100.00
2⅜". BTM. Single drop tin burner. McKearin 110-4 .... 100.00
3⅜". Free blown font. Trefoil scalloped pressed base. Single drop burner. McKearin 189-19 150.00
4½". Free blown globular font. Knob stem. Waffle cup plate base. Single drop burner 325.00
Student Lamps
24" high. Double. Brass. Green cased shades 750.00
24" high. Single. Brass. 7" milk glass shade 425.00
40" long. Hanging-type. Double. 10" diam. cased green shades. Burnished. Electrified 1200.00
Tiffany Lamps See "Tiffany Glass"
Whale Oil Lamps. Also see "Sandwich Glass"
Brass. 7". Single burner 125.00

Dolphins
Petticoat (McKee)
Canary. 6½''. Fiery opalescent sockets 450.00
Electric Blue. 6½" 425.00
Electric Blue. 6½''. Opalescent sockets 475.00
Scalloped (Mid-West)
Canary
6½". Slim 500.00
8½" 400.00
Clambroth
6½" 450.00
8½" 375.00
Clear. 8½" 125.00
Jade Green. (one color) 6½" 850.00
Translucent Blue. 6½". Slim 450.00
Steps (Boston and Sandwich)
Canary. 10⅛". Single 425.00
Clambroth. 10⅛". Single 400.00
Clear. 10⅛"
Double 125.00
Single 125.00
Overlay Glass
Amethyst. 11"high. Marble base 750.00
Cranberry. 11½" high. White base 275.00
Patterned Glass
Acanthus Leaf. 9". Brilliant blue font. Brass stem. Marble base .. 300.00
Bigler. 10¼''. Cobalt blue. Square base. McKearin 198-14 750.00
Bull's Eye and Fleur de lis. 9". Clear. Pewter collar. Hexagonal baluster stem and base 125.00
Harp. 10½". Clear. Hexagonal stem and base 100.00
Loop. 9½". Cobalt blue. Pewter collar. Hexagonal base. Double drop burners 350.00
Sandwich Star. 10½". Clear. Brass collar. Hexagonal baluster stem and base 150.00
Waffle and Thumbprint. 4½". Fingertype. Clear. Mold blown. Pewter collar 95.00
Pewter. 7½". Double burner. "Smith and Co." 125.00
Tole
6½". diam. base, 7½" high. Handled 175.00
11" high. Six 3½" wick tubes. Bail handle. Workshop-type 225.00
*Reproduced Item

LAMPS, MINIATURE

Miniature oil and kerosene lamps, often called "night lamps," are diminutive replicas of larger lamps. . .they may measure as high as 12 inches or as small as 2½-inches.
The first glass miniatures were manufactured at Sandwich, Mass. in 1825. By 1850, glass chimneys were added to small kerosene lamps.

During the Victorian period, beautiful fine art glass shades were introduced in miniatures.

Simple and utilitarian in design, these lamps were used primarily as "night lamps" and also in the parlor as "courting lamps" and in sickrooms.

Though elaborate in decor, small glass lamps were simply constructed of several separate parts. . .base, collar, burner, chimney and shade. A careful study of these individual parts can help determine the age of the lamp, country of origin and also if the miniature is all original or had certain parts replaced.

NOTE: Figure numbers refer to illustration figure number in the book, "Miniature Lamps" by Frank R. and Ruth E. Smith.

CAUTION: More and more reproductions of miniature lamps are appearing on the market. These "new" lamps are similar to the originals in shape, design and color. The only real difference seems to be height. To date, Smith figure numbers 85, 149, 150, 203, 228, 336, 400, 403, 419, 434 and 482 have been reproduced.

Figures:

4—"The London Lamp." Pale green glass. Tin burner and reflector . . $ 85.00
5—"Handy." Clear glass. Acorn burner 60.00
12—"Evening Star." Handleless . . 100.00
15—"Little Harry's Night Lamp." Clear glass base. Milk glass chimney. Olmsted burner 95.00
20—"Improved Banner." Milk glass 95.00
24—Milk Glass. Shell decor. String-type burner 75.00
29—"Nutmeg." Cobalt blue 75.00
31—Brass saucer. Nutmeg burner 70.00
33—Santa Claus. Brush painted . . 1500.00
36—"Little Buttercup." Cobalt blue. Applied handle 95.00
59—Hanging-type. Brass with reflector. Hornet burner 65.00
83—Student, Single. Brass with Bristol shade. Olmsted burner 950.00
84—Student, Single. Brass with milk glass shade. Nutmeg burner 250.00
94—Tin. Painted. Acorn burner 17.50
105—Stem. Clear. Nutmeg burner 60.00
106—Stem. Embossed Block. Clear 100.00
112—"Daisy and Bull's Eye." Amber 110.00
128—Milk glass. Pewter base. Acorn burner 195.00
175—Clear. Acorn burner 90.00
193—"Apple Blossom." Milk glass. Acorn burner 235.00
195—"Apple Blossom." Milk glass. Embossed. Nutmeg burner. Northwood 295.00
208—Milk glass. Embossed flowers, painted. Nutmeg burner 225.00
219—"Nellie Bly." Milk glass. Hornet burner 250.00
257—Custard. Gold gilt. Hornet burner 300.00
284—Satin. Red. Embossed petal-type shade. Nutmeg burner . . 300.00
286—"Cosmos." Milk glass. Embossed, fired on paint. Nutmeg burner 265.00
302—Satin. Red. Brass base. Nutmeg burner. 375.00
326—Peg. Milk glass. Decorated shade 375.00
367—End-of-Day. Hornet burner . . 300.00
396—Satin. Blue. Embossed flowers and scrolls. Nutmeg burner . . 500.00
431—"Ivy." Cranberry and crystal. Nutmeg burner 500.00
440—Amberina. Nutmeg burner . . 325.00
477—"Hobnail." Blue. Nutmeg burner 275.00
497—Owl. Milk glass. Embossed,

Swan. #499. White milk glass. Missing shade $250.00

fired on paint. Nutmeg burner 650.00
534—Cut Velvet. Blue. Nutmeg burner 750.00
536—Cranberry. Applied glass feet. Nutmeg burner 750.00
580—Verre Moire. White. Foreign burner 1500.00
626—"Glow Night." Clear 75.00
630—"Vapo-Cresolene." 50.00

LAMP SHADES

Art Nouveau art glass shades created by Durand, Quezal, Steuben and other glass makers of the early 20th century have become recognized. These glass shades will probably never be used as they were originally intended since most collectors consider them shelf or cabinet pieces. Numbers refer to Roberts' "Art Nouveau Shades."

Quezel. Similar to Roberts' #10. $175.00

Burmese. 2" collar. Scalloped edge. Acid finish. Mt. Washington $ 250.00
Duncan and Miller. 2¼" collar, 4½" long. "Mardi Gras." Crystal and satin finish 22.50

Durand
- #283. "King Tut." Orange iridescent. Opal lined 300.00
- #284. 8" high. Lily-shaped. Threads over opal 250.00
- #286. 3½". Candle shade 100.00

Fostoria
- #289. "Zipper." Green pulled decor on opal. Gold lined 175.00
- #290. Green and gold leaves, vines on opal. Gold lined 110.00
- #334. Gold and green leaves, vertical vines on opal glass. Gold lined. Pair 200.00

Lalique, Hanging-types
- 12". Amber. Shallow. Molded shells. R. Lalique 500.00
- 13". Crystal. Molded ivy. Green stain. R. Lalique 750.00
- 14". Crystal. Frosted. Block panels. Molded leaves. R. Lalique 650.00

Leaded, Hanging Dome-types
- 20". Eight slag panels. Original crown 650.00
- 20". Red and pink flowers with green, brown and amber background 1000.00
- 21". Lily pad in floral pattern. Shades of blue, pink and white 1000.00
- 22". Two color panel. Geometric 550.00
- 25". Purple and red grapes. Flowers on brown and green ground 1750.00

Lustre Art
- #136. Set of 5 650.00
- #276. Yellow band on white 100.00
- #278. Gold iridescent. Ribbed 125.00
- #281. Blue hooked feather on opal. Gold lined 225.00

Imperial-Nuart
- Cameo Satin. Floral border 30.00
- Crystal. Engraved. Electric 15.00
- Crystal. 4" collar. Gas 25.00
- Stalacite. Electric 30.00
- Venetian Satin. Bell-shaped. Paneled 25.00
- White Carnival. #78-shape. Pair 75.00

Northwood. 4½x5" square. Peach opal 85.00

Quezel
- #234-shape. 2¼" collar, 4¾x7" high. "Optic Rib" 250.00
- #253. 4½" high. Lily-shaped. Iridescent gold 185.00
- #255. Gold hooked feather on opal. Gold lined 175.00
- #259. 3¼ high. "Zipper." Gold on opal 150.00
- #261. Blue pulled feather on opal. Gold lined 150.00
- #263. 3½x5¼". Green pulled feather outlined in gold on opal ground. Ribbed. Gold lined 165.00

Steuben
- #94-shape. 5¼". Blue aurene on calcite. Pair 125.00
- #221. "Drag Loop." Brown aurene on calcite. Gold lined 150.00
- #223. Green pulled feather on gold aurene 185.00
- #240-shape. 5" high. Dark green pulled feather outlined with gold on reactive clear to white. Ribbed 125.00

Student. 3" collar. (for miniature lamp) Green 25.00

Tiffany
- #127. "Diamond Optic." Silver pulled decor on green iridescent. Signed and no'd 350.00
- #131. Candle lamp shade. Signed and no'd. 350.00

#270. Gold hooked feathers on green iridescent. Opal lined. Signed and no'd. 250.00
#273. Green feather on reactive glass. Signed L.C.T. 450.00
Waterford. 4x6½". Crystal 75.00

LANTERNS

A lantern is an enclosed, portable candleholder, attached to a bracket or pole to illuminate an area. It allegedly derived its name from early times when candles were placed in thin animal horns and were called "Lantern Horns." They were developed into portable lighting devices with glass sides or chimneys as we know them today.

Candle. 12½" high. Glass panes. Painted black tole. New York State. Mid 19th century $100.00

Auto Lanterns. See "Auto Items"
Bicycle. 6". Early ....$ 60.00
Buggy. Kerosene-type. Dietz 50.00
Carriage
- 15" long. Beveled glass panes. Brass trim 200.00
- 34½" long. Painted metal. Ornate brass trim. Eagle finial. Six beveled glass panes............ 350.00

Candle
- 13½". Paul Revere-type. Pierced tin. Cone-shaped top 100.00
- 15". Pierced tin. Square-shape with glass door. Pa. 19th century 350.00
- 17½". Pierced copper 175.00

Hearse. 31". Silverplated 300.00
Magic Lanterns. See "Magic Lanterns"
Miners'
- American. Brass. Carbide-type .. 15.00
- English 75.00

Policeman's. 3x7". Tin 40.00
Railroad Lanterns. See "Railroad Items"
Ship Lanterns
- 12". Brass. Tin reflectors. Port and Starboard. Pair 300.00
- 12". Galvanized tin with old red paint. Clear beveled cylindrical lense. Kerosene burner 100.00
- 22½". Brass and steel. Early 19th century 185.00

Skater Lanterns
- Brass. All original 65.00
- Brass and Tin. 7x8". Mold blown globe 100.00
- Tole. Square. Glass panels 85.00

Street Post. 22" high. 13" canopy. Opalescent globe. 11" high, 8" wide. Gas burner 175.00
Wagon. Tin. Square red lense. Original oil burner 30.00
Whale Oil. Pierced tin with glass panel. All original 125.00

LEEDS

The original Leeds factory in Yorkshire, England opened in 1760 and closed in 1820, although operation continued under various owners until about 1880. Noted for its cream-colored wares; either plain, salt glazed or painted with various colored enamels, Leeds also produced black earthenwares and glazed and unglazed redwares.

Much admired by other potteries, Leeds' creamware was made by other makers, including Wedgwood, and many are sold today as Leeds or Leeds-type.

Early examples are unmarked, but later pieces may bear the LEEDS POTTERY mark sometimes followed by Hartley-Green & Co., or the letters LP. Any or all of these marks may be found on reproductions.

Found in many forms, Leeds' tea wares are among the most popular. Well glazed and artistically decorated, all Leeds pottery remains one of the most beautiful of its era . . .the 18th century ware most eagerly sought by collectors.

Bowls
- 6½". Blue decoration ....$ 165.00
- 7¼". Polychrome decoration 185.00

Nut Dish. 4¾" long. Leaf-shaped. Blue oriental decor on white ground $125.00

7½". Blue decoration 210.00
Cups and Saucers, Handleless
Polychrome. Blue, orange 165.00
Polychrome. Brown, green, yellow 110.00
Jugs, Polychrome
4½" 135.00
7¾" 285.00
Mugs, Polychrome
4¾" 365.00
5" 200.00
5½" 165.00
Plates
7½". Peafowl. Blue edge........ 325.00
8¼". Peafowl. Green edge 550.00
9". Floral center. Green edge 265.00
Shaker. 4". Green decoration 110.00
Soup Plates
9¾". Blue edge. Leeds-type 48.00
10". Blue edge. Leeds-type 55.00
Soup Tureen. With ladle and tray.
Decorated. Blue edge 575.00
Sugars, Covered
Blue. Lion's head handles 135.00
Polychrome. Small. Creamware .. 110.00
Tea Pots, Polychrome
Large. Blue, green, ochre, Pearlware 245.00
Medium. Blue, orange. Pearlware 185.00
Small. Green, pink. Creamware. C. 1765 .... 550.00

LENOX

Jonathan Cox and Walter Scott Lenox established The Ceramic Art Company, Trenton, New Jersey in 1889. The factory was best known for its American Belleek. In 1906, the factory became the Lenox Company and Walter Scott Lenox fulfilled his dream to produce quality American made porcelain.

Initially only decorative pieces were produced. Tablewares were introduced later and in 1918 the first American made china ever to grace the dining tables at the White House bore the Lenox mark.

Two early marks are the 'palette' or a 'green wreath.' The company is still in existence today and the current mark is stamped in gold.

Basket. 5½ x 7". Ivory. Gold handle.
Green wreath ....$ 75.00
Bowls
6". "Ming".................. 10.00
6" long, 4" wide. Nautilus-shape. Fluting and beading. Drip edge of gold. Green mark 35.00
9". Ivory with silver overlay. Green wreath 75.00
10" long, 3¾" deep. Handled. Ivory with turquoise enameled peacocks. Signed Hicks. Palette mark 195.00
Boxes
4x5". Handpainted floral decor .. 35.00
4x5". Pate-sur-Pate-type birds on cover. Green wreath 60.00
Candlesticks. 6". Ivory with silver overlay. Green wreath. Pair 125.00
Compotes
2¾x9" diam. "Mystic." 42.50
4½x7" diam. Oval-shaped. Ivory with silver overlay. Green wreath 40.00

Cream and Sugar. 3½" high. Oval-shaped. Brown with silver overlay. Set $100.00

Cream and Sugar. 3½" high. Oval-shape. Brown with silver overlay.
Set 100.00
Cups and Saucers.
Bouillon. Garlands. Gold trim. Green wreath 20.00
Chocolate. Footed. Ivory with gold trim 25.00

Demitasse. Ivory inserts. Sterling holders and saucers. Set of 4 .... 125.00

Figurines

4". Bust of girl. Art Deco style. White. Green wreath 60.00

14". Girl dancing. Art Deco style. White. C. 1937 .... 300.00

Honey Pot. Beehive-shape. Ivory. Gold bee. Green wreath 50.00

Pen Holder. 4" wide. 2" high. Pink, white ruffled top. Gold trimmed. Sheaffer fountain pen 50.00

Pitchers

8½". Handpainted. Apples and foliage. Palette mark 125.00

14½". Tankard-shape. Berry decor on pastel ground. Gold base and handle. Palette mark 275.00

Plates

5¾". Handpainted floral decor .. 12.00

8¼". "Washington-Wakefield." .. 20.00

9". "Ming" 25.00

Salt Dips

Handpainted roses. Palette mark. Set of 4 .... 25.00

Scalloped shell and coral design. Green wreath 10.00

Swans

3" long. Coral. Green wreath 25.00

5" long. Ivory. Green wreath 30.00

9" long. Ivory. Green wreath 65.00

15" long. Ivory. Green wreath .. 100.00

Teapot. Brown. Sterling overlay 85.00

Tea Set. Sterling overlay in design of flying geese. Sunset background. Palette mark. 3 pieces 300.00

Tea Set. Silver overlay in floral design on ivory. Green mark. 3 pieces 250.00

Tobacco Humidor. 5½" high. Shades of tan coloring. Decor of hanging corn leaves. Palette mark 150.00

Toby Jug. 6". high. William Penn. Indian handle. Green mark 175.00

Urn. 11" high. Square pedestal base. Rose decor. Swan handles. Green wreath 125.00

Vases

4". Cobalt with silver overlay 55.00

6". Handpainted golden grapes. Art Nouveau trim. Palette mark .. 75.00

8". Bulbous. Ivory with sheafs of wheat in gold on front. Green wreath 45.00

8½". Trumpet-shape. Four handpainted ovals of pink roses on white. Silver overlay 175.00

11¼". Handpainted. Green and yellow daffodils. Palette mark .. 100.00

11¼". Handpainted. Five peacocks on limb. Black on ivory. Palette mark 150.00

15½". Handpainted roses on soft green ground. Palette mark 225.00

LIBBEY GLASS

In 1888, the New England Glass Works, W. L. Libbey and Son, Proprietors, Cambridge, Ohio closed and Edward Libbey established the Libbey Glass Company in Toledo, Ohio. The firm produced quality cut and intaglio cut glass for the "Brilliant Period." In 1930, Libbey's interest in art glass production was renewed. A. Douglas Nash was employed as a designer. Perhaps his "Animal Fair" stemware is best known. The factory continues production today as Libbey Glassware,adivisionofOwens-Illinois,Inc.

Fruit Bowl. 4½" high x 14" diam. Sterling silver rim. Signed $350.00

Candlesticks

5¼". Camel stem ....$ 150.00

10". Copperwheel cut florals on foot and stem. Signed 115.00

Shakers, Salt and Pepper. Egg-shaped. Blue and white. "Columbian Expo, 1893." Signed. Pair .. 225.00

Slipper. Frosted. "Columbian World's Exposition, 1893." 50.00

Stemware. "Animal Fair" C. 1933.

Champagne. Bear stem 100.00

Claret. Bear stem. Signed 150.00

Cocktail. Kangaroo stem 95.00

Cordial. Greyhound stem. Signed 125.00

Goblet. Cat stem 95.00

LIMOGES

Limoges porcelain has been produced in Limoges, France for over a century by numerous factories other than the famed Haviland. One of the most frequently encountered marks is "T. & V. Limoges" which is the ware made by Tressman and Vought. Other identifiable Limoges marks are "A. L. (A. Lanternier), J.P.L. (J. Pouyat, Limoges), M.R. (M. Reddon), Elite and Coronet.

For additional information see "Haviland China."

Cake Set. 12¼" plate, four 8½" plates. White ground with floral rims. Signed J.P.L. Set $85.00

Cake Stand. 4 x 9½" diam. Handpainted portrait center .... $ 65.00
Candlesticks. 9". Handpainted berries, flowers, foliage. Gold trim. Artist signed. Pair 50.00
Chocolate Pot. 8½" high. Embossed gold on ivory 75.00
Chocolate Set. Covered pot, sugar, creamer, 6 cups and saucers. Gold leaves on ivory. Heavy gold trim. Set 350.00
Cream and Sugar, Covered. Handpainted violets. Gold handles. Set 45.00
Cups and Saucers
  Coffee. 8 oz. Handpainted flowers, leaves. Gold trim. Signed A. Taylor 65.00
  Demitasse. Handpainted roses. Gold trim 20.00
Dinner Set. Floral decor. A. L. 80 pieces 1500.00
Diptych. 12¼ x 19". Depicts bishops within architectural setting. 19th century 1250.00
Dresser Sets
  3 pieces. Handpainted violets. Gold trim 100.00
  6 pieces. Apple blossom decor. J.P.L 175.00

Hair Receiver. Handpainted roses on blue ground. Artist signed 25.00
Pitchers
  7¾". Bulbous. Handpainted berry decor. Gold trim 125.00
  12". Tankard. Handpainted currants. Gold trim. J.P.L 150.00
  13½". Tankard. Monk pouring wine. Artist signed 275.00
Plaques. 9½ x 13". Large pink, red and yellow roses. Pair 300.00
Plates
  9". Oyster. Gold trim on white .. 25.00
  10". Asparagus. Molded asparagus separate well. Irregular gold rims. D & C. Set of 6. 225.00
  10". Handpainted portrait. Signed Dubois 135.00
  11". Service. 22K gold medallion borders on white. Set of 12 .... 750.00
Punch Bowl. 14", 9" high. Grape decor interior. Portrait medallions on exterior. Heavy rococo gold trim. T. V. 2 pieces 500.00
Punch Cup. Handpainted grape motif. Set of 6 .... 180.00
Ramekin. Handpainted red roses .. 25.00
Tea Set. Handpainted pink roses. Gold trim. T & V. 3 pieces........ 125.00
Tile. 6½" square. Pink and green florals 25.00
Tray. 13x 16". Scalloped rim. Handpainted pastel flowers on white. Gold trim 85.00
Tureen, Covered. 8x 16" oval. Rose decor. Gold and green bands 175.00
Vases
  3½". Handpainted roses 30.00
  10". Handpainted cherries. Signed Burghoff. C. 1895 .... 150.00
  12½". Handpainted red roses. Gold ball feet, handles and scrolled top. Artist signed 225.00

LITHOPHANES

Lithophanes are highly transulent porcelain panels with impressed designs. The design is formed by the difference in thickness of the plaque. Thin parts transmit an abundance of light while thicker parts represent shadows. They were first made by the Royal Berlin Porcelain Works in 1828. Other factories in Germany, France and England later produced the items. The majority on the market today were probably made between 1850 and 1900.
Be careful of reproductions!

Candle Shields
  5¾". "Pandora's Box." In candle stand .... $ 300.00
  19½" high. "Petraca." KPM 375.00

Lamp. 19" high. 6-panels, 5¼". Black metal frame. Urn-shaped base on square plinth. Plaques marked KPM $2000.00

Lamps
- 4 panels. 4 x 6". Brass frame. Hanging-type 1000.00
- 5 panels. Colored. Iron frame 2500.00
- 5 panels. Iron frame. Signed. KPM 1750.00

Lamp Shade. 3½" Egg-shape. 3 panels. Children's scene. P.R. Sickle 250.00

Plaques. Marked "KPM"
- #110-ST. Mosque type building. Man kneeling. 4¾ x 6½" 200.00
- #172-G. Dog flushing bird. Trees in background. 3¼ x 4¼" 250.00
- #173. Couple in woodland setting, with dog 200.00
- #308-G. Girl with rose. 6x 7½" .. 250.00
- #761. Semi-nude in front of fireplace. 5½ x 6¼" 275.00
- #1335. "View from West Point." 2½ x 3¼" 150.00
- #1473. "Rheinstein." Colored. 4⅝ x 6¼" 300.00

Plaques. Marked "P.R. Sickle"
4 1/8x5 1/10"
- #894. Woman gazing at ocean .. 150.00
- #1422. Woman in flowing robe .. 150.00
- #1788. Monk and girl 150.00
- #1803. Nymph and flowers 150.00
- #1849. Cupid and girl fishing .. 150.00

Plaques. Unmarked
- Children at play. Leaded frame. 6x 7" 150.00
- Girl with cat. 7¼ x 9" 175.00
- Horses, riders at sunset. 6½ x 8½" 175.00
- Madonna and Child. 6x 7½" 175.00
- People in forest. 4 x 4½" 100.00

Women. "The Tempest." 4½ x 6" .. 125.00
- Young maiden picking fruit in orchard. 4½ x 5¼" 125.00

Tea Warmers
- 4x5". Nickleplated holder. 4 panels 350.00
- 4½x5". 4 panels in nickleplated holder 350.00
- 5" square. Brass holder. 4 panels 400.00
- 7" square top. 4 panels. Original burner 500.00

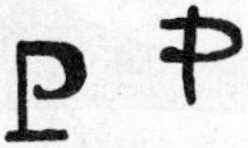

LIVERPOOL

Liverpool is the name given to products made at several potteries in Liverpool, England from 1750 to 1840. Among the early producers were Seth and James Pennington and Richard Chaffers who made tin-enameled earthenwares. By the 1780's, the tin glazed earthenwares gave way to cream colored wares decorated with cobalt, enamel colors, or blue or black transfers. These are the Liverpool pieces one is most likely to encounter on the market today.

The Liverpool glaze is characterized by bubbles and most often there is clouding under the foot rims. Early examples tend to be grayish with a milky blue glaze; while later pieces have a greenish blue glaze.

Although the late 18th century black transfer bowls and pitchers (many of historic interest) are eagerly collected; they are only a small part of the total Liverpool production. By the turn of the century, about 80 potteries were working in the town producing not only cream ware; but soft paste, soapstone and bone porcelain.

Bowls
- 4½". Black transfer ....$ 110.00
- 9". Polychrome 450.00

Charger. 15". Blue. Handpainted .. 265.00
Coffee Pot. Polychrome 365.00
Cream Jug. Polychrome 75.00
Sugar, Covered. Polychrome 275.00

Mug. 4½" high. "Mariner's." . . $375.00

Tea Services
11 pieces. Black transfer. Hand-painted moldings 575.00
15 pieces. Black transfer with silver lustre 450.00

LOCKS
(See "Padlocks")

LOETZ GLASS

Loetz is a type of iridescent art glass made in Austria by J. Loetz Witwe in the late 1890's. Loetz was a contemporary of L.C. Tiffany and worked in the Tiffany factory before establishing his own operation. Therefore, much of the wares are similar in appearance to Tiffany's. Some pieces are signed "Loetz", "Loetz, Austria", or "Austria."

Biscuit Jar. Bulbous melon-shaped. Iridescent tree bark. Metal lid and bail handle. Unsigned ....$ 195.00

Bowls
3", 8½" diam. Rose iridescent. Crimped turned in top. Applied threading. Signed 375.00
3½", 5½" diam. Cranberry crackle finish. Ormolu base. Signed 275.00
3½", 10" diam. Iridescent amber. 3-footed bronze base with 3 spiraled ring handles. Unsigned. 275.00
3⅝", 5⅝" diam. Covered. Lemon yellow ground, flowers and leaves in deep blue. Blue finial on cover. Acid cut. Signed Loetz, Austria .. 395.00
4", 7" diam. Amber iridescent. Five pinched sides. Signed 375.00

Vase. 11¾". Teardrop base with slender neck. Iridescent green. Signed. $650.00

Inkwells
3¼" high. Iridescent amber with Art Deco type design. Sterling hinged lid. Signed 350.00
5½" wide. Iridescent purple. Applied threads. Bronze cap. Unsigned 250.00

Paperweight. 2½ x 3¼" diam. Blue aurene with lacy white feather. Signed 250.00

Pitcher. 6". Iridescent green. Vertical ribbed. Signed 250.00

Rose Bowls
4½" high. Blown out. Iridescent green. Applied red threading. Signed 300.00
5", 6" wide. Clear with amber iridescent splashings. Unsigned .. 100.00

Shaker, Salt. 3½". Blue iridescent. Sterling top. Signed 225.00

Vases
4¼". Bulbous. Iridescent blue. Pinched sides. Signed 300.00
4¾". "King Tut." Iridescent blue. Pinched bulbous body. Ruffled top. Unsigned 195.00

6". Five finger. Red interior. Iridescent blue. Mottled exterior. Signed 450.00

6". Flower arranger top. White iridescent with applied iridescent green swirl. Unsigned 250.00

6". Footed. Blue iridescent with sterling overlay in floral design. Unsigned 265.00

7". "Lava." Deep red iridescent. Signed 400.00

8½". Blue "Damascene" on red. Signed 650.00

9". Green iridescent tree bark. Bulbous base. Pinched sides. Signed 350.00

11". Amethyst iridescent. Silver overlay. Unsigned 350.00

11". Emerald iridescent. Scalloped rim. Signed 400.00

11½". Gourd-shaped. Iridescent green in "Diamond Quilt." Bronze collar and band of leaves and grapes. Signed 750.00

13". Iridescent green swirl design with bronze collar. Unsigned 350.00

LOTUS WARE

Lotus ware is a lightweight porcelain with a warm white hue and rich glossy glaze. It was made by the Knowles, Taylor & Knowles Pottery Co., East Liverpool, Ohio, between 1890 and 1900. It was named "Lotus Ware" by Mr. Knowles because it resembled the bloom of the lily. The first mark was "KTK". This was later changed to the above illustrated mark.

Tea Set. Pink blossoms in relief on white. Gold handles and rims. "KTK." Three pieces $500.00

Bonbon. 5 x 5½". Shell-shaped. All white. "KTK" ....$ 225.00

Bowls

4". Footed. Leaves and berries in high relief. Leaf ends form rim ... 350.00

4x5x6½". Gold florals. Ornate top. Open handles 225.00

5½ x 11" diam. Handpainted floral decor 400.00

7½". Boat-shaped. Pink and gold openwork. Pink cherry blossoms on front and back. "KTK" 475.00

Chocolate Pot. Handpainted sunflowers 395.00

Cup and Saucer, Bouillon. Blue floral decor 75.00

Pitchers

4½". All white. Molded leaf decor 125.00

5". Bulbous. Handpainted violets in panels. Gold fish net 300.00

Rose Bowls

4½ x 5". Handpainted floral decor. Enameled turquoise and gold jewels. Gold drape top. "KTK" 450.00

4½ x 5". Handpainted floral decor. Gold fishnet 400.00

Sugar. 4 x 6" wide at handles. "Feather." "KTK" 450.00

Teapot. All white. Embossed flowers. "KTK" 300.00

Tea Set. Blue handpainted flowers. Gold fishnet. Three pieces 650.00

Vases

4½". Bulbous. Handpainted florals. Turquoise handles. Gold beaded trim 425.00

7½". Pitcher-type Bulbous. Floral decor with gold. "KTK" 600.00

LOWESTOFT

This soft paste porcelain was made at Lowestoft, Suffolk, England from about 1757 to 1803. For many years Lowestoft was a misnomer used to describe Chinese Export porcelain and unfortunately it continues in many instances.
Much Lowestoft resembles Worcester porcelain and the Worcester mark (crescent) was actually copied by the factory. Some of the initials found on examples are: H,S,R,Z,W, and R.P. The earliest examples were decorated in underglaze blue with molded reliefs; later the blue was underglazed and the enamels overglazed. The paintings are often sketchy or crude . . .and many were in the Chinese 'style' as were most wares of the period.

Cup and Saucer, Blue underglaze $ 185.00

Sauce Boat. Molded relief. Blue underglaze 275.00

Sugar. Polychrome enamel 165.00

Sugar, Covered. Polychrome enamel. C. 1770-80 ....$165.00

LUTZ GLASS

Lutz glass is a type of art glass made in the Venetian manner employing rods known as Striped Glass.

In 1860, Nicholas Lutz was one of the many French glassworkers invited to America by Charles Dorflinger. Lutz is not only recognized for his striped or cane glass but also threaded glass. He was employed by Boston and Sandwich from 1870 until its closing in 1888, then Mt. Washington Glass Co. and still later Union Glass Works.

Lutz glass is difficult if not impossible to attribute to him positively as other glass makers in the fore mentioned factories also produced similar wares.

Basket. 5¼" long. Clear with pink, red and white threads ....$ 150.00
Bottle. 9" high. Gold iridescent. Swirled threaded design 400.00
Bowls
4", 3" deep. Amethyst to clear. White threads 100.00
6¼". Clear with red, white and green threads 175.00
Compote. 3x 6" diam. Flared and ruffled top. Latticinio-type colored ribbons on clear 65.00
Cruet. Emerald, teal, goldstone. Applied reeded handle............ 300.00

Bowl. 2 x 4¼" diam. Latticinio-type. Blue, clear and goldstone. Flared and ruffled top $95.00

Cup and Saucer. Clear. Applied handle. Filigree panels of white, blue with gold 125.00
Ewers
8½" high. Pink ribbon panels laced with goldstone and white filigree. Applied handle 325.00
12". Stoppered. Clear with goldstone and white threads 300.00
Finger Bowl with Underplate. Crimped rims. Pink threads on clear to opalescent................... 150.00
Pitcher, Water. Gold threading on clear. Applied rigaree trim 350.00
Plates
6½". Filigree canes in pink, blue, yellow, green on clear 125.00
7¼". Gold spiral threading on clear 125.00
Tumbler. 3¼" high. Footed. White, gold, blue threading on clear 85.00
Vases
3½". Clear with white diagonal threads 100.00
8½". Stick. Latticinio-type ribbons in blue on clear with goldstone. Applied rigaree 250.00
Whiskey. 2½" high. Latticinio-type in pink, white, goldstone........ 85.00

MAASTRICHT WARE

P. REGOUT
Aº 1836
MAASTRICHT

Maastricht ware was made in Holland from about 1835 to near the end of the 19th century. English workmen and methods were employed. The product found a ready market in the United States and sold in competition with the English ware of the period.

Plate. 9". "Hong." $30.00

Bowls	
7½" diam., 4¼" deep. "Slamat" ....$	35.00
8½" diam. "Indian Traffic." Blue transfer	35.00
8½" diam., 4" deep. "Hong." ..	40.00
Breakfast Set. Plate, cup, saucer. "Slamat."	25.00
Chocolate Pot. Transfer of children ..	50.00
Cup and Saucer. Red, blue, green decor on white ground	15.00
Plates	
7¾". Bird and floral center in blue. Gold trim on fluted edge ..	20.00
8¼". Butterflies and insects on border. Flower center	25.00
9". Blue and white transfer	30.00
9½". Game. Mallard Duck	35.00
Platter. 11½" long. Red, green, yellow flowers on white	40.00

MAGAZINES

(See "Catalogues and Magazines")

MAGIC LANTERNS

Magic Lanterns were the forerunners of the home movie projector. Glass slides were inserted between a light source and a lense to project the images on a wall or cloth. The earlier ones used kerosene lanterns which were housed inside the machine. The majority were manufactured in Germany between 1890-1910. Prices for Magic Lanterns vary depending on manufacturer, size and condition. Slides range in price from $2.00 to $5.00 depending on subject matter.

Tin. 13" o.h. Kerosene burner ..$100.00

2¼x 8". Tin and brass. Original box. Dated 1893. Germany ....$	150.00
3½ x 5 x 7". Tin. Original kerosene burner. Milk glass chimney	75.00
4½ x 9". Cylindrical. Tin	50.00
10½" o.h. "Triumph Lanterna Magician." Tin with brass. Mounted on wooden base	125.00

MAJOLICA

Majolica is the name given to tin-glazed earthenwares; first made in Spain in the 12th century and shortly thereafter, Italy. Subsequently, it was produced by many potteries in England and Europe; including Minton and Wedgwood. The first production in the United States is credited to E. & W. Bennett, Baltimore, Maryland in the 1850's. The best known American made ware was made by Griffen, Smith & Hill, Phoenixville, Pa. marked "Etruscan" or "G.S.H." In 1880, this type of Majolica was given as premiums by the Atlantic and Pacific Tea Co.

Basket. 8½ x 13". Reticulated. Green and turquoise oak leaves. $	65.00
Bowls	
8". Shell and Seaweed. Etruscan ..	85.00

Fish Platter. 11½ x 25" long. "Shell and Seaweed." Wedgwood $150.00

15". Lily and Fern. Hollcroft	150.00
Cake Stand. 5½ x 10" diam. Tree trunk standard. Leaf effect top. Etruscan	60.00
Compote. 5 x 8½" diam. Leaf decor. Etruscan	65.00
Cream and Sugar. Covered. Cauliflower. Etruscan. Set	125.00
Cups and Saucers	
Bamboo. Etruscan	75.00
Shell and Seaweed. Etruscan	65.00
Mug. Frog. C. 1880	85.00
Pitchers	
Basketweave. 6"	30.00
Corn. 4¼"	35.00
Corn. 6½"	50.00
Fish. 10". Calder Portugal. 1880's.	75.00
Grape Leaf. 7". Vine handle. Cobridge-Hampton	45.00
Hawthorne. 9". Etruscan	85.00
Owl. 10". C. 1880	100.00
Parrot. 9"	100.00
Shell and Seaweed. 6". Etruscan. .	100.00
Plates	
Cauliflower. 9". Etruscan	75.00
Oyster. 8". Minton	50.00
Shell and Seaweed. 8". Etruscan.	65.00
Water Lily. 9". Etruscan	50.00
Platters	
Basketweave. 9x 12". Wedgwood.	150.00
Leaf. 9x 12"	65.00
Shell and Seaweed. 9½ x 13". Etruscan	85.00
Shakers, Salt and Pepper. Cauliflower. Etruscan. Pair	85.00
Sugars	
Basketweave	85.00
Cauliflower. Etruscan	95.00
Pineapple	100.00
Syrups	
Bamboo. Etruscan	95.00
Basketweave. Wedgwood	135.00
Sunflower. Etruscan	125.00
Teapots	
Bamboo. Etruscan	150.00
Cauliflower. Etruscan	125.00
Owl. Tricorner	100.00
Vases	
6". Floral decor. Sanded-type	65.00
8". Handled. Vintage decor in relief	75.00
12". Figural. Nubian Boy	95.00

MANTEL LUSTRES

Mantel lustres are glass vases with attached hanging cut glass prisms. They were usually displayed on the mantel . . .thus, the name. Colored overlay glass is the most desirable, but lustres made of Bristol glass, enameled and-or gilded are collectible. Numerous mantel lustres were produced in Bohemia and England during the mid 19th century.

14" high. Handpainted floral decor on pale green ground. Gold trim. 14 cut prisms. Pair $350.00

Bristol	
10" high. Gray ground. White and orange floral decor. 5 cut glass prisms. Pair .... $	200.00
11" high. White. Enameled decor. Cut glass prisms. Pair	300.00
14½" high. Gray. Ten 9½" cut crystals on each. Pair	350.00
Cased	
11½" high. Pink. Two rows of cut glass prisms. Pair	500.00
15" high. Pink. Enameled decor. Two rows of cut glass prisms. Pair.	650.00
Cranberry	
10½" high. All over gold decor. Handpainted portrait of woman. Ten 8½" cut glass prisms. Pair ..	750.00

13½" high. Gold enameled decor. 9" cut glass prisms. Pair 450.00

Cut Overlay. 11" high. Cranberry cut to clear. 5" cut prisms. Pair .. 600.00

MARBLEHEAD POTTERY

This hand thrown pottery had its beginning in 1905 as a therapeutic program introduced by Dr. J. Hall for the patients confined to a sanitarium located in Marblehead, Massachusetts. In 1916, the operation was removed from the hospital to another site and the factory continued under the directorship of Arthur E. Baggs until its closing in 1936.

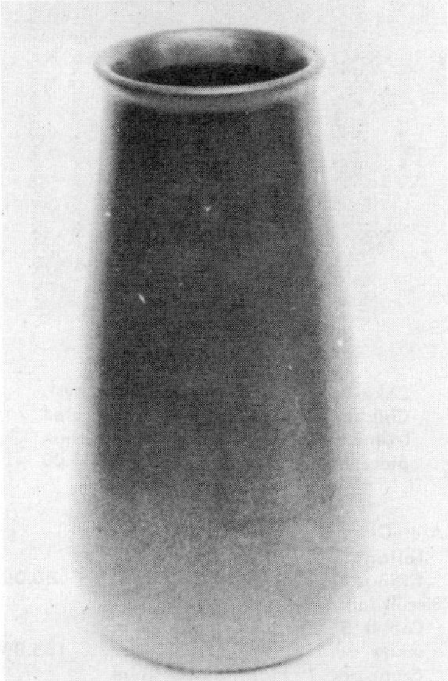

Vase. 8". Tapered, cylindrical-shape. Blue matte glaze. Signed $175.00

Bowl. 5" diam., 2" deep. Two color glaze. Leaf decor. Artist signed ...$ 300.00

Tile. 4¾" square. "Trademark" 250.00

Vases

- 3½ x 4¼" diam. Gray matte glaze. Handpainted grape decor in medallions. Artist signed 350.00
- 4". Bulbous. Green matte glaze .. 95.00
- 4 x 4½" diam. Gray matte glaze. Handpainted blue roses. Artist signed 300.00
- 8". Tapered cylindrical-shape. Blue matte glaze. Undecorated .. 175.00

MARBLES

Marbles were known to the Egyptians, the Romans and the American Indians. Early marbles were made from a variety of materials . . . unglazed clay, porcelain, semi-precious stones, etc., and varied in size from less than one halt inch to five inch carpet balls.

Most marbles were imported from Europe until the early 1900's when commercial manufacturing of "glassies" were produced by glass factories in Ohio and Pennsylvania. Today, millions of glass marbles are made in plants in Clarksburg and St. Mary, West Virginia.

Sulphide. Monkey $75.00

Akro Agate. Three sizes in bag. 96 count ....$ 100.00

Bennington 10.00

Bennington-type. ¾". Brown 2.00

Comic Strip-type 25.00

Spatterglass. 2" 75.00

Sulphides. Various animals. Approximately one to two inch diameters. Each ....55.00 to 75.00

Swirls

- Candle. 2⅞" 60.00
- Latticinio. 1⅞" 45.00
- Onionskin. 1¾" 45.00

MARINE ITEMS

This list is comprised of items used by seamen or removed from dismantled ships.
Also see "Bells" and "Lanterns."

Bells

- American. 10 x 13" high. Bronzed metal. 20th century ....$ 125.00

Compass. Alcohol. C. 1900 ..$300.00

English. 10 x 10" high. Brass. C. 1880's 300.00

Compasses

Alcohol. C. 1900 .... 300.00

Lifeboat-type. English. C. 1920's. 175.00

Half-Hulls

Motor Launch. New York. C. 1910. 50.00

Sloop. C. 1910 .... 60.00

Octant. With case. English. 18th century 500.00

Sextants

Box. Brass with leather case. English. C. 1920's 175.00

Nautical. Cherry case. American. C. 1856 .... 275.00

Reflecting. Brass. Complete. C. 1915 .... 200.00

Teaching-type. 20th century 75.00

Ship in Bottle. Sailing. Complete with 3-mast, rigging and flags. English. C. 1870 .... 300.00

Telescopes, Draw-type

Brass. 18 to 33". Complete 200.00

Leather covered. 5½ to 14". C. 1920 .... 75.00

Wheels

18½". Wooden. 19th century 125.00

24". Wooden with brass hub and caps 250.00

35". Wooden with brass hub and caps 500.00

MARY GREGORY GLASS

Mary Gregory (1856-1908) was employed by Boston and Sandwich Glass Company, Massachusetts as an artist. Her charming designs of frolicking children were delicately painted with white enamel on transparent clear and colored glass items. A positive identification of items personally decorated by her is controversial. In the late 1880's and early 1900's, other glass manufacturers employed this type of decoration in America, England and Europe and it would be more correct to refer to their wares as "Mary Gregory-type."
Current Reproductions are readily identified by seasoned collectors.

Cake Basket. 9¼ x 10¼". Amethyst. Children in white. Ornate silverplated frame and bail handle. Presentation piece. Middletown. C. 1889 ..$575.00

Ale. Olive green. 6" high. Girl, foliage in white. Silverplated fittings ....$ 60.00

Biscuit Jars

Cobalt. 5" high. Cherub, florals in white 165.00

Cranberry. 7" high. Crystal finial on self cover. Cherubs, florals in white 195.00

Bottles, Barber

Amethyst. Girl in white 195.00

Cobalt. Girl in white 175.00

Olive green. Girl in white, picking flowers. Rough pontil 150.00

Bottles, Perfume

Clear. Gold hinged top with chain and pull ring 125.00

Green, Light. Faceted stopper. Boy in white 150.00

Bowl. Azure blue. 10" diam., 4" deep. White decor 250.00

Boxes
- 2½ x 3½ x 4". Sapphire blue. Girl with kite in white. Brass fittings .. 195.00
- 4". Cobalt. Covered hinged lid. Girl and flower decor in white .. 175.00
- 5 x 5". Cranberry. Girl in white with musical instrument. Brass handles and feet 325.00

Cruet. Cranberry. 8". Girl in white. Clear stopper 195.00

Decanters
- Clear. 8¾" high. ITP. Girl in white. 175.00
- Electric blue. 10" high. Crystal stopper. Girl with tinted face 125.00
- Green, Light. 10". Girl and boy in white, dancing 165.00

Ewers. Emerald green. 10" high. Boy and girl in white. Matching pair 375.00

Goblets
- Cranberry. Boy with tinted face .. 40.00
- Sapphire. Girl in white 65.00

Lamps, Oil
- 11" high. Clear. Boy in white. Electrified 275.00
- 11¼" high. Cranberry. White enameled decor. Electrified 350.00
- 14½" high. Amethyst. Drummer boy in white. B & S 650.00

Liqueur Set. Clear. Decanter 10" high. Four glasses, 2½" high. Two with girl decor, two with boy. Tinted faces. Set 175.00

Mugs
- Cranberry and clear. Girl in white. Clear applied handle 75.00
- Honey amber. Boy in white 100.00

Pitchers
- 6¼". Green, Light. Clear handle. Boy in white 145.00
- 6¾". Cranberry. IVT. Clear applied handle. Girl in white 225.00
- 9". Clear. Bulbous. Crimped top. White decor. Blown glass 250.00
- 11". Green. Bulbous. Applied green handle. Collar base. Girl and foliage in white. Blown glass. 285.00
- 11½". Cranberry. Tankard-shape. Girl with tinted face. Gold trim .. 195.00
- 11½". Sapphire blue. Bulbous. Boy in white 295.00

Plaque. Cranberry. 10½". In brass hanger. Girl and scenery in white. 275.00

Rose Bowl. 3 x 3¼". Cranberry. Ribbed. Boy in white 195.00

Sugar Castor. Clear. Girl, butterfly in white 125.00

Syllabub. Amber. IVT. White figures. Complete with underplate, lid and ladle 500.00

Tea Warmer. 7½ x 10" high. Nickelplated with four clear panels. Boy and girl in white. Complete 295.00

Tray. Amber. 6½ x 9". Two girls in white 250.00

Tumble-Up. Emerald. 9¼" high. Girl in pink dress. White Lily of the Valley. Gold trim 175.00

Vases
- 4". Cranberry. Boy and girl in white 100.00
- 6". Amber. Boy and girl with tinted faces 65.00
- 6½". Cranberry. Stick-type. Girl holding leaf sprays in white 195.00
- 8¼". Amethyst. Girl in white. B & S 500.00
- 8¼". Cranberry. Boy in white .. 175.00
- 12". Cranberry. Tinted features .. 150.00
- 12". Emerald green. Boy and girl in white 275.00
- 12". Ice blue. Girl in white 250.00
- 14". Electric blue. Boy and girl in white, flying kite 265.00
- 15". Black amethyst. Girl in white in garden scene 295.00

Wine Glasses
- Clear. Child in white 40.00
- Cranberry. Child in white 50.00

MASONIC ITEMS

Masonic items are primarily the souvenir-type glass ware made to commemorate the Syria Temple AAONMS organization's important meetings or conventions. These collectibles date from the 1890 and early 1900 period.

Bottle, Figural. Camel. Cleveland, Ohio. 1931. Pottery ....$ 175.00

Chalices
- Pittsburgh, Pa. 1899 .... 65.00
- San Francisco. 1902 .... 60.00
- Washington, D.C. 1900 .... 65.00

Champagne. New Orleans. 1910 .. 75.00

Coverlet. Double. Woven. Blue and white 400.00

Cup and Saucer. Pittsburgh, Pa. 1906 .... 75.00

Gavel. Wood. Hand carved 40.00

Handkerchief. 10" square. Silk. Knights Templar, Boston. 1895 .. 15.00

Match Safe, Pocket-type. Masonic symbols. 1904 .... 35.00

Mugs
- Atlantic City. July 13, 1904 .... 55.00
- Pittsburgh, Pa. 1898. 3-handles .. 75.00

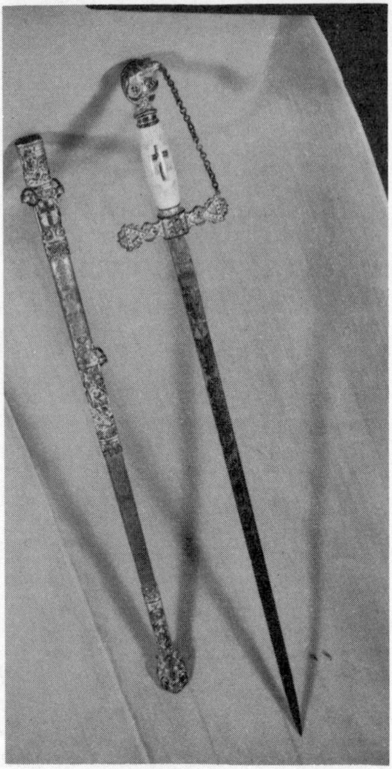

Dress Sword. 36¾" long. Engraved blade and ornate case. Ivory handle $75.00

Pittsburgh, Pa. 1903. Indian in relief 75.00
Pittsburgh, Pa. 1905. 2-sword handles. 65.00

Pins
Eastern Star. 14K gold. 3-diamond chips 50.00
32nd. Degree. 14K gold 30.00

Pitchers
5¼". Pink lustre. Masonic symbols and verse 225.00
9". Pink lustre. Pilgrim Commandery #55. East Liverpool, Ohio. With lid 275.00

Plates
6". Los Angeles. May 1906 ...... 60.00
8". Pittsburgh Commandery #1. K.T. Saratoga, N.Y. 1907 ...... 55.00
10". 54th Annual Conclave Grand Commandery, Knights Templar, Harrisburg, Pa. 1909 .... 85.00

Pocket Knife. 3¾" long. Silvered symbols. Germany 30.00
Slippers, Degree. Blue leather. C. 1910. Pair 65.00
Sword. Pittsburgh. 1909 .... 65.00
Trowel. Souvenir-type. Springfield, Mass. 1924 .... 25.00
Watch Fob with Chain. Masonic Knights Templar. Goldplated 75.00
Wine. St. Paul, Minn. 1908 ...... 65.00

MATCH HOLDERS

In the days of the so-called "barnburner" matches, match holders were a household necessity. Many styles, types and shapes were made.

Wall-type. Embossed cast iron. 1 x 2½ x 4" $30.00

Brass
Bacchus. Grape and leaf base ..$ 50.00
Banjo. 5". Double 45.00
Beetle. Hinged lid. 4" 35.00
English Bobby 85.00
Fireplace. With striker 40.00
Skull. With striker 65.00

China
Boots. 4 x 4". Pink and green on white ground 30.00
Man with cane by tree stump. 6½" high 25.00
Negro. 7". Sitting on bridge. Majolica 95.00
Peacock. 6" high. Majolica 65.00

Clear Glass
Bear Head 45.00
Charlie Chaplin 65.00
Elephant 35.00

Jenny Lind	55.00
Iron, Cast	
Advertising-type. 4″ high	25.00
Bird, Mechanical. 4″ high	40.00
Boy on tree stump, with hat. 2 x 4 x 4″	30.00
Coal Scuttle. 4 x 5″	25.00
Dog with paw on tail of rat. 6½″ long	30.00
Hunting scene. Game, hunters, guns, bugle. 5 x 9″	55.00
Scroll design. 7½″ long	30.00
Shoe, Lady's. High button style. 3¾ x 5″	35.00
Milk Glass	
Butterfly. 5″. Painted. Wall-type	35.00
Indian Head. 5″. Table-type. With striker	35.00
Jester, Black. 4¼″. Pat. date, June 13, '76	75.00
Little Jack Horner. 5¼″. Wall-type.	40.00
Uncle Sam's Hat. With stars. Painted	50.00
Urn. Saucer base	25.00
Silverplated. Picnic Basket. Meriden	50.00
Sterling. Egg-shaped. Sheaf of wheat base	50.00
Tin	
Advertising-type. 4 x 6″. C. 1900's	20.00
Crimped. 8″. Early	40.00
Wooden. Hawk. With striker	35.00

MATCH SAFES-POCKET

Before safety matches, and the 'flick of your Bic,' friction matches were carried in a safe. As the name implies, the container was a safety item. Early jewelry catalogues of the 1890's-1900's offered pocket match safes.

Advertising and Commemorative	
Arm & Hammer Baking Soda. Gutta Percha	$ 25.00
Atlantic City. Leather covered. C. 1912.	25.00
BPOE. Engraved. Silverplated	30.00
"Pan Am Expo, Buffalo, 1901." Silverplated	35.00
"St. Louis World's Fair, 1904." Sterling	50.00
Brass	
Elephant. Ivory tusks	75.00
Horseman	25.00
Pig. Enameled	40.00
Pig. Jeweled	85.00
Skull. With striker	150.00
Celluloid. Shoe	18.50
Gold. 9K. English	30.00
Gutta Percha. Horseshoe. With striker	30.00
Mother of Pearl	35.00

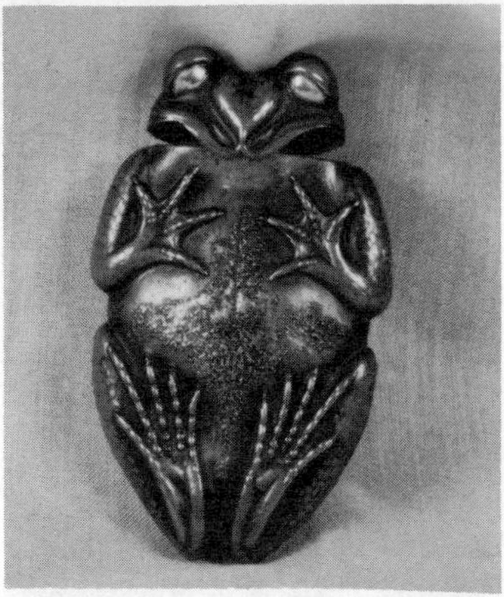

Frog. Copper $175.00

Silverplated. Fox Head. Glass eyes	75.00
Sterling Silver	
Art Nouveau. Acorns	45.00
Art Nouveau. Figure of woman	50.00
Fisherman	60.00
Flowers, leaves, scrolls. Reticulated	55.00
Golfer. Porcelain medallion	60.00
Hunter with dogs	65.00
Pan with nymphs	65.00
Plain. Monogrammed	35.00
Scrolls. Embossed	40.00
Tortoise Shell. Turtle	85.00

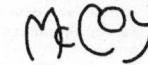

McCOY POTTERY

McCoy

McCoy Pottery, Roseville, Ohio had its beginning in 1899. Art Pottery was made after 1926 by one of its successors, Nelson McCoy Company. This firm was taken over by Mt. Clements Pottery, Michigan in 1967.

Baskets	
9″. Basketweave. Green	$ 20.00
9″. Pineapple. Yellow	25.00
Cookie Jars	
Antique Stove. 1963	18.50
Apple. 1950-1964	15.00
Aunt Jemima. 1948-57	40.00
Bear. White. 1943-45	35.00
Clown Head. 1943-49	25.00
Dog on Basket. 1956	15.00
Kitten on Basket. 1956-69	20.00
Lollipop. 1958-60	20.00

Pitcher Vase. 9". Pale green grapes on ivory ground $35.00

Mr. and Mrs. Owl. 1953-55	30.00
Rocking Horse. 1950	35.00
Windmill. 1961	25.00
Creamer. Pine Cone	7.50
Jardiniere. 6". Tan and green. Unmarked Loy-Nel	30.00
Lamp. 6½". Bulbous. Blue high glaze. Sculptured berries and leaves. Unmarked Loy-Nel	50.00
Planters	
Baby Shoe. 2¾"	6.50
Pelican. 7½". 1941	15.00
Spinning Wheel. 1953	15.00
Turtle. 8". 1955	15.00
Wishing Well. "Grant Me a Wish." 1950	20.00
Tea Sets	
English Ivy. 3 pieces	35.00
Pine Cone. 3 pieces	35.00
Vases	
6". Butterfly. 1956	10.00
6¾". Lily. Yellow	18.50
7". Rose. Embossed berries, leaves. Unmarked Loy-Nel	22.50
9". Iris. Loy-Nel	85.00
9½". Swan. Aqua. 1949	18.50
Wall Plaques	
Lily, Single. Bud-type. 1948	10.00
Oranges	15.00
Violin. 1957	12.00
Wash Sets	
Pitcher, 12". Bowl, 14". Rose	125.00
Pitcher, 12". Bowl, 14". Sponged in blue on white. Brush McCoy 1910	150.00

McKEE GLASS

The name McKee has been associated with glass making since 1834. In 1852, a factory was established in Pittsburgh, Pa. for the production of pressed glass objects. In 1888 the factory relocated about 25 miles east of Pittsburgh (the town was named Jeannette for Mrs. McKee) and continued production, almost uninterrupted, until 1951 when the firm was sold to Thatcher Glass Manufacturing Co.

Many types of glass were produced by McKee from the very first . . .bottles and window panes . . .to pressed glass tablewares (flint and non-flint), Depression glass, Milk glass objects and a variety of bar and utility wares. Also see specific categories i.e. "Candlesticks," "Lamps," "Milk Glass," etc.

Childrens Dishes. Custard with red trim. 10 pieces $75.00

Bowls	
9¼". Rainbow. Green ....$	40.00
10½". Jade	20.00
11". Custard	45.00
Creamer. Individual. Laurel. Custard	15.00
Cream and Sugar. Rock Crystal. Amber	85.00
Egg Cup. Double. Opaque green ..	6.50
Goblet. 5½". Rock crystal. Red	25.00
Pitchers, Water	
Aldine. Crystal	30.00
Snowflake. Crystal	35.00

Server. Cheese and Cracker. Rock crystal. Red	75.00
Shakers. Opaque green. Pair	16.00
Tom and Jerry Set. Custard with black lettering. 13 pieces	75.00
Toothpick. Aztec. Crystal	17.50
Tumblers	
Cobalt blue. Gladiator. Gold trim	45.00
Custard	10.00
Whiskeys. "Bottom-Up"	
Caramel	40.00
Custard	30.00
Opalescent green	40.00

MECHANICAL BANKS

(See "Banks")

MEDICAL ITEMS

Early medical instruments and related items are of interest to special collectors, especially those in the professions.

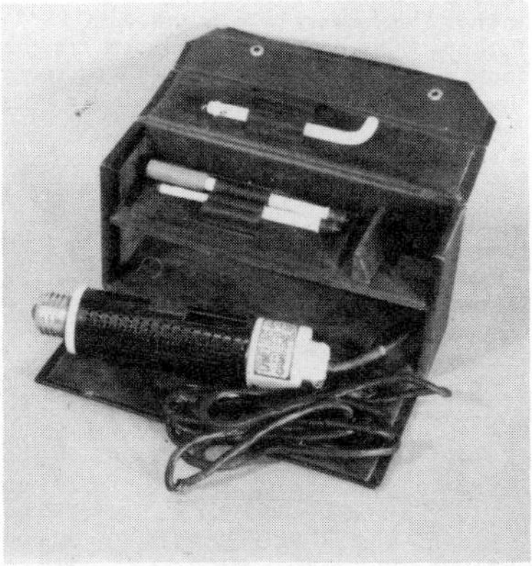

Probe Light. C. 1890 ....$75.00

Amputating and Trepanning Set. Brass bound Rosewood case. Brass handle. American. C. 1880. Complete. 40 pieces ....$	600.00
Bullet Forceps. American	35.00
Dental Cabinet. 23½ x 35½ x 50". Oak. Unrestored condition	350.00
Dental Cabinet, Harvard. 79" high. Golden oak. Restored and refinished	1000.00
Dental Chair. Hydraulic. Ritter. C. 1916. Good condition	300.00
Dental Drill, Foot power-type. Workable condition. 20th century. Complete	150.00
Dental Forceps. C. 1900	6.50
Dental Tools. (Scalers, chisels, files, etc.) C. 1900. Each	3.50
Dental Tooth Key. Iron. Wood handle. C. 1889	50.00
Doctor's Bag. 6½ x 11" high. Grain leather. Brass fittings	65.00
Electro Therapeutic Machine. 6x 7 x 9". Walnut case. Nickelplated metal works. C. 1880	75.00
Eye Cups	
Clear glass	5.00
Cobalt	10.00
Milk glass	7.50
Eye Speculum. C. 1915	3.00
Hearing Aids	
Dipper Trumpet	50.00
Long Japanned Ear Trumpet	40.00
Microscopes	
Brass. Student-type. English. C. 1880	150.00
Enameled iron and brass. Spencer. C. 1915	200.00
Enameled iron and chrome. Student-type. Spencer. C. 1938	85.00
Obstetrical Forceps. C. 1915	25.00
Percussion Hammer. C. 1880's	25.00
Physician's Pill Case. Combination-type. 6x 6x 16". Incomplete	75.00
Ophthalmic Lamps	
Brass. Moveable hand lantern. Electric	150.00
Brass with glass font and shade. Oil	300.00
Pleximeter. C. 1880's	20.00
Retractor. 11" long	3.00
Scarificator. Ten-bladed. Brass. Tieman & Co. C. 1890	95.00
Stethoscope. Mohair tubing, hard rubber bell, nickelplated metal parts	75.00
Table, Boston. Golden oak. Leather top cushion. C. 1915	500.00
Thermometer Cases	
Gutta Percha	10.00
Silverplated. With chain	25.00
Tongue Depressor. Steel. C. 1915	5.00
Tonsillectome. C. 1915	20.00
Trepanning Instruments. C. 1880s	
Hey's Saw	35.00
Lenticular Knife	35.00
Pope's Antrum Drill	45.00
Trepanning Scalpel	30.00
Trephine, Handle and Crown	50.00

MERCURY GLASS

Mercury glass is a light bodied, double walled glass that was 'silvered' by applying a solution of silver nitrate to the inside of the object through a hole in the base of the formed object.

F. Hale Thomson, London, patented the method in 1849. In 1855, New England Glass Co. filed a patent for the same type of process. Other glass makers soon followed suit. The glass did not reach popularity until the early 20th century.

Vases. 12". Green with bird and floral decor. Pair $100.00

Bowl. 5 x 2½" deep 42.50
Candlesticks
  Chamber-type. 3". Pewter holder. 50.00
  13" high, 5" diam. base. Floral decor. Pair 125.00
Compotes
  5½" high. Gold interior. Decorated with flowers and birds in white 75.00
  8" high. Scroll and leaf design in white 50.00
Cream and Sugar. Gold interior. C. 1830. Set. 125.00
Figurine. Birds. 5". Germany 25.00
Goblet. 5¾". Vintage 45.00
Lamp. 10" high. Single step marble base. Pewter connections. Vintage design 150.00
  *Lamp Reflector 45.00
Pitcher. 6". Applied handle 75.00
Rose Bowl. 5". Melon-shaped 65.00
Salt, Master 30.00
Sugar Shaker. 5½" high. Pear-shaped on standard. Original pewter screw-on top. Leaves and flowers 65.00
Tie Backs
  Plain. 2½" diam. 10.00
  Rose. 3½" diam. Pair 50.00
  Vintage. 3" diam 25.00
Toothpick. Gold interior 25.00
Vases
  4¼". Bud. Horizontal ribbing ... 18.50
  8". Bird decor in white 30.00
  10½". Bulbous. Pedestaled. Floral decor 50.00
  12". Undecorated 25.00
Wig Stand. 10" high 75.00
Wine. Vintage decor 18.50

*Reproduced Item

METTLACH

Mettlach pottery was manufactured at the Villeroy & Boch Pottery located in Mettlach, Germany. The factory was founded in 1841. Perhaps their best-known products are the famous Mettlach Steins. They also produced a line of plaques, beakers, punch bowls and other items.
Also see "Villeroy & Boch".

Beakers
  #2327-1023. ¼L. PUG ....$ 75.00
  #2368-1032. ¼L. PUG 65.00
  #2368-1108. ¼L. PUG 55.00
  #2390. ¼L. Pedestal 60.00
  #2439. ¼L. Monocolored 35.00
Plaques
  #167A. 11" diam. PUG 325.00
  #280. 8" diam. PUG 125.00
  #699. 7x7" 275.00
  #737. 8½" diam. PUG. Set of 3 .. 125.00
  #1032. 4¾" diam. PUG. Set of 6 250.00
  #1044. 16" diam. PUG 325.00
  #1044-170. 17" diam. PUG 350.00
  #1044-1122. 17" diam. PUG 350.00
  #1260. 9" diam. 175.00
  #1376-1405. 9" diam. Pair 395.00
  #1410-1490. 22" diam. Pair 1500.00
  #1652. 11" diam. Incised 450.00
  #2031. 14½" diam. PUG 200.00
  #2288. 16" diam. Incised 750.00
  #2350. 18" diam. Incised 400.00
  #2507. 17" diam. Incised 850.00
  #3084. 12" diam. PUG 125.00
  #3236. 15" diam. PUG 200.00
  #5155. 9" diam. PUG 150.00
  #7026. 9x16" 1500.00
Punch Bowls
  #418. 2 Quart. Underplate and lid. Relief 650.00
  #1969. 2 Quart. Relief 450.00

#2088. 2 Quart. PUG	500.00
#2595-1072. 1 Quart. PUG. No plate	300.00

Pitcher. 9½". Cream ground. Blue and tan tree design. Signed. #2947. $250.00

Steins

#6. 3L	600.00
#812. IL	300.00
#1028. 3L	450.00
#1100. ¼L	275.00
#1146. ½L	500.00
#1180. ½L	225.00
#1577. 5L	2500.00
#1649. 1L	450.00
#1675. ½L	450.00
#1740. ½L	225.00
#1794. ½L	425.00
#1821. 3L	425.00
#1932. ½L	495.00
#2035. ½L	450.00
#2049. ½L	600.00
#2057. ½L	425.00
#2090. ½L	500.00
#2204. 1L	750.00
#2231. ½L	475.00
#2394. ½L	500.00
#2441. Musical	1000.00
#2531. ½L	450.00
#2784-6130. 3L	550.00
#2828. ½L	1250.00
#2833B. ½L	400.00
#2891. ½L	325.00
#2936. ½L	425.00
#2958. 3L	1200.00

Miscellaneous

Jardiniere. 6x6. Bacchalian scene	350.00
Mug. Plain	40.00
Planter. 5x14". Etched. Art Deco motif	125.00
Toothpick. 2" high. Matte blue and high glazed brown	15.00
Vases	
7¾". Blue ground. Turquoise enameling on incised design. Additional decor in gold, terra cotta, white	150.00
10". Blue and white decor. Castle mark	85.00
10½". Castle scene. #2856	225.00
12¾". Children. Etched and enameled. #1591. Castle mark	385.00
14". Blue and white. #2915	250.00

MILK GLASS

Milk glass, an opaque-white glass, was introduced in England in the 18th century to fulfill the need for a less-expensive ware that resembled porcelain. It was not original because a fine opaque white glass was made in Murano, Italy as early as the 15th century.

In America, milk glass had its greatest popularity in the 1850-1900 period. Today, reproductions of some of the best patterns and designs of the Victorian era serve a purpose, but not for the true milk glass collector.

Easter Egg. 6½". Hand decorated $15.00

Animal Dishes, Covered. See "Animal Dishes, Covered."

Bell, Smoke. 7" diam	$ 20.00
Bottles, Figural	
Bear, Sitting. 11" high	175.00
Columbus Column. 18½" high	150.00

*Plate. 7". 'Three Kittens." Open edge border. Tinted $25.00

Bowls	
Acanthus Leaf. 10"	85.00
Beaded Rib. 10½"	50.00
Dutch Windmill. 3 x 8¾"	55.00
Lattice, Closed. Trumpet vine. Atterbury. 9".	95.00
Lattice, Open. 8½"	85.00
Scroll. 7½"	75.00
Square Lacy Edge. 3½ x 8½ x 9½"	75.00
Butter, Covered. Scroll. Chartreuse	125.00
Cake Stand. Flowers. 9½"	30.00
Candlestick. Crucifix. Hexagonal base. 10"	95.00
Celery. Loop Sandwich	100.00
Compotes	
Atlas, Open-Edge. 7¾ x 7¾"	125.00
Basket Weave. Blue. 7"	85.00
Jenny Lind. 7½ x 8"	95.00
Loop Sandwich. 4¼ x 8"	150.00
Scroll. 8x 8"	85.00
Scroll. Chartreuse. 8 x 8"	175.00
Creamers	
Marble. Green and white. Atterbury	500.00
Marquis and Marchionese	75.00
Owl. 3½"	35.00
Dishes, Covered	
Battleship, Dewey	65.00
Battleship, Maine	65.00
Battleship, Uncle Sam	65.00
Conestoga Wagon	100.00
Hand and Dove. Atterbury	150.00
Moses in the Bulrushes	225.00
Fish Tray. 10". Dated June 4, 1872. Atterbury	85.00
Hat. Uncle Sam's. Painted	50.00
Mustard Jar. Swan	45.00
Pitchers	
George Washington. 7"	85.00
Owl. Glass eyes. 7½"	225.00
Scroll. 11½". Tankard-shape	125.00
Plates	
Angel and Harp. 7"	25.00
Angel Head	30.00
Backward. C. 8"	15.00
Chick and Eggs. Lily of Valley border. 7¼".	40.00
Columbus. Shell and Club border. 9½"	35.00
Easter Ducks. 7½"	40.00
Gothic. 8"	17.50
Hare and Clover Leaf	35.00
Heart-shape. Heart border. 8"	45.00
Indian Head. 7½"	27.50
Rabbit and Horseshoe. 7½"	40.00
Rooster and Hens. 7¼"	35.00
Spring Meets Winter. 7¼"	50.00
Three Kittens. Square. 8½"	40.00
Platters	
Retriever. 13½"	150.00
Rock of Ages. 13"	125.00
Shakers, Salt and Pepper. Pairs	
Beehive	45.00
Billiken	175.00
Owls	150.00
Rabbits. Egg-shaped	75.00
Scroll	40.00
Shakers, Sugar	
Acorn	45.00
Beaded Swirl	50.00
Forget-me-not	55.00
Roman Cross	60.00
Spooner. Loop Sandwich	85.00
Sugars, Covered	
Basket Weave. Atterbury	125.00
Cherry. Blue	15.00
Diamond, Fan and Leaf	100.00
Swan and Cat tail	125.00
Syrups	
Beehive. Pewter top	95.00
Tree-of-Life. Blue. Pewter top	150.00
Sweetmeat, Covered. Marquis and Marchionese.	150.00
Tumblers	
Scroll	30.00
Scroll. Blue	40.00
Single Rose	25.00
Vases	
Flowers. 9½"	25.00
Hand. 8½"	50.00
Poppy. 8"	45.00
Wild Rose. 4"	35.00

*Reproduced Item

MILLEFIORI

Millefiori (thousand flowers) is an ornamental

glass. The glass is composed of bundles of colored glass rods fused to become canes. The canes were pulled while still ductile to the desired length, sliced, arranged in a pattern and again fused together. This technique was developed by the Egyptians in the first century B.C. Millefiori glass making was revised in the 1880's. It is again being produced by Master Artisans in desired articles such as paperweights, napkin rings, toothpicks, etc.

Lamp, Miniature. 12" high. Brass fittings. Electrified $600.00

Bottle. 4½" high .... $	5.00
Bowls	
3½" diam., 2" deep. 2 handles ..	100.00
6". Handled	125.00
Box. 3" high. Covered	150.00
Creamer. 4½"	165.00
Cruet. Cut crystal stopper	300.00
Cup and Saucer	75.00
Goblet. 7½" high. Clear stem and base	175.00
Lamp Base. 18" high	500.00
Lamp Shade. 6" diam. Dome-shaped	200.00
Rose Bowl. 6"	150.00
Salt, Master	85.00
Slipper. 5½" long	150.00
Toothpick. Pinched sides	150.00
Urn. 2½"	75.00
Vases	
4". Scalloped top	125.00
7½". Urn-type. 3 applied handles	250.00

MINIATURE LAMPS

(See "Lamps, Miniature")

MINIATURE PAINTINGS

The art of miniature portrait paintings began in the 16th century and was no doubt inspired by illuminated manuscript paintings. Most authorities on the subject are of the opinion that they began in Italy, then moved to France and England and later to America. They were usually painted on porcelain or ivory.

Portraits on ivory. Edgar and Ann Smit. Gold leaf frames. 3½ x 4". C. 1770. Pair $800.00

Ivory

Adelaide d'Orleans. 2½ x 3". Brass frame. Signed Dorces .... $	225.00
Gentleman. 2½ x 3". Framed. French	150.00
Jean Guy. 3" diam. Bronze frame. Signed	250.00
Lady. 4½ x 5½". Ivory frame. Signed N. Wulf	200.00
Lady and Gentleman. 2½ x 3". Original gilted frame. Pair	600.00
Mona Lisa. 2½ x 3¼". Ornate brass frame. Signed da Vinci	275.00
Mother and Children. 2¼ x 3½". Gold leaf frame	225.00
Napoleon's Sister. 3¼ x 4". Unsigned	175.00
Nude. 2 x 6½". Ivory frame. Artist signed	275.00
Pearl. 2½ x 3¼". Ivory and tortoise shell frame. Signed Palmer	275.00

Russian. 2½" oval. Black walnut frame 200.00
Victorian Lady. 2¼ x 3½". Artist signed 195.00
Young Napoleon. 2" oval. Unsigned 125.00

Porcelain

Basket. 3½ x 4" oval. Woman seated. Framed. Royal Vienna .. 250.00
Gentleman. 2¼ x 3¼". Pendant-type. Black frame. 18th century .. 350.00
Lady. 1½" oval. Square frame. Unsigned 100.00
Lady. 3¾" oval. Signed Lavalliere ... 250.00
Mademoiselle Lebrun. 3½ x 4½." Florentine frame, 7½ x 11½". Signed Sontag 500.00
Missy. 3¾ x 5" oval. Blue enamel with bronze trim inside. Bronze frame, 5½ x 8¾". Signed Bernardt 300.00
Napoleon. 2½" oval. Brass frame. Unsigned 250.00
Plumes. 2¾ x 3½". Woman wearing plumed hat. Ornate brass frame. Unsigned 175.00
Princess Louise. 2¼ x 3". Papier mache frame 125.00

MINIATURES

The term 'miniature' in the collecting field, is confusing and controversial. Some collectors prefer to classify them as children's items, others as salesman's samples and still others as miniatures! No matter the classification, miniatures are popular . . .either because the examples can be displayed in limited space or just the natural human love of small things.
Also see "Doll and Doll House Furniture."

Blanket Chest. 4½ x 5½ x 8½" long. Elm and walnut. Dovetailed. Wooden escutcheons $225.00

Andirons. Ball tops. Brass. 1¾" .. $ 25.00
Anvil. "The Famous Anvil Gretna Green." Brass. 1½" 15.00
Apothecary Jars. Blown glass with labels, corked. 1½". Pair 10.00
Baskets
- Market. Plaited splint. Alternating green and red with natural, rigid handle. 2¾ x 3¾ x 3" deep 12.50
- Picnic. Splint, metal fittings. Swing handles. 5 x 3½ x 5" o. h. .. 20.00

Bell, School. Brass. 1¼" 15.00
Bird Cage. Pewter with singing bird. 2¾" 50.00
Candelabra. 4-lite. Brass. 5¾" 40.00
Candlesticks
- Brass. Classical form. 1½". Pair .. 20.00
- Cast white metal. Chamber-type. Ornate. 1" 6.50
- Pewter. 1⅝" 20.00
- Sterling silver. Chamber-type. Border in relief. Marked Durgin. 1¾ x 2½" diam 35.00

Cannon. 3" barrel. 4 fixed wheels. Cast iron and brass. Original black paint 20.00
Carpenters Tools. Brass. C. 1930's. 1½". Set of six 12.50
Castor Sets. 4-Bottles
- Pewter frame. All original. 7¾" ... 85.00
- Twisted wire frame. All original. 5¼" 75.00

Cauldron. Bail handle. Brass. 1½" ... 7.50
Coffee Mill. Lap-type. Wood with cast iron handle. One drawer. 3½" o. h. 65.00
Cookware. Cast iron round and square skillets, dutch oven, covered; and corn stick pan. Individually marked Germany. 4 pieces 125.00
Dollie. Workable wheels. Brass. 5½" 35.00
Dust Pan. Pressed tin. 4¼" o.l. 3.50
Frying Pan. Cast iron. 1" diam.,¾" handle 7.50
Goblets
- English sterling. 1⅛" 16.00
- Pewter. 1⅛" 15.00

Hatchet. Iron. 4" 7.50
Kettle. Brass. 2" 25.00
Meat Grinder. Clamp-type for table. Cast metal. Embossed, "Made in U.S.A." 3" long. 15.00
Mortar and Pestle. Brass. 2" 20.00
Overshoes. Rubber. Marked, "American Rubber Co." 10.00
Pistol, Deringer. Silvered metal. Completely operable. Marked Austria. 1¾" long 35.00
Pitcher, Water. Bulbous shape. Sterling. 1½" 18.50

Playing Cards. With gold edges. Leather case. 2 x 2½" 15.00
Sadirons. Boat-shaped, cast iron. Single interchangeable wooden handle. 3¾" long. Pair 40.00
Samovar. Cyrillic marks. Brass. 7" ... 65.00
Scales, Grocer's. Countertop-type. Brass pans. 2 x 4" 35.00
Scissors. Brass. 1½" 2.00
Sewing Machines
  Sheet metal. Original gold stencil. Working model. Boxed with original instructions. Germany. 4½ x 5" 42.50
  "Singer". Moveable treadle. 1¼" 10.00
Shakers, Salt and Pepper. Copper. Includes tray. ¾" high. Set 25.00
Shovel. Pressed tin. 2 x 3¾" 3.00
Stein. Gray and blue stoneware with pewter lid. Germany. 3" .. 25.00
Stove, Gas. Sheet metal. 3¼ x 4½" high 22.50
Tea Kettles
  Brass. 1" high 20.00
  Iron. Swinging lid. ½ cup size .. 15.00
Teapot. Tin, lap seaming, hinged top. Blue japanning. C. 1850. 2¾" 85.00
Tea Set. Sterling. Tray, 6¼" long. 6 pieces 250.00
Tray. Handled. English silver gilt. 4" oval 50.00
Trunk. Cotter-pin hinges. Original paint. C. 1800. 3⅛ x 6" 175.00
Umbrella. Embossed flowers on plated brass. 1¾" long 8.50

MINTON CHINA

Minton earthenwares were first made by Thomas Minton in 1793 in the Staffordshire district, England. Porcelain was introduced in 1798, but was not made in any quantity until about 1825. Minton also made Parian, used a Majolica-type glaze, and employed the Pate-sur-Pate technique. Many date marks were used to identify the years of production. Minton is still in operation today.

Bowl. 11 x 3" deep. Flared. Mottled turquoise exterior. Mottled pink interior with fruit decor medallion ....$ 150.00

Tea Pot. 7" o.l. Squat-type. Gray. Floral decor in relief $150.00

Charger. 14". Cats on roof top. Blue and white Delft-type 125.00
Cheese, Covered. Floral festoons, medallions with raised turquoise bows and jewels 135.00
Cups and Saucers
  Handpainted florals. Gold butterfly handle. Gold trim 65.00
  White with heavy gold bands and handle 65.00
  White with gold band. Demitasse . 25.00
Dessert Set. 6, 7½" plates; 2, 7½ x 10" servers. Green. Scenic reserves. Gold trim. C. 1830. Set .. 750.00
Dinner Set. "Gower." C. 1881. 47 pieces 500.00
Figurines. C. 1930
  Bather 300.00
  Mary 150.00
Jug. 8". "Silenus." C. 1860 ..... 175.00
Pitchers
  8". Embossed lavender floral sprays on white. Gold trim. C. 1840 .... 175.00
  9". "Bacchus." Green. Salt glaze. C. 1840 .... 195.00
Plates
  8¾". Portrait. Gentleman. Gold trim. Signed A. Boullemier. C. 1880's 175.00
  9". Oyster. Majolica-type 55.00
  9½". Handpainted children centers. Reticulated rims. Gold trim. Signed Boullemier. C. 1873. Pair .. 550.00
  9½". Handpainted enameled floral center. Embossed rim. Gold trim. Signed W. Mupil. C. 1868 .. 225.00
  10". Handpainted Millefiori pattern. C. 1911 .... 40.00
Tiles-King Lear. Much Ado About Nothing, Temptress, Timon of Athens, Twelfth Night. Late. Each .. 40.00
Vases
  5½". Bulbous. Handled. Green with white cameo 95.00

6". Pillow form. Turquoise. Prunus blossom decor 125.00
7". Moon form. Celadon with pate-sur-pate cherubs. Gold handles 450.00
9". Bulbous. With 4" neck. Two handles. Cream ground. Handpainted flowers, butterflies 225.00

MOCHA

Research, plus the number of examples of this ware available, now demand a broader definition of Mocha. Mocha refers to the types of decoration found on Creamware, Yellow Ware and plain Earthenware; to name only the types most commonly found. Both Creamware and Yellow Ware are earthenware, but it is necessary to clarify that not all Mocha (not even all examples of Seaweed) is Creamware. Types of decoration vary greatly; from those done in a combination of motifs such as "Cat's Eye" with "Earthworm" . . .to a plain pink mug decorated with green ribbed bands. Most forms of Mocha are hollow; such as mugs, jugs, bowls and shakers. Cups and saucers and at least one plate are known. Although French and German examples of Mocha are known to exist, the majority are English and fall into three essential dated groupings: 1780-1820, 1820-1840 and 1840-1880. Marked pieces are extremely rare and usually bear the name of the owner and not the manufacturer.

Jug. 4". "Seaweed." Brown, ochre and green translucent bands. Earthenware. C. 1780-90. Rare $385.00

Bowls
6½". Earthworm. Blue and black on gray ground ....$ 175.00
6½". Earthworm. Blue and black on ochre ground 265.00
7½". Connected white circles on black ground 185.00
8½". Earthworm. Black and white on gray ground 195.00
9". Covered. Earthworm. Gray, green, brown and white 350.00
9". Seaweed. Blue bands 195.00
9¾ , 4¾" deep. Footed. Earthworm. Blue bands 225.00
10". Seaweed. Blue on yellow ware 120.00
10¼ , 4½" deep. Seaweed. Ochre ground. Green bands 250.00
10½". Seaweed. Green on yellow ware 185.00
14¾". Seaweed. Ochre ground .. 300.00
Chamber Pot. 5½" high, 9½" diam. Tree 150.00
Cup. 4½" diam. Cat's Eye 150.00
Cup and Saucer. Cat's Eye. Ochre and brown with brown bands .. 135.00
Jugs
4". Seaweed. Dark brown on ochre ground. Green ribbed bands. Earthenware................ 385.00
5". Seaweed 175.00
5". Tree. Straight sides. Blue and black bands 175.00
5½". Earthworm on ochre. Barrel-shaped. Rust red, white and dark brown 275.00
6½". Seaweed. Brown, blue and white 175.00
7½". Earthworm. Gray, black and ochre 225.00
8". Cat's Eye. Green, blue, gray, white 275.00
9". Seaweed. Yellow ground. Wide white band. Blue fern and rose. Hairline 375.00
Muffineer. 4½" high. Seaweed. Gray and ochre 100.00
Mugs
2¾". Baluster. Seaweed. Brown and ochre ground 145.00
3". Seaweed. Black on blue ground. No bandings 155.00
3½". Earthworm. Yellow and black bands 95.00
4". Seaweed. Green band at top .. 125.00
5". Tree. Blue bands 150.00
6". Earthworm. Dark brown and black 195.00
6". Twig. Black, brown, blue, white. Black bands 150.00
Mustard Pots, Covered
Earthworm. Brown and blue 255.00

Plain bands. Blue 125.00

Salts, Master, Footed

Earthworm and Cat's Eye. Black, blue, ochre 185.00

Plain band with 7 white lines. Black and white line top. Pumpkin-shaped 65.00

Sauce. 4½". Footed. Marbleized, brown, black, gray and white .. 135.00

Shakers

Earthworm 85.00

Seaweed. Ochre ground 165.00

White vertical lines on black and blue ground 125.00

Sugar, Covered. 5" high. Tree. Black and green 300.00

MONART GLASS

Monart glass is a heavy, simply-shaped art glass in which colored enamels are suspended in the glass during the glassmaking process. This technique was originally developed by the Ysart family in Spain in 1923 and John Moncrief, a Scottish glassmaker, discovered the glass while vacationing there. He recognized the beauty and potential market for such a glass and began production in his Perth, Scotland glassworks in 1924. The name "Monart" is derived from the surnames Moncrief and Ysart. Two types of Monart were manufactured . . .the "commercial" line which incorporated colored enamels and a touch of adventurine in crystal; and the "art" line in which the suspended enamels formed designs such as feathers or scrolls. Monart glass, in most instances, is not marked since the factory used paper labels.

Vase. 8½". Urn-shape body, flared top. Clear with goldstone. Cluthra ..$95.00

Bowls

3¾ x 1¼" deep. Swirled blue, pink and green with goldstone. $ 100.00

6x 2¼" deep. Orange and brown . 65.00

7x 2" deep. Green swirls, goldstone 145.00

Lamp Base. 9¾". Vase-type. Multicolored enamels in crystal. Electrified 295.00

Vases

5½". Bulbous. Mottled reddish-brown base shading to green 95.00

6½". Bulbous. Blue and rose mottling 125.00

7½". Cylindrical. Blue to white with multicolored enamels 125.00

12½". Green, yellow, heavy goldstone 195.00

MOORCROFT POTTERY

W Moorcroft

William Moorcroft established the Moorcroft factory in 1913 in Burslem, England. Practically all items were hand thrown . . .therefore no two pieces are exactly alike. The founder died in 1945 but the operation continued under his son Walter.

Plate. 11½". Multicolored stylized floral decor. Signed. Late $35.00

Bowls

4¼ x 2" deep. Blue. Pansies in relief ....$ 40.00

6". Covered. Green. Amaryllis decor 75.00

9¼ x 4" deep. Leaf and berry decor. Flambe' glaze. Script signed ... 125.00
10". Red, yellow blossoms on white ground. Script signed ... 135.00

Boxes
3x 5". Covered. Gladiolus floral design. Script signed ... 100.00
3¾ x 5". Cobalt. Floral decor on lid ... 65.00
6". Covered. Pink floral decor ... 130.00

Biscuit Jar. Blue base with deep blue top. Silver lid and bail. MacIntyre ... 375.00

Candlesticks
3½". Lime green ground. Floral decor. Pair ... 65.00
7". Blue. Fruit and leaf decor. Pair ... 125.00
10". Dark blue ground. Trees in shades of yellow. Script signed ... 125.00

Chocolate Pot. 7". Tan ground. Blue and green decor. MacIntyre C. 1899 ... 295.00

Cup and Saucer. Green. Fruit decor. Script signed ... 50.00

Inkwell. 3". Square. Blue ground. Floral decor. Script signed ... 95.00

Jar, Covered. 5¼". Blue. Orchid decor ... 95.00

Lamp. 27" overall height with shade. Blue and green. Floral decor. Signed base ... 375.00

Lamp Base. 13" high. Green. Orchid decor. Paper label ... 175.00

Pitchers
3". Berries and leaves. Flambe' glaze ... 110.00
8". Bulbous. Blue. Poppy decor. Script signed ... 195.00
16½". Cylindrical. Flambe' glaze. Floral decor. Script signed ... 750.00

Teapot. 4½" high. Cobalt. Plums and lemons. Silver rim. C. 1898 ... 175.00

Vases
2½". Cobalt. Fruit and leaves in color. C. 1897 ... 125.00
4½". Pomegranate decor. Trimmed interior. C. 1920's ... 95.00
5¾". Blue to green. Floral decor in color. Script signed. "Potter to the Queen." ... 175.00
7". Gourd-shaped. White with blue flowers. Script signed. C. 1897 ... 250.00
9". Blue. Pomegranate decor. Script signed ... 200.00
13 x 8" diam. Mottled green with cornflowers. Script signed. C. 1916 ... 500.00

MORIAGE

Moriage is the term the Japanese use to designate all their clay decorated ceramics.
After 1861, clay decorated Japanese export porcelain was mainly executed by two methods . . . slip trailing or coralene beading.
Slip trailing was carried out by applying slip (liquid clay) with a tube or syringe to the formed ware in a continuous trail. This was done when the ware was either in the leather-hard or biscuit stage and occasionally overglaze. More sophisticated designs were first formed by hand and then tediously applied. The resulting pattern in relief was usually further decorated with enamels and-or gilted. Coralene beading was accomplished in a similar manner; but the slip was applied in small dots or beads, rather than trailing. The design formed was always enameled, usually in gold.
A later imitation and simplified process of coralene beading was done with dots of enamel rather than dots of slip.

Vase, Handled. 6½". Gold coralene beading on rose and green ground. C. 1909 ... $155.00

Basket. 8½" high. Ball-shaped. Pale green ground with stylized floral decor in shades of pink. Heavy beading ... $ 200.00

Box, Covered. 3" diam. Slip trailed ... 75.00

Cream and Sugar, Covered. Footed. Matte green ground with reserves of pink roses. Slip trailed. Set ... 150.00

Pitcher, Tankard. 13½". Light green ground. Floral decor. Coralene beading 225.00

Trays

3⅝" long. Slip trailed 65.00

10 x 11½". City landmarks in reserves. Slip trailed 175.00

Vases

8". Handled. Pedestaled. Fluted collar. Iris decor. Slip trailed 150.00

9¾". Pink and yellow roses in reserves. Heavy gold coralene beading. C. 1909 .... 285.00

10". Heart-shaped. Wisteria decor. Slip trailed 175.00

13". Dragon decor on charcoal-turquoise ground. Slip trailed .. 225.00

13". Floral decor on dark green matte glaze. Coralene beading .. 265.00

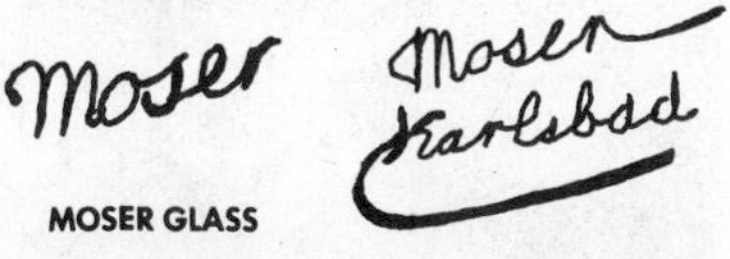

MOSER GLASS

The Moser Glassworks, Karlovy Vary, (Carlsbad), Czechoslovakia began in 1857. It was founded by Ludwig Moser whose specialty was glass engraving. Examples include Cameo, intaglio cut and enameled glass of superior quality. The firm is currently producing two-color engraved glassware.

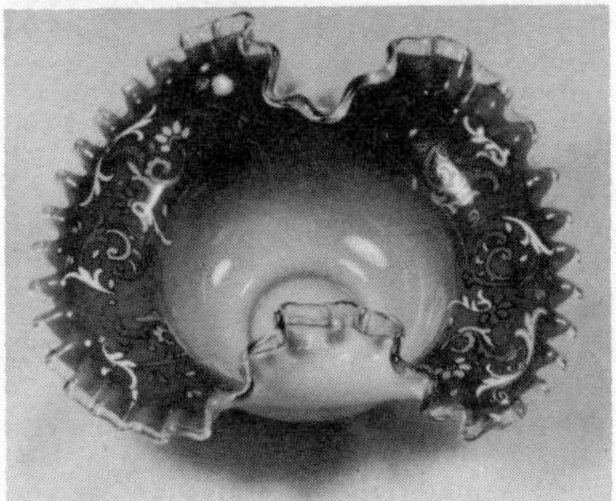

Bowl. Approx. 9". Shaded pink cased with crystal. Crimped rim. Signed T. Webb $375.00

Bottles, Perfume

Amber, Finger-type. 1¼ x 3". Gold enameled decor ....$ 150.00

Cranberry. 2¼ x 4½". Heavy gold enameling 250.00

Cranberry, Finger-type. 3¾". Heavy gold floral decor. Brass cover, ring holder and chain 125.00

Bowls

7". Amber. Gold enameled. Underwater scene with fish 300.00

10". Shell-shape. Cranberry. Enameled strawberry decor. Scalloped edge with gold beaded trim 295.00

11" oval. Footed. Cased green. Scalloped rim. Script signed 400.00

Boxes

2½ x 3¼". Blue. Heavy gold decor. 275.00

4¼ x 5" diam. Blue satin glass. Pink and white enamel decor. Gold trim. Brass bound 100.00

Compote. 5 x9" high. Amethyst. Heavy gold enameling. Script signed 350.00

Cruet. 4" high. Cranberry. Heavy gold enameling and floral decor .. 150.00

Cups and Saucers

Amber. Flowers in gold. Signed .. 150.00

Cranberry. White floral enamel .. 100.00

Emerald. Gold enameling 175.00

Emerald cut to clear. Gold trim .. 150.00

Decanters

8". Lavender. Paneled. Silvered metal mounts. Base and stopper signed 300.00

9½". Amber. White enameled insects 250.00

14". Cranberry. Stoppered, handled. All over multicolored enamels. Gold trim. Script signed .. 950.00

Ewers

5½". Cranberry to amber. Amber foot and handle. Multicolored enameled grape leaves. Gold grapes 500.00

7⅛". Cranberry. Clear applied handle. Multicolored enameled oak leaves. Applied glass acorns. Gold trim 650.00

12". Amber. Blue handle. Enameled flowers and berries. Gold trim 350.00

Finger Bowls with Underplates

Amberina. Enameled decor 450.00

Clear. Intaglio cut. Forest scene. Signed 175.00

Goblets

6½". Cranberry. Heavy gold enameling 150.00

8½". Amethyst. Panel cut. Gold band. Signed 175.00

9". Intaglio cut. Green to white. Gold rose buds on bowl and foot... 250.00

Jam Dish. 2 x 6". Cranberry. Pink and blue forget-me-nots. Gold feet and trim 175.00

Pitcher, Water. Crystal. Intaglio cut. Gold insects and vines 750.00

Plates

9". Intaglio cut. Green cut to clear. Signed 300.00

16½". Cranberry. Enameled birds. Gold trim 750.00

Rose Bowl. 4¼" high. Opalescent pink to clear base. Three amber applied feet. All over multicolored enameled oak leaves. Applied glass acorns. Gold trim. Signed in gold 1000.00

Tumblers

Amethyst. Gold enameled foliage and flowers. Signed 150.00

Cranberry. Enameled flowers. Gold trim. Signed 95.00

Vases

3¾". Blue. Heavy white enameling 175.00

4⅝". Bud. Blue cased with white. Grape decor in multicolored enamels. Applied glass grapes. Gold trim 250.00

5½". Paperweight. Crystal base. Light green top. Gold enameling .. 125.00

6½". Amber. Applied blue lizard. Enameled 350.00

9". Paperweight. Amethyst cut to clear. Gold trim 175.00

10". Rubena. Heavy gold enameling 275.00

12 x 8" wide. Fan shaped. Rubena. Gold enameling 375.00

14 x 8". Jack-in-the-Pulpit. Iridescent blue shading to amber. Gold enameled floral decor 350.00

MOSS ROSE PATTERN CHINA

The Moss Rose was a common garden flower grown in English gardens. About the mid 1800's, English potters adapted the flower's form as a decoration on their wares. The Moss Rose pattern was widely accepted and retained its popularity until the 1900's.

Box, Covered. 6½" oval ....$ 22.50

Coffee Pot. 9". E.C. & Co 65.00

Creamer 20.00

Cup and Saucer 22.50

Pitchers

6" 40.00

7¼". J.M. Co 50.00

Plates

7½" 15.00

8½". KTK 25.00

10". Cake 35.00

Platter. 12 x 18" 45.00

Sauce 7.50

Syrup. 8½". Pewter top. "KTK" C. 1872 ....$150.00

Shaving Mug 30.00

Sugar, Covered 45.00

Syrup. 8" 40.00

Teapot. 8½". Bulbous. Meakin 65.00

Toilet Chamber, Covered. Meakin .. 50.00

MUFFINEERS

(See "Sugar Castors")

MUGS

Mugs were a popular gift item in the late 19th century and continue today. They are made of various materials, decorated and-or personalized.

Also see "Children's Dishes" and specific wares.

Glass

Clear

B.P.O.E. 50th anniversary. C. 1959 ....$ 15.00

By Jingo 20.00

Cats Fighting 20.00

Dog on drum, cat on basket 25.00

Drum 25.00

Child's. Press glass. Left. Milk white $35.00

Right. Clear.................$25.00

God Speed the Plough 40.00
Heart with grapes 20.00
Lambs 25.00
Rabbits 25.00

Milk, Blue. Enameled floral decor .. 35.00

Patterned. For specific patterns such as Basketweave, Daisy and Button, Etc., refer to Section I, "Clear Glass Patterns," and Section II, "Colored Glass Patterns."

Porcelain or Pottery

"A Brother's Gift." "Josiah" on reverse. Staffordshire-type ....$ 65.00
Alphabet. Polychrome 75.00
"A Trifle for Fanny." Yellow with red transfer 65.00
B.P.O.E. 2½". Cream color. Purple transfer 30.00
B.P.O.E. 4½". Cream color. Gold lettering and trim. National Convention 1911 .... 45.00
B.P.O.E. 6¾". Blue. Gold trim 55.00
"Chit Chat." Pink decor on white .. 35.00
"Eliza." Fruit and flowers decor 40.00
"God Speed the Plow." English 40.00
"Mary." Blue transfer on white 25.00
"The Seasons." Franklin Maxim 75.00
"The Way to Wealth." Franklin Maxim 75.00
"Washington, George." Centennial. Eagles and flags. Copeland 85.00
"WX". Transfer. Staffordshire 60.00

MULBERRY CHINA

Mulberry china derives its name from the color of the decorations. The color resembles the stain of mulberry juice. Porcelains decorated as such were mainly made in the Staffordshire district, England, in the 1830-1850 period by several potteries.

Plate. "Tavoy." 9¾". T. Walker. C. 1845 ....$38.00

Bowls
Corean. 4 x 6½". P.W. & Co. ..$ 55.00
Kan-Su. 13½". T. Walker. C. 1847. 175.00
Rose. 4 x 5½". T. Walker 35.00
Vincennes. 5". Alcock. C. 1857 .. 35.00

Butter, Covered. Vincennes. J. Alcock 125.00

Coffee Pot. Udina. J. Clementson. C. 1850 .... 150.00

Creamers
Alleghany. T. Goodfellow. C. 1850 .... 75.00
Canovian. Clews 85.00
Corean. P.W. & Co 22.50
Pelew. C. Challinor 85.00

Cup Plates
Corean. P.W. & Co. 22.50
Scinde. T. Walker 22.50

Cups, Posset
Moss Rose. Furnival. C. 1850 .... 30.00
Pelew. Challinor. C. 1850 ...... 35.00

Cups and Saucers, Handleless
Corean. P.W. & Co. 35.00
Cyprus 45.00
Hong. T. Walker. C. 1850 ...... 30.00
Pelew. Challinor. C. 1850 ...... 40.00

Gravy Boat. Chusan. P. Hall 35.00

Pitcher, Milk. Pelew. Challinor. C. 1750 .... 100.00

Plates
Alleghany. 10½". Goodfellow. C. 1850 .... 35.00
Athens. 10". Wm. Adams & Sons. C. 1849 .... 35.00
Bochara. 9½". Edwards. C. 1847 35.00
Bochara. 10½". Edwards. C. 1847 40.00

Corean. 10½". Clementson 45.00
Cyprus. 9". Davenport 40.00
Dresden. 5½". Challinor. C. 1855 30.00
Hyson. 9". Clementson. C. 1845 25.00
Jeddo. 9½". Wm. Adams & Sons. C. 1845 .... 35.00
Panama. 8¼". Challinor. C. 1850 28.50
Pelew. 8". Challinor 32.50
Pelew. 10". Challinor 40.00
Peruvian. 10½". Wedgwood. C. 1849 .... 45.00
Susa. 9". Chas. Meigh & Son. C. 1855 .... 28.50
The Temple. 7½". P.W. & Co. C. 1850 .... 25.00
The Temple. 9". P.W. & Co 30.00
The Temple. 10". P.W. & Co. C. 1850 .... 45.00
Udina. 10½". Clementson 40.00
Washington Vase. 7". P.W. & Co. C. 1850 .... 25.00
Washington Vase. 8¾". P.W. & Co. 30.00
Wreath. 8¼". Furnival. C. 1845... 25.00
Wreath. 10½". Furnival. C. 1845.. 35.00

Platters
Corean. 14". Clementson 85.00
Corean. 16". P.W. & Co 125.00
Jeddo. 15½". Wm. Adams & Sons. 95.00
Percy. 16". F. Morley. C. 1850 .. 85.00
Peruvian. 14". Wedgwood 65.00
Rhone Scenery. 16". T.J. & J. Mayer. C. 1850 .... 125.00
Washington Vase. 16". P.W. & CO... 100.00

Sauce Tureen, Covered. Corean. P.W. & Co. Underplate and ladle. Set 85.00

Soap Dish, Covered. 4 x 5½". Etruscan Vase. Unknown maker. C. 1850 .... 60.00

Sugar, Covered
Alleghany. T. Goodfellow. C. 1850 .... 85.00
Athens. Wm. Adams & Sons. C. 1849 .... 100.00
Udina. J. Clementson. C. 1850 .. 85.00

Teapots
Canovian. Clews. C. 1825 ...... 175.00
Corean. 9½" high. Six sided. P.W. & Co 125.00

Vegetables, Covered
Athens. 10". Wm. Adams & Sons.. 85.00
Balmoral. 10½". Wm. Adams & Sons. C. 1855 .... 100.00
Cyprus. 12". Davenport 150.00
Jeddo. 11½". Octagon-shape. W. Adams. & Sons 125.00
Vincennes. 10". Alcock 150.00

Vegetable, Open. Corean. 8". P.W. & Co 80.00

Wash Set. Cyprus. Davenport. Bowl, pitcher, toothbrush holder, soap with drain. Set 500.00

MUSICAL INSTRUMENTS

Down through the ages people have stamped their feet, clapped their hands or were compelled to sit quietly when music was 'in the air.' Musical instruments have changed very little since the original forms. Perhaps the case design, the material used or ornamentation has changed, but a flute is a flute.

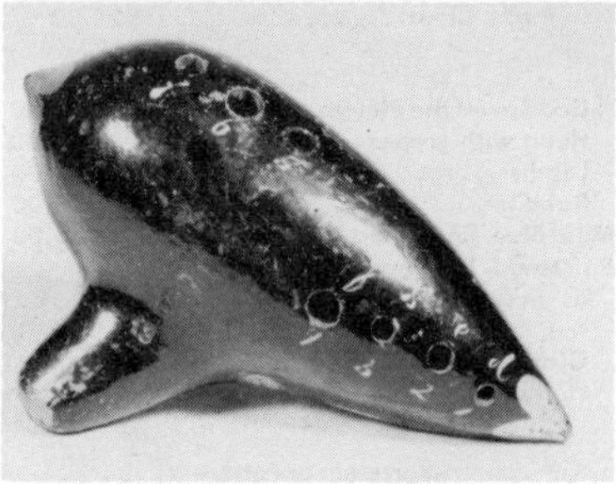

Ocarina. "Sweet Potato." Wooden $20.00

Banjo. 5 strings. Bird's Eye maple. Original case. "Howe-Stowe." ..$ 75.00
Banjo. 5 strings. Professional. Complete with velvet lined case and Tenor Tuner. "Vega." 200.00
Bugle. Boy Scout. Brass 35.00
Bugle. Military. Brass and copper .. 85.00
Clarinet. Ebony. Leather case. French 95.00
Drum. 15". Gold papered sides with American flag decor. Wooden bands. Complete. C. 1905 ...... 85.00
Dulcimer. Walnut 125.00
Fife. Rosewood and brass 100.00
Flute. Carved ivory 450.00
Glockenspiel. Two rows of steel bars supported on brass posts. Tubular brass harp with 14 bars 175.00
Guitar. "National Triolan". C. 1929. 350.00
Harmonica. Brass. C. 1875 ...... 75.00
Harmonica. Marine Band. Original box. "Hohner." 15.00
Harp. Enamel and gold 2500.00
Harp, Lap. C. 1880's 200.00
Oboe. Ivory rings, silver keys. "Korber" 300.00

Organs
Aeolian Grand. 73 keys, 20 stops.

Mahogany cabinet. Nickelplated hardware. Needs restoring 1500.00
Chicago Cottage. Ornate cabinet including spindled back, lamp holders. C. 1900. Restored 2500.00
Mason & Hamlin. 61 notes, 17 stops. C. 1900 .... 600.00
Miller. Mahogany. Restored. C. 1892 .... 2500.00

Pianos
- Aeolian. 65 note. Push up. Mechanical 500.00
- Blasius & Sons. 64 note. Mechanical 1500.00
- Franklin Ampico. C. 1923 ...... 2000.00
- Meister. Oak. C. 1904 .... 750.00
- Regent & Blasius. Upright. Mahogany. C. 1920 .... 2500.00
- Steinway. Duo Art-style. Walnut. Carved legs and molding 7500.00
- Steinway. Square Grand. Rosewood. Fruit carved legs 3500.00
- Van Dyke. 88 note. Upright. Mechanical. Restored 2500.00

Saxophone, Tenor. Brass. "Buescher." C. 1935 .... 850.00
Trumpet. Brass. Mother-of-Pearl keys 75.00
Viola. One piece back construction. Germany. 18th century 350.00

Violins
- "Edward Reichert Dresden." Bowl with MOP inlay. Case. Complete... 150.00
- Primitive-type. 7 x 21" 50.00
- "Stradivarus, Cremona." A Sears Roebuck importation of early 1890-1900 period 50.00

Zither. Late 1800's 85.00

MUSIC BOXES

Music boxes were invented in Switzerland around 1825. The instrument contained a cylinder (pin barrel) and a sounding board encased in a wooden enclosure. Later instruments used metal discs; still later ones had paper rolls resembling player piano rolls.

Album, Photo. 2-tune, tune card. Cloth cover, silvered fittings ....$ 175.00

Birds
- Single. Ornate gilted cage, 11 x 20½" 1200.00
- Two. Brass cage, 12 x 20½". Needs regulating. C. 1890's 1000.00
- Three. Brass cage, 10¼ x 15¼ x 22". 19th century 1650.00

Cylinder-type

3⅝" cylinder. 4-tunes. Mahogany case with transfer design. Tune card and mechanical tune indicator. Swiss 600.00

Cylinder-type. 6" cylinder. 8-tunes. "Butterfly." Inlaid walnut case. Swiss $650.00

6" cylinder. 8-tunes, 3 bells. Walnut case with floral inlay. Needs minor restoration. Swiss 850.00
8" cylinder. 8-tunes. Burled wood case with inlay. Swiss. C. 1880's... 1000.00
9" cylinder. 8-tunes. Painted grained case. Swiss 850.00
10½" cylinders. Interchangeable-type. 6-tunes. Mandolin attachment. Walnut case with inlay of musical instruments. Mermod Freres 3000.00
11" cylinder. 12-tunes, 6 bells. Drum attachment. Swiss 3250.00
13" cylinder. 6-tunes. Walnut case. Needs minor restoration. Heller Organ. Swiss. 19th century 2750.00
13" cylinders. Three interchangeable cylinders included. 8-tunes on each. Needs restored. Allard-Sandoz 4250.00
14" cylinder. 10-tunes. Piccolo zither attachment. Case needs refinished 1250.00
16½" cylinder. 8-tunes, lever wind brass bedplate. Mandolin attachments. Restored 2250.00
17" cylinder. 10 tunes. Piano-forte, long and short combs, tune sheet. Restored. Thibouville-Lampy 2500.00

Disc-type

Criterion. 20½" disc. Includes claw glass ball foot table. Refinished and restored 4500.00

Kalliope

7¼" disc. 4 bells. 6½ x 9 x 10¼" ... 1250.00

7¾" disc. Walnut cabinet with ivory shield inlay, 6¾ x 8¾ x 10¼". Needs restored 750.00

9¼" disc. 7 x 11 x 11½" 795.00

9¼" disc. 6 bells. Walnut cabinet with inlaid top. Underlid lithograph. 7 x 10 ¾ x 11½" 1350.00

13¼" disc. 10 saucer bells. Case needs restored 1650.00

13½" disc. Zither attachment. Walnut cabinet. Underlid lithograph. 7 x 15 x 16" 1500.00

Komet. 10¼" disc. "Komet" inlaid in ivory. 7½ x 11½ x 13". Needs restored 1000.00

Polyphon

6½" disc. Underlid lithograph. 4¾ x 7¼ x 7¼". Needs cleaned and regulated 600.00

8¼" disc. Walnut cabinet with ivory inlaid border and center design. Underlid lithograph. 6¼ x 9½ x 10¼" 850.00

9¾" disc. Walnut cabinet with underlid lithograph. 7½ x 11 x 12¼" 1000.00

11¼" disc. 7½ x 11 x 12¼" 1000.00

15½" disc. Walnut cabinet with underlid lithograph. 8¾ x 18x 21". Needs cleaned and regulated 2000.00

Regina

8¼" disc. Oak cabinet. 8 x 9¾x 12¼" 1250.00

15½" disc. Double comb. Mahogany case. Style #11 ...... 2750.00

15½" disc. Double comb, slow-fast lever. Ornate mahogany case with top gallery. Style #10. Restored 5000.00

15½" disc. Short bedplate, slow-fast lever. Serpentine case. Needs restored 3500.00

20¾" disc. Short bedplate. Banjo attachment. Style #26 .... 4200.00

Stella

17¼" disc. Double comb. Golden oak case. Disc storage in base. Mechanism needs minor adjustment 3500.00

17¼" disc. Double comb. Console model. Mahogany cabinet, 1' 10½" x 2'5½" x 3' 5000.00

Symphonion

5¾" disc. 4¾ x 6¾ x 7½". Needs cleaned 600.00

7¾" disc. Walnut cabinet with "Symphonion" inlaid on lid. Underlid lithograph. 6½ x 9 x 11" .. 750.00

11¾" disc. Double comb. Zither attachment. Walnut cabinet. 9½ x 15 x 18" 1000.00

13⅝" disc. Walnut cabinet, 9½ x 16¼ x 20". Restored 2500.00

Troubadour. 8¾" disc. Zither attachment. Walnut cabinet with "Troubadour" inlaid in ivory on lid. Underlid lithograph. 6½ x 9½ x 10½" 8500.00

Paper-type

4¼" rolls, (3) "Tanzbar Roll Playing Accordion." Case with inlay, 9 x 11 x 11" 650.00

5¼" roll. "Mignon Organette." 24 reeds. Expression flaps. Case 14 x 15 x 20½". Unrestored 850.00

MUSTACHE CUPS AND SAUCERS

Mustache cups were popular in the late Victorian period (1880-1900). The majority were made and decorated by the transfer method in Germany. The rarest items of this group are the "left-handed" cups which were especially made for lefthanded men. Left-handed mustache cups are being reproduced.

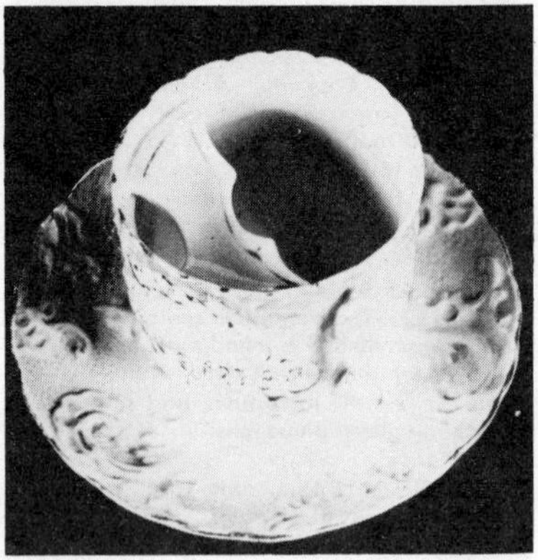

German "Love The Giver." White, shaded green. Gold trim $45.00

Austrian. Turquoise, pink, roses on white. Gold trim ....$ 55.00

German

"A Present." Handpainted florals .. 50.00

"Father." Gold florals on white .. 40.00

Flowers. Lavender, magenta and

orange on white. Gold trim 40.00
Medallion of pink roses, gold scroll work on cream and cobalt ground . 45.00
"Think of Me." Handpainted florals. Gold trim 45.00
Haviland. Handpainted florals 50.00
Nippon. Handpainted roses on blue and white ground. Gold trim. Blue leaf mark 85.00
Royal Worcester. Handpainted flowers on peach ground 125.00
Silverplated
Engraved florals. Dated 1891 .. 75.00
Engraved. Left-handed 150.00
Staffordshire. Ironstone. Flow blue decor 55.00
Sterling. American 125.00
Unmarked
Drum-shaped. "Civil War Drum" decor. Left-handed. C. 1860 .... 165.00
Owls and florals. Handpainted .. 35.00
Pink lustred 45.00
Roses. Handpainted 50.00

NAILSEA GLASS

Although glass was made in Nailsea, England, "Nailsea-type glass" was made during the late 18th and early 19th centuries by several glass makers, including glass works in America. Characteristics of Nailsea glass are its white loopings, swirls or spatters on clear or colored glass. Therefore, it is more appropriate to apply the name "Nailsea" to the decoration and technique rather than the provenance.

Bottles
Bellow. 8¾". Clear with white loops ....$ 275.00
Gemel. 8½". Clear with white loopings. Blue rim 175.00
Gemel. 10". Clear with pink and white looping 225.00
Perfume. Blue satin with white loopings. Sterling rim and lid 275.00
Bowl. 5½". Scalloped rim. Light blue with white loopings 95.00
Carafe. 7". Clear with white loopings. Attributed to Pittsburgh. C. 1840 .... 225.00
Cruets
6". Blue with white loopings. Applied frosted handle and wafer base 165.00
8". Electric blue, white loopings. Applied crystal handle and base... 125.00
Lamp Shades
6". Clear with white loopings. Blue rim 85.00
8½". Ball-shaped. Deep rose with white loopings 300.00

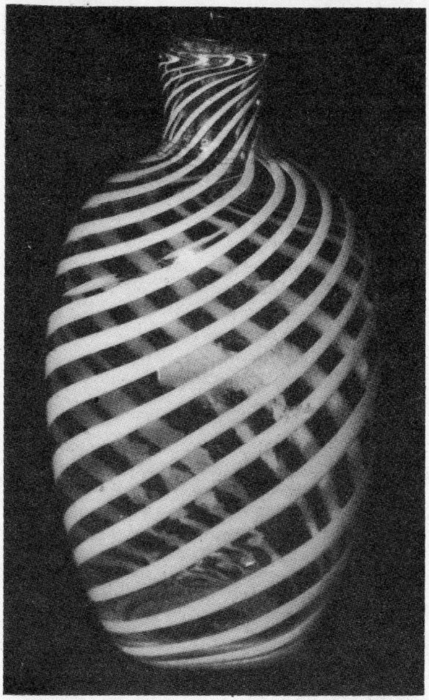

Flask. 7½". Clear with white. Original stopper $150.00

Pipes
10½" long. Curved stem. Clear with white loopings 125.00
14" long. Clear with red and white loopings 175.00
15" long. Cranberry with white loopings. English 275.00
Pitchers
8". Cranberry with white loopings. Clear applied handle .. 175.00
9½". Clear with white loopings Clear applied handle 250.00
10". Blue with white loopings. Applied handle 275.00
11¾". Tankard-type. Chartreuse with white loopings. Applied chartreuse handle 450.00
Rolling Pin. 3 x 17" long. Cranberry with white loopings 250.00
Rose Bowl. 5½" high, 6" diam. Cranberry satin with white loopings. Applied camphor satin ribbon edge 225.00
Tumbler. Green with white loopings 75.00
Vases
5½". Bud. Bulbous bottom. Clear

with white loopings 95.00
8½". Yellow with white loopings . 150.00
14½". Cranberry with white loopings. English 350.00

NAKARA
(See "Wavecrest")

NANKING

Nanking is a type of oriental porcelain made in Canton, China for export to America from the early 1800's into the 20th century. The Nanking pattern as compared with the Canton (a Chinese export porcelain of the same period) is distinguished by decoration in a darker shade of blue; and more refined and carefully painted borders. Central decoration, consisting of scenes of houses, mountains and bridges on Nanking wares, is more complex than on Canton . . .and most often shows people standing on the bridges. Green and orange variations of Nanking survived, although they are rare.
Copies of the Nanking pattern are currently being produced in China, but they are of inferior quality and decorated in lighter rather than the darker blues.

Platter. 11½ x 14½". Octagonal $325.00

Bottle, Water. 8" ....$ 450.00
Bowl, Fruit. 6 x 9" oval. Matching underplate. Reticulated 1200.00
Cups and Saucers
Baroque handle 50.00
Handleless 75.00
Loop handle 45.00
Jug, Cider. 11" 1400.00
Plates
8" 75.00
10" 110.00
Platters
13x 16". Octagonal corners 350.00
14 x 18". Well and tree 675.00

NAPKIN RINGS

Silverplated figural napkin rings were popular in the late 1800's into the early 1900's.

Kate Greenaway. Girl with barrel $225.00

Bird in flight. Pedestaled ring. Pairpoint ....$ 85.00
Bird perched on twig. Rogers, Smith & Co 125.00
Camel. Engraved. Rogers Bros 95.00
Cherub with wings. Meriden #219 . Rockford #178 .... 175.00
Cherub with wings. Meriden #219 125.00
Cherubs, Two. Kneeling. Reed and Barton 95.00
Cockatoo sits on ball attached to round fretwork base. Pairpoint #8 80.00
Dog and doghouse on side of leaf. Meriden-Britannia Co. #270 .... 95.00
Dog, Sitting. Tufts 85.00
Dogs, Two. Each side of ring. Toronto Silverplate Co 150.00
Eagles, Two. Rectangular base. Acme Silver #74 .... 85.00
Fan Base. Two butterfly wings hold ring. Meriden #209 .... 65.00
Fans, Two. With butterfly. Meriden-Britannia Co. #208 .... 100.00

Goat with flower cart. Meriden-Britannia Co. #212 .... 250.00
Horseshoe. Floral details. "Bonheur." Tufts 85.00
Kate Greenaway
Boy with baseball and bat. Babcock and Co. #202 .... 250.00
Boy with dog, cracker. Meriden-Britannia Co. #199 .... 235.00
Girl with gun on shoulder. Simpson, Hall, Miller Co. #205 ...... 250.00
Infant. #98 .... 225.00
Jack and Jill. Tufts #1667 ...... 325.00
Lily Pad. Toronto Silverplate Co 100.00
Lion. Lies on rectangular base, ring on back. Meriden #152 .... 70.00
Pansy on leaf. Meriden-Britannia Co. #162 .... 110.00
Parrot. Outstretched wings. Reed and Barton #1136 .... 75.00
Rabbits, Two. One standing; one sitting. Pairpoint #89 .... 250.00
Sailor Boy. Pushing embossed ring. Rogers Bros Co 125.00
Squirrels with nuts. Simpson, Hall, Miller 85.00
Squirrels, Two. Munching nuts. Bridgeport Silver Co. 100.00
Soldier holding shield on base. Bailey and Brainard 100.00
Stag base. Meriden 185.00
Turtle. Ring on back. Pairpoint #51 ... 225.00
Turtles, Two. Round tiered base. Meriden Silverplate Co. #216 .. 150.00
Water Lily. Rogers 50.00
Wheelbarrow. Pairpoint #10 .... 125.00
Wishbone. Four ball feet. "Best Wishes". Wilcox 45.00

NASH GLASS

Arthur Nash and his sons, Leslie and Douglas, were employed by Tiffany Furnaces, Corona, Long Beach Island in the early 1900's. It has been reported that the Nash family was responsible for designing, producing and promoting the iridescent glass for which Tiffany's received recognition.

Arthur Nash was a former member of the Woodall Gem Cameo team of Thomas Webb, England.

In the mid 1930's, A. Douglas Nash was employed as a designer by Libbey Glass, Toledo, Ohio when they introduced their art glass line. See "Libbey Glass."

Bowl. 4 x 2" deep. Amber iridescent. Signed and no'd ....$ 325.00
Candlesticks
3¾". "Chintz." 3-colors. Pair 165.00

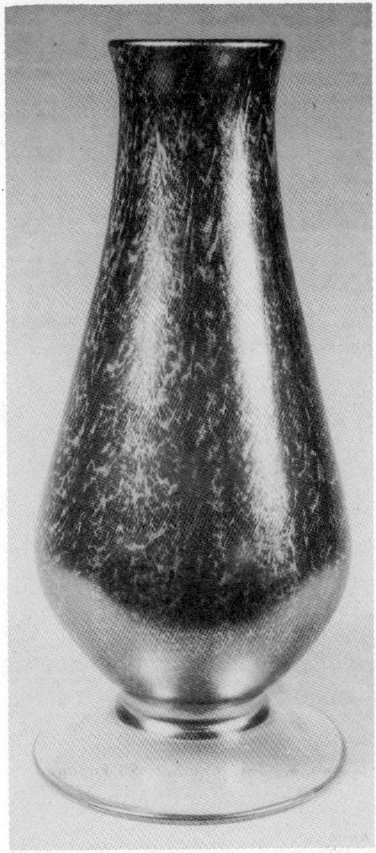

Vase. 9½". Baluster-shape. Green iridescent. Clear base. Unsigned $250.00

4½". Blue iridescent. Signed and no'd. Pair 500.00
4½". Gold iridescent. Embossed. Pair 350.00
Plates
4½". Amber iridescent. Scalloped edge. Signed and no'd 300.00
6½". "Chintz." Clear with orchid and chartreuse 95.00
8¾". "Chintz." Green and blue .. 125.00
Salt. 1¼ x 4". Gold iridescent. Ruffled top. Signed and no'd 350.00

Stemware, "Chintz"	
4" high	75.00
5" high	85.00
6½" high	100.00
Vases	
5½". Gold iridescent. Signed	325.00
6¼ x 3½" diam. at top. Trumpet-shape. "Chintz". Signed and no'd	350.00
6½ x 3" square top. Gold iridescent. Signed and no'd	350.00
7¾". Bud. Gold iridescent. Four leaves on base	375.00

NAZI ITEMS

A large number of collectors, interested in World War II items, are collecting various items of Hitler's lost cause.

Badge. Close Combat. 50 Engagements $35.00

Armbands	
Africa. Palm trees on ends ....$	55.00
Deutscher Volkssturm Wehrmacht	10.00
Red, black, swastika on white ground. 4 x 10½"	5.00
Badge. Youth Membership. Enameled	25.00
Banners	
12". Post Office	75.00
18". Triangle. Red with black swastika	50.00
Belt Buckle. With leather tab. "Gott Mitt Uns."	10.00
Bugle. 31" long. Engraved. Silver-plated. Complete with velvet banner	1500.00
Cross. Mother's. 1½ x 1¾". Blue and white enamel. Original ribbon. "Der Deuchen Mutter."	50.00
Daggers	
Air Force Officer with case	400.00
Army Medical Officer with case	450.00
Labor Corps	350.00
Luftwaffe. 1st. Model	175.00
Navy Officer with case	350.00
Youth Leader with case	500.00
Finial. RAD. For flag pole	150.00
Flags	
2 x 3'. Swastika and German Cross	150.00
2 x 3'. Battle Kriegsflagger, Navy motor launch with halyards and markings	75.00
4 x 6'. First S.S. Division	50.00
Flare Gun. Paratrooper's	75.00
Goggles. Tanker's. Amber lens. (type used in Africa)	25.00
Gorgets	
Political Leaders. No chain	200.00
RAD. With chain	350.00
Hats	
Army Officers	125.00
Army Rank	100.00
Navy Officers	175.00
Helmets	
Fire Police	75.00
M-35	50.00
Motorcyclist	200.00
Paratroopers	225.00
Police Officers	250.00
Tropical	95.00
Medals	
Cross. Swastika center, silver-plated	50.00
Serpents Death head	35.00
Overcoat, Police	150.00
Shako. Complete with plume	150.00
Stickpin. Red, white and black enameled swasitka on silverplate.	35.00
Swords	
Army Officer	150.00
Luftwaffe	250.00
Navy Officer	300.00
Transfers	
For helmets. SS, Army, Luftwaffe, etc. 14 per sheet	25.00
For Luftwaffe staff car. Eagle with 2 matching smaller types. Set of three	35.00
Tunic, Dress. Medical Officer's	250.00

NETSUKES

The traditional Japanese dress has no pockets. Daily necessities such as keys, money pouch, tobacco supplies, etc. are carried on the person by hanging them from the belt. A cord is attached and secured by a slip bead and a toggle. This toggle is known as a netsuke. . .from 'ne'-root, and 'tsuke'-to fasten. Most netsukes were carved of bone, ivory and wood. Ceramics, metals and semi-precious stones were also used. CAUTION! Recent productions are on the market. . .many carved of African ivory.

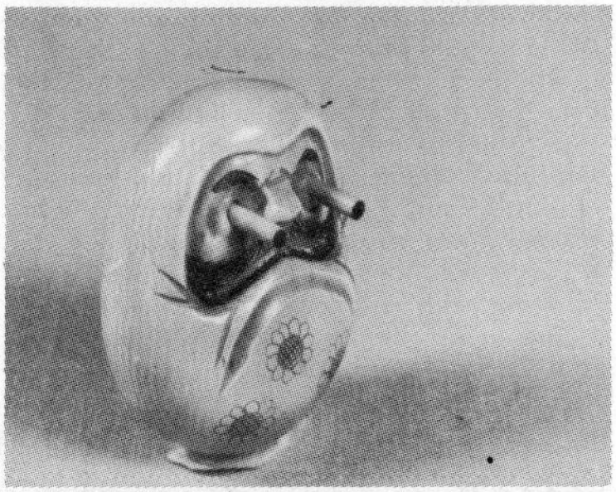

Popping Eyes. Ivory $125.00

Apple Vendor. Woman. African ivory ....$ 75.00
Boar. Kneeling. African ivory. Signed 85.00
Buddha. Ivory. 18th century 300.00
Chicken in Egg. African ivory. Signed 50.00
Devil Mask. Wood 150.00
Enshi. Ivory. Signed Meido. 19th century 500.00
Erotic. Ivory 500.00
Face. Revolving. Ivory. Happy face, sad face. Signed Suglyami 54 .. 75.00
Fish. Ivory. Signed Masoyoshi 250.00
Foo Dogs. Entwined. Ivory 150.00
Grain Man. Ivory 250.00
Horse. Ebony 275.00
Horse. Winged. African ivory 95.00
Hotei. Seated. Ivory. Signed. 18th century 850.00
Kinko. Seated on carp. Ivory. Signed. 19th century 500.00
Man. Smiling. Wood. Signed. 19th century 200.00
Man. With fish. Ivory 125.00
Marine Cluster. Ivory. Inlaid horn eyes. Signed. 19th century 650.00
Monkey. "See No Evil." Signed. 19th century 450.00
Monkey. With pod. African ivory .. 75.00
Monkeys. Mother and child. Ivory. 19th century 500.00
Mother. With two children. Wood. Signed 250.00
Popping Eyes. Ivory 125.00
Rat. Ivory. Signed 300.00
Sage. Seated. 18th century 500.00
Sculptor. With tool box. Ivory. Masaaki 650.00
Snail. Ivory. Signed. 19th century .. 350.00
Snake. Coiled. Signed Baisho 175.00
Tiger. Wood. Signed. 19th century 750.00
Turtle Group. Wood 250.00
Two Idiots. Ivory 350.00
Wolf. Resting on skull. Ivory. Signed. 19th century 300.00

NEWCOMB POTTERY

The brilliant achievements of Newcomb pottery began in 1885 in Tulane University art classes and then at the Art Pottery Co. in New Orleans. Later in 1886, the pottery was operated in conjunction with the Art Department at Sophie Newcomb Memorial College for Women in the same city.

William and Ellsworth Woodward were the founders. The two brothers directed an elective arts program at the college which was funded generously by Josephine Louise LeMonnier Newcomb and joined to Tulane University in 1887.

Students at Newcomb College worked in the pottery, producing and painting a quality art pottery with the distinctive high gloss glaze. Designs on Newcomb wares have a decidedly Southern flavor. . .such as myrtle, jasmine, sugar cane, moss, cypress, dogwood and magnolia.

The result of a unique educational "industry", Newcomb pottery is considered highly collectible today.

Bowl. 8 x 4" deep. Blue matte glaze. Undecorated. Signed J.M. $125.00

Bowls

4 x 1⅝" deep. Undecorated. Signed Hattie Joar ....$ 150.00

5½ x 2¼" deep. Blue and pink flowers on blue ground. Signed JM, Sadie Irvine 295.00

7½ x 4" deep. White daffodils, blue band on pale blue-green ground. Signed JM, CL 450.00

9½ x 3" deep. Blue narcissus on dark blue ground. Signed JM, Sadie Irvine 450.00

Candlestick. 9¾". Blue ground with pink dogwood on base. Signed JM, Sadie Irvine. Paper label 600.00

Flower Frog. 1⅝ x 4" diam. 9-holes. Pink and blue. Signed JM, Sadie Irvine 135.00

Mug. "Strive mightly, but eat and drink as friends." Florals on blue. High glaze. Signed JM, Ada Lonnegan 750.00

Vases

3¼ x 3⅛" diam. Blue flowers, green stems on dark blue ground. High glaze. Signed JM, Sadie Irvine 350.00

3½ x 3" diam. Green art nouveau-type decor on deep blue matte glaze. Signed JM, Sadie Irvine 135.00

5¼ x 5¼" diam. base, 3½" diam. top. Floral sprays in blue and pink on blue ground. Signed JM, Sadie Irvine 400.00

6". Scenic. Moon shining through trees. Blue and green. Signed JM, Sadie Irvine 450.00

7¼ x 4¼" diam. Pink narcissus, green leaves on blue ground. Signed JM, AFS 475.00

7¼ x 4½" diam. Undecorated blue. Matte glaze. Signed JM 275.00

10 x 4½" diam. Water lilies on green ground. Blue band at top. Signed JM, Sadie Irvine 600.00

11 x 8" diam. Pine cone decor. Four-color work on blue ground. Matte glaze. Signed Henrietta Bailey 700.00

NEW HALL

From 1781-1835 the New Hall China Manufactory made both Hard Paste Porcelain and Bone China using many of the same patterns and forms on both bodies, with some variations. Less famous in its day than many English factories making similar wares, New Hall was the only firm to make the transition from Hard Paste to Bone Porcelain. . .all others went from Soft Paste to Bone.

Unseasoned collectors should approach New Hall with caution since imitators abound as David Holgate warns in his book, "New Hall and Its Imitators." Although this definitive reference lists New Hall pattern numbers up to 1681, many patterns are not illustrated. However, pattern alone cannot be used to date a particular New Hall item. Shape and in some cases nature of paste and glaze are the only true guides.

It is possible that New Hall patterns exist that have not been documented and . . .such pieces, including a complete tea service, have been found recently in pattern 1278.

Tea Service. 13 pieces. Pattern 139. C. 1786. Set $750.00

Coffee Cans. Pattern 1278. Set of 4 ....$ 425.00

Cream Jug. Unknown pattern 165.00

Teapot. Pattern 173. Silver shape .. 225.00

Tea Services

15 pieces. Pattern 139 .... 750.00

26 pieces. Pattern 1064 .... 1075.00

29 pieces. Pattern 1278 .... 1250.00

NEW MARTINSVILLE GLASS

New Martinsville Glass Manufacturing Company began operation in 1901 and continued to 1931. Art glass produced during the early years of the company rivaled, in beauty and design, foreign products. Unfortunately, these pieces had limited production as a fire destroyed the plant in 1907. Thereafter, the fragile Peachblow and other types of Art glass were never again produced.

Four periods of production are noteworthy: 1901-1907-Art and opaque glass including "Peachblow," 1907-1937-Pressed pattern glass, 1937-1944-Crystal wares including the animal line, 1944-Contemporary novelties and tableware. When the company went into receivership in 1931, the plant was sold and the business was reopened as The New Martinsville Glass Company. In 1944 the entire stock was purchased by G. R. Cummings and the name was changed to The Viking Glass Company under which it still operates today.

Swan. 11½". Open back. Crystal. "Janice." $30.00

Animal Figurines
- Bear, Baby. 3" .... $ 40.00
- Dog, Police. 5" 60.00
- Hen. 5" 45.00
- Pelican. 8" 75.00
- Rabbit. 2½" 65.00
- Rooster. 8½" 75.00
- Seal, Baby. 7" 65.00
- Squirrel. 5½". On base 50.00
- Wolfhound. 8" 75.00

Basket. 9". Cobalt handle. "Janice." 45.00

Basket, Bride's. 9". "Peachblow" bowl in footed holder 250.00

Bookends
- Cornucopia. 5¾". Crystal. Pair 50.00
- Rearing Horse. Crystal. Pair 60.00
- Rearing Horse. Green. Pair 75.00

Bowls
- 10¼ x 3⅝" deep. "Peachblow." Glossy finish 175.00
- 11". "Janice." Ruby 30.00
- 11½". Etched. "Teardrop." 30.00
- 12 x 4" deep. "Janice." Crystal 25.00

Box, Covered. 8". Three compartments, #103-25. Etched #25. Crystal 30.00

Butter, Covered. "Japanese Iris." Gold trim on crystal 65.00

Candlesticks
- 6½" high. #415. Crystal. Pair 35.00
- 7¼" high. #452. Crystal. Pair 45.00

Console Set. 12" crimped bowl, two 6¼" 2-lite fan-shaped candlesticks. "Radiance." #26 etching. Blue. Set 75.00

Creamers and Sugars
- "Moondrops." Ruby. Set 25.00
- "Radiance." Blue. Set 30.00

Jam Jar, Covered. With underplate. "Janice." Blue 35.00

Liqueur Set. "Moondrops." Ruby with silver overlay. Handled tilt decanter, 8" high. Five handled liqueur glasses. Set 125.00

Pitcher. 56 oz. Etched. #2306 .... 55.00

Spooner. "Japanese Iris." #716 .... 30.00

Sugar. "Moondrops." Ruby 12.00

Swans
- 5½". Open back. Crystal 12.50
- 5½". Green bowl. Crystal applied neck 20.00
- 5½ x 10". Crystal bowl with ruby applied neck. "Janice." 30.00
- 8½ x 11½". Open back. Crystal. "Janice." 30.00

NILOAK POTTERY

Niloak (Kaolin spelled backwards) Pottery was made in Benton, Arkansas from 1911 to 1946. The hand thrown marbleized pottery developed by J. H. Hyten and his two brothers is of the greatest interest to collectors of American pottery. Molded or cast pottery was also made at the factory.

Planter. "Camel". Tan $20.00

Bowls, Marbleized
- 5 x 2¾" deep .... $ 30.00
- 5½ x 6" deep 42.50
- 10 x 3¼" deep 75.00
- 12 x 4" deep 85.00

Cup and Saucer. Square. Yellow glaze 25.00

Ewer. 10¼". Blue matte glaze. Embossed eagle and star 30.00

Figurine. "Southern Belle." 9½". Paper label 40.00

Pitchers
- 5½". Beige 15.00

10". Molded. Stylized daffodils. Red glaze with blue-green shadings 40.00
Planters
Camel. Tan 20.00
Dog. White 10.00
Dutch Shoe. Pink and green 12.50
Elephant on Drum. Blue 15.00
Swan. Blue 15.00
Vases, Marbleized
4½" 30.00
6" 35.00
8" 45.00
12" 95.00

NIPPON CHINA

Much of the Nippon porcelain seen today was manufactured by the Noritake Company, Ltd. in Nagoya, Japan. In 1891, when Congress passed a law that all imported articles must be marked as to country of origin, Japan chose to use their own name for Japan, "Nippon."
In 1921 it was decided "Nippon" was no longer acceptable and all Japanese wares must be marked with the English word Japan, thus the end of the "Nippon" period. There is quite a controversy over the many marks used on Nippon wares (over 50, some identical except colored differently). The most agreeable explanation and perhaps the most logical is that the different marks indicate the quality of the porcelain and the decorative workmanship. Other marks may identify the importer, artist or maker. Serious collectors of Nippon should familiarize themselves with these marks. All Japanese porcelains are not Nippon and all Nippon is not fine Japanese porcelain.
Also see "Noritake."

Ashtray. Queen of Clubs. 4". Bell-shaped. Green M ....$ 75.00
Asparagus Set. Serving platter with well, sauce boat with underplate, five 7½" plates. All decorated with asparagus stalks. Green M. 8 pieces 150.00
Basket. 6". Basketweave ground, plums in relief. Bisque finish 85.00
Berry Set. Master bowl, 9". Six 5¼" serving bowls. Handpainted raspberries and blossoms. Gold trim. Set 95.00
Bottle, Perfume. 5¼". Hexagonal. Handpainted violets. Green M .. 50.00
Bowls
5". Handled. Rose decor. Gold trim. Bisque finish. Green leaf mark 35.00
6½ x 2" deep. Handpainted Dutch scene in sepia. 3-feet. Green M .. 45.00

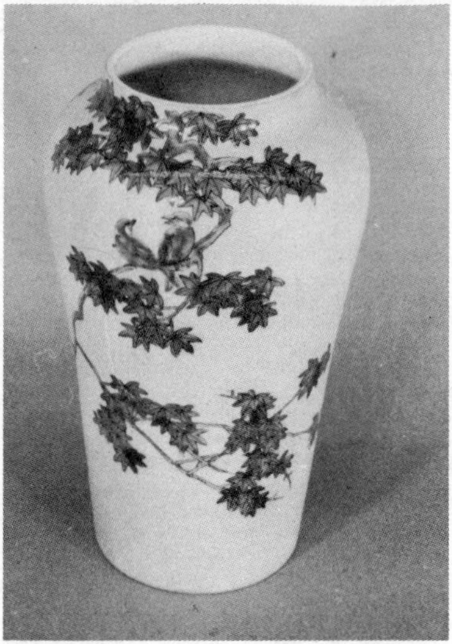

Vase. 14". Yellow. Decorated with birds and tree branches $125.00

7". Floral border. Rising sun mark . 22.00
7". Nuts in relief. Bisque finish. Green leaf mark 100.00
9¼". Footed. Handpainted roses in center. Beaded scalloped inverted rim. Green leaf mark 150.00
9¾". Handled. Handpainted harbour sunset. Gold beaded band and trim. Blue leaf mark 65.00
Boxes, Covered
3" diam. Brown florals. Gold beading and trim 20.00
3½ x 4". Handpainted harbour scene. Green M 65.00
5" diam. Portrait on lid. Gold trim . 85.00
Cake Set. 10" plate, six 7¼" plates. Scenic decor. Green M. Set 85.00
Candlesticks. 9". Gold florals on pink ground. Blue leaf mark. Pair .. 65.00
Chocolate Pots
Apple blossom decor. Cobalt and gold beaded trim. Green M 150.00
Zinnia decor. Cobalt and gold trim. Blue leaf mark 60.00
Chocolate Sets
"Flamingo." Pot, six cups and saucers. Green M 195.00
Rose decor. Gold trim. Pot, four cups and saucers. Green leaf mark .. 125.00

Creamers and Sugars
Farm scene. Green M 65.00
Jeweled. Blue leaf mark 50.00
Cups and Saucers
Geometric design. Blue M 15.00
Roses, pink with white beading. Rising sun mark 12.50
Swans. On blue ground. Jeweled gold and pink trim. Green M 35.00
Dresser Set. Handpainted pink roses, leaves. Blue border on white. Green M. 5 pieces 75.00
Ferners
3½ x 6¾" diam. Octagonal. 8-footed. Floral medallions. Gold trim. Blue leaf mark 60.00
4¾ x 7½" diam. Square. 4-footed. Florals and swags in relief. Gold beading. Green M 150.00
Hair Receiver. 5" diam. Cobalt with gold trim. Blue leaf mark 25.00
Hatpin Holder. Enameled scenic decor. Gold beading. Green M .. 85.00
Humidors
5". Deer in woods, oak trees, acorns. Green M 275.00
5". Landscape decor. Some moriage decor. Blue leaf mark .. 150.00
6". Beaded floral decor in reserves. Heavy gold trim. Green leaf mark 200.00
Mayonnaise Set, Covered. Attached underplate. Ladle. Handpainted flowers. Blue leaf mark 40.00
Napkin Ring. Handpainted multicolored florals. Gold trim on white. Green M 30.00
Nut Set. Serving bowl, six individual bowls. Handpainted pink roses. Green M. 7 pieces 65.00
Plaques
Indian portrait. 8". Green M 175.00
Lion and Lioness. In relief. Green M 450.00
Owl. Blue ground. Green beaded trim. 10". Green M 225.00
Plates
6¼". Pink roses. Green leaves. Blue leaf mark 12.50
7¼". Handpainted swans. Pink jeweled trim. Green M 50.00
Relish. 6½ x 9¾" long. Fan-shaped. 3-part, divided. Handpainted butterflies, roses. Gold trim. Green M 65.00
Ring Tree. Hand-shaped. Ship decor on base. Green M 45.00
Shakers, Salt and Pepper. Harbour scene at sunset. Green M 30.00
Shaving Mug. 3¼" high. Floral decor on white. Gold trim. Rising sun mark 55.00
Syrup. With underplate. Cottage scene. Blue M 40.00

Tea Set. Handpainted woodland scene. Some moriage-type decor. Blue leaf mark. 15 pieces 350.00
Tea Strainers
Cobalt with gold beading. Blue leaf mark 45.00
Roses. Gold trim. Rising sun mark 25.00
Vases
6". Scenic decor. Tapestry-type. Blue leaf mark 250.00
7". Pink flowers. Cobalt and gold trim on white ground. Blue leaf mark 80.00
9". Handled. Yellow florals. Gold trim. Green M 150.00
12". Handled. Poinsettia decor. Gold beaded trim. Blue leaf mark.. 80.00
14". Handled. Scenic decor on green ground. Heavy gold beading. Green M 175.00

NODDERS

Nodders are porcelain figurines with heads and-or arms attached to the bodies with wires. The slightest movement makes them "come to life." Most of them were made in the 19th century.

Dog. 4 x7". Brown $50.00

Andy Gump. 4". Germany ......$ 65.00
Boy, Revolving face. 2½" 125.00
Clown. Boy. 7". Staffordshire 150.00
Clown. Girl. 7¼". Holding dog 125.00
Dutch Boy and Girl. 3". Red outfits. Bisque. Germany. Pair 125.00
Gent, Smiling. 8½". Holding hatchet and powder horn. Bisque. Germany 175.00
Grandmother. 7". Holding fruit

basket. Germany 150.00

Man and Woman. 4". Wearing oriental style robes. Pair 175.00

Monk. 7¼". Holding four wine bottles. Germany 150.00

Monkeys on See Saw. 8½". Bisque. Germany 175.00

Moon Mullins. 3¾". Bisque. Germany 75.00

Orphan Annie. 3½". Bisque. Germany 65.00

Uncle Walt. 3". Germany 60.00

Woman. 6½". Blue and white clothing. Holding umbrella. Staffordshire 125.00

Woman. 9". Playing piano. Germany 375.00

NORITAKE

Noritake was the first Japanese firm to adapt modern production methods for ceramic dinner ware designed for export. The bulk of this ware was produced after 1900.

In addition to the dinnerware, collectible Noritake export items includes other tablewares and decorative pieces.

Major categories of Noritake decoration consist of floral, fruit, nuts, birds, heavy gold borders and designs of scenic landscapes and seascapes.

Early in the century, Noritake listed Morimura Brothers as exclusive import-export agents and early wares omit the Noritake "N" or combine it with the red or green Morimura "M" in a wreath. When Morimura closed in 1941, an "N" was substituted for the "M" in the wreath mark.

Noritake's Royal Ceramic line (marked with "RC") and Okura Art China line (marked "O.A.C.") represent the best of Noritake in body and decoration.

Noritake did supply blanks for decoration to other firms; but such wares do not carry typical Noritake marks or symbols. Dinner sets are still produced today by Noritake, Inc.

Basket. 6". Gold fleur-de-lis border and handle. Signed ....$ 35.00

Berry Set. Master bowl, 9". Six individual bowls, 5½". Handpainted poppies. Artist signed. Green wreath mark. 95.00

Bowls
- 7 x 3" deep. Nuts in relief 30.00
- 7½". Handpainted florals. Green wreath mark 20.00
- 9". Shallow. Pierced handles. "Tree at Lake." Green wreath mark 30.00
- 12 x 3" deep. Handled and footed. Chestnuts, leaves in relief . 75.00

Butter, Covered. 7¼" diam.

Bowl. 6¼". Footed. "Tree at Lake." Green wreath mark $22.50

"Rengold." Signed. 55.00

Candlestick. 8½". Orange and black trim. Green wreath mark .. 25.00

Celery Tray. 12". Handpainted sailing scene. Artist signed 35.00

Chocolate Pot. Handpainted blue birds, flowers 25.00

Chocolate Set. Handpainted roses on cream ground. Gold trim. 11 pieces 100.00

Condiment Set. Gold decor on white. Green wreath mark. 5 pieces 35.00

Cream and Sugar. "Tree in Meadow." 30.00

Creamer. "Sahara." 15.00

Cups and Saucers
- Handpainted florals 10.00
- "Tree in Meadow." 8.50

Dinner Set. "Sedan." 47 pieces 150.00

Hatpin Holder. Camel scene. Raised gold trim 35.00

Humidor. 5½". Scenic decor 45.00

Mustard. With ladle. Cottage scene . 20.00

Napkin Ring. Art Deco-style decor .. 15.00

Nut Set. "Peanuts." Master bowl, 6½". Six individual bowls. Green wreath mark 50.00

Pitcher. 6". Octagonal-shape. Art Deco-style decor. Red maple leaf mark 12.50

Plates
- 6¼". "Tree in Meadow." 5.00
- 7". Handpainted barnyard scene. Gold trim 40.00

10". Handpainted desert scene. Artist signed 50.00
10". "Linden." 12.50

Platter. 13" oval. Fleur-de-lis gold border 25.00

Snack Plate. Palette-shaped. Red flowers. Blue rim. Green wreath mark 20.00

Snack Set. Pallette-shaped plate, cup. Scrolled gold trim 25.00

Teapot. "Tree in Meadow" 45.00

Tea Sets
17 pieces. Heavy gold florals and scrolls on white ground. Green wreath mark 125.00
17 pieces. "Lucerne." 75.00
21 pieces. Multicolored florals. Orange border on white ground. Red wreath mark 65.00

Tile. "Tree in Meadow." 35.00

Vases
4". Landscape scene. Blue and gold borders. Pair 125.00
8½". Four handles. Floral decor. Green wreath mark 25.00
9½". Square. Four feet. "Dresdina." 75.00
13". Two handles. Cottage scene .. 85.00

NORITAKE-AZALEA PATTERN

One of Noritake's most commonly known patterns was "Azalea." The dinnerware was widely distributed by the Larkin Tea and Coffee Company from the 1920's to the 40's as premiums and by a mail order plan. The Larkin Club Plan enabled one on a limited budget to purchase fine china on a piece-by-piece basis.

Four different marks were used during production. The earliest was simply "Hand Painted Nippon." Two succeeding green and red marks were "M" in a wreath with the words "Noritake" and "Made in Japan" followed with symbols and the numbers "19322." The latest mark reads "Azalea Pattern" with an Azalea sprig.

Basket. 2½ x 4½" long ....$ 85.00

BonBon. 6¼". Handled 25.00

Bowl. 10" 25.00

Butter Tub. With insert 30.00

Casserole, Covered. 10¼" 55.00

Celery. 12" long. Handled 30.00

Cheese, Covered 55.00

Coffee Pot. Demitasse 400.00

Compote. 2¼x6½" diam. 50.00

Condiment Set. 5 pieces 30.00

Cream and Sugar, Open. Demitasse . 75.00

Cups and Saucers
Bouillon. Handled 15.00
Coffee 12.50
Demitasse 55.00

Plate. 7½" $8.00

Egg Cup 25.00

Gravy Boat. Attached tray 30.00

Jam Jar. 5". 3 pieces 75.00

Mayonnaise Set. 3 pieces 25.00

Pitcher, Milk. 1 Qt. 110.00

Plates
5½". Oatmeal 6.00
6½" 5.00
7½" 8.00
8". Soup. Flat 12.00
8½" 12.00
9¾" 15.00
9¾" Cake. Open handles 25.00

Platters
12" 28.50
14" 35.00
16" 300.00

Relishes
8½" oval 12.00
10". Handled. 4 sections 75.00

Shakers. Salt and Pepper. 3½" high. Pair 15.00

Sauce. 5¼" 6.00

Shell. 8" long 165.00

Syrup. With underplate 50.00

Teapots
Gold finial 150.00
Regular finial 50.00

Tile. 6" diam 30.00

Toothpick 85.00

Vase. 5½". Fan-shaped 65.00

Vegetable, Open. 10½" oval 25.00

Waffle Set. Creamer 5¾". Shaker 6½" 85.00

NUT CRACKERS

Since primitive man first cracked nuts with his teeth or with stones, inventors have been devising ways to make the task simpler and easier. Examples listed below are the fruits of their ingenuity.

*Dog. 10½". Cast iron $30.00

Alligators
- 7½". Cast iron. Painted green ..$ 25.00
- 14". Brass 50.00

Bear's Head. Wood. Glass eyes. 7".C. 1850 .... 85.00
Bowl. Turned. 9¾". Squirrel attached in center 50.00
Chicken's Head. Brass 30.00
Dogs
- *10½". Cast iron 30.00
- 11". Brass. Wooden base 50.00

Dragon. Brass 50.00
Fish. 5". Brass 30.00
Lion's Head. Brass 30.00
Monkeys. Brass 35.00
Musician. 8" high. Carved wood .. 85.00
Parrot. Brass. 5½" 35.00
Regis. Dickens' character. Silverplate 30.00
Rooster. Brass. 2 handles 50.00
Shakespeare. Brass 25.00
Squirrels
- *Cast iron 25.00
- Cast iron. Table clamp-type 25.00

Twist and Screw-type. Cast iron. C. 1910 .... 25.00
Wolf's Head. Cast iron. 4½". C. 1920 .... 25.00

*Reproduced Item

OCCUPIED JAPAN ITEMS

Items marked "Occupied Japan" were made after the surrender of Japan in World War II and during the occupation by the Allied Forces.

Ashtrays
- 2¼". Heart-shaped. White with handpainted floral sprays ....$ 5.00

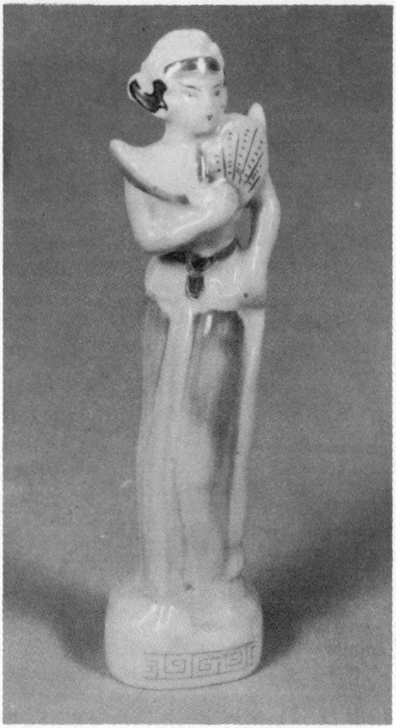

Figurine. Oriental Lady. 7¼". White and gold $15.00

- 6¾". Chrome plate. Pierced floral rim 10.00

Bookends. 5½". Oriental lady and gent. Pair 30.00
Box, Jewelry. Piano-shaped. Silvered metal 10.00
Clock. 5⅛". Grandfather-style. Bisque. Floral trim 8.50
Condiment Set. 2⅝ x 5¾". Oranges in basket. 6 pieces. Set 20.00
Cream and Sugar. Covered. Pink roses, green leaves, red trim. Set... 12.50
Fan. 8½". Red lacquered bamboo sticks. Painted roses on silk. Gold trim 20.00
Figurines
- Betty Boop. 6". Blond hair. Celluloid, moveable arms 12.00
- Boy, Singing. 4". Hummel-type .. 12.50
- Bride and Groom 3". 1920's dress . 18.50
- Cat. Fishbowl climber 12.50
- Cherub. 3". With drum and sym-

bol. Pierced pedestaled base 8.00
Duck. 2 x 4". Celluloid, brightly colored 8.00
Girl, Oriental. 4¾". Shelf sitter. Green 10.00
Lady, Oriental. 7¼". White and gold 15.00
Lady and Gentleman. 8". Oriental dress. Pair 30.00
Monkeys. 3" long. "The Three Wise Ones." 8.50

Harmonica. Butterfly-shaped 15.00
Parasol. 4" long. Paper and bamboo. 2.50
Planters
Coolie. Pulling rickshaw. 3½x5" ... 10.00
Donkey and Cart. 7" 10.00
Duck. 5 x 8" 15.00
Kitten. 3¼" 7.50

Plate. 4½". Pierced scalloped fancy rim. Silvered metal 8.50
Plate, Grill. 10". "Blue Willow." .. 7.50
Shakers, Salt and Pepper
Ducks. 2½". Original box 10.00
Flower Girls. 4¼". Hummel-type .. 20.00
Man and Woman, Oriental. 3¾" high 15.00
Tomatoes in basket. Handled tray. 2½x4¼". 3 pieces 15.00

Shelf, Curio. 19" high. Black lacquered wood. Gold decoration .. 35.00
Smoke Set. Lighter, urn, tray. Silvered metal. 3 pieces 15.00
Tea Infuser. Teapot-shaped. Metal .. 5.00
Teapot. 5" high. Violets on white .. 30.00
Tea Set. Demi-size. Blue lustre ground. Handpainted decor. 16 pieces 60.00
Tobys
Happy Holligan. 5" 25.00
Indian Chief. 2¾" 16.50
Jailer, Full figure. 7½" 35.00
Lady, Full figure. 3¼" 12.50
Man, Full figure. 2¼" 12.50
Pirate. 3¼" 16.50

Tray. 5 x 8¼". Papier mache. Brown with multicolored handpainted flowers 7.50
Vases
3" Urn-shaped. Floral bouquets ... 5.00
6⅛". Ewer-type. Handpainted flowers in relief 15.00

Wall Pockets
Colonial Lady in balcony. 1½ x 2¾ x 4" high 12.00
Cuckoo Clock. 5". Orange lustre. Pine cone weights 10.00

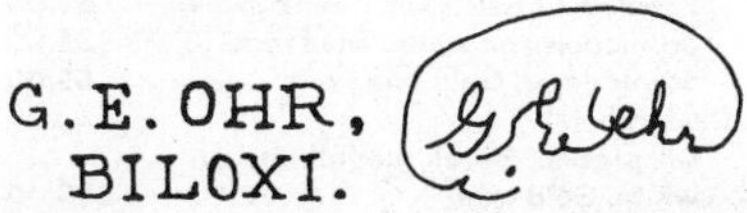

OHR POTTERY

Often a subject of controversy, Ohr pottery was produced by an authentic eccentric, George E. Ohr in Biloxi, Mississippi. There is some discrepancy as to when Ohr actually established his pottery. Biographers indicate 1878; but Ohr's autobiography indicates 1883. However, prior to 1884, Ohr had amassed 600 pieces of his work for an exhibition in that year.

A primary characteristic of Ohr's pottery is extremely thin walls often no thicker than an eggshell. Ohr's technique of twisting, crushing, folding, denting and crinkling clay into odd, grotesque and sometimes graceful wares . . . each completely unique . . .was ridiculed by the critics. They called him "The Mad Potter of Biloxi."

Critics of his day were considerably more enthusiastic about his use of glazes which were rich and varied. Ohr carefully signed all his work and most of it bears the town designation, either incised or impressed.

In 1906, Ohr closed the pottery and stored over 6,000 pieces as his legacy to his family. . .he believed it would be purchased someday by the U.S. Government. The entire collection remained in storage, undiscovered, until 1972. At this writing it has been reported that Ohr-type pottery is currently being produced.

Bank. 4½". Dome-shaped with finial. Tan. Unglazed ....$ 150.00
Bowls
4½x2" deep. Pinched. Blue mottled glaze 300.00
5½x3½" deep. Applied caterpillar. Mottled yellow and brown glaze 350.00
6x2¾" deep. Flat top. Green and brown mottled and speckled glaze 250.00

Chamberstick. 3¼x3¾". Cone-shaped with crimped rim. Gun metal and green glaze 250.00
Inkwells
Donkey's Head. 3x4½". Green glaze 350.00
Poem, Printing Press. 1½x2⅜x5". Yellow and green glaze 275.00
Shoe. 3". Mottled brown glaze .. 200.00
Symmetrical. 4⅜". Oxblood glaze. 225.00
Tiger's Head. 3½". Bright blue glaze 400.00

Mugs
4". Puzzle-type. Green mottled glaze 350.00
5½". Mottled gun metal and green glaze 225.00

Pitchers
3¾". Yellow and brown glaze .. 250.00
5½". Pinched sides, folded spout,

pleated horizontal handle. Deep blue glaze 375.00
Planter, Hanging. 3½x6½". Coiled snake inside. Mottled brown glaze exterior 450.00
Vases
- 3x3". Three horizontal ribs. Mottled black and red glaze 265.00
- 3¼x3¼". Two handled. Seaweed green, speckled with light green and orange 285.00
- 3¼x3½". Pinched rim, dimpled sides. Raspberry color glaze exterior, dark brown interior 300.00
- 3¼x5¼". Pleated and pinched. Dark brown glaze 300.00
- 5x4". Pleated rim. Dark brown glaze, speckled with yellow 350.00
- 5x4¾". Crimped. Dark blue green glaze. 500.00
- 5½x4⅛". Tan. Unglazed 195.00
- 7½x3½". Mustard glaze with brown spots. 500.00

OLD IVORY
84

OLD IVORY CHINA

This china derives its name from the ground color of the ware. The difference in patterns is indicated by a number on the base. It was made in Silesia, Germany in the latter part of the 1800's. Marked pieces usually bear the Crown Silesia mark.

Relish. 6¾". #15 ....$32.50

Berry Set. #63. 9½" bowl, six saucers. Set ....$ 250.00
Bowls
- 6". #200. Two handles 35.00
- 6½". #28, #69 .... 25.00
- 9¼". #113, #200 .... 75.00

Butter, Covered. #16 .... 150.00
Butter Pat. #11 .... 35.00
Chocolate Pot. #15, #18 .... 195.00
Chocolate Set. #16. Pot and 6 cups, saucers 450.00
Cookie Jar, Covered. #82 .... 225.00
Creamer. #15, #84 .... 50.00
Creamers and Sugars
- #10, #75 .... 85.00
- #69 .... 150.00
- #84 .... 150.00

Cups and Saucers. #7, #28, #200 40.00
Mustard, Covered. #84 .... 85.00
Plates
- 6". #10, #12, #15 .... 25.00
- 7½". #7, #16, #22 .... 30.00
- 10". Cake. #63. Open handles .. 75.00
- 11". Cake. #16. Open handles .. 100.00

Platter. 11½" long, 8¼" wide. #16. 95.00
Relishes
- 8". #75 .... 40.00
- 8¼". #16 .... 40.00

Sauce. #16 .... 18.50
Shakers, Salt and Pepper. #16. Set... 100.00
Sugar, Covered. #84, #200, #202... 95.00
Tea Tile. 6½". #15. Round 75.00
Toothpick. #16 .... 75.00

OLD PARIS CHINA

A number of French pottery and porcelain factories were situated in Paris during the 18th and 19th centuries. The finer porcelain products bore the generic name of Old Paris. The difference in the ware can be distinguished by the marks appearing under the glaze.

Bowl, Handled. 4½". With attached underplate. Pink rose decor on white ....$ 65.00
Box, Covered. 5x6". Handpainted floral decor 75.00
Busts. 11½". "Joy and Sorrow." White glaze. 19th century. Pair .. 250.00
Cake Plate. 9". Pedestaled. Floral border on white. Gold trim 75.00
Coffee Set. Pot, creamer, covered sugar. Gold trim. Set 150.00
Cups and Saucers
- Paneled. Cobalt. Gold lined cup ... 65.00
- Scenic decor on white. Gold trim ... 35.00
- Scenic decor. Gold lined cup 65.00

Dessert Sets
- 11 pieces. Floral medallions on white. Gold trim 350.00

Compote. 6¾ x 9¼" diam. Scalloped open edge top. Handpainted fruit decor on white. Gold trim $55.00

16 pieces. Brick red classical figures in reserves. Gold trim 400.00
Figurines
Boy and girl with boats. Oval bases. Pastel colors. 3½" high. Pair 250.00
Orangutans, Embracing. Gray and white. Porcelaine de Paris. Signed E. Sandoz. C. 1910 ...... 185.00
Pitchers
Milk. White. Gold trim 45.00
Water. White. Gold trim 85.00
Plaque. 12½" diam. Birds and foliage. Gold border 175.00
Plates
7". Floral decor in center. Scalloped border with gold scalloped rim 50.00
10". Fruit decor in center. Gold trim 75.00
Teapot. 8". Multicolored floral decor. Gold trim. Acorn finial 110.00
Vases, Urn-type
12½". Handpainted classical scenes in reserves. Late 19th century. Pair 500.00
13¾". White ground with chariots, horses and soldiers. Pink fluted rims. Pair 300.00
20". French blue. Vignettes. Early 19th century. Pair 950.00

OLD SLEEPY EYE

In the early 1900's, Sleepy Eye, Minnesota was the milling center of the world for production of flour in barrels. The town was named for Chief Sleepy Eye, a Sioux Indian. The pottery which is decorated with a likeness of Chief Sleepy Eye was made by Monmouth Pottery and Western Stoneware for inclusion as premiums in bags of Sleepy Eye flour. Although the pottery is the most collectible, other articles associated with the town and mill are also attracting Old Sleepy Eye collectors.

Pitcher. 6¼". Cobalt on cream. Indian head handle $150.00

Butter Crock ....$ 250.00
Centennial Items. C. 1972
Calendar 10.00
Coin. Official centennial issue ... 10.00
Newspaper. Sleepy Eye Herald Dispatch. 114 pages 15.00
Trivet 25.00
Cookbook 100.00
Pitchers
4". Cobalt on cream 75.00
4". Cobalt on gray 125.00
5½". Cobalt on cream. Indian head handle 95.00
6¼". Cobalt on cream. Indian head handle 150.00
8½". Cobalt on white. Indian head handle 185.00
Postcard 50.00
Salt Crock. 4" high, 6½" diam. Blue on gray. Marked "Old Sleepy Eye." 250.00
Stein. 7½" high. Indian head on handle. Signed "Old Sleepy Eye"... 250.00
Vases
8½". Cobalt on cream. Cattails and dragonflies 150.00
9". Cobalt on gray 300.00

ONION MEISSEN

Blue Onion or Bulb pattern is of Chinese origin and depicts peaches and pomegranates and not onions. It was originally made in the 18th century by the German Meissen factory, thus the name. . .Onion Meissen.

This popular pattern was made by several other factories in other countries; including England and Japan and is still in production today.

Onion Meissen is marked with the familiar Crossed Swords. Other makers marked their wares accordingly, and those made after 1891 with the country of origin.

Plate. 14" $85.00

Bowls
- 7" $35.00
- 9½" 65.00
- 11" 65.00

Butter, Covered. Rose finial 125.00
Candlestick. 10½" high 65.00
Cheese Dish, Covered 125.00
Coffee Pot. 9" high. Rose finial 125.00
Compote. 8¼x9" high 185.00
Cream and Sugar. Set 125.00

Creamers
- 3½" high 35.00
- 5½" high 48.50

Cruets. Oil and Vinegar. Pair 75.00

Cups and Saucers
- Bouillon 35.00
- Coffee 30.00
- Demitasse 30.00
- Tea 25.00

Egg Cup 25.00
Fruit Knives. Set of 6 .... 75.00
Grater. Vegetable. 5x9" 35.00
Gravy Boat. 10". With underplate ... 70.00
Invalid Feeder 20.00
Knife Rest 30.00
Match Holder 35.00
Meat Tenderizer. Wooden handle .. 32.50
Melon Mold. Handled 30.00
Mustard. 4¾" high. With ladle and underplate. Set 40.00
Pie Crust Crimper. Wooden handle... 22.50

Plates
- 6" 20.00
- 7½". Leaf-shaped 35.00
- 9" 40.00
- 9". Leaf-shaped 75.00
- 10". Soup 45.00
- 12" 60.00
- 14" 85.00
- 14". With hot water jacket 125.00

Platters
- 11" 85.00
- 15" 100.00
- 21" 175.00

Pot de Creme 45.00
Rolling Pin 45.00
Salt Box, Covered 65.00
Sauce. 5½" diam 20.00
Scoop. 9" long 35.00
Sugar, Covered 65.00
Teapot. 5¼" high 85.00
Tea Set. Teapot, creamer, covered sugar. Rose finials 195.00
Tea Strainer. Wooden handle 20.00
Tureen, Soup. 10½x14". Rose finial. 300.00
Vase. 5½" high. Spill-type. Scroll feet 60.00

Vegetable Dishes, Covered
- 8½" diam. 85.00
- 10". Square 125.00
- 14" diam. Divided 225.00

ONYX GLASS

Onyx glass is considered one of the most beautiful and valuable types of Victorian art glass. This rare glassware was produced in the 1890's in Findlay, Ohio by the Dalzell, Gilmore and Leighton Co. . .and is often called "Findlay Onyx." Onyx ware is plated or cased; and may consist of two or three layers of glass. The interior layer is generally an opaque white. Each of the succeeding layers are of similar color and in the end it may contain a variation of colors. There are five basic colors of onyx. . .however no two pieces have exactly the same coloring because of varied temperatures. Consequently; shades of Findlay onyx are often described as cream, rose, cranberry, raspberry and cinnamon.

Onyx was made for only a short time because of high production costs due to the fragility of the delicate glass.

Shakers, Salt and Pepper. 3" high. Cream. Pair $500.00

Bowl. 8". Cream ....$	400.00
Butter, Covered. Raspberry	750.00
Celery. 6½" high. Cream	375.00
Creamers	
Cinnamon	800.00
Cream	450.00
Shakers, Salt and Pepper. 3" high.	
Cream. Pair	500.00
Spooners	
Cream. 4½" high. Fluted rim	275.00
Raspberry	375.00
Sugar, Covered. Cream	500.00
Sugar Shaker. Original top. Cream...	450.00
Syrup Jug. 7" high. Original lid.	
Cream	450.00
Toothpicks	
Cream	200.00
Raspberry	500.00
Tumbler. Cream	300.00

OPALESCENT GLASS

Opalescent glass is a clear or colored glass with milky white decorations. When held to the light, the whitened portions show a fiery or opalescent quality. . .thus the name. The glass falls into two basic categories. . .blown or mold blown such as Coin Spot and Spanish Lace and pressed pattern glass such as Hobnail. On blown items, the pattern is made up in white. On pressed glass pieces, the opalescent effect is found on the embossed and rim edges. Novelties, Corn Vase, Pump and Trough, and Cabbage Leaf made of opalescent glass are listed as a separate category but are pressed glass. Their main distinction is that they were only made in one unique form and never a complete table set as in other pressed patterns. Opalescent glass was produced in England in the 1870's. It gained wide popularity here in America at the turn of the 20th century. It was made by several glass companies, including the early Boston and Sandwich Glass Company. Opalescent glass is currently being produced but very few of the items should be called reproductions, because many of the 'new' patterns were not originally produced in opalescent.

Also see "Colored Glass Section" for additional pressed glass patterns.

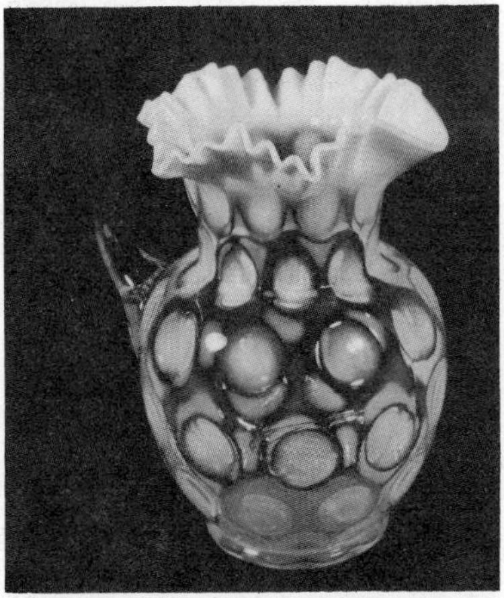

Pitcher, Water. "Coin Spot." Ruffled rim. White. Blown $100.00

Tie Backs. 4½" diam. 6 petal flower. Pair $50.00

Blown

Bowls	
Coin Spot. Cranberry. 9½" ....$	75.00
Seaweed. White. 9"	50.00

Butters, Covered	
Seaweed. Cranberry	250.00
Swirl. Cranberry. Crystal base	200.00
Celerys	
Lattice. Cranberry	85.00
Seaweed. Blue	95.00
Swirl. Cranberry	95.00
Cruets	
Coin Spot. Cranberry	75.00
Daisy and Fern. Blue	85.00
Finger Bowl. Spanish Lace. Blue	35.00
Pitchers, Syrup	
Coin Spot. Cranberry	85.00
Lattice. White	70.00
Reverse Swirl. Yellow	125.00
Spanish Lace. Blue	75.00
Stripe. Blue	75.00
Pitchers, Water	
Coin Spot. Ruffled rim. Blue	100.00
Coin Spot. Ruffled rim. Cranberry	125.00
Poinsettia. Bulbous. Blue	150.00
Reverse Swirl. Yellow	175.00
Seaweed. Blue	275.00
Spanish Lace. Ruffled rim. Blue	250.00
Spanish Lace. White	125.00
Swirl. Bulbous. Ruffled top. Cranberry	150.00
Swirl. Square top. Blue	125.00
Rose Bowls	
Daisy and Fern. Blue	40.00
Seaweed. Yellow	50.00
Spanish Lace. Yellow	60.00
Salt Shaker. Seaweed. Cranberry	35.00
Sugar Shakers	
Coin Spot. Cranberry	75.00
Lattice. Blue	65.00
Toothpick. Lattice. White	35.00
Tumblers	
Coin Spot. Cranberry	40.00
Coin Spot. White	25.00
Poinsettia. Blue	35.00
Reverse Swirl. Cranberry	50.00
Spanish Lace. Cranberry	35.00
S-Repeat. Blue	45.00
Stripe. Blue	28.00

Novelties

Cabbage Leaf. Blue	75.00
Corn. 8". Blue	100.00
"Pump and Trough." Pump, 7" high. Trough, 5" long. Blue. Pair	165.00

Pressed

Berry Sets	
Drapery. Blue. 7 pieces	300.00
Regal. Green. 7 pieces	225.00
Wreath and Shell. White. 4 pieces	95.00
Bowls	
Drapery. Blue. 8½x4" deep	65.00
Hobnail. White. 6". Ruffled top	65.00
Hobnail. Blue. 9½"	85.00
Many Loops. Blue. 6¼"	30.00
Butters, Covered	
Hobnail. Blue	100.00
Hobnail. White	85.00
Wreath and Shell. Yellow	165.00
Celerys	
Beatty Rib. White	27.50
Wreath and Shell. Green	95.00
Compotes, Jelly	
Argonaut Shell. Blue	65.00
Everglades. Blue	125.00
Intaglio. Yellow	35.00
Swag and Bracket. White	50.00
Creamers and Sugars	
Beatty Rib. Blue	150.00
Drapery. Blue	150.00
Fluted Scroll. Blue	150.00
Hobnail. Blue	150.00
Hobnail. White	100.00
Cuspidor. Wreath and Shell. Blue	95.00
Pitchers, Water	
Drapery. Blue	225.00
Intaglio. Blue	265.00
Puff Jar. Fluted Scroll. White	65.00
Rose Bowl. Beaded Swag. Green	50.00
Salt Dips	
Beatty Rib. Blue	40.00
Wreath and Shell. White	55.00
Sauces	
Drapery. White	20.00
Everglades. White	28.00
Intaglio. Blue	25.00
Spooners	
Fluted Scrolls. Blue	55.00
Hobnail. White	35.00
Intaglio. Blue	65.00
Wreath and Shell. Yellow	85.00
Toothpicks	
Beatty Rib. Blue	35.00
Hobnail. White	20.00
Tumblers	
Drapery. White	25.00
Hobnail. Blue	35.00
Hobnail. White	28.50
Hobnail. Yellow	50.00

OPALINE GLASS

Opaline or Opal glass was a popular mid-to-late 19th century European glass. The glass has a certain amount of translucency. The finished wares were often decorated with painted enamels and trimmed in gold.

Bottles, Perfume	
5" high. White. Gold trim	$ 55.00
7" high. Blue. Gold trim. In Art Nouveau-style metal holder	75.00
Bowls	
8x2" deep. Rose coloring	35.00

Mug. 4". French $90.00

10x1½" deep. Flared. Pink. Gold trim 75.00
Box. 2" diam. Raised enamel flowers on white 35.00
Cheese Dish. White with enamel decor in gold 175.00
Cruet. Applied handle. Aqua. Gold trim 85.00
Cup and Saucer. Green 50.00
Finger Bowl. With underplate. Blue .. 50.00
Goblets
- 5". White 25.00
- 7". Blue 30.00

Lamp Base. 12" high. White. French .. 95.00
Mug. White. Enameled florals. Gold trim 40.00
Pitcher. 7". Pink. Applied handle .. 125.00
Vases
- 6". Globular body, slender neck. Pink. Yellow flowers, green leaves, butterflies 85.00
- 6¾". Mauve. Gold rims. French. Pair 150.00
- 8". Jack-in-the-Pulpit. White 150.00
- 9½". Bulbous. Handpainted peacock, flowers. Beaded pedestaled base. Gold trim 165.00
- 11". Footed. White. Pale green turned down rim 150.00
- 16". Blue. Quilted 175.00

ORIENTALIA

Orientalia is a 'coined' term which is applied to articles made in Asia, especially eastern Asia which includes China and Japan.

The following list is comprised mainly of items (made for export) which do not have a specific category in this guide. Also see: "Canton", "Nanking", "Rose Medallion", "Japanese Prints" and other categories of oriental interest.

Rooster. 10". Chinese brass. 16th century. Signed $2500.00

Table. 30½ x 41½ x 59½". Mahogany. Highly carved. Close Up Of One End. 20th century $1000.00

Mug. 4½". Chinese Export. Floral decor on white. 18th century $250.00

Bottle. 7½". Decor of muted green and purple scenes. Irregular-shape. Chinese ....$ 150.00

Bowls

8¾". Pink decor on white ground. Lowestoft-type 350.00

10". Handled. Diaper pattern. Garden scenes in reserves 450.00

Cache Pot. 6". Hexagonal-shape. Footed. Handpainted blue oriental scenes. Chinese 125.00

Costume. Silk and brocade with embroidery. Pants, coat, overshirt .. 500.00

Creamer. 4". Helmet-shape. Lowestoft-type decor 195.00

Cups and Saucers, Handleless

Geometric border with basket of flowers in center. Lowestoft-type .. 175.00

Horn of Plenty decor. Wide pink border. Lowestoft-type 125.00

Desk Set. Brass. Engraved tray. Letter opener, blotter, 3½" lined wooden box. Set 125.00

Figurines

Buddha, Seated. 16". Lotus blossom base. Chinese Export porcelain 195.00

Horse. 10x13". Brass. Marked .. 185.00

Sage, Holding Child. 24". Enameled. Chinese Export porcelain 200.00

Temple Dog. 10½". Standing on plinth. Chinese Export porcelain ... 195.00

Furniture

Chair, Side. Rosewood. Solid back panel with bird and flower branch carvings 400.00

Chest, Camphor. 19x22x40". Black lacquered. MOP figures in relief. Brass straps and locks 1000.00

Chest, Camphor. 20x22x42". Figures and scenes. Highly carved . 750.00

Desk, Slant top-type. 42" wide, 22" depth, 47½" high. Carved. Scroll work 500.00

Table. 16" high x 12" top diam. Garden Seat-shape. Mahogany with porcelain insert. 250.00

Table. 16" high x 31" diam. Red and black lacquer. Figures and scrollwork decor 500.00

Table. 26" diam. top. Brass lift off tray. Folding type. Turned wooden trestle base. India. 150.00

Table. 29x50". Rectangular. Carved, pierced. 1500.00

Table. 30½x41½x59½" long. Heavy carved legs. Trestle platform base. 4 concealed drawers. 1000.00

Table. 33½x50" long. Top with blue and white porcelain insert. Straight legs, carved feet 2500.00

Ginger Jars

5" high. White porcelain. Handpainted ladies, gentlemen, horses. Pair 200.00

8¾" high. Predominately green and red decor on white ground. C. 1820. Pair 450.00

9" high. Blue and white. Teak tops. Chinese Export porcelain. Pair 175.00

9" high. Famille Jaune. Insects and flowers in reds and blues .. 300.00

12" high. Peacock, floral branch design on white ground. Polychrome. Chinese 350.00

14½" high. "Prunus." Blue and white 375.00

Incense Burner. 9½". Brass. On 4 legs. Animal decor 175.00

Lamps, Marriage

10½" high. Eggshell porcelain with varied polychrome diaper pattern rims. Two dragons in midst of flames and clouds. C. 1900 .... 500.00

13¼" high. Reticulated porcelain. Famille Jaune 1250.00

Mugs

Diaper pattern top and bottom. Black and gold florals. Lowestoft-type. 85.00

Pewter with engraved dragons.

Glass bottom. Chinese 250.00

Picnic Box. 3-tier. Brass carrier. Handles on each flowered level. Famille Jaune. C. 1800. Chinese .. 350.00

Platter. 11½". Octagonal. Red and purple decor on white ground. Ochre trim. Lowestoft-type 350.00

Printing Set. Hand carved wood. 100 pcs. Chinese. 175.00

Rice Mold. 13½ l. x 2" w. x 1½" deep. Wood. Chinese 85.00

Rice Pot, Covered. 4½ x 6 x 6". 4 post legs. Geometric decor. Jade finial. Chinese. C. 1700's 225.00

Robe. Mandarin. Gold. 19th century 500.00

Table Screen. 19x29". Needlework in MOP inlaid teak frame. 19th century 300.00

Tea Caddy. 6". Porcelain. Gold flowers. Pewter lined 125.00

Teapots

4". Lotus Blossom decor. Lowestof t type 300.00

6". Rice pattern. Blue and white. Bamboo handle and spout. 20th century 65.00

8". Brown stoneware in form of Buddha. Unglazed. C. 1840 .... 350.00

Textile. Embroidery. 9x21½". Multicolored flowers and butterfly on silver gray silk background. Magenta turquoise and black border. 450.00

Tureen. 8½ x 13". Blue and white. Rabbit handles. Chinese Export porcelain 950.00

Vases

4 x 4" diam. 2 handles. Floral decor. Lowestoft-type 175.00

12". Jaune. White flowers. Early 19th century. Chinese Export 425.00

Wedding Box. 11 x 15½ x 25". Leather. Original hardware. Handpainted flowers, birds. Polychrome. Chinese 225.00

Weed Bottle. 3½". Porcelain. Gourd-shape. Tea dust decor 350.00

ORIENTAL RUGS

The history of these rugs or carpets dates 3000 B.C.; but it was in the 16th century that they became prevalent.

Commonly referred to as "Orientals" because of their origin from regions east of Europe comprised of central Asia, Iran (Persia), Caucasus and Anatolia; these rugs can be classified into basic categories of Iranian, Caucasian, Turkoman, Turkish and Chinese. Later; India, Pakistan and Iraq produced similar rugs after the fashion of the Persians, Chinese and Turks.

The pattern name is derived from the tribes or people of these regions who produced the rugs. For example. . .from Iran we have the designs of Hamadan, Herez, Sarouk, Tabriz and others. When evaluating any oriental carpet; design, color, weave, weight and age must be taken into consideration. These same factors will also determine condition and hence the final value. This list is comprised of commonly found semi-antique rugs in good condition.

Balouchi, Prayer. 2' 10" x 3'6". C. 1915. Excellent condition $625.00

THE PRICES GIVEN ARE APPROXIMATE AND CALCULATED ON A PER SQUARE FOOT BASIS.

Afghan ....$ 30.00
Baktiari 25.00
Baluchistan 20.00
Bergamo 50.00
Bidjar 35.00
Cabistan 50.00
Dagestan 75.00
Ersari 40.00
Fereghan 35.00

Genje. 3'6" x 9'7". 19th century. Excellent condition $3450.00

Ghiordes, Prayer	100.00
Hamadan	40.00
Herez	125.00
Kashan, Silk	750.00
Kashan, Wool	200.00
Kazak	100.00
Kilim, Caucasian	75.00
Kilim, Turkish	50.00
Kirman	100.00
Kuba	40.00
Peking	100.00
Salor	50.00
Saraband	75.00
Sarouk	175.00
Senna	300.00
Shiraz	50.00
Shirvan	40.00
Tabriz, Silk	350.00
Tabriz, Wool	
Animaliers	100.00
Geometric	50.00
Hunting Scenes	400.00
Tekke	30.00
Tientsin	30.00
Yomut	35.00

OWENS POTTERY

ART POTTERY

J.B. Owens began making pottery in 1885 near Roseville, Ohio. In 1891, he built a plant in Zanesville and in 1897 began producing art pottery. In 1907, Owens added a floor and wall tile business and that segment of the company was called Zanesville Tile Co. Art pottery production continued after 1907; but with total emphasis on making only the highest quality artware, which was designated "Owens Art." Owens firm failed in the "crash" of 1929.

Due to the many artists and chemists employed by J. B. Owens, the Owens art pottery has no general characteristic other than specific glazes used on certain lines. Some of these lines are easily recognized even if they are unmarked. Much of the Owens pottery is marked, often artist signed; and the names of the various lines including "Utopian," are found impressed sometimes without the Owens name or mark.

Vase. 7" "Utopian." 3 handles. Vintage decor. Artist signed $150.00

Candlestick. 7". Utopian. Berry and leaf decor ....$ 65.00

Jardiniere. 8½ x 10". Ruffled rim.

Brown and gray matte glaze.
Tulip decor 165.00

Lamp. 4 x 9" high. Utopian. Pansy decor 150.00

Mug. 5" high. Utopian. Berries and leaves 95.00

Pitchers

6". Bulbous. Utopian. Floral decor . 95.00

7½". Lotus. Bird decor. Artist signed 250.00

10½". Utopian. Green matte glaze. Molded grapes and leaves .. 135.00

12". Tankard-shaped. Utopian. Cherry decor. Artist signed 175.00

Vases

4". Lotus. Clover decor on shaded green to pink ground 125.00

4¾". Aborigine. Matte green glaze 80.00

5". Pillow-shaped. Stick-type neck. Utopian. Rust and green foliage. Artist signed 125.00

7". Bottle-shaped. Utopian. Rose decor 150.00

8". Lotus. Fruit decor. Artist signed 225.00

8¼". Handled. Owens Art. Green 80.00

10½". Utopian. Cattails 165.00

Water Set. 12" pitcher, four mugs. Utopian. Current decor. Artist signed 500.00

PADLOCKS

Padlock collecting has become one of the fastest growing hobbies in America. Numerous people are collecting old locks not only for nostalgia and signs of the past; but are intrigued with the mechanisms. . .from simple designs to ingenious and elaborate works of art.
Although all padlocks have one basic function . . . security; they were made in numerous varieties. In a span of over 100 years, approximately 75 American manufacturers have been recorded. Some makers listed hundreds of types in production at one given time.

Brass Tumblers

A. E. Dietz. "252." 2¾" ....$ 8.50

A. & W. Co. 3⅛" 15.00

Eagle. 3¼" 8.00

Mallory Wheeler & Co. 2½" 5.00

Safe. 2½" 6.50

Winchester. 3" 25.00

Chain. Sargent. "Traveler's." 2". Brass 10.00

Chinese (Sliding-type)

Engraved. 3" long. Oriental or floral designs 10.00

Plain. 4" long. Brass 7.50

Combinations

Gougler Keyless. 3". Zinc alloy .. 1.50

W. A. Harrison, Inc. "Insurance

Railroad. Adlake. NWRR. Switch-type. Brass complete with chain $28.00

Lock." 2½". Brass 10.00

Miller

2". Four lettered brass cylinder dial, iron frame. Changeable-type 25.00

3". Pat. Nov. 29, 1910. Nickel-plated steel 2.00

Gate

Hand forged steel. Various sizes and shapes. Common variety .. 20.00

Hand wrought iron. Various sizes and shapes. American. 18th century 150.00

Kit Bag. 5" long. Brass 10.00

Levers (Push Key)

Eagle. "Favorite." 2½". Brass 7.50

Miller. "Champion." 2". 4-lever. Brass. 5.00

Yale. 2⅞". Steel 2.50

Levers (Six and Eight)

Six

Edwards, Pat. mark. Steel 5.00

Sargent. Steel 1.50

Winchester. Steel. Early 1900's 20.00

Eight

Armory. Steel. Early 1900's 6.00

Corbin. Samson. Brass 8.50

Eagle. Mammoth.

Brass 8.50

Steel 6.50

Levers (Wrought Iron)

Davenport, Mallory & Co. 3¼". Barrel key-type 6.50

Mallory Wheeler & Co. 3½" 6.50

Mallory Wheeler & Co. 3½". Flat

double key-type 8.50
Sargent & Co. 3½". Flat-key-type... 6.50
United States. 3½". Barrel key-type 7.50

Pin Tumblers
Corbin. 3". Steel with brass cylinder 3.00
Sargent. 3". Brass 4.00
Segal. 4". Brass. Rotating bolt-type 10.00
Yale. "USN." 2". Brass. Push key-type 5.00
Zeiss Ikon. 3". Brass 4.00

Railroad
Adlake. "Union Pacific." 3½". Brass. Switch-type 15.00
Dayton Mfg. Co. "A & V." 3½". Brass. Shank key-type 20.00
Shank key-type 20.00
Slaymaker. "Pan Handle." 3½". Brass 12.50

Yale
"PRR." 3". Brass. Signal 10.00
"Sante Fe." 3". Steel 6.50

Scandinavian (Barrel, Jail or Store)
J.H.W. Climax Co. 2½". Iron 6.00
Fraim. 2¼". Iron 8.50
Russel & Erwin Co. "USA" 2½". Iron 8.50
Star
¾". Nickelplated brass 2.50
3¾". Rectangular keyhole. Iron . 20.00
*Screw Key. Various sizes and shapes. Hand forged steel 10.00

*Reproduced Item

PAIRPOINT

In 1880, Pairpoint Manufacturing Co. was organized as a silverplating firm in New Bedford, Mass. The company merged with Mt. Washington Glass Co. in 1894 and became known as Pairpoint Corporation. The new company produced specialty glass items, often accented with metal frames. Pairpoint Corp. was sold in 1938 and Robert Gunderson became manager; and it operated until his death in 1952 as Gunderson Glass Works. Robert Bryden became manager of Pairpoint-Gunderson Glass Works until its closing in 1957. In 1970, Bryden reopened the factory of Cape Cod under the famous Pairpoint name. In 1978, Pairpoint Glass Company returned to its New Bedford birthplace.

Biscuit Jars
Green. Etched vintage decor. Silverplated frame ....$ 225.00
Yellow. Floral decor. Reticulated silverplated frame 250.00
Bowl. 11 x 3½". Leaf shape. Full bodied squirrel. Silverplated. Gold wash interior 175.00

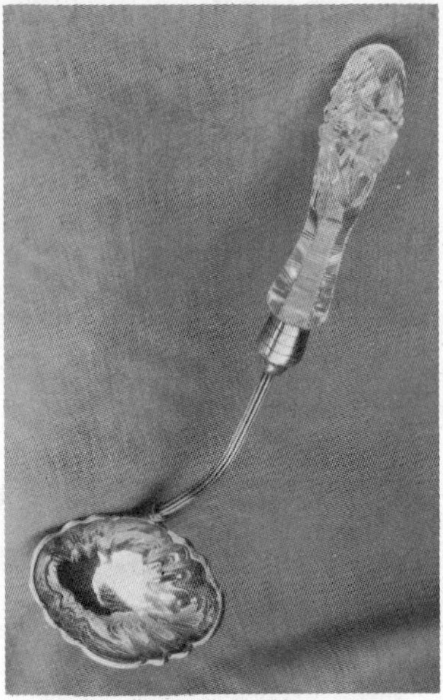

Punch Ladle. 14" long. Silver with cut glass handle. Mkd. Pairpoint Mfg. Co $350.00

Box. 6" diam. Beige ribbed opal glass with enamel decor. Footed silver body 175.00
Butter, Covered. With knife rest. Silverplated 125.00
Candlesticks
4½". Amethyst with crystal bubble-ball stem. Mushroom-shaped top 50.00
11½". Amber. Crystal bubble-ball stems. Bell-shaped bases. Pair 175.00
Champagne. 5½". "Flambo." Crystal 50.00
Compotes
6 x 6" high. Crystal. Etched leaf and floral decor on underside .. 85.00
7" high. Amber. Bubble-ball stem . 125.00
7x8½" diam. "Wexford." 135.00
Console Sets
Bowl 9½", lamps 16¾" high. With coralene shades. C. 1900-20. Signed 500.00
Bowl 14", candlesticks 12". Light green with bubble-ball stems. Cut

and etched vintage decor 350.00
Inkwell. 2¾" diam. Crystal. Paperweight-type. Hinged lid 35.00
Ladle, Punch. 14". Silver with cut glass handle 350.00
Lamps
7". Blownout flowers on shade. Tree trunk base 895.00
14". Blownout roses on shade. Tree trunk base 2500.00
Mustache Cup and Saucer. Quadruple silverplate. Hand engraved 125.00
Plateau Mirror. Baroque silverplated base. Beveled mirror 125.00
Shakers, Salt and Pepper. Eggs, Flattened. Opaque white glass. Handpainted florals. Pair 50.00
Shaving Mug. Silverplated. Engraved florals. Lift-out soap insert 85.00
Sherbet. With underplate. "Flambo." 125.00
Vases
8". Goblet-shape. Cobalt. Crystal bubble-ball stem 75.00
8⅝". Bud. Iridescent amber. Silver holder. Signed "P". C. 1895 .... 275.00
12". Trumpet-shape. Crystal bubble-ball stem 150.00

PAISLEY SHAWLS

(See "Textiles")

PAPERWEIGHTS

Although paperweights had their origin in ancient Egypt; it was in the mid 19th century that this art form reached its zenith. The classic period for paperweights was 1845-55 in France where the Clichy, Baccarat and Saint Louis factories produced the finest examples of this art. Other weights, made in England, Italy and Bohemia during this period and later in America, rarely match the quality of the French weights. Popularity peaked during this classic period and faded toward the end of the 19th century.

Paperweights were rediscovered nearly a century later in the mid 1900's. Contemporary weights are still made by Baccarat, Saint Louis, Perthshire and by many studio craftsmen in the U.S. and Europe.

Some collectors prefer to limit their collections to antique weights while others collect both contemporary and earlier editions. . .fine examples are available in both areas. Today, interest in paperweights is greater than ever and values have increased enormously.

Baccarat
Clemantis. Two buds, 7 green leaves ....$ 1000.00

Baccarat. Modern. Strawberry. Marked and dated $450.00

Millefiori Concentric 350.00
Millefiori Close Pac. Signed "B" 1848 .... 1000.00
Pansy. One bud 500.00
Rock. Faceted 175.00
Baccarat. Modern
American Beauty. Star cut base .. 500.00
Frog. Signed, dated, no'd 450.00
Garlands. Canes, ringlets, etc .. 175.00
L'Escargot. Limited edition 600.00
Strawberry 450.00
Zodiac. Complete with all signs .. 300.00
Zodiac. Individual signs 85.00
Baccarat. Modern. (Sulphides)
Bonaparte, Napoleon. Regular .. 75.00
Henry, Patrick. Regular 100.00
Jackson, President. Green base. Regular 100.00
Kennedy, John F. White overlay .. 850.00
Pope Pius XII. Regular 175.00
Pope Pius XII. Star cut base 400.00
Truman, Harry S. Faceted 100.00
Banfords
Bluebird on cat tail 225.00
Clemantis, Two. Faceted 350.00
Floral. Eight flowers, various colors. Faceted 1000.00
Roses. Three pink on yellow ground 300.00
Boston and Sandwich
Nosegay. Latticinio ground 500.00
Red poinsettia on blue and white ground. 19th century 850.00
Clichy
End-of-Day. With rose 300.00
Garland, Looped. Emerald ground.. 950.00
Millefiori. Scattered canes on clear. 500.00
Millefiori. Spaced canes on latticinio 850.00
Rose. Pink canes on clear 750.00
Swirl. Center cane 600.00
Swirl. Center cane. Miniature 850.00

D'Albert. (Sulphides)
- Audubon, John. Regular 75.00
- Hemingway. Regular 75.00
- Kennedy, J.F. Overlay 250.00
- Kennedy, J.F. and wife. Regular 85.00
- King, Martin Luther. Regular 125.00
- Lind, Jenny. Regular 75.00
- MacArthur. Overlay 195.00
- Roosevelt, F.D. Overlay 195.00
- Schweitzer, Albert. Overlay 200.00
- Twain, Mark. Overlay 200.00

Gillinder & Sons. 5¼" oval. Camphor glass. Memorial Hall 350.00

Kaziun
- Millefiori. Spaced concentric motif. Faceted. Signed "K" 1000.00
- Rose, Classic 850.00
- Rose, Stylized with canes. Signed "K" 500.00

Lundberg
- Angelfish. Cased 100.00
- Butterfly 65.00
- Butterfly. Cased 85.00
- Fighting Fish. Cased. Limited edition 150.00
- Moon and Stars 65.00
- Orchid. Cased. Limited edition .. 150.00
- Seahorse 65.00

Orient and Flume 95.00

Pairpoint
- Spiral. Red, white, blue. Paper label 85.00
- Swan. 6½" high. Amethyst. Original label 195.00

Perthshire
- Butterfly. Double overlay. Miniature 225.00
- Christmas Holly 275.00
- Christmas Rose 175.00
- Damson Plum. Strawberry cut base 250.00
- Millefiori
  - End-of-Day 85.00
  - Formal Garden 150.00
  - Nosegay. Four flowers on latticinio 200.00
  - Star-shaped pattern 85.00
- Ribbon. Red, blue on white latticinio 150.00

St. Louis
- Camomile with bud. Four leaves. Set on pink latticinio ground 2750.00
- Crown Weight. Two colorful twists radiating from central cane 1750.00
- Dahlia. Full bloom. Deep pink .. 1850.00
- End-of-Day. Typical canes 175.00
- Millefiori. Mushroom. Concentric canes 1850.00
- Nosegay. Crystal. Overall faceting 600.00
- Pom-Pom. Pink. With striped bud and green leaves. Clear crystal carpet 950.00

St. Louis. Modern
- American Eagle. Double overlay .. 300.00
- Bouquet, Upright. Double overlay . 2500.00
- Mushroom. Double overlay. Blue .. 1200.00
- Roses. Yellow. With bud, long-stemmed. Blue carpet 375.00
- Washington, George. Regular .. 375.00

Stankard
- Anthony's Fire. Single flower 300.00
- Bouquet. Full 650.00
- Meadowreath. Yellow. Faceted .. 375.00
- Wild Rose. Single flower 350.00

Steuben
- 3½". Pear. Clear 150.00
- 4½". Apple 150.00

Ysart
- Butterfly. On latticinio ground .. 350.00
- Ducks and Flower 350.00
- Fishes, Tropical 400.00
- Flowers, Stylized. Opaque pink ground 350.00

Miscellaneous

Advertising
- Acorn Gas Stoves. Cast iron 10.00
- National Cash Register. 3". Cast iron 35.00
- RCA Victor Dog. Metal. Marble base 35.00
- Royal Crown Cola. Metal. C. 1938 . 7.50
- Scranton Steel and Iron Works. Photo in glass 20.00

Apple. Applied leaves and stem. St. Claire 30.00

Bear, Standing. Snow-type 18.50

Bell. 3". Brass 15.00

B.P.O.E. Sulphide. Elk's head and lettering 150.00

Chicago World's Fair. Hall of Science. Glass 35.00

Cowboy Hat. Brass 35.00

Cut Glass. 1¾" cube 30.00

Flower Sprays, 3-tiered. Magnum .. 85.00

F.O.E. Red, white, blue eagle. Magnum 50.00

Fort Dearborn. 1933 World's Fair .. 22.50

Gibson Girl. 4". Intaglio cut and frosted 75.00

Holy Bible. 3½ x 4". Brass 30.00

Home Sweet Home. 4". Multicolored glass 45.00

Kangaroo. 3". Bronze 75.00

Lincoln, Abe. In relief. Mosaic Tile Co. 35.00

Moses in Bulrushes. Frosted oval-shape. C. 1876 .... 85.00

Pig, Sitting. 1¼x3". Cast iron 17.50

Pittsburgh Exposition. 1912. Glass .. 45.00

Plymouth Rock. 1876 .... 85.00

Remember Father and Mother 50.00

Snowman. Snow-type 18.50
Telephone. 3½". Cobalt. Solid glass 30.00
Whitefriars. 76 Bicentennial. English 450.00
Wig Stand. 11¼" high. Multicolored glass. Cone-shaped, circular base. English 300.00

PAPIER-MACHE

The literal translation of the French term "chewed paper"...papier mache is a mixture of ground paper, glue, resin and fine sand which is subjected to great pressure; then dried. The finished product is tough, durable and heat resistant. Various finishing treatments were used...lacquers, japanning, painting, enameling and inlaying with mother-of-pearl. Papier-mache articles such as boxes, trays and tables were in high fashion during the Victorian era.

Bank. 2 x 3 x 4¾" long. Black with oriental decor in red and gold ..$60.00

Basket. 10" diam. Brass handle, MOP inlay. Signed Jennens. C. 1860 ....$ 125.00
Bell. 4" 12.00
Boxes
- 1x2" diam. Silvered lid 25.00
- 1x1½x3". MOP inlay 25.00
- 3x4x10". MOP inlay 45.00

Chicken. Life size 100.00
Dog, Bull. 25" 75.00
Eagle. 11" high. 15" wingspread .. 150.00
Easter Egg. Candy container-type. Germany 17.50
Eyeglass Case. Metal trim 20.00
Funnel. 11" 25.00
Inkwell. 6½x8½". MOP trim 20.00
Lap Desk. 9½x11½". MOP inlay. Red velvet interior 125.00
Owl. 16" high 100.00
Pail, Water. Dated 1883 .... 50.00
Pitcher. 5½" 35.00
Plaque. 20" diam. Handpainted portrait of dog 50.00
Plate. 10½". Oriental design in gold and red on black 45.00
Ram. 8½x11" long. Spring legs. Beige with orange spots 40.00
Spill Holder. Floral decor 30.00
Tables
- Tier, Two. 12" top, 14" bottom. 3 bamboo-style legs. Black with chrysanthemum decor 225.00
- Tilt-top. 22x26x28". MOP inlay .. 275.00

Tea Caddy. 6x8". Black with gold and MOP inlay 250.00
Trays
- 10x12". Handled. Grape decor .. 150.00
- 10x17". Floral decor 175.00
- 12" diam. Chippendale-style. Birds, flowers, MOP inlay 200.00

Watch Holder. 4x7". Brass feet 50.00

PARIAN WARE

Parian ware is a true hard-paste porcelain known as biscuit ware; because of the lack of glaze except occasionally for the inside of pitchers or vases. Parian ware resembled white Italian marble and is sometimes referred to as "Parian Marble". Blue, rose and green were often used to tint the pure white body.

Thomas Minton is credited with perfecting Parian in England around 1845, and other Staffordshire potters produced similar ware. Bennington Pottery in Vermont is famous for Parian ware which was popular in America from 1860 until the turn of the century.

Biscuit Jar. 8". Metal lid, rim and bail. Molded florals ....$ 150.00
Bowl. 4½". Pond Lily 35.00
Boxes
- Snuff. Portrait of Lafayette. 19th century 125.00
- Trinket. Molded florals 25.00

Busts
- Beethoven. 8" 65.00
- Dante. 5" 45.00
- Dickens. 6¼" 60.00
- Edward VIII. 8". Robinson and Ledbetter 175.00
- Enid. 11". Signed Copeland 195.00
- Lincoln. 9". 19th century 85.00
- Queen Mary, King George. 5". Pair 50.00
- Scott, Sir Walter. 12" 85.00
- Shakespeare. 7½" 100.00
- Venus De Milo. 8" 85.00
- Washington, George. 9" 100.00

Cream and Sugar. Pond Lily 125.00
Creamers
- Cow 35.00
- Squirrel 30.00

Cup and Saucer. Pond Lily 55.00

Vase. 9" high. Hand-shaped . . $150.00

Figurines
- Boy and girl. 9". Pair 100.00
- Dorothea and Glorinda. 14". John Bell, Minton. C. 1868. Pair 550.00
- Girl in plumed hat. 10" 75.00
- Girl. Kneeling in prayer with open book. 9" 65.00
- Girls. One holding sheaf of wheat, other holding pitcher. 13". Pair 150.00
- Hen. 7". 19th century 125.00
- Horses. 5". On bases. Pair 100.00
- Lady and gentleman. 18th century dress. Tinted. 9". Pair 150.00
- Maidenhood. 18". Copeland 275.00
- Red Riding Hood and Wolf. 7". Tinted 85.00
- Rock of Ages. 13" 85.00

Pitchers
- 6½". Molded florals 40.00
- 7½". Classic figures in relief 75.00
- 11½". "American Independence" and "Mother" 200.00

Plate. 8". Pond Lily 50.00

Ring Tree. 6" high. Hand-shaped .. 50.00

Syrup Jug. 9". Bulbous. Paneled. Applied head of Norseman. Silverplated handle, lid 85.00

Tumbler. 4". Classic figures 25.00

Vases
- 4½ x 7". Cornucopia-shape. Cherubs standing on pillow base... 85.00
- 8¼". Vintage decor in relief 65.00
- 9". Hand-shape. Scenic medallion. 19th century 150.00

PASTILLE BURNERS

(See "Staffordshire Items")

PATE DE VERRE

Pate de Verre, translated "glass paste", is a molded glass form. Lead glass is ground into powder or crystal and then made into paste by adding a 2 or 3% solution of sodium silicate . . . the resulting mixture can be molded, fired and carved. Known to the Egyptians as early as 1500 B.C., this type of glass had its "on and off" periods of popularity through the centuries. In the late 19th and early 20th centuries, Pate de Verre was revived by glassmakers in France such as Cros, Dammouse and Daum Brothers. Contemporary artists have rediscovered this form as a medium for sculpturing.

Atomizer. 4". Turquoise with brown pine cones. "A. Walter, Nancy." $ 750.00

Bowls
- 3x 1½" deep. Cream and yellow with orange sunflower. Rayed interior. "A. Walter, Nancy." 500.00
- 3¼ x 2" deep. Scarabs, leaves and flowers. "Daum Nancy." 500.00
- 5½ x 2½" deep. Octagonal. Green and brown. "Decor chemont." 750.00
- 6". Shallow. Bacchus in relief. "A. Walter, Nancy." 2000.00

Box. 3 x 3". Violet decor. "G. Argy Rousseau" 1000.00

Compote. 1⅝ x 4" diam. Berries in relief. "G. Argy Rousseau." 650.00

Figurines
- Frog. 1¾". Green. "A. Walter, Nancy." 600.00
- Monkey. 3¼". Reading book. Green. "A. Walter, Nancy." 850.00
- Monkey. 3¾". Sitting on stump. Light amber to green. "A. Walter, Nancy and Mercier." 1000.00
- Nude. 5½". Flesh coloring. "A. Walter, Nancy" 2000.00

Inkwell. 1½ x 1½" high. Bee cover. Yellow to russet. "A. Walter, Nancy." 850.00

Lamps
- 4½" high. Flowers, leaves and berries. Orange, lavender, gold and white. Bronze base. "A. Walter, Nancy" 1000.00

11" high. Nude in white, red ground. Art Deco silvered metal base. "A. Walter, Nancy" 2000.00

Leaf Dishes

2x 5¼". Blue and green. "A. Walter, Nancy." 600.00

3x8". Iguana on leaf. Yellow, orange and green berries. "A. Walter, Nancy." 1250.00

Pen and Ink Holder. 12" long. Yellow and orange. Insert on leaf decor, flowers. "A. Walter, Nancy." 750.00

Pendants

Beetle. 2" long. Brown on gray. "A.W." 350.00

Locust. 2¾" diam. "A.W." 500.00

Pinecone. 2¼" diam. "G. Argy Rousseau." 400.00

Plaque. 4¾ x 10¾". Madonna and Child surrounded with roses in relief. "A. Walter, Nancy." 1500.00

Vase. 5¾". Purple and blue zinnias on gray ground. "G. Argy Rousseau." 850.00

PATE-SUR-PATE

Pate-sur-pate (paste-on-paste) is the French term for a slip process of decoration on porcelain. This form originated in China, but in 1863 the Sevres Manufactory succeeded in perfecting a copy under the direction of Marc Louis Solon.

Decoration in paste form was applied to the body, one thickness at a time until the desired quantity was attained; and then the piece was fired.

In 1870, Solon became ill and then homeless as a result of the Franco-Prussian War. He emigrated to England and worked at the Minton factory at Stoke-on-Trent for 35 years. It was here he produced most of his Pate-sur-pate masterpieces.

Box, Covered. 8" diam. "Ben Hur." Limoges ....$ 250.00

Lamp Base. 22½" high. Bulbous. White floral design on celadon. French 750.00

Plaques

8¾". Portrait of young woman in white on celadon. Border of pink and green flowers. Framed. Limoges. 19th century 1500.00

10" diam. Blue ground with allegorical scene in white 750.00

Vases

4½". White floral, butterflies on dark brown ground. Signed Geo. Jones & Sons 250.00

5". Moon-shaped. Celadon with white blossoms. Gold feet and trim. "Minton." 325.00

Powder Box. 6½ x 2½" high. Cameo-style lid. Blue and white with gold trim. Marked "J.P.L.-Fait Man Tharaud." $185.00

7". Sea green with mauve medallion depicting dancing nymph. Garlands of 14K gold 450.00

8¼". Blue. Lavender ground. Draped nude holding shell with cherubs 850.00

PAUL REVERE POTTERY

Paul Revere Pottery, Boston, Massachusetts was an outgrowth of a club known as "The Saturday Evening Girls." The S.E.G. was a group of young female immigrants who met on Saturday night for reading and crafts such as ceramics.

Regular production began in 1908; and the name Paul Revere was adopted by the fact that the pottery was located near the Old North Church. The firm moved to Brighton, Mass. in 1915. Known also as the "Bowl Shop," the pottery grew steadily. In spite of popular acceptance and technical advancements; the pottery required continual subsidies and as a result finally closed in January, 1942.

Items produced ranged from plain and decorated vases to tablewares to illustrated tiles. Some decorated ware was incised and glazed in Art Nouveau matte shades and occasionally a high gloss glaze.

Paper "Bowl Shop" labels were used prior to 1915 in addition to the impressed mark. Pieces can also be found dated and P.R.P. or S.E.G. painted on the base.

Plate. 7½" diam. "The Best Laid Schemes O'Mice an'Men Gang Aft Agley." Teal blue glaze. S.E.G. $125.00

Butter, Covered. Hen and chick decor. Twig handles. S.E.G. C. 1918 ....$	250.00
Bowl. 4½ x 2¼" deep. Purple. Pink band with grapes in relief. Light pink base	195.00
Candlesticks. 8". Glossy dark blue glaze. S.E.G. Pair	150.00
Creamer. 3¼". Chick decor on cream. S.E.G.	75.00
Desk Set. 4 pieces. Pink. Floral decor. S.E.G. C. 1919. Set	275.00
Paperweights	
Octagonal. Scenic decor. S.E.G. C. 1916	100.00
Swan. Yellow and white	75.00
Plates	
6". Buff. "O Don't Bother Me Said the Hen." S.E.G.	85.00
7½". Mustard color. Undecorated	30.00
8". Tree decor. Blue, green, white, black. S.E.G	65.00
Salt. 2¾ x 3¼". Figural. Chick. Dark blue glaze	50.00
Stein. 1½ pints. Blue flowers on glossy brown mottled glaze. S.E.G.	225.00
Sugar, Covered. 4" high. Handled. Buff interior. Incised band of trees. Blue glossy glaze. S.E.G.	150.00
Teapot. 4½ x 5" diam. Yellow glaze. Artist signed	75.00
Tile. 4¼" diam. Scenic woodland decor on yellow ground	65.00
Vases	
3½". Mustard color. Undecorated.	45.00
4½". Ovoid-shape. Glossy dark gray and green glaze. Lili Shapiro. S.E.G.	100.00
5½". Bulbous. Pink. Undecorated. S.E. G.	50.00
6½". Ovoid-shape. Aqua matte glaze. Lotus band. Blue and gray. Fanny Levine. S.E.G. C. 1924	150.00
10½". Ovoid-shape. Mottled dark blue glaze. Band of flying geese in blue. Edith Brown. S.E.G.	500.00

PEACH BLOW

Peach Blow is an art glass which derived its name from a fine Chinese glazed porcelain . . . described as the color of crushed strawberries or resembling the color of the peach.

Three American glass manufacturers and two English firms produced Peach Blow Glass in the late 1880's. Each firm's final product possessed its own characteristics. The following list will be helpful in identifying the makers.

Gunderson Glass Company . . .In approximately 1950 they began producing "Peach Blow"-type art glass to order. Their wares shade from an opaque faint tint of pink which is almost white to a deep rose.

Mt. Washington Peach Blow . . .Trade name for New Bedford Works. A homogeneous glass that shades from a pale gray blue to a soft rose color. Many decorative items were further enhanced with glasss appliques, enameled and gilded.

New England Peach Blow, New England Glass Works . . .The advertised name of their art glass was "Wild Rose", but the factory name was "Peach Blow." The glass is translucent, shading from rose to white acid finished or left in the original glossy state. Some of the wares were also enameled and gilded.

Thomas Webb & Sons, Stevens and Williams, England . . .At approximately the same time (1888), these two English glass makers were making a similar art glass which they termed "Peach Blow" or "Peach Bloom". It is a cased glass shading from yellow to red. Both firms occasionally employed cameo-type designs in relief on the basic objects.

Wheeling Peach Blow, Hobbs Brockunier & Co . .

An opal, glass that was plated or cased with a transparent amber glass and shades from yellow at the base to a deep red at the top. The finish can be either glossy or satin.

Wheeling. Pitcher. 7½" high. Quatrefoil top. Applied amber handle. Glossy finish. C. 1883 ...... $1750.00

Gunderson
- Bowl. 7". Tri-footed .... $ 650.00
- Cream and Sugar, Open. Decorated. Set 850.00
- Cup and Saucer 375.00
- Finger Bowl. With underplate. Crimped edge. Set 450.00
- Tumbler 150.00
- Vase. 7". Bulbous body. Slender neck 450.00

Mt. Washington
- Cruet. Rare 2500.00
- Pitcher. 7". Squat-type. Undecorated 5000.00

New England
- Bowl. 4⅜ x 2¾" deep. Glossy finish 500.00
- Darner. 5¼" long. Glossy finish .. 250.00
- Finger Bowl. 2¼" high. Acid finish 450.00
- Pear. 5". Open end stem. Glossy finish 300.00
- Plate. 5". Acid finish 250.00
- Rose Bowl. 3¾". Acid finish 395.00
- Tumblers
  - Water. Acid finish 450.00
  - Whiskey. Glossy finish 350.00
- Vase. 7¾". Lily-shape. Acid finish 750.00

Webb
- Ewer. 7" high. Applied handle. Unsigned 275.00
- Pitcher. 9½". Bulbous, tri-corn top. Applied handle. Good enameled decor. Glossy finish .. 600.00
- Rose Bowl. 3". Gold enamel decor. Acid finish 695.00
- Scent Bottle. 3¾" high. Gold enamel decor. Acid finish 500.00
- Vases
  - 5¾". Gold floral decor. Acid finish 350.00
  - 9½". Stick-type. Gold enamel decor. Glossy finish 475.00

Wheeling
- Bowl. 2¾". Glossy finish 700.00
- Butter, Covered. Glossy finish .. 1500.00
- Cruet. 6½" high. Applied amber handle. Faceted amber stopper. Glossy finish 750.00
- Cup. Glossy finish 400.00
- Lamp Base. 9" high. Brass font. Cast metal base. Glossy finish .. 1000.00
- Muffineer. 5½" high. Glossy finish 750.00
- Pitcher. 7½". Quatrefoil top. Applied amber handle. Glossy finish . 1750.00
- Syrup. 7". Glossy finish. All original 1500.00
- Toothpick. Glossy finish 350.00
- Tumbler. 3¾". Glossy finish 375.00
- Vases
  - 7". Double gourd-shape. Glossy finish 1000.00
  - 8¼". Stick-type. Bulbous base. Acid finish 1250.00
  - 10". Facsimile of "Morgan" vase. In acid holder 2000.00

PEARLWARE

Introduced by Josiah Wedgwood in 1779, Pearlware was a fashion of the late 18th century; but not a technical improvement as such. Ladies of that period tired of cream-colored china and demanded a change in coloration . . . so cobalt was added to the glaze formerly used for Creamware and the result was Pearlware. This ware bridged the gap between hard-paste porcelain, soft-paste porcelain, Creamware; and the advent of bone china. This bridge covered a span of years from 1740 to 1791, and Pearlware continued until about 1830. Marked pieces are uncommon; and there appear to be examples of Pearlware made earlier than 1779, including Bristol pottery which could not have been made later than 1778. Collectors should look for collected pools of blue or bluish green glaze on the footrim of Pearlware. Among the finest examples of this ware is the blue Staffordshire of the 1803-1820 period. Leeds, Liverpool and Swansea are among the best known makers and good examples of Pearlware include many pieces of Mocha and all Gaudy Dutch items.

Sugar, Covered. Ring handles in relief. C. 1779-80 ....$150.00

Bowls
- 5". Blue chinoiserie. Leads ....$ 165.00
- 5¾". Polychrome. Leeds 110.00
- 6". Blue chinoiserie. Leeds 210.00
- 8½". Square. Polychrome. Botanical series, Swansea 155.00
- 11½". Oval. Polychrome. Botanical series, Swansea 265.00

Coffee Pots
- Polychrome. Repaired 350.00
- Staffordshire. Blue. Repaired 225.00

Cups and Saucers
- Polychrome. Leeds. Repaired 110.00
- Polychrome. "Queen's Rose" 85.00
- Staffordshire. Blue. Small 65.00

Jugs
- 2½". Polychrome 85.00
- 4½". Pink scale. Slight damage 125.00
- 4¾". Silver shape 135.00
- 8½". Polychrome. Repaired 275.00

Mugs
- 2¾". Baluster-shaped 135.00
- 4¾". Polychrome. Spatterware. "Peafowl". Leeds 365.00
- 5¾". Polychrome. Leeds 200.00
- 5¾". Polychrome. Leeds. Damaged 120.00

Plates
- 7⅞". Polychrome. Reticulated rim. Swansea 185.00
- 8¼". Polychrome. "King's Rose."... 200.00

Plates, Soup
- 10". Blue edge. Clews 55.00
- 10". Blue edge. Stubbs and Kent... 45.00

Platters
- 9". Purple edge. Wedgwood 110.00
- 11½". Green edge 85.00
- 16½". Blue edge. Hall 45.00

Sauce. Polychrome. Chipped 45.00

Shakers
- 4½". Green. Leeds 110.00
- 4¾". Mocha. "Seaweed." 165.00

Sugars
- Blue decoration 125.00
- Ochre draping. Swan finial. Bristol. Damaged 65.00

PEKING GLASS

Peking Glass is a type of cameo glass of Chinese origin. Its production began in the 1700's and continued well into the 19th century. It is currently being reproduced, but readily identified when compared to the earlier glassware.

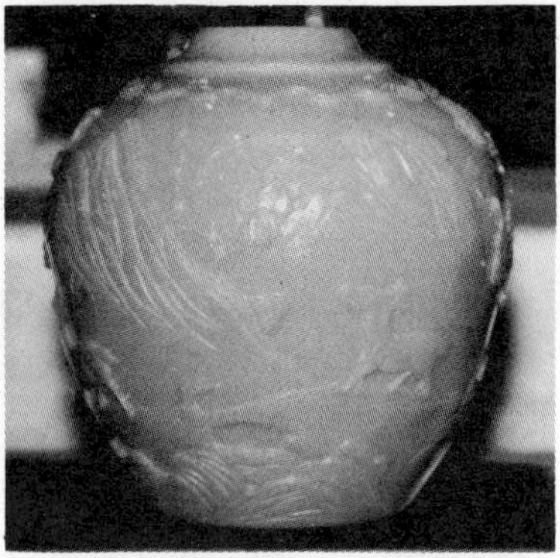

Vase. 7" high. Bulbous. Imperial yellow. Carved foliage and animal decor $600.00

Bottles
- 3½". White. Cobalt foliage ....$ 175.00
- 3½". White. Double gourd-shape. Red foliage 275.00

Bowls
- 6". White. Blue overlay carved with figures of warriors, dragons, etc. in landscape scene 600.00
- 6x 2½" deep. Flared top. Imperial

yellow. Carved birds and flowers . 400.00
6½ x 3¼" deep. White. Orange overlay. Carved birds, foliage .. 450.00
7". White. Cobalt overlay. Stylized foliage 500.00

Cup and Saucer. Blue overlay on white. Carved dragons and clouds. Sterling silver saucer 250.00

Jar, Covered. 5¾" high to top of finial. Urn-shaped. Carved geometrical pattern in cobalt 575.00

Vases
5¾". Red leopards and florals on yellow. C. 1800 .... 750.00
8" high x 5" base. Stick. Cobalt carvings on white 295.00
10". Bulbous base. Two red swans on white 850.00
10". Turquoise overlay on white. Figures, flying birds, etc 850.00

PELOTON

Peloton Glass is a novel-type art glass. It consists of small threads or filaments of opaque glass applied to translucent clear or colored glass.

To obtain the desired effect; hot glass, either pre-shaped or not, was dipped, rolled or immersed in a reservoir of the threads. The threads adhered to the surface. The glass was then reheated and remolded into the final form. Occasionally a piece was given a satin finish and-or-further decorated with enamels.

The process was patented by Wilhelm Kralik in America and England in 1888.

Biscuit Jars
Blue satin ground. Multicolored filaments. Sterling lid and bail ...$ 500.00
White satin ground. Multicolored filaments. Sterling lid and bail .. 450.00

Bowl. 8". Scalloped rim. Iridescent green. Red threads 225.00

Condiment Set. Shakers, pot, tray. Clear with multicolor filaments. 5 pieces 250.00

Cruet. Multicolored filaments on clear. Clear stopper 275.00

Pitchers
6½". Tankard. White filaments on clear 125.00
7½". Bulbous. White filaments on clear 175.00
8". Bulbous. Blue filaments on clear 175.00

Sweetmeat Jar. 7". Multicolored filaments on white. Metal lid, collar, bail handle 750.00

Tumbler. 5½". Blue filaments on clear 85.00

Vase. 7" high. Bulbous. Clear. Cranberry filaments $250.00

Vases
4". Bulbous base. Ribbed. Multicolored filaments on opaque white 350.00
6¼". White with pastel multicolored filaments. Ribbed body 300.00
7". Blue, pink, yellow filaments on clear 325.00
7". Bulbous. Clear. Cranberry filaments 250.00
8". Bulbous. Clear. Cobalt filaments 265.00

PENS AND PENCILS

Through the ages, man has recorded his thoughts, experiences and findings with some form of writing tool.

The steel pen point or nib was invented by Samuel Harrison in 1780, but was not commercially produced in quantity until the 1880's by Richard Esterbrook. The holders became increasingly elaborate . . .Mother of Pearl, gold, sterling silver and other fine materials were used to fashion holders of distinction. Many of these beautiful pens can be found intact in a velvet lined presentation box. Lewis Waterman invented the fountain pen in the 1880's. Three other leading pioneers in the field were Parker, Sheaffer (first lever-filling action, 1913) and

Wahl-Eversharp.
The mechanical pencil was patented in 1822 by Sampson Mordan. The original slide-type action developed into the spiral mechanical pencil. Wahl-Eversharp was responsible for the automatic 'clic' or repeater-type pencil which is used on ball points today. The flexible nib that enabled the writer to individualize his penmanship came to an end when Reynolds introduced the ball point pen in October 1945.

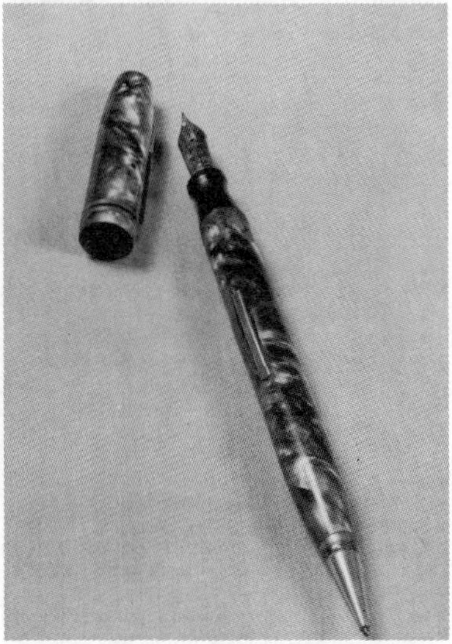

Epenco. Pen and pencil combination. Mottled green case. Lever filled. $10.00

Chilton. 1933. Pen. Black case with goldplated trim .... $ 25.00
Conklin. 1923. Pen. Hard rubber case with goldplated trim 10.00
Conklin Endura. 1925. Pen. Ring top. Mottled green with goldplated trim. Lever filled 25.00
Dunn. 1920. Pen. Black with red barrel. Goldplated trim 5.00
Eversharp
1920. Pencil. Silverplated 5.00
1931. Pen. Doric. Ladies'. "Gold Seal" 15.00
1932. Pen. Doric. Man's. "Gold Seal." 75.00
1935. Pen. Midget. Mottled green with goldplating 7.50
1941. Pen and repeater pencil. "Skyline." Set 10.00
1944. Pen and pencil. "$ 64." 14K gold caps. Lever filled. Set 55.00
1944. Pen. "Skyline." Goldplated cap 12.50
Laughlin. 1905. Pen. Silver overlay case. Eyedropper filled 45.00
Moore
1903. Pen. Non-leakable. Hard rubber case. Eyedropper filled .. 40.00
1923. Pen. Model #L-92. Hard rubber case with goldplated trim 35.00
Parker
1894. Pen. Model "6 Lucky Curve." Black with 14K gold trim 40.00
1899. Pen. Model #20. Hard rubber case. Eyedropped filled 25.00
1915. Pen. Model #48. Ring top. Gold filled barrel and cap. Button filled 50.00
1917. Pen. "Lucky Curve." Push button filler 20.00
1921. Pen. Duofold Senior "Big Red." Button filler 120.00
1923. Pen and pencil. Duofold Jr. . 50.00
1923. Pencil. Duofold Senior. Red. Propel-repel mechanism 45.00
1929. Pen. Lady Duofold. Green jade with pocket clip. Button filled 25.00
1936. Pen. Challenger. Mottled green. Lever filled 7.00
1942. Pen. "Blue Diamond" - "51". Black with goldplated cap. Button filled. 20.00
1943. Pen. "Blue Diamond" - "51". Gray with sterling silver cap. Button cap 25.00
1944. Pen. "Blue Diamond." Vacumatic. Blue and black with goldplated trim. Button filled .. 20.00
1946. Pen. Vacumatic 5.00
1948. Pen and pencil. Model "51". Goldplated case. Set 45.00
1950. Pen. Model "21". Blue with stainless cap 6.00
1956. Pen. Model "61". First edition 20.00
Ronson
1936. Penciliter. Mottled green with rodium plating 25.00
1947. Penciliter. Goldplated 35.00
Sheaffer
1916. Pencil. Goldfilled case. Propel-repel mechanism 15.00
1920. Pencil. Ring top. Goldfilled case 8.00
1923. Pen. "White Dot." Green jade with goldplated trim. Lever filled 50.00
1924. Pen. "White Dot." Ring top. Green jade with goldplated trim. Lever filled 25.00
1925. Pen. "White Dot." Ring top.

Black with goldplated trim. Lever filled 15.00
1931. Pen. "White Dot." Mottled green with goldplated trim. Lever filled 15.00
1936. Pen. "White Dot." Black with goldplated trim. Lever filled . 45.00
1942. Pen. "Triumph." Black with 14K gold band and point 30.00
1946. Pencil. "Fineline 4000". Novel point with platinum plating 4.00
1953. Pen. "White Dot" snorkel. Black with 14K gold cap and band. Plunger filled 15.00

Wahl

1918. Pen. Silver overlay case. Eyedropper filled 25.00
1922. Pen. Goldplated barrel and cap. Lever filled 10.00
1924. Pen. Goldplated case. Lever filled 25.00
1928. Pen. Goldplated case. Ball clip. Lever filled 25.00

Wahl-Eversharp

1923. Pencil. Ring top. Goldfilled case 7.50
1924. Pencil. Sterling silver engraved case 25.00

Waterman

1886. Pen. Model #12. Mottled brown with 14K gold bands 35.00
1913. Pen. Model #54. Hard rubber case with silverplated trim. Lever filled 30.00
1915. Pen. Model #452-½ V. Ring top. Silver overlay case 35.00
1918. Pen. Model #55. Hard rubber case with silverplated trim. Lever filled 65.00
1918. Pen and pencil. Model #454. Sterling silver engraved case. Lever filled. Set 175.00
1920. Pen. Model #52-½ V. Ring top. Hard rubber case with goldplated trim. Lever filled 25.00
1925. Pen. Model #71. Ripple red hard rubber case with goldplated trim. Wide clip. Lever filled 65.00
1928. Pen. "Lady Patricia." Sterling silver case. Lever filled .. 40.00
1933. Pen and pencil. Model #5. Black with goldplated trim. Lever filled. Set 30.00
1943. Pen. "Commando." 10.00
1946. Pen. Mottled gray with silverplated trim. Lever filled 5.00

PETERS AND REED POTTERY

J.D. Peters and Adam Reed Incorporated a pottery company in South Zanesville, Ohio in 1900.

Common flower pots, jardinieres and cooking wares comprised their major output in the beginning. Occasiionally, artpottery was attempted; but it was not until 1912, that their "Moss Aztec" line was introduced and widely accepted. Other art wares included "Landsun," "Chromal," "Montene," "Pereco" and "Persian."

Peters retired in 1921 and Reed changed the name of the firm to "The Zane Pottery." Marked pieces of Peters and Reed Pottery are unknown.

Also see "Zane Pottery" and "Gonder Pottery."

Jug. 4" high x 4½" diam. Gold lion's head with grapevine applique on dark brown. High glaze. Unsigned . . $50.00

Bowls

6½". "Pereco." Matte green glaze. Butterfly decor ....$ 35.00
8¼ x 2½" deep. "Landsun." Calcium interior 25.00
8¼ x 3¼" deep. "Pereco." Berry decor 65.00
8½ x 4½" deep. Sewer tile-type .. 25.00

Jardiniere. 6½ x 7½". Green lion's head decor on beige ground 65.00

Jug. 10½" high. Decorated with portraits of George Washington in slip 125.00

Mug. 5¾". Floral sprigs. High glaze . 30.00

Pitchers

6½". Tankard. "Moss Aztec." Artist signed 35.00
7¾". "Landsun." Mottled gray and brown 50.00

Vases

5". Bulbous. "Landsun." Blue, green, brown exterior. Solid blue interior 35.00

7". Portraits of George Washington	95.00
8x 5" diam. "Moss Aztec." Berry decor	45.00
9¾". "Moss Aztec." Pine cone decor	55.00
12". "Landsun." Blue glaze	85.00
Wall Pocket. 7¾" "Pereco." Egyptian decor	75.00

PEWTER

Pewter is a universal metal alloy of tin with various proportions of antimony, copper and lead. Discovered centuries ago by the Chinese, it came into extensive use in Europe and England during the 1600's; and subsequently in the early English Settlements in America.

Pewter was used extensively for tablewares, household utensils and personal items since only the more affluent families could afford fine porcelain and silverwares.

Utilitarian items were crafted in pewter by a local 'smith' to compliment the average family's limited supply of treenwares and earthenwares. From 1750 to 1850 almost every American cupboard contained a few pieces of pewter.

Since most of the American pewterers immigrated from England, their early designs show that influence. As these craftsmen advanceed, their forms became more distinguishable . . . sometimes to such an extent that, even though an object might be minus the 'touchmark' (signed) it could be readily identified as to country of origin or artist.

Pre-Revolutionary American pewter is rare because the raw-tin embargo placed on the colonies by English rulers who permitted the export of finished metals only. This embargo forced American pewterers to rely on scraps for their melting pots . . .and kept the colonies dependent on the mother country.

Pieces of pewter marked Jas. Dixon & Son, Sheffield or Dixon resemble pewter, but are made of Britannia metal, known as the hard pewter of the late 1800's. Technically, there is a difference in the formula of the two alloys; however dealers and collectors over the years have accepted pieces (with the above marks) as late pewter.

Pewter Makers-Origins-Dates Worked

American

Austin, Nathaniel. Charleston, Mass. 1763-1800

Austin, Richard. Boston, Mass. 1792-1817

Badger, Thomas. Boston, Mass. 1737-1815

Barns, Blakslee. Philadelphia, Pa. 1812-1817

Bassett, Frederick. New York, N.Y., Hartford, Conn. 1761-1800

Billings, William. Providence, R.I. 1791-1806

Boardman, Thomas Danforth. Hartford, Conn. 1805-1850

Boyd, Parks. Philadelphia, Pa. 1795-1819

Calder, William. Providence, R.I. 1817-1856

Capen and Molineux. Dorchester, Mass., New York. 1844-1854

Danforth, Edward. Middletown, Conn. 1788-1790

Danforth, Edward. Hartford, Conn. 1790-1794

Danforth, Joseph. Middletown, Conn. 1780-1788

Danforth, Josiah. Middletown, Conn. 1825-1837

Danforth, Samuel. Norwich, Conn. 1793-1803

Danforth, Thomas, III. Stepney, Conn., Philadelphia, Pa. 1777-1818

Dunham, Rufus. Westbrook, Maine. 1837-1861

Flagg and Homon. Cincinnati, Ohio. 1842-1854

Gleason, Roswell. Dorchester, Mass. 1822-1871

Griswold, Ashbil. Meriden, Conn. 1802-1842

Hall and Cotton. Middlefield, Conn. 1840's.

Hamlin, Samuel. Hartford, Conn. 1767-1801

Hamlin, Samuel, Jr. Providence, R.I. 1801-1856

Hopper, Henry. New York. 1842-1847

Jones, Gershom. Providence, R.I. 1774-1809

Kilbourn, Samuel. Baltimore, Md. 1814-1839

Lee, Richard (father and son). Mass., New Hampshire, Vermont, and Rhode Island, 1770-1820's

Leonard, Reed and Barton. Taunton, Mass. 1835-1840

Lightner, George. Baltimore, Md. 1806-1815

Manning and Bowman. Middletown, Conn. 1850-1875

McQuilkin, William. Philadelphia, Pa. 1845-1853

Morey and Co. Boston, Mass. 1852-1855

Newell, J.C. Boston, Mass. 1853

Pierce, Samuel. Greenfield, Mass. 1792-1830
Porter, Freeman. Westbrook, Maine. 1835-1860's
Putnam, James H. Malden, Mass. 1830-1835
Richardson, George, Sr. Boston, Mass. 1818-1828
Richardson, George, Sr. Cranston, R.I. 1828-1845
Savage, William. Middletown, Conn. Late 1830's
Sellew and Co. Cincinnati, Ohio. 1830-1860
Sheldon and Feltman. Albany, N.Y. 1847-1848
Smith and Co. Mass. 1850's
Smith and Feltman. Albany, N.Y. 1847-1848
Stafford, Spencer. Albany, N.Y. 1794-1830
Ward, H.B. and Co.
Wallingford, Conn. Late 1840's
Whitmore, Jacob. Middletown, Conn. 1758-1790
Wilcox, H.C. and Co. Meriden, Conn. 1850's
Wildes, Thomas. Philadelphia, Pa. 1829-1833
Wildes, Thomas. New York, N.Y. 1833-1840
Yale, H. and Co. Yalesville, Conn. 1824-1835
Young, Peter. New York. 1772-1800

English
Dixon, James and Son. Sheffield
King, Richard, Jr. London. 1745-1798
Townsend, John. London. 1777-1801
Yates, James. Birmingham. 1800-1840

Baby Rattle

Unmarked. 10¼". Three segmented. Embossed leaf decor. Turned wooden handle and finial ....$	75.00

Basins

Austin, R. 8"	450.00
Billings, W. 11¾"	1500.00
Boardman. 8"	375.00
Curtis, D. 6⅝". Albany. C. 1825	650.00
Danforth, S. 8"	400.00
Kayserzinn. 9½"	100.00
Lee, R. 6⅝"	1300.00
Pierce. 8"	425.00
Stafford, S. 8"	1500.00
Unmarked. 7¾"	225.00
Young, P. 10⅞"	2000.00

Flagon. 1 Liter. German. Late 18th or early 19th century. Engraved later $285.00

Beakers

Boardman, T. & Co. 5⅛". N.Y. C. 1822-1825	850.00
Dixon & Son. Pint	175.00
Griswold, A. Pint	500.00
Unmarked. ½ pint. American	125.00
Woodbury, J.B. 3". Philadelphia. C. 1835.	200.00

Candlesticks

Dixon & Son. Chamber-type	125.00
Dunham. 6"	250.00
Gleason. 7½". Pair	500.00
Gleason. 8". Chamber-type	250.00
Hopper, H. 10". Pair	900.00
Kayserzinn. Chamber-type	85.00
Ostronder & Norris. 4⅛". N.Y. C. 1850. Pair	750.00
Sellew-type. 9¾". Pair	500.00
Unmarked	
6". Danish. Pair	45.00
7¼". Continental. Pair	1300.00
9½". French. Pair	225.00

Teapot. 11″ high. American. D. L. Farnam. C. 1825 .... $350.00

10″. American. Baluster turned. Pair 300.00

Castor

Dixon & Son. Holder only. 5-bottle 100.00

Chalices

Boardman. 7½″ high, 3″ diam. top, 3¾″ base 400.00
Calder, W. 6⅛″ 350.00
Kayserzinn. 7″ 100.00
Unmarked. 6¾″. American 150.00

Chargers

Calder, W. 11″ 300.00
Hamlin, S. 13½″. American 595.00
Swanson, T. 16½″ 185.00
Townsend. 12″ 185.00
Unmarked
13½″ 175.00
18″. English 300.00
Whitmore, J. 12¼″ 475.00
Yates. 16½″. Hammered Booge. Late 18th century 395.00

Coffee Pots

Boardman. 12″ 375.00
Boardman & Hart. 8″ 450.00
Danforth, J. 11″ 400.00
Dixon & Son. 10½″ 220.00
Dixon & Son. 14″. Octagonal 150.00
Dunham. 10½″ 450.00
Dunham & Sons 400.00
Gleason 400.00
Homan, H. 9¾″. Flower finial. Engraved 300.00
Leonard, Reed & Barton. 9″ 300.00
Morey & Sons 250.00
Porter, A. 12″ 600.00
Richardson, G. 11½″ 400.00
Savage 300.00
Sellew & Co 500.00
Shaw & Fisher. 9½″ 100.00
Smith & Co. 10″ 250.00
Trask. 9″. Domed top 550.00
Ward, H.B. 11″. Lighthouse-shaped 425.00
Yale, H. & Co. 10½″ 475.00

Coffee Urn

Reed & Barton. 14″ 400.00

Communion Set. 11″ high. Flagon, covered. Two chalices and two plates. Unmarked. C. 1830-1850 .. 1850.00

Cream and Sugar Sets

Brewster 125.00
Winthrop 50.00

Creamers

Sheldon & Feltman. 5¼″ 200.00
Yale, H. & Co. 4″ 250.00

Cuspidors

Danforth, J. Ring handles 325.00
Derby 250.00

Flagons

Boardman, T. & Co. 11⅛″. N.Y. C. 1825-1827 .... 1200.00
Calder. 11″ 675.00
Dixon & Son. 9¾″ 225.00
Gleason. 10″ 700.00
Leonard, Reed & Barton. 11″ 550.00
Sheldon & Feltman. 10½″ 650.00

Foot Warmer

Unmarked. 7 x 11½″. Oval 175.00

Funnel.

Unmarked. 6″ 75.00

Inkwells

Kayserzinn. 10½″. Free form. With underplate 125.00
Unmarked
5½ x 8¼″. English. 18th century 225.00
7¾″ diam. base. Holds three quill pens 135.00

Ladles

Pia, G. 12″ 55.00
Unmarked
14½″ 75.00
15″. Wooden handle 75.00
Yates. 12″ 125.00

Lamps

Capen & Molineux. 7¾″. N.Y. C. 1850 .... 550.00

Gleason	540.00
Morey & Ober	500.00
Newell, J. Peg. 7". Pair	500.00
Porter, F	500.00
Putnam. 9"	425.00
Smith & Co. 7"	375.00
Unmarked	
2". Nursing	185.00
6"	200.00
Yale & Curtis. 3½"	275.00
Master Salt. Dixon & Son. Footed	85.00
Measures	
Dandre. ½ pint. Hallmarked	110.00
Yates. ½ pint	110.00
Mugs	
Danforth, J. 4½"	1500.00
Hamlin, Samuel, Jr. 6". R.I. C. 1771-1801	2600.00
Morey & Smith. Pint	250.00
Whitmore, J. 4½"	1600.00
Yates, J. ½ pint	65.00
Napkin Ring	
Kayserzinn. 2"	35.00
Pitchers	
Dunham, R. 6½"	550.00
Gleason. 6½". Covered	750.00
Porter, F. 6"	500.00
Unmarked. Covered. Gallon. American	500.00
Plates	
Austin, N. 8"	400.00
Austin, R. 8"	400.00
Badger, T. 8½"	375.00
Barnes, S. 8¾"	400.00
Barns, B. 8"	350.00
Barns, B. 9". (with an 'e')	450.00
Bassett, F. 9"	900.00
Billings, W. 8"	775.00
Blockzinn, Beindorf. 9". German	50.00
Boardman. 8"	400.00
Boyd, P. 7⅞"	350.00
Calder, W. 8"	400.00
Curtiss, I. 8½" Conn. C. 1815-1820	375.00
Danforth, E. 8"	550.00
Danforth, T, III. 8"	415.00
Danforth, W. 8"	425.00
Gleason, R. 9"	250.00
Griswold, A. 7⅞"	325.00
Kayserzinn. 10"	100.00
Kilbourn, S. 8"	450.00
King, R. Jr. 8¾"	225.00
Lightner, G. 7⅞"	325.00
Pierce, S. 8"	375.00
Townsend & Compton. 8½"	100.00
Unmarked	
7½"	85.00
9". English	95.00
9¾"	125.00
Platters	
Badger, T. 12"	600.00
Kayserzinn. 12½ x 20"	175.00
Watts & Harton. 13 x 17"	395.00
Porringers	
Boardman. 5"	400.00
Gleason, R. 3¾"	325.00
Hamlin. 5¼"	750.00
Jones, G. 7½"	2000.00
Lee, M.	
2 1/16"	750.00
3¼". Heart handle	400.00
5". Crown handle	975.00
Melville, D. 6⅝". 18th century	1500.00
Unmarked	
3"	200.00
5¼". Crown handle	300.00
6". French	125.00
7½". Tab handle. Pennsylvania.	700.00
Spoons	
Tablespoons	
Ernest, B. Wreath and Fleur-de-lis decor. Hallmarked	40.00
Yates	50.00
Teaspoons	
Boardman	30.00
Unmarked	
Fiddleback	30.00
Shellback	15.00
Sugar Bowls	
Manning & Bowman. 2¾". Open.	150.00
Richardson, Sr. 6". Covered	1500.00
Tankards	
Kayserzinn. 15"	225.00
Manning, Bowman & Co. 8½"	425.00
Unmarked. 14"	300.00
Teapots	
Boardman. T.D.5½". Acorn finial	300.00
Boardman. 8"	350.00
Boardman & Hart	
7½"	350.00
8"	425.00
Danforth, J. 6½"	325.00
Dixon & Son. 5½"	185.00
Dunham, R. 7½"	325.00
Gleason, R. 7"	425.00
Griswold, A. 7"	325.00
Morey & Ober	275.00
Porter, F.	300.00
Putnam. 8"	600.00
Richardson, G.	
7½"	550.00
11"	650.00
Richardson, G. Sr. 7½". Pear-shaped	1500.00
Savage. 10"	325.00
Shaw & Fisher. 5¾"	175.00
Smith & Co. 7½". Wood handle	275.00
Unmarked	
Pear-shaped	450.00
Plain	175.00
Wilcox	250.00

Tureen	
Kayserzinn. 11½". Covered	150.00
Wine Tasters	
Lee, R	350.00
Taunton	70.00

PHOENIX BIRD PATTERN

The Phoenix Bird pattern is a blue and white Japanese porcelain. There are seven patterns known using the Phoenix Bird as the focal point. The two most popular patterns are "Flying Phoenix" (phoenix almost always looking over his left wing) and "Flying Turkey" (looking straight ahead).

The pattern reached its peak in the early 1900's and continued until the 1930's and 1940's. After World War II, a few pieces were made and are marked "Made in Occupied Japan." SEE NOTE:

Tumbler. 2¾" high $20.00

Bowl. 8¾". M-wreath ....$	40.00
Butter Tub. 5". Handled with pierced disc insert..............	28.50
Creamer. 2½" high. Individual	6.50
Cup and Saucer	8.50
Egg Cups	
Double	10.00
Single	6.50
Platter. 10" oval. M-wreath	20.00
Salt and Pepper. Pair	18.00
Sauce Boat. With underplate	22.50
Sugars	
Covered	15.00
Open	10.00

NOTE: Newly designed items with the Phoenix Bird Patterns are currently being produced. Variations in size, design and pattern exist between the old and the new.

PHOENIX GLASS

Phoenix Glass Company, Beaver, Pennsylvania was established in 1880. Although the firm was known primarily for commercial glassware, it began producing a molded, sculptured, cameo-type line in the 1930's. This decorative ware was discontinued in the 1950's and is widely collected today.

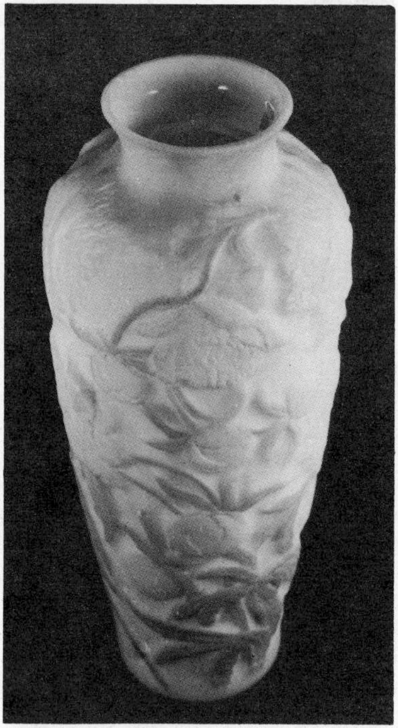

Vase. 12½" high. Ivory ground. Yellow flowers with green leaves $195.00

Basket. 4½". Pink. Dogwood ....$	35.00
Bowls	
9". Frosted and clear. Cockatoos...	65.00
10x 5½ x 4" oval. Blue	125.00
13" long. Custard and orange. Lovebirds	125.00
14 x 4¼" deep. Frosted and clear. Lily	175.00

Box. 6". Covered. Blue. Floral decor . 55.00
Candlesticks
3¼". Blue. Bubbles and swirls. Pair ... 40.00
5". Angular. "The Phoenix." Pair .. 75.00
Compote. 8½". Butterscotch. Dragonflies and water lilies 85.00
Lamps
13" high. White. Yellow roses. aqua foliage ... 250.00
22" high. White. Orange honeysuckle and green leaves .. 375.00
Planter. 3¼ x 8½". Green. Lion .. 45.00
Plates
6¾". Frosted and clear. Dancing Nudes ... 40.00
8¼". Yellow. Kumquats ... 30.00
8½". Clear and frosted. Cherries... 35.00
14". Blue. White daffodils ... 85.00
18". Green. Dancing Nudes 125.00
Vases
6¼". Frosted and clear. Lovebirds . 25.00
6¼". White. Pink peonies, green leaves ... 65.00
7". Frosted and clear. Pine cones 35.00
7". Ivory. Lavender florals ... 50.00
7¼ x 8" wide. White. Blue Praying Mantis ... 95.00
8 x 6¼" diam. Rose. White marguerites ... 75.00
8¼". Green. Grasshoppers ... 75.00
9". Pillow-shape. Blue. Fish 125.00
10 x 7" diam. Fan-shaped. Green. Bird in grape arbour ... 80.00
10". White. Bust of lady ... 100.00
11 x 10" diam. Blue. Seagulls .. 125.00
12". White. Dancing Nudes 150.00

PHONOGRAPH RECORDS

With the advent of more sophisticated recording materials, such as 33⅓ RPM long playing albums, 8-track tapes and cassettes, earlier phonograph records have become collectors' items. These records are also sought by collectors of memorabilia for past artists who recorded on different labels.

Brunswick. 10" ... $ 4.00
Capitol. 10" ... 3.00
Capitol. 12" ... 4.00
Columbia. 10" ... 3.50
Decca. 10" ... 3.50
Decca. Judy Garland ... 10.00
Decca. Al Jolson ... 5.00
Edison Blue Amberol Cylinder. 4 minutes ... 5.00
Edison Cylinder. 2 minutes ... 3.50
Edison Cylinder. 4 minutes ... 5.00
Edison Diamond Disc ... 3.50
Indestructible Cylinder. 2 minutes .. 3.50
Little Wonder. 5½" ... 2.50

RCA Victor. 12". Black label $4.50

MGM. Yellow label. 10". 78 RPM .. 5.00
Opera Disc. (German) 12". Single sided. Caruso ... 15.00
Pathe. 10", 10½", 11½" ... 4.00
RCA Victor. 10". Black label ... 3.50
RCA Victor. 10". Bluebird ... 5.00
RCA Victor. 12". Black label ... 4.50
RCA Victor. 12". Red Seal. Single sided ... 7.50
RCA Victor. 12". Red Seal. Double sided ... 7.50
RCA Victor. 45 RPM. Elvis Presley .. 10.00
Victrola. 10", 12" ... 5.00

PHONOGRAPHS

Early phonographs were commonly called 'talking machines.' Thomas A. Edison invented the first successful phonograph in 1877. Other manufacturers followed with their variations.

Amberola. Model 75. Diamond C reproducer ... $ 300.00
Baltiphone. Console. 38" high. Plays 78 RPM's ... 250.00
Britannia. Key wind. Open mechanism. C. 1910. Germany .. 175.00
Brunswick. Console. 47" high. Golden oak cabinet. Plays 78 RPM's ... 250.00
Columbia Gramaphone. 2 minute-type ... 350.00
Edison Standard. Disc-type. Built in horn in cabinet ... 300.00
Edison Standard. Disc-type. Model A. Black and gold horn ... 500.00

Victrola. Console. 48½" high. Mahogany $265.00

Edison Standard. 14" brass horn ..	350.00
Edison Standard. Morning Glory horn painted black and decorated. 2 minute or 4 minute cylinders	500.00
Edison Triumph. Plywood horn, brass. bell end. 2 minute cylinders.	950.00
Excelsior. Two minute gearing. C. 1904-08. Germany	275.00
G.C. & Co. Spun aluminum horn. C. 1900	375.00
Kameraphone. 4½ x 6½". Portable.	125.00
Keeno-Lo-Phone. Double doors conceal 2 drawers with record pockets. Bonnet is amplifier	500.00
Lyrophonwerke. C. 1908. Germany.	300.00
Pathe. Model No. O. C. 1904. French	350.00
Reginaphone. Model 150. Mahogany case	4000.00
Robeyphone. Disc-type. Large horn. English	500.00
Victor. Type III	500.00
Victor. Type V. Table model with morning glory horn. Oak cabinet..	750.00
Victrola. Table model. Oak cabinet. C. 1920. Plays 78 RPM's	250.00

PIANO AND ORGAN ROLLS

Player piano rolls were introduced at the turn of the 20th century. The first pianos were 65-note players, i.e., the rolls had 65 notes punched across the 11¼" wide paper roll. In 1901, the Melville and Clark Piano Company manufactured the 88-note player.

U.S., Imperial, Vocal style, Recordo, Cannonized and International were among the first piano-roll companies. The largest was QRS who issued over 1000 titles a year. However, piano-roll sales diminished when people began to move out of their homes for entertainment.

In 1951, player pianos were retrieved, restored and returned to the family room. A new, smaller spinet-type player piano was introduced. Two companies, Aeolian and Melodee, began producing new rolls until 1967 when they were dissolved. Music rolls are still being made today but it is the earlier ones that music collectors seek.

This list is comprised mainly of piano rolls, but others used with mechanical playing musical instruments are also included.

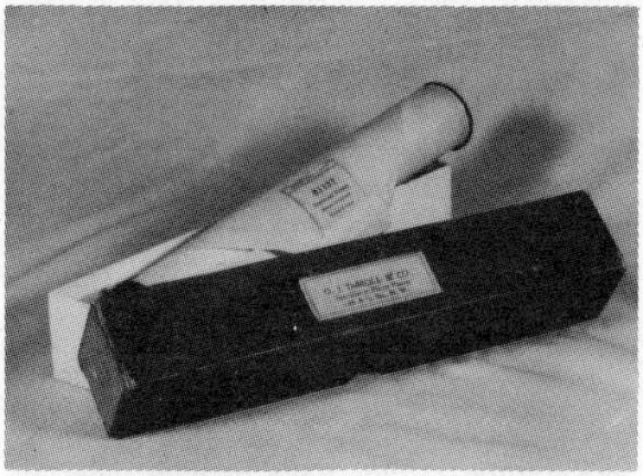

O.J. DeMolle Co. 88-note $3.50

Aeolian. 65-note ....$	2.00
Aeolian Pipe Organ. 116-note	8.00
Aeolian Reed Organ. 46-note	5.00
Ampico Reproducing A or B	7.50
Apollo Concert Grand	5.00
Automusic. 65-note	3.50
Cecilian. Organ	10.00
Columbia. 88-note	3.50
Deluxe Reproducing	7.50
Duo Art Reproducing. Organ	15.00
Gem. Organ cob	6.00
Ideal. 88-note	2.50
Imperial. 88-note	3.50
Metrostyle. 65-note	3.50
Nickelodeon. A, O, or G	20.00

Pianostyle. 88-note	3.50
Q.R.S. 88-note	2.00
Recordo	5.00
Rollmonica	6.50
Simplex	2.50
Tanzbar. 2½"	15.00
Tanzbar. 4⅛"	20.00
Tel-Electric. 65-note	5.00
U.S. 88-note	1.50
Vocalstyle. 88-note	2.50
Welte Philharmonic Organ	15.00
Wurlitzer Band Organ. 165-note	20.00

HANDPAINTED W PICKARD A CHINA

PICKARD

The Pickard China Company was founded in 1894. They were known for their fine handpainted porcelains. Originally they acquired blanks from other sources . . .namely Limoges, but now produce their own. The firm is presently located in Antioch, Illinois.

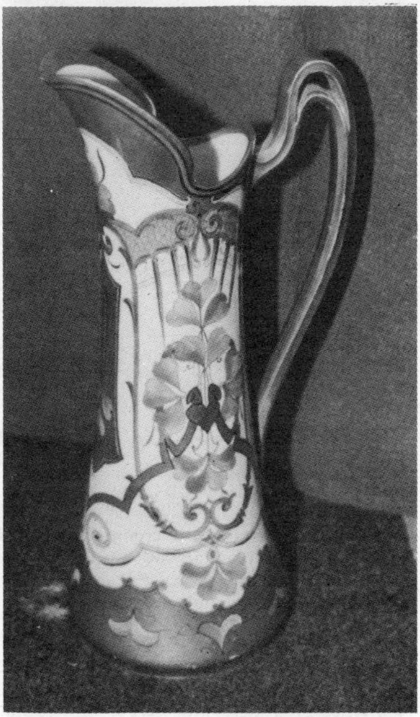

Ewer. 14" high. Magenta and green with heavy gold. Signed plus artist signature $295.00

Berry Set. 10" bowl, six 5½" bowls. Orange and yellow tulips. Heavy gold trim. Artist signed. Set .... $ 300.00

Bowls
- 6". Pierced rim. Gold florals inside, allover gold exterior 40.00
- 9½". Red roses on green and ivory ground. Scroll border in heavy gold. Artist signed. 1895-1898 mark 125.00
- 10". Yellow shaded ground, violet decor. Gold and red patterned band. Artist signed and dated 1898 ...... 150.00

Box, Covered. 2¾ x 5¾" diam. Stylized florals in gold, black and ivory 85.00

Candlesticks. 9". Floral decor. Limoges blanks. Artist signed. Pair. 100.00

Chocolate Pot. 11½" high. White pearlized ground. Orchids and leaves decor 150.00

Compotes
- 8½". Linear design. Artist signed and dated 1912 ...... 125.00
- 10½". Handled. Fruit and flower decor. Gold border and pedestal. Artist signed 165.00

Creamers and Sugers
- Allover gold. On tray. Set 65.00
- Gold beaded rims on white. Set .. 60.00
- Pink blossoms. Artist signed and dated 1905. Set 85.00

Cup and Saucer. Enamel beading. Artist signed 75.00

Hatpin Holders
- Allover gold. Etched florals. C. 1925 ...... 35.00
- Florals, gold band top. Artist signed and dated 1905 ...... 45.00

Marmalade Jar, Covered. 6" high. With underplate. Pink dogwood. Gold trim. Artist signed 75.00

Mug. 6" high. Dutch Girl decor. Artist signed. C. 1908 ...... 95.00

Pitchers
- 6". Cider. Allover etched gold decor. Gold interior. C. 1930's .. 100.00
- 6". Tankard. Art Nouveau design. Limoges blank. Artist signed 125.00
- 8". Aura Argento Linear. Artist signed 200.00
- 10". Tankard. Dark green ground, gold grapes. Gold trim. Artist signed and dated 1905 ...... 250.00

Plates
- 5½". Etched all over in gold 20.00
- 6". Violets on ground of greens and pinks. Gold scalloped border. Artist initialed. C. 1910 ...... 35.00
- 8". Humming birds and orchids.

2" embossed gold border. Hutschenreuther blank. Signed E. Challinor 100.00
8½". Reds, greens and browns with decor of gooseberries. Artist signed. C. 1905-1910 .... 65.00
8½". Scalloped with gold. Strawberries and white blossoms. Signed E. Challinor. C. 1905 .... 100.00
9". Yellow cherries on green ground. Artist signed and dated 1905 .... 75.00
10¼". Overall gold. Ornate Art Deco border 50.00
11". Cake. Open handles. Mum decor. Artist signed. C. 1910-1912 125.00
11". Service. Yellow roses in center. Bavarian blanks. C. 1930. Set of 4 .... 150.00

Salt and Pepper Shakers. Stylized floral decor. Gold tops. Artist signed. C. 1912. Pair 35.00

Stein. 7". Tankard-shape. Red poinsettias on iridescent pearlized ground. Signed N.R. Coutall. 1898-1904 mark 165.00

Swan. 3" long. Heavy allover gold, inside and out 30.00

Tea Sets
3 pieces. Scenic decor. Gold handles, spouts and finials. Artist signed. Set 350.00
4 pieces. Teapot, creamer, sugar, 16" tray. Pierced handles. Allover gold 250.00

Tray. 6½ x 12" long. Handled. Garden scene. Signed E. Challinor .. 195.00

Urn. 11½" high. Allover gold. 3" band of grapes and strawberries. Belleek blank. Artist signed 500.00

Vases
5½". Footed. Tropical scene. Gold handles. Artist signed 195.00
7". Scenic. Signed E. Challinor. C. 1905-1910 .... 250.00
8¼". Garden scene. Artist signed. C. 1912-1919 .... 235.00
10". Classic oriental scene. Artist signed 275.00
11". Enameled multicolored Peacock. Signed E. Challinor. C. 1925-30 .... 500.00
15". Peonies on pastel ground. Gold scalloped rim, base. Artist signed 295.00

PICKLE CASTORS

A pickle castor is a novelty table accessory used to serve pickles. It consists of a silverplated frame fitted with a glass insert and metal tongs. They were popular in the 1880-1900 period. Also see specific glass or patterns.

Clear. Castle $95.00

Amber .... $ 150.00
Amethyst. Enamel decor 250.00
Blue
Decorated with enameling 225.00
Enameled flowers. IVT 250.00
Clear
Barrel-shaped 150.00
Near Cut 85.00
Pressed Cut 85.00
Cranberry
Enamel decor 250.00
Undecorated 150.00

PIGEON BLOOD GLASS

Pigeon Blood refers to the orange-red colored glass wares produced around the turn of the century. Do not confuse it with any red glass. Pigeon Blood has a definite orange glow.

Bowls
8". Beaded rim .... $ 175.00
10". Boat-shaped 250.00
Butter, Covered. Metal trim 195.00
Candlesticks. 7½". Twisted stem. Pair 125.00
Champagne. Knob stem 35.00

Salt and Pepper Shakers. Pair. $100.00

Compote. 7½" high, 9½" diam.
  Scalloped edge 175.00
Cracker Jar. Melon ribbed.
  Resilvered lid, bail handle 250.00
Cruet, Stoppered. 4½" 150.00
Hat. 4½" high 75.00
Lamp, Oil 225.00
Pickle Castor 225.00
Pitchers
  7". IVT. Clear applied handle 200.00
  9". Melon ribbed. Clear applied handle 250.00
Shakers, Salt and Pepper.
  "Torquay." Pair 100.00
Sugar Castor. "Bulging Loop." 125.00
Syrup. "Torquay." 125.00
Toothpick. Melon ribbed 65.00
Tumbler, Water 40.00
Vases
  4½". Urn-shaped. Clear applied handles 65.00
  6¼". Enameled decor 125.00
  10½". Floral decor of lavender, green and gold 175.00
  12". Pedestaled. Applied clear glass rigaree 225.00

PINK LUSTRE CHINA

Pink Lustre derived its name from the color of the decoration. In 1790, Josiah Wedgwood began to experiment in decoration with a thin film of metal applied by various methods. Successors followed suit by using silver, platinum and gold (pink). Lustre decorations were often used in conjunction with enamels and transfers. Transfers used for lustre decorations covered a wide range of public and domestic subjects. These were often accompanied by pious or sentimental doggerel as well as the humors of everyday life. Also see "Sunderland Lustre."

Bowl. 6½ x 5½" deep. "House." .. $ 85.00
Creamers
  "House." 65.00
  "Strawberry." Helmet-shaped. All over lustre 150.00

Cup and Saucer. "Butterfly." Handleless $45.00

Cups and Saucers
  "Butterfly." Handleless 45.00
  "House." Handled 50.00
  "Strawberry." Handled. All over decor 165.00
  "Strawberry." Handleless. All over decor 185.00
  "Sunflower." 100.00
Goblet. All over lustre 95.00
Pitchers
  "House." 7" 150.00
  "Snapdragons." In relief. Light blue ground. Lustred rim and handles 195.00
  "Vintage." Lustred band and handle 250.00
Plates
  "House." 4" 25.00
  "House." 8" 55.00
  "Floral." 8". Lustred rim 45.00
  "Strawberry." 8¾". Soup 250.00
Sugars, Covered
  "Floral." Lustred trim 85.00
  "House." 125.00
Teapots
  "Floral." 115.00
  "House." 175.00
  "Rose." Lustred trim 100.00

PINK SLAG

The molded pattern regarded as true Pink Slag is that of an Inverted Fan and Feather. Recently pieces have come onto the market in the Inverted Strawberry and Inverted Thistle. The two patterns were made from molds of the now defunct Cambridge Glass Co. and are NOT considered 'true' Pink Slag. The price of these late patterns are only a fraction of the original Pink Slag. Quality pieces shade from pink at the top to white at the bottom. This is the most sought after of the slag wares. The glass is extremely scarce and commands a good price.

Punch Cup. Footed $375.00

Bowl. 4½ x 2½" deep. Footed	$ 600.00
Butter, Covered	1000.00
Compote. 5" high	750.00
Creamer	500.00
Cruet, Stoppered. 6½"	975.00
Jam Jar	850.00
Pitcher. 8"	1000.00
Punch Cup. Footed	375.00
Sauce, Footed	295.00
Sugar	650.00
Syrup	850.00
*Toothpick	450.00
*Tumbler	300.00

*Reproduced Item

PIPES

According to history, tobacco was introduced in England by Sir Walter Raleigh. The use of the "vile weed" quickly became popular on the continent and the need for pipes developed. Many were produced in Holland in the Gouda vicinity and were exported throughout the world.

Briar	
Amber stem. Velvet case. French	$ 45.00
Bull's Head. Glass eyes	50.00
Roosevelt, T	75.00

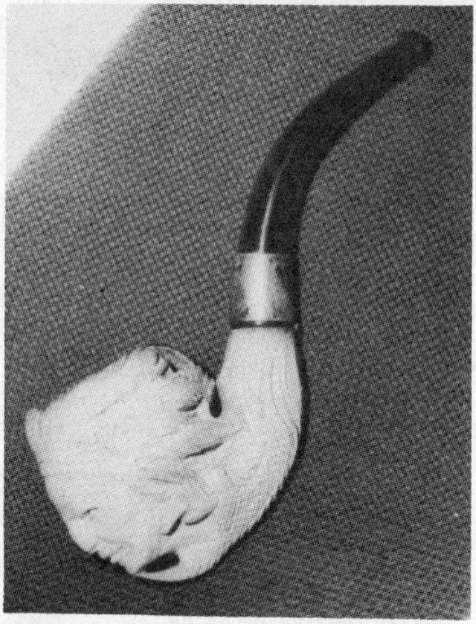

Meerschaum. Indian Head. Amber stem. 5" $125.00

Clay	
Advertising-type. Inscribed. 8" English	50.00
Bearded man. 9". French	60.00
Delft-type. Blue and white. 9"	25.00
Horn	
Deer painted on bowl, wood stem. 28"	100.00
Prussian soldier and girl. Dated 1856. 40"	125.00
Majolica. Barrel-shape bowl with dog at base. Wood stem. 11"	65.00
Meerschaum	
Cheroot. Acorn cluster. 3¾"	65.00
Cheroot. Hunter and dog. 4¾"	85.00
Deer, Antlered. 14½"	250.00
Deer pursued by dog. 7"	135.00
Devil. Leather case	175.00
Dogs, Two. Amber stem. 5"	75.00
Floral. Silk lined leather case	100.00
Hand holding fruit	85.00
Horse. Original leather and velvet lined case. 11"	350.00
Horse. Running. 5"	85.00
House, fence and man. 18"	200.00
Knight. With armour. 9"	85.00
Maiden. Art Nouveau-style. With case. 8¼"	200.00
Monk. With case	150.00
Monkey. Glass eyes	150.00
Regimented. Silver ribs, briar bottom. Dated 1862. 12"	125.00
Scholar. Tasseled cap. 7"	60.00

Ship's figure head. Silk lined case. 7" 250.00
Suede covered bowl. Leather case 60.00
Nailsea-type glass. Blown. White loops on cranberry. Curved 250.00
Opium
Brass. Chinese. 10" 50.00
Cloisonne. Black ground with blue and white water lilies and white crane with blue feathers. 15" 275.00
Water
Brass. Reptile skin covered bowl. 175.00
Porcelain. Devil's head. 17" 75.00
Porcelain. Handpainted. Landscape decor. 34". 125.00

PLAYING CARDS

Playing Cards trace the course of history and offer the collector a broad scope for exploration. Early U.S. and foreign issues, of special interest to advanced collectors include Tarots C. 1500, Educational C. 1620, General C. 1680, Transformation C. 1805 and Transparents C. 1850.
Special issues (from 1837 to today), of general interest to collectors, are Royalty Cards from 1837, Worshipful Company Cards from 1882, Cigarette Cards 1885-95, Bicycle Cards from 1885, Wide Pictorial Cards 1873-1930, and Souvenir Cards from 1893 to date.
From 1910 to 1935 other special issues include Old Flower Cards 1910-21, Narrow Named Cards 1913-25, Early Un-named Narrow Cards 1925-35 and Advertising Cards, which originated in the late 1800's and continue today in such areas as Historical and Commemorative, State Cards, Transportation, Educational Institutions and Consumer Products and Services. Additional issues of interest are Novelty Cards (unusual sizes, shapes and materials), Game Cards (educational, "fun", fortune telling and magic) and the modern series of pictorials produced since 1925.
The variety of playing cards available to the collector is almost unlimited . . .both in deck form or individual groupings such as Aces, Jokers, Court cards or Suit designs.

Advertising
"Anheuser Busch." All courts named. Wide, gold edge. 52 cards complete. C. 1899 ....$ 150.00
"El Barco Chocolates." Sunflower motif. Spanish. 40 cards complete . 100.00
"Personna" by Whitman. NFL shield backs, standard faces, narrow. 52 cards plus special joker .. 15.00
"Time." Limited edition. Unique courts, original case, 52 cards complete. C. 1962 .... 55.00
"Tropicana Hotel and Country Club." Wide, blue backs, standard faces. Simulated bullet hole through deck and case. 52 cards complete 10.00

Advertising. "Old Bridgeport Pure Rye Whiskey." 52 cards complete ..$25.00

Countries
Belgium. "Synthese" by Chas. Pry. Limited edition. 36 cards complete 18.50
England. "Old Frizzle" by DeLaRue. 52 cards complete. C. 1860 .... 75.00
England. "Oxford College Arms" by DeLaRue. Wide, standard faces. 52 cards complete plus joker 25.00
England. "Salon" by Goodall & Son. Wide, standard faces, gold edge. Backs have pictures of American Indian Chief. 52 cards complete plus joker, original case .. 15.00
France. "Blocus-I" (LeJeuDu) by Catel Et Farcy. 3 1/16 x 4 1/8", gold corners, 32 cards complete plus joker. C. 1970 .... 18.50
France. "Clavecin" by Catel Et Farcy. Courts in baroque costumes, gold corners, lattice backs. 52 cards complete, original case. C. 1955 25.00
Germany. "Master PW" reprinted by Edition Leipsig. Round cards, 5 suit game. 72 cards complete .. 35.00
Germany. "Swiss Album" by Wust. Double ended courts, 52 different back scenes. Good con-

dition. C. 1880 .... 85.00
Holland. "U.S. Movie Stars." 2¼ x 3½". 53 cards complete plus joker. 85.00
Iceland. "Historical" by Altenburg. 2⅜ x 3⅝". 52 cards complete. C. 1930 .... 45.00
India. "Hindu." 2⅛" diam. Single card. C. 1840 .... 2.00
Japan. "53 Stages of Tokaido" by Ace. P.C. Co. From the paintings of Hiroshige. 52 cards complete plus 2 jokers. C. 1950 .... 35.00
Japan. "Trains" (of different countries) 2¾ x 3¾", silver border. 52 cards complete plus 2 jokers 15.00
Spain. "Fournier," #27. 2⅜ x 3¾". 40 cards complete plus title card. C. 1962 .... 10.00
United States. "Braille" by Arrco. Narrow, backs have humming bird at flower. Special case. 52 cards complete plus joker 10.00
United States. "French Recipe Cards" by Western Publ. Co. 5 x7". Original case. 52 cards complete plus 2 index cards in French and English. C. 1969 .... 30.00
United States. "Green Cross for Safety." Narrow, gold edge. 52 cards complete plus 2 jokers 25.00
United States. "Kennedy." Faces of courts are members of Kennedy Clan. Original case. 52 cards complete 35.00
United States. "Kling" (magnetic steel playing cards) by Regal & Wade Mfg. Co. Two complete decks of 52 cards plus magnetic board 50.00
United States. "Tarot" by Morgan Press. 2 15/16 x 4 5/8" . Medieval designs. 78 cards complete. C. 1970 .... 10.00
United States. "W.C. Fields" (with famous sayings.) 52 cards complete plus joker 15.00

Games

"Constitution" (political) by Mrs. C.F. Pond. 62 cards complete. C. 1915 .... 35.00
"Fortune Telling" by H.V. Loring, Chicago. U.S.A. Military, wide backs have small design of service men's heads, original case. 56 cards complete 50.00
"Play Maid" by Playboy. Adult version of "Old Maid." 26 pairs plus one "Granny" card 12.50
"Star Baseball Game" by Wm. Ulrich. Original case. 56 cards complete. C. 1941 .... 25.00

Picture Back

"New York Girl, The" by Russell P.C.Co. Wide, gold edge. 52 cards complete 20.00
"Roosevelt, F.D., at Hyde Park." Narrow, standard faces, original case. 52 cards plus 2 jokers. C. 1940 .... 20.00

Royalty

"Commemoration of King Edward VII, June 26, 1902." by Worshipful Co. Wide, backs have 2 cupids, gold edge. 51 out of 52 cards 50.00
"Queen's Silver Jubilee." Sealed in original wrappers with case. 52 cards complete plus joker. C. 1977 15.00
"Queen Victoria" by Goodall. Named courts. 52 cards complete. C. 1897 .... 150.00
"Wedding of Duke & Duchess of Kent", June 8, 1961 by DeLaRue, Worshipful Co. Backs depict wedding, blue-maroon borders. Original seal. 52 cards complete 20.00

Souvenir

"Apollo II" by B & B. Standard faces, backs have Eagle. Original case. 52 cards complete plus 2 jokers 25.00
"Disneyland" by Walt Disney Productions. Narrow, standard faces, Magic Castle backs. 52 cards complete plus joker. Mint .. 7.50
"Fabulous Las Vegas" made in Japan. Narrow, standard faces, original case. 52 cards complete plus joker 7.50
"Florida East Coast" by U.S. P.C. Narrow, Florida State Flower with state seal backs, gold edge. Original case. 52 cards complete. C. 1922 .... 35.00
"From Sea to Summit" by Chisholm Bros. Wide, state seals of Maine and New Hampshire backs, gold edge. 52 cards complete. C. 1904 .... 30.00
"Jim Jeffries" (championship fight). 52 cards complete plus joker. C. 1909. Fair condition 100.00
"Panama" by U.S.P.C. Wide, steamship in canal backs, gold edge. 52 cards complete. C. 1923 . 50.00
"Panama Inaugural Edition" by U.S. P.C. Wide, gold edge. Original case. 52 cards complete. C. 1915 .... 50.00
"Ringling Bros., Barnum & Bailey Circus" by Western Publ. Co., U.S.A. Narrow, standard faces, two lions on backs. 52 cards com-

plete plus 2 jokers. C. 1973 .... 7.50

Transformation

"Beatrice." (originals) Background scenes on courts, plain backs, hand colored courts. 48 cards out of 52. C. 1818 .... 250.00

"Tiffany Harlequin." 2⅝ x 3¾". Gold edges. 52 cards complete. C. 1879. U.S.A 200.00

"Vanity Fair" by U.S.P.C. Unique courts, clowns' heads backs. 52 cards complete. C. 1895. U.S.A .. 165.00

Transportation

"American Export Isbrandtsen Lines, Inc." Steamship in fold on solid background. 52 cards complete plus 2 jokers. C. 1950 .... 12.50

"Japan Airlines." Standard American faces, narrow. Japanese stamp, original case. 52 cards complete 12.50

"KLM Airlines." Narrow, standard English faces. Red-blue stripes with insignia backs, original case. 52 cards complete 12.50

"Swiss Airline" by Muller. Swiss courts, original case. 36 cards complete 10.00

World's Fair and Exposition

"Columbian Exposition Chicago, 1893". Wide, backs have Columbus landing in America. Good condition. 52 cards complete 50.00

"Jamestown Exposition, 1907". Backs are stained glass window of Pocahontas' baptismal. 52 official pictures, original case. 52 cards complete 75.00

"N.Y. World's Fair, 1939." By Western Products Co. Narrow, standard faces. 52 cards complete plus joker 20.00

"N.Y. World's Fair, 1964." Spanish by Fournier. Original case. 48 cards complete 65.00

POCKET KNIVES

Over the years a wide variety of pocket knives has appeared on the market. Each had its use or mis-use

Advertising Type

"German Savings Bank". Davenport, Iowa. Sterling ....$ 35.00

"Purina." Checkerboard handle. 3-blades 15.00

Autopoint. 2-blades 10.00

Case

Bone. Long pull. Stamp XX. C. 1940-1955 .... 125.00

Bone. 10 dots. C. 1970 .... 35.00

Bone. Transition. XX to USA. C. 1965 .... 50.00

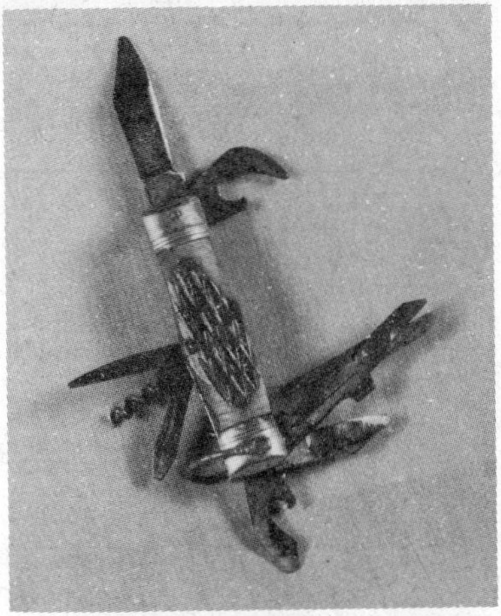

Unmarked. Simulated horn. 8 blades with corkscrew $25.00

Bone. USA. C. 1965-1970 ...... 40.00

Red Bone. Long pull. Stamp XX. C. 1940-1955 .... 185.00

Red Bone. Stamp XX. C. 1940-1955 .... 100.00

Stag. Long pull. Stamp XX. C. 1940-1950 .... 225.00

Stag. 10 dots. C. 1970 .... 125.00

Stag. USA. C. 1965-1970 ...... 85.00

Cattaragus Cutlery Co. Stag bone. 1-blade 20.00

Clover. Mother-of-Pearl. 2-blades .. 15.00

Colonial. White handle. 2-blades .. 10.00

Imperial. Mother-of-Pearl. 2-blades 25.00

Kabar Union Cut. Bone stag. 2-blades. #61106. .... 650.00

Keen Kutter. Stag-type handle. 3-blades 10.00

Pal Cutlery Co. Boy Scout-type. 4-blades 20.00

Remington, Patterns

#R-17 .... 50.00

#R-71 .... 75.00

#R-111 .... 100.00

#R-153 .... 165.00

#R-185 .... 175.00

#R-205 .... 200.00

Robenson. "Sure Edge." Bone. 2-blades 20.00

Saynor, Cooke. Redal. "Dog Leg." Bone. 1-blade 20.00

Henry Sears & Sons. Stag-type handle. 2-blades 35.00

Union Cut Co.

Circle mark. Bone stag. Pattern #61106LG 750.00

Shield Mark. Bone stag. Pattern #61106 .... 850.00
Straight line mark. Bone stag. Pattern #61106 .... 650.00

Unmarked
Gold. 14K. 3¼" long. Embossed. 2-blades 75.00
Goldplated. 2¼" long. 1-blade .. 25.00
Pewter. 2-blades 35.00
Silverplated. Floral decor. 1-blade 12.50
Stainless Steel. 2-blades 15.00
Sterling. 2" long. 1-blade 25.00
Sterling. 3" long. Embossed scroll design. 2-blades 50.00

POMONA GLASS

Pomona Glass was initiated by Joseph Locke and was first produced by the New England Glass Works in 1884. It has a frosted ground on clear glass which is frequently mineral stained in amber or pale blue.

First grind refers to the method in which the glass was etched by acid with a needle point. Second grind was a less time consuming method that consisted of rolling the glassware in acid resisting particles and then etched with acid.

Tumbler. Decorated. First grind ...$135.00

Bowls
4½ x 2¼" deep. Crimped rim. Amber stain. Second grind ....$ 85.00
5 x 2½" deep. Cornflower. First grind 150.00
8". Cornflower. Crimped rim. Second grind. New England 400.00
9½ x 4½" deep. Cornflower. Crimped rim. Second grind. New England 500.00

Cream and Sugar. 2¾" high. Crimped tops. Amber handles. First grind 395.00
Cruet, Stoppered. Pansy and Butterfly. Amber stained. Second grind. 250.00
Pickle Castor. 11½" high. Cornflower. Silverplated frame, tongs. Second grind 450.00

Pitchers
6". Trefoil top. First grind 225.00
8". Bulbous. Cornflower. Applied clear handle. First grind 650.00
8½" Tankard. Pansy and Butterfly. Applied amber handle. Second grind 500.00
8½". Undecorated. Second grind... 400.00

Plate. 6½". Ruffled rim. Second grind 195.00

Punch Cups
Acanthus Leaf. First grind. New England 295.00
Blueberries. Second grind. New England 250.00
Cornflower. Second grind. New England 125.00
Diamond Quilted. First grind 100.00

Rose Bowl. 5½" high. Cornflower. D.Q. Second grind 375.00
Shakers, Salt and Pepper. 4" high. Cornflower. Amber stain. Original tops. Second grind. Pair 350.00

Tumblers
Cornflower. First grind 175.00
Cornflower. Second grind 125.00
Diamond Quilted. Second grind .. 125.00
Pansy and Butterfly. Applied amber handle. Second grind 500.00
Undecorated. First grind 100.00

Vases
3". Fan-shape. Undecorated. Second grind 150.00
6½". Cornflower. First grind 325.00

TR&C°

PORTO BELLO WARE

This is an early pottery made by John and Thomas Astbury of Shelton in the mid 18th century. It was issued to commemorate the capture of the Porto Bello on the Isthumus of Panama. The ware was reddish brown, glazed and decorated with figures of fortification, ships, etc. in white.

The Porto Bello pottery encountered as in the market was made in Tunstall, Staffordshire after 1830 as an imitation of the Pratt-type work of Porto Bello, Scotland. The glaze is a deep brown with an allover paisley-type design in ochre.

Bowl. 5x 2¾" deep. Allover paisley decor ....$ 150.00
Jug. 5½" high. Oriental scene 225.00
Tray. 7½ x 11½". Octagonal. Open handles. Allover paisley decor. Impressed Scott 200.00
Vase. 6". Tapered square. Allover leaf decor 175.00

PORTRAIT PLATES

During the latter part of the Victorian era, plates decorated with portraits of beautiful women were an important decorative feature in many homes. The majority of the portraits were transfers produced commercially; some were hand painted and artist signed. Seldom was the subject a member of the family. Prices vary accordingly to blanks used, and the quality of the artist's or firm's work.

8½". Handpainted. Artist signed. TVL $45.00

Amicitia. 9½". Burgundy rim. Gold trim. Royal Vienna. Beehive mark $ $ 150.00
Amorosa. 9½". Facing right. Burgundy rim. Gold trim. Royal Vienna. Beehive mark 125.00
Ariadne. 9¾". Tin. Dresden Art 40.00
Constance. 9½". Cerise and mauve rim. Gold trim. Handpainted. Artist signed 75.00
Innocence. 9¾". Handpainted. Artist signed 65.00
Lady Harcourt. 11". Royal Vienna. Beehive mark 225.00
Madame Le Brun and Daughter. 9". Handpainted. Gold rim. Unsigned. 45.00
Madame Monreau. 9". Handpainted. Haviland 75.00
Mademoiselle Elisabeth. 9". Pink rim. Gold trim. Artist signed. Sevres 175.00
Madonna and Child. 9½". Brown rim. Unsigned 50.00
Queen Louise. 8¾". Limoges 40.00
Miscellaneous
9". Handpainted. Artist signed. Limoges 50.00
10". Turquoise rim. Gold trim. Unsigned. Austria 65.00
10½". Blue rim. Royal Bayreuth... 50.00
11½". Art Nouveau-style. Iridescent gold rim 85.00
11½". Burgundy rim. Gold trim. Bavaria 55.00

POST CARDS

Post card collecting is technically known as deltiology and a post card collector is called a deltiologist. Austria was the first country to put a post card in the mail in 1869. England followed suit in 1870. The well known Raphail Tuck cards were a result of Queen Victoria's request. The first colored photographic post cards were issued in 1939.

Prices listed are approximate. Artist, subject, condition, circa and desirability must be considered . . .and not necessarily in this order.

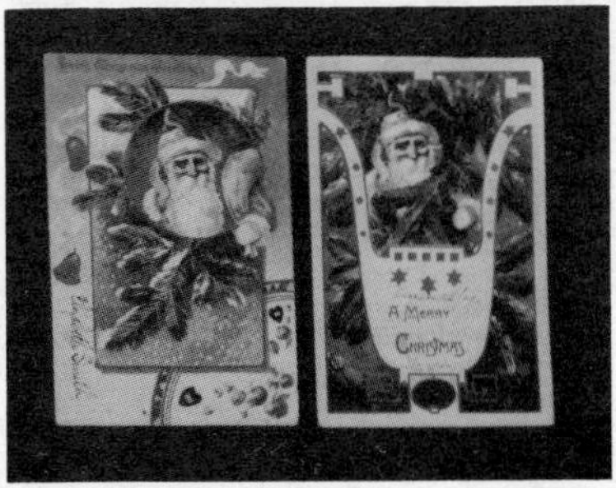

Santa Claus. Tuck. Each $7.50

Actors or Actresses. Pre-1915 ....$ 2.00
Airplanes. Early 2.00
Automobiles. After 1930 .... .75

Automobiles. Pre-1930	1.50
Billikens. C. 1908	7.50
Bridges, Covered	1.00
Capitols. (U.S. State)	1.00
Capitols. (U.S. State) With seals	3.50
Christmas. Embossed. Pre-1915	3.50
Christmas. General	1.50
Clapsaddles. Signed	5.00
Courthouses. Pre-1925	3.50
Disasters. (Floods, Tornadoes, etc.) Pre-1930	2.50
Easter	1.50
Easter. Embossed. Pre-1925	3.50
Expositions. 1900's	3.00
Florals	1.00
Foreign. Early	1.00
Fraternal Organizations	2.00
Gelatin. (Processed type)	1.75
Greetings, General	.75
Hall Mfg	1.50
Historical. Modern	1.00
Humorous	1.00
Indians. Pre-1915	3.00
Leather	2.50
Lithophanes	7.50
Mitchell. Fruit, flowers. C. 1900's	1.50
Patriotic	1.00
People, Famous	2.00
Presidents. After 1915	2.00
Presidents. Pre-1915	5.00
Religious. Pre-1930	2.50
Royalty	3.50
Santa Claus	
Bergman	3.50
Nash	3.50
Stechner	3.00
Tucks	7.50
Whitney	3.50
Winsch & Winsch	3.00
U.S.A. (Made)	1.75
Ships. After 1930	1.00
Ships. Pre-1930	1.50
Souvenir Folders. Pre-1925	2.00
States. After 1930	.50
States. Pre-1930	1.50
Thanksgiving	1.50
Trains. Early	1.50
Trolley Cars	2.50
Tucks	
Dickens	5.00
Four Seasons Bears. Set of 4	15.00
Greetings. General	3.50
Greetings. Holidays	7.50
Nursery Rhymes	3.00
School Days	5.00
Women	5.00
Valentines. General	1.50
Valentines. Sentimental. Early	5.00
World War I	3.00
World War II	1.50

POSTERS

Posters are commercially produced art works for the purpose of advertising products or services, announce events or introduce people. They were seldom considered serious works of art; even when executed by accomplished artists. Today, posters are a recognized art form and have attracted art connoisseurs.

Prices given are approximate. Condition is important and affects the final price considerably.

ADVERTISING

"Anheuser Busch Beer." 12 x 21 x 24". Eagle Brand. C. 1930's $	15.00
"Dandy For Home Made Candy." Karo. Leyendecker. C. 1920's	295.00
Fisk Tire. 10x 14". Maxfield Parrish. C. 1917	35.00
"Hello! Have You Had Your Beech-Nut Gum Today." 11 x 21". C. 1940's	20.00
Hires Root Beer. 13 x 37". Self-standing. Maxfield Parrish	275.00
"Nabisco." 11 x 22". Baker with box of cookies. C. 1910	65.00
"New Victor Records, Oct. 26, 1923." 14 x 34". Victor Records. Metal ribs	50.00
"Orange Crush." 12 x 18". Bathing beauty. C. 1930's	20.00
"Pompeian Beauty." 7½ x 28". Forbes. Metal. Autographed, "Sincerely, Mary Pickford." Dated 1917	75.00

ADVERTISING-TOBACCO

"Flyer 5c Cigar." 9x 20". Lindberg Commemorative. C. 1920's $	10.00
"I'd Walk A Mile for A Camel." 21 x 48". Litho on cloth. C. 1910	125.00
"Kool Cigarettes." 12 x 18". Willie the Penguin. C. 1940	5.00
"Prince Albert Is The National Joy Smoke." 21 x 48". Litho on cloth. C. 1910	125.00
"Red Indian Tobacco." 20 x 30". Tin rim	225.00
"True Individuality." 14 x 30". Chesterfield. C. 1929	40.00

CIRCUS

Cooper Bros. 8x 22". Double sided pictorial. C. 1920's $	10.00
Hamid Morton. 'Featuring Clyde Beatty.' Litho. Late 1940's	25.00
Ringling Bros. Barnum & Bailey. Landing of Columbus. C. 1896	150.00
Ringling Bros. Barnum & Bailey. 28 x 40". Litho. C. 1928-30	60.00
Ringling Bros. Barnum & Bailey. 20 x 30". Col. Tim McCoy. Litho. C. 1935	50.00
France. 33 x 44". Cirque D'Hiver. Winter Circus. C. 1890	115.00

POLITICAL

Blaine, James G., President and John A. Logan, Vice-president. 15 x 20". C. 1884. Pair ....$	75.00
"Johnson & Humphrey for the USA." 20x 28". Black and white photos. Folded C. 1964	15.00
McCarthy. 25 x 38". "Peace." Ben Shahn. C. 1968	100.00
"Nixon's The One." 20 x 28". Official Nat'l. Youth For Nixon-Agnew. J. Michailson. C. 1968 ..	35.00
Roosevelt, F.D., A Gallant Leader. 39 x 59". Black and white portrait. C. 1940	85.00
Wallace. 14 x 22". C. 1948	35.00

THEATRICAL

African Queen. 40x 80". Folded. C. 1952. Original ....$	175.00
Alice In Wonderland; Disney. 14 x 22". French	30.00
A Star Is Born. 30 x 45". Judy Garland and James Mason. C. 1954	75.00
Blazing Saddles. 27 x 41". Mel Brooks	10.00
Bus Stop. 27 x 41". Marilyn Monroe. C. 1956	35.00
Equus. 40 x 60". Clive Barnes quote. Broadway edition	55.00
Godspell. 30 x 45". David Byrd. Broadway edition	25.00
Gone With The Wind. 27 x 41". Classic reissue, 1968-1974	15.00
Jaws. 27 x 41". C. 1970's	10.00
Jesus Christ, Superstar. 40 x 80". Broadway edition. Original	25.00
Red Dragon, The. 14 x 22". Charlie Chan. French. C. 1937	25.00
Santa Fe Trail. 14 x 22". Errol Flynn. Litho. French	30.00
Sleuth. 40x80". Broadway edition.	25.00
The Sting. 27x41. "Richard Amsel..	15.00
Three Penny Opera. 40 x 80". Paul Davis. Broadway edition	60.00

TRAVEL

Air France. 27 x 40". C. 1935 ....$	40.00
B & O RR. 11 x 30". Mid winter excursions to Washington, D.C. C. 1891	35.00
Ile De France. Litho. C. 1915	85.00
Pa. RR. 27 x 42". Pittsburgh in the Beginning-Fort Prince George, 1754. Linen mounted. N.C. Wyeth. C. 1925	200.00

WORLD WAR I

"Clear the Way." 20 x 30". H.C. Christy. Bond ....$	125.00
"Food is Ammunition-Don't Waste It." 20 x 30". J.E. Sheridan	80.00
"Have You Answered the Red Cross Christmas Roll Call?" 28 x 40". Harrison Fisher	55.00
"I Want You for the Navy." 28 x 40". H.C. Christy	350.00
"Order Coal Now." 20 x 30". Leyendecker	350.00
"Treat 'em Rough." 14 x 22". Ahgiet Hutof	175.00
"Weapons For Liberty." Leyendecker. Bond	200.00
"Your Country Needs You. Join the Navy Now." 20 x 30"	100.00

WORLD WAR II

"Buy War Bonds." 28 x 40" ......$	60.00
"Give 'em Both Barrels." 28 x 40". Jean Carlu. Mint	275.00
"Keep 'Em Flying. 28 x 40". Ivan Dimitri	45.00
"Remember Dec. 7th." 28 x 40". Saalburg	65.00
"This Is the Enemy." 20 x 30"	65.00
"We Have Just Begun to Fight!" 30 x 40"	35.00

POT LIDS

Pot lids are just 'that' . . .lids from pots or containers. The pots originally held ointments, pommades or soap. The lids were decorated with transfers of various scenes.

The majority of these ceramic containers were made by Pratt, Fenton, Staffordshire between 1845-1888.

Although a complete set; pot and lid is desirable to some collectors . . .lids are the most collectible.

It has been reported that some of these lids with the original designs have been reissued by Kirkman Pottery, England.

"The Thinker."................$65.00

Blue Boy $100.00
Cavalier, The 75.00
Charing Cross 85.00
Crabbing on Ordic Beach 65.00
Cries of London 60.00
Crystal Palace 125.00
Game Bag, The 75.00
Garibaldi 75.00
Golden Hour. Constantinople 100.00
Good Dog 65.00
Hamlet and His Father's Ghost 125.00
Harbour of Hong Kong 65.00
Hide and Seek 75.00
Landing the Fare, Pegwell Bay 125.00
Master of the Hounds 95.00
Ning Po River 65.00
On Guard 100.00
Pair, A 100.00
Persuasion 75.00
Picnic, The 110.00
Residence of Ann Hathaway 85.00
Rifle Contest. Wimbledon 100.00
Second Appeal 85.00
Seven Stages of Man. "As You Like It." Act II 95.00
Shakespeare's Home 95.00
Shepherdess with Dog, 3 sheep 100.00
Shrimpers, The 75.00
Thirsty Soldier, The 55.00
Uncle Toby 85.00
Village Wedding 125.00
War 95.00
Westminster Abbey 150.00
Wolf and Lamb 75.00

POTTERY, EARLY

(See "Stoneware")

POWDER FLASKS AND HORNS

Early containers for carrying gun powder were made of animal horns, especially those of cattle and buffalo . . .thus the name Powder Horns. Patented containers made of copper, brass, pewter and other materials came into use much later.

Brass
- Dead Game. 8½". James Dixon Co $75.00
- Eagle. 4" 85.00
- Eagle. With gun and flask. 4½" 150.00
- Fleur-de-Lis 65.00
- Floral.5" 55.00
- Rabbit. 8" 65.00
- Shell. 8" 65.00
- Undecorated. 9½". American 50.00
- Wreath and Shell. American Brass and Cap Co 60.00

Copper
- Eagle. 5". Brass dispenser 85.00
- Gunstock-type. James Dixon Co 95.00
- Hunting Scene. 8". Ameladk and Capio 60.00
- Ribbed 55.00

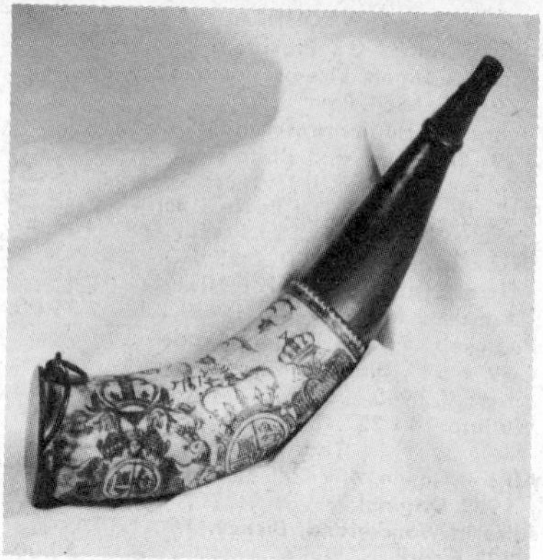

Horn. 13" long. Scrimshaw. German. 18th Century $750.00

- Stag. 8" 65.00
- Undecorated 50.00

Horn
- 8" 45.00
- 8½". Brass dispenser. Leather shoulder sling. Complete. All original 95.00
- 13" 65.00
- 15". Pewter plug 75.00
- 15". Scrimshaw. Map of New England. C. 1650-1700 .... 650.00

Leather Covered
- Flora and Fauna. 9" 75.00
- Undecorated. 9". Brass dispenser 45.00

Pewter. 7". Brass dispenser 85.00

PRATT

PRATT
FENTON

PRATT WARE

The earliest Pratt earthenware was made by William Pratt, Lane Delph in the late century. In 1810-1818 Felix and Robert Pratt, sons of William, established their own firm known as F. & R. Pratt, Fenton, Staffordshire. The wares consisted of relief molded jugs, commercial pots and tablewares with transfer decoration. (See "Pot Lids") Much of the early ware is unmarked. The mid-nineteenth century wares bear several different marks in conjunction with the name Pratt, including "&Co."

Plate. "Philadelphia Public Building, 1876." 8½" $110.00

Candlestick. 7⅜". Figures. Roman Key border .... $ 75.00
Compote. 9¼" diam., 5" high. Transfer of English castle 150.00
Cream and Sugar. 4". Scenic transfer decor. Set 100.00
Creamer. 3". Basalt. White figures in relief 65.00
Dessert Set. Eight 5½" plates. Oval handled bowl. Scenic transfers .. 350.00
Mugs
Frog. 5¼ 125.00
Satyr Mask. 4¼". C. 1810 ...... 225.00
Pitchers
4¾". "Mischievous Sport." Polychrome 225.00
5¼". Wellington. Pink lustred trim 195.00
6½". Transfer of hunt scene. Blue and gold. C. 1850 .... 125.00
11". Pewter cover. Beige background. Colorful seashells in relief. C. 1810 .... 500.00
Plates
Battle of the Nile. Basketweave border. 9½" 65.00
Game Bag. Basketweave border. 9½" 65.00
Hop Queen. Acorn and oak border. 10" 150.00
Laundry Woman. Tan border. 8½". 60.00
Philadelphia Exposition 1876. 8½" 110.00
Picnic, The. Maroon border. 8½" .. 60.00
Roman Ruins. Roman Key border. 8½" 55.00
Shakespeare's Birthplace. Basketweave border 75.00
Times, The. 7" 55.00
Trooper, The. Basketweave border 65.00
Pot Lids, See "Pot Lids"
Snuff Jar. 4". Blue with tan and black transfer of men, animals .. 30.00
Toby Jug. Englishman. 3½". Multicolored 85.00
Vase. Urn-shaped. Handles. 4½". Classical figures. Orange with gold 95.00

PRIMITIVE PAINTINGS

Primitive painting was a special art school in America during the 19th century. Many of the artists had no formal art education; but had God-given talent and a desire to create. Charming portraits . . .especially of children were executed. Many times they were out-of-proportion with unusual facial expressions and an interesting palette. Some of these portraits were painted in stages. The artist would prepare the background and figure of a subject in his studio; sans the head. He would then travel the countryside seeking prospective clients. The head and features of the chosen model were then painted in to complete the portrait. Seldom are these paintings artist signed.

Primitive type painting continues. Twentieth century artists, namely Grandma Moses are bringing record breaking prices at auctions.

Prices given are for paintings offered and-or sold. Prices will vary according to desirability, quality and condition.

Apples and Book. 8x 10" .... $ 400.00
Boy with Dog. Gold leaf frame. 42 x 54" 3000.00
Child with Butterfly. Gold frame. 14 x 18" 750.00
Farm Scene. Walnut frame. 20 x 30". 850.00
Fruit. Still life. Unframed. C. 1835. 18x 24" 650.00
Girl, Young. Gold gilt frame. 37 x 50" 2000.00
Girl Pouring tea. Gold leaf frame. 26 x 30" 2500.00
Girl with Flowers. 17 x 20". C. 1840. 750.00
Lady and Gentleman. Framed. 28x 34". Pair. 500.00
Three Children. 26 x 45". C. 1825 .. 2000.00

PRINTS

Prints are intended reproductions of an artist's original painting, drawing, design, etc.

Recently, prints have come into their own because of the surging interest in the arts, and the almost "untouchable" prices of original works. It is possible to gather good works of art at a fraction of the cost of the originals through prints. Be careful of the 'reproductions' of the 'reproductions'; know your prints or know your dealer!

For the most complete, comprehensive price guide of Currier and Ives and contemporaries, consult "4th Print Price Guide" published by E.G. Warman Publishing, Inc.

Kellogg. "The Morning Prayer." $50.00

Baillie, J.
- Christ Blessing Little Children ... $35.00
- Eliza ... 30.00
- Iron Steamship, The ... 125.00
- Polk, James ... 45.00
- Young Bride, The ... 40.00

Currier and Ives
- American Country Life. "October Afternoon." Large folio ... 550.00
- Burning of Chicago. Small folio ... 220.00
- Clipper Ship. Red Jacket. Small folio ... 425.00
- Life and Age of Man, The. N.C. Small folio ... 60.00
- Portraits. Small folios. Each approximately ... 40.00
- Presidents. (Washington to Polk) Small folio. Each approximately ... 100.00
- Seasons. Small folio. Set of 4 ... 200.00
- Washington Crossing the Delaware. Small folio. N.C. ... 275.00

Godey. Fashion Print ... 15.00

Gutmann. (Bessie Collins Pease) 14 x 21". Children's scenes ... 25.00

Haskill and Allen
- Fannie ... 30.00
- Smuggler ... 75.00

Icart, Louis
- Alms ... 425.00
- Apache Dancer ... 375.00
- Bathing Beauties ... 850.00
- Carmen ... 600.00
- Cinderella ... 500.00
- Coach, The ... 550.00
- Daisy ... 350.00
- Goldfish Bowl ... 350.00
- Lamp, The. (Blonde) ... 350.00
- Mardi Gras ... 1100.00
- Mealtime ... 400.00
- Model I ... 1200.00
- Rainbow ... 1200.00
- Smoke ... 600.00
- Speed ... 850.00
- Tosca ... 450.00
- Venus in the Waves ... 1500.00
- White Lilies ... 650.00
- *Winter ... 300.00
- Wisteria ... 900.00
- Zest ... 1000.00

Kellogg, E.C. Uncle Tom and Little Eva ... 60.00

Kellogg and Bulkeley. Little Sissy ... 40.00

Kellogg and Thayer. Three Kittens ... 50.00

Nutting, Wallace (Matted and Framed)
- Along the Wall. 6 x 9¼" ... 25.00
- Brookside Blossoms. 9 x 12" ... 35.00
- Coming Out of Rosa. 18 x 22" ... 45.00
- Decked as a Bride. 7 x 9¼" ... 20.00
- Flowering Time. 4½ x 13" ... 30.00
- Jane. 4½ x 9½" ... 50.00
- Larkspur. 14 x 16" ... 45.00
- Sparkling Blaze, The. 10 x 12" ... 55.00
- Stitch in Time ... 75.00
- Summer Vale. 7 x 9" ... 25.00
- Thanksgiving Goodies. 14¾ x 16¾" ... 85.00
- Unbroken Flow, The. 12 x 21" ... 35.00
- Waterfall Curve, A. 7 x 9" ... 30.00

Parrish, Maxfield
- Atlas. 10x 12" ... 25.00
- Cleopatra. 6½ x 7½" C. 1917 ... 75.00
- Daybreak. 12 x 15". C. 1922 ... 75.00
- *Daybreak. 18 x 30". C. 1954 ... 30.00
- *Ecstasy. 7 x 11". C. 1970 ... 10.00
- Evening. 13 x 16". Framed ... 75.00
- *Garden of Allah. 9 x 18". C. 1954 ... 25.00
- Garden of Allah. 12 x 20" ... 50.00
- Lute Players. 16 x 20". Vertical ... 100.00
- Old King Cole. 10x 27". Famed ... 100.00
- Page, The. 9½ x 13". (Knave of Hearts) C. 1925 ... 60.00
- Pied Piper, The. 15 x 30". Framed ... 175.00
- Prince, The. (Not from Knave of Hearts) C. 1925 ... 125.00

Romance. 18 x 30". (Not from Knave of Hearts) Framed 250.00
*Stars. 7 x 11".C. 1970 .... 25.00
Twilight. 18 x 20" 150.00
*Twilight. 18 x 22". C. 1954 .... 25.00

Prang, Louis. Untitled. Approximately 12 x 15". Each 25.00

Rockwell, Norman, See "Rockwell, Norman"

Sarony and Major
Death of Montgomery 75.00
Wedding Day 50.00

Sarony, Major & Knapp
Big Blackfoot Valley. 9 x 11½" .. 15.00
Fort Benton. 9 x 11½" 15.00

*Reissued

PRINTS, JAPANESE

Japanese woodblock prints of the 18th and 19th century are considered 'sleepers' in the collecting field; but interest is rising.
Values range from a few dollars to thousands of dollars depending on artist, subject, quality and condition. A popular print had many editions. First and second editions command the highest price.

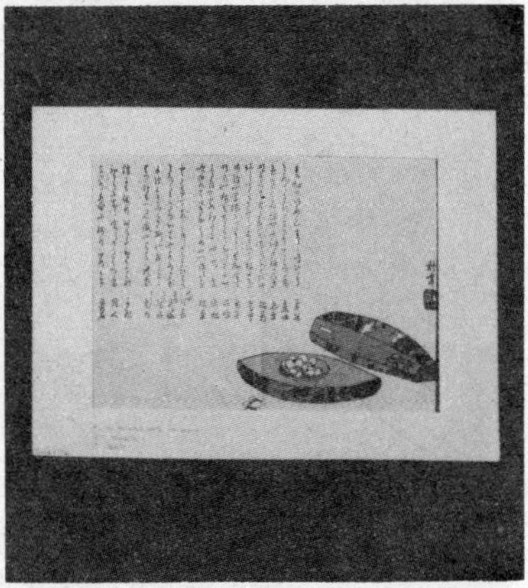

Shutei "Plum Blossom in box." C. 1860. H,C. $125.00

Explanation of abbreviations
D-Diptch
H-Horizontal
T-Triptych
V-Vertical
Sizes
A-Aiban 9 x 13½"
C-Chuban 7 x 10"
K-Koban 6 x 9"
O-Oban 10 x 15"

Azechi
Portrait of a woman. 46-100, 1955. V,C ....$ 40.00

Chikanobu
Beauty wearing blue kimono, Shin Bijin, 1897. V,O 125.00
Second Industrial Exposition, Yokohama, 1881. V,O.T 175.00

Eisen
Beauty holding a tea cup. C. 1825. V,O 250.00
Courtesan and Samurai. C. 1825. V,C. B-W 100.00

Eishi
Standing beauty with cat at her feet. C. 1785. Hashira-e (Pillar print) 850.00

Eisho
Two beauties lounging on veranda. C. 1785. Hashira-e. (Pillar print) 1500.00

Hashimoto, Okiie
Rock garden, 1960. H, 18" x 23". (29-60) 200.00

Hironobu
Police breaking up party 40.00
Priest seeing serpent in fire 40.00

Hirosada (Osaka)
Bust portraits. 1845-50. V,C. Each...................... 125.00

Hiroshige I
Famous Views of the 60 Odd Provinces, 1853-1856. V,O.
Chikuzen-Boats.............. 350.00
Iyo-Flying Geese 400.00
Kii-Cranes flying over water .. 650.00
Omi-Moonlit night scene 500.00
Snow at Skukiyagashi in Edo .. 1250.00
Scene at an inn at Akasaka, Hoeido Tokaido, 1832. H,O 675.00
Snow at Seki, Reisho Tokaido, 1848-50. H,O 1000.00

Hiroshige II
48 Views of Edo, C. 1860. V,C. Each 60.00

Hiroshige III
A tour of Western Japan, 1877. V,O, T 175.00

Elizabeth Keith
Outside the Hata-Men, Peking, 1922. V, O 125.00
Returning from the funeral, Korea, 1922. V, O 125.00

Kunisada
Actors as circus performers-a samisen player and horseback rider, 1852. V,O 150.00
Beauties enjoying cherry blossoms in evening, 1849-53. V,O,T 275.00

Four actors in kabuki play with dialogue above them, 1862. V,O,D 150.00
Seated beauty, C. 1820, V,O 275.00
Warrior climbing out of large box, 1840's. H,O 85.00
Kuniyoshi
Edo Nishiki Imayo Zukushi (Scenes in the 60 Odd Provinces), 1852. V,O. Each 200.00
69 Stations of the Kisokaido, 1852, V,O.
Ageo-Woman being weighed against gold pieces 225.00
Kawado-Procession of blind travelers 225.00
Sadahiro I (Osaka)
Bust Portraits, C. 1850, V,K. Each. 75.00
Sadanobu (Osaka)
Maple trees at Bridge to Heaven, Famous Views of Kyoto, C. 1850. H,C 100.00
Nobles seated in front of Emperor and Empress, C. 1875. V,O,D 150.00
Saito (Kiyoshi)
Girl looking through flowers, Autumn, 1950. V, 22" x 32". 11-30 .... 275.00
Sekino
Girl and rooster, 1958. V, 19" x 24". 12-50 .... 325.00
Owls and Woods, 1957. H, 19" x 24". 5-100 .... 325.00
Shijo School
Surimono, C. 1860. H,C. Each .. 75.00
Shunga (Erotic Prints)
Chikanobu-Erotic paintings on silk, C. 1900. H, 8" x 9½". Color ... 175.00
Kunisada-Erotic scene, 1850's. H, 8" x 7". Color 100.00
Kunisada-Erotic scenes, C. 1850. H, 10" x 13". Color 150.00
Shunsen
Beauties on a veranda, surimono, C. 1820. H,O 250.00
Toyohiro
Lion, C. 1800. V,C. B-W 75.00
Woman in a boat, C. 1810. V,C. B-W 85.00
Toyokuni I
Sawamura Gennosuke as young man Tomojiro, C. 1800. V,O 300.00
Tea house woman holding a teapot, C. 1800. Hashira-e. (Pillar print) 895.00
Toyokuni II
Segawa Kikunojo as a waitress, C. 1825. V, O 175.00
Three actors fighting over a banner, C. 1820. V,O,T 725.00

Yoshitsuya
War Stories of the wars of 16th Century, 1864. V,O. Each 75.00

Quezal

QUEZAL

Quezal Art Glass was produced in Brooklyn, N.Y., from 1901-1920 by Martin Bach, a former Tiffany employee. After the death of Bach in 1920, his son-in-law, Conrad Vohlsing, opened a small shop near Elmhurst, L.I. New York, where he produced the same type of ware until 1929. Vahlsing marked his glass "Lustre Art Glass."
Named after the Central American bird, Quezal Glass has an iridescent finish featuring contrasting colored glass threads. While still in the cooling stage, the threads were pulled up and drawn into various designs, often a drape with a peacock eye at the end of the feather. Gold, green and white colors are most often found.

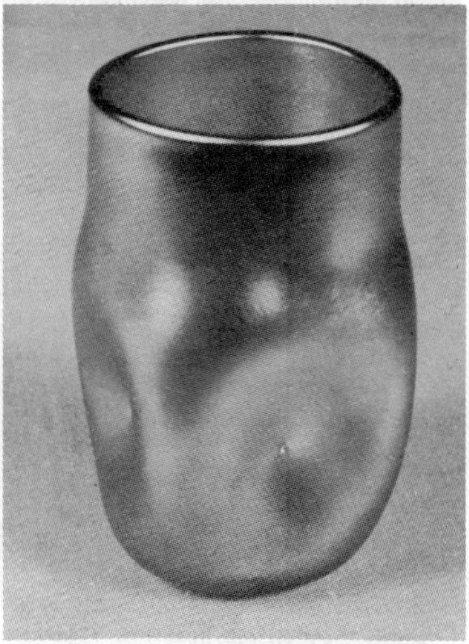

Vase. 3". Dimpled. Gold iridescent. Signed $350.00

Bowls
5½ x 3¾" deep. Blue iridescent. $ 450.00
10 x 5" deep. Gold iridescent with flowers and leaves in green iridescent 1000.00
Candlestick. 10". Blue iridescent .. 450.00
Cologne Bottle, Stoppered. 7¾". Cone-shaped. Ribbed. Gold irisdescent 350.00

Compotes

6x 8" high. Gold iridescent 500.00

7½ x 4½" high. Blue iridescent .. 650.00

Lamp Shades-See "Lamp Shades"

Plate. 11¼". Iridescent gold 650.00

Rose Bowl. 4¼". Iridescent blue .. 500.00

Salts

3" diam. Ribbed. Gold iridescent... amethyst 300.00

3" diam. Ribbed. Gold iridescent 225.00

Tumbler. 3½". Gold iridescent 195.00

Vases

5". Melon-shaped. Iridescent green and rose. Cased with opalescent white 650.00

5½". Iridescent blue-green base, gold iridescent top. Silver overlay... 1500.00

6". Chalice-shaped. Gold iridescent. Cased in white 650.00

6". Trumpet-shaped. Ruffled top. Gold iridescent. Signed and numbered 600.00

6¾". "Pulled Feather." 650.00

9". Gold iridescent. "Pulled Feather." 850.00

10". Gold iridescent. "King Tut." 850.00

10½". Gold iridescent in ornate brass holder. Signed 1000.00

15". Rainbow iridescent. Floral silver overlay 3000.00

QUILTS

(See "Textiles")

QUIMPER

Quimper earthenware has been made in Quimper, France for over 300 years; but it was in the early 1800's when Jules Henriot, Finistere, France introduced the Breton peasant-type decoration that the ware gained recognition.

Two companies continue to produce this pottery . . .James Henriot, Quimper and so marked and the Fainceries Bretonne de la Grande Maison factory marked "HB Quimper." Pieces made after 1891 also bear the country of origin, "France."

Bell. 3". France ....$ 25.00

Bowls

6½" 15.00

9". Square 25.00

10"......................... 35.00

Box, Covered. 2½ x 4½ x 6" 35.00

Butter, Covered. France 15.00

Butter Pat. France 75.00

Candleholder. 5¼". Chamber-type 40.00

Creamer 30.00

Cruet Set. 2 bottles. With holder .. 50.00

Cup and Saucer. Demi. France 22.50

Bowl. 8 x 2" deep. Scalloped rim. Marked Henriot Quimper, France. . . .$45.00

Egg Cup 30.00

Figurals

Goose. 5¼" 40.00

Peasant. 5¼" 45.00

Inkwells

8" long x 4½" wide. With tray .. 50.00

12" long. Double 125.00

Heart-shaped 150.00

Knife Rest. 3½" long 35.00

Mug 40.00

Nappie. 5¾" 18.50

Pitchers

6½" 35.00

8" 50.00

Plates

5" 10.00

6½" 20.00

7½". Flowers only 22.50

8". Hexagonal 30.00

9½". Soup 55.00

9¾" 30.00

11"........................ 45.00

Platter. 15". Hanging-type 65.00

Relish. 16½" long. 3-sections 65.00

Salts

Diamond-shaped. Double 30.00

Diamond-shaped. Single 15.00

Oval 10.00

Swan-shaped 25.00

Sugar, Covered 35.00

Tea Tile. Four feet............... 35.00

Teapot. Small 85.00

Tray. 8½ x 15". Open handles 65.00

Tumbler. 4½" 20.00

Tureen, Covered. 9 x 14"......... 125.00

Vase. 6" 40.00

R.S. GERMANY
R.S. POLAND
R.S. PRUSSIA
R.S. SUHL
R.S. TILLOWITZ

(See "Schlegelmilch Porcelain")

RADIO RECEIVERS

A growing number of collectors have taken an interest in early items from the electronics field. At present, radio receivers are one of their favorites.

Atwater Kent. Model 318. Beehive-type. Table model $75.00

Angeulus. Cathedral case ......$	125.00
Clapp Eastman. R 4	95.00
Crosley. Ace B3	50.00
Crosley. Pup. C. 1925	300.00
Eveready. Table model. Metal cabinet. C. 1932	100.00
Grebe. Table model with separate speakers. Type CR5. C. 1920's ..	275.00
Magnavox. TRF. C. 1925	250.00
Marconiphone. Model 42. Table top. C. 1930's	125.00
Philco. Beehive-type. C. 1930's	75.00
Philco. #551. C. 1928	125.00
RCA. Aeriola, Jr. C. 1922	125.00
RCA Radiola. Model #26	500.00
RCA Radiola III. Box-shape. Bakelite. Complete. C. 1924	195.00
RCA Victor. Traveler. Battery operated. Complete. C. 1925	125.00
Westinghouse. Aeriola, Sr. Receiver-type. RF. Battery operated. C. 1920's	150.00

RAILROAD ITEMS

With the passing of railroads for transportation of people for business and pleasure, many of the items used on and for the maintenance of the trains have become collectible, especially the tableware that graced the well appointed dining cars of the past.

Platter. 11". B&ORR. Warwick ..$18.00

Ticket case. 8½ x 16 x17½" high. Connellsville, Pa. Railroad Station. Oak with tin ticket holders $75.00

Badges
"Baggageman." PRR. Gold

colored ....$ 20.00
"Investigator." NYCRR. Enameled logo 50.00
"Police Shield." ERR. Eagle top .. 60.00

Bell, Locomotive. 17". Brass. Hand and Air actuated 750.00

Book. Rules and Instructions. C. 1915-1930. Each ....2.00 – 5.00

Buttons, Uniform. Brass
C. 1870-1900. Each 5.00
C. 1900-1952. Each 3.50

Dining Car-Tablewares
Ashtray. NYCRR. 24 K gold trim .. 22.00
Bowls
6" oval. Serving. RIRR. "Golden Rocket." Shenango 50.00
6". NPRR. "Villard." Shenango 35.00
7". GNRR. Silverplated 40.00
Castor Set. 3-bottles. NY, NH, HRR. 6½" long boat-shaped frame. Silverplated. Reed & Barton 75.00
Celery. 4½ x 10". MRR. "Peacock." 11.75
Coffee Pot. 14 oz. PRR. "Broadway Service." Trenton 34.95
Cream and Sugar, Covered. NY, NHRR. Silverplated. Reed & Barton. Set 60.00
Crumber. NHRR. Silverplated .. 15.00
Cups and Saucers
"Centennial." B&ORR 25.00
"Flambeau." Demi. CNRR 25.00
Egg Cup. SPRR. "Poppy." 15.00
Finger Bowl. With underplate. Wabash RR. Silverplated 55.00
Flatware. Silverplated
Boullion spoon 7.50
Cocktail fork 6.50
Dinner fork................... 10.00
Knife 8.00
Tablespoon 8.50
Teaspoon 7.50
Serving spoon 15.00
Goblet. UPRR 7.50
Ice Bucket. YCRR. Silverplated .. 75.00
Menu Holder. PRR. With applied Keystone crest 27.50
Napkins. With logo. Each 7.50

Plates
7". SRR. "Peach Blossom." Buffalo 17.50
7¼". NYCRR. "Mercury." Syracuse 22.00
7½". Pullman Co. "Indian Tree." Syracuse 40.00
7½". Soup. MRR. "Traveler." Syracuse 12.50
8". Soup. MRR. "Peacock." Syracuse 13.75
9". C&ORR. "George Washington." 325.00
9". NPRR. "Yellowstone." Shenango 35.00
9¼". Soup. B &ORR. "Derby." H.P. Chandlee Sons 20.00
9½". SFRR. "Mimbreno." Syracuse 45.00
9½". PRR. Broadway Service. "Mt. Laurel." 30.00
11". ICRR. Glass. Showing seven different locomotives 85.00

Platters
8½" oval. GNRR. "Mountains and Flowers." Syracuse 20.00
10". With cover. WPRR. Silverplated 27.50
18½". GNRR. "Glacier." 150.00
Sherbet. 3¼" diam. NHRR. Silverplated 16.00

Tablecloths with logos.
36x 36" square 15.00
42 x 58" 20.00

Tray. 5¼ x 8¼". NHRR. Silverplated. International Silver Co .. 15.00

Wine Glass. NYCRR 15.00

Firebucket. Canvas with folding metal frame. Bail handle 40.00

Lanterns, Hand
Adams & Westlake. Etched globe. Ring bottom 40.00
Adlake-Kero. Clear globe. Ring bottom 45.00
Adlake-Reliable. Embossed globe. Ring bottom 75.00
Armspear. Embossed globe. Brass drop pot. Ring bottom. C. 1889 .. 75.00
Dietz Vesta. Clear globe. Single ring 65.00
Handlan. Embossed globe. Double ring. Ring bottom 75.00
M.M. Buck. Clear globe. Brass top. Bell bottom. C. 1908 .... 125.00

Lanterns, Marker
Adlake. Blue lens. Brass plated. C. 1906 .... 125.00
Armspear. 4 lenses 150.00
Handlan. Amber lens 85.00

Lanterns, Switch
Armspear. 4 lenses. (2-green, 2-red) 125.00
Dressel. 4 lenses 65.00
Handlan. 4 lenses. (2-amber, 2-green) 125.00

Money Bag. Railway Express Agency. Gray canvas 10.00

Oil Can. 24" o.h. Large spout. Copper 60.00

Passes. C. 1890-1915. Each 7.50-12.50

Sign, Crossing. 36" diam. Metal. Black letters with reflective yellow crystals. C. 1920's 50.00

Switch Control Box. 19" Oak with brass trim 125.00

Switch Key 10.00

Telegraph Key. Brass. Early 25.00

Ticket, Punch. Conductors 5.00
Tickets. C. 1890-1930. Each 5.00-7.50
Tie Bars. Goldplated. C. 1920-1930's. Each. 5.00
Timetables
Pre-1900 .... 10.00-15.00
C. 1900-1930 .... 5.00-10.00
C. 1930-1965 .... 3.00-7.50
Torch. 7½" spout, 7" loop handle. 7" high. Tin. Pint. Pre-1860 .... 45.00
Water Dispenser. NY, NH, HRR. Gallon. Milk can-shaped. Tin. Handled cover. Loop handles. Brass spigot 55.00
Way Bills
C. 1840. Each 10.00-15.00
C. 1880's. Each 5.00-10.00
Whistle, Caboose. Steam operated. Brass. Embossed Sherburne Co., Boston. Pat. 1890212. C. 1930 .. 75.00

RAZORS

Razors date back several thousand years. The Egyptians, Greeks and Romans had metal razors. Earlier man used sharpened stones for the purpose.
Early metal razors were made of hand-hammered steel such as Damascus steel. Later, in the 19th century, razors were made of machine steel and hard tempered to hold their edges. The best known in this country were those made by various companies in the Sheffield area of England. Razors of equal quality were also imported from Germany.
The invention of the safety razor has practically 'edged out' the straight-edge razor. Today the electric shaver is fast replacing the safety razor.

"Ideal Safety Razor." Reg. #67745. Pat's. Simulated leather case ..$15.00

"Arlington." Electric Cutlery Co ..$ 7.50
"Army and Navy." Imperial, Germany 20.00
"Chip-A-Way." Chip-A-Way Cutlery Co 12.50
"Clean Clipper." Rector & Wilhelmy & Co 6.50
"Columbian Exposition." Dated 1893 .... 25.00
"Extra Superb." Solinger, Germany 7.50
Griffon. Carved ivory handle 30.00
"Ideal." Elsener, Switzerland 7.50
"Osgar." Sheffield 15.00
"Red Imp" 6.50
Rogers, Joseph 10.00
Sears, Henry and Co. Wooden handle 5.00
"Statue of Liberty" 25.00
"The Celebrated." Wade and Butcher, Sheffield 10.00
"The Palmer." Ivorine handle 6.50
Unmarked. Barber shop-type. Set of 7. Straight edge razors in original box 50.00

REDWARE

From the late 1600's on; the availability of clay, the same used to make bricks and roof tiles accounted for the great production of red earthenware pottery in the American colonies. Redware examples are mainly utilitarian . . .bowls, crocks, jugs, etc.
Lead-glazed redware retained its reddish color, but a variety of colored glazes were obtained by the addition of metals to the basic glaze. Streaks and mottled splotches in redware items resulted from impurities in the clay and or uneven firing temperatures.
"Slipware" is a term used to describe redwares decorated by the application of slip, a semi-liquid paste made of clay. Slipwares were made in England, Germany and elsewhere in Europe for decades before becoming popular in the Pennsylvania Dutch country and elsewhere in colonial America.

Bowl. 10¾ x 6" deep. Tapered sides. Glazed. Cogglewheel decor. New England. 19th century ....$ 200.00
Butter Churn. 10½". Earred handles. Glazed. Cogglewheel decor on shoulders. Original wood dasher 335.00
Candle Sconce. 6½" high. Glazed. Yellow slip decor 250.00
Colander. 7½". One handle. Glazed interior. Pa. C. 1850 .... 225.00
Flower Pots with Saucers
6¾". Crimped rims. Unglazed. Pa. 125.00
8½". Crimped rims. Glazed. Cogglewheel decor. New England. 19th century 350.00
Jars
5¾". Glazed. Cogglewheel decor. 150.00
8¾". Earred handles. Glazed. Cogglewheel and manganese splotches 200.00

Jugs
- 5¾". Bulbous. Manganese glaze. 95.00
- 10½". Glazed 250.00

Milk Pan. 16". Glazed 175.00

Plates
- 9". Glazed. Cogglewheel edge. Yellow slip trailings 275.00
- 10¼". Glazed. Slip decorated "ABC." 375.00
- 12". Notched rim. Glazed 100.00
- 13½". Notched rim. Yellow slip trailings 400.00

Porringer. 3½". Handled. Manganese glaze. 75.00

Sugar Bowl, Open. 4½". Two handles. Glazed. Yellow slip trailings 150.00

Tray. 8¾ x 12½". Notched rim. Yellow slip trailings 450.00

Washboard. 12 x 22". Wooden frame. Tin glazed with manganese splotches 275.00

RED WING POTTERY

There were several potteries located in Red Wing, Minnesota in the late 1800's. The parent company was the Red Wing Stoneware Co. A merger with other local potteries resulted in the formation of the Red Wing Union Stoneware Co. in the early 1900's. The firm was one of the largest producers of stoneware utilitarian wares ...crocks and jugs. ..in the United States. In 1930, when the desirability for stoneware items diminished, a line of art pottery was introduced and the company was renamed Red Wing Potteries, Inc. Production of stoneware continued in limited quantities until 1947. The art line flourished until 1967 when the stockholders voted to liquidate the establishment due to labor disputes.

Bean Pot, Covered. Interior glaze. Provincial ware. #28 ....$ 25.00

Beater Jar. Stoneware 35.00

Bowl. 8 x 3¼" deep. Tab handles. Pink 12.00

Canning Jar. 1 quart. Stoneware .. 35.00

Coffee Server. 12¾". Green. "Waffle." 25.00

Compote. 6 x 9" diam. Green and ivory. Cherubs in relief 25.00

Console Sets
- Square-shaped. Bowl 9", candlesticks 3¾". White with pale green interior 25.00

Pot. 4 x 5" diam. Handled. Brown high glaze interior, tan matte exterior. Impressed $20.00

- Bowl 10", candlesticks 2 x 5" long. Ivory with brown accents. Vintage decor 30.00

Cookie Jars. Figural
- Apple 22.50
- Baker 25.00
- Dutch Girl 35.00
- Monk 30.00

Cornucopia. 7½". Green and yellow 15.00

Crock Pot. 4 x 5". Handles. Unglazed tan exterior, glazed interior 25.00

Pitchers
- 4". "Waffle." 10.00
- 7". "Swirl." 25.00
- 10". "Griffin." Cobalt 45.00

Planter. 5 x7½ x 14". Green. Deer and lady decor 20.00

Teapots
- Chicken. Yellow 35.00
- Handpainted florals on cream ground. Flower finial 25.00

Vases
- 6". Bulbous base. Slender neck. Handles. White matte glaze 15.00
- 6½". Ivory. Gardenia in relief. Brown stain 27.50
- 7½". Conch shell-shape. Turquoise and white 17.50
- 8". Green. Bird of Paradise in relief 18.50
- 8". Yellow. Free form 12.00
- 9". Green. Dancing maiden, trees. High glaze 45.00
- 10". Blue mottled glaze 22.50
- 10½". Five finger-type. Brown and green 30.00
- 12". Bamboo. Yellow 30.00

Wall Pocket. 8". Flower form. White 15.00

RELIGIOUS ITEMS

Objects for the worshipping or expression of man's belief in a superhuman power are being collected by many people for many reasons.

Bank. 8½" high. Cast iron. Christ Child with Lamb. Painted yellow $30.00

Bible, Family. Leather with brass fittings . . . . $ 50.00

Fonts, Holy Water

- Angel. 3½ x 8" Porcelain. French 100.00
- Cross. 2½ x 5". Porcelain. Handpainted 65.00
- Madonna. 14". Parian 150.00

Icons

- 1¼ x 1½". Traveling-type. Goldwashed silver. 19th century 300.00
- 6x 6½". Brass. Greek. 19th century 350.00
- 9¾'' o.h. Triptych. Steeple-shaped. Carved wood with Madonna and Child medallion center, angels on outer panels. Handpainted 100.00
- 10½ x 12". Silver gilt. Greek. C. 1850 . . . . 500.00

Rosary with case. Goldplated 25.00

REVERSE PAINTING ON GLASS

Reverse painting on glass is non-indigenous. Although studied in parts of Europe in the 17th century and a similar technique applied by the Chinese as early as the 13th century; reverse painting on glass did not reach any significance in America until the 18th century.

European artists preferred classical and mythological scenes. In America, the subject matter was usually confined to patriotism, family mourning pictures and traditional still life.

Quality and demand for such paintings decreased with the advent of less expensive methods of print making. By the 1850's, most reverse paintings on glass were executed by non-professionals and are rarely signed.

Jerome Napoleon. Framed. 12¾ x 15¾" $275.00

Basket of flowers, birds. Gold frame. 18½ x 22½" . . . . $ 300.00

Country Scenery. Walnut frame. 21 x25" 195.00

Floral with birds. Red painted frame. 18¼ x 22½" 350.00

Jersey Beauty, The. Portrait. Framed. 10¾ x 13½" 250.00

Lady in Blue Gown. Framed. 7½ x 10" 225.00

Lafayette. Framed. 12½ x 15½" . . 350.00

Oriental Scene. Mother-of-Pearl frame. 7¾ x 10" 125.00

Sweet Little Dear. Full length portrait of girl. Framed. 6½ x 10" ..	250.00
U.S. Capitol Building. C. 1916. 17½ x 23"	45.00
Washington, George. Portrait. Framed. 7 x 10"	300.00
Washington, George. Full length portrait. Framed. 10 x 12"	500.00
Young Cavalier. Framed. 8 x 10" ..	225.00

RIDGWAY

The name Ridgway has been prominent in English pottery since the early 1800's. Two firms, J. & W. Ridgway and William Ridgway, operated in Shelton during the 1800's producing a series of historical scenes. Most early wares marked "Ridgway" were made by one of these two firms.
See "Staffordshire." Ridgway Potteries, Ltd. continues operation today in England.
The following listing is comprised of other "Ridgway" potteries' production . . .items made after the 1840's.

Plate. "Coaching Days and Coaching Ways." 9" $35.00

Bowl. "Racing the Mail." 8 x 4" deep $	55.00
Chocolate Pot. "Ursas." Sepia	85.00
Creamer. "Giraffe." Sepia. 19th century	45.00
Mugs	
"Changing Horses." Sepia	42.00
"Christmas Eve."	50.00
"Eloped."	35.00
" Salisbury Cathedral."	30.00
Pitchers	
Bacchus with Pan handle. Pewter lid. 11"	250.00
Cattails in relief. Green salt glaze. Pewter lid. 10"	165.00
"Henry VIII, Abbot of Reading." 4"	35.00
"Tam O Shanter." Gray salt glaze. 6¼"	85.00
"Waiting for Coach." Tankard. 9¾"	50.00
Plates	
"A Morning Delight." Black. 9" ..	45.00
"Asiastic Palaces." Blue. Set of 6 ...	125.00
"Giraffe." Blue. 10"	50.00
"Maidenhair Fern." 4½"	10.00
"Paying Toll." Sepia. 9"	35.00
Turkey. Blue. 10½"	45.00
"Winter Day's Amusement." 9" ..	35.00
Platters	
"Maidenhair Fern." 8"	30.00
"Tyrolean." Green. 14¾"	85.00
Teapot. "Old Derby." 5"	150.00
Vegetable, Covered. Delft-type. Blue	40.00

RING TREES

Small, tree-like objects of glass, metal or porcelain with branches for hanging or storing finger rings are known as "ring trees."

Sterling silver with cornelia stone in center. Marked Chiaravalli Milano $75.00

Glass	
Cobalt. Gold decor of flowers and leaves. 4¼" ....$	55.00
Cranberry. White enamel decor. Gold trim. 4"	50.00
Crystal. Pear-shape. Blue rose in center	100.00
Gray. Bristol-type. Handpainted florals	35.00
Milk. Pink roses. Green leaves. 3" ..	37.50
Metal	
Gold tone. Shape of hand, heart-shaped tray. 3½"	35.00
Silver, Sterling. Tiffany and Co. 2½ x 3½" diam	125.00
Porcelain	
Austrian. Handpainted floral decor	25.00
Austrian. With attached hatpin	

holder. White with pink roses. Gold trim 50.00
Bavarian. Handpainted floral decor. Gold trim. 3" 27.50
Copeland. Morning glory, bee decor 40.00
Haviland. Handpainted floral sprays on white. Gold trim 25.00
Limoges. Hand-shaped. Gold ring, bracelet. Pink roses. Gold trim .. 35.00
Nippon. Hand-shaped. Hand-painted roses 30.00

ROCKINGHAM WARE

Rockingham earthenware was first produced on the estate of the Marquis de Rockingham, Yorkshire, England in 1745. A succession of potters followed for almost 100 years. The well-known dark brown high glaze pottery known as "Rockingham" was introduced by Brameld & Company, Swinton, England in 1788. Porcelain of great artistic beauty was also made at the same factory in the 1820's and continued until the firm was dissolved in 1842.
The well-received Rockingham-type glaze was used in the United States by various potteries including the Bennington, Vermont works.
See "Bennington."

Salt Shaker. 4½" high. Brown glaze $95.00

Bed Pan. Brown glaze ....$ 100.00
Bird Whistle. 3" long. Brown glaze 65.00
Bowl. 9 x 4¼" deep. Brown glaze .. 65.00
Compote. 8". Low standard. Turquoise flower border on white porcelain 85.00
Creamers
- *Cow, Covered 150.00
- Silver lustred on white porcelain 75.00

Cup and Saucer. Rose and gold decor on white porcelain 50.00
Cuspidor. 8 x 3½" high. Scalloped shell with embossed ribbing. Brown glaze 125.00
Figurines
- Cat. 5½" high. Brown glaze 125.00
- Dog. 10½" high. Brown glaze .. 225.00
- Lion. 5¼ x 8¾" long. Reclining on base. Brown glaze 150.00

Foot Warmer. Brown glaze 100.00
Mug. 3¾". Brown glaze 50.00
Pastille Burner. 5 x 5¼". Encrusted with mossy grass and pastel flowers. 4 columns. C. 1820's 375.00
*Pitcher. 9". Hound handle. Brown glaze 225.00
Plates
- 6". Floral center. Green rim, gold trim 35.00
- 9¾". Pie. Brown glaze 55.00
- 11". Pie. Brown glaze 75.00

Tea Service. Teapot, sugar, creamer, 6 cups and saucers. Florals on white. Gold trim 650.00
Tureen, Covered. 6 x 6½" diam. Flower panels. Gold trim. C. 1825 200.00

*Reproduced Item

ROCKWELL, NORMAN

Norman Rockwell's influence on many forms of creative production . . .from bells and plates to coins and figurines . . .requires this separate category of Rockwell "collectibles." These items are not antiques as such; but they demand attention because of the popularity of the artist and the increased demand for reproduced versions of his work since his death on November 8, 1978.
Born in 1894, Norman Rockwell was America's best known and prolific artist and illustrator. He produced over 3000 works, including 323 "Saturday Evening Post" covers, "Boy's Life" covers and calendars, plus over 1,500 paintings for various advertisers. Rockwell works, with the most value, are the original illustrations and limited edition lithographs.
In the months following his death, prices began to skyrocket. In 1979, they have tended to fluctuate; and some time will pass before values of various Rockwell "collectibles" will stabilize.

1978. Gorham Fine China. "Triple Self Portrait." $37.50

Bells

Danbury Mint Series No. 1. 1975-1977 issues. Each ...... $ 55.00
Danbury Mint Series. 1979 issues. Each 35.00
Gorham. Sweet Song So Young. 1974. F.E. 80.00
Grossman Designs, Ltd. Faces of Christmas. L.E. 35.00
River Shore, Ltd. Children's Series. No. 1. 1977. Set of four 300.00

Coins

Ford Motor Company-50th Anniversary 20.00
Four Freedoms. Kennedy Mint. Set of four 150.00
Four Seasons. Hamilton Mint. L.E. Set of four 80.00

Figurines

Gorham Fine China
At the Vets. RW-4 ...... 50.00
Big Decision. RW-25 ...... 100.00
Pride of Parenthood. RW-18 ...... 90.00
Tiny Tim. RW-3 ...... 55.00
Triple Self Portrait. RW-27 ...... 150.00
Gorham Fine China. "Four Seasons." Sets of four.
1972. Boy and His Dog 1750.00
1973. Boy and His Girl 1200.00
1974. Four Ages of Love 1500.00
1975. Grandpa and Me 1000.00
1976. Me and My Pal 1000.00
1977. Grand Pals 750.00
1978. Going on Sixteen 750.00
1979. Tender Years 600.00
Franklin Mint. Porcelain
1976. Joys of Childhood. Series of ten. L.E. Each 150.00
Grossman Designs, Inc. L.E.-1000
1974. Baseball. NR102. (Closed) 500.00
1975. Barbershop Quartet. NR23 350.00
1976. Tom Sawyer Series No. 1. (Closed) 250.00
1977. Tom Sawyer Series No. 2 or No. 3. (Closed) 225.00
1978. Tom Sawyer Series No. 4. (Closed) 200.00
Grossman Designs, Inc. (Retired)
1973. Lazy Bones. NR8 ...... 250.00
1973. Leapfrog. NR9 ...... 400.00
1973. Marble Player. NR11 ...... 350.00
1973. Red Head. NR1 ...... 150.00
1973. Schoolmaster. NR10 ...... 200.00

Igots

Franklin Mint
Mark Twain
Bronze. Set of ten 175.00
Sterling. Set of ten 350.00
Hamilton Mint
Christmas
1974. Sterling 30.00
1975. 24K gold on fine silver 40.00
1976. Sterling 30.00
1977. 24K gold on fine silver 55.00
1978. Sterling 40.00
Fondest Memories. Sterling. Set of ten 500.00
Four Freedoms. Fine silver. Set of four 225.00
Portraits of America. Fine silver. Set of 24 ...... 850.00

Medals

Franklin Mint
Boy Scouts of America. Spirit of Scouting. Sterling. Set of 12 ...... 300.00
Girl Scouts of America.
Bronze. Set of 12 ...... 250.00
Sterling. Set of 12 ...... 500.00

Ornaments

Hallmark Cards, Inc.
1975 ...... 12.00
1976 ...... 10.00
1977 ...... 10.00
Gorham
1979. Tiny Tim. F.E. 20.00
Grossman Designs, Inc.
1975. Faces of Christmas. No. 1. L.E. 20.00
1976. Santa Planning Visit. No. 2. L.E. 10.00
1977. Rocking Horse. NRO-3 ...... 6.50
1978. Santa's Road Map 5.00
1978. The Carrolers. NRX-3. L.E. (Closed) 40.00
1979. Drum for Tommy. NRX-24. L.E. 25.00

PLATES

Brown and Bigelow
- 1977. F.E. Runaway. Clown Series 60.00
- 1978. F.E. Traveling Salesman. Salesman Series 50.00
- 1979. F.E. Grand Pals. Grandpa and Me Series 55.00

Franklin Mint
- 1970. F.E. Bringing Home the Tree. Sterling 500.00
- 1971. Under the Mistletoe. Sterling 200.00
- 1972. The Carrolers. Sterling 200.00
- 1973. Trimming the Tree. Sterling 225.00
- 1977. American Sweethearts. Crystal. Set of six 950.00

Gorham Fine China
- 1970. F.E. Family Tree 200.00
- 1974. F.E. Christmas. Tiny Tim 40.00
- 1976. Dwight D. Eisenhower 50.00
- 1976. Four Freedoms. Set of four 250.00
- 1976. John F. Kennedy 50.00

Gorham Fine China. "Four Seasons." Sets of four.
- 1971. A Boy and His Dog 600.00
- 1972. Young Love 225.00
- 1973. Ages of Love 375.00
- 1974. Grandpa and Me 225.00
- 1975. Me and My Pal 200.00
- 1976. Grand Pals 200.00
- 1977. Going on Sixteen 225.00
- 1978. Tender Years 125.00
- 1979. Helping Hand 125.00

Grossman Designs, Inc.
- 1976-1979. Tom Sawyer Series. Set of four 250.00

Lake Shore Prints
- 1973. F.E. Butter Girl 225.00

River Shore, Ltd.
- 1976-1979. Famous American Series. Copper. Set of four 750.00

Rockewell Society of America
- 1974. F.E. Christmas. Scotty Gets His Tree 150.00
- 1976. F.E. Mother's Day. A Mother's Love 85.00
- 1977. F.E. Heritage. Toymaker 125.00

Royal Devon
- 1975. F.E. Christmas. Downhill Daring 60.00
- 1975. F.E. Mother's Day. Doctor and Doll 85.00

Prints

Circle Gallery, Ltd.
- Children At the Window. 20 x 26". Lithograph 1750.00
- Critic, The. 28x 32". Collotype 4000.00
- Doctor and Doll. 29 x 35". Collotype 12500.00
- Family Tree. 20x 35". Lithograph 4500.00
- Four Seasons Folio. 20 x 21". Lithograph. Set of four 4800.00
- Freedom From . . .Fear, Religion, Speech, Want. 29x 35". Collotype. Each 5000.00
- Marriage License. 28x 32". Collotype 5500.00
- Prescription. 24 x 30". Lithograph 3500.00
- Schoolhouse. 15 x 18". Lithograph 1500.00
- Tom Sawyer Folio. 20x 26". Lithograph. Set of eight 17500.00
- Wet Paint. 24 x 30". Collotype 1800.00

Eleanor Ettinger, Inc.
- After the Prom. 24 x 26¾". Lithograph 4500.00
- Ben Franklin. 21 x 28". Lithograph 4000.00
- Buttercup. 21x24". Lithograph 3250.00
- Gilding the Eagle. 21x 25½". Lithograph 2750.00
- Puppy Love Folio. 20x 21½". Lithograph 8500.00
- Sports Folio. 20¼x24½". Lithograph 8500.00
- Swing, The. 20x 21". Lithograph 3000.00
- Young Lincoln. 19 x 34". Lithograph 7500.00

Miscellaneous

Ads, Individual. Approximate value.
- 1915-1920. Each 20.00
- 1920-1940. Each 15.00
- 1940-1970's. Each 10.00

Bowl. 8½ x 5½" deep. Ben Franklin. Danbury Mint 125.00

Display Cards. Individual ads. Approximate value. Each 125.00

Magazine Covers. S.E.P. including other publications. Approximate value.
- 1920-1930. Each 35.00
- 1930-1940. Each 25.00
- 1940-1960. Each 10.00

Posters
- Freedom From . . .Fear, Religion, Speech, Want. One sheet. World War II. Each 100.00

Steins. Gorham. L.E.
- 1976. Pride of Parenthood 85.00
- 1977. A Boy Meets His Dog 65.00
- 1978. The Mysterious Malady 55.00
- 1979. Adventures Between Adventures 50.00

Toby Mugs. Grossman Designs, Inc.
- 1979. NR1 thru NR6. Each 40.00

Trays
- 1975-1976. Various designs and producers. Approximate value. Each 20.00

ROGERS' STATUARY

John Rogers, born in America in 1829, studied sculpturing in Europe and produced his first plaster-of-paris statue, "The Checker Players" in 1859, followed by "The Slave Auction" in 1860.

His works were popular parlor pieces of the Victorian era. He published at least 80 different subjects and the total number of groups produced from the originals is estimated to be over 100,000.

One of his best and largest pieces is "The Council of War" which shows President Abraham Lincoln, Gen. U.S. Grant and Edwin M. Stanton.

It has been determined that "Romeo & Juliet," "Is That You Tommy?" and "A Capital Joke" were never listed in Rogers' catalogue. Some authorities attribute them to Casper Henneke, one of Rogers' contemporaries.

"First Love." $325.00

Camp Fire .... $	500.00
Checker Players, The	850.00
Checkers up at the Farm	550.00
Coming to the Parson	600.00
Council of War (hands behind head)	1000.00
Council of War (hands at side)	1000.00
Council of War (hands forward of head)	1000.00
Favored Scholar, The	500.00
Fetching the Doctor	650.00
First Love	325.00
Football	850.00
Going for the Cows	500.00
"Is it So Nominated in the Bond?" ..	500.00
Neighboring Pews	600.00
Parting Promises	400.00
Phrenology at the Fancy Ball	650.00
Playing Doctor	600.00
Rip Van Winkle at Home	500.00
School Days	650.00
School Examinations	500.00
Shaughram and Tatters	400.00
Slave Auction	1250.00
Town Pump (canteen in front)	500.00
Traveling Magician	550.00
Uncle Ned's School	675.00
Union Refugees	750.00
We Boys	400.00
Weighing the Baby	650.00
"Why Don't You Speak for Yourself"	500.00
Wounded Scout, The	650.00

ROOKWOOD POTTERY

Rookwood Pottery was founded in 1880 by Mrs. Marie Longworth Nichols Storer, Cincinnati, Ohio. The name of this outstanding American art pottery was derived from the family estate, "Rookwood", named for the 'rooks' or crows which inhabited the wooded grounds.

From 1880 to 1941, when it was sold, Rookwood Pottery changed with the times and the variety of the wares is endless . . .in glazes and designs. In the 1930's alone at least 500 different types of glazes were used.

There are 5 distinctive Rookwood marks: the clay or body mark, the size mark, the decorator mark and the factory mark. Rookwood art pottery can best be dated from factory marks.

In 1880-82 the factory mark was the name "Rookwood" incised or painted on the base. Between 1881 and 1886 the firm name, address and year appeared in an oval frame. Beginning in 1886, the impressed "RP" monogram appeared and a flame-mark was added for each year until 1900. After 1900; a Roman numeral, indicating the last 2 digits of the year of production, was added at the bottom of the "RP-flame mark" monogram. This last mark is the one most often found on Rookwood pottery encountered today.

Ashtrays	
Bat. 6". Blue matte. 1942 .... $	65.00
Fox. 6¾". Brown. 1931	55.00
Nude. 4". Green. 1948	65.00
Bookends, Pairs	
Elephants. White matte. 1920 ..	175.00
Lions. Brown. 1925	150.00
Rooks. Green matte	195.00
Bowls	
4 x 4" o.h. Covered. Two handles. Shape 554. Floral sprays on standard glaze. Sally Coyne. 1894 ..	225.00
5¾x 2½" deep. Covered. Embossed florals. Matte maroon glaze. 1909	65.00

Penquin. 5x 5½" high. Black matte glaze. Artist signed. C. 1934 . . $225.00

Vase. 8½" high. Bulbous base, slender neck. Incised design on gold. Green matte glaze. 1910 . . . . $125.00

6x 1½" deep. Pink porcelain glaze. 1916 . . . . 85.00
8 x 3" deep. Reticulated. Shirayamadani design. 1912 . . 55.00
12". White roses on peach ground. 1891 . . . . 295.00
15". Scalloped. High glaze turquoise interior. White matte exterior. 1926 . . . . 95.00

Boxes, Covered.
2x3x4½". Fruit, flower decor. White matte glaze. 1936 . . . . . . 75.00
5½" diam. Handled. Leaves, twigs decor. A.M. Valentine. 1893 250.00

Candleholders
2". Blossom shaped. Yellow matte glaze. 1923 . . . . 75.00
3½". Paneled. High glaze green. 1946. Pair 50.00
5½". Shape 508. Yellow daffodils. 1891. . . . . 150.00
10". Cattail decor. Rose matte glaze. 1922. Pair 65.00

Console Set. Pedestaled bowl, 5½ x 11" diam. Candlesticks 4½" high. Elephant decor. Celadon glaze. 1929 . . . . 175.00

Creamers and Sugars
Cherries and berry decor. 1901 . . 275.00
Floral decor on salmon glaze. H. Wilcox. 1890 . . . . 350.00

Dinnerware. "Blue Ship." 1920's
Bowl. 10 x 3" deep. Shape M29 . . 85.00
Butter, Covered. Shape M13 . . . . 60.00
Cream and Sugar 75.00
Plates
6". Shape M7 . . . . 25.00
14". Shape 2701L 85.00
Platter. 7 x 10". Shape M30 . . . . 45.00

Ewers
4". Pansy decor. Sara Saxe. 1897 225.00
5¾". Berry decor. Brown-yellow, orange glaze. 1904 . . . . 175.00
10½". Vintage decor. Browns, greens, yellow. Valentine. 1892 . . 350.00

Figurines
Bird. 5". Red, white, blue high glaze 125.00
Dog. 5". Brown. 1946 . . . . 125.00
Donkey. 3⅝". Green. Louise Abel. 1922 . . . . 165.00
Rabbit. 3¼". White. 1910 . . . . . . 175.00
St. Francis. 11½". Beige high glaze. Artist signed. 1947 . . . . . . 125.00

Humidors
5 x 9" high. Yellow glaze. 1940 . . 150.00
6x 6¾". Decor of pipes, cigars, leaves. LNL. 1899 . . . . 650.00

Inkwell. 3½ x 6" diam. Incised geometric design. Green glaze. 1903 . . . . 100.00

Jardinieres
- 4½". Flower spray. Sallie Toohey. 1889 .... 225.00
- 7¾". Yellow roses, buds. Van Briggle. 1899 .... 500.00

Jugs
- 4½". Bamboo. Black, gold highlights. 1884 .... 500.00
- 4½". Hops and leaves. 1896 .... 275.00
- 9". Crocus. Silver overlay. Valentine. 1892 .... 1500.00

Lamps
- 8½". Dolphin decor. Shape 2289. White matte glaze. 1920 ...... 95.00
- 24". Green glaze. Flowers in high relief. Shape 2613. 1923 ...... 500.00

Mugs
- 4½". Portrait of Monk. Matthew Daly. 1892 .... 1250.00
- 5". Advertising-type. 1945 .... 150.00
- 7½". Commemorative-type. 1885 275.00
- 7½". Starkville Period. 1963 .... 75.00

Paperweights
- Flower Basket. 2½ x 3 x 5". Toohey. 1929 .... 125.00
- Lizard and Cocoon. 2 x 6". Rose matte glaze 85.00

Pitchers
- 4". Clover decor on brown glaze. Lenore Ashbury. 1895 .... 275.00
- 6". Floral decor. Pink and blue. Wax matte glaze. KWT. 1930 .. 225.00
- 7½". Green high glaze. Animal head handle. 1927 .... 75.00

Plaques
- "Evening." 9½ x 11½". Original frame. E.F. McDermott 1000.00
- "In the Tropics." 14 x 16¼". Epply. 1912 .... 1250.00
- "Snow Scene." 4½ x 8¾". Vellum. Coyne. 1919 .... 1250.00
- "Sunset Scene." Framed. 9 x 13". Hurley 1000.00

Plates
- 8½". Pastel floral design. H.E.W. 1900 .... 250.00
- 8½". White blossoms. Orange high glaze. A.B.S. 1889 .... 265.00

Rose Bowls
- 3". Footed. Blue matte glaze. 1928 .... 85.00
- 4½". Iris. 1904 .... 275.00

Tiles
- 5½" square. Matte ivory and blue ground, slate blue rook. 1945 .. 75.00
- 5¾" square. Cockatoos. W.E.H. 1913 .... 125.00
- 6" square. Dark blue matte glaze. Undated 45.00

Trays
- 3x 8". Red flowers. Green matte glaze. R.F. 1905 .... 150.00
- 10½ x 16½". Corn cob pipes, matches. Brown glaze. Ed Diers. 1898 .... 500.00
- 11¾". Three angels, clouds. H.E.W. 1891 .... 1500.00

Vases
- 4". Bulbous. Handles. Pink to gray-green. Porcelain. 1917 .... 75.00
- 5". Commemorative-type. Blue glaze. 1934 .... 165.00
- 5". Narcissus. Iris glaze. Irene Bishop. 1904 .... 175.00
- 5". Scenic. Vellum. S. Coyne. 1922 450.00
- 5½". Ovoid-shape. Embossed band of flowers. Turquoise high glaze. 1950 .... 20.00
- 6". Flared. Blue porcelain. 1916 ... 85.00
- 7". Bud Blossoms. Aqua matte glaze. 1934 .... 50.00
- 7". Floral. Orange. Leona Van Briggle. 1902 .... 325.00
- 7¼". Amphora-type. Aqua matte glaze. 1933 .... 65.00
- 8". Tulip decor. Green to lavender. Wax glaze. 1936 .... 300.00
- 8". Floral decor. Mauve matte glaze. Elizabeth Lincoln. 1920 .. 150.00
- 8". Tiger Eye. 1885 .... 350.00
- 8½". Berries and leaves. Greens, yellows, browns. S. Coyne. 1902 250.00
- 9". Incised design. Green matte glaze. 1928 .... 55.00
- 9". Mistletoe. Red and green. Sallie Toohey. 1903 .... 195.00
- 10½". Seascape at Sunset. Vellum. E.T. Hurley. 1904 .... 500.00
- 12". Dandelions. Lenore Asbury. 1899 .... 275.00
- 15". Scenic. Blue and gray. E.T. Hurley. 1913 .... 400.00

ROSALINE GLASS

Rosaline glass is a product of the Steuben Glass Works, Corning, N.Y. It is a rose-colored jade glass. Because of this distinction; Rosaline has been separated into its own classification.

Bowls
- 4¾". Handled. Ormolu trim ..$ 150.00
- 5". Flared. With underplate. Set 175.00
- 8½". Flared. Alabaster ring base 275.00
- 12". Flared. Alabaster ring base 550.00

Compotes
- 6" diam. Alabaster standard and wafer foot 250.00
- 8". Alabaster standard 350.00

Cordial. 3½". Conical cup, alabaster stem and wafer foot. Signed Carder 195.00

Decanter. 15½". Alabaster stopper. Fleurde-lis. Signed 500.00

Goblet, Water 275.00

Ladle, Mayonnaise. Alabaster handle 125.00

Rose Bowl. 3½" high 250.00

Salt Dip 185.00

Sherbet. 5½". Crystal stem, wafer foot 175.00

Vases
- 8". Bud. Alabaster wafer base .. 195.00

8¾". Stick-type	225.00
9". Amphora-type. Alabaster base	500.00
Wine. 5½"	225.00

Cruet. Alabaster neck and stopper $195.00

ROSE BOWLS

A Rose Bowl is a decorative open bowl with a crimped or pinched top used to contain fragrant rose petals and a potpourri. The bowl was placed on a table top within a room and the emitting pleasant aroma scented and 'freshened' the air in the room.

A popular room accessory in the late Victorian-Art Nouveau period; Rose Bowls were made in a variety of patterns by practically every glass manufacturer of the period; including fine art glass. See specific categories i.e. "Carnival Glass," "Durand", "Peachblow", etc.

Amethyst. 4½". Handpainted pansies ....$	50.00
Amethyst. 8½". Enameled flowers. Gold trim	150.00
Apple Green. 7¼". Hobbed	35.00
Bristol-type. 4¼". Undecorated ..	30.00
Crystal. Cased. 4". Optic ribbed. Floral decor	75.00

Crystal. 3". Spatter-type decor of tortoise shell with applied gold ..$125.00

Crystal. 4". Floral decor. Gold trim	35.00
Emerald Green. 7". Gold enameled flowers	150.00
Iridescent. 5½". Melon ribbed. Brass trimmed top	50.00
Porcelain. 5". Handpainted florals. Inscribed	55.00
Vaseline. 3"	40.00

ROSE MEDALLION

Rose Medallion or Rose Canton porcelain was first made in China in the 18th century. Originally it was made exclusively for the head of the household called "Mandarin." Later, it was made available to the court people and the feeling was expressed by the groups of people in reserves. Even later, it was made with birds and butterfly decor for the general populous of China.

Rose Medallion pattern is being reproduced today; but obvious to the knowledgeable.

Vegetable, Covered. 8¼ x 9½". Nut finial. Mandarin. C. 1775 ....$700.00

Basket. 4 x 10½" long. Reticulated $	500.00
Bottle. 16" high. Stoppered	525.00
Bowls	
4¾x 2½" deep	85.00
7¼ x 1½" deep. Flanged	165.00
8¼". Shallow	150.00
9x 4" deep	450.00
9½ x 10¾". With tray. Reticulated. Flared rim. Set	750.00
10x 4" deep	500.00
Bowls, Punch	
11¾"	1200.00
14½". C. 1820	1800.00
15½ x 7½" deep. Floral reserves	2200.00
Brush Holders	
3½ x 7". Rectangular	325.00
4¼" high. Cylindrical	225.00
Candlesticks	
8". Pair	750.00
10". C. 1870. Pair	650.00
Chargers	
12". C. 1840	225.00
14½". C. 1790	650.00
16". C. 1840	750.00
Creamers	
Bulbous	185.00
Helmet-type	195.00
Crocus Pot. C. 1870	500.00
Cups and Saucers	
Bouillon, Lidded	75.00
Demitasse	50.00
Handleless	70.00
Hexagonal	85.00
Tea	85.00
Cuspidor	375.00
Ginger Jar. 3½". Covered	225.00
Jug. 5". C. 1820	375.00
Leaf Dish. 8". C. 1820	225.00
Mug. 5". Strap handle. C. 1820	425.00
Pitchers	
4". Bulbous. Rose reserves	195.00
6½". Octagonal	225.00
8½". Bulbous	325.00
Plates	
6½"	60.00
7½"	75.00
8½"	85.00
10⅛"	150.00
Platters	
7½ x 10½"	250.00
9½ x 12"	300.00
14½ x 17½". C. 1790	500.00
Pomade Jar. Lidded. 3½"	125.00
Sauce Boat. 3¼ x 8". Medallion within boat	200.00
Shrimp Dish. 10" long. C. 1820	400.00
Soap Dish. 4¼ x 5½". Covered. 3" high to gold finial. Inner drip dish. Rose reserves	275.00
Spill. 4¼" high. C. 1850	175.00
Spoon, Rice	30.00
Sugar. 5½". Covered. Berry finial. Two handles	325.00
Teapots	
5"	225.00
6". Twig handle	175.00
7". Drum-shaped	300.00
9½". Domed lid	600.00
Teapot and Cup. In original wicker basket. C. 1880	300.00
Teapot and 2 cups. In wicker basket. C. 1880	395.00
Vases	
3½". C. 1820	95.00
6". C. 1820	225.00
8". C. 1870	175.00
8½". Bottle-shaped	325.00
10¼". C. 1870	225.00
12". C. 1830	425.00
14". Hexagonal. Pair	1800.00
17". Hexagonal-shaped. Lidded. Foo Dog finial. C. 1800	1500.00
36". Temple	3000.00
Vegetables	
Covered. 8½ x 10½". Berry finial	500.00
Open. 8½ x 10¾"	375.00

ROSE O'NEILL ITEMS

Rose O'Neill created "Kewpie" in the early 20th century. The pixie-like character was first introduced to the public in the "Ladies' Home Journal." An immediate success, Kewpie dolls and various items decorated with the 'imps' were soon in wide production. Early dolls and china decorated with "Kewpies" were produced in Germany. Later, other manufacturers followed suit. The popularity of the frolicking figures continues as a decorative motif.

Bank. 3". Glass $	95.00
Bowls	
6". Shallow. Six kewpies. ABC border. Germany. Signed	125.00
7½". Shallow. Eight action kewpies. Royal Rudolstadt. Signed	150.00
Box. 3". Green Jasperware. Pink kewpies. Signed	250.00
Candlestick. 4". Applied kewpie	125.00
Clock. Blue Jasper. Signed	275.00
Cream and Sugar. 2½". Green lustre on white	165.00
Creamers	
2½". Blue Jasperware. Seven kewpies. Signed	195.00
3". Action kewpies	85.00
Cup and Saucer. Royal Rudolstadt. Signed Rose O'Neill Wilson	135.00
Figurines	
Baby on Scale. 5¼". Bisque. Signed	95.00

Toothpick Holder. 3" o.h. Glass . . $50.00

Bride and Groom
- 2½". Bisque. Signed 85.00
- 4½". Bisque. Signed 150.00
- Doll. 4½". Celluloid. Signed 45.00

Doll. 5". Bisque. Germany. Signed 100.00
Doll. 10½". Bisque. Signed heart label 350.00
Farmer, The. 4". With rake. Bisque. Signed 250.00
Huggers, The. 2½". Japan. C. 1912 . . . . 45.00
Huggers, The. 3⅝". German. Original bouquet 150.00
Soldier. 4¾". Dressed. Signed . . 225.00
Thinker, The. 6¼". Original heart label. 185.00
Traveler, The. 3½". Bisque. Signed 135.00

Flannels. 5 x 5¾". Signed. C. 1914. Each. 20.00
Hair Receiver. Green Jasperware. Pink kewpies. Signed 175.00
Hat Pin Holder. Blue Jasperware. Signed 175.00
Mug. 3". Pearl lustre. Signed 85.00
Paperweight. 1¼ x 2". Cast iron . . 35.00
Pin. 1½ x 1¾". Porcelain. Pink kewpie with tennis racket 75.00
Plaque. 8 x 10". Wood. Callus. C. 1973 . . . . 20.00

Plates
- 5". Two kewpies. Royal Rudolstadt. Signed 60.00
- 6". Six action kewpies. Royal Rudolstadt. Signed 75.00
- 7½". Deep. Eight action kewpies 125.00
- 8". Nine action kewpies 150.00
- 10". Christmas Plate. Callus. C. 1973 . . . . 25.00

Post Card. Greetings 15.00
Poster. 7⅜ x 18". Framed. "Kewpie Baseball Team". Signed 175.00
Sand Bucket. 3" high. Tin. Lithographed "Kewpie Beach." . . 60.00
Shakers, Salt and Pepper. 3". Silver-plated. Signed. Pair 185.00
Tea Set. Teapot, covered sugar, creamer, 6 cups and saucers. Green lustre bands. Signed 500.00

Toothpick Holders
- Glass 50.00
- Porcelain. Signed 75.00

Trays
- Dresser. Cloverleaf-shape. Five kewpies on green Jasperware. Signed 250.00
- Ice Cream. 11¼ x 17½". Advertising-type 175.00

Vase. 6½". Blue Jasperware with four kewpies. Signed 150.00

ROSENTHAL

Rosenthal Porcelain Manufactory began operating at Selb, Bavarian in 1880. Specialties were tablewares and figurines. According to recent reports, the firm is still in operation.

Server. 9¾". Scalloped and ruffled edge. Handpainted floral decor. Gold ring handle and trim. Artist signed $75.00

Biscuit Jar. 7". Pate-sur-Pate. White flowers on green ....$ 175.00
Bowls
10". Closed handles. Handpainted Dutch scene 85.00
13". Handpainted roses on shaded green, white ground 75.00
Candlesticks. 2¾". White with gold trim. Pair 35.00
Chocolate Set. Pot, creamer, covered sugar. Violets in relief on white. Gold finials and handles 150.00
Coffee Set. Demitasse. Blue and white decor. Gold trim. 18 pieces 250.00
Compote. 10 x 4" high. Handpainted floral center. Fruit border 85.00
Cream and Sugar. Pink florals. Gold trim 35.00
Cups and Saucers, Demitasse.
Ivory with gold bandings and handles. Set of 4 .... 100.00
Silver Overlay. Art Nouveau 35.00
Dinnerware. "Alda." 5 piece place setting 35.00
Figurines
Colt. 7". C. 1946 .... 85.00
Dachschund, Puppy. 6 x 6". Karner 125.00
Fish. 4 x8". On seaweed stand .. 85.00
Goat. 7½". Orange glaze 150.00
Horse. 7". "Dapple Grey" 85.00
Nude. Woman. 4 x 5 x 8". White. Signed L.F.G. 115.00
Rabbit. 2½" 35.00
Scotty, Sitting. 5" 125.00
Wire-haired Terrier, Sitting. 5". Signed 125.00
Mug. 5½". Lustred Art Nouveau style decor 100.00
Pitcher. 5½". Pink roses on white .. 40.00
Plates
8½". Handpainted grapes and roses 45.00
9¼". Oval. Handpainted purple flowers, green leaves. Gold closed handles 40.00
10". Handpainted pink roses on white. Open handles 65.00
Tureen, Covered. 10". Gold trim on white 65.00
Vases
5". Handpainted orchids on black ground. Gold trim 95.00
6". Handpainted pink roses on white 65.00
9". Art Nouveau style decor. Artist signed 150.00

ROSE TAPESTRY

Rose Tapestry was made by Royal Bayreuth, Germany in the late 19th century. The surface of the ware feels and looks like woven cloth. This was accomplished by applying fabric to the porcelain before it was decorated and glazed.

Pitcher. 5" high. Sheep, mountain scene $250.00

Basket. 5 x 5". Roses ....$ 350.00
Bowl. 5¾". Sheep, mountain scene 225.00
Boxes, Covered
4" diam. Three gold ball feet. Roses 200.00
6" long. Kidney-shaped. Roses .. 250.00
Chocolate Pot. 8½". Roses 375.00
Hair Receivers
Roses. Three gold feet 195.00
Turkey decor 225.00
Hatpin Holders
Portrait 300.00
Roses 250.00
Pitchers
3½". Roses 185.00
3½". Tavern scene 200.00
3½". Turkey decor 195.00
4½". Roses 225.00
Plates
4 x 5". Leaf-shaped 150.00
6". Roses 165.00
7". Roses. Three colors 200.00
10". Roses. Three colors 300.00
Relish. 4¼ x 8". Open handles. Roses 225.00
Sauce. 5". Roses 85.00
Shakers, Salt and Pepper. Roses. Gold tops. Pair 225.00
Sugars, Covered
Lady equestrian. Gold handles .. 500.00

Roses. Gold handles 400.00
Tray. 8 x 11". Roses. Three colors .. 375.00
Vases
4". Castle scene 195.00
4½". Roses 165.00
6½". Farm scene 300.00
7½". Portrait 600.00
9½". Pink roses. Two gold handles 450.00

Roseville U.S.A.

ROSEVILLE POTTERY

Incorporated in 1892 at Roseville, Ohio, Roseville Pottery originally produced only utilitarian wares at plants in Roseville and, after 1898, in Zanesville, Ohio. In 1910 work ceased at the Roseville plant and continued in Zanesville until 1954.

In 1900, art pottery was introduced and the popular glazed "Rozane" line was developed. Roseville art wares were made with many types of decoration . . .slip, decals, free hand, incised and embossed designs. In 1918, a new trademark, "Roseville U.S.A." was adopted.

In 1920 machine-made pottery replaced the hand-made wares; and very little free hand decoration was used.

Much of the early Roseville production is decorator signed. Factory marks, impressed, ink stamped or paper stickers, may be used to date Roseville art wares.

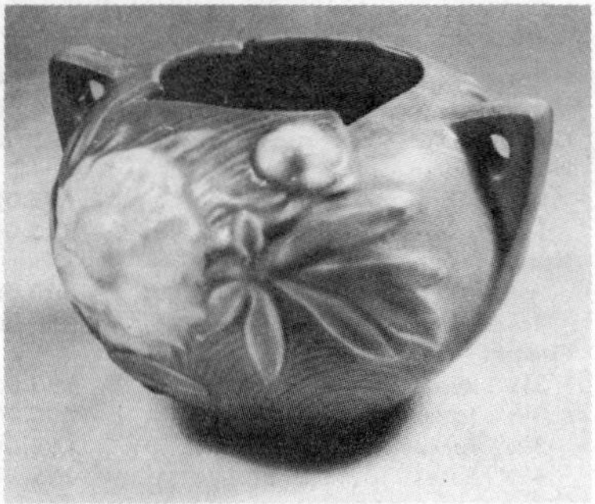

Bowl. "Peony." Green and white. Handled. 6½" $25.00

Ashtray. Snowberry. Green ......$ 17.50
Baskets
Clematis. Blue. 7" 40.00
Columbine. Apricot and green. Handled. Embossed. 14" 65.00
Foxglove. Blue. Footed. 8¼" 45.00
Gardenia. Gray. 10" 60.00
Wincraft. Green. Handled. 8" .. 45.00

Bookends, Pairs
Ming Tree. Turquoise 45.00
Wincraft. Tan. Floral motif. #259 35.00
Bowls
Bushberry. Blue. 2½ x 10¾" 30.00
Carnelian. Pink and green. Footed and handled. 5 x 11¼" 60.00
Imperial. With flower arranger. Handled. 6½" 35.00
Pine Cone. Brown. 12" 50.00
Rosecraft. Ivory with multicolored roses. Handled. 8" 25.00
Snowberry. Blue. Handled. 8½" 25.00
Candlesticks, Pairs
Apple Blossom. Green. 4½" 40.00
Lotus. Lime and green. 2½" 55.00
Silhouette. Turquoise. 2¾" 25.00
Snowberry. Blue. 4¾" 35.00
Cookie Jars
Clematis. Blue. 8" 85.00
Magnolia. Green. 8" 65.00
Cornucopias
Bittersweet. Green 30.00
Gardenia. Green 35.00
Cuspidor. Donatello. 6½" 100.00
Ewer. Fuschia. Green. 10" 50.00
Inkwell. Egypto. "In Hoc Signo Vinces." 3⅛ x 5" 175.00
Jardinieres
Cameo. Rust and green with gold trim. Dancers. 10" 395.00
Donatello. Cherub decor. 9½" .. 150.00
Moss. Blue and brown.5" 65.00
Lamp Base. Rozane. Pansy decor on blended brown, green and yellow high glaze 225.00
Pitchers
Cow. Embossed. 7" 150.00
Grape. Beige, yellow, purple. Embossed. 6¼" 50.00
Magnolia. Blue. Water, with ice lip 75.00

Planters
Apple Blossom. Green. 2½ x 3x 9" 30.00
Silhouette. Turquoise. 3⅜ x 4½ x 10⅞". 35.00
Whirlpool. Green. 9" long 25.00
Teapots
Granny. 5¼" 250.00
Irishman. 5" 225.00
Tea Set. Peony. 4 pieces 75.00
Tray. Peony. Rose, green. Handled. 10¾" 60.00
Vases
Bushberry. Blue. Handled. 15" .. 85.00
Carnelian II. Rose mottled in ivory and gold. Handled. Bulbous base, short neck. 9" 100.00
Clematis. Orange, green, yellow. Open handles. 10" 50.00
Clematis. Light blue buff with

pink, white, blue. Scalloped top.
Handled. 12" 85.00
Cosmos. Handled. 4" 35.00
Dogwood II. Green. 10" 75.00
Egypto. 10" 300.00
Falline. 7½" 175.00
Gardenia. White. 12" 85.00
Jonquil. 7¼" 65.00
Laurel. Green. 9" 65.00
Luffa. 7" 40.00
Monticello. Blue, green. Handled.
7" 75.00
Peony. Bud, double. Rose, green.
4½" 20.00
Pine Cone. Green. 9" 45.00
Rosecraft. Blue. Hexagon. 5" 100.00
Snowberry. Pink. 12" 75.00
White Rose. Handled. 6" 40.00
Wisteria. Blue. Shoulder handles.
6" 65.00
Zephyr Lily. Brown. 10" 50.00
Wall Pocket. Cosmos 40.00

Royal Bayreuth
PRN. 1794
BAVARIA

ROYAL BAYREUTH

The Royal Bayreuth factory founded in Tettau, Bavaria in 1794 has continued production through the present. Currently, the factory is producing dinnerware with no attempts to duplicate their earlier wares; mainly the figural line.
The figural series were introduced in 1885, as inexpensive souvenir items. Designs included animals, people, fruits, vegetables and others in a wide array of tablewares.
Not all wares were marked or the 'stamped' mark did not prove permanent. The Royal Bayreuth crest mark varied in design and color over the years and it is impossible to verify the chronological years of production; due to the lack of authentic records.
Also see "Rose Tapestry" and "Sunbonnet Babies."

Ashtrays
Art Nouveau Lady. 4¾" long ..$ 200.00
Clown 125.00
Corinthian 65.00
Devil 135.00
Eagle 65.00
Elk 65.00
Bell. Children scene 75.00

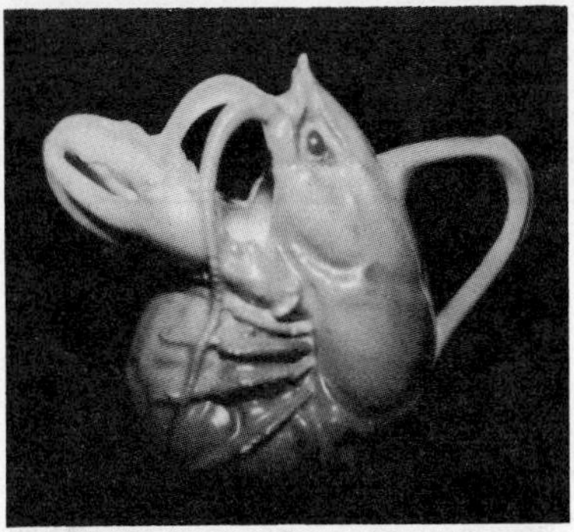

Creamer. "Lobster." $75.00

Bowls
Corinthian. Covered. 2 handles.
6" 125.00
Little Jack Horner. 5¾" 50.00
Poppy. Red. 9½" 135.00
Poppy. White. 6" 85.00
Boxes, Covered
Devil 175.00
Little Bo-Peep 125.00
Rose. Red. 1¾" x 4" 250.00
Scenic. Romantic. 2¾" 75.00
Shell. Murex 50.00
Spade-shape. Turkey center 50.00
Storks, Three 50.00
Breakfast Set. Nursery decor. 3
pieces 150.00
Butter Sauce Pot with ladle. Lobster.
4¼" 65.00
Candleholders
Clown. With match holder 175.00
Corinthian 75.00
Jack and Jill 85.00
Violets. Handpainted. Gold trim 75.00
Celery. Brittany Girls 50.00
Cracker Jars or Humidors
Elk 275.00
Lobster 225.00
Santa Claus. Large 350.00
Tomato 125.00
Creamers
Apple 85.00
Buffalo, Water. Black 135.00
Butterfly. Closed wings 165.00
Cat. Black 150.00
Cavaliers. Portrait 75.00
Children 85.00
Clown 135.00
Coachman 135.00
Conch 75.00
Corinthian 65.00
Cows in meadow 60.00
Crow. Black 125.00

Dachshund	125.00
Devil and Cards	165.00
Eagle	125.00
Frog. Red	95.00
Grape	85.00
Jack and Jill	85.00
Lemon	60.00
Lobster	75.00
Monkey. Green	195.00
Old Man of the Mountain	75.00
Orange	55.00
Pansy	85.00
Parakeet	135.00
Poppy. Red	75.00
Robin	125.00
Strawberry	85.00
"To Bed by Candlelight"	75.00
Tomato	55.00
Cups and Saucers	
Deer scene	35.00
Devil	175.00
Elk. Demi	85.00
Poppy. Red	95.00
Rose. Red. Demi	225.00
Tomato. Leaf saucer. Demi	65.00
Hair Receivers	
Barnyard scene	75.00
Roses. Handpainted. Artist signed	65.00
Hatpin Holders	
Bell Ringer	250.00
Dachshund	350.00
Hunting scene	85.00
Owl	275.00
Poppy. Red	150.00
Match Holders	
Clown. Hanging-type	150.00
Devil and Cards	95.00
Mayonnaise Sets	
Poppy. Red	65.00
Strawberry	85.00
Mugs	
*Devil and Cards	195.00
Elk	195.00
Mustache Cup. Elk	175.00
Mustard Jars	
Apple	85.00
Farm scene. With tray	60.00
Grapes	55.00
Lobster. Leaf spoon	75.00
Orange	60.00
Tomato. With ladle	62.50
Pitchers	
Bell Ringer. Milk	265.00
Cavaliers. Milk	150.00
Chimpanzee. Milk	250.00
Clown. Water	350.00
Dachshund. Milk	225.00
Fish Head. Milk	150.00
Girl feeding chickens. Cider	125.00
Lemon. Water	400.00
Lobster. Water	195.00
Poodle. Milk	250.00
Robin. Milk	250.00
Seal. Milk	355.00
Strawberry. Water	375.00
Tomato. Water	150.00
Watermelon. Water	500.00
Plates	
Cavaliers. 10". Dixon	150.00
Farmer with chickens. 9"	85.00
Jack and Jill. 10½". Open handles	125.00
Jack and the Beanstalk. 6"	50.00
Leaf. With loop handles. 5½"	30.00
Tomato. 6"	35.00
Shakers, Salt and Pepper. Pairs	
Conch	75.00
Devil and Cards	150.00
Grapes	100.00
Lobster	75.00
Shoes	
Man's. Oxford	100.00
Woman's. High top. Button	125.00
String Holder. Rooster. Hanging-type	150.00
Sugars, Covered	
Apple	60.00
Grapes	85.00
Lobster	65.00
Shell. Murex	35.00
Tomato	60.00
Sunbonnet. See "Sunbonnet Babies"	
Tea Sets. 3 pieces	
Apple	225.00
Poppy. Red	300.00
Tomato	225.00
Teapots	
Apple	150.00
Little Bo-Peep	100.00
Tomato	125.00
Toothpick Holders	
Coachman	150.00
Devil and Cards	110.00
Elk	65.00
Trays	
Art Nouveau Lady. 10"	400.00
Conch. 12"	100.00
Handpainted. 11". Pink roses. Gold trim	85.00
Hunting scene. 11"	100.00
Lobster. 12"	
Vases	
Boy with turkeys. 4¼"	50.00
Cavaliers. 4". Dixon	75.00
Cows in pasture. 8"	175.00
Hunting scene. 7"	150.00
Portrait. 4"	75.00
Queen Louise. 7"	85.00

*Reproduced Item

ROYAL BERLIN
(See "KPM China")

ROYAL BONN

The Bonn Factory was established by Clemers August in the mid-eighteenth century in Bonn, Germany. Subsequently known as Royal Bonn, the majority of this porcelain encountered on today's market is from the late 19th century. These later wares are usually marked Mehlem, a castle or with the initials FM.

Vase. 10¼" high. 46" circum. Lady and gentleman in period dress. Multicolored with gold trim. Tapestry finish. Mkd. "Bonn." $750.00

Biscuit Jar. 5". Multicolored florals on ivory ground. Gold trim ....$ 95.00
Bone Dish. Blue and gold 15.00
Bowls
9". "Wild Rose." 75.00
10x 5" deep. Handpainted roses. Heavy gold trim 200.00
Cheese Dish, Covered. Wedge-shaped. Roses on white. Gold trim........................ 125.00
Ewer. 14". Red and white roses. Brown foliage. Gold handle 150.00
Jam Jar. 5". Silverplated lid and bail. Floral decor on beige ground. 55.00
Jardiniere. 6½ x 7½". "Persian Cashmere." 125.00
Plates
8". "Wild Rose." 40.00
9½". Portrait 75.00
14". Portrait. Fruit border. Artist signed 150.00
Relish. 10". Handled. Three sections. Handpainted florals. Gold trim .. 125.00
Urn. 13½". Handpainted florals. Tapestry finish. Gold handles and base 225.00
Vases
4". Red roses on green ground. Gold trim 35.00
5". Garden scene. Tapestry finish. 100.00
9½". Handpainted pastel florals. Animal head handles in gold 175.00
12". Cavalier Portrait. Gold trim. Artist signed 225.00
12". Floral decor. Transfer with handpainted accents 125.00
15". Portrait. Leaf stem gold handles 285.00
17". Multicolored floral decor. Ornate gold handles, base 225.00

ROYAL COPENHAGEN

Royal Copenhagen was actually established in 1773 when Franz Mueller produced his first piece of porcelain.

In 1779, the Danish king acquired ownership of the factory, named Mueller manager and adopted the name Royal Copenhagen. The Crown sold its interest in 1867 and the company remains privately owned to this day.

Royal Copenhagen's most famous pattern "Blue Fluted" was created in 1780. It is of Chinese origin, comes in 3 types: (1) smooth edge (2) closed lace edge (3) perforated lace edge (full lace), and was copied by many other factories. "Flora Danica," named for a famous botanical work and introduced in 1789, remains Royal Copenhagen's most unique and exclusive pattern. Botanical illustrations were done free-hand and all edges and perforations were cut by hand.

All Royal Copenhagen porcelain is marked with three wavy lines which signify ancient waterways and a crown which was added in 1889 ...the stoneware does not carry the crown.

Bon Bon. Blue Fluted ....$ 35.00
Bottle. 10". Medallions. "Frederiksborg Castle." 80.00
Coffee Pot. 8½". Blue Fluted. Flower finial 125.00

Robins. 2¾" and 1¾" high. Pair $100.00

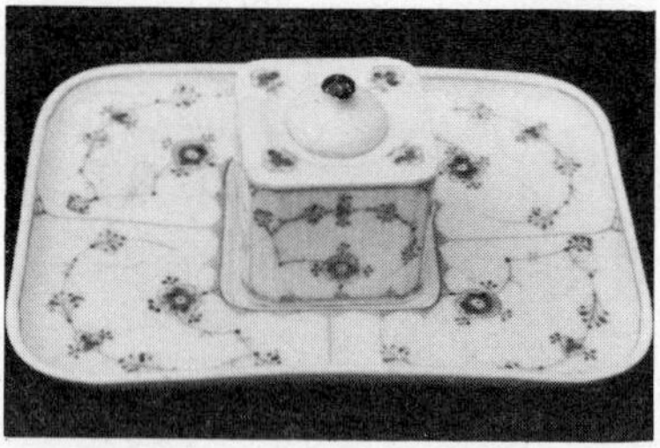

Inkwell with tray. 6 x 8½" long. "Blue Fluted." $100.00

Cruet, Stoppered. Blue Fluted 85.00
Cups and Saucers. Blue Fluted
Demi 25.00
Dinner 35.00
Figurines
Boy with Pig. 6½" 85.00
Cat. 5½". Sitting. Gray, white. Green eyes 75.00
Goose Girl. 9½" 150.00
Robin. 8" 85.00
Scottie. 4" 75.00
Squirrel. 3½" 35.00
Woman knitting 250.00
Inkwell with Tray. 6 x 8½" long. Blue Fluted 100.00
Jar, Covered. 9". White. Figures in relief. Milkmaid finial 80.00
Jardiniere. 7". Bulbous. Blue Fluted. Snail handles. C. 1897 .... 175.00
Plaque. Cupids, Three. 14" diam. Blanc de Chine 750.00
Plates
7¾". Soup. Blue Fluted. Perforated lace edge 35.00
8". Fruit center. Hand decorated... 35.00
9". Leaf-shape. Handled. Blue Fluted 35.00
9¼". Blue Fluted 30.00
10¾". Portrait. Josephine. 1923 .. 85.00
Platters. Blue Fluted. Smooth edge
8 x 10" 65.00
9 x 12" 80.00
12 x 16" 110.00
Syrup. Blue Fluted. Spring-type lid... 100.00
Tile. 5 x 6". Blue Fluted 35.00
Trays. Blue Fluted
5½ x 10" 75.00
9½ x 15" 100.00
11x 17½" 125.00
Tureen, Covered. 18" long. Blue Fluted. C. 1897 .... 195.00
Vases
5". Florals. Green and white. Crackle glaze 35.00
6". Bulbous. Molded leaves, applied frog on celadon ground. 19th century 175.00
8". Sailboat. Blue on white 75.00
12". Gold decor on green. Crackle glaze. Pair 300.00

ROYAL CROWN DERBY

Derby Crown Porcelain Co., established in 1875 in Derby, England had no connection with earlier Derby factories which operated in the late 18th and early 19th centuries. In 1890, this new and distinct company was appointed "Manufacturers of Porcelain to Her Majesty" (Queen Victoria); and from that date to the present has been known as "Royal Crown Derby".

Derby porcelains from the 1878 to 1890 period carry only the standard crown printed mark. From 1891 on, the mark carries the "Royal Crown Derby" wording; and in the 20th century, "Made in England" and "English Bone China" were added to the mark.

A majority of these porcelains, both tableware and figures, were hand-decorated; but a variety of printing processes were used for additional adornment. Today, Royal Crown Derby is a part of Royal Doulton Tableware. Ltd.

Bowl. 11 x 3¾" deep. Handpainted florals, cobalt rim ....$ 85.00
Box, Covered. 4½ x 5" diam. Multicolored flowers on white .. 55.00
Cups and Saucers
Demitasse. Florals. Blue, gold and

Ewer. 9¾" high. Chinese red ground. Gold leaf and floral decor $225.00

green decor	37.50
Demitasse. Sailboat. Cobalt	45.00
Tea. Blue chinoiserie decor	50.00
Tea. Imari-type decor	55.00
Dessert Set. Imari-type decor. 35 pieces	500.00
Ginger Jar. 10½". Berry branches on red ground. Gold trim	300.00
Mug. 2¼". Gold handle. Imari-type decor	65.00
Plates	
9". Floral medallions. Green border	45.00
9½". Imari-type decor	85.00
Platter. 8½ x 11½". "View of North Wales." Cobalt with gold trim	175.00
Service Plates. 10½". Floral centers, rose and green borders. Gold bands. Set of 12	1000.00
Tea Service. Imari-type decor. C. 1919. 18 pieces	400.00
Tea Set. Pot, covered sugar, creamer. Ovoid-shaped. Imari coloring. Heavy gold	200.00
Tray. 13 x 17". Closed handles. Blue flowers in swag design on white. Gold trim	165.00
Vases	
4½". Gold handles. Flowers and insects on yellow. Gold trim. C. 1900	125.00
7½". Imari-type decor	150.00
9". Blue and ivory panels. Overlay design. Gold trim	295.00

ROYAL
DOULTON
FLAMBE

DOULTON LAMBETH

ROYAL DOULTON

Doulton pottery began in 1815 under the direction of John Doulton at the Doulton & Watts pottery in Lambeth, England. Early output was limited to salt-glazed industrial stoneware. John Watts retired in 1854; the firm became Doulton and Company and production was expanded to include hand decorated stoneware such as figurines, vases, dinnerware and flasks. In 1872, the firm began marking their ware Royal Doulton.

In 1878, John's son, Sir Henry Doulton, purchased Pinder Bourne & Co. in Burslem and the companies became Doulton & Co., Ltd. in 1882. Decorated porcelain was added to Doulton's earthenware production in 1884 and the Royal Doulton mark was used on both wares.

Most Doulton figurines were produced at the Burslem plants from 1890 until 1978, when discontinued. A 'new' line of Doulton figurines was introduced in 1979. Beginning in 1913, an "HN" number was assigned to each new Doulton figuine design. The "HN" numbers refers to Harry Nixon, a Doulton artist. "HN" numbers were chronological until 1940; after which blocks of numbers were assigned to each modeler. From 1928 until 1954, a small number appeared to the right of the crown mark . . .this number added to 1927 gives the year of manufacture of the figurines.

Dickensware, in earthenware and porcelain, was introduced in 1908. The ware was decorated with charcacters from Dicken's novels. The line was withdrawn in the 1940's, except for plates which continued until 1974.

Character jugs, a 20th century revival of early Toby models, were designed by Charles J. Noke for Doulton in the 1930's. They come in 4 major sizes and feature fictional characters from Dicken's, Shakespeare and other English and American novelists; and historical heros.

Doulton's Rouge Flambee (aso Veined Sung) is a highly glazed, strong colored ware noted most for the fine modeling and exquisite colorings, especially in the animal items. The process used to produce the vibrant colors in this ware is a Doulton secret.

Doulton ceased production of stoneware at Lambeth in 1956, but porcelain production continues at the Burslem factories today.

Character Jug. "The Poacher." Large $125.00

Figurine. "Fair Lady." 2193 ....$95.00

Teapot. 9½" high. Silverplated lid. Floral decor on white, cobalt and gold trim. Burslem. C. 1886 ......$195.00

Animal Models

Airdale. 1023 ....$	55.00
Bull Dog. White. 1074	35.00
Elephant, Fighting. 2640	350.00
Elephant. 2644..............	65.00
Fox, Sitting. 2634	350.00
French Poodle. 2631	65.00
Huntsman Fox. 6448	30.00
Kittens, Various. 2579-2584. Each	30.00
Lion on Rock. 2641	600.00
Pekingese. 1012	35.00
Pheasant. 2632	300.00
Pointer. 2624	200.00
Siamese, Various. 2655, 2660, 2662. Each	45.00
Tiger. 2646	375.00

Bank. Bunny.................	150.00

Biscuit Jars

5⅛". Incised horses on gray, white body. Applied flowers, leaf border. Silver hallmarked. Lambeth. C. 1880	375.00
9¼". Birds, foliage on beige ground. Signed F. Barlow. C. 1878	475.00

Bowls

9½". Gaffers series	50.00
10". Octagonal. "Babes in Wood."	195.00
11". Robin Hood	45.00
12 x 7" deep. Cobalt with gold decor exterior. Light blue and white interior	225.00

Cake Stand. 9½ x 4¼" high. Pastel

florals, gold trim 85.00
*Character Jugs, TINY. 1¼"
Auld Mac 195.00
Cardinal 225.00
Fat Boy 95.00
John Peel 200.00
Mr. Micawber 95.00
Mr. Pickwick 165.00
Old Charlie 85.00
Paddy 85.00
Sairey Gamp 85.00
Sam Weller 95.00

*Character Jugs. MINIATURE. 2¼ to 2½"
Arriet 65.00
Auld Mac "A" 35.00
Captain Hook 225.00
Cardinal "A" 55.00
Dick Turpin 50.00
Fat Boy "A" 55.00
Fortune Teller 250.00
Gladiator 300.00
John Barleycorn "A" 55.00
John Peel "A" 55.00
Mikado 225.00
Mr. Micawber "A" 50.00
Paddy "A" 50.00
Punch and Judy 350.00
Regency Beau 350.00
*Character Jugs. SMALL. 3½ to 4"
Ard of Earing 550.00
Farmer John 65.00
Fortune Teller 250.00
Gladiator 250.00
Gondolier 250.00
Jester 85.00
John Barleycorn "A" 60.00
Mephistopheles 650.00
Old King Cole "A" 85.00
Paddy "A 55.00
Parson Brown "A" 65.00
Ugly Duchess 185.00
*Character Jugs. LARGE. 5¼ to 7"
Ard of Earing 750.00
Captain Hook 225.00
Cardinal "A" 110.00
Cavalier "A" 110.00
Clown. White hair 1000.00
Jockey 125.00
Johnny Appleseed 225.00
Lord Nelson 225.00
Mr. Pickwick "A" 125.00
Robin Hood 110.00
Sairey Gamp "A" 75.00
Sam Johnson 225.00
Scaramouche 375.00
Touchstone "A" 195.00
Cheese Dish. 6½ x 7½ x 5½" high. White ground with blue, yellow decor 85.00
Cream and Sugar. 3" Melon ribbed.
Blue and white 50.00
Cups and Saucers
Canterbury Pilgrims 45.00
Coaching Days 25.00
Nursery Rhyme Series 35.00
Decanters
Old Crow 65.00
Zorro 40.00

Dickensware
Bowls
Fagan. 5¼" 65.00
Sairey Gamp. 8 x 11" 85.00
Sam Weller. 6¾" 40.00
Box, Covered. Mr. Micawber. 3½" 75.00
Cream and Sugar. Mr. Pickwick. Set 125.00
Creamer. Fat Boy 30.00
Cup and Saucer. Mr. Micawber 45.00
Pitcher. Sairey Gamp. 8" 85.00
Plates
Bill Sykes. 13" 150.00
Mr. Pickwick. Octagonal. 8¾" 60.00
Sairey Gamp. 10½" 50.00
Tony Weller. 8" square 37.50
Relish. Little Nell. 5" 50.00
Tray. Mr. Pickwick. 7¼ x 9" 85.00
Vases
Poor Jo. 5¼" 40.00
Sairey Gamp. 5" 75.00
Ewer. 10". Incised cats and dogs. Stoneware. Lambeth 425.00

Figurines
Alice in Wonderland Series. Each 25.00
*Autumn Breeze. 2147 .... 195.00
*Balloon Man. 1954 .... 95.00
Beatrix Potter Series. Each 17.50
Bunnykins Series. Each 20.00
Child (Williamsburg) 2154 .... 65.00
Christmas Parcels. 2851 .... 125.00
Debbie. 2385 .... 60.00
Dickens Series. Each 20.00
*Eliza. 2543 .... 200.00
Fair Lady. 2193 .... 95.00
Flower Seller's Children. 1342 .... 250.00
*Grandma. 2052 .... 200.00
Helmsman. 2499 .... 110.00
Jester. 2016 .... 125.00
Kate Greenaway Series. Each 60.00
King Charles. 2084 .... 750.00
*Little Bridesmaid. 1433 .... 100.00
Make Believe. 2225 .... 65.00
*Mr. Micawber. 7½". 2097 .... 275.00
My Love. 2339 .... 100.00
Old Balloon Seller. 1315 .... 100.00
*Phyllis. 1620 .... 300.00
*Sairey Gamp. 7½". 556 .... 275.00
St. George and the Dragon. 7½". 2051 .... 200.00
Sweet Seventeen. 2734 .... 100.00
*Tinkle Bell. 1677 .... 50.00
*Victorian Lady. 1345 .... 200.00

Votes for Women. 2816 .... 150.00
Young Love. 2735 .... 400.00

Flambee

Animals

- Cat. 9 .... 40.00
- Drake. 137 .... 50.00
- Duck. 112 .... 35.00
- Duck. 395 .... 35.00
- Elephant. 489A 55.00
- Fox. 14 .... 50.00
- Fox. 5". Veined Sung. C. 1920 225.00
- Hare. 656A 40.00
- Penguin. 84 .... 40.00
- Penguin. 8½". Veined Sung. Signed Noke 350.00
- Rabbit. One ear up. 113 ...... 50.00

Bowl. 10". Woodcut. Scenic decor 125.00

Vases

- 3". Oval. Narrow neck. Straight line mark. C. 1910 .... 50.00
- 5". Veined Sung. 1605 ...... 40.00
- 7". Woodcut. Castle scene 125.00
- 11⅛". Woodcut. Pastoral scene. Signed Noke 195.00

Humidors

- Birds, dogwood branches. Brown salt glaze. F. Barlow 195.00
- Stylized florals in off white and turquoise on chocolate ground. Silicon Lambeth. C. 1891-1932 .. 100.00
- Three Musketeers. Cream 150.00

Jars, Covered

- 4½ x 6". Floral decor. gold trim. Artist signed. Burslem 185.00
- 5½ x 6½". Horses. Blue and brown. H. Barlow. C. 1884 ...... 400.00

Jardinieres

- 7½ x 8½". Gallant Fishers 125.00
- 10x 11". Tapestry 250.00

Jugs

- Boston Motto. 6 x 14". C. 1902 .. 125.00
- Herons, bulrushes, water. Blue slip on white. Lambeth. C. 1874 350.00

Luncheon Set. Coaching Days. 42 pieces 700.00

Mugs

- Dr. Johnson at the Cheshire Cheese. 4½". 30.00
- Lord Nelson. Miniature 50.00

Pitchers

- Doc Berry's Watch. 8" 100.00
- Doctor Johnson. 9" 165.00
- Lamplighter, More Than Enough, Is Too Much. 4" 75.00
- Leatherware. 11¾". C. 1891 .... 250.00
- Sir Andrew Acuecheek. 7½" 75.00
- The Gleaners. 4½" 50.00
- Tudor Rose. 5¾" 85.00

Plaques

- Summer and Winter Scenes. Cobalt, gold trim. 14" oval. Burslem. C. 1880's. Pair 500.00
- The Jackdaw of Rheims. 15" diam. 175.00

Plates

- Coaching Days. 10½" 35.00
- Dogs. Handpainted. 10". Pair .. 85.00
- Jackdaw of Rheims. 6½" 30.00
- Robin Hood. 8¾" 40.00
- Shakespeare. 10" 55.00
- The Gaffers. 10½" 30.00

Salad Set. Bowl 10" diam. Two servers. Hand decorated. Cobalt and gold. Burslem. 3 pieces 275.00

Service Plates. 10½". Ivory. Flower basket within cobalt medallion border. Gold trim. Set of 12 .... 500.00

Soap Dish. With drain. Rose and gold decor on white 45.00

Teapot. 4½". Tudor Rose 85.00

Tile. 9" square. Floral decor. Faience. Lambeth 50.00

Toby Jugs, Full Seated

- Captain Cuttle. 4½" 200.00
- Fat Boy. 4½" 185.00
- Old Charley. 5½" 175.00
- Old Charley. 8¾" 250.00
- Sairey Gamp. 4½" 175.00
- Sam Weller. 4½" 225.00
- Squire, The. 6" 275.00

Tumblers

- Leatherware. Sterling rim. 10". C. 1891 .... 85.00
- Stoneware. Leaf decor. F. Barlow. Lambeth. C. 1877 .... 150.00

Vases

- 6". Handled. Scenic. Monasteries, river. J.A. Bailey. C. 1924 ..... 65.00
- 7" Chocolate ground with applied off-white and turquoise decor. Silicon Lambeth. C. 1880-1891 85.00
- 7½". Babes in Wood. Cobalt, gold trim. Burslem 185.00
- 9". Stylized leaves and scrolls. Green with deep red trim. Lambeth 175.00

Wall Mark. Jester. 11" 250.00

*Discontinued Item

ROYAL DUX

Royal Dux was porcelain made in Dux, Bohemia (Czechoslovakia) at the Duxer Porzellan-Manufaktur established in 1860.

Many items were imported to the United States. A relatively inexpensive porcelain in the beginning; the ware is gaining in recognition . . . to the point of being reproduced.

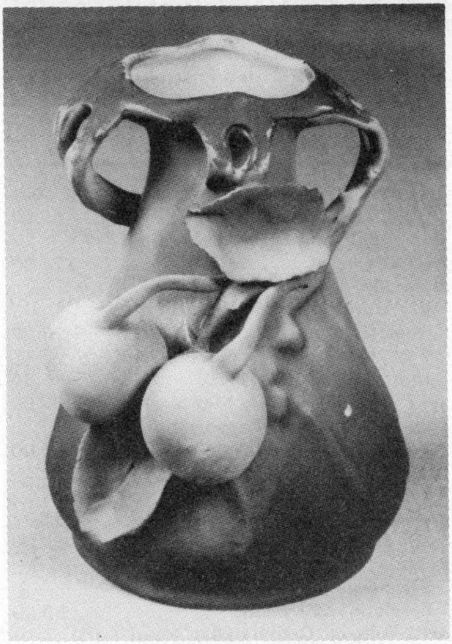

Vase. 5" high. Handled. Applied peaches and leaf decor $50.00

Basket. 2¼ x 4 x 4½". Brown basketweave pattern. Applied cherries ....$	125.00
Bowls	
6x 9½". Open handles. Applied rose spray on green ground	100.00
7". Full figure maiden reclines on edge	160.00
Bust. Lady. 17". Flesh tones, pink and green	850.00
Centerpieces	
Atlantis Survivors. 11 x 12". Man holding woman. Waves form bowl	375.00
Girl with basket and umbrella. Flower bowl base. 7¼ x 8"	350.00
Maiden holding seashell. Sea waves forms base. 8½ x 11"	350.00
Ewer. 10". Applied fruits and flowers. Natural coloring	185.00
Figurines	
Bird Dogs. 8 x 10½". Pink triangle mark	100.00
Boy with Basket. 5½ x 7½"	150.00
Boy with Fish, Girl with Basket. 10⅜". Natural coloring. Gold highlights. Pink triangle mark. Pair	450.00
Camel. With rider. 17½"	350.00
Dancers, Tango. Blue and white costumes. Gold trim. 14"	175.00
Horse. Rearing. 8"	125.00
Woman with Water Jar. 11½". Ivory with gold base and trim ..	135.00
Vases	
5". Handled. Applied roses on green ground	50.00
11". Maiden holding conch shell. Green, rose and ivory	300.00
16". Ornate handles. Applied plums	185.00
19". Ornate twig handles. Pale green with applied roses and foliage	250.00

ROYAL FLEMISH

Royal Flemish is a transparent, acid etched and stained art glass. The areas of colors are divided with gilt lines and further decorated.
The glass was made at the Mt. Washington Glass Works, New Bedford, Massachusetts in 1889. The process was patented by Albert Steffin in 1894.

Vase. 6" high. Globular-shape with short flaring neck. Gold pansy decor. Unsigned $2250.00

Biscuit Jar. 7". Roman coins, medallions, dragon motifs. Heavy raised gold. Lid marked and no'd ....$	2250.00
Vases	
8½". Globular-shape. Two handles. Classical decor within medallions. C. 1890	2800.00
9¾". Globular-shape with inverted rim. Scrolls and leaf decor. Coat of Arms on reverse	2950.00
12". Expanded cylindrical base, cup-shaped top. Two loop handles. "Sea Lion."	3500.00

12". Stick-type. Bulbous base, slender neck. Black and gold floral medallions on deep pink and amber ground 2750.00

14¼". Expanding cylindrical base, straight neck. Multicolored sections divided by five pointed stars and rays. Geese in flight on reverse. C. 1895 .... 3000.00

ROYAL RUDOLSTADT

This hard paste porcelain was made in Rudolstadt, Thuringen, East Germany. The first factory was established by Ernt Bohne in 1854. A second factory was opened by L. Straus & Sons, Ltd. in 1882.

The ware was never originally labeled "Royal Rudolstadt"; but the word 'Royal' was probably added by dealers because of the connotation of the word.

The early mark was a hayfork representing the arms of Johann Fredrich von Schwarzburg-Rudolstadt, the patron. Later, crossed two-prong hayforks were used to imitate the Meissen or Dresden mark. In 1800, the letter "R" was used. Still later, variations of the hayfork were used. Modern marks show a shield with the latters "RQ", a crown on top, with the word "Crown" above and the name "Rudolstadt" below the shield. Another mark has the word "Germany" in place of the word "Crown" which indicates the ware was made after 1891.

Basket. 4½ x 6¾". Gold handle. Floral design on ivory ....$ 85.00

Biscuit Jar. 8". Corset-shaped. Paneled with multicolored flowers 125.00

Bowls

9". long. Shell-shaped. Cupid seated on edge 150.00

9". Scalloped rim. Deco style decor in multicolors. Artist signed 65.00

11". Cream ground. Pink, yellow roses. Green foliage. Artist signed 125.00

Cake Plate. 12". Gold handles. Pink, white roses. Gold trim 50.00

Cheese Dish. Wedge-shape. Rose decor 95.00

Chocolate Set. Pot, four cups, saucers. Handpainted roses on cream ground, gold trim 250.00

Cup and Saucer. Handpainted roses. Gold trim 20.00

Dresser Set. Tray, hatpin holder, hair receiver, ring tree, covered jar. Rose decor. 6 pieces 250.00

Ewer. 9½". Floral decor. Scrolled gold handle 75.00

Hatpin Holder. Decor in lavender and roses 25.00

Pitchers

4½". Flower spray medallions. Gold serpent handle 65.00

11". Bulbous. Floral decor. Gold handle 125.00

Plates

6". Handpainted multicolored roses. Gold trim 25.00

8½". Handpainted poppies. Gold trim 45.00

11". Rose decor. Gold trim 75.00

Shakers, Salt and Pepper. Handpainted floral decor. Pair 50.00

Trays

8¼ x 11½". Pink roses on ivory ground 55.00

10" diam. "Corn." Gold trim 65.00

Vases

7¼". Gold handles. Handpainted florals on ivory ground 60.00

9". Bulbous. Gold handles. Handpainted florals 125.00

11½". Baroque style. Flowers, berries, foliage on ivory ground .. 150.00

ROYAL VIENNA

The production of this hard paste porcelain commenced in 1720 with Claude Innocentius du Paquier, a runaway employee of the Meissen Works. The factory was located in Austria, Vienna. In 1744, Empress Maria Theresa brought the factory under royal patronage and subsequently the ware became known as Royal Vienna. The establishment went through many administrative changes until its closing in 1864; but the quality of workmanship was always maintained. The majority of this ware encountered on today's market was probably made by other Austrian or German firms who continued to produce a reasonable facsimile of Royal Vienna; including using the distinctive and distinguished 'Beehive' mark.

Bowl. 5". Handled. Portrait. Blue with gold trim ....$ 75.00

Chocolate Pot. 10". Cupids on shaded purple ground 250.00

Compote. 8¼ x 4½" high. Floral decor in blue and green on white 175.00

Cup. Portrait. "De Bourgogne." Gold interior. C. 1870 .... 175.00

Vase. 8½" high. Portrait of Lady. Gold and yellow ground, gold trim. Loop foot $175.00

Cup and Saucer. Demitasse. Portrait. Maroon with gold. Artist signed 150.00

Ewers

4¼". "Trauman." Green lustre. Gold handle. Signed Wagner 475.00

12". "Die Hochzeit." Red ground. Gold handle. Signed Huber 750.00

15½". Mythological scene. Maroon ground. Signed Schulers 1000.00

Jar, Covered. 12". Portrait. Burgundy ground. Gold trim. Jeweled. Signed Wagner 850.00

Plates

8⅞". Handpainted scene of children. Cobalt border. Gold trim. Signed Ahne 450.00

9½". "Amorosa." 250.00

9½". Scalloped edge. Handpainted roses in pink, yellow and white. Gold trim 85.00

13¾". "Pearl." Green and maroon border. Gold trim. Signed Carl Larson 450.00

14". Classical garden scene. Maroon border. Gold scrolled trim 350.00

14". Nude with three cupids. Heavy gold. Signed Frichling 450.00

Service Plates. Floral center. Burgundy rims. Gold trim. Set of 12 .... 1500.00

Tea Caddy. 7" high. "Amor Und Cephiste" and "Rinaldo Und Almeido." Signed C. Herr. C. 1820 500.00

Tray. 8¼ x 12". Handpainted violet decor on pale green ground. Gold trim 175.00

Urns

6½". "Erbluht." Burgundy. Gold trim. Signed Wagner 400.00

10". Covered. "Josephine." Green ground. 18K gold trim. Signed Wagner 750.00

11¼". Covered. "Ann Gitana." Signed Wagner 850.00

13". Portrait of sleeping lady, cupids. Gold beading 250.00

15¼". Classical scene 375.00

Vases

4½". Portrait of Lady. Signed Wagner 300.00

5". Multicolored flowers, insects, etc. Four gold feet. C. 1881 ...... 225.00

7¼". Bottle-shaped. Portrait center. Heavy applied allover gold. Signed Pold 450.00

8½". Bulbous. Scenic. Story of Moses, Mother holding child, children riding lions 500.00

14". Cherubs. Applied flowers. Drilled for lamp 350.00

ROYAL WORCESTER

The porcelain works was established in 1751 by Dr. John Wall and 14 partners. Dr. Wall died in 1776 and the entire business was sold to Thomas Flight in 1783. Martin Barr was admitted as a partner in 1793 and the firm was known as Flight and Barr. In 1807 the name was changed to Flight, Barr and Barr. It was changed again in 1813 to Barr, Flight and Barr, or "B.F.B." and continued as such until 1840 at which time Chamberlin and Son and Barr, Flight and Barr were consolidated. The works moved to Dighlis, the home of Chamberlin and Son. The company was sold to Kerr and Binn in 1852. Most of the earlier ware encountered are of the 1870-1900 period. Current Royal Worcester wares are available on the modern market.

Basket. 8 x 9". Beige. Basketweave design. C. 1908 ....$ 195.00

Biscuit Barrel. Handpainted pheasant. Silverplated lid and bail 300.00

Bone Dish. Blue floral decor 45.00

Bowls

4¾ x 2¼" deep. Swags of fruits, insects and butterfly decor. Gold border. C. 1765 .... 500.00

Teapot. 6½" high. Bulbous. Cream ground, multicolored floral decor. Gold spout, handle, base and ring finial $300.00

9" square. Butterfly and floral spray decor. 19th century 300.00
Butter, Covered. Blue and white. C. 1770 .... 375.00
Cache Pot. 2¼ x 2½" deep. White with decor of roses, blue bells, berries, dragonfly, etc. Gold trim. Three gold feet. C. 1908 .... 200.00
Cake Stand. 10¼" diam. x 5¼" high. Lilac with narrow gold bands. Scalloped edge. C. 1908 ... 200.00
Candle Snuffers
  Nun. 6½". C. 1920 .... 95.00
  Toby and Punch. C. 1882. Pair .. 350.00
Chocolate Pot. 8¾". Floral decor on beige satin ground. Gold handle and trim. C. 1894 .... 250.00
Cup, Handleless. Blue and gold. C. 1770 .... 95.00
Cups and Saucers
  Demitasse. Cream ground, rust flowers. C. 1890 .... 60.00
  Handleless. Brown lines, flowers, leaves. C. 1770 .... 195.00
Ewers
  7". Florals on front and reverse. Beige ground. Gold handle. C. 1900 .... 250.00
  11½". Serpent handle. Multicolored floral decor. C. 1908 . 450.00
  12½". Bulbous base. Ornate gold handle. Floral decor on quilted base. C. 1920 .... 400.00
Figurines
  Beagle. 7". Doris Linder 175.00
  Children. Days of the Week. (Monday, Tuesday, etc.) 7½". F. Doughty. Each 85.00
  Flower Seller. 4". F. Doughty 250.00
  Grandma's Dress. 6½". F. Doughty 85.00
  Joy and Sorrow. 10½". J.Hadley. Pair 500.00
  The Satyre. 30". J. Hadley 1500.00

Humidor. Sabrina ware. C. 1906 .. 195.00
Leaf-shaped Dish. 3½ x 4½". Gold turtle. C. 1909 .... 195.00
Mug. 5". Blue and white. C. 1770 .. 300.00
Pitchers
  5". Bulbous. Handpainted florals outlined in gold on beige ground. Gold reeded handle. C. 1908 .... 125.00
  8". Bulbous. Gold handle and ring base. Allover gold sprays on yellow ground 150.00
  8¾". Bulbous. Ornate gold handle. Florals in blue, pink, lavender. Purple mark 350.00
Plates
  7". Decorated in the Imari manner. Panelled. Gilt background. C. 1765 .... 1250.00
  8½". "Royal Lily." C. 1785 ...... 175.00
Rose Bowl. 3". Handpainted bluebird. Gold trim 150.00
Sweetmeat, Covered. 8". Pedestaled. Beige to gold. C. 1903 250.00
Teapots
  5". Bulbous. Floral decor. C. 1770 375.00
  6 x 7½". Blue and white. Melon-shaped. C. 1770 .... 395.00
  7". "Royal Lily." C. 1785 .... 350.00

Tureens, Covered
  4½ x 9½" long. Blue, white oriental decor. Gold finial, gold feet. Gold elephant head handles. C. 1880 .... 225.00
  14½ x 10½" long. Blue and white. Crow's feet, elephant handles. With underplate. C. 1880 .. 550.00
Vases
  4¼". Bulbous. Pansy decor on beige. Gold trim. C. 1912 ...... 95.00
  4¼". Handled. Florals on beige ground. Gold trim. C. 1902 .... 100.00
  7". Bulbous base. Hexagonal neck. Reticulated cover. Natural colored flowers. Signed Cole. C. 1908 .... 450.00
  10". Gold handles. Floral sprays on beige ground. C. 1902 ...... 300.00
  10½". Blue molded cabbage leaves in relief. C. 1760 .... 450.00
  19½". Classical scene of woman with water jug................ 500.00

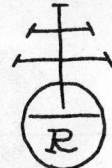

ROYCROFT ITEMS

Elbert Hubbard, founder of the Roycrofters in East Aurora, New York during the turn of the 19th and 20th centuries, was considered a genius in his day. He was author, lecturer, manufacturer, salesman and philosopher.

Hubbard established a campus, including a printing plant where he published "The Philistine," "The Fra" and "The Roycrofter." His most famous book was "A Message to Garcia", 1899. His 'community' also included a furniture manufacturing plant, a metal shop and a leather shop.

Pamphlet. 40 pages. September 1918 .... $3.00

Ashtrays
- 4". Hammered copper $22.50
- 6¾". Handled. Hammered copper. Center design 40.00

Bean Pot. Pottery. Brown glaze 30.00

Books
- American Bible. Leather bound. 1911 .... 25.00
- Dictionary. 1914 .... 15.00
- Little Journeys to the Homes of the Great. Memorial Edition. 10 volumes 100.00
- Message to Garcia. Leather bound. 1908 .... 25.00
- Myth in Marriage. Leather bound. 1912 .... 15.00
- Note Book. 1927 .... 25.00
- Scrap Book. 1923 .... 25.00

Bookends, Hammered copper. Pairs
- Cut-outs 25.00
- Florals 30.00
- Owls 45.00
- Sailing Ships 50.00

Bowl. 5½". Hammered copper. Crimped top 35.00

Candleholder. 2 x 3½". Hammered copper. Footed and handled 30.00

Compote. 4¼ x 5¼". Hammered copper 45.00

Desk Set. Hammered copper. 4 pieces 65.00

Inkwell, Covered. 3½" square. Hammered copper 35.00

Jug. 5½" high. Mottled brown glaze 25.00

Trays, Hammered copper
- 10". Octagonal 65.00
- 15" long 75.00

Vases
- 4¾". Hammered copper 35.00
- 5". Hat-shaped. Detailed handles. Enameled band 50.00
- 10½". Riveted base 75.00

Wastebasket. 11½ x 13". Weathered oak 85.00

RUBENA GLASS

Rubena crystal is a flashed transparent glass that shades from red to clear. It was made by several glass manufacturers. One of the first was Hobbs, Brockunier & Company, Wheeling, W. Va.

Vase. 5" high. Floral coralene decor. Gold trim $375.00

Biscuit Jar. 6½" high. Silverplated cover and bail .... $ 225.00
Bon Bon. Tricorn. 6". Applied ring handle. "D. Q." 85.00
Bottles, Perfume
- 4½". Square-shaped. Clear cut stopper 85.00
- 8". Triangular-shaped. Sterling top 125.00

Bowls
- 5". "Hobnail." In two handled silver holder 195.00
- 7". Ribbed 125.00

Cruet. 7½". "Hobnail." 125.00
Finger Bowl. Plain 50.00
Mustard Jar. Enameled daisies. Silverplated lid and underplate .. 85.00
Pickle Castor. "IVT". Enameled decor. Silverplated frame 295.00
Pitchers
- 4". Bulbous. Square top. "Hobnail." Applied clear handle 150.00
- 7". Applied clear handle. "Overshot" 195.00
- 10". Applied clear handle. "IVT". Enameled flowers 300.00

Rose Bowls
- 4". Ribbed 55.00
- 5". Ribbed. Enameled floral decor. Gold trim 125.00
- 5". Ribbed. "Overshot" 225.00

Sugar Castor. 4". Square-shape. Silverplated top 125.00
Syrup Pitcher. 6". Hinged lid. Acid etched floral decor 150.00
Tumblers
- "Hobnail." Frosted 50.00
- "IVT" 30.00

Vases
- 7". "Swirl". Applied clear feet .. 65.00
- 10". Ruffled top. Enameled flowers. Gold trim 125.00

Water Set. 9¾". Tankard pitcher. Six tumblers. "Overshot." 350.00

RUBENA VERDE GLASS

Rubena Verde is a flashed yellow green to cranberry glass of the Victorian period. It is now considered art glass. It was originally produced by Hobbs, Brockunier & Co., Wheeling, W. Va.

Bottle, Cologne. 6½". Original clear cut stopper. Cut panels outlined in gold .... $ 100.00
Bowls
- 8x 4" deep. White and yellow enameled flowers, gold leaves .. 175.00
- 9¾ x 6" deep. Scalloped rim 200.00

Compote. 6 x 9½". Silverplated pedestal base 195.00
Cruet. 6½". "IVT". Applied clear crystal handle. Cut crystal stopper 150.00

Vase. 4" high. Bulbous base. Collared top. "Webbed." $225.00

Finger Bowl. "IVT." 85.00
Mustard Pot. 3". "IVT". Metal spring top, handle. Complete with spoon 125.00
Pickle Castor. Enameled decor. Silverplated frame 350.00
Pitchers
- 4". Bulbous. "IVT." Square mouth 175.00
- 5¾". Bulbous. "Melon Ribbed" .. 195.00
- 8". Bulbous. "Hobnail." Clear applied handle 350.00

Punch Cup. Enamel decor 75.00
Rose Bowl. 5". "Melon Ribbed" 125.00
Sauce. 4½" square. "Hobnail." 65.00
Tumbler. "IVT." 65.00
Vases
- 5¾". Ruffled top. "Ribbed." Clusters of gold leaves 185.00
- 8¾". Trumpet-shaped. Scalloped top 185.00
- 9". Trumpet-shaped. White, green enameled flowers 225.00
- 11". "Drapery." 250.00
- 12". Ruffled top. Applied enameled flowers on ribbed body. Gold outlining 325.00

RUBY STAINED GLASS
(Souvenir-Type)

Ruby-stained glass, a late Victorian introduction used to decorate souvenir items, was produced primarily in Pittsburgh, Pa. during the 1880's and 1890's.

These items were fashioned from clear glass pressed in one of several thousand patterns; and then a ruby-red staining material was painted on the annealed glass for a decorative effect. Very often, a factory would press the glass and sell it to various decorating companies where different parts of the same pattern would be stained.

Ruby-stained glass souvenir items were sold at fairs and expositions; and often 'etched' with the name of a place, person, date or event.

Also see "Pattern Glass Sections I and II" in this guide.

Cordial. "Syracuse Fair, 1905." . . $ 27.50
Goblet. "Plymouth, Pa." 25.00
Mugs
"Atlantic City." 3" 20.00
"Cincinnati, Ohio". 2½" 20.00
"Clinton, Ok." 3" 25.00
"Virginia 1915". 3" 25.00
"Winona, July 1970." 2½" 25.00
"World's Fair, 1893." 3" 35.00
Pitchers
"Cushing, Ok." 4" 30.00
"Gettysburg." 4" 30.00
"Mt. Clemens 1901." 4" 35.00
"Pond, Vermont." 3¾" 25.00
"Revere Beach, 1905". 2½" 20.00
"World's Fair, 1893." 2¼" 30.00
Toothpicks
"Christmas, 1906" 30.00
"Helen, 1900." 20.00
"Muskegon." 20.00
Tumblers
"Alton Bay, N.H." 25.00
"Great Bend, Kan." 18.50
"Irwin, Pa." 20.00
Wine. "Green City, Mo." 25.00

RUSSIAN ITEMS

Works of Russian artists and craftsmen are highly regarded by collectors. Russian enamels are one of the most exquisite examples of the Russian arts executed during the Czarist period. The items were fashioned of precious metals, elaborately enameled and encrusted with precious and-or semi-precious stones.

Enamels

Basket, Strawberry. 4¼" diam. x 1½" deep. Multicolored enamels. Bail handle. Signed . . . . $ 2700.00
Bowl. 2½ x 1" deep. Sloped sides. Bead trim. Multicolored enamels. Signed 1600.00
Boxes
1¾" diam. Covered. Red, green, white rose decor. Sunburst bottom 1200.00
2½" diam. Domed, hinged lid. Multicolored florals and scroll decor. C. 1890 . . . . 1850.00
3¾ x 7''. Rectangular. Multicolored florals and scroll decor 3000.00

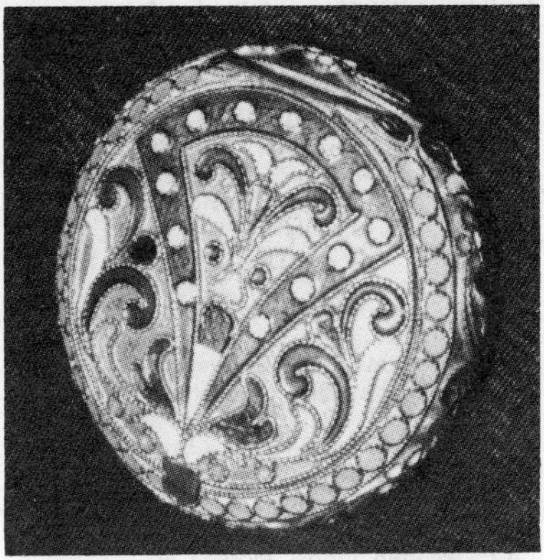

Box. 2¼" diam. Domed, hinged lid. Multicolored scroll decor. C. 1890 . . . . $1850.00

Candlesticks. 12" high. Silver. C. 1885. Pair $850.00

Cane Head. 4¼" long. Multicolored scroll decor 1250.00

Cigarette Case. 2¾ x 4". Allover scroll work. Amethyst clasp 3000.00

Demitasse Cup. 3½" high. Multicolored enamels. Marked H.C. 84, St. George 1250.00

Egg Cup. 3" high. Multicolored scrolls. Marked Saltykov, 84, St. George 950.00

Eggs

2½ x 4" Hanging-type. Allover decor on gold 10000.00

2 x 3 1/3" . Multicolored enamels on silver gilt. Marked Kucmitchev. C. 1890 .... 6500.00

Fork. 5" long. Blue and white enameling on gold washed sterling. Gustav Klingert 750.00

Letter Opener. 3" enameled handle, 12" wooden blade. Marked on handle 750.00

Napkin Ring. 2" oval. Multicolored enamels 750.00

Salts

1 x 2" diam. Enamels on silver gilt. Marked F.R. 88 .... 600.00

2¾" diam. Enamels on silver gilt. Marked 84, St. George 750.00

Spoons

2½". Multicolored enamels 350.00

4¼". Multicolored pastel enamels. Marked Kokoshnik, 11 Attel, 84, St. George 450.00

5". Red, white, blue enamels on gold wash 750.00

6¾". Pastel florals and scrolls on silver gilt. Marked Khelebnikov, Kokoshnik, 88 .... 850.00

Spoon Set. 13 spoons in original satin lined leatherette case. 12 four inch long spoons; one 6" long spoon. Multicolored enamels. Marked 84, St. George 4500.00

Sugar Scoop. 6" long. Pastel enamels. Marked 84, St. George .. 850.00

Tie Pin. 1 x 2¼" long. Multicolored enamels. Marked 84, St. George .. 1250.00

Tongs. 5" long. Blue and white on silver gilt. Signed 750.00

Tumbler. 4¾" high. Coronation of Nicholas II. C. 1896. Signed 500.00

Vodka Cup. 2½" high. Multicolored enamels on body and base. Marked 84, St. George 1500.00

Silver

Belt Buckle. Niello. Dagger clasp. Marked AA, 84 .... 450.00

Candlesticks. Pairs

12". C. 1885 .... 850.00

15". Ornate bases and stems. Engraved with grapes and leaves 950.00

Dispatch Case. 4 x 5½". Shield-shape. Hinged lid. Chased with silk tassel 350.00

Match Safe. Pocket-type. Chased. Marked 84, St. George 250.00

Napkin Rings

Niello. Hallmarked 250.00

1½" diam. Bird decor 175.00

Pin, Bow Knot. 2½" long. Marked 84, St. George, KL 350.00

Salt Dip. Ball feet. Etched florals. Marked 84, St. George 150.00

Spoon Set. Six 4¼" long spoons in original satin lined box. Twisted handles. Engraved bowls. C. 1886 600.00

Miscellaneous

Box. 3⅝". Brass. Troika in relief .. 200.00

Bread Plate. 11" diam. Carved wood 85.00

Candlesticks. 9". Brass. Cossack stems. Pair 150.00

Coffee Pot. 9 x 12" high. Brass. Double eagle mark 300.00

Cup and Saucer. White with delicate gold floral rims. Ribbed and swirled. Lamanosox Factory ... 85.00

Eggs

Porcelain. 3¼". Handpainted decor of Bible in panel. Heavy gold borders. Signed 650.00

Wood. 3". Hand decorated in allover pattern 65.00

Tea Caddy. 2½ x 3 x 4". Papier Mache. Scenic decor. Three medallion seal 450.00

Tray. 14 x 23". Hammered copper. Double eagle mark 350.00

Umbrella Stand. 8 x 21" high. Brass. Ring handle. Double eagle mark ... 500.00

Vases

10". Covered. Woodpecker handle, pine cone finial. Gardner. C. 1850 .... 750.00

12". Copper. Tankard-shape. Step joint construction. Two handles. Hallmarked 300.00

SABINO GLASS

SABINO-PARIS

Sabino figurines were made of opalescent glass in the Art Deco manner. Each piece was created from the original hand sculptured mold by the artist Sabino, "The Sculptor in Crystal." All items are signed "Sabino, Made in France."
At this writing it has been reported that Sabino

died in 1971 and never disclosed his original glass formula. An attempt was made to reproduce the fiery opalescent glass; but to no avail. It also has been reported that the factory is no longer producing glass objects but manufacturing brass articles.

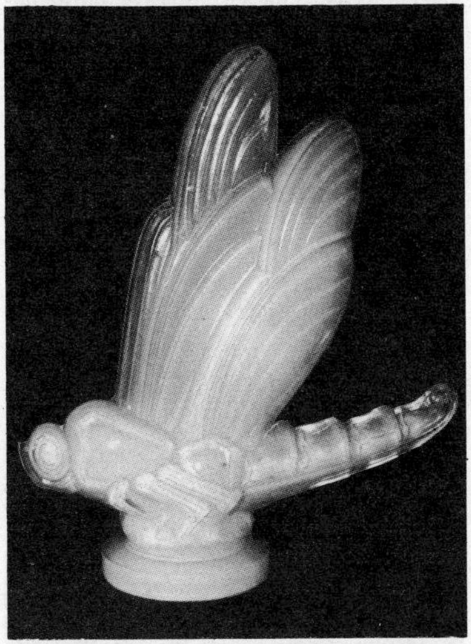

Dragonfly. 5¼x6" $80.00

Ashtrays	
Shell. 3½x5½" ....$	25.00
Shell. 4 x 7"	45.00
Swallow. 3½"	20.00
Swallow. 4¾"	35.00
Violet. 4½"	28.50
Birds	
Branch of 5. 7x8"	500.00
Cluster of 2. 3½x4½"	100.00
Cluster of 3. 5x5"	150.00
Feeding. 1½x2"	22.50
Fighting. 2x2¾"	25.00
Jumping. 3¼x3½"	30.00
Kingfisher. 4½". On stump	65.00
Mini. ½". Wings up or out	15.00
Mocking. 4½x6"	75.00
Teasing. 2½x3". Wings down or up	50.00
Wren. 1½"	18.50
Bottle, Perfume. 3¼x5½"	55.00
Bowls	
Beehive. 7x7" deep	150.00
Berry. 5¾". Shallow	50.00
Fish 5"	50.00
Box, Powder. 3" diam.	45.00
Butterflies	
2¾". Wings closed	22.50
2¾". Wings open	30.00
6"	125.00
Cherub. 2"	20.00
Chick. Drinking. 3¾"	42.50
Dogs	
German Shepherd. 2"	22.50
Pekinese. 2¾x3¾"	65.00
Scotty. 1½x3x4"	60.00
Dove. 1¾". Head up or down	20.00
Dragonfly. 5¼x6"	80.00
Fish	
2x2"	25.00
4x4"	50.00
Heron. 7½"	100.00
Knife Rest. Various-types. Each	22.50
Madonnas	
3"	30.00
5"	65.00
Mouse. 3"	50.00
Napkin Ring. Birds. 2¼" diam	20.00
Panthers, Grouping. 5¾x7¾"	200.00
Pigeon. 6¼"	125.00
Rabbit. 2"	20.00
Roosters	
3½"	30.00
7"	200.00
Snail. 1x3"	25.00
Snail Shell. 2x3"	50.00
Squirrel. 3"	28.50
Statues	
Draped. 7¼"	225.00
Nude. 6¾"	150.00
Stork. 7¼"	125.00
Swan. 2"	25.00
Turkey. 2"	28.50
Turtle. ¾x2"	20.00
Venus de Milo. 2¾"	25.00
Venus de Milo. 4½"	50.00
Zebra. 5½x5½"	125.00

C S SALOPIAN

SALOPIAN WARE

Although Salopian is the name applied to this ware, it is a misnomer. 'True' Salopian is a semi-vitreous porcelain that was made at Caughley Pot Works, Salop, Stropshire, England in the 18th century by Thomas Turner. The Salopian referred to here is earthenware made by several potters including Davenport, Stubbs and Woods in the Staffordshire district of England in the 1810-1820 period. The ware is polychrome on transfer. The named patterns have many variations. It has been reported that the blue banded ware was made for immediate export and the orange rim for the English market.

The name Salopian was derived from the fact that the wares were sold from the Salopian Warehouse, London, England. At one time it was classified as Polychrome Transfer; but regained the more popular name Salopian.

Plate. 8¾''. Octagonal. "Oriental." $175.00

Bowls. 6" diam., 2¾" deep	
Bird and Flowers ....$	450.00
Milkmaid and Cow	400.00
Creamers	
Cottage	325.00
Deer, Single	350.00
Cups and Saucers	
Bird and Flowers. Handled	350.00
Cottage. Cup, handleless. 1⅞" high x 3¼" diam.; saucer, 5¼" diam.	250.00
Cottage. Cup, handleless. 2¼" high x 3¼" diam.; saucer, 5¼" diam.	300.00
Deer, Double. Handleless	275.00
Deer, Single. Handeless	250.00
Oriental. Cup, handleless. 1⅞" high x 3" diam.; saucer, 5" diam.	150.00
Mug. Milkmaid and Cow. 4"	240.00
Plates	
4⅛". Cottage	325.00
8½". Cottage	250.00
8¾", octagonal. Oriental	175.00
Sauce. 4⅞". Cottage	175.00
Sugar, Covered. Milkmaid and Cow. 4¾" high x 7¼" long	450.00
Teapots	
Bird and Flowers	475.00
Cottage	525.00
Deer, Single	525.00
Deer, Double	600.00
Milkmaid and Cow	425.00

SALT GLAZED WARES

Salt glazed wares have a distinctive "pitted' surface texture. The result came about by throwing salt into the hot kiln during the final firing process. The salt vapors produced sodium oxide and hydrochloric acid which reacted on the glaze.

Many Staffordshire potters produced large quantities of this type of ware during the 18th and 19th centuries. A relatively small quantity was produced in the United States. Salt glazed wares continue to be made today.

Pitcher. 9" high. Gray. Bamboo design. Ridgway & Co., England $95.00

Bowl. 8 x 4½" deep. White. Undecorated. English. C. 1860 ....$	125.00
Jugs	
10½". White. Bacchanalian decor in relief. Hinged pewter lid. Chas. Meigh. C. 1845	400.00
15¼". Gray. Blue stylized floral decor. Hinged pewter lid. Unmarked	200.00
Pitchers	
7½". White. Lily and foliage in relief. American. C. 1890	125.00

8". Bulbous. White. Hunt scene in relief on base. Blue banded top with vintage decor in relief. Wedgwood. C. 1780 .... 750.00
8¼". Pale green. Game in relief. Envitte 150.00
11½". White. Muenster-type. C. 1846 .... 500.00

Syrups
6". White. Undecorated. Hinged pewter lid. C. 1870 .... 175.00
7". White. Berries and foliage in relief. C. 1890 .... 150.00
7½". Melon ribbed. White with blue bands. Hinged pewter lid. W.B. Flouger 195.00
9½". White. Bacchanalian decor in relief. Hinged pewter lid. English. C. 1860 .... 225.00

Teapot. 8". White. Neptune in relief. Shell finial. C. 1835 .... 425.00

Tea Set. White. Apostle-type. Chas. Meigh. C. 1842. 3 pieces 750.00

Vase. 7¾" White. Blue vintage decor in relief 175.00

SALTS

Salt, as an essential food, has always required some sort of dispenser or salt dish. In Feudal days, banquet seating was arranged "above the salt" for lords and ladies and "below the salt" for common people.

Salt dishes were made of various materials. Glass salts were blown, molded, cut or pressed of flint and non-flint glass. There are two types of open salts. . .the master salt which is larger and the individual salt, usually placed before each person's setting at the table. Pressed glass salts of elaborate designs produced in the United States and abroad from 1825-1850 era are called "Lacy." Major American producers include Boston and Sandwich, Mt. Vernon or Saratoga and New England Glass Company.

When the salt shaker was introduced in the mid 19th century, a mechanical agitator was invented to break and pulverize the 'caked' salt. The most common of these agitators was patented on Dec. 25, 1877; and all such glass shakers came to be known as "Christmas Salts."

NOTE: Numbers used in "Lacy" listing refer to illustrations in the book, "Pressed Glass Salt Dishes of the Lacy Period 1825-1850", by L. W. and D. B. Neal.

Salt dishes of more common patterns in flint and non-flint, clear and colored glass can be found in Section One and Section Two of this guide.

Christmas

Amber
Original top and breaker ......$ 75.00

Christmas. Amber. Original top and breaker $75.00

Lacy. CT1. Chariot. Silver opaque blue $500.00

Pewter pepper shaker top 60.00

Amethyst
Original pewter top with breaker .. 125.00
Pewter tops on salt and pepper with breakers. Mounted in original brass holder 250.00

Apple Green, Pale. With period top and breaker 75.00

Clear
Covered. With agitator. Top dated . 35.00
Nickelplated brass pepper shaker top 35.00

Master. Fiery opalescent. Six panel. Flared $165.00

Cobalt Blue. Original pewter top and breaker 110.00
Electric Blue. Pewter top. Agitator .. 125.00
Pink. Milk glass fired on. Breaker and period top 65.00
Sapphire Blue. Original pewter top and breaker 110.00
Vaseline. Period pewter top. Frozen into position 40.00

Lacy

BT 5. Boat. Clear. Boston & Sandwich Glass Co. Rare ....$ 135.00
BT 8. Boat. Clear. Boston & Sandwich Glass Co. 110.00
BT 8. Boat. Fiery opalescent medium blue. Boston & Sandwich Glass Co. 900.00
CN-1A. Clear 80.00
CT-1. Chariot. Silver opaque blue .. 500.00
CT-1A. Chariot. Clear 125.00
EE6. Clear. Rectangular. Chamfered corners 175.00
EE-3A. Eagle and Shield. Clear 175.00
EE-3B. Eagle. Clear. Boston & Sandwich Glass Co. 125.00
EE-8A. Eagle. Clear. Boston & Sandwich Glass Co. Very rare 250.00
HL-2. George Washington. Clear. Extremely rare 750.00
MV-1. Aqua. Mt. Vernon or Saratoga Glass Works 125.00
NE-1. Fiery opalescent. New England Glass Co. 250.00
NE-4. Clear. Boston & Sandwich Glass Co. 75.00
NE-6. Basket of Flowers. Light green. New England Glass Co. .. 135.00
OL-4. Emerald green. Oval. Belgian . 250.00
OL-12. Clear. Oval. Boston & Sandwich Glass Co. 90.00
OL-12A. Purple-blue. Oval. Boston & Sandwich Glass Co. 325.00
00-13. Clear. Octagonal and oblong. Boston & Sandwich Glass Co. 65.00
PO-5. Peacock Eye. Clear. Oval. Boston & Sandwich Glass Co. 100.00
RP-3. Silvery violet-blue. Round and pedestaled. Boston & Sandwich Glass Co. 650.00
SD-12. Strawberry. Deep cobalt blue. Boston & Sandwich Glass Co. 175.00
SL-1. Shell. Cobalt blue. Boston & Sandwich Glass Co. 165.00
SN-1. Stag's Horn. Cobalt blue. Boston & Sandwich Glass Co. 200.00

Master
(Flint)

Apple Green.
Oblong. Horizontal ribbing around sides and scalloped rim.
New Jersey ....$ 125.00
Six-panel 150.00
Blue Amethyst. Six-panel. Flared. Boston & Sandwich Glass Co. 175.00
Canary
Hexagonal pedestal 125.00
Mushroom. Six-scallop base 150.00
Sixteen-scallop. 20 ray base 85.00
Stiegel-type. 14-diamond mold .. 75.00
Cobalt
Six-sided 125.00
Six-panel. Round base 150.00
Fiery Opalescent
Six-panel. Flared 165.00
Six-scallop base with diamond top 175.00
Peacock Blue
Six-sided 150.00
Sapphire Blue. Hexagonal. Footed. Sandwich-type 150.00
Smoky Translucent Electric Blue. Boston & Sandwich Glass Co. 350.00
Translucent Blue. Mushroom. Six-scallop base 350.00

SAMPLERS

Samplers were originally a reference sheet of hand stitches or a practice panel for a beginner.

Examples of samplers date back to the 1700's. The earliest ones were long and narrow and simply done with only the alphabet and numerals. Later examples were square. Before the 'art' lost its popularity, about the 1900's, the shape changed again to rectangular. Flowers, birds and houses, were incorporated into the completed design. Mottoes usually indicate the sampler is Victorian.

1836. 15" square. Alphabet, numerals, verse. Unfinished $75.00

Dates

1744. Alphabet, numerals, birds and animals. Homespun linen. Signed ....$ 450.00
1799. 11½x13". Alphabet, numerals, verse 275.00
1802. 12" square. Birds, animals, flowers 125.00
1807. 17" square. Alphabet, numerals, trees 250.00
1812. 13x16". Alphabet, numerals, flowers. 175.00
1813. 15x19". Strawberry vine border. Signed 285.00
1815. 12¾x17". Adam and Eve under apple tree. Biblical quotation 300.00
1818. 12x20". Alphabet, trees, birds, house. Signed 195.00
1818. February 24. 13x16". Alphabet repeated 3 times, numerals once. Signed 150.00
1826. 10x18". Red and green alphabet and numerals. Homespun linen. English 200.00
1830. 9x12". Strawberry border with house. Alphabet and verse. Signed 375.00
1831. 8x17". Alphabet only. Signed 125.00
1834. 15½" square. Unfinished .. 100.00
1835. 21" square. Alphabet, verse, flowers 200.00
1836. April 21. 13x17". Alphabet, numerals, verse. Signed 225.00
1837. 17x18". House, birds, flowers. Religious verse. Signed .. 225.00
1838. Alphabet, flower pots and trees. Signed 195.00
1848. 12x13". Alphabet and numerals 150.00
1848. 23" square. Birds, flowers, lions, buildings and verse. Signed . 275.00
1849. 20½" square. Church, flowers, fruit baskets. Signed 395.00
1850. 25½x27½". "The Happy Family." Verse with floral and vine border 195.00

SANDWICH GLASS

The term Sandwich Glass applies to the large variety of glass, including lacy (1825-1850) made by The Boston and Sandwich Glass Company from 1822 to 1888. Although the company is best known for its pressed glass, it also manufactured art glass in the 1870's and 1880's.

Bottles. See "Bottles"

Bowls, Shallow

Acanthus. Clear. 6¼" ....$ 125.00
Eagle and 13 Stars. Clear. 7" octagonal 395.00
Oak Leaf. Clear. 8¼" 125.00
Princess. Clear. 6¼" 125.00
Rayed Peacock Eye. Clear. 6½" .. 75.00
Roman Rosette. Clear. 6½" 50.00
Tulip. Clear. 6¼" 135.00

Candlesticks

Canary. 2". Hexagonal base 225.00
Canary. 6¾". Petal and Loop 325.00
Clambroth. 7". Petal and Loop. Pair 300.00
Clear. 6¾". Square base. Stepped concentric rings. Lacy socket 250.00
Clear. 7". Trefoil paw foot base. Lacy socket 450.00
Fiery Opalescent. 12½". Crucifix .. Hexagonal base 375.00
Fiery Opalescent. 12½". Crucifix 275.00
Peacock Blue. 6⅞". Petal and Loop 750.00
Translucent Blue top with white fluted base. 9½" 500.00
Translucent Blue and White dolphin base. 10¼" 450.00
Vaseline. 10¼". Dolphin 350.00

Celery Vase. Canary. Octagonal base with wafer $450.00

Carafe. 9½". Overlay blue to white to clear. Star-cut stopper. Enamel decor in panels 250.00
Casket, Covered. Clear. Lee. Plate 168 .... 350.00
Celery Vases
  Blue Amethyst. Octagonal base with wafer 550.00
  Canary. Octagonal base with wafer 450.00
Cream and Sugar. Ivy. Clear. Miniature 100.00
Creamers
  Lacy. Clear. Miniature 95.00
  Lacy. Opaque silver blue 750.00
  Peacock Eye. Purple blue 750.00
Dishes
  Double Horn of Plenty. Clear. 5½x8" 150.00
  Gothic. Clear. 8⅜" 85.00
Ewer. 12½". Pink at top shading into white at bottom. Amber thorn handle 295.00
Finger Bowl. 5". Overshot 75.00
Honey. Fiery Opalescent. 3½" 65.00
Lamps, Whale Oil. Also see "Lamps"
  Acid Finish Blue. 10½". Acanthus Leaf. Reeded brass stem. Marble base 350.00
  Amethyst
    8½". Brass base 395.00
    11". Cut to clear. Double marble base 350.00
  Clear
    4". Blown and pressed. Miniature 175.00
    10½". Star and Punty 225.00
    11". Sweetheart. Pair 300.00
    12". Tulip. Column base 185.00
  Peacock Blue. 8½". Petal and Loop. Square base 950.00
Paperweight. 2½". Candy-type .. 225.00
Pitchers
  1⅞". Clear. Miniature 250.00
  5½". Tankard-shape. Clear 80.00
  7". Blue overshot glass. Square mouth. Bulbous body. Applied amber handle in ribbed shell. Blown 250.00
  7". Syrup. Star and Buckle. Clear. Hexagonal body. Applied handle.. 185.00
  8½". Icicle. Amber. Enameled .. 1500.00
  8½". Overshot amber glass. Cloverleaf-shaped top. Amber, ribbed shell applied handle. Blown 250.00
  11". Tankard-shape. Overshot cranberry. Applied crystal ribbed handle 295.00
  11½". Overshot clear. With ice insert. C. 1865 .... 295.00
Plates, Clear
  Beehive. 9¼" 125.00
  Beehive. 9¾" 95.00
  Bust of Napoleon. 6" 150.00
  Hairpin. 6" 65.00
  Heart. 6" 55.00
  Leaf and Scroll. 6" 55.00
  Oak Leaf. 6" 35.00
  Peacock Eye. 5¼" 75.00
  Peacock Eye and Thistle. 8" 125.00
  Thistle and Beehive. 9¼" octagonal 150.00
Pomade. 3¾" high. Bear. Black amethyst 275.00
Pulls, Drawer
  Canary. Set of six 225.00
  Clear. Set of six 75.00
Salts. See "Salts"
Sauces
  Beaded Scale and Eye, Daisy center. Clear 65.00
  Oak Leaf. Clear 35.00
  Peacock Eye. Clear 40.00
  Roman Rosette. Fiery Opalescent 50.00

Shell Medallion. Octagonal. Clear . . . 65.00
Variant Eye. Clear 15.00

Spills
- Canary. Inverted Diamond with Thumbprint 650.00
- Canary. Star and Punty 550.00
- Clambroth. Vine 350.00
- Clear. Star 75.00
- Electric Blue. Star 750.00

Sugars, Covered
- Acanthus. Clear 175.00
- Gothic. Clear 135.00

Sugar Shaker. Diamond Quilted. Clear. Original top 125.00

Tie Backs
- Amber. 4¼". Pair 35.00
- Canary. 3". Pair 75.00
- Clear. 4½". Pair 40.00
- Opalescent. Pair 85.00

Tray. 5x6½". Scrolled Leaf and Fleur de Lis. Clear 65.00

Tumbler. 3⅝". Six Panel. Fiery Opalescent 175.00

Vases
- 7½". Loop. Amethyst 600.00
- 9". Paneled. Amethyst 750.00
- 9¾". Bigler. Canary 450.00
- 10". Three Punty. Canary 450.00

Whiskey Tasters
- Lacy. Fiery Opalescent 150.00
- Loop. Canary 135.00

SARREGUEMINES

SARREGUEMINES

Sarreguemines ware is a faience type, i.e., tin-glazed earthenware. The factory was established in Lorraine, France in 1770 under the supervision of Utzcheider and Fabry. The factory was regarded as one of the three most prominent manufacturers of French faience. Most of the wares found today are of the 19th century. Later wares are impressed Sarreguemines and Germany due to a change of boundaries and location of the factory.

Bowl. 10x11". Scalloped shell-shaped. Pink . . . .$ 60.00

Character Jug. 6½". "The Judge."... 100.00

Jam Jar, Covered. 4". Basketweave. Applied fruit finial 40.00

Oyster Plate. 8½". Pink, green and white 40.00

Pitchers
- 4¾". Pink interior. Green-yellow exterior 30.00
- 8¼". Pewter top. Cherub decor in relief 65.00
- 9¾". Tankard. Green exterior, aqua interior. Figures in relief . . 150.00
- 13". Figural. Dog with gaping mouth forms spout. Cobalt handle . 175.00

Character Jug. "Lawyer." $100.00

Plates
- 7½". Nursery Rhyme. Colored transfer center 20.00
- 7½". Strawberries on deep gold ground 35.00
- 8". Monk. White and pink ground . 35.00
- 8". Birds, branches, cherries on blue ground 35.00
- 8½". "Napoleon." Black transfer . . 40.00
- 12". Fruit decor in muilticolors . . 55.00

Platter. 12x15½". Transfer of Brittany people in center. Floral border 65.00

Vases
- 5". Bulbous. Three handles. Incised Art Deco-style leaves and geometric designs. Red and blue with gold trim 55.00
- 13½". Bulbous base, slender neck. Art Deco-style decor in cobalt, green and gray 95.00

Wine Jug. 11". Pewter lid with thumbrest. "Hanoi." 125.00

SATIN GLASS

The term "Satin Glass" refers to all opaque colored glassware with a soft velvety surface finish. The glass was treated with hydrofluoric acid to produce the dull satin surface. Vases and rose bowls are the decorative items found most frequently in plain satin glass; and the range of colors is broad with blue, yellow and pink being favored. Tableware and nightlights were also made in this plain finish, but they were produced in larger volume in the beautiful Mother-of-Pearl finish.

Similar to plain satin glass in respect to the plating (or casing), Mother-of-Pearl differs in that it displays integral or indented designs in the glass and has a distinctive surface finish. This finish (also called Pearlware or Pearl Satin Ware) was perfected in 1885 by an Englishman, Joseph Webb. He patented his process while working at the Phoenix Glass Co., Beaver, Pa.

A great number of ornamental and utilitarian pieces in many shades were produced by various firms. . .rainbow is considered a choice color.

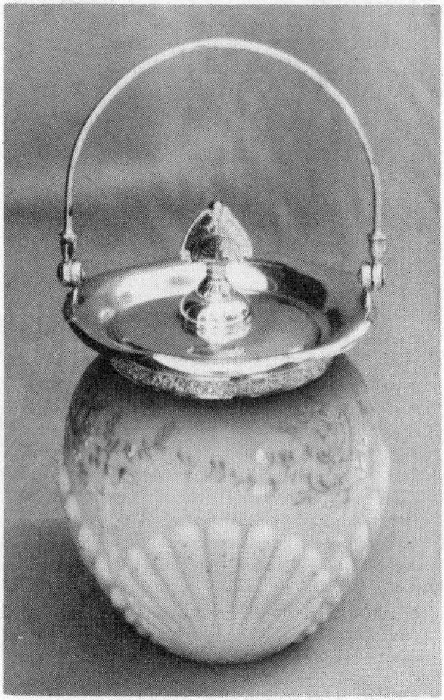

Biscuit Jar. 7¾" high. Pink. MOP. Enamel decor. Silverplated lid and bail $350.00

Basket. 5" high. "Herringbone." Blue. MOP. Two circular formed handles ....$ 375.00

Biscuit Jars
- 6½". "Blown-out DQ." Pink 150.00
- 7½". "Melon Ribbed." Pink. MOP. Enameled floral decor 275.00

Bobeches. 5" diam. "Swirl." Pink with applied camphor. Fluted rims. Pair 75.00

Bowls
- 7x5" deep. "DQ". Blue. MOP. Enameled gold florals. Webb 650.00
- 7½x3½" deep. "Melon Ribbed." Blue. MOP 350.00

Box. 5¼" square. White. Enameled with pink and blue florals 185.00

Cologne Bottle. 5". "Peacock Eye." White. Challinor 175.00

Egg. 3½" high. Blue 125.00

Ewers
- 7". "Melon Ribbed." Rose to pink. Camphor handle and stopper .. 350.00
- 10". "Raindrop." White. MOP. Camphor handle 350.00

Finger Bowl. Chartreuse to cream. With underplate. Folded-down, crimped camphor rim 250.00

Mustard Pot. 3". "Melon Ribbed." White. Enameled floral decor. Silverplated lid and bail handle .. 125.00

Pickle Castors
- "DQ." Green. MOP. Silverplated frame 300.00
- "Swirl." Blue. Silverplated frame .. 225.00

Pitchers
- 8". "Peacock Eye." MOP. Yellow. Clear reeded handle. Webb 375.00
- 10". "DQ." Blue. Ruffled top 425.00
- 10½". "Raindrop." MOP. Pink and blue applied camphor handle .. 800.00
- 12¾". Rainbow. MOP. Applied camphor handle 1500.00

Plate. 6". Rainbow. MOP. Crimped rim 500.00

Punch Cup. Rainbow. Applied camphor handle 375.00

Rose Bowls
- 3". MOP. Pink. Shell and Seaweed embossing 125.00
- 3½". "DQ." MOP. Blue 150.00
- 4". MOP. Blue 85.00
- 5". MOP. Blue. Coralene decor. Applied camphor feet 275.00
- 5½". Egg-shaped. "DQ." MOP. White. Enameled yellow florals. Applied camphor thorn feet 325.00
- 6". "DQ." Rainbow 350.00

Sugar Castor. Blue. Silverplated top . 150.00

Tumblers
- "DQ." Yellow 165.00
- "DQ." MOP. Yellow. Enameled florals 300.00
- "Herringbone." Blue 125.00
- "Swirl." MOP. Blue 150.00

Vases
- 5". "DQ." MOP. Rainbow 750.00
- 6". "Raindrop." MOP. Rainbow. Applied camphor handles and feet 950.00
- 6½". Triangular-shape with crimped tops. MOP. Apricot. Applied camphor thorn handles. Pair 500.00
- 8½". "Melon Ribbed." MOP. Rainbow. Gold enameled florals 850.00
- 10½". "D.Q." Yellow. Bulbous base, slender neck 350.00

SATSUMA

Satsuma, named for a war lord who brought skilled Korean potters to Japan in the early 1600's, was a hand-crafted Japanese faience glazed pottery. It is finely-crackled, has a cream, yellow-cream or gray-cream color and is decorated with raised enamels in floral geometric and figural motifs. Figural Satsuma was made specifically for export in the 19th century. Later Satsuma, referred to as Satsuma-style ware, is Japanese porcelain also hand-decorated in raised enamels. From 1912 to the present, this Satsuma-style ware has been mass-produced and much of the ware on today's market is of this later period. Satsuma-style wares are still being produced.

Tea Set. 3 pieces. "Thousand Flowers." C. 1900 .... $175.00

Bottles
- 8½". Peonies and clouds. C. 1885 $ 200.00
- 10½". Phoenix bird and clouds. Awaji. C. 1830 .... 1000.00

Bowls
- 4" square. Arhats with phoenix bird. C. 1920 .... 275.00
- 4¾ x 2" deep. Overall floral motif. Early 19th century 650.00
- 6". Arhats and Kwannon. Crackled. Gold trim. C. 1925 .... 175.00

Boxes
- 2¼ x 5". Fan-shaped. Figural and floral decor. C. 1935 .... 65.00
- 3 x 5". Melon-shaped. Florals and butterflies. C. 1840 .... 300.00

Buttons. 1" diam. Face on each. Set of six 85.00

Charger. 12½". Thousand Warriors. Diapered border of dragons in multicolors. C. 1850 .... 1500.00

Cups and Saucers
- Arhats on black. 19th century .. 60.00
- Scenic. Diapered. 3-legs. C. 1900 75.00

Figurines
- Elephant. 3". C. 1935 .... 25.00
- Hotei. 3½". C. 1935 .... 35.00
- Kwannon. 7½". 19th century .. 400.00

Incense Burners (Koro)
- 2½". Bulbous. Birds and peonies on oxidized cobalt. C. 1875 .... 450.00
- 6". Bulbous. 3-legs. Wisteria decor on black. Lion dog handles and finial. C. 1900 .... 375.00

Jars, Covered
- 3½". Thousand Faces. 19th century 85.00
- 8½". 3-legs. Scenic decor with figures. Heavy gold. C. 1875 .... 450.00
- 10". 3-legs. Lion dog handles and finial. C. 1920 .... 75.00
- 17½". 3-legs. Peonies in medallions. Awata. C. 1900 .... 300.00

Pitchers
- 4½". Fruit and flower decor on tan ground. C. 1840 .... 85.00
- 4½". Warrior scene. Gold scrolled handle. C. 1920 .... 225.00

Plate. 4". Jeweled iridescent scrolling. C. 1800 .... 175.00

Teapots
- 4½". Bulbous. Peony decor. Tortoise finial. C. 1800 .... 350.00
- 7". Elephant-shaped. Pagoda finial. C. 1930's 75.00

Tea Sets
- 7 pieces. Enameled florals on white. Handleless cups. C. 1920 .. 225.00
- 21 pieces. Arhats, Kwannon, dragon scales. Dragon handles, spouts, finials. Handled cups. C. 1925 .... 500.00
- 27 pieces. Thousand Faces. Gold dragon handles. 19th century .. 2250.00

Vases
- 5". Square-shaped. Arhats with halos in panels. C. 1930 .... 150.00
- 6". Double gourd-shaped. Figures in reserves. Late 19th century 595.00
- 7¼". Baluster-shaped. Peacock with trees in background. White ground, heavy gold trim. Early 19th century 650.00
- 7½". Jeweled leaf decor. C. 1800 450.00
- 10". Enameled flowers and leaves on pale ground. Gold clouds. C. 1810 .... 1000.00
- 12½". Baluster-shaped. Chrysanthemums and foliage on white ground. Heavy gold trim. C. 1910 . 125.00
- 15". Baluster-shaped. Arhats with halos. C. 1925 .... 250.00
- 18". Ring handles. Figures. Dotted enamel trim 300.00
- 23". Sleeping sage, attendants, court people. Diaper borders. C. 1850 .... 1500.00

SCALES

Prior to 1900, the simple balance scale was commonly used for measuring weights. Since that time, scales have become more sophisticated in design and more accurate. Scales in a variety of styles and types, used by farmers, storekeepers and druggists, include beam, platform, postal and pharmaceutical.

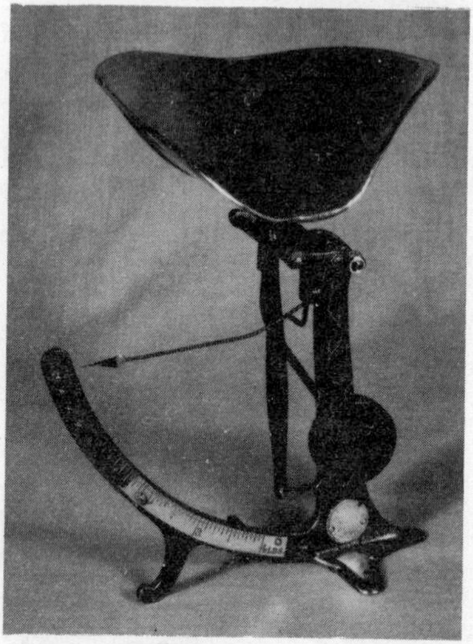

Gravity-type. Cast iron base with brass pan. Dated 1880 ....$125.00

Candy. 4 lbs. 14½ x 18" long. Cast iron, painted and stenciled. Brass pan ....$ 125.00
Egg. Cast iron. "Zenith." 15.00
Jeweler. Brass pans, marble-top base with drawer 125.00
Letter. Desk-type. Tin 15.00
Money. 2 x 7". Complete. All original. 18th century 250.00
Pharmaceutical. 15½ x 16½". Cast iron. Marble pans. Brass weights... 150.00
Photographer. German silver pans. Brass weights 125.00
Platform. 50 lbs. Counter-top-type. Cast iron 75.00
Platform. 300 lbs. Floor model-type. Cast iron. Single or double beam... 150.00
Pocket. Folding. English. 18th century 200.00
Postal. Brass. Includes nest of weights, ½ oz. to 4 lbs. Wooden base 175.00
Postal. Cast iron. Brass beam, sliding weight 75.00
Spring balance
- 5 lbs. Hanging-type. Brass 25.00
- 10 lbs. Tin. Brass dial 50.00
- 15 lbs. Hanging-type. Steel 25.00
- 25 lbs. Hanging-type. With tray. Brass dial 65.00
- 30 lbs. Hanging-type. Tin with white porcelain dial 75.00

SCHLEGELMILCH PORCELAIN

From 1861-1918, production of this porcelain . . . marked R.S. Germany, R.S. Poland, R.S. Prussia, R.S. Suhl and R.S. Tillowitz . . .was directed by two brothers, Erdmann and Reinhold Schlegelmilch at their respective factories in the Germanic provinces of Prussia, Thuringia and Silesia.

All Schlegelmilch porcelain is of the finest quality with exquisitely molded forms and unique decoration. A majority of it was factory-decorated; but blanks were produced for home-decorating and occasionally, artist-signed examples are found.

In the past, the famous "red mark" R.S. Prussia was valued above the "green mark" pieces. Today, as prices soar on R.S. Prussia, so it is also with the R.S. Germany scenic, portrait and floral examples, plus the R.S. Suhl and R.S. Tillowitz items. R.S. Poland is commanding high prices due to the scarcity of the red mark which was manufactured only from 1916-1918.

The "animal" pieces are much sought after by collectors because production of these particular patterns were limited.

CAUTION: A great many "fake" Schlegelmilch are appearing on the market. These reproductions are new decal marks, transfers or recently handpainted animals on old, authenic R.S. pieces.

R.S. GERMANY

Ashtray. 1½ x 3¾". Pinecone decor $ 25.00
Berry Set. 9¼" master bowl. Four 5" bowls. Floral decor. Set 75.00
Bowls
- 7¼". Pedestaled. Handpainted orange, white flowers, green ground 35.00
- 8¼". Hexagonal. Underplate 9½". Floral decor. Gold trim. Set... 75.00
- 9¼". Wild rose decor. Lustred ground 45.00
- 10". Cottage scene. Gold lustred top 150.00

Cake Set. 10" plate. Six 6" plates. Handpainted floral decor. Satin finish. Set 125.00

R.S. Germany. Vases. Pitcher-type. 11¼" high. Floral decor on blue ground. Gold trim. Pair $750.00

Candlestick. 5". Lilies on beige, green ground 35.00
Celery Tray. 12¼". Lily decor 35.00
Cheese and Cracker Plate. Lilies on gray ground 45.00
Chocolate Pots
5". Blue, pink florals on light green ground. Gold handle and trim 55.00
9". Handpainted carnations on cream ground 75.00
Chocolate Set. Pot, 6 cups and saucers. Tulips. Blue with gold trim 250.00
Cracker Jars
Geometric decor in aqua, black. Gold trim 85.00
Tulips. Satin finish 65.00
Creamers and Sugars, Covered
Lilies on off-white ground. Set .. 50.00
Silver Lustre. Hexagonal-shape. Set 85.00
Hatpin Holder. Orange poppies ... 35.00
Jam Jar, Covered. Orchids 25.00
Nappies
5½". Handpainted daisies. Gold trim. Green mark 25.00
6¾". Pink roses, green to beige background. Scalloped rim. Satin finish 35.00
Pitchers
Cider. Pink roses on blue-green ground 85.00
Syrup. White hydrangea. Gold trim. Satin finish 45.00
Plates
6". Orange poppy on green 8.50
7½". Scenic. Shepherd boy, farmhouse, tree 38.50
8½". White clematis. Gold trim .. 25.00
10". Classical scene. Saxe mark .. 75.00
10". Petaled flowers with raised centers. 50.00
11". Open handles. Multicolored poppies on white. Gold trim 60.00
Relish. 9". Three sections. Handpainted pink blossoms, gold handle and trim. Signed L. S. Huxley ... 45.00
Sauce. With tray. Pink roses, gold leaves. Gold trim 30.00
Shaving Mug. With soap drain. Undecorated 35.00
Sugar, Covered. Two handles. Pink and orange florals 22.50
Sugar Castor. White dogwood on green. Gold trim 45.00
Tea Service. 16 pieces. Pink roses on tan lustre. Set 250.00
Toothbrush Holders
Pink roses on green 55.00
White. Undecorated 35.00
Toothpicks
2 handles. Roses. Gold trim 25.00
3 handles. Pansies on pastel ground. Gold trim 40.00
Trays
3¼ x 5½". White dogwood. Scalloped edges. Gold trim 35.00
5 x 14". Handled. White flowers with gold centers, green leaves on tan 50.00
Vase. 4½". Iris on white ground .. 30.00

R.S. POLAND

Bowl. Crane. 9" .... $ 900.00
Hatpin Holder. Floral decor on shaded ground 95.00
Plate. Portrait. 9½" 1000.00
Vases
7". Lion and Lioness 1000.00
9". Scenic decor 850.00

R.S. PRUSSIA

Berry Sets
7 pieces. 11½" bowl, six 5¾" bowls. Handpainted orchids. Gold trim. Set .... $ 425.00
7 pieces. Master bowl, six serving bowls. Swan decor. Icicle molded edges. Set 1000.00
Bowls
5". Green ground. White, yellow poppies 475.00
5½". Red ground. Floral center. Portrait medallions 225.00
9½". Green. Multicolored flowers. Gold trim 150.00
10". Boat scene. Pearlized finish .. 600.00
10". Cabbage mold. Satin finish .. 500.00
10½". Melon Eaters. Jewel molded edge 1000.00
10½". Portrait center 850.00

R.S. Prussia. Compote. 7" diam. x 4½" high. Scalloped edge. Pink floral decor on white ground. Gold trim . . $235.00

11". Floral center. Shaded green ground. Gold trim 225.00
11". Stage center. Beaded molded edge. Gold trim 1800.00
12" Oval. Open handles. Roses . . 175.00

Boxes, Covered
Jewel. Pink and white flowers . . 125.00
Powder. Rose decor on white 95.00

Chocolate Pots
Castle Scene. Ball feet 1250.00
Florals. All white flowers on shaded green ground. Gold beaded trim 350.00
Snowbird. Icicle molded edge . . 1750.00
Swan. Gold beaded edge 500.00

Chocolate Sets. 7 pieces
Farmyard. Icicle molded edges . . 2750.00
Floral. Carnation molded edges. Gold trim 850.00
Portrait 3000.00
Swallows 1200.00

Compote. 6½" diam., 7" high. Roses on shaded green ground . . 200.00

Cracker Jars
6½". Pink and white flowers. Scalloped base 175.00
7". Green florals. Satin finish 300.00

Creamers and Sugars, Covered
Castle. Ball feet 600.00
Floral. Ball feet 275.00
Swans 350.00

Hair Receivers
Florals. Diamond-shape. Pearlized 150.00
Roses. Shaded green ground 95.00

Hatpin Holder. Roses on shaded yellow-green ground 95.00

Jam Jar. With underplate. Pink roses. Gold trim. Beaded edge . . 150.00

Mug. Roses on yellow ground 125.00

Pitchers, Tankard-shaped
Fall Season. Carnation molded edges 4000.00
Lilies. Shaded violet ground. Satin finish 500.00
Roses. Pink and yellow on shaded green ground 325.00
Swans. Icicle molded edges 1500.00

Plates
Castle. Petaled edges. Gold trim. 8¾" 500.00
Farmyard scene. 10½" 950.00
Floral. Shaded ground. Carnation molded edge. 10" 300.00
Melon Eaters. Jeweled molded edge. 10½" 1000.00
Mill Scene. 10" 400.00
Portrait. Plain rim. 10" 650.00
Sheepherder. 10½" 700.00
Ship. Orange. 10½" 650.00

Ring Tree. Florals. Gold trim 110.00

Sauce. 5". Mill Scene 55.00

Shaving Mug. Roses. Yellow and pink. Beaded edge 125.00

Sugar Castors
Apple Blossoms. Shaded green ground. Gold trim 135.00
Roses. Three handles. Satin finish. 175.00

Syrup. With underplate. Pink roses on shaded green ground. Gold trim 175.00

Tea Sets. 3 pieces.
Daffodils. Shaded green ground 300.00
Swans. Icicle molded borders 1000.00

Toothpick Holder. Floral decor. 2 handles 125.00

Trays
6x12". Swans 500.00
6 x 12½". Open handles. Waterlilies 250.00
7½ x 11". Pink roses on green ground 175.00
7½ x 12". Snowbirds 1500.00

Vases
Cage, The. Handles. 8" 1000.00
Cottage Scene. 4½" 250.00
Farmyard Scene. 9" 950.00
Florals. Pink and white on yellow ground. 8" 175.00
Hummingbirds. 5" 625.00
Melon Eaters. Handles. Jeweled. 10" 1500.00
Mill Scene. Handled. Cobalt. Gold trim. 9" 1000.00
Peace Bringing Plenty. Green. 7" 950.00
Roses, Pink. Handles. 9" 325.00
Ships. Handles. 9" 600.00
Winter Season. 8¼" 650.00

R.S. SUHL

Bowl. Mill and Sheepherder (combination). 10" . . . . $ 850.00

R.S. Suhl. Vase. 8". "Mill Scene." . . $600.00

Box, Covered. Nightwatch	650.00
Plate. Lion and Lioness. 9"	750.00
Tea Service. Nightwatch. 15 pieces	1000.00
Vases	
Nightwatch. 12"	850.00
Three by Dawn. 8"	600.00

R.S. TILLOWITZ

R.S. Tillowitz. Chocolate Set. 10 pieces. Multicolored floral and leaf decor on ivory ground. Signed $295.00

Basket. 5 x 2½" high. Octagonal. Handpainted multicolored florals. Gold handle and trim . . . . $	60.00
Bowls	
7½". Shallow. Handled. Poinsettias on white	60.00
9¼". Roses on shaded green ground. Gold trim	40.00
Cake Plate. 10". Open handles. Orange poppies	55.00
Cake Set. 7 pieces. Blue handpainted roses. Gold trim	175.00
Cream and Sugar. 3" high. Poinsettia decor on white ground. Set . .	45.00
Teapot. Pastel florals	40.00
Tea Tile. 6". White sweetpeas on orange	45.00
Tray. 6¼". Handled. Handpainted florals. Artist signed	30.00
Tray. 9 x 13" oval. Pastel peonies on blue ground	50.00
Vase. 6" ovoid. Roses on shaded tan ground	45.00

SCHNEIDER GLASS

Schneider

Charles and Ernest Schneider founded the firm known as Cristalerie Schneider in Epinay-sur-Siene, France. Their art glass, can be identified by the distinctive mottled colors. This type of Schneider glass was made from 1913 to 1933. According to the latest reports, the firm currently operating is producing crystal tablewares.

Compote. 10¼" diam. x 8¾" high. Mottled blue with citron edge. Metal frame. $350.00

Compotes

- 3½ x 5" diam. Mottled orange. Wrought iron frame ....$ 150.00
- 5 x 14" diam. Mottled rose. Amethyst stem and wafer foot .. 275.00
- 8½ x 9½" diam. Mottled violet and yellow bowl. Wrought iron frame 300.00

Ewer. 6½" Mottled blue and gray. Applied black amethyst handle .. 200.00

Finger Bowl. With underplate. Mottled orange 175.00

Pitchers

- 6½". Mottled orange and yellow .. 185.00
- 11". Mottled yellow. Applied amethyst handle and wafer foot .. 350.00

Plate. 4". Mottled deep pink 60.00

Vases

- 4½". Ribbed body. Applied petal feet. Mottled orange and yellow .. 175.00
- 8¼". Trumpet-shaped. Mottled yellow and cobalt. C. 1925 .... 250.00
- 13". Double. Pear-shaped. Mottled orange. Crystal standard and domed base 450.00
- 15½". Baluster-shaped. Mottled orange. Applied crystal convex circles on shoulder. Amethyst wafer foot 395.00
- 17¾". Bulbous base, slender neck. Applied handles. Mottled blue and orange. 450.00

SCHOENHUT TOYS

Albert Schoenhut, son of a toymaker was born in Germany, 1849. In 1866, he ventured to America to work as a repairman of toy pianos for Wanamaker's, Philadelphia, Pa. Finding the glass sounding bars inadequate, he perfected a toy piano with metal sounding bars. His piano was an instant success and the A. Schoenhut Company had its beginning. From then on, toys seemed to flow out of the factory. Each of his six sons entered the business at the appropriate time. Under the firm, yet loving, tutelage of their father the business prospered until 1934, when misfortune forced the company into bankruptcy. In 1935 Otto and George Schoenhut contracted to produce the Pinn Family Dolls.

At the same time, the Schoenhut Manufacturing Company was formed by two other Schoenhuts. Both companies operated under a partnership agreement that eventually led to O. Schoenhut, Inc. which continues today.

Some dates of interest: 1872-toy piano invented; 1903-Humpty and Dumpty and Circus patented; 1911-1924-wooden doll production; 1928-1934- composition dolls.

Animals

- Alligator. Glass eyes ....$ 235.00

"Ballerina." 8½" high $175.00

- Alligator. Painted eyes 175.00
- Bear. Brown painted eyes 125.00
- Buffalo. Glass eyes 195.00
- Buffalo. Painted eyes 135.00
- Bulldog. Brown painted eyes. (rare) 225.00
- Camel. Glass eyes, one hump .. 225.00
- Camel. Painted eyes, two humps .. 175.00
- Camel. Painted eyes, one hump .. 200.00
- Deer. Glass eyes 275.00
- Donkey. Large. Glass eyes 110.00
- Donkey. Small. Painted eyes 45.00
- Elephant. Glass eyes 95.00
- Elephant. Painted eyes 50.00
- Giraffe. 11" high. Glass eyes 250.00
- Goat. Glass eyes 110.00
- Goose. Painted eyes 200.00
- Hippopotamus. Glass eyes 250.00
- Hippopotamus. Painted eyes 185.00
- Horse. Painted eyes 125.00
- Lamb. Painted eyes 150.00
- Leopard. Glass eyes 225.00
- Lion. Glass eyes 125.00
- Monkey. Painted eyes 150.00
- Ostrich. Painted eyes. (rare) 200.00
- Pig. Glass eyes 150.00
- Poodle. Glass eyes 175.00
- Poodle. Painted eyes 115.00
- Spark Plug. All original 150.00
- Tiger. Glass eyes 225.00
- Tiger. Painted eyes 150.00

Zebra. Glass eyes 200.00

Blocks

"Auto Build 5 in 1." Original box. Complete. C. 1925 .... 125.00

"Building Blocks." Original box. Complete 150.00

Circus. "Humpty Dumpty." Glass-eyed figurines, poster. Original box. Incomplete, 22 pieces 1000.00

Circus. "Humpty Dumpty." Animals with glass eyes. Complete with tent. 52 pieces 5000.00

Circus Accessories

Barrel.................... 7.00

Chair 9.00

Platform 10.00

Tent. 25 x 35" 400.00

Circus Performers

Acrobat, Lady 140.00

Acrobat, Lady. Bisque 225.00

Clown. Cotton suit. Large 95.00

Bare back rider on white horse. 6½" 250.00

Lion Tamer. Wooden head 175.00

Ringmaster. 8". Bisque head. All original. Complete 275.00

Ringmaster. 8½". Wooden head .. 135.00

Strong Man. Bisque head 275.00

Dirigible. 13". Original box. C. 1929. 50.00

Doll House—Garage. 14 x 19 x 20" high. Two stories, stairway, hinged roof, swing-away sides. C. 1920's 350.00

Dolls

Baby Face. 14". Baby body, wooden head. Painted hair, eyes. Dressed 225.00

Baby Face. 16". Toddler body. Wooden jointed body. Painted hair, eyes, closed mouth 250.00

Clothespin Boy. Yarn hair, painted features. Suitably dressed 85.00

Character. 16". Wooden. Intaglio eyes, molded hair with pink ribbon 475.00

Nature. 11". Sitting, original wig .. 175.00

Walking. 14". All wood. Painted eyes, mohair wig, open mouth. Suitably dressed. 425.00

Personalities

Barney Google 125.00

Farmer 125.00

Hobo 125.00

Jiggs 300.00

Maggie with rolling pin 400.00

Max and Moritz. Replaced coats. Pair 500.00

Teddy Roosevelt with hat 350.00

Teddy Roosevelt without hat 300.00

Pianos

8½ x 9½ x 16". 15 keys 100.00

11 x 21 x 23". Brass pedals 150.00

17x 24 x 27". Grand 275.00

17x 29 x 31". 29 keys 200.00

Piano Stools

Double 150.00

Single 65.00

Roly Dolly. Drummer Boy 125.00

Trinity Chimes 125.00

SCONCES

A sconce is a utilitarian or decorative wall bracket used to hold candles or lights.

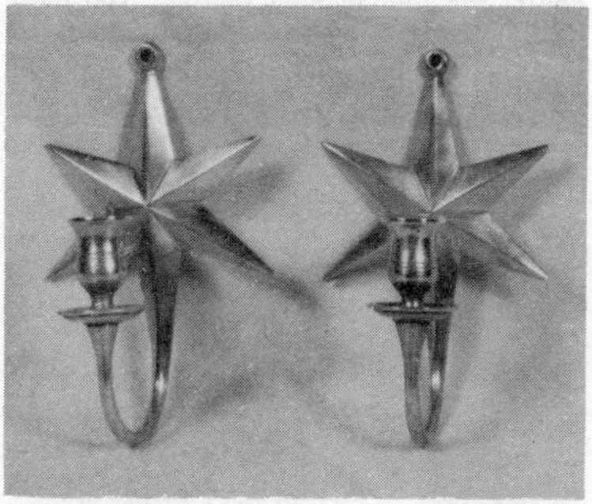

Brass. 1-Candleholder. Star-shaped backs. Pair $75.00

Brass

1-Candleholder. Dolphin finial. Mirrored back ....$ 100.00

2-Candleholders. American. Pair . 250.00

2-Candleholders. Ornate. Beveled mirror. Decorator's type 150.00

2-Candleholders. Queen Anne-style. English. Pair 350.00

2-Gaslights. 10¼ x 13½". Calcite shades. Bradley and Hubbard .. 400.00

3- Candleholders. Lyre-shaped backs. Pair 275.00

Cast iron. 2-Candleholders. Pair .. 125.00

Tole. Single candleholder

8¼" 150.00

9". Ribbed reflector. C. 1820. Pair . 350.00

16½". Pierced and decorated 250.00

SCRIMSHAW

Scrimshaw, a true form of American folk art, dates back over 150 years. During the 19th century, whaling was an important industry and sailors occupied idle hours by carving and engraving whale and walrus tusks and other bits of bone and ivory. Most items were decorated with intricate designs of ships, nautical adventures or a loved one's likeness. A few articles were carved for utilitarian purposes; but most were purely ornamental and presented as homecoming gifts. Like so many primitive arts, scrimshaw disappeared. This almost forgotten art is being revived today, with modern technology, in reproductions of past designs. The only acceptable modern scrimshaw is that of new forms created for tomorrow's treasures and heirlooms.

NOTE: Though the ban on importing some ivories has been lifted; whale and walrus ivories are excluded. If you are engaged in trading in any of the "endangered species," you must familiarize yourself with the new bill that was passed in November, 1978.

Whale's Tooth. Polar Bear. 3¼" $350.00

Buttons. ¾". Incised. Geometric design. Set of 5 ....$	75.00
Corset Stay. 1½" wide, 14" long. Heart-shaped top. Scene of birds being fed in a nest	75.00
Mallet. 6½" long. Dolphin head handle	195.00
Ostrich Egg. Portrait, compass, etc ..	500.00
Pie Crimper. Star decor. Wood handle	75.00
Spoon. 8". Carved handle. Stag in bowl	75.00
Walrus' Tusk	
6¼". Indians by tree	450.00
14". Primitive carvings	300.00
Whale's Tooth	
6". Eagle and flag	400.00
7½". Robert E. Lee, Dixie, Flag ..	600.00

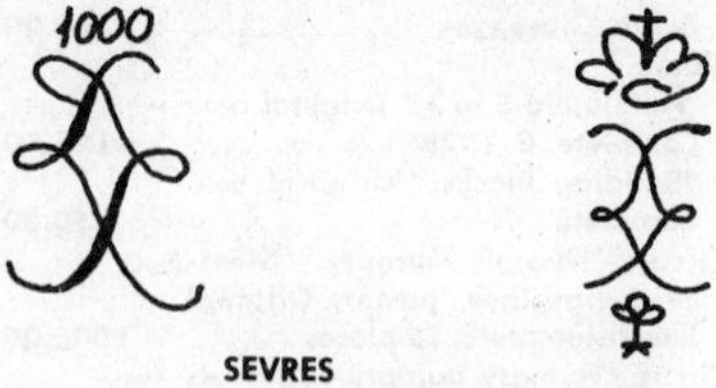

SEVRES

Sevres is a superb porcelain made in Sevres, France since the middle 1700's. Originally sanctioned by royalty, some of the finest porcelain ever made was produced in the early years. The name now applies to all wares made in Sevres, France.

Posset Cup with underplate. 6¼" o.h. including cherry finial. Robin egg blue. Handpainted scenic decor $250.00

Bowl. 13" long. Ornate handles. White with multicolored roses ..$	500.00
Box, Hinged. 5" diam. White with floral decor. C. 1771	300.00
Compote. 8¾". Classicial scene. Signed Watteau	400.00
Condiment Set. 8". Trefoil-shaped. Three containers. White with floral sprays, gold trim. C. 1760 ...	500.00
Cup and Saucer. Demitasse. Cobalt and gold	35.00
Figurine. 12". Cherub. Lavender, gray, gold trim. C. 1880	300.00
Plates	
8". Four diamond-shaped reserves with "LP", three oval reserves with floral bouquets. Gold trim	135.00
9". Classical scene of lady and gentleman. Blue rim with florals, gold trim. Signed Watteau	200.00
9½". "LP" crown in center. Gold vines around celeste blue border. C. 1844. Set of 6	750.00

9½". Portrait. "Mme Elisabeth, Duc de Burgogne." Signed Debrie . 195.00
Salt, Master. White, turquoise, gold jeweled. Gold interior. C. 1850 . . 150.00
Tazza. 10½ x 17½". Portrait center plate. Ormolu frame 450.00
Urns
14½". Cobalt with gold scrolls, flowers. Center medallion of young girl and boy. Signed Callard 375.00
19". Cobalt. Lady and gentleman on front, scenic design on reverse. Ormolu base and handles 600.00
Vase. 28". Baluster-shaped. Multicolored roses on cobalt. Heavy gold trim. Artist signed . . 750.00

SEWING ITEMS

As late as 50 years ago, a wide variety of sewing items were found in almost every home in America. Women, of every economic and social status, were skilled in sewing and dress making.

Even the most elegant ladies practiced the art of embroidery with the aid of jeweled gold and silver thimbles.

Sewing birds, an interesting convenience item, were used to hold cloth (in the bird's beak) while sewing. Made of iron or brass, they could be attached to table or shelf with a screw-type fixture. Later models featured pin cushions.

Pin Cushion. Valise-shaped. Sterling flap and handle $50.00

Bodkins
MOP. 3" ....$ 7.50
Sterling. Fish-shaped. Set of three in silk case 35.00
Buttons. Approximate 1" diam.
Brass. English .... .75

Sewing Machine. "Wheeler & Wilson." Oak case. Electrified $100.00

Enameled 2.00
Glass 3.00
Chatelaine. Sterling. Scissors, note pad with 5 ivory inserts, thimble, thimble case, needle holder. 19th century 500.00
Crochet Hook. Bone 15.00
Darning Eggs
Glass. "End-of-Day." Blown 95.00
Ivorine 10.00
Wood. Embossed sterling handle . . 30.00
Wood. Walnut 15.00
Emery. "Strawberry." Sterling top . . 15.00
Glove Darner. Sterling 25.00
Machines
Busy Bee. Hand-type. 3¼ x 6" base. New England 50.00
Singer. Model 29K71 .... 150.00
White Sewing Machine Co., Cleveland, Ohio. Last patent date June 3, 1913 .... 65.00
Wilcox & Gibbs. Model 1502. Pat. 1882 .... 100.00
Needle Cases
Ivory. Cylinder-shaped. Carved. Basketweave pattern 60.00
Ivory. Umbrella-shaped 35.00
Pewter. Key-shaped 40.00
Tortoise Shell. Trunk-shaped 85.00
Wood. Urn-shaped. Mechanical . . 35.00
Pin Holder. 1¾" diam. Embossed sterling, mirrored back. Holds 24 pins 85.00
Rule. 4". Embossed sterling 50.00
Scissors
Brass. 7". Art Nouveau motif 85.00
Silverplated. 3". Stork handles . . 25.00
Steel. 3½". H. Boh. 19th century . . 30.00
Sterling. 4¼". Embossed handles. C. 1890 .... 50.00

Sewing Birds

Brass. One cushion	50.00
Brass. Two cushions. C. 1850	100.00
Cast Iron. Two cushions	35.00
Silver. Two cushions	75.00

Shuttles

Ivorine. Tatting	5.00
Silver, German. Tatting	8.50
Wooden. 11" Netting	15.00

Stiletto. 1¾". Arrow-shaped. MOP	18.50

Thimbles

Aluminum. Advertising-type	5.00
Brass	15.00
Cloisonne. 20th century	30.00
Gold. 14K. Embossed florals. Ketcham and McDougall	250.00
Gold. 14K. Embossed "Walls of Troy." Simmons	175.00
Gold. 14K. Jeweled with 5 diamond chips. Simmons	250.00
Gold. 14K. and Sterling. Embossed scrolls	50.00
Ivorine	5.00
Porcelain. Bird motif on ivory ground. Gold trim. Royal Worcester	250.00
Porcelain. Pink and white roses on white. Gold trim. Unmarked	75.00
Silver	
Coin. Wide band. Touchmarks	175.00
Continental. Embossed florals	50.00
English. Waffle design band	25.00
Sterling	
Chased. Three rubies. Ketcham and McDougall	100.00
Engraved. Leaf and berry decor. Simmons	150.00
Milled. Faceted	25.00
Paneled. H. Muhr Sons	35.00
Plain. Wire rim	30.00
Topless	20.00
Tortoise Shell. Sterling band	85.00
Steel. Plain base. Early	20.00

Thimble Holder. Egg-shaped. Wooden	15.00

Thread Holders

Ivory. Acorn-shaped	65.00
Silverplated. 14½" high. Manning & Borman. C. 1890	250.00
Sterling. Cherubs	85.00

Thread Winders

Bone	7.50
Ivory. Pierced, scalloped border	35.00
MOP. Scalloped border	35.00

SHAKER ITEMS

The Shakers (so named because of a dance used in worship) is the oldest communal organization in the United States. This religious group was founded by Mother Ann Lee who emigrated from England and established the first Shaker community near Albany, New York in 1784. The Shakers reached their peak populus in 1850 with 6,000 members and continued to decline since . . . with less than ten Shakers living today. Shakers lived celibate and self-sufficient lives. Their philosophy stressed cleanliness, order, simplicity and economy. Highly inventive and motivated; the Shakers created the first flat broom, common clothespin, water systems and many other utilitarian items. Their furniture reflects their striving for quality and purity in design; and is considered the only pure American furniture. In the early 19th century, Shakers began to produce many items for commercial purposes . . . chairmaking and the herb and packaged seed businesses thrived. In every endeavor and enterprise, the members followed Mother Ann's advice: "Put your hands to work and give your heart to God."

Shaker Items.

Baskets

8¼ x 8¾ x 11¼". Oval. Covered. Chatham, N.Y. C. 1870	$ 85.00
15". Apple. Side handles. Crisscross laced top	85.00

Bean Sorter. Wooden. Adjustable slatted bottom	75.00

Booklet, Advertising. "Dorothy

Cloak." 4-pages, 4-views of garment. Includes 1938 photograph of three Shakers working. Canterbury, N.H. 35.00
Bottle. 4". Aqua. Embossed "Bimal-Shaker Anodyne Enfield, N.H." .. 40.00
Boxes
4" to 10". Graduated. Set of 5 .. 1500.00
9¼". Covered. Pantry-type. Dark green paint 45.00
4 x 6¾ x 14". Hinged lid. Dovetailed. Original black finish. "Wait and the boys." Signed 145.00
6x 14 x 19". Oval. Natural finish. Wallpaper lining interior 225.00
Box Mold. 8" oval. Solid wood. Used for making finger lapped bentwood boxes 65.00
Firkins
Gray paint. Canterbury, N.H 130.00
Green paint. 11½". Buttonhole laps. Worn 70.00
Jar Opener. 8½" 35.00
Knife Box. Yellow. Mt. Lebanon, N.Y. 325.00
Picture. 8 x 10". Framed. Sister Sarah Colline. Mt. Lebanon, N.Y. 85.00
Postcard. Photo-type. Sister Rebecca. Canterbury, N.H. C. 1938 ...... 15.00
Rolling Pin. 14¼". Wooden. Shaped handles 30.00
Rug Whip. Wireware with spring action. Maple grip handle. Original label. "Shaker Rug Whip-Mfg. by Levi Shaw, Mt. Lebanon, N.Y." .. 85.00
Sign. 16 x 20". "Shaker Cloaks." Broadside 1200.00
Stocking Driers. 24". Wooden. Pair .. 50.00
Swift. Yellow. Mt. Lebanon, N.Y ... 125.00
Tongs. 23". Fireplace-type. Wrought iron 50.00
Verse. "I Remember-I Remember." Composed by Sister Mary Alice. Handwirtten in pen and ink. Canterbury, N.H. C. 1908 .... 25.00
Whale Oil Filler. 5½ x 6". Tole. Early lapped seaming. Side handle, graceful spout 65.00

Furniture

Candleholder. 24". Clamp on lighting device. Cherry and maple with red wash. Tole candle holder. Hancock, Mass. C. 1840-50 ....$ 1200.00
Candle Stand. 18" top diam. Adjustable from 18" to 36". Cherry and birch. Harvard, Mass 3400.00
Chairs
Enfield, N.H. Three-slats, rush seats. Ash and maple. C. 1820-40. Set of 4 .... 2000.00
North Union, Ohio. Child's. Original finish 200.00
Chests
Enfield, Conn. 18 x 44 x 45". Bonnet drawer on top. Yellow. C. 1850-60 .... 3200.00
Harvard, Mass. 18 x 35 x 63". Tailor's. 12 drawers. Pine. C. 1810 6500.00
Tyringham, Mass. 18 x 40". Four drawers. Red paint 3200.00
Watervliet, N.Y. 18 x 40 x 62". Six drawers. Cherry, pine and birch. Dated 1827 .... 6200.00
Cupboards
Hancock, Mass. 18 x 31 x 43". Pine. Signed. C. 1850-60 ...... 1800.00
Mt. Lebanon, N.Y. Jelly. Old red paint. C. 1820-30 .... 900.00
North Union, Ohio. 42½ x 50". Walnut. Old gray paint. Replaced feet 650.00
Tyringham, Mass. 11 x 17x 32". Red paint 1200.00
Desk. Table top-style. Old red paint. Mt. Lebanon, N. Y. 400.00
Drying Rack 375.00
Rockers
Groveland, N.Y. Splint seats and backs. Matched pair 450.00
Mt. Lebanon, N.Y. Nine spindles .. 350.00
Mt. Lebanon, N.Y. Slat back 450.00
Stand. 17x 17 x 26". One drawer. Brass pull. Black cherry painted black 1200.00
Tables
Canterbury, N.H. Sewing. 27 x 28 x 50". Two drawers. Pine and cherry painted green. C. 1830 .. 5700.00
Mt. Lebanon, N.Y. Dining. One drawer. Seats four. Pine top, cherry base. C. 1830 .... 3800.00
South Union, Ky. Work. Walnut and cherry 2200.00

SHAVING MUGS

A shaving mug was an essential item in the Victorian gentleman's toiletry. The container held soap and hot water to be used with a soft bristled brush to lather the face before shaving. During the period of 1870-1924, shaving mugs of porcelain or pottery were manufactured and decorated with the owner's name and occupation. They were usually kept at the owner's favorite barber shop for his exclusive use.

Scuttle shaving mugs get their name from their general appearance, resembling somewhat the early European coal scuttles. Most scuttles were European imports and few are handpainted, but rather have transfer decorations. A few were American made. Scuttles are 2-compartment receptacles (one for water and one for soap). The earliest ones are without drain holes in the soap (top) compartment. The lower compartment has a spout for pouring off the water after use.

NOTE: Many reproductions are currently imported from England and Japan.

FRATERNAL
K. of P $35.00

Fraternal Emblems (with owner's name)

A.O.U.W	$ 40.00
B.P.O.E.	35.00
F.O.E.	45.00
G.A.R.	65.00
I.O.O.F. (Odd Fellows)	35.00
K.K.K	90.00
K.G.E.	65.00
K. of C	45.00
K. of L	65.00
K. of P	35.00
K.T	35.00
L.O.O.M	35.00
M.W.A	30.00
Masonic	35.00
O.of I.A.	90.00
Shrine	80.00
W.O.W.	35.00

Occupational

Architect Emblem	135.00
Artist. Painting picture	135.00
Athlete. Track runner	130.00
Bakery Wagon	165.00
Baseball Players. Batter and catcher	180.00
*Bartender. Men drinking	130.00
Blacksmith. Shoeing horse	185.00

OCCUPATIONAL
Blacksmith. Shoeing horse $185.00

Bricklayer. Working	165.00
Butcher. Steer head and tools of trade	120.00
Carpenter Tools	165.00
Cooper. Making barrels	165.00
*Cowboy. Lassoing steer	130.00
Dairy Wagon	140.00
*Dentist. Pulling teeth	185.00
*Dentist. False teeth	145.00
Drayman. Horse drawn cart	100.00
Express Wagon	185.00
Farmer. Plowing	145.00
Fireman. Motorized engine	225.00
*Fireman. Steam engine	200.00
*Dry Goods Store	110.00
Grocery Wagon	150.00
Harness Maker. Working	165.00
Hunter. With bird-dog	165.00
Jockey	160.00
Miner. With tools	175.00
Minister. In pulpit	200.00
*Mortician. Horse-drawn hearse	475.00
Musician. With violin	135.00
Notary. Pen in hand	110.00
Painter	130.00
Pharmacist. Mortar and pestle	115.00
Photographer. With camera	170.00
*Policeman	180.00
Printer. With printing press	150.00
Railroad. Caboose	100.00
*Railroad. Locomotive engine	135.00
Seaman. Captain of saling vessel	170.00
Stationary Engine	160.00
Surveyor. With instruments	150.00
Sulky Race	180.00
*Tailor. Sewing	135.00
Telegrapher. With key	100.00
Watch Maker. Watch and chain	120.00
Whiskey Distributor. With wagon	150.00

SCUTTLES

Molded leaf form. White pearlized with gold trim $55.00

Scuttles

Cream pitcher-shaped	28.00
*Fish-shaped	35.00
Ironstone. Floral transfer	35.00
Ironstone. Plain	28.00
Lady's Portrait. Transfer	48.00
Porcelain. Pat. Sept. 20, 1870	38.00
Porcelain. With drain hole in handle.	35.00
R.S. Prussia	95.00
R.S. Prussia. With mirror inset	120.00
Seashell-shaped	30.00
Silverplated. Pairpoint	90.00
Swan-shaped	45.00
Wedgwood-type decor	45.00

*Reproduced Item

SHAWNEE POTTERY

Organized in 1935 in Zanesville, Ohio, Shawnee Pottery was not an art pottery. The factory produced in expensive commercial pottery... kitchenware, dinnerware and premium items.. for the American mass-market until early 1961. At first, Shawnee pieces carried an Indian-on-an-arrowhead trademark. Later production was marked "Shawnee" or "Kenwood"; and many items were marked with paper labels.

Bowl. 8". Corn King ....$	15.00
Casseroles, Covered	
Basketweave base, fruit lid	27.50
Corn King. Large	27.50
Corn King. Individual	20.00
Cookie Jars	
Corn King	30.00
Dutch Girl	28.50
Farmer Pig	28.50
Reclining Clown	35.00

Cookie Jar. "Corn King." $30.00

Winnie Pig	30.00
Cream and Sugar. Corn King	25.00
Creamers	
Elephant	10.00
Puss 'N Boots	10.00
Mug. Corn King	22.50
Pitchers	
Bo-Peep. 8"	28.00
Corn King. 8"	30.00
Little Boy Blue. 7½"	28.00
Planters	
Cockatoo. 3½ x 4"	5.00
Train. 4 pieces. Set	35.00
Platter. 11¾". Corn King	10.00
Shakers, Salt and Pepper. Pairs	
Corn King. 5"	15.00
Dutch Boy and Girl. 5"	12.50
Fruits. 3½"	10.00
Puss 'N Boots. 3"	10.00
Winnie Pig	12.00
Teapots	
Corn King	28.50
Granny Ann	30.00
Tom, The Piper's Son	25.00

SHEET MUSIC

If you can't play a note or sing on key, collecting sheet music can be an informative and rewarding experience. Much of our history is recorded in music . . .time of war, depressions, fashions and glimpses of our romantic trends. People collect sheet music by composers, favorite stars, musicals, movies, colorful covers or just for memories. A few years ago old sheet music could be bought for a "song." Today prices range from one dollar for the ordinary to several dollars for the earlier lithographed covers.

Chopin. "Funeral March." Large format. C. 1914 ....$5.00

Ballads. Large format. Star on cover. C. 1900-1920 ....$ 2.00
Ballads. Small format. Star on cover. C. 1925-1945 .... 1.50
Berlin, Irving. Large format. C. 1910-1915 .... 10.00
Berlin, Irving. Regular format. C. 1920-1945 .... 5.00
Dixieland. Large format. C. 1900-1915 .... 5.00
Jolson, Al. Regular format. C. 1920's 7.50
Marches, Waltzes, Fox Trots. Small format. C. 1900-1940 .... 1.00
Movie Melodies. Small format. C. 1925-1950 .... 2.00
Piano Solos. Small format. C. 1925-1945 .... 2.00
Western. Small format. C. 1930-1950 .... 1.50
World War I. Large format 5.00
World War I. Small format 1.50
World War II. Regular format 3.00

SHIRLEY TEMPLE ITEMS

(See, "Character and Personality Items")

SILHOUETTES

Popular during the 18th and 19th centuries, silhouettes (or "shades") are shadow profiles; either cut, mechanically-traced or painted. The name "silhouette" came from a French Minister of Finance, Etienne de Silhouette who tended to be tight with money and cut "shades" as a pastime. Since "shades" or shadow portraits were inexpensive, they became known as "silhouettes."

Silhouette portraiture dropped in popularity with the introduction of the daguerreotypes prior to the Civil War. In the 1920's and 1930's, this art form had a brief revival when it became popular for tourists in Atlantic City and Paris to have their profiles "cut" as souvenirs of their visit.

Andrew Jackson. Painted. 6½ x 10" $125.00

Child. 4¾". Hollow cut ....$ 85.00
Gentlemen
3¼". Revolutionary General 125.00
3¾ x 4¾" oval. James Monroe .. 150.00

4½" diam. Hollow cut. Pencil details 95.00
4 x 5". Brushwork on hair, coat .. 100.00
4 x 5". Lincoln and T. Roosevelt. Signed Guttenamy. Pair 225.00
5 x 6". Colonial 75.00
5⅛ x 6". Inked. Gold. Brushwork details 125.00
9½ x 13½". Young man, in frock coat, holding book. Signed Aug. Edouard 1810 .... 275.00

Ladies
4 x 4¾". Bonnet, ruffled collar. Pencil details 125.00
5" diam. C. 1820 .... 150.00
7 x 9". Hat, high neck gown, with cut work. Dated April 20, 1904 .. 95.00
10½". Wearing bonnet, full skirt, leg-o-mutton sleeves 125.00

Ladies and Gentlemen
4 x 5". Hollow cut. Ink details. Signed F.P. Jones. C. 1830. Pair .. 150.00
5¼ x 6". George and Martha Washington. Black reverse painting on glass. 20th century 75.00

SILK PICTURES

(See "Stevengraphs")

SILVER

Silver is a lustrous white metallic element which is ductile and malleable. Because of its beauty and scarcity, it is highly valued for its use in fashioning jewelry, tablewares, objects d'art, and as a medium of exchange.

******

SILVER, COIN

Silver objects designated as "Coin Silver" were made from melted silver coins.

There was a period in the United States (1800-1850) when pure silver was not readily available and silversmiths turned to using melted coins to obtain their media.

The silver content in coin silver will vary depending on the coins used. Many early English coins were debased with alloys and did not meet the standard proportion. Later, silver coinage was regulated and the quantity of silver in coin silver items were usually nine parts silver to one part alloy.

Basket. 4½ x 6½" high. Embossed florals, shell and scroll feet, beaded border. Lincoln & Foss. Boston. C. 1850 ....$ 400.00
Beaker. 3½". Barrel-shaped. Banded. Wm. Gale & Son. N.Y. 500.00
Butter, Covered. With drain. Cupid final. Egg and Dart border. California Seal mark 850.00

S. Kirk & Son. Cream and Sugar. "Repousse." 2" $175.00

Cream and Sugar, Covered. Butterfly finial. Gorham. C. 1850 .... 195.00

Cream Jugs
David, John Jr. Philadelphia. 4½". Inverted pear-shape. Double scroll handles. C. 1785 .... 1250.00
Erwin, Henry. Philadelphia. 6¾". C. 1825 .... 300.00

Flatware

Forks
Gordon, George. Augusta. Dinner. "Fiddle Thread." 42.00
Hyden Bros. & Co. Charleston. Luncheon. "Beaded." C. 1850's . 42.00
Kinsey, D. Cincinnati. Serving. C. 1865 .... 150.00
Krider, P.L. Philadelphia. Serving. Engraved tines 100.00
Tucker. J.W. San Francisco. Luncheon. "Beaded with Oval and Shell." C. 1860 .... 85.00
Wilson, R. & W. Philadelphia. Luncheon. C. 1830 .... 55.00

Knives
F. & H. Boston. Master butter 45.00
Lewyn, Gabriel. Baltimore. Hollow handles. coin silver blades. C. 1795. Pair 185.00

Ladles
Crosby, S. T. Boston. 13". "Beaded." C. 1840 .... 195.00
Griffin, George. Louisville. 13¼". "Fiddle Thread." C. 1840 . 300.00
Sayre, John. N.Y. 15". Bright cut and engraved. C. 1800 ...... 575.00
Tucker, J.W. San Francisco. 13½". "Beaded". C. 1860 .... 350.00

Marrow Spoon. 7¾". Bull's Head crest. Irish. C. 1750 .... 175.00
Mote Spoon. 5¼". English. C. 1775 .... 125.00

Salt Spoons
Gregg & Hayden. Charleston. "Fiddleback." C. 1840. Pair 85.00
Kirk, S. Baltimore. "Fiddleback."

Shell bowl. C. 1830 .... 30.00
Serving Spoon. Fletcher & Gardiner. Philadelphia. 13". "Fiddle Thread & Shell." C. 1825 ... 375.00
Stuffing Spoon. 11½". Oval bowl with double drop. English. C. 1750 .... 175.00

Sugar Shells
Elias Baker. New Brunswick. Fluted bowl with embossed handle. C. 1860 .... 45.00
Robert Tait & Co. "Thread and Shell." Pat. 1855 .... 30.00

Sugar Tongs. Wilson, R. & W. Philadelphia. "Shell." C. 1830 . 125.00

Tablespoons
Clark, G.D. Baltimore. "Fiddleback." C. 1840 .... 50.00
Hall, David. Philadelphia. Rattail. 8¼". C. 1779 .... 375.00
Hastings, B.B. Cleveland. "Fiddleback." C. 1830 .... 35.00
Hill, E. H. Kentucky. Pinched Waist. "Fiddleback." C. 1840 .. 45.00
Jaccard & Co. St. Louis. "Fiddleback." C. 1850 .... 35.00
Jarvis, Munson. Stamford. 8¾". C. 1765-1783 .... 180.00
Kinsey, David. Cincinnati, Pinched Waist. "Fiddleback." C. 1840 .... 45.00
Kirk. S. & Son. Baltimore. "Fiddleback." C. 1840. Pair 75.00
Richardson, Joseph. Philadelphia. 8⅛". Rib front, upturned end, rounded drops with shells. C. 1750 .... 275.00
Tucker, J.W. San Francisco. "Beaded Oval and Shell". C. 1860 .... 100.00
Warner, Joseph. Wilmington. C. 1780. Pair 400.00

Teaspoons
Clayton, Richard. Cincinnati. "Fiddleback." C. 1830. Pair 40.00
Elliott, John Aaron. Sharon. "Fiddle." C. 1810 .... 25.00
Faris, William. Annapolis. C. 1760 .... 100.00
Kirk, S. Baltimore. "Fiddleback." C. 1830. Set of 6 .... 125.00
Lynch, L. Baltimore. "Fiddleback." C. 1820 .... 25.00
Pittman, I. Baltimore. C.1795 . 35.00
Tanner, John. Newport. Rattail. C. 1735 .... 75.00
Weaver, E.T. Philadelphia. C. 1795. Set of 6 .... 425.00
Wilson, R. & W. Philadelphia. "Sheaf of Wheat." C. 1830. Set of 8 .... 450.00
Wingate, F. Augusta. Coffin end. C. 1810 .... 30.00

Mugs
Boyce, G.C. 3½". C. 1835 ...... 185.00
Pearce, Walter, 3¼". Strap handle. C. 1830 .... 500.00
Radcliffe, Thomas W. 3⅝". C. 1830 .... 375.00

Pitchers
Bard, C. and Son. Philadelphia. 10½". "Vintage." C. 1850 ...... 600.00
Wilson, R. & W. Philadelphia. 14½". 30 oz. 850.00

Porringer. 5 x 1⅞" deep. Engraved handle. Jacob Hurd. Boston. C. 1740 .... 3500.00

Salt Cellars
Edwards, Thomas. Boston. Three cabriole legs, pad feet. Engraved. C. 1735 .... 2500.00
Kirk. Baltimore. 3½". "Repousse." Chinese motif. Cabriole legs, pad feet. 11 oz. 450.00

Sugar Castor. 1⅞ x 5⅜" high. Cylindrical with inverted pear-shaped base, splayed feet. Domed cover with pine cone finial. Samuel Minott. C. 1776 .... 1250.00

Tea Caddy. 5½" high. "Repousse." S. Kirk. Baltimore 650.00

Teapots
Fletcher and Gardiner. Philadelphia. 8". C. 1820 ...... 1800.00
Gorham. Butterfly finial. 5". C. 1850 .... 200.00

Tea Set. "Greek Key." William Thompson. N.Y. C. 1810. 3 pieces .. 3000.00

Tray. 28½" o.l. including fluted handles with acanthus leaves. Gadrooned scalloped rim with shells. Arms and crest center. 134 oz. Richard Sibley. London. C. 1816 .... 3000.00

Waste Bowl. "Repousse." J. Conning. Mobile 600.00

SILVER, PLATED

Plated silver production by an electrolytic method is credited to G.R. and H. Elkington, England, in 1838.

In electroplating silver, the article is completely shaped and formed from a base metal before it is coated with a thin layer of silver. In the early years, the base metal was Britannia, an alloy of tin, copper and antimony. Other bases used were copper and brass; and today, nickel silver is used as the base.

In 1847, the electroplating process was introduced in America by Rogers Bros., Hartford, Connecticut. By 1855 a number of firms were using this method to mass-produce silver plated items in large quantities.

Cake Server. Strawberry decor. Wallace $25.00

Baskets

- 8x 13" long. Decor of full bodied strawberries. Vine-like handle, ornate feet. C. 1890's .... $ 225.00
- 8 3/4 x 16" long. Ornate. Quadruple plate. Forbes, Meriden, Conn 125.00

Bowls

- 11 x 3½" deep. Leaf-shaped. Squirrel with nut in full relief. Gold washed interior. Pairpoint .. 200.00
- 15 x 9" deep. Repousse border. Meriden 275.00

Boxes, Covered

- Collar Button. 3". Dachshund finial. C. 1890's 55.00
- Hairpin. 1 x 2½ x 3". Hairpin on lid. Wm. Rogers 35.00

Butters, Covered

- Cow finial. With knife rest. Meriden 85.00
- "Greek Key." Engraved. Insert. Simpson, Hall, Miller & Co 85.00

Candelabras

- 14½". Three branch. Fluted, beaded accents. English. 20th century 600.00
- 19". Ornate. Three branch. Victorian 275.00

Candlesticks

- 9". Gadroon border. Reed and Barton. Pair 45.00
- 10". "Adam-style". English. 20th century. Pair 200.00

Castor Sets, See "Castor Sets"

Chafing Dish. 1½ qt. Alcohol burner. F.B. Rogers Silver Co. 95.00

Champagne Bucket. Handled. 8½" high. Reed and Barton 150.00

Coffee Pot. 13". "Repousse." James Tufts 85.00

Coffee Server. 6 x 12". Ring handles on sides. Spigot dispenser 150.00

Coffee and Tea Services

- "Fern." Engraved. Oval-shaped with straight spouts. J.D. & S. English. C. 1850. 5 pieces 850.00
- "Lancaster Rose" Poole. 4 pieces ... 250.00
- "Marquise". Rogers Bros. C. 1847. 4 pieces 225.00

Cracker Jar, Covered. 7½". Ornate bail and finial. "Crackers" engraved on front 75.00

Cup and Saucer. Quadruple. Meriden 30.00

*Egg Cooker. 11" high. Hen finial. Insert for 4 eggs. Victorian 125.00

Flatware

- Baby Spoon 2.50
- Butter, Master. Rogers Bros 3.50
- Ladle. Gravy. Oneida Community 7.50
- Sugar Shell 5.00
- Tablespoon 5.00
- Teaspoons. "Grape." Rogers Bros. C. 1881. Set of 8 .... 35.00

Flatware, Pearl Handled

- Dinner Knives. 9". Embossed ferrules. English. Set of 6 .... 60.00
- Fruit Knives. Set of 6 .... 35.00
- Luncheon Knives. Rogers. C. 1847. Set of 6 .... 45.00

Goblet. 6¾". Plain. Resilvered. Meriden 30.00

Knife Rest. Cherub ends 45.00

Pickle Castor, See "Pickle Castors"

Platter. 23". Fish-shaped. Detailed. Reed and Barton. C. 1934 .... 175.00

Salvers

- 8". "Chippendale-style." English. 20th century 85.00
- 10". "Vintage." Victorian 75.00

14". "Georgian-style". English. 20th century ... 185.00

Sugars

7½" high. Covered. Ornate handles and finial. 4 feet. Queen City Silver Co ... 65.00

10½" high. With spooner holding 12 spoons. Rogers Silver. Pat. Nov. 3, 1925 ... 125.00

Syrup Pitcher. Hinged lid. Ornate bands. Bright cut decor in center. Rogers Bros ... 35.00

Teapot. 7½". Ribbed bowl. Rose band in relief. Ornamental spout and handle ... 50.00

Toast Rack. English ... 30.00

Trays

10½ x 16". Gallery-type. English. 150.00

15x 20". Octagonal. "Queen Anne-style". English. 20th century 375.00

Vase. 11". Pierced handles. Ornate embossing. James Tufts. C. 1909 .. 50.00

Vegetable Dish, Covered. 11½" long. Divided. Ornate removable finial. English ... 75.00

Water Coolers

13½". Allover etched florals. Derby ... 225.00

20½". Full looped handle, underplate and goblet. Ornate ... 275.00

*Reproduced Item

SILVER, SHEFFIELD

Sheffield silver (or "Old Sheffield Plate") was a fusion method of silverplating used from the middle of the 18th century until the mid-1800's when the silver electroplating process was introduced.

Sheffield plate was discovered in 1743 when Thomas Boulsover of Sheffield, England accidentally fused silver and copper. The process consisted of sandwiching a heavy sheet of copper between 2 thin sheets of silver. The result was a plated sheet of 'silver' which could be pressed and rolled to a desired thickness. All Sheffield plate articles were "worked" from these plated sheets.

Most of the silverplated items found today marked "Sheffield" are not early authentic Sheffield plate. They are later silver wares made in Sheffield, England.

Biscuit Warmer. 8½ x 9x 14½". Melon ribbed ... $ 300.00

Candelabras. 3-lite. C. 1850. Pair .. 1500.00

Candle Snuffer. With tray ... 125.00

Candlesticks. Telescopic-type. 4" closed to 9" extended. Pair ... 350.00

Chamberstick. 6¼" diam. saucer. C-shaped handle ... 85.00

Coffee Pot. 8½" ... 300.00

Tray. 19¼". Footed. Embossed and engraved ... $500.00

Desk Set. Inkwell, sander, stamp box ... 250.00

Kettles, Swinging

14". Vintage decor in relief ... 300.00

18". Plain. Ivory handle ... 350.00

Pitcher, Covered. 13". Urn-shaped. C. 1800 ... 500.00

Sugar Castor. 8". Octagonal-shaped 85.00

Tea Service. C. 1820. 4 pieces ... 2000.00

Toast Rack. 6" long ... 75.00

Trays

16". C. 1850 ... 350.00

19". Pierced border. C. 1840 ... 500.00

Tureens, Covered

Adams. C. 1790 ... 1500.00

Baroque decor. C. 1840 ... 750.00

Wine Coaster ... 225.00

Wine Coolers. C. 1810. Pair ... 1200.00

SILVER, STERLING

Sterling silver is a highly refined metal which derived its name from an English coin of the same name. The word "sterling" is believed to be a contraction of the word "Easterlings," which was the name of a band of traders of the 12th century during the reign of Richard I. They came from the eastern part of Germany and in trading, offered tokens in exchange for goods. These tokens were made of a silver alloy with a standard of 925-1000 fine.

Animal Figurines

Dachshund, Sitting. 2½ x 3½" $ 150.00

Elk. 4½ x 5½" ... 225.00

Pig, Sitting. 1¼ x 2" ... 75.00

Bell. 3¼". Paneled with floral decor. 55.00

Cordial. "La Paglia." Wt. 18 oz. One of 12. Set $375.00

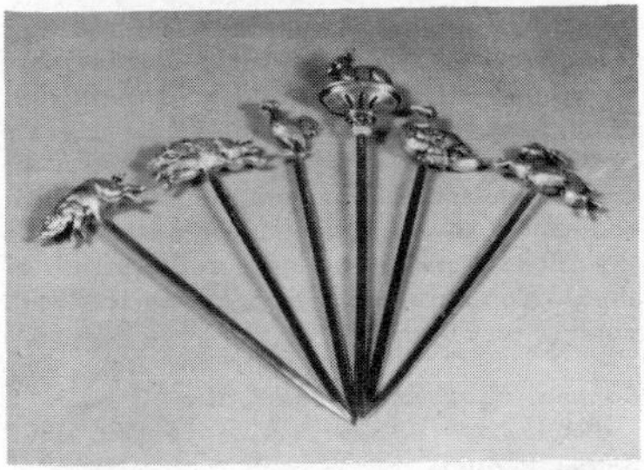

Skewers. 8" long. Figural animal tops. C. 1770-1800. Set $300.00

Box, Covered. 3 x 4½". "Repousse." Gorham 225.00
Bowls
6¾". Chased and engraved scenic decor with florals, foliage, etc. S. Kirk. Baltimore. C. 1850 .... 395.00
7". Edinburgh-style. Wt. 19 oz. English. 20th century 500.00
Bread and Butter Plates. 6". Gorham. Set of 12 .... 300.00
Button. 1". Ornate. C. 1902 ...... 20.00
Button Hook. 7". Ornate handle .. 25.00
Candelabra. 14" high. 3-lite. "Adams-style". English. 20th century 1500.00
Candle Snuffer. 10½". Cone-shaped. Turned wooden handle. English. 20th century 55.00
Candlesticks
3½". "Prelude." International. Pair 100.00
7". Classical design. Square bases. English. 20th century. Pair .. 375.00
Castor Set. "Judaic." 6¾" high. Five turrets. Allover embossed decor .. 400.00
Coffee and Tea Services
"Melon." J. Charles Edington. London. C. 1837. 4 pieces 5000.00
"Queen Anne-style." English. 20th century. 4 pieces 3750.00
"Repousse." House, horseman, florals. C. 1860. 6 pieces 10,000.00
"Repousse". Kirk. 20th century. 6 pieces 5000.00
Simple Designs. Major American makers. 20th century. 5 pieces .. 1000.00
Creamers
4½". "Starfish." Gold washed interior. English. C. 1786 .... 400.00
4½x 6½". "Cow." Hand chased .. 450.00
4¾". "Beaded." J. Richardson, Jr. Philadelphia. C. 1800 .... 800.00
Demitasse Pot. 9". Chased florals. Simpson, Hall, Miller 400.00
Dresser Set. Comb, brush, mirror. Signed Tiffany. 20th century 250.00
Entree Server. 8½ x 12¼". Gadroon border. Benjamin Smith. London. C. 1820 .... 2500.00
Flatware
Demitasse Spoon. "Apostle." English 18.50
Forks. "Fiddle." Crested. A.B. Savory. London. C. 1830. Set of 6 . 400.00
Knife and Fork. MOP handles. Sterling ferrules. Set 50.00
Tablespoon. "King's." TKB. London. C. 1893. Set of 6 .... 450.00
Teaspoons. "Fiddle." George Adams. London. C. 1865. Set of 6 . 150.00
Flatware. Place Settings
"Fairfax." Engraved. Gorham. 172 pieces 3500.00
"Laureate." Towle. 5 pieces 100.00
"Leicester." International. 74 pieces 975.00
"Repousse." S. Kirk. 5 pieces 100.00
"Rose." Steiff. 120 pieces 2500.00
"Fiddle." Handmade. English. 3 pieces 175.00
Flatware. Serving Pieces
Asparagus Tongs. "King's" English. C. 1900 .... 300.00
Asparagus Tongs. "Lily." Whiting 175.00

Basting Spoon. 12¾". "Hanoverian." English. C. 1754 .. 375.00
Berry Spoon. "Rose." Steiff. Embossed strawberries in gold washed bowl 175.00
Butter Spreaders. MOP handles, sterling ferrules. Set of 6 .... 65.00
Cake Knife. 11¼". Winthrop." Tiffany 135.00
Carving Set. "Rose." Steiff. 2 pieces 125.00
Fish Serving Set. "Fiddle Thread." George Adams. London. C. 1847 .. 375.00
Grape Shears. Ornate handles. Gorham 100.00
Ice Tea Sippers. Tiffany. Set of 8 .. 160.00
Ice Tongs. "Repousse." Kirk 100.00
Marrow Spoon. Crested fox, rattail back. English. C. 1901 .... 110.00
Mote Spoon. "Shell." English. C. 1780 .... 185.00
Punch Ladle. 13". English. C. 1925 . 225.00
Punch Ladle. "Louis XV". Gold washed bowl. Whiting 225.00
Salad Set. Jensen. Denmark 295.00
Salad Set. "Old Baronial." Gorham 200.00
Salad Set. "Persian." Tiffany 350.00
Salt Spoon. "King's Hourglass." H. & H. Lias. London. C. 1849 .... 35.00
Sardine Fork. "Raleigh." Alvin .. 30.00
Serving Spoon. 8½". "Lily." Whiting 75.00
Serving Spoon. 9". "Old English." Peter, Ann & William Bateman .. 100.00
Sugar Spoon. "Queen's." English. C. 1872 .... 85.00
Sugar Tongs. "Fiddle." English. C. 1831 .... 50.00
Tea Caddy Spoon. "Georgian." English. C. 1910 .... 75.00

Glove Stretcher. Ornate handles .. 50.00
Goblets
Random patterned bowl. English. 20th century 150.00
"Repousse." S.Kirk 250.00
Ice Bucket. 6½". Hand hammered finish. Wt. 30 oz. 250.00
Julep Cup. Wallace 65.00
Knife Rest. 2⅞" long. Spiral bar, V-shaped legs. Gorham 20.00
Labels. "Georgian-style" Various engravings. English. 20th century. Each. 25.00

Letter Opener.
Jensen. Denmark 150.00
9¼" long. English. 20th century .. 60.00
Mugs. 2½-3" high
Leaf and Scroll engravings. Beaded base. English. C. 1859 .. 265.00
Undecorated. Gorham. C. 1915 .. 40.00
"William and Mary-Style." English. 20th century 100.00
Pitcher, Water. 9½". "Repousse." Kirk. 750.00
Salvers
"Georgian-Style." 10" square. English. 20th century 500.00
"Repousse." 8". S. Kirk 225.00
"Rosepoint." 17". Wallace 500.00
Skewer. 12" long. Tiffany 50.00
Sugar Castor. 6½". Urn-shaped. "Repousse." S. Kirk 125.00
Tea Infuser. Acorn-shaped. C. 1910 40.00
Toast Rack. 6" long. English. 20th century 300.00
Trays
6". Beaded edge. Caldwell 95.00
10". "Arabesque." Tiffany. C. 1870 .... 600.00
28½". Handled. Chased surface, shell and leaf border, shell feet. Paul Storr. London. C. 1817 .... 5000.00
Wedding Cup. 5¼". Figure of lady with hoop skirt holding smaller cup over head 200.00
Wine Coaster. English. 19th century.. 500.00
Wine Taster. 2¾". Plain. English. 20th century 85.00

SILVER DEPOSIT GLASS

Silver Deposit Glass, so-named because a thin coating of silver was actually deposited on glass via an electrical process, was popular at the turn of this century. The process was simple . . .glass and a piece of silver were placed in a solution; and an electric current was introduced which caused the silver to decompose, pass through the solution, and remain only on those parts of the glass on which a particular pattern had been outlined previously.

Bonbon. 7". Crystal. Footed, handled ....$ 50.00
Bottles, Perfume
4". Emerald 45.00
5½". Crystal 35.00
Bowls
5½ x 3" deep 45.00
9 x 2" high. Crystal. Flared turned over rim 85.00
Box, Puff. 4¼ x 3½" high. Crystal 50.00
Cream and Sugar. 2¾" creamer, 2½" open sugar. Crystal. Set 65.00
Cruet. 6¾". Fluted stopper. Crystal . 60.00
Decanter. 9". Crystal 75.00
Marmalade Jar. 4¾". Crystal 40.00
Pitcher. 8". Cobalt 65.00
Plates
7". Crystal 35.00
7½ x 10". 3-part divided. Handled. Footed 50.00

Vase. 16". Green. C. 1920 .... $75.00

Salt Shaker. 4" high $80.00

12". Crystal. Fruit decor 75.00
Sherbets. With underplates. Crystal.
Set of 6 .... 250.00
Toothpick Holder. 2½". Crystal 25.00
Vases
4¼". Emerald 35.00
5½". Flared top. Crystal 40.00
6". Cobalt 50.00
8". Bud. Crystal 45.00
8". Bulbous bottom, long neck with flared rim. Crystal 55.00

SILVER LUSTRE

This metal-surfaced earthenware was made in large quantities in the Staffordshire district of England between 1805 and 1840. In this process, the item to be silvered was first covered completely with a thin coating of a "steel lustre" mixture containing a small quantity of platinum oxide; then an additional coating of platinum, worked in water, was laid on before the item was fired. With the introduction of electroplating in 1840, there was a sharp decline in demand for such metal-surfaced earthenwares.

Bowl. 6". Festoon and Shell. C. 1840 $ 85.00
Candleholder. Chamber-type. 6" saucer. Embossed scroll decor 65.00
Cream and Sugar. 3". Queen Anne-style 150.00

Creamers
4½". Ribbed 75.00
5½". Hexagonal 85.00
Goblet. 4 x3½" diam. bowl. Copper lustre lining 65.00
Mug. 4½ x 4" diam. C. 1840 ...... 75.00
Sugars, Covered
Scroll design 150.00
Ribbed design 125.00
Teapot. 6". Six ball feet. Queen Anne-style. Paneled 195.00
Tea Set. Queen Anne-style. Teapot, creamer, covered sugar 350.00

SILVER OVERLAY

Silver overlay differs from silver deposit and silver resist in that the sterling silver ornamentation is much heavier and it is applied in a more direct manner. Since sterling is a malleable metal, the silver decoration on this ware is cut out; then laid on or molded around the object. Such embellishments (most often floral in design) were applied to crystal or colored glass and, occasionally, porcelain. Lenox employed silver overlay on some of their decorative wares. Most of the designs are indicative of the Art Nouveau and Art Deco periods.

Bottles, Perfume. Stoppered
3". On crystal ....$ 40.00
3¼". On emerald 75.00
6". On cranberry 150.00
6½". On crystal 85.00
Bottles. Pinch
10½". On amber 175.00
10½". On amethyst 195.00
11". On crystal 165.00

Perfume Bottle. Stoppered. 2⅛". On crystal $35.00

Bowls

7¾ x3¾" deep. Tapered. Floral decor on emerald	400.00
10x 6¼" deep. Pedestaled. Florals and vines on emerald	500.00
Decanter. 8½". Stoppered, handled. Wheat on crystal	275.00
Liqueur Set. Decanter 12". Stoppered. 6 glasses. Leaf pattern on cranberry	500.00
Nut Dish. 6½". Oval. Footed. On white porcelain	45.00
Teapot. 8" long. On dark brown porcelain	225.00

Vases

3½". On emerald	100.00
4½". Gourd-shaped. On iridescent	150.00
8". On emerald. Flared top Wafer foot	250.00
10". On cranberry	300.00
12". On emerald	400.00
12½". On cobalt	500.00

SILVER RESIST

This metal-decorated earthenware, first produced in 1805, is similar to Silver Lustre with respect to the silvering process. However, it differs in that, instead of an allover coating, a definite metal design appears on the surface of the ware.

A particular design was drawn or stenciled on the body and then a sugar-glycerin adhesive was brushed over parts of the item which would remain unlustred. After the lustre solution was applied and allowed to dry; the adhesive was washed off and the item was fired in the kiln. Obviously, the name of the ware comes from the fact that all parts of the item coated by the adhesive would "resist" the lustre solution thereby producing a decorative metal pattern.

Cup and Saucer. 2½". "Greek Key." $75.00

Chalice. 4½". Leaf decor ....$	165.00
Cup and Saucer. 2½". Handled. "Greek Key."	75.00

Jugs

4½". Vintage decor on tan ground	200.00
5". Leaf and foliage decor. C. 1815	275.00
5½". Commodore Decatur, Major General. Brown transfers. Floral sprays under spout	875.00
6". Bird on floral spray. Scrolled border. C. 1810	275.00
6¼". Black Memorial transfers in medallions. Silver trim	275.00
7". Black scenic transfer on tan ground. Monogrammed and dated 1812	350.00
Mug. 5". Floral vine decor on green ground	145.00

Plates

7". Vine decor	100.00
9½". Soup. "Greek" border. Sunburst center	150.00

SINCLAIRE GLASS

H. P. Sinclaire and Company was founded in 1904. They were the twelfth glass works to locate in the "Crystal City," Corning, New York. In 1920, H.P. Sinclaire began his own glass blowing factory in Bath, N.Y. Prior to this, Sin-

claire's cut and engraved designs were done on other glassmakers' blanks.
Sinclaire produced some of the most beautiful glass of the "Brilliant Period." Many of his designs were based on nature . . .fruits, flowers and foliage . . .and he approached them from an architectural viewpoint.

Console Set. 6 pieces. Amethyst. Two candlesticks 12", two bowls 9½" and 8½". Two compotes 7".
C. 1920 .... $1250.00

Bowls
- 12". Green. Amber foot ...... $ 125.00
- 13". Canary. Etched florals 175.00
- 13½". Crystal. "Pansy." 395.00

Candlesticks
- 8½". Crystal. Engraved on Steuben blanks. Pair 225.00
- 10". Twisted blown stems. Topaz. Unsigned. Pair 125.00
- 10". Spiral stems. Topaz. Pair .. 250.00

Console Sets
- 5 pieces. Green. Etched. Four candlesticks 3¼", bowl 14¼" 450.00
- 6 pieces. Amethyst. Two candlesticks 12", two bowls 9½" and 8½". Two compotes 7" 1250.00

Cruet. 8½". Crystal. Engraved and cut 150.00
Nappy. "Adam II" 60.00

Plates
- 8". Amethyst. Set of 6 .... 200.00
- 10½". Green. Footed 65.00

Relish. 4½ x 11". Cut. "Cane." 225.00
Rose Bowl. 5". "Fan and Stars." Engraved florals 225.00

Tumblers
- Copperwheel engraved 50.00
- Etched 35.00

Vases
- 8". Bulbous. Wafer foot, ring top. Copperwheel engraved #40 and "Grapes." Olive 450.00
- 10½". Fan-shaped. "Plateau." Elfin green 400.00
- 14". Cylindrical. Crystal. Intaglio florals, leaves 175.00

SMITH BROS. GLASS

Alfred and Harry Smith were employed as decorators by the Mt. Washington Glass Works in the early 1870's. In 1874, the brothers established their own operation in New Bedford, Massachusetts. They created an outstanding line of decorated glasswares.

Biscuit Jar. 8½". Pink florals on cream ground. Silverplated bail and lid $225.00

Biscuit Jars
- 6½". Daisy decor on cream .... $ 300.00
- 8". Melon ribbed. Gold medallions, blue geometric designs on white 375.00

Bowls
- 3½". Melon ribbed. Enameled pink and blue wisteria. Gold trim . 165.00
- 7". Melon-shaped. Cream ground.

Pink and orchid florals 225.00
10½". Melon ribbed. Yellow daisies on white satin ground. Metal collar 325.00

Boxes, Covered
3". Melon ribbed. Enameled daisy decor on white ground 225.00
4". Melon ribbed. Gold enameling 300.00

Chandelier. 14" diam. shade. Pink roses on white. Blue prisms, brass trim. Complete 850.00

Finger Bowl. Handpainted florals on white. Handled silverplated holder 165.00

Mustard Pot. 3½". Barrel-shaped. Butterflies, foliage decor on white 75.00

Rose Bowl. 4". Melon ribbed. Enameled florals on cream ground 195.00

Salt, Master. Enameled florals on cream 55.00

Salt Shakers. 2½". Squat. Melon-shaped. Shaded pink. Pewter tops. Pair 125.00

Sugar Castor. 6". Melon ribbed. All-over florals on cream satin ground. Blue beading trim 195.00

Toothpick. Melon ribbed. Floral decor. Beaded rim 65.00

Vases
3½". Bulbous. Enameled florals on white. Unsigned 150.00
5¾". Melon ribbed. Enameled daisies 250.00
6". Bulbous base, slender neck. Enameled gold daisies on white satin glass 350.00

SNOW BABIES

Snow Babies are small bisque figurines, originally made in Germany, that came onto the market in the early 1900's. There are several theories on their origin. One is that German doll makers copied the designs from their traditional Christmas candies. Another theory . . .the most accepted; is that they were made to honor Admiral Peary's daughter who was born in Greenland, 1893 and was called the "Snow Baby" by the Eskimos.
CAUTION: Reproductions.

Babies
Hiking. 4½" ....$ 65.00
Hugging, Two. 3" 65.00
Lying on tummy. 3½" long 95.00
Playing accordion. 2¾" 50.00
Playing drums. 2¾" 50.00
Playing musical instruments. Seven babies, 2" 300.00
Playing trumpet. 2¾" 50.00
Pulling sled. 2" 60.00
Santa's helpers. Red hats and coats. 2½" 65.00

Baby Seated. 3¼" high $125.00

Seated
1" 35.00
2" 65.00
3¼" 125.00
Skater. 1½" 55.00
Skier. 1½" 55.00
Sledding
1½" 45.00
1½ x 3". Baby turns on wooden peg 150.00
2" 50.00
2¾". Pulled by huskies 75.00
3" 65.00

Bear. 2¼" 50.00
Elf. 1½" 45.00
Kitten. 1½" 35.00
Matchholder. 3½" 125.00
Santa with Angel. 2" 65.00
Sheep. 2" 40.00

SOAPSTONE

The mineral steatite, a type of rock, is often referred to as soapstone because of its soapy feel. The intricately detailed carved novelty ornaments most often originated in China and were popular during the late Victorian period.

Ashtray. Monkeys. (2) 8" long ..$ 35.00

Bookends
Bird and tree. 5½". Pair 65.00
Chrysanthemums and foliage. 4x5". Pair 85.00

Box. 3½ x 5". Oriental scene 55.00

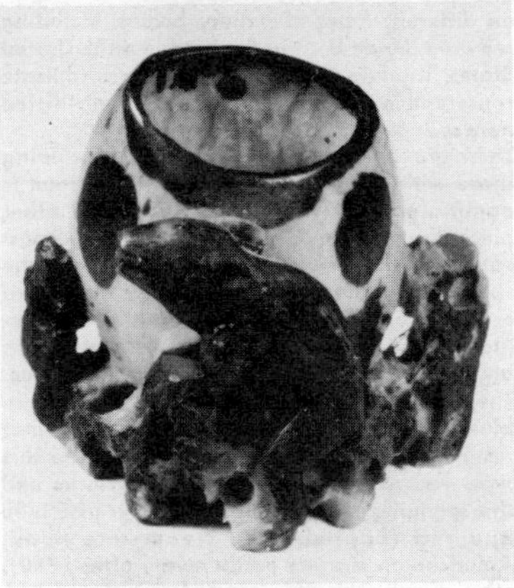

Vase. 2½" high. Rodent $65.00

Candleholder. 4½ x 9". Three-lite ..	55.00
Figurines	
Bear. 3¾"	35.00
Buddha. 4½". Light green	45.00
Chicken. 4"	35.00
Elephant, Seated. 5½"	65.00
Eskimo. 6 x 6¾". Black	150.00
Foo Dogs. 7". On pedestals. Green. Pair	175.00
Kwan Yin. 10½". Green on tan base	135.00
Woman, Oriental. 5¾". On pedestal. Tan	55.00
Vases	
2½". Rodent	65.00
5". Fish and underwater foliage ..	45.00
6 x 7¾". Cranes	95.00
7 x 5" base. Monkey and Dog	125.00
8¾". Floral	95.00

SOUVENIR-TYPE GLASS
(See "Ruby Stained Glass")

SOUVENIR SPOONS
(See "Commemorative and Souvenir Spoons")

SPANGLE GLASS
(See "End-of-Day Glass")

SPANISH LACE GLASS
(See "Opalescent Glass")

SPATTER GLASS
(See "End-of-Day Glass")

SPATTERWARE

The earliest examples of Spatterware were made about 1780, however most items found will date after 1800. A careful examination of damaged pieces of Spatterware will reveal that they are made of common earthenware, though some examples are Creamware. Today, collectors are primarily concerned with the decoration of Spatterware. Some very attractive pieces have nothing more than decorated borders if they are flat; or edges if they are hollow . . these were done in various colors. Such examples are believed to have been decorated with a brush, requiring several hundred touches of the brush to a square inch of decoration to achieve the spatter effect. Many Spatterware pieces have the entire surface covered with spatter and a great many have borders or edges dominated by blue, red or green, in that order; often combined with pictorial motifs, such as the "Rose," "Tulip," "Peafowl," "Castle," "Thistle," or "Cannon" . . .all in the center. On hollow pieces this decoration often occurs on both sides. Uncommon colors; such as yellow, black, purple and brown may also appear combined with any of the above motifs. Pieces of this ware are rarely marked. Harvey and Cotton and Barlow are among the known makers.

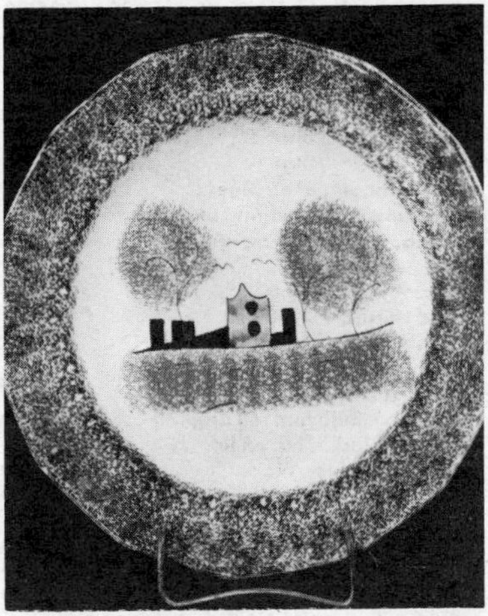

Plate. "Fort." 9½". Blue $265.00

Bowls, Small	
Eagle and Shield. Blue. Hairline .$	165.00
Open Flower. Purple	155.00
Peafowl. Red. Chipped	185.00
Bowl, Medium. Rainbow. Green,	

yellow and brown. Chipped 225.00
Coffee Pot. Flowers. Purple 250.00
Cup Plate. Peafowl. Red 165.00
Cups and Saucers
Eagle and Shield. Blue 185.00
Fort. Blue 220.00
Peafowl. Highly stylized. Green branches. No other spatter. Small . 225.00
Peafowl. Red.................. 230.00
Rainbow. Green, red and blue mottled. Four petal center. Harvey 325.00
Rainbow. Red and blue 165.00
Rose, Adam's. Red 175.00
Jugs
Blue. 10" 250.00
Rainbow. 3½". Red and blue 275.00
Rainbow. 6¼". Barrel-shaped. Green and blue. Repaired 450.00
Rainbow. Large. Red, green, yellow, blue and black. Repaired .. 650.00
School House. Large. Blue. Repaired 450.00
Wild Horses. Medium. Octagonal. Red 265.00
White Circles. 4⅝". Purple. Early form. Open circles in 3 rows 225.00
Plates
Blue. 10¼" 155.00
Daisies. 8½". Blue 110.00
Eagle and Shield. 7". Blue 125.00
Flora. 8¾". Blue 95.00
Holly Berry. 7⅞". Purple. Damaged 125.00
Oriental Scene. 9". Blue 85.00
Peafowl. 7½". Blue 185.00
Peafowl. 8½". Blue 220.00
Pomegranate. 8¾". Blue 155.00
Rainbow. 8½". Red and blue 275.00
Rainbow. 10". Blue, green and red 245.00
Star. 9½". 13 Points 145.00
Wild Horses. 9¼". Blue 95.00
Sugars
Coxcomb. Hexagonal. Blue. Slight damage 80.00
Rainbow. Blue and red draping .. 210.00
Stripes. Black. Chip on lid 185.00
Transition piece. Black 155.00
Tulip. Blue. Minor repair 245.00
Teapots
Eagle and Shield. Purple 350.00
Peafowl. Large. Blue. Repaired .. 550.00
Peafowl. Small. Green 275.00
Peafowl. Small. No lid. Leeds. Early 245.00

SPONGEWARE

The term Spongeware indicates a specific type of decoration; not a type of pottery or glaze and this decoration was not necessarily done with a sponge. Examples of this decoration are found on different types of pottery bodies, including redware. Made both in England and the United States, marked pieces of Spongeware indicate conservative dating from 1815 on. Items listed here are no later than 1880.

There are many types of Spongeware, including those with space decoration where the item is dominated by white underglaze; and other pieces that appear to have been sponged almost solidly on both sides. On later pieces, the sponging appears in either a circular movement or in a streaked or horizontal technique. Examples may be blue and white; multicolored in browns, greens and ochre and greenish-blue. The greenish-blue may have been sponged in blue and then overglazed in a pale yellow that resulted in the final effect. Some forms of this type were overglazed in red on the exterior and the sponging appears black or navy; also blue and red (English-on a creamware body, American-on a crude earthenware after 1880), gray, greyish green, red, dark green on stark white, dark green on a mellow yellow, and rarely purple. Spongeware should not be confused with Classic "Spatterware" or "Design Spatterware." (See these two classifications under separate headings.)

Coffee Pot. Blue and white. Unmarked. C. 1830 ....$275.00

Baking Dishes
7". Round. Greenish blue. Red outerglaze. Redware ....$ 155.00
7½". Oval. Greenish blue. Red outerglaze 135.00
9½". Oval. Greenish blue. Red outerglaze 165.00

Banks

- Pig. Green, blue, ochre 135.00
- Pig. Green. Stoneware-type 185.00
- Tudor. Red and blue. 6 x 6¾" high. C. 1800 .... 450.00

Bowls, Mixing

- Large. Blue and white. Blue band. 145.00
- White band 130.00
- Relief exterior 235.00
- Smooth exterior 225.00

Bowl, Mixing. Medium. Blue and white 130.00

Bowl, Mixing. Small. Blue and white 125.00

Bean Pots

- Green, brown, ochre 165.00
- 4Quart. No lid. Blue and white .. 185.00
- 4 Quart. Blue and white 250.00

Butter Crocks

- Large. No lid. Blue and white 165.00
- Medium. No lid. Blue and white .. 145.00
- Small. Blue and white 210.00

Compote. 8½". Shallow. Blue and white 325.00

Crocks

- 7½" diam. Wire bail. Blue and white 135.00
- 8½" diam., 5½" high. Grayish green. Straight sides. Wire bail .. 215.00
- 9" diam., 4½" high. With lip. Bluish green. Wire bail 210.00
- 10½" diam. Covered. Wire bail. Blue and white 250.00

Cups and Saucers

- Curved side. Blue and white 120.00
- Small size. Blue and white 95.00
- Straight side. Blue and white 135.00

Honey Jar, Covered. Two handles. Blue and white. Rare form 125.00

Ink Wells

- Blue and White. Rare form 225.00
- Green 185.00

Jugs

- 3". Green, ochre, brown 145.00
- 4". Bluish green 65.00
- 4¾". Blue and white 145.00
- 5". Bluish green 85.00
- 5¼". Baluster. Blue and white .. 185.00
- 5½". Baluster. Purple. Creamware 245.00
- 7". Tankard. Blue and white 115.00
- 8½". Deer in relief on both sides. Blue and white 195.00
- 9". Baluster. Blue and white 130.00
- 9". Barrel-shape. Grayish-green... 135.00
- 9". Solid blue flower on both sides. Sponged top and bottom. Blue and white 155.00
- 9". Tankard. Blue and white 145.00
- 9¼". Baluster. Blue and white .. 195.00
- 9¼". Miss Liberty and Eagle and Shield in relief on both sides. Blue and white 225.00
- 9½". Geometric relief. Green, ochre, brown 145.00
- 10½". Baluster. Green sponging on shoulder and lip only 135.00

Mugs

- 1¾". Red 125.00
- 3½". Red and green 135.00

Mustard Pot, Covered. Blue and white 165.00

Nappies

- 8½". Rectangular. Sponged interior only. Blue and white 175.00
- 10½". Oval. Sponged both sides. Blue and white 165.00

Planter. 8". Swirled fluting. Blue and white. Rare form 315.00

Plates

- 6¾". Scalloped rim. Overall sponging in cobalt on both sides. Ott & Brewer-type. Blue and white 85.00
- 10½". Scalloped rim. Overall sponging. Ott & Brewer-type. Blue and white 135.00
- 10½". Sponged on interior only. No interior rim. Blue and white .. 130.00
- 10½". Sponged on both sides. Interior rim. Plain edge 115.00

Plates, Soup

- Red and green. Hairline. Early .. 275.00
- 9". Blue and white 135.00
- 9". Blue and white. Set of 8 .... 875.00
- 10". Blue and white. Marked 155.00

Platters, Blue and white

- 9½". Oval. Sponged on both sides 115.00
- 9½". Rectangular. Sponged on both sides 120.00
- 11½". Rectangular. Sponged on both sides 135.00
- 13½". Rectangular. Sponged on both sides 165.00
- 17½". Marked. Minor chips 235.00

Pots

- Coffee. Marked. Blue and white... 325.00
- Tea. Flat lid. 1¾" flange. Blue and white. Chipped 265.00
- Tea. Green and brown on yellow glaze. Elongated flange. (Reproductions on Market--no elongated flange) 225.00
- Tea. High dome lid. No flange. Chipped 325.00

Rum Jug. Marked. Blue and white. Rare form 235.00

Salt Crock. Hanging-type. Blue and white 210.00

Soap Dish. Red and blue 125.00

Sugars

- Blue and green 235.00
- Blue and red 185.00
- Blue and raspberry 235.00

Tea Set. Small. 15 pieces. Blue and white. Rare form 650.00

Vase. Baluster. Green and blue 335.00
Vial. 4½″. Blue and white. Rare form 135.00

SPOONS,
("See, "Commemorative and Souvenir Spoons")

STAFFORDSHIRE

The Staffordshire district of England had an abundance of fine clay for pottery making. There were 80 different establishments operating there in 1786; by 1802 the number increased to 149. The district included Burslem, Cobridge, Etruria, Fenton, Foley, Hanley, Lane Delph, Lane End, Longport, Shelton, Stoke and Tunstall. Among the many famous potters located there were Adams, Davenport, Spode, Stevenson, Wedgwood and Wood.

W ADAMS & SONS ADAMS

ADAMS

The Adams family from the Staffordshire district of England has been associated with ceramics from the mid 17th century. In 1802, William Adams of Stoke-upon-Trent produced American views. Two of his cousins, both of whom were named William Adams, were also potters. One operated at Greengates, Tunstall, and the other at the Brick House Works, Burslem and Cobridge. Neither of the cousins is reported to have made American historical views.
In 1819, a fourth William Adams, son of William Adams of Stoke, became a partner with his father and was later joined by three brothers to form the firm of William Adams & Sons. In 1829, the father died and William, the eldest of the sons, became manager. The company operated four potteries at Stoke and one at Tunstall. American views were produced at Tunstall in black, light blue, sepia, pink and green in the 1830-40 period. William Adams died in 1865 and all operations were moved to Tunstall. The firm continues today under the name of Wm. Adams & Sons, Ltd.

Creamer. "Palestine." Pink ......$ 120.00
Cups and Saucers
"Columbus." Pink.............. 100.00
"Garden Sports." Light blue 75.00
"Log Cabin", with medallions. Pink 225.00
"The Sower." Pink.............. 70.00
Pitchers
7½″. "Seal of U.S." Dark blue .. 1000.00
10″. "Bologna." Pink 150.00
Plates
6″. "New York, U.S." Pink 125.00
6″. "Palestine." Medium blue 65.00
7″. "Montevideo, Conn." Pink .. 75.00

Plate. 10″. "Mitchell & Freeman's China & Glass Warehouse, Chatham Street, Boston." Dark blue $450.00

7¼″. "Columbus." Green border, pink center 150.00
7½″. "Caledonia." Pink 75.00
7½″. "Palestine." Pink.......... 55.00
7⅞″. "St. Paul's School London." Dark blue. 125.00
8″. "Shannondale Springs, Va." Pink 110.00
8″. "Andalusia." Pink 65.00
8½″. "Caledonia." Dark blue 150.00
9″. "View Near Conway, N.Y." Pink 175.00
9½″. "Bologna." Mulberry 45.00
10″. "Mitchell and Freeman's China and Glass Warehouse." Dark blue 450.00
10¼″. "Catskill Mountain House." Pink 150.00
10½″. "Caledonia." Pink 75.00
10½″, Soup. "Columbus Fleet." Black 55.00
10½″, Soup. "Headwaters of the Juanita." Sepia. 120.00
10½″, Soup. "Headwaters of the Juanita." Pink 150.00
10½″. "Palestine." Pink 55.00
10¾″. "Landing of Columbus." Black........................ 165.00
Platters
10″. "Schenectady of the Mohawk." Pink 275.00
15½″. "Harper's Ferry, U.S." Black. 375.00
17″. "Landing of Columbus." Pink. 395.00
21″. "Lyme Castle Kent." Dark blue 495.00

Sugar. "Log Cabin," with medallions. Pink 325.00

Vegetables

8 x 10". "Bologna." Pink 125.00

9½ x 13". "Lake George, U.S." Open handles. Black 300.00

9¾". "Schenectady at Mohawk." Pink 165.00

CLEWS

From sketchy historical accounts that are available, James Clews took over the closed plant of A. Stevenson in 1819, with his brother Ralph entering the business later. The firm continued until about 1836 when James Clews came to America to enter the pottery business at Troy, Indiana. The venture was a failure because of the lack of skilled workmen and the proper type of clay. He returned to England but did not re-enter the pottery business.

Plate. 7¾". "Winter View of Pittsfield, Mass." Dark blue $300.00

Bowl. 5½". "Christmas Eve." Dark blue ....$ 200.00

Creamers

4½". "Landing of Lafayette." Dark blue 500.00

5½". "Eagle on Urn." Dark blue .. 500.00

"Christmas Eve." Dark blue 225.00

Cup Plates

3½". "Peace and Plenty." Dark blue 350.00

3⅞". "Hudson River View." Pink .. 65.00

Cups and Saucers

"Eagle on Urn." Dark blue 400.00

"Hunting Dogs." Dark blue 100.00

"Landing of Lafayette." Dark blue 400.00

Pitchers

6½". "Double View, One New York City Hall." Dark blue 750.00

7½". "Near Fort Miller, Hudson River." Pink 325.00

Plates

4½", Toddy. "Peace and Plenty." Dark blue 500.00

4½", Toddy. "Pittsfield Elm." Dark blue 450.00

5¾". "Fort Montgomery." Black .. 150.00

6". "Dr. Syntax, The Garden Trio." Light blue 250.00

6¾". "Dr. Syntax and a Blue Stocking Beauty." Dark blue 250.00

6¾". "Junction of the Sacandaga and Hudson River." Black 175.00

6¾". "Pittsfield Elm." Dark blue 275.00

6¾". "States." Building in distance, women foreground. Dark blue 225.00

7¼". "Dr. Syntax Turned Nurse." Dark blue 225.00

7½". "Landing of Lafayette." Dark blue 250.00

7¾". "Near Fishkill." Dark blue .. 250.00

7¾". "West Point, Hudson River." Sepia 125.00

8". "Baker Falls." sepia 85.00

8". "Near Sandy Hill, Hudson River." Mulberry 75.00

8". "Pittsfield Elm." Dark blue .. 275.00

8½". "Dr. Syntax Star Gazing." Dark blue 225.00

8¾". "Dr. Syntax Returned from His Tour." Dark blue 250.00

8¾". "Meeting of Sancho and Dapple." Dark blue 225.00

9". "Christmas Eve." Dark blue .. 225.00

9". "Hobart Town. "Dark blue .. 300.00

9". "Landing of Lafayette." Dark blue 275.00

9". "Near Fort Miller, Hudson River." Light blue 175.00

9", Soup. "Peace and Plenty." Dark blue 275.00

9⅛". "Bakers Fall, Hudson River." Light blue 125.00

10", Soup. "Dr. Syntax Mistakes a Gentleman's House for an Inn." Dark blue 185.00

10". "Knighthood Conferred on Don Quixote." Dark blue 250.00

10¼". "Fishkill, Hudson River." Black 95.00
*10½". Dr. Syntax Bound to a Tree by Highwaymen." Dark blue 250.00
10½". "Pittsburgh, Pa." Black .. 225.00
10½". "States." Dark Blue 325.00
10½". "Three Story Building and Observatory." Dark blue 400.00
10½". "Winter View of Pittsfield, Mass." Dark blue 325.00

Platters
13". "States." Castle Center. Dark blue 850.00
13". "Winter View of Pittsfield, Mass." Dark blue 750.00
13½". "Hudson River, Hudson." Black 275.00
14½". "Columbus, Ohio." Dark blue 2500.00
15". "Landing of Lafayette." Dark blue 750.00
16". "Dr. Syntax Advertising for a Wife." Blue 500.00
16". "Penitentiary in Allegheny near Pittsburgh." Mulberry 450.00
17". "Dr. Syntax, A Noble Hunting Party." Dark blue 500.00
17". "Land of Lafayette. "Dark blue 850.00
17½". "Little Falls of Luzerne, N.Y." Sepia. 350.00
17½". "Newburg, Hudson River." Sepia 325.00
18½". Detroit, Mich." Dark blue 3000.00
18½". "Sancho Panza and the Duchess." Dark blue 500.00
19". "Dr. Syntax Amused with Pat in the Pond." Dark blue 650.00
19". "Landing of Lafayette." Dark blue 1000.00

Teapot. "Christmas Eve." Dark blue 350.00

Tureens
Gravy. "Dr. Syntax Stopped by Highwaymen." Dark blue 500.00
Gravy, with underplate. "Landing of Lafayette at Castle Gardens, N.Y. Aug. 16, 1824." Dark blue .. 850.00
Sauce, lid and underplate. "Landing of Lafayette." Dark blue 750.00
Soup. 14" long. "Louisville, Kentucky." Dark blue 3500.00

Vegetables
10", rectangular. "Near Hudson, Hudson River." Black 250.00
12½". "The Escape of the Mouse." Dark blue 350.00

*Reiussued in 1890 to fulfill a size which was not made originally. "Laidacker" ...

J. & J. JACKSON

J.&J. JACKSON

Job and John Jackson began operations at the Churchyard Works, Burslem, about 1830. The works had formerly been owned by the Wedgwood family. The firm did not produce dark blue transfer scenes but made black, light blue, pink, sepia, green, maroon and mulberry. In all, approximately 40 different American views of Connecticut, Massachusetts, Pennsylvania, New York and Ohio were issued. The firm is believed to have closed about 1844.

Plate. 10½". "View of Canal, Little Falls, Mohawk River." Black $250.00

Bowls
5". "University Hall, Harvard." Black ....$ 350.00
12⅜". "Albany, New York." Black. 325.00

Plates
6". "Girard's Bank, Philadelphia." Pink 175.00
7". "At Richmond, Va." Black 125.00
7". "At Richmond, Va." Sepia 150.00
8". "Battery & Co., N.Y." Sepia .. 200.00
8". "Battery & Co., N.Y." Pink 225.00
8". "Race Bridge, Philadelphia." Light blue. 175.00
9". "Battle Monument, Philadelphia." Mulberry 225.00
9". "Water Works, Phila." Medium blue 350.00
9". "Water Works, Phila." Sepia .. 225.00
10½". "Hartford, Conn." Pink .. 150.00
10½". "The President's House, Washington." Sepia 250.00
10½". "The President's House, Washington." Medium blue 265.00
10½". "View of Canal, Little Falls, Mohawk River. "Black 250.00

Platters
17". "New York." Light blue 500.00
17½". "Newburgh, New York." Black 350.00
Sauce Boat. 3½ x 9" long. "Fort Ticonderoga." Medium blue 600.00
Tureen. 6¼ x 9". "Lake George." Green 400.00
Vegetable. 8 x 9½". "Upper Ferry Bridge." Black 450.00

THOMAS MAYER

In 1829 Thomas Mayer and his brothers John and Joshua purchased Stubbs' Dale Hall Works of Burslem. They continued to produce a superior grade of ceramics.
Thomas Mayer produced the American Series of the Arms of the States at Stoke. Teapots and sugar bowls depicting Lafayette at the Tomb of Franklin and at the Tomb of Washington were also his designs.

Platter. 19". "Arms of New Jersey." Medium blue $3000.00

Bowls
8¾". Open. "Arms of Mass." Dark blue ....$ 3000.00
12". "Arms of Maryland." Medium blue 3500.00
Plate. 8½". "Arms of Rhode Island." Dark blue 600.00
Platter. 21". "Arms of Pennsylvania." Dark blue 6500.00

Vegetable, Covered. 12", oval. "Arms of Virginia." Dark blue .. 4000.00

CHARLES MEIGH

The Meigh pottery began with Job Meigh in 1780 in the Old Hall Pottery, Hanley. Later his sons and grandson entered the business. The firm's name is recorded as Job Meigh & Sons, 1823; J. Meigh & Sons, 1829; Charles Meigh, 1843. The American Cities and Scenes series were produced by Charles Meigh between 1840-1850.

Pitcher. 8¾". "Albany." Light blue $ 275.00
Plates
9½". "Yale College, New Haven." Light blue 295.00
10". "New York, City Hall." Light blue 120.00
Platters
10". "Schuylkill Water Works." Light blue 300.00
16". "Baltimore." Light blue 325.00
Sugar. 6½ x 7½". "Utica, N.Y." Light blue 275.00

MELLOR, VENABLES & CO.

Little information is recorded on Mellor, Venables & Co. except that they were listed as potters in Burslem, 1843. Interest in their series of American views increased when their white wares with the State of Arms included New Hampshire. This proved that the view did exist and renewed hope to locate Thomas Mayer's missing "Arms of New Hampshire" to complete his series of the original thirteen states.

Pitcher. 6". "Arms of Pennsylvania." White ....$ 425.00
Plates
7½". "Arms of Maryland." White 225.00
7½". "Washington's Tomb, Mount Vernon." Light blue 275.00
8¼". "Fort Hamilton, New York." Seven design border. Light blue .. 275.00
10½". "Lake George Caldwell." Light blue 175.00
Teapot. "Arms of Maryland." White 500.00

J.W.R.

J. & W. RIDGWAY

Stone China

John and William Ridgway, sons of Job Ridgway and nephews of George of Bell Bank Works (1792) and Cauldon Place Works (1813) produced the only recorded American views "Beauties of America" from their firm at Cauldon, near Hanley. The partnership was dissolved in 1830. John continued operations at Cauldon. William managed the Bell Bank Works until 1854 and issued additional American series in light blue, brown and black.

Platter. 14¾". "Deaf & Dumb Asylum, Hartford, Conn." Medium blue $850.00

Plates	
6¼". "Antheneum, Boston". Dark blue .... $	250.00
7". "Insane Hospital, Boston." Dark blue	300.00
8". "Library, Philadelphia." Dark blue	250.00
8¼", Soup. "Staughton's Church, Philadelphia." Dark blue	300.00
9¾", Soup. "Octagon Church, Boston." Dark blue	250.00
Platters	
6½". "Bank of Savannah," mismarked Charleston. Medium blue	700.00
9½". "St. Paul's Church, Boston." Dark blue	1500.00
10½". "Court House, Boston." Dark blue	750.00
12½". "Hospital, Boston." Dark blue	500.00
20½". "Capitol, Washington." Dark blue	1250.00
20½". "Capitol, Washington," with well. Dark blue	1500.00
Sauce Boat. "Boston State House." Medium blue.	450.00
Vegetable, Covered. 11". "Hospital, Boston." Dark blue	500.00

W. RIDGWAY

WILLIAM RIDGWAY & CO.
NARROW LACE BORDER

After the partnership between the Ridgway brothers, John and William was dissolved in 1830, William continued operating the Bell Bank Works in Hanley until 1854. He produced two series of American views from Bartlett's "American Scenery." The first series had three various borders . . .including narrow lace. The marks consisted of a printed eagle, title and W.R. or impressed lions with plaque, "Opaque Granite China, W.R. & Company." The other series is known as "Catskill Moss" and is so marked.

Cup and Saucer. "Crow's Nest from Bull Hill," and "Valley of Shenandoah from Jefferson's Rock." .. $	200.00
Custard Cup, Covered. 2¾", footed. "Narrows from Staten Island." Light blue	350.00
Plate. 8". "Washington's Tomb." Mt. Vernon. Light blue	250.00
Platters	
9¾". "Peekskill Landing, Hudson River." Light blue	265.00
15½". "View from Fort Putnam." Black	375.00
19". "Capitol at Washington." Light blue	1200.00
Sugars, Covered.	
"Narrows from Staten Island" and "Undercliff near Coolspring". Light blue	250.00
"Peekskill Landing, Hudson River." Black	300.00

ROGERS

ROGERS

John Rogers and his brother George established a pottery near Longport in 1782. After George's death in 1815, John's son Spencer became a partner in which the firm operated under the name of John Rogers & Son. John was deceased in 1816, but his son continued the use of the name until he dissolved the pottery in 1842.
The firm produced only three distinct American views . . .the battle between the U.S. Frigate "Chesapeake" and the British Frigate "Shannon", "Boston State House" (with variations of cows; one tree or two trees, no cows) and the so-called "Boston Harbour."

Cup and Saucer. "Boston State House." Dark blue .... $	450.00
Plates	
4", Toddy. "Boston Harbour". Dark blue	425.00
7½". "Boston State House." Dark blue	225.00
10". "Boston State House." Dark blue	250.00
10", Soup. "Boston State House." Dark blue	200.00

Platters

13". "Boston State House." Dark blue 500.00

19". "Boston State House." Dark blue 650.00

22½". "Chesapeake and Shannon." Medium blue 750.00

Sugar. "Boston Harbour." Blue 450.00

Teapot. "Boston State House." Medium blue 600.00

R.S.W.

STEVENSON

As early as the 17th century the name Stevenson has been associated with the pottery industry. Andrew Stevenson Cobridge (1808-1829) introduced American scenes with the flower and scroll border. Ralph Stevenson, also of Cobridge (1815-1840), used a vine leaf border on his dark blue wares of historical views and a lace border on his series executed in pink, mulberry, sepia and black. The initials R.S. & W. indicate Ralph Stevenson and Williams are associated with the acorn and leaf border. It has been reported that William was Ralph's New York agent and the wares were produced by Ralph Stevenson.

Plate. 10". "Park Theatre, New York." Acorn and oak leaves border. Medium blue. RSW $265.00

Pitcher. 9". "Hartford Deaf and Dumb Asylum" and "Alms House, N.Y." Acorn and oak leaves border. Dark blue ....$ 850.00

Platter. 16¼". "Alms House, Boston." Vine border. Dark blue. Stevenson $750.00

Plates

4½", Toddy. "Octagon Church, Boston." Acorn and oak leaves border. Dark blue 600.00

6½". "Columbia College, New York." Acorn and oak leaves border. Dark blue 450.00

6¾". "Battery N.Y." Acorn and oak leaves border. Dark blue 350.00

6¾". "Harvard College." (end of hall) Acorn and oak leaves border. Dark blue. RSW 1000.00

7½". "Columbia College." Acorn and oak leaves border. Dark blue . 550.00

8½". "City Hotel, N.Y." Acorn and oak leaves border. Dark blue 300.00

8½". "Harvard College." (with horseman) Acorn and oak leaves border. Dark blue. RSW 550.00

8½". "Nahant Hotel near Boston." Acorn and oak leaves border. Dark blue. RSW 300.00

9". "Hospital, Boston." Vine border. Dark blue. RSW 300.00

10". "Capitol, Washington." Vine border. Dark blue. RSW 350.00

10". "New York From Brooklyn Heights." Floral border. Medium blue 750.00

10", Soup. "Park Theatre, N.Y." Acorn and oak leaves border. Dark blue. RSW 225.00

10". "Park Theatre, New York" (Erie Canal View B) Four Portrait Medallions. Dark blue 1500.00

10". "Water Works, Phila." Acorn and oak leaves border. Dark blue. RSW 400.00

Platters

10½". "Brooklyn Ferry." Vine border. Dark blue 1500.00

16¼". "Alms House, Boston." Vine border. Dark blue 750.00

17". "State House, Boston." Acorn and oak leaves border. Dark blue 750.00

Teapot. "State House, Hartford." Floral border. Dark blue 750.00

Tureen, Soup. 2 pieces. "Pennsylvania Hospital, Philadelphia." Acorn and oak leaves border. Dark blue 5000.00

STUBBS

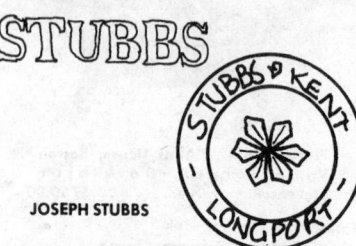

JOSEPH STUBBS

In 1790, Stubbs established a pottery works at Burslem, England, which he operated until 1829 when he retired and sold his works to Mayer Bros. It is believed that he produced his views of America about 1825. Many of his scenes were from Boston, New York, New Jersey and Philadelphia.

Plate. 10". "Fairmount Near Phila." Spread Eagle border. Dark blue $150.00

Creamers

4½". "Boston State House." Rose border. Medium blue ....$ 325.00

5½". "City Hall, N.Y." Rose border. Dark blue 375.00

Cup Plate. 3¼". "Woodlands near Phila." Spread Eagle border. Dark blue 350.00

Cups and Saucers

"Boston State House." Rose border. Medium blue 300.00

"City Hall, N.Y." Rose border. Dark blue 350.00

Custard Cup, Covered. "Hoboken in New Jersey." Spread Eagle border. Dark blue 400.00

Mug. 3½ x 3½". "Boston State House" and "New York." Rose border. Medium blue 450.00

Plates

6". "Park Theater, N.Y." Spread Eagle border. Dark blue 325.00

6½". "City Hall, N.Y." Spread Eagle border. Dark blue 350.00

6¾". "Woodlands near Phila." Spread Eagle border. Dark blue .. 300.00

7¾". "Hoboken in New Jersey." Spread Eagle border. Dark blue .. 250.00

8½". "Nahant Hotel near Boston." Spread Eagle border. Dark blue .. 275.00

8¾". "Upper Ferry Bridge." Spread Eagle border. Dark blue .. 250.00

9". "Nahant Hotel near Boston." Spread Eagle border. Dark blue .. 275.00

10". "Fairmount near Phila." Spread Eagle border. Dark blue .. 150.00

10". "Bank of the U.S. Phila." Spread Eagle border. Dark blue .. 325.00

Platters

10½". "Woodlands, Near Philadelphia." Spread Eagle border. Dark blue 600.00

14½". "State House, Boston." Spread Eagle border. Medium blue 600.00

16½". "Mendenhall Ferry." Spread Eagle border. Dark blue .. 750.00

18". "Upper Ferry Bridge." With Conestoga. Spread Eagle border. Medium blue 750.00

18". "Upper Ferry Bridge." Without Conestoga 650.00

20". "Fairmount near Phila." Spread Eagle border. Dark blue .. 850.00

Teapot, Covered. 10". "N.Y. City Hall." Rose border. Medium blue . 600.00

S. TAMS & CO.

The firm operated at Longton, England. The exact date of its beginning is not known but is believed to be around 1810-1815. The company produced American views including the United States Hotel, Philadelphia; the Capitol, Harrisburg, Pa., and the Capitol, Washington, D.C. About 1830 the firm became Tams, Anderson and Tams.

Bowls
- 8½". "The Capitol, Washington." Dark blue ....$ 750.00
- 11¾", flat. "Capitol, Washington." Dark blue 1500.00

Pitcher. 9". "The Capitol, Washington." Dark blue 850.00

Plate, Soup. 10". "United States Hotel, Phila." Dark blue 750.00

ENOCH WOOD & SONS BURSLEM

WOOD

Enoch Wood, sometimes referred to as the "Father of English Pottery," began operating a pottery in 1783, Fountain Place, Burslem. A cousin, Ralph Wood was associated with him. In 1790, James Caldwell became a partner and the firm was known as Wood and Caldwell until 1819 when he and his sons took full control of the business. Enoch died in 1840, but the pottery continued under the name Enoch Wood & Sons. It was during the years in which the sons were affiliated with the business that the American views were produced. It is reported that the pottery produced more signed historical views than any other Staffordshire firm and perhaps even many views listed as unknown maker. Marks vary . . .although always with the name Wood; occasionally" & Sons" was omitted. The establishment was sold to Messrs. Pinder, Bourne & Hope in 1846.

WOOD
SHELL BORDER, CIRCULAR CENTER

Cup Plate. 3¾". "Castle Garden, Battery." Dark blue ....$ 325.00

Plates
- 6½". "Highlands near Newburg." Light blue 150.00
- 7½". "Pass in the Catskill Mountains." Dark blue 250.00
- 7½". "The Capitol, Washington." Dark blue 375.00
- 7½". "View of Trenton Falls". Dark blue 275.00
- 8½". "B. & O. Railroad, Incline." Dark blue 650.00
- 8½". "B. & O. Railroad, Level". Dark blue 650.00
- 8½". "City of Albany." Dark blue 375.00
- 9", Soup. "Fall of Montmorenci, near Quebec." Dark blue 225.00

Plate. 7½". "Pass in the Catskill Mountains." Dark blue $250.00

- 9". "Gilpins Mills on Brandywine Creek." Dark blue 325.00
- 9". "Transylvania University." Dark blue 375.00
- 9¼". "Fall of Montmorenci, near Quebec." Dark blue 275.00
- 9¾". "Marine Hospital, Louisville, Ky." Dark blue 325.00
- 10". "Pine Orchard House." Dark blue 275.00
- 10". "Table Rock Niagara." Dark blue 375.00
- 10", Soup. "B. & O. Railroad, Level." Dark blue 550.00

Platters
- 15". "Niagara from the American Side." Dark blue 1200.00
- 16½". "Lake George." Dark blue .. 850.00
- 20½". "Castle Gardens" and "Battery, N.Y." Dark blue 1200.00

WOOD
SHELL BORDER, IRREGULAR CENTER

Cup Plate. 3½". "Cadmus." Dark blue ....$ 325.00

Plates
- 6½". "MacDonough's Victory." Dark blue 250.00
- 8". "MacDonough's Victory" Dark blue 275.00
- 8". "Chief Justice Marshall. Troy Line." Dark blue 375.00
- 9". "Marine Hospital, Louisville." Dark blue 325.00
- 9¼". "The Union Line." Dark blue . 325.00

10". "Cadmus." Dark blue 375.00
10". "MacDonough's Victory." Dark blue 325.00

Platter. 18½". "Christianburg, Danish Settlement on the Gold Coast of Africa." Dark blue 850.00

Teapot. "Commodore MacDonough's Victory." Dark blue 750.00

Plate. 10¼". "The Union Line." Dark blue $375.00

WOOD
IRREGULAR BORDERS

Bowl. 11". "Lafayette at Franklin's Tomb." Floral border. Dark blue $ 800.00

Cup and Saucer. "Lafayette at Washington's Tomb." Floral border. Dark blue 450.00

Cup Plates
3½". "Castle Garden Battery, N.Y." Trefoil border. Dark blue .. 275.00
3⅝". "Cottage in the Woods, Ruggles Home." Trefoil border. Dark blue 225.00

Pitcher. 9". "Lafayette at Franklin's Tomb." Dark blue 1000.00

Plates
9". "Franklin's Birthplace." Floral border. Dark blue 175.00
10". "Lafayette at Washington's Tomb." Floral border. Dark blue .. 500.00
10". "Landing of the Fathers at Plymouth." Trefoil border. Medium blue 150.00

Platter. 18½". "La Grange, the Residence of the Marquis Lafayette." Flower and grape border. Dark blue 800.00

Sugar. "Wadsworth Tower." Dark blue 425.00

Teapot. "Washington Standing at Tomb, Scroll in Hand." Floral border. Dark blue 750.00

UNKNOWN MAKERS

Plate. 10". "Dam and Water Works at Phila." Floral and fruit border. Dark blue $375.00

Teapot. 6¼ x 9¼". "Basket of flowers with chain." Green $375.00

Cup Plate. 3½". "Holliday Street Theatre, Baltimore." Fruit and flower border. Dark blue ......$ 550.00

Jug, Cooling. "The Residence of the Late Richard Jordan, New Jersey." Mulberry 850.00

Plates
6¾". "Philadelphia from the Great Tree." Dark blue 425.00
6¾". "Vevay, Indiana." Fruit and flower border. Dark blue 750.00

8½". "Baltimore Court House." Fruit and flower border. Dark blue 350.00
9", Soup. "Hobart Town." Light blue 275.00
10". "Baltimore Exchange." Fruit and flower border. Dark blue. 425.00

Platters
9½". "Chillicothe," with cows. Flowers and scroll border. Dark blue 2500.00
12½". "Louisville, Kentucky." Flower and scroll border. Dark blue 1750.00
16½". "Sandusky." Flower and scroll border. Dark blue 2200.00
Tureen, Soup. 14½". "Louisville, Kentucky." Dark blue 4500.00

STAFFORDSHIRE ITEMS

A wide variety of ornamental pottery items were made in the Stafforshire district of England. Trinket boxes, pastille burners, animal figurines and groups of people (sometimes called Chimney ornaments) were produced in abundance in the 19th century.

Cats. 7½" high. Pair $275.00

Animals
Cats
7½" high. Black and white. Orange bases. Pair ....$ 275.00
12" high. Gray. Green glass eyes 200.00
Cow. 6¾" long. Russet spots on cream colored body. Green base 85.00
Dogs
4" high. Spaniel. Russet spots on white. Pair 125.00
5" high. Poodles. White. Gold collars. Pair 150.00
5½" high. Dalmations. Black markings on white. Pair 175.00
9½" high. Poodles. Russet spots

Trinket Box. Pocket watch-shape $65.00

on cream. Black chains, gold collars, lockets. Pair 200.00
10½" high. Spaniels. Russet markings on white. Black chains, gold lockets. Pair 250.00
12" high. Spaniels. Brown and tan. Brown glass eyes. Pair 395.00
Lion. 9½ x 11" long. Brown 85.00
Swan. 6" high. White 185.00

Chimney Ornaments
Bacchus. 7" 125.00
Children with lambs. 7". Pair 125.00
Farmer and Wife. 13½" 125.00
Going to Market. Returning Home. 8½" high. Polychrome colors. Pair. 175.00
Huntsman. 15" 175.00
Musicians. Lady and gentleman. 17". White with gold trim 125.00
Pastoral scene. 7½". Grazing sheep 95.00
Peace on Earth, Good Will Toward Men. 12¾" high 175.00
Prince and Princess of Wales. 8". Standing next to clock 95.00
Prince of Wales. 18". White ground, painted face, orange robe. C. 1875 195.00
Rivals. 15" high. Three figures 125.00
Sankey. 15½" high. Black and white 150.00
Shakespeare. 18" high. Standing 195.00
Uncle Tom and Eva. 9¾" 250.00
Vicar and Moses. 8¼" 85.00

Pastille Burners
Castle. White with two towers, center turret 150.00
Cottage. White, blue roof, green shrubbery 125.00
Woman with dog. On pedestal 125.00
Shoe. 5½" long. Gold sanded rose on front. Scalloped top 65.00

Spill Holders
- 5½". Boy and girl. Pair 125.00
- 6". Cow and calf. Russet with green accents. Pair 250.00

Trinket Boxes, Covered
- Books and Vase 55.00
- Child sleeping in high chair 75.00
- Clock and Vase 60.00
- Marriage Bed Series 75.00
- Red Riding Hood and Wolf 65.00
- Table and chairs 60.00

STAINED AND-OR LEADED GLASS PANELS

Stained glass is transparent, translucent or opaque colored glass. Leaded glass panels are constructed of glass put together with lead cames and these are soldered together to produce a design. The Egyptians are credited with using the first stained glass windows. With the advent of Christianity, stained glass windows became a major form of religious art. The best known stained glass artist of the 20th century was Louis C. Tiffany. A standard formula for determining the value of a stained and-or leaded glass panel is as follows:
Count the number of glass panes per square foot for base number. Double the base number if decorative. Subtract 2 points for each damaged pane and halve the base number for missing panes or other major damage. Multiply the result by the total square feet of the complete panel to arrive at an approximate value. Subject of the design and quality of the workmanship are important factors in determining value.

22 x 42". Semi-circular. Torch center. Lead cames. Original frame ..$275.00

- 19 x 44". Tulip center ....$ 150.00
- 30 x 48". Rectangular center of birds, flowers and leaves. Multicolored 650.00
- 33 x 43". "Whiskey." Lead cames .. 750.00
- 36 x 42". "CAFE" in white letters on red background 250.00

STANGL POTTERY

Stangl Pottery acquired Fulper Pottery in the late 1920's. Stangl birds are their most collectible items; but other objects such as planters, vases and bowls were produced.

Plate. 9⅛". "Thistle." $5.00

Birds
- Bird of Paradise. 3408 ....$ 60.00
- Bluebird. 3276 .... 50.00
- Cardinal. 3596 .... 45.00
- Cockatoo. 3580 .... 85.00
- Hummingbird. 3626 .... 40.00
- Orioles, Double. 3402 D 65.00
- Titmouse. 3592 .... 35.00
- Warbler, Prothnaty. 3447. Early mark 55.00
- Warbler, Red Faced. 3594 ...... 40.00
- Wren. 3401 .... 25.00

Bowls
- 6x 2¼" deep. Leaf handle. Terra Rose. Green 10.00
- 7x 4" deep. Covered. Terra Rose .. 15.00
- 8". Petal-shaped. White 15.00

Candlesticks. 3 x 4½ x 6". Calla Lily on blue leaf. Pair 30.00

Carafe, Stoppered. 8" high. Ribbed. Yellow and blue. Wooden handle . 20.00

Cigarette Box, Covered. 5¾". Leaf-shaped 10.00

Cornucopia. 8¾". Terra Rose. Green. 15.00

Creamer. 2½". Thistle. Brown and white 5.00

Dinnerware. Terra Rose. 17 pieces .. 85.00

Planter. 5¾ x 6". Open blossom. Terra Rose 20.00

Relish. 8 x 2" deep. Cloverleaf-shaped. Three part. Terra Rose .. 10.00

Vases

7". Milk can. Terra Rose. Tan 8.00

7". Handled. Reeded and scalloped. Blue to yellow 18.00

8". Sunflower-shaped. Terra Rose. Green 15.00

11". Urn-type. Black and gold .. 50.00

Water Set. Pitcher, 2 quart. Four tumblers. Horizontal rib. Blue .. 35.00

STATUES AND FIGURES

The technical difference between a statue and figure is the material. A statue is made of stone or metal. A figure is composed of wood or clay (porcelain, pottery). Large or important figures are sometimes classified as statues. The terms figurine and statuette are used to distinguish size. Using the human figure as a guide, if the statue measures one-fourth life size, it is known as a statuette. If a figure is less than approximately one-fourth life size it is referred to as a figurine. Bronzes, See "Bronze"

Classical figures. 18" high. One with harp, other with book. Bronzed pot metal. Pair $175.00

Boy and Girl. 12". Bisque. Playing. Heubach ....$ 500.00

Boy and Girl. 13". Porcelain. Germany. C. 1900. Pair 175.00

Dog. 3". Bisque. Heubach 65.00

King and Queen. 8". Porcelain. Meissen. Pair 375.00

Knight. 10½". Sterling. Vermeil work and embossed. Ivory face .. 500.00

Napoleon. On horseback. 10 x 11". Porcelain. Dresden 450.00

Peasants. 12". Enamel over wood. Pair 150.00

Rabbit. 7". Porcelain. White. Meissen 275.00

St. Joseph with Christ Child. 60". Wood 650.00

Woman, Seated. 3¾ x 3¾". Porcelain. Playing musical instrument. Child standing near by with hat. Meissen 500.00

STEINS

Basically, a stein is a mug especially made to hold beer or ale. Most steins are fitted with a metal hinged lid with thumblift. The earthenware character-type steins are attributed to German origin.

Lithophane-type. 11". Porcelain with pewter lid. Gruss aus Aschback. $150.00

Art Nouveau-style decor. 14". Copper and brass. Germany ......$ 95.00

Bacchus. 11½". Silverplated. English 150.00

Bismarck. 1½ L. Porcelain. Radish finial. Musterschutz	400.00
Clown. ½ L. Lithophane	350.00
18th Infantry. 1L. Regimental	275.00
Father John. 1L. Musterschutz	1500.00
Field Artillery. 1L. Regimental	275.00
Flower. 1L. Gesetzlicht	295.00
Glass, Pressed. ½ L. Handpainted porcelain. Inlaid pewter lid with red fox finial	85.00
Indian. ¼ L. Musterschutz	450.00
Ivory. 25". Highly carved. French. 19th century	6500.00
Judge. ½ L. Musterschutz	650.00
Mandarin. ½ L. Merkelbach & Wick	175.00
Monk. ½ L. Lithophane	250.00
Monks. ½ L. Gesetzlicht	175.00
Monkey. 1L. Musterschutz	450.00
Munich Maid. ½ L. Lithophane	450.00
Nun. 7". Lithophane	250.00
Pixie. 1L. Musterschutz	850.00
Ram, Seated. 1L. Musterschutz	650.00
Rolandbrannen Park. 1L. Lithophane. Dresden	400.00
Satan. ½ L. Musterschutz	800.00
Village Dancers. ½ L. Musterschutz	225.00

STEREOSCOPE VIEWERS AND CARDS

First marketed in 1854, the stereoscope was a popular Victorian parlor ornament . . .almost every home in America had one. This optical instrument had two eyeglasses which enabled the viewer to see the double picture cards as a single view with true feeling of depth and distance. Stereoscopes were hand held and fitted to the face; and the picture cards were contained in a slide (or rack) 10 inches away at the other end of the instrument. Scenes of far away places and people, foreign cities, cathedrals and other architectural wonders were popular subjects. Millions of stereoscopic views were published, often in large issues of hundreds or thousands. As the first truly pictorial medium, stereoscopes remained available into the late 1930's; however interest in the medium had begun to decline with the advent of the picture postcard, movies and radio.

Viewers

Binocular-type. With light bulb ..$	30.00
Double-type. 18 x 10" wide. American	150.00
Double-type. 10½ x 6½". French	150.00
Eye Comfort. With stand	40.00
Hand-type. With sliding adjustment	35.00
Keystone, Junior	35.00
Keystone View Co. Leather, velvet trim	50.00
Stereosconse	50.00

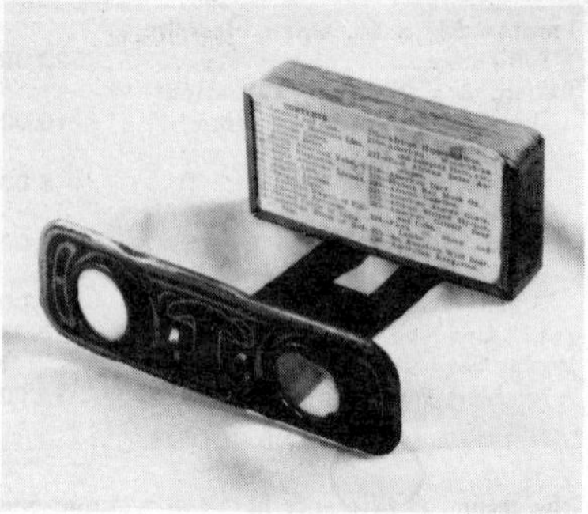

Viewer. Hand-type. Sliding adjustment $35.00

Cards

Sets

Countries. 75	75.00
Egypt. With map and book. 100	50.00
Germany. 100	50.00
Italy. With maps and book. 100	50.00
Panama. 100	40.00
San Francisco Earthquake. 50	75.00
Sears Roebuck. 50	35.00
Sweden. 50	30.00
World War I. 100	65.00

Singles .. .Prices quoted are approximate for cards in good condition. Folded, mutilated or badly soiled cards are of little or no value to collectors.

Advertising-type	.75
Alaska Gold Rush	3.00
City Scenes	1.00
Civil War	10.00
Comics	1.50
Disasters	1.50
Expositions	2.00
Indians	3.50
Oil Wells	2.50
Panama Canal	1.50
Presidents	3.00
Railroads	5.00
Sentimentals	1.00
Ships	2.00
Spanish American War	3.50
States	1.00
Tissues. American and French	5.00
Transportation. Early	2.50

STERLING

(See "Silver")

STEUBEN GLASS

The Steuben Glass Works commenced in 1904 with Frederick Carder, an Englishman and Thomas G. Hawkes of Corning, New York. In 1918, the Corning Glass Company purchased the Steuben Works. Carder remained with the company and designed many of the pieces bearing the Steuben mark. The firm continues operating, producing glass of exceptional quality.

Vase. 6" high. "Pulled Feather." Iridescent blue with sterling overlay. Handles with stained glass inserts $1500.00

Atomizers

6½". Crystal. Black and gold rings. Complete .... $ 95.00
7". Iridescent gold. "Devilbiss." Complete 250.00

Basket. 8 x 12" o.h. Iridescent gold with magenta hi-lights. Signed and no'd 1250.00

Bowls

5½ x 2⅛" deep. Flared. Ivrene .. 65.00
8¾ x 3⅛" deep. Jade Green. Signed and no'd 75.00
10½ x 2½" deep. Iridescent gold and amethyst. Calcite obverse .. 375.00

Box. 3¼ x 5¾ x 9" long. Green Jade, acid-cut back. Pine cone decor 300.00

Cake Stand. 10". Pedestaled. Celeste Blue 95.00

Candlesticks

7½". Crystal. Deep socket, knob stem, bell-shaped base 125.00
7¾". Aurene. Pink and blue hi-lights. Signed and no'd. Pair 500.00
10". Jade Green and calcite. Optic Twist. Pair 600.00

Claret. 4¾" high. Celeste Blue 75.00

Compote. 8". Jade Green. Alabaster stem. Signed and no'd 500.00

Darner. Multicolored. Cased 95.00

Decanter, Stoppered. Amethyst 275.00

Finger Bowl. With underplate. Jade Green 100.00

Goblets

6¼". Topaz. Controlled bubbles, threading. Hollow stem 100.00
6¾". Selenium Red. Ball stem .. 60.00
7". Jade Green. Twist stem 90.00

Jar, Covered. 6" high. Threaded and ribbed body 175.00

Mug. 2⅝". Crystal. Applied handle. Applied blue and black threading. 125.00

Pitcher. 10½". Bristol Yellow. Black threading 185.00

Plate. 8½". Jade Green 75.00

Salt, Master. Jade Green 125.00

Shades, See "Lamp Shades"

Sherbets

Aurene and Calcite. With underplate 300.00
Jade Green. With underplate .. 150.00

Vases

5". Bulbous. Jade Green 250.00
5½ x 9" long. Rectangular. Jade Green acid-cut back. "Calla Lily." Signed Carder 550.00
7½". Urn-shaped. Crystal. "Moonlight." Applied threading and prunts 175.00
8". Bud. Blue Aurene 325.00
8". Fan-shaped. Selenium Red .. 200.00
8¼". Rose. Iridescent silver swirls. 750.00
8½ x 9" diam. Ivrene. Flared top. Ribbed body 325.00
10¼". Aurene. Blue and pink hi-lights. Shape #2548 .... 600.00
11". Amethyst. Cluthra 1000.00

Whiskey. 2¾". Jade Green 150.00

Wines

Green. Blown 65.00
Selenium Red. Intaglio cut 150.00

STEVENGRAPHS

All miniature silk weavings should not be classified as "Stevengraphs."

Thomas Stevens of Coventry, Warwickshire, England established his business to produce woven silk designs in 1854. He produced his first bookmark in 1862 and introduced his first Stevengraph in 1874. Stevens' bookmarks are relatively longer than they are wide and have mitred corners at one end and finished with a tassel. Stevens' name is ALWAYS woven into the silk at a mitred corner.

True Stevengraphs are miniature silk pictures, matted, framed and produced by Stevens.

Stevens' name was NEVER woven into a Stevengraph. His name may appear on the mat, along with the title of the picture.

Contrary to past information, Stevens' bookmarks were never sold at the New York Crystal Palace Exposition in 1853, simply because they did not exist at that time.

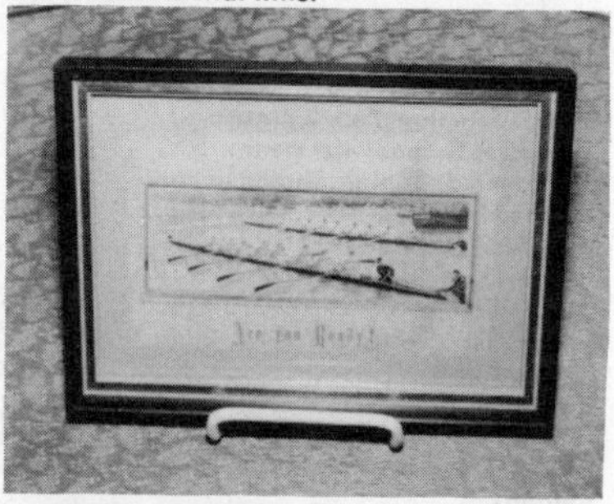

"Are You Ready." $150.00

EXAMPLE SHOWING REVERSE OF STEVENGRAPH

Bookmarks

Birthday Greetings	$ 150.00
*Centennial, Washington	165.00
Christmas Verse	85.00
Daughter	40.00
Home Sweet Home	125.00
The Lord Watch Between Me and Thee	65.00
To a Dear Friend	50.00

Stevengraphs

Are You Ready	150.00
Called to the Rescue	275.00
Crystal Palace, The. (exterior)	300.00
Crystal Palace, The. (interior)	750.00
Dick Turpin's Last Ride	350.00
Finish, The	225.00
First Set, The	450.00
First Touch, The	400.00
For Life or Death	350.00
Forth Bridge, The	500.00
Full Cry	250.00
God Speed the Plough	350.00
Good Old Days, The	325.00
Lady Godiva Procession	250.00
Landing of Columbus, The	350.00
Last Lap, The	350.00
Madonna and Child	1500.00
Meet, The	275.00
Present Time, The	500.00
Souvenir of the Wild West	750.00

*Reproduced Item

STEVENS AND WILLIAMS

In the late 19th century, the firm of Stevens and Williams, Stourbridge, England became one of the pioneers in producing a less expensive and commercial cameo glass. The original or earlier cameo glass was handcarved. It was produced mainly for exhibition purposes or for the wealthy. But as the demand increased, Stevens and Williams revised the method by employing the wheel and acid for the engraving. This hastened the production and subsequently made the glass available to more people. While the earlier cameo glass was of the classical design. Stevens and Williams' designs were influenced by the Orient. One of their foremost artists was also a botanist, which accounts for the many beautiful nature designs.

Biscuit Jars

Peachblow coloring. Applied glass feet. Ornate silver bail and cover $	400.00
8½" o.h. Melon-shaped body. Blue interior, white exterior. Applied flower and leaves. Amber thorn handle and feet	350.00

Bowls

7". Tortoise shell coloring. Scalloped rim. Applied birds and flowers	350.00

Sauce. 5½". Crystal with red strawberries. Gold leafed $150.00

10". Crystal. Applied apple, pear and leaves	450.00
Cologne Bottle. 8¾". Paneled. Green cut to crystal. Crystal stopper	225.00
Compote. 5¼ x 8¾" diam. Blue cut to crystal. "Willow."	450.00
Ewer. 12¼". Rose and white looped design. Applied frosted handle ..	600.00
Parfait. 5½" high. Jade green with alabaster stem and foot. Signed	75.00
Pitcher. 9". Amber. Blue handle and feet. Applied green leaves	350.00
Rose Bowl. 3". Arabesque. Cranberry and white	150.00
Vases	
3¾" diam. Light green, white interior. Deep pink loop pattern ..	450.00
5¾". Ruffled top. Pink and white loop pattern. Applied frosted rigaree, three feet	450.00
8". Ribbed. White to blue. "Morning Glory." Frosted	1250.00
8 x 6" diam. Cobalt cut to white. Dragonfly, flowers and etc	1500.00
10". Ruffled top. Green. Applied red cherries and flowers. Amber feet and handles	750.00
18½". Bulbous base. Slender neck, flared top. Amberina with light blue interior. "Swirl." Frosted	1000.00

STIEGEL-TYPE GLASS

America's first flint glass factory was founded by "Baron" Henry Stiegel at Manheim, Pennsylvania in the 1760's. Decorated bar and tableware were the main products of the establishment. Business thrived for a number of years; but extravagant living by Stiegel and the import of European glass caused the enterprise to fail.

Bottle. 6½". Clear. All over floral decor. Primary colors. Pewter collar ..$325.00

Bottles	
4⅜". Opaque blue. Floral decor in primary colors ....$	375.00

5⅜". Clear. Pewter collar. All over floral decor in primary colors 250.00
7". Clear. Enameled with distelfink bird, hearts and flowers in multicolors 295.00

Flip Glasses
3⅛". Clear. Polychrome decor of birds and flowers 225.00
3¾". 27 rib panels. Engraved leaf pattern 300.00
4". Distelfink bird with heart. Enameled in primary colors 400.00

Mug. 6¾". Clear. Applied strap handle. Engraved floral design .. 450.00

Pot. 4" high. Amethyst. Expanded Diamond and Daisy 1800.00

Salt, Master. Cobalt blue. Diamond Quilted. Applied foot 325.00

STONEWARE

Made from dense kaolin clay and commonly salt-glazed, stonewares were hand-thrown and high fired to produce a simple, bold vitreous pottery. Stoneware crocks, jugs and jars were produced for storage and utility purposes. This use dictated shape and design . . .solid, thick-walled forms with heavy rims, necks and handles with little or no embellishment. When decorated, the designs were simple . . .brushed cobalt oxide, incised or slip trails; also stamping or tooling.

Stoneware has been made for centuries and the early American settlers imported stoneware items at first. As English and European potteries refined their eathenwares, colonists began to produce their own wares. Two major North American traditions emerged based mainly on the location or type of clay. North Jersey and parts of New York were the first area . . .the second was eastern Pennsylvania spreading westward and into Maryland, Virginia and West Virginia. These two distinct locations, style of decoration and shape are discernible factors in classifying and dating early stoneware.

By the late 18th century, stoneware was manufactured in all sections of the country. During the 19th century, this vigorous industry flourished until glass 'fruit jars' appeared and the wide spread use of refrigeration. By 1910, commercial production of salt-glazed stoneware came to an end.

Bottle. 9¼". Impressed and blued "M. Robinson, 1879." ....$ 35.00

Butter Tub, Covered. 4¾ x 8¼". Brushed leaf decor 135.00

Canning Jars
"A. Conrad & Co., New Geneva, Pa." 45.00
"Hamilton & Jones, Greensboro, Pa." 45.00

Canning Jar. "Jas. Hamilton & Co. Greensboro, Pa." $45.00

Unknown maker. Brushed blue bands and flowers 75.00

Chicken Watering Pots
10". Brown glaze 35.00
10". Brushed blue bands 100.00

Chimney Pots
"Jos. Eneix Evans, New Geneva, Pa." 850.00
Unknown maker. Sewer tile 75.00

Churns
3¼". Miniature. Brown glaze. Complete 50.00
18½". "Whites, Utica, N.Y." Blue slip flower. Complete 750.00
3-Gallon. Brushed blue leaf decor. 250.00
4-Gallon. Brushed blue fish and banner. Attributed to Lyons, N.Y. 1250.00
6-Gallon. "Harrington & Burger. Rochester, N.Y." Bird of Paradise on daisy 900.00

Colanders
9". Brown glaze 75.00
14". Incised "Brotherton & David-ford, Patented Baltimore, Md." Brushed blue florals 275.00

Pitcher, 5½". Tanware. Pa. . . $300.00

Coolers

9¼ x 13¼". Lug handles. Brush blue leaf sprays. Impressed "3" . . 300.00

11 x 21½". Double. Covered. Lug handles. Brushed blue leaves on both pieces. Complete with pewter bung 700.00

Crocks

2-Gallon. "Cowden & Wilcox, Harrisburg, Pa." Man in the Moon . . 750.00

2-Gallon. "S. Hart and Son, Fulton, N.Y." Brushed blue leaves . 175.00

2-Gallon, "Frank B. Norton." Blue floral and swirl decor 175.00

2-Gallon. Unknown maker. Stencil of blue eagle and banner 350.00

3-Gallon. "C.W. Braum, Buffalo, N.Y." Brushed blue bird decor . . 375.00

3-Gallon. Covered. "S. H. Sonner, Strasburg, Va." Brushed blue leaves and trim 250.00

3-Gallon. "Warne & Letts, S. Amboy." Impressed and blued holly leaves 1500.00

3-Gallon. "Whites, Utica." Brushed blue bird 300.00

3-Gallon. Unknown maker. Blue slip bust of man 500.00

4-Gallon. "Jas. Hamilton & Co., Greensboro, Pa." Blue floral decor. 250.00

4-Gallon. T.F. Reppert, Greensboro, Pa." Stenciled blue eagle . . 500.00

4-Gallon. "Williams & Reppert, Greensboro, Pa." 185.00

4-Gallon. Unknown maker. Blue grapes 250.00

5-Gallon. "E.S. & B., New Brighton, Pa." Blue slip leaves . . 200.00

5-Gallon. "West Troy, N.Y." Deer decor 850.00

6- Gallon. Unknown maker. Brushed blue Mennonite figures; two women and child within wreath 1500.00

8-Gallon. Incised "J. Hamilton, Beaver Co." Cogglewheel marks 500.00

8- Gallon. "Hamilton & Jones, Greensboro, Pa." Brushed blue leaves 350.00

10-Gallon. "Williams & Reppert, Greensboro, Pa." Eagle decor 950.00

20-Gallon. "Donaghho Co., Parkersburg, W. Va." 250.00

Foot Warmer. 5½ x 11". "Pig." Cream glaze 100.00

Jars

1-Gallon. "F.B. Norton & Co., Worcester, Mass." Blue slip floral decor. 75.00

5-Gallon. "Hamilton & Jones, Greensboro, Pa." Blue stenciled eagle, brushed blue bands and leaf spray 300.00

Jugs

1-Gallon. "Hamilton & Jones, Greensboro, Pa." 65.00

2-Gallon. "Hagg & Abbott, Nashua, N.H." 100.00

2-Gallon. Nichols & Boynton, Burlington, Va." Blue floral sprays. 150.00

2-Gallon. "E. & L. P. Norton, Bennington, Vt." 225.00

3-Gallon. "N. Crawley, Wheeling, W. Va." Brushed blue florals, vines 300.00

4-Gallon. "Goodwin, Hartford" . . 125.00

5-Gallon. "Hoxton Ottman & Co., Ft. Edwards." Blue floral spray . . 200.00

Milk Pans

11½ x 4½" deep. Brushed blue leaves 100.00

13 x 5" deep. Cream glaze 75.00

Mug. 4". Brushed blue bands and leaves 75.00

Pitchers

5½". Tanware. Pa 300.00

9". "E. W. Farrington, Elmira, N.Y." Albany slip 35.00

9". Unknown maker. Brushed blue bands and flowers 250.00

10½". "James Hamilton & Co." Brushed blue bands 200.00

10½". Incised "W. H. Lehew, Strasburg". Repaired 500.00

10½". "Rabb & Rehm, Bloomsburg, Pa." Brushed blue flowers . . 125.00

12¾". Unknown maker. Brushed blue bands, cogglewheel marks ... 275.00
Spittoon. 5½ x 10". Brushed blue flowers ... 125.00

STRAWBERRY CHINA

This ware takes its name from the distinctive decorative motif . . .the Strawberry. There are three primary types; strawberries and strawberry leaves (often called Strawberry Lustre), green feather-like leaves with pink flowers (often called Cut Strawberry, Primrose or Old Strawberry) and a third type with the decoration in relief. The first two types are characterized by rust red moldings. Often called Strawberry Soft Paste, which it is not; all examples of this ware are handpainted on Creamware.

Strawberry was produced by many manufacturers, but Davenport created some of the finest forms of excellent quality. Marked pieces are uncommon.

"Strawberry" ranges from complete tea services to serving pieces; including platters. While the hollow wares are highly prized, flat pieces are more rare.

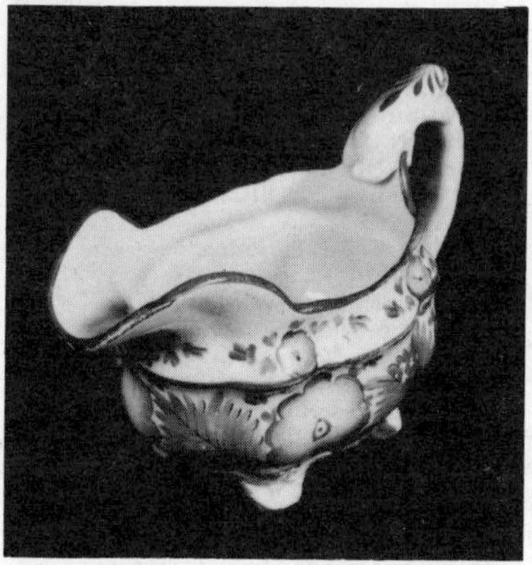

Creamer. 6¼'' long. ''Cut Strawberry." $300.00

Bowl. 6½" top diam., 3½" deep ..$ 350.00
Creamers
- 4½" long. Strawberries in relief .. 450.00
- 6¼" long. "Cut Strawberry." 300.00

Cup and Saucer. Handleless 325.00
Plates
- 5½" ... 225.00
- 6½" ... 275.00
- 8¼" ... 450.00
- 8¼". "Cut Strawberry." 275.00
- 10" ... 400.00

Soup Plate. 8¼" ... 295.00
Sugar, Covered. Footed. "Cut Strawberry." ... 250.00
Teapots
- 4¼ x 9½" ... 450.00
- 6 x 10½" Strawberries in relief. Repaired finial ... 400.00
- 7½ x 11". Footed. Sculptured handle ... 500.00

STRETCH GLASS

Stretch glass was produced by many glass manufacturers in the United States from the early 1900's through the 1920's. The most prominent makers were Cambridge, Fenton (who probably manufactured more Stretch glass than any others), Imperial, Northwood and even Steuben. Stretch glass can be identified by its iridescent, onionskin-like effect. Look for mold marks. Imports are blown and show a pontil mark and are not American Stretch Glass.

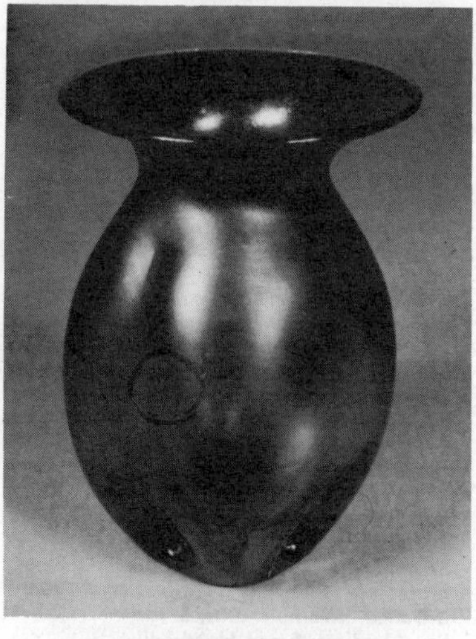

Vase. 8" high. Teardrop-shape with collar rim. Orange iridescent. Unsigned..................$65.00

Basket. 10¼" o.h. White ....$ 125.00
Bobeches. Scalloped. Vaseline. Pair . 35.00
Bowls
- 6½ x 2½" deep. Ribbed. Blue. Rolled edge ... 50.00
- 10x 2¾" deep. Black amethyst .. 100.00
- 10 x 4½" deep. Yellow iridescent. Imperial ... 85.00

Candlesticks. 8½". Blue. Pair 65.00
Compote, Covered. 9½ x 6" diam. Green. Imperial 50.00
Perfume Bottle, Stoppered. 5½". Bulbous, footed. Blue 75.00
Plates
- 8¼". Red. Paneled 60.00
- 12". Light green. Reticulated border 75.00

Rose Bowl. 3½ x 5". Melon ribbed. Pink 50.00
Sherbet. 4". Red. Melon ribbed 50.00
Tumble-Up. 6". Blue. Unsigned 75.00
Vases
- 5½". Pink. Signed Imperial 65.00
- 8½". Amberina. Signed Imperial . 125.00
- 14½". Blue. Flared scalloped rim. Unsigned 75.00

STRING HOLDERS

Grocery and dry goods stores found string holders to be useful items. Usually made of iron, there were two common types . . .the hanging holder and counter-top-type.

Iron. Beehive. 6½" $30.00

Glass
- Beehive. 4¾". Tin closure ......$ 35.00
- Beehive. 4¾ x 5¼" base. Clear with applied cobalt rim and collar. 150.00
- Sandwich 150.00
- Zipper and Prism. Cut. Sterling top 85.00

Iron
- Ball. 6½" 30.00
- Counter-type. 12" Pyramid cone .. 25.00
- Hanging-type. 4" 28.50

Pottery. 9¾". Cone-shaped. Brown glaze 35.00

SUGAR CASTORS

Muffineers, sugar shakers or sugar castors . . . all served the same purpose . .to 'sugar' muffins, scone or toast. They were much in vogue in the late Victorian era. Larger than salt or pepper shakers, ranging in sizes from four to six inches high, they were made in a variety of materials.

Milk Glass. Handpainted floral decor $25.00

Bisque. Pink. Art Nouveau decor in relief. Self top ....$ 65.00
Cranberry
- Cut Bands. Silverplated top 55.00
- Optic. Bulbous base. Silverplated top 75.00
- Ribbed, Ten. Silverplated top 55.00
- Venetian Diamond. Ornate silverplated top 85.00

Cut Glass. Six panels separated with deep cut notches. Sterling top 85.00
Emerald Green
- Paneled. Sterling top 85.00
- Ribbed. Enameled flower decor. Silverplated top 75.00

Leaf Mold
- Blue satin. Northwood 150.00
- Cranberry, Cased. Spattered with mica flecks 175.00
- Yellow, Cased. Original top. Northwood 145.00

Milk Glass
Acorn
Blue 75.00
Pink 125.00
Apple Blossom 65.00
Forget-me-not
Blue. Cased in silver filigree .. 125.00
Green 85.00
Pink 95.00
White 55.00
Opalescent. See "Opalescent Glass"
Quilted Phlox
Amethyst 95.00
Pink 75.00
Sapphire blue 85.00
Rubina. Optic 85.00
Satin Glass
Butterscotch, Cased. "Raindrop". Shades to pink to white. 2-piece sterling top 250.00
Green. Egg-shaped. Blue and purple decor. Original top 165.00
Pink. Shading to yellow. Decorated with white florals, green leaves. Original pewter top . 175.00
Silver
Continental. Ribbed and scroll decor in relief. C. 1800 .... 275.00
Sterling. Signed Theodore B. Starr . 125.00
Silverplated. English. Hallmarked ... 55.00

SUNBONNET BABIES

Molly and Mae, the Sunbonnet Babies were created in the early 1900's by Bertha Louise Corbett. Although she was a talented artist, Miss Corbett had no confidence in her ability to draw faces . . .so she tried hiding the faces of her little darlings under large bonnets and the Sunbonnet Babies were born. The "Babies" were an instant success . . .illustrations of them were first used on postcards and greeting cards; then story books, quilts, porcelains and prints. "The Sunbonnet Babies Primer" was the first school primer printed in four colors. Royal Bayreuth China Co. in Germany produced most of the porcelain. Interest in all these items continues to this day and in recent years, Royal Bayreuth has brought out new Sunbonnet Babies plates and bells. Postcards are being reproduced and applique-embrodery patterns have been reprinted.

Books
ABC. 1935 edition ....$ 50.00
At Work. 1906 edition 85.00
In Italy. 1922 edition 65.00
In Mother Goose Land. 1936 edition 50.00
Primer. 1902 edition 125.00
Bowls
1¾". Miniature. "Mending." R.B. 135.00

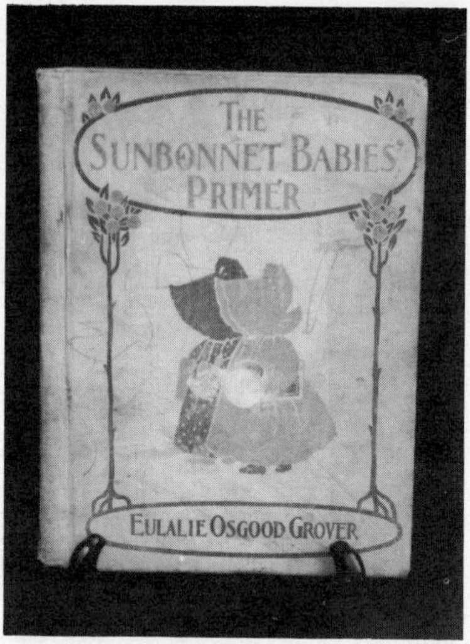

Primer. 1902 Edition $125.00

6". "Ironing." R.B. 150.00
8". Three ball feet. Gold trim. "Ironing." R.B. 195.00
Candlestick. "Fishing." 185.00
Chamberstick. Ring handle. "Cleaning." 225.00
Cup and Saucer. Gold handle. "Fishing." R.B. 175.00
Egg Cup. Double. "Sewing." 75.00
Feeding Dish. "Washing." 250.00
Nappy. 5". "Washing." 175.00
Pitchers
3". "Fishing." R.B. 125.00
3¾". "Cleaning." R.B. 150.00
5¾". "Washing." R.B. 185.00
Plates
6¼". "Washing." R.B. 95.00
7". "Ironing." R.B. 135.00
8". "Ironing." R.B. 155.00
10½". Cake. Open handles. "Washing." R.B. 250.00
Post Cards
Days of the Week. Ullman Mfg. Co. C. 1905. Set of 7 .... 150.00
Months of the Year. Set of 12 .... 200.00
Prints
Days of the Week. Series 106. Signed Corbett. Set 275.00
Months of the Year. 6 x 8". Ullman Mfg. Co. C. 1906. Each 35.00
Relish Dish. 4 x 9½". "Fishing." R.B. 195.00
Rose Bowl. 4". "Cleaning." R.B. 150.00

Sugar Castor. 5½". "Cleaning." R.B. ... 285.00
Sugar, Open. "Ironing." R.B. 150.00
Tile 6". "Fishing" R.B. 150.00
Toothpick. "Cleaning." R.B. 150.00
Trays
5½". Diamond-shaped. "Mending." R.B. 100.00
7 x 10". "Washing." R.B. 250.00
Vases
3½". Footed. "Washing." R.B. .. 185.00
4¼". "Ironing." R.B. 200.00
6¼". "Mending." R.B. 275.00

SUNDERLAND LUSTRE

Sunderland ware is a course type of cream-colored earthenware with a marbled or spotted pink lustre decoration which shades from pink to purple. A solution of gold compound applied on a white body developed the many shades of pink lustre . . .shades were determined by thickness of metallic film. Decorated with transfer prints of commemorative and sentimental scenes and inscriptions, these wares were produced by Adams, Bailey & Batkin, Copeland and Garrett, Wedgwood, Enoch Wood and many others. Also see "Pink Lustre China."

Pitcher. "The Lots of Gold is much, Etc." 5½" $325.00

Boxes, Covered
2½ x 3½ x 5". Comic black transfer on cover. ....$ 95.00
2½ x 4 x 6". Black transfer of English scene 125.00
Bowls
"Sailor's Farewell" and "Sailor's Return." 10" 425.00
View from the Cast Iron Bridge. 10" 275.00
Chalice. 4½". "Cloud." 100.00

Cups and Saucers
"Babes in the Woods" 125.00
"Cloud." Handled. Allerton 50.00
Jugs-Pitchers
"Christ is my pilot-wise, etc." 4¾." 175.00
"Home is a name of more than, etc." 5" 275.00
Hunting scene in black transfer. Allover pink lustre. 6" 185.00
"Sailor's Departure." 5¾" 295.00
"Success to the Tars of Old England." 5½" 375.00
Mugs
"Cloud." 65.00
"Faith, Hope." 150.00
Frog. Mariner's compass and John Bull 250.00
"Peace and Plenty." Ship on reverse 150.00
"Sailor's Tears." 150.00
Mustache Cup. Ship transfer and verse in black 125.00
Plaques. 8½ x 9½"
"Farmer's Prayer." 175.00
"Peace and Plenty." 250.00
"Prepare to Meet Thy God" 150.00
Salt Dip. "Cloud." 25.00
Shakers. Salt and Pepper. "Cloud." Pair 75.00
Sugar Castor. "Cloud" 75.00
Teapots
"Cloud." Medium 195.00
"Cloud." Large 175.00

SWANSEA

This superb pottery and porcelain was made at Swansea (Glamorganshire, Wales) as early as the 1760's and production continued until 1870; but the most highly collectible examples are those made before 1830.
Marks on Swansea vary . . .the earliest was SWANSEA impressed under glaze to DILLWYN under glaze after 1805. CAMBRIAN POTTERY was stamped in red under glaze from 1803-1805. Many fine examples, including the Botanical series in Pearlware, are not marked but may have the botanical name stamped under glaze.
Dark brown mouldings at the rim of plates and serving dishes is a characteristic of Swansea porcelain, but not a sure mark of identification. Often, fine examples of Swansea may show imperfections such as firing cracks . . .these pieces must be considered mint because this is the way they left the factory.
Documented examples have not appeared in enough numbers to make Swansea popular, although it is eagerly sought by advanced collectors.

Serving Dish. Botanical Series. Lily, Pink. 11½". Oblong. C. 1805 ......$325.00

Plates

7¾". Creamware. Reticulated. Handpainted flowers. Marked Dillwyn. C. 1805 ....$ 185.00

9". "Gaudy Welsh." Marked Dillwyn. C. 1810 .... 125.00

Punch Bowl. Earthenware. In manner of Oriental porcelain. Marked Cambrian Pottery. C. 1803-05 .. 950.00

Serving Dishes, Botanical Series.

Pearlware

Lily, Pink. 11½". Oblong. C. 1805 .... 325.00

Nightshade. 8". Square. C. 1805 .... 155.00

Sweetpeas. 8". Square. C. 1805 165.00

Tray, Dessert. 9½". Creamware. Handpainted. Polychrome with gilding. Marked Swansea under glaze. C. 1780 .... 275.00

TEA CADDIES

Tea was a precious commodity in the past. Special boxes or caddies were used as containers to accommodate different teas, including a mixing cup for blending. Elegant caddies, storing rare teas, were placed in the dining room apart from the easy accessibility of kitchen servants.

Brass. 5¼" high. Cylindrical ....$ 50.00

Lacquered. 6½ x 9". Black, gold stenciling, shaped corners, pewter interior. Chinese 350.00

Mahogany. 6 x 6½ x 10". Complete with glass mixing cup 175.00

Mahogany. 6 x 6x 10½". Brass handle, lock. 18th century 265.00

Porcelain. 4 x 5". Ivory ground, berry decor on front panel, gold trim. Royal Worcester 165.00

Sheffield-type. 4½" high. Silver on copper. Children in relief. English ..$85.00

Rosewood. 5 x 6½ x 10". Fruitwood inlays, ivory pulls, brass hinges, 2 compartments 150.00

Satinwood. 5 x 7½". Shell inlay, 2 compartments. C. 1790 .... 350.00

Tole. 4" high. Cylindrical. Floral decor. Early 195.00

TEA LEAF LUSTRE

Tea Leaf Lustre also known as Lustre Band with Sprig is the name given to white ironstone decorated with a stylized copper lustred tea leaf. It was produced by various American and English potteries.

Sauce Boat. With underplate. Burgess $45.00

Bone Dish. Scalloped rim. Meakin.	$ 35.00
Bowls	
9½". Square. Clementson	60.00
10". Oval. Scalloped. Johnson	75.00
Butter, Covered. With insert. Meakin	75.00
Butter Pat. Meakin	15.00
Coffee Pot. 9". Meakin	125.00
Cups and Saucers. Handleless	
Meakin	35.00
Shaw	55.00
Pitchers	
Milk. 8". Mayer	45.00
Water. 12". Shaw	95.00
Plates	
7¾". Burgess	20.00
8½". Meakin	15.00
9". Grindley	17.50
10". Cake. Meakin	55.00
Platters	
12". Meakin	35.00
13". Shaw. Open handles	55.00
14". Burgess	40.00
Sauce. Meakin	10.00
Sauce Boat. With underplate. Shaw	50.00
Shaving Mug. Shaw	50.00
Sugar, Covered. Meakin	60.00
Teapot. Meakin	85.00
Vegetables, Covered	
6¼ x 9". Wilkinson	40.00
5 x 10½". Furnival and Sons	55.00

TEA WAGONS

(See "Furniture")

TELEPHONES

Telephones are designed to modulate, transmit and reproduce audible sounds at a distance. The basic principle of this type of communication was developed in Germany as early as 1854. Alexander Graham Bell was granted the first American patent in 1876 for his electromagnetic telephone.

Since that time, the telephone has gone through many evolutions . . .improving in structure, design and function. Many so-called improvements occurred earlier than is commonly thought . . .in 1892, Automatic Electric Co. developed the first push-button phone using telegraph keys.

In that same year, Almon Brown Strowger invented the dial phone and his patent for automatic switching still holds today. By 1900 there were over 300 phone manufacturers including such companies as Ericsson, B&B, Chicago and Western Electric.

Early telephones came in two basic model types . . .the candlestick phone and the cased wall phone.

Candlestick-type	
Dean Electric. Non-dial	$ 75.00

Wall-type. "Long Distance Telephone Mfg. Company." Straight oak case $200.00

Kellogg. Dial	65.00
Kellogg. Non-dial	50.00
Stromberg. Nickelplated trim. Dial	100.00
Western Electric. Non-dial	85.00
Desk-type	
Cradle. Black bakelite. C. 1930's	10.00
French-style. C. 1920's	50.00
Lineman's. Western Electric. Oak case. Complete with leather strap.	75.00
Wall-type	
American Electric. Oak case, plain front.	200.00
Automatic Electric. Improved rotary. C. 1905	450.00
Centralia. Chicago Parts. Wet battery. Carved oak case	1000.00
Centralia. Ericsson Parts. Wet battery. Carved oak case	3000.00
Chicago Gibson Girl. Glass front	1500.00
Ericsson. Fiddleback. Copper-plated. Plain front. Sweden	350.00

Ericsson. Fiddleback. Copper-plated, chrome trim. Sweden 400.00
J.E. Atkinson. Oak case. All original. Swedish-American. C. 1910 .... 400.00
Kellogg. Oak case. Brass trim 250.00
Monarch. Straight walnut case. Plain front 175.00
Stromberg. Oak case. Plain 200.00
Western Electric. Fiddleback. Hook and switch and hand set 650.00
Western Electric. #4. With cow bells 450.00
Western Electric. Oak case with cathedral top. Double box 375.00
Western Electric. Straight oak case. Single box 275.00

TEPLITZ

Teplitz wares were manufactured in the Bohemian province of Czechoslovakia, the location of the city of Teplitz. They reached their peak of production when this area was part of the Austrian-Hungarian Empire. An early 1900 industrial directory lists 26 ceramic manufacturers in Teplitz. Teplitz wares consisted of four main bodies . . .pottery, low-fired stoneware, true vitreous stoneware and porcelain. The wares were molded, cast and hand decorated. Transfer decorations were not used. The general shapes and decor have an Art Nouveau or Art Deco style with an influence of the Viennese School of Secession.

There may be exceptions but most wares were marked "Teplitz", "Turn-Teplitz" or "Turn" (a city near Teplitz). As in any of the arts, superior and inferior grades of work exist.

Basket. 5½ x 8". Basketweave body. Applied multicolored flowers ....$ 175.00

Bowls

5". Bulbous. Blossoms on ivory ground. Gold trim 65.00
5½ x 11". Rectangular. Acorns with jeweled centers 200.00

Bust. 8½" high. Lady 150.00

Candlestick. 13". Applied flowers. Gold trim 65.00

Ewers

6½". Portrait decor on front 200.00
8¾". Bulbous base. Insects and flowering branches on cobalt ground 100.00

Vase. 14½". Florals in relief. "Crown-nookware." Artist signed $195.00

Lamp. 13" high. Art Nouveau-style. Multicolored base and shade. C. 1895 .... 175.00

Vases

6". Gray-green. Berries in relief .. 65.00
6". Amphora-type. Woodland scene and jeweled florals 100.00
8". Handled. Lady's portrait. Gold trim. Signed Stellmacher 200.00
9". Thistle and leaf decor. Emerald ground. Gold trim 185.00
12½". Bulbous base. Two ornate handles. Handpainted tulip decor on cream ground 135.00
15". Bulbous. Maroon with gold trim. Silver jewel teardrops. Marked "Teplitz Turn" 225.00
19½". Cream ground. Red florals, green leaves. Gold trim 325.00

TERRA COTTA WARE

Terra Cotta is another name applied to wares made of a hard, semi-fired ceramic clay. The color of the pottery ranges from a light orange-brown to a deep brownish-red.

Art objects, utilitarian wares and architectural elements were made of this material. The finished products were usually left unglazed, but they may be found partially or completely glazed, and-or decorated with slip designs, incised or carved.

Figurine. 9¼x9¾". Costumed Orientals. Seal signed. Chinese. C. 1830-40 .... $750.00

Cup and Saucer. Glazed. Undecorated .... $ 40.00

Figurines. 9½" high. Oriental man and woman. Glazed. Pair 225.00

Foot Bath. 10 x 18". Yellow glazed interior 65.00

Mug. 6½". Raised dragon decor. Dragon tail handle 85.00

Plaques. 7 x 9". Dutch Fishermen. Pair 125.00

Teapot. 3⅛". Green and yellow enamel decor. C. 1900 .... 50.00

Tobacco Jar. 10". Man in swallow-tail coat, white vest, skull cap .. 125.00

Vases

5". Dragons in relief 65.00

5". Urn-shaped. Threaded. Unglazed 50.00

12". Dragons in relief 100.00

TEXTILES

Textiles are cloth or fabric items, especially anything woven or knitted. Within the recent period of collecting called nostalgia, certain textiles are sought by those who wish to remember elegant household appointments of the past and such items as coverlets, table covering, domestic linens and quilts demand new attention.

Quilt prices will vary considerably according to age, condition, artistic design and use of color, workmanship and fabric. For example; a contemporary quilt, made of older fabric, will be of more value than one fashioned of more recent materials. Pattern of the quilting is also important . . .imaginative designs and shapes such as hearts and flowers, etc. are valued over straight-line quilting.

Coverlet. 84" square. With two pillow shams. "YoYo". C. 1920. Set .. $175.00

Bedspreads

Crochet. "Petal Medallion." Off white. 94 x 111" .... $ 250.00

Linen. Hand embroidered. Floral design. 72 x 102" 195.00

Coverlets, Woven

73 x 76". Beige ground with green, red and blue. Fruit trees, wreaths and medallion decor. Eight-sided stars on bottom and top edge. Signed and dated 1861 500.00

Wall Hanging. Crewel. Framed. 23½" diam. $250.00

74 x 88". Eagles. "Independence, Virtue, Liberty." Red, tan and ivory	850.00
84 x 103". "Snail Trail." Three sections. Blue and white overshot ..	250.00
Handkerchief. Battenburg Lace. 12" square	15.00
Lace	
4½" wide. Crochet. Ecru. One yard	10.00
5½" wide. Worked on Linen. Ecru. One yard	15.00
Pillow Cases. Muslin	
Bolster-size. White satin stitch embroidery. Scalloped edges. Monogrammed	10.00
Tatted inserts and edging. Pair ..	10.00
Pillow Shams. Linen. Hemstitched. Pair	30.00
Quilts	
Axe. Pink and white. 78 x 84" ..	100.00
Checkerboard. Red and white. 66 x 82". Amish. C. 1920	275.00
Crazy. Silk and satin. 62 x 78" ..	125.00
Irish Chain, Double. Green on white. 72 x 79"	225.00
Log Cabin. 78" square. Pa. Mennonite. C. 1925	375.00
Maple Leaf. Green on burgundy. 78" square. Ohio Amish. C. 1940.	250.00
Nine Patch. Red, white and blue. 68 x 78". Lancaster County, Pa ..	175.00
Patchwork. Silk on velvet. Embroidery. 43 x 67"	150.00
Star of Bethlehem. Purple, lavender, dark sea green, maroon and pink. 66 x 76". Amish	500.00
Tic Tac Toe. Pink and blue. 68 x 75". C. 1908	100.00
Wedding Ring. Yellow. 72 x 84"	175.00
Quilt Tops	
Hexagon. Printed cotton with pink centers. 76 x 82"	50.00
Patchwork. Hand sewn. White cotton border. 76 x 96"	75.00
Ribbon. Satin. 1" wide. White with hand embroidered violets and green leaves. One yard	15.00
Rug, Braided. Wool. Reversible. Multicolored. 54 x 82"	75.00
Rugs, Hooked	
Black with flowers and initialed. 30 x 64"	125.00
Stained glass pattern. Multicolored. 30 x 40" Signed. C. 1900	95.00
Winter scene. 30 x 40". New England	55.00
Runner. Battenburg Lace. 18 x 60"...	75.00
Shawls	
Paisley. Wool. Self fringed. 62 x 63"	125.00
Silk, woven. Yellow. Six inch self fringe. 51" square	100.00
Sheets, Linen	
Hemstitched border. 72 x 100" ..	50.00
Homespun. Seamed center. Full size	85.00
Tablecloths	
Battenburg Lace. 48" diam	85.00
Damask. "Holly." 70 x 72". Six napkins. Hand hemmed. Set	75.00
Linen. 66x 100". Twelve napkins. Hand hemstitched. Set	250.00
Towel. Linen. Homespun. White. Knotted fringe. 22 x 35"	15.00
Wall Hangings	
Crewel. Framed. Flowers in vase. Animals in foreground. 19th century. 17¼ x 19¾"	350.00
Needlepoint	
Floral design. Framed. Signed and dated 1842. 23½ x 24" ..	300.00
"Rebecca at the Well." Wool. 24½ x 32"	200.00
"The Flight Into Egypt." Wool. 20 x 24"	150.00

THREADED GLASS

Glass decorated with applied threads is called Threaded Glass. The process was used extensively both aboard and in the United States during the 19th century.

In the beginning, the glass threads were applied by hand. In 1876, an Englishman patented the first apparatus to apply the threads mechanically.

Threaded Glass was produced in quantity and

varying degrees of quality by practically every major glass factory and definite attribution is almost impossible.

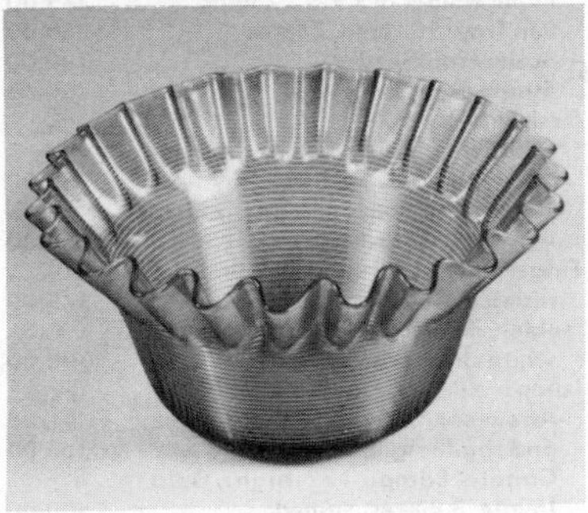

Finger Bowl. Chartreuse on clear. Fluted edge $65.00

Berry Set. 10" bowl, six 4" bowls. Cobalt on clear. Set .... $ 225.00

Biscuit Jar. 5" high. Rose on clear. Applied feet 135.00

Decanter. 10". Blown, ground stopper. Gold on clear 165.00

Ewer. 7½". Applied crystal leaf form handle. Applied cyrstal petal-shaped feet. Cranberry on clear 125.00

Finger Bowls. With underplates
- Cranberry on clear. Gold trim 75.00
- Cranberry on clear. Fluted edge. Sandwich 175.00
- Teal Blue on clear 55.00
- Vaseline on clear 85.00

Jam Jar. Silverplated lid and handle. Pink on clear 85.00

Pitchers
- 5¼". Tankard-shaped. Applied handle. Cranberry on clear 125.00
- 11½". Bulbous. Applied handle. Cranberry on clear 225.00

Tumblers
- Juice. Green on clear 20.00
- Lemonade. Applied handle. Pink on clear. Sandwich 100.00
- Water. Cranberry on clear. Sandwich 85.00

Vases
- 3". Bulbous. Clear rigaree top. Cranberry on green 95.00
- 4". Tear-drop shape. Ruffled top. Blue on clear 35.00

TIFFANY ITEMS

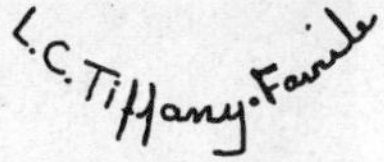

Louis Comfort Tiffany (1849-1934) established a glass house in 1878 primarily to make stained glass windows. It was here he developed a unique type of colored glass called Favrile . . .the name derived from the old English "Fabrile" meaning handmade. His Favrile glass differed from other art glass in manufacture as it was a composition of colored glass worked together while hot. The essential characteristic is that ornamentation is found within the glass. Favrile was never further decorated . . .different effects were achieved by varying the amount and position of colors which project movement in form and shape. In 1890, in order to utilize surplus materials, at the plant, Tiffany began to design and produce "small glass", such as iridescent glass lamp shades, vases, stemware and tableware in the Art Nouveau manner. Almost all of the early blown glass reportedly went to museums. Commercial production began in 1896. Most Tiffany wares are signed with the name L.C. Tiffany or the initials L.C.T. Some pieces also carry the word "Favrile" as well as a number.

Tiffany items marked with an "X" were not for sale. An "O" indicated a special order, and "A-Coll" indicated Tiffany had selected that piece for his own collection.

Prefix and suffix marks can be used to date Tiffany pieces. Prefixes A through N (1896-1900), P through Z (1901-1905) and suffixes A through N (1906-1912), P through Z (1913-1920).

Louis Tiffany and the artists in his studio are also well-known for fine work in other art areas . . . bronzes, pottery, jewelry, silver and enamels.

Compote. 7". Low standard. Bronze. MOP inlay $275.00

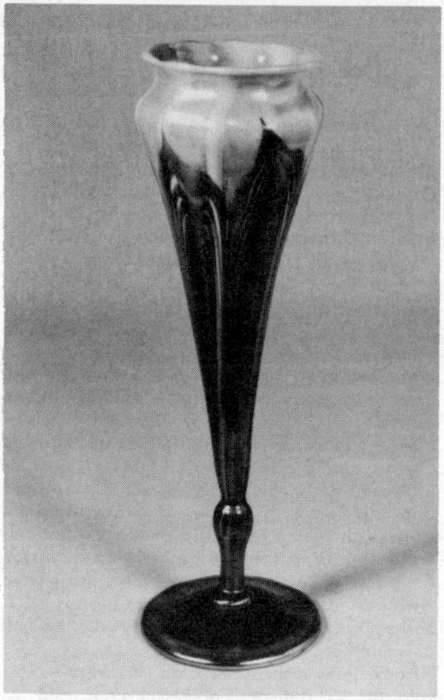

Vase. 11¾". "Pulled Feather." Green $850.00

Bowls
- 5". Scalloped rim. Blue iridescent $ 350.00
- 8¼". Blue iridescent. Favrile 750.00
- 12". With flower frog. Green lily pads and vines 1250.00

Candlesticks
- 4½". Gold and blue iridescent .. 350.00
- 11½". Gold iridescent 500.00
- 19". Bronze 750.00

Champagnes
- 5½". Intaglio cut 250.00
- 7½". Pastel pink. Venetian green foot 300.00
- 8". Turquoise iridescent 350.00

Compote. 6". Low standard. Iridescent blue. 600.00

Cordial. Gold iridescent 250.00

Cream and Sugar. 3". Tankard-shaped. Gold iridescent. Set 750.00

Cup. 2¼" high. Amber. Green lily pads. Favrile 750.00

Desk Accessories
- Blotter. Rocker-type. Adams 125.00
- Blotter-ends. 12". Zodiac. Pair .. 175.00
- Calendar Holder. Zodiac 175.00
- Inkwell. 2½ x 3¼ x 3¼". Pine Needle 150.00
- Inkwell. Double. Venetian 300.00
- Letter Opener. 10½" long. Zodiac 95.00
- Letter Rack. 5 x 6½". Pine Needle 175.00
- Match Box Holder. Pine Needle .. 75.00
- Paper Holder. 6 x 9½". Zodiac .. 275.00
- Pen Tray. 10" long. Zodiac 250.00
- Scale. Pine Needle 300.00
- Stamp Box. Grapevine 150.00

Desk Sets
- American Indian. Blotter, calendar, holder, inkwell, pen tray 750.00
- Geometric. Blotter-ends, clock, inkwell, pen rack, tray 1850.00

Finger Bowl. With underplate. Gold iridescent 375.00

Goblet. 9". Flower form. Pink with white striations 300.00

Lamps
- Arrowroot. 20" diam. shade. Base and shade signed 20000.00
- Candle Lamp. 12" high. Gold favrile. 3 pieces. Signed 1500.00
- Dragonfly. Hanging Head. 22½" diam. shade. Base and shade signed 45000.00
- Lily. 3-lite. Signed 2600.00
- Lily. 12-lite. 4' 7" high. Signed .. 18000.00
- Pine Needle. 11¾" high x 16¼" diam. shade. Signed 3500.00
- Poinsettia. 22½" diam. shade. Base and shade signed 45000.00
- Roman. 25" diam. shade. Base and shade signed 19500.00

Parfait. 5" high. Gold iridescent. Favrile 275.00

Perfume Bottle. 3½". Molded floral form. Iridescent blue and amber. Matching sterling stopper 1650.00

Pitcher. 10". Green. Etched with grapes and leaves. Favrile 1000.00

Plates
- 6". Gold iridescent 325.00
- 8". Iridescent turquoise 295.00
- 8½". Iridescent blue. Leaf decor in center 375.00

Salts
- 2½" diam. Ruffled edge. Gold iridescent 135.00
- 3". Footed. Ruffled rim. Gold iridescent 200.00

Vases
- 3½". Ribbed. Gold iridescent 175.00
- 6". Bud. Pink pulled feather 500.00
- 6¾". Baluster-shaped. Paperweight-type. Muted greens, ochre base. Blue and green leaf decor .. 3500.00
- 7½". Red swirled and feather on gold iridescent 2500.00
- 8½". Ovoid-shaped. "Tel El Amarna". Green with black and gold bands. Favrile 5000.00
- 9¼". Iridescent blue. Pulled-up green leaves and stems. Favrile .. 1500.00

10½". Urn-shaped. Handled.
Gold iridescent 1250.00
11". Flower form. Gold iridescent with red and blue highlights 2000.00
12". Paperweight-type. "Narcissus" 9500.00
12". Pottery. Blossoms in relief .. 1750.00
15½". Trumpet-shaped. Iridescent amber and green. Bronze base 3000.00

Wines
Iridescent gold. Favrile 300.00
Opalescent to green 250.00

TIFFIN GLASS

The Tiffin Glass Company, a subsidiary of U.S. Glass Company continues operating in Tiffin, Ohio.

During the period between 1923-1926, they produced a line of black glassware . . . sometimes referred to by collectors as "Black Satin." Although the black glass seems to be the most favored; the firm also produced other colored glass, manufactured blanks for other concerns and did a limited amount of cutting themselves.

Vase. 5". Bulbous. "Poppy." Black satin $35.00

Box, Covered. 5" diam. Black Satin $ 35.00
Candleholder. Saucer-type. Black Satin 35.00

Compotes
5 x 7" diam. Crystal. Paper label .. 25.00
7 x 8¾" diam. Optic. Blue with crystal stem. Paper label 40.00

Console Set. Bowl with base, 9½". Two candlesticks, 8½". Frosted yellow 95.00

Cornucopias. 8 x 13"
Blue 45.00
Crystal 35.00

Dog, Seated. 7" high. Amber. Jeweled eyes 75.00
Goblet. Fuschia 20.00
Jar, Covered. 4½ x 8" diam. Black Satin with red and yellow coralene 95.00
Pheasant. 13" high. Blue 95.00

Rose Bowls
Canterbury. Crystal 25.00
Poppy. Black Satin 40.00

Stemware. Optic. Blue and crystal. 36 pieces 350.00
Tumblers. Black Satin. Set of 8 .... 100.00

Vases. Bulbous
5". Poppy. Black Satin 35.00
7". Optic. Light blue 30.00
8". Jonquil. Frosted and clear .. 35.00
8½". Poppy. Frosted blue 35.00
10". Iris. Black Satin 50.00
11". Poppy. Black Satin 75.00

TILES

Decorative and utilitarian tiles have been made through out the years by various potteries in the United States and abroad. Their usages are varied . . .from small tea tiles or table-top protectors to fireplace facings, floors and walls.

Wedgwood. "Jonathan." $85.00

American Encaustic Tile Co. Monk seated at table holding tankard. 6" ....$ 45.00
Copeland. Two related country scenes. W. Yale. 6 x 12". Pair 150.00

Delft-type. Blue frigate on white ground. 6" 10.00
Grueby Faience & Tile Co. Green matte finish. 3" 15.00
Hamilton Tile Works. Grecian Woman holding jug over shoulder. Green plaque. 7¼ x 13". 115.00
Low, J.G. Art Tile Works. Bust of Grover Cleveland. Carmel brown glaze. 1885. 4¼ x 6" 100.00
Mintons China Works. "A Midsummer Night's Dream." 35.00
Moravian Pottery & Tile. Castle, swan and verse. 4" 35.00
Moravian Pottery & Tile. Zodiac. 4" . 25.00
Mosaic Tile Co.
  Bear. Black. 5¾ x 10¼" 95.00
  Floral decor 15.00
  Geometric decor 15.00
  Lincoln, A. White on blue 40.00
Murdock Parlor Grate. Lady beside fireplace, verse, etc. Golden amber. Stove-type 25.00
Provententical Tile Works. Girl's portrait. 6" 55.00
Tiffany. Medallions. Orange and black. 4" 175.00
Wedgwood
  Calendar. C. 1900 .... 75.00
  Memorial Hall, Harvard University. C. 1919 .... 65.00
  U.S. Navy Yard, Boston. C. 1917 .. 50.00

TIN CONTAINERS

Tin containers were used in the early part of the 20th century for the packaging of tobacco, medicines, chemicals, powders and various foodstuffs. Tins were manufactured in countless shapes, sizes and colors by U.S. and foreign companies.

Many were made plain and the companies would put on their own labels. On others, the name of the company was embossed or stamped into the tin.

Tin container collecting has become popular in the past several years. Old tins can be found almost everywhere. Prices vary greatly depending on the age and condition of the tin, and the location in which the tin is found.

CAUTION: A variety of tin containers are currently being produced in England exclusively for a United States firm. They are marked accordingly.

Baking Powder. Calumet. 12 oz. ..$ 7.50
Biscuit. Huntley & Palmer
  Artist's Studio. 7½ x 9" 150.00
  Books. Set of seven. With bookends 125.00
  Egyptian Scenes 55.00
  Grand Prizes. Paris 1878-1900 .. 85.00
  Lantern. 10" 95.00

Tin Containers. "Coffee."

  Wicker Hamper. C. 1904 ...... 125.00
  World Globe. C. 1900 .... 125.00
Biscuit. Loose-Wiles. Statue of Liberty. 3⅜ x 9⅜" 20.00
Candy
  Benson's English Toffee. S.S. Queen Mary. 2½ x 4 x 7" 15.00
  Hershey's Chocolate. Canister. 5 x 12¼" diam 25.00
  Tootsie Roll. 5c. 10 x 12½" 75.00
  Whitman's Prestige Chocolates. 1 lb. box. 7.50
Coffee
  Bower & Bartlett. Lithographed. Red, blue and gold. Bin 250.00
  Campbell's. Desert scene. 4 lbs. C. 1920 .... 50.00
  Golden Rule. Black with gold lettering. 12 x 12 x 16" 50.00
  Luzianne. Sample size. 3". C. 1938 .... 35.00
  Schottens. 13 x 19 x 19" 150.00
  Yale. Blue and white. 1 lb 15.00
Lard
  Straight, seamless edges. Bail handle. 3 lbs 5.00
  Straight, seamless edges. Side handles. 50 lbs 10.00
Peanut Butter
  Haligan's. 25 lb. pail 75.00
  Monarch. With Teenie Weenies. 1 lb. pail 95.00
  Squirrel. 10 lb. pail 65.00
  Sultana 1 lb. pail 40.00
Peanuts
  Cream Dove Salted Peanuts. Blue and yellow. 8½ x 10" 30.00
  Nut House Nuts. House and ship decor. 1 lb 30.00
  Pickaninny Brand Jumbo Salted Nuts. Yellow and red. 10 lbs. C. 1909 .... 75.00
  Planter's Peanuts. Blue label, red banner. 10 lbs 50.00
Spices. A.P. Paper labels. Each 3.00

Tea

English Breakfast. Oriental lady in garden. Black and gold. 13 x 16" 125.00
Lipton. Gathering tea leaves. 5 lbs 100.00
Tetley's. Yellow and green florals on red. 3" 10.00

Tobacco

Bond Street. Sample Pocket 50.00
Bull Dog. Pocket 35.00
Central Union. Lunch box 65.00
Chesterfield. Flat. 50's 7.50
Dutch Master's Cigars. Flat 3.50
Edgeworth Pipe. Canister 5.00
Fashion. Lunch box 150.00
Game Fine Cut Plug. Bin 175.00
Half & Half. Pocket 6.50
H-O Cut Plug. Lunch box 55.00
Lorillard's. Lunch box 30.00
Lucky Strike Roll Cut. Pocket 25.00
Mayo Roly Polys
  Dutchman 500.00
  Mammy 300.00
  Satisfield Customer 500.00
  U.S. Marine Storekeeper 650.00
Players Navy Cut. Flat. 50's 35.00
Prince Albert. Pocket 2.00
Sweet Clover Fine Cut. Bin 325.00
Sweet Cuba. Green. Bin 125.00
Tiger Bright Sweet Chewing Tobacco. Lunch box 75.00
Velvet. Sample pocket 45.00

TINSEL PICTURES

Tinsel pictures (or 'paintings') are basically a form of "cottage art" which enjoyed great popularity during the mid-19th century. The 'painting' was created by using bits and pieces of colorful foil as the primary media. A mother and her children worked on tinsel pictures as a family project. Designs are usually simple . . . still life, fruit, flowers and birds. Occasionally, an exceptionally talented artist produced a more sophisticated design. The prices quoted below are general since the value of a particular 'painting' is determined by quality of the art-work and intricacy of design.

Biblical Scene. 9½ x 12" $300.00
Bowl of Flowers. 9½ x 12" 95.00
Butterflies and Flowers. 8 x 10" 75.00
Floral Arrangement in Urn-shaped Vase. 15½ x 20" 250.00
Peacock on Wall. 25½ x 27½" 350.00
Wreath of Roses. 12½ x 16½" 150.00
Wreath of Roses with Birds. 17½ x 21½" 250.00

"Floral Arrangement in Vase." 28x35" $350.00

TINWARE
(See "Tole")

TOBACCO CUTTERS

Before pre-packaging, tobacco was delivered to merchants in bulk form. A special tool was used to cut the tobacco into desired sizes.

Unmarked. Wooden base with cast iron cutter $40.00

Arrow $28.50
*Black Beauty 45.00
Brown Mule 30.00
*Drummond Tobacco Co., St. Louis 40.00
Five Brothers Tobacco Co., Louisville, Kentucky 50.00
*Imp 85.00
P. Lorillard & Co 50.00
Piper Heidsieck Tobacco Works. Bottle-shaped 85.00

Spearhead. P.J. Sorg & Co 75.00
Standard. Reading Hardware 50.00
Star 60.00
Triumph 35.00

*Reproduced Item

TOBACCO JARS

A tobacco jar is a container for storing tobacco. Early tobacco humidors were made of various materials and shapes including figural-types.

"Caricature." 5¾". Majolica-type. German $50.00

B.P.O.E. Nakara...............$ 350.00
Baker. Majolica-type 75.00
Boy. 6¾". Cossack hat. Bisque 150.00
Bulldog. "Old Sport." Bristol-type glass 75.00
Cut Glass. Silverplated lid 150.00
Elephant. Majolica-type 100.00
Flowers. Handpainted on white ground 65.00
Frog. Smoking pipe. Majolica-type .. 85.00
Gnome. Woodlike texture 75.00
Human Skull. White 100.00
Indian. 5". Majolica-type 85.00
Jester with dog. 9½" high. Staffordshire 275.00
Jockey. Majolica-type 125.00
Maiden's Head. Art Nouveau-style... 175.00
Man with Derby. Austrian 65.00
Monkey. Pipe and sports hat. Majolica-type 100.00
Monkeys. Papier Mache 150.00
Owl. Majolica-type 65.00
Owl. Handpainted. Signed Handel . 395.00
Pirate. Majolica-type 100.00
Pouch. Drawstring-type. Place for pipe 65.00
Sea Captain. Majolica-type 100.00
Silverplated. Fitted interior. Embossed decor. Meriden Silver Co 175.00

TOBY JUGS

A Toby Jug is a drinking vessel usually depicting a full-figured, robust, genial drinking man. They originated in England in the late 18th century and the term "Toby" probably related to the character Uncle Toby from "Tristran Shandy" by Stern which reads: "Old Toby Philpot, A Thirsty old soul, As e'er drank a bottle, Or fathomed a bowl."

Within the last 100 years or more; Tobies have been copiously reproduced by many potteries in the United States and abroad. They are available in a wide price range and even the new versions of good quality are desirable.

Czechoslovakia
- Sairey Gamp ....$ 15.00

England
- Beswick. Winston Churchill. C. 1950 .... 100.00
- Burlington. Captain Hook. C. 1950 .... 75.00
- Burlington. Humpty Dumpty. C. 1950 .... 30.00
- Chelsea. Beefeater. C. 1950 .... 75.00
- Copeland-Spode. Winston Churchill 125.00
- Kirkman. Squire 50.00
- Ralph Wood. Martha Gunn. C. 1770-1780 .... 750.00
- Ralph Wood. Sailor. C. 1770-1780 750.00
- Royal Doulton. See "Royal Doulton"
- Royal Staffordshire. Woodrow Wilson. C. 1914 .... 225.00
- Shorter. Old King Cole. C. 1950 .. 75.00
- Shorter. Old Salt 45.00
- Staffordshire. Falstaff. 19th century 300.00
- Staffordshire. Toby Philpot. Brown high glaze. 19th century 125.00
- Wain. The Cardinal. C. 1950 .... 100.00
- Wood & Sons. Betsy 50.00

Germany
- Goebel Hummel. Santa Claus. C. 1940 .... 50.00
- Unmarked. Admiral Perry. C. 1900 .... 150.00

Staffordshire. "Hearty Good Fellow." $275.00

Match Safe. 6". Wall-type. Yellow with original decor $125.00

Japan
- English Character. Pre-1940's .. 25.00

United States
- Apgar Americraft. Long John Silver. C. 1960 .... 125.00
- Bennington. Benjamin Franklin .. 375.00
- Lenox. William Penn. Pink. C. 1938 .... 165.00
- Lenox. George Washington 450.00
- Syracuse. Herbert Hoover 125.00

TOLE
(Tinware)

Tole is the original name given to tinwares used for many household items such as boxes, pots and trays. The complete name is to'le peinte . . . French for sheet iron. Today, the term is the generic name applied to stenciled or hand decorated tinwares.

Candle Box. 14". Stenciled. Strap handles ....$ 150.00

Candle Snuffer with 8" tray. Stenciled. C. 1850 .... 95.00

Coffee Pots
- 6½". Black ground, gold stenciling, wood handle. C. 1860 .... 100.00
- 9". Tapered cylinder, flat lid, straight spout. Free hand decor, brown japan 550.00
- 11". Tapered cylinder, dome lid, goose neck spout, strap handle. Free hand florals 395.00

Creamer. 4". Free hand fruit decor, brown japan 135.00

Cutlery Tray. 3½ x 9½ x 14½". Center divider, handled. Original stenciling 85.00

Deed Boxes
- 3¾ x 4½ x 8". Free hand decor of red berries, leaves, etc. Hasp clasp, domed lid. C. 1825 ...... 135.00
- 6x 9x13". Red and gold stenciling, black japan 195.00

6½ x 7½x9½". Stenciled strawberries and flowers, brown japan 250.00
9x10½". Book-shaped. Red and yellow stenciling 250.00

Foot Bath. 27" diam. C. 1840 .... 165.00

Foot Warmer. 6½ x8½x8½". Original stenciling. Complete with pan. C. 1850 .... 250.00

Horn, Stagecoach. 59½". Trumpet-shaped. C. 1840 .... 295.00

Inkwell. 4½" oval. Yellow fretwork, 4-lion feet. With sander. C. 1810... 195.00

Match Safe. 6". Wall-type, fluted edges. Original stenciling 125.00

Mug. 4". Strap handle 65.00

Spice Box. 6 round cans, 2¾" high within a 3x6½x9" sliding container. Black with gold and red stenciling 100.00

Sugar, Covered. 3½ x4" diam. Free hand florals, brown japan 165.00

Sugar Castor. 5½" high. Original free hand decor 185.00

Tea Caddy. 4" high. Cylinder-shaped. Free hand leaf decor, brown japan 235.00

Trays
8½x12½". Apple. Flaring sides, free hand decor. C. 1840 ...... 275.00
19x25". Chippendale-style. Original stenciled gold leaf and scroll border, free hand floral center 295.00
20x30". Free hand and stenciled. Floral border, scenic center. Artist signed 350.00

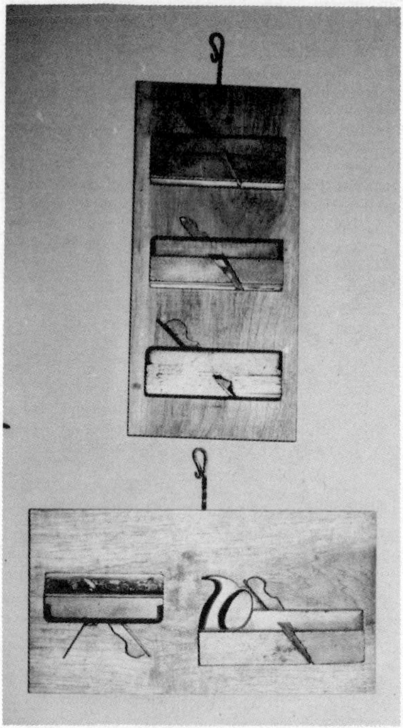

"Planes"

TOOLS

Before the advent of assembly line-mass production; practically everything required for living was hand made at home or by a local tradesman or craftsman. The cooper, the blacksmith, the cabinet maker . . .all had their special tools. Early examples of these hand tools are collected for their workmanship, ingenuity or design.

Adzes
Bowl. C. Whitehouse ....$ 75.00
Gutter. Hand-forged. Early 75.00

Auger. Hand-forged 10.00

Axes
Broad. Beatty. C. 1890 .... 75.00
Felling. Black Raven 50.00
Goosewing. Hand-forged. Early Pa 300.00
Hewing. Beatty 75.00
Mortise. Sample 150.00
Side. Cooper 75.00

Belt Slitter. Rosewood and brass. Osborn 75.00

Brace. Cooper. 4½" pad. Brass ferrule. Beech 200.00

Bung Hole Bore and Reamer 25.00

Caliper. 20". Unmarked 25.00

Chisel, Corner. Hand-forged. Early Pa 40.00

Croze. Sawtooth-type. Brass wear plates 65.00

Fence Stretcher. Complete 35.00

Froe, Curved. Hand-forged 85.00

Gauges
Primitive. Cherry 45.00
Stanley. G-4 .... 85.00

Hacksaw. Hand-forged. Rosewood handle 45.00

Hammers
Brass. Head 75.00
Snow Knocker. Hand-forged 35.00

Howel. Cooper. Small 75.00

Jointer. 4" square x 5' long. Cooper . 175.00

Knives
Crooked. Drop handle. Early 40.00

Draw. 13". Hand-forged 20.00
Race. Rosewood 35.00

Levels
- Marples & Sons, Sheffield, England 35.00
- 10". Stanley. #3 .... 25.00
- 12". Adjustable. Brass filagree. Davis 85.00

Line Reel. Box-type. Early Pa 30.00

Mallets
- Bookbinder's. Burl 75.00
- Carpenter's. Lignam Vitae 30.00

Planes
- Beltmaker's. Maple 65.00
- Bullnose. 5/8". Rosewood and brass 150.00
- Circular. Stanley #113. C. 1897 ... 65.00
- Coachmaker's. Walnut 60.00
- Dado. 1/2" width. Stanley #39 .. 25.00
- Plow. Adjustable. Boxwood 75.00
- Rabbit, Side. Cast brass. Mahogany handle 225.00
- Rabbit, Side. Stanley #98 ...... 40.00
- Smoothing. Brass lever cap and screw. Rosewood handle. Unmarked 175.00
- Sun. Cooper 75.00
- Tongue and Groove. Cherry 50.00
- Witchet. Adjustable 200.00

Router. Snaggle tooth. Mahogany ... 35.00

Rules
- 24". Folding. Boxwood. Brass edge and fittings 38.00
- 36". Folding. Boxwood 50.00
- 36". Folding. Boxwood. Brass edge and fittings 75.00
- 36". Straight. Tiger maple 50.00

Saws
- Bow 50.00
- Frame. Early 35.00

Scraper, Veneer. Rosewood handle. Stanley 25.00

Shave. Brass wear plate 10.00

Travelers
- Brass disc. Connolly. English 150.00
- Hand-forged iron 50.00
- Wood disc. Early Pa 50.00

Wrench. Hand-forged 5.00

TOOTHPICK HOLDERS

Toothpick holders are small containers used to hold toothpicks. They were an important table accessory during the Victorian era.

Alligator. Milk glass ....$ 75.00
Basket. Amber 30.00
Book. Blue 25.00
Boot. Amber 25.00
Bulldog. Silverplated. Glass eyes, all over embossing. Rogers & Bros. #2304 .... 150.00

"Take Your Pick." Silverplated ..$40.00

Cherub with Hat. Bisque 15.00
Chick with Egg. Silverplated 40.00
Clown. Porcelain 25.00
Coal Scuttle. Clear 22.50
Cupid with Barrel. Clear 25.00
Dog with Hat. Clear 40.00
*Elephant's Head. Amber 35.00
Frog. Milk glass 85.00
Hat. Blue crackle glass 35.00
Heart. Amber 35.00
Indian Chief. Milk glass 50.00
Iris with Meander. Green 50.00
Jefferson. Blue 55.00
Kettle. Green marble glass 50.00
Leaf Umbrella. Yellow cased glass ... 85.00
Monkey and Log. Blue 35.00
Pig on Railroad Car. Amber 175.00
Saddle. Amber 45.00
Top Hat. Silverplated 35.00
*Tree Trunk with Owl. Amber 45.00
Urn. Sterling silver 50.00
Valise. Amber 45.00
Wheelbarrow. Amber 85.00

NOTE: For additional items see "Pattern Glass Sections I and II" for pressed glass patterns, and "General Section" for specific wares.

*Reproduced Item

TORTOISE SHELL ITEMS

The shell or back of the tortoise was once used as material to fashion small articles such as boxes and combs. Genuine tortoise shell items are scarce on today's market and command relatively high prices.

NOTE: Anyone dealing in the sale of tortoise shell objects must be familiar with the Endangered Species Act and Amendment in its entirety. As of November, 1978, antique tortoise shell objects can be legally imported and sold with some restrictions.

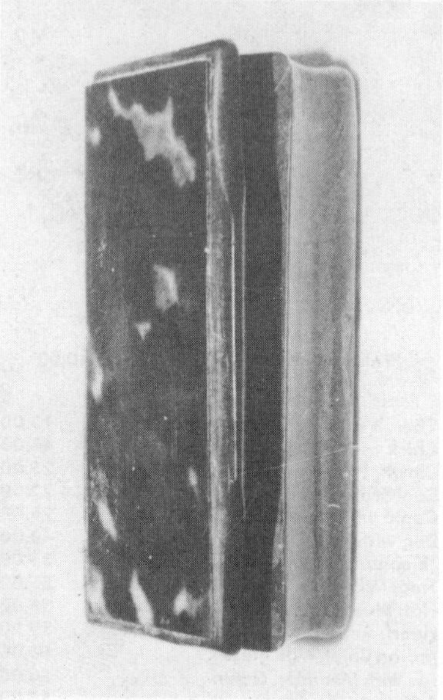

Box. 1½x3½". Hinged lid $125.00

Boxes	
1½ x 2½". Hinged lid. Silver pique work ....$	125.00
1½ x 3". Heart-shaped. Sterling trim	385.00
4 x 5". Grand piano-shaped. Mother of Pearl and silver inlay work	450.00
4½ x 5¾". Hinged lid. Brass fittings	195.00
Calling Card Cases	
Mother of Pearl inlay	195.00
Reticulated	175.00
Silver inlay	375.00
Cigarette Case. 2¾ x 4½". Hand decorated with enamels	350.00
Lorgnettes	
Carved and reticulated	250.00
Plain. With slide	185.00
Mustache Comb. In sterling case ...	50.00
Page Turner. Silver trim	135.00
Vase. 8¾". Pedestaled base, flared top	125.00

TOYS

Toys are a reflection of what is happening in any given era . . .and it seems there have always been toys. Archaeologists have unearthed the remains of a 5,000 year old toy factory in India. Centuries ago, Asian and Egyptian children enjoyed dolls and toy animals. Toys of wood, pottery and metal have been found in the tombs of royal children.

Toys were slow in becoming established in America since early settlers came from Northern Europe where the spirit of Puritanism frowned on such frivolities. When the Dutch arrived, the fun began . . .they brought Santa Claus, plus a variety of toys and games.

During the early 19th century almost every town had a toymaker who handcrafted primarily wooden playthings. During the 1830's and 1840's metals became plentiful and toymakers used tin and iron. Just after the Civil War, mechanical tin toys became popular as did the non-mechanical cast iron varieties.

Today's toys continue to reflect the times in such things as outer space, communication and scientific discoveries.

Hubley. Motorcycle. 6¾" long. With driver. "Harley Davidson." $100.00

American Flyer Trains	
Locomotive. "S". #350. B&O ....$	65.00
Silver Bullet. "S". #356. Set	100.00
Streamliner. "O." #556 with tender, two #495 coaches, #494 baggage car. Set	200.00
Arcade	
Bus. 8¾" long. C. 1940	75.00
Dump Truck. 6". C. 1927	85.00
Farm Wagon. Driver with two horses	125.00

Marx. "Spic & Span-The Hams What Am." $175.00

Cap Gun. "Sharp Shooter." $15.00

Farm Wagon with team. McCormick-Deering	250.00
FireTruck.13½"long.C.1936	125.00
Ice Truck. 6½"	100.00
Model T Coupe. 5". C. 1920	100.00
Sedan. 4". Mkd. 774B. C. 1930	100.00
Spreader. With team of horses. McCormick	400.00
Tractor. John Deere	40.00
Yellow Cab. #3	50.00
Yellow Cab. 9" long. C. 1927	300.00

Buddy L

Concrete Mixer. C. 1926	125.00
Coupe. Model T	150.00
Dump Truck. Ford. Model T	200.00
Express Truck. C. 1920's	100.00
Fire Truck. Hook and Ladder. C. 1925	125.00
Ice Truck. C. 1926	150.00
Steam Shovel. C. 1930	150.00

Dent

Bus. 6¼". Cast iron	125.00
Dray Wagon. With driver and two horses	45.00
Dump Wagon. 15" long. Two horses	75.00
Fire Ladder Truck. 8½" long. With driver	65.00
Fire Truck. Hook and Ladder. Three horses	375.00
Ice Wagon. 12" long. Two horses	75.00

Hubley

Bulldozer. 10¼" long. C. 1950	30.00
Chrysler Air Flow. 6". C. 1938	75.00
Dump Cart. 13" long. Driver and one horse. C. 1906	350.00
Dumpo Truck. 7½". C. 1938	75.00
Fire Pumper. 20" long. Two horses and three figures	125.00
Hook and Ladder Wagon. 32" long. Three horses	300.00
Log Wagon. 15" long. Driver and two oxen. C. 1905	275.00
Motorcycle. 6¾" long. With driver. Harley Davidson	100.00
Tractor. 7" long. Allis Chalmers	250.00

Ives

Fire Patrol. 20½" long. Two horses and seven figures. C. 1900	400.00
Train. Wind-up. "O". #17. Tender, three cars. Olive. Set	350.00

Kenton

Band Wagon. "Overland Circus." 15½" long. Two horses, five figures	200.00
Bus. "Coast to Coast."	65.00
Cart. 5". With rabbits	85.00
Cattle Truck. 8". C. 1938	110.00
Dump Wagon. 10" long. Driver and two horses	60.00
Fire Wagon. 17" long. Drivers, three horses and two ladders	175.00
Grader. 6" long	75.00
Milk Wagon. Driver and one horse.	125.00
Salky. With driver	65.00

Lehmann

"Adam the Porter." 8". C. 1912	375.00
Alabama Coon Jigger. 10". C. 1920's	175.00
Alligator	225.00
Balking Mule. "Jennie." C. 1930	100.00
Bucking Bronco. 6½". With rider	250.00
Car. 5½". Women passengers and dog	325.00

Happy Drunk 650.00
Paddy Pig 300.00
Tut Tut Man. 6¾". C. 1910 ...... 300.00

Lionel Trains
Flying Yankee. "O". #616 with two 9167 coaches, one #618 observation car. Gun metal. Set 300.00
Junior Set. Wind-up. Engine, tender and two cars. Set 200.00
Locomotives. "O"
#225E with #225W tender 225.00
#249 with tender. Black and nickel trim 150.00
Locomotives. "S"
#318E. Green. Electric 175.00
#384. 2-4-0. Black with green stripe. Steam 275.00

Marx
Big Parade. C. 1929 .... 225.00
Charleston Trio Dancers. C. 1921 300.00
Dapper Dan. C. 1910 .... 250.00
Honeymoon Express. C. 1929 .... 175.00
Honeymoon Express. C. 1947 .... 60.00
Looping Plane. #182 .... 50.00
"Merry Merrymakers." Mouse bank. C. 1929 .... 375.00
Motorcycle Trooper. C. 1935 .... 100.00
Racing Car. 12". C. 1940 ...... 50.00
Sparkling-Climbing Tank. C. 1939 75.00
Sparkling Tractor. C. 1939 ...... 50.00
Sunny Service Station. C. 1939 .. 250.00
Tidy Tim. C. 1933 .... 150.00
"Toylands Milkwagon." C. 1930 100.00
Train Set. Locomotive and seven cars. 50" long. Lithographed. Includes transformer and 12½' of track. C. 1953 .... 100.00
Zeppelin. 27" long 120.00

Strauss
"Alabama Coon Jigger." 9¾". C. 1910 .... 275.00
"Big Trixo." 10" 35.00
Bulking Mule. "Jenny." 10" 60.00
Interstate Bus. Double decker with driver 295.00
"Jazzbo Jim." C. 1921 .... 250.00

Tootsietoy
Ambulance. Graham. C. 1932 .. 40.00
Army Jeep. ¼ ton 15.00
Automobiles
Buick. Coupe. 1926 .... 30.00
Cadillac. Roadster. 1926 ...... 50.00
Chevrolet. Sedan. 1926 ...... 35.00
Ford. Model A. 1929 .... 25.00
Ford. V-8. Sedan. 1935 ...... 15.00
Graham. Convertible. 1932 .. 40.00
LaSalle. Coupe. 1935 .... 85.00
Oldsmobile. Roadster. 1926 .. 35.00
Packard. 1950 .... 10.00
Mack Car Transporter. With three cars. C. 1932 .... 100.00
Mack Coal Truck. C. 1922 ...... 20.00
Motorcycle. "Smitty." 85.00
Steam Roller. C. 1932 .... 40.00

Unique Art
"Dandy Jim." C. 1921 .... 200.00
Dogpatch Four. C. 1945 .... 200.00
G.I. Joe. 9". With K-9 pups 50.00
Jazzbo Jim. C. 1921 .... 150.00
Nodding Goose 30.00
Rollover Motorcycle Cop. C. 1935 175.00
Sky Ranger. C. 1933 .... 125.00

Miscellaneous

American Logs. Longest log, 14" long. Textured logs, machine dovetailed. Wooden box. Halsam. 328 pieces. Set 125.00
Cap Guns. Cast Iron
Automatic Kilgore. 6 shot 25.00
Daisy 25.00
Master 35.00
Cash Register. "Tom Thumb." Western Stamping Co 15.00
Chicken. Mechanical. 3¼ x 7 x 8". Lithographed tin. Wyandotte Toys. 55.00
Erector Set. A.C. Gilbert. Set No. 2. Complete 65.00
Lincoln Logs. Large set. Boxed. C. 1940 .... 50.00
Match Box Series. Each 5.00
Soldiers
Auburn. Rubber. Each 5.00-10.00
*Barclay. Lead. Each 5.00-10.00
Britains. WWI. Diarama. 150 pieces. C. 1916. Set 2500.00
Manoil. Lead. Each 5.00-10.00
Mignot. WWI. Americans. 13 pieces. C. 1910. Set 350.00
Stove. "Little Orphan Annie." 4¾x 5¼ x 9¾" long. Lithographed tin.. 50.00
Typewriter. Symplex. Model R. C. 1900 .... 50.00
Teddy Bear. 18". Hump back. Mohair, straw filled, glass eyes. Fully jointed 75.00
"The Star." Paddlewheel steamer. Penney Toy 25.00

*Reproduced Item

TRAMP ART

Tramp art is the term applied to a type of chip-carving used to enrich the surfaces of decorative and utilitarian wooden objects. Tradition states this craft was initially practiced by hoboes or tramps who wandered about the countryside doing odd jobs. Picture frames, boxes and furniture were fashioned in this "folk" media from the Civil War era to the 1930's. The tramp art technique was simple . . .V-shaped pieces of wood were cut, usually from cigar box tops, and glued in layers in three-dimensional patterns which were then joined together to form various types of objects. As with most primitive art, items are neither signed nor dated.

Sewing Box. 5½x7". Pin cushion top. One drawer $65.00

Bird Cage. 10½ x 15½ x 20½". Black with gold and green trim $	500.00
Boxes	
3½ x 6¼ x 9½". Hinged, flattened pyramid-shaped, lid. Red paper lining	75.00
8x 11 x 15". House-shaped. Lift-off roof	100.00
Chest. 6x 10x 16". Two small drawers at top, three drawers below. Porcelain knobs	200.00
Comb Case. Hanging-type. 8 x 12½". White porcelain nail heads.	40.00
Dresser. 5 x 9½ x 10". Three drawers, porcelain knobs	125.00
Frame. 17 x 19"	75.00
Magazine Rack. Wall-type. 17 x 24".	125.00
Sewing Box. 6½ x 10½". Pin cushion lift-off lid. Fitted interior, one drawer	75.00

TRIVETS

A trivet is a three-legged stand used to support hot vessels, either in an open fireplace, in workrooms or on table tops. The popular collectible trivets are those which were used to hold the early hand irons. These trivets were usually very ornate, incorporating designs of animals, birds, flowers, fruits, etc.

All listed are cast iron, unless otherwise designated.

Bar and Holes. Open railings ....$	18.50
Cathedral	22.00

Washington, George. Cast iron. $125.00

Chevrons	25.00
Christmas Tree	25.00
Crab. With legs	65.00
Crisscross	45.00
Eastern Star	35.00
Enterprise	45.00
Fern	35.00
Fireplace. 8½ x 23". Adjustable ..	150.00
Fox and Geese Tracks	45.00
Fox and Grapes. Brass	95.00
Good Luck. (no horseshoe) Brass ..	65.00
Harp	55.00
Harp. Brass	95.00
Hearts	
Double	45.00
Double. Brass	95.00
Single. Hand wrought. 18th century	200.00
Single. With star center	45.00
Triple. Brass	125.00
Hex Sign. Hand wrought	175.00
Horseshoes	
Eagle and Globe	45.00
Good Luck. Eagle. Brass	110.00
Masonic Emblem	45.00
Masonic Emblem. Brass	125.00

Rose	35.00
Jenny Lind	65.00
Lacy Urn. Plain railing	25.00
Lacy Urn. Wavy railing	50.00
Leaf and Scroll. Brass	95.00
Letters. In center	25.00
Love Birds. Brass	140.00
Lyre. Brass. English	65.00
Shield. Brass	175.00
Spade. Lacy	75.00
Star. Brass	75.00
Star and Sunburst	45.00
Sunflower	45.00
Swastika	25.00
Target	35.00
Triple-eight. Brass	75.00
Turtle	35.00
Turtle. Brass	75.00
Waffle. Octagonal. No railing	35.00
Washington, George	125.00
Washington, George. Brass	225.00

TRUNKS

Trunks are portable boxes or containers that clasp shut for the storage or transportation of personal possessions. Many trunks arrived in America during the immigration movement. These early trunks are now being sought out; restored and used for a multitude of purposes.
Prices will vary considerably depending on size, shape and condition.

Dome Top. Metal. C. 1890 . . . . $150.00

Dome Top

Leather covered pine, brass studs, wrought iron hardware . . . . . . $	100.00
Metal covered pine or poplar. Wooden slats	75.00
Wood. Ladies' hat trunk. Fitted interior	125.00
Wood. Metal slats	85.00
Wood. Wooden slats. Completely refinished, new leather handles, relined with cloth	175.00

Flat Top

Canvas covered pine. Wooden slats. C. 1910	75.00
Leather covered pine. Metal slats, brass studs, corner protectors and handles. Chinese	135.00
Paper covered poplar. Iron hardware	50.00
Wood. Oak. Dovetailed and pegged construction	350.00

TUCKER CHINA

Tucker china was the first porcelain made in America on a commercial basis. William Ellis Tucker, son of a Quaker china merchant, produced his first porcelain in Philadelphia in 1825. Thomas Hulme joined Tucker in 1828 in a partnership that lasted over a year . . .their wares were marked Tucker & Hulme.
In 1831, a brother, Thomas Tucker joined the firm as an artist and the family business continued to produce fine china until Williams death in 1832. At this time, another partnership was formed with Judge Joseph Hemphill and his two sons. Financial difficulties, not the least of which was the great bankfailure of 1833, continued to plague the small company and in 1837 the Hemphills withdrew from the firm. Finally Thomas Tucker was forced to close the factory in 1838.

Pitcher. 9⅝". Vase-shaped. Sepia landscape on both sides. Unsigned. $1250.00

Tucker porcelain, made during this short span of years, 1825-1838, was of exceptional quality and comparable to Sevres. All Tucker wares were handpainted and no transfer prints were used. Although dinner services comprised a large part of the firm's production, urns and vases were also made. Tucker china, because of its brief history, short production and fine quality, is considered rare . . .today few pieces can be found outside museums and private collections.

Pitcher. 11⅝". Vase-shaped.
  Polychrome floral decor. Unsigned $ 1500.00
Pitcher. 11⅝". Vase-shaped.
  Polychrome floral decor. Signed . . 4000.00

VALENTINES

Many myths and mysteries surround the origin of Valentines Day, February 14.
Esther Howland was the first American artist to create Valentine Day messages commercially. As the custom to send affectionate greetings on this special day developed, other artists and printers followed suit. The Victorians delighted in receiving and sending elaborately decorated cards and the majority of the collectible cards are from this era.
The price range for early Valentines is wide... from a few dollars to hundreds of dollars. Quoted prices listed are general and will vary according to composition, condition and size.

Artists

Addenbrooke	$35.00 -50.00
Brundage	15.00 -20.00
Dobb	50.00 -100.00
Greenaway	25.00 -50.00
Howland	50.00 -100.00
Meek	10.00 -20.00
Nester	15.00 -25.00
Tuck	15.00 -25.00
Whitney	15.00 -10.00

Types

Comic	3.00 -5.00
Comic. Mechanical	10.00 -15.00
Fold-out	15.00 -25.00
Handmade	5.00 -10.00
Lithographed	10.00 -20.00
Mechanical. Lacy	15.00 -20.00
Sailor's	25.00 -50.00
Theorems	100.00 -200.00

Comic-type. "The Boss of the Family."
8¾x10¾" framed $7.50

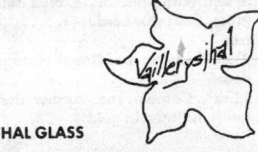

VALLERYSTHAL GLASS

Vallerysthal (Lorraine) France has been a glass producing center for centuries. In 1872 two major factories merged and produced art glass from 1898. Later pressed glass covered animal dishes were introduced. The factory continues operation today.

Box. 3 x 3½". Diamond Quilted.
  Blue milk glass . . . .$ 60.00
Candlestick. 11". Square floral base. Grecian girl stem, urn forms candle cup. Frosted crystal 125.00
Dishes, Covered
  Beehive. 5". Clear glass 65.00
  Cow and pasture scene on cover. 7". Clear glass 75.00
  Dog. 3½ x 5". Amber glass 85.00
  Dog. 4½". White milk glass 55.00
  Duck. 5". White milk glass 45.00
  Duck. 6". Blue milk glass 55.00
  Hen. 2½". Pink 40.00
  Hen. 7". White milk glass 75.00
  Hen. 7½". Frosted clear glass 85.00
  Pig. 3¼". Clear glass 40.00
  Shell. 6". White milk glass 100.00

Duck. 4½". Painted brown and green $75.00

Squirrel. 5". White milk glass .. 75.00
Egg Cup. Chicken decor. White milk glass 35.00
Sherbet. With underplate. Blue milk glass. Gold star border 50.00
Vases
9½". Cameo-type. Green vintage decor 385.00
11½". Cameo-type. Amber daffodils outlined in gold 450.00

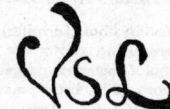

VAL ST. LAMBERT

Val St. Lambert Cristalleries of Belgium was established in the early 1800's. They feature exquisite cased glass, heavily cut and engraved. The company is still in existence.

Ashtray. 4½". Opalescent. Crane and fish decor ....$ 150.00
Bowls
8¾" square. Footed. Deep blue. Seated nude female figures. C. 1930 .... 250.00
12x4" deep. Flared top. Crystal .. 75.00
Boxes
3½" diam. Cameo lid. Cranberry cut to crystal 175.00
4¾" diam. Mother and child cameo-type lid. Gray-green 125.00
Coasters. Intaglio cut Zodiac signs.

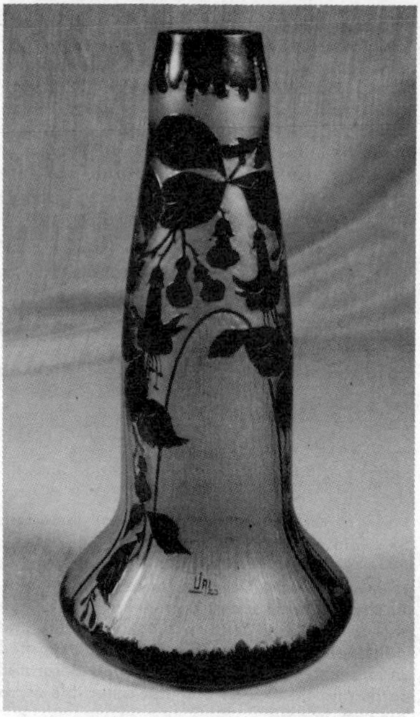

Vase. 13¾". Pink with purple floral decor $395.00

Set of 12 .... 200.00
Perfume Bottle, Stoppered. 6". Pink cut to clear 175.00
Ring Tree. Crystal and amber 50.00
Tray. 3½ x 5". Crystal. Gold trim .. 65.00
Vases
7". Cobalt cut to crystal. Floral decor 250.00
12". Baluster-shaped. Mottled blue overlaid with blue green. Intaglio cut Venetian scene. C. 1910. .... 500.00
12½". Frosted. Purple floral decor. Amethyst rim and base 350.00

VAN BRIGGLE POTTERY

Born in 1869, Artus Van Briggle was a talented Ohio artist who studied in Paris for three years prior to working at Rookwood. In 1901, he moved to Colorado for his health and established his own pottery in Colorado Springs.

In that same year, he produced his famous "Despondency" vase.

Van Briggle's work was heavily influenced by the Art Nouveau "school" he saw in France; and he produced a great variety of matte glazed wares in this style. Glazes varied, but the most famous were Ming and Persian Rose.

In the beginning, "AA" mark was incised by hand on each piece along with the date and words "Van Briggle". Later, stock numbers were stamped on items and the letters "U.S.A." followed the mark from 1922 to 1929. After 1920, the words "Colorado Springs, Colorado" (or an abbreviation) were added.

When Artus died in 1904, his wife Anne continued the pottery operation. Van Briggle Pottery continues to be made today.

Vase. 2½". Bulbous. Leaf decor. Ming $35.00

Bookends

Bear. Dark green. Pair $125.00
Peacock. Ming. Pair 150.00

Bowls

2¾ x 8¾". Dragonflies. Persian Rose. C. 1922 .... 70.00
3 x 5½". Acorn and oak leaves. Green and brown. C. 1910 .... 175.00
5 x 10". Triangular leaves. Ming. C. 1917 .... 120.00
7x11". Four handles. Daisy. Ming 85.00
10½ x 11 x 15". Kneeling Nude. Maroon and blue 195.00

Candlesticks

2¾". Leaf base. Brown. Pair 45.00
3½". Tulip-shaped. Persian Rose. Pair 65.00
4¼". High glazed black with blue and white drip. Signed Anne Van Briggle. Pair 1500.00
10½". Flowers and vines. Ming. C. 1906 .... 200.00

Console Set. Siren of the Sea, with frog, two dolphin candlesticks 600.00

Figures

Dog. 2". Persian Rose 75.00
Elephant. 4⅛ x 7½". Maroon 125.00
Rabbit. 2½". Plum. C. 1917 .... 175.00

Flower Frog. 1¾ x 4". Dome-shaped. Oak and leaf. Ming 25.00

Lamp Bases

6". Mission-style. Bluish gray. C. 1914 .... 150.00
10". Bird on tree. Ming 175.00

Planter. 4¼ x 12½". Shell-shaped. Persian Rose 65.00

Vases

2½". Lotus. Royal blue. C. 1908 .... 85.00
3". Bulbous. Mistletoe. Deep green and brown. C. 1907 .... 300.00
4½". Leaf decor. Ming 65.00
7". Vertical line. Yellow and green. Shape #690. C. 1915 .... 225.00
8". Urn-shaped. Floral decor. Ming. C. 1917 .... 175.00
9¼". Lorelei. Ming. C. 1919 .... 150.00
9½". Daffodils and foliage. Ming. C. 1920 .... 125.00
11½". Indian heads. Persian Rose. 150.00
12". Urn-shaped. Two handles. Maroon. C. 1920 .... 200.00
13". Maroon and dark blue. Shape #748. C. 1930 .... 175.00

VASA MURRHINA GLASS

Vasa Murrhina glass was produced by the Vasa Murrhina Art Glass Company, Sandwich, Mass. in the late 1800's.

The name Vasa Murrhina was derived from Roman Murrine which was a glass embedded with precious metals and stones.

Basically, Vasa Murrhina glass was made by incorporating metallic flakes and particles of colored glass into a ball of transparent glass and heating it sufficiently to cause the mica to become embedded within the glass. A similar type glass was produced in England in the late 19th century.

Basket. 10½". Applied clear loop handle. White hobnailed exterior, blue interior. Ruffled edge $200.00

Bowl. 9". Cased pink. Ruffled and fluted rim 175.00

Cruet. 8½". Pink. Applied amber handle and stopper 150.00

Decanter. 12½". Hourglass-shaped. Applied clear reeded handle. Cranberry with gold flecks 185.00

Ewers

6½". Cased apricot. Applied clear handle 95.00

Cheese Dish, Covered. "Swirl". 6¼x9½" diam. Cased pink with silver flecks. Hobb's. C. 1880's. $225.00

10". Cased pink. Applied clear leaf handle and shells 225.00

Finger Bowl. With underplate. Ruffled and scalloped rims. Cranberry with gold flecks. Set 100.00

Mug. Amber with gold flecks 75.00

Pitchers

5½". Bulbous. Mottled green, red and yellow. Cased. Applied reeded clear handle 125.00

8". Cased cranberry. Applied clear handle 195.00

10½". Molded cabbage rose. Cased red. Applied clear handle .. 325.00

Rose Bowls

3½". Cased pink 125.00

5". Shaded blue and white 150.00

Shakers. Salt and Pepper. 4". Cased pink. Pair 275.00

Syrup. 6". Pewter lid. Applied clear handle. Mottled green, pink and white 150.00

Toothpick. 2". Cobalt. Gold flecks .. 50.00

Tumblers

4". Pink 50.00

5½". Multicolored. Gold flecks .. 65.00

Vases

3¼". Melon ribbed. Cobalt 65.00

4½". Rainbow colors. Gold and silver flecks 100.00

6½". Cased mottled red, yellow and green 95.00

7". Cased light blue. Blown 200.00

7". Jack-in-the-Pulpit. Cased multicolors 150.00

8". Tri-cornered crimped rim. Green, white with gold flecks .. 175.00

8¼". Fan-shaped, turned down top with applied clear ribbon edging. Cased rainbow colors .. 175.00

9". Bulbous base. Stick top. Yellow and brown with gold flecks 185.00

12". Petaled top. Light green with gold flecks 150.00

VASART

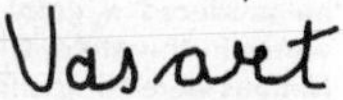

Vasart is a contemporary art glass made in Scotland by the Streathearn Glass Co. The colors are mottled and sometimes shade from one hue to another. It is readily identified by an engraved signature on the base.

Basket. 5x8¼". Mottled green shading to pink $85.00

Baskets

3 x 5". Mottled orange .... $ 55.00

4 x 6". Mottled blue 65.00

Bowls

4 x 2" deep. Mottled yellow shading to blue at top 60.00

7". Flared. Wafer foot. Orange, black and clear 55.00

9 x 3½" deep. Orange, black and clear 75.00

Hat. 2¼". Mottled green and white . 55.00

Mug. Mottled blue and white 45.00

Rose Bowl. 4". Mottled lavender and white 55.00

Tray. 4 x 12". Mottled blue shading to green 75.00

Vase. 8½". Mottled blue shading to pink 95.00

VENETIAN GLASS

Venetian glass has been made on the Island of Murano, near Venice, since the 13th century. Most of the wares are thin walled. Many types of decoration have been used . . .embedded gold dust or lace work and applied fruits or flowers.

Basket. 5½ x 8 x 10½". Crystal .. $ 195.00

Bowls

9½". Crystal. Gold trim 85.00

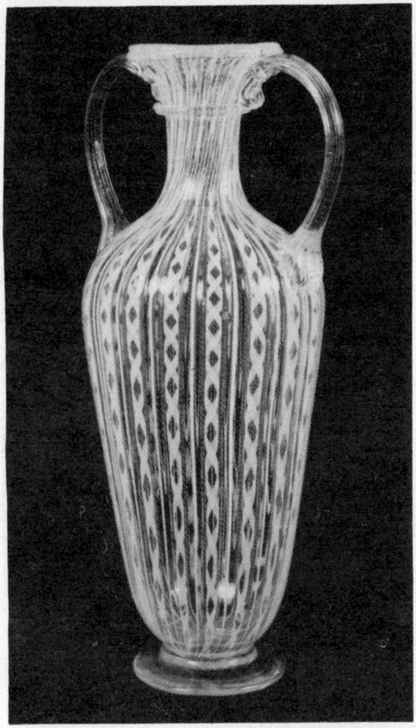

Vase. 10¾". Handled. Alternating white ribbons on clear. Gold dust $195.00

4 x 7x 10". Rubina, crystal base. Applied amber flowers	165.00
Candlesticks	
5". Dolphin. Crystal with gold dust	55.00
12". Crystal with gold dust. Red trim. Pair	125.00
Candy Jar, Covered. 10½". Ribbed. Enameled floral decor	100.00
Chandelier. Five arms. 30 x 34" long. Applied pink and blue decor on crystal. Gold washed	2000.00
Cologne Bottle. 7½". Crystal with applied rigaree on neck	75.00
Compotes	
7 x 6½" high. Cranberry. Crystal dolphin stem	150.00
10 x 8" high. Cobalt blue. Gold overlay	185.00
Ewer. 12". Crystal. Pink ribbons, gold dust	225.00
Finger Bowl. With underplate. Diamond Optic. Dolphin handles .	50.00
Goblets	
8". Dolphin. Ruby	35.00
8". Ribboned and gold dust. Applied dragon	185.00
Perfume Bottle, Stoppered. 4". Alternating white ribbons and gold dust	85.00
Pitcher, Water. Bulbous. Crystal. Enameled lillies	100.00
Plates	
7½". Pink. Gold dust	25.00
8½". Diamond Optic. Pink	20.00
Salt. Swan-shaped. Pink. Gold trim .	25.00
Vases	
9½". Rose shading to peach. Ruffled top. Applied green leaves ..	165.00
10½". Hourglass-shaped. Enameled winter scenes and leaves	85.00
11". Urn-type. Pink. Gold dust ..	195.00
18". Red shading into clear. Enameled white flowers. Gold trim	225.00
Wine. Dolphin. Pink, green. Gold dust	55.00
Wine Set. 11" decanter, six 5½" wines. Crystal	250.00

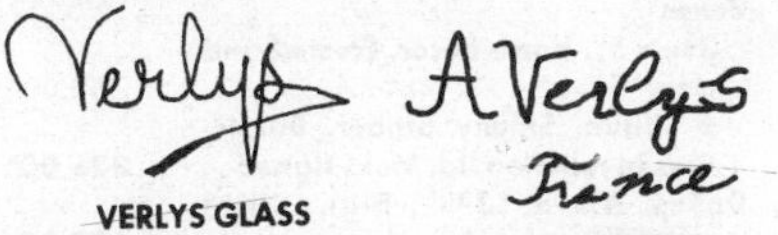

VERLYS GLASS

Verlys Glass is a type of art glass originally made in France after 1930. For a period of a few months, Heisey Glass Co., Newark, Ohio produced the identical glass having obtained the rights and formula from the French factory. The French-produced glass can be distinguished from the American product by the signature . . . French is mold marked, the American is etched script signed.

Ashtrays	
3¾ x 4¾". Frosted doves on base, frosted floral border. Script signed .	$ 45.00
4 x 5". Penguin perched on one end. Script signed	50.00
Bowls	
6". Cupid with bow and arrow and hearts in center. Mold signed . .	100.00
6". Oriental scene in center. Script signed	75.00
6¼". Thistle. Blue. Mold signed . .	125.00
11⅓". Frosted birds and bees in relief. Script signed	175.00
11¼". Tassel. Script signed	125.00
12". Thistle. Mold signed	175.00
14". Lily pad decor. Script signed . .	125.00
14¾". Dragonfly. Etched clear crystal. Script signed	150.00

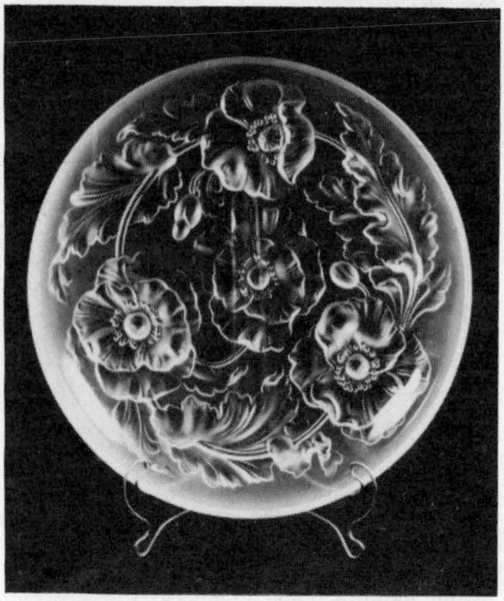

Bowl. 13½". "Poppy." Script signed $125.00

Boxes

3¾ x 5". Horse decor. Frosted and clear 50.00

6" diam. Smoky amber. Butterflies in relief on lid. Mold signed .. 325.00

Doves. 4½ x 13¾". Blue. Script signed 125.00

Planter. 4¼ x 6¼ x 10⅛". Chrysanthemum. Frosted and clear. Script signed 100.00

Plaque. 5½". Madonna of the Roses. Frosted and clear. Script signed .. 150.00

Plates

6¼". Pine Cone. Frosted and clear. 80.00

9". Three Swirling fish. Frosted and clear. Mold signed 135.00

13½". Child and sheep in relief. Frosted and clear. Script signed .. 150.00

Vases

5". Butterflies. Frosted and clear. Script signed 95.00

9". Thistle. Rolled out rim. Script signed 200.00

9½". Frosted and clear Thistle. Mold signed 225.00

9½ x 5⅛" diam. Mandarin. Script signed 235.00

VERRE DE SOIE GLASS

Verre de Soie (glass of silk) is an iridescent type of glass. This iridescence was produced by using a metallic chloride spray which caused the glass to develop a satiny finish with the appearance and feel of silk.

Verre de Soie glass was produced by the Steuben Glass Company around the 1905-10 period. Its development was reportedly under the supervision of Frederick Carder who originated Aurene glass shortly after the turn of the present century. Production was discontinued about 1930.

Bowl. 8x3¼" deep. Flared $135.00

Basket. 8 x 11" excluding handle. Steuben ....$ 325.00

Bowls

5 x 4½" deep. Applied plums and leaves 195.00

8". Three footed. Steuben 165.00

12 x 2½" deep 150.00

Candlesticks

10". #379. Steuben 125.00

10". Rose edges. Steuben. Pair .. 400.00

Cologne Bottle. 7". Steuben 250.00

Compotes

4 x 4½" diam 95.00

5¼ x 6". Engraved. Signed Hawkes 275.00

Cup and Saucer. Demitasse. Steuben 100.00

Finger Bowl. With underplate. Steuben 120.00

Goblet. Steuben 150.00

Perfume Bottle. 4½". Blue flame-shaped stopper. Steuben 185.00

Pitcher. 9¾" 250.00

Plate. 7½" 40.00

Rose Bowl. 3½". Steuben 125.00

Salts

Individual. Pedestaled. Steuben .. 50.00

Master. Pedestaled. Steuben 100.00

Sherbet. With underplate. Steuben. Set 185.00

Vases

6". Squat bulbous base, narrow throat ending in wide ruffled top .. 95.00
7". Bulbous base, short neck with 3¼" diam. flaring rim. Steuben .. 300.00
7¼". Amphora-type 150.00
8". Engraved. Unsigned 125.00
9". Steuben 400.00
11 x 4" diam. Engraved 200.00

Water Set. Decanter pitcher, 12½" high. Spray of large orchids in shades of lavender. 6 matching tumblers 500.00
Wine. Etched. Hawkes........... 125.00

VILLEROY & BOCH

The founder of one of the original potteries that eventually became Villeroy and Boch was Pierre Joseph Boch who established a factory near Luxemburg, Germany in 1767. His son Jean Francis attained the distinction of introducing the first coal fired kiln in Europe and perfecting a water power driven potter's wheel. Other potteries in the area were those of Mettlach, managed by Pierre's grandson Eugene and Nicholas Villeroy's factory.

A consolidation of these three firms was effected in 1841 and became known as Villeroy and Boch. Early production included a hard paste earthenware comparable to English Ironstone. This ware continues to be made today for their line of tablewares.

It was the combined talents and efforts of this organization that initiated decorated stonewares known the world over as Mettlach. See "Mettlach."

Bowls

8". Floral decor ....$ 50.00
10½". Handled. Blue floral decor. 95.00

Bread Board. 5½ x 8½". White 95.00
Butter, Covered. Design in relief. Tan and green 125.00
Cider Set. Tankard pitcher, six tumblers. Baseball theme. Set 225.00
Cruet. 8½". Blue and white 55.00
Fish Mold. 8" long. Brown and white. 60.00
Mustard Pot. 4". Tan glaze 30.00

Pitchers

4". Vintage decor. Blue on white... 55.00
7½". Florals in relief. Handpainted 75.00
9". Tan ground with pink flowers in relief 95.00

Plaque. 13¾". White portrait center on blue. Decorated tan border. Impressed #879. C. 1885 ....$395.00

Plaque. 15". Ocean scene. Black on white. C. 1900's 300.00
Plate. 12". Blue and white 55.00
Platter. 12 x 18". Red and green flowers on white 85.00
Ramekin. With underplate. Blue and white 30.00
Syrup Jug, Lidded. 4". Blue and white 40.00
Teapot. 6¼". White with blue decor. 100.00
Tile. 6 x 6". Dutch scene. Blue on white 25.00
Tureen, Soup. Covered. 12½". With underplate. Blue and white 275.00

Vases

5½". Amphora-type. Apples and leaves. "Yorkshire." 55.00
7½". Beige figures in relief on tan ground. Silver lustre trim 225.00
9". Cherubs in relief. White 125.00
14". Bulbous base, slender neck. Maroon. Ormolu trim 300.00

WARWICK

Warwick China Manufacturing Company, Wheeling, W. Va. began operation in 1887 and continued until 1951. They were one of the first manufacturers of vitreous glazed wares in the United States. Their production lines were extensive . . tablewares, garden ornaments, decorative and utilitarian items. Many of their wares were decorated with decals, few were handpainted and some designs combined decals and hand decorations.

Mug. "Seaman." IOGA $75.00

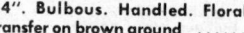

Ale Set. 10¼" pitcher, six handled mugs. Fishermen's portrait decor on brown ground ....$	500.00
Bowl. 5 x 9 x 12". Scroll work in relief. Cherry transfer	60.00
Chocolate Set. 11" pot, six cups and saucers. Floral decor on blue-green ground. Gold trim	225.00
Humidor. Poppy transfer..........	100.00
Mugs	
F.O.E. on brown ground	65.00
Hobo. Playing guitar	75.00
Monk	75.00
Seaman......................	75.00
Pitchers	
7½". Monk transfer on brown ground	150.00
10½". Tankard-shaped. Cardinal transfer	150.00
Plates	
9½". Monk. Brown ground	75.00
11". Bulldog. Artist signed IOGA	100.00
Trays	
6½ x 9". Dark green border. Red roses	30.00
12". Windmill. Flow blue	85.00
Vases	
10". "Lady of the Night" portrait. Gray. IOGA	150.00
12". Monk. IOGA	275.00
12". Portrait-type. Twig handles. Moss green ground shading to dusty rose	175.00
13". Stork. White ground. IOGA	100.00
14". Bulbous. Handled. Floral transfer on brown ground	125.00

WASH SETS

Before the advent of indoor plumbing, the wash set was an essential part of every household. The water pitcher and wash basin were the basic set. More complete sets comprised of other essentials were available. They were made by practically every major ceramic manufacturer in the United States and abroad in varying degrees of quality.

Unmarked. Multicolored floral decor on white. Gold trim. Two examples illustrated. 7 pieces $500.00

Burleigh. Blue shading to off white. Yellow handles and trim. 4 pieces $	225.00
Laughlin, Homer. Holly transfer on white ground. Gold trim. 2 pieces .	125.00
Limoges. Handpainted floral decor. 2 pieces	250.00
Maddock, John. Green leaves and scrolls. 7 pieces	425.00
Meakin. Pink hollyhocks, leaves and buds. 4 pieces	250.00
Minton. Blue and white ground. Green decor. 2 pieces	300.00
Ridgway. Blue and green floral decor on white. 2 pieces	250.00
Royal Doulton. Blue and white "Willow". 2 pieces	250.00
Unmarked Sets	
Begonias, leaves in natural colors. Gold handles and trim. 12 pieces.	750.00
Brown roses, wine decor on white. 5 pieces	300.00
Green ivy vines and leaves on white. 5 pieces	350.00
Ironstone. White. Plain. 2 pieces	125.00

WATCHES, POCKET

The first watch, basically a miniature table clock, was made in Germany in 1500 and Nuremberg, Germany and Blois, France became early production centers. Later Geneva, Switzerland and London, England were prominent watchmaking centers; while in the United States, watchmaking was practiced by the clockmakers of the period on a very small scale.

Early watches were regarded more as jewelry than time pieces. When the balance spring was introduced in 1675, accuracy increased and watches achieved a new image.

Abraham Louis Brequet, a Swiss born genius who worked in Paris in the late 18th century, is called the finest watchmaker of all times. He developed, invented and improved many watch components and changed the appearance of the pocket watch. From this time on, the watch went through a metamorphisis of dramatic change-culminating in the quartz-crystal electric watch. In recent years, Japan and the U.S. have challenged the Swiss in mechanical watch production, but to most the Swiss remain unassailable for quality.

Abbreviations used . . . DAMK-Damaskeened movement, DS-Double sunk, HB&B-Hinged back and bezel, HC-Hunting case, j-jewel, K-Karat, KWKS-Key wind and Key set, LS-Lever set, MRR-Montgomery Railroad, OF-Open face, R-Railroad, SB & B-Screw back and bezel, SS-Single sunk, WFG-White gold filled, YFG-Yellow gold filled.

El Kohinoor. 16s, OF, YFG case. Presentation-type $175.00

Ball (Hamilton) 18s, silveroid case. 19j, LS, SB&B, SS dial .... $ 375.00

Ball (Illinois) 12s, OF, WFG Keystone case. 19 j 200.00

REVERSE OF ILLUSTRATED POCKET WATCH

Ball (Waltham Gold Seal). 16s, OF Keystone case. 21j, LS. Adjusted to 5 positions 225.00

Bunn (Illinois). 16s, OF, YGF case. 19j, SB&B, DS dial. Adjusted to 5 positions 225.00

Bunn Special (Illinois). 18s, OF, YFG case. 21j, SB&B 175.00

Elgin Father Time. 18s, silveroid case. 21j, LS, DS dial, DAMK movement. Locomotive engraved on reverse 285.00

Elgin National. 18s, OF, coin silver case. 7j 50.00

Elgin National. 18s, coin silver case. 21j, Roman numeral dial. KWKS . 150.00

Elgin Veritas. 18s, silveroid case. 23j, DS, RR dial. Locomotive in relief on reverse 400.00

Gallet & Co. 14s, gold washed, sterling case. 7j. Swiss 100.00

Hamilton 940. 18s, Royal 20 year case. 21j, DS porcelain dial. Adjusted to 5 positions 150.00

Hamilton 996. 16s, OF, YGF case. SB & B, DS dial 175.00

Hampden. 18s, OF, silveroid case. 21j, SB&B, DS dial 200.00

Howard. Railroad Chronometer. Series 11. 16s, OF, YGF case. SS dial, LS 375.00

Illinois Lincoln. 18s, YGF Star case. 21j, LS, engraved moment 300.00

Illinois Victor. 16s, silveroid Star case. 21j, MRR dial. Adjusted to 3 positions 150.00
Lepine. 16s, OF, silver case. KWKS. French 175.00
New England Watch Co. 16s, silveroid case with glass front and back 225.00
New York Standard. 12s, OF, Philadelphia silveroid case. 15j, DAMK movement 50.00
Omega. 16s, OF, YGF case. 17j. Swiss 40.00
Regina. 12s, OF, YGF case. 17j 50.00
Rockford. 18s, HC, YGF engraved case. 15j, SW, LS. Micrometer regulator 250.00
Rockford. 18s, OF, Keystone silveroid case. 21j, DS, RR porcelain dial. Adjusted to temperature and 5 positions 325.00
Seth Thomas. 18s, HC, coin silver case. 7j, LS 150.00
Southbend Studebaker. 16s, YGF engraved case. 21j, SB&B, DS dial. Adjusted to 8 positions 250.00
Tavannes. 12s, 10K, WG case. 17j .. 75.00
Waltham. 6s, HC, YGF engraved case. 7j. Ornate hands 115.00
Waltham Crescent Street. 16s, YGF case. 21j, Up-Down winding indicator 550.00
Waltham. 18s, OF, 14K, YG case. HB&B 450.00

Watches, Miscellaneous

Character

Cinderella. Grosgrain strap. C. 1940 .... 75.00
Dick Tracy. C. 1940 .... 100.00
Donald Duck. Pocket-type. C. 1939 300.00
Elvis Presley. Limited edition. C. 1978 .... 75.00
Lil Abner. Animated 125.00
Mickey Mouse. C. 1930 .... 175.00
Mickey Mouse. C. 1940 .... 100.00
Mickey Mouse. Pocket-type. C. 1935 .... 200.00
Spiro Agnew. Original 250.00

Lapel, Lady's

Platinum with diamond bar pin. Total weight 3.5K 1500.00
WGF pin, 1" oval. Set with semi-precious stones. C. 1900 .... 100.00

Wristwatch, Lady's

Enameled rose gold. Art Deco-style 200.00
Platinum with diamonds. Total weight 3K. C. 1918 .... 4000.00

Wristwatch, Man's

Patek Phillippe. 14K, YG. C. 1900 600.00

WATCH FOBS

A watch fob is a useful and decorative jewelry item attached to a man's pocket watch. Fobs have been of interest to men since the Victorian age. The advertising-type fob became popular in the 1870's and continues today. The majority of these fobs are metal that have been die-struck. Companies gave these fobs as a media of advertising or to announce a new product.
Special fobs were also designed to commemorate events, places and people.
Watch fobs continue to be made today . . .some are restrikes of the earlier ones; others are totally new designs. All serve a 'purpose' to collectors.

Link-Belt Speeder. Shovel-Crane. C. 1960's $15.00

Art Nouveau Maiden. Advertising on reverse ....$ 30.00
Atlas Life Insurance Co., Tulsa, Okla 25.00
BPOE. C. 1912 .... 35.00
Bowling 10.00
Boy Scout. C. 1915 .... 25.00
Bryan 40.00
Buick. Enameled. C. 1920 .... 75.00
Caterpillar. C. 1954 .... 20.00
Case Power Farming Machinery .. 75.00
Columbia Expo. 1893 .... 50.00
Copper Clad Ranges. Original ribbon 30.00
Dr. Pepper. Oval. C. 1910 .... 75.00
Fireman's Convention. C. 1936 .... 15.00
Fish. Enamels on sterling silver 45.00
Football Player. C. 1925 .... 15.00
Gamewell Fire Alarm Telegraph Co. Copper 25.00
Horseshoe. Cut-out 15.00
Indian. Sterling 50.00
Initials. Cut-out. Brass 20.00
International Harvester. C. 1960 .. 20.00

Iowa State Traveling Men's Association. Enamels on nickel. Original strap	20.00
Mack Trucks. C. 1960	20.00
Magcobar Drilling Mud. Original strap	25.00
Memphis Furniture Mfg. Co. Enameled. Original strap	40.00
National Letter Carriers Association. C. 1970	15.00
National Sportsman. C. 1920	50.00
OVB. Souvenir-type	30.00
"Over Sea . . .to Give Kaiser Hell." C. 1917	45.00
Pennsylvania. C. 1915	25.00
Pepsi Cola, New Bern, N.C.	40.00
Pioneer Coal & Timber Co. Oklahoma City. Okla	35.00
Roosevelt-Cox. C. 1919	55.00
Tractomotive	15.00
Vol. Fireman. C. 1948	15.00

WATERFORD

Waterford crystal is quality flint glass commonly decorated with cuttings.

The original factory was established at Waterford, Ireland in 1729. The early glass made before 1830 was darker than the brilliantly clear glass of later production. The factory closed in 1852 and after 100 years reopened and continues production today.

Biscuit Jar. Silverplated cover and bail. Band of cuttings	$ 275.00
Butter, Covered. Mushroom finial. Ovoid. Early	250.00
Celery Vase. 8". Footed. Turned down rim.	150.00
Compote. 12½". Mushroom-shaped cover. Diamond cut. Signed	850.00
Cornucopia. 15". Silverplated holder	500.00
Cruet. 9". Stoppered. Applied handle	125.00
Decanters. 10". Mushhroom stoppers. Pair	300.00
Jars, Covered	
7". Signed	175.00
8". Heavy cuttings. C. 1820	850.00
Lamps, Hurricane. 27". Cut base, stem and bobeches. Double button cut prisms. Early 19th century. Pair	1500.00
Mantel Lustres. 12½". 9" button cut prisms. Pair	750.00
Pitcher. 10½". Applied handle	195.00
Plate. 8". Center cut	65.00
Punch Bowl. 7½ x 10x 14". Oval-shaped. Turned out rim	650.00
Salts	
Individual. Boat-shaped. C. 1820	65.00
Master. Footed. Diamond-shaped	50.00
Sugar Shaker. Silver top	125.00

Pitcher. 10½". Ribbed. Applied handle $195.00

Tumbler. Allover cuttings	65.00
Urn. 9½". Plinth base	350.00
Vases	
7¾". Cylindrical. 20th century	150.00
10¾". Allover cuttings. C. 1810	500.00
12¼". Flared, scalloped top	350.00
Wine. 5½". Diamond cut	35.00

WAVE CREST WARE

WAVE CREST GLASS

Wave Crest is a decorated opal or milk white glass produced by the Pairpoint Manufacturing Company, New Bedford, Massachusetts. All of the articles were blown in full-sized molds. The blanks were decorated by the C. F. Moore Company, Meriden, Connecticut.

Biscuit Jars	
Brass cover and bail handle. Blue Forget-me-Nots. Unsigned	$ 225.00
Silverplated cover and bail handle. Enameled floral decor. Signed	285.00
Bowls	
3½". Footed. Signed	150.00

Planter. 2¾x4¼x5¼". Puffed. Pink floral decor. Ormolu rim $250.00

7½ x 6" deep. Brass ring handles and feet. Unsigned	225.00
Boxes, Covered	
3" diam. Hinged lid. Blue floral decor. Satin lined. Red mark	175.00
3¾" diam. Portrait-type with cherubs. Signed	225.00
4" high. Floral decor on front. "CIGARETTES" in raised gold on reverse	250.00
4" square. Round beveled mirror on cover. Pink flowers on sides ..	300.00
4 x 6x 9½". Glove. Pale pink with white flowers in relief. Hand-painted flowers on lid	650.00
5¼ x 5½". Hinged lid. Ormolu dolphin footed stand	450.00
7" diam. Hinged lid. Pink, floral decor and jeweled	500.00
Card Holder. 1¾ x 2½ x 4". Pink enamel flowers. Ormolu frame ..	100.00
Cigar Humidors	
4 x 6". "Cigars". Shell lid. Aqua, pink flowers. Paper label. Red mark	375.00
6 x 6½". Indian Chief. Red mark	450.00
Cream and Sugar. Sets	
3¼". Swirl design with pink roses. Unsigned	150.00
3½". Swirl. Silverplated rims and sugar lid. Red mark	425.00
Jardiniere. 7 x 8½". Enameled flowers, jeweled rim. Signed	500.00
Letter Holder. 3¼ x 4 x 6". Floral decor with raised enamel accents. Ormolu frame	225.00
Planters	
3 x 5¾". Scrolled. Lake scene. Brass rim and insert	250.00
3⅝ x 6¾" square. Puffed. Fern decor	225.00
Shakers. Salt and Pepper. Pairs	
Daisy Petal. Unsigned	125.00
Erie Twist. Blue. Enameled	175.00
Sugar Castor. Erie Twist. Beige and white	165.00
Syrup Jug. 8". Silverplated lid	300.00
Trays	
3¼" diam. Florals. Gold trim. Red mark	75.00
7" diam. Blue and pink flowers ..	250.00
Vases	
6¼". Pink and blue pansies. Raised shell. Gold trim. Ormolu holder	325.00
6½". Stick-type. Unsigned	175.00
7". Bulbous. Ormolu butterfly side handles. Leaf decor	350.00
7". Ormolu footed holder. Blue enameled scrolls. Red mark	450.00
9". Pink blossom decor. Ormolu holder	450.00
Wig Holder. Red mark	375.00

WEATHER VANES

A weather vane indicates wind direction. It is uncertain when the first vane was made in the United States.

The earliest known examples were found on late 17th century structures in the Boston area of Massachusetts. The first weather vanes were handcrafted of various materials. Some wooden models were used as patterns to produce cast iron forms and molds which enabled the coppersmith to hammer out full bodied figures.

The 'champion' is the rooster . . .in fact the name weathercock is synonymous with weather vane.

Whirligigs are a variation of the weather vane. Constructed of wood and metal by unschooled sculpters, these dimensional vanes not only indicate the direction of the wind and its velocity but their unique movements served as entertainment to children, neighbors and honest balt of Sleepy Hollow.

NOTE: Authentic reproductions of early models exist.

Weather Vanes

Arrow. 23". Filigree brass, cranberry glass. Owner's name ....$	175.00
Automobile. 26" long. Copper. Full bodied. C. 1920	400.00
Cow. 15". Tin. Painted black. Copper bar	195.00
Cow. 15 x 24". Copper. Full bodied. Complete with standard, orbs, directionals	2000.00
Eagle. 15". Copper. Full bodied. Complete with orb and directionals	1000.00

Horse. 32" long. Cast iron. Massachusetts. C. 1830's $1200.00

Whirligig. Windmill. 16½". Wood. Original paint $100.00

Eagle. 37". Zinc. Complete with directionals	750.00
Fish. 27". Wooden. Original silver paint	400.00
Fox. 30". Copper. Full bodied	250.00
Goose. 23" wing span. Cast iron ..	500.00
Horse. 10½ x 28½". Copper. Full bodied	750.00
Horse. 33" long. Copper. With rod and standard	400.00
Horse with Rider. 32". Copper. Full bodied. Complete with directionals	1800.00
Rooster. 20 x 22". Cast iron. Original gold paint. New England	500.00
Rooster. 21 x 21". Copper. Full bodied	600.00

Whirligigs

Blacksmith. 12 x 20". Wood	250.00
Farm Scene. 30 x 32". Barn, horses and figures. Wood and metal. Original paint. C. 1900	750.00
Fisherman. 14½". Wood. Original paint. C. 1930	150.00
Flying Goose. 21". Wood. Conn. C. 1900	200.00
Man Sawing Wood. 12 x 19". Wood. Pa. C. 1900	350.00
Men Working Under Tree. With stand. 27 x 45". Metal and wood. Original paint. Pa. C. 1920	300.00
Wash Woman. 11 x 15". Wood. Painted. Maine. C. 1915	250.00

WEDGWOOD

WEDGWOOD

Josiah Wedgwood founded the famous Wedgwood Pottery at Burslem, England in 1759. Wedgwood's history is complex and confusing.

Although Wedgwood is probably associated more with Basalt and Jasperware, the factory produced many wares including creamware, drabware, redware and a fine quality porcelain. In 1920 Fairyland Lustre was introduced. This porcelain is decorated with colorful, fantasy-like decals with gold detail. Lustreware production ceased in 1932. The firm in Wedgwood, England is still active and produces fine quality dinnerware and accessories.

Also see "Basalt", "Jasperware" and "Pearlware".

Plate. Majolica. 8¾". "Email Ombamnt''. Wedgwood only. C. 1878 .... $195.00

Tea Pot. Caneware. ''Sheaf of Wheat" $185.00

Bottle, Scent. Jasperware. Blue. White cameos. Glass stopper. 18th century .... $ 250.00
Bough Pots
  Creamware. 8x 7" top diam. C. 1820 .... 450.00
  Drabware. 7½". C. 1790-1800 .. 400.00
  Queensware. 10". Pierced grid. Embossed. C. 1845 .... 300.00
Bowls
  Basalt. 10". Basketweave design. Engine turned. C. 1790 .... 300.00
  Creamware. 15¼ x 14¼" deep. Green scenic decor 225.00
  Drabware
    7½ x 3¼" deep. Abrabesque .. 165.00
    9". Fluted. Smearglaze with deep banding of Tudor Rose relief in white. C. 1790-1817 .. 280.00
Lustres
  Butterfly
    3⅛ x 4¾" high. Pedestaled. Z4832 .... 350.00
    8½ x 5½" high. Pedestaled. Orange lustre interior and MOP exterior. Z4832 .... 850.00
  Dragon. 5". Z4828 .... 175.00
  Fairy
    7 x 3½" deep. "Castle on Road," "Bird in Hoop." 1250.00
    9¼". "Thumbelina." Z5200 .. 1800.00
    10½ x 5" deep. Octagonal. Bead border. Z5125 .... 2500.00
  Fish. 4¼". Z4920 .... 250.00
  Flame. 3⅞ x 2" deep. "Leap Frogging Elves." Z5360 .... 950.00
  Hummingbird. 4". Z5294 ...... 325.00
  Night Time. 5 x2⅜" deep. Z4968 . 900.00
Tricolor. Two handles 350.00
Boxes, Jasperware
  3¼ x 2½" high. Black. Sterling rim. C. 1900 .... 175.00
  7" diam. Terra Cotta. Spiked lid .. 185.00

Butters, Covered
  Drabware. Blue leaves 195.00
  Jasperware. "Lady Templeton." Light blue. Engine turned. 18th century 750.00
Busts, Basalt
  Lincoln. 8". Limited edition 100.00
  Mercury. 18½" 1250.00
  Napoleon. 9". C. 1850 .... 850.00
Candlesticks. Basalt. 11". Defined sacrifice relief. Etruria, England. C. 1900. Pair 375.00
Charger. Majolica. 11½ x 25½". Hanging-type. Sea life motif. C. 1882 .... 300.00
Compote. Majolica. 7½ x 9¾". Dolphin base 395.00
Condiment Dish. Queensware. 8½". 125.00
Cup, Peche Melba. Fairy Lustre. 4 x 3½" deep. Moonlight exterior. Sunlight interior. Z4968 .... 850.00

Cups and Saucers
  Creamware
    Twig handle. C. 1790 .... 95.00
    Vintage motif in sage green relief. C. 1820 .... 300.00
  Jasperware. Terra Cotta. Medallion decor 150.00
  Pearlware. Miniature 125.00
Ewer, Wine. Basalt. 17½" high. C. 1840 .... 850.00
Flower Holder. Basalt. 6½". "Putti." 800.00
Game Dish. Caneware. 4½ x 7". With insert 300.00

Hair Receiver. Jasperware. Blue. Classical relief. C. 1880 .... 175.00

Honey Pot. Jasperware. 4½". Light blue. Silverplated cover, handle. "Domestic Employment and Sacrifice" in relief. C. 1865 ...... 150.00

Inkwell. Basalt. 1½ x 2⅝" 150.00

Jardinieres

- Basalt. 7¼". Classical decor. Wedgwood only 350.00
- Jasperware. 8½". Black. Wedgwood, England 300.00
- Majolica. 7". Polychromed. Ram's heads. Ball feet. Wedgwood only. C. 1866 .... 250.00

Jugs

- Caneware. 7". Smearglaze with banding of white Tudor Rose relief. C. 1790-1817 .... 300.00
- Drabware. "Arabesque." C. 1790-1817 .... 195.00

Muffineer. Jasperware. 5½" high. Dark blue. Self dome lid. Wedgwood only 175.00

Mustard Pot. Creamware. 3¾" high. Covered. Chinoiserie decor in reds, oranges, yellow and blue. C. 1780 150.00

Pitchers, Jasperware

- 4". Yellow. White classical figures. Wedgwood, England 350.00
- 4½". Terra Cotta 135.00
- 5". Blue with white classical figures. Wedgwood only 195.00

Plaques

- Fairy Lustre. 10¾ x 14½". White steps and torches leading to castle in sky. Framed. Limited edition .. 1750.00
- Jasperware
  - 5½ x 7½". Light blue. Classical figures. Framed. C. 1840 ...... 250.00
  - 8 x 10¾" oval. Light blue. Classical figures. Wedgwood, England 125.00

Plates

- Caneware. 8". C. 1810 .... 100.00
- Creamware. 9½". Ribbon edge. Gilted. C. 1790 .... 75.00
- Majolica
  - 7". White. Multicolor floral designs in relief. Set of 6 ...... 210.00
  - 8½". Cabbage Leaf. Wedgwood only. Set of 6 .... 175.00
  - 9". "September." 135.00
  - 10½". "January." Polychromed. Etruria, England 65.00

Sugars, Covered

- Caneware. Smearglaze. Prunus blossoms. C. 1790-1817 .... 275.00
- Jasperware. Terra Cotta. Classical relief. Acanthus leaves on lid. C. 1850 .... 165.00

Teapots

- Caneware. 4-cup size. Octagonal. Twig finial. Applique work on spout. Gray-green vintage in relief. C. 1790-1817 .... 750.00
- Drabware. White Tudor Rose border on teapot and lid. Wedgwood only 295.00
- Salt Glaze. White. Arabesque Spaniel finial 175.00

Tea Sets

- Jasperware. Dark blue. Silverplated rims and lids. 20th century. 300.00
- Queensware. Blue. Edward VIII Coronation. C. 1937 .... 375.00

Tile. Calendar. C. 1900 .... 75.00

Tray. Jasperware. 7½ x 10". Dark blue. Classical scenes. Wedgwood, England 125.00

Trivet. Jasperware. 7" diam. Dark blue. C. 1920 .... 75.00

Urn. Tricolor. 6¼" high. Covered .. 1000.00

Vases

- Creamware. 5½". Stick-type. Worcester decoration. Wedgwood only. C. 1880 .... 225.00
- Jasperware
  - 3½". Lilac. Bacchanalian. Wedgwood, England 200.00
  - 6". Dark blue. Portland 350.00
- Lustres
  - Butterfly. 5½". Z4825 .... 280.00
  - Butterfly Women. 6⅛". Black. Z4968 .... 1250.00
  - Candlemas. 7½". Z5157 .... 2250.00
  - Dragon. 8½". Deep blue exterior. Z4616 .... 450.00
  - Rainbow. 8½". Z5366 .... 2000.00

Wall Pocket. Majolica. 11½" top diam. Bird nest-shape. With birds. C. 1872 .... 385.00

WELLER

In 1873 Samuel A. Weller opened a small factory in Fultonham, Ohio to produce stoneware jars and flower pots. In 1882 he moved his facilities to Zanesville and 1893 formed a partnership with W. A. Long. Within the year, they began to produce "Lonhuda" . . .a shaded brown ware with decoration underglaze. After Long left the company in 1895, Weller continued to make similar art ware under the name "Louwelsa", plus a large variety of other art pottery lines. By 1915 Weller claimed to be the largest pottery in the world.

At the end of World War I, many prestige lines were discontinued and Weller concentrated on more commercial wares. During the Depression, the art lines became even less elaborate. Even though business prospered again briefly during World War II; foreign competition forced the factory to close in 1948. Many lines were offered by Weller and it is impossible to list all here. Most of the pottery was marked "Weller" . . .either impressed, incised or rubber-stamped; and some art pottery was also artist signed.

Vase. "Louwelsa." 2½". Squat-type. Pansy decor $75.00

Vase. "La Sa." 11½". Amphora-type $500.00

Baskets
- Forest. 6¼ x 8½". C. 1918-28 . . $65.00
- Woodcraft. 9". Strap handle, footed. C. 1920-33 . . . . 95.00

Bowls
- Burntwood. 4". Fish decor. C. 1910 . . . . 55.00
- Floral. 8". Wild Rose. C. 1930's . . 25.00
- Lonhuda. 6¼". Yellow and orange florals. Standard glaze. C. 1895 . . . . 225.00

Cornucopia. Oakleaf. 4 x 10". Green and brown. C. 1935 . . . . 25.00

Figural. Frog on Lily Pad. 3½" 100.00

Fountain. Graystone. 11 x 11" base, 10" high top. C. 1920 . . . . 375.00

Jars, Covered
- Chase. 8". Blue. C. 1928 . . . . 185.00
- Evergreen. 11½". Mottled terra cotta. C. 1930 . . . . 75.00

Jardinieres
- Chelsea. 30". Pedestaled. C. 1933 165.00
- Dickensware 1st line. 7". Mum decor on green ground. Artist signed. C. 1897 . . . . 200.00
- Knifewood. 6". Glendale. C. 1918 . 100.00
- Louwelsa. 9". Bell-shaped. Poppy decor. C. 1896-1924 . . . . 225.00
- Roma. 6¼ x 7¾". Garland of fruits and flowers. C. 1914-20 . . 100.00
- Woodrose. 9 x 10½". Pre-1920 . . 100.00

Mugs
- Art Nouveau. C. 1903 . . . . 150.00
- Louwelsa. Berry decor. C. 1896-1924 . . . . 175.00

Pitchers
- Etna. 5¾". Purple flowers. C. 1906 . . . . 75.00
- Zona. 7½". Dark blue. C. 1920 . . 85.00

Planters
- Sabrinian. 4 x 5¼". Scalloped shell, fish feet. C. 1928 . . . . 75.00
- Sicardo. 2¾ x 6". Dark green and purple. C. 1902-07 . . . . 300.00

Tankards
- Dickensware 2nd line. 12". Cavalier. Artist signed. C. 1900-05 . . . . 750.00
- Louwelsa. 14". Blackberry decor. C. 1896-1924 . . . . 275.00

Tyg. Dickensware 2nd line. 6½". Three handles. Monk. C. 1900-05. 350.00

Vases
- Alvin. 6". Double tree trunk. C. 1928 . . . . 40.00
- Aurelain. 6¾". C. 1898-1910 . . 200.00
- Baldwin. 6". Apples in relief. C. 1915 . . . . 80.00
- Blueware. 3½ x 7⅜". Lady. Pre-1920 . . . . 65.00
- Burntwood. 5½ x 11¾". Birds and flowers. C. 1910 . . . . 100.00

Cameo. 6½". Urn-shaped. C. 1935	35.00
Chengtu. 10". Red. C. 1925-36	100.00
Coppertone. 10". Ovoid. C. 1920	125.00
Eocean. 8". Toadstools. Artist signed. C. 1898-1918	325.00
Floretta. 5½". Pansy decor. C. 1904	65.00
Hudson. 7". Two handles. Mum decor. C. 1920-30's	150.00
La Sa. 5". Ovoid. Desert scene. C. 1920-25	200.00
Lonhuda. Orange and green flowers. C. 1895	185.00
Louwelsa. 11". Thistle decor. Artist signed. C. 1896-1924	225.00
Lustre. 6½". Bulbous base, slender neck. Violet blue. C. 1920	60.00
Marbleized. 9½". C. 1914	165.00
Sicardo. 8". Ovoid. Melon-shaped panels. Cloverleaf decor. C. 1902-07	400.00
Sicardo. 18". Bottle-shaped. Iridescent purple to green	1000.00
Silvertone. 5 x 7". Berry and floral decor. C. 1920's	75.00
Softone. 5½". Ovoid. Ribbed. Yellow. C. 1930's	25.00
Wall Pockets	
Dupont. 10½". Basket with roses. C. 1918	75.00
Woodcraft. 5 x 11". C. 1920-33	125.00

WHIELDON

WHIELDON

So associated with Thomas Whieldon and his experiments, this mid 18th century agate-tortoise shell type of earthenware is now the generic term used for similar wares made by other potters in the Staffordshire and other districts of England.

By employing a lead glaze that was more successful than preceding glazes and limiting the range of colors (green, brown, blue, yellow and green) the combination produced some of the most appealing and collectible English pottery of the 18th century with production continuing to the early 19th century.

It is difficult to determine which examples were made by Whieldon or by his followers at other factories. But it does not require expertise to ascertain which pieces are of finer quality and with the most successful mottling.

Tea wares and dinner plates are good utilitarian examples of Whieldon; but figurines, cradles and decorative pieces were also produced.

Cradles	
Three colors ..$	325.00
Two colors	265.00
Figurine. 8¼"	425.00
Plates	
8¾". Octagonal. Molded border	250.00

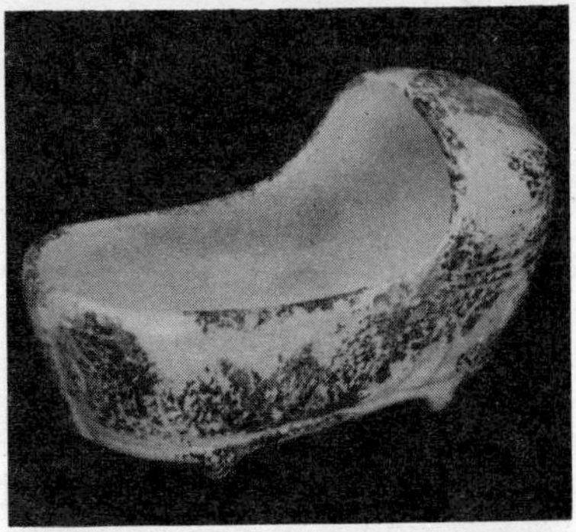

Cradle. 3¾''. Two-colors. C. 1760-70 ....$265.00

9". Dot-diaper-and-basket border	225.00
9". Feather edge. Brown only	135.00
Teapot. 4"	475.00

WHITE PATTERNED IRONSTONE

Ironstone is a heavy earthenware first patented by Charles Mason, Staffordshire, England in the late 18th century. Most White Patterned Ironstone found today dates from 1850 to 1880. Those pieces with coded registry marks will date 1853-1865.

Though the range of patterns seems endless, a mere dozen dominate the market. Two general classifications are used . . .the floral motif and the geometric motif. Some patterns, such as "Fig," combine the two motifs. Demand is beginning to change because collectors are discovering that the less popular yet attractive patterns can be collected at reasonable prices.

White Patterned Ironstone was and continues to be produced by several potteries in the United States and abroad. Weights and glazes will vary according to the manufacturer. Fired at a very high temperature, ironstone is durable and can be used and enjoyed daily.

Caution: Reproductions are on the market and late pieces are being offered as early ones with 'early prices'.

Chocolate Pot. Ceres. Rare form ..$	145.00
Coffee or Tea Pots	
Blackberry	110.00
Ceres	120.00
Pankhurst Ribbed	125.00
Sydenham. Round. Repaired	75.00
Cups and Saucers	
Calla Lily	26.00
Laurel Wreath	28.00

Coffee Pot. "Grape and Medallion" $175.00

Wheat 26.00
Hot Plate. Chinese. Rare form 145.00
Jugs
Bands, raised with lion's head brace. Extra large 110.00
Ceres. 5¼" 55.00
President. Batter 45.00
Sydenham. 4¾" 85.00
Sydenham. Octagonal. Large 65.00
Wheat. 8½" 60.00
Nappies
Gothic. 10½". Octagonal 52.00
Laurel Wreath. 8½". Oval 28.00
Lily of the Valley. 11". Round 48.00
Pankhurst Broad Fluted. Square... 35.00
Wheat. 9". Oval 45.00
Plates
Corn. 9¾" 18.00
Dover. 10" 18.00
Hexagonal Loop. 10" 28.00
Laurel Wreath. 9¾" 26.00
Morning Glory. 10" 28.00
Paris. 9⅞" 16.00
Pankhurst Broad Fluted. 10¾" .. 22.00
President. 7½" 12.00
Sydenham. 7½" 9.00
Wheat
7½" 12.00
8¼" 15.00
9¾" 20.00
Plates, Soup
Ceres. 9¾" 34.00
Chinese. 10" 18.00
Pankhurst Broad Fluted. 9½" 20.00
Paris. 9⅝" 22.00
Wheat. 9¾" 32.00
Platters
Fig. 16" 55.00
Hexagonal Loop. 16½" 65.00
Lily of the Valley. 16½" 55.00
Paris. 17½" 70.00
St. Louis. 16½" 32.00
Sydenham. 12" 45.00
Server. 3-tier. Assembled in 7 pieces by metal bolt. Rare form 165.00
Soap Dishes, Covered
Fig. With drain. Hairline in lid ... 38.00
Wheat. With drain 48.00
Soap Dishes, Open
Oblong 22.00
Oval 18.00
Sugars
Ceres 45.00
Grape and Medallion 58.00
Lily of the Valley 65.00
Pankhurst Ribbed 72.00
Syllabubs
Lily of the Valley 18.50
Pankhurst Broad Fluted 16.00
President 16.00
Sydenham 20.00
Tazzas, Lily Pad
High foot. Rare form 155.00
Three feet. Rare form 75.00
Tea Sets
Grape and Medallion. Coffee pot, creamer and sugar 265.00
Pankhurst Ribbed. Small. 14 pieces 250.00
Tureens, Sauce
Pankhurst Fine Ribbed. Tray and ladle 110.00
Pearl. Ladle and no tray 80.00
Sydenham Tulip. Tray and ladle .. 145.00
Tureens, Soup
Fig. Tray and ladle 335.00
Prairie Flower. Tray and ladle 235.00
Sydenham Tulip. Tray and ladle 375.00
Tureens, Vegetable
Ceres 90.00
Floral. (Unidentified) 58.00
Pankhurst Broad Fluted 45.00
Pearl. Large 185.00
President 125.00
Wheat. Small 85.00

WILLOW WARE

This popular ware derives its name from a design which is in the Chinese tradition. Willow ware had its inspiration from early Canton ware brought to Europe from China in the 16th century. An early willow transfer pattern, said to be

the first ever transfer-printed, is credited to either Thomas Tucker or his apprentice Thomas Minton . . .both of whom worked at Caughley Pottery in the Staffordshire district of England. The first (1780) under-glaze transfer design did not contain all the Chinese-legend motifs found in the later 'standard' willow pattern developed in 1810 by Josiah Spode. The 'standard' willow pattern has several distinctive features . . .a willow tree, two pagodas, a rail fence with finials, two birds and a three-arch bridge with three figures crossing it. In the late 18th century, willow ware was made in England and Germany. By the 19th century it was produced in the United States, France, Japan, Holland and Ireland; and it is still produced today in many countries.
Most commonly produced in blue; occasional pieces can be found in pink and green.

Pitcher. 7". Buffalo Pottery. C. 1905 ....$150.00

Butter, Covered. Ridgway ......$	50.00
Butter Pat. Ridgway	7.50
Cream and Sugar, Covered. Buffalo .	50.00
Cup and Saucer. Allerton	25.00
Plates	
7". Ridgway	15.00
9". Allerton	20.00
10¼". Buffalo	20.00
Platters	
11". Buffalo	20.00
13½". Allerton	40.00
16". Ridgway	55.00
Sauce Boat. With attached underplate. Allerton	30.00
Sugar, Covered. Ridgway	45.00
Teapot. Royal Doulton	55.00
Vase. 8". Mason	45.00

REVERSE OF ILLUSTRATED PITCHER

Vegetables	
9". Open. Allerton	25.00
10". Covered. Ridgway	45.00
Wash Set. Ridgway. 2 pieces	125.00

WITCH BALLS

A witch ball is simply a hollow sphere of colored or multicolored glass. There are various myths surrounding the origin and purpose of the witch ball. Some say they were displayed by the fireplace to catch demon spirits as they descended the chimney or that they were used to store salt and placed in the chimney to keep the salt dry. Others maintain that witch balls were never suspended (or had hangers); but were placed in containers with the open end up to catch "evil spirits", taken outdoors to release the spirits and replaced in the vase after such "cleansings."
In all probability a witch ball was merely a glassmaker's whimsey . . .used strictly for decorative purposes atop an unfilled flower vase.
Erroneously categorized with other blown glass balls such as Christmas tree ornaments, target balls, floats and early glass fire extinguishers; witch balls came in a variety of sizes and were blown by several glassmakers.

Amethyst. 4½" diam ....$	150.00
Blue, Medium. 4½" diam ball, 9" matching vase. Attributed to Pittsburgh	500.00

Nailsea-type. 10½" o.h. Clear with white loopings $750.00

Bowl, Burl. 16¾x5¾" deep ..$500.00

Hat Block. Walnut. 2 pieces $35.00

Cranberry. 6" diam. Pontil stem. C. 1840 .... 500.00

Nailsea-Type

Aquamarine with white loopings. 6½" diam. Suncook, New York .. 300.00

Clear with white loopings. 6½" diam. ball, 12" matching vase. Attributed to South Jersey 750.00

Clear with white and cranberry loopings. 3½" diam. Attributed to South Jersey 200.00

WOODENWARES

This list serves as a 'catch all' for all wooden items not specifically categorized. Also consult individual categories such as "Boxes," "Kitchen Collectibles," etc.

Barber Pole, Hanging. 22" long. Original paint ....$ 350.00

Barrel Spigots. 10" 4.00

Blueberry Picker. Wood and tin 165.00

Bottle Corker. 10½" 20.00

Bowls, Burl

7x 2½" deep.................. 250.00

9¼ x 3½" deep 325.00

18x 6" deep 500.00

Buckets

Grain. 10" diam. Stave construction 35.00

Grease. Conestoga Wagon 150.00

Paint. Iron hoops, bail handle .. 28.50

Sap 40.00

Sugar, Covered................ 45.00

Water. Bentwood handle 45.00

Butter Churn. Also see "Kitchen Collectibles".

Dog-type. All original. Eastern .. 500.00

Candle Dryer. 20" high. Pine 95.00

Ceiling Fan. 22" blades	300.00
Cigar Mold. 23". 25-units	30.00
Corn Planter	15.00
Cranberry Picker	175.00
Eagle. Carved, on ball. 7½" high, 11" wingspread	250.00
Egg Carrier. 24 dozen size. Slat construction	35.00
Farm Seeder. 3 x 3½ x 45". Wheelbarrow-type. All original	125.00
Grain Scoop	25.00
Grain Shovel. One piece	150.00
Hat Stretcher. Brass sizer	30.00
Hay Forks	
2-prong	75.00
4-prong	95.00
4-prong. Hand crafted, mortised tines, pegged. Early 1800's	125.00
Human Yoke. One piece construction	45.00
Keg, Water. 6¼ x 10" diam. Eyelet lock, lapped hoops, raised bung hole	150.00
Measures. Nesting-type. Pint, quart, ½ gallon, 1 gallon. Bentwood. Set	60.00
Mill Spindles. 7". Maple	1.50
Mouse Traps	
2½ x 5½". Early 1800's	95.00
7 x 14". Pine	25.00
Ox Yokes	
With bows	125.00
Without bows	95.00
Shoe Last	3.00
Shuttle. 18" long. Maple	12.50
Smoothing Boards	
American. 7½ x 10½". Hand carved maple	40.00
German. 6½ x 19½". Heavy carvings. Dated 1781	500.00
Snowshoes. Hand crafted, all original. C. 1880. Pair	50.00
Soap Mold. 3 x 3½ x 6"	25.00
Tape Loom Board. 7¾ x 30". Pine. 18th century	250.00
Wagon Jack. Conestoga	250.00

YELLOW WARE

Yellow Ware is a fairly heavy earthenware of varying weight and strength. Not to be confused with English Yellow-Glazed Earthenware; Yellow Ware, when broken, will show yellow completely through; not just a yellow overglaze. Pieces of this ware vary in color from a rich pumpkin to lighter shades with more tan than yellow. Kitchen pieces are most prevalent; although plates, nappies and custard cups can also be found. There are both English and American examples available; however the English pieces appear to have had additional ingredients added to the earthenware to make a harder body. Derbyshire and Sharp's were foremost among English manufacturers and the Bennington, Vermont factory was one of the first among American producers. Yellow Ware is widely collected and used . . .and prices of this ware are rising.

Humidor. 6''. Banded. C. 1830-40 ....$65.00

Baking Dishes	
10". Oblong. White interior ....$	72.00
10½". Oblong	75.00
11". Oval	85.00
Bowls, Milk	
8"	35.00
10"	45.00
14"	65.00
Bowls, Mixing. Relief exterior	
8"	38.00
12"	65.00
13½"	55.00
14"	60.00
15¼"	70.00
Crocks, Covered	
Medium. Brown bands	55.00
Medium. White bands	65.00
Custard Cups	
Extra Large	28.00
Medium	18.00
Small	16.00
Ginger Jar. 8". Rare form	35.00
Molds	
Corn	42.00
Geometric	35.00
Rabbit	38.00
Mortar. 5½". White bands. Rare form	65.00
Mugs	
Brown bands. Slight damage	32.00
Plain	40.00
White bands	45.00
Nappy. 9¾". Oval. Scalloped edge.	45.00

Pie Plates

8″	40.00
8½″	30.00
9¼″. Pie crust edge	65.00
9½″	45.00
Plate. 8½″. Rare form	55.00
Soap Dish. Round. Rare form	45.00

ZANE POTTERY

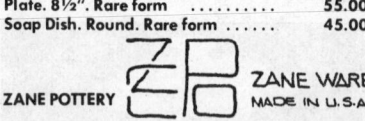

ZANE WARE
MADE IN U.S.A.

Adam Reed and Harry McClelland bought the Peters and Reed Pottery located in Zanesville, Ohio in 1921.

The firm continued production of garden wares and introduced several new art lines . . . "Sheen", "Powder Blue", "Crystalline" and "Drip". The factory was sold in 1941 to Lawton Gonder. See "Peters and Reed" and "Gonder"

Jardiniere with Stand. 34″. Green matte glaze. Frank Ferreu $275.00

Bowls

5″. Green. Moss Aztec	$ 25.00
6″. Landsun glaze	25.00
Jardiniere. 14½″. Two handles. Variegated green semi-matte glaze. Montene	125.00

Vases

7″. Ribbed body. Green	30.00
8″. Handled. Ribbed body. Powder Blue. C. 1925	50.00

ZANESVILLE POTTERY

LA MORO

Zanesville Art Pottery, one of several potteries located in Zanesville, Ohio, began production in 1900. A line of utilitarian products was first produced. Art pottery was introduced shortly thereafter. The major line was La Moro . . . hand-painted and decorated under glaze. The impressed block print mark La Moro appears on the high glazed and matte glazed decorated ware. The firm was bought by S. A. Weller in 1920 and became known as Weller Plant No. 3.

Bowl. 7″. With flower frog. Dark blue matte glaze	$ 35.00
Jardiniere. With stand. 28″. Blue	85.00
Tankard. 13½″. Floral decor. La Moro	195.00

Vases

6″. 3 -handles. Floral decor. La Moro	125.00
7″. Clover blossoms. Artist signed. La Moro	175.00
8″. Indian. La Moro	250.00
9½″. Pansy decor. La Moro	225.00
14″. Wild rose decor on brown high glaze. Unmarked	125.00
Whiskey Jug. 5½″. Floral decor. La Moro	125.00

ZSOLNAY PÉCS
TJM
ZSOLNAY PÉCS

ZSOLNAY

Zsolnay is a Hungarian ceramic ware. Vilmos Zsolnay (1828-1900) took over his brother's factory located in Pe'cs, Hungary in the mid 1800's. Zsolnay's son Miklos became manager in 1899. Characteristically, the ware possesses a cream-colored ground and is highly ornamental and glazed. 'Eosin' glaze, a deep rich play of colors reminiscent of Tiffany's iridescent wares, was developed by Zsolnay in 1820. This technique was awarded the Gold Medal at the 1900 World Exhibit in Paris.

No trademark was used in the beginning. From 1878 on, the blue mark depicting the five towers of the Cathedral of Pe'cs was used. The letters "T. J. M.", incorporated into the other known trademark, are reported to be the initials of Miklos Zsolnay's three children.

Of more recent origin are the iridescent glazed figurines appearing on the market. These figurines initially sold for small sums; however, after catching the attention of Zsolnay collectors, they are beginning to increase in value.

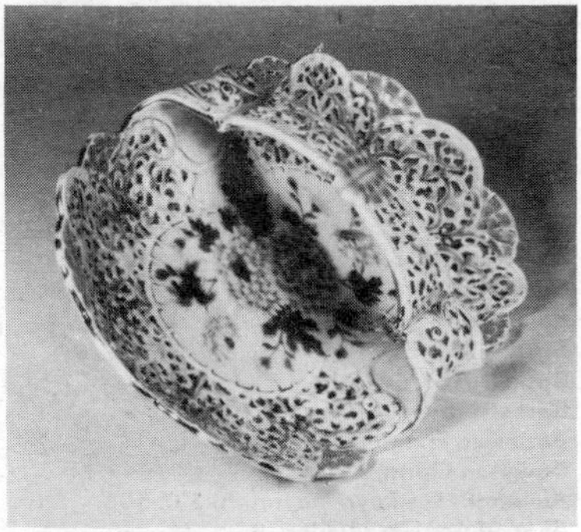

Cake Basket. 14½" long. Reticulated. Floral center. Pink and gold trim $225.00

Figurine. Iridescent. "Bears on Rock." 5x8" $95.00

Bowls
- 5¼". Irregular pinched rim. Blue lustred exterior with molded fish decor. Deep red interior ......$ 500.00
- 6". Oval. Reticulated. Multicolored floral medallions on ivory ground. Gold trim 125.00
- 8". Iridescent green 195.00
- 10". Oval. Two handles. Reticulated. All over floral and scrolls on ivory ground. Gold trim .. 225.00

Cache Pot. 4½". Reticulated. Multicolored flowers on ivory ground 125.00

Cup and Saucer. Pink and blue flowers on ivory ground 65.00

Ewer. Stoppered. 6½". Pink lustred handle and spout. Pink and green scrolls on ivory ground 175.00

Figurines. Iridescent
- Bears on rock. 5 x8" 95.00
- Deer. Reclining. 4½ x 5¼" 125.00
- Frog. 6 x 6" 75.00
- Owl. 3" 35.00
- Rooster. 5 x 8" 85.00

Pitcher. 5". Animals and figures on ivory ground. Lustre trim 150.00

Puzzle Jug. 6¼". Multicolored florals on ivory ground. Gold trim . 175.00

Vases
- 3". Ball-shaped. Iridescent green. 125.00
- 7¼". Cone-shaped. Turquoise and gold swirls on cobalt blue ground. C. 1900 .... 250.00
- 10". Handled. Iridescent green .. 275.00
- 11¼". Molded leaves. Green. iridescent. C. 1900 .... 600.00

Index

-C-

-D-

-G-

-H-

-I-

-J-

-K-

-L-

-M-

-S-